Let's Go writers travel on your budget.

"Guides that penetrate the veneer of the holiday brochures and mine the grit of real life."

—The Economist

"The writers seem to have experienced every rooster-packed bus and lunar-surfaced mattress about which they write."

—The New York Times

"All the dirt, dirt cheap."

—People

Great for independent travelers.

"The guides are aimed not only at young budget travelers but at the independent traveler; a sort of streetwise cookbook for traveling alone."

—The New York Times

"Flush with candor and irreverence, chock full of budget travel advice."

—The Des Moines Register

"An indispensible resource, *Let's Go*'s practical information can be used by every traveler."

—The Chattanooga Free Press

Let's Go is completely revised each year.

"Only *Let's Go* has the zeal to annually update every title on its list."

—The Boston Globe

"Unbeatable: good sightseeing advice; up-to-date info on restaurants, hotels, and inns; a commitment to money-saving travel; and a wry style that brightens nearly every page."

—The Washington Post

All the important information you need.

"*Let's Go* authors provide a comedic element while still providing concise information and thorough coverage of the country. Anything you need to know about budget traveling is detailed in this book."

—The Chicago Sun-Times

"Value-packed, unbeatable, accurate, and comprehensive."

—Los Angeles Times

Let's Go Publications

Let's Go: Alaska & the Pacific Northwest 2001
Let's Go: Australia 2001
Let's Go: Austria & Switzerland 2001
Let's Go: Boston 2001 **New Title!**
Let's Go: Britain & Ireland 2001
Let's Go: California 2001
Let's Go: Central America 2001
Let's Go: China 2001
Let's Go: Eastern Europe 2001
Let's Go: Europe 2001
Let's Go: France 2001
Let's Go: Germany 2001
Let's Go: Greece 2001
Let's Go: India & Nepal 2001
Let's Go: Ireland 2001
Let's Go: Israel 2001
Let's Go: Italy 2001
Let's Go: London 2001
Let's Go: Mexico 2001
Let's Go: Middle East 2001
Let's Go: New York City 2001
Let's Go: New Zealand 2001
Let's Go: Paris 2001
Let's Go: Peru, Bolivia & Ecuador 2001 **New Title!**
Let's Go: Rome 2001
Let's Go: San Francisco 2001 **New Title!**
Let's Go: South Africa 2001
Let's Go: Southeast Asia 2001
Let's Go: Spain & Portugal 2001
Let's Go: Turkey 2001
Let's Go: USA 2001
Let's Go: Washington, D.C. 2001
Let's Go: Western Europe 2001 **New Title!**

Let's Go *Map Guides*

Amsterdam	New Orleans
Berlin	New York City
Boston	Paris
Chicago	Prague
Florence	Rome
Hong Kong	San Francisco
London	Seattle
Los Angeles	Sydney
Madrid	Washington, D.C.

Coming Soon: *Dublin* and *Venice*

Let's Go

TURKEY

2001

Elizabeth S. Daniel editor
Siobhan K. Quinlan associate editor

researcher-writers
Caitlin Aiko Harrington
Peter Henninger
Inga Hunter
Andrew Laming
Alexander D. Schrank
Selin Tüysüzoğlu

Filip Wojciechowski map editor

Macmillan

Published in Great Britain 2001 by Macmillan, an imprint of Macmillan Publishers Ltd, 25 Eccleston Place, London, SW1W 9NF, Basingstoke and Oxford.
Associated companies throughout the world
www.macmillan.com

Maps by David Lindroth copyright © 2001, 2000, 1999, 1998, 1997, 1996, 1995, 1994, 1993, 1992, 1991, 1990, 1989, 1988 by St. Martin's Press.

Published in the United States of America by St. Martin's Press.

ISBN: 0-333-90143-6
First edition
10 9 8 7 6 5 4 3 2 1

Let's Go: Turkey is written by Let's Go Publications, 67 Mount Auburn Street, Cambridge, MA 02138, USA.

HOW TO USE THIS BOOK

Welcome to Let's Go: Turkey 2001! You're undoubtedly thrilled to be on the road (again), but before you go, take a few moments to cop a squat and read what we're all about. The following paragraphs give you the lowdown on how we've organized this guidebook, so you'll feel even more comfortable. confident, and ready to roll.

THIS BOOK'S ORGANIZATION

INTRODUCTORY MATERIAL. Discover Turkey, the first chapter, provides you with an overview of travel in the country, including **Suggested Itineraries** that give you an idea of what you shouldn't miss and how long it will take to see it. The **History and Culture** chapter blesses you with a general introduction to the art, literature, cuisine, and an abridged history of Turkey. Meanwhile, the **Essentials** section outlines practical information you'll need to prepare for and execute your trip.

THE "MEAT". This book's chapters are divided regionally, beginning with our unbeatable coverage of İstanbul. From this hub of all urban hubs, our coverage traces next the outlines of the country: the northwestern region, then the Aegean, Black Sea, and Mediterranean coasts before winding into Central Anatolia, Turkey's heartland, and finally to the wild, wild East. Our unique coverage of Northern Cyprus gives you an edge for a true off-the-beaten path experience, and our coverage of Greek Islands allows you to continent-hop with ease. The **black tabs** in the margins will help you to navigate between chapters quickly and easily.

APPENDIX. The appendix contains useful **conversions**, a **phrasebook** of handy Turkish, and a **glossary** of foreign and technical (e.g. architectural) words.

A FEW NOTES ABOUT LET'S GO FORMAT

RANKING ESTABLISHMENTS. In each section (Accommodations, Food, and so forth), we list establishments in order from best to least good. Our absolute favorites are graced with our highest honor: the *Let's Go* thumbs-up (🌑).

PHONE CODES AND TELEPHONE NUMBERS. The **phone code** for each region, city, or town appears opposite the name of that region, city, or town, and is denoted by the ☎ icon. The ☎icon also comes before **phone numbers** in text.

GRAYBOXES AND WHITEBOXES. Grayboxes at times provide wonderful cultural insight, at times simply crude humor. In any case, they're usually amusing, so enjoy. **Whiteboxes,** on the other hand, provide important practical information, such as warnings (**M**), helpful hints and further resources (**S**), and border crossing information (☎).

CONTRACT AND EXPAND. This year, our 🌑 researchers (independent contractors) did such a fabulous job that we're adding even more Turkish delights for you. Eastern Turkey has recently become far more accessible than it once was, allowing us to expand coverage of cities like Van, and add beauties like Diyarbakır. We've pumped up our pre-existing coverage everywhere else, too, from the striking Central Anatolian heartland to Ankara's modern sophistication. Have a blast!

A NOTE TO OUR READERS The information for this book was gathered by *Let's Go* researchers from May through August of 2000. Each listing is based on one researcher's opinion, formed during his or her visit at a particular time. Those traveling at other times may have different experiences since prices, dates, hours, and conditions are always subject to change. You are urged to check the facts presented in this book beforehand to avoid inconvenience and surprises.

RESEARCHER-WRITERS

Caitlin Aiko Harrington   *Western Mediterranean, Konya*

Caitlin's perseverance and brilliant competence in the face of scorching record heat and a sprained ankle earned her a reputation as our most resilient researcher—her coverage of Turkish hospitals went far beyond the call of duty. With a keen eye for aesthetics, Caitlin found hidden beauty in small villages, honed her bartering skills in Mediterranean markets, and marveled at the backdrop of many, many Lycian rock tombs, all the while delivering clear, concise copy.

Peter Henninger   *İstanbul and Northwestern Turkey*

This tireless urbanophile extraordinaire fled his East Coast confines to "summer" in İstanbul, where, after putting down an attempted coup by his stomach, Peter launched into exhaustive coverage of everything under the burning Turkish sun. Whether engaging local kids in a pickup game of *futbol*, attaining Nirvana on a mountain summit, or making friends with the trendiest bouncers, Peter left no stone–or *bir bira*–unturned, sending back flawless copy, and music suggestions, that never failed to put his editors in a good mood.

Inga Hunter   *Northwestern Turkey, Aegean Coast*

Having fallen in love with the country while teaching in İstanbul, Inga put her passion and language skills to use on the road and left the Aegean Coast reeling. *Let's Go*'s most avid time traveler, she hungrily dug into some of the world's most impressive ruins and sights, revamping our coverage of Ephesus with vision and clarity. Her meticulous, conscientious research and spotless writing cut through any touristy veneer to find the best *lokantasi*, *pansiyons*, and people around.

Andrew Laming   *Eastern Black Sea Coast, Eastern Anatolia*

Probably the only researcher who can claim both to have wrestled a bull and treated heart failure, Andrew combined a staggering travel background with effortless, brilliant prose. This hard-core Australian jack-of-all-trades scoured one of the most off-the-beaten track routes of the entire *Let's Go* series, wowing us with insightful coverage of regional trekking, hidden ruins, previously inaccessible towns, and fresh Turkish history, and he nearly summited Mt. Ararat before World Bank duties called him back to the States.

Alexander D. Schrank   *North Central Anatolia, Ankara, Black Sea Coast*

Unflagging energy and meticulous, professional research characterized Alex's copy, as this student of Turkish became the confidant of tourism directors all along the Black Sea coast. His background in diplomacy and Turkish international affairs complemented our coverage of port cities' pristine beauty and strategic importance. Alex spectacularly overhauled our coverage of Ankara with sophisticated insight and a sharp eye for the hottest nightlife and classiest culture around.

Selin Tüysüzoğlu   *Cappadocia, Northern Cyprus, Eastern Mediterranean*

This no-holds-barred social dynamo left nary a stranger in her wake as she covered one of our most demanding (and swinging) itineraries, flying through Cappadocia, Northern Cyprus, and most of the Mediterranean Coast. Selin's contagious *joie de vivre* helped us live vicariously through the record-breaking heat wave, several Anatolian weddings, and a bar-hopping bonanza, and she even paused long enough to spice up our phrasebook with her native Turkish.

ACKNOWLEDGMENTS

Beth and Siobhan thank Aarup, for his inexhaustible patience and editing prowess; our  RWs, for smashing coverage; Anup, for revisiting Turkey; Team Turkey '00, for an excellent base; Amélie, Bede, Ankur, Brady, John, Sunny, Marly, Valerie, Nora, Naz, Alice, Nathaniel, Nick, Sarah, Anne C., Chris, Melissa R., Fiona, and countless others in the office for help in our moment of need. A special thanks to our Greek partners in crime, Nora and Jen.

Beth thanks Siobhan, for hard work and hilarity. Bisous to Jana and Zoë, Jason and Joe, and lemon cookies, for making #14 a wonderful place to live; thanks to Crystie, for Tuesday lunches and sanity; to the inimitable Dr. Julie Hartlé, Julia, Bo, Lila, Eijean, Desirée, Sarah, Rachel, Etty, Mani, Anjali, and Lidwien, for encouragement; to Alicen and Maya, for letters and inspiration from afar; Verna's donuts; the folks at the Globe Corner Bookstore; and all others at Beth, Inc. Thanks especially to my ▨ Daniel clan: Dad, Mom, Carl, and David.

Siobhan thanks Beth for guidance and daily doses of laughter. Thanks to my family for their encouragement, for putting up with my crazy schedule, and for not renting my room out in my absence; to Amie for her support, for getting me out of the office from time to time, and for letting me crash on her lovely couch. Special thanks to Adam for his moral support, cures for "cases of the mondays," and flowers; and to the purveyors of Magic Coffee and Bangkok Wraps.

Selin thanks her family, Hamgi, Serkan, Ruth, Raab, Anneciğim, and Sümbül. **Peter** thanks Mom and Dad, Maura, Paul, Eli, Loonam and Swanson. **Caitlin** thanks Whitney for her spice, her Turkish mom, Monica, and her wonderful parents. **Alex** thanks Ahmet Baykal, Elvan Evren, and Bulent Eroğlu. **Andrew** thanks Bron "Bronster" Magdulskit, Dawn "Boxer" Lay, and Telli-Kellie Farr.

Editor
Elizabeth S. Daniel
Associate Editor
Siobhan K. Quinlan
Managing Editor
Aarup Kubal
Map Editor
Filip Wojciechowski

Publishing Director
Kaya Stone
Editor-in-Chief
Kate McCarthy
Production Manager
Melissa Rudolph
Cartography Manager
John Fiore
Editorial Managers
Alice Farmer, Ankur Ghosh,
Aarup Kubal, Anup Kubal
Financial Manager
Bede Sheppard
Low-Season Manager
Melissa Gibson
Marketing & Publicity Managers
Olivia L. Cowley, Esti Iturralde
New Media Manager
Jonathan Dawid
Personnel Manager
Nicholas Grossman
Photo Editor
Dara Cho
Production Associates
Sanjay Mavinkurve, Nicholas
Murphy, Rosa Rosalez,
Matthew Daniels, Rachel Mason,
Daniel Visel
(re) Designer
Matthew Daniels
Office Coordinators
Sarah Jacoby, Chris Russell

Director of Advertising Sales
Cindy Rodriguez
Senior Advertising Associates
Adam Grant, Rebecca Rendell
Advertising Artwork Editor
Palmer Truelson

President
Andrew M. Murphy
General Manager
Robert B. Rombauer
Assistant General Manager
Anne E. Chisholm

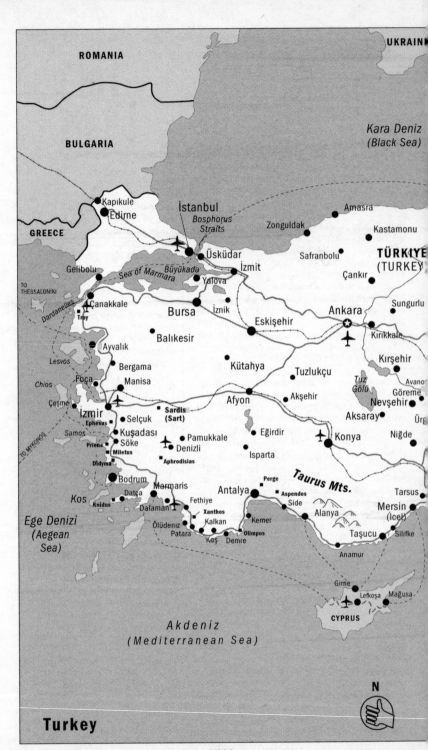

Turkey

CONTENTS

When To Go 1
Things To Do 1

DISCOVER TURKEY 1
Suggested Itineraries 4

HISTORY AND CULTURE 6
History 6
The Arts 20
Society 25

ESSENTIALS 39
Facts for the Traveler 39
Getting There 59
Getting Around 64
Additional Information 68

İSTANBUL 75

NORTHWESTERN TURKEY 137
THRACE 138
Edirne 138
GALLIPOLI PENINSULA AND THE DARDANELLES 144
Eceabat 144
Gelibolu 146
Battlefields of Gallipoli 147
Çanakkale 148
THE EASTERN MARMARA REGION 152
Bursa 152
Yalova 159
İznik 161

AEGEAN COAST 164
NORTHERN COAST 164
Truva (Troy) 164
Bozcaada (Tenedos) 167
Behramkale (Assos) 169
Akçay 170
Ayvalık 171
CENTRAL COAST 174
Bergama (Pergamon) 174
Foça 179
İzmir 182
Çeşme 189
EPHESUS REGION 193
Efes (Ephesus) 193
Selçuk 197
Kuşadasi 202
Priene, Miletus, and Didyma 207
Altinkum Beach 209
PAMUKKALE AND APHRODISIAS REGION 209
Pamukkale (Hierapolis) 209
Denizli 212
Geyre (Aphrodisias) 213
Aydin 215
BODRUM PENINSULA 217
Bodrum 217
Milas 225
Labranda (Labraynda) 226
Euromos 227
Akyaka (Bay of Gökova) 228

GREEK ISLANDS 230
RHODES 230
City of Rhodes 230
KOS 235
Kos Town 236
SAMOS 239
Vathy (Samos Town) 239

MEDITERRANEAN COAST 242
MARMARİS COAST 243
Marmaris 243
İçmeler 249
Bozburun 250
Datça 251
Köyceğlz 254
Dalyan and Kaunos (Caunus) 256
Dalaman 258
Göcek 259
FETHİYE COAST 260
Fethiye 260
Ölüdeniz 266
Patara 269
Kalkan 272
KAŞ COAST 274
Kaş 274
Demre and Myra 278
Olimpos 279
ANTALYA GULF COAST 281
Phaselis 281
Antalya 282
Side 289
EASTERN MEDITERRANEAN COAST 291
Alanya 291
Anamur 294
Taşucu 297
Silifke 298
Kizkalesi 299
Mersin 301
Adana 302
Antakya (Hatay) 306

CENTRAL ANATOLIA 310
CAPPADOCIA 311
Nevşehir 312
Göreme 314
Üçhisar 318
Underground Cities: Kaymakli and Derinkuyu 319
Çavuşin-Zelve 320
Ürgüp 320
Mustafapaşa 323
Avanos 324
Niğde 325
Ihlara 327
Güzelyurt 328
Aksaray 329
Hacibektaş 330
Kayseri 332
KONYA AND ENVIRONS 337
Konya 337
WESTERN ANATOLIA 344
Eğirdir 344

CONTENTS

Afyon 346
Kütahya 348
Eskişehir 351
NORTH-CENTRAL ANATOLIA 352
Ankara 352
Boğazkale 366
Sungurlu 369
Tokat 370
Sivas 373

BLACK SEA COAST 377
WEST OF TRABZON 377
Safranbolu 379
Amasra 383
İnebolu 385
Abana 385
Kastamonu 386
Sinop 388
Samsun 390
Amasya 393
Ünye 396
Ordu 397
Giresun 400
Tirebolu 402
Trabzon 403
EAST OF TRABZON 409
Uzungöl 410
Rize 410
GEORGIAN FRONTIER 412
HEMŞIN VALLEY 413
Şenyuva Valley 413
Ayder 414
Artvin 416
Yusufeli 417

The Çoruh Valley 418
Trekking in the Kaçkars 419

EASTERN ANATOLIA 422
Erzurum 422
Erzincan 428
Kars 429
Doğubeyazit 432
Van 434
Tatvan and Environs 438
Van's North Coast 439
Diyarbakır (Amed) 439
Mardin 441
Malatya 442
Nemrut Dağı 443
Şanlıurfa 444
Gaziantep 448

NORTHERN CYPRUS 451
Essentials 451
GIRNE AND THE NORTH 456
Girne (Kyrenia) 456
Lapta (Lápithos) 463
LEFKOŞA AND ENVIRONS 464
Lefkoşa (North Nicosia) 464
MAĞUSA AND THE KARPAZ 468
Mağusa (Famagusta, GAZİMAGUSA) 468
Karpaz Peninsula 474

PHRASEBOOK AND GLOSSARY 476
Turkish Phrasebook 476
Glossary 480

MAPS

Turkey viii-ix
Turkey: Regions xv

İSTANBUL
İstanbul 76-77
Central İstanbul 78-79
İstanbul Overview 81
Sultanahmet and Süleymaniye 92-93
Tünel and Taksim 97
Topkapı Palace 105
South of the Golden Horn 113

NORTHWESTERN TURKEY
Northwestern Turkey 137
Edirne 139
Gallipoli Peninsula 145
Çanakkale 149
Bursa Overview 152
Bursa 155

AEGEAN COAST
Aegean Coast 165
Troy Site Plan 166
İzmir 183
Ephesus 195
Selçuk 199
Kuşadasi 203
Bodrum 219

MEDITERRANEAN COAST
Mediterranean Coast 242-243
Marmaris 245
Fethiye 261

Kaş 275
Antalya Gulf Coast 281
Antalya Center 283
Adana 303
Antakya 307

CENTRAL ANATOLIA
Central Anatolia 310
Kapadokya (Cappadocia) 312
Nevşehir 313
Göreme 315
Kayseri 333
Konya 339
North Ankara 354
South Ankara 355

BLACK SEA COAST
Black Sea Coast 378-379
Safranbolu 380
Trabzon 405

EASTERN ANATOLIA
Eastern Anatolia 424
Erzurum 425
Kars 431
Van 435

NORTHERN CYPRUS
Northern Cyprus 452-453
Girne 457
Lefkoşa (North Nicosia) 465
Mağusa (Famagusta) 469

✚ Hospital	✈ Airport	⛪ Church	Pedestrian Zone
🚓 Police	🚌 Bus Station	🏛 Museum	Park
✉ Post Office	🚂 Train Station	🏨 Hotel/Hostel	
ⓘ Tourist Office	Synagogue	⛺ Camping	Beach
🏦 Bank	Hamam	🍎 Food & Drink	
Embassy/Consulate	(207) Highway	🛍 Shopping	Water
■ Site or Point of Interest	⚓ Ferry Landing	♪ Arts & Entertainment	
☎ Telephone Office	🕌 Mosque	Nightlife	The Let's Go thumb always points NORTH.
Theater	▲ Mountain	Internet Café	

ABOUT LET'S GO

FORTY-ONE YEARS OF WISDOM

As a new millennium arrives, *Let's Go: Europe*, now in its 41st edition and translated into seven languages, reigns as the world's bestselling international travel guide. For over four decades, travelers criss-crossing the Continent have relied on *Let's Go* for inside information on the hippest backstreet cafes, the most pristine secluded beaches, and the best routes from border to border. In the last 20 years, our rugged researchers have stretched the frontiers of backpacking and expanded our coverage into Asia, Africa, Australia, and the Americas. This year, we've introduced a new city guide series with books on San Francisco and our hometown, Boston. Now, our seven city guides feature sharp photos, more maps, and an overall more user-friendly design. We've also returned to our roots with the inaugural edition of *Let's Go: Western Europe*.

It all started in 1960 when a handful of well-traveled students at Harvard University handed out a 20-page mimeographed pamphlet offering a collection of their tips on budget travel to passengers on student charter flights to Europe. The following year, in response to the instant popularity of the first volume, students traveling to Europe researched the first full-fledged edition of *Let's Go: Europe*, a pocket-sized book featuring honest, practical advice, witty writing, and a decidedly youthful slant on the world. Throughout the 60s and 70s, our guides reflected the times. In 1969 we taught travelers how to get from Paris to Prague on "no dollars a day" by singing in the street. In the 80s and 90s, we looked beyond Europe and North America and set off to all corners of the earth. Meanwhile, we focused in on the world's most exciting urban areas to produce in-depth, fold-out map guides. Our new guides bring the total number of titles to 51, each infused with the spirit of adventure and voice of opinion that travelers around the world have come to count on. But some things never change: our guides are still researched, written, and produced entirely by students who know first-hand how to see the world on the cheap.

HOW WE DO IT

Each guide is completely revised and thoroughly updated every year by a well-traveled set of nearly 300 students. Every spring, we recruit over 200 researchers and 90 editors to overhaul every book. After several months of training, researcher-writers hit the road for seven weeks of exploration, from Anchorage to Adelaide, Estonia to El Salvador, Iceland to Indonesia. Hired for their rare combination of budget travel sense, writing ability, stamina, and courage, these adventurous travelers know that train strikes, stolen luggage, food poisoning, and marriage proposals are all part of a day's work. Back at our offices, editors work from spring to fall, massaging copy written on Himalayan bus rides into witty, informative prose. A student staff of typesetters, cartographers, publicists, and managers keeps our lively team together. In September, the collected efforts of the summer are delivered to our printer, who turns them into books in record time, so that you have the most up-to-date information available for your vacation. Even as you read this, work on next year's editions is well underway.

WHY WE DO IT

We don't think of budget travel as the last recourse of the destitute; we believe that it's the only way to travel. Living cheaply and simply brings you closer to the people and places you've been saving up to visit. Our books will ease your anxieties and answer your questions about the basics—so you can get off the beaten track and explore. Once you learn the ropes, we encourage you to put *Let's Go* down now and then to strike out on your own. You know as well as we that the best discoveries are often those you make yourself. When you find something worth sharing, please drop us a line. We're Let's Go Publications, 67 Mount Auburn St., Cambridge, MA 02138, USA (email: feedback§letsgo.com). For more info, visit our website, www.letsgo.com.

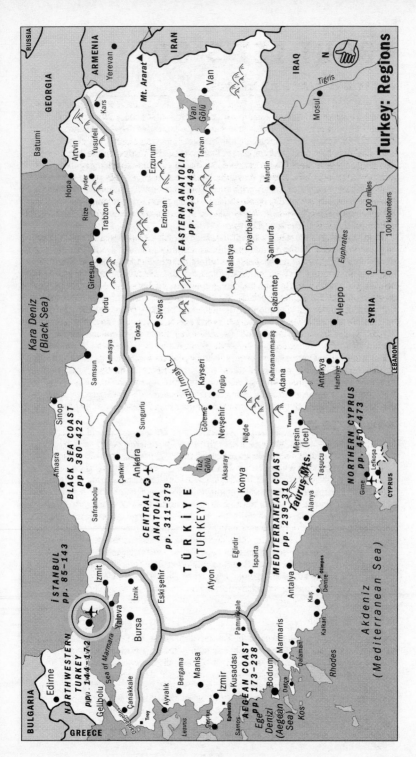

Turkey: Regions

DISCOVER TURKEY

Ten thousand years of stunning historical riches, vibrant modern cities, and exquisite natural wonders grace the modern Republic of Turkey. From the Ancient Greeks to the Romans, the Byzantines, and the Ottomans, Asia Minor has hosted the advance and retreat of numerous great civilizations and their cultural traffic. Humanity's influences on the region are retained in its diverse religions, languages, and architectural wonders, among them İstanbul's majestic mosques and Eastern Anatolia's Armenian churches. Mother Nature has done her part too, from the glittering Aegean and Mediterranean beaches to northern *yayla* plateaus, central deserts, and Mt. Ararat towering in the East. Well-trodden tourist paths grace İstanbul's Sultanahmet district, the coasts, and Cappadocia. The rest of Anatolia remains a purist backpacker's paradise, filled with pristine alpine meadows, cliffside monasteries, medieval churches, tiny fishing villages, and countless cups of *çay* offered by people who take pride in their tradition of hospitality.

FACTS AND FIGURES

CAPITAL Ankara

TYPE OF GOVERNMENT Republican Parliamentary Democracy

POPULATION 66m, and counting

SUFFRAGE 18 yrs. old, universal

ADULT LITERACY 81.6%

LIFE EXPECTANCY women 71.7 years; men 66.5 years

LANGUAGE Turkish (official), Kurdish, Arabic

CURRENCY Turkish lira (TL)

INFLATION RATE 54%

RELIGIONS 99.8% Muslim (Sunni), .02% Christian and Jewish

TOTAL KM. OF HIGHWAYS 10,386

NATIONAL DRINK *raki*

WHEN TO GO

Turkey's high tourist season is concentrated in the summer months (especially in July and August), when major cities and coastal resorts are infiltrated by hordes of boisterous backpackers. By contrast, in the late spring and early fall temperatures are far milder, many regions of the country are quieter, and prices in the resort areas may be at least 10% lower; unfortunately, a few facilities and sights may also be closed in the off-season. During Ramazan, the Islamic holy month, travel may be trickier for non-Muslims, since public eating, drinking, and smoking are generally taboo during daylight hours. For a temperature chart, see **Climate**, p. 39. For details on all the religious holidays and festivals in Turkey, see **Festivals**, p. 37.

THINGS TO DO

The sheer diversity of travel options in Turkey makes it attractive to visitors with a wide range of interests. Outdoor enthusiasts, beach bums, gourmets, history buffs, and urban clubhoppers alike will leave Turkey with warm memories of its incomparable local hospitality, deep sense of tradition, and spectacular landscapes. For more specific regional attractions than the ones listed below, see the **Highlights of the Region** section at the beginning of each chapter.

URBAN LEGENDS

As both the cradle and the crossroads of civilization, Turkey's cities are bursting at the seams with history, modernity, and humanity. **İstanbul** (p. 75) lays claim to its position as historic head of the mammoth Ottoman Empire, while today it's the country's cosmopolitan champion and ultimate tourist destination. **Ankara** (p. 352), Turkey's sophisticated capital, embraces its leadership in a combination of diplomacy, cultural events, and unbeatable museums. Beach cities **Bodrum** (p. 217) and **Antalya** (p. 282) lure thousands with their relaxed daytime atmospheres and raging nightlife. A bit farther off the beaten path, **Trabzon** (p. 403), a major Black Sea port city, is an important commerce hub surrounded by lush highlands.

ON THE WATERFRONT

Bordered on three sides by sea, Turkey offers up every imaginable flavor of coastline. **Alagadi Beach** (p. 460), on Northern Cyprus, and **Patara** (p. 269) are two of the last preserves of the endangered loggerhead turtles. Munch on fried mussels in **Çengelköy** (p. 129), or try the catch of the day at **Sinop's seaside restaurants** (p. 388). Learn why it's called the "Turkish Riviera": by day, windsurf at **Altınkum Beach** (p. 209), chew on Turkish taffy-like ice cream in **Antalya** (p. 282), or bronze with the beautiful people at **İçmeler** (p. 249). By night, play it cool in a boater's bar in **Dalyan** (p. 256) or gyrate to bass-heavy beats in **Marmaris's open-air discos** (p. 243). Get set for a trans-national nautical booty call in **Bodrum** (p. 217), the "Bedroom of the Mediterranean."

EXCELLENT ADVENTURES

Turkey's otherworldly landscapes will make even the most peak-weary rambler's jaw drop. Hikers of all abilities can meet their match among the alien rock clusters of **Cappadocia** (p. 311), the **yaylas** (alpine plateaus of northern Turkey; p. 397), or the serene waterfalls of **Butterfly Valley** (p. 268). For a more in-depth experience, join a trek through Turkey's stunning **Kaçkar Mountains** (p. 419). Adrenaline junkies can reach new highs river rafting in the **Çoruh Valley** (p. 418), parasailing over the Mediterranean in **İçmeler** (p. 249), gawking at **Kirkpinar grease wrestlers** (p. 143), skiing on a budget at **Mt. Uludağ** (p. 159), or witnessing bloodless bullfights in **Artvin** (p. 416). From Mediterranean pine groves to Black Sea villages, *Let's Go* gives you the low-down on the best places to pitch a tent and commune with the great outdoors.

BLAST FROM THE PAST

Life in ruins? Come to Turkey! Ancient foreign conquests pay off for history buffs today, as Turkey boasts the world's most outstanding collection of Greek ruins. Some, like **Ephesus** (p. 193) and **Troy** (p. 164), are well-placed on the tourist stampede (and for a good reason—don't miss them). At emptier **Miletus** (p. 208) and **Aphrodisias** (p. 213), you'll have some of antiquity's best temples and theaters to yourself. A visit to the **Çatalhöyük** (p. 343), the world's oldest settlement, or the Hittite capital of **Hattuşaş** (p. 367) puts the Greeks' leftovers to shame. Beam ahead a few years to the incomparable Ottoman mosques in **Bursa** (p. 152), **Edirne** (p. 138), and **İstanbul** (p. 75), all former Ottoman capitals. Gawk shamelessly at Edirne's **Selimiye Camii** (p. 142) and İstanbul's **Süleymaniye Camii** (p. 114), built by master of the universe architect Sinan.

RUNNING WITH THE PACK

Backpackers have taken over İstanbul's most historic neighborhood, **Sultanahmet** (p. 101). Hip international types trade war stories in the shade of Aya Sofia before moving on down the coast. The beaten track leads to **Kuşadası** (p. 202), with a detour to the Greek island of **Samos** (p. 207); **Bodrum's discos** (p. 223), with a jaunt to Greek **Kos** (p. 236); **Ölüdeniz's serene shores** (p. 266); **Fethiye's Mediterranean boat trips** (p. 263); and **Olimpos's treehouses and mysterious mountaintop flame** (p. 279). From the coast, backpackers head inland to the surreal landscapes of **Cappadocia** (p. 311), where they congregate in bars carved out of the soft tufa rock and **belly dance** with the pros at **Göreme's infamous "Turkish Nights"** (p. 320).

YOUR BAD SELF

While true "off the beaten path" probably doesn't exist, there are plenty of less-touristed options to explore. In İstanbul, avoid the Sultanahmet backpacker bars and take the ferry to **Kadıköy** (p. 127), a thoroughly Turkish hotspot. Hone your *tavla* (backgammon) skills in cafes overlooking the Black Sea. Pamper yourself with a *kese* (exfoliation) and massage at a *hamam* (Turkish bath; p. 131). Cheer for the home *futbol* team with thousands of **Turkish soccer *fanatiks*** (p. 132). Head out to Turkey's wild, wild East to explore the ancient Armenian capital of **Ani** (p. 430) and to roam around a ruined **Kurdish palace** in full view of **Mt. Ararat** (p. 431). Ferry yourself to the practically undiscovered beaches and ruins of **Northern Cyprus** (p. 451). And, to make it all go a little smoother, brush up on your Türkçe with the help of our **phrasebook and glossary** (p. 476). Even the most heinously pronounced *teşekkür ederim* is appreciated.

▨ LET'S GO PICKS

BEST WONDERS OF THE ANCIENT WORLD: Turkey boasts a whopping two of the seven: the once-colossal **Temple of Artemis** near Selçuk (p. 200) and the ruins of the **Mausoleum of Halicarnassus** in Bodrum (p. 221).

BEST PLACES TO DEFY GRAVITY: Revel in an unforgettable **hot-air balloon** ride over Cappadocia's surreal landscape (p. 314). Commune with the clouds and an occasional bird on the silent summit of Bursa's **Mt. Uludağ** (p. 159).

BEST WAY TO CLEAR YOUR SINUSES: Indulge in regional specialty *Adana Kebap* (p. 302), a spicy strip of soft meat served with tomatoes, peppers, and bread.

BEST EVENT FOR GETTING DIRTY: Artvin's annual **Kafkasör Wrestling Festival** (p. 417) is a testosterone-heavy mix of bulls, men, sweat, saliva and olive oil.

BEST PLACE FOR CLEANING UP: The **Termal Hot Springs** near Yalova (p. 160) have cleaned grime off Roman conquerors and Ottoman sultans—why not you?

BEST SITE TO COMMUNE WITH YOUR INNER SHEPHERD: On the slopes of Erciyes Dağı (p. 336), join scores of shepherds who pitch their tents on the hillsides and graze their sheep during the summer.

BEST FESTIVALS IN ALL TARNATION: Hang with the *VosVoscus* at the **Volkswagen Beetle Festival** in Ordu (p. 398). Feeling carsick? Try Manisa's **Sugar and Gum Festival** (p. 187), where boiled gum is hurled from minarets to heal hopeful crowds. You'll find leather pants and oil aplenty at the annual **Kirkpinar Grease Wrestling Festival** (p. 143) in Edirne. Not to be outdone, Selçuk hosts its very own **Camel Wrestling Festival** (p. 197).

BEST WAY TO DRINK FOR FREE: Cappadocia's famous wineries in Gorëme (p. 314) and Ürgüp (p. 320) allow you to "sample" new and vintage wines.

BEST NATURAL HISTORY: Scuba dive at the **site of WWI battles** on the Gallipoli Peninsula and search for real bullets and shells (p. 147).

BEST SPOTS FOR 40 WINKS: Snooze amid clouds of nocturnal butterflies in **Butterfly Valley** (p. 268). Relive your Peter Pan fantasies in **Olimpos's treehouses** (p. 280). Cuddle (so to speak) with endangered loggerhead turtles under the stars at North Cyprus's **Alagadi Beach** (p. 460). Dream of days past in a **Cappadocian cave** (p. 316) or a 16th-century Edirne *kervanseray* (p. 140).

DISCOVER

SUGGESTED ITINERARIES

BEST OF TURKEY

Göreme (see p. 314) and Ürgüp (see p. 320) end your Turkish visit with the grand finale that is Cappadocia: geological wonder of underground cities, cave churches, and fairy chimneys.

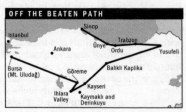

OFF THE BEATEN PATH

THE BEST OF TURKEY (3 WEEKS)

Begin in **İstanbul** (see p. 75), the traditional gateway to Turkey. Bargain for baubles at the Grand Bazaar (see. p. 110), marvel at luxurious Ottoman palaces, and stand awed in Aya Sofia (see p. 101). For evening sweets, tea, and backgammon, head to one of İstanbul's hippest waterfront cafes. Need a break from the city? The Bosphorus ferry lets you kick back and admire the behemoth burg from a distance, stopping for fresh fish sandwiches and fried mussels along the way. **Edirne** (see p. 138), the majestic former Ottoman capital, is now famous for tea gardens and breathtaking architecture, including the finest mosque in all of Turkey. Then step off the beaten track and enjoy the serene beaches and small-town atmosphere of **Bozcaada** (see p. 167), a useful Aegean island that has been producing wine since antiquity. Craving something older than aged wine? The sparkling Aegean Coast houses the sun-bleached ruins of some of the ancient world's most powerful cities, **Bergama** (see p. 174), **Foça** (p. 179), and the eternally-popular **Ephesus** (see p. 193). **Kuşadası** (see p. 202) is barhopping at its best, but it's above all **Bodrum** (see p. 217) that knows how to get down, every night, all night. As a daytrip from **Fethiye** (p. 260), visit the waterfalls and wings at the nearby Butterfly Valley. For a change of pace from the roaring Mediterranean, Turkey's holiest city, **Konya** (see p. 337) is home of the whirling dervishes. In

OFF THE BEATEN PATH: OUTDOOR ADVENTURES (2 WEEKS)

Start with a laid-back trip up Bursa's Mt. Uludağ. Move further inland to take in the surreal landscapes of **Cappadocia** (see p. 311) as you hike amid the other-worldly fairy chimneys of the **Rose Valley** (see p. 318), the underground cities (see p. 319) of **Kaymaklı** and **Derinkuyu,** and the breathtaking beauty of the church-dotted **Ihlara Valley** (see p. 327). Marvel at the spectacular frescoes in **Göreme**'s Byzantine cave churches (see p. 314). After a hike up **Erciyes Dağı** (p. 336), the tallest mountain in central Turkey, soothe yourself in the hot springs of **Balıklı Kaplıca** (p. 376), where friendly flesh-eating fish bring new meaning to exfoliation. Feeling better? Go for another adrenaline rush of whitewater rafting along the rivers of the Çoruh Valley, near **Yusufeli** (see p. 417) and trek through the pristine **Kaçkar mountains** (see p. 419). Then head back west to **Trabzon** (p. 403), a thriving Black Sea port town. Perched on a cliff outside of this city, the awe-inspiring **Sumela Monastery** (p. 409) may cause monk-envy. Give up those dreams of celibacy and follow the Black Sea coast to the pristine **Çambaşı Yayla** (highland plateau) outside of **Ordu** (see p. 397), and further to **Ünye** (see p. 396), where you can pamper yourself with a divine bath and massage at the hamam (Turkish bath) that was once a Byzantine church. End your adventure with a campout on the beaches of stunning **Sinop** (see p. 388) before catching a ferry to **İstanbul.**

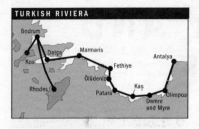

TURKISH RIVIERA

THE TURKISH RIVIERA (12 DAYS) A wonder of the party world, **Bodrum** (see p. 217) is the place to pursue hard-core hedonism, whether on a sun-soaked beach or in an open-air dance club. Recover aboard a relaxing Blue Journey boat ride to one of the many nearby Turkish islands and beaches (see p. 224). Or hop a continent via a short ferry to the Greek isles of **Kos** and **Rhodes.** Once back on shore, bronze your bod on the secluded beaches of **Datça,** a quiet and charming little town away from it all (see p. 251). Get vertical long enough to reach the backpackers' gathering ground of **Fethiye** (see p.260), which works well as a base for daytrips further along the Mediterranean coast to **Ölüdeniz** (see p. 266) and the serene **Butterfly Valley** (p. 268). For even more natural wildlife, head to the beaches of **Patara,** where endangered loggerhead turtles lay their eggs (p. 269). Visit **Demre**'s basilica of St. Nicholas (see p. 279) and climb among the Lycean rock tombs of **Myra** (see p. 278) before being drawn to the eternal flame of **Olimpos** (see p. 280). After a night in a treehouse, finish off with a stay in **Antalya,** capital of the Turkish Riviera (see p. 282).

352), which hosts Turkey's premier Museum of Anatolian Civilizations (p. 363). Hoof it to the ancient Hittite capital Hattuşaş (see p. 368), near **Sungurlu** (see p. 370), before moving on to the Aegean coast and the splendid ruins of some of the most important of Greco-Roman cities. Make like Achilles and head for **Troy** (see p. 164), city of Iliad fame. Though the Trojan remains are quite literally ruins, **Assos** (see p. 169) and **Bergama** (see p. 174), further down the coast, remain stunning even today. **Ephesus** (see p. 193) is a historical highlight; amble down the colonnaded Arcadiane (see p. 195), with its 2-storied library and ancient brothel. Close to Ephesus, **Priene** (see p. 207) rests perched on a high plateau. The sanctuary at **Didyma** (transit through **Söke**) lies nearby (see p. 208). After all that scrambling over marble and rock, move inland and rest your tired limbs at the **Pamukkale** hot springs (see p. 209), site of Hierapolis and a good base for a visit to the stunning but little-known ruins at **Aphrodisias** (see p. 213). Back on the coast, see the ruins of ancient **Termessos** (see p. 288) scattered among pine trees above **Antalya** (see p. 282), the sun-soaked capital of the Mediterranean coast. Moving east, test the acoustics at **Aspendos** (see p. 287), one of the best-preserved Roman theaters in the world, and finish your tour near Syria. **Antakya** (see p. 306), né **Antioch,** remains barely discovered by tourists despite its rich holding of perhaps the world's finest collection of Roman mosaics.

ANCIENT ASIA MINOR

Istanbul
Troy
Assos (Bahramkale)
Bergama (Pergamon)
Ankara
Sungurlu
Efes (Ephesus)
Priene
Söke
Pamukkale
Didyma
Aphrodisias
Aspendos
Antakya (Hatay)

ANCIENT ASIA MINOR (2 WEEKS)
Life in ruins? Come to Turkey! Begin your tour of ancient Asia Minor with the most modern of Turkey's cities, **Ankara** (see p.

HISTORY AND CULTURE

HISTORY

Since the first human settlements in Anatolia, Turkey has hosted the greatest civilizations, each waxing with exuberance and then fading with despair. A journey through Turkey is a chance to retrace steps of armies, to relive the magnificence of great courts, and to pause for a moment where tragedy has unfolded. Timeless religious, ethnic, and cultural tensions live on here, as they have in every Asia Minor empire before it. The pride and confident nationalism of Turkey today cost the blood and torture of thousands. Despite being the custodian of Hellenic and Roman heritage as well as of the roots of Christianity, it has forever represented foreign intrigue for Europe. Neither a comfortable neighbor nor a suppressible foe, it is the only regional power that walks unhumbled in the Arab world yet demands accord from the west.

ANCIENT ASIA MINOR

FROM HITTITES TO HELLENES

The Neolithic Revolution in 7000 BC ushered in settled life, cultivation, and non-cave habitation. Though the oldest evidence of settlements in Turkey is at **Hacilar,** 25km southeast of Burdur, the most impressive is **Çatalhöyük** (p. 343) on the Konya Plain, which traded razor sharp obsidian blades in the pre-metalworking era. **Çayönü,** near present-day Elazig, began smelting copper tools, a trade that involved Mesopotamia and the northern Aegean and underwrote the Early Bronze Age (3200-2000 BC) wealth of the Asia Minor cities of **Troy** and **Alacahöyük.**

By the Middle Bronze Age (2000 BC), Anatolia's **Hatti** people were trading with the Assyrians to the south, who delivered clothing and textiles in exchange for much needed gold, silver, and iron. More importantly, the Assyrian traders introduced the first written records here; their cuneiform tablets were left behind in the Hatti capital of **Kanesh,** now Kultepe.

2nd millennium BC
The Hittite Empire is established in Central Anatolia.

Eventually the Hatti merged with the iron-forging **Hittites,** who migrated south from the Caucuses, adopting Hatti language and religion. The Hittites' devotion to warfare would dominate central Anatolia for 600 years. From their capital Hattuşaş (modern **Boğazkale,** see p. 366), they waged a series of campaigns against their Mesopotamian and Egyptian neighbors. In 1286 BC at Kadesh, the Hittites defeated Egyptian pharaoh Ramses II and acquired Syria. The description of this battle and the subsequent international treaty are regarded as firsts in recorded history. Later, Tutankhamun's widow would petition unsuccessfully for a royal Hittite husband. The Hittites are remembered for their revolutionary fortifications, humane legal code, and ground plans with neither columns nor capitals.

1286 BC
Hittites defeat Ramses II and acquire Syria.

Despite Hittite dominance in central Anatolia, other groups established themselves in the area of present-day Turkey. Made famous by Homer and Virgil, the **Trojans** built their city at the mouth of the Dardanelles. Archaeological excavations at the site suggest that the war recounted in the *Iliad* occurred around 1250 BC. Scholars believe that the fall of Troy (see p. 164) coincides with the Doric invasions, the mass migration of Sea Peoples across the Aegean, and the end of the Bronze Age. Greek Mycenae, Cyprus, northern Mesopotamia, and Hittite rule of Anatolia ended by 1190 BC, heralding three archaeologically empty centuries until the unification of Urartu around Lake Van in 875 BC. With their capital at Tušpa (modern Van, see p. 434), the Urartu demonstrated their engineering skill in the construction of fortresses and canals. However, the Urartu were ultimately defeated by the Medes in 580 BC.

Among the invading "Sea peoples," the **Phrygians** were related to the Greeks and built their capital at **Gordion** (see p. 366). In the 8th century BC, King Midas, the man with the golden touch, ruled Phrygia at its most prosperous period. At the same time, **Ionia,** the central western coast of Anatolia, was a center of trade, science, and culture. Escaping the Doric invasion, Mycenaean Greeks emigrated here in 1100 BC and flourished in cities like Miletus until subjugated by Croesus of Lydia in 546 BC. From 1000 BC, Hellenic city-states extended from Spain to the Crimea and included the influential cultural centers of Smyrna, Miletus, and Ephesus. It was in Smyna (modern İzmir, p. 182) that **Homer** wrote the *Iliad* and the *Odyssey* in the Ionian dialect. Miletus, whose original settlers were the Minoans of Crete, became an early center of Greek philosophy and pre-Socratic thought (see p. 208). In the realm of architecture, the enduring Ionic style includes the colossal Temple of Artemis, one of the Seven Wonders of the Ancient World (see Ephesus, p. 193). The **Lydians** eventually defeated Miletus and the Ionians, setting up their capital in Sardis. They were a Hittite-related people, famous for huge royal tombs and the invention of dice and coined money. Their final monarch, the fabulously wealthy Croesus was routed by Persian king Cyrus in Cappadocia in 547 BC, ending the 140-year-old Lydian empire.

In the absence of any political cohesion between the Greek city-states, Cyrus II rapidly extended the Achaemenid Empire of Persia along the coast of Asia Minor and made forays into Greece. Cyrus replaced the city-states with a structure of subordinate satrapies (administrative regions) ruled by wealth-hoarding tyrants. Persian culture rarely spread beyond its courts, and apart from the Mausoleum of Halicarnassus (see p. 221) there is little to see from this period today. Greek dislike of Persian rule precipitated the fateful Ionian Revolt of 499 BC. Though the ring-leading city-state Miletus was ruthlessly crushed, the resistance kindled anti-Persian sentiment in Ionia (see p. 208) sustained until Alexander's arrival a century later.

After failed attempts to conquer mainland Greece, Cyrus's successors Darius I and Xerxes temporarily lost control over the Greek cities of Asia Minor. Though it briefly regained them, the Persian Empire was conquered by Alexander the Great in 333 BC, with his routing of Darius III's huge army in the Gulf of İskenderun. It was symbolic of his campaign that Alexander chose to slice rather than untie the mythical Gordion knot, thereby becoming the master of Asia (see Gordion, p. 366). Alexander's conquests disseminated Greek language and traditions across Asia Minor, from Egypt to the Indian Ocean. Yet

1250 BC
Troy falls.

1190 BC
Hittite dominance in Central Anatolia comes to an end.

9th century BC
The Urartu Kingdom is established in the Lake Van region.

8th century BC
Phrygians invade Anatolia and establish their capital at Gordion.

7th century BC
Lydians establish their capital at Sardis in Western Anatolia.

6th century BC
Cyrus II begins expanding the Persian Empire in Asia Minor.

499 BC
Ionian cities are crushed in the unsuccessful Ionian Revolts

333 BC
Alexander the Great kicks butt, bringing down Darius I and Xerxes.

323 BC
Alexander the
Great kicks the
bucket.

with no obvious successor, Alexander's kingdom died with
him. On his deathbed in 323 BC, his words, "The kingdom shall
go to the strongest," precipitated a carve-up by his generals. To
Ptolemy went Egypt and its capital at Alexandria, Lysimachus
took Thrace, and Seleucus established control over Syria and
much of Asia Minor from Antioch (modern Antakya, see p.
306). The **Attalids** of Pergamon (modern Bergama, see p. 174)
won their independence from the Seleucid kingdom 20 years
later. Under the Attalids, Pergamon evolved into a cultural center marked by the impressive Altar of Zeus and its library that
rivaled Alexandria's, until Marc Antony seized its contents as a
wedding present for Cleopatra. The Hellenistic Era continued
until the arrival of the Romans.

PAX ROMANA

2nd century BC
Romans establish
dominance in
Asia Minor.

63 BC
Pontus falls to
Pompey.

20 BC to 180 AD
The Pax Romana
ushers in peace.

From Rome's defeat of the Greeks at Pydna in 168 BC, it was
clear a new era was nigh. Most feared Rome's military prowess;
Attalus III bequeathed his Pergamon to Rome, rather than wage
a war he could not win. Only King Mithradates of Pontus, now
modern Amasya (see p. 393), and nearby Tigranes the Great of
Armenia, offered significant resistance. Pontus fell in 63 BC to
the Roman general Pompey, while Armenia swayed between
allegiance to Rome and Parthia to the east.

Despite Rome's military and administrative success, its 400-
year empire actually perpetuated Greek art and philosophy.
Pax Romana was a time of relative peace, in which local governments enjoyed autonomy so long as they kept the Romans
happy, paid their taxes, and let them play soldier. Such tranquility allowed Asia Minor to amass great wealth, finance construction, and revitalize many Aegean trading centers. Such was the
fertile soil that allowed the roots of Christianity to take hold.

CHRISTIANITY AND THE BYZANTINE EMPIRE

1st century AD
St. Paul journeys
through Asia
minor, spreading
Christianity.

4th century AD
The Roman Empire
is divided up. Con-
stantine becomes
the first Christian
ruler in Asia Minor.
Foundation of the
Greek-speaking
Byzantine Empire.

476 AD
Goths sack Rome.

In 36 AD, the apostle St. Paul traveled through Asia Minor, sowing the seeds of the Christian faith and establishing the seven
Churches of Revelation. From Antioch to Cappadocia and then
Greece, he converted Gentiles while raising the ire of Jews and
pagan silversmiths. Persecution only lessened in 251, with the
third century, following the conversions of the first king, Abgar
of Edessa (now **Şanlıurfa**, p. 444), and of Gregory the Illuminator
in Armenia in 310. Destabilized by economic tumult and invasions from the north, Diocletian's (284-305) structure of four caesars collapsed Rome into civil war. Out of the scramble,
Constantine emerged in 324 as the sole ruler and became Rome's
first Christian Emperor, founding his capital exactly where Byzantium had stood. Constantine's successors, however, could not
preserve the unity of the empire. In 395 Theodosius partitioned
the empire into Hellenistic east and Latin west. Rome was sacked
by the Goths just fifteen years later, and collapsed in 476 AD.

Things were different in the east, where the Byzantine
Empire dominated for the next 600 years. Constantinople
remained secure behind its fortifications built by Theodosius II,
until the Fourth Crusade in 1204. The Theodosian Walls can
still be seen in modern İstanbul (see **Yedikule,** p. 120). Mass conversion to Christianity created an imperial ideology of univer-

salism and a proliferation of evangelical missions and monasteries. The emperor, the Church, taxation, and the Greek language bound together a cosmopolitan Byzantine culture of Greeks, Syriacs, Egyptian Copts, Armenians, and Slavs.

Between the 4th and 7th centuries, **Seven Ecumenical Councils** established the structure and clarified the doctrine of the Church. The **Council of Nicaea** in 325 (see **İznik,** p. 161) and the Council of Constantinople in 381 appointed the emperor as the head of both Church and State, exempted the clergy from taxation, and organized the Church into five **patriarchates** (diocese)—Rome, Constantinople, Alexandria, Antioch, and Jerusalem. Each had its own patriarch (pope) who performed religious duties and functioned as a sort of local governor.

4th-7th centuries
Seven Ecumenical Councils establish church infrastructure.

These early years of the Church were filled with doctrinal debate, heresy, and name-calling. Nestorius, patriarch of Constantinople, suggested that Mary was the mother of Jesus and not the mother of God. **Arians** believed that rather than consubstantial with God, Jesus was created merely for the purposes of reincarnation. The Alexandrian patriarch St. Cyril emphasized the single divine nature of Christ **(Monophysitism)**—straying from the accepted belief that Christ was both divine and human. These debates prompted the **Nicene Creed,** a summation of Church doctrine, that emphasized a belief in the Trinity; specifically, that Jesus is simultaneously human and divine.

This religious dispute caused immense turmoil between the imperial seat in Constantinople and the empire's Monophysite southern and eastern territories. Indeed, it was the persecuted Monophysite provinces of Egypt and Syria that first welcomed the tolerance of Islam during the Middle Byzantine period (610-1081 AD). Heraclius defeated the Persians only to lose Palestine, Syria, and Egypt to the Arabs. These defeats prompted **Iconoclasm;** a Byzantine belief that their own icons were idolatrous and that defeat was divine punishment. For sixty years starting in 726, all holy images were demolished by imperial order. To the relief of aesthetes, this order was rescinded in 787. Unfortunately, it was too little too late; the Byzantine treasures were gone forever, and the empire's three-century decline had begun. Civil wars, as well as those with Slav and Arab neighbors, slowly weakened the empire. At the same time, the patriarchates and Rome became increasingly estranged. This culminated in the **schism,** the establishment of separate Greek Orthodox and Roman Catholic Churches in 1054.

1054
Schism confirms separation of Roman Catholic and Greek Orthodox churches.

THE GREAT SELÇUK SULTANATE

THE ARRIVAL OF THE TURKS

In the early 11th century, a new group added their names to the Byzantine guest register. The **Selçuks'** ancestors are first recorded on 7th-century Mongolian funerary inscriptions (stelae), which testify to a Goturk empire that stretched across the Central Asian steppes. Subsequently, the Goturk split into the Mongols, the Kirgiz, and the Oguz confederacy of Turks in the west (the Turkmen). The Selçuks belonged to one of these 24 original Oğuz clans that migrated westward in the 9th century.

11th century
The Selçuks arrive in Anatolia.

Based on the Aral Sea, several clans of the Oğuz under the leadership of their chief, **Selçuk,** broke away from the confederacy and settled near the lower reaches of the Syr Darya River in Central Asia, where they were gradually converted to Sunni Islam. Described by Armenian historians of the day as "long haired Turkmen armed with bow and lance on horses which flew like the wind," they had, by the middle of the 11th century, amassed an empire stretching from Afghanistan to the borders of Fatimid Egypt. Pushing up against the eastern frontier of the Byzantine Empire, they were poised to win Anatolia for Islam.

Under the leadership of Selçuk's grandson, the Selçuk Turks crossed into today's Iran, successfully invading Persian lands. The **Abbasid Caliphate** in Baghdad, protector of the **Sunni** faithful, was at that time in a severely weakened state—a virtual puppet of the **Shi'ite** Buyid rulers in Iraq. At the behest of the embattled Caliph, **Tughril-Beg** (1038-1063), Selçuk's grandson, defeated the Buyids in 1055. In gratitude, the Abbasid Caliph vested him with the **Sultanate** ("government": "sultan" literally means "power"). It was the Sultan's duty to defend the *umma* (the Muslim community), eliminate schism and heresy, and to carry on the *jihad* (struggle) against the nations who rejected God and his prophet Muhammed.

1055
Selçuks are granted the Sultanate.

While the Great Selçuk Sultans established a state in Persia (today's Iran), the crossing of the Oxus River opened the way for other unruly Turkmen tribes to threaten the borders of the Byzantine Empire. In 1071, Alp Arslan crushed the Byzantine army near Van at the **Battle of Manzikert,** capturing the Christian Emperor and leaving Byzantine's Anatolian frontier helplessly open to Turkmen whim. The defeat was so disastrous that it was thereafter referred to by Byzantines as "that dreadful day."

1071
The crushing Battle of Manzikert leaves Byzantine Empire's Anatolian frontier wicked vulnerable.

Meanwhile, back at the ranch, the Anatolian Selçuks became increasingly independent from the Persian Great Selçuk Sultanate. In 1075, Süleyman, son of Alp Arslan, captured Nicaea from the Byzantines and renamed his new capital İznik (see p. 161). Within a decade, his Sultanate of Rum had seceded—Anatolia was known to Selçuks as the land of the Romans.

1075
Süleyman captures Nicaea (İznik) and organizes the Sultanate of Rum.

WE'RE ON A MISSION FROM GOD

1097
First Crusade nabs İznik.

Though the Crusaders dealt the Selçuks a series of temporary setbacks, they ultimately succeeded only in destroying Christianity in Asia Minor. The **First Crusade** of French and Norman knights took İznik from the Turks in 1097, forcing them to reestablish their capital and Selçuk culture at **Konya** (see p. 337). Though the Crusaders had taken Antioch and Jerusalem by 1099, the Selçuks recovered it all by 1176. The **Second Crusade** in 1146 provoked the Turks to attack Byzantine Empire; the result was a second Manzikert, with Constantinople losing the Balkan states just as they had lost Armenia a century before. If the German Barbarossa's **Third Crusade** was only a minor worry for the Byzantine empire, the **Fourth** in 1204 eviscerated it. Conceived in Venice, the plan was to neutralize a trading rival in Constantinople before reclaiming Jerusalem from the infidels. Instead, the invaders desecrated the most magnificent city of their time and forgot about Jerusalem. The ruin of Constantinople has been described as among the greatest crimes in recorded history. The legacy was short, with Nicaean Greeks recapturing Constantinople and reestablishing the empire in

1146
The Second Crusade: Turks lose Balkan states in an attempt to conquer Constantinople.

1190
The Third Crusade: No biggie.

1204
The Fourth Crusade: Constantinople is destroyed.

1261. In all, the Crusaders left behind around 100 fortresses and took home Islamic medicine, philosophy, and science. This came at the expense of hardened Muslim attitudes and skepticism at home regarding God's will and Papal authority.

Taking advantage of a weakened Byzantine empire, Sultan **Kay-Khosrow I** (1192-1205) recaptured Konya in 1205 with the aid of the frontier Turkmen. The Sultanate of Rum was reunified and expanded vigorously to the west and to the north, absorbing the remnants of the Byzantine Empire. The conquest of the Mediterranean port of Antalya in 1207 marked a significant political and economic moment in the evolution of the Sultanate—the Selçuks were no longer confined to the interior of the Anatolian plateau, and they were ready to sprawl.

1207
Selçuks capture Antalya, setting the stage for further conquests.

THE ROARING 13TH CENTURY

By its heyday in the 13th century, the Sultanate of Rum had developed into one of the most important Islamic states of its time. The Sultanate brought stability to its heterogeneous, war-torn population of Greeks, Armenians, Syrians, and Persians through religious and racial tolerance. Unlike prior outside colonizers, this was the first empire to unify and settle in Anatolia.

Under the Selçuks, trade, agriculture, and the arts thrived. The Crusades opened the market for Eastern products in Europe, and the sultans were eager to reap the benefits. Seizing control of the **Silk Route** and Byzantine ports, they built a vast infrastructure to accommodate passing caravans. Hundreds of inns (*kervansaray* or *han*) sprung up along the Anatolian highways, as did fortifications, bridges, and harbors, many of which can still be seen in Turkey today (see **Selçuk Architecture and Decorative Arts,** p. 22). Revenue was channeled into the building of theological seminaries (*medrese*), mosques, hospitals, asylums, and medical schools. The tremendous Karatay Medrese in Konya (see p. 342), the Çifte Minare Medrese in Erzurum (see p. 426), and the brilliant Gök Medrese in Tokat (see p. 372), stand as architectural testaments to the magnificence of Rum.

The Rum Selçuks were also prodigious patrons, supporting, in addition to architects, Islamic philosophers such as **Suhrawardi** and **Ibn al-Arabi,** and Turkish and Persian poets like **Yunuş Emre** and **Celeddin-İ-Rumi** (see **I Was Raw,** p. 341). They established insurance for the losses of tradesmen. Attracted by the cultural boom, many Islamic craftsmen, theologians, and Sufi dervishes migrated to the Selçuk realm, where they aided the spread of Islam in Anatolia. The Goturks mummified their dead in tents for six months before burial. This tradition gave way to the beautiful domed tombs (*türbe*) of central Anatolia.

Drawing upon ancient Iranian notions of centralized authority, the Sultanate was largely run by Persian-speaking bureaucrats, with Arabic the academic language and Turkish spoken day to day. Led by local chiefs (*beyerli*), Turkmen tribes made up the military and lived along the Byzantine border. Some served as vassals to their Selçuk lords, and were assembled when needed for expeditions against the Byzantines. By the end of the 13th century, these mercenary tribesmen had become increasingly independent, engaging with the Byzantines on their own initiative.

THE OTTOMAN EMPIRE

THE EARLY YEARS

The **Beylik Period,** which began after Selçuk centralized power collapsed in 1335, featured fragmented politics and competing fiefdoms (*beylik*). In the free-for-all land-grab that followed the disintegrating Sultanate of Rum, **Osman** claimed the northwest corner near Bursa in 1326 and expelled the Byzantines. Though the Selçuk empire was rapidly drawing to a close, it had laid the foundations for one of the greatest empires in the history of civilization: the *Osmanlı*, or Ottoman Empire.

1326
Osman's capture of Bursa expels Byzantines. Collapse of centralized power lays the foundation for the Ottoman Empire.

They established capitals first in Bursa (p. 152) and then Edirne (p. 138) in 1364, where mosques and elaborate tombs still testify to the early magnificence of the Ottoman state. After defeating the Crusaders in 1396, their expansion was temporarily halted by the meteoric rise of Tamerlane in 1402. The mid-13th century Mongol onslaught also threatened Selçuk sovereignty. Mongol leader **Bayju** took Erzurum in 1242 and plowed on to crush the Selçuks in 1243 and 1256. From this point until 1335, Mongol troops were permanently stationed in Anatolia, and the Selçuk sultans were mere figureheads. Following this period, the Ottomans relentlessly dismantled the Byzantine empire by encirclement.

Mehmet the Conqueror completed the empire with his conquest of Constantinople in 1453. First, he murdered all his brothers to eliminate rivals and then built his own castle on the Bosphorus overlooking the defiant city. His army outnumbered the Byzantine defenders by ten to one. When the 54-day siege ended, so did the Byzantine Empire. Mehmet converted the Aya Sofia basilica into a mosque and renamed the Ottoman's fourth capital, İstanbul.

1453
Mehmet the Conqueror takes Constantinople, renames it İstanbul, and crowns it the jewel of his growing empire.

The early territories of the Ottoman Empire included Greece, Cyprus, and the Balkans as far as Belgrade. Post-Mehmet, the Ottoman armies of **Selim I** (1512-1520) conquered Syria, Palestine, Egypt, and Arabia. This meant that in a single, tremendous military campaign, the Ottoman Sultan became the guardian of Islam's three holiest cities: Mecca, Medina, and Jerusalem.

1512
Sultan Selim I nabs present-day Levant, Egypt, and Arabia, including Islam's top three holy cities.

Non-Muslims in the empire were generally left to practice their religions freely. Many of the empire's minorities, including Greeks and Jews, were peacefully incorporated into Ottoman society, and most fared better under Muslim authority than they had under the crusading Franks and the Spanish Monarchs. Expansion was characterized by retaining defeated Christian princes as vassals in exchange for loyalty and the absorption of their military. Aside from the occasional ruthless suppression of rebellions, the early days of the Ottoman Empire brought relative peace and prosperity to most.

Mehmet II (1451-81) and his predecessor **Murat II** (1421-51) created the Janissaries (from *yeni çeri*, "new army"), the first standing army in Europe. Young Christian males from the Balkan region were conscripted under the *devşirme* system, converted to Islam, and educated. Many advanced to the highest ranks of the military and bureaucracy, including the great architect Sinan and many Grand Viziers (Prime Ministers).

The sheer size of the Ottoman Empire made central government impossible. Instead, the Porte (as the Ottoman government was known) retained only limited contact with satellite provinces through tax collection and military conscription. Such autonomy among the diverse Ottoman states would ultimately contribute to the decline of the empire.

HOW SÜLEYMAN THE MAGNIFICENT GOT HIS NAME

Süleyman inherited an Ottoman Empire, fresh from conquests in Egypt, Syria and the Arabian peninsula. As Sultan (1520-66), the land-hungry Süleyman doubled the empire's size again, securing borders from the Balkans to Iraq and south to the Arabian Peninsula and Africa. He even gained Hungary for the Ottomans before being halted at the gates of Vienna in 1529. "Magnificent" referred both to his military prowess and to his lavish lifestyle: Süleyman's administrative, artistic, literary, and architectural legacies were equally sensational. As a legislator, he earned the title of **Kanuni** (the Lawgiver), and his patronage of Mimar Sinan, the great Ottoman architect, resulted in some of the most renowned of Ottoman monuments (see **Ottoman Architecture**, p. 23) including 41 mosques in Istanbul alone.

1520-1566
Süleyman the Magnificent doubles the empire's size, adds some European flavor, and builds like crazy.

TROUBLES AT HOME, TROUBLES ABROAD

Süleyman's most influential wife, **Roxelana,** convinced the Sultan to name her less-than-magnificent offspring as his successor. **Selim the Sot** turned virtually all matters of state over to the Grand Vizier. After his death (drunk, he drowned in his tub in 1574), the palace was rife with infighting. This period has been dubbed the **"rule of the women,"** as mothers of potential sultans vied for power by knocking off rival sons. Such tiffs in İstanbul only worsened the government's already vulnerable condition.

1566-1574
Süleyman's loser son Selim the Sot marks the beginning of the end.

The sultanates were increasingly transient and inexperienced. Most were crowned without any knowledge of or background in administration, having whiled away years in the harem. With an end to fratricide in 1609, sultans safeguarded their sovereignty by encaging rather than killing their male relatives. At times, the women of the harem and the *vezirs* (officials) stepped in to fill the vacuum left by incompetent sultans. Janissaries gained power and made their privileges hereditary, attacking any threats to their status with generalized terror and hooliganism. The word of the sultan became law; he commanded the army, appointed statespersons, and supervised the cabinet ministers *(Divan)*. All land was owned by the state, which collected revenue and reclaimed land that was ineffectively farmed for three consecutive years. Enderun was the education system for statespersons, while *medreses* diversified from religious studies to include language, philosophy, and the sciences. Students lived in cells, studied a fixed set of books rather than for a fixed period of time.

On the economic front, the British and Dutch had ditched Middle East trade routes in favor of new Asian ones. Moreover, the discovery of precious metals in the Americas caused hideous inflation in the Ottoman provinces. The Porte (no Alan Greenspan) responded by debasing the currency, causing serious long-term consequences for an exploding population already living in poverty.

The first major blow to the empire's international reputation came with the **Battle of Lepanto** in 1571. Austria's Don Juan led a Holy League that sank 200 of the 245 Turkish ships in an unprecedented naval demolition derby. Afterwards, the pace of Ottoman expansion slowed (Tunis 1574, Azerbaijan 1576, Morocco 1578, and Crete in 1669) and then reversed, with defeat at St. Gotthard (1664) followed by repulsion from Vienna

1571
At the Battle of Lepanto, the Ottomans lose over 80% of their naval fleet and a lot of credibility.

by a Polish-led European coalition in 1863. (According to lore, two mainstays of continental cuisine emerged from the Ottoman siege of Vienna: coffee, which the retreating troops left by the sackful, and croissants, invented by Viennese bakers in the shape of the Turkish standard.) After this series of humiliating Ottoman defeats, the 1699 **Treaty of Karlowitz** surrendered much of their European territories. Catherine the Great sought to liberate fellow-Orthodox nation Greece in 1770. Nearly a century of losses to Russia followed, ceasing only with western intervention in the 1856 Crimean War.

While the Ottoman borders crumbled, the sultans ran down the empire like the proverbial cash cow. "Let us laugh, let us play, let us enjoy the delights of the world to the full," wrote one court poet, summing up the mentality of the times. Sultan Ahmet III (1703-30) reigned over the Tulip Period, a brief aesthetic revival of the arts. Back in the real world, Ottoman provinces continued to gain increasing autonomy as power slipped through İstanbul's fingers.

THE 19TH CENTURY: REFORM AND REACTION

Well-intentioned **Selim III** tried to stem the tide when he became sultan in 1789. His program, called **Nizam-i-Cedid,** or the "New Order," concentrated on Westernizing the army. The Janissary corps, threatened by these new developments, deposed the sultan in 1807 and murdered him for good measure. By 1812, the picture for the Janissaries was grim. All territory north of the Black Sea was lost, Serbia and Greece had rebelled, and Egypt was becoming increasingly independent. Following their defeats of the Ottomans, Russia and Austria were authorized by treaty to intervene on behalf of non-Muslim Ottoman subjects.

Mahmut II succeeded Selim III with great caution. He spent 20 years waging disastrous wars abroad, meanwhile quietly appointing his followers to positions of domestic power. With strong backing assembled by 1826, Mahmut II eliminated the havoc-wreaking Janissaries and their supporters by burning them alive in their barracks (the "Auspicious Event"). Next, he established a secular bureaucracy to effectively replace the traditional Islamic leadership **(ulema).**

Mahmut II had set the stage for the **Tanzimat** (reorganization). Begun in 1839 by sultans **Abdülmecid I** and **Abdülaziz,** it revamped the army, freed education and media, reduced tax corruption, and changed the administration of the provinces.

THE PLOT THICKENS

During the 19th century, the Ottoman Empire was dubbed "the sick man of Europe." Most powers preferred it remain a buffer state, rather than invade and provoke hostility among other Western powers. Russia seized as much as it could (Greece, Serbia, Wallacia, Georgia, and Danube ports) before cold stares from the West precipitated a begrudging treaty in 1833. When Egypt seceded in 1838, the Ottomans were too weak to take it back. Thankfully, England fought the Crimean War (1853-56) on the Ottomans' behalf, restoring some gloss at the price of civil unrest and slowed domestic reform.

In addition to military support, European banks and financiers lent the Porte colossal sums of money for war, reforms,

1699
The Treaty of Karlowitz wrenches half the European territories from Ottoman control.

1789
Sultan Selim III implements a "New Order" program to save face and territory; he is rewarded by being deposed and murdered.

1826
Euphemistic "Auspicious Event" eliminates the power-hungry Jannisary corps.

1839
Tanzimat (reorganization) Period: reform is accelerated to westernize defense and clean up corruption.

and new palaces (see **Dolmabahçe Palace**, p. 123 and **Beylerbeyi Palace**, p. 129). Inevitably, the Ottoman government spiraled further and further into debt. In 1875, it declared bankruptcy and lost financial authority to the European-controlled Ottoman Public Debt Administration. Seizing the moment, virtually every independence-minded province sought to jump the sinking ship, including the Greeks, Serbs, Bulgarians, Armenians, Bosnians, Lebanese, Egyptian, and Cretans.

This crisis inspired a group of bourgeois intellectuals to form a group known as the **Young Ottomans (Yeni Osmanlılar)**. One of the most prominent members was **Namık Kemal** (see **Literature**, p. 24), a poet and young functionary convinced that the 19th century "reforms" were both a poor imitation of Europe and an insult to Turkish tradition. The Young Ottomans hoped to save what was left of the empire, and drafted a constitution for Sultan **Abdülhamid II** (1876-1909), only to have him suspend it two years later and assume autocratic rule. Abdülhamid reformed the financial system, shrewdly developed pan-Turkik and Islamic alliances, and courted numerous European powers.

Mounting dissatisfaction and the sultan's forced recall of parliament was too little too late. Though the Young Turk Revolution of 1908 was put down, Mustafa Kemal (Atatürk) and Sevket Paşa's 1909 march on İstanbul earned a different reception. Parliamentary deputies met them outside İstanbul and agreed to depose the sultan. Though a new one was appointed, the Young Turks would now have their moment in the sun.

YOUNG TURKS AND WORLD WAR I

After a few years of infighting, the CUP managed to establish a stable government in 1913, led by powerhouse trio **Talat Paşa, Ahmed Cemal Paşa**, and **Enver Paşa**. Domestically, their efforts were aimed at amending past failed reforms. This meant a focus upon legal secularization, industrialization, standardization of education, and centralization of power.

These reforms were unable to stem further military humiliation, however. Albanian uprisings and the Italian invasion of Ottoman North Africa were followed by alliances among the Balkan states of Serbia, Montenegro, Bulgaria, and Greece that lead to the bloody Balkan Wars (1912-13). Just as they ended, an Ottoman Empire minus all of its European territories was confronted with World War I. Seeing Russia as the principal threat, CUP leaders tried to woo Britain and France, who flatly rejected them. Next on the dancecard was Germany, who agreed to an alliance in 1914, the eve of World War I. Under Mustafa Kemal, the Turks blunted an early Allied assault at **Gallipoli** (see p. 147) by committing all their troops to the high ground and bluffing until reinforcements arrived. Their battle for the Dardanelles restricted the Allies to a kilometer-wide piece of scrub at the price of over 280,000 deaths on both sides. Mustafa Kemal's tactical brilliance and front-line leadership catapulted him to hero status and reignited Turkish nationalism. Apart from this phase, the war was a total disaster, a humiliation mitigated only by the nationalistic spur it provided and the new nation it would soon inspire.

More significant in this period was the Armenian genocide of 1915. The decision of Armenian Turks to align with Orthodox Russia during the war ended centuries of peaceful coexistence

1875
Faced with crippling debt from a century of reforms, the empire loses financial control to the European-controlled Ottoman Public Debt Administration.

1876
Young Turks propose new constitution; Sultan Abdülhamid II ditches it.

1912-1913
Balkan Wars claim the rest of Ottoman-controlled European territories.

1915
Both the defending Turks and especially the invading Allies sustain huge losses at the Battle of Gallipoli.

1915
1.5 million die in Armenian genocide.

within Turkey and unleashed a genocide. Civilians proved easy prey for the otherwise struggling Turkish army; the result was as many as 1.5 million Armenians force-marched, bayonetted off cliffs, incinerated, buried alive, or summarily executed (see **Armenians,** p. 30). Simultaneously, Turkish authorities encouraged their other disliked minority, the Kurds, to harass Armenians, only to list Kurdish casualties as Turkish victims.

THE CULT OF MUSTAFA KEMAL

1918
Turkey surrenders to the Allies. The Treaty of Sèvres proposes carving up Anatolia for European powers.

In 1918, Turkey surrendered to the allies at Lemnos. The **Treaty of Sèvres** gave Turkey's coast back to Greece and created an independent Armenia and Kurdistan. In March 1920, Britain placed İstanbul under military occupation, breaking up Parliament and exiling its members. The sultan accepted his "empire" of just İstanbul and hinterlands in exchange for keeping his throne. Such a capitulation was anathema to the nationalists, setting the stage for the Turkish War of Independence.

The rebels regrouped in Ankara under Mustafa Kemal, whose successes at Gallipolli and Syria were already legendary. He established a Grand National Assembly and the **National Pact,** which outlined what is modern day Turkey, promised to protect minority populations, and demanded the end of European spheres of influence. At the same time, Turkish nationalists were hard at work, fighting the French in the southeast, the Italians in the southwest, the Armenians in the northeast, and the Greeks (by far the greatest threat) in western Anatolia. First, the nationalists reclaimed the newly independent Armenia. Next, Mustafa Kemal routed the Greeks, who no longer had Allied support. Trapping 60,000 on the quay at İzmir, an international flotilla was needed to transfer the refugees to safety in Greece. After an armistice was signed on October 11, 1922, Mustafa Kemal and his Grand National Assembly abolished the sultanate, leaving their assembly as the sole ruling power.

November 1922
After the two-year Turkish War of Independence, Mustafa Kemal and the Grand National Assembly abolish the sultanate.

THE TREATY OF LAUSANNE

1923
Allies recognize Turkish gains in the Treaty of Lausanne. Greece and Turkey agree to a population exchange.

Acknowledging their defeat, the Allies bowed to the Turkish demands in the 1923 **Treaty of Lausanne.** This document recognized newly established Turkish frontiers, demilitarized the Dardanelles and paved the way for an independent Turkey. The **Population Exchange** of 1923, sought to eliminate anti-minority violence and unrest by removing Greeks from Turkey, and viceversa. Approximately 500,000 Turkish Muslims left Greece and were replaced by 1.3 million Greek Christians from Turkey, at the price of property loss, upheaval, dislocation, and alienation.

MODERN TURKEY

1923
Mustafa Kemal Atatürk becomes the first president of the Turkish Republic and begins a campaign to westernize the country.

ATATÜRK'S AGENDA: REDUCE, REUSE, REFORM

Mustafa Kemal became first president of the Turkish Republic in 1923. As part of his campaign to westernize Turkey, he required that all Turks adopt surnames, adding **Atatürk,** or "father of the Turks," to his own in 1934. He helped implement a Western-style **constitution** and adopted the **Gregorian calendar** and the metric system. Many of his reforms focused on secularization. This meant abolishing **polygamy,** doing away with

Islamic courts, and instituting secular law codes. In addition, he prohibited the use of the **fez** (traditional Islamic headwear), closed religious schools, and legalized alcohol. By 1928, Islam was no longer the official state religion. New labor codes, agricultural reform, and five-year plans were introduced and new banks established to encourage commerce and investment.

Culturally, Atatürk sought to make the country distinctly Turkish. He mandated the Turkification of city names: Angora was changed to Ankara, Smyrna to İzmir, and Adrianople became Edirne. He stepped up his Turkification program by attempting to purge all Arabic and Persian influences. In 1924, Kurdish was banned and the *adhan* (call to prayer) was to be recited in Turkish rather than in classical Arabic.

Though Atatürk's reforms were earth-shaking for all Turkish citizens, they had the greatest impact on **women.** Previously prohibited from holding jobs, women were granted equality with the new **civil code.** He overturned a 1917 bill that had legalized marriage for girls as young as nine and condoned polygamy. Whereas women were once legally under their husbands' control, the **1923 Suffrage Act** regulated their education and incorporation into society.

It wasn't always smooth sailing for Atatürk. His radical abolishment of the veil fired a debate that still burns today. In 1923 Trabzon's Ali Sukru attacked Atatürk's drinking and legalization of alcohol; his body later turned up in a shallow grave near Atatürk's villa. A plot to assassinate Atatürk ensued, resulting in a mini-purge and 12 public hangings in İzmir. Experimentation with two-party politics allowed the germination of the reform-slowing PRP in opposition to Atatürk's Peoples' Party in 1924. Citing Kurdish unrest, Atatürk invoked emergency powers and had the PRP banned the following year.

Atatürk's reforms had delivered Turkey from Ottoman lethargy to the twentieth century. He had replaced the Arabic alphabet with a Latin version by decree in the space of two months. Within a generation, Turks could no longer read the texts, letters, and books of their ancestors. Ties to the old order had been severed forever.

TESTING THE WATERS: A YOUNG NATION-STATE

Shortly before WWII, Atatürk died and was replaced by his associate **İsmet İnönü.** Turkey remained neutral throughout World War II, until it was compelled to join the Allies in the final weeks of the war.

1938
Atatürk dies.

The Cold War made Turkey a geopolitical gem for both the United States and the Soviet Union. Not only was it within firing range of the Soviet Union, but it also had control over the strategically vital Bosphorus. It was only the financial aid of the Marshall Plan that repelled Russian claims to the eastern parts of Turkey in 1945. Since then, the United States' military and economic aid to Turkey has remained rather freehanded. Turkey became a full member of NATO in 1952. It didn't oppose Greece's membership in 1970 to its chagrin today, as Greece has impeded its EU membership efforts.

1952
Turkey is accepted as a full member of NATO.

Turkey made a surprisingly peaceful transition from a one-party state to a multi-party democracy. The 1950s were controlled by the Democrats, with Atatürk's former party, the People's Party, in opposition and strongly censored. From 1960, Turkey appeared to herald each new decade with a military coup. Rising domestic output was undone by public debt and inflation, resulting in a People's Party parliamentary walk-out and closure of universities in protest. Though the ensuing coup was bloodless, the trials of nearly 600 Democratic Party members led to fifteen executions.

The 1960s represented a leftist and anti-American shift in Turkish politics, with calls for social sector and land reform to address rapid industrialization. The 1970s were even more turbulent. Kurdish violence and public sector protests ground the government to a halt in 1971, and brought a return of the military and martial law, dissolution of the Labor Party, and four years of ineffectual non-party government. The military's handling of political violence and terrorism in this period attracted international human rights condemnation.

It was during this time that **Abdullah Öcalan** formed the Workers' Party of Kurdistan (PKK is its Kurdish acronym) in order to fight for Kurdish sovereignty. Although the PKK does not represent all Kurds (see p. 29), the PKK would gain prominence among the Kurdish population in the southeast of the country in the following decades.

1974
Turkey invades
Northern Cyprus.

Turkey's foreign relations didn't fare much better. Fearing that Cyprus would be annexed by Greece, Turkey invaded the island in 1974, in response to a pro-Greek attempted coup. Economic and arms embargoes were imposed by the West, to which Turkey responded with closure of foreign military installations. By the end of the 70s, however, tensions decreased and normal foreign relations resumed (see **Cyprus in the 20th Century,** p. 455). The 70s ended with unemployment, inflation, twenty political murders per week and impotent governance.

RECENT YEARS

General **Kenan Evren** led a bloodless military coup in September 1980, placing both political leaders under house arrest and dissolving political parties. Muslim fundamentalist leader Erbakan was tried for political agitation and 43,000 others arrested and in some cases tortured. The new 1982 constitution provided for a president who could choose a prime minister, and held that political parties could attain seats in Parliament only if they could claim at least 10% of the vote.

1983
Three-year martial
law ends as Turgut
Özal is elected
president and
enacts initial
reforms.

Martial law ended by 1983 with the election of the center-right **Motherland Party** (ANAP) and its leader **Turgut Özal.** Though economic reforms, free-market principles, and emphasis upon trade was promising at first, the decade's worldwide recession sent Turkey into massive inflation, deficit, and unemployment.

Throughout the 1980s, security in eastern Turkey became increasingly precarious. Based in Syria and Iraq, the **PKK** (Kurdistan Workers' Party) increased its forces and directed a guerilla war against the Turkish state. Civilians were caught in the crossfire: Turkish troops razed villages suspected of helping the PKK, and the PKK razed villages suspected of being pro-government. Meanwhile, the use of the Kurdish language in schools or in the media was banned, as was any expression of sympathy for the Kurds.

Only the 1990 outbreak of the Gulf War shifted the spotlight, with Özal opening Turkish airbases for the Allied air offensive. This was a robust demonstration of Western alignment, but was undone by further PKK terrorism and the retaliatory bombing of Iraqi Kurd villages by the Turkish airforce in 1992.

In May 1993, following Özal's sudden death, the True Path Party elected **Tansu Çiller,** Turkey's first female prime minister. That might have seemed progressive, but later elections showed support for Islamic parties, largely in reaction to a growing income gap between the rich and the poor. Ultimately Çiller was removed after a sub-par performance as leader.

May 1993
Tansu Çiller is elected as Turkey's first female Prime Minister.

Class tensions mounted in January 1998, when Turkey's highest court dissolved the Islamic Welfare Party and banned its leader, **Necmettin Erbakan,** from politics for five years. Welfare Party members then reorganized themselves into the allegedly secular **Virtue Party,** or **Fazilet,** focused on freedom of expression and democratization. Suspicious opponents of the former Welfare Party, however, believe that the new party's agenda is still Islamically centered. In April 1998, İstanbul mayor and Fazilet supporter **Tayyib Erdogan** was sentenced to ten months in jail for reading a poem describing minarets as "our bayonets."

January 1998
Islamic Welfare Party dissolved in the name of secularism.

Turkey's secular **dress code** has also sparked controversy, with the government attempting to curb the wearing of head scarves in universities. Under a new law, a bare head is a requirement for a student ID card photo and, hence, the ability to enter final exams. Religious women students have protested and sidestepped this rule by wearing showy blond wigs over their head scarves and by holding street demonstrations.

As the **European Union** finalized its members list, Turkey's role remained unclear. In 1987, it had applied for full membership, but was rejected in 1989 because its market wasn't developed enough by European standards. Other factors included Turkey's less-than-stellar human rights record, high inflation, and control of Northern Cyprus. European nations also feared that the number of Turkish immigrants working in the rest of Europe would increase if visas were made unnecessary. In early 1995, Turkey was accepted into the European Customs Union, but on the condition that the Turkish Parliament make hundreds of new laws and changes to the constitution by that October. The European Union again denied Turkey candidacy for membership in December 1997. That same year, the EU's selection of Cyprus as a potential candidate angered Turkey, which threatened in late March 1998 to begin a new war with Cyprus (see **Cyprus in the 20th Century,** p. 455).

After several years of unstable coalitions and frequent charges of political corruption, Turkey went to the polls in April 1999 for the first general election since 1995. The results were surprising to most analysts. As expected, the Democratic Left Party (DSP), the party of veteran politician and caretaker **Prime Minister Bülent Ecevit,** triumphed, but he could not form government alone. The surprise runner-up was DSP's old political foe, the right-wing National Action Party (MHP), led by **Develt Bahçeli.** The Islamic inclined party, **Fazilet,** performed poorly given its overwhelming successes just a few years ago.

April 1999
Bülent Ecevit is elected Prime Minister. Abdüllah Öcalan is put on trial.

THE HERE AND NOW

Nature has not been kind to Turkey in the last year. On August 17, 1999, a devastating **earthquake** hit İzmit, near İstanbul. In a space of 45 seconds, it killed approximately 18,000 people, left tens of thousands injured, destroyed 60,000 buildings, and left 200,000 homeless. A series of **aftershocks** plagued the area for

TURKEY

August to November 1999
Massive earthquakes ravage northwestern Turkey, killing 20,000.

weeks afterwards. While neighboring countries and international relief groups raced to the rescue, the Turkish government was seen as slow and disorganized. A **second major quake** struck in mid-November, centered in Duzce, less than 100km from the first epicenter. This one claimed more than 700 lives, injured over 5000, left 80,000 people homeless, and destroyed approximately 750 buildings. Severe winter weather worsened the suffering of homeless refugees from both quakes.

While concentrating on the relief efforts domestically, Turkey received encouraging news from the European Union. The Helsinki European Council meeting in December 1999 nominated Turkey as a full **candidate for membership** to the EU. However, the Turkish government protested the prerequisite of peace with **Greece** for approval, though relations between the two (especially since the earthquake tragedies) have been improving. Also threatening its membership is Turkey's intransigence on the **Northern Cyprus** issue.

December 1999
Turkey becomes a full candidate for EU membership.

Overall, tensions in the southeast decreased since the spring 1999 capture, arrest and death sentence of PKK leader **Abdullah Öcalan**. His capture triggered public demonstrations of joy in many of Turkey's cities, and Kurdish demonstrations of outrage throughout Europe and in Turkey. In light of Öcalan's failing health and his status as an icon for many Kurds, his death sentence is unlikely to ever be carried out. In June 2000, Parliament voted to lift the state of emergency for certain mostly Kurdish southeastern provinces, including Van, which had been in place since fighting with Kurdish guerillas in 1987.

Spring 2000
Ahmet Necdet Sezer elected 10th president of the Turkish Republic.

In April 2000, the Turkish parliamentary vote denied seven-year president **Süleyman Demirel** the right to run for a second term. In early May, the Turkish Grand National Assembly elected **Ahmet Necdet Sezer** the 10th president of the Turkish republic. A judge who had advanced his career up the ranks of the Turkish court system, Sezer stated in his May 16 inaugural speech that he planned to concentrate on higher standards for democracy, secularism, and rule of law.

THE ARTS

VISUAL ARTS

A heart in love with beauty never grows old.
——Turkish proverb

THE GRECO-ROMAN HERITAGE

Of the **Seven Wonders of the Ancient World,** Turkey boasts two—the **Temple of Artemis** in Ephesus (see p. 193) and the **Mausoleum of Halicarnassus** in Bodrum (see p. 221). Traces of these and other ruins from the Hellenistic and Roman periods (mid-4th century BC to 3rd century AD) dot Turkey's coast. Although the Romans did introduce new architectural elements—the arch, the vault, the forum, and *thermae* (baths)—they borrowed heavily from their Greek predecessors, effectively ensuring an artistic continuity between these two periods.

Ancient sites such as Ephesus, Miletus, Smyrna, and Pergamon illustrate the organization of Greek political and social life around the *polis* or city-state. The existing ruins also highlight the civic role of Hellenic art and architecture; independent city-states sought to foster civic pride and to outdo one another by erecting impressive monuments and edifices. But it wasn't all about whose obelisk was bigger: buildings typically served more practical civic functions, supplying the public spaces of citizens' daily lives. **Temples** dedicated to the city-state's patron deity marked the center of religious life. Often, they occupied commanding positions, and where geography cooperated, as in Pergamon, they were perched upon the highest point of the city, known as the acropolis. The **agora** (marketplace) was the center of commercial and political life. A large open space, the *agora* housed countless shops under the **stoas** (colonnades) which lined its sides. In oligarchic and democratic city-states, the open space of the *agora* and the nearby **bouleuterion** (council house) functioned as the meeting places for the local government.

The surviving ruins also provide a glimpse into the culture of the period. A society that valued athletics and the athlete, the Greeks built **gymnasia** for physical education and **stadia** for athletic competitions. They also celebrated the human form in the famous naturalistic sculpture scattered throughout the city on pedestals and friezes. For entertainment, the residents of the *polis* attended musical performances in the **odeon** (theater) and theatrical performances in the ubiquitous and semi-circular **amphitheater.** In the Hellenistic period, the auditorium of the amphitheater was built into the hillside, while the Romans used free-standing walls to support the weight of this structure.

THE TIMELESS VISION OF BYZANTIUM

The Byzantine emperor administered his holy city in the image of God ruling the cosmos. The structure and decorations of the emperor's palace reflected the overwhelming focus of Byzantine art and architecture on religious expression. The artistic achievements of Byzantine culture were developed within rigid theological parameters. First codified under the emperor Justinian (527-65 AD), stylized and abstract representations were more important than naturalistic representation.

Byzantine art evolved homogeneously up to and beyond the fall of Constantinople in 1453. The Byzantine style later spread to Italy, by way of trade through Venice, where it continued to flourish through the 13th century and served as a model for Italian artists. Because of the influence of the Eastern Orthodox Church, Byzantine artistic traditions prevailed through the 17th century in Eastern Europe.

ARCHITECTURE. In the fourth century, when the early Christians were finally afforded the right to establish their own places of worship, the Byzantine church emerged. This church was based on a longitudinal **basilica** plan with its central **nave** oriented along an east-west axis. The entrance of the basilica was approached on the western side from a colonnaded outer courtyard. On the eastern side, at the other end of the nave, was the semi-circular **apse** and the altar. Arched colonnades separated the nave from two parallel side aisles, and the wooden ceiling of the nave was raised above that of the side aisles to incorporate a series of clear windows admitting light to the central part of the building.

The most eminent symbol of Byzantine architecture is İstanbul's **Aya Sofia,** built between 532-37 over the remains of a church from the era of Constantine (see p. 101). The Aya Sofia features a domed roof centered over a square base, rather than the conventional octagonal kind. By the reign of **Basil I** (867-886), the domed basilicas of Justinian had evolved into a **cross-in-square** plan, featuring four vaulted arms of equal length extending from the domed center. Smaller domes occasionally replaced the vaulted roofs above the four arms of the cross, producing a five-domed church known as the **quincunx.**

DECORATIVE ARTS. Byzantine artistry ran the gamut of artistic media, from illuminated manuscripts to carved ivory panels, embossed bronze doors, and exquisite jewel-encrusted enamels. The dazzling mosaics and icons decorating Byzantine churches mark the pinnacle of Byzantine craftsmanship. Artists underwent years of spiritual and technical training before portraying sacred subjects. Byzantine icons aimed to transmit—not just represent—the spiritual power of the subject.

Byzantine icons used many different materials: mosaic, enamel, ivory, gold, and wood. Mosaics were made of **tesserae,** small cubes of stone or ceramic covered in glass or metallic foil. The unique shimmering effect of Byzantine mosaics was achieved by setting gold and silver tesserae at sharp angles to enhance the reflection of light. Excellent examples of Byzantine mosaics can be seen in the Aya Sofia and the **Kariye Camii** (see p. 119).

ISLAMIC ART AND ARCHITECTURE

Because Islam developed in wildly disparate areas with differing cultural traditions, Islamic art encompasses a tremendous variety of motifs, materials, and styles. One element common to all Islamic art is the absence of human form. Any attempt to imitate God's divine creation is considered idolatrous and blasphemous. As a result, Islamic artists developed a non-representational artistic language. Calligraphy, floral arabesques, and geometric motifs cover everything from mosques and pottery to metalwork and wood carvings.

THE MOSQUE. The mosque (**cami** in Turkish) represents the most significant architectural manifestation of Islamic art. As the religious, political, and social center of the Islamic world, mosques often had schools and libraries attached to them. The earliest mosques, based on the layout of the prophet Muhammed's house in Medina, were simple and functional: large, square prayer halls with open central courtyards. The expansion of the Islamic empire saw the assimilation of Persian, Roman, and Byzantine motifs. Greek, Syrian, Iranian, and Armenian craftsmen and architects helped transform the simple Arabian mosque into a complex affair of tiled domes, squinches, vaults, and arches.

The minaret **(minare)** is attached to the outside of the mosque. Originally a small elevated platform, but now a conical tower, it is used by the *müezzin* (crier) to belt out the *adhan* (call to prayer). The minarets of most mosques are now equipped with speakers for extra amplification. The mosque courtyard often features a fountain **(şadirvan)** for the ritual wash before prayers. Inside, the congregation faces the **mihrab**, a niche in the **qibla**, or wall that the congregation faces when praying. To the right of the *mihrab* is the **minber**, a wooden staircase from which the **imam** (spiritual guide) gives the sermon.

All mosques place great emphasis on spacious, oasis-like interiors, either an airy domed space or an open-air courtyard flanked by cool porticoes. With their roots in Persian and Byzantine models, **domes** are a common feature of mosques. They use a dazzling variety of structural supports to transform the corners of the square base into an octagonal opening for the dome.

Mosques often formed the centerpiece of a larger complex of buildings. The **medrese** (theological seminary) and **türbe** (tomb) are two structures often flanking mosques. Under the Ottomans, the complex surrounding a mosque developed into a vital social center that served all of a community's needs.

SELÇUK ARCHITECTURE AND DECORATIVE ARTS. During the heyday of the Sultanate of Rum, Selçuk architects kept busy with extensive public works projects. Using the abundant Anatolian stone and clay, they built mosques, *medrese*, and *türbe*. Rum Selçuk architects modified the designs they inherited from their Iranian counterparts with elements of Syrian and Byzantine architecture. They kept the strict Iranian rectilinear mosque and *medrese* plan, as well as the highly decorated minarets, but roofed over the courtyard.

To safeguard their profitable trade in silks, spices, and slaves, and to provide rest for merchants, the Rum Selçuks built over 100 **kervansaray**, or *hans*, along Anatolian highways, spaced a day's ride away from each other. Rather than fast-food restaurants and gas stations, these rest stops featured mosques, storage rooms, stables, coffeehouses, hamams, private rooms, and dormitories. The most impressive example of Selçuk *hans* is the **Sultan Han** (see p. 336) outside Kayseri.

Rum Selçuk buildings were characterized by their elaborate stone carvings. Earlier carvings reflect the geometrical asceticism of Syrian and Persian designs. In later carvings, such as those on the façades of Sivas buildings (see p. 373) or on Konya's İnce Minareli (see p. 343), these designs burst into exuberant arabesques and Baroque flourishes. In addition to carvings, the Selçuks enhanced their mosques and *medreses* with glimmering *faïence* (glazed earthenware). The fruit of Iranian craftsmen, Selçuk *faïence* was used to cover walls or minarets. The best examples of Selçuk *faïence* are at Konya in the Karatay Medrese (see p. 342).

Under Selçuk patronage, decorative arts enjoyed a boom, only halted by the 13th-century Mongol invasion. **Glassware** and **textiles** were regular staples of commerce, while new techniques in ceramics and lustre painting created more opportunity for the use of *faïence*. The school of Selçuk **metalworking** was particularly important, churning out engraved, silver-inlaid candlesticks, kettles, and bowls.

OTTOMAN ARCHITECTURE. The first Ottoman capital, **Bursa,** is a museum of 14th- and 15th-century Ottoman architecture (see p. 152). Its mosques and tombs combine elements borrowed from Selçuk and European architecture.

With the capture of İstanbul in 1453, Ottoman architects were challenged to respond to the vaults and pendentives of the Aya Sofia's spectacular dome (see p. 101). Ottoman architecture reached its pinnacle under the unprecedented patronage of Sultan Süleyman. During his rule alone (1520-66), over 80 major mosques and hundreds of other buildings were constructed. **Divan Yolu,** İstanbul's processional avenue, boasts a spectacular collection of these structural wonders. The master architect **Sinan** served Süleyman and his sons as Chief Court Architect from 1538 to 1588, during which time he created a unified style for all of İstanbul and for much of the empire. Trained as a military engineer, Sinan forged an architecture influenced by early Islamic and Byzantine styles. His masterpieces, the **Süleymaniye Camii** in İstanbul (see p. 114) and the **Selimiye Camii** in Edirne (see p. 142), exemplify the harmonious, multi-domed Ottoman trademark style.

Many Ottoman mosques stand at the center of a **külliye** (complex) designed to serve all of a community's needs. *Külliyes* often included a *medrese*, a market, a soup kitchen, a *kervansaray*, and a medical center, all integrated architecturally into a single whole. The most impressive *külliyes* are the Süleymaniye, in İstanbul (see p. 114), and the Beyazıt, in Edirne (see p. 142). Most *külliyes* were established as charitable foundations. Although massive inflation has jeopardized these institutions financially, many of them are still functioning.

Sixteenth-century Ottoman architects set a powerful precedent. Buildings like the **Blue Mosque** were mere imitations of the Sinan blueprint (see p. 102). In the 18th and 19th centuries, Ottoman architecture, perhaps inspired by the fashions of the Austro-Hungarian Empire, appropriated a highly ornate Europeanized **Baroque** style, evident in İstanbul's flashiest eyesore, the **Dolmabahçe Palace** (see p. 123).

OTTOMAN DECORATIVE ARTS. The height of Ottoman decorative arts was **tile-work.** From the 14th-17th centuries, the Ottomans imported Persian craftsmen in the 14th century to develop their ceramic industry in **İznik** (see p. 161), though by 1800 manufacture had virtually stopped. **Kütahya** had also experienced a 400-year boom, and in recent years, however, the ceramics in Kütahya have experienced a tourist-driven renaissance (see p. 348).

MODERN TURKISH ART. Long before Atatürk's revolution, Ottoman painting had gradually begun to adopt Western forms, thanks to the influence of European artists were working at the Ottoman court. In 1883, the **Academy of Fine Arts** was founded by Ottoman artist, museum curator, and archaeologist **Osman Hamdi Bey.** Osman Hamdi was thoroughly Westernized in his painting technique and educational philosophy. Referred to as *the* Academy, it has had a huge influence on the Turkey's major artistic movements: the **Çallı group** of the 20s, the **'D'** Group of the 30s, and the **New Group** of the 40s, 50s, and 60s. Many of the artists who created these movements later became professors at the Academy. Their work can be seen at the **Painting and Sculpture Museum** in Ankara (see **Other Museums,** p. 365).

In 1914 the Ottoman government, in response to demands of the elite, opened an Academy of Fine Arts for Women headed by the painter **Mihri Müşfil Hanım,** whose work blended İstanbul's conservatism with the Parisian flair for Levantine fashions. In 1926 the Women's Academy merged with the Academy of Fine Arts, and has since produced four generations of recognized women painters.

LITERATURE

Early literature consisted primarily of oral performance. Poems would be recited, sometimes with musical accompaniment. Traces of this art form may be seen in the *türkü* (modern Turkish folk song).

Although modern Turkish literature has adopted the Western literary forms of the novel and the essay, it often looks back to its pre-Ottoman origins. The Sufi poetry of **Celeddin-i-Rumi** and **Yunuş Emre** survived the Ottoman centuries relatively unscathed, as did *The Book of Dede Korkut*, a collection of 12 legends, recounting the travels and trials of the noble Oğuz Turks, the ancestors of modern Turks. This epic provides the modern reader with a good introduction to an important genre in Ottoman literature. Many such epics were rediscovered during the 19th century. With this renewed interest in folk literature came a propagation of the tales of **Nasrettin Hoca**, an amiable, anti-authoritarian, religious man whose parables and fables are known by all Turkish school children (see **Wise Ass,** p. 346).

Satire has historically been an important element in Turkish literature. A prominent modern Turkish poet, **Namık Kemal,** is famous for his satire of the Ottoman Empire during its final years. **Nazım Hikmet's** critical poetry brought him both literary fame and exile, a common fate for writers with politically contentious views. A fervent republican and free speech advocate, **Aziz Nesin,** is the provocative Alevi writer around which the 1993 Sivas incident occurred (see **Otel Madımak,** p. 376). One of the better known Turkish writers is **Yaşar Kemal,** author of *Memed, My Hawk.* Thrice nominated for the Nobel Prize for Literature, his work has been critical of Turkish society and government. Not without recourse: the government recently charged Kemal with anti-Turkish activities. **Orhan Pamuk,** the best-selling author in Turkish history and one of the few Turkish writers to have received international acclaim, explores the concept of identity through magical realism. His three major novels are *The White Castle, The New Life,* and *The Black Book.*

MUSIC

During the early Republican period, the only forms of Turkish music that had government approval were classical music and "authentic Turkish" folk music. However, musical life in Turkey today is varied and exciting, presenting a wide range of forms and styles. The two most common forms, **arabesk** and **taverna,** often have a canned, insipid quality; *arabesk* (called *"minibüs müziği"* for its proliferation on vehicles of all kinds) is an offspring of Arabic pop, while *taverna* combines the influence of Greek music with Turkish cabaret.

Moving beyond these two types, however, are the urban forms of *sanaat, Türkü,* and *özgün.* **Sanaat,** or "art" music, has preserved 18th-century vocal styles. The late **Zeki Müren** was its most famous performer, although a bit earlier **Bülent Ersoy** had made a name for herself before having her music banned in 1980, the year she had a sex-change operation. Based in folk music, **Türkü** is performed on a diverse mixture of Arab, Western, and Turkish instruments. **Özgun** music is Turkey's protest music, and it often contains political, left-wing lyrics.

On top of the pop music scene is **Tarkan,** the fabulously popular "Turkish Ricky Martin." Also livin' la vida loca is **Kenan Doğlu. Sertap Erener** combines pop and soulful female vocals. **Sezan Aksu,** whose concerts draw hordes of screaming devotees, is considered Turkey's most talented musician; in addition to producing her own music, she acts as a mentor for many up-and-coming singers. **Athena** is a popular Turkish ska band that even does the occasion Cake cover. In summer, live concerts are held in outdoor amphitheaters. An annual Pop Song Festival and competition is held in Çeşme in the 3rd week of August (see **Çeşme,** <u>p. 189</u>).

Folk music is celebrated in a variety of local festivals throughout Turkey (see **Music,** p. 24), and it forms the basis for festive rural occasions like weddings. The troubadour tradition, which has continued for 1000 years, is still practiced by the **aşıks** in central Anatolia. These traveling minstrels perform poetry set to music on the lute-like *saz,* whose three sets of strings represent the three points of the

Bektaşi/Alevi faith (see p. 28 and p. 31). Along the Black Sea coast, the *tulum* (a two-piped bagpipe) and the *kemençe* (a three-stringed fiddle), are common. **Kurdish folk music** engages its own particular instruments, which include the *blur* (wooden flute), the oboe-like *düdük*, and the *def* (bass drum). The bards of Kurdish music, repositories for Kurdish legend and culture, are the **dengbeys**. Many of them, including the well-known artists **Temo** and **Şivan Perwer,** have been exiled because of their politically controversial lyrics.

Ottoman classical music and the ritual music of the Mevlevi dervish order are based on a series of *makams* (500-year-old modal systems) that use a unique tonal system. The compositions of **Abdülkadir Meraği** (15th century), **Prince Dimitiri Cantemir** (17th-18th century), and **Sultan Selim II** and **Tanburi Cemil Bey** (both 19th-20th century) are drawn upon most frequently. Live performances of classical music are given by the Klasik İcra Heyeti of the İstanbul Municipal Conservatory. The annual **Mevlâna Festival,** held in Konya in December, is an excellent opportunity to hear live Mevlevi music (see **Konya,** p. 340).

SOCIETY

ISLAM

About 99% of Turks are Muslim. Jews and Orthodox Christians of Greek, Armenian, and Syrian backgrounds compose the remaining population. Turkey does not have an official state religion, but every Turkish citizen's national identification card states his or her creed. Although Atatürk set Turkey on a secular course, Islam continues to play a key role in the country's political and cultural evolution.

UNDERSTANDING ISLAM

The monotheistic religion of Islam was founded by the Arab prophet **Muhammed** in the 7th century. At the heart of the Islamic faith is the Arabic word *islam* (submission). The believer, or *muslim* (from the active participle of *islam*), accepts complete submission to the will of **Allah** (God) as embodied in the sacred scriptures of Islam, the **Koran** (recitation). The Arabic text is held to be perfect, immutable, and untranslatable—the words of God embodied in the human language.

Informed of his prophetic calling by the Archangel Gabriel, Muhammed became the "seal of the prophets," the end of a long chain of visionaries including such Biblical luminaries as Abraham, Moses, Elijah, and Jesus. While most Christians view Jesus as both human and divine, Muslims consider Muhammed only as a human messenger of God's word. As opposed to the Christian belief in the Trinity, Islam's rigorous monotheism holds that God is one and unique. Described as omnipotent and omniscient, dearer to human life than the jugular vein, the God of the Koran can be a stern judge when faced with ingrates. Yet for a Muslim, the majesty of God's justice lies in unbounded mercy—all but one of the 114 Koranic *suras*, or chapters, begin, "In the name of God the most Merciful and Compassionate." In Islam, Allah is above all a God of uncompromising love, guiding all those who sincerely invoke His name.

THE FIVE PILLARS OF ISLAM

All Muslims are charged to adhere to the five pillars of Islam: the profession of faith, prayer fives times daily, alms-giving, fasting during the month of Ramazan, and, if able, the once-in-a-lifetime pilgrimage to Mecca.

The first pillar, upon which membership in the *umma* (community) depends, is the proclamation of faith, the **shahadah:** *La ilaha illa Allah. Ashadu anna Muhammedan rasul Allah.* (There is no god but God. I swear that Muhammed is God's messenger.) Any person who wishes to convert to Islam may do so by reciting the *shahadah* aloud and with heartfelt sincerity.

The second pillar of Islam is **salat** (prayer), performed five times daily, preferably following the *müezzins'* call to prayer *(adhan)*. Prayers, preceded by ablutions, begin with a declaration of intent and consist of a set cycle of prostrations and recitations in the direction of Mecca. Communal prayer on Fridays, led by the local mosque's *imam* (leader), is particularly encouraged.

The third pillar is the paying of the religious tax known as **zakat** (purification). Every Muslim who can afford to is required to give 2.5% of his or her income to the poor. Before the secularization of Turkey, the state collected the *zakat*, but it has now largely become a matter of individual responsibility.

Muslims believe that Muhammed received the Koran during the month of **Ramazan** (Ramadan). Fasting during this holy month is the fourth pillar of Islam. Between dawn and sunset, Muslims are forbidden to smoke, have sex, or let any food or water pass their lips. Exceptions exist for travelers, the sick, and women who are pregnant or menstruating. However, travelers should respectfully refrain from eating or drinking during the day. Ramazan inspires a sense of community among Muslims. They break the fast after the evening *adhan* is heard and begin a night of feasting, visits to friends and relatives, and revelry. Fasting is intended to be an invigorating spiritual exercise, teaching self-control and resistance to desire. The experience of hunger encourages Muslims to be both compassionate toward those less fortunate and grateful for the sustenance that God has provided them. During Ramazan, offices and businesses may close or keep shorter hours.

The last pillar, required only once in a lifetime, is the **hajj** (pilgrimage). Only those Muslims who are financially and physically able to fulfill this obligation make the journey to **Mecca** and **Medina** during the last month of the Muslim calendar. The *hajj* is a metaphorical reenactment of the Prophet Muhammed's path, and it serves to unite Muslims. Regardless of gender, wealth, race, or nationality, all pilgrims wrap themselves in white cloth and perform the same rituals.

As with any religion, degrees of interpretation and observance produce a wide range of practices. For more information, try *An Introduction to Islam* by Frederick Denny, *Islam: The Straight Path* by John Esposito, *Vision of Islam* by Sachiko Murata and William Chittick, or *Ideals and Realities of Islam* by Seyyed H. Nasr. Kenneth Cragg and Marston Speight's *Islam from Within* provides a sampling of Islamic texts. If you feel inspired enough to read the Koran, try Muhammed Pickthall's translation, *The Meaning of the Glorious Koran*.

THE HISTORICAL EVOLUTION OF ISLAM

Monotheistic Islam met with staunch opposition in 7th-century polytheist Arabia. In 622, Muhammed fled persecution in his native city of Mecca and escaped to nearby Medina, where he was welcomed as a mediator of a long-standing blood feud. This *hijra* (flight) marks the beginning of the Muslim community and of the Islamic (lunar) calendar. For the next eight years, Muhammed and his community defended themselves against raids, later battling the Meccans and neighboring nomadic tribes. In 630, Mecca surrendered to the Muslims, and numerous Meccans converted to the new faith. This experience established the pattern for *jihad* (struggle), referring first to the spiritual struggle against one's own desires, then to the struggle to make a righteous Muslim community, and lastly to the struggle against outsiders wishing to harm this community. Sadly, most Westerners have heard only of this last aspect of *jihad*, often removing it from its larger context.

Islam continued to grow after the Prophet's death. The stories and traditions surrounding the Prophet's life have been passed on as *sunna*, and those who follow the *sunna* (from which the term "Sunni" is derived) in addition to the teachings of the Koran are considered especially devout. The primary source for *sunna* is the **Hadith,** a collection of sayings attributed to Mohammed. A *hadith* was rigorously verified before it was accepted as true; the tale had to be verified (preferably by those who saw the action), and the greatest weight was given to testimony by Mohammed's followers and relatives.

Of the four Rightly Guided Caliphs *(Rashidun)* who succeeded Muhammed, the fourth, Muhammed's nephew and son-in-law Ali, was the catalyst for the major present-day split between Sunnis and Shi'ites in the Muslim world. After Ali slowly lost power and was murdered in 661, the *Shi'at Ali* (Party of Ali), or **Shi'ites,** believed him to be the only legitimate successor to Muhammed. Contrary to popular Western perception, Shi'ism is not a creed of fanaticism, but is Islam with a sharp focus on **imams.** These divinely inspired mystical guides are spiritual and sometimes blood descendants of the Prophet through Ali and his wife, the Prophet's daughter Fatima. While most Turkish Muslims today are Sunni, the Shi'ite Alevi form a sizeable minority (see **Alevi,** p. 31).

SUFISM

Sufism is the mystical Islamic practice in which Muslims seek divine love and knowledge through a direct personal experience with God. Sufism began in opposition to the material excess of the **Umayyad caliphate** (661-750), and it sought to refocus the Islamic community on the spiritual goals of Islam. Yearning for an illuminating communion with God, Sufis thought the outer path of obedience to Islamic law *(shar'ia)* inadequate, though still essential, and increasingly affirmed the interior path *(tariqa)* of Sufi mysticism. Guided by the Sufi master, the *murid* (disciple) achieves the *tariqa* (path) of Sufism through a strict regimen of ascetic practices. Sufis believe that self-denial, through acts like fasting, permits victory over the ego, the elimination of all thoughts of self in the quest for *fan-fi-Allah* (annihilation in God). Emphasizing universal love between God and humans, Sufi followers are a tolerant and peaceful people, marked by compassion and humility.

Sufism has been vitally important in the development of Islam. Thanks to the efforts of traveling Sufi dervishes, Islam spread into Central Asia, India, Turkey, and Sub-Saharan Africa. The flowering of Sufi literature, most notably mystical love poetry, reflects a golden age among the Arabic, Persian, and Turkish languages. Though the Sufis were outside the mainstream of orthodox Islam and though some of their more esoteric practices were never far from heresy, the orders enjoyed great privileges in the Ottoman Empire. Under the Ottomans, the Sufi orders lived in lodges *(tekke* in Turkish) that were endowed by the state, rich patrons, and charity. Under Atatürk's 1925 secular reforms, however, all ceremonies, meetings, and costumes associated with the Sufi orders were officially banned. But the government was unable to suppress such an established religious tradition, and Turkey has witnessed the gradual reemergence of Sufi customs and practice. The English language cannot always adequately translate terms describing Sufism, so consider words like "mystic" and "order" to be approximations.

MEVLEVI ORDER

Since in order to speak, one must first listen, learn to speak by listening.
——Celeddin-i-Rumi

The Mevlevi order was founded in Konya in the late 13th century by the Persian mystic and poet **Celeddin-i-Rumi** (see p. 341), whose popular title, *Mevlâna* (our master), gave the order its name. Known to the West as the **Whirling Dervishes** because of their ritual dance ceremony, the disciples of the order lived in *tekke,* which included living quarters, prayer room, kitchen, and a galleried *semahane* (dance hall). The Mevlevi's ritual whirl, or *sema,* is an esoteric spiritual exercise that allowed disciples to attain a state of union with God. The dancers' tall camelhair hats represent tombstones, the black cloaks signify tombs, and the white robes a death shroud. In casting off the black cloaks, the dancers set aside all worldly ties and step out of the tomb of the self. Their arms extended—the right palm facing the heavens, the left the ground—the dervishes whirl slowly, channeling the mystical energy that makes the world turn.

The Mevlevi impact on poetry, **calligraphy,** and the visual arts from the 14th to 20th century is profound. Perhaps an even more important contribution to Ottoman culture is their development of a **religious music,** as music was frowned upon by Orthodox Islam. In 1954 the Turkish government allowed the Mevlevi ritual dance *(sema)* to be performed for tourists during the week preceding the anniversary of Rumi's death on December 17. Since then, the Mevlevi have gained more freedom to display their dance, and *sema* can be seen almost every other week at the **Galat Mevlihane** in İstanbul (see **İstiklâl Caddesi,** p. 100). Today the Mevlâna's *türbe* (tomb) in Konya, officially a museum, attracts the faithful (see p. 340).

BEKTAŞI ORDER

> We have recognized the unity of Allah... We have been the intoxicated
> ones from all eternity—we are butterflies in the divine light.
> ——Jevad Paşa

The Bektaşı order of Sufism was founded by **Haci Bektaş Veli,** who was born around 1248 in Iranian Khorasan. Haci Bektaş came to Anatolia in the late 13th century and lived in Kayseri, Kirşehir, and Sivas before founding his monastic complex in Suluca Karahöyük, where he died in 1337. The teachings of Haci Bektaş helped popularize Islam in pre-Ottoman Anatolia, finding a particular resonance among soldiers and peasants. Haci Bektaş espoused a folksy brand of Sufism characterized by maxims like "seek and you shall find." His best selling self-help book **Makalat** touted the **"Four Doors,"** or steps to enlightenment.

The Bektaşı, originally Sunni, began to assimilate Shi'ite practices in the 16th century. This explains the close ties between the Bektaşı and Shi'ite Alevi communities. The white-capped Bektaşı were famous for their slightly unorthodox behavior, including ritual wine swilling, dancing, and Christian practices such as bread-sharing and the confession of sins. They rose from a rural base to political importance in the 15th century, when their order began to dominate the elite Janissary Ottoman military corps (see p. 13). Bektaşı influence waned after 1826, when the "Auspicious Event" (see **The 19th Century: Reform and Reaction,** p. 14) eliminated the Janissary corps. Today, at an annual mid-August gathering, thousands still gather in Hacibektaş to commemorate its namesake with dancing and merriment.

WOMEN IN TURKEY

Rapid social change in 20th-century Turkey has transformed the traditional roles of many women, especially those of the urban upper classes. In rural areas and in lower social classes, traditional practices persist. In the move to create a progressive republic, **Atatürk's reforms** (see p. 16) gave women nearly the same legal status as men. In 1934 women were granted suffrage and could office. Before and during WWII, women entered the workforce as teachers, clerical workers, and industrial laborers, and after the 1950s more became employed in industry. By the 1970s, many women held positions in education and health care. In cities, some women held more elite positions in such fields as law and medicine. In fact, more Turkish women worked in these fields than did their French and American counterparts in the early 1980s. In 1993, **Tansu Çiller** became Turkey's first female prime minister.

In the early days of the Republic, **abortion** and sterilization were illegal, as they went against the government agenda of population increase. However, a 1965 family planning law extended birth control information and services. In 1967, abortion was legalized for up to 10 weeks after conception, in public hospitals.

In less modernized areas, traditional family and social roles are still widespread, especially within the customarily **male-dominated family.** However, women continue to gain societal and familial power. The wedding code of the early Republic decreed an end to traditional marriage rituals such as bride fees and parentally arranged marriages, emphasizing the personal contract of two individuals and a woman's right to demand a divorce. Today, in rural areas, two ceremonies are sometimes enacted—one religious and family-oriented, the other civil—in order to attain the best of both worlds. In urban areas, marriage is a very Western institution. For information on travel for women in Turkey, see **Women Travelers,** p. 68.

MINORITIES

KURDS

The capture and conviction of Kurdish guerilla leader Abdüllah Öcalan has brought increasing international attention to the Kurds, the largest ethnic group in the world without its own nation. An estimated 20 million Kurds live in the regions of eastern Turkey, northern Syria, Iraq, and northern Iran. Twelve-fifteen million live in Turkey alone, comprising nearly 25% of the population. Estimates date the ancestors of the Kurds to the 3rd millennium BC, though the first mention of them comes from the 7th century when they converted to Islam. Divided by international borders and along religious, linguistic, and political lines, the Kurds are far from forming a homogenous group. While most Kurds are Sunni, others subscribe to Sufism or to the smaller and unconventional Yezidi and Ahl-i-Haqqi sects. The **Kurdish language,** which is related to Persian, has its roots in northwestern Iran. Of the three mutually unintelligible dialects spoken by Kurds today, **Kermanji** is the most widely spoken in Turkey. Traditionally, the Kurds pursued a **nomadic lifestyle** of pastoralism, herding sheep and goats and raising horses. After WWI, urbanization and the division of Kurdish lands into disparate nations prevented customary migrations and forced many to settle in towns. However, nomadic lifestyles persist within the more remote regions of Eastern Turkey.

The Kurdish nationalist movement began in urban intellectual circles after the collapse of the Ottoman Empire and was influenced by Marxist and Leninist ideology. Although the **1920 Treaty of Sèvres** provided for an autonomous Kurdistan, the Treaty of Lausanne that supplanted it in 1923 included no mention of the Kurds or of a Kurdish nation-state. After the Kurds joined Atatürk's forces to fight for a Turkish state, they were repaid not with the foundation of an independent Kurdistan, but with the new Turkish government's policy of **enforced Kurdish assimilation.** Kurdish revolts in the 20s and 30s were met with the executions, deportations, and razing of villages that began **armed control** of Eastern Turkey. By 1925 the government had outlawed the Kurdish language, forbidden traditional dress in cities, and encouraged Kurdish migration to the country's urbanized western regions. The publication of Kurdish newspapers and the broadcast of Kurdish television and radio were also prohibited. Refusing to recognize their distinct ethnicity, the Turkish government referred to Kurds as "mountain Turks" until the 1991 Gulf War.

Disaffected by their plight, many Kurds sought to voice their objections and demands through political means. Kurdish separatist goals, however, were incompatible with mainstream Kurdish leftist parties, and the rightist rise to power in 1971 and again in 1980 further alienated Kurds in the east. Throughout the 70s and 80s many Kurds felt forced to form political groups of their own. The most famous and extremist of these is the **PKK,** or **Worker's Party of Kurdistan.** Founded by political science student **Abdüllah Öcalan** in 1978, the PKK pledged itself to armed struggle in hopes of forming an independent and Marxist Kurdish state.

In the mid-80s, the PKK began to attack Turkish towns in the east and prominent Turkish officials. In response, the government declared **martial law** in the affected areas and armed loyal Kurds to create a defensive force known as the **village guards.** By taking advantage of the lack of Kurdish unity, the government helped to turn Kurds against one another, and the PKK increasingly attacked Kurds who had associated with the Turkish system. In the early 1990s the PKK undertook a series of bombings in heavily touristed coastal cities. These bombs were meant to bring attention to the Kurdish cause by bruising the country's high-revenue tourist industry. The government responded harshly with its own bombings, village evacuations, jailings (often in violation of international human rights legislation), and executions (often under mysterious conditions). By 1999, the continuing conflict had claimed over 30,000 lives.

International perception of the Kurdish issue in recent years has changed from anti-PKK sentiment to criticism of Turkey's human rights policies. The state is torn between its desire to completely quell Kurdish separatism and its interest in placating the international community and the European Union. There has, for instance, been some progress for the Kurds. Though the Kurdish language is still banned in schools and broadcasts, a 1991 decision now permits its use in unofficial settings. However, the Turkish army has maintained its tough stance against terrorist activities, launching offensives to eradicate the PKK. As a testament to the army's success in weakening the PKK, Öcalan was preparing for a compromise before his capture in February 1999. Though throughout his trial he offered to broker a ceasefire in exchange for his life and Kurdish minority rights, the court sentenced him to death in June. After the verdict, there was a renewed outbreak of bombings, but the PKK has announced that it would no longer target civilians. Still, the potential for violence exists (see **The Here and Now,** p. 19).

ARMENIANS

Though some scholars disagree, many Armenians trace their roots four millennia back to the Urartian peoples. Despite systematic destruction of cultural remains, the ruins of **Ani** (50km east of Kars), a city that rivalled its western brother Constantinople in size, grandeur, and population, still remain to prove the millenial legacy of Armenians in Eastern Anatolia (see p. 430). The exquisite, 10th-century Akdamar Church (see p. 436) is one of the last of thousands of churches that speckled the countryside. Today there are almost no Armenians left in Eastern Anatolia. The few that remain may not even be aware of their original ethnicity as older generations quickly assimilated to Kurdish or Turkish identities.

Until the 19th century Armenians coexisted with Kurdish peasants, also under Ottoman rule. Armenian nationalism arose in the 1890s, when Armenians comprised about 10% of the Anatolian population. The first **Armenian separatist groups,** founded in 1887 and 1890, aimed to promote their cause through acts of terrorism.

The Armenians found themselves handicapped by their small numbers, and their cause fell upon deaf European ears; the Great Powers jealously guarded their own interests in the partitioning of the Ottoman Empire. Undaunted, Armenians seized and occupied the Ottoman Bank in İstanbul in August 1896. The resulting slaughter of more than 50,000 Armenians cemented this attempt as another failure.

At the outset of WWI, the **Russian cause** offered hope for Armenian independence, and a few thousand Armenians enlisted in the Russian armed forces. On April 20, 1915, Armenians revolted in **Van,** seizing the city's fortress in anticipation of Russian back-up. Fearing the Armenians' alliance with Russia, the Ottoman government (or the military acting independently) initiated a program of **deportation,** relocating Armenians to the Syrian desert. Hundreds of thousands were later killed outright in the process of relocation, while many more died on the march.

Today, both sides dispute the facts, causes, and repercussions of this event. Armenian **casualties** are estimated at 2 million, though the Turkish government suggests that they are much lower. The Turkish government denies that the program was officially sanctioned, and claims that it was a spontaneous military response to the threat posed by the Armenians' treasonous alliance with Russia. They assert that the high death count was largely a result of intercommunal warfare between Armenians and Kurds, and that many Turks were killed as well. In any event, the Turkish government claims that all state records of orders and decrees concerning the slaughter, known as *tercih* in Turkish, have been lost or corrupted. Other international sources believe that the incident was the first state-sanctioned genocide of the 20th century. Armenians and their supporters demand that Turkey officially recognize the genocide and provide some form of apology or compensation. In the 1980s a group known as the Armenian Secret Army for the Liberation of Armenia (ASALA) murdered over 30 Turkish diplomats to bring attention to these demands. Many Turks today, however, feel that it is unrealistic and impossible for them to assume responsibility for actions of the Ottomans of almost a century ago.

JEWS

The earliest evidence of Jewish culture in Turkey is among the synagogue ruins of **Sardis,** dating back to about 220 BC. Today, 96% of Turkish Jews are of **Sephardic** descent, tracing their lineage back to those who fled Iberia in the 15th century. Some fled the Inquisition, but the majority were expelled after the Christian *reconquista* of Spain and Portugal in 1492. (The term "Sephardic" comes from the Hebrew word for "Spain," though it was originally applied to the area around Sardis to which Jews fled after Nebucchadnezzar's conquest of Jerusalem.) Under the Ottomans, Jews led relatively untroubled lives. Viewed by Muslim authorities as "people of the book," they received the same privileges as Christians. Many attained high social standing, becoming diplomats, doctors, and writers.

Jews represent a population of about 26,000 in Turkey today, concentrated mainly in İstanbul and with large communities in İzmir and Ankara. The remaining population is mainly Ashkenazi (Jews living in Germany up until the 11th-13th century Crusades), though there is a handful of Karaites, those who do not subscribe to the authority of the chief rabbi. The older generation of Sephardic Jews still speaks **Ladino,** a variant of the 15th-century Judeo-Spanish language, while the Ashkenazis speak Yiddish and the Karaites speak Greek. One newspaper survives, the eight-page weekly ŞALOM, which includes seven pages in Turkish and one in Ladino. Dating to the early 15th century, the Ahrida Synagogue in the Balat neighborhood is the oldest of İstanbul's 16 synagogues in use today.

Throughout the **Holocaust,** Turkey extended open refuge to Jews fearing Nazi persecution, and notable Jewish intellectuals were invited to find safety behind Turkish borders. However, Turkey has been accused, along with Switzerland, Sweden, Portugal, Spain, and Argentina, of helping to prolong WWII by supplying Germany with wartime goods in return for looted gold. After the war, Turkey's gold reserves had jumped from 27 to 216 tons, none of which has been returned. A committee is currently investigating these allegations. Upon the establishment of an Israeli state in 1948, 30,000 Jews emigrated from Turkey, and the population has continued to decline steadily over the past few decades.

ALEVİ

The term "Alevi" does not actually refer to a single group of people. Rather, it refers to numerous heterodox communities with a wide range of belief structures, rituals, languages, and practices. The Alevi can be divided into four primary groups based on language: Azerbaijani Turkish speakers of Eastern Turkey, the Arabic speakers of southern Turkey (with ties only to communities in Syria), and the more populous Kurdish- and Turkish-speaking groups. The Turkish Alevi are concentrated in central Anatolia, while Kurdish Alevi are settled in southeastern Anatolia. The Alevi are estimated to comprise between 15-25% of the population.

The Alevi are Shi'ite Muslims (see **The Historical Evolution of Islam,** p. 26) who adhere to simple moral norms rather than the *Sharia* (Islamic law) and the traditional pillars of Islam. Elements of pre-Islamic Turkish and Persian religions infuse Alevi practice with more mysticism than is present in Sunni Islam. The Alevi believe in direct communion with God without the intermediary of the prayer leader. Thus, the only religious figure is the advice-giving *dede* (wise man). Much like the dervishes, the Alevi celebrate their religion through music and dance in religious ceremonies known as *cem.* That men and women perform these dances together has traditionally been a source of contempt among Sunni Muslims, who emphasize the potential for unholy activities.

There is some indication that the Alevi were discriminated against under the Ottoman Empire. Forced to settle in isolated mountain villages, they began to emigrate only as recently as the 1950s. This mistreatment by the ruling Sunni majority had transformed the Alevi into ardent supporters of the secularization of the state; they embraced Kemalism since it allowed them to fit into mainstream Turkish society. In fact, the Kurdish Alevi, who tend to identify with their religious group rather than their ethno-linguistic one, had helped the state to oppose the Kurdish rebellion of 1925. More recently, the Alevi became increasingly politicized as Sunni-Alevi clashes in the 1970s demonstrated to Turkish officials the difficulty of realizing the unified, homogenous, secular state that Atatürk envisioned. Sivas, a town with a large Alevi population, has been the site of many of these clashes. The most recent, in 1993, began as a protest against a provocative Alevi writer and claimed the lives of 37 Alevis trapped in a burning hotel (see **Otel Madımak**, p. 376).

The early 1980s saw a major government effort to homogenize Turkish Islam and to incorporate the distinctive Alevi. The **Turkish-Islamic Synthesis** doctrine promulgated by a group of conservative intellectuals, fused Islam with Turkish nationalism and became a sort of state ideology. Because of their greater visibility the Alevi have become increasingly vulnerable to violence from certain conservative groups, inspiring some radicalized Alevis to draw parallels between their own situation and that of the Kurds; both stand as obstacles to the nationalistic, antipluralistic conservative agenda of Turkey's most extreme factions.

THE LAZ, THE HEMŞİN, AND THE CIRCASSIANS

The **Laz,** though present throughout Turkey, are concentrated largely in the eastern regions of the Black Sea coast near the border with Georgia. Numbering approximately 250,000, the Laz have a reputation for being successful businesspeople, as they own and operate many of the Black Sea shipping companies. Their relative affluence often makes them the subject of envy and ethnic jokes among young Turks. It seems likely that they migrated from the war-torn region of **Abkhazia,** the westernmost province of the Republic of Georgia, in the 16th century when they were driven west to Turkey by Arab invaders. Christians until the 16th century, the Laz gradually converted and became so assimilated that most have completely forgotten their religious heritage. Related to Georgian, the Laz language, *Lazuri*, was purely a spoken one until the 1960s, when its alphabet was codified as a combination of Georgian and Latin letters.

The **Hemşin** people, historically concentrated around Ayder in northeastern Anatolia, are Caucasians like the Laz. Traditional Hemşin villages are suffering from the flight of their youth to urban centers—there are only about 15,000 Hemşin people left in the Ayder region. There is some speculation that the Hemşin might have originated in the area of modern-day Armenia. Like the Laz, the Hemşin people were originally Christian, and even now, their version of Islam is much more relaxed than that of most of their ethnic Turkish neighbors. The Hemşin are traditionally beekeepers and pastry makers (see **Hemşinli,** p. 415).

The **Circassians** (*Çerkes* in Turkish) originated in the northern Caucasus region. With several hundred thousand members, this is the largest of the Caucasian minority groups in Turkey. Most Circassians today are descendants of refugees forced to leave their homelands during the 19th-century Russian occupation. The fall of the Soviet Union seemed at first to be a likely catalyst for Circassian repatriation, but the 1992 war in Abkhazia and the subsequent wars in Chechnya served as major deterrents. During the last decade, the Turkish Circassian communities have become more visible and are experiencing a revitalization.

LANGUAGE

Once thought to be related to Finnish, Hungarian, and Mongolian, Turkish is now classified in a distinct Turkic language group. This group includes such widely spoken tongues as Azerbaijani, Kazakh, Khirgiz, Uyghur, and Uzbek. Turkish dominates the group. In his 1928 effort to forge a secular Turkish identity, Atatürk instituted the use of a romanized alphabet and purged Turkish of many of its Arabic and Persian borrowings. This linguistic cleansing was not absolute; common Arabic and Persian words such as *merhaba* (hello) remain.

Visitors with little or no experience with Turkish should not be intimidated. Any attempt at speaking Turkish will be much appreciated by the Turks. (For **pronunciations** and a brief **glossary,** see p. 476). English is widely spoken wherever tourism is big business—mainly in the major coastal resorts. In the rest of Anatolia, only university students tend to know English. A small phrasebook will help greatly during your travels. For more in-depth study, consult *Teach Yourself Turkish* by Pollard and Pollard (New York, 1996).

CUSTOMS AND ETIQUETTE

Turks value **hospitality** and will frequently go out of their way to welcome travelers, commonly offering to buy visitors a meal or a cup of çay (tea). Do not refuse tea unless you have very strong objections; it provides a friendly, easy way to converse with locals. If you are invited to a Turkish house as a guest, it is customary to bring a small gift such as flowers or chocolates and to remove your shoes before entering. A pair of slippers will usually be provided. When chatting with Turks, do not speak with any disrespect or skepticism about Atatürk, founder of modern Turkey, and avoid other sensitive subjects. In particular, do not discuss the Kurdish issue and the PKK, Northern Cyprus, and Turkey's human rights record.

BODY VIBES. In Turkey, **body language** often matters as much as the spoken word. When a Turk raises his chin and clicks his tongue, he means *hayır* (no); this gesture is sometimes accompanied by a shutting of the eyes or the raising of eyebrows. A sideways shake of the head means *anlamadım* (I don't understand), and *evet* (yes) may be signalled by a sharp downward nod. If a Turk waves a hand up and down at you, palm toward the ground, she is signaling you to come, not bidding you farewell. In Turkey the idle habit of snapping the fingers of one hand and then slapping the top of the other fist is considered obscene. It is also considered rude to point your finger or the sole of your shoe towards someone. Though public displays of affection are inappropriate, Turks greet each other with a kiss on both cheeks.

Turks often stare at one another more than visitors are used to, and women in particular may feel uncomfortable by the stares. Try not to feel threatened by the usually harmless interest. Smiling, regarded in the West as a sign of confidence and outgoing friendliness, is sometimes associated in Turkey with a lack of sincerity or an element of deception. Often, what might appear to be grimness in some Turks may be a mistranslation of an everyday interaction or gesture.

DRESS. Shorts are a sure way to attract a tourist label. Most Turkish men, and especially Turkish women, do not wear shorts. Women will find a head scarf or a bandana handy, perhaps essential, in more conservative regions of the country. Except in İstanbul and the resort towns of the Aegean and Mediterranean coasts, where such dress is much more widely accepted, scanty clothing sends an audacious or flirtatious signal. Long skirts and lightweight pants are most acceptable. They are also comfortable and practical, especially in summer. T-shirts are fine, though you should cover your arms in the more religious parts of the country. While topless bathing is common in some parts of the Aegean and Mediterranean coasts, it is not acceptable in other regions of the country. Nude sunbathing is officially illegal.

> # VISITING MOSQUES
> Many of Turkey's greatest architectural monuments, including tombs and mosques, have religious significance. Visitors are welcome, but they ought to show their respect for the holiness of these places by dressing and acting appropriately. Shorts and skimpy clothing are forbidden inside mosques. Women must cover their arms, heads, and legs, and both sexes should take off their shoes and carry them inside. There are usually shoe racks in the back of the mosques, or caretakers will provide plastic bags for carrying your shoes. Do not take flash photos, never take photos of people in prayer, avoid visits on Fridays (the holy day) and during prayer times, announced by the call to prayer from the mosque's minarets.

TURKEY

LEISURE

Many popular Turkish pastimes still take place in all-male enclaves. A favorite is visiting the local *kıraathane* (coffeehouse), where customers sip coffee or tea over games of *tavla* (backgammon). Another popular game is *OKEY*, which is basically gin rummy played with tiles instead of cards. Men can be found smoking *nargile*s (hookahs) in some corners of Turkey. If you decide to purchase a *nargile* as a souvenir, make sure customs officials do not mistake it for a *water pipe* or *water filtration device* (bong).

THE HAMAM. Because of the Islamic emphasis on cleanliness (pious Muslims perform ablutions before each of the day's five prayers), the baths have been a customary part of daily life since medieval times. They have traditionally functioned as social meeting places, especially for women, who otherwise wouldn't leave the house often. Men and women use separate bathhouses, or the same ones on different days. A sign on a hamam door gives a schedule for women *(kadınlar)* and men *(erkekler)*. For more information, check out **Hamam-o-Rama**, below.

SPORTS. A passion for *spor* proves itself the common denominator among Turks, transcending religious, cultural, and social lines. Although Turks do follow other sports, particularly American basketball, they are **futbol** (soccer) fanatics. Of Turkey's numerous soccer teams, only four have risen to national significance: Fenerbahçe, Beşiktaş, Galatasaray, and Trabzon Spor. Fans living outside İstanbul or Trabzon generally root for one of the four in addition to their smaller home clubs. All four play very fast, very scrappy, world-class soccer. **Fenerbahçe,** hailing from an Asian İstanbul suburb, is immediately recognizable by its blue and yellow team shirts. Nobody, not even die-hard fans of the European Bosphorus counterpart Beşiktaş, really dislikes Fener, the first foreign team ever to beat Manchester United *in* Manchester, in 1997. Commanding the most respect abroad, yellow and red **Galatasaray** is an old, venerated outfit and the reigning Turkish champ. In May of 2000, they made headlines worldwide with their defeat of Britain's Arsenal in the UEFA Cup finals, bringing the trophy and pride to the people of Turkey. **Beşiktas,** the "Black Eagles" in black and white, play very tight soccer, and purple-and-blue **Trabzon Spor** (see p. 408) is the upstart of the bunch, with a zealous fan base consolidated in eastern Turkey. Because of past violence at matches, large numbers of riot police now patrol the scene, confiscating lighters at the entrance.

Traditional spectator sports such as *cirit oyunu* (tossing javelins at competitors on horseback) and *deve güresi* (camel wrestling) enjoy a very local following and are generally practiced during festivals. One exception is the Kırkpınar Grease Wrestling Festival (see p. 143), held in Edirne in the second and third weeks of July; it draws a huge crowd and enjoys TV broadcasts throughout Turkey.

HAMAM-O-RAMA Hamams can be intimidating for first-timers, but they're well worth the effort. Pay the entrance fee plus massage and *kese* (see below). Bring your own shampoo, soap, and towel, or pay to use the bath's. Some hamams have cubicles *(camekan)* for personal storage. You will be given a large towel *(peştemal)*. Men generally strip and wrap the *peştemal* around their waists, but don't drop that sucker! Turkish women frequently strip naked (in the hamam).

Some hamams have a hot, sauna-like room. After you've worked up a sweat, proceed to the warm main room with its large, heated stone *(göbek taşı)*. Mix hot and cold water and pour it over yourself with the bowl provided.

A wash and **massage** on the large, heated marble stone costs a little more. Usually, the masseuse is your gender; female visitors may request a female masseuse. The massage is often very vigorous; try the phrase *"lütfen daha yumuşak"* (gentler please) if need be. The *kese* (abrasive mitt) used can also be purchased at pharmacies. Following the massage and *kese*, you will usually be sponged gently and shampooed. When you're clean as a whistle, rehydrate with water and a have a nap.

FOOD AND DRINK

Contemporary Turkish cuisine reflects its Ottoman heritage. Popular dishes such as *kebap* (kebab) and *pilav* (rice) derive from the traditions of nomadic Central Asian tribes and other civilizations that have swept through Asia Minor. An Assyrian cookbook found during recent excavations showed that similar dishes have been served for thousands of years. Fans of Greek, Armenian, and Middle Eastern food will recognize favorite dishes on Turkish menus, but these neighboring traditions have been reinterpreted and recombined to forge a unique cuisine.

Although Turkish food varies from region to region, some staples will turn up in just about any Turkish kitchen: yogurt, olive oil, bread, rice, lamb, spices, and, above all, fresh produce. Pre-packaged and processed food items are rarely used.

Turks typically start the day with a **breakfast** of freshly baked bread, thick honey, jam, olives, cheese, a soft-boiled egg, sliced tomatoes, and cucumbers, complemented by strong Turkish tea. Many *pansiyons* (small hotels) will offer breakfast for a small sum or free of charge.

APPETIZERS AND ACCOMPANIMENTS. Lunch and dinner often begin with *meze*, hot or cold appetizers which can be a meal in themselves. *Meze* come in many forms, from simple *beyaz peynir* (feta cheese) to complex vegetable dishes. Most menus feature *dolma*, a kind of *meze* whose name comes from the verb meaning to fill or to stuff (not coincidentally the same verb that gives the *dolmuş* its name). *Dolma* include peppers, grape leaves, and tomatoes stuffed with rice or meat. *İmam bayıldı* (literally, "the priest fainted") is a stuffed eggplant dish. *Börek* is another common *meze* item—a flaky pastry either filled with *kıyma* (meat), *peynir* (cheese), or *ıspınak* (spinach). *Börek* can be *sigara* (long crispy fried rolls which resemble cigarettes), *su* (lasagna-like noodles with cheese filling), or *normal* (flaky pastry dough with filling). Other *meze* include salads and soups.

Lettuce makes only rare appearances in Turkish salads. More common varieties of salad include *çoban salatası* (chopped tomato and cucumber salad), *patlıcan salatası* (pureed eggplant), *yeşil salatası* (green salad, also called *mevsim salatası*—the closest you'll come to an American-style side salad), *cacık* (thin yogurt with cucumbers, often spiced with garlic), and *Amerikan salatası*–an ill-named mixture of peas, carrots, potatoes, and mayonnaise.

Çorba (soup) changes with the seasons. Thicker soups like *mercimek çorbası* (lentil soup) and *domates çorbası* (tomato soup with shredded *kaşar* cheese) are a mainstay in the winter months, while cool, minty yogurt soups dominate summer menus. Inebriated Turks coming back from a wild night on the town often head straight to the nearest *çorba* joint to have a piping-hot bowl of *kırmızı mercimek çorbası* (red lentil soup) or *işkembe çorbası* (tripe soup). Lord knows stomach always tastes better after a good night of drinking.

MAIN DISHES—AAAHH, MEAT. Ubiquity, thy name is **kebap**. Almost every meal in Turkey involves meat, and meat in Turkey usually means lamb. Many restaurants specialize in **köfte** (small, spiced meatballs), **mantı** (tiny meat-filled ravioli), or other meat dishes, and the varieties of this staple are limitless. Coastal Turkey travel merits at least a stop at one of the fish restaurants. Selections vary according to season, region, and the catch of the day; diners choose their *balık* (fish) from the display. Eating fish requires nimble teeth: it's cooked and served whole, with bones, head, and tail.

VEGETABLES AND FRUIT. Fresh produce, grown along the western and southern coasts, is the secret ingredient in Turkish cuisine. Fruits and vegetables are not grown out of season. To find the best produce available, join the basket-toting women at any of the markets listed in this book. **Carefully wash all produce with bottled or boiled water before taking a bite.** An even better rule of ▧ thumb is only to eat peelable fruit. Take the plunge and treat your taste buds to a combination of *karpuz* (watermelon) and *beyaz peynir* (feta cheese).

PLEASE PASS THE KEBAP

Sure, the meaty kebap was a treat at first, but after 75 identical meals in a row, you'd rather eat glass. Aside from upscale restaurants, which often offer the same tired menu for Trump-ish prices, your best bet for a wider variety of cheap Turkish cuisine is the *lokanta* (sometimes *lokantası*). These restaurants lie off the tourist path and cater mostly to working men. Their style is usually cafeteria-like: seven or eight dishes will have been prepared for the day, of which two or three are meat-based. The rest are mainly vegetarian (though some may contain unexpected pieces of meat). Everything comes in sized portions and is extremely cheap ($1-2 per serving). For real sampling, request a half-serving. The only drawback to *lokanta*s is that women may feel a tad uncomfortable joining the rows of male patrons. Some *lokanta*s have an *"aile"* section upstairs, reserved for families and single women, which is usually much cleaner and airier than the men's section. In any case, don't worry about unwanted social contact in the *lokanta*. People usually eat quickly and with no conversation, knowing they soon have to head back to work.

SWEETS. Save room for dessert, which is almost always sticky and sweet. Highlights include *baklava* (a flaky, sweet nut pastry, usually with pistachio), *kadayif* (shredded pastry dough filled with nuts and drenched in syrup), *tavukgöğsu* (a creamy sweet made of pulverized chicken fibers), and *helva* (sesame paste). The *dondurma* (ice cream) manages to be chewy and sticky and frozen all at the same time. Keep an eye out for pudding shops, where you can try the *aşure* (fruit pudding), *sütlaç* (rice pudding), *krem karamel* (crème caramel), and *profiterol*.

STREET FOOD. Taking advantage of street food is one of the joys of adventures in Turkish cuisine: it varies with season, region, quality, and freshness. Baked goods like *simit* (a sesame bread ring), *poğaça* (flaky pastry often served with a layer of cheese), and *börek* are safe, as are most dried fruit and nuts. However, buying ice cream on the street may be a bad idea. As always, be cautious, and remember that your stomach may not be used to the benign bacteria found in Turkish food.

Besides the snacks sold on Atatürk Caddesis throughout the nation, Turkey offers the budget traveler a delicious array of inexpensive fast food. Instead of a Big Mac (although there's that, too), try *gözleme*, a crêpe-tortilla hybrid, filled with cheese, potatoes, spinach, or meat; *kokoreç*, fried, chopped tripe (a cow's stomach lining), usually in sandwiches with tomatoes; *lahmacun*, often called Turkish pizza, a thin rounded bread topped with ground spiced meat; *tost*, a grilled cheese sandwich; or *kumpir*, baked potatoes piled high with toppings.

DRINKS. When in Turkey, do as the Turks do and **always drink only bottled or purified water.** A half cup full of pure caffeine, *kahve* (Kick-Me-In-The-Face-Turkish coffee) can be ordered *sade* (black), *orta* (medium sweet), or *şekerli* (very sweet). Despite the fame garnered by Turkish coffee, Turkey's national drink remains, without a doubt, *çay* (tea). Served in small, hourglass-shaped glasses, *çay* is strong, black, and everywhere. *Elma çayı* (apple tea), which tastes like warmed apple juice, is an alternative to conventional Turkish tea's strong brew. Turks drink *çay* with new acquaintances, old friends, and potential carpet buyers.

Ayran, a salty yogurt drink, is usually drunk with meat dishes and in hot weather. *Meyva suyu* (fruit juice), *maden suyu* (mineral water), and *cola* (Coca-Cola) are all common beverages. *Sahlep*, available only in winter, is a warm, sweet, milky drink made of pulverized orchid root and served with cinnamon.

Alcohol, though widely available, is frowned upon in the more conservative parts of the country. Restaurants that post *içkisiz* in their windows have none, but those with *içkili* are taking special pains to announce alcohol's availability. *Bira* (beer) is ever-popular: *Efes Pilsen* and *Tüborg* are the leading brands, with the former is better. The best domestic white wines are *Çankaya*, *Villa Doluca*, and *Kavaklıdere*, made in Cappadocia. The best red wines are *Yakut* and *Kavaklıdere*. Ice-cold *rakı*, a clear anise-seed liquor with the taste of licorice, is Turkey's national alcohol. Mixed in equal parts with water, which clouds it, *rakı* is similar to Greek *ouzo*, but even stronger. İstanbul's local specialty is *balyoz* (sledge hammer/wrecking ball). Getting wrecked will not be difficult: *balyoz* consists of *rakı*, whiskey, vodka, and gin mixed with orange juice. Yipes.

HOLIDAYS AND FESTIVALS

In Turkey, these are of three kinds: national secular, national religious, and local. Since religious holidays are dependent on the lunar calendar, the day they fall on varies from year to year. Local festivals are often dependent upon the harvest, the weather, or the moon, and as such it is difficult to predict exact dates. For specific dates of a given festival, contact the town's tourist office. If you anticipate traveling in a town or region during festival time, check ahead on accommodations, since hotels and pensions in many towns can fill up quickly. For more specific information about the holidays, see the appropriate city section.

Turkey's religious holidays, festivals, and traditions are sometimes overwhelming for travelers. **Ramazan,** which occurs during a different one-month period every year, is a time of fasting for observant Muslims (see **The Five Pillars of Islam,** p. 25). Though tourists are not expected to comply with the holiday, it is important to remember that this is the holiest month of the year for many Turks, and that respect for their customs is imperative. If you're in Turkey during Ramazan, be aware that many restaurants are closed. In those that are open, the clientele will be largely foreign. It is advisable that you not drink, eat, or smoke cigarettes on the street until sunset. *Oruç tutmak* (fasting) is a test of faith, and it is considered disrespectful to tempt the faithful in this way. At sundown, *Ramazan pidesi*, a special, dense flatbread, is used to break the daily fast. The three-day festival of **Şeker Bayramı** (Sugar Holiday) occurs at the end of Ramazan, and is celebrated with family gatherings, the giving of sweets to children, and general festivity. **Kurban Bayramı** (Sacrifice Holiday) usually occurs a few months after Ramazan, and involves the large-scale slaughter of sheep. Families with enough money purchase sheep, which are sold during that week on streetcorners throughout the country. The animals are slaughtered on the appointed day and distributed to the poor.

DATE	FESTIVAL	CITY/OBSERVANCE
Nov. 27, 2000 Nov 17, 2001	Ramazan (Ramadan)	National (religious) Duration is one month; date given is first day. Starting date may vary by one day depending on the moon.
Eve of the 28th day of the month of Ramazan	Kadır Gecesi (Eve of Power)	National (religious) Varies with Ramazan.
December 27, 2000 December 16, 2001	Sugar Holiday (Şeker Bayramı)	National (religious) Date may vary by 1 or 2 days depending on the moon.
December 10-17, 2000	Rumi Commemoration—Mevlâna Festival	Konya
January 1	Yılbaşı—New Year's Day	National (secular)
3rd weekend in January	Camel Wrestling Festival	Selçuk
March	Film Festival	Ankara
March 5-9	Festival of the Sacrifice (Kurban Bayramı)	National (religious) Date varies with the moon.
March 16	Day of the Hajj	National (religious) Varies with Ramazan.
March 18	Sea Victory Celebration	Çanakkale
4 days around the vernal equinox (March 21)	Mesir Macunu ("Power Gum") Festival	Manisa
March/April	Bald Ibis Festival	Gaziantep, Şanlıurfa, Birecik
Last 2 weeks of April	Film Festival	İstanbul
April 23	Independence Day and Children's Day	National (secular)

DATE	FESTIVAL	CITY/OBSERVANCE
April 25	ANZAC DAY	Gelibolu Peninsula
Late April	Power Gum Festival	Manisa
2nd week of May	Ephesus Performance Festival	Ephesus
2nd week of May	Yacht Festival	Marmaris
May 19	Youth and Sports Day—Atatürk's Birthday	National (secular)
May 20	Black Sea Giresun Aksu Festival	Giresun
May 29	Anniversary of İstanbul's capture in 1453 by Mehmet the Conqueror	İstanbul
Late May/Early June	Song Competition	Pamukkale
June	International Tea Festival	Rize
June	İzmir Music and Dance Fair	İzmir, Çeşme, Ephesus
June	Kuşadası Music Festival	Kuşadası
June	Cherry Festival	Tekirdağ
June 4	Birth of the Prophet (Peace Be Upon Him)	National (religious) Date varies with the moon
3rd week of June	Bull Wrestling/Caucasus Culture and Arts Festival	Artvin
Last week of June	International Golden Pomegranate Festival	Kemer-Antalya
Late June/Early July	Aspendos Opera and Ballet Festival	Antalya
Late June/Early July	Golden Hazelnut Festival	Ordu
June/July	Music Festival	İstanbul
July	VW Beetle Festival	Ordu
July	Folk Dance Festival	Samsun
July	Nasreddin Hoca Festival	Akşehir
July	Hittite Festival	Çorum
July 1	Navy Day	National (secular)
1st week of July	Kırkpınar Grease Wrestling Festival	Edirne
Early July	Bursa Festival	Bursa
2nd or 3rd week of July	Apricot Harvest Festival	Malatya
July/August	Highland Festivals	Trabzon
August 16-18	Hacibektaş Veli Commemoration Ceremony	Hacibektaş
August 26	Armed Forces Day	İstanbul
August 30	Celebration of Turkish Defeat of Greece (1922)	National (secular)
End of August	International Pop Song Contest	Çesme
August/September	İzmir International Fair	İzmir
September	Architectural Treasures and Folklore Week	Safranbolu
September	International Efes Festival	Efes (Ephesus)
1st week of September	Golden Apple and Silver Fish Festival	Eğirdir
September 9	Liberation Day (speeches marking the end of the Independence War)	İzmir
Late September	Meerschaum (White Gold) Festival	Eskişehir
Late September	Wine Competition	Ürgüp
September/October	Golden Pistachio Festival	Gaziantep
September/October	Plastic Arts Festival	İstanbul
September/October	Mediterranean Song Contest	Antalya
October	Atatürk Dam Sailing Competition	Alanya
End of October	Yacht Festival/Race Week	Marmaris
October 29	Republic Holiday—Celebration of Atatürk's Declaration of the Republic	National (secular)
November 10, 9:05am	Anniversary of Atatürk's Death (nationwide moment of silence)	National (secular)

ESSENTIALS

FACTS FOR THE TRAVELER

CLIMATE

Avg Temp	January		April		July		October	
	°C	°F	°C	°F	°C	°F	°C	°F
Ankara	0	32	11	51.8	23	73.4	13	55.4
Antalya	10	50	16	60.8	28	82.4	20	68
Erzurum	-9	15.8	5	41	19	66.2	9	42.8
İstanbul	5	41	12	53.6	23	73.4	16	60.8
İzmir	9	48.2	16	60.8	28	82.4	18	64.4
Trabzon	6	42.8	11	51.8	22	71.6	15	59
Van	-2	28.4	7	44.6	23	73.4	10	50
Lefkoşa, Cyprus	10	50	18	64.4	29	84.2	21	69.8

Avg Rain mm	Jan	Feb	Mar	Apr	May	Jun	July	Aug	Sep	Oct	Nov	Dec
Ankara	48.7	52	43.5	43	56	36.6	13.5	4.5	27	22	26	64
Antalya	244	164	96	43.3	23	8	2.4	3	12	61	117	253
Erzurum	25	28	34.5	53.7	72.4	52	27.3	11	23	46	35.6	23.1
İstanbul	93	68	62	46	30	26	14	32	47	63	92	112
İzmir	127	94	74	41	31	9	3	4	16	34	86	133
Trabzon	81	66	59	57.4	59.2	55	32	44	74	108	94.7	76.1
Van	33	32	43	55	47	18	6.5	3	12.5	44	46	33
Lefkoşa	71	49.5	36.5	19	25	9	1	2.5	4.5	21	39	73.5

DOCUMENTS AND FORMALITIES

TURKISH CONSULAR SERVICES ABROAD

Australia: Embassy: 60 Mugga Way, Red Hill, **Canberra** ACT 2603 (☎(02) 6295 0227 or 6295 0228; fax 6239 6592; email turkembs@ozemail.com.au). **Consulates:** 24 Albert Rd. South, 8th fl., **Melbourne** VIC 3205 (☎(03) 9696 6066 or 9696 6046; fax 9696 6104; email turkcons@eisa.net.au); 66 Ocean St., P.O. Box 222, Woollahra, **Sydney** NSW 2025 (☎(612) 9328 1155, 9328 1239, or 9326 1618; fax 9362 4533).

Canada: Embassy: 197 Wurtemburg St., Ottawa, ON, K1N 8L9 (☎(613) 789-4044 or 789-3440; fax 789-3442; email turkish@magma.ca).

Ireland: Embassy: 11 Clyde Rd., Ballsbridge, **Dublin** 4 (☎(01) 668 5240 or 660 1623; fax 668 5014; email turkemb@iol.ie).

New Zealand: Embassy: 15-17 Murphy St., Level 8, **Wellington** (☎(04) 472 1290 or 472 1292; fax 472 1277; email turkem@xtra.co.nz).

South Africa: Embassy: 1067 Church St., Hatfield, **Pretoria** 0181 (☎(012) 342 6053 or 342 6057; fax 342 6052; email pretbe@global.co.za). **Consulate:** 6 Sandown Valley Crescent 2nd fl., Sandown-Sandton, **Johannesburg** 2001 (☎(011) 884 9060 or 884 9061/2/3; fax 884 9064).

UK: Embassy: 43 Belgrave Sq., **London,** SWIX 8PA (☎(020) 7393 0202; fax 7393 0066; email turkish.embassy@virgin.net). **Consulate:** Rultand Lodge, Rutland Gardens, Knightsbridge, **London,** SW7 1BW (☎(020) 7589 0949, 7589 0360, or 7584 1078; fax 7584 6235; email trcons@globalnet.co.uk).

US: Embassy: 2525 Massachusetts Ave. NW, Washington, D.C. 20008 (☎(202) 612-6706; fax 612-6744; email info@turkey.org). **Consulates:** 360 N. Michigan Ave., #1405, **Chicago,** IL 60601 (☎(312) 263-0644 or 263-1295; fax 263-1449; email chicago@tr.consulate.org); 1990 Post Oak Blvd., #1300, **Houston,** TX 77056 (☎(713) 622-5849, 622-0324, or 622-3205; fax 623-6639; email turcon@ix.netcom.com); 4801 Wilshire Blvd., #310, **Los Angeles,** CA 90010 (☎(323) 937-0118; fax (323) 932-0061; email lacg@turkiye.net); 821 United Nations Plaza, 5th fl., **New York,** NY 10017 (☎(212) 949-0159, 949-0160, or 949-0161; fax 983-1293; email tcbkny@worldnet.att.net).

CONSULAR SERVICES IN TURKEY

Australia: Embassy: 83 Nenehatun Cad., Gaziosmanpaşa, **Ankara** 06700 (☎(312) 446 11 80/87; fax 446 11 88). **Consulate:** 58 Tepecik Yolu, Etiler, **İstanbul** 80630 (☎(212) 257 70 50 or 257 70 53; fax: (212) 257 70 54).

Canada: Embassy, 75 Nenehatun Cad., Gaziosmanpaşa, **Ankara** 06700 (☎436 12 75; fax 447 21 73). **Consulate:** 107/3 Büyükdere Cad., Bengun Han, Gayrettepe, **İstanbul** 80300 (☎(212) 272 51 74; fax 272 34 27).

Ireland: Embassy: Ugur Mumcu Cad. MNG Binasi, B Bloc, Kat 3, Gaziomanpaşa, **Ankara** 06700 (☎(312) 446 61 72; fax (312) 446 80 61). **Consulate:** 26/A Cumhuriyet Cad., Pegasus Evi, Harbiye, **İstanbul** (☎(212) 246 60 25; fax (212) 248 07 44).

New Zealand: Embassy, 13/4 İran Cad., Kavaklıdere, **Ankara** (☎(312) 467 90 56; fax 467 90 13).

South Africa: Embassy: 27 Filistin Sok., Gaziosmanpaşa, **Ankara** (☎(312) 446 40 56; fax 446 64 34; email saemb@ada.net.tr). **Consulate:** Servetci is Merkezi, Kat:15, 106 Büyükdere Cad., Esentepe, **İstanbul** (☎(212) 288 04 28; fax (212) 275 76 42).

UK: Embassy: 46/A Şehit Ersan Cad., Çankaya, **Ankara** (☎(312) 468 62 30/42; fax 468 66 43; email britembank@ankara.mail.fco.gov.uk). **Consulates:** Ucgen Mahallest Dolaplidere Cad., Pirilti Sitesi Kati ilit, Sauna Karisi, **Antalya** (honorary; ☎(242) 247 70 00; fax (242) 243 14 82); Kızılsaray Mah., Dolaplıdere Cad., Pırıltı, Sitesti, Kat 1, **Bodrum** 48400 (☎(252) 316 49 92; fax 313 00 52); Catoni Maritime Agencies, 28 Maresal Cakmak Cad., **Iskenderun** (☎(326) 613 03 61/2/3; fax 613 03 64); Meşrutiyet Cad. #34, Tepebaşı, Beyoğlu, PK 33, **İstanbul** 80072 (☎(212) 252 64 36; fax 245 49 89); Mahmut Esat Bozkurt Cad. 1442 Sok. No. 49, Alsancak, PK 300, **İzmir** (☎(232) 463 51 51; fax 421 29 14); Yesil Marmaris Tourism and Yacht Management Inc. 118 Barbaros Cad., P.O. Box 8, **Marmaris** 48700 (☎(252) 412 64 86; fax 412 50 77); Catoni Maritime Agencies SA, Cakmak Cad. Mersin Orta Okulu Sok. No. 3/B, **Mersin** (☎(324) 232 12 48 or 237 86 87; fax 232 29 91).

US: Embassy: 110 Atatürk Bul., Kavaklıdere, **Ankara** 06100 (☎(312) 468 61 10; fax (312) 768 61 31). **Consulates:** Atatürk Cad. Vali Yolu, Bossa Apt. Kat 1, **Adana** (☎(322) 453 91 06; fax 457 65 91); 104-108 Meşrutiyet Cad., Tepebaşı, **İstanbul** 80050 (☎/fax (212) 251 36 02). Consular Agent, Kazim Dirik Cad., Atabay İş Merkezi 13/8, Daire 805, Pasaport, **İzmir** (☎(232) 441 00 72).

PASSPORTS

REQUIREMENTS. Citizens of Australia, Canada, Ireland, New Zealand, South Africa, the UK, and the US need valid passports to enter Turkey and to re-enter their own countries. Turkey does not allow entrance if the holder's passport expires in under six months. Returning home with an expired passport is illegal, and may result in a fine.

PHOTOCOPIES. Be sure to photocopy the page of your passport with your photo, passport number, and other identifying information, as well as any visas, travel insurance policies, plane tickets, or traveler's check serial numbers. Carry one set of copies in a safe place, apart from the originals, and leave another set at home. Consulates also recommend that you carry an expired passport or an official copy of your birth certificate in a part of your baggage separate from other documents.

LOST PASSPORTS. If you lose your passport, immediately notify the local police and the nearest embassy or consulate of your home government. To expedite its replacement, you will need to know all information previously recorded and show identification and proof of citizenship. In an emergency, ask for immediate temporary traveling papers that will permit you to re-enter your home country. For most of the embassies and consulates in Turkey, these can be issued within three to four working days.

NEW PASSPORTS. File an application from your local post office or passport authority. Applications for new passports or renewals should be filed several weeks or months in advance of your planned departure date. Most passport offices offer emergency passport services for an extra charge.

VISAS AND WORK PERMITS

As of August 2000, citizens of Australia, Ireland, the UK, and the US require a visa—a stamp, sticker, or insert in your passport specifying the purpose of your travel and the permitted duration of your stay—in addition to a valid passport for entrance to Turkey. A visa costs US$45 for Americans; it is valid for a year from the date of issuance, and allows multiple entry to Turkey for a period not exceeding three months. A three-month visa costs AUS$20 for Australians, £10 for British citizens, and £5 for Irish citizens. Citizens of Canada, New Zealand, and South Africa do not need visas to enter Turkey. New Zealanders may stay for up to three months with a valid passport, South Africans for up to one month. Though visas can be obtained from the Turkish embassy or consulate in your home country, it is most convenient (and cheapest) to get them upon arrival in Turkey. US citizens can take advantage of the **Center for International Business and Travel (CIBT;** ☎ (800) 925-2428), which secures visas for a variable service charge. Visas can be purchased at the airport or at the border upon entry to Turkey.

Visitors traveling on a tourist visa are not permitted to work, which is authorized only by a **work permit.** Students must obtain a **student visa.** Unlike tourist visas, work permits and student visas **must** be obtained from the nearest Turkish embassy or consulate prior to arrival in Turkey.

IDENTIFICATION

When you travel, always carry two or more forms of identification on your person, including at least one photo ID. Many establishments, especially banks, may require several IDs in order to cash traveler's checks. Never carry all your forms of ID together; split them up in case of theft or loss. It is useful to bring extra passport-size photos to affix to the various IDs or passes you may acquire along the way.

STUDENT AND TEACHER IDENTIFICATION. The **International Student Identity Card (ISIC),** the most widely accepted form of student ID, provides discounts on sights, accommodations, food, and transport. The ISIC is preferable to an institution-specific card (such as a university ID) because it is more likely to be recognized (and honored) abroad. All cardholders have access to a 24-hour emergency helpline for medical, legal, and financial emergencies (in North America call ☎ (877) 370-ISIC, elsewhere call the US collect ☎ 1 (715) 345-0505); US cardholders are also eligible for insurance benefits (see **Insurance,** p. 53). Many student travel agencies issue ISICs, including STA Travel in Australia and New Zealand; Travel CUTS in Canada; usit in the Republic of Ireland and Northern Ireland; SASTS in South Africa; Campus

Travel and STA Travel in the UK; and Council Travel (www.counciltravel.com/idcards/default.asp) and STA Travel in the US (see p. 61). The card is valid from September of one year to December of the following year and costs AUS$15, CDN$15, or US$22. Applicants must be degree-seeking students of a secondary or post-secondary school and must be at least 12 years old. Because of the proliferation of fake ISICs, some services (particularly airlines) require additional proof of student identity, such as a school ID or a letter attesting to your student status, signed by your registrar and stamped with your school seal. The **International Teacher Identity Card (ITIC)** offers the same insurance coverage as well as similar but limited discounts. The fee is AUS$13, UK£5, or US$22. For more info, contact the **International Student Travel Confederation (ISTC),** Herengracht 479, 1017 BS Amsterdam, Netherlands (☎31 (20) 421 28 00; fax 421 28 10; email istcinfo@istc.org; www.istc.org).

YOUTH IDENTIFICATION. The International Student Travel Confederation issues a discount card to travelers who are 26 years old or under, but are not students. This one-year **International Youth Travel Card** (**IYTC;** formerly the **GO 25** Card) offers many of the same benefits as the ISIC. Most organizations that sell the ISIC also sell the IYTC (US$22).

CUSTOMS

Upon entering Turkey, you must declare certain valuable items from abroad and pay a duty on the value of those articles that exceed the allowance established by Turkey's customs service. It is wise to make a list, including serial numbers, of any valuables that you carry with you from home; if you register this list with customs before your departure and have an official stamp it, you will avoid import duty charges. Be careful to document items manufactured abroad. Although not all merchants participate, Turkey does have a value-added tax (see **Taxes,** p. 45). For more specific information, **www.turkey.org,** Turkey's official website, has an itemized list of duty-free allowances.

Upon returning home, you must declare all articles acquired abroad and pay a **duty** on the value of articles that exceed the allowance established by your country. Goods and gifts purchased at **duty-free** shops abroad are not exempt from duty or sales tax at your point of return; you must declare these items as well.

MONEY

If you stay in hostels and prepare your own food, expect to spend anywhere from $15-30 per day. **Accommodations** start at about $5/$10 per night for a single/double, while a basic sit-down meal costs $3-5 per person. Carrying cash with you, even in a money belt, is risky but necessary; though banks will exchange traveler's checks, most establishments in Turkey do not accept them (see **Traveler's Checks,** below).

CURRENCY AND EXCHANGE

The Turkish lira (TL) is the main unit of currency in Turkey. The currency chart below is based on published exchange rates from August 2000. Check a large newspaper or the web (e.g. finance.yahoo.com or www.bloomberg.com) for the latest exchange rates.

Notes are in denominations of 10,000,000; 5,000,000; 1,000,000; 500,000; 250,000; and 100,000TL. Coins are in values of 100,000; 50,000; 25,000; 10,000; and 5000 TL. As a general rule, it's cheaper to convert money in Turkey than at home. The PTT (post and telephone office) and banks generally have the best rates. Using an ATM or a credit card (see p. 44) will often get you the best possible rates. Elsewhere, watch out for commission fees. A good rule of thumb is only to go to banks or *döviz (bureaux de change)* that have at most a 5% margin between their buy and sell prices. The most reliable large **banks** in Turkey include Akbank, Koçbank, Garanti Bankası, Yapı ve Kredi, TC Ziraat Bankası, and

CURRENCY		
US$1 = 645,250 TL	100,000 TL = US$0.15
CDN$1 = 435,127 TL	100,000 TL = CDN$0.23
EUR€1 = 583,969 TL	100,000 TL = EUR€0.17
UK£1 = 969,165 TL	100,000 TL = UK£0.10
IR£1 = 737,823 TL	100,000 TL = IR£0.14
AUS$1 = 373,567 TL	100,000 TL = AUS$0.27
NZ$1 = 291,524 TL	100,000 TL = NZ$0.34
SAR1=92,159 TL	100,000 TL = SAR1.09

A NOTE ON PRICES. Throughout the guide, *Let's Go* quotes prices effective in the summer of 2000. With fluctuating exchange rates and Turkey's high inflation rate, this could lead to price increases of an additional 10-30% by 2001. Prices are quoted in US dollars to minimize unexpected increases.

Türkiye İş Bankası. Since Turkey has a high inflation rate, it's best to convert money on a more regular basis despite the one-time commission charges. Keep the receipts in case they become necessary upon departure.

In Turkey, Western currency, particularly US dollars and German marks, will will sometimes be accepted. Still, avoid using Western money when you can since throwing it around for preferential treatment may be offensive. It also marks you as a foreigner and invites many locals to jack up prices.

TRAVELER'S CHECKS

Traveler's checks are one of the safest means of carrying funds, since they can be refunded if stolen. Several agencies and banks sell them, usually for face value plus a small percentage commission. Though **American Express** and **Visa** are the most widely recognized, particularly along the Aegean and Mediterranean coasts, traveler's checks are not readily accepted at most establishments. Instead, you will have to cash them at banks or at the post office (PTT).

Carry checks in small denominations (US$50 or less). They will be easier to cash, and they are especially useful for times when you are forced to exchange money at disadvantageous rates.

In case you need to collect a **refund for lost or stolen checks,** keep your check receipts separate from your checks and store them in a safe place or with a traveling companion. Record check numbers when you cash them, leave a list of check numbers with someone at home, and ask for a list of refund centers when you buy your checks. Never countersign your checks until you are ready to cash them, and always bring your passport with you when you plan to use the checks.

American Express: In Australia call ☎(800) 251 902; in New Zealand ☎(0800) 441 068; in the UK ☎(0800) 521 313; in Ireland ☎(800) 626 000; in the US and Canada ☎(800) 221-7282; elsewhere call the US collect ☎1 (801) 964-6665; www.aexp.com. To report lost or stolen checks, in Turkey call ☎00 (800) 4491 48 20. Checks can be purchased for a small fee (1-4%) at American Express Travel Service Offices or banks. American Automobile Association (AAA) members may purchase checks commission-free at AAA offices (see p. 67).

Citicorp: In the US and Canada call ☎(800) 645-6556; in Europe, the Middle East, or Africa, call the London office at ☎44 (020) 7508 7007; from elsewhere, call the US collect ☎1 (813) 623-1709. Commission 1-2%. Call 24hr.

Thomas Cook MasterCard: From the US, Canada, or Caribbean call ☎(800) 223-7373; from the UK call ☎(0800) 622 101; from Turkey call ☎00 (800) 4491 48 95; elsewhere, call ☎44 (1733) 31 89 50 collect. Checks in 13 currencies. Commission 2%.

Visa: In the US call ☎(800) 227-6811; in the UK ☎(0800) 895 078; from elsewhere, call ☎44 (1733) 31 89 49 collect.

ESSENTIALS

CREDIT CARDS

Credit cards are accepted in the larger and more established businesses in Turkey. **Mastercard** and **Visa** are generally more widely accepted than **American Express.** Major credit cards—particularly MasterCard and Visa—can be used to extract cash advances in Turkish lira from associated banks and teller machines throughout Turkey. Credit card companies get the wholesale exchange rate, which is generally 5% better than the retail rate used by banks and other currency exchange establishments *(döviz)*. However, transaction fees on credit card advances (up to US$10 per advance, plus 2-3% on foreign transactions after conversion) tend to make credit cards a more costly way of withdrawing cash than cash cards or traveler's checks. All ATMs require a **Personal Identification Number (PIN).** You must ask your credit card company for a **four digit** PIN before you leave; without it, you will be unable to withdraw cash with your credit card outside your home country. If you already have a PIN, check with the company to make sure it will work in Turkey. Be aware that MasterCard is sometimes called "EuroCard" in parts of the country. Credit cards often offer an array of other services, from insurance to emergency assistance. Check with your company to find out what is covered.

CASH CARDS

Cash cards—popularly called ATM (Automated Teller Machine) cards—are widespread in Turkey. Depending on the system that your home bank uses, you can probably access your personal bank account whenever you need money. Be aware, though, that some ATM cards only work at certain Turkish banks. ATMs get the same wholesale exchange rate as credit cards. However, there is often a limit on the amount of money you can withdraw per day (usually about US$500, depending on the type of card and account), and computer networks sometimes fail. If you're traveling from the US or Canada, memorize your PIN code in numeral form since machines elsewhere often don't have letters on their keys. Also, if your PIN is longer than four digits, ask your bank whether you need a new number.

The two major international money networks are **Cirrus** (US ☎(800) 4-CIRRUS (424-7787)) and **PLUS** (US ☎800 843-7587). Cirrus and Plus are usually accepted at the larger banks, including Akbank, Koç Bank, Türkiye İş Bankası, and TC Ziraat Bankası. Generally, banks in Turkey do not charge a transaction fee, but your home bank may charge for international withdrawals. To locate ATMs around the world, use www.visa.com/pd/atm or www.mastercard.com/atm.

GETTING MONEY FROM HOME

Turkish law requires that cash advances, money wiring, and the replacement of lost cards or checks be done through a bank. If you are in a bind and need cash immediately, the following organizations may prove helpful.

Western Union: Travelers from the US, Canada, and the UK can wire money abroad through Western Union's international money transfer services. In the US, call ☎(800) 325-6000; in Canada ☎(800) 235-0000; in the UK ☎(0800) 833 833. For a complete list of Western Union agents in Turkey visit www.westernunion.com. The rates for sending cash are generally US$10-11 cheaper than with a credit card, and the money is usually available at the place you're sending it to within an hour.

American Express: Cardholders can withdraw cash from their checking accounts at any of AmEx's major offices and many of its representatives' offices, up to US$1000 every 21 days (no service charge, no interest). AmEx's agent is **Akbank.**

US State Department: In the direst of emergencies, US citizens can have money sent via the State Department for a US$15 fee. Contact the Overseas Citizens Service, American Citizens Services, Consular Affairs, Room 4811, US Department of State, Washington, D.C. 20520 (☎(202) 647-5225; nights, Sundays, and holidays 647-4000; fax (on demand only) 647-3000; http://travel.state.gov).

TIPPING AND BARGAINING

Even though Turkish salaries often do not take **tipping** into account as a form of income, tipping is widely expected and accepted. Leaving a bit of small change (around US$1 regardless of the total price) at your table after a meal or with a taxi driver or hotel porter is appreciated as a friendly gesture and a sign of gratitude. Fifteen to twenty-percent tips are only required in very deluxe restaurants. In these establishments, service may be included in the bill *(servis dahil)*, but an additional small tip is usually required.

Bargaining occurs in outdoor food markets, bazaars, some carpet and souvenir shops, and hotels. Walk-in stores that stock conventional goods such as groceries, pharmaceuticals, and clothes have fixed prices. When bargaining, do not be the first to name a price; wait until the salesperson does. Generally, start from a price that is lower than what you intend to pay, but don't offer to pay less than half of the seller's price. Proceed to haggle up from your initial price for something between the two prices. Do not bargain for items that depend upon a guarantee of authenticity or antiquity unless you are an expert in such matters.

TAXES

Not all shops participate, but Turkey does have a 10-20% value-added tax (VAT) known as the *katma değer vergisi* or KDV. It is included in the prices of most goods and services (including meals, lodging, and car rentals). Before you buy, check if the KDV is included in the price to avoid paying it twice. Theoretically, it can be reclaimed at most points of departure, but this requires much persistence. An airport tax of $15 is levied only on international travelers, but it is usually included in the cost of the ticket.

SAFETY AND SECURITY

EMERGENCY NUMBERS IN TURKEY. These 24-hour phone numbers can be dialed from any phone in Turkey. At card-operated public phones, you can dial them without inserting a card. At coin-operated phones, you must insert a coin, but it will be returned to you after the call.

Police: ☎ 155
Ambulance: ☎ 112
Fire: ☎ 110
Jandarma (state police in rural areas): ☎ 156

Each year, thousands of visitors return home from Turkey with nothing but happy memories. Nonetheless, there are some very real safety concerns about travel to Turkey. Road safety is an oxymoron, and tensions in the country are still present, though they have decreased over the past year since the capture of PKK leader Abdullah Öcalan (see **The Here and Now,** p. 19). Stay informed of recent developments (see **Staying Informed,** p. 46).

PERSONAL SAFETY

Crime is mainly an issue in large cities in Turkey. Particularly if you are a woman, never admit that you are traveling alone. Extra vigilance is always wise, but there is no need for panic when exploring a new city or region.

To help avoid unwanted attention, try to **blend in** as much as possible. Respecting local customs (usually, dressing more conservatively) may placate would-be hecklers. Low-profile, conservatively dressed foreigners are less obvious targets for petty theft than gawking camera-toters. You may want to carry a **whistle** to scare off attackers or attract attention if attacked; memorize the emergency numbers above. Whenever possible, *Let's Go* warns of unsafe neighborhoods and areas, but there are some good general tips to follow. When walking at night, stick to busy, well-lit streets and avoid dark alleyways. Buildings in disrepair, vacant lots, and unpopulated areas are all bad signs. The distribution of people can reveal a great deal about the relative safety of the area; look for children playing, women walking in the open, and other signs of an active community.

There is no sure-fire way to avoid all the threatening situations you might encounter when you travel, but a good self-defense course will give you concrete ways to react to unwanted advances. **Impact, Prepare, and Model Mugging** can refer you to local self-defense courses in the US (☎(800) 345-5425) and Vancouver, Canada (☎(604) 878-3838). Workshops (2-3hr.) start at US$50 and full courses run US$350-500. Both women and men are welcome.

TERRORISM

The **PKK** (Kurdistan Workers' Party) and the DHKP/C (formerly Dev Sol) commit most of the terrorist acts in Turkey. Though the Turkish police and military have responded with sometimes brutal effectiveness, terrorism still maintains a presence in Turkey. When PKK leader Abdullah Öcalan was captured in February 1999, the number of terrorist acts in Turkey increased for a few months. In July 1999, the PKK vowed to stop targeting civilians, and in August 1999, it declared a cease-fire. Since then, tensions have decreased significantly and the Turkish tourism industry is enjoying a small boom (see **The Here and Now,** p. 19). Tourists have not been significant targets, although some believe that in the future the PKK might target tourists in an attempt to hurt Turkey's economy. Most terrorist attacks have occurred in Eastern Turkey. The scattered incidents that have occurred have taken place in İstanbul, Ankara, Adana, and Elazığ.

It is wise to stay away from large crowds. Foreign visitors should absolutely steer clear of all political demonstrations. Travelers to Turkey should inform themselves of the latest developments.

STAYING INFORMED. Before you go, read up on Turkey's most recent events and check some of the following websites for the latest travel advisories. Once you're in Turkey, continue to gather information by talking with fellow travelers and reading news stories on-line. Those considering travel to Eastern Turkey should be in touch with their embassies or consulates in Turkey.

Australian Department of Foreign Affairs and Trade: ☎(02) 6261 1111; www.dfat.gov.au.
Canadian Department of Foreign Affairs and International Trade (DFAIT): In Canada call ☎(800) 267-8376; elsewhere call ☎1 (613) 944-6788; www.dfait-maeci.gc.ca.
United Kingdom Foreign and Commonwealth Office: ☎(020) 7238 4503; fax 7238 4545; www.fco.gov.uk
New Zealand Ministry of Foreign Affairs: ☎(04) 494 8500; fax 494 8511; www.mft.govt.nz/trav.html.
UK Foreign and Commonwealth Office: ☎(020) 7238 4503; fax 7238 4545; www.fco.gov.uk.
US Department of State: ☎(202) 647-5225; auto faxback (202) 647-3000; http://travel.state.gov. For *A Safe Trip Abroad,* call ☎(202) 512-1800.

SOUTHEASTERN TURKEY

Travel to southeastern Turkey should only be undertaken after careful consideration of the risks involved. Some provinces are effectively in a state of civil war as Kurdish guerillas fight for separation from Turkey. Incidents of terrorism are much more frequent in southeastern Turkey than in other parts of the country. Most of southeastern Turkey is under martial law, and while some cities will present few safety issues for foreigners, others are part of ongoing conflict and should not be visited. As of the summer of 2000, the provinces of Van, Hakkarı, Şırnak, Tunceli,

Dıyarbakır and Sıırt were designated as being in a "state of emergency," while the provinces of Muş, Mardin, Batman, Bingöl, and Bıtlış were considered "sensitive areas," one level below state of emergency. Access to Mt. Ararat is now officially prohibited, but it is still possible to get near it. In parts of these regions, you can run the remote risk of being kidnapped or even caught in the cross-fire.

Although certain towns in these regions are included in this book (including Muradiye, Van, Diyabakir, Doğubeyazıt, and Mardin), exercise extreme caution if you decide to visit. Above all, be aware of recent developments both before you leave and while on the road (see **Staying Informed,** p. 46). Keep in mind that locals may be inclined to under-emphasize safety precautions and present a more rosy picture of a given town or area than that which actually exists. In most militarized cities, roads close in the afternoon; plan ahead before you travel by bus or car. Do not travel at night. Do not venture away from towns into the hills and mountains or into restricted areas. In order to travel within 5-10km of the borders of Iran, Armenia, and Georgia, you must have a special permit.

Expect to be questioned by authorities as to your traveling intentions, and always have your passport on you to present in such situations. Routine police checks become common around some cities: on buses, all men disembark from the bus and stand in a single-file line while officers ask questions and sometimes frisk. Women stay in the bus. Do not adopt a hostile attitude with the authorities—they will do everything in their power to protect you. Do not take photographs of military installations, bridges, power stations, or any other structure which might have military significance. While you should not engage locals in any political discussions, do not be afraid of speaking and interacting with Kurdish civilians.

Eastern Turkey poses much risk, difficulty, and hassle for **women traveling alone.** *Let's Go* does not recommend that women travel alone in this region.

In **Northern Cyprus,** do not use blocked-off roads or cross the Green Line between North and South Cyprus unless you're looking to be deported or imprisoned.

ROAD SAFETY

Road conditions in Turkey call for extreme concentration, caution, and defensive driving. About 15 people are killed in Turkey every day in traffic accidents, and Turkey has one of the world's worst traffic safety records. Almost half of all vehicular accidents occur in İstanbul and Ankara; of those, a large percentage happen during evening rush hour. Driving after dark is particularly hazardous, especially given that some drivers do not use their headlights. Drivers are also prone to making sudden traffic moves without warning, including cutting in front of other vehicles from the right and passing on blind curves. Always wear your **seatbelt.** Although many Turks consider it a sign of distrust if passengers fasten their seatbelts, travelers who value their lives will risk the *faux pas* and **buckle up** anyway. Turkish pedestrians often make dastardly attempts at crossing busy streets; be ready to stop suddenly at all times. Accident rates increase in bad weather: roads offer less traction than European roads, becoming oily when wet and icy in winter. Children under 18kg (40lb) should ride only in a specially designed car seat, available for a small fee from most rental agencies.

Road travel in Turkey is dangerous by European and American standards. Whether taking a bus or driving, travelers in Turkey should educate themselves about road conditions. Only travel on reputable bus companies such as Ulusoy and Varan (see **Getting Around: By Bus,** p. 64). Avoid road travel at night and in inclement weather. For more information, consult:

US Embassy Driver Safety Briefing: www.usis-ankara.org.tr/sec/secdsb.htm.
Association for Safe International Road Travel: ☎(301) 983-5252; fax 983-3663; email asirt@erols.com; www.asirt.org. Provides free information on road safety in Turkey.

ESSENTIALS

Sleeping in your car is one of the most dangerous ways to get your rest. If your car breaks down, wait for the police to assist you. Sleeping out in the open can be even more dangerous—camping is recommended only in official, supervised campsites or in wilderness backcountry.

FINANCIAL SECURITY

In large cities and touristed areas, especially İstanbul, pick-pocketing and purse-snatching are quite common. Follow the suggestions below to avoid street crime.

PROTECTING YOUR VALUABLES. There are a few steps you can take to minimize the financial risk associated with traveling. First, bring as little with you as possible. Leave expensive watches, jewelry, cameras, and electronic equipment at home; chances are you'd break them, lose them, or get sick of lugging them around anyway. Second, buy a few combination **padlocks** to secure your belongings either in your pack—which you should never leave unattended—or in a hostel or train station locker. Third, carry as little cash as possible; instead carry traveler's checks and ATM/credit cards, keeping them in a **money belt**—not a fanny pack—along with your passport and ID cards. Don't put a wallet with money in your back pocket. Fourth, keep a small cash reserve separate from your primary stash. This should entail about US$50 sewn into or stored in the depths of your pack, along with your traveler's check numbers and important photocopies.

SCAMS. Be careful of in-your-face hustlers, *avcılar* ("hunters") in Turkish, who will try to sell you items, souvenirs, transportation, or lodging. They can make up to 50% commission for each deal. When arriving in a town, have a hotel or pension name in mind. Hawkers and taxi drivers, who will more than likely be working on the same system, will tell you that they know of a better place. They may even say the place you want is full, has burned down, or is experiencing a deadly disease outbreak. Stand firm, carry yourself with confidence, and keep walking. Contact the police if a hustler is particularly insistent.

In large cities such as İstanbul, **street children** may ask for money. Difficult as it is to walk away from a child who appears needy, most Turks believe that giving money will only encourage their parents to keep them in rags on the streets.

DRUGS AND ALCOHOL

Turkey plays a key role in European drug trafficking, and 75% of drugs seized in Europe have passed through the country. The Turkish government has adopted a stringent policy (including fines and jail sentences) against those caught with drugs. If caught, a meek "I didn't know it was illegal" will not suffice. Remember that you are subject to the laws of the country in which you travel, not to those of your home country, and it is your responsibility to familiarize yourself with these laws before leaving. If you carry **prescription drugs** while you travel, it is vital to have a copy of the prescriptions themselves and a note from a doctor.

Avoid public drunkenness; it is culturally unacceptable in most parts of Turkey and can jeopardize your safety. Since Islam prohibits the consumption of alcohol, it is improper to drink in some of Turkey's more traditional towns and during the holy period of Ramazan (for dates of Ramazan, see **Festivals,** p. 37).

HEALTH

Common sense is the simplest prescription for good health while you travel. Travelers complain most often about their feet and their gut, so take precautionary measures: drink lots of fluids to prevent dehydration and constipation, wear sturdy, broken-in shoes and clean socks, and use talcum powder to keep your feet dry. To minimize the effects of jet lag, "reset" your body's clock by adopting the time of your destination as soon as you board the plane.

Hmm, call home or eat lunch?
With
you can do both.

Nathan Lane for YOU℠.

No doubt, traveling on a budget is tough. So tear out this wallet guide and keep it with you during your travels. With YOU, calling home from overseas is affordable and easy.

If the wallet guide is missing, call collect 913-624-5336 or visit www.youcallhome.com for YOU country numbers.

Dialing instructions:
Need help with access numbers while overseas? Call collect, 913-624-5336.

Dial the access number for the country you're in.
Dial 04 or follow the English prompts.
Enter your credit card information to place your call.

Country	Access Number	Country	Access Number	Country	Access Number
Australia **v**	1-800-551-110	Israel **v**	1-800-949-4102	Spain **v**	900-99-0013
Bahamas **✚**	1-800-389-2111	Italy **✚ v**	172-1877	Switzerland **v**	0800-899-777
Brazil **v**	000-8016	Japan **✚ v**	00539-131	Taiwan **v**	0080-14-0877
China **✚ ▲ v**	108-13	Mexico **u v**	001-800-877-8000	United Kingdom **v**	0800-890-877
France **v**	0800-99-0087	Netherlands **✚ v**	0800-022-9119		
Germany **✚ v**	0800-888-0013	New Zealand **▲ v**	000-999		
Hong Kong **v**	800-96-1877	Philippines **T v**	105-16		
India **v**	000-137	Singapore **v**	8000-177-177		
Ireland **v**	1-800-552-001	South Korea **✚ v**	00729-16		

Service provided by Sprint

v Call answered by automated Voice Response Unit.   **✚** Public phones may require coin or card.
▲ May not be available from all payphones.   **u** Use phones marked with "LADATEL" and no coin or card is required.
T If talk button is available, push it before talking.

Pack the Wallet Guide
and save 25% or more* on calls home to the U.S.

It's lightweight and carries heavy savings of 25% or more* over AT&T USA Direct and MCI WorldPhone rates. So take this YOU wallet guide and carry it wherever you go.

To save with YOU:
- Dial the access number of the country you're in (see reverse)
- Dial 04 or follow the English voice prompts
- Enter your credit card info for easy billing

Service provided by Sprint

BEFORE YOU GO

Preparation can help minimize the likelihood of contracting a disease and maximize the chances of receiving effective health care in the event of an emergency.

In your passport, write the names of any people you wish to be contacted in case of an emergency, and also list any allergies or medical conditions you would want doctors to be aware of. Obtain a full supply of any necessary medication before the trip. Matching a prescription to a foreign equivalent is not always easy, safe, or possible. Carry up-to-date prescriptions or a statement from your doctor stating the medication's trade name, manufacturer, chemical name, and dosage. While traveling, be sure to keep all medication with you in your carry-on luggage.

IMMUNIZATIONS. Take a look at your immunization records before you go. Travelers over two years old should be sure that the following vaccines are up to date: MMR (for measles, mumps, and rubella); DTaP or Td (for diptheria, tetanus, and pertussis); OPV (for polio); HbCV (for haemophilus influenza B); and HBV (for hepatitis B). Below is a list of recommended immunizations for travel to Turkey. Check with a doctor for guidance through this maze of injections.

 INOCULATION RECOMMENDATIONS. While there are no required vaccinations for travel to Turkey, Hepatitis A vaccine and/or immune globulin (IG) is recommended. Typhoid is suggested for travelers to the less-developed areas away from the Aegean and Mediterranean coasts. Adults traveling to Turkey should consider an additional dose of Polio vaccine if they have not already had one during their adult years. Those traveling for longer periods (more than 6 months) should be inoculated for Hepatitis B, and those intending to hike and camp in Turkey should also be immunized for rabies.

USEFUL ORGANIZATIONS AND PUBLICATIONS. The US **Centers for Disease Control and Prevention** (CDC; ☎(877) FYI-TRIP; www.cdc.gov/travel), an excellent source of information for travelers, maintain an international fax information service. The CDC's comprehensive booklet *Health Information for International Travelers*, an annual rundown of disease, immunization, and general health advice, is free on the website or US$22 via the Government Printing Office (☎(202) 512-1800). The **US State Department** (http://travel.state.gov) compiles Consular Information Sheets on health, entry requirements, and other issues for various countries. For quick information on health and other travel warnings, call the **Overseas Citizens' Services** (☎(202) 647-5225; after-hours 647-4000), contact a US passport agency or a US embassy or consulate abroad, or send a self-addressed, stamped envelope to the Overseas Citizens' Services, Bureau of Consular Affairs, #4811, US Department of State, Washington, D.C. 20520. For information on medical evacuation services and travel insurance firms, see http://travel.state.gov/medical.html. The **British Foreign and Commonwealth Office** also gives health warnings for individual countries (www.fco.gov.uk).

For detailed information on travel health, including a country-by-country overview of diseases, try the **International Travel Health Guide,** Stuart Rose, MD (Travel Medicine, US$20; www.travmed.com). For general health info, contact the **American Red Cross** (☎(800) 564-1234).

 For **medical emergencies** in Turkey and Northern Cyprus, dial ☎112 or call your consulate. If your difficulties are not urgent, go to the nearest tourist office before trying the police; they can ease communication.

MEDICAL ASSISTANCE ON THE ROAD. If you are in need of medical care in Turkey, an embassy or consulate can provide you with a list of English-speaking doctors. Payment with cash or a credit card is expected at the time of treatment. Serious medical problems should be taken to the *klinik* or hospital *(hastane)*.

ESSENTIALS

Private hospitals, located in the more urban areas, tend to provide much better care than state-run ones *(devlet hastanesi)*, and they are not much more expensive for foreigners. Cash payments are expected. Most doctors speak some English. Turkish **pharmacies** *(eczane)* will have remedies for minor troubles. Pharmacies in each town stay open all night on a rotating basis; signs in their windows and in newspapers tell which is on duty *(nöbetçi)* on a particular night. *Eczane* also sell *esem mat*, small rectangles of mosquito repellent that burn slowly on heat pads that plug into the wall.

If you are concerned about being able to access medical support while traveling, there are special support services you may employ. The *MedPass* from **Global Emergency Medical Services (GEMS)**, 2001 Westside Dr., #120, Alpharetta, GA 30004, USA (☎ (800) 860-1111; fax (770) 475-0058; www.globalems.com), provides 24-hour international medical assistance, support, and medical evacuation resources. The **International Association for Medical Assistance to Travelers** (IAMAT; US ☎ (716) 754-4883, Canada ☎ (416) 652-0137, New Zealand ☎ (03) 352 2053; www.sentex.net/iiamat) has free membership, lists English-speaking doctors worldwide, and offers detailed info on immunization requirements and sanitation. If your regular **insurance** policy does not cover travel abroad, you may wish to purchase additional coverage (see **Insurance,** p. 53).

Those with medical conditions (diabetes, allergies to antibiotics, epilepsy, heart conditions) may want to obtain a stainless-steel **Medic Alert** ID tag (first-year US$35, $15 annually thereafter), which identifies the condition and gives a 24-hour collect-call number. Contact the Medic Alert Foundation, 2323 Colorado Ave, Turlock, CA 95382, USA (☎ (800) 825-3785; www.medicalert.org).

POTENTIAL HAZARDS ON THE ROAD

ENVIRONMENTAL HAZARDS

Heat exhaustion and dehydration: Heat exhaustion, characterized by dehydration and salt deficiency, can lead to fatigue, headaches, and wooziness. Avoid it by drinking plenty of fluids, eating salty foods (e.g., crackers), and avoiding dehydrating beverages (e.g., alcohol, coffee, tea, and caffeinated soda). Wear a hat, sunglasses, and a lightweight long sleeve shirt in hot sun, and take time to acclimate to Turkey's hot summers before seriously exerting yourself. Avoid the mid-afternoon heat; try to venture outdoors in the mornings and evenings, when it is cooler. Continuous heat stress can eventually lead to **heatstroke,** characterized by a rising temperature, severe headache, and cessation of sweating. Victims should be cooled off with wet towels and taken to a doctor.

Sunburn: If you're prone to sunburn, bring sunscreen with you (especially in Eastern Turkey, where it is nearly impossible to find) and apply it liberally and often to avoid burns and the risk of skin cancer. If you are planning on spending time near water, in the desert, or in the snow, you are at risk of getting burned, even through clouds. If you get sunburned, drink more fluids than usual and apply Calamine or an aloe-based lotion.

Hypothermia and frostbite: These are problems only in winter and in the more mountainous regions of Eastern Turkey. A rapid drop in body temperature is the clearest sign of overexposure to cold. Victims may also shiver, feel exhausted, have poor coordination or slurred speech, hallucinate, or suffer amnesia. *Do not let hypothermia victims fall asleep,* or their body temperature will continue to drop and they may die. To avoid hypothermia, keep dry, wear layers, and stay out of the wind. When the temperature is below freezing, watch out for frostbite. If skin turns white, waxy, and cold, do not rub the area. Drink warm beverages, get dry, and slowly warm the area with dry fabric or steady body contact until a doctor can be found.

High altitude: Travelers to the higher altitudes of Eastern Turkey must allow their bodies a couple of days to adjust to less oxygen before exerting themselves. Note that alcohol is more potent and UV rays are stronger at high elevations, even in cold weather.

INSECT-BORNE DISEASES

Many diseases are transmitted by insects. Be aware of insects in wet or forested areas, especially while hiking and camping. **Mosquitoes** are most active from dusk to dawn. Wear long pants and long sleeves, tuck your pants into your socks, and buy a mosquito net. Use insect repellents, such as DEET, and soak or spray your gear with permethrin (licensed in the US for use on clothing). Consider natural repellents that make you smelly to insects, like vitamin B-12 or garlic pills. To stop the itch after being bitten, try Calamine lotion or topical cortisones (like Cortaid), or take a bath with a half-cup of baking soda or oatmeal.

Malaria: Transmitted by *Anopheles* mosquitoes that bite at night. Though mosquitoes chomp away throughout Turkey, the disease is only a risk in the southeast. The incubation period varies and can last months. Early symptoms include fever, chills, aches, and fatigue, followed by high fever and sweating, sometimes with vomiting and diarrhea. See a doctor for any flu-like sickness that occurs and get tested immediately. Left untreated, malaria can cause anemia, kidney failure, coma, and death. It is advisable to use mosquito repellent when outdoors. The oral prophylactics **mefloquine** (sold under the name Lariam) or **doxycycline** are usually prescribed before travel to protect against malaria. Both these drugs can have very serious side effects, including slowed heart rate and nightmares.

Leishmaniasis: A parasite transmitted by sand flies that can occur in Turkey. Cutaneous leishmaniasis, characterized by skin lesions that include sores, ulcers, and wart-like bumps, occurs in southeastern Turkey and in the Tigris-Euphrates basin. Visceral leishmaniasis *(kala azar)* is found along the Aegean, Mediterranean, Sea of Marmara, and Black Sea coasts. It affects the internal organs and bone marrow, and common symptoms are fever, weakness, and swelling of the spleen. There is a treatment, but no vaccine, for both forms of the disease.

FOOD- AND WATER-BORNE DISEASES

Prevention is the best cure: be sure that everything you eat is cooked properly and that the water you drink is clean. In Turkey, where the risk of contracting traveler's diarrhea or other diseases is high, you should never drink unbottled water unless you have treated it yourself. Bottled water, avaliable almost anywhere, is very cheap, and a large bottle typically sells for less than $0.50. To purify your own water, bring it to a rolling boil or treat it with **iodine tablets.** In risk areas, don't brush your teeth with tap water or rinse your toothbrush under the faucet, and keep your mouth closed in the shower. Peel your fruits and veggies and avoid tap water (including ice cubes and anything washed in tap water, like salad). Watch out for food from markets or street vendors that may have been cooked in unhygienic conditions. Other culprits are raw shellfish, raw meat, unpasteurized milk, and sauces containing raw eggs. Always wash your hands before eating, or bring a quick-drying purifying liquid hand cleaner. Your bowels will thank you.

Traveler's diarrhea: Results from drinking untreated water or eating uncooked foods; a temporary (and fairly common) reaction to the bacteria in new food ingredients. Symptoms include nausea, bloating, urgency, and malaise. Try quick-energy, non-sugary foods with protein and carbohydrates to keep your strength up. Over-the-counter antidiarrheals (e.g., Imodium) may counteract the problems, but can complicate serious infections. The most dangerous side effect is dehydration; drink 8 oz. of water with ½ tsp. of sugar or honey and a pinch of salt, try uncaffeinated soft drinks, or munch on salted crackers. If you develop a fever or your symptoms don't go away after 4-5 days, consult a doctor. Consult a doctor for treatment of diarrhea in children.

Hepatitis A: A viral infection of the liver acquired primarily through contaminated water. Symptoms include fatigue, fever, loss of appetite, nausea, dark urine, jaundice, vomiting, aches and pains, and light stools. The risk is highest in rural areas and the countryside, but it is also present in urban areas. Ask your doctor about the vaccine (Havrix or Vaqta) or an injection of immune globulin (IG; formerly called gamma globulin).

ESSENTIALS

Parasites: Microbes, tapeworms, etc. that hide in water and food. **Giardiasis,** for example, is acquired by drinking untreated water from streams or lakes. Symptoms include swollen glands or lymph nodes, fever, rashes or itchiness, digestive problems, eye problems, and anemia. Boil water, wear shoes, avoid bugs, and eat only cooked food.

Schistosomiasis: Also known as bilharzia; a parasitic disease caused when the larvae of flatworm penetrate unbroken skin. It occurs along the Euphrates River (near the Syrian border). Swimming in fresh water, especially in rural areas, should be avoided. Symptoms include an itchy localized rash, followed in 4-6 weeks by fever, fatigue, painful urination, diarrhea, loss of appetite, night sweats, and a hive-like rash on the body. If exposed to untreated water, rub the area vigorously with a towel and apply rubbing alcohol. Schistosomiasis can be treated with prescription drugs.

Typhoid fever: Caused by the salmonella bacteria; common in villages and rural areas in Turkey. While mostly transmitted through contaminated food and water, it may also be acquired by direct contact with another person. Early symptoms include fever, headaches, fatigue, loss of appetite, constipation, and a rash on the abdomen or chest. Antibiotics can treat typhoid, but a vaccination (70-90% effective) is recommended.

OTHER INFECTIOUS DISEASES

Hepatitis B: A viral infection of the liver transmitted via bodily fluids or needle-sharing. Symptoms may not surface until years after infection. Vaccinations are recommended for health-care workers, sexually-active travelers, and anyone planning to seek medical treatment abroad. The 3-shot vaccination series must begin 6 months before traveling.

Hepatitis C: Like Hep B, but the mode of transmission differs. IV drug users, those with occupational exposure to blood, hemodialysis patients, and recipients of blood transfusions are at the highest risk, but the disease can also be spread through sexual contact or sharing items like razors and toothbrushes that may have traces of blood on them.

AIDS, HIV, AND STDS

Though **Acquired Immune Deficiency Syndrome (AIDS)** is a growing problem around the world, the HIV virus doesn't have a large presence in Turkey. Only 2000 adults (ages 15-49) in Turkey, 0.01% of the population, were infected with the virus in 1999. The largest share of HIV-infected individuals is in northeastern Turkey (around Trabzon) where prostitution is more widespread (see **Nataşas,** p. 400).

For detailed information on **Acquired Immune Deficiency Syndrome (AIDS)** in Turkey, call the **US Centers for Disease Control's** 24-hour hotline at ☎ (800) 342-2437, or contact the **Joint United Nations Programme on HIV/AIDS (UNAIDS),** 20 av. Appia 20, CH-1211 Geneva 27, Switzerland (☎ 41 (22) 791 36 66; fax 791 41 87). Council's brochure, *Travel Safe: AIDS and International Travel,* is available at all Council Travel offices and on their website (www.ciee.org/Isp/safety/travelsafe.htm).

Sexually transmitted diseases (STDs) such as gonorrhea, chlamydia, genital warts, syphilis, and herpes are easier to catch than HIV and can be just as deadly. **Hepatitis B** and **C** are also serious STDs (see **Other Infectious Diseases,** above). Though condoms may protect you from some STDs, oral or even tactile contact can lead to transmission. Warning signs include swelling, sores, bumps, or blisters on sex organs, the rectum, or the mouth; burning and pain during urination and bowel movements; itching around sex organs; swelling or redness of the throat; and flu-like symptoms. If these symptoms develop, see a doctor immediately.

WOMEN'S HEALTH

Women traveling in unsanitary conditions are vulnerable to **urinary tract** and **bladder infections,** common and very uncomfortable bacterial diseases that cause a burning sensation and painful and sometimes frequent urination. To avoid these infections, drink plenty of vitamin-C-rich juice and plenty of clean water and urinate frequently, especially after intercourse. Untreated, these infections can lead to kidney infections, sterility, and even death. If symptoms persist, see a doctor.

Vaginal yeast infections may flare up in hot and humid climates. Wearing loosely fitting trousers or a skirt and cotton underwear will help. Yeast infections can be treated with an over-the-counter remedy like Monostat or Gynelotrimin. Bring supplies from home if you are prone to infection, as they may be difficult to find on the road. Some travelers opt for a natural alternative such as plain yogurt and lemon juice douche if other remedies are unavailable.

Tampons and **pads** are easy to find in any pharmacy (see **Medical Assistance on the Road,** p. 49). However, since your preferred brands might not be available, you may want to take supplies along. **Reliable contraceptive devices** will be difficult to find. Women on the pill should bring enough to allow for possible loss or extended stays. Bring a prescription, since forms of the pill vary a good deal. Women who use a diaphragm should bring enough contraceptive jelly. Condoms are also hard to come by and are only available in the bigger cities.

PACKING

Pack according to the extremes of climate you may experience and the type of travel you'll be doing. **Pack light:** a good rule is to lay out only what you absolutely need, then take half the clothes and twice the money. The less you have, the less you have to lose (or store, or carry on your back).

LUGGAGE. If you plan to cover most of your itinerary by foot, a sturdy **frame backpack** is unbeatable. Toting a **suitcase** or **trunk** is fine if you plan to live in one or two cities and explore from there, but a very bad idea if you're going to be moving around a lot. In addition to your main piece of luggage, a **daypack** (a small backpack or courier bag) is a must.

CLOTHING. No matter when you're traveling, it's always a good idea to bring a **warm jacket** or wool sweater, a **rain jacket** (Gore-Tex@ is both waterproof and breathable), sturdy shoes or **hiking boots,** and **thick socks. Flip-flops** or waterproof sandals are crucial for grubby hostel showers. Shorts are acceptable in the more touristed regions along the Aegean and Mediterranean coasts, but completely inappropriate in other parts of Turkey. Men should bring light, breathable slacks, and women should bring loose-fitting pants or long skirts. For both sexes, short sleeves and loose-fitting T-shirts are fine, but tank tops will stand out. It is also a good idea to bring a slightly dressier pair of clothes and, if you have the room, a nicer pair of shoes. Also keep in mind that when visiting religious sites, appropriate attire is required. For more information on women's dress, see **Women Travelers,** p. 68.

SLEEPSACK. Some hostels require that you either provide your own linen or rent sheets from them. Save cash by making your own sleepsack: fold a full-size sheet in half the long way, then sew it closed along the long side and one of the short sides.

ADAPTERS AND CONVERTERS. In Turkey, electricity is 220 volts AC, enough to fry any 110V North American appliance. 220V electrical appliances don't like 110V current either. Visit a hardware store for an adapter (which changes the shape of the plug) and a converter (which changes the voltage). Don't make the mistake of using only an adapter (unless appliance instructions explicitly state otherwise). **New Zealanders** and **South Africans** (who both use 220V at home) as well as **Australians** (who use 240/250V) won't need a converter, but will need a set of adapters.

TOILETRIES. Toothbrushes, towels, cold-water soap, talcum powder (to keep feet dry), deodorant, razors, tampons, and condoms are often available, but may be difficult to find, so bring extras along. **Contact lenses,** on the other hand, may be expensive and difficult to find, so bring enough extra pairs and solution for your entire trip. Also bring your glasses and a copy of your prescription in case you need emergency replacements. If you use heat-disinfection, either switch temporarily to a chemical disinfection system (check first to make sure it's safe with your brand of lenses), or buy a converter to 220V.

FIRST-AID KIT. For a basic first-aid kit, pack bandages, aspirin or other painkiller, antibiotic cream, a thermometer, a Swiss Army knife, tweezers, moleskin, decongestant, motion-sickness remedy, diarrhea or upset-stomach medication (Pepto Bismol or Imodium), an antihistamine, burn ointment, and a syringe for emergencies (get an explanatory letter from your doctor)

sultan's inn

This modern luxury hotel situated in
the heart of Istanbul's old city is within an
easy walk of all of Sultanahmet's major historical
sights. The roof terrace offers a panoramic 360 degree
view taking in the Blue Mosque, the Sea of
Marmara and the Bosphorus Strait.
All rooms are beautifully appointed.
All have bathrooms en suite.

low season from $20 high season from $25

email: sultansinn@hotmail.com
url: www.sultansinn.com
tel: +90 212 638 2563 fax: +90 212 638 3922

alp guesthouse b&b

*In the heart of Istanbul's Old City,
this family run guesthouse has a relaxing atmosphere,
panoramic views, and is within easy walking distance of
the Blue Mosque, the Church of St. Sophia, Topkapý Palace
the underground cistern and the Grand Bazaar.
All rooms en suite.*

*Akbiyik Cad, Adliye Sok. No. 4, Sultanahmet
Tel: +90 212 517 9570 Fax: +90 212 638 3922*

email: alpguesthouse@turk.net web: www.alpguesthouse.com
Low season: Double and triples from $15pp High season: Doubles and triples from $20p

FILM: Film in Turkey costs $3-4 for a 200 speed roll of 36 color exposures. It may be more convenient to bring film from home and develop it at home. Also, it may be very difficult to find APS (Advantix) film, and very expensive if you do. Despite disclaimers, airport security X-rays *can* fog film, so either buy a lead-lined pouch, sold at camera stores or ask the security to hand inspect it. Always pack it in your carry-on luggage, since higher-intensity X-rays are used on checked luggage.

OTHER USEFUL ITEMS. For safety purposes, bring a **money belt** and small **padlock.** Basic **outdoors equipment** (plastic water bottle, compass, waterproof matches, pocketknife, sunglasses, sunscreen, insect repellent, hat) may also prove useful. **Quick repairs** of torn garments can be done on the road with a needle and thread; also consider bringing electrical tape for patching tears. Doing your **laundry** by hand (where it is allowed) is both cheaper and more convenient than doing it at a laundromat—bring detergent, a small rubber ball to stop up the sink, and string for a makeshift clothes line. **Other things** you're liable to forget: an **umbrella**, sealable **plastic bags** (for damp clothes, soap, food, shampoo, and other spillables), an **alarm clock,** safety pins, rubber bands, a flashlight, earplugs, garbage bags, and a small **calculator.**

ACCOMMODATIONS

HOSTELS

Hostels are generally dorm-style accommodations, often in large single-sex rooms with bunk beds, though most in Turkey, known for their welcoming atmosphere, also offer private rooms for families and couples. They sometimes have kitchens and utensils, bike or moped rentals, storage areas, and laundry facilities. Hostels in Turkey generally do not have daytime "lock-out" hours or a curfew. A bed in a hostel will average around $5-8.

There are very few accredited International Youth Hostels in Turkey, and if you ask for a hostel (*yurt*), you will most likely be directed to university dormitories. The web page for the umbrella organization of **Hostelling International (HI)** (www.iyhf.org) as well as www.hostels.com and www.eurotrip.com/accommodation may still be of some use as you research hosteling in Turkey.

HOTELS AND PENSIONS

Clean, cheap accommodations are available nearly everywhere in Turkey in hotels (*otel*) and pensions (*pansiyon*). Basic rooms generally cost $6-8 for a single and $12-16 for a double in Turkey. Some establishments may have dorm-style rooms; some may even allow frugal travelers to sleep on their roofs for reduced rates. In most situations, you should have little trouble finding a room; it is still wise, however, to make reservations at accommodations along the Aegean and Mediterranean coasts during the peak season.

Pensions, by far the most common form of accommodation, provide a cozy alternative to impersonal hotel rooms. Often they are private homes with rooms available to travelers. Hosts will sometimes go out of their way to be accommodating by giving personalized tours or offering home-cooked meals. On the other hand, many pensions do not provide phones, TVs, or private bathrooms. Pensions that call themselves **aile** (family-style) try to maintain a wholesome atmosphere, and may be the preferred choice for women traveling alone in remote parts of Turkey, particularly the East and the Black Sea coast. In the more touristed areas along the Aegean and Mediterranean coasts, Turks are accustomed to **unmarried male-female couples** staying together. However, such relations are often culturally unacceptable in rural and conservative regions, including the Black Sea coast and southeastern Turkey. In these parts of Turkey, unmarried couples may have trouble finding a room together without proof of their marital status, such as wedding rings, a certificate, or the same last name on passports. It is generally a good idea to wear rings to help gain admittance. Men may be turned away from pensions if there are no other men staying in the house.

DORMS

Many **colleges and universities** open their residence halls to travelers when school is not in session—some do so even during term-time. These dorms are often close to student areas in larger cities such as Ankara and İstanbul. Getting a room may take a couple of phone calls and require advanced planning, but rates tend to be low. *Let's Go* lists colleges which rent dorm rooms in the **Accommodations** sections of cities and towns when applicable.

CAMPING AND THE OUTDOORS

Camping is more than just a viable means of travel in Turkey, particularly along the Black Sea and Mediterranean coasts and in the East. Since Turkish families on vacation form the bulk of the campers, camping in designated campgrounds is often safe for all travelers. If you have your own tent, the cost per night per tent is $2.50-$4. Tents can usually be rented for an additional charge. In some places, usually the *yayla* (highland plateaus), camping is free. Generally, camping is not permitted on beaches or in non-designated areas, but you can sometimes secure permission from a member of the *jandarma*.

For eco-friendly camping, make sure your campsite is at least 150 ft. (50m) from water supplies or bodies of water. Similarly, if there are no toilet facilities, do as nature intended far from any water supply or campsite. Always pack your trash in a plastic bag and carry it with you until you reach the next trash can.

WILDERNESS SAFETY

Stay warm, stay dry, and stay hydrated. The vast majority of life-threatening wilderness situations can be avoided by following this simple advice. Prepare yourself for an emergency by always packing raingear, a hat and mittens, a first-aid kit, a reflector, a whistle, high-energy food, and extra water for any hike. Dress in wool or warm layers of synthetic materials designed for the outdoors; never rely on cotton for warmth, as it is absolutely useless when wet.

Check **weather forecasts** and pay attention to the skies when hiking, since weather patterns can change suddenly. Whenever possible, let someone (a friend, your hostel, or a park ranger) know when and where you are hiking. Do not attempt a hike beyond your ability—you may be endangering your life. See **Health,** p. 48, for information about outdoor ailments and basic medical concerns.

ADVENTURE TRIPS

Organized adventure tours offer another way of exploring the wild. In Turkey, activities include hiking, biking, skiing, kayaking, rafting, climbing, and archaeological digs. Begin by consulting tourism bureaus, which can suggest parks, trails, and outfitters. *Let's Go* lists agencies in Cappadocia and the Eastern Black Sea region (see **Trekking in the Kaçkars,** p. 419).

KEEPING IN TOUCH

MAIL

SENDING MAIL TO TURKEY. Airmail letters under 1 oz. between North America and Turkey take 4-7 days and cost US$1 or CDN$1.45 (sending a postcard costs about $0.50). Allow 6-7 days from Australia (postage AUS$1 for up to 20 grams), 4-8 from Britain (postage £0.36 for up to 20 grams), 6-8 days from Ireland (postage IR£0.32 for 25g), and 6-8 from New Zealand (postage NZ$1.80 for 20g). Mark envelopes "air mail" or "par avion" to avoid having letters sent by sea.

There are several ways to arrange pick-up of letters sent to you by friends and relatives while you are abroad, and most involve the **PTT** (post, telegraph, and telephone office), which are well-marked by their yellow signs. Large PTTs in major urban areas are open M-Sa 8am-midnight, Su 9am-7pm. Major PTTs in İstanbul are open 24 hours. Smaller post offices share the same hours as government offices (M-F 8:30am-12:30pm and 1:30-5:30pm). *Let's Go* lists post offices in the **Practical Information** section for each city and most towns.

General Delivery: Mail can be sent to Turkey through *poste restante* (the international phrase for General Delivery) to almost any city or town with a PTT (post, telegraph, and telephone office). To send a letter to someone in Bodrum, address it *poste restante* to: Anita CARTER, Postrestant, Merkez Postanesi, Bodrum 48400, Türkiye. The last name should be capitalized and underlined. The mail will go to a special desk in the central post office *(merkez postanesi)*, unless you specify a post office by street address or postal code. As a rule, it is best to use the largest post office in the area, and mail may be sent there regardless of what is written on the envelope. When possible, it is usually safer and quicker to send mail express or registered. When picking up your mail, bring a form of photo ID, preferably a passport. Some PTTs may charge a small sum for *poste restante*, but it generally does not exceed the cost of domestic postage. If the clerks insist that there is nothing for you, have them check under your first name as well. Some of the smaller PTTs may send you with a slip to a larger PTT in the same city.

American Express: AmEx's travel offices act as a mail service for cardholders if you contact them in advance. Under the free **Client Letter Service,** they will hold mail for up to 30 days and forward upon request. Address the letter in the same way shown above. Some offices offer these services to non-cardholders (especially those who have purchased AmEx Traveler's Cheques), but call ahead to make sure. Check the **Practical Information** section of the cities you plan to visit; *Let's Go* lists AmEx offices in most large cities. A complete list is available free from AmEx (☎(800) 528-4800).

SENDING MAIL FROM TURKEY. Aerogrammes, printed sheets that fold into envelopes and travel via airmail, are available at post offices. It helps to mark "*uçak ile*" if possible, though "par avion" and "air mail" are universally understood. Tell the vendor the mail's destination: *Avustralya, Kanada, Büyük Bretanya* (Great Britain), *İrlanda, Yeni Zelanda* (New Zealand), *Güney Afrika* (South Africa), or *Amerika*. Most post offices will charge exorbitant fees or simply refuse to send aerogrammes with enclosures. Airmail from Turkey averages one to two weeks, although it takes longer when sent from smaller towns.

If regular airmail is too slow, there are a few faster, more expensive, options. The fastest option is usually *Acele Posta Servisi* (APS), though this may not be available in every PTT. Companies including DHL and Federal Express can also send packages from their offices in the larger Turkish cities.

TELEPHONES

CALLING TURKEY. To call Turkey direct from home, dial:

1. The **international access code** of your home country. International access codes include: Australia 0011; Ireland 00; New Zealand 00; South Africa 09; UK 00; US and Canada 011. Country codes and city codes are sometimes listed with a zero in front

(e.g., 033), but after dialing the international access code, drop successive zeros (with an access code of 011, e.g., 011 33).

2. 90 (Turkey's country code).

3. The city code (found across the header for each city and town listed) and local number.

CALLING FROM TURKEY. A **calling card** is probably your best and cheapest bet. Calls are billed either collect or to your account. Many phone companies provide travelers with additional services, such as legal and medical advice, exchange rate information, and translation services. **To obtain a calling card** from your national telecom service before you leave home, contact the appropriate company below.

Australia: Telestra **Australia Direct** (☎ 13 22 00).
Canada: Bell Canada **Canada Direct** (☎(800) 565-4708).
Ireland: Telecom Éireann **Ireland Direct** (☎(800) 250 250).
New Zealand: Telecom New Zealand (☎(0800) 00 00 00).
South Africa: Telkom South Africa (☎09 03).
US: AT&T (☎(888) 288-4685); **Sprint** (☎(800) 877-4646); **MCI** (☎(800) 444-4141).
UK: British Telecom **BT Direct** (☎(800) 34 51 44).

ACCESS NUMBERS. To **call home with a calling card,** dial the appropriate access numbers in Turkey:

AT&T: ☎00 (800) 12277.
Sprint: ☎00 (800) 14477.
MCI WorldPhone Direct: ☎00 (800) 11177.
Canada Direct: ☎00 (800) 16677.
BT Direct: ☎00 (800) 44 1177.
Ireland Direct: ☎00 (800) 353 1177.
Australia Direct: ☎00 (800) 61 1177.
Telekon South Africa Direct: ☎00 (800) 27 1177.

You can usually make direct international calls from public pay phones at the **PTT** (post and telephone office), but if you aren't using a calling card you may need to drop your coins as quickly as your words. Note that a **prepaid card (telekart)** or a token-like **jeton** (both available at the PTT) must be deposited to activate the phone. No credit will be deducted from your card, and your *jeton* will be returned.

If you do dial direct, you must first insert the *telekart* or *jeton*. Since **Turkey's international access code is 00,** you must then dial 0, wait for the tone, and dial 0 again followed by the country code and the number, without pausing. For a helpful list of country codes, see **International Calling Codes,** below. *Telekarts*, which are cheaper and more widely used than the *jeton*, are available in denominations of 30, 60, 100, or 120 *köntur* (credits). Some calls cost more units than others, and during international calls, one credit lasts 2-10 seconds. Regular coins are not accepted. Magnetic-card public phones, abundant in big cities and resort areas, have on-screen instructions in English, French, and German. Calling card calls usually terminate after three minutes if you are calling from a public phone. You can also make use of the **kontörlü telefon** located in the PTT. The officer tells you how much you owe at the end of your call. Since there may be long lines for these phones, especially during the day, try to use one at night at one of the 24-hour PTTs. The same kind of phone is available at some hotels and restaurants, but it may cost you 20-500% more.

The expensive alternative to dialing direct or using a calling card is using an international operator to place a **collect call.** For an international Türk Telekom operator dial ☎115. An English-speaking operator from your home nation can be reached by dialing the access numbers of the appropriate service provider listed above, and they will typically place a collect call even if you don't have one of their phone cards. Although incredibly convenient, in-room hotel calls invariably include an arbitrary and sky-high surcharge (as much as US$10).

INTERNATIONAL CALLING CODES			
Australia	61	N. Cyprus	90 392
Austria	43	Turkey	90
Canada	1	Greece	30
Ireland	353	Italy	39
New Zealand	64	Spain	34
South Africa	13	France	33
United Kingdom	44	Germany	49
United States/Canada	1	Syria	963

CALLING WITHIN TURKEY. With few exceptions, even the smallest village is acessible by phone. Local numbers all have seven digits, and all area codes have three. (In small towns, numbers start with the same three digits, so you may occasionally be given a four-digit phone number). The number for **directory assistance** in Turkey is ☎ 118. For operator-assisted calls within Turkey call ☎ 131. The simplest way to call within the country is to use the prepaid *telekart*, which carry a certain amount of credits depending on the card's denomination (see above). When making a **long-distance** call within Turkey, insert the card into the phone, dial 0, wait for the tone to change to a lower pitch, and dial the area code and the number. A computer indicates how many credits you have left on your card. Phone rates are highest in the morning, lower in the evening, and lowest on Sunday and late at night.

EMAIL AND INTERNET

Internet access is available in most regions of the country, particularly in the more touristed areas of İstanbul, Cappadocia, and the Aegean and Mediterranean coasts. Access, however, thins out along the Black Sea and in Eastern Turkey. Prices typically range from US$1-2 per hour. *Let's Go* lists establishments that provide Internet access in the **Practical Information** sections of cities and towns. Web sites, including www.cybercafe.com, can also help you find cybercafes in Turkey.

Though it's sometimes possible to connect to your home server, in most cases this is a much slower (and thus more expensive) option than taking advantage of free **web-based email accounts** (e.g., www.hotmail.com and www.yahoo.com).

TIME ZONES

Turkey and Cyprus are both two hours later than GMT, seven hours later than EST, and 10 hours later than PST. When it is noon in New York, it is 7pm in Turkey and Cyprus. When it is noon in California, it is 10pm in Turkey and Cyprus. When it is noon in London, it is 2pm in Turkey and Cyprus.

GETTING THERE

BY PLANE

When it comes to airfare, a little effort can save you a bundle. Tickets bought from consolidators are good deals, but last-minute specials, airfare wars, and charter flights often beat these fares. Unfortunately, there are no courier flights to Turkey. The key is to hunt around, to be flexible, and to ask persistently about discounts. Students, seniors, and those under 26 should never pay full price for a ticket.

DETAILS AND TIPS

Timing: Airfares to Turkey peak between June and September. Midweek (M-Th morning) round-trip flights run US$40-50 cheaper than weekend flights, but the latter are generally less crowded and more likely to permit frequent-flier upgrades. Return-date flexibility is usually not an option for budget travelers; traveling with an "open return" ticket can be pricier than fixing a return date when buying the ticket.

Route: Round-trip flights are by far the cheapest. "Open-jaw" (arriving in and departing from different cities) and round-the-world, or RTW, flights are pricier but reasonable

ESSENTIALS

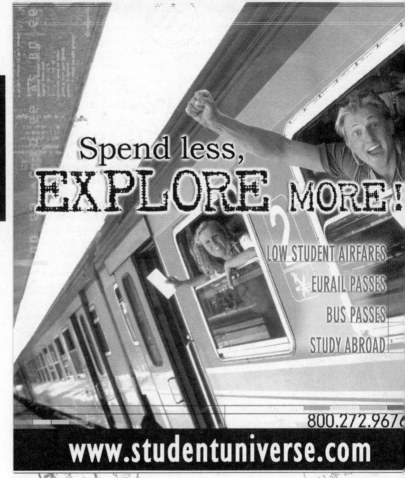
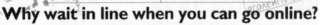

alternatives. Patching one-way flights together is the least economical way to travel to Turkey. Flights to İstanbul will offer the most competitive fares, although some airlines will add a connection to İzmir, Antalya, or Ankara for free.

Boarding: Pick up tickets well in advance of the departure date, and confirm by phone within 72 hours of departure. All of the major carriers to Turkey require that passengers arrive at the airport at least 2 hours before departure. One carry-on item and 2 pieces of checked baggage are the norm. Consult the airline for weight allowances.

Fares: Round-trip fares to Turkey from the US range from US$750-1000. Fares between November and March (excluding late December) may drop to as low as $500. Round-trip fares from Europe typically cost US$300-600.

BUDGET AND STUDENT TRAVEL AGENCIES

While knowledgeable agents specializing in flights to Turkey can make your life easy and help you save, they may not spend the time to find you the lowest possible fare—they get paid on commission. Students and under-26ers holding **ISIC and IYTC cards** (see p. 41), respectively, qualify for big discounts from student travel agencies. Most flights from budget agencies are on major airlines, but in peak season some may sell seats on less reliable chartered aircraft. For budget travel agencies in Turkey, see individual city listings under **Practical Information.**

A.T.C. Anadolu Tours, 420 Madison Ave., New York, NY, 10017 (☎(888) 262-3658 or (212) 486-4012). Specializes in consolidator tickets to Turkey.

usit world (www.usitworld.com). Over 50 **usit campus** branches in the UK (www.usitcampus.co.uk), including 52 Grosvenor Gardens, **London,** SW1W 0AG (☎(0870) 240 1010); **Manchester** (☎(0161) 273 1721); and **Edinburgh** (☎(0131) 668 3303). Nearly 20 **usit now** offices in Ireland, including 19-21 Aston Quay, O'Connell Bridge, **Dublin** 2 (☎(01) 602 1600; www.usitnow.ie), and **Belfast** (☎(02890) 327 111; www.usitnow.com). Offices also in Athens, Auckland, Brussels, Frankfurt, Johannesburg, Lisbon, Luxembourg, Madrid, Paris, Sofia, and Warsaw.

Council Travel (www.counciltravel.com). US offices include: Emory Village, 1561 N. Decatur Rd., **Atlanta,** GA 30307 (☎(404) 377-9997); 273 Newbury St., **Boston,** MA 02116 (☎(617) 266-1926); 1160 N. State St., **Chicago,** IL 60610 (☎(312) 951-0585); 931 Westwood Blvd., Westwood, **Los Angeles,** CA 90024 (☎(310) 208-3551); 254 Greene St., **New York,** NY 10003 (☎(212) 254-2525); 530 Bush St., **San Francisco,** CA 94108 (☎(415) 566-6222); 424 Broadway Ave E., **Seattle,** WA 98102 (☎(206) 329-4567); 3301 M St. NW, **Washington, D.C.** 20007 (☎(202) 337-6464). **For US cities not listed,** call ☎(800) 2-COUNCIL (226-8624). In the UK, 28A Poland St. (Oxford Circus), **London,** W1V 3DB (☎(020) 7437 7767).

CTS Travel, 44 Goodge St., **London,** W1 (☎(020) 7636 0031; fax 7637 5328; email ctsinfo@ctstravel.com.uk).

STA Travel, 6560 Scottsdale Rd. #F100, Scottsdale, AZ 85253 (☎(800) 777-0112; fax (602) 922-0793; www.sta-travel.com). A student and youth travel organization with over 150 offices worldwide. Ticket booking, travel insurance, railpasses, and more. US offices include: 297 Newbury St., **Boston,** MA 02115 (☎(617) 266-6014); 429 S. Dearborn St., **Chicago,** IL 60605 (☎(312) 786-9050); 7202 Melrose Ave., **Los Angeles,** CA 90046 (☎(323) 934-8722); 10 Downing St., **New York,** NY 10014 (☎(212) 627-3111); 4341 University Way NE, **Seattle,** WA 98105 (☎(206) 633-5000); 2401 Pennsylvania Ave., Ste. G, **Washington, D.C.** 20037 (☎ (202) 887-0912); 51 Grant Ave., **San Francisco,** CA 94108 (☎(415) 391-8407). In New Zealand, 10 High St., **Auckland** (☎(09) 309 0458). In Australia, 366 Lygon St., **Melbourne** Vic 3053 (☎(03) 9349 4344).

Travel CUTS (Canadian Universities Travel Services Limited), 187 College St., **Toronto,** ON M5T 1P7 (☎(416) 979-2406; fax 979-8167; www.travelcuts.com). 40 offices in Canada. Also in the UK, 295-A Regent St., **London,** W1R 7YA (☎(020) 7255 1944).

ESSENTIALS

FLIGHT PLANNING ON THE INTERNET. The Web is a great place to look for travel bargains—it's fast and convenient, and you can spend as long as you like exploring options without driving your travel agent insane.

Many airline sites offer last-minute deals on the the Web. You can check out the websites of each airline that flies to Turkey—among them Turkish Airlines (www.thy.com) and many European and North American carriers—or have other sites compile the best deals; try www.bestfares.com, www.onetravel.com, www.lowestfare.com, and www.travelzoo.com.

STA (www.sta-travel.com) and **Council** (www.counciltravel.com) provide quotes on student tickets, while **Expedia** (msn.expedia.com) and **Travelocity** (www.travelocity.com) offer full travel services. **Priceline** (www.priceline.com) allows you to specify a price, and obligates you to buy any ticket that meets or beats it; be prepared for antisocial hours and odd routes. **Skyauction** (www.skyauction.com) allows you to bid on both last-minute and advance-purchase tickets.

Just one last note—to protect yourself, make sure that the site uses a secure server before handing over any credit card details. Happy hunting!

COMMERCIAL AIRLINES

The commercial airlines' lowest regular offer is the **APEX** (Advance Purchase Excursion) fare, which provides confirmed reservations and allows "open-jaw" tickets. Generally, reservations must be made seven to 21 days ahead of departure, with seven- to 14-day minimum-stay and up to 90-day maximum-stay restrictions. These fares carry hefty cancellation and change penalties (fees rise in summer). Book peak-season APEX fares early; by May you will have a hard time getting the departure date you want.

Although APEX fares are probably not the cheapest possible fares, they will give you a sense of the average commercial price, from which to measure other bargains. Specials advertised in newspapers may be cheaper but have more restrictions and fewer available seats. **Turkish Airlines** (THY, *Türk Hava Yolları;* www.thy.com) is the national carrier, with offices in: **Chicago** (☎(312) 943-7858), **New York** (☎(212) 339-9650), **Sydney** (☎(02) 92 99 84 00), **London** (☎(020) 7766 9300 or 7766 9933), **Capetown** (☎(021) 251 967), and **Johannesburg** (☎(011) 883 3771). THY offers outstanding discounts during the low season (particularly Nov.-Mar., excluding late Dec.). Most flights are direct to İstanbul, but they allow you to add on a connection to Ankara, İzmir, or Antalya at no additional charge. Other carriers with significant service to Turkey include: Delta Airlines, Northwest Airlines, KLM, United Airlines, Lufthansa, and British Airways.

OTHER CHEAP ALTERNATIVES

CHARTER FLIGHTS. Charters are extra flights a tour operator contracts with an airline to fly during peak season. They can sometimes be cheaper than flights on scheduled airlines, some operate nonstop, and restrictions on minimum advance-purchase and minimum stay are more lenient. However, charter flights fly less frequently than major airlines, make refunds particularly difficult, and are almost always fully booked. Schedules and itineraries may also change or be cancelled at the last moment. As always, pay with a credit card if you can, and consider traveler's insurance against trip interruption. **Discount clubs** and **fare brokers** offer members savings on last-minute charter and tour deals.

TICKET CONSOLIDATORS. Ticket consolidators, or **"bucket shops,"** buy unsold tickets in bulk from commercial airlines and sell them at discounted rates. Consolidators often place tiny ads in the Sunday travel sections of major newspapers. Call quickly, as availability is typically extremely limited. Not all bucket shops are reliable, so insist on a receipt that gives full details of restrictions, refunds, and tickets, and pay by credit card so you can stop payment if you never receive your tickets. For more information, check out www.travel-library.com/air-travel/consolidators.html or pick up Kelly Monaghan's *Air Travel's Bargain Basement* (Intrepid Traveler, US$8).

> **FURTHER READING: BY PLANE.**
> *The Worldwide Guide to Cheap Airfares,* Michael McColl. Insider Publications (US$15).
> *Discount Airfares: The Insider's Guide,* George Hobart. Priceless Publications (US$14).
> *Air Traveler's Handbook* (www.cs.cmu.edu/afs/cs.cmu.edu/user/mkant/Public/Travel/airfare.html).
> *TravelHUB* (www.travelhub.com). A directory of travel agents that includes a searchable database of fares from over 500 consolidators.

BY TRAIN

Trains run directly to İstanbul from Athens and Bucharest. Some lines may be suspended due to political crises in the Balkans. Eurail passes are not valid in Turkey, but InterRail passes are. The Under 26 InterRail Pass (from US$239) allows either 15 days or one month of unlimited travel within one, two, three, or all of the seven zones into which InterRail divides Europe; the cost is determined by the number of zones the pass covers. The Over 26 InterRail Pass (also zone-based) offers unlimited second-class travel for 22 days for US$344. For information and ticket sales in Europe contact **Student Travel Centre,** 1st fl. 24 Rupert St., London, W1V 7FN (☎(020) 7437 0121, 7437 6370, or 7434 1306; fax 734 38 36; http://student-travel-centre.com). If you have a Eurail pass and are traveling from Greece to Turkey, take the train as far as Alexandroupolis, and ride the bus from there. Beware: the 38-hour ride from Athens will wear out even the most seasoned traveler.

BY FERRY

Ferries connect Turkey to Greece, Northern Cyprus, and Italy. Reservations are recommended, especially in high season. Be warned that ferries run on irregular schedules. If you sleep on deck, bring warm clothes and a blanket. Don't forget motion sickness medication, toilet paper, and a hand towel. Bring your own food to avoid high prices on board, and check in at least two hours in advance.

Connecting Turkey and **Greece,** ferries run between Ayvalık and Lesvos (see **Ferries,** p. 172), Çeşme and Chios (see p. 190), Kuşadası and Samos (see p. 202), Bodrum and Kos (see p. 218), and Marmaris and Rhodes (with connecting ferries to southern Cyprus and Israel; see p. 244). Between **Italy** and Turkey, ferries connect İzmir and Venice (see p. 184), and Çeşme and Brindisi (see p. 190). Ferries to **Northern Cyprus** leave from Alanya, Taşucu, and Mersin (see p. 452). Individual city listings, referenced above, contain specific information about schedules and fares.

BY THUMB

Let's Go does not recommend hitchhiking. Those who **hitch** between Turkey and Greece usually try to get to İstanbul in one ride from Alexandroupolis or Thessaloniki; there isn't much traffic, and people are not permitted to walk across the border (see **Border Crossing: Greece,** p. 144). Hitchhikers have said they made sure the license plate number did not get stamped in their passports (but rather on some other, disposable piece of paper), so that they wouldn't have to produce the car to leave the country.

GETTING AROUND

BY AIR

Turkish Airlines (*Türk Hava Yolları*, THY) flies to over 30 cities in Turkey, including Adana, Ankara, Antalya, Bodrum, Dalaman, Erzincan, Erzurum, İstanbul, İzmir, Kars, Kayseri, Malatya, Nevşehir, Samsun, Sivas, Trabzon, and Van. **İstanbul** and **Ankara** are the hubs for domestic flights. See individual city listings for schedules and prices. Domestic flights average about US$90 one-way, but passengers ages 12 to 24 may receive a discount. It is often cheaper to purchase tickets for domestic flights in Turkey. In some cities, an airport shuttle bus leaves from the downtown ticket office 30 to 90 minutes before flights (for an extra fee). There are reduced fares for passengers who book an international flight with THY.

BY BUS

Frequent, modern, and cheap **buses** run between all sizeable cities. In large cities, the *otogar* (bus station) is often located quite a distance from the city center, but many bus companies have branch offices downtown. Free shuttles called *servis* take ticketed passengers to the *otogar*. Buy tickets in advance from local offices, or purchase them directly at the station. Tickets are sometimes available on the bus, though you should ask ahead of time—some drivers allow only ticketed passengers aboard. You will need to go from booth to booth to piece together a complete schedule; one company may not divulge competitors' schedules. Many lines provide a 10% discount to ISIC-carrying students. Fares may increase during summer and religious holidays. Passengers are expected to remain in their assigned seats for the duration of the trip.

Because road safety is a serious concern in Turkey (see **Road Safety,** p. 47), *Let's Go* strongly recommends that you **only travel on reputable bus lines,** particularly for long trips. Although these are the most expensive tickets, they are still cheap. The extra money you pay allows the companies to take safety precautions such as giv-

ing the drivers rest breaks. Reputable companies include: **Varan, Ulusoy,** and **Kamıl Koç.** Whenever possible, *Let's Go* quotes prices from these companies.

Long routes are often served by **overnight buses.** For greatest comfort, request a window seat in the middle of the bus, away from the driver's radio and behind the overhead window. Every so often, a steward will come around spraying cologne; stretch out your palms to receive a squirt, then rub it over your face and neck. Once or twice during the trip, the bus will stop at a rest area where you can stretch your legs, use the toilets (10¢; paper extra), pray, and purchase overpriced cafeteria grub. The driver will announce the duration of the stop in Turkish, but it might vary by as much as 15 minutes either way, so keep an eye on your bus. If you are stranded, another bus going your way will probably visit the rest complex within a few hours; find the steward to buy a ticket. Nighttime travel is more risky than daytime bus travel. Beware of tourist bureau advice to travel at night in order to maximize touring time. Take care not to travel through poor weather conditions.

In rural parts of Turkey, it is customary to flag buses down from the roadside without reserving a seat in advance. Try to spot the bus's destination sign in the front window. Drivers, who keep an eye out for passengers, stop only if they have an empty seat. A steward hops off to stow your baggage and collect your fare.

Fez Travel, Turkey's flexible "backpacker bus" service, runs around a long loop encompassing İstanbul, Çanakkale, Gallipoli, the Aegean and Mediterranean coasts (including Ephesus, Troy, Kuşadası, Bodrum, Marmaris, Pamukkale, Antalya, and Side), Konya, Cappadocia, Ankara, and Bursa. A season pass (June-Oct. US$175, under 26 US$165) allows you to get on and off along the route at your own whim. There are also various scheduling alternatives, including cheaper passes that cover smaller portions of the route. Buses have English-speaking staff who offer info on accommodations and activities. Contact **Fez Travel,** 15 Akbıyık Cad., Sultanahmet, İstanbul (☎(212) 516 90 24; fax 638 87 64; email fextravel@escortnet.com; www.fez-travel.com. Tickets can also be purchased through STA in the UK (see **Budget and Student Travel Agencies,** p. 61).

BY DOLMUŞ

Extensive *dolmuş* (shared taxi) service follows fixed routes within larger cities and between small towns. These are usually vans or minibuses, though occasionally cars are in service as well. They leave as soon as they fill up (*dolmuş* means stuffed), and are almost as cheap as municipal buses (which do not exist in some towns). Best of all, you can get on and off anywhere you like.

BY FERRY

Ferries do not serve the west coast, but a **Turkish Maritime Lines** (TML) cruise ship sails between İstanbul and İzmir (21hr., 1 per week). A weekly boat connects İstanbul with destinations on the Black Sea Coast; for more information, see **The Black Sea Ferry,** p. 378. İstanbul has frequent service to Bandırma and Yalova. Larger ports have ship offices; otherwise, just get on the boat and find the purser.

Most Turkish ferries are comfortable and well-equipped; the cheapest fare class sometimes includes a reclining chair or couchette where you can sleep. Avoid the often astronomically priced cafeteria cuisine by bringing your own food. Fares jump sharply in July and August. Student discounts are often available.

BY TRAIN

Despite low fares, trains within Turkey are no bargain, as they are slow and follow circuitous routes. The Turkish rail system is rivaled only by the Greek system as Europe's most antiquated and least efficient. First-class gets you a slightly more padded seat, but most Turks travel second-class. Since couchettes are available, overnight train trips are preferable to overnight bus trips. Lock your compartment door and keep your valuables on your person. Make reservations at least a few hours in advance at the train station. There is no rail system in Cyprus.

DOLMUŞ DOS AND DON'TS To the uninitiated, mastering this quintessentially Turkish mode of transportation can appear daunting. Travelers can avoid a *dolmuş faux pas* by following these suggestions.

Dolmuş flexibility and price is somewhere between those of taxis and buses. They run along set but unpublished routes, usually beginning from a secret hub somewhere in the city. *Dolmuş* post their final destinations in their front windows, but if you're headed to an intermediate destination, you'll probably need to ask locals which is the right one for you: *"Bu dolmuş [destination] gidiyor mu?"* (Does this *dolmuş* go to X?). If you're at a hub, there should be a queue of people waiting to board a queue of *dolmuş* to your destination. Hop in line and exude savvy.

If you've just jumped on a *dolmuş* en route, don't stand precariously and fish for your money as the driver pulls away—you'll just make everybody nervous. There's no rush. Take a seat. Keep in mind that you should generally sit next to somebody of the same sex, though as the *dolmuş* fills up the rule is inevitably broken.

Ask your neighbor or the driver how much it costs to go to your destination: *"X kadar ne kadar?"* (How much is it to X?). Then pass the cash up to someone in the next row, saying the name of your destination and adding "öğrenci" if you're a student. The driver, while racing his stick-shift minibus through tricky traffic, will change your money and pass it back to you. If money is passed to you by somebody else, send it on its way with the same instructions you received.

The driver may remember your stated destination and stop there without any reminder on your part. Otherwise, clearly say *"inecek var"* (getting off) and, as the driver pulls to a stop, calmly squeeze out of your seat and hop off.

BY MOPED AND MOTORCYCLE

Motorized bikes offer an enjoyable, relatively inexpensive way to tour coastal areas and countryside, particularly where there are few cars. They don't use much gas, can be put on trains and ferries, and are a good compromise between the high cost of car travel and the limited range of bicycles. Exercise extreme caution— driving in Turkey can be tricky at best. Your trip to Turkey is not the best time to learn how to ride a moped or motorcyle. They're uncomfortable for long distances, dangerous in the rain, and unpredictable on rough roads and gravel. Always wear a helmet, and never ride with a backpack. Expect to pay about US$20-35 per day; remember to bargain. Motorcycles normally require a license. Ask if the quoted price includes tax and insurance, or you may be hit with an additional fee. Avoid handing your passport over as a deposit; if you have an accident or mechanical failure you may not get it back until you cover all repairs.

BY THUMB

 Let's Go strongly urges you to seriously consider the risks before you choose to hitch. We do not recommend hitching as a safe means of transportation.

Those who decide to **hitchhike** in Turkey generally offer to pay half of what the trip would cost by bus. Most Turks, however, refuse payment. Hitchers in Turkey signal with a hand wave or the standard thumb. Travelers in remote parts of Turkey will find that drivers may offer them rides even when they're just waiting for a bus. No one should hitch without careful consideration of the risks involved. After all, any bozo can drive a car.

If you're a woman traveling alone, **do not hitch.** It's just too dangerous. Safety issues are always imperative, even for those who are not hitching alone. Safety-minded hitchers avoid getting in the back of a two-door car and never let go of their backpacks. They will not get into a car that they can't get out of again in a hurry. If they ever feel threatened, they insist on being let off, regardless of where they are. Acting as if they are going to open the car door or vomit on the upholstery may get a driver to stop. Hitchhiking at night is particularly dangerous.

BY CAR

Turks drive on the right-hand side of the road, except in Northern Cyprus, where traffic runs on the left side. The speed limit is 50kph (31mph) in cities, 90kph (55mph) on the highways, and 130kph (80mph) on *oto yolu* (toll roads). Road signs in English make driving somewhat easier. Archaeological and historical sites are indicated by yellow signposts with black writing; village signs have blue writing. Before taking your own car to Turkey, consider the effects of poor roads. If you get into an accident, you must file a report with the police (traffic police ☎118). The **Touring and Automobile Association of Turkey** (TTOK) can provide more information. Their İstanbul office is at I. Otot Sanayi Yanı, Çamlık Cad. 4, Levent, ☎(212) 282 81 40; fax (212) 282 82 40; email turing@turing.org.tr; www.turing.org/tr/Turing/emain.html. For safety information, see **Road Safety,** p. 47.

DRIVING PERMITS AND CAR INSURANCE

INTERNATIONAL DRIVING PERMIT (IDP)

If you plan to drive a car while in Turkey, you should have an International Driving Permit (IDP). Though Turkey allows travelers to drive with a valid American or Canadian license for a limited time, it may be a good idea to get an IDP anyway in case you're in a situation (e.g., an accident or stranded in a small town) where the police do not know English; information on the IDP is printed in 10 languages.

Your IDP, valid for one year, must be issued in your own country before you depart. An application for an IDP usually needs to include one or two photos, a current local license, an additional form of identification, and a fee.

Australia: Contact your local Royal Automobile Club (RAC) or the National Royal Motorist Association (NRMA) if in NSW or the ACT (☎(08) 9421 4444; www.rac.com.au/travel). Permits AUS$15.

Canada: Contact a Canadian Automobile Association (CAA) branch office or write to CAA, 1145 Hunt Club Rd., #200, K1V 0Y3. (☎(613) 247-0117; www.caa.ca/CAAInternet/travelservices/internationaldocumentation/idptravel.htm). Permits CDN$10.

Ireland: Contact the nearest Automobile Association (AA) office or write to the UK address below. Permits IR£4. The Irish Automobile Association, 23 Suffolk St., Rockhill, Blackrock, Co. Dublin (☎(01) 677 9481), honors most foreign automobile memberships (24hr. breakdown and road service ☎(800) 667 788; toll-free in Ireland).

New Zealand: Contact your local Automobile Association (AA) or their main office at Auckland Central, 99 Albert St. (☎(09) 377 4660; www.nzaa.co.nz). Permits NZ$8.

South Africa: Contact the Travel Services Department of the Automobile Association of South Africa at P.O. Box 596, 2000 Johannesburg (☎(011) 799 1400; fax 799 1410; http://aasa.co.za). Permits SAR28.50.

UK: To visit your local AA Shop, contact the **AA Headquarters** (☎(0990) 44 88 66), or write to: The Automobile Association, International Documents, Fanum House, Erskine, Renfrewshire PA8 6BW. To find the location nearest you that issues the IDP, call ☎(0990) 50 06 00 or 44 88 66. For more info, see www.theaa.co.uk/motoringandtravel/idp/index.asp. Permits UK£4.

US: Visit any American Automobile Association (AAA) office or write to AAA Florida, Travel Related Services, 1000 AAA Drive (mail stop 100), Heathrow, FL 32746 (☎(407) 444-7000; fax 444-7380). You don't have to be a member to buy an IDP. Permits US$10. AAA Travel Related Services (☎(800) 222-4357) provides road maps, travel guides, emergency road services, travel services, and auto insurance.

CAR INSURANCE

Some credit cards cover standard insurance. If you rent, lease, or borrow a car, you will need a **green card**, or **International Insurance Certificate**, to certify that you have liability insurance and that it applies abroad. Green cards can be obtained at car rental agencies, car dealers (for those leasing cars), some travel agencies, and some border crossings. Rental agencies may require you to purchase theft insurance in countries that they consider to have a high risk of auto theft.

ORIENTATION AND STREET ADDRESSES

Since few Turkish cities follow a grid plan, maps can be difficult to use. To avoid confusion, a three-tiered addressing system is used. *Mahalle* refers to the neighborhood, *cadde* or *bulvar* are avenues or boulevards, and a *sokak* is a street. A slash after the street number, or the word *kat*, introduces the number of the floor, if applicable. *Mahalle(si)* is abbreviated to **Mah.**, *Cadde(si)* to **Cad.**, *Bulvar(ı)* to **Bul.**, and *Sokak* (or *Sokağı*) to **Sok.** Thus, a complete street address in Turkey might look like *Çiğdem Mah. Atatürk Bul. Söğüt Sok. 6/2*. This book, which prints street numbers directly before the streets to which they refer, would list this address as *Atatürk Bul., 6/2 Söğüt Sok, Çiğdem Mah.* It means the second floor of 6 Söğüt St., off Atatürk Ave., in the Çiğdem District. Few addresses will contain all of these parts. In towns and rural areas, the street names may not appear on maps. Rather than searching for street names and building numbers, ask for the place you're seeking: *"Aya Sofia nerede?"* (Where is Aya Sofia?).

ADDITIONAL INFORMATION

SPECIFIC CONCERNS

WOMEN TRAVELERS

Foreign women, especially those traveling alone, attract significant attention in Turkey. Catcalls and other forms of verbal harassment are common; physical harassment is rare. Regardless of whatever signals a foreign woman intends to send, her foreignness alone may suggest a liberal openness to friendly or amorous advances. Because Western movies and TV often depict women as seductive sex symbols, female travelers are frequently perceived as likely sex partners. However, as long as women expect plenty of attention and take certain common sense precautions, there is no need for paranoia.

More touristed parts of Turkey—İstanbul, Northwestern Turkey, the Aegean and Mediterranean Coasts, Cappadocia, and Ankara—may be more comfortable for women travelers. Female travelers in Anatolia, along the Black Sea, and in Eastern Turkey should be confident and experienced in developing-world travel.

DRESSING FOR SUCCESS. A lot of harassment can be avoided by dressing conservatively. Shorts, short skirts, tight T-shirts, and revealing clothes are unacceptable in all areas of Turkey, including İstanbul, except in the most touristy of Aegean and Mediterranean towns. Women traveling alone might want to avoid such threads even in the latter regions. Generally, the less you look like a tourist, the better off you'll be. Carry a kerchief or scarf to cover your head in mosques and more conservative towns. Wearing a conspicuous **wedding band** may help prevent unwanted overtures. Some travelers report that carrying pictures of a "husband" or "children" is extremely useful to help document marriage status. Even a mention of a husband waiting back at the hotel may be enough to discount your potentially vulnerable, unattached appearance.

ACCOMMODATIONS AND FOOD. Sometimes more expensive, slightly more upscale accommodations with single rooms are more secure for a woman traveling alone; however, cheap dorm-style accommodations are often equally good and also can provide invaluable opportunities for meeting other travelers with whom to venture out after dark. Stick to centrally located accommodations to avoid solitary late-night treks or metro rides. For comfortable restaurants, look for establishments with the word *"aile"* ("family") in their names. Although you're free to sit wherever you choose, Turkish women and couples will always sit in the *aile* room, which tends to be furnished better than the men-only "main" room.

STREET SMARTS. On the street, avoid eye contact, and appear confident and directed. Consider approaching older women or couples for directions if you're lost or feel uncomfortable. Customarily, Turkish women seldom walk outside alone, especially after dark. Always carry extra money for a phone call, bus, or taxi. Women and men usually do not sit next to one another on buses and *dolmuş*. To avoid insinuating interest in her driver, a female traveler should not sit in the front seat of a taxi. **Hitching is never safe** for lone women, or even for women traveling together. Choose train compartments occupied by other women or couples; ask the conductor to put together a women-only compartment if he or she doesn't offer to do so first.

HARASSMENT. The best answer to verbal harassment is no answer at all; feigned deafness, sitting still, and staring straight ahead will do a world of good that reactions usually don't achieve. Alternatively, you can attract attention and show your displeasure by making a scene, perhaps using the expression *"ayıp!"* ("shame!"). A phrase like *"haydi git"* ("go away") may also come in handy. Don't hesitate to seek out a police officer or a passerby if you are being harassed.

Rape and other violence against women are still relatively new to Turkish culture, and their incidence is much more rare than in most Western countries. If, at any time, unwanted attention becomes physical and/or threatening, you should yell, scream, and make getting away your first priority. In Turkish, holler *"imdat"* ("eem-DAHT," help) or *"polis"* ("PO-lees," police). Carry a **whistle** or an airhorn on your keychain, and memorize the **emergency number (☎ 155).** An **IMPACT Model Mugging** self-defense course will not only prepare you for a potential attack, but will also raise your confidence and your awareness of your surroundings (see **Personal Safety,** p. 45). Women also face some specific health concerns when traveling (see **Women's Health,** p. 52).

FURTHER READING: WOMEN TRAVELERS.

A Journey of One's Own: Uncommon Advice for the Independent Woman Traveler, Thalia Zepatos. Eighth Mountain Press (US$17).

Adventures in Good Company: The Complete Guide to Women's Tours and Outdoor Trips, Thalia Zepatos. Eighth Mountain Press (US$7).

Active Women Vacation Guide, Evelyn Kaye. Blue Panda Publications (US$18).

Travelers' Tales: Gutsy Women, Travel Tips and Wisdom for the Road, Marybeth Bond. Traveler's Tales (US$8).

TRAVELING ALONE

There are many benefits to traveling alone, among them greater independence and more rewarding challenges. As a lone traveler, you may find that Turks are more inclined to help you. On the other hand, any solo traveler is a more vulnerable target of harassment and street theft. Lone travelers need to be well-organized and look confident at all times. If questioned, never admit that you are traveling alone. Maintain regular contact with someone at home who knows your itinerary.

For more tips, pick up *Traveling Solo* by Eleanor Berman (Globe Pequot, US$17) or subscribe to **Connecting: Solo Travel Network,** P.O. Box 29088, Delamont RPO, Vancouver, BC V6J 5C2 (☎/fax (604) 737-7791; www.cstn.org; membership US$25-35), or the **Travel Companion Exchange,** P.O. Box 833, Amityville, NY 11701, USA (☎ (631) 454-0880 or (800) 392-1256; www.whytravelalone.com; US$48).

OLDER TRAVELERS

Older travelers may find traveling in Turkey a bit difficult. Many opt for senior group travel agencies, which are growing in enrollment and popularity. The following organize trips to Turkey:

ElderTreks, 597 Markham St., Toronto, ON, M6G 2L7, Canada (☎(800) 741-7956 or (416) 588-5000; fax 588-9839; email eldertreks@eldertreks.com; www.eldertreks.com) Adventure travel programs for the traveler over 50.

Elderhostel, 75 Federal St., Boston, MA 02110, USA (☎(617) 426-7788 or (877) 426-2166; email registration@elderhostel.org; www.elderhostel.org). Organizes 1- to 4-week "educational adventures" in Turkey on varied subjects for those over 55.

Walking the World, P.O. Box 1186, Fort Collins, CO 80522, USA (☎(970) 498-0500; fax 498-9100; email walktworld@aol.com; www.walkingtheworld.com). For those over 50.

> **FURTHER READING: OLDER TRAVELERS.**
> *No Problem! Worldwise Tips for Mature Adventurers,* Janice Kenyon. Orca Book Publishers (US$16).
> *A Senior's Guide to Healthy Travel,* Donald L. Sullivan. Career Press. (US$15).
> *Unbelievably Good Deals and Great Adventures That You Absolutely Can't Get Unless You're Over 50,* Joan Rattner Heilman. Contemporary Books (US$13).

BISEXUAL, GAY, AND LESBIAN TRAVELERS

Although homosexuality is legal in Turkey and Northern Cyprus, social conservatism and religious and social dictates keep most homosexual activity discreet. Homophobia can be a problem, especially in remote areas. If problems arise, expect authorities to be unsympathetic.

Turkey's urban centers do not lack bars or informal cruising areas (men only), although they may be less obvious. Contact Turkey's gay and lesbian organization **Lamartin,** c/o İbrahim Eren, Lamartin Cad. 23/6, Tuslim, İstanbul for more details. Gay and lesbian travelers will benefit from the close contact that Turks maintain with same-sex friends. Public displays of affection should be avoided.

For more information on gay and lesbian travel, contact the **International Gay and Lesbian Travel Association,** 4331 N. Federal Hwy., #304, Fort Lauderdale, FL 33308, USA (☎(954) 776-2626; fax (954) 776-3303; email IGLTA@aol.com; www.iglta.com), an organization of over 1350 companies serving gay and lesbian travelers worldwide. Call for lists of agents, accommodations, and events.

> **FURTHER READING: BISEXUAL, GAY, AND LESBIAN TRAVELERS.**
> *Spartacus International Gay Guide.* Bruno Gmunder Verlag. (US$33).
> *Damron's Accommodations* and *The Women's Traveler.* Damron Travel Guides (US$14-19). For more information, call US ☎(415) 255-0404 or (800) 462-6654 or check their web site (www.damron.com).
> *Ferrari Guides' Gay Travel A to Z, Ferrari Guides' Men's Travel in Your Pocket, Ferrari Guides' Women's Travel in Your Pocket,* and *Ferrari Guides' Inn Places.* Ferrari Guides (US$14-16). For more information, call ☎(602) 863-2408 or ☎(800) 962-2912 or check their website (www.ferrariguides.com).
> *The Gay Vacation Guide: The Best Trips and How to Plan Them,* Mark Chesnut. Citadel Press (US$15).

TRAVELERS WITH DISABILITIES

Turkey and Northern Cyprus are only slowly beginning to respond to the needs of travelers with disabilities. Some hotels, train stations, and airports have installed facilities for the disabled; many of the archaeological sites throughout the region, however, are still not wheelchair accessible. It may be difficult for people with disabilities to travel on a budget in Turkey.

Those with disabilities should inform airlines and hotels of their disabilities when making arrangements for travel; some time may be needed to prepare special accommodations. Call ahead to restaurants, hotels, and other facilities to find out about the existence of ramps, the widths of doors, the dimensions of elevators, etc. The following organizations provide helpful information or publications:

Mobility International USA (MIUSA), P.O. Box 10767, Eugene, OR 97440, USA (☎ (541) 343-1284 voice and TDD; fax 343-6812; email info@miusa.org; www.miusa.org). Sells *A World of Options: A Guide to International Educational Exchange, Community Service, and Travel for Persons with Disabilities* (US$35).

Moss Rehab Hospital Travel Information Service (☎ (215) 456-9600 or (800) CALL-MOSS; email netstaff@mossresourcenet.org; www.mossresourcenet.org). An information resource center on travel-related concerns for those with disabilities.

Society for the Advancement of Travel for the Handicapped (SATH), 347 Fifth Ave., #610, New York, NY 10016, USA (☎ (212) 447-7284; www.sath.org). An advocacy group that publishes the quarterly travel magazine *Open World* (free for members, US$13 for nonmembers). Also publishes a wide range of info sheets on disability travel facilitation and destinations. Annual membership US$45, students and seniors US$30.

MINORITY TRAVELERS

In Turkey, Caucasians are a minority. However, while Turks have a well-deserved reputation for hospitality and openness to strangers, travelers of African, Asian, or Latin American descent, especially those traveling alone and/or in non-touristy areas, may have an experience different from that of their Caucasian counterparts. Turks often have no qualms about staring at the unfamiliar, be it beautiful, intriguing, or repulsive. If you're in less-traveled towns and cities, be ready for a few terrified children, puzzled old women, or snickering teenagers. Probably the worst you can expect is a derisive over-the-shoulder remark. You may be faced with a few amusing or even offensive questions, but keep in mind that it's mostly from plain curiosity, without malice or contempt.

A few caveats: dark-skinned travelers should know that, thanks to the power of Hollywood, a distorted cultural representation awaits them, associated with violence and crime. People of East Asian descent are automatically assumed to be Japanese. This may lead to extra deference from people in the tourist industry, as the Japanese have a reputation for lavish spending. Travelers to **Northern Cyprus** may notice quite a few South Asians and Africans on city streets due to the island's ties to the British Empire. Most speak fluent Turkish, so travelers of similar appearance may find themselves expected to do the same.

TRAVELERS WITH CHILDREN

Turks and Cypriots adore children. Expect a stream of compliments, advice, candy, and discounts on transportation throughout Turkey and Cyprus. Children under two generally fly for 10% of the adult airfare on international flights (this does not necessarily include a seat). International fares are usually discounted 25% for children from two to 11. Family vacations will be most enjoyable if you slow your pace and plan ahead. Be sure that your child carries some sort of ID in case of an emergency or if he or she gets lost, and arrange a reunion spot in case of separation when sightseeing. Consider using a papoose-style device to carry your baby on walking trips. Baby foods are usually only available in pharmacies.

DIETARY CONCERNS

Vegetarians should have no problem finding suitable cuisine in Turkey. **Vegetarian dishes** in Turkey and Cyprus include succulent fruits, colorful salads, tasty breads, *fasülye* (beans), and *börek* (cheese-filled pastry). Vegetarian *meze* (appetizers) are plentiful. In summer, fresh vegetables, fruits, and interesting cheeses abound in the outdoor markets. In well-traveled areas of Turkey, Turks understand the concept of vegetarianism; simply explain, "*Vejetariyanım*" ("I am a vegetarian.") In other areas ask, "*Etsiz yemek var mı?*" ("Do you have food without meat?")

Travelers who keep **kosher** will be hard-pressed to find a kosher restaurant. If you are strict in your observance, consider preparing your own food on the road. **The Jewish Travel Guide,** which lists synagogues, kosher restaurants, and Jewish institutions in over 100 countries, including Turkey, is available from Vallentine-

Mitchell Publishers, Newbury House 890-900, Eastern Ave., Newbury Park, Ilford, Essex, IG2 7HH, UK (☎ (020) 8599 8866; fax 8599 0984). Buy it in the US ($16.95 plus $4 S&H) from ISBS, 5804 NE Hassallo St., Portland, OR 97213 (☎ (800) 944-6190).

ALTERNATIVES TO TOURISM

For an extensive listing of "off-the-beaten-track" and specialty travel opportunities, try the **Specialty Travel Index**, 305 San Anselmo Ave., #313, San Anselmo, CA 94960, USA (☎ (888) 624-4030 or (415) 455-1643; www.spectrav.com; US$6). **Transitions Abroad** (www.transabroad.com) publishes a bimonthly on-line newsletter for work, study, and specialized travel abroad.

STUDYING ABROAD

Foreign study programs in Turkey vary tremendously in expense, academic focus and quality, living conditions, degree of contact with local students, and exposure to culture and language. If you plan on staying in Turkey for more than three months, you will have to obtain a student visa, available from the Turkish consulates and embassies listed on p. 39.

Most American undergraduates enroll in programs sponsored by US universities. Because English is the language of instruction at many Turkish universities, it is also possible to enroll directly as a special student. Doing so might be less expensive than enrolling in an American university program. Schools that offer study abroad programs to foreigners are listed below.

American Field Service (AFS), 310 SW 4th Ave., #630, Portland, OR 97204, USA (☎ (800) 237-4636; fax (503) 241-1653; email afsinfo@afs.org; www.afs.org/usa). Summer, semester, and year-long homestay international exchange programs in Turkey for high school students and graduating high school seniors. Financial aid available.

Beloit College, World Affairs Center, 700 College St., Beloit, WI 53511, USA (☎ (608) 363-2269; www.beloit.edu). A semester program at Marmara University in İstanbul.

Summer Program at Boğaziçi University, İstanbul. Contact Illinois Programs Abroad, 115 International Studies Building, 910 S. 5th St., Champaign, IL 61820, USA (☎ (800) 531-4404 or (217) 333-6168; fax (217) 244-0249; email ipa@uiuc.edu). Students choose 2 or 3 seven-week classes on the culture, language, and history of Turkey, Central Asia, and the Middle East, taught at one of Turkey's foremost universities.

Council on International Education Exchange, 205 E. 42nd St., New York, NY 10017, USA (☎ (888) 268-6245; fax (212) 822-2699; email info@ciee.org; www.ciee.org). Summer programs at Ankara's Middle East Technical University and Bilkent University.

Study Abroad at Middle East Technical University, Ankara. Contact Dr. Shirley Epir, Director, International Relations Office, Rektorluk 501, Middle East Technical University, Ankara 06531 (☎ 90 (312) 210-2000; email shirleyj@rorqual.cc.metu.edu.tr; www.metu.edu.tr/MIA/summersc). A 6-week program providing college students with 2 3-credit courses. Offers a wide range of courses on Turkish history, politics, and culture.

Pitzer College in Turkey. Contact the Office of External Studies, Pitzer College, 1050 N. Mills Ave., Claremont, CA 91711, USA (☎ (909) 621-8104; fax 621-0518; www.pitzer.edu/academics/ilcenter/external_studies/turkey.htm). 4-month field study program, usually mid-Feb. to mid-June.

School for International Training, College Semester Abroad, Admissions, Kipling Rd., P.O. Box 676, Brattleboro, VT 05302, USA (☎ (800) 336-1616 or (802) 258-3267; www.sit.edu). Semester- and year-long programs in Turkey run US$9500-12,900.

State University of New York/Binghamton, Office of International Programs, N.A. Rockefeller Center G-1, P.O. Box 6000, Binghamton University, Binghamton, NY 13902, USA (☎ (607) 777-2336; fax 277-2889; email oip@binghamton.edu; www.binghamton.edu). Semester, year, and summer programs at İstanbul's Bosphorus University.

TÖMER, 18/1 Ziya Gökalp Cad., Kızılay, Ankara (☎ (312) 435 97 81; fax 433 81 90). Teaches Turkish in cities across Turkey, including İstanbul, Antalya, Bursa, and İzmir.

ESSENTIALS

FURTHER READING: STUDYING ABROAD.
www.studyabroad.com
Academic Year Abroad 2000/2001. Institute of International Education Books (US$45).
Vacation Study Abroad 2000/2001. Institute of International Education Books (US$43).
Peterson's Study Abroad 2001. Peterson's (US$30).
Peterson's Summer Study Abroad 2001. Peterson's (US$30)

ESSENTIALS

WORKING ABROAD

Finding work in Turkey and Cyprus is difficult, as the government tries to restrict employment to citizens. Foreigners who wish to work in Turkey must obtain a **work permit,** issued by the Ministry of the Interior; contact a Turkish diplomatic mission for more information. The brightest prospect for working in Turkey is probably **teaching English.** Students with university credentials might fare quite well, but having your credentials verified can take some time. Various organizations in the US will place you in a (low-paying) teaching job. University foreign language departments may have connections to job openings abroad.

International Schools Services, Educational Staffing Program, P.O. Box 5910, Princeton, NJ 08543, USA (☎(609) 452-0990; www.iss.edu). Recruits teachers and administrators for American and English schools in Turkey. US$150 application fee.

Office of Overseas Schools, US Department of State, Room H328, SA-1, Washington, D.C. 20522 (☎(202) 261-8200; fax 261-8224; www.state.gov/www/about_state/schools/). Keeps a comprehensive list of schools abroad and agencies that arrange placement for Americans to teach abroad.

VOLUNTEERING

Volunteer jobs are readily available, and many provide room and board in exchange for labor (on archaeological digs, community projects, etc.).

Archaeological Institute of America, 656 Beacon St., Boston, MA 02215 (☎(617) 353-9361; www.archaeological.org). The *Archaeological Fieldwork Opportunities Bulletin* (US$16 for non-members) lists field sites throughout Europe (call for info on Turkey). Purchase the bulletin from Kendall/Hunt Publishing, 4050 Westmark Dr., Dubuque, Iowa 52002 (☎(800) 228-0810).

Gençtur Turizm ve Seyahat Ac. Ltd. (Tourism and Travel Agency), Head Office: Professor K. İsmail Gürkan Cad., No. 14 Flat 4, Sultanahmet, İstanbul 34100 (☎(212) 520 52 74; fax 519 08 64). Taksim Branch (handles workcamps): İstiklâl Cad., Zambak Sok. 15/5, Taksim, İstanbul 80080 (☎(212) 249 25 15; fax 249 25 54; email workcamps@gentur.com.tr; http://genctur.com.) Organizes teenage, group, or international voluntary 2-week summer workcamps and year-round study tours in Turkey.

Volunteers for Peace, 1034 Tiffany Rd., Belmont, VT 05730, USA (☎(802) 259-2759; www.vfp.org). Arranges placement in workcamps in Gençtur, Turkey. Annual *International Workcamp Directory* US$20. Registration fee US$200. Free newsletter.

FURTHER READING: VOLUNTEERING.
International Jobs: Where They Are, How to Get Them, Eric Koocher. Perseus Books (US$17).
Work Abroad: The Complete Guide to Finding a Job Overseas, Clayton Hubbs. Transitions Abroad (US$16).
International Directory of Voluntary Work, Louise Whetter. Vacation Work Publications (US$16).
Teaching English Abroad, Susan Griffin. Vacation Work (US$17).
Overseas Summer Jobs 2001, Work Your Way Around the World, and *The Directory of Jobs and Careers Abroad.* Peterson's (US$17-18 each).

WEB RESOURCES

Turkey is becoming as wired as a carpet salesman on seven cups of *çay*. The World Wide Web allows travelers to consult official and unofficial sources of information in Turkey and throughout the world and to browse through a vast library of literature and multimedia material about Turkey's past, present, and future. The following is a grab-bag of useful resources.

All About Turkey (www.balsoy.com/Turkiye/index.html). The name says it all.

Center for Middle Eastern Studies (www.fas.harvard.edu/~mideast/inMEres/countries/turkey.html). A spectacular listing of multi-lingual Turkey links.

Learn Practical Turkish (www2.egenet.com.tr/~mastersj/). Covers the language basics and then some. The section on "Off-color Turkish" is not for the faint of heart.

Let's Go (www.letsgo.com/Thumb/mideast/index.htm#). Useful travel-related links.

Republic of Turkey (www.turkey.org). The web site of the Turkish Embassy in Washington. Information on travel, history, and current events, from the government's point of view.

Shoestring Travel (www.stratpub.com). A budget travel e-zine that features listings of home exchanges, links, and accommodations information.

Turkish Daily News (www.turkishdailynews.com). Turkey's only English-language daily. Don't believe everything you read.

Turkish Republic of Northern Cyprus (www.trncwashdc.org). Web site of the Northern Cyprus Representative Office, with a variety of semi-helpful information and links.

Türkiye on the Web (www.columbia.edu/cu/libraries/indiv/area/MiddleEast/Turkey.html). Provides a lifetime's worth of Turkey-related web sites.

İSTANBUL

Straddling two continents and almost three millennia of history, İstanbul exists on an incomprehensible scale. The city unfolds against a densely historic landscape of Ottoman mosques, Byzantine mosaics, and Roman masonry. The Bosphorus Straits have proven to be the city's lifeline and its curse: the strategic location between two seas and two continents gave birth to the city, but also attracted countless sieges from covetous neighbors. Having withstood innumerable demographic shifts, devastating wars, natural disasters, and foreign occupations, İstanbul is naturally composed of a unique mix of civilizations, a melange evident not only in architecture and religious practice, but also in everyday life. Conservative women wearing black veils merge in the swelling crowds with younger women in western dress, and major religious and historical sights double as the stunningly beautiful backdrops for love scenes in Turkish pop videos.

In its current incarnation, İstanbul is the most crowded and cosmopolitan city in the Turkish Republic. This urban supernova explodes out into the surrounding countryside behind an ever-expanding front of new construction sites, as no crane or cement truck could possibly hope to keep up with the pace of İstanbulian life, the city remains crowded. New immigrants from the Anatolian hinterland live in shanties on the fringes of the city. These dwellings, called *gecekondus* because they are hastily erected, as if in a single night *(gece)*, were some of the first structures to be leveled in the devastating earthquake of August 1999.

The poverty of İstanbul's *gecekondus* coexists with an ambitious commercialism as audacious and ostentatious as any to be found in New York or London. Yet every level of the city's burgeoning economy remains distinctly İstanbulian: posh, modern nightclubs lend their space to raucous traditional weddings, and modern fast food competes neck-and-neck with boatmen selling fried fish sandwiches.

Even as İstanbul's centuries-long sprawl has engulfed entire towns, each neighborhood of the city retains a distinct character. Some sections of the city are easily accessible to the visitor. The challenge is to see beyond the Ottoman palaces, carpet salesmen, and backpacker bars, and venture out into neighborhood produce markets, back-alley tea shops, and Byzantine fortifications.

İSTANBUL HIGHLIGHTS

TOUR the **Topkapı Palace,** one-time residence of Süleyman the Magnificent and his harem, and pore over the visual archives of the Islamic World (p. 104).

VISIT the **Blue Mosque,** the six-minareted wonder whose creation once threatened the singularity of the mosque at Mecca (p. 102).

WANDER ACROSS creaky boards and among ancient columns through the eerie underground cistern to the partially submerged **Gorgon heads** (p. 111).

NAVIGATE the labyrinthine **Grand Bazaar** (p. 110), and bargain for gold, silver, silk, and carpets as you drink bottomless cups of *çay.*

BROWSE through Ortaköy's Sunday **silver market** (p. 125) and spend the afternoon playing backgammon with bohemians at a colorful waterfront cafe.

SAMPLE *lokum* at the **Egyptian Spice Bazaar** (p. 117), whose air is thick with the pungent aroma of tea and spices.

HOP on the Tünel Metro (p. 85), the oldest subway in the world, to watch a **Whirling Dervish show** at the Galat Mevlihane on İstiklâl Cad.

BOARD a vintage ferry to the **Prince's Islands** and bike among Greek monasteries before collapsing on the beach to work on that tan (p. 130).

İSTANBUL

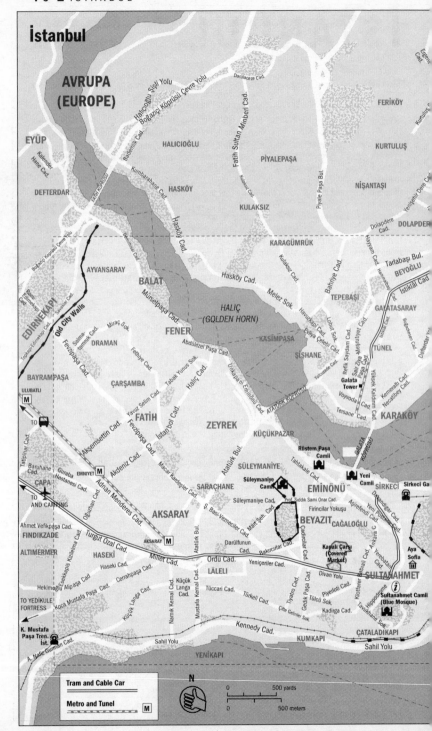

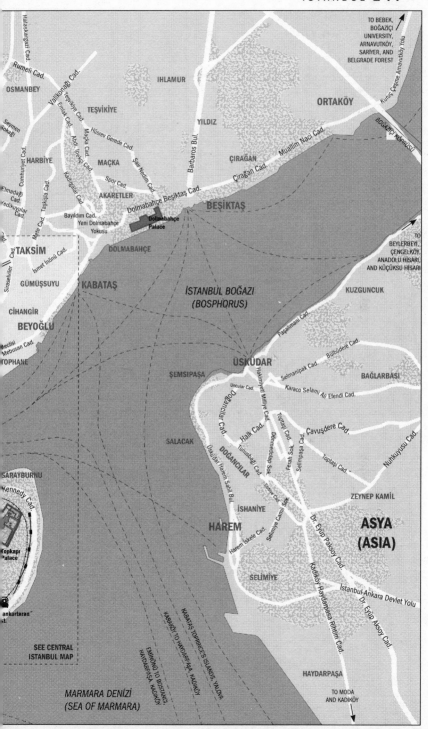

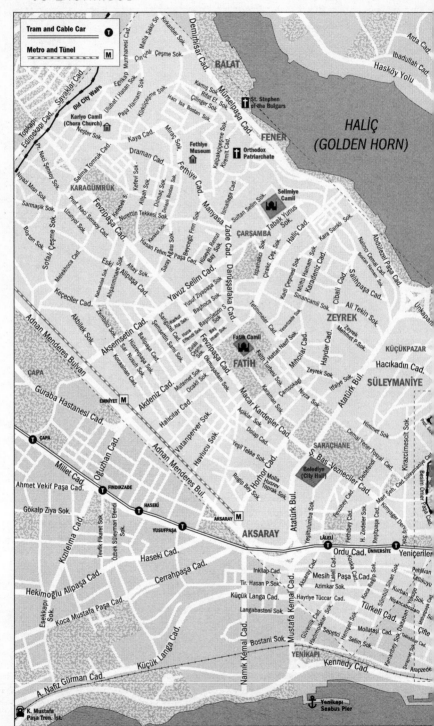

Central İstanbul

HISTORY

The traces of the first known settlement in the İstanbul area date to the Paleolithic age. **Mycenaeans** established themselves on the site of modern İstanbul around the 13th century BC. Two hundred years later, settlers founded several fishing villages in the area, one of which occupied the exact site of the Topkapı Palace. It was not until **Megarian** colonists from Greece landed on the Asian shore of the Bosphorus around 700 BC, however, that the city's history was first recorded.

Legend has it that in the 7th century BC, **Byzas,** a Greek speculator looking for prime real estate, consulted the infallible Oracle at Delphi, who told him to settle "opposite the Land of the Blind." As Byzas sailed the Bosphorus, he spotted the Megarian settlement on the Asian shore at Chalcedon (now Kadıköy, one of the centers of Asian İstanbul). Overcome by the glory of the Golden Horn's harbor on the European shore, he decided that the folks at Chalcedon must have been blind to have ignored this site. Byzas and his crew settled here in 667 BC, and Byzas's sister Ramona gave the city its first name in his honor: **Byzantium.**

Roman infighting at the beginning of the 4th century AD determined the city's fate for the next millennium. The abdication of Diocletian in 305 prompted a power struggle between Constantine, Emperor of the West, and his rival Licinius in the East. The victorious Constantine declared Byzantium **"New Rome,"** renamed it Constantinople, and made it the capital of what came to be known as the Byzantine Empire. Constantine's enthusiasm for Christianity led to the building of the city's first Christian churches. During the 5th century, Theodosius I supervised the construction of a massive set of fortified walls around the city.

In 532, Emperor Justinian was nearly overthrown by the **Nika Revolt,** a dispute among factions of the Hippodrome. He was on the verge of abdicating when his wife, Theodora, reproached him for his cowardice. "Purple makes a good shroud," she quipped. Purple being the symbol of imperial honor, Justinian got the message. After five days of bloodshed, he emerged triumphantly to face a ruined city. He eventually restored Constantinople to twice its former glory, undertaking such building projects as the Aya Sofia (see p. 101). In the decades following Justinian's reign, besieging Persian, Avar, and Slav armies kept Constantinople continually on her toes. The 7th and 8th centuries saw Arab raiders join the fray, but Theodosius's walls held fast. Finally, the Fourth Crusade broke through Constantinople's seemingly impregnable defenses in 1204. The Crusaders breached the sea walls and plundered the city, occupying it for 60 years. Following Latin rule, the Empire was further weakened by internal crises and skirmishes. The decline of the Byzantine Empire was paralleled by the rise of the Ottoman Turks, whose conquests in the 14th century marked the beginning of the Ottoman Empire.

By 1451, **Mehmet II,** known as "Fatih," or "the Conqueror," came to lead the Ottomans. The Byzantine emperor controlled little besides the coveted capital city; Anatolia and most of the Balkans were already in Ottoman hands. In 1452, a confident and careful Mehmet commissioned the building of two fortresses on the Bosphorus in anticipation of the conquest. **Rumeli Hisarı** and **Anadolu Hisarı** (the fortresses of Europe and Asia) stood on opposite banks of the Bosphorus and enabled the Ottomans to control the straits. The Byzantine emperor tried to block the Golden Horn but could not foil Mehmet, who had his boats transported by slides to the other end of the straits at night. For his final bombardment of the Theodosian city walls, Mehmet cast the largest cannon in existence.

Constantinople fell to the Ottomans on May 29, 1453. The prophet Muhammed foretold that a commander who bore his name would one day conquer the city, and thus Mehmet (Turkish for Muhammed) secured for himself a place in heaven with his victory. The new sultan took to rebuilding and repopulating the city, transforming İstanbul into the exalted administrative, cultural, and commercial center of his empire. Under Ottoman rule, the city developed into an architectural treasure trove, best known for its collection of Imperial mosques. As the Ottoman Empire expanded to Eastern Europe, the Middle East, and North Africa, the capital became one of the world's major cosmopolitan centers. Neighborhoods such as Galata and Pera were populated almost entirely by foreigners. After more than four centuries, however, the city's fortunes waned along with those of the Empire, and following WWI, Western powers occupied İstanbul.

Upstart Ankara became the capital of the Republic of Turkey in 1923, but İstanbul remains the cultural heart of Turkey. Between 1960 and today, the city's population has increased tenfold, to over 13 million inhabitants.

⚒ ORIENTATION

Waterways divide İstanbul into three sections. The **Bosphorus Strait** (Boğaz) separates Asia from Europe. Turks call the western, European side of İstanbul **Avrupa** and the eastern, Asian side **Asya.** The **Golden Horn,** a river originating outside the city, splits Avrupa into northern and southern parts. Directions in İstanbul are usually further specified by city precinct or district (i.e. Kadıköy, Taksim, or Fatih).

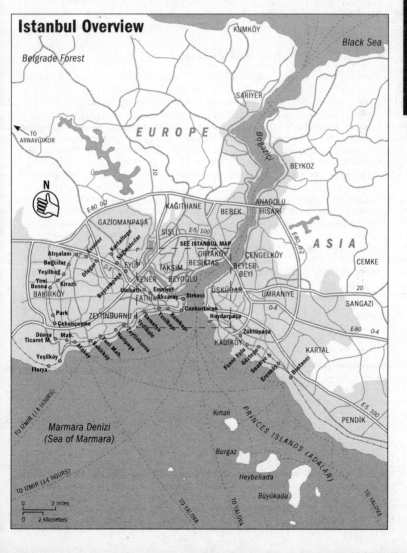

Istanbul Overview

Most of the famous mosques, historical sites, and tourism facilities are south of the Golden Horn and towards the eastern end of the peninsula, which is framed by the Horn and the Sea of Marmara. The other half of "Europe" is focused on Taksim Square, the commercial and social center of the northern European bank. Two main arteries radiate from the square: **İstiklâl Caddesi,** the main downtown shopping street, and **Cumhuriyet Caddesi,** which is lined with airline offices and hotels. The Asian side of İstanbul is primarily residential, but it offers plenty of rewarding wandering and a more relaxed pace.

Each district is defined much more by its center than by its often unclear borders. Many of these districts were once outlying towns, long since swallowed up by metropolitan İstanbul's insatiable expansion. European Sultanahmet and Taksim, and Kadıköy (on the Asian side), will be the most relevant for most visitors to the city, but memorizing the location of even a few more areas on the map will prove immensely helpful. With help from a map and a keen eye for the many landmarks, you can navigate yourself through the maze of alleys that make up the city.

This chapter is arranged by **discrete neighborhood units.** *Let's Go* recommends that you organize your visit according to those approximate guidelines.

✖ GETTING IN AND OUT

Flights: İstanbul's airport, **Atatürk Havaalanı,** is located 30km from the city. The domestic and international terminals are 800m apart and are connected by bus (every 20min. 6am-11pm). For information on **visas and entering Turkey,** see **Visas,** p. 41.

To **Sultanahmet** from the **Airport:** Take a Havaş shuttle bus from either terminal to Aksaray (every 30min. 6am-9pm, $7). At Aksaray, walk 1 block south to Millet Cad. and take an Eminönü-bound tram to the Sultanahmet stop. The tram is a gray train with orange and blue stripes that runs along the electrical wires overhead. Alternatively, cab it ($4) to the Yeşilköy train station and take the commuter rail (*tren*) to the end of the line in Sirkeci. A taxi to Sultanahmet costs $17-20.

To **Taksim** from the **Airport:** Take a Havaş shuttle to the end of the line (every ½hr. 6am-9pm, $7).

To the **Airport:** Have a private service such as **Karasu** (☎638 66 01) or **Zorlu** (☎638 04 35) pick you up from your hostel ($5.50; about every 1½hr.; most hostels can arrange this service), or take the Havaş airport shuttle from the McDonald's in Taksim (45min., every 30min., $6.75).

Cheap fares: Many travel agents offer cheap airfares on charter flights to international destinations out of Atatürk Airport. Sample 1-way airfares include: Amsterdam $145, Berlin $118, London $210, Rome $178, Athens $116, Budapest $110, Tel Aviv $155. See **Travel Agencies,** p. 88, for more information.

Buses (domestic and international): Inter-city buses leave from the Esenler Otobüs Terminal (☎658 00 36) in Esenler, several kilometers from central İstanbul. The otogar is laid out like a giant set of parentheses around the metro stop in the center. Bus companies sell tickets from their offices on the ground floor of the 2 parenthetical buildings, facing inward. Buses depart from the outer side of the building. Each company has a number corresponding to their place along the ticket arcade, from 1 to 167.

To the **Bus Terminal:** Take the tram to Yusufpaşa (1 stop beyond Aksaray; $.50), cross the overpass from the platform, walk 1min. to the Aksaray metro station on broad Adnan Menderes Bul., and take the metro to the otogar (15min., $.40). Most companies have courtesy buses, called *servis,* that run to the otogar from Eminönü, Taksim, and other points in the city (free with bus ticket purchase).

Bus companies: Hundreds of buses leave daily for virtually every point in Turkey and for some neighboring countries. Service tends to vary widely in quality and safety, so be careful when choosing a company. It is best to get to the station with 30min.-1hr. to spare, shop around for the best price to your city, then buy your ticket. For trips within Turkey, **Ulusoy** (☎658 30 00; fax 658 30 10; No. 127 in the terminal), **Varan** (☎658 02 74 or 658 02 77; No. 15-16), **Kamil Koç** (☎658 20 00 or 658 20 02; No. 147) and **Metro** (No. 51) are professional and enjoy good reputations. Unfortunately, they don't run to many towns in Eastern Turkey. To get there, you can take a slightly less reputable bus direct from İstanbul (see below) or simply go as far as you can with one of the major companies and then switch over to more reliable regional service. Reservations are recommended, and tickets can be bought in advance at the bus company offices in central İstanbul. Fares increase by about 10-15% during the summer and over religious holidays.

BUS SCHEDULES

Destination	Company	Duration	Times (daily)	Price	Students
Adana	Varan	14hr.	6, 7pm	$29	$25.50
Afyon	Pamukkale	7hr.	7 per day 8:30am-11:45pm	$15	$13.50
Ankara	Kamil Koç	6hr.	every hr. 6:30am-6:30pm, 8:30pm-2:45am	$22	$20
Ankara	Ulusoy	6hr.	every 2hr. 9am-1am	$25	$22
Ankara	Varan	6hr.	7 per day 8:15am-1am	$25	$23
Antalya	Ulusoy	12hr.	8:30, 9:15, 10pm	$30	$26
Antalya	Varan	11hr.	8:30, 9:30pm	$30	$26.50
Bodrum	Ulusoy	13hr.	8:30, 9:15, 9:30pm	$31	$27
Bodrum	Varan	14hr.	8:30, 9:30pm	$31	$28.50
Bursa	Kamil Koç	4hr.	every 30min.	$9	$8.25
Eskişehir	Pamukkale	6hr.	2:30pm	$12	$11
İzmir	Ulusoy	9hr.	9am, 1:30, 10:30, 11pm	$28	$24
Pamukkale	Pamukkale	10hr.	7 per day 8:30am-11:30pm	$21	$19
Trabzon	Ulusoy	18hr.	1, 5:30, 6:30, 8:30, 10:30pm	$35	$31
Yalova	Kamil Koç	3hr.	every 30min.	$8.50	$6.50

TRAIN SCHEDULES

Name	Destination	Duration	Departs	Price
Eskişehir Express	Eskişehir	4½hr.	M, W, F, 6:55pm	$9
Boğaziçi Express	Ankara	9hr.	daily 1:30pm	$6
Başkent Express	Ankara	6½hr.	daily 10am	$9
Fatih Express	Ankara	7½hr.	daily 11:30pm	$9
Başarı Express	Ankara	7¼hr.	daily 1pm	$12
Ankara Express	Ankara	9½hr.	daily 10:30pm	$10; sleeper $33
Anadolu Express	Ankara	9hr.	daily 10pm	$6
Doğu Express	Kars	13½hr.	daily 8:35am	$15
Yeni Doğu Express	Kars	11hr.	M, W, F 9am	$10
Meram Express	Konya	12¾hr.	daily 7:20pm	$5; sleeper $14
Toros Express	Gaziantep	27hr.	Tu, Th, Su 8:55am	$5
Balkan Express	Budapest	40hr.	daily 2:52pm	$90
Bosfor Express	Bucharest	17½hr.	daily 11:55pm	$30
Ege Express	Athens	24hr.	daily 8:20am	$60

Eastern destinations: Companies with service to more "exotic" locales tend to cluster at the far end of one of the "parentheses," generally in the terminal's highest numbers (look for a big yellow sign for "Van"). **Mar-Soy** (☎ 658 13 90 or 658 13 91; No. 163) has buses to: **Gaziantep** (12hr.; 1, 4pm; $23); **Mardin** (18hr.; 1, 4pm; $33); **Şanlıurfa** (15hr.; 1, 4pm; $25). **Sivas** has buses to **Erzurum** (18hr.; 2, 4, 7, 10pm; $30) and **Sivas** (13hr.; 5:30, 7:30, 9:30, 11:30pm; $23). **Yeni Van Seyahat** (☎658 33 65 or 658 33 66; No. 163) runs to **Van** (24hr.; 10:30am, 3pm; $32).

International Buses: Unlicensed companies have been known to offer substantial discounts on trips to Western European destinations and then abandon their passengers in Eastern Europe, so choose your company carefully. **Ulusoy** runs to **Athens** (21hr.; Th, Sa 10am; $60, students $51). **Parlak Tur** (☎ 658 17 55 or 658 17 56; No. 164) runs relatively cheap buses to **Prague** (2 days; Sa 4pm; $100, students $95). For service to **Tehran**, try **İgdir** (No. 165-6), next door to Mar-Soy and Van (36hr., daily 1pm, $30). **Nur** (☎ 58 05 43 or 658 05 44; No. 47-48) has buses to **Amman** (26hr.; 1:30, 4:30, 7:30pm; $45, students $40); **Damascus** (23hr.; 1:30, 4:30, 7:30pm; $40, students $30); **Sofia, Bulgaria** (12hr., 6pm, $25).

Trains: In virtually every case, it's quicker and cheaper to take the bus. All trains to Anatolia leave from Haydarpaşa Garı (☎(216) 336 04 75 or 336 20 63), on the Asian side. To get there, take the ferry from Karaköy pier #7 (every 20min. roughly 6am-midnight, $.65). The pier is halfway between Galata Bridge and the Karaköy tourist office, where rail tickets for Anatolia can be purchased in advance at the TCDD (Turkish Republic State Railway) office upstairs. To reach both, make a right at the end of the bridge if walking from Eminönü, and walk along the waterfront. The office accepts couchette (kuşet) reservations for Ankara (2 days in advance, if possible). Haydarpaşa ticket office open daily 7:30am-11:30pm. Tickets also available at the Sirkeci station. Europe-bound trains leave from Sirkeci Garı (☎(212) 527 00 50 or 527 00 51), in Eminönü (downhill from Sultanahmet towards the Golden Horn). Connections to most European cities must be made in Athens or Bucharest. Some lines may be temporarily suspended due to Balkan political crises. Call ahead for information and student fares.

Ferries: Turkish Maritime Lines (☎249 92 22), near pier #7 at Karaköy, to the left of the Haydarpaşa ferry terminal. Look for a building with a blue awning marked *Denizcilik İşletmeleri*. The Samsun-Trabzon ferry traverses the Black Sea, leaving from Sarayburnu in İstanbul (M 2pm). (See **The Black Sea Ferry,** p. 378, for details.) Ferries also leave for **Bandırma,** with train connection to İzmir (combination ticket $10-25). Ferries and seabuses cross the Sea of Marmara to **Yalova,** from where you can connect to **Bursa** and other points inland (see Yalova: **Practical Information,** p. 160). To **Yalova** from: **Bostancı** (45min.; 6:25am, 5:55pm; $6.50); **Kabataş** (1hr., 6 per day 7:20am-8pm, $7.10); **Kartal** (35min., 8 per day 6:50am-8:15pm, $4.75). The slower ferry, *yolcu vapürü* (☎814 10 20) runs from Kabataş (2½hr.; 9:30am, 2, 6:30pm; $3) and Kartal (4 per day 9am-9:15pm). For local ferry info, see **Getting Around: Ferries,** p. 86.

☞ GETTING AROUND İSTANBUL

Getting around İstanbul proves fairly easy during the day and evening, with dirt-cheap ferries, buses, shared-taxi dolmuş and trams all making good substitutes for the comparatively expensive private taxis that swell the streets. Even so, the city is gargantuan, and navigating it can be frustrating even for native İstanbulians. The metropolis must be considered a **series of neighborhoods** rather than a system of coherent streets. Very often streets will change names unannounced as they move from one neighborhood to the next. As the city has grown and aged, the borders between neighborhoods have become nearly transparent, and streets appear to change on a whim. Keep the tram and metro in mind as you organize your travel plans. They can usually get you within walking distance of where you want to go, or at least cut down on the eventual cab fare. If you know the names of your home and destination neighborhoods, finding a bus or dolmuş should be fairly simple. Very heavy traffic can significantly prolong travel time between far-flung neighborhoods, so it's best to focus your day's itinerary on one particular neighborhood or area of the city and explore from morning to evening.

AKBİL AND TICKETS. İstanbul's transportation systems have become somewhat more integrated with the introduction of AKBİL, an electronic ticketing system that works on municipal ferries, buses, trams, seabuses, and the subway (but not dolmuş). Anyone staying longer than three or four days should definitely consider springing for an **AKBİL tab.** After an initial deposit of $5, you can add money to your tab (a little plastic key ring with a magnetic button on the end) in 1,000,000TL increments and save 15-50% on fares when you hold the tab against a reader on the bus or at the station. Deposit credit to your AKBİL from any of the white IETT public bus booths which has the sign "AKBİL satılır." Such kiosks are located at most sizeable bus and tram stops, such as Eminönü, Beyazıt, Taksim, Sariyer, Kadıköy, etc. The Kabataş and Eminönü seabus terminals (among other spots) have automated AKBİL 24 machines, which are open 24 hours. These are good to use for seabus trips, since using AKBİL on the boat can save you 15-20% on pricey seabus tickets.

To use the machines, press your tab into the reader and remove it, insert a 1,000,000TL note, and press once more. If you have enough on your tab, the machine beeps once and you may board; otherwise it sounds a lower note and a red light blinks on. Regular tickets are not interchangeable, meaning that you can't use a bus ticket (bought at a kiosk) for the tram or on a bus with a ticket seller on board. Tickets for trams and buses without ticket sellers are available from little white booths, while ferries and seabuses take *jeton* (tokens) available at ferry stops. Always be sure to carry plenty of small lira notes so that if you are on a bus with a ticket seller, you won't have to clog up traffic.

BUSES. İstanbul's bus system is a dream, not because of its organization or punctuality, but because there are simply so many buses, with one going wherever you need to go about every 10 minutes. Bus service runs from approximately 5am to midnight, dropping off markedly after about 10:30pm. The real difficulty for newcomers is figuring out where to catch a given bus. The bus system centers around several major stops, from which all buses serving a certain part of the city leave. Hubs include **Eminönü** (in the parking lot on the seaward side of the Egyptian Spice Bazaar), **Aksaray** (Yusufpaşa tram stop), **Beyazıt** (near the tram stop), **Taksim, Beşiktaş,** and **Üsküdar.** It is generally best to go to one of these hubs and then catch the next bus you need from there, although there are a few much-traveled routes along which you can be sure to find the bus you need. Signs on the front of buses indicate the endpoints of the route, and signs on the right-hand side list the major places that the bus passes. Smaller stops aren't always posted. If you do not see your destination listed in the front window, step in and ask the driver: *"Bu otobus [destination] gider mi?"* ("Does this bus go to [destination]?") That should do the trick, or you can simply get on, look a bit lost and say the name of your destination. This will usually get the job done as well.

From Sultanahmet, bus #210 leaves from the Aya Sofia Meydanı, crosses the Galata Bridge, and heads up the European Bosphorus shore to Ortaköy and Bebek (every 20min.). From Aksaray and Beyazıt, multiple buses serve districts to the northwest along the Golden Horn (Yedikule Fortress, Zeyrek, Fatih, Fener, Balat, Edirnekapı, Eyüp). In the big bus lot at the foot of the Galata Bridge in Eminönü, six platforms *(peron)* serve different areas to the north and along the Bosphorus: Yeşilköy (#81) and Ataköy (#71) from *peron* #1; Karaköy, Beşiktaş, Bebek (all #22c) from *peron* #3; and Taksim (#46h) from *peron* #5. From Taksim Square, most buses head either north into the suburbs or southwest across the Atatürk Bridge to Aksaray and Beyazıt. Any given route has buses running in the reverse direction as well, and many routes are largely repeated by other buses. When the bus nears your stop, push the button on top of the door to alert the driver.

Even if you are using AKBİL, be sure to have a few spare bus tickets in the event of unexpected bus changes. By the same token, remember to have extra money in case you take a private bus—impossible to differentiate from a public one—which will require that you buy a ticket on board. A final note on buses: when riding the bus, passengers should give their places to elderly riders and women with children if there are no available seats.

DOLMUŞ. Dolmuş, a venerable Turkish tradition, are minibuses that run along a fixed local route. Like buses, they're cheap, and the endpoints of their routes are posted in the front window. Because stops are not announced, it's easiest if you know what your stop looks like or if you want to get off at the end of the line. Dolmuş are generally unnecessary within most of İstanbul since buses are plentiful (with the exception of Kadıköy), but they can be helpful and are much more comfortable than city buses. Dolmuş run only during daylight hours and the early evening, and they are most active at the end of the workday, when people congregate on curbs all over the city, waiting for their ride home. They can be found near most of the major bus hubs, including Aksaray and Eminönü. Dolmuş also congregate around the Hippodrome in the early evening and in front of Aya Sofia throughout the day. The largest and most useful collection of dolmuş is in the side streets north of Taksim Square, where you can catch one to Beşiktaş, Sariyer, Karaköy, Kadıköy, or Aksaray. In neighborhoods far from the bustle of Taksim and Sultanahmet they serve as local group taxis, and it is best to hail them down as they crawl along streets picking up passengers on their way back into the center of İstanbul. For more information on dolmuş travel, see **Dolmuş Do's and Don'ts,** p. 66.

TRAMS, COMMUTER RAIL, AND METRO. The *tramvay* (tram) runs from Eminönü to Zeytinburnu (\$.50 per ride). Since it's easy enough to follow the tracks, the tram is very useful for finding your way back to Sultanahmet even if you don't actually take it. A second tram begins behind the large mosque at the Yusufpaşa tram stop in the middle of Adnan Menderes Bul., and it heads to the outer suburbs of İstanbul (Zeytinburnu, Bakırköy, etc.) via the new **otogar** (intercity bus station). Built with consideration for modern İstanbul's sprawling expanse, the tram weaves through many of the city's major neighborhoods. Though there are only a couple of lines, the tram can drop you off within close proximity to many popular destinations.

The city continues to run a beautifully ramshackle **commuter rail** (known locally as *tren*) between Sirkeci Gar and İstanbul's far western suburbs. The upshot of the cars' age is that many of the windows have become stuck halfway down or are missing altogether, making for blessed ventilation and exhilarating views of the sea and ancient city walls along the southern coast of the European side. Watch your step getting on though, as there are often gaps between the door and the edges of the platform. Despite its defects, the commuter rail is a safe option, and many locals use it for a daily commute. For most visitors, the *tren* is good for two things: a more pleasant ride from Sultanahmet to Sirkeci and a cheaper route to the airport. To find the Cankurtaran station near Sultanahmet, head downhill and left from the Blue Mosque. The tracks run on an elevated path parallel to the coastal road. It's a one-stop ride to Sirkeci along the seaside tracks. In the other direction, a 30min. ride goes to Yeşilyürt (near Yeşilköy), from where a cab to the airport is a mere $4. The *tren* runs the same hours as the tram and is just as cheap. Use AKBİL or a *jeton*. The combination of the two-stop **metro** and a trolley along İstiklâl Cad. makes for an easy way to get up to Taksim Square if you want to walk across the bridge from Eminönü and then catch the metro on the other side.

TAXI. Most cabs can be spotted from miles away, since the little yellow street bees have chrome wheels, lots of glittering evil eye protectors, and multiple hood ornaments with names like "saloon" or "sport." Given the chance, taxi drivers are even more reckless and speed-crazed than other İstanbul drivers. This is particularly true after midnight, when all public transportation is closed, roads are more empty, and drivers are eager to give their cars a workout after a day of traffic-jam crawl. Many Turkish taxi drivers are devoid of fear and eager to show off their ability to make their vehicles do maneuvers previously thought possible only on skateboards. If at any point you feel uncomfortable in a taxi, you can and should ask the driver to slow down (*Yavaş lütfen*) or to stop (*Dur!*). That said, high-speed cab rides late at night are good fun, and probably the only way you're going to see the blur of neon club signs and headlights of an İstanbul evening at 150mph.

Though İstanbul's cabbies should by no means be considered generally corrupt, **scams** are widespread. Be especially alert if you don't speak Turkish and are catching a cab in Sultanahmet or Taksim. A common trick is to use the night rate (30% more after midnight) during the day. One light on the meter means day rate; two lights mean night rate. Other common scams are to give foreigners incorrect change, taking advantage of their unfamiliarity with the currency, or to intentionally not reset the cab's meter when you enter. Feel free to fix a price if you don't trust the driver or your ability to recognize an excessively long route. A ride between Sultanahmet and Taksim should be no more than $5 for a group of 3, and few rides in the central İstanbul area should cost more. You can shave $3-4 off a trip from Sultanahmet to Taksim by walking ½km up the tram tracks to Beyazıt and catching a cab there, where it's a straight shot to Taksim. Or if the tram is still running, ride it to the end of the line, get off at Eminönü, and hail one of the many cabs that sits by the waterside around the Galata Bridge.

FERRIES. Closer to a respite from the metro grind than a part of it, İstanbul's ferry system transforms mundane public transport into a scenic mini-cruise. They can also shave nearly an hour off transit between İstanbul's European and Asian sections. Ferries run primarily between Europe and Asia, though there is same-side service up the Bosphorus and to more remote points such as Yalova and the Prince's Islands (Adalar). Among the many boats that cluster around this port, the ferries are large white and green ships with yellow smokestacks that often spew a thin black smoke. Timetables are posted at each terminal. Before leaving for a far-off destination, be sure to check that there is a return ferry later in the day.

The following boats depart from the piers clustered around Galata Bridge in Sirkeci (each dock is labeled with the destination): **Üsküdar** (pier 1, every 15-20min. 6:30am-10pm, $.75); **Kadıköy** (pier 2, every 15-20min. 7:30am-8:30pm, $.75); **Prince's Islands** (Adalar) and **Yalova** (from a dock down past pier 1, on the other side of the car ferry; Yalova $3, Adalar $1.50); **Harem** (from a pier labeled "Posta" in large red print among the above piers, every 20min, $.75). To get to Balat and the Haydarpaşa train station, take a ferry across the Golden Horn to Karaköy, then catch a boat down to these points. Ferries to Karaköy leave often from the piers on the far side of the Galata Bridge and cost less than a dollar. From the car ferry near the Adalar dock, other ferries connect the various İstanbul suburbs every half hour ($1-4). For details, buy a timetable (*feribot tarifesi*; $.60) at any pier.

Points on the Bosphorus are served by less frequent and more expensive day cruises. Some of the ferries to the north shore of the Golden Horn are commuter ferries. Since they leave in the morning and return in the evening, taking an evening ferry out could leave you stranded. There is a day cruise that floats up the Golden Horn, docking at places like Fener and Balat and a couple of points further north. But if you're planning for a day in these neighborhoods rather than a day on the boat, it is best to reach these points by land.

Fast Seabus catamarans, each carrying up to 250 passengers, also run along the ferry routes. The seabus generally disembarks in the same area as the ferry, as the two dock in the same place at many destinations. Seabuses (recognizable by their leaping dolphin emblem) are twice as fast as ferries and cost about three to four times as much (average $4-5). Free timetables are available at the booths. You can get the latest updates from Seabus Information (☎(216) 362 04 44).

COMMON ROUTES. To simplify matters, *Let's Go* offers the following İstanbul connection suggestions:

FROM THE AIRPORT TO:

SULTANAHMET: From the international terminal, catch a Havaş bus to Aksaray (every 30min. 6am-9pm, $7). From there, catch an Eminönü-bound tram to Sultanahmet (walk uphill along the overpass to the Lâleli tram stop). Alternatively, split a cab ($17-20). Or pick up İstanbul's commuter rail in Yeşilyürt, *tren* to Sirkeci, and tram to Sultanahmet. It's cheaper and cooler than the Havaş, though less direct.

TAKSİM SQUARE: Stay on the Havaş bus. Airport-bound Havaş buses leave from the Havaş office on Cumhuriyet Cad., right off the square.

CAMPGROUNDS (FLORYA/ATAKÖY): They're not far from the airport and you need only take a cab once ($3), as the campgrounds are right next to a stop on the commuter rail running frequently to the Sirkeci train station. From here you can either walk or catch buses to most everywhere else.

ASIAN İSTANBUL: Go either to Taksim, from which most of the Asia-bound buses leave, or to Eminönü (see Sultanahmet directions, above), from which both the Üsküdar and Harem Kadıköy ferries leave.

FROM SULTANAHMET TO:

TAKSİM SQUARE: Bus #61B runs infrequently between Beyazıt and Taksim. For faster transport, take the tram (Zeytinburnu-bound) to Yusufpaşa. From the platform, go up onto the overpass, head left, and catch the bus from the stop at the bottom. Taksim-bound buses pass at least every 5min. Alternatively, take a 5min. walk across the Galata Bridge and then catch the metro and then the trolley up to the square–a pleasant way with little hassle or crowds.

EMİNÖNÜ (Spice Bazaar, Ferries, Yeni Cami): Tram it to the end of the line, or walk (20min.) along the line. The *tren* (commuter rail) runs from Cankutaran station down the hill from the Blue Mosque to Sirkeci Gar, a stone's throw from Eminönü.

EUROPEAN BOSPHORUS (Kabataş, Beşiktaş, Arnavutköy, Ortaköy, Bebek; some buses follow inland routes to Rumeli Hisarüstü and Sariyer): Either take bus #210 from Aya Sofia Square (*Meydanı*) or buses #20-25 from Eminönü platform 3. Bus #40KT runs express from Taksim to the ferry port at Kabataş.

YEDİKULE: Take the commuter train from Cankurtaran station in Sultanahmet ($.40). Buses also leave from Eminönü, but from the stop on the waterfront side.

İSTANBUL

FATİH, FENER, EDİRNEKAPI, BALAT, EYÜP: Buses run between Beyazıt and Edirnekapı, but it's quickest to tram to Yusufpaşa and then head to the Aksaray bus stop near the Aksaray Metro station on Adnan Menderes Bul. Bus #39E runs to Eyüp. The bus passes through the districts in the order listed above. Eyüp and Eyüp Sultan are essentially the same place.

YALOVA: Use the ferry or the less frequent seabus service from Kabataş. Otherwise, take the hourly seabus from Yeni Kapı on the *tren* line.

ASIAN BOSPHORUS TOWNS (Beylerbeyi, Anadolu Kavağı, Kanlica, Paşabahçe): Take a ferry to Üsküdar ($.60). From the main bus stop across from the *iskele* (ferry stop), catch a #15 bus, which will head up the Bosphorus.

PRINCE'S ISLANDS (ADALAR): Take the *"Adalar İskelesi"* ferry from Eminönü, the one closest to Sirkeci train station, next to the car ferry. High-speed catamarans to *Adalar* depart the Kabataş dock in late afternoon and early evening ($4).

SELİMİYE BARRACKS (Florence Nightingale's chambers): Take a ferry to Üsküdar ($.60). Catch one of the many buses ($.50) or a cab ($2) down to the Harem *iskele*/otogar. For an easier trip, take the ferry to Harem. The barracks can be seen uphill from the water.

KUMKAPI (where all the fish restaurants are located): A very short, hot walk along Sahil Yolu during the day can be avoided by catching the *tren* from Sirkeci or Cankurtaran stations.

🛈 PRACTICAL INFORMATION

❗ İSTANBUL STREET SMARTS. Visitors to İstanbul should exercise the same common sense they would use in any large city (see **Personal Safety,** p. 45). Touts, the men who call out to foreigners (particularly in Sultanahmet), are annoying but ultimately harmless. Feel free to ignore these hawkers; there's no need to even make eye contact (see **Financial Security,** p. 48).

More serious are the reports of tourist scams. One scenario involves Turkish men befriending male tourists and leading them to bars where they are soon joined by bands of women. After ordering drinks, the women scram, leaving the tourist with an exorbitant bill. Purchasing drinks for women can also be a front for a prostitution ring. That "drink" might cost you $50, and you may be getting more for your money than you had bargained for. There are also reports of tourists being given drugged drinks and subsequently robbed. Exercise caution before accepting drinks from strangers.

TOURIST AND FINANCIAL SERVICES

Tourist Office: In Sultanahmet, 3 Divan Yolu (☎/fax 518 87 54), in the **white metal kiosk,** at the north end of the Hippodrome. Open daily 9am-5pm. In Taksim the main office (☎233 05 92; open daily 9am-5pm) is in the **Hilton Hotel Arcade** on Cumhuriyet Cad., and another, less-useful branch is near the **French consulate** (☎245 68 76; open M-Sa 8:30am-5pm). There is a particularly comfortable and helpful office in the **Sirkeci train station** (☎511 58 88; open daily 8:30am-5:30pm) and a reasonably extensive one at **Atatürk Airport** (☎663 07 93; open 24hr.). **Karaköy Maritime Station** (☎249 57 76) has a small, gruff booth, open daily 8:30am-5pm.

Travel Agencies: Tourist agencies line the beginning of Divan Yolu Cad. and Akbıyık Cad., the main backpacker drag in Sultanahmet. Compare prices before sitting down to make a reservation, since there are often special deals at particular agencies, and prices tend to vary in general. That said, *Let's Go* recommends a few: **7-Tur,** 37 Gümüşsuyu Cad., 2nd fl., is İstanbul's STA Travel equivalent, and does all STA ticket changes. ISICs available ($15). From Taksim Sq., walk downhill to the right of Atatürk Cultural Center. **Gençtur,** Prof. K. Ismail Gürkan Cad., Cağaloğlu Hamamı Sok., Kardeşler Iştlanı, 4th fl. (☎520 52 74 or 520 52 75; fax 519 08 64), a 5min. walk from Aya Sofia Meydanı up Yerebatan; the entrance is around the corner from the sign hanging on Yerebatan. Sells ISICs ($10) and GO25 cards ($10). Open M-F 9:30am-5pm, Sa 9:30am-1pm. Taksim branch of Gençtur, 15/5 İstiklâl Cad. (☎249 25 15), organizes volunteer work programs in villages. Open M-Sa 9:30am-6pm. **Indigo Tourism and Travel Agency,** 24 Akbıyık Cad. (☎517 72 66; fax 518 53 33; email www.indigo-tour.com), is in the heart of the hotel cluster in Sultanahmet. Open in summer daily 8:30am-7:30pm; in winter M-Sa 9:30am-6pm. Sells GO25 cards ($10) and ISIC cards only with valid student ID ($15). Services include bus, ferry, and plane tickets for Europe and the Middle East, airport shuttle service, city and Turkey tours, as well as *poste restante.* Internet upstairs ($1.50 per hr.).

Consulates: All open M-F. Area code ☎212. **Australia,** 58 Tepecik Yolu, Etiler (☎257 70 50; fax 257 70 54); visas 10am-noon. **Canada,** 107/3 Büyükdere Cad., Bengün Han, Gayrettepe (☎272 51 74; fax 272 34 27). **Ireland** (honorary), 25/A Cumhuriyet Cad., Mobil Altı, Elmadağ (☎246 60 25); visas 9:30-11:30am. **New Zealand,** Level 24, 100-102 Maya Akar Center, Büyükdere Cad., Esentepe (☎275 28 89; fax 275 50 08). **South Africa,** Serbetci ış Merkezi, 106/15 Büyükdere Cad., Esentepe (☎288 04 28; fax 275 76 42); visas 9am-noon. **UK,** 34 Meşrutiyet Cad., PK33, Beyoğlu/Tepebaşı (☎293 75 40; fax 245 49 89); visas 8:30am-noon. **US,** 104-108 Meşrutiyet Cad., Tepebaşı (☎251 36 02; fax 251 32 18); visas 8:30-11am.

Banks: Currency exchange counters open M-F 8:30am-noon, 1:30-5pm. Most don't charge commission. V/MC **ATM cards** work almost everywhere, and nearly all ATMs have an English-language option. **Pamukbank** machines at the airport, Taksim Sq., and Sirkeci accept practically every kind of card, as do **Garanti Bank** machines. **Şekerbank** (1 location on Yenicirler Cad. in Çemberllitaş) and **Akbank** (1 location on Divan Yolu) are also good. Akbank and Vakıf Bank machines also take AmEx. **Yapı ve Kredi, Türkiye İş Bankası, TC Ziraat Bankası,** and **Vakıf Bank** are scattered throughout the city and accept most cards. Traveler's checks can be changed at any sizeable branch of the above banks, though the process often takes about 10-15min. and more paperwork than seems necessary. Change windows in Sultanahmet offer poor rates and charge 2-4% commission, but are often open late and on the weekends.

American Express: Türk Express, 47/1 Cumhuriyet Cad., 3rd fl. (☎235 95 00), uphill from Taksim Sq., handles lost checks and cards as well as other related AmEx business. Open M-F 9am-6pm. Their office in the Hilton Hotel lobby (☎230 15 15), Cumhuriyet Cad., offers *poste restante* and deals with lost cards when the main office is closed. Open daily 8:30am-8:30pm. Neither branch actually handles the financial side of replacing lost cards or checks, nor do they give cash advances or accept wired money, as Turkish law requires it be done through a bank. AmEx's agent is **Akbank,** with branches across the city. Money is wired without fee if you accept Turkish lira; 1% fee for other currencies. To get a cash advance on your card, you must have a personal check or know the account number and address of your bank. Cardholder services until 4pm only.

LOCAL SERVICES

English-Language Bookstores: In Sultanahmet, **kiöşks** at the Blue Mosque, on Aya Sofia Meydanı, and on Divan Yolu sell international papers, as does **International Press Büfe** in front of 91 İstiklâl Cad. in Beyoğlu. **Galeri Kayseri,** 58 Divan Yolu (☎512 04 56; email galerikayseryi@ihlas.net.tr), caters to thinking tourists. Its helpful owner keeps the shop open daily 9am-9pm. **Balkaya İnşaat Bookstore** at the exit of the Underground Cistern (see p. 111) has a good but sometimes pricey selection of books on the history, poetry, and arts of the region. You can visit on your way out of the Cistern or walk in the Cistern's exit down the hill from Aya Sofia on Alemdar Cad., along the tram tracks. For more travel books and contemporary novels there is the tasteful **Robinson Crusoe,** 389 İstiklâl Cad. (☎293 69 68), where texts in English are on the right side of the store. Open M-Sa 9am-9pm, Su 10am-9pm. Off Galatasaray Sq., **Homer Kitabevi,** 28A Yeniçarşı Cad. (☎249 59 02), aims for academic comprehensiveness; you'd be hard-pressed to find an English-language "Gender Theory" section anywhere else in the city. Open M-Sa 9:30am-7:30pm. Walk through a small underwear shop to get upstairs to **Literatür,** 133 İstiklâl Cad. (☎292 41 20). The store has a wide-ranging collection, from art to finance. Open M-Sa 9am-8pm.

Laundromat: Star Laundry, 18 Akbıyık Cad. (☎638 23 02), below Star Pension in Sultanahmet. Wash and dry $1.50 per kg; 2kg min. English spoken. Open daily 8am-8pm.

İSTANBUL

EMERGENCY AND COMMUNICATIONS

Tourist Police: In Sultanahmet, at the beginning of Yerebatan Cad. (24hr. hotline ☎527 45 03 or 528 53 69; fax 512 76 76). They speak the best English of all local cops, and their mere presence causes hawkers and postcard-selling kids to scatter. In an **emergency**, dial 155 from any phone.

Pharmacies: The Turkish word for pharmacy (or chemist) is *eczanesi*. All of them offer the basics of personal hygiene (deodorant, toothbrush and paste, hair products, tampons, etc.) and all can fill a prescription. In many cases the pharmacists do not speak English. **Çemberlitaş Eczanesi,** No. 46 Vezirhan Cad. (☎522 69 69), off of Divan Yolu by the Çemberlitaş tram stop, is among the most professional and helpful in the neighborhood. The pharmacy also services glasses if you break yours or think you could use a new pair. Open M-Sa 7:30am-8pm. **Ayasofya Eczanesi,** No. 28 Divan Yolu (☎513 72 15; fax 511 80 04), near the main sights, is stocked with all the necessities. Open M-Sa 8:30am-7:30pm. Across the Golden Horn, **Taksim Eczanesi** (☎244 31 95), right off the square on İstiklâl Cad., is a well-run pharmacy in a central location. Stocks most everything you could wish for or need. Fills prescriptions. Open M-F 9am-7pm.

Hospitals: American Hospital, Admiral Bristol Hastanesi, 20 Güzelbahçe Sok., Nişantaşı (☎231 40 50), is applauded by İstanbul natives and tourists and has many English-speaking doctors. The **German Hospital,** 119 Sıraselviler Cad., Taksim (☎251 71 00 or 251 71 01/2/3/4), also has a multilingual staff and is more conveniently located for Sultanahmet hostelers. **International Hospital,** 82 İstanbul Cad., Yeşilköy (☎663 30 00). Payment with cash or a credit card is expected at time of treatment at all of the above. The state-run **Taksim İlkyardım Hastanesi** (Taksim First Aid Hospital), 112 Sıraselviler Cad. (☎252 43 00), offers cheaper services.

Internet Access: In low-rent corners and hostels all over Sultanahmet and Taksim. **The Antique Internet Cafe,** 51 Kutlugün Sok., offers a fast connection—despite its name—and big plush chairs in a relaxing spot. Antique also serves tea, cold sodas, and tasty meals (omelettes and salads from $1.50). $1.50 per hr. Open daily 24hr. **The Sinem Internet Cafe,** 16 Dr. Emin Paşa Sok. (☎513 62 77), in an alley off Divan Yolu by the metro stop, 3 floors up from street level. Waits are rare at this pleasant Sultanahmet cafe with tapestries, cushions, and full drink service. $1.25 per hr. Open daily 9am-midnight. **Cafein Internet Cafe,** 21A Bekar Sok. (☎252 18 66), near the upper end of İstiklâl Cad. Cheap at $1.20 per hr. Open 10am-11:30pm. The nearby **British Council Library,** 253 İstiklâl Cad., 3rd fl., offers a wider-screen connection. $1.80 per hr. Open Tu 10:30am-8:30pm, W 10:30am-6:30pm, Th-F 10:30am-5:30pm, Sa 9:30am-2:30pm.

PTT: İstanbul has more than 100 post offices. The most convenient for Sultanahmet-dwellers is the yellow booth opposite the entrance to Aya Sofia on Aya Sofia Meydanı, where you can change money and get stamps. **Main branch** in Sirkeci, 25 Büyük Postane Sok. Stamp and currency exchange services open 8:30am-midnight. 24hr. phones. A branch off the north end of Taksim Sq., at the mouth of Cumhuriyet Cad., is convenient for mailing packages or making calls. 24hr. international phone office, but no collect calls allowed. Open M-F 8am-8pm, Sa 8am-6pm. All PTTs accept packages; if a customs officer is not present, you may be directed to the Kadıköy, Beyazıt, or Tophane (on Rıhtım Cad.) offices. Keep larger packages open so the customs or postal officials can check them if they want. Card phones are a convenient way to make phone calls. You can buy cards with 30, 60, or 100 *kontür* (credits). 1 credit lasts 2-10 seconds during international calls. **Sirkeci postal code:** 5270050 and 5270051.

▮ ACCOMMODATIONS

İstanbul's budget accommodations are mainly in touristy **Sultanahmet,** clustered on a few streets just steps away from the city's most awe-inspiring sights. The **Taksim** district, home to many of the city's five-star hotels and a smattering of budget lodgings, is less touristy than Sultanahmet. The side streets around **Sirkeci** railway station and **Aksaray** offer dozens of dirt-cheap hotels, but these neighborhoods are not pleasant places to stay. **Lâleli** is the center of prostitution in İstanbul and should be avoided. Rates sometimes rise by 20% in July and August.

SULTANAHMET

This small neighborhood, bounded by the Blue Mosque, Aya Sofia, and the walls of the Topkapı Palace, is the tourism capital of İstanbul. Hostel accommodations are fairly generic here, and according to some owners, the better hostels tend to fix prices among themselves. The main differences between the hostels usually involve hot water and available facilities. Most establishments request that you pay one night at a time, and $5-7 is the average going rate for a bed in a dormitory room. Belly dancer performances and *Efes*-sodden happy hours are common evening events in the hostels, whose guests tend to be short-term transients in the city on their way to points east in Turkey, the Greek Islands, or back into Europe. But while the high density of travelers in this four-block area will provide you with a wealth of international acquaintances, getting away from the numerous basement bars and terrace cafes will give you a better chance to experience one of the world's best collection of historic architectural behemoths. In the off-season, usually November through March, prices tend to drop by 10-15%.

CHEAP SLEEPS

▩ **İstanbul Hostel,** 35 Kutlugün Sok. (☎516 93 80; fax 516 93 84; email info@valide.com). From the path between Aya Sofia and the Blue Mosque, walk south down Tevfikhane Sok., past the Four Seasons Hotel to Kutlugün Sok; the hostel is on your right. This large hostel offers all major amenities, and its marble-floored bathrooms are the cleanest in town. The rooms are standard but a little worn in. Internet $2 per hr. 24hr. hot water. Lockers and luggage storage free. Travel agency connected to hostel. Happy hour 6:30-9:30pm at Downstairs "Buzz Bar" (beer $2), including music, nightly movies and satellite TV. Lunch and dinner $3. Breakfast $2. 9 rooms. Dorms $7 per person, 4-8 beds per room; doubles $16. Traveler's checks and cash only.

▩ **Orient International Hostel,** 13 Akbıyık Cad. (☎517 94 93; fax 518 38 94; email orienthostel@superonline.com; www.hostels.com/orienthostel). 2 blocks south of Aya Sofia, along the main backpacker strip. Happy hour daily until 10pm (beer $1.50), but blaring music, darts, dancing, and plenty of drinks keep the party going into the morning. The Orient's goods include a travel agency, cable TV, backgammon, videos, and free luggage storage and safe deposit box. Less-than-spotless communal bathroom. For peace and quiet, ask for a room *not* facing the bar. Free belly dancing (M, W, F at 10pm), and *nargile* (water pipe) use Th, Su 9pm. Email $1 per hr. Cafe open 7am-11pm. Breakfast $2; dinner $3. Dorms $7; doubles $17, deluxe with TV and bath $35; quads $28. V, MC.

▩ **Moonlight Pension,** 87 Akbıyık Cad. (☎517 54 29 or 518 85 36; fax 516 24 80; email moonlight@superonline.com). Inexpensive pension a few blocks away from the hustle and bustle of the backpacker scene. Clean, spare rooms and a kind staff. Clear rooftop views, bar, communal kitchen. Cable TV in reception. Fax available; internet $1.50 per hr. Laundry service $4 per load. Snacks (pizza, burgers) $3. Breakfast $2. 15 rooms; with shower same price as those without. Dorms $5; doubles $16; triples $21. V, MC.

▩ **Nayla Palace Pansion,** 22 Kutlugün Sok. (☎516 35 67; fax 516 63 06; email nayla@superonline.com). Walk past the Four Seasons, turn right on Kutlugün, head down 2 blocks on the right. A homey atmosphere and quiet garden courtyard make this a good backpacker hideaway. Great view of Marmara from rooftop lounge. Internet $1 per hr. Breakfast included. Dorm beds $5; singles with bath $15; doubles $25, with bath $30; triples with bath $35.

Sultan Hostel, 3 Terbıyık Sok. (☎516 92 60; fax 517 16 26; email sultan@fez-travel.com). Off Akbıyık Cad., around the corner from Orient Hostel. Great views of the Sea of Marmara from the rooftop restaurant and large bar (sandwiches $1.50-3; beer $1.50). The happy hour gets very happy (5-8pm). In-house travel office. TV and VCR in common room, with nightly movies. Internet $1.50 per hr. Belly dancing Tu and Sa; water pipe nights M and Th; BBQ on F ($2). Breakfast $2. Free safe-deposit, luggage storage. 100 beds. Dorms $6.50; singles $13; doubles $9; quads $7. V, MC.

Yücelt Hostel/Interyouth Hostel, 6/1 Caferiye Cad. (☎513 61 50 or 513 61 51; fax 512 76 28; email info@backpackersturkey.com; www.yucelthostel.com). From the tram stop

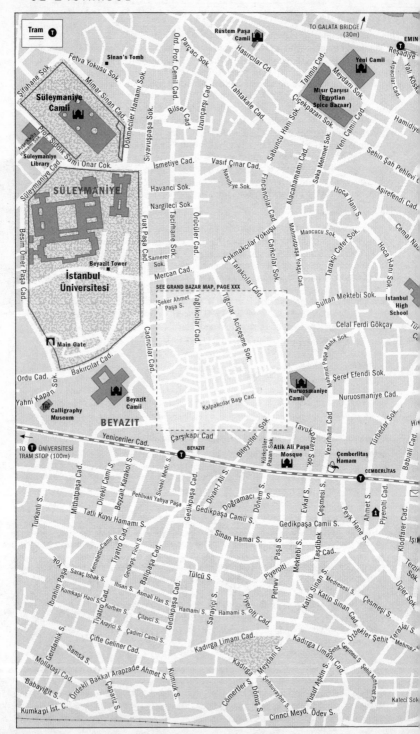

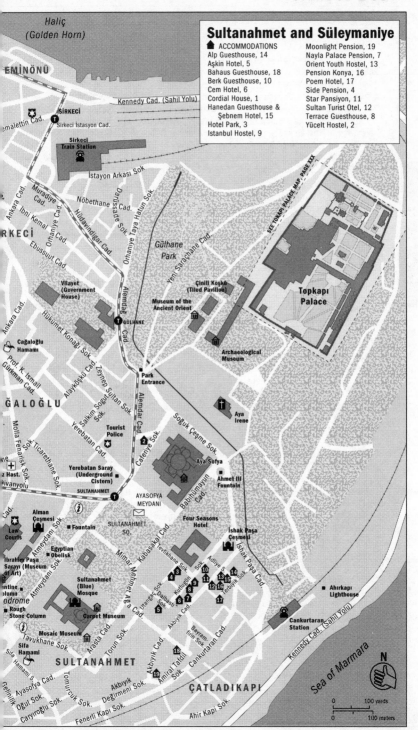

Sultanahmet and Süleymaniye

♦ ACCOMMODATIONS
Alp Guesthouse, 14
Aşkin Hotel, 5
Bahaus Guesthouse, 18
Berk Guesthouse, 10
Cem Hotel, 6
Cordial House, 1
Hanedan Guesthouse &
  Şebnem Hotel, 15
Hotel Park, 3
Istanbul Hostel, 9

Moonlight Pension, 19
Nayla Palace Pension, 7
Orient Youth Hostel, 13
Pension Konya, 16
Poem Hotel, 17
Side Pension, 4
Star Pansiyon, 11
Sultan Turist Otel, 12
Terrace Guesthouse, 8
Yücelt Hostel, 2

Haliç
(Golden Horn)

EMİNÖNÜ

Kennedy Cad. (Sahil Yolu)

SİRKECİ
Sirkeci İstasyon Cad.

Sirkeci
Train Station

İstayon Arkası Sok.

İstayon Arkası Sok.

Kemalettin Cad.

İRKECİ

Ankara Cad.

Muradiye Cad.

İbni Kemal Cad.

Ebussuut Cad

Osmaniye Cad.

Hüdavindigar Cad.

Nöbethane Cad.

Darüssade Sok.

Ormaniye Taya Hatun Sok.

Alemdağ Cad.

Yeni Saraçhane Cad.

Gülhane
Park

Çinili Köşkü
(Tiled Pavilion)

Museum of the
Ancient Orient

Topkapı
Palace

SEE TOPKAPI PALACE MAP, PAGE XXX

Ankara Cad.

Vilayet
(Government
House)

Hükümet Konağı Sok.

Zeynep Sultan Cad.

GÜLHANE

Cağaloğlu
Hamamı

Prof. K. İsmail
Gürkman Cad.

Archaeological
Museum

ĞALOĞLU

Molla Fenarisk Sok.

Ticarethane Sok.

Salkım Söğüt Sok.

Alayköşkü Cad.

Yerebatan Cad.

Alemdar Cad.

Park
Entrance

Soğuk Çeşme Sok.

Aya
İrene

Tourist
Police

Catferiye Sok.

z Hast.

Hast.

Yerebatan Saray
(Underground
Cistern)

SULTANAHMET

Divanyolu

AYASOFYA
MEYDANI

Aya Sofya

Babıhumayun Cad.

Ahmet III
Fountain

Alman
Çeşmesi

SULTANAHMET
SQ.

Fountain

Law
Courts

Atmeydanı Sok.

Egyptian
Obelisk

İbrahim Paşa
Sarayı (Museum
of Art)

entine
olumn

Atmeydanı Sok.

odrome

Rough
Stone Column

Mimar Mehmet Ağa Cad.

Tevfikhane Cad.

Kabasakal Cad.

Four Seasons
Hotel

İshak Paşa
Çeşmesi

Sultanahmet
(Blue)
Mosque

Adliye Sok.

Terbiyik Sok.

İshak Paşa Cad.

Ahırkapı
Lighthouse

Carpet Museum

Utangaç Sok.

Dalbastı Sok.

Kutlugün Sok.

Akbıyık Cad.

Cankurtaran
Station

Mosaic Museum

Tavukhane Sok.

Arasta Cad.

Torun Sok.

Bayram
firin Sok.

Cankurtaran Cad.

Kennedy Cad. (Sahil Yolu)

Sifa
Hamamı

SULTANAHMET

Akbıyık Cad.

Amiral Tafdil
Sok.

ÇATLADIKAPI

Sea of Marmara

Sifa Hamamı S.

Ayasofya Cad.

Oğul Sok.

Tomurcuk Sok.

Değirmeni Sok.

Akbıyık

Caryroğlu Sok.

Fenerli Kapı Sok.

Ahir Kapı Sok.

N

0   100 yards
0   100 meters

at Sultanahmet Sq., walk down Caferiye Cad. on the left side of Aya Sofia. This massive, 3-building complex has free billiards, table tennis, computer service, travel library, book exchange, safe boxes, and luggage storage, as well as videos in the rooftop lounge. Clean bathrooms and friendly staff make this a backpacker favorite. Laundry $1.50 per load. Reception claims to speak German and French. HI member. Dinner $3. Breakfast $3. 320 beds. Dorms $7-9; singles $18; doubles $18; triples $27. V, MC.

Cordial House, 29 Peykhane Sok., Divan Yolu (☎518 05 65; fax 516 41 08; email cordial@dominet.in.com.tr; www.cordialhouse.com). Combination hotel/hostel in nearby Çemberlitaş. Walk up Divan Yolu Cad. and turn left on Peykhane Sok. Clean but cozy dorms. The fluorescent lights can be a bit harsh, but windows provide light. There's an indoor bar with a pool table, internet access ($1.50 per hr.), TV room, and laundry service. Safe boxes free. Breakfast $2. 44 rooms. Dorms $6-8; singles $17, with bath $35; doubles $22, with bath $45; triples $33, with bath $60. V, MC, AmEx.

Konya Pansiyon, 15/2 Terbıyık Sok. (☎517 36 77). Walk down Adliye Sok., 1 block past Akbıyık Cad., and turn right around the corner. Probably the cheapest place in Sultanahmet; expect to get what you pay for: the only furniture you'll find here is the beds. Quiet and tidy, however, and only a block from the "action" on Akbıyık Sok. Dingy guest kitchen off concrete "garden." Internet $1 per hr. Free safe box. Breakfast $2. Basement dorm $4; regular dorm $5; doubles $14, with shower $30.

Cem Hotel, 30 Kutlugün Sok. (☎516 50 41; fax 517 65 76). Pass the Four Seasons, turn right on Kutlugün, walk 2 blocks down and look on your right. Tidy and cheap, this hotel provides an inexpensive alternative to the hostel grind. Breakfast included on tiled terrace bar (beer $1.50) with a panoramic view of the Marmara. Free airport pick-up if you stay longer than 3 days. Laundry $.50 per load. 15 rooms. Singles $15, with bath $20; doubles $20, with bath $25; triples with bath $30. V, MC, AmEx.

MID-RANGE

🖾 **Side Pension/Hotel Side,** 20 Utangaç Sok. (☎517 65 90; fax 517 65 90; email info@sidehotel.com; www.sidehotel.com). Near the entrance of the Four Seasons Hotel. Look for the giant bearded heads on the street. This hotel/pension combination occupies the 2 handsome wooden buildings by the corner of Tevfikhane Sok. and Utangaç Sok. The pension in the newer building offers simple rooms with brightly painted walls, while the hotel provides better furnished rooms with private bathrooms. Breakfast included on rooftop terrace. 24hr. hot water. 40 rooms. Pension singles $20; doubles $25; triples $35. Add $10 for clean, modern bathroom. Hotel singles $40; doubles $50; triples $60. Basement apartment with kitchen, bath, TV also available. Subtract 20% from all prices in winter. V, MC.

Alp Guesthouse, Akbıyık Cad., 4 Adliye Sok. (☎517 95 70 or 518 57 28; email alpguesthouse@turk.net). Head down Tevfikhane Sok., turn left after the Four Seasons, take the first right. The guesthouse is down 2 blocks on your left. Family-run hotel with Mediterranean ambiance. Spacious, spotless rooms with minibar and international telephone, some with fine views of the Marmara. Barbecues held often; drinks until 11pm on one of area's finest terraces with superb views of Aya Sofia. Free airport transport with 3-day stay. Free internet, safe, and basement luggage room. All 12 rooms with bath. Singles $30; doubles $50; triples $60.

Bahaus Guesthouse, Akbıyık Cad., 11 Bayram Fırını Sok. (☎517 66 97; fax 517 66 97). From the front of the Blue Mosque, strut down Mimar Mehmet Ağa Cad. 2 blocks, and turn left on Akbıyık Cad. The guesthouse is on your left. This bright yellow hotel has spare, standard rooms and a terrace view of the Sea of Marmara. Free backgammon courses from the owner. Cable TV in lobby. International phone service. Terrace has various musical instruments for the traveler in need of a tune-up. Breakfast included. 16 rooms. Singles $20; doubles $30, with bath $35; triples $40.

Hotel Park, 26 Utangaç Sok., Cankurtaran Mah. (☎517 65 96; fax 518 96 02; email hotelpark@ihlas.net.tr). Right across the street from the Four Seasons on Tevfikhane Sok. Quiet lobby, flowered terrace, and great views of Aya Sofia and the Blue Mosque. Rooms have bath, international phone, and cable TV. Large windows let in plenty of

AHH...THE LUXURY OF A TURKISH PRISON

Before its present incarnation as İstanbul's most luxurious (and expensive) accommodation, the ochre-colored Four Seasons Hotel was a less-than-glamorous high-security Turkish prison. Converting it into a four-star hotel a mere three years ago, interior designers maintained the original size of each room and used furniture sparingly in order to harken back to the building's more glorious days. The prison yard used for the inmates' daily exercise now hosts a deluxe restaurant with an Italian chef, and the old watchtower doubles as a site for wedding banquets. Other prison elements have also been restored; one central marble column bears an etched-in prisoner's name with a 1935 date and a pierced heart scribble. While architects left much of the original building intact, one thing that has changed is the price: rooms range from $200-2000 and the 65 available rooms are booked solid. What an escape!

light. Breakfast included. Singles $25; doubles $40; triples $55. Ask about a 10% discount for long stays (10+ days). Off-season prices 20% lower. V, MC, AmEx.

Aşkın Hotel, 16 Dalbastı Sok. (☎638 86 74; fax 638 86 76). From Sultanahmet Sq., walk down Mimar Mehmet Ağa Cad., turn left on Utangaç Sok., and take the 1st right. 20 rooms decorated in the style of old Ottoman houses, complete with ornate furniture. Private toilets and clean bathtubs offer the most peace and quiet you'll get in İstanbul outside of a hamam. Reception is happy to set up tours and cruises of the Bosphorus. Bar in lobby with pleasant sitting room. Breakfast included. All 20 rooms with A/C. Singles $35; doubles $50; triples $65.

Hanedan Hotel, Akbıyık Cad., 3 Adliye Sok. (☎516 48 69; fax 517 45 24; www.hanedanhotel.com). Walk down Tevfikhane Sok., turn left after the Four Seasons, and take the 1st right. The hotel is down 2 blocks on the right. Pleasant view from terrace, a beautiful cafeteria, and currency exchange. 24hr. free airport pick-up with minimum 3-day stay. Ultra-friendly staff offers travel advice and free nightly movies and drinks (beer $2). Breakfast included; other meals ($3-5) on roof in the summer. Most rooms have bathroom; 2 with view of the water. Singles $25; doubles $35; triples $45.

Star Guest House, 18 Akbıyık Cad. (☎638 23 02; fax 516 18 27). Located opposite the Orient Hostel, above the Star Laundry. Spartan rooms look a bit worn around the edges. 13 rooms, all with bath. Doubles $20; triples $30. Extra bed $10. V, MC.

THE BUDGET SPLURGE

▨ **Poem Hotel,** Akbıyık Cad., 12 Terbıyık Sok. (☎/fax 517 68 36; email hotelpoem@superonline.com). Quiet, luxurious rooms are marked with titles of Turkish poems instead of room numbers; all have Bosphorus views. Turkish breakfast (included) served in garden. Female owned, female friendly. Free internet. Lunch, dinner $10. Welcome drink on the house. 12 rooms with safe, TV, A/C, superb full bath. Singles $55; doubles $70-95; triples $90-115. Subtract 25% in winter. V, MC.

▨ **Terrace Guesthouse,** 39 Kutlugün Sok. (☎638 97 33; fax 638 97 34; email terrace@escortnet.com). Charming and peaceful hotel with carpet-lined walls (carpets sold for $125-1000), which hush the noise from outside. Attentive staff. Rooms offer great views of the sea. Small library/book exchange. Coffee and tea always available. Breakfast included in rooftop lounge. Reservations recommended. All 6 rooms with private bath. Doubles $50; triples $60. V, MC.

Sebnem Hotel, 1 Akbıyık Cad. (☎517 66 23; fax 638 10 56; email sebnemhotel@superonline.com; www.sebnemhotel.com). Walk down Tevfikhane Sok., turn left after the Four Seasons, and take the first right. Sebnem is down 2 blocks on your right. This pink-walled, converted house has 15 rooms, each with a private, tiled bathroom, canopy bed, and dark wood furniture. Super-deluxe yacht tours ($100) can be arranged. Safe provided at desk. Breakfast (included) on terrace. A/C, fridge, and international phone in all rooms. Singles $35; doubles $50; triple $60. V, MC.

Berk Guesthouse, 27 Kutlugün Sok. (☎517 65 61; fax 517 77 15; email reservations@berkguesthouse.com). Family-run, clean, quiet, and comfortable. Deluxe rooms with chandelier, fancy bedding, A/C, TV, and minibar. All rooms with modern bath and phone. Breakfast included. 8 rooms, 2 deluxe. Doubles $50; deluxe $95. Discounts for stays over a week. Traveler's checks accepted with 3% commission.

TAKSİM

☒ **Hotel As,** 26 Bekar Sok., (☎252 65 25; fax 245 00 99). Off upper İstiklâl Cad. Unbeatable price and location make the minor wear and tear charming. Singles and doubles have plenty of elbow room, though their private baths are cramped. Tiny balconies overlook busy cafe alleys. All rooms with bath. Singles $10; doubles $20; triples $30.

☒ **Hotel Plaza,** 19-21 Aslanyataği Sok. (☎245 32 73; fax 293 70 40). Down Arslanyata Sok., the small side street of Roxy fame, which is off Siraselviler. Bear left when Arslanyata turns right. The Plaza is a big, rambling building, foundering in a shady courtyard perfectly removed from Taksim's hustle—a good place to write your novel. Quiet, tattered, but classy rooms, some with great Bosphorus views, sitting rooms, fridges, glass tables, large windows. Breakfast included. Singles $40; doubles $60; "student rooms" (rooms showing their age) $10. Who knew a night at the Plaza could be so cheap?

Oriental Hotel, 60 Cihangir Cad. (☎252 68 70; fax 251 93 21). After leaving Taksim Square, take the 3rd left off Sirasilever onto Soğanci Sok., then a left when the road ends. Follow the road down a short hill, where the hotel is on the left side of a quiet residential street. Clean rooms with telephone. Singles $50; doubles $70; extra bed $20. When staying 10 nights or more: singles $40; doubles $50.

Hotel Nural, 12 Abdülhakamit Cad. (☎235 15 11). The closest you can get to Taksim Square without a goldcard. Nural is also directly in front of the stop for dolmuş to Aksaray. Unremarkable upscale rooms have A/C, phone, and TV. Singles $25; doubles $50. Haggling may be productive.

CAMPING

The slight savings is hardly worth the hassle and ugliness of city camping. İstanbul's remote campgrounds lie along the commuter rail tracks near the airport. From the airport, take a taxi ($3). From town, take the commuter rail from Sirkeci.

Londra Camping (☎560 42 00). On Londra Asfaltı Süt Sanayi Karşısı, 1km from the airport, along the noisy and nerve-grating highway to İstanbul. No bus stop; take a taxi. Far from the center of town, but not from its sounds. Includes cafeteria, bar, and showers. $5 per tent; 2-person bungalows $15.

Ataköy Tourist Village (☎559 60 00). About 2km from the airport. $4 per tent.

🗂 FOOD

The dining options in İstanbul cover the full quality and value spectrum. İstanbul's restaurants, like its clubs and bars, often stick with the golden rule that if it's well advertised or easy to find, it's not worth doing. Poking around side streets is always worthwhile. Though İstanbul's budget cuisine (under $5) is diverse, a certain amount of creativity is necessary to avoid getting stuck in the *pide*, kebap, and *lahmacun* rut. Light dinners of hot or cold *meze* (appetizers), *çorba* (soup), and *salata* (salad) can be inexpensive and satisfying, both for your stomach and your curiosity (see **Food,** p. 35).

Sultanahmet's heavily advertised "Turkish" restaurants aren't difficult to find, but they often have few Turkish patrons. Much better meals can be found on İstiklâl Cad. and around Taksim. The small Bosphorus towns such as Arnavutköy and Sariyer (on the European side) and Çengelköy (on the Asian side) are the best places for fresh **fish.** In the streets off Cumhuriyet Cad. north of Taksim, the city's high-end ($20-30 per person) restaurants are worked in amongst the Hilton and other ritzy hotels. Kanlıca, on the Asian side, reputedly has the city's best **yogurt.**

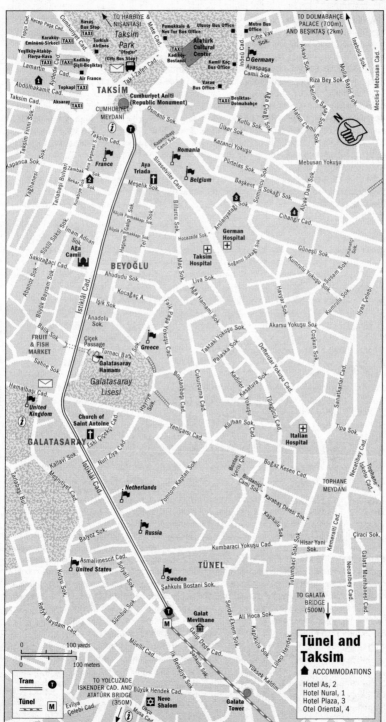

ISTANBUL

Tünel and Taksim

⚑ ACCOMMODATIONS

Hotel As, 2
Hotel Nural, 1
Hotel Plaza, 3
Otel Oriental, 4

A lamentably overlooked option is food sold by street vendors. Eminönü, like Karaköy across the water, is home to covered boats that fry up **fish sandwiches** on board ($1.50). These are almost always made safe by the vigorous cooking process, despite the questionable composition of the local waters. There are, however, unfortunate exceptions. Good **kebap** shops are everywhere, but quality tends to be better in more residential areas. Now and then, kebap carts roll by, usually with a small wood fire inside, serving sandwiches with lamb, tomatoes, lettuce, onions and spices—a very tasty, very cheap option. Ortaköy is the place to go for **baked potatoes** stuffed with all kinds of fillings from nacho cheese and salsa to goat cheese and sprinkles of lamb. **Vişne suyu** (sour cherry juice) is sold by vendors in Ottoman dress bearing big steel teapots on their backs. Since the sale of these three foods is supervised by the municipality, prices are fixed at around $.20-.30 for cherry juice and $1 for kebaps and potatoes.

Excellent **leblebi** (roasted and salted chickpeas) are often available around the Beyazıt bus stop ($.20-30 per serving). **Dondurma** (Turkish ice cream) stands are ubiquitous, particularly around Ortaköy. They are hard to miss, as the vendors often clatter their tongs like castanets or play with the scoop of ice cream at the end of their meter-long ice cream scoops. In winter, street offerings differ somewhat, as *vişne suyu* gives away to **sahlep** (a sweet, milky drink made of pulverized orchid root and sprinkled with cinnamon) and corn, everywhere during the summer months, is replaced with baked goods, fruits, and nuts.

Travelers who prepare their own food should know that because of space considerations and cultural differences, İstanbul has very few supermarkets. Migros is one of the most well known of Turkish supermarket chains, but there are only a couple in the city. A good alternative is the neighborhood market. Found on corners all over the city, these small shops sell cheese, bread, produce, and drinks, all at rock-bottom prices. Meat is invariably expensive (about $4 for 250g of chicken). A large and fresh selection of produce can be found in the city's **open-air markets;** the best is the daily one in Beşiktaş, near Barbaros Cad. Every Wednesday there is a very good fruit, vegetable, nut, and cheese market along Akbıyık Cad. in Sultanahmet. Two other large open-air markets are centrally located—a general one (including fish), next to Çiçek Pasajı in Beyoğlu, and a **fruit market** next to the Egyptian Spice Bazaar *(Mısır Çarşısı)*, which sells mouthwatering sweets.

SULTANAHMET AND DİVAN YOLU

By no means the gastronomical center of İstanbul, Sultanahmet's restaurants are mostly tourist troughs. A simple Turkish meal in this district shouldn't cost much more than $4-5 in any of the cafeteria-style restaurants. There are a number of pricier places scattered throughout the neighborhood and the side streets off Divan Yolu, but for your lira the less expensive eateries can provide just as much flavor as the upscale. Many restaurants have no menu, and hungry customers are encouraged to point and pick from trays of mouth-watering options.

■ **Doy-Doy,** 13 Şifa Hamamı Sok. (☎517 15 88). From the south end of the Hippodrome, walk down the hill around the edge of the Blue Mosque and look for the blue and yellow sign high in the trees. Easily the best and cheapest of Sultanahmet's crop of cheap eats, 3-story Doy-Doy keeps locals and backpackers coming back for more. Tasty kebap and refreshing salads ($3.50 and under). The *İskender kebap* ($2.50) is sublime. From the 4th-story terrace, enjoy an excellent view of the Marmara, the Blue Mosque, and a school yard where local kids play pick-up soccer. Open 8:30am-late.

■ **Dârüzziyâfe,** 6 Şigahane Cad. (☎511 84 14 or 511 84 15; fax 526 18 91). Behind the Sultanahmet Camii on the Hippodrome. Tour groups abound. Mellow atmosphere and attentive service. The specialty, *Süleymaniye çorbası* (meat and veggie soup; $2), is a must, as is the *çilek keşül* (strawberry pudding; $1.50). Main courses $4.50-$6; meals

$12-15. Live Ottoman music on Saturday nights. No alcohol, but try the rosehip nectar or the *nargile* pipes and apple tobacco. Open noon-11pm. Sister restaurant at 6 Şifahane Cad., next to the Süleymaniye Mosque, serves the same food at the same prices.

■ **Cennet,** 90 Divan Yolu (☎ 513 14 16). On the right side of the road as you walk from Sultanahmet toward Aksaray, 3min. from the Sultanahmet tram. Try on "traditional" Ottoman costumes as you watch women make *gözleme* (Anatolian pancakes) on a griddle in the center of the restaurant. The cheese pancake ($1.75) and the mixed meat one ($2) are divine, but the adventurous palate might enjoy a combination pancake with everything the place has to offer in one piece of fried dough. Kebaps of all sorts are fresh as well ($3). Live Turkish music and dancing every night. Have a tip ready; the musicians are not shy and don't quit. Open daily 10am-midnight.

■ **Can Restaurant,** 10 Divan Yolu (☎527 70 30). Across the street from the tourist information office at the north end of the Hippodrome. This no-nonsense, dirt-cheap cafeteria offers inexpensive line fare out front and dining tables in the rear. Veggie combination plates start at $1.75, while meat costs a bit more ($2.50-$5). The green beans in tomato sauce ($1) are to die for, and the tomatoes stuffed with rice and lamb ($1.25) are tasty and filling. Open 8am-9pm.

Pudding Shop, 6 Divan Yolu (☎522 29 70; fax 512 44 58). A major pitstop for those on the Hippie Trail to the Far and Middle East during the 70s, this family-owned establishment was the setting for the drug deal scene in *Midnight Express*. It is now a self-serve restaurant (meat dishes $2-2.50; veggie dishes $1.50) and super dessert stop whose walls are lined with newspaper clippings and notes about its storied past. Finish up with a *creme caramel, keşkül* (vanilla pudding), or cappuccino (each $1). Continental breakfast served mornings ($2). Air-conditioned upstairs.

Med Cezir, 16 Tevkifhane Sok. (☎517 22 67). Across from the Four Seasons Hotel. One of the better breakfast options in Sultanahmet, this narrow but nicely decorated spot does big Turkish breakfasts for $5. Daytime fare tends toward sandwiches ($2-3), pizza ($5), and various stuffed potatoes ($4). Come nightfall, the place becomes a pleasant cafe, perfect for watching the high-speed antics of both the taxi drivers and the rich and famous staying at the Four Seasons. 10% service charge. Open 8:30am-midnight.

Pandeli Restaurant, 1 Egyptian Spice Bazaar (☎/fax 522 55 34). The stairs to the 2nd-floor restaurant are right inside the entrance to the bazaar facing the water. Check the walls for celebrity endorsements, including Burt Lancaster's. Extensive wine list. Tasty *yaprak dolması* (stuffed vine leaves) and *hünkâr beğendi* (eggplant with kebap; $5.75) are specialties. Starters $3-8; main courses $6-12. Open M-Sa noon-4pm.

House of Medusa Restaurant, Yerebatan Cad., 19 Muhteremefendi Sok. (☎511 41 16 or 513 14 28; fax 527 28 22). A 2min. walk up Yerebatan Cad. from Aya Sofia. This 4-floor, internationally renowned eatery is a must-see half-restaurant, half-museum. Delicious *piliç* (chicken stuffed with vegetables; $6) and lamb kebap ($5), savory vegetarian specials $3-6, and tasty pudding $2.50 are best capped by their delicious Turkish coffee. Open daily 8am-midnight. V, MC, AmEx.

Cafe Magnaura, 27 Akbıyık Cad. (☎518 76 22). Down the street from Orient Youth Hostel and Star Pansiyon. Attentive staff serves typical Turkish fare in a romantic, wood-lined interior that opens onto the street in mild weather. The chicken roll with almonds and pistachios ($6) and the wide array of vegetarian options ($4-7) are delectable. Menu also features international fare (steak and fries $8). Universally enjoyed by backpackers looking for a sit-down meal with a clean tablecloth. Open daily 9am-10pm.

Ayışığı Çay Bahçesi, on Alemdar Cad. Between the tram tracks and Aya Sofia, right next to the Interyouth Hostel. This tree-lined garden cafe features shady outdoor dining, water pipe use any time of day, and good-sized snacks for carnivores. The kebaps ($3) are fresh and juicy, and the atmosphere is relaxing. Open daily noon-12:30am.

İSTİKLÂL CADDESİ AND TAKSİM

The famed **Çiçek Pasajı** (Flower Passage), home of classy but increasingly pricey restaurants, branches off İstiklâl Cad. Look a bit harder in the side streets off İstiklâl Cad. for cheaper bars and cafes where the clientele is mostly Turkish. Hit Taksim Square only if you are missing the Golden Arches.

■ **Haci Baba,** 49 İstiklâl Cad. (☎ 244 18 86 or 245 43 77), has perfected a wide range of Turkish standards in its nearly 80 years. The unassuming entrance hides a large dining room with a terrace overlooking the courtyard of Aya Triada in back. The menu is extensive, but it's easier to pick something from the deli case in front or help yourself to the immense, vegetarian *meze* selection (entrees about $7). Open 10am-10pm.

■ **Naregatsi Cafe.** Upstairs at the mouth of Sakizağacı Cad., across from the Ağa Camii. Perhaps the weirdest spot in the Taksim area, Naregatsi serves gourmet cafe fare in the midst of a galactic, high-speed collision of kitsch and concept art. Warhol would feel right at home. Inflatable superheroes, a collection of board games, and the occasional live accordion complement the cappuccino (4 flavors, $3.50). Open noon-11:30pm.

■ **İnci Pastahanesi,** 126 İstiklâl Cad. (☎ 243 24 12), has served the neighborhood for 53 years under the same owner. The specialty is the scandalously cheap *profiterol,* a creme-filled cake smothered in chocolate sauce ($1.40). Open daily 7am-9pm.

■ **Great Hong Kong Restaurant,** 12B İnönü Cad., 100m off Taksim Square. A red gateway leads to this lavish Chinese restaurant marooned in Taksim. The full spread of favorites, from wonton soup ($2.50) to Huajiao prawns ($8.50). Open noon-3pm, 6-11:30pm.

Afacan, İstiklâl Cad. 2 locations, one at the top end by the 1st movie theater and the 2nd at the bottom end, past the Galatasaray Lisesi. Despite the linoleum interior, this is one of the street's better restaurants, serving seriously good kebaps and *dolma* ($3-4). Top restaurant open 10am-midnight; bottom open 8am-11pm. V, MC.

Cafe Gramafon, 3 Tünel Meydanı (☎ 293 07 86), on the left as you come out of the Tünel station, offers divine *Gramafon* filet ($8-10) and *tost* (sandwiches with veggies or meats; $4-8). Turkish coffee $1.50; cappuccino royal with amaretto, brandy, and cacao $3.75; various liquors $6-10. Live jazz (W-Sa after 10:30pm, $5 cover waived if you come before 11pm) attracts diverse crowds. Open daily 11am-2am.

Şampiyon, Balık Pazarı. Next to Çiçek Pasajı. Famous across Turkey for the country's best *kokoreç* (grilled tripe cooked with spices and tomatoes). Try the smallest portion, the *çeyrek ekmek kokoreç* ($1.50). For something quick, stand out front for skewers of fried mussels ($1.50) or fresh mussels with lemon ($.25 each). Open 8:30am-midnight.

Cumhuriyet Meyhanesi (☎ 252 08 86). At the far end of the fish market. In the evenings Turkey's top poets, artists, and journalists migrate between here and the cafes to discuss politics, culture, and other intellectual matters. Serves delectable items such as eggplant salad for $3. Open daily 10am-1am, sometimes later.

Duran Sandwich, 9 İstiklâl Cad. (☎ 243 52 30). Turkish sandwiches reach a rare level of intrigue at this small counter. More than 30 varieties, including caviar and roast beef. Prices range from $.50 to $4. Open daily 9am-10pm.

Borsa Fast Food, 87 İstiklâl Cad. This 3-story fast food restaurant serves quick-fix variations on traditional Turkish cuisine. Try the soup ($1) and artichokes ($2). Vegetarian options. Beer on 3rd floor. Clean, air-conditioned, and raucous. Open 8am-midnight.

Patisserie Gezi, 5 İsmet İnönü Cad. Right next to the Atatürk Cultural Center. A taste of Viennese luxury on Taksim Square. Great service compensates for higher prices. Try the delicious *rübli torte* (almond carrot cake; $3) or sample from their large assortment of truffles ($4 per 100g). Open 9am-10pm.

Saray Muhallebicisi, 102 stiklâl Cad. A fixture on the street for over 50 years, this pastry shop has expanded to 5 locations all over İstanbul. Marble floors and dark wood tables belie low prices, which keep a constant stream of locals moving through the door. Try the chocolate cake with pistachio ($1.25 a slice). Open daily 6am-midnight.

Ali Muhiddin Haci Bekir, 129 İstiklâl Cad. This place claims to have invented *lokum.* Colossal but pricey Turkish Delight selection ($8-10 per kg). Open 8am-9pm. Another branch at 76 Dolayoba Cad., behind Yeni Camii. V, MC.

🖼 İSTANBUL'S NEIGHBORHOODS

İstanbul's incomparable array of churches, mosques, palaces, and museums can keep a tireless tourist busy for weeks, but five or six days of legwork should be enough to get acquainted with the best of the city's thousands of years of history. Students will find that an ISIC sometimes allows entry to major museums for free. Before touring any working religious facilities, see **Visiting Mosques,** p. 33.

SULTANAHMET

Most budget travelers spend a lot of time in **Sultanahmet,** the area around the Aya Sofia mosque, south of and up the hill from Sirkeci and down to the southwestern tip of the old city. The area is dominated by three of the city's major sights: the Blue Mosque, Aya Sofia, and Topkapı Palace. Within a few hundred yards of each other, the three create a visible testament to the region's varied and full history, as well as a gigantic tourist trap. Post-sightseeing, re-energize with a pick-up soccer game on the Marmara, or wander up Divan Yolu to get lost in the merchant's maze of the Grand Bazaar.

AYA SOFİA (HAGIA SOPHIA)
Museum open Tu-Su 9:30am-4:30pm. Gallery open Tu-Su 9:30am-4pm. $6.50.

Aya Sofia was built by Emperor Justinian after the **Nika Riots** of 532, in which Hippodrome hooligans had destroyed an earlier structure (see **Christianity and the Byzantine Empire,** p. 8). To prove his power and restore order, Justinian commissioned the mathematicians **Anthemius of Tralles** and **Isodorus of Miletus** to design and build the church. After five years of construction, the exterior of the church was painted blood-red to serve as an unambiguous warning to would-be revolutionaries. The church opened in December 537. Covering an area of $7570m^2$ and rising to a height of 55.6m, it was then the grandest building in the world. Upon entering the church and marvelling at its girth, which was even greater than that of King Solomon's temple in Jerusalem, Justinian reportedly exclaimed, "Solomon, I have outdone you!" Twenty years later, an earthquake revealed a fatal miscalculation on the part of the original architects, bringing the dome crashing to the ground. The task of rebuilding fell to Isador the Younger, nephew of Isadorus. Isador completed his work in 563, having added clumsy exterior buttresses to support the new dome.

From then on, the church began its millennium-long tenure as the most impressive building in the Byzantine world, though it was plundered and desecrated in the 13th century by Catholic soldiers of the Fourth Crusade. The Crusaders looted the holy relics, destroyed the exquisite carvings, and seated a prostitute on the patriarch's throne in order to ridicule the Eastern Church. Despite this humiliation, the Byzantines regained Constantinople and Aya Sofia for another 200 years before they fell to the Ottomans in 1453.

Mehmet the Conqueror converted Aya Sofia to a mosque, removing all representational art and images and adding a wooden minaret. In the late 16th century, the architect Mimar Sinan undertook a renovation program that included the addition of four minarets. Aya Sofia remained a mosque from then until 1932, when Atatürk established it as a museum.

Aya Sofia's austere interior amplifies its awesome size. Walking through the main entrance will bring you into the ruins-strewn exonarthex, a long, transverse hall common in Byzantine architecture (see **Architecture,** p. 21). The nave, reached by crossing the hall, is overshadowed by the massive, gold-leaf mosaic dome. The **mihrab,** the calligraphy-adorned portal pointing towards Mecca, stands awkwardly in the **apse,** whose two rows of stained glass windows made for a traditional backdrop to the altar during the mosque's Orthodox incarnation. The **minber,** or platform used to address the crowd at Muslim prayer, is the stairway to the right of the *mihrab.* Like the *mihrab,* it was added to the building as part of its reconsecration as a mosque. The elaborate marble square in the floor of the Aya Sofia's main space marks the spot where Byzantine emperors were once crowned.

If you move out of the nave towards the south wall of the main floor, you can peer into the library of Sultan Mahmut I, built in the 1730s. The blue İznik-tiled room features a collection of 18th-century furniture and Koran stands. Crossing back through the nave to the north side of the building, you will reach the **narthex,** a quiet hallway with lace-like column capitals. At the back end of the narthex is the the famed **sweating pillar,** sheathed in bronze. The pillar has a hole where you can insert your finger to collect the odd drop of water, believed to possess healing powers. Be prepared to wait, though—the perspiration is slow in coming. When you are done here, the climb up to the second floor gallery begins at the north end of the exonarthex.

The **gallery** contains Byzantine mosaics uncovered from beneath a thick layer of Ottoman plaster, laid over these pieces centuries ago in accordance with regulations on Islamic art. At the end of the climb, turn right, walk down one side of the second floor and turn the corner to the mosaics. Badly damaged from its years under the plaster, the first mosaic depicts Christ listening to the pleas of his mother and John the Baptist. The mosaic on the right depicts Emperor John II Komnenos, his wife Empress Irene, and their son Alexios around Mary and the Christ child. The final mosaic shows Jesus with the Empress Zoë and Constantine Monomachus. The story goes that each time one of Zoë's husbands died, his face would be carved out of the mosaic and the new husband's face would replace it.

▨ BLUE MOSQUE (SULTANAHMET CAMİİ)

Open Tu-Sa 8:30am-12:30pm, 1:45-3:45pm, and 5:30-6:30pm. The Blue Mosque is a working religious facility. Please be courteous—don't attempt to visit during prayer times, which are marked by the call to prayer issued five times daily from all six of the mega-phoned minarets. Dress appropriately—head coverings for women and no shorts or tank tops—and speak quietly once inside. On your way out, expect to make a small donation. Tomb open Tu-Su 9:30am-4:30pm. Tomb $1, students free.

Located across Sultanahmet Park from Aya Sofia and next to the Hippodrome, the Blue Mosque, or Sultanahmet Camii, is a six-minareted, multi-domed structure. Though not blue on the outside, the mosque takes its name from the beautiful blue İznik tiles inside. Completed in 1617, it was Sultan Ahmet's response to the architectural challenge of Aya Sofia. Though the Blue Mosque is huge, its dimensions don't compete with those of Aya Sofia. Both elegantly and intelligently designed, the mosque is buttressed by an internal framework of iron bars across its domes, enabling the entire structure to bend in earthquakes. So far, it has withstood 20. An underground pool moderates the mosque's interior temperature, keeping it cool in the summer and warm in the winter.

Follow the signs posted along the outside of the mosque to the visitor's entrance on the south side, past the fountains reserved for ceremonial washing. Before entering you will be asked to remove your shoes, and women will be provided with necessary head coverings. Once inside the mosque's carpeted quiet, you will find yourself directly under the giant İznik-tiled hemispheres. It's best to visit on a sunny day, when shafts of light enter through the windows along the cupola. Six-teenth- and 17th-century Kütahya tiles in characteristically Ottoman floral and geometric patterns grace most of the mosque's surfaces (see **Kütahya,** p. 348).

The barely-visible wires hanging from the ceiling support a set of giant light-studded rings. Originally lit with candles, the **chandelier** structure was intended to create the illusion that tiny starlike lights floated freely in the air. The understated *mihrab*, covered with red and white tile and calligraphic inscriptions, is located along the wall of 17th-century stained-glass windows. A small stone from the **Ka'aba** at Mecca is almost invisible from the tourists' area.

The entrance to the courtyard is in the wall facing away from Mecca. In typical Ottoman style, the rectangular **courtyard** has a central **fountain** and a colonnade with small domes above the arches. The courtyard also holds a **sundial** that was used to determine prayer times. In honor of Sultan Ahmet, the sixth sultan after the Turkish conquest of Constantinople, the **six minarets** are the reason for the mosque's fame. Only the mosque at Mecca had six minarets at the time of the Blue

Mosque's construction, and the thought of equaling that sacred edifice was considered heretical. Sultan Ahmet got around this difficulty by financing the construction of a 7th minaret at Mecca. The mosque has 16 balconies, symbolizing Ahmet's role as the 16th sultan since the beginning of the Ottoman state.

The small, square, single-domed structure in front of the Blue Mosque is **Sultanahmet'in Türbesi,** or Sultan Ahmet's Tomb, which contains the sultan's remains as well as those of his wife and his sons, Osman II and Murat IV. Contrary to popular belief, the high ratio of small coffins to large ones is not a product of ritual fratricide committed by jealous would-be sultans. Though fratricide was a frequent Ottoman practice, it was officially abolished by Sultan Ahmet himself. The small tomb's main attractions are its İznik tiles. The cases of holy relics in the back include strands of the Prophet Muhammed's beard and several Koran stands.

In summer evenings, the daily light show romanticizes the history of the mosque's construction. The show is narrated in a different language every night (Turkish, English, French, and German rotate in that order), and even if you don't understand the language of the day, the blue-lit mosque and powerful music make the experience worthwhile.

THE HIPPODROME

Though all of the major Sultanahmet sites provide insight into pre-Ottoman and Ottoman history, few conjure images of the glory of Byzantine Constantinople like the **Hippodrome** *(At Meydanı)*. Behind the Blue Mosque, the remains of this ancient Roman circus form a pleasant park whose tranquility contrasts with its turbulent history. Built by the Roman Emperor Septimus Severus in the year 200, it was the site of chariot races and public executions. Constantine, the first Byzantine Emperor, enlarged the racetrack until it was 500m on each side.

The Hippodrome played an integral part in the political life of Byzantine Constantinople. The **Hippodrome Factions,** named by color, arose out of the Hippodrome's seating plan, which was determined by social standing. The "blues" were wealthy citizens seated in the front rows and the "greens" were urban plebians in cheap seats. In one particularly violent demonstration in 532, a protest against the exorbitant taxation policy turned into the bloody **Nika Revolt.** About 30,000 rioters were eventually subdued (read: massacred), but not before they managed to demolish much of the city.

Two parallel streets, both called Atmeydanı Sok., mark the Hippodrome's long straightaways, while the little semi-circular alley behind the Marmara University rectorate is the only surviving bend. Taxis still race around the Hippodrome's edges, so watch your step on the curb. The park in the center with the three columns and a gazebo at the north end was a high-walled median divider, against which many unfortunate charioteers were fatally crushed. Along with gladiatorial contests, racing provided an ample supply of corpses from which ancient doctors were able to develop knowledge of human anatomy and medicine.

The northernmost column with hieroglyphics is the **Dikili Taş,** the **Egyptian Obelisk** erected by the Pharoah Thutmosis III in 1500 BC and brought from Egypt to Constantinople in the 4th century by Emperor Theodosius I. At that time, the base was carved with depictions of the life of Theodosius, Byzantine chariot races, and war victories. A few meters away stands all that is left of the **Serpentine Column.** Once an impressive piece of plunder, the column now stands short, its top cut and its bronze gone black. Originally placed at the Oracle of Delphi, the statue consisted of three intertwined snakes whose heads pointed in different directions until Mehmet I conquered the city and decapitated one of them. (A 17th-century print of Mehmet tackling the statue and one of the original serpent heads is displayed in the "İstanbul Through the Ages" exhibit at the Archaeological Museum (p. 109). The southernmost column is the deteriorating **Column of Constantine,** whose original gold-plated bronze tiling was looted by members of the Fourth Crusade during the sack of Constantinople. The small gazebo with fountains around its base at the other end of the Hippodrome is **Kaiser Wilhem's fountain.** On the east side of the Hippodrome along Atmeydanı Sok. is **İbrahim Paşa Sarayı,** the **Museum of Turkish and Islamic Art** (p. 111).

Today, the park's many benches provide a relaxing place to take a break. Vendors there sell everything from ice cream to boiled and salted corn. On the weekends, enjoy people-watching families, small soccer games, and young people out for a stroll with their friends.

TOPKAPI PALACE (TOPKAPI SARAYI)

Open Tu-Su 9am-4:30pm. Each day's open galleries are posted next to the ticket window. Palace $6.50. Harem closes at 4pm. Mandatory tours of the Harem leave every 30min. 9:30am-3:30pm. Harem $4.

Towering from the high ground at the tip of the old city and hidden behind walls up to 12m high, Topkapı Palace *(Topkapı Sarayı)* was the nerve center of the Ottoman Empire from the 15th through the 19th century. This sprawling collection of buildings, gardens, and colonnades, their arrangement disobeying the rules of symmetry and mathematics that traditionally govern Islamic architecture, served as a monument to Ottoman power and glory. The palace is the greatest structure in Islamic secular architecture, combining a number of different styles within its miles of outer walls. Topkapı offers unparalleled insights into the wealth, excess, cruelty, and artistic vitality of the Ottoman Empire throughout its rise to, and fall from, continental eminence. Built by **Mehmet the Conqueror** between 1458 and 1465 on the strategic Seraglio Point overlooking the Marmara, the palace was originally intended as an administrative center for the Ottoman Empire. When the palace became an imperial residence during the reign of **Süleyman the Magnificent,** the administrative offices were converted into the Harem, the Sultan's private residence and the living quarters for his family and wives.

The palace is divided into a series of courts, all surrounded by the palace walls. These walls also encompass **Gülhane Park,** whose entrance lies at the Gülhane tram stop, on Alemdar Cad. The palace's main entrance is on Babıhümayun Cad., the cobblestone street off Aya Sofia square. From here, visitors pass machine gun-toting members of the military and enter into the first of four courtyards, a large walled-in park that also contains the **archaeological museums** (p. 109). The second court makes up the bulk of the palace and was used for carrying out the business of ruling the empire. The third court is the site of the palace school and the sultan's library, and the fourth houses a set of pavilions with amazing views of the Sea of Marmara beyond Gülhane's forest canopy.

THE FIRST COURT. Follow Babıhümayun Cad. to the Bab-ı-Hümayun, the **Imperial Gate.** At the top are the *tuğra* (seals) of the builder, Mehmet the Conqueror, as well as those of Mahmut II and Abdülaziz, who restored the palace. Mehmet would sit and watch his troops from a pavilion which originally stood atop the gate but has since collapsed.

The first courtyard, located through the gate, was the popular center of the Palace. The general public was permitted entrance to watch executions, to trade, and to view the nexus of the Empire's glory. The first court is comprised mostly of a shady park and scattered gardens. On the left stands the **Church of Divine Peace** *(Aya İrini Kilisesi),* a Byzantine church and a former palace armory. The only way to see the inside of the church is to catch a concert there during either the **İstanbul Festival** or the summer music festivals. The summer music festivals are a pretty good bet, as the concerts are frequent in June and early July, and the tickets can run as low as $6. Next door is the **Imperial Mint,** occasionally open for scholarly symposia and art shows. Its design incorporates an utterly random collection of architectural styles ranging from classical Ottoman to proto-Bauhaus, connected by a narrow-gauge rail line used for transporting bullion. Here coins were minted and the Imperial silverware cast.

THE SECOND COURT. At the end of the first courtyard, the capped conical towers of Bab-üs-Selam (the Gate of Greeting) mark the entrance to the second court. The design for the two octagonal towers was derived from the battlements of medieval

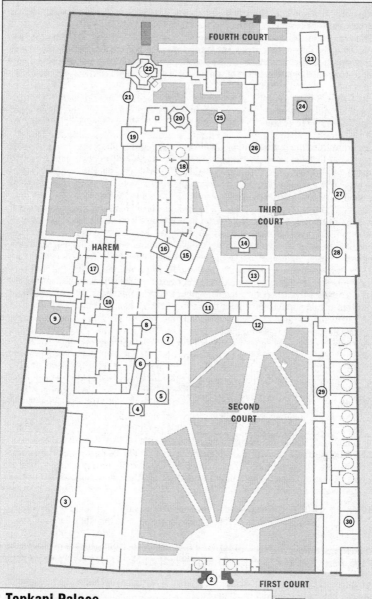

İSTANBUL

Topkapi Palace

Ahmet III Library, 14
Audience Chamber, 13
Baghdad Pavilion, 22
Circumcision Room, 19
Collection of Calligraphy,
    Miniature Paintings and
    Portraits of the Sultans, 26
Court of the Black Eunuchs, 6
Dormitory of the Expeditionary
    Pages, 28
Entrance, Ticket Office, &
    Bathrooms, 1

Former Mosque for the Kitchen
    Staff, 30
Gate of Felicity, 12
Gate of Greeting, 2
Harem Entrance, 4
Harem Garden, 9
Harem Mosque, 16
Iftar Porch, 21
Inner Treasury, 7
Kitchens (Porcelain & Glass
    Collections), 29
Library, 15
Main Harem Gate, 8

Meeting Hall of the Privy
    Council, 5
Palace Treasury, 27
Pavilion of Holy Relics, 18
Restaurant, 23
Revan Pavilion, 20
Sleeping Quarters of the
    White White Eunuchs, 11
Sofa Mosque, 24
Stables of the Sultans, 3
Throne Room, 17
Tulip Garden, 25
Valide Salon, 10

European castles which Süleyman saw during his Eastern European campaigns. The gate itself was built by Sultan Mehmet II in 1542.

The area where guards check tickets and maintain security is the **Kapı Arası.** In Ottoman days, viziers and other emissaries were detained here before receiving permission to enter the palace. In the days of the sultans' rule, the second courtyard formed the business center of the palace. Here, the Janissaries were paid, the Sultan received foreign heads of state, and meetings were held. Inside the gate, six paths lead to different locations within the court. The first path on the left leads to the stables and dungeons. The second path leads to the entrance to the Harem, the Palace's residential center. The third path leads to the **Privy Chambers** (*Kubbealtı*) and the **Inner Treasury,** both situated along the left wall alongside the Harem entrance. With its window grilles, awnings, walls, and ceilings slathered in gold leaf, the privy chambers were the sight of the Divan council's Tuesday meetings, a gathering of high-ranking Ottoman officials. The privy chamber is composed of a few rooms. The **Council Chamber,** closest to the Harem entrance, retains its original classical Ottoman *faïence* and calligraphic decor. Of the two grilles here, the one mounted high on the wall contains a peep-hole through which the Sultan could observe his council's deliberations from the Harem. When he felt his advisers had said enough, he would rap his hand on the grille to conclude the meeting. The plush Rococo-style room abutting the Council Chamber was where the **Grand Vizier** received foreign dignitaries. Both of these rooms lost their prominence after the 18th century, when the Grand Vizier became autonomously powerful and the importance of his council diminished. Next door, the **Inner Treasury** holds the sultans' swords and various other instruments of cutting, bludgeoning, and hacking. Regrettably, this popular portion of the palace is often closed.

The fifth and sixth paths from the second gate lead to the opposite wall and the **Imperial kitchens,** with their distinctive conical and vaulted chimneys. The kitchens house three collections of porcelain and silver. From the narrow alley, the door that is closest to the entrance to the third court leads into the confectioners' kitchen, displaying glass and porcelain collections. The pastry rolling stone bearing the Imperial seal is the only remaining piece of original kitchen equipment in the building. Back outside on the narrow street, the doors along the opposite, court-side wall lead into the **silver and European porcelain collections,** worth visiting if only to pay homage to the herniated spirits of those who had to schlep the loot in. The last set of doors on the left of the alley open into the palace's deservedly world-famous **Chinese and Japanese porcelain collections.** The Chinese collection is among the largest in the world, featuring pieces from all the major porcelain eras, from the Song through the Ch'ing Dynasties. Also worth noting are the kitchen chimneys; one of **Mimar Sinan's** minor commissions, they were built after a fire in 1574 gutted the kitchens.

THE THIRD COURT. Officially known as **Enderun** (literally *inside*), the third court is accessible through the **Gate of Felicity,** also referred to as the **White Eunuchs' Gate** (*Akağalar Kapısı*). On the second courtyard side of the gate, the white stone in the ground underneath the awning is all that remains of the pedestal which held the sultan's standard whenever he held audience here. The gate shows the beginning of the architectural change from the intricate classical Ottoman order to the showiness of Dolmabahçe Palace (see p. 123). It also reveals that while in use, the Topkapı Palace remained a work in progress.

The building whose awning attaches to the gate is the **Arz Odası,** an **audience chamber** where the sultan met privately with his viziers and high-ranking advisers. While it is closed to the public, you can peer inside for a glimpse of the sultan's loveseat-sized throne. The buildings attached to either side of the gate are the quarters and school of the *Enderva Ağas* (Boys of the Inside). Recruited from foreign countries, these boys received preliminary education elsewhere in the empire before being brought to the palace to prepare for a life in the service of the sultan. In the center of the courtyard is the **Library of Ahmet III,** also closed to the public. To the right of the library sits the **School of the Expeditionary Pages,** which houses the Palace's **costumes collection.** Follow the evolution of imperial dress from the early days of *kaftans* (long tunics) to the introduction of *şalvar* (baggy trousers) in the late 18th century, right through to the adoption of the fez with Western clothing under Mahmud II.

Moving down along the colonnade brings you to the **Palace Treasury,** subdivided into four rooms of bulletproof display cases covered with nose prints. The first of these is the **gold objects** room, containing the **chain mail** armor of Murat IV and the sultan's throne. The second hall is reserved for objects embellished with emeralds, including the **legendary Topkapı dagger.** Sultan Mahmut I intended to present it to Nadir Shah of Iran in return for the solid-gold throne displayed elsewhere in the treasury, but Nadir Shah was assassinated before the gift could be received. The next room features various gifts to Ottoman Sultans from European countries. The **Spoonmaker's Diamond,** the world's 7th largest, earned its nickname because it was traded to a spoonmaker in exchange for three spoons. The highlight of the medals case is the diamond-encrusted anchor, awarded by the German *Kaiser* to a daring Ottoman sea captain. Also note the silver hand; the small glass compartment reportedly contains some of John the Baptist's bones.

Walking counter-clockwise along the colonnade, you will reach the **Hall of the Treasury,** which now houses 37 portraits, one for each of the 37 sultans. The pride of this collection is the three works commissioned by Murat II: the Shahanshah-name (Book of the King of Kings), the Surname (Book of Festivals), and the Hür-name (Book of Accomplishments). The **Treasure Dormitory** next door displays a sizeable collection of Islamic Art cataloguing the evolution of Selçuk and Mamluk art, particularly calligraphy. Also check out the **shadow theatre display,** with English captions explaining the central role of these figures in Turkish folk culture (see **No Strings Attached,** p. 158).

Just on the other side of the courtyard lies the elegant **Pavilion of Holy Relics,** housing the booty snatched by Selim the Grim after the Ottoman capture of Egypt, as well as gifts sent by the governor of Mecca and Medina upon Selim's victory. The interior is lavishly covered in blue İznik tile, with the names of God and Muhammed on calligraphic seals in the upper corners of the main room. Two further rooms feature extensive Muhammed memorabilia. In the third room is a soundproof glass cubicle from which the *muezzin* sounds the call to prayer.

HAREM. Cashing in on the associations of debauchery and intrigue conjured up by the word harem, the Topkapı officials require the purchase of a separate ticket for this, the museum's most popular attraction next to the Spoonmaker's Diamond. The word harem is actually Arabic; the Turks use the word *darüssade*, or house of felicity. The harem's 400-plus rooms housed the sultan, his immediate family, and a small army of servants, eunuchs, and general assistants. Because it was forbidden for men other than the sultan and his sons to live here, the harem became a fount of intrigue and gossip. The crazy rumors included one that claimed the sultans' wives and concubines had to crawl on their hands and knees to his bed. Unfortunately, the guided tour of the harem can be anywhere from quite decent to thoroughly useless, depending on the pace and the distortion of the guide's voice brought on by the building's echoing acoustics. Stand close to the guide or look out for explanatory signs to get the lowdown on the down and dirty.

The harem breaks down into three main sections: the Eunuchs' section, the Women's section, and the Sultan's section. The mandatory guided tour proceeds through the harem in roughly that order. The tour begins in the **courtyard** with the **Black Eunuchs' Dormitory** on the left, where the lowest ranking eunuchs lived on the top floor, the higher ranking eunuchs lived on the lower floors, and the chief eunuch lived on the ground floor. The Black Eunuchs, so named because they were specially recruited from Africa, were charged with the administration of the harem. They acted as bodyguards for the sultan and his women, controlled traffic in and out of the harem, and handled other mechanics of harem life.

SLEEPING YOUR WAY TO THE TOP
Though often billed as Hugh Hefner's seventh heaven, the activities of Ottoman **harems** went far beyond his trade. Often, the women inhabitants had been captured in foreign countries or bought as slaves at age five. Concubines were sorted into two groups: the beautiful, who personally served the sultan, and the rest, who started out as rookies *(açemis)*. During their stay at the harem, women were educated in religion, philosophy, and state affairs, and were taught to read and write. At first, they could leave the harem to visit İstanbul, and after nine years they were done with harem service and could ask the sultan for permission to marry. However, if a concubine attracted the sultan's affections or if the sultan spent a night with her, she was promoted to odalisque. This position meant she lost her privilege to leave the harem, but her standards of living were upped, and she had chances for further advancement. If she carried the sultan's first son, she was practically guaranteed to be Valide Sultan. If she bore the sultan any son, there was a good chance of becoming Kadın Efendı, or wife of the sultan (he could have up to 8 of these). Through this system of prestige, the harem women became a powerful, cohesive unit, competently running the affairs of state in the event that the sultan was too mad, weak, or young to rule effectively on his own.

The women's section of the harem begins with the chambers of the **Valide Sultan,** the sultan's mother. Easily the most powerful of the harem women, the Valide Sultan was greatly influential on her son. Roxelana, the wife of Süleyman the Magnificent, induced her husband to kill his first son in order to pave the way for the accession of her son, Selim the Sot (see **How Süleyman the Magnificent Got His Name,** p. 13). The first to move her living quarters to Topkapı, she was also the harem's inaugural member. The tour makes its way through the **Queen Mother's chambers** and the smaller apartments of special concubines who served the Queen Mother.

After the Concubines' Courtyard, the tour dives into a maze of unremarkable sitting rooms and bathrooms. You'll pass through the bedroom of Murat III, designed by famed architect Mimar Sinan. Further on, admire the **Fruit Room,** so named because pictures of fruit adorn every imaginable surface. Before ending, the tour goes through **Hunkon Sofrası,** where the sultan and his esteemed guests delighted in watching belly dancers and tumbling midgets (who lived in the Harem Dwarves' Dormitories). The decor here is eclectic to say the least, with İznik, Ming, and Rococo influences all cluttered together. As is typical of Ottoman palace playrooms, the balcony on the far side of the room was for the orchestra.

THE FOURTH COURT. Three passageways lead into the fourth and final palace courtyard. It was among these pavilions, gardens, and fountains that the (in)famous merriments and sordid garden parties of the Tulip Period took place (see **Troubles at Home, Troubles Abroad,** p. 13). Directly in front of the covered entrance to the courtyard, the **Tulip Garden** is now filled with other flowers in well-manicured plots. The courtyard's main attraction is the broad marble terrace with a large central pool and fountain around which the Baghdad, Revan, and Sünnet *kiöşk*s stand. From here you can take in the uninterrupted breathtaking vistas of the Sea of Marmara and the Bosphorus.

The İznik-tiled **Revan Pavilion,** the first room at the top of the stairs to the terrace, was built in 1635 to commemorate Sultan Murat IV's Revan campaign in Iran. The back wall of the Pavilion of the Holy Relics, adjacent to the Revan Pavilion, features a sampler of further 15th-century İznik tiles. At the other end of the portico is the **Circumcision Room,** an octagonal chamber that overhangs the edge of the pavilion, built by Ibrahim the Mad. Young princes would be clipped into adulthood in this chamber lined with beautiful (and easy to clean) İznik tiles, including panels with white- and tomato-colored flowers ascending on a blue background (as opposed to the more typical blue flowers on white background). The golden canopy overlooking the Sea of Marmara is the **İftariye Köşku,** also built by İbrahim the Mad. It was before these beautiful views that İbrahim and his successors broke the

Ramazan fast after sunset. At the far end of the L-shaped terrace stands the **Bağdat Köşku,** Murat I's monument to his capture of Baghdad in 1638. Inside, identical stained-glass windows, matching carpets, and identically paneled doors create an astounding example of radial symmetry. The symmetry is said to be such that if you were to close the door and spin around, you would forget which door you entered through.

THE ARCHAEOLOGICAL MUSEUM COMPLEX

The museum complex lies through the gate marked "Archaeological Museums," about 100m downhill from the palace's first courtyard. When the Topkapı Palace is closed, it is possible to enter through Gülhane Park, where a separate road next to the park ticket booths leads to the museum complex. A single ticket theoretically gets you into all 3 museums, although one or another is often closed at any given time. Museum complex open Tu-Su 9:30am-5pm. $5.

TILED PAVILION (ÇİNLİ KÖŞK). The tiled pavilion was built in 1472 by Mehmet the Conqueror to view the athletic competitions below. Originally covered from floor to ceiling in İznik tiles, the sultan's superbox suffered fire and an earthquake which destroyed much of the original *faïence*. The opulent fountain tucked in the corner of the room, off to the right as you enter the *köşk*, is still fringed by its original, delicately patterned İznik tiles. The display covers the full spectrum of Ottoman tilemaking, including some rare early İznik tiles.

THE MUSEUM OF THE ANCIENT ORIENT. This smaller cement building adjacent to the Tiled Pavilion houses treasures so rare that the museum seems reluctant to let anyone see them. Should you have the luck to arrive when it's open, you can expect to find an excellent collection of large stone artifacts from Anatolia, Mesopotamia, and Egypt, dating from the 1st and 2nd millennia BC. The pride of this museum is the **Treaty of Kadesh,** the world's oldest-known written treaty, drafted after a battle between Ramses II of Egypt and the Hittite King Muvatellish ended in a stalemate. A copy of this document graces the entrance to the United Nations.

THE ARCHAEOLOGY MUSEUM (ARKEOLOJİ MUZESİ). Though cursed with an unfortunately generic name, the Archaeology Museum contains one of the world's great collections of Classical and Hellenic art. Built in the middle of the 19th century, the treasures inside were organized into a coherent collection under the curatorship of Ottoman archaeologist Osman Hamdi Bey. To the right of the museum's entrance stands a copy of the famous **tear column** in the Yerebatan Cistern, though this one lacks the original's green algae. To the left of the entrance is a couple of **Roman sarcophagi,** noteworthy for their distinct seals showing a letter "p" superimposed on an "x." The two Greek letters, "chi" and "rho," are the first two letters in Jesus' name. The symbol was an early Christian icon.

In the room directly in front of the entrance stands a great statue of **Beş,** the demigod of inexhaustible strength. Heading right leads through the evolution of classical statuary. You can get a good sense of Roman imperial hubris by noticing the heightened similarities between the busts of the Caesars and those of Heracles and Alexander the Great. In the last room of the section are some immense sculptures of Roman gods, including an gigantic statue of Zeus from the 2nd century BC and a well-preserved statue of Oceanus, god of the rivers. From the entrance, a left turn leads to the **Sidon Sarcophagi** section. Excavated by the same Osman Hamdi Bey, the Sidon Sarcophagi are among the most important archaeological finds of all time. Eighteen sarcophagi were found in the royal necropolis of Sidon in Lebanon, and though seven were left in the tomb for various reasons, the remaining 11 were all brought back to İstanbul. The pieces date from the 6th to 4th centuries BC. In the second room of the Sidon Hall rests the **Alexander Sarcophagus.** Modeled on a Greek temple and covered with intricate carvings, the tomb actually holds the Sidonese king Abdalonymous. As a peripheral member of the Sidonese royal family, Abdalonymous was constantly aware that he owed his position to Alexander. His sarcophagus, created long before his death, is an attempt to legitimize his rule through association with Alexander and the kingly sport of lion-hunting.

Follow the stairs to the **"İstanbul Through the Ages"** and the **"Ancient Turkey"** exhibits, the former the winner of a European Museum award. The well-explained İstanbul exhibit describes the city's history from the Bronze Age to the last few centuries. The Ancient Turkey exhibit has artifacts from Troy, made a lot more interesting by the background **movie** (at 10, 11:30am, 1:30, and 3:30pm).

GRAND BAZAAR AND ENVIRONS

To reach the bazaar from Sultanahmet, follow the tram tracks toward Aksaray for five minutes until you see the Nuruosmanıye Camii on the right. Walk down Vezirhanı Cad. for one block, keeping the mosque on your left. Follow the crowds left into the bazaar (www.grand-bazaar.com.). Open M-Sa 9am-7pm. A small number of stores tend to close an hour or two before the rest of the bazaar.

Consisting of over 4000 shops, several banks, mosques, police stations, fountains, and restaurants, the enormous **Grand Bazaar** (*Kapalı Çarşısı*, "covered bazaar") could be a city in itself. Now the largest of its kind in the world, the Grand Bazaar began in 1461 as a modest affair during the reign of Mehmet the Conqueror. Today, the enormous Kapalı Çarşısı forms the entrance to the mercantile sprawl that starts at Çemberlitaş and covers the hill down to Eminönü, ending at the **Egyptian Spice Bazaar** (*Mısır Çarşısı*) and the Golden Horn waterfront. This chaotic, labyrinthine world combines all the best and worst of shopping in Turkey. Though the bazaar is loosely organized according to specific themes, much of it is a jumble of shops selling hookah pipes, bright baubles, copper filigree shovels, Byzantine-style icons on red velvet, Turkish daggers, embroidered pillows, carpets, amber jewelry, silver flintlock guns with mother-of-pearl handles, musical instruments, chess sets, hand puppets, ornaments, and the ubiquitous evil-eye keychains. Through banter and barter, haggle and hassle, a day spent at the Kapalı Çarşısı is bound to tempt and tantalize even the most experienced traveler.

Navigating through the corridors of the Kapalı Çarşısı is no easy task. There are street signs to help you find your way, but unless you're looking for a particular item, you might want to surrender yourself to the pandemonium and simply wander among the merchants' calls. But don't despair—in the event that you have limited time or specific interests, there is some method to the madness. If you enter through the **Nuruosmaniye Kapısı,** the gate near the Çemberlitaş tram stop, you will find yourself on **Kalpakçılarbaşı Cad.,** the goldsellers' avenue that forms the primary east-west spine of the market. The street is lined with jewelers and gold merchants until it opens out onto the **Beyazıt Kapısı,** the gate near the Beyazıt tram stop. The **Kürkçüler Kapısı,** the entrance off Beyazıt Square, feeds into **Kürkçüler Çarşısı,** a giant leather goods bazaar. Takkeciler Cad. and Kuyumcalar Cad. are the main streets running perpendicular to Kalpakçılarbaşı Cad., and also frame the **Old Bazaar,** which holds most of the bazaar's old silver and valuable antiquities. The Old Bazaar begins two blocks below Kalpakçılarbaşı Cad., its entrances marked by painted metal signs, some wrapped in broken, colored light bulbs. The gold merchants continue on Kuyumcalar, but fine carpets can be found on Takkecelir Cad. as well as the two other streets that wrap around the Old Bazaar.

Around the outside of the bazaar are other interesting opportunities to browse, explore, and empty your pockets. **Fesciler Kapısı,** like both the Beyazıt and Yorguncılar gates, opens onto the open-air clothing market. The market runs along the outside of the bazaar's western wall and is close to the **Sahaflar Çarşısı,** the antique book bazaar. A wide selection of books is available here, along with Koranic inscriptions and university texts. The majority of the books are Turkish, but the few English titles are absolute bargains, starting at about $1 for new paperbacks. When walking out of the Fesciler Kapısı, turn right to find the books. The entrance is just a few meters down on the left. Opposite the book market stands the huge entrance gate of **İstanbul University** (see **Beyazıt,** p. 112). The **Çarşıkapı** entrance, facing Divan Yolu, leads out onto Yağlıkçılar Cad., where ceramics are sold.

OTHER SULTANAHMET MUSEUMS

■**MUSEUM OF TURKISH AND ISLAMIC ART (İBRAHİM PAŞA SARAYI).** This superb museum, housed in the palace of Süleyman the Magnificent's Grand Vizier, features a large Islamic art collection organized by period (see **Islamic Art and Architecture,** p. 22). One of the foremost museums of its kind in the world, the museum houses over 40,000 pieces of art, covering nearly every period in Islamic art. The museum's main wing consists of a long hall with stone artifacts from the early Islamic world, cases of ceramics, carpets, and silver displays. Off the hall lie rooms containing works from specific periods in Islamic and urban development. Among these, the Selçuk exhibits and the Ottoman calligraphy display with *tuğras* (seals) of various Ottoman sultans are particularly impressive. This main corridor leads into what was the palace's **Great Hall,** which features a well-lit, genuinely interesting collection of old carpets in decent repair, explained by plaques detailing the origins of certain patterns and motifs. Admire the Koran stands and beautiful, handwritten copies of the Koran itself. The Great Hall leads outside into a courtyard that also features a tea garden serving *çay* ($.75) and pastries ($2). From here you can see the modern steel and glass renovations that somehow complement the original red brick structure. Off the courtyard is the newly opened ethnographic wing. The exhibit provides detailed displays of Turkish life and artistic techniques from various time periods. Life-size dioramas include Anatolian village life and 19th-century İstanbul interiors, both clearly explained. *(Museum and cafe open Tu-Su 9:30am-4:30pm. $2, students $1.20.)*

YEREBATAN SARAYI (UNDERGROUND CISTERN). This subterranean "palace" is actually a vast cavern whose shallow water eerily reflects the images of its 336 supporting columns, all illuminated by pulsating colored lighting. The echoing sounds of constantly dripping water and the muted strains of classical tunes will accompany your stroll across the elevated wooden walkways. Watch your step: dripping water makes the floor slippery. Don't miss the pair of columns in the far corner, whose pedestals are a pair of giant **Medusa heads.** Underground walkways originally linked the cistern to Topkapı Palace, but they were blocked to curb rampant trafficking of stolen goods and abducted women. This was also the site of one of the battles between Mahmut II's forces and the Janissaries at the time of the Auspicious Event (see **The 19th Century: Reform and Reaction,** p. 14). The cistern is used as the backdrop for various art exhibitions, and the cafe near the exit has a small stage on which local actors perform. Check with the tourist office for show information. At the top of the exit stairs you'll find a small but well-stocked bookstore. Though expensive, the shop has many English-language books on history, poetry, and Islamic art. *(As you stand with your back to Aya Sofia, the entrance is about 175m from the mosque in the small stone kiosk on the left hand side of Yerebatan Cad. Open daily 9:30am-5:30pm. $4, students $3.25.)*

THE MOSAIC MUSEUM. On the site of Emperor Justinian's palace, this museum displays the mosaic from the palace's main hall. Plaques on the wall provide a detailed history of the mosaic, originally laid as a decorative pavement in the palace's main space. The tiles depict nature scenes, hunting, and traditional legends. To get a good look, walk left around the viewing balcony when you enter and pay attention to the explanatory notes along the wall. *(From the exit of the Blue Mosque, walk out into Sultanahmet Sq., turn right, and look for the sign for Arasta Bazaar and the museum. The entrance is on the street side of the carpet bazaar. Open Tu-Su 9:30am-4:30pm. $1.75.)*

THE CARPET MUSEUM. Strictly for hard-core carpet enthusiasts, this small, dimly lit facility displays four centuries' worth of worn-out carpets from all over the Muslim world. With very few display plaques explaining the importance of each carpet fragment, only those with knowledge of the history of Turkish carpets and *kilims* will enjoy this one. The museum serves primarily to lure unwitting tourists to the cluster of carpet shops nearby. Be warned: the dealers here are notorious for overcharging. *(At the exit from the Blue Mosque, a ramp about 20m to the right leads up to the museum. Open M-Sa 9am-noon, 1-4pm. $2, students $1.)*

İSTANBUL

SOUTH OF THE GOLDEN HORN

BEYAZIT

Divan Yolu Caddesi., the Ottoman processional avenue, leads from Sultanahmet to Beyazıt Meydanı, Beyazıt's main square. A large student district, Beyazıt is home to İstanbul University's main campus and the magnificent Süleymaniye Camii.

ALONG DİVAN YOLU. Walking down the tram line along Divan Yolu from Sultanahmet to Beyazıt, you will pass a number of historical tombs, small graveyards and charming rose-filled tea gardens. The tomb of **Sultan Mahmud II** is housed in a block-long marble structure right before the Çemberlitaş Hamamı (see **Hamams,** p. 131). Although simple compared to earlier burial sanctuaries, the tomb is an example of Ottoman design near the end of the empire. *(Donation required. Dress appropriately.)* The **Press Museum (Basım Müzesi),** displays massive printing presses from Turkey's 100 years of modern publishing history. On the 2nd floor, the **Katta Sanat Gallery** highlights artwork and handicrafts from contemporary Turkish artists. The gallery often displays work by both local youth and serious university students. *(84 Divan Yolu Cad. ☎ 513 84 58. Free.)* Follow Divan Yolu Cad. to the **Tomb of Sinan Paşa,** and pay tribute to the Ottoman Grand Vizier by drinking a cup of *çay* in the adjoining tea garden. Move from caffeine to nicotine at the **Çorlulu Alipaşa Medresesi,** a Koranic school-turned-shopping complex where *nargile* pipes can be smoked in a co-ed environment.

BEYAZIT SQUARE. Continuing along the tram line brings you to the Beyazıt tram stop. On the right sidewalk, amid jewelry and soccer clothing stalls, are the stone stairs up to the large cobblestoned expanse of Beyazıt Meydanı (Beyazıt Square). You can also continue past this small path to the square's main stairs a few meters up the road. The square is full of pigeons, fed by the tourists and young kids who purchase small tins of seed from old men and women around the square ($.10). There are a number of places to go off the square, beginning with the **Calligraphy Museum** to the left of the main stairs. Located in an old *medrese*, the museum houses a collection of *tuğra*s (embellished royal seals) and Korans. Small and dimly lit to preserve the artwork, the museum contains a smaller and older collection than that of the İbrahim Paşa Sarayı (see **Museum of Turkish and Islamic Art,** p. 111). The Calligraphy Museum's permanent collection is primarily from the 13th century, but it also houses temporary exhibits by local artists. On a sunny day of walking, the museum also offers a cool respite, and the inner courtyard has a beautiful garden with benches. *(Open Tu-Sa 9am-4pm. $1.50, students $1.)*

BEYAZIT CAMİİ. Opposite the museum, on the right side of the square, Beyazıt Camii, commissioned by Sultan Beyazıt II (1481-1512), offers a good example of the pre-*faïence* period of Ottoman mosque decoration. It also provides a barricade-free opportunity to view one of the oldest standing Imperial mosques in its entirety. Enter the courtyard used for washing up before prayer and take a right, walking around the *şadirvan* to enter the mosque. Though the door is usually covered by a heavy green curtain in the day, the mosque is still open, and the curtain is easily pushed aside. The adjoining courtyard, located in the perpetual shade of the mosque, is popular with bead sellers, young men hawking cellular phones, students, and *çay*-drinkers. On the right side as you move toward the used book bazaar is the **Tomb of Sultan Beyazıt II** (1481-1512). The tomb itself is underwhelming, with only a solitary casket and a painted dome. *(Open Tu-Su 9:30am-4:30pm.)*

İSTANBUL UNIVERSITY. The entrance to İstanbul University, to the left of Beyazıt Camii, is a massive arch embellished with gold calligraphy against a deep green background. Originally, a wooden statue of an artillery piece stood guard over the small ridge leading up to the entrance. Nowadays, riot police take up this position since the university is a hotbed of both Muslim and secular student activism, which occasionally flares up into large, violent demonstrations. Protests and riots, when they do happen, generally occur on Friday afternoons, immediately after

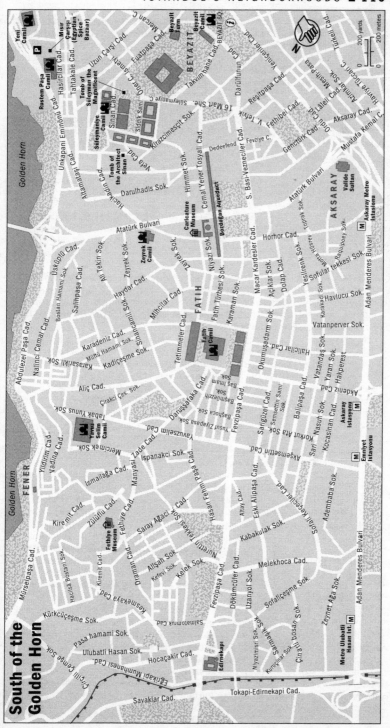

İSTANBUL

prayers. Guards at the gate check IDs, but an ISIC should be more than sufficient. The main entrance leads to a long, tree-canopied driveway flanked by a forested park that is frequented by young couples and the occasional stray dog looking for a cool place to sleep. In the center of the main walkway and directly in front of the main campus building, a statue of Atatürk in all his glory points out the path of knowledge to a rather muscular male flag bearer and a female torch bearer. To the right of the Atatürk statue is the **Beyazıt Tower,** which serves as a lookout and meteorological station. The building's somber façade reflects its original use as a part of the Ministry of War during the late Ottoman period. Follow the path around to the right to the only public basketball court for miles around. You'll eventually come to a park where students gather to smoke and eat. *(Do not attempt to go in the main campus building without a student escort, since students themselves must pass through metal detectors to enter the building, and the guards are less than friendly.)*

SÜLEYMANİYE KÜLLİYESİ (SÜLEYMANİYE COMPLEX)

From the university, head out the northwest gate and take a right on to Besim Omar Paşa Cad. Follow that past the painted walls of the grammar school and take another right when the street ends onto Süleymaniye Cad. Walk straight. From Sultanahmet, either walk along the tramvay (15min.) or take the tramvay to the "Üniversite" stop, walk across the square, and take Besim Ömer Paşa Cad. past the walls of the university to Süleymaniye Cad. Open Tu-Su 9:30am-4:30pm, except during prayers.

To the north of İstanbul University sits the massive and elegant **Süleymaniye Camii,** one of architect Sinan's two great masterpieces. The other is Selimiye Camii in Edirne (see p. 142). Süleyman was a great lawmaker and one of the Ottoman Empire's greatest leaders, who more than doubled the size of the empire (see **How Süleyman the Magnificent Got His Name,** p. 13).

The Süleymaniye Camii is part of a larger **külliye** (complex), which includes **tombs,** an **imaret** (soup kitchen), and several **medreses** (Islamic schools). The mosque's charitable and educational institutions served as an integral part of both the complex and everyday life (see **Ottoman Architecture,** p. 23). Prof. Sıddık Sami Onar Sok. runs between the university and the mosque. The street was formerly known as Tıryakı Çarşısı (The Addicts' Market), after the once-flourishing hashish trade. An entrance on S.S. Onar Sok. leads into the royal cemeteries, where each person has two tombstones: one for the body and one for the soul, with cylindrical-shaped tombstones for men and board-like tombstones edged with flowers for women. Passing through the graveyard brings you to the similarly decorated **royal tombs** of Süleyman I and his wife, Haseki Hürrem. Süleyman's tomb incorporates all three of Sinan's decorative signatures: İznik tiles, stained glass, and painted patterns. The tomb is a superb example of the Ottoman integration of these three elements; fans of İznik tile will appreciate the band of deep blue tile with calligraphy tracing the middle of the room. *(Open Tu-Su 9:30am-4:30pm. Donation required.)*

Walk along the Süleymaniye Camii's southwest side to the large arch just below the dome. With three columns of honeycomb windows, this arch mirrors those of Aya Sofia. Enter the mosque's central courtyard through the smaller tourist entrance to the left of the main door. Sinan used balconied minarets attached to the main part of the mosque to mark the corners of this courtyard. Columns made from the stones of the royal box at the Hippodrome (see **The Hippodrome** and **The Museum of Turkish and Islamic Art,** p. 103) support the courtyard's 24 domes.

In the spirit of Aya Sofia, the mosque's main attraction is its vast space. The impression of perfect proportions is no accident: the height of the dome (53m) is exactly twice the length of the mosque's walls. The arches' red and white stones highlight their vast size and draw attention to the lines of the dome. The stained-glass windows are the work of the master **Sarhoş İbrahim** (İbrahim the Drunkard), whose great skill, reflected in his exquisite windows, must have surpassed his vice. The area around the *mihrab* showcases Sinan's first experiment with İznik tile decoration. The wooden lattice curtain in the back left side of the mosque marks off the section where women recite their prayers.

Pick up your shoes on the way out of the mosque, turn right through the gardens along the outside of the courtyard, and, turning left, exit onto Şifhane Sok. **Sinan's Tomb** can be reached by following Şifhane Sok. past the excellent restaurant Dârüzziyâfe (see **Food: Sultanahmet,** p. 98), to the intersection with Mimar Sinan Cad. The architect's modest tomb is overshadowed by a neighboring **playground.**

The **Süleyman Library** is located behind the busy cafes along the Prof. Sıddık Sami Onal Cad. Originally built by Sinan to store all the old texts scattered throughout the city, the library now stores ancient texts on microfilm.

ZEYREK

Zeyrek and Şehzadebaşı, two neighborhoods located at either end of the **Aqueduct of Valens** and separated by Atatürk Cad., mark the beginning of greater Fatih, the religiously conservative quarter of İstanbul. Any bus heading from Aksaray to destinations on the Taksim side of the Golden Horn stops at the top of the hill right before the aqueduct at Şehzadebaşı, in front of the broad **İstanbul City Hall.** Buses stop again immediately after the aqueduct. From Sultanahmet and any other part of the old city, take the tram to the Lâleli stop (one after the University), continue walking along the tracks, and turn right before the large overpass of Atatürk Cad.

Stretching from Fatih to Beyazıt, the **aqueduct** was built in the 4th century to augment the Roman water system running from the Belgrade forest. Diligent maintenance by emperors and sultans kept it in use for 1500 years before it fell into disrepair. Although its brick façade has chipped and faded over the millennia, it still rises high above the surrounding neighborhood as traffic zips through its central arches. When facing the Atatürk bridge and the Golden Horn, the neighborhood on the left side of the street is **Zeyrek,** a conservative Muslim district of İstanbul that is also one of the city's major meat processing areas. Sides of lamb, big buckets of tripe, chickens naked of head and feathers, and kebap are displayed in the windows of butcher shops along İtfaiye Bul. (Fire Station St.), the main street which connects the neighborhood's sights. The area of Zeyrek that's worth seeing weaves in and out of the shade of the aqueduct and the buildings nearby.

Starting from the City Hall, cross Atatürk Bul. and head right toward the aqueduct and through the lovely little **Saraçhane Park.** The Fatih monument stands on the right-hand side of the park. This bronze **statue of Sultan Mehmet II** (a.k.a. Fatih) astride a leaping horse is flanked on either side by scholars and a group of Janissaries (see p. 12) with their feet firmly planted on the ground. Housed in the Ganzafer Medrese, which presses up against the aqueduct, the **Karikator ve Mizah Müzesi** (Caricature Museum) is one of the city's more delightful small museums. It can be reached by following Atatürk Cad. under the aqueduct and taking the first left onto Kovacılar Sok. The museum is immediately on the left. The first section exhibits Turkey's more venerated comics from the 50s until the present day, such as *Dolmuş, Girgir, Avni,* and *Nasreddin Hoca* (see **Wise Ass,** p. 346). The collection also contains a number of politically oriented panels from both the Ottoman and Young Turk periods (see **The Young Turks and World War I,** p. 15). Also featured are some rare, less-than-flattering strips of Mustafa Kemal (see p. 16) before his glory days. (✆ 521 12 64. Open daily 9am-4pm. Free.)

FATİH

Fatih, meaning "the conqueror" in Turkish (and an anagram for "faith"), is an enclave of strict Muslim conservatism surrounded on all sides by secular, modern İstanbul. As such, it's a pretty insular community, holding fast to such Muslim traditions as full *chador* with head scarves for women and wool caps and beards for men, earning it the nickname *Küçük Iran* (little Iran). Tourists need only take the usual steps to cover up—no shorts, long sleeves for women, etc. Fatih is also a stronghold of the **Fazilet Party,** Turkey's most Islamic-leaning Party. Fazilet, like the banned Welfare Party before it (see p. 19), has been trying to boost its image through its community's success—there is low crime, good trash collection, and a cleanliness that contrasts with that of its northern neighbors, Fener and Balat (see

The Here and Now, p. 19). Tourists are rarely targeted here for moneymaking schemes, and street merchants sell prayer beads, wool caps for men, and copies of the Koran. The walk up to Yavuz Selim Camii passes through the district of **Çarşamba** (Wednesday), named after the **market** that fills these streets on, uh, Wednesdays. It's a shopping experience far more vivid and authentic than anything at the Grand Bazaar or the Egyptian Spice Bazaar. Fatih is easily reached by a westward walk on Şehzadebaşı Cad. (which turns into Macar Kardeşler Cad. once over Atatürk Cad. and then changes names again to Fevsi Paşa Cad. when the road reaches the mosque complex) or a Fatih-bound bus from Aksaray.

FATİH CAMİİ. With its high walls and tree-lined entrance boulevard, Fatih Camii serves as the hub of the community. Unlike İstanbul's other great mosques, which often lie dormant outside prayer times, Fatih Camii still functions as the primary meeting place and social center of the neighborhood. Kids run free on the wide walkways that surround the mosque on all sides, flying kites or kicking around a soccer ball with friends while old men, resting with prayer beads, watch from seats along the walls. The stunning mosque was built in 1463, completely destroyed by an earthquake in 1766, and rebuilt according to the original design, though the interior remains unfinished. While the mosque's outer precincts can be easily visited and explored, visiting the inside requires appropriate clothing and a spot of patience close to prayer times, as the mosque is often full of worshippers. Once inside, however, the mosque is an airy, open, colorful space. Stained glass windows look more like intricately cut mosaics, their small panes winding a wall of design around the *mihrab*. The four corners at the base of the dome have been newly painted, with similar intertwinings of blue, green, vermilion, and a deep orange. *(Open Tu-Su 9am-5:30pm. Donations encouraged.)*

YAVUZ SELİM CAMİİ. Named in honor of Sultan Selim the Grim, Yavuz Selim Camii is Fatih's other impressive mosque. When approached from the west, it dominates the view for several hundred meters. Although renovations are afoot, there is nothing new to see on the inside. The **tomb of Selim the Grim** is frequented by local visitors coming to pray and leave beads in memory of the sultan. Nicknamed "the Grim" for his fierceness and military success, Selim paved the way for Ottoman guardianship of the three holy cities of Islam. The giant, rectangular hole in the ground in front of the mosque is the last remnant of the **Cistern of Aspar,** one of the city's three Byzantine reservoirs. Formerly a squatter village and shantytown, the reservoir has been converted into basketball and tennis courts with a couple of soccer fields on the far side. *(The mosque, tomb, and cistern lie northwest of Fatih Camii and can be easily reached from there by following Fevzi Paşa Cad. (formerly Kardeşler Cad., né Şehzadebaşı Cad.) west (uphill) and then turning right on Yavuz Selim Cad. Tomb open Tu-Su 9:30am-4:30pm. Donation suggested; $.20 may be required.)*

AKSARAY-LÂLELİ

If you come to İstanbul from Europe, or vice versa, you are bound to encounter this bustling section of the old city, since it's a major bus hub and the departure point for the otogar-bound subway. Its streets are lined with display windows, and its sidewalks are full of merchants on the prowl for stragglers looking to buy. The neighborhood is a shopper's paradise for those in the market for leather jackets or *Nataşas* (see p. 400). Incidentally, it also has a very large Bulgarian and Russian community. Consequently, many of the signs and advertisements are written in Cyrillic. Stores cater to Russian and Eastern European clothing manufacturers who buy Turkish leather and fabrics to import back home, but you can find anything here among the hodgepodge of happy capitalists. At night the area is one of İstanbul's centers of prostitution, and its small back streets, windows covered with dark iron shutters, ought to be walked with caution.

Despite its seedier side, the Aksaray-Lâleli area, like most of İstanbul, is safe during the day, with two attractive mosques. **Kalenderhane Camii,** formerly the Byzantine **Church of Kyriotissa,** is a 9th-century church converted first into a monastery by the Kalender dervishes and subsequently into a mosque. Although it sits unadorned and aging on the outside, the interior is striking in its gray and pink marble simplicity. *(From the "Üniversite" tram stop, walk 20m or so downhill along Ordu Cad., take the 1st right after the tram platform onto Büyük Reşit Paşa Cad., walk past the university, and then make a slight right onto Kalender Camii Sok., from where you can see the mosque.)* **Lâleli Camii,** downhill along Ordu Cad. from the "Üniversite" tram stop, also lies immediately next to the "Lâleli" tram stop. This classical Ottoman mosque has a covered **bazaar** *(arasta)* below. Light filtering in from the large windows around the dome creates a particularly dramatic effect. The **tomb of Sultan Mustafa III,** who commanded the mosque's construction, lies at street level near the entrance to the bazaar. This market is much smaller than the Grand Bazaar, and it sells mostly clothing for local shoppers. Look for a cafe downstairs.

EMİNÖNÜ

Alive with the bustle and energy of commerce, Eminönü might be called the home of the real Grand Bazaar. To reach Eminönü from Sultanahmet, head through the northern exits of the Grand Bazaar and downhill through narrow, hawker-lined streets or take the convenient Zeytinburnu-Eminönü tram to the end of the line. From Taksim, take any bus marked Eminönü, or take the trolley that runs along İstiklâl Cad. down to the end of the line, hop on the one-stop metro and walk across Galata Bridge into the heart of the neighborhood.

Pigeons, buses, and people swarm the waterfront area. With traffic flying down Kennedy Cad. on one side and the busy port on the other, Eminönü's winding merchant strip can be overwhelming. Watch yourself and your wallet. With your back to the water, Eminönü's three major attractions are, from left to right, Yeni Camii, the *Mısır Çarşısı* (Egyptian Spice Bazaar), and Rüstem Paşa Camii.

YENİ CAMİİ. Home to tens of thousands of pigeons, Yeni Camii was the last Imperial Classical mosque built by the Ottomans. It is considered to be of lesser quality than some of İstanbul's grander mosques since its tiles are not from İznik and its architect wasn't Sinan. However, for the non-expert, the color and quantity of tiles along the *mihrab* and the *minber* are still impressive. On Fridays at 1pm, the most important Muslim prayers of the week crowd the Yeni Camii so much that worshippers congregate on the stairs to pray. While tourists are not allowed to enter the mosque during prayer time, this overspill provides a good opportunity to observe unobtrusively the recitation of Muslim prayers.

MISIR ÇARŞISI. Sacrelicious odors from the *Mısır Çarşısı* (Egyptian Spice Bazaar) may distract you from the mosque. On your way there, exit west from the mosque into Eminönü Square, where you can buy a saucer of birdseed (\$.10) from a vendor and experience Hitchcockian fear while the pigeon flocks move in. A stroll through the Mısır Çarşısı's halls is always a sensory overload and one of the most memorable ways to spend an İstanbulian hour or two. The bazaar once handled customs and excise taxes, but today the 80 or so vendors in the L-shaped building sell a mind-boggling array of spices, gold, tea, sticky sweets, honeycombs, nuts, dried fruit, some ▨ natural Turkish Viagra, and a bit of unlicensed soccer team merchandise. The bazaar's high-vaulted ceilings, saffron and curry-scented air, and relative lack of tourist-related merchandise, lend it an atmosphere more authentic than that of the Grand Bazaar. Vendors even give away free samples. If you are looking for a bite to eat, **Pandeli Restaurant** (p. 99) sits at the far end of one hallway, right above the seaside entrance.

RÜSTEM PAŞA CAMİİ. Leaving the Spice Bazaar by the waterfront entrance and turning left leads you back to Eminönü Square and the small but breathtaking Rüstem Paşa Camii. Designed by the illustrious Mimar Sinan, the mosque was constructed in 1561 at the behest of Rüstem, a Grand Vizier. Stunningly beautiful tiles arranged in rare circular patterns, said to be among İznik's finest, cover practically every surface. The unique main entrance features a nested arch design showcasing all the basic arch forms found in Islamic architecture: first a normal shallow cusp

İSTANBUL

shape, then a tulip shape, and finally a circular shape. Another attractive aspect of the mosque is its small size. Because of the limited space, there is no roped-off section for tourists, so have a close look at the İznik tiles that are more accessible than those in the larger mosques. (*Either cut a path through the densely populated bazaar or walk along Reşadiye Cad.—the entrance is on the far side of the mosque, down a small alley. Be on the lookout for a gate marked "Rüstem Paşa Kapısı," through which stairs lead to the mosque. The tourist entrance is to the left of a small courtyard that faces the main entrance.*)

FENER AND BALAT

When advancing his original plan for the attack on the Dardanelles, Winston Churchill asked the war cabinet to imagine the confusion and terror that would fill the "tumbledown wooden houses and narrow cobblestone streets of the Golden Horn" at the sight of British warships. Though most of İstanbul has been developed, paved and concreted in the post-war 20th century, Fener and Balat have retained some of this pre-modern sprawl. İstanbul's Greek and Jewish neighborhoods preserve the look and feel of a town from the 1800s, and despite ramshackle cement houses, the narrow old cobblestone streets remain. There's a definite sense of melancholy and emptiness here, as the last flickering embers of a once thriving Greek and Jewish community appear to be dying out.

The easiest way to see Fener and Balat is to take a bus from Eminönü to Unkapanı (a stop on Abdülezel Cad., the wide road that runs along the Golden Horn). Unkapanı-bound buses leave from the Eminönü bus stop. From the Unkapanı bus stop, **Gül Camii** (Church of St. Theodosia) can be reached by continuing along Abdülezel Cad. for 300m in the same direction as the bus and then turning left onto Kara Sarıklı Cad. After this, take the second left and then the second right (the streets are unmarked) up the stairs to the mosque. The 12th-century Greek Orthodox church earned its name, Gül (Rose) Camii, in 1453, when the soldiers of Mehmet's army entered the church and found it strewn with roses. The mosque is usually open only for prayers, but the staff can open it for visitors at other times. About 500m farther up Abdülezel Cad. lies the **Greek Orthodox Patriarchate of Phanar.** "Phanar," as Fener was once known, derives from the Phanariots, a group of wealthy Greek families that lived in the area and served as prominent advisors and administrators in the Ottoman Empire. These rather modest buildings are in fact the Orthodox Christian church's equivalent to the Vatican; the church's patriarchs preside from here. It was also here that the Greek War of Independence began, when the Ottomans hanged patriarch Gregory V in front of the church's gates. Unfortunately, the church and its dependent buildings are generally closed to casual visitors. About 300m past the patriarchate, **St. Stephen of the Bulgurs** is sandwiched between the two roads as the highway splits in two. The church's shiny, magic-castle appearance comes from its completely cast-iron construction.

From the Bulgarian church, **Balat,** the city's Jewish quarter, is only 300m ahead and inland. In marked contrast with Turkey's Greek community, which has had a sometimes difficult relationship with the outside, Jews have always received hospitable treatment. Fleeing persecution during the 1492 Spanish Inquisition, Spanish Jews were encouraged by Beyazıt II to settle in İstanbul (see **Jews,** p. 31). Çincınlı Cad. branches off of Demirhisar Cad. (the continuation of the shoreline road) and leads to the 500-year-old **Ahvida Synagogue,** the city's oldest synagogue.

EYÜP

At the far western end of the Golden Horn lies the necropolis of Eyüp, a major Muslim pilgrimage site with added significance for Turkish Muslims. It was here that Eyüp (Job), a companion of the Prophet Muhammed, died in battle during the first Arab siege of Constantinople. When Eyüp's tomb was rediscovered after the Ottoman conquest, Fatih Mehmet had a mausoleum and mosque complex built on the site. Modern Eyüp is synonymous with religious ceremony. Young boys are brought here, accompanied by their celebrating families, for a final prayer before circumcision. The hills overlooking the city are thick with the turban-capped headstones of Ottoman graves, and smaller mausolea line the streets near the two main mosques. It is considered a great privilege to be buried in Eyüp. Numerous prayer bead shops and stores specializing in Korans surround the complex.

EYÜP CAMİİ AND THE TOMB OF EYÜP. Eyüp's primary attraction, Eyüp Camii is the second mosque to grace the site. It dates from 1800, after the one built by Fatih collapsed. With a Baroque exterior and gobs of gold on the inside, its excess is characteristic of later Ottoman art. A long line of the soon-to-be-circumcised boys and their fathers often forms before the *mihrab*, as they wait to pray in this choice spot. The boys wear satin capes of blue and white, detailed in gold sequin and a regal plumed hat. After reading *"Maşallah,"* they usually pose for pictures in front of the tomb or in the mosque itself. Directly across from the mosque, in the **Tomb of Eyüp**, lavishly sheathed in İznik tiles and spookily lit in an emerald green light, rests a very large footprint of Muhammed. Women should wear head scarves, long sleeves, and long skirts. *(Tomb open daily, no hours posted. Free.)*

CAMİİ KEBIR AND THE NECROPOLIS. Camii Kebir, the cobblestone street heading from Eyüp to the Golden Horn and the ferry stop, is the main thoroughfare of the old necropolis. Numerous domed mausolea line the street on either side. Regrettably, only the **tombs of Sokollu Mehmet Paşa** and **Siyavus Paşa** are open to the public. The former is the more impressive, with deftly crafted stained glass typical of some of Sinan's other works. The excellent İznik panels of Siyavus Paşa's tomb feature an intense, earthen-red hue that modern synthetic dyes have been unable to reproduce. *(Necropolis open Tu-Su 9:30am-4:30pm. Donations encouraged.)*

PIERRE LOTI CAFE. During the very end of the Ottoman period, Eyüp had a large community of artists and writers. The most famous was the French novelist and travel writer **Pierre Loti,** a.k.a. Julian Marie Viaud (1850-1923). His Orientalist romance *Aziyade* tells the story of the tragic love affair between a young and daring Loti and a married harem woman during the Ottoman Empire's last days. The Turkophile opened up a coffeehouse on the hill overlooking the Golden Horn. This cafe, reached via a web of winding cobblestone roads, happily capitalizes on its famous associations. From the tiny tables at this graveyard perch the view extends all the way to the Süleymaniye Camii and Beyazıt tower at İstanbul University. The tea ($.60) and coffee are great. An adjacent gift shop is the only place in İstanbul where the prices are listed in French francs. *(To get there from the Eyüp bus or the ferry stop, walk away from the Golden Horn along Camii Kebir Sok. until it turns into another street that runs into Silahtarağa Cad. Head right for 100-200m, where you'll spot yellow signs showing the way. Alternatively, follow a cobblestone switchback through the graveyard directly to the cafe. The path, a far quicker (but steeper) route than the road, begins to the left of the main entrance to Eyüp Camii. Hailing a cab is another option ($2-3). Open daily 9am-11pm.)*

EDİRNEKAPI AND KARİYE CAMİİ

A fairly quiet, typical İstanbulian neighborhood at the fringes of Fatih, modern Edirnekapı would hardly merit mention if it were not the site of **Kariye Camii,** formerly the **Church of St. Saviour** or **Chora Church,** now a museum. Hidden in the back streets of Edirnekapı, the church has some of the best-preserved Byzantine mosaics in the world. Although every gilded tile goes against Islamic strictures concerning representational art, the church managed to escape the fate of Aya Sofia, whose mosaics were either plastered over or torn down. During the 1453 siege, the church's location in Edirnekapı, a defensive nightmare and the weakest spot in the Theodosian walls, made the odds of Kariye's survival even more improbable. Situated at the base of a small hill outside the walls, Edirnekapı's low location gives the advantage to an attacker's artillery—a position that Mehmet quickly exploited.

Enough of St. Saviour Church survived Mehmet's artillery to be repaired and converted into a mosque. Or perhaps the shells, like many visitors, got lost and couldn't find the place, hidden away in the twisting streets off Fevzi Paşa Cad. *(Start at the Edirnekapı otogar, heading downhill along Fevzi Paşa Cad., turn left onto Salma Tomruk Cad., then take the second left onto Arat Sok., and continue onward. If you miss Arat Sok., stay on Salma Tomruk Cad. until the road forks, then make a left onto Kariye Torbesi Sok., and another left on Kariye Camii Sok. Most people in the area will be able to direct you.)*

The church's mosaics, crafted with gold-leaf tiles, narrate the life of Christ (see **The Timeless Vision of Byzantium,** p. 21). When viewed in the dim light of a candle, the figures appeared much more lifelike, as the candlelight moving over the image gave the illusion of motion. The mosaics provide an excellent example of a later strain of Byzantine art whose realism and expressiveness influenced Giotto and other Italian painters. If there is no available curator or an English-speaking tour group to listen in on, start your own tour in the narthex with the birth of Christ, and continue around the church to behold scenes from the life of Mary, portrayals of Christ's family tree, and portraits of saints, including the pen- and manuscript-toting St. Kosmas the Poet, patron saint of writers. *(Open Th-Tu 9am-4:30pm. $4.)*

YEDİKULE

At the intersection of Sahil Yolu and Belgrat Kapısı Demirhane Yolu. Yedikule is most conveniently reached by commuter rail from Sirkeci Garı or from the Cankurtaran in Sultanahmet, below the Blue Mosque down by the water. The walk between Yedikule and Topkapı (the region, not the palace) along Belgrat Kapısı Demirhane Yolu, which runs north parallel to the walls for about 1¼km, can be scorching in summer; fortunately there's very good dolmuş service from gate to gate. Museum open Tu-W 9am-4pm. $1, students $.60.

The Theodosian land walls and the Yedikule (Seven Towers) fortress are the last remnants of the old city's ironclad defenses. This system once included sea walls that ran from Yedikule to the former Byzantine palace of Buceleon and continued around to present-day Eminönü. There, a great iron chain was strung across the Golden Horn whenever invaders threatened. In 1453, the land walls proved to be the weak link in the system when they crumbled under Mehmet's artillery. Ironically, these walls are the only pieces of the city's defenses that survive today.

The current Yedikule fortifications comprise the Byzantine **Golden Gate** and five newer towers which Mehmet added after capturing the city. Theodosius I built the Golden Gate, the two towers with three large brick and stone arches between them, as a triumphal arch through which he and later emperors would enter the city. The arch, sheathed in white marble with gold-plated gates, once served the city as both defense and decoration. Mehmet's five towers were connected to each other and to the Golden Gate by high walls. To reach the **Marble Tower,** the southernmost section of the Theodosian land walls, turn left outside the Yedikule museum doors and follow the fortress walls to the Yedikule gate. From here, walk along the exterior of the fortress across the train tracks to the sea. More than the Golden Gate, the tower gives a clear sense of the original fortifications.

The two towers directly to the left of the entrance served as a maximum-security **prison** during the early part of the Ottoman Empire. The first tower, used for prisoners serving long sentences, has their names carved into the wall. The second tower was used for incarceration and beheadings. Though somewhat hard to see from the ground floor, the infamous "well of death," the hole into which heads would roll, still survives. *(Wear sturdy shoes, bring a flashlight, and watch your head.)*

The thin ribbon of land between Belgrat Kapısı Demirhane Yolu and the land walls is home to much of İstanbul's **gypsy community,** which subsists on farming.

NORTH OF THE GOLDEN HORN

TAKSİM SQUARE AND BEYOĞLU

Taksim Square, home of the ritzy Marmaris Hotel and the mammoth Atatürk Cultural Center, draws the rich, the bohemian, and the curious. The square leads into İstiklâl Cad., a cosmopolitan shopping area by day and fast-paced bar and club scene by night. The word *"taksim"* means "distribution" in Turkish, referring to the days when the city's water supply was parceled out from a giant cistern at the top of İstiklâl Cad. Under the approving gaze of the giant Atatürk banner that graces the far end of the main square, Taksim serves as a cement monument to Turkey's modernization, an area of bright lights, big banks, and the industrious insomnia of a great metropolis. Taksim also showcases many of the city's disparate elements: affluent Beyoğlu, poor Galatasaray, İstanbul's independent artistic community, multinational banks, and consulates.

Present-day Taksim, Beyoğlu, and Galatasaray, through which the İstiklâl Cad. tram runs, stand in what was once known as Pera (Greek for "beyond"). Across the Golden Horn from the old city, this area owed its unique demographics to an obscure Byzantine treaty. In the 12th century, when Constantinople began to feel threatened, the emperor allowed the Genoese to set up a colony on the other side of the Golden Horn. Despite the understanding that the Genoese would contribute to the city's defense, they remained neutral when Fatih Mehmet struck in 1453. They were allowed to keep their colony, and over the course of the following three centuries, it became the city's foreign quarter, where Greeks, Armenians, Jews, and Russians lived together. The takeover of the Young Turks introduced a pro-Turkish agenda, largely as a hedge against the European powers who were slowly dividing up the Empire (see **The Young Turks and World War I,** p. 15). Though not overly persecuted, the minority communities of Pera felt ill-at-ease, and some emigrated. By the time of the population exchange in the early 1920s (see **The Treaty of Lausanne,** p. 16), the end of Pera was near, and a general campaign of Turkification took place, resulting in the area's new name, Beyoğlu.

İSTİKLÂL CADDESİ

Formerly *Le Grand Rue de Pera,* İstiklâl Caddesi (Freedom Street), unlike any of the other streets radiating off Taksim Sq., still retains the appearance and some of the character of its Ottoman and pre-Republican days. Navigating here is easy, as almost all the sights, restaurants, and cafes are either on İstiklâl itself or immediately visible from it. The best way to see the street is to start at Taksim Square, work your way down to the end, and catch either the historic Tünel metro to Karaköy and the Galata Bridge (which stretches over to the old city) or hop on the 1915 İstiklâl streetcar back up into Taksim.

At the top of İstiklâl Cad., the **tram turnaround** and the **French consulate,** both classic İstanbulian rendezvous spots, are excellent for people-watching. At the center of the square stands one of the finer (among the numerous) monuments to Atatürk and the country's independence. The monument consists of four sculptures each depicting different participants in the country's struggle for freedom. Atatürk himself faces down İstiklâl Cad., surrounded by 15 figures, including politicians, members of the military, and peasants holding children. Slightly down the hill from the French consulate on the avenue's first side street, the silvery onion domes of **Aya Triada** peak out among the surrounding skyscrapers and hotels. This 19th-century Greek church is particularly beautiful at night when its spot-lit domes are surrounded by graceful, high-flying seagulls. The terrace of Haci Baba restaurant is a good place to contemplate the scene over *çay.* Visit the church's beautiful interior, accessible from Meşelik Sok., on Sunday (service 9-11am), as the sanctuary, like that of many Greek churches in Turkey, is locked the rest of the time. About 100m down İstiklâl Cad., on the left, are **Kücük** and **Büyük Parmakkapı Sok.,** two of Taksim's principal **nightlife** streets. Another 200m farther on the right is the **Çiçek Pasajı,** a recently restored cluster of cafes and somewhat pricey restaurants under a high glass roof. Next door, the **Balık Pazar** (fish market) makes for some pleasant meals. On the left, past the **Galatasaray Lisesi,** a leading candidate for the World's Most Beautiful, Best-Located High School, the Roman Catholic **Church of St. Antoine** survives under the care of Franciscan monks. The original St. Antoine was torn down during the construction of the streetcar line, but the present church, built in 1913, is an exact replica containing original paintings and valuables. The sanctuary is especially peaceful in the afternoon, when members of İstanbul's tiny Roman Catholic community drop in for silent prayer in the pale, colored light of the many stained glass windows. *(Church open for visitors daily 8am-noon, 3-7pm. Mass conducted in English at 10am on Sundays.)*

İstiklâl Cad. rambles downhill for 500m until **Tünel Meydanı,** the northern terminus of the two-stop Tünel Metro that links İstiklâl Cad. with Yüzbaşı Sabhattin Euren Cad., near Galata Bridge to the west ($.35, with AKBİL $.25). Tünel Meydanı is packed with musical instrument stores, from traditional shops catering to long-time local players to rock-and-roll outfits full of aspiring youth practicing their

İSTANBUL

heavy-metal chops. This is a prime area if you're in the market for traditional Turkish instruments; some shop owners will even point you towards a good instructor.

Just off Tünel Meydanı, to the left when facing the Tünel station, Galip Dede Cad. plunges into the heart of Galata. **Galat Mevlihane,** the Mevlevi dervish house, is 30m down Galip Dede on the left. The entrance is easy to miss, consisting only of a single gate with a gilded Ottoman *tuğra* (calligraphic seal) above the door. Once a Sufi lodge housing the Mevlevi Order (see **Mevlevi Order,** p. 27), Galat Mevlihane features a well-restored octagonal ceremonial hall dating from the 18th century. Two tiers of seats surround the eight-sided floor, with the upper tiers reserved for the *derviş* orchestra, which plays in the box directly above the main entrance during ceremonies. The audience sits in the lower level, surrounded by displays of musical instruments and dervish costumes. The Galat Mevlihane is one of the best places this side of Konya to catch an authentic *sema,* or **whirling dervish show.** Shows are advertised at the ticket booth and usually take place every other Sunday from 3-5pm and on December 17, the anniversary of Mevlâna's death and an important Sufi holiday. Much longer and more authentic than the free ones in Gülhane Park, the shows here are well worth the $4 admission. *(Museum open W-M 9:30am-4:30pm. $1.75, students $1.)*

About 100m down Galip Dede and one street over (look right), the 62m-high **Galata Tower** rises as the area's most prominent landmark, with the best views of the city from the European side. The tower, built by Justinian in 1348, was intended as part of the defensive fortifications around the Genoese colony. When Mehmet II took Constantinople, he allowed the Genoese to keep the tower, but demanded that the walls be torn down. The tower has recently been assaulted by change, with extensive scaffolding and an 8th-floor nightclub ominously promising an "evening that can never be forgotten." The walkway surrounding the nightclub, however, still offers incredible views of Beyoğlu, Taksim and the many mosques of the old city across the water. *(Open daily 9am-8pm. $3.25, $2.50 on Mondays.)*

MILITARY MUSEUM (ASKERİ MÜZESİ)

Any Mecidiyeköy- or Harbiye-bound vehicle from Taksim Square goes to the museum. Buses and dolmuş leave from the bus stop where Cumhuriyet Cad. hits Taksim Square, in front of the McDonald's. Open W-Su 9am-5pm. $.65, students $.25; taking a camera into the exhibits requires an extra $1.50.

With its large collection of artifacts from two military millennia and its unparalleled air conditioning system, the superb Askeri Müzesi more than makes up for its location 2km from Taksim Sq. Housed in the former Harbiye Military Academy, which was built as a school 1841 and later converted into the Ministry of War by alum Atatürk when the academy moved to Ankara, the museum is divided into two floors. The first is devoted to weapons, and the second to Turkish military history. It's organized so that visitors must pass through the "Hall of Martyrs," featuring a billboard-size frieze and a list of all the wars in which Turks have fought. The hall also has five or six display cases containing the martyrs' freshly pressed and cleaned uniforms, with the holes of their fatal wounds left chillingly unmended.

Highlights of the weaponry floor include **Atatürk's classroom,** now a shrine to the leader's memory, complete with the obligatory oversized bronze bust. Mustafa Kemal's report cards show the extent to which he managed to conceal his military genius before Gallipoli. The lower floor also features a display of wartime cloth, with intriguing displays of battlefield tents and flags. At one end of the lower floor is an alleged section of the great chain that was once strung across the Golden Horn to keep attacking ships out. Upstairs, the exhibits on Turkish military history, full of medals and uniforms, are very impressive, though a bit inaccessible without knowledge of Turkish. The **Gallipoli exhibit** offers the Turkish version of the battle through a number of exhibits with English explanations. More impressive is the **War of Independence** section, containing a copy of Atatürk's "To the Mediterranean" order (and other original documents). A skilled Janissary band, the **Mehter Band,** plays traditional military music in the courtyard (daily 3-4pm).

EUROPEAN BOSPHORUS SHORE

BEŞİKTAŞ

Locals agree that Beşiktaş marks the frontier between westernized İstanbul and the rest of the city. Though the district is less touristy than Sultanahmet and Eminönü, it has a lively and upscale community. Except for the naval museum, housed in a small modern building by the main bus stop, the sights are largely hidden behind giant walls built during the twilight of the Ottoman Empire, when the imperial center was moved from the old city onto the banks of the Bosphorus.

DOLMABAHÇE PALACE

From Taksim Sq., follow İnönü Cad. around the Atatürk Cultural Center, down to the waterfront, and take a left on Dolmabahçe Cad. The palace is up 400m. Alternatively, catch any Sariyer-bound bus for Taksim Sq. Open Tu-W, F-Su 9am-4pm. $8.50 for mandatory tour of Harem or Selâmlık alone, $13 for a combination ticket. Tickets may sell out in summer months. Call ahead to reserve (☎ 227 34 41).

Dolmabahçe's extravagant entrance fee is only the tip of the decadence iceberg. The building borrows its excess indiscriminately from French Baroque, Rococo, and Neoclassical styles. It sits atop the space that Mehmet the Conqueror used as a harbor when he prepared to conquer Constantinople. Sultan Ahmet I filled in the harbor to make a garden, and hence the palace got the name Dolmabahçe (literally "filled garden"). From 1843 until 1856, Sultan Abdul Mecid commissioned the architect Kavabe Balian to design and build a new palace here.

The obligatory guided tour, which thankfully covers only some of the 285 rooms (combined tour 2hr.), begins before the **grand staircase**, where a crystal balustrade and an 1800kg chandelier set the tone for the rest of the tour. The aesthetic merits of the collection are measured in tons of crystal, square meters of handwoven carpet, and pounds of gold leaf. The tour arrives next in the **reception hall**, a room complete with bear-hide mats from Tsar Nikolai, clocks from the Napoleons, and other gifts from the likes of Kaiser Wilhelm and George II. From here, the tour is a gilded blur until the **throne room**, where a 36m dome supports the largest chandelier in the palace, a 3500kg Waterford novelty presented by Queen Victoria.

After the throne room, the focus turns domestic in the **Harem**, the former home of the Imperial family. The Harem's attractions include the **circumcision recovery room**, where young princes would spend about five days in post-operative convalescence (and pain). While there, check out the **giant gold crown** mounted atop the recovery bed and the old black-and-white photo of a prince and his surgeon.

Atatürk's rooms include his death bed, now covered by a silver-filigree Turkish flag, and his clock, which stopped on the day of his death, November 10, 1938. On this day each year, at exactly 9:05am, the entire country ceases activity for a full minute of commemorative silence.

FLIGHTS OF PASSION In the 17th century, the Galata Tower became the world's **first intercontinental airport**, when an Ottoman daredevil by the name of Hezarfen Ahmet Çeleb flew a hang glider from the top of Galata across to the Asian shore, becoming the first man to fly since the mythical Icarus. He was initially handsomely rewarded by Sultan Murat IV, but the *ulema* (official Ottoman Islamic clergy) predictably proclaimed his project satanic, and the suspicious sultan banished the aviator to Algeria. In 1997, Turkish director Mustafa Altioklar made the wildly successful film "İstanbul Beneath My Wings" about the legendary flight. The movie's implication that the sultan's change of heart might have been related to a homosexual relationship between the two men enraged conservative Turks, for whom the idea of homosexuality in the Ottoman Porte is an inconceivable sacrilege.

İSTANBUL

YILDIZ PARKI COMPLEX

Park open daily 9am-10pm; in winter 9am-6pm. Free; $2 more if you take a taxi or drive to the köşks or palace. Belediye Müzesi (City Museum) open Tu-Su 9:30am-5pm. $3. Yıldız Şale open Tu-W, F-Su 9:30am-5pm. $5. Malta Köşkü open daily 9am-6pm; winter 9am-5:30pm.

On the far side of central Beşiktaş from Dolmabahçe (about 1km farther down the coastal road) is the main entrance to **Yıldız Parkı,** a heavily wooded park that served as the nerve center of the Ottoman Empire during the 30-year reign of Abdülhamid II (see **The Plot Thickens,** p. 14). Large, sprawling, and uphill in every direction, the park is filled with tall trees that block out the sounds of the nearby city. The **Yıldız Palace Complex,** a collection of *köşk*s (pavilions) and other buildings, is scattered throughout the park. After first serving as the palace of Sultan Abdülhamid II, who retreated to Yıldız from the excesses of Dolmabahçe, the buildings became part of the War Academy during Atatürk's presidency. The main building fell into disrepair until its restoration by the Turkish motoring club and subsequent conversion into two museums, a theater, and offices.

From the park entrance, a steep road leads almost a kilometer uphill to a T-junction. To the left is Çadır Köşk, and to the right are Yıldız Şale and Malta Köşk. Built in three chunks in the last two decades of the 19th century, **Yıldız Şale** (Star Chalet) was the Sultan Abdülhamid II's palatial guest house. Though the overall decor is relatively understated, the guest house is home to what is unofficially one of the largest carpets in the world; an entire exterior wall was knocked down in order to install it. The luxury lodge also housed Atatürk during the early period of his rule and contains bedrooms that housed various foreign heads of state (including de Gaulle, Ceaucescu, and Kaiser Wilhelm) until the 1970s, when the palace was turned into a museum. The **Belediye Müzesi** contains a medium-sized collection of random household effects from the late Ottoman period, a couple of cabinets worth of *Karagöz* (shadow puppets; see **No Strings Attached,** p. 158), and a rotating exhibit on local handicrafts. About 100m downhill from the palace entrance is the **Malta Köşkü,** a former palace *köşk* turned cafe/bar/*büfe* with an expansive, tree-framed view and an irresistible sweets buffet. **Çadır Köşk** is a pink building with a pond in front. Local nannies bring kids here to feed the ducks.

OTHER SIGHTS IN THE BEŞİKTAŞ AREA

If you leave Dolmabahçe Palace and follow Dolmabahçe Cad. along the walls for about 500m, *voilà* **Deniz Müzesi,** the Naval Museum, immediately recognizable by the garden full of torpedoes, mines, and the skeletal, scarred hull of an old submarine that sank in the Black Sea a while back. A favorite of both military enthusiasts and the casually curious, the Naval Museum is a quiet and curious side-show amid the larger package tour sights in the vicinity. Classical music gushes from dozens of speakers (the *1812 Overture* seems a perennial favorite) as the museum is adamant about taking itself seriously, down to the hand-fitted brass and oak display cabinets. Most of the first building is given over to captured flags and uniforms, though the basement houses stone **lithograph plates** once used for printing Ottoman maps and training manuals. Other sections include a collection of Ottoman **naval memorabilia** and furnishings taken from Atatürk's official yacht (including items as mundane as a few of his butter knives, all labelled with archaeological precision), a mine garden, and a building with imperial **caiques,** the long galleys used by the sultan. The stars of the caique collection are the two very long 17th-century boats with magnificently decorated *köşk*s. These were used for ceremonial occasions when the sultan made his entrance on water. (☎ 261 00 40. Open Su-Tu, F-Sa 9am-12:30pm, 1:30-5pm. $.85, students $.25.)

On the right, 100m down Dolmabahçe Cad. (which becomes Beşiktaş Cad.), stands the **Barbarossa Memorial,** consisting of a large blackened statue of the Barbary Pirate and admiral of the Ottoman Fleet (a.k.a. Redbeard) who captured Algiers and Tunis. His tomb lies across from the statue. In summer, the smooth pavement near the memorial attracts hordes of skateboarders and inline skaters.

Back along the shore road further from Dolmabahçe, you will eventually run into **Çirağan Sarayı** (Çirağan Palace), across from Yıldız Parkı. Now an *über*-luxury hotel, the building has been marked by idleness and disuse. Built in 1874, it served as the scene of Sultan Abdul Aziz's murder and then as a prison for Murad IV before being used briefly by the Turkish parliament and finally burning to the ground in 1910. In 1991, the palace was restored as a hotel. While the guards provide a veneer of exclusivity, the palace grounds are open to the public. The interior, however, is neither particularly interesting nor welcoming to sightseers.

ORTAKÖY

Set right on the water, hip Ortaköy positively rages with upper-class partygoers on summer nights (see **Nightlife,** p. 135). The town is essentially one grand cafe, surrounded by old wooden houses and painted in cheerful greens, oranges, and reds. The looming Bosphorus Bridge shades the town by day and provides a dramatic backdrop for the all-night revelry at Paşa Beach. Though pricey, Ortaköy is a perfect place to chill, play backgammon, and drink yet another cup of *çay*.

The relative dearth of sights and the inconvenience of the narrow coastal road insulate Ortaköy from the bustle of more downtown areas like Beşiktaş and Taksim. And despite its proximity to Dolmabahçe Palace and the other big Bosphorus attractions, few tourists go the extra kilometer to get here. The town remains a thriving center for young Turks, intellectuals, and socialites. Along the pedestrian path by the water are many places to stop for a small meal or a drink. Further away from the shore, in the few blocks of winding streets between the water and the center of town, small boutiques sell everything from fine jewelry to pricey foreign magazines. Wedged in among the cafes along the main street, the town's Greek Orthodox church and synagogue abut each other about 300m from the ornate stonework of the seaside Ortaköy Camii.

While the food is mouthwatering, cheap it is not. The *kumpir* stands at the mouth of the pedestrian area hawk baked potatoes filled with toppings of your choice, including cheese, meat, and various assorted vegetables ($2). Stands selling *gözleme* (crêpes) operate out of the canopied parking lot right off the main road ($2.50). The waterfront establishments serve meals for about $10, while the inland side of the road is crowded with traditional kebap and *lahmacun* joints.

ARNAVUTKÖY

Tiny Arnavutköy, squished between Ortaköy and Bebek and a pleasant walk from either area, is all about ambience and **fish**. Arnavutköy means "Albanian Village" in Turkish, and after the Albanians, Greeks formed the last minority community to occupy the town. Their *yalıs* (wooden waterfront houses) still stand as an elegant architectural testimony to their fading legacy. Originally, boats were moored under the overhanging parts of the houses. Several very good fish restaurants serve the day's catch from the cleaner, upstream end of the Bosphorus. There is also a **Greek Orthodox church** in good repair and open to visitors. Follow the street that runs parallel to the coast road and turn at the "Etiler" signs. *(Open daily 9am-4:30pm.)* The area has several pleasant cafes, and locals stroll along what has become İstanbul's de facto marina for cruising and touring boats.

BEBEK

Smack dab in the middle of the chain of small European Bosphorus districts, Bebek is a university town, home to the south gate of Bosphorus University and many of its professors. Bebek is spread along a narrow waterfront hemmed in by very tall hills. The Ortaköy end of the town is thick with stores, offices, and *dondurmacılar* (ice cream sellers). Up the Bosphorus past the small *camii* are some pricey shops and a few gentrified cafes. A good portion of İstanbul's rich, famous, and numerous American and European expats call Bebek home, taking advantage of the English-language bookstore and the university scene.

Boğaziçi Üniversitesi (Bosphorus University), originally founded as Robert College by American missionaries in the 1800s, is a short walk along the coastal road until you reach the Boğaziçi bus stop. From there you will see the university entrance gate. Don't worry about the guard—you don't need identification to enter on foot. The long, winding trek up to the main campus leads past the school swimming pool and the boys' dormitory. This green oasis in the middle of a chaotic city is the physical embodiment of the campus spirit: an enclave curiously removed from the tensions that plague İstanbul's other major universities. Frisbee-tossing students lounging on the grassy knoll surrounded by brick buildings make Boğaziçi seem like a realized college idyll. The *çay* garden near the cash machine is a great place to recover from the exertion of the climb.

The **Fortress of Rumeli Kavağı (Rumeli Hisar)** lies about a kilometer or so upstream from Boğaziçi and is impossible to miss. Mehmet the Conqueror built the fortress in 1452 as he prepared to besiege Constantinople, and the Ottomans later used it to shield the artillery battery used to control naval traffic at the narrowest point of the Bosphorus. The massive fortifications are still impressive, even in their state of disrepair. At the entrance, turn right to the crowded theater or left and uphill to the maze of steps and turrets. The views of the Bosphorus from atop the high walls at the back of the fort are staggering. All that remains of the fortress's mosque is the large central space surrounded by the amphitheater. Minor Turkish pop concerts are held here in the summer. *(Fortress open Th-Tu 9am-5pm. $2.)*

SARİYER

Sariyer is one of the last bus stops on the European Bosphorus road, and it can take anywhere from 1-2 hours to reach by bus (from Eminönü) or dolmuş (from Taksim or Beşiktaş). While architecturally less interesting than Arnavutköy, it does share the "Albanian Village's" laid-back, low-key ambience, as if it still hasn't gotten over its hypnotically beautiful Bosphorus views. Swimmers and picnickers line the shore walls, workday or not. The most serious citizens seem to be the fishermen staring reflectively at the cliffs across the water. Sariyer also enjoys the distinction of hosting an excellent small museum, the **Sadberk Hanım Müzesi,** Piyasa Cad. 25-29, 400m from the Sariyer dolmuş stop in the direction of Bebek. Built in honor of the wife of a Turkish entrepreneur and housed in a cream-colored Armenian house, the museum has an eclectic collection of the artistic and ethnographic items of the late Sadberk Hanım. The collection includes engrossing embroidery, calligraphy, and illustrated manuscript displays. The highlight, however, is the *faïence* collection, which features fine İznik pieces. *(Museum ☎ 242 38 13. Open Oct.-Mar. Th-Tu 10am-5pm; Apr.-Sept. 10:30am-6pm. $1.50, students $.25.)*

THE BELGRADE FOREST

As İstanbul's last and only old-growth forest, this is where the nature-lovers go to hike, picnic, wash their cars (the water's free here), and loll in the cool shade of the tall pines. A former Ottoman hunting ground, Belgrade Forest is also the site of a remarkable network that supplied İstanbul with water for centuries. The forest gets its name from a community of Serbian prisoners, brought here after the capture of Belgrade in 1521 to maintain the water supply system.

Built in stages from the Byzantine period through the reign of Süleyman the Magnificent, the water system remained in use until the beginning of the 1900s, a testimony to the sturdy simplicity of the system's design and the ingenuity of its Serbian caretakers. Scattered around the park are a number of **bends** (large dammed reservoirs) and the remains of the **su terazı** (water towers). These water towers replaced the need for unwieldy aqueducts, and since they worked on the same principle as a gas siphon, they solved the problem of getting water over hills. Water was sent through underground passageways where enough pressure was built up to force it up into a water tower. When the tank filled up, the water was sent back down through the underground channels with enough force to rise up into the next water tower and so on until the water reached the city.

The best and by far the easiest way to check out the forest and the water works is to catch bus #153, which runs between Sariyer and Bahçeköy every 20 minutes. The end of the line is the town square of Bahçeköy, a village so small that the *müezzin* belts out the call to prayer without amplification. To orient yourself, face uphill with the little tea garden to your right. Behind you and one block downhill is a cheap supermarket, the perfect place to score a bottle of water, *dikmen* wine, or whatever else sustains your wanderlust. Once equipped, there are three ways to get to the forest. To the left and downhill about 45m is the street with signs reading **"Site Bend."** Follow these signs to the edge of the forest, where you can pick up one of the narrow trails up a small, steep hill. At the top, there is a well-worn jeep trail running through the woods. With your back to the forest entrance, head right along the trail for a quarter mile to the *bend*, a large dam made of massive stone blocks with Arabic inscriptions. The second option is to head right from the main square and backtrack along the bus route. Follow the signs marked **"Bentler"** 2½km to the entrance of the **Belgrade Forest National Park.** Immediately after the ranger's little hut, the road forks. The right fork leads 1½km past Ottoman springs with cold, refreshing water to the impressive **Valide** and **Yeni Bentler.** The other fork leads to the **Neşet picnic ground** and the **Büyük Bend,** which is larger but farther (45min. walk each way) than the other bends. Of course, you can also catch a cab from Bahçeköy to the bend for $5 (including $.50 parking fee).

ASIAN İSTANBUL

Any #15 bus (buses go from 15A to 15T, but any will do) from Üsküdar heads to Kanlıca, Emirgan, and Anadoluhisarı ($.50).

New by İstanbulian standards, the Asian side, like much of the European Bosphorus, is an aggregate of villages that fell outside the old city walls. Because of its residential nature and the relative youth of its few sights, Asian İstanbul remains undiscovered country for most visitors. As such, *Asya* enjoys a certain reflective distance, both physical and mental, from the rest of the city—the perfect antidote for the Sultanahmet-weary. An entire day can be spent walking the busy streets and local bazaars without hearing a single "Yes, please!," "Carpet! *Kilim!*," or "Where are you from?" By virtue of its location on the Bosphorus, Asian İstanbul is also the place to watch the sun set over the old city. The whole deal is sweetened by the ease of transit—ferries run every 10-15 minutes from Eminönü to Kadıköy for a lovely 15-minute cruise. **Çengelköy's** excellent, inexpensive fish restaurants, **Anadoluhisarı's** small dockside cafes, and **Emirgan's** old-style Turkish houses are each worthy of a visit.

KADIKÖY AND MODA

Kadıköy is the commercial heart of Asian İstanbul and the principal shopping district. There are few tourist sights; instead, Kadıköy offers an honest slice of modern İstanbulian life. The neighborhood's relative lack of pretension make its crowded markets and narrow stone streets great places to shop for everyday items. And without the tourist tax of more traveled sections of the city, list prices tend to be less ambitious. Kadıköy sits along the Asian Bosphorus shore; south of Üsküdar and Harem, but considerably north of Bostancı. The best way to get there is a ferry from pier 2 in Eminönü (every 15-20min. 7:30am-8:30pm, $.75)

Apart from wandering the back streets off Söğütlüçeşme Cad., home to most of the cheap and fairly decent restaurants, Kadıköy's main attraction is **Gen. Azim Gündüz Cad.,** a pedestrian street to the left off Söğütlüçeşme Cad. as you head uphill. The street has slightly cheaper stores than those found along İstiklâl, and has one of the highest concentrations of movie theaters anywhere in İstanbul. These show primarily American films, almost always in English with Turkish subtitles. Turkish movies, unfortunately, are almost never subtitled (tickets $4-6).

A second area for indulgent wandering lies across Söğütlüçeşme Cad. from the dock (on the right as you walk uphill). A small pedestrian square (by the Yapı ve Kredi bank), visible from the dock, leads to a small side street. On the left and 100m up is

Aya Efimia, an unusual Roman Orthodox church open to visitors (daily 9:30-4:30). A right at the church leads onto Mütürder Cad., off of which run the small market streets that comprise Kadıköy's "old city." The first street on the left off of Mütürder Cad. is Serasker Cad., home to a luscious fruit market and the ▩ **Kent Otel** (No. 8), an excellent retreat for a few relaxing days in small-town Asia. The small hotel is brand new, and the rooms have balconies, some with views out over the old town and across to Topkapı Palace. Though the rooms do not have their own baths, the shared facilities are modern and exquisitely kept. Haggling may be helpful. (☎337 45 18. Singles $18; doubles $36; triples $48). Continue up Mütürder Cad. and turn left onto Dumlupınar Sok. to tightly packed, ivy-terraced cafes serving up cappuccinos, old jazz, and to the tiny shops displaying obscure books and Turkish comics. In this direction, a right and then a left onto Sakizgülü Sok. leads up to Kadife Sokaği., a street lined with some of Asia's coolest and most obscure bars and cafes. One of the better places, housed in a basement-level enclave and terrace, is anonymous apart from the **metal crow.** Kadife Sok. can also be found by asking for the adjoining Reks Cinema.

The *bat pazarı* **(bazaar)** off Üzelik Sok. (to the right off Söğütlüçeşme Cad. about 100m uphill) is far cheaper than the Grand Bazaar, and sells much more eclectic wares, including icepicks, surfboard leashes, and racks upon racks of black leather shoes. Muvakithane Cad. is another open-air bazaar street, the third right off of Üzelik Sok., where the **Otantik Restaurant** at No. 62 serves freshly-prepared traditional Anatolian *gözleme* (crêpes; $3). (☎330 71 44. Open daily 9am-8pm.) Further up is Dellalzade Sok., which branches uphill to the left off Üzelik Sok. The street is occupied solely by antique dealers selling mostly copper and silver goods, and is one of the cheaper places to acquire antiques, real or otherwise.

Moda, right next to Kadıköy (a 15min. walk), is one of the city's chief gallery districts, along with Teşvikiye and Nişantaşı. To reach it, face uphill at the Kadıköy ferry dock, head right to the unmistakable mother of all dolmuş lots, and follow the street that curves uphill from the end of the lot. From here, signs point the way. A surplus of galleries lines Moda Cad., selling entry-level priced modern Turkish art, some of it very good (and very expensive: $1000-7500; see **Modern Turkish Art,** p. 23). Further down Moda Cad., away from Kadıköy, is **Yürt and Dunya Gallery** at No. 272, which will open the door for casual visitors. From here, Moda Cad. continues to a windy point overlooking the Bosphorus. Right by Yürt and Dunya, Feritlek Sok. forks to the right off Moda Cad. and heads to a shady point with park benches perfect for watching local windsurfers flying across the water.

ÜSKÜDAR

After Kadıköy, Üsküdar is Asian İstanbul's other big suburb. It is accessible from Eminönü by a ferry as quick as it is frequent. Like Fatih on the European side, Üsküdar is relatively devout, though the somewhat more laid-back atmosphere of the Asian peninsula tempers Üsküdar's conservatism just as enjoyably as it does Kadıköy's commercialism. Long, busy commercial streets connect the district's mosques (where visitors are more than welcome) and the atmosphere, while hectic, is pleasant. The streets off İskele Meydanı are perfect for buying big *dondurma* (there is no "Sultanahmet surcharge" for foreigners) and aimless wandering while chewing the taffy-like ice cream.

İskele Meydanı, the square across the street from the ferryboat landing, contains several mosques. If you face inland, the one to the right is the **Yeni Valide Camii,** built by Sultan Ahmet III for his mother. Surrounded by a shady, quiet courtyard with a well-tended garden and exotic flowers, this mosque is a standard example of late Classical Ottoman architecture. The metal cage built into the wall on the Hakimiyet-i Milliye Cad. side, once the tomb of the Valide Sultan, occasionally houses a solitary olive oil dealer, who passes the cans and bottles of oil through the bars. On the other side of İskele Meydanı is the **İskele** or **Mihrimah Camii,** which was designed by Sinan in 1547. With its waterfront position and large prayer area, the mosque is architecturally reminiscent of Rüstem Paşa Camii in Eminönü, and is the only Ottoman mosque with an odd number of semidomes (three).

The **Çinli Camii** (Tiled Mosque) contains some of the city's finest İznik tilework, second only to Rüstem Paşa (see p. 117), but it has seen at least one shoddy restoration job. Catch a cab heading inland from Hakimiyet-i Milliye Cad. ($1.50-2, perhaps a bit more from İskele Meydanı or Harem Sahil Yolu, the shore road). If you decide to make the short, steep walk, follow Hakimiyet-i Milliye Cad., turn left onto Eski Toptaşı Sok., and continue about 1km as the road becomes Dr. Fahri Alabey Cad. The mosque dates from 1640 and the tiles here are generally better than those in Sultanahmet. The unique luster of their terra-cotta and sea-green tints has eluded even the most advanced glaze makers. The mosque is usually kept locked, but either the caretaker or *imam* is always nearby and will show you around. For a small donation, he may even let you climb up the minaret ($1-1.50). About 10m from the mosque, down the hill towards the water, lies the **Çinli Hamam**, one of İstanbul's better small baths (see **Turkish Baths,** p. 131). The prices are reasonable, and though the interior is no architectural masterpiece the facilities are as elaborate as they come (bath $4; *kese* $3; massage $9).

Near Üsküdar rises **Büyük Çamlıca,** the highest point in İstanbul. Take any Ümraniye-bound dolmuş from İskele Meydanı and ask to be dropped off at "Çamlıca." From here, yellow signs point the way to Turistik Çamlıca Cad., the final steep 1½km approach to the hill. The view from the top is fantastic, as the hill lies above the blanket of smog that sometimes clings to the city. On clear days, it's possible to see parts of İstanbul through the haze, and the Uludağ mountain range to the southwest. There's also a great cafe at the summit, serving chocolate-topped *gözleme* and tea by the double-decker pot. (Open daily 9am-midnight.)

NEAR ÜSKÜDAR: SELİMİYE BARRACKS

Looming large over the port and bus station in Harem, the stone and terra-cotta colossus of the **Selimiye Barracks** is also a museum open to the public, containing **Florence Nightingale's chambers** in the same state that they were during her stay here in the Crimean War. It can be reached either by taking the Sirkeci ferry to Harem or any Kadıköy-bound dolmuş from Üsküdar. The barracks are a short walk from the docks. This behemoth was constructed in 1799 by Selim III as part of a failed effort to undermine the power of the Janissaries by creating a separate, parallel corps. The Janissaries voiced objection to this plan by murdering Selim and torching the barracks. Not to be undone, Mahmut II responded by rebuilding the barracks after slaughtering the Janissaries in a puddle of green slime (see **The 19th Century: Reform and Reaction,** p. 14). The British used the barracks as a hospital during the Crimean War, and it was here that Florence Nightingale earned fame as a nurse by reducing the hospital's death rate by 90%. According to the tourist office, the barracks are open to visitors on Saturdays from 9am to 4pm; however, this seems to mean nothing to the soldiers on duty if all you can say is "Florence Nightingale." Your best bet is to bring a Turkish speaker along to plead the case, as there's no specific visitors' entrance to the military installment.

ASIAN BOSPHORUS

North up the Asian Bosphorus are a number of small fishing communities, most notably **Çengelköy.** The waterfront fish restaurants here are perfect for eating the day's catch and watching the sun sink over Rumeli Hisarüstü with the old city in the background. Navigation is pretty straightforward, as all the towns lie along the route of any #15 bus from Üsküdar. The first large village along the shore is **Beylerbeyi,** the former summer residence of the Ottoman sultans and the present home of many of İstanbul's super-rich, who live behind big steel gates with portals for machine guns. Downhill and toward the Bosphorus Bridge from the Beylerbeyi bus stop, the massive pink **Beylerbeyi Palace** and its lovely magnolia garden is hard to miss. To get there, jump off the bus at the Çayırbaşı stop, one before the main Beylerneyi stop. Beylerbeyi is a less orgiastic (and less exhausting) version of Dolmabahçe Palace. It was built in little over a year to the melodious strains of an orchestra that Sultan Abdülaziz hired to motivate the workmen. The thoughtful sultan allowed his passion for ships and things nautical to inspire the interior decoration, as paintings of ships adorn many ceilings. Another room takes the naval motif to an absurd climax, with all the furniture and molding decorated with gilded knots and mooring ropes. Many of the ceilings are engraved with romantic poetry in Arabic script. *(Open Tu-W, F-Su 9:30am-5pm. $5 mandatory guided tour.)*

The next village, **Çengelköy,** is *the* place for **fish** in İstanbul, with a dense pack of well-established *balık* restaurants along the waterfront. The village is also respected for its goat cheese and a special strain of miniature cucumbers. After Çengelköy, **Anadolu Hisarı** is a village built around the Ottoman fortress of the same name. Lying on the Küçüksu Deresi River, this was the Harem ladies' picnic and recreation site, who came only when accompanied by a eunuch bodyguard. From Anadolu Hisarı, head back toward Üsküdar, cross the bridge over the Küçüksu Paresi, and turn left onto Küçüksu Cad. to get to **Küçüksu Kasrı,** yet another late Ottoman palace used as a hunting lodge by Sultan Abdülaziz. French Baroque on the inside, the house offers an excellent view of the Bosphorus. A visit includes a tour of four or five large salons. *(Open Tu-W, F-Su 9am-5pm. $2.75, students $1.)*

PRINCE'S ISLANDS (ADALAR)

The craggy Prince's Islands, which locals know simply as the *Adalar* (islands), are a retreat for middle-class İstanbul families looking to escape the metropolis. People do live on the four islands, but the majority run tourist-oriented businesses there or limit their stay to posh summer houses built far up in the hills, away from the shops and hotels around the island's main ports. **Büyükada** is by far the busiest, with the largest selection of markets, hotels, restaurants, and bars. It's also more strictly regulated than the others; while there are more navigable woods and beaches, these areas are often only barely "natural." Since **Heybeliada** is a giant step downward from Büyükada in terms of facilities, its giant step up in peace and scenery is somewhat inaccessible. It's best visited as a day trip from Büyükada, via the 5-minute ferry (about twelve throughout the day, free). The other two islands, **Kıalıada** and **Burgazadası,** are even smaller and almost entirely residential, with little more than restaurants. The two islands are the first stops along the ferry's island route; Heybeliada, the third, is the largest, and the most distant of the islands; Büyükada is last. Prices are high on all the islands, though the food quality is almost worth it (especially the fruit). It's a good idea to bring lunch with you.

Ferries depart from the north side of Eminönü or Kabataş; look for signs saying "Sirkeci Adalar" (from Eminönü, 3-4 per day, round-trip $2). A faster and slightly more expensive alternative is the **seabus** (from Bostancı and Kabataş in summer).

BÜYÜKADA ☎ 216

Büyükada is the largest and most enjoyable of the islands. Superb fish restaurants dot the shore, and delicious kebap restaurants and *pastane* (pastry shops) line the streets in every direction. A big-time summer retreat, Büyükada offers pine-forested scenery, swimming spots, and peaceful walks beyond the busy main drag, making it an excellent daytrip from İstanbul.

Once off the ferry, you're in the heart of the commercial district. Mercifully, there are no cars or buses on the island; most people are **walking, biking,** or taking **horse-and-buggy rides.** Starting from İsa Çelebi Sok., horse-and-buggy prices range from $2.50 for a short ride to $20 for an entire island tour; bike rentals run about $1.50-3 per hour, depending on the bike you choose for your ride. As most of the streets are cobblestone, a more comfortable bike is a good investment in the end. For **police,** go to the corner of Lala Hatun Cad. and Kadiyoran Cad., only a block from the main square in a two-story white building. (☎382 50 10 or 382 60 36). The **hospital** is **Adalar Devlet Hastanesi** (☎382 6228), at 41 Lala Hatun Cad., a five-minute walk up the street from the police station. The **PTT** is at 17 Balık Cad. (Open in summer M-F 9am-9pm, Sa-Su 9am-1pm; in winter M-F 9am-6pm, Sa-Su 9am-1pm.)

Most of the hotels here are expensive, luxurious summer retreats. The ▨ **Ideal Aile Pansiyon,** 14 Kadıyoran Cad. is the exception: a haunted house-style masterpiece with huge rooms. (☎382 68 57. $13 per person.) A horde of restaurants occupies the central commercial area by the dock. In the area around the clock tower, small restaurant-cafes spill out onto the street. On the uphill side are more standard kebap and *çay* places, while slightly more expensive (around $7 per meal) eateries line the downhill side. Unbeatable seafood restaurants line the waterfront. These offer various kinds of *şiş,* local specialties like stuffed mussels, and alcohol. Small groceries also sell fresh fruit. Don't miss the great ice cream sold on the main street from the ferry to the clock tower.

Yöruk Ali and **Dil Uzantısı** are good picnic or beach spots. Swimming off the rocks is a tricky but possible alternative. Another option is to take the buggy to **Luna Park** (no more than $7.50; 10-15min.), the local amusement park on the far side of the island. **Donkeys** can be rented as well ($10 for ½hr.). **St. George's Monastery** claims the highest point on the island. A fully functioning Greek Orthodox monastery complete with a cafe, it can be reached by a 20-minute walk up a steep cobblestone path, or by buggy leaving from Yöruk Ali ($1.50 from Yöruk Ali, $7 from the town center). Luna Park, the donkey rentals, and the path up to St. George's Monastery are all clustered around **Birlik Square,** a spot near the middle of the island where all roads converge before separating out towards the far coast.

HEYBELİADA

For some reason, the TML ferries (but not the seabus) heading outbound from Büyükada to Heybeliada are free, making a great excursion from Büyükada. Like much of İstanbul, the island once housed a large Greek population, which left a legacy of wooden houses. Heybeliada means "saddle bag" in Turkish, though the island is shaped more like a saddle, with Heybeliada in one of the stirrups.

Bikes can be rented from Trakya Gida, right off Ayyıldız Cad. ($1 per hr.; handdrawn maps $.20). The coastal road runs along the beaches, of which the German one is reportedly the best. İstanbul's cycling teams train on the hilly terrain. Another option is a **horse-drawn carriage** *(fayton)* ride around the island. Carriages stop near the *iskele:* face inland, head to the right, and look near the basketball courts. Try haggling, particularly if you know the specific stops you want and don't opt for the guided tour. The **Prenset Pension,** 74 Ayyıldız Cad. (☎351 81 83), is one of the least expensive places to stay on the island, but its quality is as good as elsewhere. All of the clean, large rooms have bath and phone. Breakfast included. Haggling is a must; otherwise you'll pay $40 per double regardless of occupancy.

The **Greek Orthodox School of Theology,** atop one of the island's two large hills, is a must-see *(fayton* there and back $10). The school also contains the **Aya Triada Monastery,** whose church features some Byzantine relics and a collection of silver inlay and oil paintings as striking as those at St. George's, its sister school on Büyükada

⬚ ENTERTAINMENT

HAMAMS (TURKISH BATHS)

İstanbul baths cover the entire quality spectrum. Since this might be your first or only opportunity to experience a Turkish bath, choosing the right hamam is of critical importance. Remember that while most İstanbul baths have either separate women's sections or women's hours, not all have designated female attendants. Women should specifically request female washers. Self service is always an option, and this desire is best indicated by showing the attendants your bar of soap and wash cloth. Before you go, read **Hamam-o-Rama,** p. 34.

▨ **Çemberlitaş Hamamı,** 8 Verzirhan Cad. (☎522 79 74). Just a soap-slide away from the Çemberlitaş tram stop. Though a touch touristy, Çemberlitaş is one of the better spots for cleanliness and service. Built by Sinan in 1584, it's also one of the most beautiful inside. Both the men's and women's sections have marble interiors under identical domes. Vigorous "towel service" after the bath requires a tip of $1.50-3. Bath with your own towel and soap $9; with a sudsy rubdown, massage and wash (tip included) $15. Open daily 6am-midnight.

⬛ Çinli Hamamı. In Fatih, near the butcher shops at the end of Itfaiye Cad. Built for the pirate Barbarossa, this bath is excellent and authentic. It retains a few of its original İznik and Kütahya tiles. Large facilities mean ample space on the hot stone. Bath $5; massage $6. Both sections open daily 8am-8pm.

⬛ Mihrimah Hamamı (☎ 523 04 87). Right next to Mihrimah Mosque on Fevzi Paşa Cad., about 50m from Edirnekapı. Definitely one of the better local baths: it's large, quiet, clean, cheap, and hot. Women's facilities are good, though smaller. Bath $4; massage $3.50. Men's section open 7am-midnight; women's section 8am-7pm.

Galatasaray Hamamı (men ☎ 244 14 12; women ☎ 249 43 42). At the end of Turanacıbaşı Sok., off İstiklâl Cad., just uphill from Galatasaray. Pricey, a bit touristy, and the place to go if you plan to spill serious lira for a scrub down in opulence. Bath and massage $22. Men's section open daily 7am-11pm; women's section 8am-8pm.

Cağaloğlu Hamamı (☎ 522 24 24). On Yerebatan Cad., 2km up from Yerebatan Cistern in Sultanahmet. This famous hamam, where scenes from *Indiana Jones* were shot, is somewhat disappointing if you like your stone and water ultra-hot—both can tend toward the lukewarm here. $8 for self-service; $30 for the "Sultan treatment" (massage and scrubdown). Men's section open daily 7am-10pm; women's section 8am-8pm.

FILMS

Movie theaters showing Hollywood blockbusters and world cinema line İstiklâl Cad. Showings are prominently advertised on billboards outside of the theaters and listed in the nation's large newspapers: *Hürriyet, Sabah, Radikal,* and others. Advertisements list theater and showtime information for each film. Most foreign films are shown in the original language with Turkish subtitles, though be sure to ask at the window before you purchase your ticket, as theaters occasionally have films dubbed in the local language. Tickets are $4-6 depending on the showtime, usually cheaper for the matinee.

FUTBOL

Futbol (football, soccer), Turkey's national sport, is centered in İstanbul (see **Sports,** p. 34). It's not too expensive to cheer on one of the teams with the rest of the *fanatiks:* ticket prices for İstanbul *futbol* matches rarely exceed $15-20 each for very good seats, and can be as low as $3. Tickets are sold at the stadiums. In İstanbul, two easily-accessible stadiums are **İnönü Stadium** in Beşiktaş, just off Dolmabahçe Cad., and **Fenerbahçe Stadium,** best reached by taking a $2 cab ride from Kadıköy. Show up about an hour early to secure a good view, as tickets in the cheap seats are numbered.

CHEAP SETS AND FLOPPED STUNTS Yedikule's dramatic possibilities—high walls to scale, towers to throw people from, and a courtyard for staging pitched battles between armies of extras—have not been lost on Turkish directors. The fortifications are the default "Ottoman castle" set for many low-budget Turkish movies. Footpaths running along the tops of the walls have no handrails and do not run the whole length of the castle's perimeter. This results in several deep, 3m wide chasms whose comic possibilities were more than realized in the Cüneyt Arkın low-budget cinema classic, **Ottoman Eagle.** In the climactic final battle, staged over the sounds of car horns on Sahil Yolu, with the tall buildings of modern İstanbul visible in the background, the hero (played by Arkın) gets thrown down one of these shafts, only to bounce back up on a trampoline barely kept off camera.

◪ NIGHTLIFE

But this is a decadent city of loveless lusts,
ready to give up the ghost,
a city of young whores, dead sultans, and the sick
an İstanbul debased.
　　　—İlhan Berk, "İstanbul"

A USER'S GUIDE

Contrary to popular misconceptions, İstanbul does have a great nightlife, with the scope and diversity that one would expect in a city of 13 million. Unfortunately, the best clubs and bars are neither well-advertised nor particularly organized, and as a result, bars often have unmarked entrances and clubs are woefully unlisted. Unplanned attempts at club-hopping are ill advised, as they will likely prove fruit-less. Women heading out alone at night, aside from taking care to exercise the cau-tions suggested in the **Safety and Security** section (see p. 45), should consider taking cabs. It's also wise to team up with a few other foreigners, Turkish women, or Turkish men you know well. Establishments in Taksim and certainly in Ortaköy tend to be upscale enough to be relatively safe, though there are always excep-tions. Cafe-bars and backpacker bars tend to be less threatening than rock bars or clubs. (See **İstanbul Street Smarts,** p. 88.) Men heading out alone or in a pack will have a tough time getting into some of the more upscale clubs and bars. Especially on weekends in the later hours, many places require every man to be accompanied by at least one woman. Although many people, including locals, find this frustrat-ing, clubs insist it is the only way to keep the dance floors "sufficiently" co-ed.

Turkish nightlife generally falls into one of three categories. The first includes male-only çay houses, backgammon parlors, and dancing shows. In addition to being boring, they tend to be dingy, poorly lit, and even somewhat unsafe for men as well as women. Though usually not prohibited, women are unwelcome, and should avoid these places. *Let's Go* does not recommend patronage of this sort of establishment. The second category includes **cafe-bars, rock bars,** and **backpacker bars.** Cafe-bars serve light fare, tea, and cappuccino in the afternoon and alcohol in the evening. Generally smaller and more relaxed than the sometimes cavernous rock bars, they play less invasive sounds—often jazz or Latin. Rock bars provide clean fun and in general are one of two types. The first include loud, dark halls that tend to blast American and Turkish metal anthems. They can be fun, if you can get over the repetition of watching well-dressed young people banging the gel out of their hair alongside shaggy metalheads. The second are more laid-back establish-ments that play a mix of classic rock, modern pop, and funk to a young crowd of people looking to relax with a beer. Backpacker bars, probably the best places to meet fellow travelers, are concentrated in the Sultanahmet area and are usually associated with hostels. These bars are convenient and cheap, but they hold a markedly familiar, non-Turkish clientele. **Clubs and discos** make up the third night-life category. The hippest İstanbul clubs often move from unlisted locations in Taksim in the winter to unlisted open-air summer locations throughout the city. Even taxi drivers can't keep up with the itinerant İstanbul night scene. Clubs can be a blast, though often only subtly Turkish and sometimes prohibitively pricey.

SULTANAHMET AREA

Most of the bars listed here are within 100m of each other on Akbıyık Cad., the main backpacker strip, and many standardize their beer prices at $1-1.50 for local brew. Others are a short walk up towards the Sultanahmet tram stop.

◪ **Mordi Cafe Bar,** 47 Akbıyık Cad. Down the street from the Orient Hostel. Leagues above the other backpacker bars in cleanliness and ambiance, this spot was created from a pri-vate residence. Dark wood decor and candles enhance the mood, and the waitstaff is extraordinarily friendly. If you're on the prowl for a nice place to relax with a beer, quiet conversation, and some good jazz, rock or folk, head here. Happy hour until 10pm.

Orient Bar, 13 Akbıyık Sok. (☎ 517 94 93). In the Orient Youth Hostel. Revelry and dancing abound in this social and boisterous basement bar. *Nargile* (water pipe) nights (Th, Su 9pm) attract international types, while evening belly dancing shows (M, W, F 10pm) are inauthentic but entertaining. Decked out DJ plays both Turkish and international dance hits, and a dart board entertains the non-dancer. A/C. Open 8pm-2am; happy hour until 10pm.

Sultan Hostel Roof Bar, Terbıyık Sok. Around the corner from the Orient Hostel, right off Akbıyık Sok. Party every night; belly dancing Tu and Sa, water pipes M and Th; on W the bar serves "punch." Much less smoky than other places. Beautiful evening view of the Golden Horn and the Sea of Marmara. Sizeable, well-stocked bar. Open 8am-2am.

Soldier Cafe and Bar, 37 Ticarethane Sok. (☎ 511 36 21). Turn right at Vitamin Restaurant, then take first left; the club is on the left. The only true dance club in Sultanahmet, this basement bar alternates between techno, hip hop, Turkish pop, and Celine Dion. A student crowd grooves on weekends, some attempting to breakdance to anything and everything the DJ spins. The walls are covered with murals of soldiers in combat. No worries, though—the dance floor promotes inter-cultural harmony. $2.50 beer. No cover.

Corlulu Alipaşa, 35 Yeniceriler Cad. Walk 100m toward Sultanahmet from the Beyazıt tram stop. This combination *çay/nargile* (tea/water pipe) garden is unabashedly cool, though touristy and a bit too brightly lit. Skilled waiters glide between cushioned benches, refilling glasses and adding coals to water pipes. Well-stuffed bowl of apple tobacco $2.50. *Çay* $.75. Open 8pm-1am.

TAKSİM SQUARE AND İSTİKLÂL CADDESİ

İstanbul night action is centered around Taksim and İstiklâl Cad., where the bar scene kicks in around 8pm and finishes at about 2 or 3am, while the clubs shut down a few hours later. If you take a bus or a dolmuş to the Taksim area, wandering down İstiklâl Cad. is sure to lead you to a fine club or bar. The density of bars in this area is staggering, with many quality places hiding out in narrow side streets. The list below is certainly not exhaustive, and should serve merely as a starting point for your adventures.

▨ **Jazz Stop.** At the end of Büyük Parmakkapı Sok. A mixed group of music lovers mostly sit while live bands lay the funk, blues, and jazz on thick. The owner, an immensely talented drummer from one of Turkey's oldest and most respected rock groups, occasionally takes part in the jams. Live music nightly at 11pm. Beer $3; liquor $6 and up. June-Aug. no cover; Sept.-May F-Sa cover $10. Open 11am-4am.

▨ **Peyote** (☎ 293 32 62). İmam Adnan Sok., next to Leman Kültür. This humble spot is one of Taksim's cheapest venues for live music. Popular with artists, it's a great place to hear local rock bands performing funky original tunes. Beer $1.25. Cover F-Sa $7.50, one drink included. Live music Tu-Sa at 11:30pm. Open M-Sa 6pm-4am.

▨ **Riddim,** 6 Büyük Parmakkapı Sok. If you are looking for Jah, he is here, in the only bar in Taksim dedicated to spinning reggae all night long. Crowd is a mixed group that likes to dance, and the DJs are generally great, spinning the Jamaican export as well as other African and island music. Unattended men will be turned away on weekends. Beer $2.50. Open F-Sa 8pm-4am, Su-Th 8pm-2am.

▨ **Madrid Bar,** İpek Sok. Off Küçük Parmakkapı Sok., which is off İstiklâl Cad. An understated bar with a fascination for surrealist Spanish paintings. This small, mellow spot is popular with Turkish students and young foreigners looking for one of the cheapest pints in Taksim ($1.25). Open 2pm-2am.

Kemancı (☎ 251 30 15), consists of 2 clubs 150m down Siraselviler Cad. on the right, up a small flight of stairs in a big archway. The most popular of Taksim's rock bars, this immense downstairs venue draws a large crowd of high-schoolers and college students who come to watch local bands tear through sped-up U2, Judas Priest, and Poison covers. Upstairs, a slightly older crowd cheers as bands pound out loud covers of American tunes. Beer $2.50. Cover F-Sa $12.50, Su-Th $3. Open noon-4am.

Caravan Rock Cafe Bar (☎243 42 47). In the fish market beside the Çiçek Pasajı off İstiklâl Cad. One word: wow. Loud, cavernous and cheap, this is where Turks go to consummate their love affair with heavy metal. Think crowd surfing, diving off tables, and enough headbanging to make your own head spin. Beer $1.50. Live bands in summer W-Sa 11pm-1am, in winter nightly at 11pm. Open F-Sa noon-3am, Su-Th noon-1am.

Mojo Club, 26 Büyük Parmakkapı Sok. (☎243 29 27), off İstiklâl Cad. An upscale rock bar that caters to a more sophisticated crowd. Easter Island-style sculptures look on as live bands dish out flavors of rock, pop, and blues (after midnight). Beer $3.25. Cover F-Sa $7.50, Su-Th $2.50 cover after midnight; includes one drink. Open 9pm-4am.

Leman Kültür, 8 Imam Adnan Sok. Off İstiklâl Cad. down the street from Büyük Parmakkapı Sok. on the other side of the road. A fine 2-story bar owned by Leman, Turkey's leading cartoonist. The entire bar is covered with his strips. Check out the cool light shades shaped like giant pen nibs. Fairly low-key and quiet. A nice place for a few drinks with some friends. Beer $2.50. Open 7pm-3am.

Home Bass, 15 Sadri Alısıik Sok. (☎251 00 07). Down İstiklâl Cad. on the left. Hip hop heads ought to head to this downstairs club, which keeps it heavy on the low end. Though the clientele might not always know the words, the DJ knows the hits and spins until late. Live tunes on weekends include all sorts of "global music." Cover $4 for live performance. Beer is cheap at $1.50. Open daily 5pm-4am.

Sefahatname (☎251 22 45). In the Atlas Pasajı on İstiklâl Cad. One of the loudest parties along İstiklâl. The open, friendly, and mostly twenty-something crowd spills out into the elegant marble *pasaj,* where people dance and chat. Beer $3. Open 10am-2am.

Hayal Kahvesi (☎244 25 58). Büyük Parmakkapı Sok. Mild-mannered coffeehouse by day, live music bar by night. Burly bouncers and a steep weekend cover create an air of elegant exclusiveness. Unaccompanied men cannot get past the door. Live music nightly at 11:30pm. Pricey beer $3. Cover F-Sa $12.50. Open noon-2am.

2019. A huge, hip techno club, whose summer location has been Maslak for the last few years. Turks know it as "twenty." Maslak is pretty far from Taksim, and you must take the Bosphorus road to get there. Be prepared to pay for a pricey cab ride. Winter location is in Taksim. The cover is high—about $30. Open until 4am.

ORTAKÖY, THE COASTAL ROAD, AND ETİLER

The Beşiktaş end of Ortaköy is a maze of upscale hangouts, with hundreds of small cafes and bars offering drinks under the lights of the Bosphorus Bridge. Along the coastal road toward Arnavutköy are a string of open-air clubs, frequented by rich Bosphorus University students, *nouveau riche* swingers, and Turkish celebrities. This scene affords the best people-watching in the city, as İstanbul's jet set lets loose beyond the prying eyes of the hoi polloi. The cover charges can be astronomical ($18-45), and the bouncers highly selective. Unaccompanied men are unlikely to get past the door. If you're money enough to hit this scene, dress well, be confident, and abuse any out-of-the-ordinary ID you have. Lines outside these places can be long, but if you pick the right one, the rigmarole can be more than worth it.

The following bars and clubs are between Ortaköy and Bebek, and they are listed in the approximate order that they appear along the coastal road. ПУХ ("Nick's"), an indoor/outdoor techno club in Ortaköy, is a notch below the inaccessible decadence of Paşa, but only a few steps down the road. The $30 cover charge is a steal by Ortaköy standards. **Paşa Beach Club** is a world-famous İstanbul open-air club boasting the longest lines, a latest-model Ferrari lot, the most arrogant bouncers, and the highest cover in the city ($40). Rumor has it that they'll waive the cover if you pull up in your yacht. The club is laughably hard to get into, since you can't even pay the cover without a membership card, for which you must be recommended. Befriending a member or spinning extravagant lies about yourself and your net worth are the best bets here. Across from ΠYX, **Civeli** alternates between a relaxed indoor/outdoor bar and restaurant and a scene of bacchanalian mayhem (their logo is a cracked, spilling wineglass). A lot depends on the live (generally Turkish) band and the special events, like wedding receptions. Drinks here are half the price of those at Paşa or ΠYX (about $5).

Around Arnavutköy, **SHE** Bar is a great, hip spot—particularly in the off-season when wealthy, corpulent businessmen bring their young girlfriends. This bar blasts British punk. Astronomical drink prices ($10) more than compensate for the lack of a cover charge. **Desperado,** right next door, is a favorite of Bosphorus University students. It's dim but fun, and the scene is innocent and laid back. **Purple Bar,** close to Bebek on the same road, is marked with a weird black-lit purple sign with almost indecipherable lettering. An exclusive crowd, including, among others, models, actors, and fashionable transvestites, packs the cramped confines. At $12 the cover isn't too bad, and the $5-7 drinks are reasonable.

NORTHWESTERN TURKEY

The cradle of the Ottoman Empire, Northwestern Turkey wraps around the Sea of Marmara with a diverse collection of cities and towns. Most of these locales—Mt. Uludağ's ski slopes, Marmara's beach resorts, Termal's hot springs, Bursa's bazaars, and Edirne's mosques—make fantastic quick escapes from İstanbul's urban sprawl. As the dusty streets of the Bosphorus city filter into winding highways, pavement gives way to terra cotta soil, and silvery olive groves and fields of peach trees take over like the countryside's own city blocks. This is, after all, the region that nourished the young Ottoman Empire, and it has two Ottoman capitals, Bursa and Edirne, to show for it. The artistic achievements, including Edirne's masterful architecture, İznik's ceramic tilework, and Bursa's silk, are world-famous. The Gallipoli Battlefields remain a major pilgrimage site for those commemorating the bloody World War I battle for control of the Dardanelles. Whether ferrying the Marmara, bussing through golden sunflower fields in Thrace, or riding a cable car up the heights of Uludağ, traveling in this region allows for a game of rich and eclectic cross-continental hopscotch.

HIGHLIGHTS OF NORTHWESTERN TURKEY

WANDER through Edirne's streets and behold some of the finest Ottoman architecture, including **Selimiye Camii** (p. 142), considered to be Sinan's magnum opus and the most spectacular mosque in Turkey.

GRILL your own meal from the high mountain plateau of **Mt. Uludağ** (p. 159) while the sun sets vermilion over snowfields.

EXPLORE the **Gallipoli Battlefields** and contemplate the bloodshed at ANZAC Cove (p. 147) as you witness the site of the 1915 conflict.

FOLLOW in the footsteps of emperors and sultans to the **Hot Springs of Termal,** and soak your well-traveled bones in the baths of champions (p. 160).

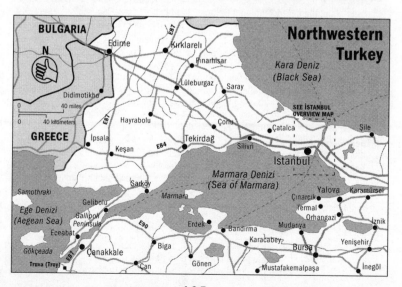

THRACE

EDİRNE   ☎ 284

In almost 2000 years of historical prominence, Edirne has enjoyed a mixed and fickle fate, ranging from imperial splendor to hostile occupation. It has been a Roman outpost, an Ottoman capital, and a modern Greek military possession. Its status as a border town—the source of the city's historically variable fortunes—remains an important part of Edirne's character today.

In 125 AD, the Roman Emperor Hadrian founded Adrianople (Hadrianopolis) and named it, Alexander style, in his own honor. Under Roman sway, Adrianople was an important garrison town and center of armor production. Crusaders dominated the city for a brief period in the 12th century, but it did not fall permanently from Byzantine hands until Sultan Murat I conquered it in 1362. Pleased with his latest European possession, Murat made Edirne the capital of his rapidly expanding empire, beautifying it with lavish architecture. Today Edirne's three remarkable mosques, the Eski Cami (Old Mosque), the Üç Şerefeli Camii (The Three-Balconied Mosque), and the incomparable Selimiye Camii, all recall this splendor.

When the capital of the Ottoman Empire shifted to Constantinople in 1453, Edirne retained its prominence as a major stop on the eastern caravan route. In the 19th century, Edirne was still the 7th-largest city in Europe. Now the city has a frontier town feel, removed from the rest of Turkey. Edirne sits less than 20km from Bulgaria and barely 7km from Greece, though crossing the borders from Edirne is inconvenient. Trakya University, the university for European Turkey, keeps Edirne young. Not coincidentally, the finest brand of *rakı* is made nearby.

▐ TRANSPORTATION

Buses: Numerous bus companies cluster around the parking lot, all selling similarly priced tickets to the region's major cities. Be sure to shop around. *Let's Go* offers the following suggestions, including bus companies: **Ankara** (Edirne Ece Turizm; 9hr.; 9:30pm, $20); **Antalya** (Edirne Ece Turizm; 17hr., 7:45pm, $23); **Bursa/Mt. Uludağ** (7hr., 5pm, $16.50); **Çanakkale** (Edirne Ece Turizm; 4hr., 7:45pm, $8.25); **Hatay** (Edirne Ece Turizm; 21hr.; 5:30, 7:30pm; $28.25); **İstanbul** (Edirne Ece Turizm; 3½hr., 5:30, 7am, then every ½hr. until 6:30pm; $5) or (Lüx Edirne Express; 2hr., every ½hr. 7am-7pm, $8.25); **İzmir** (Edirne Ece Turizm; 9hr., 7:45pm, $15.50).

Trains: Edirne has 2 train stations. Trains for **İstanbul** (6 hr., 7:40am, $4; 4hr. express, M-F 3am, $9) leave from the **Edirne Garı** (☎225 11 55 or 212 09 14), outside Edirne on the İstanbul road. To get to the station, take dolmuş #1 (see dolmuş listing for directions) past the otogar toward İstanbul. Ask to be let off at the train station or, if this fails, at Migros, a supermarket opposite the station. Trains to **Sofia, Bulgaria** (8hr., 3:30am, $19) leave from the **Kapıkule station** (☎238 23 12). To reach Kapıkule, take a dolmuş from the stand behind Rüstempaşa Kervansaray Otel (every 10min., $.75) or a bus (every hr. until 6pm) from the local station (see listing below).

Local Buses: Although the dolmuş is almost always the cheapest option for local travel, it's sometimes convenient to take the local bus to the border towns **Kapıkule** ($1) or **Karaağaç** ($.75). The local bus station lies 50m up Mimar Sinan Cad., on the left just past the City Hall. Kapıkale and Karaağaç each have their own clearly marked platform.

Dolmuş: Dolmuş leave from the dusty gravel lot behind the Rüstem Paşa Kervansaray Hotel. Each dolmuş travels on one of 4 different circuitous routes, indicated by the colored number in the dolmuş window. Signs posted around the lot indicate the routes denoted by each number. Rides cost $.25-$.45.

Taxis: In the small square off Talat Paşa Cad., past the tourist office (walking from the center of town). Another stand sits between Sera Park and Üç Şerefeli Camii. Dial ☎213 56 90 to order a taxi; if you do not speak Turkish it is easier to hail one on the street.

⬟ ORIENTATION

Two of Edirne's major roads, **Mimar Sinan Cad.** and **Talat Paşa Cad.**, converge on the fountain at the center of city. From the fountain, with its water-spouting earthenware jugs, you can see the city's three main mosques, and nearly everything of interest is a short walk away. To the south sits **Eski Cami**, the **Bedesten,** and one of the city's central cafe squares. **Talat Paşa Cad.**, the city's main east-west thoroughfare, starts at the fountain and runs through town to the Tunca River. The other half of **Talat Paşa Cad.** begins behind Eski Cami, runs southeast out of the city, and continues on to İstanbul. **Mimar Sinan Cad.** runs up toward the main mosque and Edirne's major **museums.** The city's shops are on **Saraçlar Cad.**, reached by walking on Talat Paşa Cad., away from Selimiye Camii, and making the first left. Further down Talat Paşa Cad. at the intersection with **Maarif Cad.**, you'll find the tourist office and a variety of cheap accommodations. The magnificent **Selimiye Camii,** Edirne's symbol, towers above the city, visible from several kilometers away.

🛈 PRACTICAL INFORMATION

TOURIST AND FINANCIAL SERVICES

Tourist Office: 17 Talat Paşa Cad. (☎ 213 92 08), 300m down the road from the center of town. Friendly, helpful staff offers free city maps. Open M-F 8:30am-5:30pm, occasionally later and on weekends during June-Aug.

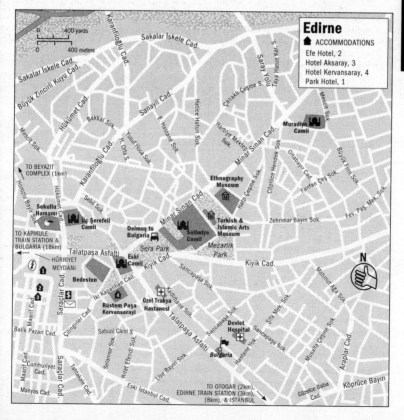

Edirne

▲ ACCOMMODATIONS

Efe Hotel, 2
Hotel Aksaray, 3
Hotel Kervansaray, 4
Park Hotel, 1

Bulgarian Consulate: 31 Talat Paşa Cad. (☎225 10 69), about 1km from the center of town down the road to the otogar. 30-day tourist visas: 1-week processing $55, same-day service $70. Multiple-entry visas: 3 months $66, 6 months $93, 1 year $126. Transit visas: single-entry $44, double-entry $63. Open M-F 9am-noon. For information on the Bulgarian border crossing, see p. 143.

Greek Consulate: (☎235 58 04). In a blue and white apartment building in a remote residential region. Take dolmuş #1 to Mega Park (10min., $.25) and find the police station in a new, gray building. Take the road that doubles back to the main road on the other side of the police station. After 3min., you will see the blue and white Greek flag flying 30m down one of the side streets on the left. Open M-F 10am-noon. For information on the Greek border crossing, see p. 144.

Banks: Türkiye İş Bankası, on Saraçlar Cad.and **Vakıfbank,** further down on Saraçlar Cad., exchange traveler's checks and has a V/MC/Cirrus/Plus ATM. Both open M-F 9am-12:30pm, 1:30-5:30pm. **Akbank,** on Talat Paşa Cad., near the tourist office, has a full-service ATM and can exchange AmEx **Traveler's cheques.** Open M-F 9am-5:30pm. 50m further down on Talat Paşa Cad., **Garanti** posts its exchange rates in the window (cash only), and has an ATM that accepts all major cards. Open M-F 9am-5pm.

EMERGENCY AND COMMUNICATIONS

Police: (☎213 92 40), far away from the center of town on Mega Park, in a residential area. Take dolmuş #1 to the Mega Park stop (10min., $.25).

Pharmacy: Şifa Eczanesi (☎225 46 36; fax 213 17 77), across the street and down 50m (heading away from town) from the tourist office on Talat Paşa Cad. Open M-F 8:30am-7:30pm. Better-located **Güven Eczanesi** (☎224 65 24) is on Saraçlar Cad., 25m from Talat Paşa Cad. Open M-F 8:30am-7:30pm. V/MC.

Hospitals: Özel Trakya Hastanesi (private, ☎213 92 00), just before the Bulgarian consulate on Talat Paşa Cad. **Edirne Devlet Hastanesi** (public, ☎225 46 03), is immediately up the hill from the Bulgarian Consulate.

Internet access: Lider Internet Cafe (☎214 67 28). Take an immediate left after the Türkiye İş Bankası on Saraçlar Cad. and walk 250m. The cafe is on the left on the 2nd floor. Modern and well-kept with good, fast connections. ($.65 per hr. Open 8am-midnight.) **Eska İletişim Internet Cafe,** 3 doors down from the Kervansaray Hotel. ($.85 per hr. Open 10am-midnight.) **Kervansaray Hotel** also has an Internet room, which tends to be busier ($1 per hr.).

PTT: 17 Saraçlar Cad. Post 8:30am-5pm, phones until 10pm. **Postal code:** 22100.

▌ ACCOMMODATIONS

Plenty of places to spend the night are scattered along Maarif Cad., the first left after passing over Saraçlar Cad. on Talat Paşa Cad. Travelers to Edirne during the Kırkpınar Grease Wrestling Festival should call ahead, since the town is filled with spectators for the week-long event in the first week in July. When the flow of travelers through the city tends to fall off, bargaining can be productive.

▨ Hotel Kervansaray (☎225 71 95; fax 212 04 62), a.k.a. Rüstempaşa, runs the length of Hürriyet Meydanı on Eski Cami Altı. It was built in the 1550s as a resting place for camel caravans trudging between Europe and the East. The exquisite gardens, cloistered courtyard, and stone hallways recall early Ottoman days, but the history doesn't keep guests from enjoying the hotel's modern facilities, including bath, TV, phone, and carpet in each of its 79 rooms. There's also a hamam, parking, 2 bars, and a billiards/internet parlor. Worth the extra expense. Singles $30; doubles $60; triples $90. V/MC.

Hotel Aksaray (☎225 39 01), at the intersection of Maarif Cad. and Ali Paşa Ortakapı Cad., a few doors down from the Efe Hotel. Cheap and basic, this well-worn Ottoman house offers small, plain rooms, most with TV, phone, and sink in the room. Singles $8.25; doubles $15, with bath $16.50; triples $20, with bath $21.50.

Park Hotel, 7 Maarif Cad. (☎213 52 76). Nondescript clean, modern rooms have bath, phone, and TV. Breakfast included. Singles $20; doubles $33; triples $41.50.

Efe Hotel, 13 Maarif Cad. (☎213 61 66; fax 213 60 80). Offers luxurious rooms with modern bathrooms, phones, and satellite TV that shows American movies. Air-conditioned lobby and "American Bar" with live music. Pricey but not overpriced. Breakfast included. Singles $50; doubles $70; triples $90; suite $100.

Camping: Fifi Camping and Motel (☎226 01 01), on the İstanbul road, 8km from the center of town. Offers a restaurant, bar, and pool. The motel rooms have modern bathrooms (singles $20, doubles $40). The camping is cheaper ($5 per person; price doubles with a car). Dolmuş service exists but is infrequent at this distance from the city.

🍴 FOOD

TEA GARDENS AND CAFES

Şera Park Cafe (☎212 66 30), on Selimiye Meydanı in the park between the Selimiye Camii and Eski Cami, has a breathtaking view of both mosques. The cafe's relaxed atmosphere and elegant central fountain make it a favorite. Çay is served either in a traditional small Turkish tea glass ($.25) or in a larger cup ($.40). Ayran and tost each $.40. Open M-F until midnight, Sa-Su until 2am.

Antik Park Cafe, 22 Tahmis Cad. (☎212 22 53), farther down from the Selimiye Camii, covers most of the Hürriyet Meydanı. Bordered by the Eski Cami and Kervansaray on 2 sides. Its romantic atmosphere and table umbrellas create an intimate dining space. Selections are nearly identical to those at the other cafes but with slightly better prices and a greater variety of quick snacks (karışık tost $.60; hamburger $1).

RESTAURANTS

Saray Restaurant (☎212 13 92). Directly behind the PTT on a short, nameless street. Identifiable by its dirty red awning, the Saray stands out as a local favorite. As you walk in, choose from 8 or 9 dishes prepared for the day ($.50-$1 per serving). Fresh bread and pitchers of cold water come free in endless supply. Open only for lunch.

Yudum Tava Ciğer Salonu (☎212 43 52). Faces the square bounded by Talat Paşa Cad., the Eski Camii, the Hotel Kervansaray, and the row of stores stretching down from the Bedesten. On the Bedesten side, the Yudum serves Edirne's specialty, Tava Ciğer, a beef dish prepared in a large pan ($1). Open 4am-10pm.

Edirne Lahmacun (☎225 10 13). Across the square from Eski Cami, just down the street from Kervansaray Hotel. A bit of a brightly lit eyesore on the otherwise subdued square. Huge servings of top-notch kebaps at low prices ($2 per portion). Also serves pastries, just as cheap (baklava $1.25). Open daily 10:30am-10:30pm.

Villa Restaurant (☎225 20 67). On the far bank of the Meriç River beside a picturesque Ottoman bridge. Follow Saraçlar Cad. away from town as it curves around the stadium and crosses first the Tunca River and then the Meriç; the restaurant is to the right of the Meriç River bridge. The walk to the restaurant takes about 20min. (cab ride $2). Like the several other restaurants on the river, the Villa opens only for dinner and is a notch above small restaurants in town, serving a wide range of delicious dishes on order (appetizers $1-2; main courses $3-5). Live music plays regularly.

SWEETS

Final Pastaneleri, 30 Saraçlar Cad. (☎225 42 27). An old standard, with 3 locations in the city. Ice cream at the door, cases full of sweets inside and cafe seating upstairs. This sweet shop serves puddings, cake, pastries and an array of cookies that are a cut above the rest on the street ($2.50 per kg.). Open daily 9:30am-midnight.

Roma Pastanesi, 99 Saraçlar Cad. This sweet shop has 3 floors, a dondurma (ice cream) machine at its entrance, and killer cake ($3 per kg.). Open daily 7am-11pm.

📷 SIGHTS

Edirne's three main mosques illustrate the architectural transition from the Selçuk style of Konya and Bursa to the more distinctively Ottoman style of İstanbul. All are packed around the city center, as are Edirne's two museums.

ESKİ CAMİ. Completed in 1414, the Eski Cami, or Old Mosque, is a prime example of an Ottoman mosque built before the conquest of Constantinople. Built in the style of Bursa's Ulu Camii (see **Bursa Sights,** p. 156), the mosque's rows of arches and pillars capped by nine small domes form a perfect square. Inside, spellbinding calligraphic inscriptions adorn the walls, and the front domes are adorned in intricate floral and botanical scenes. The marble *mihrab* is exquisitely crafted. The interior of the Eski Cami has been under restoration since 1995, but part of it can still be visited. *(Located on Talat Paşa Cad. at Hürriyet Meydanı.)*

ÜÇ ŞEREFELİ CAMİ. Built of Burgaz limestone on orders from Murat I, the Üç Şerefeli Cami illustrates an intermediate stage in the development of Ottoman architecture. When completed in 1447, it replaced the Eski Cami as Edirne's mosque for Friday prayers. The mosque, named for the three balconies *(üç şerefe)* gracing its minarets, features a fine fountain *(şadirvan)*, a tall northwest minaret (overshadowed only by the Selimiye, built two centuries later), and a dome 23m in diameter, the largest Ottoman dome at the time of its construction. A long restoration process was completed in the spring of 2000. The domes, painstakingly redone, are painted in different combinations of geometric and floral designs. At the front of the mosque, on either side of the *mihrab*, are two sets of handmade wooden doors, showcasing the mosque's best craftsmanship. *(On Hukumet Cad., the first right off of Talat Paşa Cad., opposite Şaraclar Cad.)*

SELİMIYE CAMİİ. The superb Ottoman architect Sinan's self-proclaimed masterpiece, the Selimiye Camii is considered to be the finest mosque in all of Turkey (see **Ottoman architecture,** p. 23). Because Edirne was near the front line of the campaign against Hungary, the colossal sultanic mosque was to be a standard-bearer of Islam. Sultan Selim II ordered construction to begin in 1567, the year after Sinan died; the mosque was completed in 1575.

In his design, Sinan surpassed the Aya Sofia (Hagia Sophia) in size, structural stability, and aesthetic unity. Eight massive columns support a dome slightly taller and larger in diameter than Aya Sofia, without relying on semi-domes and side-aisles for support. On the exterior, Sinan augmented the skyward orientation with four slender minarets, each 71m tall. Inside, he illuminated the massive vertical space with 999 windows, giving the interior a weightless, airy feel. The eight potentially awkward columns are seamlessly integrated into the interior design.

The artistic decoration of the mosque—the carving, painting, and tile work—suggest a similarly untouchable mastery. Because Sinan has planned closely with his artisans and craftsmen, he knew what he could demand in his designs. The 32m-wide interior dome is covered with colorful lace patterns and calligraphic inscriptions. The intricate craftsmanship of the *mimber* and the exquisite tile-work of the *mihrab* are equally breath-taking. Be sure to approach the mosque from the west, as Sinan intended, passing through the **Kavaflar Arasta** (cobbler's market) and up a small stone staircase (marked *Camii Giriş*) to the courtyard.

BEYAZIT KÜLLİYESİ (BEYAZIT COMPLEX). Built in the late 1480s by the court architect of Beyazıt II, the Beyazıt Külliyesi was a charitably endowed spiritual and physical welfare facility a few kilometers from the center of town. The centerpiece of the complex is the **Beyazıt Camii.** Multi-domed buildings, once used as schools, hospitals, and asylums surround the mosque with their handsome courtyards. Only the wing used for medical purposes is open, now housing Trakya University's **Museum of Health.** The cells of the asylum contain displays of medieval and modern medicine, including a room of herbal guidebooks and a graphic display about genital diseases. The teaching hospital that once occupied these buildings stood out as one of the foremost centers of medicine in its time. The long, narrow wing housed the mentally ill, who were soothed who were soothed by the sounds of running water from courtyard fountains. The polygonal wing, designed to encourage sociability, housed the patients with physical ailments. A platform here indicates where musicians stood to play the prescribed music therapy. Incidentally, Trakya University is known in Turkey for its medical school. *(Follow Horozlu Bayır Cad. from its origin near the Sokullu Hamamı. After it crosses the Tunca River, the road passes through a small thicket and past some fields before it crosses another bend in the river and affords the most picturesque view. Museum open Tu-Su 8:30am-5:30pm. $1.50.)*

OTHER SIGHTS. There are several sights in the center of town which merit a quick look. The **Bedesten,** on Hürriyet Meydanı, is a 500-year-old covered market where leather goods, books, stationery, linens, and postcards can be purchased. On the other side of Hürriyet Meydanı is the **Rüstem Paşa Kervansaray.** This multi-domed structure, designed in the style of the Eski Cami, was built as a resting place for medieval caravan trains. It now serves as a splendid hotel.

Near the Selimiye Camii are two museums of minor interest. In the former *medrese* of the Selimiye Camii, the **Turkish and Islamic Art Museum** contains marble plaques and monumental inscriptions, manuscript Korans, weapons, glass work, weaving, Ottoman furniture, and a special room cataloguing the history of the Kırkpınar Wrestling Festival (see below). *(Open Tu-Su 8am-noon, 1:30-5:30pm. $1.50, students $1.)* The **Ethnography Museum,** across the street, exhibits clothing, carpets, china, coins, and almost every imaginable household item from Ottoman days. *(Open Tu-Su 8:30am-noon, 1:30-5:30pm. $1.50, students $1.)*

If you are tired, relax at one of Edirne's historic hamams. Sinan's 16th-century **Sokullu Hamamı,** beside the Üç Şerefeli Camii, is the best and most beautiful. *(☎ 225 21 93. Open daily 7am-11pm for men, 9am-6pm for women. $2.50, with massage $6.25.)*

KIRKPINAR GREASE WRESTLING FESTIVAL. Once a year, competitors from all over Turkey travel to Edirne, don giant leather breeches, slather themselves in oil, and hit the mats. The champions of the Kırkpınar Grease Wrestling Festival are assured lasting fame and a portrait in the wrestling room of the Turkish and Islamic Art Museum (see above). Ahmet Taşci won in 2000, earning 9 titles since 1990 and tying the all-time record. Musical performances, crafts, and folk dancing add to the festive atmosphere. *(The festival is held during the first week of July. At the time of publication, the dates for the 2001 festival weren't available. Call the tourist office for information.)*

✂ BORDER CROSSING: BULGARIA

To cross into Bulgaria from Turkey, it is by far most efficient and convenient to take a direct bus from İstanbul. Trying to cross any other way is likely to be a hassle. However, there are a few options for those determined to leave from Edirne.

The border crossing, 18km west of Edirne, is to the left off the road from Edirne to Kapıkule. Either take the local bus into Kapıkule and walk out of town to the crossing zone, or have a dolmuş drop you directly at the entrance (both $1; see **Transportation,** p. 138). Although going on foot is possible (if the guards on duty allow it), the distance of several kilometers between the two border towns makes walking impractical. Turkish taxis will not cross the border or any of the three border checkpoints (passport control, customs, and police, though they run frequently past the Turkish side of the border in search of someone to ferry to Edirne, a $20-25 trip). Some travelers hitch a ride on one of the Bulgaria-bound buses from İstanbul or elsewhere. This will make things a lot easier on the Bulgarian side as well, since the first town, Andreevo, has no accommodations. Sofia can be reached via Plovdiv, accessible only by taxi from Andreevo.

◤ BORDER CROSSING: GREECE

Near Pazarkule and just past Karaağaç, the Greek border is less than 7km south-west of Edirne. The border crossing has extremely limited hours of operation (9am-noon). Without private transport, the best way to cross by road into Greece is a direct bus from İstanbul. Nevertheless, the crossing at Pazarkule is possible.

From Edirne, take a taxi to **Pazarkule** (15min., $6.25) or save money by catching the local bus to **Karaağaç** (frequent during the day, $.50, see **Transportation**, p. 138) and walking the remaining 2km to Pazarkule and the border. Between the Turkish and Greek border posts is a 1km no-man's land. Because Greece has declared the border area a military zone, no one may walk this 1km stretch without a military escort. Although Turkish taxis do not drive through to the Greek side, Greek taxis routinely wait at the border to ferry travelers across and on to the next Greek town, Kastanies, where bus and train connections are available.

GALLIPOLI PENINSULA AND THE DARDANELLES

> Pilgrim, be still! The soil you walk upon once engulfed the end of an era. Listen carefully! In this now quiet mound there once beat the heart of a nation.
> —Necmettin Halil Olan

The strategic position of the Gallipoli Peninsula (Gelibolu in Turkish) on the Dardanelles made it the target of a major Allied offensive in WWI. Eighty thousand Turks and more than twice as many soldiers of the British Empire—Englishmen, Australians, New Zealanders, and Indians—lost their lives in the hideous, entrenched stalemate that came of poor planning. Today, much of the peninsula and its numerous memorials and cemeteries are Commonwealth property, owned and maintained jointly by the British, Canadian, Australian, New Zealand, and Indian governments. The battlefields are best visited as a daytrip from the nearby towns of Eceabat, Çanakkale, and sometimes Gelibolu.

ECEABAT

Forty-five kilometers southwest of Gelibolu, Eceabat sits a short ferry ride (every hour on the hour, $.75) across the straits from Çanakkale and is the closest major town to the Gallipoli battlefields. The town's excellent tour company and hostel, combined with its location, make it the best base for exploring the battlefields.

◰ TRANSPORTATION. In the main square, Eceabat has both a Çanakkale Truva office and a Radar Tur office for bus connections to: **Ankara** (10hr., 2 per day 9am-9pm, $14.50); **Aydın** (9hr.; noon, 11pm, midnight, 1:15am; $10); **Bursa** (5hr., 9 per day 8am-12:30am, $7.50); **İstanbul** (5hr., every hr. 7:30am-1:30am, $10.50); **İzmir** (5hr., every hr. 6am-2am, $9); **Selçuk** (7hr.; 10:30, 11:30pm, 1:15am; $11:50). The buses to Selçuk continue on to **Antalya, Bodrum,** and **Marmaris. Dolmuş** to **Gelibolu** depart about every hour until early evening ($1).

◰◰ ORIENTATION AND PRACTICAL INFORMATION. Eceabat's main square is bordered on one side by the sea and ferry docks. The road running parallel to the sea is Cumhuriyet Cad. Facing away from the sea, the road running off to the left one block beyond Cumhuriyet Cad. is Zübeide Hanım Cad. İlhami Gezici, nick-named TJ because of his resemblance to singer Tom Jones, owns and runs ◪ **TJ's Tours** (☎814 29 40; fax 814 29 41; email TJs_TOURS@excite.com). TJ himself gives the tours of the battlefields ($19), tours of Troy when there are sufficient people ($14), and general advice for tourists. Few people in the Turkish tourist industry rival the kindness and helpfulness of the well-known and well-loved TJ. Also available are snorkeling tours of WWI seaside battle sites where adventuresome tourists frequently find unfired bullets, shells, and other war remains. The **PTT** is about a 5-minute walk along Cumhuriyet Cad. with the sea on your right. Another PTT branch is at the ferry dock. **ATMs** can be found at Is Bankası in the main square and at Ziraat Bankası, located past the Gul Restaurant.

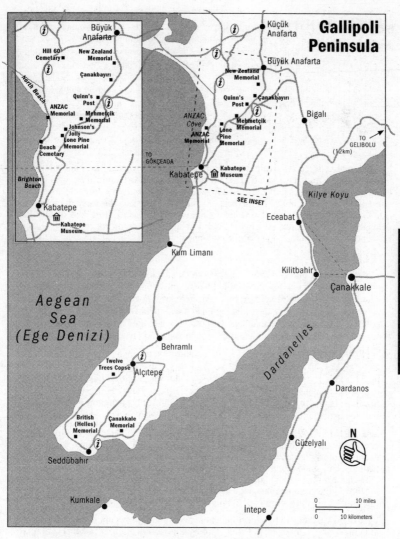

Gallipoli Peninsula

ANZAC Cove
Kabatepe

Aegean Sea (Ege Denizi)

Dardanelles

Kilye Koyu

TO GELIBOLU (12km)

Büyük Anafarta
Küçük Anafarta
Hill 60 Cemetary
New Zealand Memorial
Çanakbayırı
Quinn's Post
ANZAC Memorial
Mehmetçik Memorial
Johnson's Jolly
Lone Pine Memorial
Beach Cemetary
Brighton Beach
Kabatepe
Kabatepe Museum

New Zealand Memorial
Quinn's Post
Çanakbayırı
Mehmetçik Memorial
Lone Pine Memorial
ANZAC Memorial
Bigalı
Kabatepe Museum

TO GÖKÇEADA

SEE INSET

Kum Limanı
Eceabat
Kilitbahir
Çanakkale
Behramlı
Twelve Trees Copse
Alçıtepe
British (Helles) Memorial
Çanakkale Memorial
Seddübahir
Dardanos
Güzelyalı
İntepe
Kumkale

N

0   10 miles
0   10 kilometers

NORTHWEST

⚑ ACCOMMODATIONS. The refurbished **Down Under Hostel** (☎814 10 65 or 814 29 40; fax 814 29 41; email d.under@mailexcite.com), on Cumhuriyet Sok. to the right of the square (1min. walk), offers breakfast ($1.50), home-cooked meat and vegetarian dinners ($2 without drink), internet access ($2 per hr.), laundry service ($3.25), and spotless doubles and triples, each with towels and modern bathrooms ($5 per person). **Hotel Eceabat,** on the main square, offers average rooms with bathrooms and old TVs for $10 per person. (☎814 24 58; fax 814 24 61. Breakfast $2. V, MC, AmEx.) The **Vegemite Bar** (see **Food**) offers free camping and showers.

◐ FOOD. For a quick and inexpensive meal, the **Gül,** on the waterfront 20m to the left of the square (facing inland) on Cumhuriyet Cad., serves traditional Turkish pizzas ($2) and pick-and-choose appetizers ($1.50) in both indoor and outdoor dining areas. The **Vegemite Bar** on Zübeide Hanım Cad. is an Aussie joint, which offers travelers free camping land and hot showers in addition to Western food and drink. The **Boomerang Bar,** another little piece of Australia, serves Western fare

REIS-A-RONI Statues all over Gelibolu celebrate the achievements of the town's local hero Piri Reis, a seaman and cartographer born in Gelibolu in 1470. As an admiral in the Ottoman Navy, he collected new charts and maps from the bazaars of his many ports-of-call. In 1513, he used his extensive library of charts to draw a map of the world. Reis's map resurfaced in 1929, when a group of historians discovered it while poking around in İstanbul's Topkapı Palace. They were astonished to discover that the 1513 map showed the coastal outlines of South and North America and included precise data on Antarctica, supposedly not discovered until 1818. Further studies of Reis's map have suggested that his reference charts may have been drawn from aerial pictures; the rivers, mountain ranges, islands, deserts, and plateaus are drawn with unusual accuracy.

(hamburger $1.20), Australian specialties (Vegemite toast $1.20), and plenty of beer ($1.60; imported alcohol $5). To get there, follow Cumhuriyet Cad. to the right from the main square. At a slightly higher price but with tablecloths and an excellent view, the **Murat Restaurant,** on the water next to the ferry dock, serves the best seafood in town (fixed menu including fish, salad, fruit, and drink $12). Eceabat's two bars are shrewdly placed at the far ends of the town away from potential complaints of noise and rowdiness.

GELİBOLU ☎286

Though the Battle of Gallipoli actually occurred many kilometers away at ANZAC Cove and Hellas Point, the town of Gelibolu became the namesake of the entire peninsula. Gelibolu is a pleasant destination in its own right, with its quiet atmosphere, fresh fish, and beach. However, it is the most expensive and inconvenient base for touring the battlefields. Eceabat and Çanakkale are both closer to the battlefield sites and better equipped for budget tourism. Gelibolu is probably best seen as a daytrip from Eceabat.

▐ TRANSPORTATION. From the main square, facing away from the harbor, the otogar is 1km to your left, the museum directly in front, and the Yelkenci and Yılmaz hotels to the right. From Gelibolu, **Radar Tur** (☎566 64 24) offers non-stop buses to **İstanbul** (4½hr., every hr. on the hr., $8) and **İzmir** (6½hr., 4 per day, $10). A minibus runs every hour to **Eceabat** (30min., $1) from the otogar. Ferries service **Lapseki**, northeast of Çanakkale on the mainland (every hr. 9am-midnight, $.75).

▐▐ ORIENTATION AND PRACTICAL INFORMATION. Across from the Yılmaz Hotel in the main square, **Atatürk Cad.** leads up to the secondary town square near the top of the hill. Services include the **PTT,** 3 Cumhuriyet Okulu Cad. (open M-F 7am-12:30pm, 1:30-8:30pm for post and money exchange; daily 7am-12:30pm, 1:30-10:30pm for phone cards); **pharmacies** (all open daily 9am-7pm) and grocery stores on Atatürk Cad.; an **Akbank** with a V/MC/Cirrus **ATM** near the harbor and to the right of the tower museum (open daily 9am-12:30pm, 1:30-5pm).

▐ ACCOMMODATIONS. Gelibolu's best accommodations are a short walk from the main square. Down from the square by the water, the **Otel Yelkenci** on Liman Meydanı offers hospitable rooms without bath, but most with a good view of the small harbor (☎566 10 22. $8 per person. V, MC.) **The Yılmaz Hotel,** 8 Liman Mevkii, offers singles with shower. It also organizes daily tours of the battlefields ($25) but they're led by a tape-recording. (☎566 12 56, 566 35 98 or 566 35 95. Breakfast included. $10. 10% *Let's Go* discount.) The **Oya Hotel** is slightly more expensive. Each room has its own bath and TV. (Breakfast included. $15 per person.)

▐ FOOD. For meals, the local seafood can't be beat. The **Boğaz Restaurant,** 22 Liman Meydanı (☎566 16 06), and neighboring **Imren Restaurant,** Liman Meydanı (☎566 23 22), have views of the harbor and the daily fish market from their outdoor tables. Seafood dishes run $4-6; sardines are a local specialty. If fish doesn't float your boat, **Yarımada Lokantası,** 34 Atatürk Cad. (☎566 12 25), is an excellent family restaurant with an uncommonly large selection of dishes. For after-dinner *dondurma*, there is no shortage of ice cream shops throughout the city. **Roma,** at the base of Atatürk Cad. across from the Yılmaz Hotel (and also in a kiosk along the waterfront halfway to the bus station), makes cones while you watch.

🕐 **SIGHTS.** Gelibolu's only legitimate historical sights are the **fortifications** that surround the back side of the harbor. Inside the two-story stone tower, the most distinctive part of the fortification is a small, dimly lit, dusty **museum** which displays Byzantine terra-cotta lamps, faded reproductions of photographs, and rusted WWI bullets from Gallipoli. *(Open daily 9-5. Free.)*

BATTLEFIELDS OF GALLIPOLI

About 10km northwest of Eceabat lie the battlefields of **Gallipoli**. Shortly after the beginning of WWI, Britain's young First Lord of the Admiralty, **Winston Churchill,** proposed that Britain use its superior naval forces to launch an attack on the Dardanelles, drive Turkey out of the war, and open communications with Russia. After a few unsuccessful attempts on the straits in late 1914 by an Anglo-French fleet, the Allies returned in March 1915, determined to penetrate the waterway. Badly scattered by Turkish mines, the Allied fleet regrouped on the Greek island of Limnos and shifted tactics, preparing for an amphibious assault on Turkish forces on the peninsula. The several months spent preparing the Allied expeditionary forces backfired, allowing the Turks time to secure their defenses. Bad move.

The Allies resolved to land an Anglo-French force at Hellas Point, the mouth of the straits, while **ANZAC** (Australian-New Zealand Army Corps) troops simultaneously invaded the beach north of **Kabatepe.** At daybreak on April 25, 1915, the Anglo-French regiment landed and, at great cost, established a beachhead which they were hard-pressed to expand throughout the rest of the campaign. The ANZACs suffered even more casualties but managed to drive inland slowly, aiming to threaten the Turkish stronghold of **Conkbayırı.** In the face of fierce Turkish resistance, the battle dissolved into a bloody stalemate. The battle of Gallipoli launched its hero, **Atatürk,** on a rapid rise toward his status as Turkey's founding father, while temporarily endangering Churchill's career. By the time the unsuccessful Allies withdrew in December of 1915, the campaign had claimed over 80,000 Turkish soldiers and more than 200,000 Allied troops.

The disproportionate sacrifice of the ANZACs heightened the sense of sovereignty for Australia and New Zealand within the British Commonwealth. Each year, thousands of Australians and New Zealanders make pilgrimages to Gallipoli's war cemeteries, and April 25, the date of the Allied landing, is an important day of remembrance in both countries. Thousands of Australians and New Zealanders pack every hotel in Çanakkale and Eceabat for the anniversary.

🕐 **SIGHTS**

Gallipoli's battle sights and accompanying memorials are spread out, so your best bet is to take an organized tour, many of which provide lunch, excellent English-speaking guides, and transportation to each of the memorials. Tours are available from Çanakkale (see Çanakkale: Tourist Agencies, p. 149), Eceabat (see p. 144), and Gelibolu (see p. 146). Bring along your swimsuit, since tours often make a short stop for a swim. If you want to visit the area on your own, take a dolmuş to the Kabatepe Müzesi (☎814 12 97) from Eceabat. The museum has a good collection of photographs from the battle, as well as old uniforms, weapons, skeletal remains, and, to demonstrate the intensity of the fighting, two bullets which collided in midair. (Museum open daily 8:30am-noon, 1-5:30pm. $1.20.)

ANZAC COVE. Four kilometers from the museum is ANZAC Cove, where the Australia-New Zealand Army Corps first landed on April 25th. The ANZACs had intended to land on the wide shore to the south called Brighton Beach, but their landing boats were carried on north by a combination of strong ocean currents and bad leadership. Instead of wide beaches, they found themselves on a preposterously narrow strip whose heights were dominated by heavily entrenched Turkish forces. Undeterred, the ANZAC troops forced their way slowly uphill, dying in droves as they went. Eventually they fought their way to a stalemate, and both sides hunkered down in anticipation of the long and bloody battle ahead. In the ANZAC Cove, you can see a stone monument inscribed with a moving tribute by Atatürk to the young men of all nationalities who died fighting.

NORTHWEST

THE LONE PINE MEMORIAL. Seven kilometers uphill from the museum, this marks the site of an unsuccessful Australian attempt to break the stalemate. The graveyard and monument commemorate the thousands of lives lost in the effort.

JOHNSTON'S JOLLY. A short walk north from the Lone Pine brings you to Johnston's Jolly, where the still-visible opposing trenches of the Australians and the Turks are so close together that they actually line both sides of the road. The site is so named because the Australian commander Johnston amused the nearby Turkish soldiers with his jovial antics.

OTHER SIGHTS. More memorials and battle-sites line the road uphill to Conkbayırı, the highest point of the battlefield, controlled throughout by Atatürk's forces. The **New Zealand Memorial** shares the hilltop with a statue of Atatürk.

Tours don't always include the memorials at the southern tip of the peninsula (some 30km from **Kilitbahir,** the town directly across from Çanakkale at the Dardanelles's narrowest point), but these can easily be seen on a separate trip. Take the smaller ferry from Çanakkale to Kilitbahir and then ride one of the regular minibuses to the **Çanakkale Memorial** at **Melles Point,** at the tip of the peninsula.

ÇANAKKALE ☎286

Modern Çanakkale presides over the mythic and eternally strategic Dardanelles, straits which have seen poets and soldiers come and go for centuries. In 1915, Winston Churchill ordered an ultimately unsuccessful naval operation to take the straits. His goal was to keep Turkey out of WWI by bringing British gunboats into İstanbul. The prospect of storming the fields where the fates of Hector and Achilles were decided, not to mention raising the Union Jack over the great city of Constantinople, kindled the British Empire's romantic spark. The outcome of the battle is well known: the naval operation's failure forced the army to land on the peninsula and fight an almost year-long battle in disease-ridden trenches, ultimately ending in the Allied withdrawal (see **Battlefields of Gallipoli,** p. 147). Nonetheless, Çanakkale and the Dardanelles have carried on in legend as the birthplace of the sagas of both Atatürk and ANZAC.

With its inexpensive accommodations and frequent bus connections to nearby sights and cities, Çanakkale is an easy base from which to explore Gallipoli and Troy. Though not the most scenic locale, it appears to be improving as the central Cumhuriyet Meydanı is refurbished and local tourist establishments are expanded. If you intend to visit only Gallipoli and not Troy, Eceabat (see p. 144) is a more peaceful base since it is smaller and less frantic. Nevertheless, Çanakkale is particularly hospitable to New Zealanders and Australians, compatriots of the thousands who lost their lives in the battle. Every year, thousands of Australians and Kiwis make the pilgrimage to Gallipoli, particularly around ANZAC Day (April 25th), when every accommodation in town is sure to be overbooked.

▐ TRANSPORTATION

Those approaching from the European side (on a ferry from Eceabat) arrive at the ferry dock while those approaching from the Anatolian side arrive at the otogar. To get to the ferry area from the otogar turn left along **Atatürk Cad.,** after a short 30m make a right onto **Demircioğlu Cad.,** and follow signs marked "Feribot."

Buses: The **Kamil Koç** bus company offers the greatest number of trips daily. To: **Ankara** (11hr., 10 per day 7am-1am, $15); **Bursa** (4½hr., 5 per day 6:15am-5pm, $6.50); **Edirne** (5hr., 4 per day 1pm-10pm, $8); **İstanbul** (5hr.; every hr. until 7pm, every 2hr. afterwards; $10); **İzmir** (5hr., 16 per day 6:45am-2:30am, $8); **Selçuk** (6hr., 16 per day 6:45am-2:30am, $8.75). **Dolmuş** ($.50-$1) run from under the small bridge over the Sarı Çay inlet to **Troy** (25 min., leaving throughout day when the dolmus fills, $.80).

Ferries: To **Eceabat** (30 min., 5am and every hr. 7am-1am). Buy a token ($1) at the window next to the PTT booth. The smaller ferry to **Kilitbahir** is left of the main docks when facing the sea (about every 15min., $.40). Board the ferry; a porter will collect the fare.

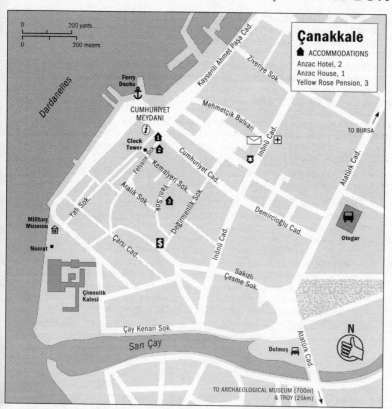

Çanakkale

⌂ ACCOMMODATIONS
Anzac Hotel, 2
Anzac House, 1
Yellow Rose Pension, 3

✳ 🛈 ORIENTATION AND PRACTICAL INFORMATION

Practically everything relating to budget travel (food, accommodations, and travel agencies) lies within the one-block area around the **ferry dock** and the clock tower.

Tourist Office: 67 İskele Meydanı (☎/fax 217 11 87). English-speaking staff distributes maps and helps find rooms in the high season. Open M-F 8am-7pm, Sa-Su 10am-6pm.

Tourist Agencies: Tours of the Gallipoli battlefields and the city of Troy are available through both the **Hassle Free Travel Agency** based in Çanakkale and **TJ's Tours** based in Eceabat. The afternoon tours include lunch, and both afternoon and morning tours include an English-speaking guide, transportation, and admission to the sights. **The Hassle Free Travel Agency,** 61 Cumhuriyet Meydanı (☎213 59 69; email hasslefree@anzachouse.com) provides daily Gallipoli tours (Apr.-Nov. 11:45am, Dec.-Mar. 10:45am; $19) and almost-daily Troy tours (Apr.-Nov. 8:45am, Dec.-Mar. 7:45am; $14) that depart from Anzac House. ◪**TJ's Tours** (☎814 29 40; fax 814 29 41; email TJs_TOURS@excite.com) provides daily Gallipoli tours (12:30pm, $19) and Troy tours (8:45am, $14) when sufficient demand. Call ahead to reserve a space.

ATMs: Several **banks** with Cirrus/Plus ATMs stand on a 4-way intersection in a secluded part of the city. To get there, walk up Demircioğlu Cad. away from the ferry docks, and turn right onto Değirmenlik Sok., the 4th right after Anzac House. Follow this street for a few minutes to the intersection. All 3 banks open M-F 9am-12:30pm, 1:30-5:30pm.

Police: (☎212 14 66), off İnönü Cad. next to the PTT.

Pharmacy: Pelini Eczanesi (☎217 12 60), on Demircioğlou Cad. just down from Anzac House (towards the ferry dock). Many more pharmacies on the right hand side of Demircioğlu Sok. as you walk away from the ferry docks.

Hospitals: Devlet Hastanesi (public, ☎217 10 98), off İnönü Cad. across from the PTT. **Özel Hastanesi** (private, ☎217 74 61), on Atatürk Cad., about a 20min. walk from the bridge over the Sarı Çay, away from town.

PTT: Central location on İnönü Cad. Traveler's check and money exchange. Open 8:30am-12:30pm, 1:30-5pm. Small satellite PTT in front of ferry docks. Useful for buying stamps and telephone cards. Open daily 8am-midnight. **Postal code:** 17100.

ACCOMMODATIONS

Budget accommodations cluster around the clock tower, with many good restaurants and bars only a few steps away.

Efes Hotel, 5 Aralık Sok. (☎217 3256). Walk to the left of the clock tower, then turn left onto Aralık Sok. Completely tiled, spotless hotel with relatively spacious rooms, each with bath. Operated entirely by one lovely English-speaking Turkish woman. Parking spots in front. Particularly welcoming to single female travelers. Breakfast $2.50. Singles $10; doubles $13; triples $15. 25% discount for *Let's Go* readers.

Anzac House, 61 Cumhuriyet Meydanı (☎213 59 69; fax 217 29 06; email hasslefree@anzachouse.com; www.anzachouse.com). When facing Cumhuriyet Meydanı with your back to the ferry docks, it's located immediately on your right. A popular spot with Aussie and Kiwi backpackers. Minimalist rooms with spotless sheets and clean communal bathrooms with hot showers. Laundry service ($2.80) and internet access ($4 per hr.). Arranges daily Gallipoli and Troy tours through the Hassle Free Tour Agency. *Gallipoli* starring Mel "Kanga" Gibson shown nightly at 9:30pm. Breakfast $2; $5 BBQ every evening on the rooftop overlooking the Dardanelles. 24 hr. reception. Dorms $5; singles $9.75; doubles $14.50; triples $18; quads $24. V, MC, AmEx.

Yellow Rose Pension, 5 Yeni Sok. (☎/fax 217 33 43; email yellowrose1@mailexcite.com; www.yellowrose.4mg.com). Turn left onto Kemal Yeri at the clock tower and then right onto Yeni Sok. A popular backpacker hangout, the Yellow Rose has moderately clean, cramped single-sex dorm rooms, each with its own bath. Other features include table tennis in the shaded garden, window screens, laundry service ($5), and international phone and fax services. *Gallipoli* starring Mel Gibson shown each morning before the Gallipoli tour. Breakfast $1.50. Internet $2 per hr. Dorms $4; single $7; 2 twin beds $6; double bed $5.

Anzac Hotel, 8 Saat Kulesi Meydanı (☎217 77 77; fax 217 20 18). Next to the clock tower. Spotlessly unremarkable rooms in this higher-end hotel feature TV and tiled bath. Elevator. Attractive, warmly lit dining area. English-speaking receptionist only in evenings. Singles $40; doubles $50; triples $66. $10 discount for *Let's Go* readers.

FOOD

Many of Çanakkale's restaurants serve the catch of the day along the waterfront. You can also find the standard Turkish fare infused with some Australian flare.

Doyum Pide ve Kebap Salonu (☎217 48 10). On the right side of Demircioğlu Cad., a few minutes from the Anzac House (away from the ferry docks). Excellent *Iskender kebap* ($2.50) and *lahmacun* ($.45) make this restaurant a local favorite. A few English-speaking waiters facilitate ordering off the Turkish menu. Open 10am-midnight.

Boğaz 2000, 4 Saat Kulesi Meydanı (☎214 08 88). On your left when facing the clock tower. Buffet-style restaurant. Step inside, choose small portions, and then sit. The waiter will bring you your meal. Very tidy with antique photos on the walls and a calming atmosphere. Specialties are *döner kebap* ($2.50) and *Kemal Paşa Tatlısı* (a dessert with cheese inside; $.75). Open daily for lunch and dinner.

The Yeni Entellektüel, 7 Iskele Meydanı, Eski Balıkhane Sok. (New Intellectual; ☎214 16 44), a minute walk from Cumhuriyet Meydanı along the waterfront towards the Military Museum. An indoor/outdoor cafe on the waterfront with fresh flowers and an inspiring view of the ships in the harbor. Serves Turkish breakfast ($2.50), an array of starters ($1.20 each), and meat and fish entrees ($2.50-3.50). Open 8am-2pm. V, MC.

Aussie/Kiwi Restaurant, 32 Yalı Cad. (☎212 17 22). Walking towards the clock tower from Cumhuriyet Meydanı, veer to the right at the tower; it's on your right a couple of blocks up. Standing outside the restaurant, armed with a convincing Australian accent, owner Kemal lures many a plastic dollar-toting traveler (Australian bills are made of plastic). Meals ($3) are a combination of Western and Turkish cuisine: lamb şiş kebap comes with french fries. English magazines and newspapers offered for perusal. Free Milo (hot chocolate) with every meal. Happy hour 5-7pm. Open daily 8am-about 2am.

SIGHTS

ÇIMENLIK KALESI (GRASSY CASTLE). About 200m downstream from the harbor lies a combined city park and naval museum. Its shady groves reveal nothing of its significance in the early part of the Gallipoli campaign. The castle, originally built by Mehmet the Conqueror and reinforced by Abdul Aziz in the 19th century, was a major Turkish battery, containing what little heavy artillery the Turks had. Several Turkish guns from the battle of Gallipoli lie scattered around the park. The Turkish mine layer **Nusrat**, with its decks full of racked mines, is also in the park. As a result of Nusrat's daring missions, three large Allied battleships, *Ocean*, *Irresistible*, and *Bouvet*, were destroyed, crippling the Allied attack.

MILITARY MUSEUM. The exhibit displays such novelties as a pair of bullets that collided in mid-air, as well as drawings by Mehmet Ali Laga, the first Turkish soldier-artist. Among these is a charcoal drawing of Çanakkale's clock tower as it appeared in 1915. The museum has excellent English translations throughout, and if you have questions, the young Turkish men doing their military service staffing the museum are glad to share their knowledge. *(In the small white house by the park entrance. Open Tu-W and F-Su 9am-noon, 1:30-5pm. $.75; students $.30.)*

ARCHAEOLOGICAL MUSEUM. This well-displayed collection features items from many local excavations, including those at Troy. Particularly exceptional are several cases of excellent Hellenistic and Roman glassware, including a few especially colorful Phoenician vessels. Also notable are a large, well-preserved statue of the Roman Emperor Trajan and several cases of Hellenistic funerary objects. The Trojan collection primarily features well-preserved ceramics and household items from each of the various Trojan settlements (see **Truva**, p. 164). One of the most notable objects recently arrived from the excavation field: an exquisitely crafted sarcophagus. It is the very last piece in the museum (in the museum you must move essentially in one direction). Though badly damaged, it still shows traces of paint. This museum also displays the wares from which Çanakkale took its name. You can view a number of earthenware bowls *(çanak)* produced locally in the 19th century. *(Kale* means "castle.") To see these, you'll have to head to the waterfront. Unfortunately, the placards are not translated into English. *(100 Yuzuncu Yıl Cad. Walk on Atatürk Cad. away from the otogar, about 2km past the bridge. ☎217 67 40. Open daily 8:30am-5pm. $1.25, students $.75.)*

ENTERTAINMENT

The city's ever-changing body of short-term visitors and the prevailing quiet during the long off-season make Çanakkale nightlife a lot like the Troy dolmuş: it only really goes if there are enough people.

The TNT Bar/Garden (☎217 07 74), on Saat Kulesi Meydanı, is probably the best of the bars, drawing in the hostelers to drink and play pool ($4 per hr.) to the beat of Turkish and Western rock in a big wooden house. The garden in back serves drinks and quality fare ($4-6) in a romantically lamp-lit, tree-canopied space. Many vegetarian options. Open daily in summer 3pm-2am; in winter 3pm-midnight. V, MC, AmEx.

Carıklı, 20 Fetuahane Sok. Across the street from Depo Disco Bar. When you tire of foreign tunes blaring from the speakers, you can walk up to the 2nd floor here and get groovy with live Turkish music every night. No food, but plenty of alcohol (foreign and local) served. Open daily in summer 8pm-2am; in winter 8pm-midnight.

Depo Disco Bar, 19 Fetuahare Sok. (☎212 68 13). Veer to the left of the clock tower when walking from Cumhuriyet Meydanı. Great for all-out dancing and getting down with foreign hits and Turkish favorites like Tarkan. Depo and the yellow-fronted satellite club across the street overflow with revelers on roaring nights around Anzac Day (April 25). Open in summer 8:30pm-2am; in winter 6:30pm-midnight.

Alesta, 4 Yalı Cad. (☎217 87 32). Next to the clock tower. This tiny joint serves as the town's low-key dance bar, playing REM and other introspective pop in the early evening before plugging in the woofers for bass-heavy dance music. Happy hour 10pm-midnight (4th beer is free). Open daily in summer 2pm-2am; in winter 2pm-midnight.

THE EASTERN MARMARA REGION

BURSA ☎224

At the base of the 2km high slopes of Mt. Uludağ, Bursa is both one of Turkey's holiest cities and a major industrial center. Surrounded by fertile plains and blessed with vast gardens and parks, the city has earned the moniker "Green Bursa." Since green is also the symbolic color of Islam, the nickname has a double meaning. While the city's 14th-century mosques and tombs still receive visitors, Bursa's robust economy has fueled the development of a wealthy resort area among the towering mountains, including one of Turkey's hottest skiing spots.

Osman, founder of the Ottoman *(Osmanlı)* dynasty, besieged Bursa for nearly a decade before his son Orhan seized the town in 1326 and made it the empire's first capital. The mosques and tombs scattered around the city harken back to the formative stages of Ottoman architecture, when Selçuk influence was still strong.

Despite the relocation of the capital to Edirne and then to İstanbul, Bursa remained an important Ottoman city, bolstered by its role as a center of fine silk production. Today, silk trade remains a major industry in Bursa; the bi-annual silk worm cocoon harvest is held here every June and September. The city is also the home of Turkish shadow theater, an art that then spread all over the Ottoman Empire. Bursa boasts a museum, monument, theater, and annual festival all dedicated to the performance and preservation of the show. The town also claims a number of culinary triumphs: the *İskender kebap* (lamb meat with tomato sauce served on a bed of bread chunks with yogurt) and *İnegöl Köfte* (a kind of meatball) were both invented here. Perhaps anticipating the gastric misery resulting from eating too much kebap, Sultan Süleyman's Grand Vizier commissioned several mineral baths only a few minutes outside of central Bursa.

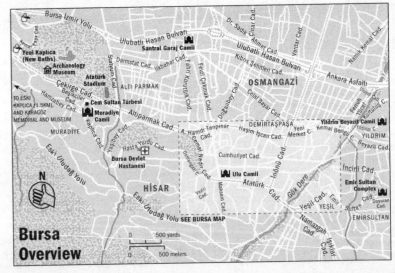

Bursa Overview

NORTHWEST

▐ TRANSPORTATION

Buses: Bursa's terminal is 20km outside the city center. Local bus #90/A goes directly downtown ($.45). To get back to the bus station, pick up the same bus by the PTT on Atatürk Cad. (every 30min. 6:20am-midnight, $.45). The ride takes about 30min., as the bus tends to make a number of stops along the way.

Destination	Company	Duration	Times (daily)	Price
Afyon	Kamil Koç	5hr.	6 per day 8:30am-10pm	$10
Amasya	Yeni Amasya Tur	8½hr.	6:30pm	$14.30
Ankara	Kamil Koç	5½hr.	every hr. 6am-3am	$9.25
Ayvalık	Kamil Koç	5hr.	10 per day 9am-2am	$9.25
Bodrum	Kamil Koç	9hr.	8:30pm, midnight	$16
Çanakkale	Kamil Koç	5hr.	very frequent	$8.50
Çeşme	Kamil Koç	8hr.	2pm, 1:30am	$11
Datça	Kamil Koç	12hr.	10:30pm	$18
Denizli	Kamil Koç	8½hr.	12:30am	$14
Eskişehir	Kamil Koç	2½hr.	every hr.	$5.50
Fethiye	Kamil Koç	10hr.	8:30, 9:30pm	$17.50
Giresun	Ulusoy	16hr.	1, 3, 5, 7pm	$26.50
İstanbul	Kamil Koç	3½hr.	very frequent	$8.25
İzmir	Kamil Koç	5hr.	every hr.	$8.25
İznik	Atan Kardeşler	1½hr.	every hr. 7am-7pm	$2.40
Konya	Kontur	8½hr.	9am, 11pm	$8.50
Kuşadası	Kamil Koç	7½hr.	noon, 10pm, midnight, 2am	$11
Kütahya	Has Tour	2½hr.	1:30, 7pm	$6
Marmaris	Kamil Koç	9½hr.	10:30am, 10:30pm, 1am	$16
Ordu	Ulusoy	14hr.	1, 3, 5, 7pm	$25
Samsun	Ulusoy	12hr.	1, 3, 5, 7pm	$23
Trabzon	Ulusoy	18hr.	1, 3, 5, 7pm	$30
Yalova	Yalova Seyahat	50min.	every ½hr. 6am-10:30pm	$2.50

Ferries and Seabuses: This is an excellent way to travel from İstanbul. Ferries and seabuses connect İstanbul and Bursa via Yalova. (For ferry information to Yalova, see **Yalova: Practical Information,** p. 160.) Buses make the hour-long trip from the ferry docks at Yalova to Bursa's Terminal every 30-40min. (8am-10pm, $2.50).

Dolmuş: Bursa has an extensive dolmuş system. Each car takes 4 passengers ($.40-$.60 per person) and leaves from either Atatürk Cad., behind the *Adliye,* or from further down the street, before the Atatürk statue in Heykel. Destinations and stops in between are on a sign on the roof. The city has many garages *(garaj)* from the days before the construction of its *terminal.* Don't assume that a dolmuş marked "*garaj*" will take you to the one you want. Most garages, however, are a short walk away from Atatürk Cad.

◢▞ ORIENTATION AND PRACTICAL INFORMATION

Except for the Ulu Cami, all of Bursa's sights lie about 1½km east and west of either end of **Atatürk Cad.,** while all of the hotels and restaurants, except those in the Arap Şükrü district, are within a block of Atatürk Cad. in the area called **Heykel.**

Tourist Offices: To get to the main tourist office (☎220 18 48), head to the Ulu Cami side of Atatürk Cad., walk past the fountain toward the Atatürk statue, and go down the stairs on the left. Signs point the way. Helpful, English-speaking staff can help with hotel bookings and offers a city guidebook with a detailed map for $1. Open daily May-Sept. 8:30am-6pm; Oct.-Apr. 8am-5pm. A 2nd tourist information booth next to the Yeşil Türbesi provides the same. Open July 1-Sept. 15 M-Sa 9am-6pm, Su 11am-5pm.

Banks and Currency Exchange: Numerous banks line Atatürk Cad. **Akbank, VakıfBank, Garanti,** and **Pamukbank** all have branches along the main street that can **change foreign currency,** and all have **ATM** machines that accept V/MC/Cirrus/Plus.

English-Language Bookstores: Elt Kitabevi (☎ 223 41 80), Eski Adliye Karşısı, up Konaaltı Sok. by the old government building, has a selection of periodicals and Penguin and Wordsworth classics. Open daily 9am-8pm. **Santana,** 12 R. Şefik Bursalı Cad. (☎224 56 42), has a small but carefully selected collection of music. The owner might even dig into his own stacks if you're looking for something specific. Open 10am-9pm.

Police: (☎221 35 12 or 155 in an emergency.) There are 2 police stations minutes off Atatürk Cad.; one 2 blocks down İnönü Cad. and the other a 5min. walk on Cemal Nadir Cad., the continuation of Atatürk Cad., toward the tombs of Orhan and Osman Gazi.

Hospitals: Hayat Hastanesi (private, ☎225 08 50), just a few blocks from Atatürk Cad. on İnönü Cad. There are signs all the way down the street from the Atatürk statue. **Vatan Hastanesi** (private, ☎220 10 40), further down İnönü Cad. **Devlet Hastanesi** (state, ☎220 00 20). Take a dolmuş from Atatürk Bul., or dial ☎111 for an ambulance.

Internet Access: Elite Internet Cafe, 37 Yeşil Cad. (☎327 03 34), before the overpass leading to the Emir Sultan Cami. $1.30 per hr. 1 per hr. Open daily 10am-1am.

PTT: Across the street from Ulu Cami. Open daily 8am-11pm. Airmail services 8am-5:30pm. **Currency exchange** that cashes **traveler's checks.** Open M-F 8:30am-5:30pm. **Postal code:** 16300.

▌ ACCOMMODATIONS

A number of Bursa's budget hotels lie off Atatürk Cad., to the south of the PTT. Hotels closer to the main street tend to be noisy.

Otel Güneş, 75 İnebey Cad. (☎222 14 04). 8 basic rooms with linoleum floors and large, clean, shared baths. Tidy and quiet. Plants in the humble lobby give the place a friendly atmosphere. Singles $10; doubles $16.50; triples $21.50; quads $24.

Otel Deniz, 19 Tahtakale Veziri Cad. (☎222 92 38). Keeping the Ulu Cami on the right, walk along Atatürk Cad. and turn left after the Sümerbank. Walk 2 blocks to the end of this street, take a right onto Veziri Cad., and walk 75m. 12 comfortable, quiet rooms around a pleasant courtyard. Shared bath and free laundry. Owner locks up between midnight and 1am, though it is possible to get in later. Singles $8; doubles $14.

Çeşmeli Otel, 6 Gümüşçeken Cad. (☎/fax 224 15 11). Down a street across from the Atatürk statue and a block towards Ulu Cami. This is the place to go if you're willing to spend some extra money. Sparkling, well furnished rooms with couches, fridges, and TV. Cleaning staff leaves *lokum* on your pillow. Female owners and friendly staff. Some rooms with A/C. Breakfast included. Singles $30; doubles $50; triples $60.

Lâl Otel, 79 Maksem Cad. (☎221 17 10). Follow Atatürk Cad. towards Ulu Cami with the mosque on your right, and turn left after the PTT. 21 large, unremarkable rooms with common baths. Hot shower $2. Singles $10; doubles $16.50; triples $21; quads $24.

◖♫ FOOD AND ENTERTAINMENT

You've been eating it all over Turkey, but now you've come to the birthplace of the famous *İskender kebap.* Restaurants specializing in the dish cluster in between the Atatürk statue and the Green Mosque. Bursa's **Kültür Parkı** district also has decent, though pricier restaurants and cafes. (Take a dolmuş from Heykel, $.30.) The Arap Şükrü district, next to Tophane Parki and centered around Sakarya Cad., a cobblestone side street off of Cemal Nadir Cad., features fish restaurants, bars, and pubs. To get to Arap Şükrü, follow Atatürk Cad. 1½km west, and after passing the park containing the Orhan and Osman Gazi tombs., bear left onto Sakarya Cad.

▨ **Kebapçı İskender** (☎221 46 15) has two locations: a large, posh restaurant at 7 Ünlü Cad. and a smaller one by the Cultural Center on Atatürk Bul. Claims to have invented the *İskender kebap* ($2.50 for a single portion) in 1867. Once served, don't dig in until they bring the pan of browned butter and apply the final fixin'. Open daily 11am-9pm.

Bursa

▲ ACCOMMODATIONS

Otel Deniz, 1
Otel Güneş, 2
Lâl Otel, 3
Çeşmeli Otel, 4

N

150 yards
150 meters

NORTHWEST

TO EMİR SULTAN COMPLEX (400M)
TO YILDIRIM BEYAZIT COMPLEX (800M)

Sevindik Sok.
Sible Cad.
İnce Ar.
Emir Sultan Cad.
Yeşil Camii
Yeşil Türbe
Alan Sok.
Yeşil Alan Sok.
Sağlık Sok.
Turkish & Islamic Arts Museum
Müze Sok.
Çelebi Mehmet Bul.
Değirmen Sok.
Akdemir Sok.
Yeşil Cad.
İncirli Cad.
Adliye Sok.
Cumhuriyet Cad.
Yeşil Cad.
Karakol Cad.
Gök Deresi
Alncak Cad.
İsfagu Cad.
Kütüphne Sok.
Selçuk Halun Sok.
Selçuk Halun Cad.
Hocaisabey Cad.
Atatürk Cad.
Ünlü Cad.
İnönü Cad.
Kerestecller Cad.
Kayan Cad.
Demirciler Cad.
Devociler Cad.
Sidika Halun Cad.
Yeni Merkez Cad.
Ar Sok.
Apşak Sok.
Celal Bayar Cad.
Tahil Cad.
Cumhuriyet Cad.
Cancilar Cad.
Tuzpazarı Cad.
Boyathane Sok.
Abdal Cad.
Ürün Cad.
Haşım İşcan Cad.
Elmalık Cad.
İsmail Hakkı Cad.
Tavşadan Cad.
Bekirdede Sok
Reyhan Cad.
Mantıcı Cad.
Şehreküstü Cad.
A. Hamdi Tanpınar Cad.
TO OTOGAR (1KM)
Sakarya Cad.
TO MURADİYE COMPLEX (1.5km), ARCHAEOLOGY MUSEUM (2km), KARAGÖZ MEMORIAL (3km), AND BATHS (2.5km)
Cemal Nadir Cad.
Clock Tower
Osmangazi Tomb
Orhangazi Tomb
Durak Cad.
Fevzi Çakmak Cad.
Ulucami Cad.
Cemal Nadir Cad.
Osmangazi Cad.
Orta Pazar Cad.
Kavakli Cad.
Konur Alp Cad.
Temiz Cad.
Muradiye Dolmuş
B. Çarşısı Cad.
Şeker Hoca Cad.
Çelebiler Cad.
Çeşmeli Otel
Flower Market
Çömlekciler Cad.
Belediye Cad.
Gümüşçeken Cad.
Orhan Sok.
Paris Çık Sok.
Belediye
Vilayet
R. Şefik Bursalı Cad.
Alb. Bekir Sami Cad.
Heykel
Kültür Sok.
Tuzpazarı Sok.
Tek Sok.
Fedrlci Sok.
Kültür Sok.
Borsa Sok.
Uzun Çarşı Cad.
D.K. Çarşısı Cad.
Koza Han
Orhan Camii
Emir Han
Bedesten
Ulu Camii
Atatürk Cad.
Taşkapı Cad.
Akbıyık Cad.
Maksem Cad.
İnebey Cad.
Yeşil Cad.
Işıklar Cad.
Fışkırık Cad.
Kızıkulu Cad.
İbrahim Paşa Cad.
Konaklı Sok.

Çiçek Izgara, 15 Belediye Cad. (☎221 65 26). In the square behind the large brick and wood building (town hall) on Atatürk Cad. One of Bursa's better restaurants. Sit-down service and uniformed waiters. Carnivore-oriented menu, with delicious *köfte* and *kasarlı köfte* (meatballs and cheese; $4). Roast tomatoes and peppers ($2.50) are excellent on the side. Open daily 11am-4pm, 6-9:30pm.

Hanzade Bar/Restaurant, 43 Sakarya Cad. (☎221 00 52). One of the many similar fish restaurants with outdoor seating along the narrow, cobblestone road. Serves fresh fish ($6-8) and *köfte* ($3). Open daily 4pm-1am.

Lalezar, 14/C Ünlü Cad. (☎221 84 24). Across from Kebapçı İskender, featuring a special dish for each day of the week. Try the tasty vegetarian appetizers ($1.40) and desserts, including *kadayıf* in milk and nuts ($1). Open M-Sa 7:30am-9:30pm.

Gedelek Turşuları. On R. Şefik Bursalı Cad. Sells nothing but pickled items, including pickled peppers, pickled beans, pickled raspberries, and of course, pickles and pickle juice. Try a glass for $.20 and send your stomach on an adventure.

Kafkas, 31 Atatürk Cad. (☎221 55 49). On the corner of Atatürk Cad. and R. Şefik Bursalı Cad., down from Pizza Hut. A Bursa institution, with several city locations. Delectable and reasonably-priced chocolates, pastries, and the self-proclaimed best *kestane şekeri* (candied chestnuts) in Bursa ($8.30 for 800g). Open daily 7:30am-11:30pm.

Çevriye Bar, 47 Sakarya Cad. (☎224 71 10). In the Arap Şükrü district. Hosts live music every night in its blacklit space with swirling painted walls. Beer $2.50; whiskey from $4.70. Open daily noon-1am.

👁 SIGHTS

Bursa's examples of early Islamic architecture are some of the most stunning in all of Turkey. Largely because the city's Ottoman layout still exists today, most of Bursa's sights lie roughly in a long row along Atatürk Cad. and its continuations.

ULU CAMİ. The immense Ulu Cami stands in the center of town on Atatürk Cad. Though Selçuk in style, with an interior *şadırvan* (fountain), puffy minaret caps, and a sprawling, column-filled interior, the unique layout is the result of a compromise between Sultan Beyazıt I and God. Before the Battle of Nicopolis in 1346, Beyazıt promised God that he would build 20 mosques in exchange for victory. After routing his Hungarian foes, the Sultan changed his plans, opting instead to build one mosque with 20 domes. The domes are arranged in four rows of five, with the center made of glass. Beneath the dome is a large fountain, one of the more unique features of the mosque. When the land for the mosque was chosen before the start of construction in 1398, one woman refused to move her house from the plot. She was eventually removed, but one cannot pray on a piece of land not given willingly, so the traditional saying goes. To avoid any problems, the architects built the fountain where the woman's house once stood. The three main entrances to the mosque feature large, Persian-style *eyvan*, and the interior columns and walls are adorned in Selçuk calligraphic Koran excerpts. The *mihrab* contains an astronomical guide with pictures of the planets. *(Donation expected.)*

YEŞİL TÜRBE AND MOSQUE. The gorgeous Yeşil Türbe (Green Tomb) stands atop a hill, its blue-green tile-sheathed octagonal base and dome rising high above the surrounding buildings. Inside, everything is covered with beautiful tiles, even the sarcophagus. Sultan Mehmet I, who pulled the Ottoman Empire back together after Tamerlane swept through, is buried here.

Across the street from the tomb stands the 15th-century Yeşil Camii, whose Selçuk influence is apparent in its brick and stone construction and in its onion-shaped minaret caps. The mosque's real beauty lies within, where intricately-stenciled İznik tiles adorn the walls. The blue and gold mihrab demands attention simply for its size (6m wide and almost 11m tall). The **balcony** that hangs low above the entrance is generally only found in large, important mosques. Here, the sultan could enter and pray unobserved, while keeping his eyes peeled for potential assassins. The cylinders embedded in the side walls by the entrances to the domed chambers were (and are) used to check the "health" of the building. If they spin freely, then all's well; if not, the supports are bearing undue pressure. This dome is one of the first large, central domes used in Ottoman architecture. *(From Heykel, head east along Atatürk Cad., bear right, and continue along Yeşil Cad. following the signs marked "Yeşil." Tomb open daily 8:30am-noon, 1-5:30pm.)*

MURADİYE NECROPOLIS AND MOSQUE. *Şehade* (royal sons) are buried in tombs which surround the Muradiye Camii, a testament to the early Ottoman practice of fratricide. In order to ensure a smooth succession, the eldest son would execute his younger or weaker brothers. The complex includes 12 tombs, but at the time of publication, only four were open to the public. Some are spectacular inside, particularly Cem Sultan's tomb, covered in the finest İznik tiles. Adjacent to the tomb is the Muradiye or Murat II Camii, built in the same style as the Yeşil Cami in 1425-6. *(Catch one of the frequent "Muradiye" dolmuş or buses from the Atatürk Cad./ Heykel area. Tombs and mosque open daily 8:30am-noon, 1-5:30pm. $.60.)*

THERMAL BATHS. Bursa's fabled mineral baths are in the *Çekirge* ("Grasshopper") area, to the west of the city. The three-bath complex, **Yeni Kaplıca** (New Baths), is the closest, about 300m past the Kültür Parkı. Three adjacent baths, fed by natural thermal springs, feature cavernous bathing pools with tiling and mosaic work on the walls and floors that is, by itself, worth the admission fee. Bathing options involve varying degrees of service and privacy. The first bath of the complex, called Yeni Kaplıca, is a men's hamam, built by Süleyman the Magnificent's Grand Vizier, Rüstem Paşa, atop the remains of an even older bath built by Justinian. (Bath $3-5.25; massage $3.50; *kese* $2. Open 5am-11pm.) The **Kaynarca** is a women's bath. (Bath $3; massage $3.50; *kese* $2. Open 7am-10:30pm.) **Karamustafa**, the family bath, has 2- and 4-person cabins available with the special water on tap. (2-person cabin $6.60 per hr.; 4-person $14.30 per hr. Open 7am-11pm.) Karamustafa also has special **mud baths,** where you can soak in a tub of smooth, pasty earth for as long as you like. ($4. Men's mud baths open 7am-5pm; women's mud baths open 8am-4pm.) *(Take bus #40 or any dolmuş from Heykel with a "Çekirge" sign ($.60). Get off on Çekirge Cad. by the Atatürk Museum, continue walking away from the city center, and bear right at the fork onto Yeni Kaplıca Cad. From here, signs point down the stairs toward the baths.)*

Further west on Çekirge Cad. is the shinier and less crowded ■ **Eski Kaplıca** ("old bath"). This bath was originally built by Murat I, but got its name when ancient Roman baths were discovered around the grounds. Restored by the posh Kervansaray Hotel, this is one of the finest Turkish baths in the country, featuring a hot pool, a hotter pool, and a great massage room. *(On Çekirge Meydanı. Take bus #40 or a Çekirge dolmuş and ask to be let off at the Eski Kaplıca. ☎ 233 93 00. Men $7.50, women $6; kese $5.50; massage $5.50.)*

BURSA MUSEUMS. Built in 1424 as a *medrese*, the **Turkish and Islamic Arts Museum** *(Turk İslam Eserleri Musezi)* retains its original style, consisting of a rectangular portico with a central garden and classrooms off the sides. The collection is ceramics-oriented, with several beautiful İznik pots and vases. The museum also has a costume display in the main lecture hall and a hamam exhibit containing such items as silver bath clogs and a sultan's towel. Outside are Selçuk and Ottoman stelae and gravestones; the relief work emphasizes the difference between the angular, raised Selçuk lettering and the flowery, carved Ottoman style. *(On Yeşil Cad., just before the tomb and mosque. Open Tu-Su 8:30am-noon, 1-5pm. $1.50, students $1.)*

On the opposite end of town, the **Bursa Archaeology Museum** *(Arkeoloji Müzesi)* has a decent collection of artifacts pulled from local soil, with a heavy emphasis on Roman items. One of the newer exhibits features an assortment of artifacts and reproductions from the Üçpınar tomb at Balıkesir, but the real highlight is the reconstructed chariot complete with life-size plaster horses. Descriptions and labels are predominantly in Turkish. *(In Bursa's Kültür Parkı on Çekirge Cad. From Heykel, take bus #40 to the Archaeological Museum and Batı Garajı. Open Tu-Su 8:30am-noon, 1-5:30pm. $1.50. Additional $.50 per person to enter Kültür Parkı, $1.50 for cars.)*

NO STRINGS ATTACHED Turkish folk shadow puppet theater supposedly began during the reign of the Sultan Orhan Gazi (1324-1359) when two workmen, the stonemason Karagöz and his foreman Hacivat, engaged in conversations so ribald and witty that the entire crew stopped work on the sultan's new mosque in order to listen. An enraged Orhan ordered the execution of the two jokesters, but finding himself bored without their humor, he grew to regret his rash move. An inventive Persian dervish, Mehmet Küscteri, attempted to entertain the melancholy sultan with figures of the late twosome made from transparent camel skin and manipulated from behind a screen lit with oil lamps. Handed down from one puppet-master to the next, Turkish "Karagöz" shows evolved into bewitching spectacles of color, music, bawdy comedy, subtle word-play, and clever political satire. The knavish, amorous, and uneducated character Karagöz ("Black Eye") is recognizable by his black eye and the huge turban that covers his bald head. His polar opposite Hacivat tries to appear erudite, peppering his speech with words of obscure origin that Karagöz perpetually misunderstands. Somehow, Karagöz's street-smart cunning always outdoes everyone, including his pretentious pal. The vignette plots include ludicrous money-making schemes (the two friends once tried to sell the heat of summer and the cold of winter in bottles), or ribaldry (Hacivat in his absence asked the lusty Karagöz to protect the virtue of his none-too-faithful wife). Karagöz enthusiasts are reviving the tradition in Bursa with an annual shadow theater festival, held each year in November (see Karagöz, p. 158).

HANS AND BEDESTEN. On Atatürk Cad., behind the Ulu Cami, stand the **Koza and Emir Hans,** the centers of the city's silk *(ipek)* trade for the past 500 years. Originally built in 1492 by Beyazıt II and later restored by the Aga Khan, the **Koza Han** (cocoon *han*) draws silk cocoon dealers every July and September. During the rest of the year, the *han* is home to a slew of nearly 100 silk shops, which sell the fine local fabric by the bolt, tie, and scarf. In the center of the two-story market's large courtyard is a *masjid* (small mosque). The **Emir Han** concerns itself strictly with the sale of the finished product.

Both *hans* open into the **bedesten** (covered market), architecturally similar to İstanbul's Grand Bazaar. Organized as they were in the 1300s, when Beyazıt commissioned the marketplace, the shops all sell the same merchandise. *(Hans and bedesten open daily 9am-7am, though some stores close an hour or two earlier than others.)*

KARAGÖZ (SHADOW THEATER). Every year, in the third week of November, the city holds a week-long shadow theater festival, inaugurated at the **Karagöz and Hacivat Memorial** on the road to Çekirge (see **No Strings Attached,** p. 158). The festival includes performances of Turkish shadow theater and of other puppeteering groups from around the world. Across the street from the memorial is the **Karagöz Sanat Evi,** with exhibitions on shadow theater from around the world. The museum also displays traditional clothing and crafts from the villages surrounding Bursa. (☎ 232 87 27. Open M-Sa 11am-4pm. $1.50, students $.80.)

The **Karagöz Antique Shop** is one of the few stores that sells shadow puppets. The master puppeteer R. Sinasi Çelikkol, who owns the shop, gives performances at the Karagöz Sanat Evi every Wednesday and Saturday at 11am. *(12 Eski Aynalı Çarşı, in the Eski Aynalı Çarşı, a marketplace off the bedesten. A former hamam, it's identifiable by its domed ceiling dotted with little lights. ☎ 221 87 27. Open M-Sa 8:30am-7:30pm.)*

TOMBS OF ORHAN AND OSMAN GAZİ. These tombs were ruined in the earthquake of 1855 and restored in the Baroque style, but perhaps most spectacular is the view over Bursa from the perch by the Bursa clocktower, which was built in 1906. *(Follow Atatürk Cad. to where it fizzles out and becomes Cemal Nadır Cad., and turn left onto Orhangazi Cad., a very steep street marked by "Muradiye" signs. The park will be on you right after leaving Atatürk Cad. Open daily 8:30am-noon, 1–5:30pm. Free.)*

OTHER SIGHTS. The mosque in the **Emir Sultan complex,** very popular with devout Muslims, is where fathers take their young sons before circumcision. The buildings are bright and well-preserved. There's a wonderful view of the city from the park behind the mosque. *(To get there, walk along Yeşil Cad. past the Yeşil Camii to a large underpass on the right. Head to the right of the tunnel, following the sidewalk over the tunnel, and continue uphill to Emir Sultan Cad., which leads to the complex.)*

The **Yıldırım Beyazıt Camii** and complex includes an *imaret* (soup kitchen), multiple *medrese*, tombs, and a hospital recognized as the first Ottoman hospital ever built. The complex was built by Sultan Beyazıt Yıdırım, "the Thunderbolt," towards the end of the 14th century. Beyazıt earned his sobriquet for the *Blitzkrieg*-like tactics he employed in capturing Yugoslavia and Hungary. He died quickly enough in captivity after succumbing to Tamerlane. Note the so-called "Bursa arch" between the courtyard and the mosque—this architectural device crops up repeatedly in subsequent Ottoman buildings. *(The complex is accessible via the Heykel-Beyazıt Yıldırım dolmuş, the Heykel-Fakulte dolmuş, or any bus with Yıldırım on its route list. The fairly large mosque is the only one in the neighborhood.)*

Back on Atatürk Cad. near the Atatürk statue is the site of the annual **Bursa Festival,** which kicks off during second or third week of June with a parade down Atatürk Cad. Dancers and musicians from various nations make their way through the city, and afterwards the mayor delivers a speech in front of the Atatürk statue. During the festival, concerts and plays are also held in the Kültür Merkezi.

▓ DAYTRIP FROM BURSA: MT. ULUDAĞ

One of many peaks in the ancient world once called Olympus, this towering, snow-capped mountain is now known as Uludağ, literally "Great Mountain." In winter, the south face (the side away from Bursa) is a popular ski area (lift tickets $5) surrounded by a cluster of hotels. The ski season runs from December to April, with peak season from January to March. In summer, the Teleferik cable car in Bursa shuttles visitors up the north face to the campgrounds and picnic areas at the Sarıalan plateau. From here, the views are absolutely stunning. The summit remains snow-covered for most of the year.

Food and fire are both available at the **et mangal restaurants**, which sell meat in grams ($4.30 for 500g) and cook your food on personal, table-side barbecues. While these places don't offer much for vegetarians other than salad, potatoes, and yogurt, food markets in the area sell fresh fruits and vegetables. Camping is only permitted at the campground, **Sarıalan Kamp Yeri,** equipped with toilets, showers, phones, and hot water three days a week. ($2.40 per tent; $3.50 per caravan. Open June 1-Sept.) From Sarıalan dolmuş make the 8km trip, otherwise a two-hour walk, to the hotels on the south face (15min.; 8:30am-10:30pm, depart when full; $1), from where it's a challenging two to three hour hike to the summit. From Sarıalan a second cable car runs to another picnic and camping area, **Çobankaya.** As there's little of interest in Çobankaya, the primary attraction is the 35-minute ride offering views of Bursa. (Daily 11am-8pm, round-trip from Sarıalan $3.50.)

From Bursa, there are two ways of reaching the Uludağ cable car station. The easier method is to take a bus from Peron 1 on Atatürk Cad. Buses 3-C, 3-İ, or any with a "Teleferik" sign in the front window run this route (every 5-10 min., $.40). Otherwise, you can catch the dolmuş from behind Adliye and Heykel ($.60). From there, the Teleferik cable car leaves every 40 minutes for the midstation, Kadıyayla, whose only attraction is its gift shop (8min.; runs daily 8am-10pm; round-trip to Kadıyayla $3.50; one way to Sarıalan $3.25, round-trip $7.) Another car then continues to Sarıalan about 10 minutes later.

YALOVA
☎ 226

Though Yalova is an unattractive warren of forgettable architecture, sub-par restaurants, and hairdressers, its glut of cheap accommodations makes it the best base for visits to the nearby baths at Termal and the beaches of Çınarcık.

▣ TRANSPORTATION. The square is the site of the bus hub and Yalova's only bus company office, **Yalova Seyahat,** housed in a white office near the bus parking lot. The **Seabus** *(deniz otobüsü)* or **passenger ferry** *(yolcu vapürü)* leaves from the **car ferry port,** about 400m down the coast in the direction that Atatürk is facing.

Hızlı Feribot İskelesi, as the port is called, has its own dolmuş and bus hub. Buses for Bursa stop here as well as near Cumhuriyet Meydanı. **Buses** run to: **Ankara** (6hr., 5 per day 8:30am-12:30am, $10); **Antalya** (10hr.; 10:30am, 9:30pm; $15); **Bursa** (1hr., every 30min. 6:30am-9pm, $2.50); **Eskişehir** (4hr.; 8:30, 11am; $6.75); **İstanbul** (3hr., every hr. 8:30am-6:30pm, $5); **İzmir** (6hr.; 10:30, 11:30am, 10:30pm; $8.25). There is also frequent dolmuş service to **Termal** from the square (25min., 7:15am-10:30pm, $.50). **Minibuses** run to **İznik** from the bus parking lot next to the ferry port (1hr. 20min., about every hr., $4). **Ferries,** including the *ekspres vapur* and *deniz otobüs,* run between İstanbul ports and Yalova. The faster **Seabus** (☎812 04 99), identifiable by its dolphin logo, departs for: **Bostancı** (45min., 6:25am, $7); **Kabataş** (1hr., 4 per day 8:30am-6:25pm, $7.50); **Kartal** (35min., 9 per day 7:30am-8:30pm, $4). The **car ferry,** *hızlı feribot* (☎811 13 23) runs from the main dock to **Yenikapı** in İstanbul (9 per day 7:15am-9pm; $8.30 per person, $30 per car). On weekends and holidays, ferries leave later in the day and run later into the evening.

■■🖪 **ORIENTATION AND PRACTICAL INFORMATION.** The stern-faced **statue of Atatürk** in **Cumhuriyet Meydanı** serves as an excellent reference point. The **tourist office** is in front of Atatürk, about 50m down Yalı Cad., the main road along the waterfront. The 2nd-floor office is on the right side of the road when walking away from the square, marked with a small, yellow "Tourist Information" sign. The English-speaking staff can help find lodging. (☎814 21 08; fax 812 30 45. Open in summer daily 8am-noon, 1-5pm; in winter M-F 8am-noon, 1-5pm.) There is a second office right behind the bus station in Cumhuriyet Meydanı. (Open in summer daily 8am-noon, 1-5pm; in winter M-F 8am-noon, 1-5pm.) Though the office staff speaks little English, they can provide maps and guides. To Atatürk's right, along Cumhuriyet Cad., lie the **banks, pharmacies, ATMs,** and **currency exchanges. Nirvana Internet,** 1 Gazi Paşa Cad. is on the 2nd floor of an office building in the main square (☎811 44 99. $1 per hr. Open 10am-midnight.) **Postal code:** 77100.

🖪🖪🖪 **ACCOMMODATIONS AND FOOD. Çiftçi Otel 2,** Cumhuriyet Meydanı, 8 Huzur Sok., inland from the main square, offers 30 reasonably-priced rooms with bath and TV, many of them newly renovated. (☎814 22 36. Singles $8.30; doubles $14.25; triples $17.50; quads $23.25.) For identical prices, **Erdinç Otel,** 8 Yalı Cad. (☎814 40 99), down the street to Atatürk's right, has 13 rooms, all with bath and TV. In both cases, ask for a room not facing the noisy street. Though a bit more expensive, **Fatih Hotel,** 27 Cumhuriyet Cad., is removed from the square to ensure a quiet sleep. Cleaner than the other hotels around the square, each room has TV, phone, and bath. (☎814 95 14. Singles $13.25; doubles $16.75; triples $25.)

Yalova has many kebap restaurants and pastry shops on Cumhuriyet Cad. Try the **Şehir Lokantası** (☎814 28 05), İskele Meydanı, in the main square, for a bowl of soup ($.70) and *kuzu tandır* (oven roasted lamb; $4.30). (Open 8am-midnight.)

🖪 **DAYTRIP FROM YALOVA: TERMAL HOT SPRINGS.** Having successfully cleansed grime off ancient Greeks, Roman Emperors Constantine and Justinian, Ottoman Sultans, and Atatürk, the springs at Termal have entered their third millennium of providing relief from the dusty bustle of İstanbul. Tucked away in the forest 15km south of Yalova, the Termal resort shows no signs of its proximity to either Yalova or İstanbul. The foliage is thick and healthy, and the air is heavy with the scent of ginger. Seizing upon the possibilities offered by this beautiful location, Ottomans built the 16th-century baths, which remain in use today.

Termal's main attractions are its baths and saunas, which serve the precious waters in a variety of ways. **Valide Banyo** is a classic Turkish hamam, with separate sections for males and females. The hot room contains a pool full of the special water. ($1.75, children's discount available. *Kese* $6; massage $6. Open in summer 8:30am-5pm; in winter 8:30am-4pm.) The **Sultan Banyo** has private rooms with big tubs and a traditional hamam wash basin, as well as a separate room for changing. (☎675 74 00. 1 person $5 per hr.; 2 people $8.25 per hr.; 3 people $10.75 per hr. Open daily 8am-6pm.) **Kurşunlu Bath,** in the middle of the complex, down by the stream, is the place to enjoy a large open-air pool, sauna, and bath. Arrows point the way to the baths from all parts of the resort. (Pool $4.10; baths and sauna $3.25; private saunas $50 for 1½hr. Open 8:30am-10:30pm.) *(For all practical purposes, Termal can only be reached via Yalova (see p. 159). Frequent dolmuş leave Yalova from the dolmuş hub in front of the car ferry terminal and make a stop along the curb in front of Cumhuriyet Meydanı (25min., 7:15am-10:30pm, $.60). The Termal resort is the last stop on the route.)*

İZNİK
☎224

In terms of religious, artistic, and historic significance, the sleepy hamlet of İznik ranks among the most important cities in the world. Archaeologists have found traces of different peoples living on the banks of what is now İznik Lake as far back as 2500 BC. The city fell into Greek hands in the wave of conquest under Alexander the Great. Later, in 74 BC, the Romans controlled the settlement. A religious center under the great empire, Nicaea, as the town was called, was the site of ground-breaking councils of the early Christian Church. In 325, Emperor Constantine convened the First Council of Nicaea, condemning the Arian heresy, the belief that Christ was inferior to God. The Council formulated the Nicaean Creed, setting the Orthodox record straight on Christ's omnipotence (see **Christianity and the Byzantine Empire,** p. 8). The bishops returned in 787, gathering in the local Aya Sofia for the Seventh Ecumenical Council, which settled the issue of Iconoclasm.

In 1081 the Selçuk Turks conquered Nicaea, renamed the city İznik, and made it the capital of the Sultanate of Rum (see **The Great Selçuk Sultanate,** p. 9). Reclaimed by the Byzantines in 1097, the city became part of the nascent Ottoman Empire when Orhan Gazi, son of Osman, drove the Byzantines out for good in 1331. With the fall of Constantinople in 1453 and the relocation of the Ottoman capital, İznik lost its political importance. However, it gained renown as an artistic center, producing *faïence* on a par with Delft porcelains and Ming china.

The discovery of large deposits of kaolin (glossy clay) and silicon in the area around İznik and the import of Persian craftsmen by Mehmet Çelebi I, began the golden age of İznik pottery (see **Ottoman Decorative Arts,** p. 23). Sultan Selim the Grim gave the İznik tile industry further impetus when, after conquering parts of Persia in the early 16th century, he sent the skilled potters of Tabriz westwards. At its height, İznik boasted 300 ateliers producing tiles that were used on all the major buildings of the Ottoman Empire. Sadly, by the end of the 1700s, almost all the kilns and workshops had shut down, and the town spent the next two centuries sliding into obscurity, with the war of 1922 sealing its fate.

Today, İznik is a passive lakeside town. Speed bumps and laws against honking keep motorists from disturbing the peace of the townsfolk as they drink infinite cups of *çay* in İznik's tea houses and gardens. The scene is even more mellow by the lake, where the natural beauty of a sunset borders on a religious experience.

▐▔ TRANSPORTATION

Bursa and Yalova are the two main approaches to İznik. Frequent seabus service means arriving from İstanbul via Yalova is no problem (see **Yalova,** p. 160).

Buses: From the otogar to: **Ankara** (5½hr., 9:30am, $10); **Bursa** (1¼hr., every ½hr. 6am-7:45pm, $2.40); **İstanbul** (3½hr., 7:45am, $10); **Yalova** (1hr. 20min.; 7:45am, every hr. 9am-7pm; $3).

Ferries: From Yalova (58km away) to **Kabataş, Kartal,** and **Bostancı** in **İstanbul.** See **Transportation,** p. 160.

◢*▮*◤⁊ ORIENTATION AND PRACTICAL INFORMATION

The city's grid-like street plan makes for easy navigation. Two main boulevards, **Kılıçaslan Cad.** and **Atatürk Cad.,** divide İznik into quarters, meeting in the center at Aya Sofia. Most of İznik is enclosed by its ancient walls. The lake *(İznik Gölü)* lies along **Sahil Yolu,** outside the town's western walls.

Tourist Office: (☎757 14 54; fax 757 19 33). Near Aya Sofia inside the large modern building off the park. Friendly staff speaks some English and offers free maps and town guides. In summer daily 8:30am-noon, 1-5:30pm; in winter M-F 8am-noon, 1-5pm.

Banks: Türkiye İş Bankası, across the street from Aya Sofia, has a V/MC/Cirrus/Plus ATM. Open 9am-12:30pm, 1:30-5:30pm. There is also a **Yapı ve Kredi** a block from the square on Atatürk Cad. with a V/MC/Cirrus/Plus ATM as well. Open 9am-12:30pm, 1:30-5pm. **Akbank** can change AmEx **traveler's checks** at its branch, one block off the square on Kılıçaslan Cad, away from the lake. Open 9am-12:30pm, 1:30-5:30pm.

Hospital: Devlet Hastanesi (public, ☎757 75 80), a 10min. ride out of town. **Vatan Hastanesi** (private, ☎757 55 50; fax 757 27 22) is 2 blocks away from the central square on Atatürk Cad. English speaking staff. Accepts some insurance plans.

PTT: (☎757 18 15), 150m down Kılıçaslan Cad. towards the lake. Open 8am-12:30pm, 1:30-7pm. **Postal code:** 16860.

▰ ACCOMMODATIONS

Burcum Motel, Kemalpaşa Mah., 20 Sahil Yolu (☎757 10 11; fax 757 12 02). A pleasant place to stay, with clean rooms and terraces facing the lake. All 25 rooms have shower, toilet, and phones. 24hr. hot water when full, otherwise available morning and night only. Breakfast included. $12.50 per person, regardless of room size.

Cem Pansiyon, 34 Göl Kenarı (☎757 16 87; email cempansiyon@mynet.com.tr). After reaching the lake via Kılıçaslan, take a right and walk 300m. Well-kept rooms with superb views. Communal bathroom and shower on every floor. Breakfast $1.80. Singles $8.25, with a view of the lake $12.50; doubles $13.25, with view $20; triples $25.

Hotel Babacan, 104 Kılıçaslan Cad. (☎757 12 11). At the center of town, on the same side of the square as the tourist office. 42 modest rooms vary in quality; rooms with bath are nicer, but more expensive. Singles $10, with bath $12.50; doubles $16, with bath $20; triples $21, with bath $25; quad $28.25.

Camping is possible at a completely facility-less grassy patch, where visitors can pitch a tent for free. Follow Kılıçaslan Cad. toward the lake, turn left at Sahil Yolu, and continue about 275m past Çamlık Restaurant. Anything along the shore there is fair game.

◉ FOOD

Kar-pi Fast Food (☎757 42 24). Across from the Aya Sofia. Cheap, large portions of kebap and *lahmacun* ($2-3). Outstanding kebap selection. Choose between open-air seating and the air-conditioned interior. Open 11am-midnight.

Çamlık Restaurant, 15 Göl Sahil Yolu (☎757 16 31). At the intersection of Göl Sahili and Kılıçaslan. *Taratör* (spiced garlic yogurt) $1.20; grilled *yayın balık* (catfish, a regional specialty) $4. Open 9am-1am.

Ceren Pastanesi, 72 Atatürk Cad. (☎757 13 79). This popular pastry shop serves *poğaça* (pastry with cheese) and tea for less than $.30. Open 6am-midnight.

◉ SIGHTS

AYA SOFIA. Built as a Christian church by the Byzantines in the 4th century, the Aya Sofia (Saint Sofia or Church of the Holy Wisdom) was converted to a mosque in 1331 by Osman, the founder of the Ottoman dynasty. After the occupying forces of Tamerlane damaged the building in 1402, it was renovated during the reign of Süleyman the Magnificent (1520-1566) by Sinan, the court architect. Today, it is decrepit and surprisingly small with only a few pieces of religious art. *(Aya Sofia is located at the town's central intersection. Open daily 9am-noon, 1-4:30pm. $1.65.)*

İZNİK MUSEUM. Sultan Murat I built the **Nilüfer Hatun İmareti** in 1388 in honor of his mother Nilüfer Hatun, but the building now functions as İznik's museum. Serving as a charitable house, the *imaret* offered food and shelter to traveling students, dervishes, and artisans. Today, it contains İznik porcelain wares and various local stelae, reliefs, and Islamic gravestones. The display case full of ancient coins is a real treat. Look out for the Lysimachean tetradrachm coins bearing the image of Alexander the Great on one side. These coins were used for trade as far away as India and Saudi Arabia. There is also a case of pottery used by the people of Ilıpınar, a part of northwest Anatolia, that dates from 6000-5500 BC. *(Follow Kılıçaslan Cad. away from the center of town. Open daily 8:30am-noon, 1-5pm. $1.65.)*

YEŞİL CAMİ. Across from the museum stands the Yeşil Cami, "Green Mosque." Designed by Haci Musa in 1371, the well-proportioned building is mostly uninspiring, except for the tiled minaret with bands of various geometrical patterns.

MURAT HAMAMI. Just south of Aya Sofia, the sagging Murat Hamamı offers cheap baths in a made-to-last facility. The center stone is original and so old that its edges have been rounded from use. The furnace behind the sauna still burns wood rather than propane. *(Standing with your back to the gate of Aya Sofia, turn left, walk 2 blocks, and take another left. The bath is down a block on the left. ☎757 14 59. Open for men 8am-1pm, 5pm-midnight; for women 1pm-5pm. Bath $2.50; massage $1.75.)*

ÇİNİ KILNS. The large, overgrown clearing across the street from the baths is all that remains of the original, world-famous **İznik kilns.** Excavations in the late 1970s discovered these two kilns and confirmed that they had been in service during İznik's prime tile-making days. Follow İstiklâl Cad. down one block to Kekket Sok., where artisans make modern reproductions of old İznik tile patterns. The tiles are cheap, starting at $2 for simple designs.

ROMAN THEATER. Although the theater was designed to seat 15,000, the remaining ruins offer little hint of the sheer size of the original structure, as most of the theater lies buried under several feet of dirt and crumbled brick. It was supposedly hit by Greek artillery when the city was razed in 1922. Four of the entrance arches still rise out of the rubble. Excavations of the theater site have revealed that the enclosure was used in later years as a sight for kilns, a church, a palace, and ceramic workshops. *(From the center of town, head south along Atatürk Cad. to Tiyatrosu Cad., on the right, where signs point the way to the ruins.)*

CITY GATES. Tiyatrosu Cad. leads through one of the city's seven remaining gates and along the **city walls.** The walls are doubled and even tripled in places with a fosse (water-filled ditch) in between each section. This degree of fortification, a concrete testament to İznik's former importance, is matched only by the Theodosian Sea Walls in İstanbul. Follow the walls around the city to the four main city gates, of which only three survive. Of these, the **İstanbul Gate** *(İstanbul Kapısı)*, at the north end of Atatürk Cad., is the most impressive. Built at the emperor Vespasian's request, it consists of three concentric gates flanked by high walls.

OTHER SIGHTS. Some of İznik's more ghoulish sights, such as the **Yeraltı Mezar** (an ancient tomb) and the **Byzantine Catacombs,** lie outside the city walls. Visiting these requires a guide from the İznik Museum. Unfortunately, not too many people at the museum speak English. Your best bet is to make arrangements through the tourist office a few days in advance. İznik has two other historical sights of interest. The brick-and-mortar **Süleyman Paşa Medrese,** built by the brother of Orhan I on the site of a former Byzantine monastery, is the oldest standing *medrese*, or seminary, in Turkey. Students' cells lined the cramped, porticoed courtyard. *(On Kekket Sok., off İstiklâl Cad.)* The tiny, brick **Haci Özbek Camli,** dingy on the inside and not much better on the outside, is noteworthy for being the oldest Ottoman mosque whose construction date (1333) can be verified. *(On Kılıçaslan Cad.)*

NORTHWEST

AEGEAN COAST

Fabulous classical ruins and a sinuous coastline concealing sublime beaches have helped transform Turkey's once-tranquil Aegean coast into an increasingly popular destination. Framed by 5000-year-old mythology and history, the region's intensely rich culture offers an eye-full for photographers, archaeologists, nature-lovers, and hedonists alike. The coast's first foreign visitors were the ancient Greeks, who established several ports in the area. As Alexander the Great and subsequent Hellenic rulers pushed their empire east, the ports became the nerve centers of commerce in the ancient world. Today, Hellenic ruins—especially extensive at Pergamon, Ephesus, Aphrodisias, and Pamukkale—stand as weathered testaments to the coast's glorious heritage.

Far from just cordoned-off tourist traps, the Aegean's ruins are a natural backdrop to modern life. Broken columns and statuary fill the natural sulfur swimming pools in Pamukkale hotels, standing exactly where they fell when earthquakes toppled them centuries ago. Many restaurants in Aegean coastal towns respectfully reserve their basement floors for mini-exhibits of the ruins on which their foundations were laid. This makes for a spectacular fusion of the booming modern Aegean region with its unparalleled ancient legacy.

HIGHLIGHTS OF THE AEGEAN COAST

VISIT the remains of the ancient city of **Bergama** (Pergamon; p. 174), and contemplate Galen, the doctor of the ancient world at the **Asclepion,** a healing-center and shrine to the Roman demi-god Asclepius.

SCAMPER about the ruins of the Temple of Artemis in **Ephesus** (p. 193) and the Mausoleum of Halicarnassus in **Bodrum** (p. 217) to see two of the Seven Wonders of the Ancient World.

FOLLOW in the footsteps of hundreds of thousands of weary travelers and witness the calcium covered travertines of **Pamukkale** (p. 209), one of the most beautiful natural baths in the world.

EMBARK on a "Blue Voyage" for a day to explore and swim in the otherwise inaccessible caves, coves, and islands around the **Bodrum Peninsula** (p. 217).

SPEND a day or two amidst the reds and blues of **Ayvalık** (p. 171), a former Greek fishing village with olive groves, Neo-Classical architecture, and fantastic beaches.

NORTHERN COAST

TRUVA (TROY)

Site open daily in summer 8:30am-7:30pm; in winter, spring, and fall 8am-5pm. $2.50.

For the casual visitor with no romantic attachment to Homer, Troy's jumbled, partially excavated ruins may well prove a disappointment. The site is confusing and not immediately striking to the romantic imagination. A hokey wooden horse and the academic dryness of the displays in the excavation house don't help either. For these reasons, a tour of the site (provided by the Hassle Free Tour Agency) is advisable as a tour guide's explanations of Troy's complicated history and the excavation process enliven the views. For those interested in archaeology as a discipline, in particular, Troy is a rare gold mine among ancient sites, and for everyone, a "must-see" for any trip to the Aegean Coast.

HISTORY

When Heinrich Schliemann rediscovered Troy in the 1880s, the city had been uninhabited for at least 13 centuries. However, the previous 35 centuries of almost continuous

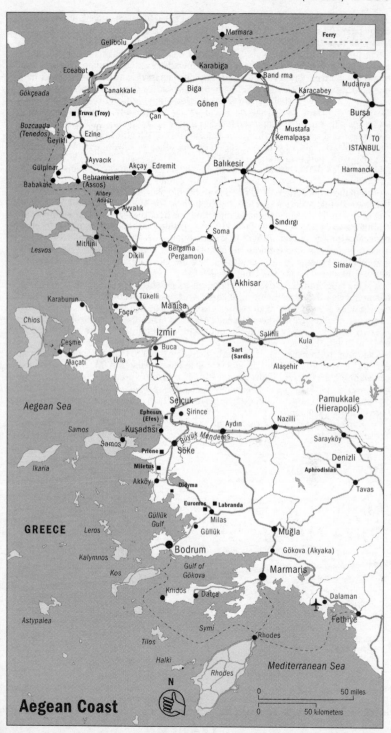

Aegean Coast

habitation span a huge continuum of civilization, stretching from the early Bronze age to the later Roman Empire. During 110 years of sporadic excavation, archaeologists have split these periods into comprehensible, clearly numbered units.

The first of these smaller units, labeled **Troy I,** dates from about 3000-2500 BC. Once a small fishing settlement, it now consists of walls made of fairly small stones in a huge bone pattern. On top of the first Trojan city lies **Troy II,** an affluent city-state dating from 2500-2200 BC, which Schliemann mistook for the city of the Trojan War. Schliemann believed that the stone ramp, close to which he found the so-called "Treasure of Priam," was used to lead horses up into the city. While there are certainly signs that invaders captured the city, modern scholarship suggests that these conquerors hailed from Asia Minor instead of Greece. After the fall of Troy II, **Troys III-V** (2300-1800 BC) were small, unfortified fishing villages. Newcomers of non-Trojan origin moved into the area around 1800 BC to build the great city of **Troy VI.** The financial successes of this city are visible in the considerably finer workmanship of the smooth walls, often made of sloped, square stones rather than the fitted, uncut stones of the other settlements. Turkish archaeologists hold this city to be the one of epic fame, while American archaeologists believe **Troy VIIa** (1275-1240 BC) to be the city of Priam. The main evidence supporting this hypothesis is the large number of storage vessels found within Troy VIIa, suggesting that the city prepared for and endured a long siege. Yet no swords, spears, shields, or other signs of war have been unearthed, raising doubts about the famous Trojan War. Nevertheless, the city fell and remained vacant for four centuries until **Troy VIII,** another fishing/farming community, appeared on the site from 700-350 BC.

For the next four centuries, great conquerors passing back and forth across Asia bestowed wealth and attention upon the town, hoping to associate themselves with the Homeric legend. Among the earliest to do this was **Alexander the Great.** After his campaign of conquest crossed into Asia, Alexander traveled to Troy where he sacrificed to **Achilles,** staged games in his honor, and supposedly took the warrior's armor and shield as he headed east to subdue the Persians. **Julius Caesar,** the next superhero to visit Troy, toured the city's remains in 48 BC. He ordered that the ruined temple of Athena be reconstructed and the city rebuilt as **Ilium Novum (Troy IX).** Troy held a special significance for the Julian clan, for—aided by Virgil's poetic imagination—they believed themselves to be the descendants of the Trojan hero Aeneas. The senatorial and land-owning classes of Imperial Rome followed suit, claiming lineage from members of the Trojan pantheon.

As Rome collapsed and a Christianized Empire shifted east to Constantinople, Troy fell once again into decline. While there is record that the site was inhabited in

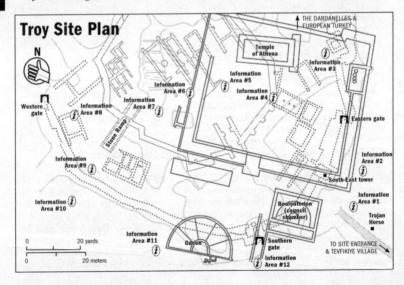

Troy Site Plan

N

THE DARDANELLES & EUROPEAN TURKEY

Temple of Athena

Information Area #3

Information Area #5

Information Area #6

Information Area #4

Western gate

Information Area #8

Information Area #7

Stone Ramp

Eastern gate

Information Area #9

Information Area #2

South-East tower

Information Area #10

Information Area #1

Bouleuterion (council chamber)

Trojan Horse

0   20 yards

0   20 meters

Information Area #11

Odeon

Southern gate

Information Area #12

TO SITE ENTRANCE & TEVFIKIYE VILLAGE

the time of Justinian, the city seems to have been largely ignored by royalty and nearly forgotten. Carrying on the tradition of the conqueror/pilgrim, **Sultan Mehmet,** who viewed the ruins in 1444, vowed bloody revenge upon the Greeks for their cruelty towards the people of Asia.

Schliemann's chapter in the story starts in the mid-19th century. Having amassed huge wealth before the age of 40, he promptly left his business to pursue his boyhood dream of finding Troy. Following Frank Calvert's hunch as to the city's location, he broke ground in the 1880s. The ensuing years of excavation produced many treasures and uncovered most of the important features of today's site. In his motives and methods, Schliemann has long been controversial, straddling the line between amateur archaeologist and crazed looter. Although he did document his work and pay some attention to strata, he still concentrated his efforts on the pursuit of treasure. When his work uncovered the magnificent so-called "Treasure of Priam," he dressed his teenage wife in the gold jewelry and took photographs before sending his finds back to Berlin wholly without government permission. Apart from a few minor pieces in the museum in İstanbul, the treasure disappeared from Berlin at the end of WWII. It resurfaced in Russia a few years ago and can now be seen at the Pushkin Museum of Fine Art in Moscow.

🛈 PRACTICAL INFORMATION

🖼 **TJ's Tours** (☎ 814 29 40; fax 814 29 41; email: TJs_TOURS@excite.com) based in Eceabat has excellent tours conducted by İlhami "TJ" Gezici ($14) when there are sufficient tourists. **Anzac House** in Çanakkale offers tours through the **Hassle Free Tour Agency** (☎ 213 59 69; email hasslefree@anzachouse.com). If you decide to visit the site on your own, avoid the cabs ($20-30) and instead take a Troy-bound dolmuş that leaves from the Çanakkale dolmuş lot under the bridge on Atatürk Cad. every half hour for most of the daylight hours ($.80). It's a good idea to start early to avoid missing the last dolmuş back to Çanakkale.

BOZCAADA (TENEDOS)

Sandy coves, rolling hills, a perpetual cool breeze, and plentiful wine make Bozcaada a natural paradise. The charm of the white-washed, pastel-trimmed houses of the island's only town provides a distinctively Greek feel. Though the island is short on residents (pop. 2500), the summer months see an influx of İstanbulian tourists, recognizable by their number "34" license plates. Even these arrivals aren't enough to crowd the place, though—there's no lack of beach. And there's enough wine to go around; this tiny island supplies more than 10% of Turkey's wine. In antiquity, Tenedos's wine was considered some of the finest in the world. Unfortunately, today's product standard has dropped a little, but it's cheap ($4-5 per bottle) and available everywhere except (maybe) the post office.

⌷ TRANSPORTATION. Ferries run from **Geyikli** (Yükyeri dock) to Bozcaada (daily in summer 10am, 2, 7pm, midnight) and back to Geyikli (daily in summer 7:30am, noon, 5:30, 11pm). **Minibuses** run from the **Çanakkale** otogar (1hr., every hr., $1.50) and arrive in Geyikli near, but not at, the ferry dock. To get to the dock, take a dolmuş from the bus stop to the Yükyeri dock (5min., $.35). Like the several large buses traveling to **İstanbul** and **İzmir, dolmuş** wait for ferries coming back from the island before heading to **Çanakkale** (20min., $.60) and other local destinations.

🖿🛈 ORIENTATION AND PRACTICAL INFORMATION. Bring extra money with you: Bozcaada is a bad place to go broke. The only ATM in town is a **Yapı ve Kredi** that doesn't take foreign cards. The **PTT** in the main square, inland from the ferry dock and to the right, changes money and cashes **traveler's checks.** (Open mid-June to mid-Sept. daily 7am-11pm; winter M-F 8:30am-5:30pm, Sa 8:30am-1pm. Money exchange M-F 8:30am-5:30pm.)

While Bozcaada can be navigated by dolmuş at the peak of the tourist season (end of June through August), it is perhaps better explored by **bike. Ada Cafe,** in the main

AEGEAN COAST

square (to the right as you face away from the ferry), rents bikes and also provides free maps and an English speaking staffer. (☎ 697 87 95. $1.30 per hr., $6.50 per day. Open 8:30am-2am.) Because the afternoon heat, combined with steep hills, is brutal in the summer, cyclists should head out early, wear a hat, and bring a bottle of water. There are two main roads out of town, one running around the southern side of the island and one around the north. Of the two, the southern route is longer and better, as its views are closer to the shoreline. Nevertheless, it is possible to combine the two by criss-crossing through the vineyards and forests in the center of the island. Dolmuş to the far side of the island (where the other branch of Ada Cafe lies) leave from the large çay gardens in front of Ada Cafe, though these take a shorter, less scenic inland route (summer only, 10 min., $1).

▐▐▐ ACCOMMODATIONS AND FOOD. The cheapest and coolest way to stay on Bozcaada is to camp. Camping is permitted in most places that aren't privately owned provided that you don't litter, build campfires, or otherwise spoil the land. There is an official campsite, **Kiraz Camping,** about 3km down the coastal road that offers showers, toilets, a public barbecue, and a food stand. Campers stay in the provided tents or bring their own. Free transport is provided between the center of town and the campsite. (☎ 697 04 60. Open June 20-Aug. $5 per person.)

Many different pensions operate out of private homes. The majority of these, which provide a double or the occasional triple, are clean and affordable ($8-13 per room; very negotiable). Sometimes the owners will wait at the ferry dock to approach possible guests. It's worth the effort of checking out the rooms, which are usually cheaper than comparable hotel options. To avoid bargaining, however, stay at the **Otel Güler Ada,** on the second street running parallel to and behind the PTT. New, still spiffy, and relatively spacious (except for the 3rd floor), it provides private bath and bug-free surroundings. (☎ 697 88 99. $12 per person.)

The **Ada Cafe,** to the left as you face the PTT, offers excellent quality breakfast ($2), snacks, and red poppy syrup (a juice-like drink diluted with water; $1.50 per glass). (☎ 697 87 95. Open daily 8:30am-2am. V, MC.) Another good option is the outdoor **Hafiz Çamlik Restaurant,** in the forested area between the soccer field and the square in front of the PTT. In addition to excellent fish ($2-4), it serves the whole range of traditional dishes at decent prices (beans $1; *köfte* $2.50). (☎ 341 81 67. Open daily 6am-midnight.) Good **fish and meat restaurants** line the small boat harbor, directly across from the ferry landing. The higher prices (salad with meat or fish $5-6) are worth it for the exceptional views of the mainland across the straits and of the tiny fishing craft that fly postcard-sized Turkish flags.

◙ SIGHTS. The well-preserved **castle** dominates the area around the harbor. The edifice was constructed in the Byzantine period and renovated by the Venetians, Genoese, and Ottomans. Climbing or scrambling (carefully) is permitted on the battlements. The **museum** is fairly weak, exhibiting mostly unremarkable 19th century Turkish household items. The museum does, however, contain examples of old Turkish money, so you can see pre-inflation one and five lira coins. *(Castle open daily 10am-1pm, 2-7pm. $1.20, students $.40.)* The island's main attractions, however, are its beaches and cliffs, from which you can gaze out over the cobalt sea.

To tour the island by bike, take a left at the first fork in the road out of town and follow the more scenic, southern route (refer to the map from the Ada Cafe). The first 10km of the ride involve huffing and puffing up and racing down the steepest and ugliest of the island's coastal hills, passing the old **lighthouse** at Tuzburun Feneri and the tiny cove with its pebbled beach at **Mermer Burnu.** After this, it's a long, winding descent to Ayana, the first in a 7km stretch of sandy beaches. The beautiful beaches of **Ayana, Ayazma, Solubahçe,** and **Habbele** are the best on the island and the most popular, though they are rarely crowded. Turning right onto the only paved road between Solubahçe and Habbele beaches leads to some of the island's vineyards, where you can get a glimpse of tomorrow's wine today. At Habbele, the paved coastal road peters out, and a left turn takes you down a short dirt road to the other branch of the Ada Cafe. There is no better place on the island to have a meal (with salad $4-5) or a glass of cold water or beer ($1.25). *(Open daily in summer 24hr.)* All of the roads that lead inland in this vicinity pass through a small but pleasant pine forest. About 1km inland, dirt roads off to the left lead to a lighthouse, forested areas, and vineyards at the northwest tip of the island.

The north side of the island is smaller and less impressive. While it has lots of caves, its beaches are narrower and less sandy. This easier ride leads past the **Horoz Taşları,** where large rocks poke dramatically out of the water.

BEHRAMKALE (ASSOS)   ☎ 286

Despite its stunning ruins and pristine blue water, Assos remains a largely unspoiled tourist destination, catering mostly to wealthy Turkish and German visitors. For the moment, attractive, tasteful hotels far outnumber lurid souvenir shops, but it's difficult to believe that this will last much longer. Apart from the delicate veil of fog that hangs over the narrow stretch of water between the town and the Greek island of Lesbos, there's little to complain about in Assos.

Assos's remote location has been one of its major selling points since its founding in the 6th century BC by Methymnian refugees fleeing Lesbos. During the period of its greatest glory in the 4th century BC, the city became a sort of mecca for intellectuals, including Aristotle, who taught here before moving on to the Macedonian capital of Pella to tutor the young Alexander the Great. After Alexander's untimely death in 323 BC, Assos declined, eventually falling under the rule of Pergamon. The city slipped into oblivion under the Byzantines and Ottomans.

E⁊ TRANSPORTATION AND PRACTICAL INFORMATION. Modern Assos is a strangely divided community. Half the residents live by the acropolis in the village at the top of the hill, and the remainder stay 2km down the hill in the little cluster of buildings by the ancient harbor. The **upper town** contains the local population and the cheaper pensions and restaurants, while the **lower town** caters exclusively to affluent tourists, featuring a number of posh hotels and expensive restaurants. Although the ruins are more accessible from the upper town, the lower town offers amazingly beautiful pebble coves. While dolmuş run every hour from mid-June to August, only fickle service connects the towns during the rest of the year, and walking the steep 2km is out of the question.

To get to Behramkale, take a **dolmuş** from **Ayvacık** (every hr. mid-June to Sept., usually more sporadic). They stop in the upper town first and then continue to the lower half, picking up passengers to take back to Ayvacık. The **PTT,** in a kiosk right next to the upper town dolmuş stop, exchanges traveler's checks. (Open July-Aug., Sa-Th, 9am-6pm). **Postal code:** 17860.

⊓⊓⊐ ACCOMMODATIONS AND FOOD. Accommodations and food prices are inversely proportional to altitude; the only inexpensive way to stay on the beach is to camp, and given the superlative quality and abundance of campgrounds, it's also the best option. The six campsites are all beyond the glitzy hotels as you walk with the sea on your right. They vary minimally, each providing bungalows with toilet and shower ($8-18 per person). Prices vary according to how crowded the grounds are, so if you want to save, come before the middle of June or after August, when you can bargain to reduce the fee. Each campground has access to the sea with a dock from which to swim. Some provide tents as well ($5-6), but you can bring your own. Breakfast is usually included. Tidy but bare rooms with cramped bathrooms can be found at the **Antik Pansiyon,** behind the Assos Hotel in the lower town. (☎ 721 34 52. Breakfast included. Singles $8; doubles $16.)

At the top of the mountain, right at the dolmuş stop, the **Dolumay Pension** provides lodging built in the same stone-and-mortar style as the mosque and ruins. (☎ 721 71 72. Breakfast included. Singles $12.50; doubles $25. Open year-round.) At the summit, beside the entrance to the Acropolis, is the **Timur Pansiyon,** where you can unload if you want the most stunning views in town. Of the four rooms, two are 200-year-old originals, though their bathrooms have been remodeled. (☎ 721 74 49. Breakfast included. Singles $12.50; doubles $25. Open year-round.)

In the lower town, attached to the Antik Pansiyon is the relatively cheap **Antik Restaurant,** offering various starters ($1.25 each), fresh fish, and grilled meat ($4). (☎721 34 52. Open 8am-3:30am.) Other lower town restaurants, all doubling as hotels, include the **Assos, Nazlihan,** and **Behram** (open 24hr.). All dish out tasty meals ($13 for three courses) under umbrellas or covered canopies.

The upper town's oldest restaurant, the **Cengiz,** features quality traditional cuisine at excellent prices. The owner has collected 20 volumes of guest books over the 32 years he's been in business. He'll gladly show them over a cup of tea. (☎721 70 04. Salad, meat, and dessert $3. Open all year 8:30am-midnight.)

■ **SIGHTS.** The humpbacked bridge to the left of the modern road into town was once the only way into Assos by land. At the top of the hill, overlooking the village from the edge of a small cliff, is the **Murat Hodavendigar Camii.** Built in 1359 at the behest of Sultan Murat I, it was the first Turkish mosque in Assos and stands as a well-preserved example of very early Ottoman architecture. The rectangular, elevated stone patio beneath a large awning and the *mihrab* covered with *muqarna* (decorative vault with stalactite decoration) show marked Ottoman influence, but the interior is quite simple, having been built at a time when the Empire's fortunes could not indulge a more elaborate creation. The Greek inscription over the door acts as a reminder that many of the building materials, including the marble door frame, are *spoglia* (recycled parts; lit. "spoils") from a 6th-century church. The mosque is supposed to be open at all times, but if it is locked, simply ask the ticket-booth attendants to open it for you.

Next to the mosque lies the entrance to the **acropolis,** the only part of the ruins that charges admission. The pillars on top of the plateau are the remnants of the **Temple of Athena** (c. 530 BC), partially rebuilt with funds from *Efes Pilsen*, which has financed all of the excavations in the ancient city. The best part of the visit is the view, since much of the temple, including the reliefs, has been sent to the Archaeological Museum in İstanbul. Locals collect the greenish-tan plants that grow here and dry them for tea, which is sold along the road ($.25 for a 50g bag). *(Open daily 8am-8pm; in winter 8am-5pm. $2.)*

From the village, walk down the hill 300-400m beyond the Cengiz Restaurant. On the left side of the road stands the main gate to the **excavation site** (the "No Admittance to the Excavation Site" signs only apply when people are digging). The archaeologists rarely mind visitors as long as they don't interfere with the day's work. The long, stone-paved road that runs through the gate up into the city walls are the remains of the city's Hellenic and Roman **necropolis.** A few stone **sarcophagi,** whose lids were left ajar by Medieval grave robbers, lie along the broad street. Assos gained great fame for its sarcophagi after Pliny the Younger, as governor of Bithynia, claimed that the local stone could fully dissolve a corpse's flesh within 40 days. The term sarcophagus refers to this very property, deriving from the Greek words for "flesh" (or body) and "to eat."

To the right of the necropolis are the Hellenic **city walls,** fashioned of precisely cut and finished andesite, the igneous rock that provides the building material for almost everything in Assos. A walk on the stone-paved path, through the necropolis and the main gate of the Hellenistic walls, leads into the ancient city. Unlike many other ancient cities, Assos is blessed with never having been built over, and the extent of the site provides insight into its archaeological potential. Marked with *Efes Pilsen* signs, the **gymnasium, Agora Temple, Roman bath, stoa, bouleterion,** and early Christian **churches,** all down the hill through the brush, are far from well-preserved (the partially restored **theater** is an exception). Stick to the clearly trodden path and don't climb on any of the ruins. It is not permitted to approach the theater from above, where the theater is in its weakest state of preservation. Instead, exit the fenced area and walk down the road to approach it from below.

AKÇAY ☎266

This small coastal resort, with its expansive sand beaches and typical resort amenities, including countless ice cream shops and tea gardens, lures mostly Turkish tourists and can work well as a daytrip. The town's streets and buildings feel austerely clean, the searing sun having burned away any potential filth. Akçay will delight sun bunnies craving a cold drink and an occasional ice cream cone.

TRANSPORTATION AND PRACTICAL INFORMATION. The otogar sits along the main coastal highway about 1km from the beach and city center. It is easy to walk into town along **Edremit Cad.**, which becomes **Çamiyol Cad.** as it passes to the left of the Atatürk statue in the main square, **Barbaros Meydanı.** Because the main coastal highway passes by Akçay, bus service to and from the city is frequent. To: **İstanbul** (8hr., 12 per day 9am-9pm, $15); **İzmir** (3½hr., 12 per day 7:30am-6:30pm, $5). Some İstanbul buses stop at **Çanakkale** (2 hr.; noon, 2, 4pm; $5) and other major cities as they head north. **Edremit,** the next town down the coast, has more extensive and frequent bus service, and it can be reached by taking any dolmuş that runs up and down Edremit Cad. and past the otogar ($.35).

The **tourist office** is on the left side of Edremit Cad. as you approach the sea, 200m from the water. (Open daily 8:30am-noon, 1:30-5:30pm.) **TC Ziraat Bankası,** farther down Edremit Cad., before the otogar, has an **ATM** and exchanges currency. (☎ 385 13 95. Open M-F 8:30am-5:30pm.) **Pharmacies** full of exorbitantly priced sunscreen are on virtually every corner. From the main square, walk to the right of the Atatürk statue toward the beach; the **police station** is on the left, opposite the central **PTT** (open daily 8:30am-12:30pm, 1:30-5:30pm, 8-11pm). The PTT kiosk next to the police station changes money until 5pm. **Postal code: 10390.**

ACCOMMODATIONS AND FOOD. From Barbaros Meydanı, facing the beach, you can spot **Otel Palmiye** to your left. Marked by two palm trees, the Palmiye offers clean, spacious rooms with large bathrooms and balconies facing the sea. The shade from the surrounding trees keeps the rooms on the first two floors cool. (☎ 384 10 08. Rooftop breakfast included. Singles $12. V, MC, AmEx.) Past the Palmiye and to the right along the beachfront walkway is **Otel Özsoy.** Though not as clean, this beachfront hotel provides rooms with televisions, baths, and balconies looking toward the sea (☎ 384 11 90; fax 384 21 90. Breakfast included. $12 per person.) The upper rooms are bound to be sweltering during July and August.

Akçay 1 Pide Salonu (☎ 384 59 54), along Barbaros Meydanı, serves tasty and cheap standards. **Tuana,** on the sea 500m down from the police station (with the water on your left), has a more refined and expensive selection, including *şiş* ($3.75), calamari ($4.25), fish ($4.25), and salad ($.75). Tablecloths and an excellent sea view raise it a step above the *pide* and kebap joints in the center of town.

SIGHTS. Akçay's main attraction is, of course, its sand beaches. Dotted with umbrellas and bodies in summer, they stretch for over a kilometer in both directions. In July and August, the unbearable sun makes the evening the best time to be out. When you've had your fill of *dondurma* (ice cream; $.50-.75), the numerous gift boutiques lining the whole length of the beach offer refuge from the heat.

Get some culture at the **Private Ethnographic Gallery of Tahtakuşlar Koyu** (Tahtakuşlar Village). Though the exhibits are not in English, the life-size displays of village life can be appreciated without explanation. *(☎ 387 33 40. Open daily 8am-sunset. $.80, students $.40.)* The museum can be reached by minibuses that stop opposite the Tahir Yenicag supermarket *(10min.; M-F 8 per day 7am-5pm, Sa-Su 4 per day; $.35).* Ask for the *Tahtakuşlar Koyu Ozel Etnografya Galerisi.*

AYVALIK
☎ 266

Ayvalık's decaying old-world charm and host of exceptional accommodations make it an attractive destination from which to explore the surrounding beaches, olive groves, and 25 small islands. Known for its ornate Neoclassical buildings, Ayvalık was a wealthy Greek settlement until the 1923 population exchange. Hidden away in a maze of narrow cobblestone streets are pastel houses, markets, shops, and people whose traditional lifestyle disappeared in most of Turkey decades ago. For all its old-fashioned charm though, the prevailing impression is one of decay: unlike other

Aegean resort towns, Ayvalık's streets are dirty and many of its buildings are uninhabited ruins. In the daytime, the sandy beaches of Sarımsaklı and the austere beauty of Alibey Island are enough to keep you busy.

⌐ TRANSPORTATION

Buses and Dolmuş: Buses from the otogar go to: **Ankara** (10½hr.; 9, 10:30, 11:30am, 8, 9:30, 10:45pm; $16.50); **İstanbul** (8½hr., 11 per day 8:30am-midnight, $16.50); **İzmir** (2½hr., every hr., $4). City buses for **Sarımsaklı beach** ($.50) and **Altınova** ($.80) leave continuously from Cumhuriyet Meydanı near the Tourist Society booth. Minibuses for **Bergama** (6 per day 8:30am-6pm, also 7:15pm in summer, $2.25) leave from the otogar and also stop at a seaside bus stop (a few minutes' walk from Cumhuriyet Meydanı with the sea on your right).

Ferries: Jale Tur (☎ 312 27 40), on the docks in Cumhuriyet Meydanı. All year to the Greek Island of **Lesbos** (2hr.; W, Th, Sa 6pm; $50). $20 port tax when exiting Greece.

✴ 🛈 ORIENTATION AND PRACTICAL INFORMATION

Atatürk Bulvarı, the main road, runs parallel to the coastline and becomes **İnönü Cad.** to the left of the small information booth as you face the sea. The other main street, **Cumhuriyet Cad.,** runs parallel to İnönü Cad. and Atatürk Cad. one block up the hill and away from the sea. Tourist information, dolmuş, city buses, police, taxis, and several banks can be found in **Cumhuriyet Meydanı,** the main square. With the sea on your left, the **otogar** comes about 1km after this main square.

Tourist Office: The main office (☎ 312 21 22) is just beyond the hospital as you walk away from Cumhuriyet Meydanı with the sea on your right. Open all year M-F 8:30am-5:30pm. A small booth (☎ 312 31 58) in Cumhuriyet Meydanı on the docks is open May-Oct. M-Sa 10am-2pm, 3-7pm. Both distribute free maps.

Banks: Türkiye İş Bankası (☎ 312 22 10 or 312 26 08), in Cumhuriyet Meydanı, **exchanges currency** and has a 24hr. Cirrus/Plus/MC/V **ATM**. Open M-F 9am-12:30pm, 1:30-5:30pm.

Police: On İnönü Cad. in Cumhuriyet Meydanı, next to Türkiye İş Bankası.

Pharmacies: Many in Cumhuriyet Meydanı and on İnönü Cad. **Gültekin Eczanesi** (☎ 312 12 28) is across from the water in Cumhuriyet Meydanı. Open 8am-7:30pm.

Hospital: Ayvalık Devlet Hastanesi (public, ☎ 312 63 00), 500m from Cumhuriyet Meydanı with the water on your right. Across from and just beyond a Migros grocery.

Internet Access: Ayvalık Internet Cafe, Atatürk Cad. Nazar Pasaj 14 (☎ 312 22 75), on the left before the PTT as you walk out of Cumhuriyet Meydanı with the sea on your left. $1.60 per hr. Open daily 9am-9pm, in summer 9am-11pm.

PTT: (☎ 312 60 41), on İnönü Cad., about 300m from Cumhuriyet Meydanı as you walk with the sea on your left. Open daily 8:30am-11pm. **Traveler's checks** cashed 8:30am-5:30pm. **Postal code:** 10400.

⌐ ACCOMMODATIONS

Ayvalık's accommodations are undoubtedly some of the best in Turkey. Its top pensions, located up the hill in the old town's maze of narrow, cobblestoned streets, are without doubt *Let's Go* picks.

🏨 **Bonjour Pansiyon,** 5 Maraşal Çakmak Cad. (☎ 312 80 85). Follow the road directly across the PTT entrance uphill and into the old city. Originally the home of a French priest acting as the French ambassador to the Sublime Porte, this pension has been recently restored in turn-of-the-century style. The ceiling paintings are worth seeing even if you are not staying here. Laundry service $3.25. Breakfast $3.25. $8 per person.

🏨 **Beliz Pansiyon,** 28 Mareşal Çakmak Cad., Fethiye Mahallesi (☎ 312 48 97). Follow Talatpaşa Sok. (the 1st street on your right as you exit Cumhuriyet Meydanı with the sea on your left) for 5 blocks away from the sea until you come to the Beliz Pansiyon signs. Run by the vivacious and chic former TV actress Beliz, this pension sports bright yellow walls and colorful pillows. Enjoy the homemade Turkish dinners cooked by Beliz herself, and bring your bathing suit for the daily boat tours she offers of 5 nearby islands ($8). Breakfast included. Bungalow rooms $10 per person; house rooms $12 per person.

Yalı Pansiyon, 25 Balıkhane Sok. (☎312 24 23 or 312 38 19). Behind the PTT. The oldest pension in Ayvalık, Yalı abuts the waters of the Aegean such that guests can admire the sunset on the horizon from the chairs in the garden, from the balconies of their rooms, or from the water. The setting is tranquil and the location easily accessible. Laundry service $3.50-5. Public kitchen. Breakfast included. $12 per person.

Taksiyarhis Pansiyon, İsmetpaşa Mah., 71 Maraşal Çakmak Cad. (☎312 14 94). Take the 2nd street on the left after the PTT (when walking toward the main square with the sea on your right) and follow it uphill to the signs, which will direct you farther through the old town. Decorated with carpets, sitting pillows, and other knick-knacks, this eclectic pension has a guest kitchen and book exchange. Remember to remove your shoes upon entering. Bike rentals ($8 per day) include a map of Alibey Island. Laundry service $8. Enormous breakfast $3.25. $8 per person.

 FOOD

Enjoy some *iskender* ($3) at the **Osmanlı Mutfağı,** two blocks away from the hubbub on Cumhuriyet Cad. Take a left at the Yapı Kredi bank, about a minute walk from Cumhuriyet Meydanı with the sea on your left. (☎312 54 27. Open daily noon-10:30pm. V, MC, AmEx.) Otherwise, the extremely clean **Kardeşler** restaurant has two branches, one on the docks in front of Cumhuriyet Meydanı (☎313 00 81), which dishes out fresh seafood, an array of salads ($1.50), and meat dishes ($2.50-$3.50) along with a harbor view. Another branch, called **Kardeşler Kebapci,** on the right side of Cumhuriyet Cad. as you walk out of Cumhuriyet Meydanı with the sea on your left, specializes in kebaps and other meat selections and features an air-conditioned dining room on the upper level. (☎312 18 57. Open daily 8am-10pm. V, MC, AmEx.) For *çorba, lahmacun,* and *baklava,* visit the **Dayım Ocakbaşı,** across from Kardeşler on İnönü Cad. (Open noon-11pm.)

 SIGHTS

There are few sights to speak of within the town itself. On the walk to the Taksiyarhis Pansiyon is **Saatli Camii** (Clock Tower Mosque), the former **Church of Agios Yannis** (Church of St. John). The splendor and grace of its former life as a 19th-century Greek church shines through the flaking paint and eroded details. At the time of publication it was closed for a long overdue renovation. Farther inland and visible on its hillside from Saatli Camii is **Agios Yorgos** (St. George's Church) or **Çinanlı Camii,** which boasts Old and New Testament frescoes. Unfortunately, this mosque too is closed for renovation. Next to the Taksiyarhis Pansiyon, off Maraşal Çakmak Cad., the **Taksiyarhis Church** exhibits paintings on fish skins. It is usually closed, but you may be able to peek inside if you find the right moment. Beware the small, ferocious dog who guards the place. Every Thursday the town has an **open-air market** covering the streets around Cumhuriyet Cad. and Barbaros Cad. In the finest Turkish market tradition, 99% of the stuff for sale is impractical junk, but that in no way takes the fun out of browsing for potential souvenirs.

 DAYTRIPS FROM AYVALIK

ŞEYTAN SOFRASI. To the south of Ayvalık lies the Şeytan Sofrası (Devil's Dinner Table), a large rock formation that resembles a dinner table only in the sense that pretty much any flat surface can double as a table. Local legend has it that the hell raisers met here to feast, citing a giant footprint-shaped dimple in the rock as evidence of the devil's presence. The panoramic view of Cunda and the Sarımsaklı area is impressive, particularly at sunset. The supremely located **Şeytan Cafe** provides the best spot to watch the sunset, serving reasonably priced beverages (big beer $1). The **devil's footprint** lies at the corner of the table farthest from the dolmuş lot, beneath a steel cage on whose bars napkins and bits of cloth are tied. This practice is evidence of non-Orthodox Islamic ritual, wherein visitors make wishes and leave a knotted fabric or paper as an offering. Throwing coins must be an acceptable substitute for tying napkins, as the Lord of the Underworld's footprint has been all but filled with five and ten thousand lira coins. *(During July and August dolmuş to the site leave daily at 6pm from the Tansaş supermarket, a short walk from Cumhuriyet Meydanı with the sea on your right. The dolmuş wait for visitors to watch the sunset before returning ($.80).)*

SARIMSAKLI BEACH. About 6km south of Ayvalık, Sarımsaklı has some of the best beaches between Bozcaada and Altınkum, with lots of clean, fine sand. The same can't be said for the town of Sarımsaklı, which occupies a formidable spot in the great pantheon of tacky beach towns. It's always a quarter past Miller Time here, with no spot on the beach more than 5m from either the *Efes* chest or one of the numerous beach or dance techno bars. But the beaches themselves, particularly the parts near the shore and away from the central area, have clean sand and warm water without any strong currents or other unexpected surprises. In the low season, Sarımsaklı is eerily deserted. *(It is accessible from Ayvalık by dolmuş (every 5-10min. 10am-3pm; $.50) that depart from the Tansaş supermarket and by buses departing from in front of the harbor in Cumhuriyet Meydanı (every hr., $.50). The beach is not the final destination; let the driver know that you want to go to the plaj (beach).)*

ALİBEY ISLAND (CUNDA). Alibey (Sir Ali's) Island is a beautiful escape from the noise and filth of Ayvalık. With good beaches on the north side, a deserted monastery, and several pleasant fish restaurants along the waterfront in the town of Cunda, there is enough here for an entire day. Provided the heat isn't too bad, the best way to explore Alibey Island is by **bike.** The **Taksiyarhis Pension** (see **Ayvalık: Accommodations,** p. 173) rents bikes and provides a map showing a much-recommended scenic route. This path passes over the bridge connecting the island to the mainland and then continues on through the island's olive groves to the monastery and secluded beaches (bikes $8 per day).

In the town of Cunda, the old and hauntingly beautiful **Church of Nicolaus,** lies about 300m inland. Pigeons fly through its nave, and thick, deeply fissured columns support its domes. Having suffered during the 1922 war with Greece and a 1944 earthquake, the church has more recently been forced to endure graffiti. *(Buses also leave from Ayvalık from in front of Türkiye İş Bankası in Cumhuriyet Meydanı (every 30min., $.50) and head to the town of Cunda. You can purchase bus tickets at the small ticket window to the right of Türkiye İş Bankası. On Alibey Island, you can buy your bus ticket in the office behind Artur Motel Restaurant, on the cafe-lined seafront. Church open daily during daylight hours. Donations welcome.)*

CENTRAL COAST

BERGAMA (PERGAMON)   ☏ 232

The physical layout of Bergama, formerly ancient Pergamon, seems to reflect directly the ebb and flow of the city's prosperity over time. A dazzling center of cultural activity in antiquity, Pergamon became the capital of the Roman province of Asia and had one of the two largest libraries in the ancient world. The ruins of this great Hellenistic and Roman city dominate the top of the hill, while buildings from later eras, when the city's stature and importance declined, cling lower down at the hill's feet. Greek houses, remnants of the more prosperous days of the late 19th century, cluster around the tiny hills of the river banks before giving way to the cement buildings of modern Bergama. Unfortunately, in spite of having some of the most extensive and important ruins in Asia Minor, Bergama is often overlooked. The quiet, attractive town suffers from severe economic desperation, mostly due to its location off the main coastal highway and away from the sea.

HISTORY

Pergamon traces its roots back to the Aeolian Greeks, who built a settlement here in the 9th century. Like many other ancient cities, Pergamon blossomed from the spoils of Alexander the Great's conquest of the Persian empire. Alexander's successor in the region, Lysimachus, deposited a hefty booty in the city under the care of **Phile-taerus,** who rose from treasurer to ruler when Lysimachus did not return from battle. Philetaerus ruled fairly and generously, maintaining good relations with neighboring cities, and beautified Pergamon with temples and other new buildings. When he chose his nephew Eumenes I to succeed him in 263 BC, he established a royal dynasty that would last for five generations. This dynasty expanded Pergamon's empire into Central Anatolia as far as Konya. By the 2nd century BC Pergamon had gotten itself into bed with the increasingly powerful Romans, and in 133 BC King Attalus II bequeathed the city to the Roman Empire. Under the Romans, Pergamon became the prosperous capital of the province of Asia. An earthquake in the 2nd century brought the city into a period of irreversible decline, however, and over the next several centuries it passed through the hands of the Byzantines, Crusaders, Lascarids, Arabs, and finally, Ottomans.

⌐ TRANSPORTATION

Buses: At the *garaj* (☎ 633 15 45), across from Çamlı Park, about 1.5km south of the old town on İzmir Cad. This distance is walkable, but taxi may be preferable ($2). To: **Ankara** (10hr.; 9:30am, 8:45pm; $18); **İstanbul** (10hr.; 9:30am, 9:25pm; $19.50); **İzmir** (2hr., every 30min. 6am-7:30pm, $3.25). When traveling to Bergama, especially from the north, ask for a direct bus since some stop only at the Bergama turnoff on the main highway, 7km from the city. If you arrive at the main highway, you can take a dolmuş to the center of town and avoid the heavy cab fare.

✴ ❼ ORIENTATION AND PRACTICAL INFORMATION

The Pergamene Acropolis is across the river from the modern city of **Bergama,** while the Asclepion is uphill from **Atatürk Meydanı,** in the modern area. The city's main road runs north-south, winding its way to the ancient ruins at the northern end. From İzmir to the bus station it is called **İzmir Cad.** From the bus station to the northern end of Atatürk Meydanı, it is called **Cumhuriyet Cad.,** and from the northern end of Atatürk Meydanı to **İstiklâl Meydanı,** it is called **Bankalar Cad.** Most of the pensions and restaurants are located around İstiklâl Meydanı.

Tourist Office: (☎ 633 18 62). From the bus station, take a right onto İzmir Cad. and walk 1km to Cumhuriyet Meydanı, located on the left side of the road. Distributes a helpful map with all hotels and pensions labeled. Open Apr.-Sept. daily 8:30am-noon, 1-7pm; Oct.-Mar. M-F 8:30am-noon, 1-5:30pm.

Banks: On the left side of İzmir Cad., about 200m up from the PTT (away from the bus station) is **TC Ziraat Bankası** and on the right side **Türkiye İş Bankası.** Both exchange currency and have Cirrus/Plus/MC/V **ATMs.** TC Ziraat open M-F 8:30am-4:30pm. Money exchange closed noon-1pm. Türkiye İş open M-F 9am-5:30pm.

Hamam: The historic **Çarşı Hamam,** 32 Bankalar Cad. (☎ 632 10 75), is across from the banks. Reasonably clean, it serves Turkish men and tourists of both genders. Bath $3.25; massage $8. Open daily 6am-11pm. Newly tiled and very clean, the **Sprinter Sauna,** 88 İzmir Cad. (☎ 632 36 48), south of the *garaj,* serves men and women, and is more welcoming to single female travelers than Çarşı. Sauna, bath, and steam bath $5.50. Turkish massage $2.50. Full body massage $5.50. A cafe on the upper level serves hot and cold drinks. Take a dolmuş from the *garaj* and ask for the Serapion or Efsane Hotel as both are nearby. Alternatively, walk south 500m on İzmir Cad. from the otogar. Open daily 1-5pm for women; 8:30am-1pm, 5pm-midnight for men.

Hospital: Bergama Devlet Hastanesi (☎ 631 28 97 or 631 28 94). Walk from the bus station towards the PTT, turn left where the park ends, go uphill, and turn right.

Police: (☎632 70 01), on İzmir Cad.

Internet Access: Köşe Internet, on the road to the Asclepion, Galenos Cad., near the center of town. 10 computers. $1 per hr. Open daily 10am-midnight.

PTT: (☎632 39 90), on İzmir Cad. Some English spoken. **Currency exchange** (1% commission). Open daily 8am-11pm. **Postal code:** 35700.

▌ ACCOMMODATIONS

Pension Nike, 2 Tabak Köprü Çıkmazı, Talatpaşa Mah. (☎633 39 01). Walking from the otogar, pass İstiklâl Meydanı, bear left, and go over a small bridge to this 300-year-old turquoise stone house. Lush flower garden and newly refurbished, brightly colored and spacious rooms with hardwood floors. Ask about the histories of the rooms, as each is unique in its original purpose. Kind owners offer hand-drawn maps of town and of ancient sites. Homemade Turkish dinner, vegetarian or meat, $4-7. Breakfast included. Open Mar. through Nov. $7.50 per person, with bath $10.

Pension Athena, 5 Imam Cıkması, Barbaros Mahallesi (☎633 34 20; aydinathena@hotmail.com). Housed in a restored Ottoman home on the winding road beyond İstiklâl Meydanı. 24hr. hot water, living room with cable TV, public kitchen, and enclosed çay garden. Free map of town. Laundry $6. Rooms $5, with shower $7; a place to throw your sleeping bag out on the roof $2.50. 10% discount for *Let's Go* readers.

Acroteria Pension, 10 Bankalar Cad. (☎633 24 69). On the right as you walk north on Bankalar Cad. from the otogar. Moderately clean, fairly dark rooms surround an inner court that's lush with plant life. The view of the acropolis from the rooftop breakfast table makes up for the poor view from the rooms. Laundry machine available for free use. Public kitchen. Lunch and dinner available in busier summer season. Breakfast included. $6.50 per person, with bath $10 per person.

Pergamon Pension, 5 Bankalar Cad. (☎632 34 92). Near Atatürk Meydanı. Housed in an old, Ottoman brick building with an inner courtyard. Rooms are cramped and not exactly spic and span. Owners have diverted their energy into the restaurant, one of the better eateries in town. Unfortunately, if you stay in a room without a bathroom, you must pass through the restaurant to reach the facilities. Laundry service $6. Breakfast included. Rooms $6 per person, with bath $7.

Berksoy Camping (☎633 25 95). Walk south on İzmir Cad for 20-30min. No English spoken, so it's probably best to inquire at the tourist office about availability. Amenities include pool and tennis courts. $5 per person.

◖♬ FOOD AND ENTERTAINMENT

Bergama's dining options, mostly family-style kebap and *pide* restaurants clustered around İstiklâl Meydanı, are often quite pleasant.

Arzu Pide Salonu, 10 İstiklâl Meydanı (☎631 11 87). 5 kinds of *pide* ($1), *köfte* ($1.50), *lahmacun* ($.50), and nothing else, with bigger portions than elsewhere in town. Dining area in back. Open daily 8:30am-11pm.

Sağlam 2 Restaurant, 3 İstiklal Meydanı (☎633 20 46). The Sağlam family, who has all but cornered the dining market, run 2 restaurants in Bergama and 3 more in other cities. Sağlam 2 offers southeastern Anatolian cuisine, which you can watch being cooked in the traditional brick oven. *Meze* ($1) per plate, *pide* ($1-2.50), and kebaps ($2-2.50). Live Turkish music nightly 10pm-1am in upstairs bar. Open daily 8am-1am.

Sağlam 3, 29 Hükümet Meydanı (☎632 88 97). On the right side of the street before the PTT as you walk north from the otogar. Expansive garden-style seating and 2 authentic Ottoman dining rooms upstairs with rug-covered seats. Open daily 8am-midnight, sometimes later. V, MC, AmEx accepted at both Sağlam locations.

Café Manolya, 48 Hükümet Cad. (☎633 25 83 or 632 05 49). Past the PTT on the way to the acropolis. Serves up sweets and tea. Perfect for ice cream and lemonade or a cup of *salep* ($.70), a hot chocolate-like drink, in winter. Open daily 8am-midnight.

Call the USA

"feel free to call"

1-800-COLLECT

When in Ireland
Dial: 1-800-COLLECT (265 5328)

When in N. Ireland, UK & Europe
Dial: 00-800-COLLECT USA (265 5328 872)

Member of
Dublin Tourism

Australia	0011	800 265 5328 872
Finland	990	800 265 5328 872
Hong Kong	001	800 265 5328 872
Israel	014	800 265 5328 872
Japan	0061	800 265 5328 872
New Zealand	0011	800 265 5328 872

Pergamon Pension Restaurant, 5 Bankalar Cad. (☎632 34 92). Soft chairs, bright floral tablecloths, a small pool, and natural lighting from skylights add to the charm of this court-yard restaurant housed in an old Ottoman building designed like a *kervansaray*. Prices average $2-3 per dish. Open daily 8am-2am.

 SIGHTS

ACROPOLIS

Wear long pants to avoid the relentless thorn bushes and bring a big bottle of water. Site open daily 8:30am-5:30pm. $3.50, ISIC-toting students free.

The acropolis of Pergamon looms over the city like a giant and inaccessible brick-and-marble storm cloud, its treasures protected by a high barbed-wire fence and steep hills. From a lower gate, the ancient, stone-paved road climbs the hill, passing all the ruins and the current excavation sites. The walk up is better than a taxi ride ($5), which follows the modern paved road and misses half the sights. Start at the river (near the Athena Pension), cross the bridge, and proceed through the maze of the old town diagonally to the right and up the hill. Eventually you will meet the paved road that leads to the top. Follow it for a short distance until you reach a gate and a cluster of concrete buildings on the right, in which the German excavation team lives and works. To the right of this gate, a little path runs between the road's chain-link fence and the perimeter fence of the archaeological compound, eventually becoming a fairly easy-to-follow trail that threads its way through the ruins. Hand-drawn maps showing the way to the lower entrance are at the front desk of the Pension Nike (see **Accommodations,** p. 176).

Stay on this former **Royal Road** by following the blue dots painted on steps, walls, and other pieces of stone. The first set of rectangular ruins on the left is the **lower agora,** the center of the ancient city's commercial trade. The trail here clings to two of the *agora*'s sides before making a sharp switch back to the right. Farther along is the **gymnasium,** a massive three-tiered complex of exercise halls and baths built on the hillside. In addition to providing a venue for physical exercise, Greek gymnasia also functioned as schools, training young men in philosophy and oratory. Young boys began in the lower gymnasium, the least impressive and worst preserved of the three, and moved up to the middle level at around age 13. The upper level, built around a large, colonnaded exercise area, included a small theater, a lecture hall, and two bath complexes. In the center of the gymnasium, the largest room and the most impressive of the ruins, was used for track and field competitions. The remains of the **Temple of Demeter,** marked by a few inscriptions, lie on the path uphill from the upper gymnasium. At the west end, animals were slaughtered as sacrifices to Demeter, goddess of rebirth, harvest, and fertility.

From here, the road winds uphill, growing wider and more evenly paved up to the now tree-covered **Altar of Zeus,** built by Eumenes II in commemoration of Attalus' victory over the Gauls. All that remains today are the first four or five tiers of steps on the base, the Germans having carted off the columns and giant friezes to Berlin, where they have been incorporated into an impressive restoration of the temple (see **Der Zeusalter gehört zu Bergama-wir möchten ihn zuruck,** p. 178). While the lower portion of the museum is free, visiting the Temple of Zeus requires a ticket. The ticket booth is off to the right, facing the big temples and the city walls. The **precinct of Athena,** the rectangular ruin closest to the ramp leading from the entrance gate, was the site of Pergamon's famed **library** (see **Fahrenheit 640,** p. 179).

Carved into the hill for an impressive effect when viewed from the road, the **Hellenistic theater** once seated 10,000 in nosebleed comfort. Above the theater, the giant **Temple of Trajan** was built for both the cult of Zeus and the imperial cults of Trajan and Hadrian. It is currently undergoing restoration. On the steep bluffs behind the temple were the foundations of the various **royal palaces** of the Attalids, which used to extend into the area now covered by the Temple of Trajan and a **wishing well.** Wishers throw three coins at the column in the well, and their wish comes true if one lands on top. Fortunately, the rapid devaluation of the Turkish lira has seriously lowered the price of happiness, as one or two dollars can buy enough 5000 lira coins for an afternoon's worth of wishing.

ASCLEPION AND BERGAMA MUSEUM

Asclepion open same hours as Acropolis (see p. 177). $2.50, students $1.25. The refurbished Bergama museum is toward the bus station about 100m from the Bergama tourist office. Open Tu-Su 8am-5pm. $1.25, students $.75.

Pergamon's famed Asclepion lies on the west side of town, a relatively easy uphill walk marked by yellow signs off Atatürk Meydanı. The Asclepion was a shrine to the Greek (and later Roman) demi-god of healing, Asclepius. After the center at Epidauros in Greece, Pergamon's Asclepion was the most famous healing center in the ancient world, and its native son **Galen** was the foremost doctor of his time. An avid promoter of animal dissection and vivisection, Galen spent much of his life here serving as chief physician and conducting anatomical research. His treatises and theories became the foundation for medical thought in Europe and the Middle East until the mid-17th century.

The site opens with the **Via Tecta,** a broad, colonnaded street connecting the Asclepion with Pergamon proper. The Via Tecta leads to the cylindrical **Temple of Asclepius,** modeled on the Roman Pantheon, and the **healing center,** which consists of six semicircular chambers radiating in a flower-like arrangement from the central domes. Ailing visitors to the Asclepion took part in a kind of dream therapy known as **incubation:** sleeping in the temple, they would be visited in dreams by Asclepius. These dreams, later interpreted by one of the Asclepion's priests, revealed the appropriate treatment, usually a changed diet, hot or cold baths, mud bathing, and exercise. An impressive and perfectly preserved underground tunnel links the healing center to the rest of the complex. Lining the courtyard at the other end of the tunnel is the **Propylon,** a small, square building thought to have contained a cult statue of Asclepius. Next door is the **library,** which houses a number of stelae covered in Greek inscriptions. The **theater,** which held 3500, staged lectures and other entertainment for the benefit of patients and local citizens.

The museum, arranged like a Roman Villa, surrounds a small, perfectly maintained central courtyard. Grave and dedicatory stelae line the halls surrounding this courtyard. The main room of the museum, at the far end off of the courtyard, presents an eclectic collection that includes several sculptures, glassware, an extensive coin collection, and a large, world-renowned Medusa mosaic. The adjacent **Ethnography Museum** was closed for renovation at the time of publication.

DER ZEUSALTER GEHÖRT ZU BERGAMA-WIR MÖCHTEN IHN ZURUCK

Like more than a few other famous ancient sites scattered throughout the eastern Mediterranean, Pergamon is missing its finest piece, the famous Altar of Zeus. No, marauding Vandals did not raze it, nor did crusading Christians topple it. No, it remains safe and sound—in Berlin. During their early excavations in the late 19th century, German archaeologists carted off the colossal and extremely well-preserved Altar of Zeus, reassembling and restoring it in the Pergamon Museum in Berlin. No one knows for sure how this came about. In the absence of surviving written documents, some maintain that the Sultan gave the Germans permission to remove the building and its precious friezes from Turkish soil. Others claim that, in an uncontrollable bout of European imperialism, the Germans took it without asking. It is difficult to say to whom the treasures actually belong, since the Turks have little cultural connection to Pergamon's ancient inhabitants. Although many Turks believe that the Altar of Zeus belongs to Bergama, they might be hard-pressed to justify all of the mid-Eastern and North African ruins which Turkey has hung onto since Ottoman days—now proudly exhibited in İstanbul's Archaeological Museum.

FAHRENHEIT 640 In ancient times, only the library in Alexandria surpassed Pergamon's, which contained more than 200,000 volumes in repositories all over the city. So great was Alexandria's jealousy over the Pergamenes' literary hoard that they made what they thought was a brilliant strategic move: they limited the flow of Egyptian papyrus to Pergamon. The Pergamenes countered by writing all their subsequent volumes on parchment pages made from goat hide, an exponentially more durable, though more expensive material. The scheming Alexandrians, however, were only temporarily foiled. When the Alexandrian library's fire suppression mechanism experienced a system-wide failure, Marc Antony plundered Pergamon's shelves and presented the whole library to Cleopatra, presumably as a token of his love. In 640, the ill-fated collection was put to the torch by the Caliph Omar and his lieutenant, the aptly named Amr ibn al-Ass. Subscribing to a kind of witch-trial logic, Omar decreed that if the books agreed with the Koran, they were unnecessary, and if they disagreed with the Koran, they were heretical and fit for combustion. Innumerable works of ancient literature went up in flames and were lost forever, including dozens of plays by Sophocles, Euripides, and Aeschylus.

KIZIL AVLU (RED HALL)
Open daily 8:30am-5:30pm. $2.50, ISIC students free

The remnants of Kızıl Avlu, a pagan temple, stand near the river, İstiklâl Meydanı, and the old part of Bergama. "This is where Satan has his altar," declares Revelations (2:3), citing Kızıl Avlu as one of the Seven Churches of the Apocalypse. This mammoth structure was built in the first half of the 2nd century AD and is dedicated to the Egyptian trio of gods Serapis, Isis, and Harpocrates. At its far end once stood a talking statue of Serapis; priests would climb into the hollow figure to make it "speak." With the advent of Christianity, Kızıl Avlu was converted into the Church of St. John, receiving its twin towers sometime during the Byzantine period. One of these is now a mosque.

FOÇA   ☎ 232

Small, quiet, and attractive, Foça is the North Aegean's other summer resort, rivaling Kuşadası and Ayvalık as the non-Bodrum summer escape. With its large fishing fleet and clear, blue waters, Foça offers a more refined and welcome variation on Aegean resort towns. Foça's strategic location near the gulf of İzmir has made it both a popular resort and a large military center. The navy controls the land south of Foça and the *jandarma* training school hugs most of the land on the interior.

In antiquity, Phokaia, as it was called, was a major trading and seafaring center. Herodotus reports that Phokaian shipbuilders built 50-oared galleys capable of ferrying 500 people across the Mediterranean and the Black Sea. On trips like these, they founded both the Frech city Marseilles and Samsun, on the Black Sea coast. Recent archaeological excavations have revealed segments of the massive walls Herodotus described. Though Foça has declined in importance, it remains true to its ancient character in at least one respect: in ancient Greek, "phokia" means "seal." The town still has a close relationship with its small population of endangered monk seals, who have won official protection for Foça's austerely beautiful landscape of scree-covered hills and rocky coastline. They have become the town's mascot, their black eyes keeping watch from posters, pamphlets, and T-shirts. Some scholars say that the legend of the Sirens, the tantalizing sea nymphs whose songs lured sailors to their deaths, derives from the barking of Foça's seals.

▐ TRANSPORTATION

Buses: From the Foça otogar, buses run to **İzmir** (1½hr., every 30min. 6am-11pm, $2.50), some of which stop along the way in **Yeni Foça** (30min., every hr. 8am-8pm, $1.20). **Hanedan**-bound dolmuş are useful for reaching the beach/camping area to the north (every 15min., 8am-midnight, $.50). To reach Foça from the south, catch the direct bus either from İzmir or en route. Approaching from the north, you'll be dropped off at the Foça junction, where either a dolmuş or a coach from İzmir can take you the last 20km ($1.10). The bus/dolmuş stop at this junction is located on the road perpendicular to the north-south highway.

ORIENTATION AND PRACTICAL INFORMATION

Foça lies 20km west of the north-south highway connecting the North Aegean (Çanakkale, Ayvalık, etc.) with İzmir. The town is divided into two main sections. Only **Eski (old) Foça** is covered in this guide. The less attractive **Yeni (new) Foça**, about 10km north, is a big resort town complete with Club Med. Eski Foça consists of a wide strip between the hills and the shore around two harbors—the **Küçük Deniz** (Little Sea) and the **Büyük Deniz** (Big Sea). Most restaurants, accommodations, and other necessary establishments are clustered near the Küçük Deniz, while many sights lie along the Büyük Deniz. Street addresses are largely useless, as Foça, like İzmir, numbers its streets rather than naming them. However, the main street, running through town from the otogar down to and along the right side of the Küçük Deniz harbor, does have a name: **Küçük Deniz Sahil Caddesi.** Leaving the otogar, you'll see the tourist information office to your left. Küçük Deniz Sahil Cad. runs to the right of the office.

Tourist office: (☎ 812 12 22), near the otogar end of Küçük Deniz Sahil Caddesi. Extremely organized and well-run. Competent staff can arrange summer boat tours, recommend sights, provide maps and pamphlets, and check for hotel/pension vacancies. Open M-F 8:30am-5:30pm; also open Sa-Su 10am-1pm, 3-6pm in summer.

Boat Tours: A dozen or so full-day summer boat tours leave in the mornings from Küçük Deniz. The tourist information office has details about the price, schedule, route, and capacity of each boat.

Bike Rental: (☎ 812 19 69), at the "Motor-rent" sign across from the bus station. Bikes $8 per day; mopeds $16 per day; motorcycles $24 per day. Open daily 8am-9pm.

Banks: V/MC/Cirrus/Plus **ATMs** are at **Türkiye İş Bankası,** on the left side of Küçük Deniz Sahil Caddesi as you walk from the otogar to the harbor, and at **T.C. Ziraat Bankası,** down from Türkiye İş Bankası. They'll also exchange currency and cash traveler's checks (for an exorbitant $8.50 each). Open daily 9am-12:30pm, 1:30-5:30pm.

Pharmacy: Merkez Eczanesi (☎ 812 12 31), on the right side of Küçük Deniz Sahil Cad. as you walk towards the harbor, across from Türkiye İş Bankası. Pharmacist Önder Aytuğ speaks French, Italian, and English. Open M-Sa 8:30am-7:30pm.

Hospital: The main hospital (☎ 812 14 29) is 30m beyond the Karaçam Hotel on Küçük Deniz Sahil Cad.

Internet: Mouse Internet Cafe, just beyond Türkiye İş Bankası. Listen to American Top 40 hits while you email. $1.60 per hr. Open daily 9am-midnight.

PTT: Across from the tourist office. Exchanges currency, cashes traveler's checks (when currency is available), and offers *poste restante*. Metered phones inside and Türk Telekom phones outside for international calls. Open daily 8am-11pm. **Postal code:** 35680.

ACCOMMODATIONS

Depending almost exclusively on summer tourism, Foça's pensions charge according to the volume of business, and, in most cases, prices are somewhat negotiable. Foça's hotels, all located on the waterfront, tend to have a higher opinion of themselves than they ought to, though most are clean.

Siren Pension, İsmet Paşa Mah. 161 Sok. (☎ 812 26 60 or 812 62 20). Follow Küçük Deniz Sahil Cad. to the right of the harbor and take a right at the "Ensar" sign pointing inland. A large, well-kept family pension with a terrace view of the mountains and the sea. The owners of this mom-and-pop operation speak German and some English. Guest kitchen and private baths. Free use of washing machine. Bar, TV, and A/C in living room. $8 per person; $13 per person in July and Aug. Open May-Oct.

Ensar Pension, İsmet Paşa Mah. 161 Sok. (☎812 17 77; fax 812 61 59). Beside and similar to Siren. Has additional mirrors, carpeting, and bright pink sheets. Also caters to a family crowd. No booze available. 24hr. hot water and guest kitchen provided. Internet $1.60 per hr. Laundry service $3.25 per load. Breakfast on terrace $1.60. $8 per person; $10 in July and Aug. V, MC.

İyigün Pension, Sahil Cad. 155 Sok. No. 1 (☎812 11 82). Right on the waterfront with a refreshing swim just 20m from the door. White lighting and cement floors lend a somewhat institutional feel, but rooms have balconies with great views. Most have private bath. Guest kitchen on rooftop. Breakfast $1.60. $12.25 per person.

Ferah Camping (☎812 11 42). No-frills camping on the beach. Electricity, showers (no hot water), and a little restaurant next door. Owners are very generous, especially to those weary travelers with slender wallets. Take any "Hanedan" dolmuş from the Foça otogar and ask to be dropped off at Remzi'nin Yeri ($.50). Walk to the beach and continue heading away from Foça for about 500m. Pitch your tent ($3.25 per day) or rent a tent ($8 per day). Travelers come to camp or just to swim.

FOOD

There is no shortage of fresh fish restaurants along the harbor on Küçük Deniz Sahil Cad., nor of *pide*, kebap, and even pizza restaurants. At most harbor-front establishments, you can browse the menu first. Be mindful to ask for prices when they are unlisted because once you've been served and given the bill, complaints are futile. The farther inland you go, the more economical the dining becomes.

Rıdvan Usta'nın Yeri (☎812 74 64). Büyük Deniz Cad. On your left as you exit the otogar and head towards the harbor on Küçük Deniz Sahil Cad. Classic Turkish dishes on shiny wooden tables. *Döner kebap* ($2), *lahmacun* ($.50), and especially delicious *macar kofte* (meatballs in a cheese sauce; $2). Open daily 24hr. V.

Kordon Restaurant, 8 Küçük Deniz Sahil Cad. (☎812 61 91). In the pedestrian zone on the waterfront. A cut above the rest, Kordon offers foreign specials (chicken schnitzel $2.80) and fresh fish (priced daily) in a very attractive setting. On important *futbol* days, a TV is displayed in the front window so outdoor diners won't miss a move. Open daily 9am to about 1am. V, MC.

Venedik Pizza (☎812 64 14). Aşıklar Yolu Cad. On your left about 50m beyond Deniz Restaurant. If you need a slice of the West for a change, Venedik bakes pan pizzas to order. Varieties range from vegetable to sausage, tuna, or egg pizzas ($2-3). Open daily 8:30am-midnight or 1am. V.

SIGHTS

A number of sights can be seen simply by strolling around Küçük Deniz. Start at the tourist information office, turn right, and walk on Eski Adliye Sokagı, which is one block from the sea. You'll pass a sculpture of Atatürk and two children on your left. The **Fatih Camii** appears next on your right. Built sometime between 1455 and 1570, this mosque has undergone extensive repair and thus no longer looks as it originally did. If you walk down to the waterfront and continue with the sea on your left, you'll arrive at the **Beşkapılar (Five Doors) and city walls,** immediately in front of the Temple of Athena. These walls formed the earliest fortifications of Phokaia in the 6th century BC. The walls have survived intact because of repairs done in the Byzantine era, then later by the Genoese in the late 13th century, and finally by the Ottomans in the 16th century.

Up a small hill and to your right is Foça's local high school, on the far side of which is the excavation site for the **Temple of Athena,** built in the early 6th century BC. Her temple's location on raised ground, as well as her presence on ancient coins and in ancient inscriptions, demonstrates Athena's importance to the Phokians. To the left

AEGEAN COAST

on the small hill is the **Kayalar Camii.** This mosque too has undergone numerous renovations since it was first constructed in the 16th or 17th century, and thus, it too has lost its original appearance.

A bit farther along on your right is the Phokaia Port, containing the **Kybele Açık Hava Tapınağı** (the Cybele Open Air Temple), a sanctuary carved from stone and dedicated to the goddess Cybele in 580 BC. For the Anatolians, Cybele was the guardian of life and fertility, but the powers that came to be associated with her are manifold. Continue walking and turn right immediately after the Tansaş grocery store and right again onto 196 Sokak.

Apart from the Byzantine **mosaics,** a block from the Aydın Motel, which are currently under excavation and not visible, the rest of Foça's sights must be reached by boat since they are in the military zone. The well-restored **Dış Kale** ("Outer Castle") clings to the tip of the point occupied by the navy, and it is more impressive than the fortress. The **siren rocks** are far off in the ocean near Orak Island. Most boat trips include lunch and stops at the castle, the rocks, and Orak Island.

İZMİR ☎ 232

İzmir (pop. 3 million), formerly ancient Smyrna, has risen from a tumultuous past to become Turkey's third-largest city and second-largest port. Reputedly the birthplace of Homer, Smyrna gained prominence in the 9th century BC and thrived before the Lydians from Sardis destroyed it about 300 years later. In 334 BC, Alexander the Great conquered the city and refounded it atop Mt. Pagus, now called Kadifekale. During the Roman and Byzantine periods, Smyrna re-emerged as a prosperous port. The diversion of the River Hermes protected the harbor from silting up, saving Smyrna from the landlocked fate of its stagnating neighbors. In 1535, Süleyman the Magnificent signed a treaty with France, bringing trade to Smyrna. Beginning with the influx of Christian and Jewish merchants, Smyrna, by the 19th century, had become a haven for migrants from mainland Greece. After the Ottoman Empire's defeat in WWI, the Greek army occupied İzmir in hopes of uniting the area with mainland Greece. Turkish nationalist leader Mustafa Kemal (later Atatürk) defeated the weak, overextended Greek forces who had exhausted themselves in the Anatolian heartland. Greek troops left Smyrna on September 9, 1922, when the city's minority quarters burned. The Asia Minor Disaster, as the events of 1922 came to be called, meant the end of Greek presence in İzmir.

Along the waterfront, İzmir is a cosmopolitan city with wide boulevards, plazas, and plenty of greenery. Fast cars, luxury hotels, and other signs of conspicuous wealth distinguish the coast. Away from the water, much of İzmir is a bleak, factory-laden wasteland; on the outskirts, poverty and uncontrolled industrial expansion combine to produce heartbreaking urban squalor. Still, the city is worth visiting for a few days, especially in June, July, and August, when it hosts the International İzmir Festival, attracting world-renowned musical, dance, and theater performers. In the summer of 2000, the bill included the Waterbury Chorale, the Russian Army Chorus and Dance Ensemble, and the El Paso Texas Symphony Orchestra, along with the Borusan İstanbul Philharmonic Orchestra.

▛ TRANSPORTATION

Flights: Airport Adnan Menderes, 20km south of İzmir, connects Turkey to most major European cities. To get to the airport take the Havaş bus from the tourist office (30min., every 1½hr., $2.80). Many major airlines serve the airport, but **Turkish Airlines** (airport office: ☎ 274 24 24 or 274 28 00; fax 274 20 33) often has the cheapest flights. The sales office, 1/F Gazi Osman Paşa (information ☎ 484 12 20; reservations ☎ 445 53 63; fax 483 62 81), is just up from the tourist office. Open daily 8am-7pm. To: **İstanbul** (45min.; $85, students $58) and **Ankara** (1hr.; $85, students $58).

Buses: For major intercity travel, go to the new airport-like **Yeni Garaj.** Times and prices vary, and buses head just about everywhere. Major destinations on **Kamil Koç** and **Pamukkale**

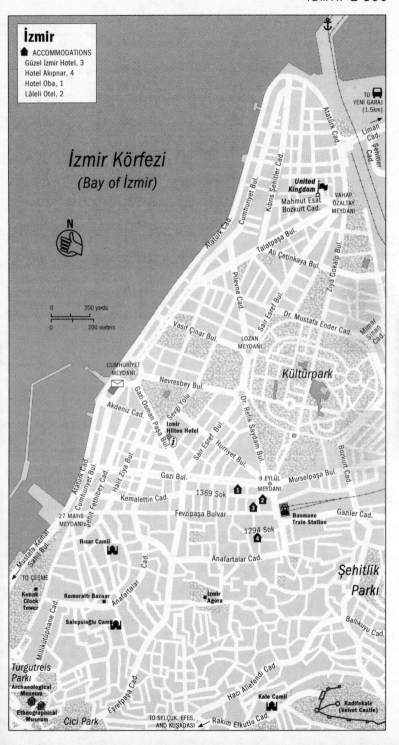

İzmir

ACCOMMODATIONS
Güzel İzmir Hotel, 3
Hotel Akıpnar, 4
Hotel Oba, 1
Lâleli Otel, 2

İzmir Körfezi
(Bay of İzmir)

N

0   200 yards
0   200 meters

İZMİR Körfezi

TO
YENİ GARAJ
(1.5km)

Atatürk Cad.

Liman Cad.
Şehitler Cad.

Cumhuriyet Bul.

Kıbrıs Şehitler Cad.

United
Kingdom
Mahmut Esat
Bozkurt Cad.

VAHAP
ÖZALTAY
MEYDANI

Atatürk Cad.

Talatpaşa Bul.

Ali Çetinkaya Bul.

Ziya Gökalp Bul.

Pilevne Cad.

Şair Eşref Bul.

Dr. Mustafa Ender Cad.

Mimar
Sinan
Cad.

Vasıf Çınar Bul.

LOZAN
MEYDANI

Kültürpark

CUMHURİYET
MEYDANI

Nevresbey Bul.

Sevgi Yolu

Akdeniz Cad.

Gazi Osman Paşa Bul.

İzmir
Hilton Hotel

Şair Eşref Bul.

Hürriyet Bul.

Dr. Refik Saydam Bul.

Bozkurt Cad.

Atatürk Cad.

Cumhuriyet Bul.

Şehit Fethibey Cad.

Halit Ziya Bul.

Gazi Bul.

Kemalettin Cad.

1369 Sok

9 EYLÜL
MEYDANI

Mürselpaşa Bul.

Gaziler Cad.

Fevzipaşa Bulvar

Basmane
Train Station

27 MAYIS
MEYDANI

Hısar Camii

Anafartalar Cad.

1294 Sok

Mustafa Kemal

Sahil Bul.

TO ÇEŞME

Konak
Clock
Tower

Kemeraltı Bazaar

Anafartalar Cad.

İzmir
Agora

Şehitlik
Parkı

Salepsioğlu Camii

Balıkuyu Cad.

Millikütüphane Cad.

Turgutreis
Parkı

Archaeological
Museum

Ethnographical
Museum

Cici Park

Eşrefpaşa Cad.

TO SELÇUK, EFES,
AND KUŞADASI

Hacı Aliefendi Cad.

Rakım Elkutlu Cad.

Kale Camii

Kadifekale
(Velvet Castle)

AEGEAN COAST

include: **Ankara** (8hr., every hr. 9am-1am, $13.75); **Antalya** (8hr., every hr. 4am-1am, $13); **Bodrum** (4hr., every hr. 7am-1am, $10); **Bursa** (5hr., every hr. 9am-1am, $8); **İstanbul** (9hr., every hr. 9am-1am, $18); **Kuşadası** (1hr., every 90min. 8:30am-5:30pm, $3.25); **Marmaris** (5hr., every hr. 7am-1am, $10); **Selçuk** (take a Bodrum- or Kuşadası-bound bus and ask to be let off at Selçuk; 1hr.; $4). For more local destinations including **Manisa** (1hr., every 30min. 6am-9pm, $1.60) and **Sardis** (1½hr., every 30min. 6:25am-10:20pm, $2.50), go to the upper level of the terminal to purchase your ticket and board the bus.

Trains: From Basmane station to: **Ankara** (13hr.; 6:20, 7pm; $11.50); **Denizli** (6hr.; 9am, 3:10, 6:50pm; $4); **Söke** (3hr., 7:20pm, $2). Trains stop en route in many other towns. They are currently not running to İstanbul.

Ferries: (☎ 464 88 89 or 464 88 64; fax 464 78 34), at the Yeni Liman. One ferry per week to **İstanbul** (20hr.; Su 2pm; from $18.75, students $15). There is a weekly ferry to **Venice, Italy** (3 days; from $590 in summer, $490 otherwise, students 15% off).

Car Rental: Niyazoğlu Turizm Company, 1/E Gazi Osman Paşa Bul. (☎ 483 93 00; fax 483 17 00), rents to those 21 and older. From $40 per day.

✳ ORIENTATION

İzmir's principal boulevards radiate from roundabouts, called *meydan*. **Cumhuriyet Meydanı,** on the waterfront, is the city's financial center and the home of several travel agencies, fashionable restaurants, consulates, and the PTT. Many budget hotels and inexpensive restaurants, along with several bus company offices and the **Basmane train station,** are located around **9 Eylül Meydanı,** the center of the Basmane district. To get there from İzmir's new intercity bus station (Yeni Garaj), walk two flights down from the upper level where buses arrive to the ground level where city buses and dolmuş depart. Take city bus #601, 605, 50, 51, 53, 54, or 60. All of these pass through 9 Eylül Meydanı, but the best way to make sure you get off in this square is to sit near the bus driver and tell him you want "Basmane Meydanı." Buy bus tickets from the kiosk before boarding ($.50). To return to the Yeni Garaj, purchase your bus tickets in one of the bus company offices in 9 Eylül Meydanı and take the company shuttle to the station. If the bus company does not provide service to your destination, they will still allow you to use their shuttle.

🔢 PRACTICAL INFORMATION

TOURIST AND FINANCIAL SERVICES

Tourist Office: Tourism Information Office, 1/1D Gazi Osman Paşa Bul. (☎ 445 73 90 or 489 92 78; fax 489 92 78). From 9 Eylül Meydanı, walk down Gazi Bul. to the 1st main intersection, then turn right onto Gazi Osmanpaşa Bul. Look to your right, about 30m up from the İzmir Hilton Hotel. Some English spoken. Great free maps and other information. Open in summer M-F 8:30am-6:30pm, Sa-Su 9am-5pm; in winter M-F 8:30am-5:30pm, Sa 9am-5pm.

Travel Agencies: The 3 recommended agencies offer a variety of tours that include an English speaking guide. **Ramtur,** Gazi Osman Paşa Bul., 3/312 Yeni Asır İşhanı (☎ 425 27 10 or 483 34 36; fax 483 34 36; email info@ramtur.com), is on the 3rd floor. Arranges daily tours of İzmir; Ephesus; Pergamon; Jewish heritage of İzmir; Priene, Miletus, and Didyma; Pamukkale; İstanbul; and Cappadocia. Also assists with airline tickets and İzmir tourist information. Open M-F 8:30am-6pm, Sa 8:30am-4pm, Su 8:30am-noon. **Opal Travel Agency,** 1 Gazi Osman Paşa Bul. (☎ 445 67 67; fax 489 88 65), is in the basement of the Büyük Efes Oteli. Daily tours to Bergama, Efes, and Pamukkale. Open M-F 9am-7pm, Sa 9am-6pm. **Bintur Travel Agency,** 10/1A Gazi Osman Paşa Bul. (☎ 489 41 00; fax 489 65 64). Deals with hotel reservations. Open in summer M-F 8:30am-7pm, Sa 8:30am-5pm; in winter M-F 8:30am-6pm, Sa 8:30am-1pm.

Consulates: UK, 49 Mahmut Esat Bozkurt Cad. (☎ 463 51 51; fax 421 29 14), in Alsancak. **US,** American Consular Agency, 13 Kazim Dirik Cad., Flat 805 (☎ 441 00 72 or 441 22 03; fax 441 23 73).

AEGEAN COAST

Banks: All national banks and a number of foreign banks have large offices along the water-front. Smaller banks have offices around Basmane, including a **T.C. Ziraat Bankası,** on the left side of Gazi Bul. when walking east, just before your arrive in 9 Eylül Meydanı. Cirrus/MC/V **ATM** and **currency exchange.** Open M-F 8:30am-5pm.

American Express: 270 Atatürk Cad. (☎ 463 65 93; fax 422 67 20). In the Pamfilya Travel Agency, 15min. from Cumhuriyet Meydanı. Open M-Sa 9am-noon, 1:30-6:30pm.

LOCAL SERVICES

English Language Bookstore: Net Bookstore, 142/B Cumhuriyet Bul. 142/B (☎ 421 26 32). At the intersection of Cumhuriyet Bul. and 1375 Sok., 1 block north of Cumhuriyet Meydanı. Decent selection of novels and tourist books on Turkey. Open daily 9am-7pm.

Hamam: Hoşgör Hamamı, 360 Sok. No. 10, in the Mecidiye district south of Basmane. The hamam is shown on the detailed map distributed at the tourist office. Somewhat far from the Basmane area, but walkable (30min. from 9 Eylül Meydanı). Foreigners are advised to make an appointment. Mixed gender groups as well as single males and females welcome. Male masseurs only. Bath and massage $20. Open daily 7am-11pm.

EMERGENCY AND COMMUNICATIONS

Pharmacies: On almost every corner in the downtown areas. **Aşıkoğlu Eczanesi,** 103 Gazi Bul. (☎ 483 79 63), on the corner of Gazi Bul. and 1362 Sok., 3 blocks west of 9 Eylül Meydanı. Open daily 8am-8pm.

Hospitals: Ege Üniversitesi Tıp Fakültesi (☎ 343 43 43), in Bornova. 2 state hospitals include **Alsancak Hastanesi** (☎ 463 64 65), on Talat Paşa Bul. **Yeşilyurt Devlet Hastanesi,** a.k.a. **Atatürk Hastanesi** (☎ 243 43 43), Gazeteci Hasan Tahsin Cad., Yeşilyurt.

Internet Access: Seçkin Internet Cafe, 16 Mimarkemalettin Cad. (☎ 482 14 37; fax 445 15 11; email seckin.cafe@secsan.com.tr; www.secsan.com.tr), on the left side of the street near the intersection with Cumhuriyet Bul. (when walking towards the water). New computers and a reliable, if slow connection. To avoid an inflated fee, make sure to establish the price and starting time when you arrive. $1.25 per hr. Open daily 24hr.

PTT: In Cumhuriyet Meydanı. Open M-F 8:30am-10pm. 24hr. **currency** and **traveler's check exchange** and sale of **phone cards. Postal code:** 35000.

▌ ACCOMMODATIONS

▓ **Hotel Oba,** 1369 Sok. No. 27 (☎ 441 96 05 or 441 96 06; fax 483 81 98). 4 blocks west of 9 Eylül Meydanı, away from the train station. A rare find combining relatively cheap, clean lodgings with great amenities, including a lobby bar, private bath, TV, and A/C in each room. Laundry service is pricey (about $8), but clothing is beautifully cleaned and folded. Unfortunately, no hot water between 10am and 8pm. Breakfast served 7:30-9:30am. Singles $12; doubles $16.

Lâleli Otel, 1368 Sok. No. 5-6 (☎ 484 09 01 or 484 09 02). Walk 1 block from 9 Eylül Meydanı on 1369 Sok. and turn left. Comfortable rooms, all with showers and ceiling fans. English-speaking staff always available. Breakfast $1.60. 1 person $10; 2 people $17.85; 3 people $24.50. Beds $12, in dorm-style quads $10. V, MC, AmEx.

Hotel Akpınar, 1294 Sok. No. 13 (☎ 446 38 96 or 484 16 34; fax 489 46 88). Walk south from 9 Eylül Meydanı on Anafartalar Cad., pass the train station on your left, and turn right onto 1294 Sok. Akpınar is quiet, cool, and clean. Every room has a window, though some have views of an airshaft, so it's good to preview them. TV in each room. Shared baths for bathless guests are conveniently located. Self-service laundry free, full service $3.25. Singles $5, with bath $8; doubles $8, with bath $11.50.

Güzel İzmir Hotel, 1368 Sok. No. 8 (☎ 483 50 69 or 484 66 93). 1 block away from 9 Eylül Meydanı, across the street from Lâleli Hotel. Some chipping paint and cramped quarters, but a good value. TV room. Public phone in lobby. All rooms have showers and fans in the summer. Singles $9; doubles $16.25; triples $20. V, MC, AmEx.

◨ ♫ FOOD AND ENTERTAINMENT

Basmane Kebap Salonu, 157/A Fevzipaşa Bul. (☎425 50 19), a few doors down on your right as you walk away from the train station. A display case at the front of this friendly restaurant holds the meats from which you create a *şiş* mix (chicken *şiş* $2; mixed meat $2.50). The specialty is *içli köfte* (meatballs with deep-fried batter; $.75 each). *Kofte* and *şiş* come in normal or hot "*acılı*" form. Open daily 9am-midnight. V.

Çankaya Börek ve Pide Salonu, 8 Mimar Kemalettin Cad. No. 130/B (☎484 62 50). All sorts of *börek* (cheese, potato, spinach, meat; $1) and *pide* ($.50-$1) are on display so you needn't know a word of Turkish. Open daily 5am-midnight.

9 Eylül Et Lokantası, 9 Eylül Meydanı No. 5/B (☎445 05 31). A popular spot offering vegetarian options like *taze fasülye* (green beans in tomato sauce; $1.20) and exceptionally flavorful meat dishes ($2-2.50). Outdoor tables with a view of the buzzing square. Open daily 6am-11pm.

Güzel İzmir Lokantaları, 1368 Sok. No. 8/B (☎445 05 31), at the Basmane end of the 1369 Sok. Along with 9 Eylül Et Lokantası, Güzel İzmir is the best *lokanta* in the vicinity, offering traditional dishes in a cleaner-than-average setting. Excellent *moussaka* and other meat dishes $2. Vegetable dishes $1.50. Open daily 6am-midnight.

Bolula Hasan Usta, 141/B Cumhuriyet Bul. (☎464 67 26 or 464 67 93), a few minutes north from Cumhuriyet Meydanı. Parisian-style cafe offers tempting Turkish desserts, including *ekmek kadayıfı* ($1.20) and *krem karamel* ($1). Open daily 7am-1am.

Sera Cafe-Bar-Restaurant, 190/A Atatürk Cad., Alsancak (☎464 25 94 or 464 25 95). A bit pricier, Sera offers a relaxing sea breeze and a refreshing harbor view. The eclectic decor combines Egyptian and Renaissance motifs. This trendy hot spot offers Turkish, Continental, and American breakfasts ($4-5.50), though they differ very little. Burgers $2.50. Cocktails $6.50. Live Turkish and foreign music every night from 10pm until closing. Open 7am-about 3am.

Kültürpark (☎446 14 56). Between 9 Eylül Meydanı, Montrö Meydanı, Lozan Meydanı, the southern end of Ziya Gökalp Bul., and the western end of Akıncılar Cad. with entrances at each of these spots. A great center for day- and nightlife, especially during the International Fair (Aug. 15-25). Features various attractions including numerous restaurants, tea gardens, a zoo (open 9am-6pm), an amusement park (open 11am-midnight), a disco, and a casino (both open 9pm-4am). Crowds are most vigorous on weekends. Park open daily, 24hr. Entrance fee $.30.

Club 33, 1469 Sok. No. 40, Alsancak (☎464 04 70). The first right off Atatürk Cad. after 1481 Sok. The hip place to be seen. Large dance floor holds up to 1000. Beer $5. No cover. Open in summer W, F-Sa 10:30pm-3am; in winter daily 10:30pm-3am.

◉ SIGHTS

İzmir's **agora** (marketplace) was built in the 4th century BC, destroyed by an earthquake in 178 AD, and subsequently rebuilt by Emperor Marcus Aurelius. The mediocre remains of ancient columns and more interesting tombstones can be reached by walking south on Gazi Osman Paşa Bul. and turning left on Anafartalar Cad. *(Open daily 8:30am-5pm. $1.25.)* Above the city at Mt. Pagus is the **Kadifekale.** Alexander originally built it in the 4th century BC, but various conquerors frequently altered and restored it. The park within the walls of the Kadifekale is unsavory, yet intriguing. The area may be unsafe after dark. Dolmuş marked "Mezarlık" leave from in front of the agora entrance on Anafartalar Cad. and ascend the mountain, offering a thrilling panorama of the bay ($.40).

If you stroll along Anafartalar Cad. from its origin at the Basmane station, you'll pass evidence of a less-industrialized Turkey—*çay salonu* (tea houses), men smoking *nargile*, children and vendors filling the air with their cries, and colorful streets that eventually turn into İzmir's full-fledged **bazaar.** The bazaar runs at a feverish pace, crowded with shoppers and determined hawkers. Leather, jewelry, and name-brand knockoffs are the most abundant offerings. *(M-Sa 9am-8pm.)*

For a more subdued experience, İzmir's **Archaeological Museum,** near Konak Square, offers probably the finest collection of statuary outside of İstanbul. Among finds from Ephesus and other local sites are a couple of elaborate sarcophagi and a few extraordinary statues. *(Open Tu-Su 9am-5pm. $2.50.)* Directly across and just uphill from the archaeological museum, the **Ethnographical Museum** occupies a lovely old Ottoman house. It displays early Ottoman weapons and traditional folk art mostly from the last century, including *kilims,* costumes, and furniture. *(Open Tu-Su 9am-noon, 1-5pm. $1.25.)*

In the center of the Konak district lies **Hisar Camii,** İzmir's 400-year-old treasure. Decorated with beguiling floral tiling and fantastic Turkish carpets, this mosque is the most renowned site in İzmir. It is located in the **konak** itself, the late Ottoman clock tower that looms over the intersection of Cumhuriyet Bul. and Atatürk Cad. The annual highlight, the **International İzmir Festival,** best reflects the city's cosmopolitan character. Held from mid-June to early August, the festival brings a variety of Turkish and international acts to İzmir, Çeşme, and Ephesus. For tickets and information, call the numbers listed in the back of the İzmir Festival brochure distributed at the tourist office. Considering the quality and reputation of many of the performers, tickets are cheap ($10-16, students $5-8. Email izmirfestivali@superonline.com; www.iksev.org or www.izmirfestival.org.)

DAYTRIPS FROM İZMİR

MANİSA

Manisa is easily visited as a daytrip. Bus service to İzmir from the garaj (1hr., every 30min., $1.60) saves you the woe of staying in the town's accommodations. To reach the hillside with the old city's remains, catch a dolmuş from behind the bus station and ask for "Sultan Hamam" or "Müze." You'll be dropped off at the top of İzmir Cad., which connects Murat Cad. at the top of the hill and Doğu Cad. at the bottom. The tourist office, 14/3 Doğu Cad., is down the hill (☎ 236 231 25 41; open in summer M-F 8:30am-5pm), but it's much easier and more advisable to seek tourist information at the museum.

Thirty kilometers inland from İzmir, Manisa was once a beautiful city covered in orchards and springs. The modern version retains nothing of its idyllic past, presenting a long, hot, grimy strip along the İzmir highway. Most of the old city was destroyed in the Turkish War of Independence in 1922, but Manisa still contains some interesting remains, mainly on the attractive wooded hillside that overlooks the concrete jungle below. Apart from the Niobe stone and Byzantine acropolis, all the sights lie within a two to three block cluster with signs pointing the way.

The Sultan Hamam, part of the **Valide Sultan Camii** complex, scores high points for good clean fun with its authentic facilities, guaranteed female attendants for female bathers, and piping bath temperature. (☎ 231 20 51. For women, bath $5, massage add $15. Open daily 10am-9pm; in winter 10am-5pm. For men, bath $2.50, massage add $4. Open daily 6am-midnight.) Every year on the two days on either side of the spring equinox, the mosque complex continues a tradition begun by Hafise Hatun, mother of Süleyman the Magnificent. She was brought back from the jaws of death by a medicinal gum made of over 40 spices and mostly sugar, concocted by the concerned citizens of Manisa. To show her gratitude, she commissioned the construction of the complex whose *imaret* (charitable soup kitchen) still remains open on these two days. The *imaret* abides by the strict rule that the food be passed through a small window or around the corner in order to spare the recipient the humiliation of making eye contact with the cook. Other money from the estate of the Valide Sultan was used to establish an annual **Sugar and Gum Festival.** During the modern festival, at the end of April, several tons of the gum are boiled up and thrown off the Valide Sultan's minarets to a crowd of tens of thousands of umbrella- and bedsheet-wielding health seekers.

Near the dolmuş stop, close to the Muradiye Camii, is the local **Archaeological/ Ethnographical Museum,** housed in an *imaret* and *medrese* respectively. The archaeological museum, under renovation but not off-limits at the time of publication, houses a collection of artifacts from all eras of Manisa's history. The ethnographic collection consists mainly of royal personal effects. *(Museum open Tu-Su 8:30am-5:30pm. $1.60, students $1.)* Next to the museum is the **Muradiye Camii,** designed by the unparalleled Mimar Sinan and constructed in 1586. Muradiye Camii has **99 windows,** a religiously significant number in Islam symbolizing the 99 known names for God (the 100th remains shrouded in mystery). The *mihrab* and walls are covered in beautiful İznik tiles, which incorporate carnation and rose motifs, alluding to Manisa's days as a garden city. Similarly, the underside of the *hünkar sofrası* (sultan's lodge), the wooden platform above and to the left of the *mihrab,* has a border relief of the grape vines for which the city was once famous. The red marble column to the left of the *mihrab,* loosened in an earthquake, is often spun after prayers for good luck. Fine examples of *mermer* (marble) **paper prints** hang above the doors in the mosque. This technique, perfected by the Ottomans, counters the slickness of marble as a painting surface. Patterns are painted onto blotting paper, and pressed against the stone surface while the paint is still wet. The paper prevents smudges as it holds the paint in place while it dries.

Uphill from Muradiye Camii by way of the steep stairs is the **Ulu Camii,** constructed in 1336 by famed Selçuk architect Haci Ahmet. Built under the rule of Işak Bey, this mosque is trisected by columns into three roughly equal areas. Eight "elephant leg" pillars break up the mosque's interior space. The Ulu Camii complex also includes the **tomb of İsa Bey,** through the door off to the right of the mosque's entrance. The tomb's caretaker will gladly show it to you in exchange for a string of prayer beads or money. A tea garden under the trees outside the mosque takes advantage of the view of the town and countryside below (tea $.30).

With your back to the mosque's main entrance, turn left along the road and proceed up the hill, passing the ruins of the Roman and Byzantine city of Magnesia ad Sipylum until you reach the open-air theater on your left. The **Aglayan Kaya,** or **Niobe rock,** is a large stone, which, when viewed from the seats of the theater, midway between the bottom and the top, looks like a woman leaning forward and weeping. According to myth, Niobe, wife of Amphion and daughter of Tantalus, gave birth to many children (between 10 and 14 sons and daughters). The proud mother boasted that she was superior to Leto, mother of twins Artemis and Apollo. As punishment for her hubris, the two deities slew the entire brood, leaving her to weep until Zeus took pity upon her and turned her into a statue. The creek and the rocky ravine that cradles it are a relief after a few days in İzmir.

SART (SARDIS)

To reach Sardis from İzmir, take a bus bound for Salihli from the upper floor of İzmir's Yeni Garaj (1½hr., every 30min., $2.50). Ask to be let off at Sart. You will be dropped near a yellow "Sart Temple of Artemis" sign, located amidst the shops and tea houses scattered along the highway. The yellow sign points the way to the Temple of Artemis, along a road that runs off to the right of the highway. If you walk forward on the highway, the gymnasium, synagogue and baths are about 50m ahead on your left. Buses back to İzmir run with the same frequency, but may be about $.50 more expensive. Catch them from the wide, pull-off area across the road from where the bus dropped you.

Sardis (Sart to the Turks) was the capital of the Lydian Empire, which dominated Aegean Ionia from 680-547 BC. The Lydians embraced and embellished the existing Hellenic culture, giving the world dice and coin minting. Sardis was also an important *satrapy* (administrative center) in the Persian empire and home to one of the seven churches mentioned in the Book of Revelation. Apart from the remains of the temple of Artemis, most of the ruins at Sardis are Roman and early Byzantine. Though small, Sardis stands out as perhaps the best-restored site in Turkey. It is so well refurbished that it can be difficult to distinguish the replacement marble from the original.

After entering, proceed to the right along the **West Road** (a.k.a. **Marble Way**), which is lined with a row of **Byzantine shops.** At the end of the Marble Way, turn left to enter

AS RICH AS CROESUS

Known in antiquity as the richest man in the world, the Lydian king Croesus (r. 560-546BC) ruled a large Aegean empire from his capital at Sardis. He held sway over a sizeable part of Anatolia and all of the coastal Greek cities except Miletus. Although large and wealthy, his empire was far from secure, and the powerful Persian forces threatened his borders from the south. Indeed, the Persian Empire was even larger and more powerful than Croesus'. Expecting an imminent war, Croesus sent messengers to Delphi, the most famous oracle in the ancient world, to discover the outcome. In typical ambiguity, the Pythia answered "you will destroy a great empire." Confidant that the oracle foretold Persian defeat, Croesus went to battle in 547 BC against the famous Persian king Cyrus. Of course, Croesus did destroy a great empire, his own. In no time, the Persians besieged and sacked his capital, and like his kingdom, Croesus soon met his end. Still, his memory remains in the phrase, "as rich as Croesus," a testament to the wealth and conspicuous consumption of the Lydian empire.

the **synagogue,** donated by the Roman authorities to the town's Jewish inhabitants. The patterns of the synagogue's 3rd-century mosaic floors are strangely juxtaposed with the Corinthian and Doric columns above. Beside the synagogue lies the ruined **Palaestra,** where wrestling matches and other sporting events were held. The imposing and magnificently restored two-story structure is the **gymnasium,** the site of a Roman bath house, whose towering columns overshadow a long-deserted **swimming pool.**

Cross the street and enter Mahmutbey Cad., between the Akçay market and a tea shop, for a wonderful view of Anatolian landscapes. A 1km trek up the paved road brings you to the **Temple of Artemis.** This 4th century BC edifice was one of the largest temples built and is one of the Seven Wonders of the Ancient World. Today, only a few columns remain, but their scrolled capitals are exquisite. Even more impressive are the intricately carved, floral-patterned column bases. On the way to the temple, about 100m up on the left, are the remains of an ancient Roman city wall. 50m farther on the right, catch a glimpse of the ancient **Lydian gold refinery** and a dome from a 12th-century Byzantine **basilica** that was built atop a 5th-century church. On the left, about 800m ahead, you will find a trail to the **pyramid tomb.** Located in the area northwest of the acropolis, the earliest of these tombs dates from the 6th century BC, but it has since been buried by landslides. *(Old city, including the gymnasium, baths, and synagogue, open daily 8am-5 or 6pm. $1.60, students $1. Temple open daily 8am-8pm; in winter 8am-5pm. $1.60, students $1.)*

ÇEŞME

☎ 232

A breezy seaside village, Çeşme was built around a 14th-century Genoese fortress that was expanded and beautified by 16th-century Ottomans. Only one hour west of İzmir, the town has deservedly gained popularity for its cool climate, crystal clear waters, and proximity to the Greek island of Chios. Many affluent İzmirites have weekend houses here, but it is the daytrippers from Chios who keep the myriad restaurants and leather shops in business. Nightlife keeps a healthy pace in the cafes and bars along the marina. At the end of July and the end of August, Çeşme hosts the Sea Festival/International Pop Song Contest and the Çeşme Film Festival, respectively. For the song contest, bars stay packed, and primary sponsors TEKEL (the state alcohol and tobacco monopoly) and Coca-Cola set up tents along the waterfront for giveaways and contests. Information regarding exact dates for these week-long festivals is available in the tourist office.

◼ TRANSPORTATION

Buses to Çeşme stop either at the new **otogar** or at the top of **İnkılap Cad.**

Buses: The otogar (☎ 712 64 99) is at the corner of A. Menderes Cad. and Çevre Yolu Cad. Here, Turgutozal Cad. picks up and runs down to the sea. To: **Ankara** (10hr.; 10am, 9:30pm; $17.50); **İstanbul** (11hr.; 10am, 9:30pm; $20); **İzmir** (1¼hr.; every 30min. 6:30am-6pm, 9pm, midnight; $3.25). Most buses to İzmir arrive at the **Üçkuyular** otogar, not the main otogar. However, İzmir-bound buses at 7, 9, 11am, 1, 3, 5, and 7pm continue to the main otogar. Bus #605 connects Üçkuyular with the main otogar, and any bus running north heads to the center of İzmir (see **İzmir: Transportation**, p. 182).

Ferries: Buy tickets from Ertürk Tourism (see **Travel Agencies**) or any of the tourist offices in town for **Chios** (1hr.; July 1-Sept. 10 Tu, Th-Sa; June, Sept. T, Th, Sa-Su; May, Oct. Tu, Th; Nov.-Apr. Th; $30 one-way, $40 open round-trip; $10 Greek port tax for stays over 1 day). From June-Sept., ferries also depart from the **Turkish Maritime Lines** office (☎ 712 10 91), on the ferry docks on the south side of the waterfront, for **Brindisi, Italy.** (36hr.; M 11pm; Th 11am; F 11am, 11pm; $95 for the deck.) To get to the dock from the tourist office, walk along the sea with the water on your right for about 10min. until you reach the large white building inscribed with "TDİ." Open Tu-Th 8am-6pm, M, F, 8am-until boat leaves.

Car Rental: Sultan Rentacar and Motorbike (☎ 712 73 95; fax 712 82 59), on İnkılap Cad., rents the cheapest cars and motorbikes in town. For 1-2 days: Fiats $50; scooters $17; motorbikes $30-40. Open daily 8:30am-midnight.

✴ 🔃 ORIENTATION AND PRACTICAL INFORMATION

İnkılap Cad. is a pedestrian shopping street lined with many leather shops and ice cream parlors. From the otogar, follow Turgutözal Cad., which begins at the corner of the parking lot with the Kamil Koç booth, down to the sea (about 200m), turn right at the sea, and walk 300m to the main waterfront square in front of the castle. This square, Çeşme Meydanı, houses the tourist office on the left in front of the castle, the *kervansaray* next to the castle, and numerous budget accommodations. From the İnkılap Cad. stop, walk downhill 300m to Çeşme Meydanı.

Tourist Office: 8 İskele Meydanı (☎/fax 712 66 53). On the waterfront across from the castle and *kervansaray*. English spoken. Maps and accommodations information available. Open in summer M-F 8:30am-7pm, Sa-Su 9am-5pm; in winter M-F 8am-5pm.

Travel Agencies: Hanye Tours, 26 İzmir Cad. (☎ 723 33 46; fax 723 00 68), in Ilıca. Car rental, tours, and plane and ferry ticket sales. Offers jeep safaris including lunch ($34) and a 1-day trip to **Priene, Miletus,** and **Didyma** ($34) including lunch. Open daily Mar.-Oct. 8am-10pm; Nov.-Feb. 9am-6pm. Take the Ilıca-bound dolmuş from beside the tourist office to the "Ilıca Terminalı" ($.50). **Ertürk Tourism and Travel Agency,** Beyazıt Cad. No. 6-7 (☎ 712 67 68), across from tourist information and next to the *kervansaray*, sells ferry tickets. Open daily in summer 8am-9:30pm; in winter 8am-6:30pm.

Banks: TC Ziraat Bankası and **Yaşar Bank** are in the main square. **Türkiye İş Bankası** is just up İnkılap Cad. from the square on the left. All offer **currency exchange, traveler's check exchange** (M-F 9am-5pm), and V/MC/Cirrus/Plus **ATMs.**

Police: (☎ 712 66 27). In the back of the tourist office.

Pharmacy: Çağler Eczanesi (☎ 712 69 64), on the left side of İnkılap Cad. when walking away from the sea. Open daily 8:30am-midnight.

Hospital: (☎ 712 07 77), 5km east of town on Çeşme İzmir Yolu, on the right. Take the Ilıca-bound dolmuş from beside the tourist office and ask for "hastane" ($.50).

Internet: Emre Computer and Internet Cafe, 11 Kutludag Cad. (☎ 712 67 36). From where İnkılap Cad. meets the sea, walk 1 block away from sea. $.75 per hr. Open daily 24hr. **Takıl Internet Cafe,** 16 Eylül Mah., Acargorgun Sok., 6D Karaaslan blok (☎ 712 07 34), 1 block away from İnkılap Cad. When walking towards the sea from Dalyan Cad., take the 1st right. Attractive cafe with frilly decor. $1 per hr. Open daily 7am-2am.

PTT: (☎ 712 66 20 or 712 63 48), on the waterfront as you walk away from the tourist office (with the sea on your left). **Currency** and **traveler's check exchange.** Open June-Sept. daily 8am-midnight; Oct.-May M-F 8am-8pm. **Postal code:** 35930.

ACCOMMODATIONS

Tarhan Pension, 9 Çarşı Sok. (☎ 712 65 99), Musalla Mah. Walking 1 block away from the sea, turn left right after the *kervansaray* (at the "No Problem" cafe). Cozy rooms with beautifully clean, white walls and hot showers. Terrace, guest kitchen, and laundry service ($5 per load). Breakfast included. Singles $8; doubles $16; triples $24.

Filiz Pension, 16 Dellal Sok (☎ 712 67 94). 1 block beyond the shop-lined İnkılap Cad. (walking away from the sea), turn onto Mektep Sok. and then immediately right onto Dellal Sok. Refreshingly clean rooms with decorative rugs. Hot water with good pressure. Extra bathrooms and showers on each floor for guests who've checked out. Beautiful English spoken. Guest kitchen. Laundry service $5-8. Breakfast $2. $8 per person.

Alim Pension, Tarihi Türk Hamamı Yanı (☎ 712 83 19 or 712 12 38; fax 712 83 19). On the corner past the *kervansaray* and hamam as you walk with the sea on your right on Alpaslan Cad. (1 block away from sea). Carpeted rooms with phones and showers, some with balconies overlooking an overgrown patch of trees and shrubbery with a fascinating, partially collapsed Ottoman stone house beyond. Primitive guest kitchen in rear garden. Breakfast $2. Singles $6.50; doubles $13; triples $19.50; quads $26.

Yeni Kervan Pension (☎ 712 84 96), Kale Sok., Musalla Mah. Walk up the hill on the alleyway that goes beyond the Tarhan Pension, turn right at the 1st road, and continue 30m. All rooms have showers, balconies with a garden view, and fans in summer. TV lounge and private garden on basement level. Breakfast included. Singles $8; doubles $16; triples $24; quads $32.

U2 Pension, 2 Muarrem Sok. (☎ 712 63 81). Centrally located on the left side of İnkılap Cad. as you walk away from the sea, about 150m from the waterfront. Pleasant rooftop terrace overlooking the town. Rooms with tile floors, and modern, yet slightly mildewed, bathrooms. Laundry $5 per load. Guest kitchen. Homemade Turkish dinner upon request ($2.50-3.50). Breakfast $1.60. Singles $8; doubles $13; triples $16.25.

Bayram Baba Camping, Altınkum Beach. From the dolmuş stop, face the water, and Bayram Camping is just to your right. A caravan and tent campground, with electricity, water, a restaurant, and beach. Open May-Oct. Free if you eat at Bayram Baba restaurant, the cheapest restaurant around. No tents provided.

FOOD AND ENTERTAINMENT

Biz Bize Salonu, 6 İnkılap Cad. (☎ 712 17 46). On the right side of İnkılap Cad., next to the castle. A favorite among locals, Biz Bize serves some of the best and cheapest *döner* (and not much else). *İskender kebap* $3.50. Open daily 24hr. V, MC.

Mangal Restaurant (☎ 712 85 21 or 721 10 86). On the corner of Yağcılar Sok. and İnkılap Cad., 200m up from the tourist office, across from the Garden Pub. Enter on Yağcılar Sok., the side street. This 2nd-story open-air restaurant has flawless decor and high ambitions. Excellent food prepared table-side on an enormous barbecue makes it worth the slightly higher prices. Salads $1.25-1.60; pasta dishes from $3.25; meat dishes from $4. Open May-Oct. daily 10am-1am. V, MC, AmEx.

Flamingo Cafe and Restaurant, Kervansaray Karşısı (☎ 712 93 01). Right in front of the *Kervansaray*. A no-frills place offering some of the least expensive food around. Outdoor dining under parasols with a nearby TV to glance at between bites. Spaghetti plates $2.40; mushroom and chicken sautes $3.25-4; kebaps $3.25. 10% discount for parties of 5 or more. Open May-Sept. daily 24hr.

Street Bar, Uzun Sok. 4/A (☎ 712 84 76). On the right corner all the way at the top of İnkılap Cad. when you walk away from the sea. The mother of all clubs in Çeşme, with the largest dance floor, A/C, and retractable roof (open until 10pm). In July and Aug., live Turkish pop nightly until 1:30am, then foreign and Turkish hits until 4am. *Rakı* and beer $2.50; cocktails $8. Happy hour 10-11pm, drinks half-off. Open daily 7pm-4am.

Körfez Restaurant, Bar and Disco, 12 Çeşme Könfer Hürriyet Cad. (☎ 712 67 18 or 712 01 91). On the waterfront towards the PTT. A bicameral disco/fast food joint next door to a more refined restaurant serving international cuisine and Turkish standards. Disco grooves nightly. Soda $.80; beer $1.20; cocktails $5.70. Open daily 8am-4am.

◆ SIGHTS

Some of Çeşme's fabled healing **hot springs** are at Vekamp, a luxurious (by campground standards, at least) campground in the rather yuppified suburb, Ilıca (see **Accommodations**). Çeşme's other major attractions include its **beaches**, easily accessible by dolmuş. A public beach is only a short walk past the PTT (walk with sea on left). Other major beaches are at **Altınkum** (see below), **BoYalık, Ildır,** and **Erythrai.** BoYalık is a 25-minute walk from Çeşme along Çeşme İzmir Cad. or a short ride on the Ilıca-bound dolmuş. Ask for "BoYalık" ($.50).

The most impressive sight in Çeşme is the waterfront **castle** across from the tourist office. Built in 1508 by Ottoman Sultan Beyazıt II in order to spy on Chios, the castle had 50 cannons and a garrison of 185. Though it was rebuilt in the 18th century, by the 19th century it had lost its military significance. It houses a well-displayed but sparse **Archaeological Museum** of common local artifacts, including Roman and 19th-century statues accompanied by little explanation. *(Open Tu-Su 8:30am-noon, 1-5:30pm. $1.60.)*

The **kervansaray,** built under Süleyman the Magnificent and imaginatively renamed the Hotel Kervansaray, contains a typical Ottoman floor plan with a rectangular frame that opens onto a courtyard. Feel free to poke around the courtyard. Back up on İnkılap Cad., the shell of the Greek basilica of **Agios Haralambos** is now the town's exhibition center. The finals of the song contest and some of the film festival screenings are held here. It houses ongoing displays of contemporary, local art and handicrafts from June-Oct. *(Open daily 9am-11pm.)*

▒ DAYTRIP FROM ÇEŞME: ALTINKUM BEACH

Dolmuş run to Altınkum from the lot in Çeşme, by the tourist office (15min.; June-Sept. every 20min. 8am-8pm, sporadic in winter; $.75.)

With a long ribbon of clean, powder-white sand flanked by clear, warm, blue waters on one side and rolling rush-covered dunes on the other, Altınkum is probably one of Turkey's best beaches. Strong offshore winds make Altınkum one of Turkey's best **windsurfing** beaches; it hosted the '98 Quicksilver European championships, which brought such legends of the sport as Robbie Nash to brave the local gales. **Fun Club** (24hr. weather hotline and office ☎ 723 16 96), at the southern end of the beach (from the dolmuş stand, face the water and walk left 600m), is a certified windsurfing school that also rents boards and wetsuits. *(Open May-Oct. Windsurfers $10 per hr.; 12hr. basic windsurfing course $100; jet ski $24 for 10min., $55 for 30min.; catamaran rental $24 per hr.; waterskiing $24 for 12-15min.; tubing $8 for 10min.)* **Bayram Baba Camping and Restaurant** is the only place to eat, drink, or stay on Altınkum Beach as other places are far pricier. If you eat your meals (*köfte* $1.60; fish $4; *şiş* $2.25) and drink your beer ($1.25 per bottle) at the restaurant, you can camp for free, but you must bring your own tent.

EPHESUS REGION

EFES (EPHESUS)
☎ 232

Stretching from early archaic times to the 6th century AD, Ephesus' glorious prosperity has not gone the way of other notable ancient cities. To this day, Ephesus boasts a concentration of Classical art and architecture surpassed only by Rome and Athens. As both the capital of Roman Asia and the site of a large, wealthy port, Ephesus accumulated almost unparalleled wealth and splendor, the marble specter of which still leaves visitors in awe. The ruins rank first among Turkey's ancient sites in terms of sheer size and state of preservation. No piles of weed-ravaged rubble await imaginative reconstruction work here. Instead, extensive marble roadways and columned avenues create an authentic impression of this ancient, metropolitan gateway to the Eastern world. The best time to visit is early in the morning, before the scorching mid-day summer sun and throngs of tourists obliterate the last remnants of lingering nighttime cool and silence.

HISTORY

Fiery and intense, Ephesus' history has all the makings of an ancient tragedy. Out of devotion to its patron goddess Artemis, it stayed close to her colossal temple near modern Selçuk rather than sidestep certain death as its harbor steadily filled with silt from the Cayster River. The recession of the sea had sealed the city's fate by the 6th century, as the harbor deteriorated into a marshy wasteland and eventually became infested with malaria-carrying mosquitoes. A massive epidemic resulted in nearly 200,000 deaths.

Ephesus' origins are equally romantic. The Delphic Oracle had prophesied that a fish and a wild boar would determine the ideal site for the founding of the city. Soon after this proclamation, Androclus was passing through a seaside village where fish were being roasted along the shore. One fish, covered in burning wood, fell from the fire, igniting a nearby bush and upsetting a wild boar, who tore out from the foliage. Androclus slew the boar, and heeding the oracle, he founded the city on the site, now 10km inland.

The ancient traveler Pausanias deemed Ephesus the "most wondrous of the Seven Ancient Wonders" and "the most beautiful work ever created by mankind." The first major structure built entirely of marble and the largest edifice in the ancient Greek world, the **Temple of Artemis** was four times as big as the Parthenon. The 6th-century philosopher Heraclitus was so enamored of this massive monument that he deposited his enigmatic treatise on the nature of the universe in the temple instead of publishing it. He later claimed that no one but the gods could understand his theories anyway. Could be.

Remarkably, the Temple of Artemis was actually built twice. It was set afire during the reign of Mad King Hesostratos in 356 BC on the night of Alexander the Great's birth. According to legend, the pyro-king succeeded only because Artemis—watching over Alexander's birth at the time—was absent. Fittingly, Alexander himself offered to restore the temple when he passed through the city. The Ephesians, however, declined his offer and rebuilt the temple even more splendidly with their own resources and the offerings made by hundreds of thousands of pilgrims. Today, little remains of the magnificent structure. Goths sacked the sanctuary in the 3rd century, and the Byzantines followed suit. Some of the temple's columns can be seen at İstanbul's Aya Sofia and London's British Museum.

Ephesus reached its zenith after 129 BC, when the Romans established the province of Asia with Ephesus as the capital. After Rome, it was second only to Alexandria in population, with more than 250,000 inhabitants. The ruins today date primarily from this period. St. Paul, recognizing the significance of the metropolis, arrived in 50 AD and converted a small group of Ephesians to Christianity. Not surprisingly, many perceived the development of the new religion as a threat to Artemis and Cybele (mother goddess of Anatolia) and forced St. Paul and his followers to depart. Eventually, however, Ephesus became a center of Christianity in the Roman Empire, so much so that the Ecumenical Council met here in 431. Pope Paul VI visited the site in 1967 and prayed with a congregation in the ruins of Ephesus' 4th century church to the Virgin.

📧🛂 TRANSPORTATION AND PRACTICAL INFORMATION

Contrary to the signs and advice given by the tourist offices in Kuşadası, Selçuk, and Samos, the guided tours of Ephesus are not recommended. Ephesus is easily reached by regular dolmuş or by walking from Selçuk, the ruins are in good repair, and there is an abundance of explanatory material. Why spend $30 on what is often a rushed and cursory look at the 2,000-acre site? A good guidebook to Ephesus is about $2.50 in Kuşadası's souvenir shops or at the entrance to the site.

Ephesus lies about 2-3km outside of Selçuk along the main Kuşadası-Selçuk road called **Dr. Sabri Yayla Bulvarı.** The easiest way to get to Ephesus from Kuşadası or Selçuk is to take advantage of the free shuttle service offered by practically every hotel and *pansiyon*. Otherwise, to get to Ephesus from the Kuşadası otogar, take a **dolmuş** to Selçuk and tell the driver to stop at Efes (30min., $1). From the Selçuk otogar, take a Pamucak-bound dolmuş toward Kuşadası (5min.; May-Oct. every 30min., Nov.-Apr. every hr.; $.50). Taxis also run from Selçuk to Ephesus ($4) and to the House of the Virgin Mary (9km, $21 round-trip including 45min. to visit the house). The site is also an easy walk (25min.) from Selçuk along a fig tree-shaded path (beside Dr. Sabri Yayla Bulvarı) that passes by the spectacular **Ephesus Museum** (see **Selçuk: Sights,** p. 200) and the **Temple of Artemis.** The lower entrance, to which you arrive by dolmuş or on foot, has **toilets** ($.40) and a **PTT.**

Aside from the stands selling chewy Turkish ice cream, the culinary offerings at the site are pretty weak, though there are some picnic tables just outside the site. Infinitely preferable is the *gözleme* tent just outside the entrance to the Seven Sleepers. There are currently **no accommodations** in Ephesus.

🏛 EXPLORING EPHESUS

☎892 64 02. Site open 8am-6pm. $6.50. Bring a water bottle and sunscreen.

VEDIUS GYMNASIUM AND STADIUM. On the left as you walk down the road that goes from Dr. Sabri Yayla Bulvarı to the lower entrance is the Vedius Gymnasium, built in 150 AD in honor of then-emperor Antonius Pius and Artemis, the city's patron goddess. A marble path connects this structure to the Grand Theater at the head of the Arcadiane.

Beyond the vegetation visible from the road lie the horseshoe-shaped remains of the city's stadium, originally constructed by the Greek architect Lysimachus and then expanded during the reign of Nero. The dual construction highlights the fundamental differences between Hellenic and Roman public entertainment. The original Greek structure would have been a semi-circular theater whose shape followed the contours of the land to add a natural emphasis to the staged dramas. The Roman stadium was built atop the old theater for the viewing of such martial spectacles as bloody gladiator games, wild beast hunts, and public executions. As you walk past, you can see the stone supports underneath the seats and the tunnels that served as an ancient world "green room" for wild beasts and gladiators.

ON THE WAY TO THE ARCADIANE. Of the three holy Christian sites in the Efes vicinity, only the very long, skinny building of the **Church of the Seven Councils** is in the Ephesus site itself. Just inside the lower entrance, a dirt path leads to the right; follow this path and turn right where it splits to the ruins of the Church. Here, the Ecumenical Council met in 431 AD to iron out the **Nestorian Heresy,** in which the bishop Nestor called into question the humanity of Christ. This was also the site of Pope Paul VI's visit in 1967. Beside the Church of the Seven Councils is the **Archbishop's Place,** which was destroyed by Arabs in the 6th century AD.

ALONG THE ARCADIANE. Back at the main entrance gate, a tree-lined path leads straight ahead to the Arcadiane, which could loosely be termed Ephesus' main drag. Running from the Grand Theater to what was once the harbor, the magnificent, colonnaded marble avenue would have been thronging with stevedores (men who unload ships' cargoes) and carts bringing wares from ships to sell in the *agora*. The street eventually liquefied into a small marsh, and only a few marble stumps remain of the covered arcade which ran along the sides of the main road. Ephesus was one of only three ancient cities that could afford street lighting. The large expanse of column stones laid out in tidy rows to the left as you face the theater are the remnants of the **Theater Baths and Gymnasium.** This area, used in the Roman Period for training actors, is currently a focus of excavation.

Buried under nothing more than a dense swarm of tourists, the **Grand Theater** is a stunning, 30m by 145m, heavily restored beast. Its *cavea* (seating area), carved into the side of Mt. Pion, had a capacity of 25,000 people. (Archaeologists have used this

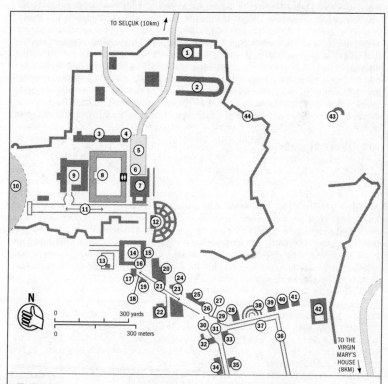

Ephesus

SIGHTS:
Agora , 14
Arcadiane , 11
Archbishop's Palace , 4
Basilica , 39
Baths and Hall of Verulanus , 8
Baths of Varius,
    restored by Scholastica , 24
Baths, brothel, & toilets , 20
Byzantine Walls , 44
Cave of the Seven Sleepers , 43
Church of the Seven Councils , 3
East Gymnasium , 42
Former Harbor , 10

Fountain of Trajan , 25
Grand Theater , 12
Hadrian's Gate , 18
Harbor Barhs , 9
Hercules Gate , 26
Inscripted Advertisement , 15
Library of Celsus , 17
Lower Gate , 6
Munumental Fountain , 27
Museum of Inscriptions , 34
Octagon, Tomb of Princess Arsinoe , 19
Odeon , 38
Parking Lot and Souvenir Shops , 5
Peristyle House built of Basilica Blocks , 40
Prytaneion , 28
Relief of Nike , 30

South Gate of Agora , 16
Square of Domitian , 31
Stadium , 2
State Agora , 37
Step houses , 22
Street of Curetes , 21
Temple of Domitian , 32
Temple of Hadrian , 23
Temple of Serapis , 13
Theater Baths with Sports Ground , 7
Tomb of Memmius , 29
Tomb of Pollio , 33
Upper Baths/The Various Baths , 41
Upper Gate , 36
Vedius Gymnasium , 1
Water Palace , 35

number to estimate the population of this and other Hellenistic cities by multiplying the theater capacity by 10.) The hard marble and the sound-catching colonnade across the top gave the theater excellent acoustics. The *skene* (where the scenery and props stand in a modern theater) is a forest of columns, stelae, and statues dating mostly from the reigns of Claudius and Trajan. Denizens of Ephesus placed 89 golden idols of Artemis here to celebrate the goddess's annual festival each April. St. Paul railed against these same false gods. Today, the **International Efes Festival** is held here in September.

THE MARBLE ROAD. From the Grand Theater, one approaches the Street of Curetes by walking along the Marble Way. To your right as you walk along the Marble Way is the **agora,** which is currently off-limits, but was once a large commercial area built during the reign of Nero. A square stone in the center marks all that remains of the city's **horologium,** a combination sundial and water clock that kept accurate time. At the southern end of the *agora* is the **Gate of Maxeus and Mithridates,** two wealthy freedmen who had the gate built and dedicated to the first Roman emperor, Augustus. About halfway to the Street of Curetes, on the right-hand edge of the Marble Way, stands a small metal barrier surrounding and protecting a rough-hewn inscription thought to be the world's first advertisement. The inscription consists of a picture of a foot, a cross, a woman, and a heart-shaped blob. The ad-wizards of the day intended this to designate the brothel down the road. The foot indicated the viewer's position as well as the need to walk to the crossroads ahead, represented by the cross. The heart above and to the left of the cross showed the house's position at the intersection, and the woman depicted is just that, a woman. Sailors could follow these clear directions to the **brothel,** which was dedicated to the love goddess Aphrodite.

THE STREET OF CURETES. A slight incline signals the beginning of the Street of Curetes, which connected the city to the Temple of Artemis, now in Selçuk. Ruts in the road are evidence of the enormous concentration of traffic between the temple and the city, and gaps between the slabs reveal glimpses of the city's **sewer system.** At the very bottom of the Street of Curetes is the **Library of Celsus,** which was restored by Austrian archaeologists. A memorial to Gaius Julius Celsus and a general fount of knowledge, the library was covered with inscriptions recording important events and once contained 12,000 scrolls. The façade's frontal curvature and the slight thinness of the peripheral columns serve to create an impression of greater width. This tempers the minimizing effect of being sandwiched between the broad *agora* and another building. Scholars suspect that the large building behind the library is the **Temple of Sarapis,** an Egyptian god associated with grain.

Walking up the Street of Curetes from the library, the **brothel** is on your left. Romantic commerce took place by oil light in the windowless side rooms, where archaeologists unearthed the infamous statue of **Priapus,** the god of fertility, now in Selçuk's Efes Müzesi (see p. 200). Near the brothel is a well, still in use, whose waters were thought to make barren women fertile. Adjacent to the brothel are the **Baths of Scholastica,** built in the 5th century at the behest of a wealthy woman. You will find a **public restroom** just beyond the brothel.

Farther up the Street of Curetes you'll see the imposing ruins of the **Temple of Hadrian** on your left. It is marked by its double-layered column construction, several friezes depicting the creation of Ephesus, and a bust of the goddess Cybele that adorns the keystone. The temple was built in 118 AD during Hadrian's rule, atypical for Romans, who usually preferred to deify their emperors only after death. Modest, no? Covering the hillside on the right are the famous stephouses, which the local bourgeoisie called home. Since they are currently under excavation, most are off-limits to tourists. A little further up the hill on the left are the ruins of the exquisite **Fountain of Trajan.** A statue of the **Emperor Trajan,** who extended the Roman Empire's borders as far as the Indian Ocean, once stood before the fountain. Today only its base remains.

Two pillars in the middle of the road mark the location of the **Gate of Hercules.** Farther uphill and to the left is the **Prytaneion.** Dedicated to the worship of **Vesta** (Hestia to the Greeks), goddess of the hearth and home, the Prytaneion contained an eternal flame that was tended by the **Vestal Virgins,** a small group of priestesses who served Vesta. Worship of Vesta was of such great significance to Romans that the Vestal Virgins were afforded social standing close to that of men.

Immediately adjacent and in fine repair is the **odeon** (bouleterion), a small, once-covered theater that seated approximately 1500 people. It was used as both a theater and a meeting place. The **state agora** on the right was the heart of political activity from the 1st century BC until the city's final demise. On the left after the odeon lie the upper **baths.**

OTHER SITES. The road that runs by the top entrance of Efes leads to the **House of the Virgin Mary** (8km, 1-1½hr. walking), where, according to a legend supported by some archaeological and literary evidence, she lived with the Apostle John and later by herself after leaving Jerusalem (see **Selçuk: Sights,** p. 200). Much closer to the Ephesus site are the **Caves of the Seven Sleepers,** easily reached by leaving Ephesus through the bottom gate, turning right at the "Seven Sleepers" sign, and walking for 10 to 15 minutes. Legend has it that seven youths fleeing religious persecution under Emperor Decius slept in the cave for what they thought to be a night. Upon waking up, they discovered that they had slept for 112 years, during which time Christianity had become the official religion of the Empire. Amazed by their story, Emperor Theodosias II built a church atop the caves and decreed that the sleepers' remains be buried there. All that remains of the church is a fence in front of the cave. It is covered with tiny napkins representing wishes. The youths' tombs are at the top of the hill, abutting the fence. (Always open. Free.)

SELÇUK ☎232

Selçuk serves as the most convenient base from which to explore nearby Ephesus, and offers several notable archaeological sites of its own. The Selçuk castle dominates the city's skyline, and the Basilica of Saint John, where the apostle John is buried, the İsa Bay Camii, and the ruins of the Temple of Artemis lie just below. The House of the Virgin Mary (*Meryemana*) can also be reached from Selçuk. Selçuk is also home to the famous Camel Wrestling Festival, held annually during the third weekend of January near Pamucak Beach, a short dolmuş ride away (contact the tourist office for more information).

▐ TRANSPORTATION

Buses: The **otogar** is at the intersection of Şahabettin Dede Cad. and Atatürk Cad. To: **Ankara** (9hr., 9:30pm, $18); **Bodrum** (3hr.; every hr. 7:30am-8:30pm, 10:30pm, 12:30am; $9); **Fethiye** (6hr., every 2hr. 8am-9:30pm, $12); **İstanbul** (10hr.; May-Sept. 7 per day 9:45am-midnight, Oct.-Apr. 3 per day; $19.50); **İzmir** (1hr., every 20min. 6:30am-8:30pm, $3.25); **Marmaris** (4hr., every 2hr. 8am-9pm, $8). **Minibuses** run to **Kuşadası** (20min.; every 20min. May-Sept. 6:30am-midnight, Oct.-Apr. 6:30am-8:30pm; $1.20). To get to **Pamukkale** go first to **Denizli** (3hr., every 30min. 8am-8pm, $5.75) and then catch a dolmuş (20min.). From May-Sept., you can take a bus directly to **Pamukkale** (3hr.; 9:30am, return 5pm; $7.30).

Trains: To: **Ayfon** (10hr., 9:30am, $1.75); **Denizli** (4hr.; 10:30am, 4:58, 8:27pm; $3); **İzmir** (1½hr., 7 per day 6:44am-7:28pm, $1.20).

✦▐ ORIENTATION AND PRACTICAL INFORMATION

The İzmir-Aydın road, **Atatürk Cad,** is one of Selçuk's main drags. **Dr. Sabri Yayla Bulvarı,** also called **Kuşadası Cad.,** meets Atatürk Cad. from the west, and **Şahabettin Dede Cad.** meets Atatürk Cad. from the east to form the town's main crossroads.

Tourist Office: 35 Agora Çarşısı, Atatürk Mah. (☎892 63 28; fax 892 69 45; email info@selcukephesus.gen.tr; www.selcuk.gov.tr or www.selcukephesus.gen.tr), at the intersection of Kuşadası Cad. and Atatürk Cad. Free city maps. English spoken. Open M-F 8:30am-noon, 1-5:30pm; Apr.-Dec. also open Sa-Su 9am-5pm.

Banks: Türkiye İş Bankası, İsabey Mah., 17 Namık Kemal Cad. (☎892 61 09 or 892 65 14), under the aqueduct. Exit the PTT, turn left, and walk 1 block. **Currency** and **traveler's check exchange** and a V/MC/Cirrus/Plus **ATM.** Open M-F 8:30am-5:30pm.

Hamam: Selçuk Hamamı, 2002 Sok. No. 3 (☎892 61 98). Bath and massage $10; special cream massage $5. Open daily 6am-midnight for men, except F noon-5pm when the bath provides a female masseur and is open to women only.

Police: (☎892 60 16), office beside Türkiye İş Bankası, and a booth at the corner of the otogar on Atatürk Cad.

Hospital: (☎892 70 36), across Kuşadası Cad. from the tourist office.

Internet Access: Australian New Zealand Pension. The cheapest in town. $1 per hr.

PTT: 1006 Sok. No. 9 (☎892 90 65 or 892 64 25), 1 block west of All Blacks Pension (walk away from train tracks) on Cengiz Topel Cad. Full service 8:30am-12:30pm, 1:30-5:30pm. **Currency, traveler's check exchange,** and **phone** open daily 8am-11pm. **Postal code:** 35920.

▌ACCOMMODATIONS

Selçuk is notorious for having some of the wiliest bus station hawkers in Turkey. Claiming to represent the better pensions, they tell visitors that all pensions in town, save theirs, are closed. Pension prices are set by the municipality and posted on a board on Atatürk Cad., on the right hand side in the direction of İzmir. Avoid anyone offering you a spot at their "slightly more expensive" pension.

▨ Artemis Guest House, Atatürk Mah., 1012 Sok. No. 2 (☎892 61 91; email jimmy@egenet.com.tr; www.artemisguesthouse.com). Guests are greeted with a refreshing drink, shown to a carpeted room complete with bath and towels, invited to join the BBQ in the garden (every other night, $5), and finally, welcomed to retire either to a cushion in the tree-house lounge to smoke fruit tobacco in the water-pipe, or to watch one of Jimmy's 100 movies. One of the few gay-friendly establishments in Turkey. Arranges group excursions to the hamam for women. Free transportation to Ephesus, and to Pamucak and Tusan beaches in the morning. Internet access $1.50 per hr. Laundry $5. Breakfast $2. $5 per person. 2 hotel-style rooms with A/C $30 per night. V.

▨ All Blacks Hotel and Pension, Atatürk Mah., 1011 Sok. No. 1 (☎892 36 57; email abnomads@egenet.com.tr; www.allblacks.8m.com). Named after the famous Kiwi rugby squad. Ultra-clean tile floors and bathrooms. Rooftop terrace with views of the fortress and the ancient Roman aqueducts. The ideal place to congregate, relax on the cushions, or eat BBQ chicken. Free transportation to and from Ephesus, Pamucak Beach, and Kuşadası harbor. Ring the bell to enter. Guest kitchen. Laundry $4 per load. Internet $2.50 per hr. Breakfast $1.60. Singles $6; doubles $12; triples $18.

Australian New Zealand Pension, 7 Prof. Miltner Sok. (☎892 60 50; www.anzturkishguesthouse.com). Behind the museum. Rooms centered around a lively garden. Terrace on roof with nightly BBQs and Turkish dinners (vegetarian options available) and a view of the Temple of Artemis. Very sociable. Free service to Ephesus and to the beach. Trips to Mary's House and Şirince for groups of 3 or more. Boat tickets to Samos (Apr.-Nov., $30) and winter trekking packages available. 20% discounts for trekking groups larger than 7. Laundry $5 per load. Internet $1 per hr. Breakfast included. Dorms $3; $5 per person, with bath $6.50. 15% discount for *Let's Go* readers.

Diana Pension, Zafer Mah., 3004 Sok. No. 30 (☎892 12 65; jesseakin@hotmail.com). Beyond the railroad tracks. After crossing the bridge, walk 50m with the track on your left, turn right onto 3008 Sok, walk 3 blocks, and turn left onto 3004 Sok. Immaculate rooms and bathrooms in a more distant and peaceful location. Views of the illuminated castle from the terrace. All-you-can-eat BBQ ($5). Free transport to Ephesus. Guest kitchen. 24hr. hot water. Laundry $5. Breakfast $3.25. $6.50 per person with bath.

Barım Pansiyon I (☎892 69 23), Müze Arkası Sok. Behind the museum. Great decor with bamboo roofing. Hanging plant life creates canopies over the entranceway and garden. The breakfast/living room tempts one to lounge all day in front of the fireplace on the pillows bordering the carpet-covered floor. Little English spoken. 24hr. hot water. Laundry $3.25. Breakfast $3.25. $6.50 per person.

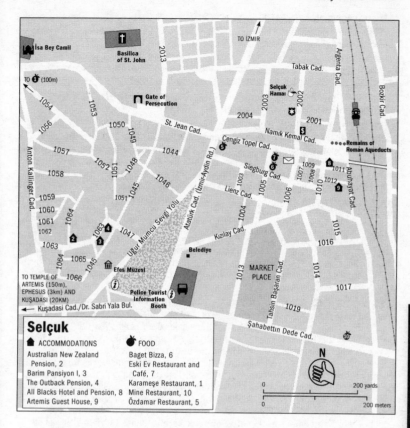

Selçuk

🏠 ACCOMMODATIONS

Australian New Zealand
  Pension, 2
Barim Pansiyon I, 3
The Outback Pension, 4
All Blacks Hotel and Pension, 8
Artemis Guest House, 9

🍎 FOOD

Baget Bizza, 6
Eski Ev Restaurant and
  Café, 7
Karameşe Restaurant, 1
Mine Restaurant, 10
Özdamar Restaurant, 5

📷 🎵 FOOD AND ENTERTAINMENT

On Saturdays and Wednesdays, locals and tourists flock to the huge open-air markets, which feature fresh fruit, cheeses, and spices.

Karameşe Restaurant (☎ 892 04 66), Tarihi İsabey Camii Önü, beside İsa Bey Camii. The decorating scheme makes this restaurant a sight in itself. A maze of stone paths wind through miniature waterfalls, fountains, and grass-covered gazebos. Bench seating or low tables surrounded by cushions available. In the rear, a miniature zoo is home to swans, monkeys, and even camels. All *ayran* and yogurt made with the milk from on-site cows. *Gözleme* $1-2; *çop şiş* $3.25; *ayran* $.50. Open daily 9am-1am.

Özdamar Restaurant, Atatürk Mah., 33 Cengiz Topel Cad. (☎892 00 97). Outdoor seating with a view of the castle. Dine on just about any Turkish dish imaginable. Choose from pizza (Italian or Turkish), fish kebaps, *döner kebap* ($2.40), cold dishes ($1), or mixed grill ($3.25). Open daily 8am-midnight. V, MC, AmEx.

Eski Ev (Old House) Restaurant and Cafe, Atatürk Mah., 1005 Sok. No. 1/A (☎892 93 57). Around the block from the PTT. Quiet dining with pomegranates hanging overhead in the garden of a century-old home. A mixed *meze* plate allows you to sample a bit of each appetizer ($1.60). *Gözleme* $1.25-1.50; lamb *şiş kebap* $2.80; bottle of Pamukkale wine $6.50. Open daily 8am-1am.

Baget Pizza, Atatürk Mah., 1005 Sok. 5/C (☎892 80 50). Near Eski Ev. This tiny place is the best in town for *döner* roll-up sandwiches, called *dürüm* ($1.20). Margherita (vegetarian) pizza $2; meat pizza $2.50. Open daily 9am-11pm.

Mine Restaurant, Atatürk Mah. 15 Şahabettin Dede Cad. (☎ 892 31 07). Standard look-and-choose restaurant at a pleasant distance from the incessant haggling of carpet vendors. *Taş kebap* (meat stew) $2; mixed grill $4; Turkish breakfast with boiled egg or omelette $1.60. Open daily 8am-midnight. 10% discount for *Let's Go* readers.

👁 SIGHTS

Selçuk's archaeological sights have always been overshadowed by the towering majesty of neighboring Ephesus. However, they should not be overlooked.

BASILICA OF ST. JOHN. The colossal and unadvertised Basilica of Saint John lies on the site of St. John's grave. The Byzantine church's entrance is inaccurately called the **Gate of Persecution.** The name refers to a frieze believed to depict a Christian being thrown to a lion, which in fact shows Achilles slaying a lion. The 6th-century church, constructed by Emperor Justinian, would be the 7th-largest cathedral in the world if it were reconstructed today. *(Open daily 8am-6:30pm. $2.50.)*

İSA BEY CAMİİ. This stunning Selçuk mosque lies at the foot of the hill on which the Basilica of St. John and the Ayasoluk Castle stand. Built in 1375 on the order of Aydınoğlu İsa Bey, it features columns taken from Ephesus, which the Ephesians had pilfered from Aswan, Egypt. Restored in 1975, the mosque has regained much of the simplicity that 600 years of wear and tear had eroded. Inside the courtyard is an enormous collection of well-preserved Ottoman and Selçuk tombstones and inscriptions. The mosque's façade features Persian-influenced geometric black and white stone inlay. *(Open 10min. before and 10min. after times of prayer.)*

EFES MÜSEZİ. Back in town, directly across from the town's tourist office, Selçuk's **Efes Müzesi (Ephesus Museum)** houses a world-class collection of recent Hellenistic and Roman finds from Ephesus. Most of the earlier finds are in Vienna. The collection includes the infamous statue of **Beş** (Priapus) that graces postcards throughout Turkey, rather tastelessly displayed in a darkened glass box, where you have to push a button for a 10-second peep at him. While this particular piece was found in the vicinity of the Ephesian brothels, the image of the erect, and generously endowed, demi-god was not a smutty novelty, but rather a fairly common piece of iconographic currency in the ancient world. The museum also houses an excellent collection of statuary, including a multi-breasted statue of Artemis, exquisite busts of Eros, Athena, Socrates, and emperors Tiberius, Marcus Aurelius, and Hadrian. You can also view a reconstructed room from one of the famous Ephesus terrace houses. *(Open daily 8:30am-noon, 1-5:30pm. $5.)*

TEMPLE OF ARTEMIS. A few hundred meters down Dr. Sabri Yayla Bul., walking away from town with the tourist office on your right, are the sad remains of the **Temple of Artemis.** Once the largest temple in the ancient world, it now consists of a lone reconstructed column twisting upwards from a bog that approximates the area of the temple's foundation. *(Open daily 8:30am-5:30pm. Free.)*

HOUSE OF THE VIRGIN MARY. Nearer to Selçuk than to any other town, but still a $21 round-trip cab ride away (9km from town), the tranquil **House of the Virgin Mary** lies 100m off the road from Ephesus to **Bülbüldağı** (Nightingale Mountain). About five years after the death of Christ, St. John is said to have accompanied the Virgin Mary to Ephesus, where they lived in a small house on the slopes of Bülbüldağı. It is a popular pilgrimage destination for both Christians and Muslims, who leave wishes and prayers in the form of tissue tied to chain-link screens.

🏃 DAYTRIP FROM SELÇUK: ŞİRİNCE

To get to Şirince, take the Şirince-bound dolmuş that runs from the Selçuk bus station (every hr., in summer 8am-8pm; in winter 8am-5pm; $.80). From Kuşadası, take the Selçuk-Kuşadası dolmuş ($1) and switch minibuses at the Selçuk station.

Şirince is a rustic enclave cradled in hills of olive and cherry trees—a perfect weekend getaway for those traveling east of Selçuk (7km) or from Kuşadası (25km). Historically interesting churches and a tradition of fine lace handicrafts reflect a local

THERE'S SOMETHING ABOUT MARY Sixteen kilometers from Selçuk, on the tranquil, leafy slopes of Bülbüldağı (Nightingale Mountain), stands what local tradition, inconclusive archaeological and literary evidence, and now the Vatican say is the House of The Blessed Virgin. It is believed that Mary came here with the Apostle John about five years after the death of Jesus to live out the rest of her life. St. John's connection to Ephesus is well established, his tomb lying in the ruined Basilica of St. John in Selçuk. According to the New Testament, Jesus commended his mother to John's care while on the cross: he said to his mother, "Dear woman, here is your son," and to John, "Here is your mother." From that time on, the disciple took her into his home (John 19:25-27). Given the quantity and strength of evidence, it seems probable that Mary did come to Ephesus and finish her life there. Locating where she lived is a bit harder. The discovery of the currently acknowledged site involved no small amount of romance and mysticism. Long forgotten to all but local Orthodox Christians who made yearly pilgrimages, the site was discovered towards the end of the 19th century by Lazarist Fathers following the visions of a bed-ridden German nun named Catherine Emmerich (1775-1824). She had never left Germany but could describe the hills surrounding Ephesus with perfect accuracy, leading the Lazarists to the ruins of a 6th-or 7th-century church built over the house. Subsequent archaeological examination has concluded that, in fact, the foundations of the church date from the 1st-century AD. Catherine Emmerich also provided rough directions and a description of the Virgin's tomb, but as yet archaeologists have found nothing. The enshrined church and nearby spring remain in the care of the Lazarists, and have produced a number of miraculous cures.

blend of Turkish and Greek influences. Şirince, meaning "charming" in Turkish, captivates visitors with cobbled lanes and breathtaking scenery.

As if Şirince's location among lush green hills weren't enough, the village also displays the remains of two 19th-century Greek churches. **St. John the Baptist Church,** under renovation at the time of publication, is marked by numerous Byzantine cupolas and a well-preserved Greek inscription which dates from 1832. *(To get here from the dolmuş stop, walk into town with the mosque on your left and take your 1st right. Pass Erdem Pansiyon on your right and turn left at the Ocakbaşı sign.)* **St. Demetrios Church** was converted from a 19th-century Greek church to a 20th-century mosque after the 1923 Population Exchange (see **The Treaty of Lausanne,** p. 16). Today it is in disrepair, but the frescoes are still visible. The steps that the *müezzin* used are to the right as you stand between the church and the cliff. *(To reach St. Demetrios, turn right instead of left at the Ocakbaşı sign and walk to the end of the path.)*

Embroidered and crocheted handicrafts are on display in Şirince's streets and in the stores of the bazaar. Some enterprising locals proffer these fineries in their homes—a sales technique usually initiated by a kindly offer of tea.

Accommodations in Şirince tend to be comfortable, but since streets are unnamed in this village, they can be a bit difficult to find. In July and August, call ahead to book a reservation at these compact pensions. Signs for **Halil Pansiyon** are up the small hill across from the Artemis Winehouse at the entrance of town. Three cool and relaxing rooms share a bathroom. (☎ 898 31 28. Laundry $1.60 per load. Breakfast included. $8 per person.) The **Huzur Pension** is at the other end of town. After getting off the dolmuş, walk straight up the hill, passing the mosque and the entrance to the covered bazaar on your left. Old wooden cupboards line the bedroom walls of this 150-year-old home. The largest room accommodates up to five people. A triple and a double with bath are also available. (☎ 898 30 60. Guest kitchen available. Breakfast $3.25. $5.75 per person.)

Şirince is best known for its strong local wine, available at many of the village's restaurants, or at the **Artemis Winehouse,** which also houses the **Şarap Evi Restaurant.** It is by far the largest and most elegant, but also the most commercial, restaurant for many miles around. From the dolmuş stop, Artemis is on your right as you walk away from town. With an unbeatable picturesque setting in a 150-year-old Ottoman schoolhouse, Artemis offers gourmet versions of traditional Turkish fare at standard prices and petite portions. (☎898 32 40. Salads $1; stuffed or baked mushrooms $1.60; beef $4.50. Open daily 9am-midnight.) **Ocakbaşı Restaurant**, on a hill overlooking town, cooks delicious traditional Turkish *gözleme* ($.50-.60) on the hearth in the center of the dining area. Stuffed grape leaves ($1) are made with leaves grown in their own garden. (☎898 30 94. Open daily 8am-midnight.)

KUŞADASI ☎256

Named for the pigeons that make their home in the town's 14th-century Genoese castle, Kuşadası ("Bird Island") could hardly have escaped the intense tourism it receives these days. Its picturesque setting on sea-sloping hills, excellent sand beaches, and proximity to the magnificent archeological wonders at Ephesus, Priene, Miletus, and Didyma ensured its transformation a few decades ago from a quiet town to a grand resort. Kuşadası's broad tourist apparatus accommodates every group. Backpackers arrive by ferry from Samos and by bus from the north, and wealthy American and European tourists flood the carpet shops whenever their luxury cruise liners dock in the small harbor, dwarfing other ships and—from a distance—the town itself. Excellent budget hotels and towering, four-star luxury palaces are surrounded by myriad high-end jewelry and carpet shops. Rumor has it that over 100 pubs dot the city. While Kuşadası is swamped with tourists of all kinds, it has not lost all of its charm.

▐ TRANSPORTATION

Buses: The *garaj* is on Kahramanlar Sok., about 2km from the center of town. Most hotels will either provide or pay for transportation from the *garaj*. Several bus companies serve Kuşadası, including **Pamukkale** (☎612 09 38). To: **Ankara** (9hr., 3 per day 8:30am-9:30pm, $21); **Antalya** (7hr.; 9:30am, 11pm; $18); **Bodrum** (2½hr.; 9:30am, 4:30pm; $9); **Denizli** (3hr., 3 per day 8:30am-9:30pm, $7.30); **Fethiye** (5½hr., 10:30am, $13); **İstanbul** (9hr., 6 per day 10:45am-11:45pm, $22.75); **İzmir** (1½hr., every 20min. 6am-10pm, $4); **Konya** (8hr., 6pm, $16); **Marmaris** (4hr., 9:15am, $11.50); **Nevşehir** (11hr., 6pm, $24.50); **Pamukkale** (3½hr.; 9am, returns 5pm; $9). Pamukkale can also be reached by dolmuş via **Denizli**. Take the İzmir bus to get to the İzmir **airport**. Call ahead for bus tickets on weekends.

Dolmuş: City dolmuş run between the dolmuş stop on Adnan Menderes Bul. and the lot adjacent to the *garaj* ($.50). Inter-city dolmuş head to **Selçuk** (30min., every 20min. 7am-11:30pm, $1.20) via Ephesus (ask to be let off) and **Söke** (30min., every 30 min. 7am-11:30pm, $1.20).

Ferries: Ekol Travel beats the official rate. Youth and student 10% discount. Flash *Let's Go* for an additional 15% discount. To **Samos** (1½hr.; in summer daily 8:30am, 4:30pm; in winter 2 per week; $30 including port tax).

✱ ORIENTATION

The duty-free shop, the tourist office, and the **customs office** are all in the port area. Visitors disembarking from ferry travel are advised to pay the port tax ($10) in US dollars. The **garaj** is about 2km south of town on **Kahramanlar Sok.** Dolmuş depart from a separate dolmuş stop on **Adnan Menderes Bul.**, a few meters southeast of the intersection of Adnan Menderes Bul. and **İnönü Bul.**, two of the main streets. **Liman Cad.** runs inland from the tourist office, passing an ancient **kervansaray** and a covered bazaar. On the other side of the *kervansaray*, the broad, pedestrian-only **Barbaros Hayrettin Paşa Bul.** is home to the PTT, travel agencies, and several banks. Farther east on Atatürk Bul., which runs along the coast, is a medieval watchtower turned modern-day **police station.**

AEGEAN COAST

Kuşadası

ACCOMMODATIONS
Hotel Sammy's Palace, 9
Golden Bed Pension, 10
Hotel Sezgin, 11

FOOD
Avlu Restaurant, 5
Seyran Restaurant, 3
Yuvam, 6

SERVICES
Art Kitabevi, 4
Bus Ticket Office, 2
Customs, 7
Eko Travel, 8
Kuydaş Kitabevi, 1

TO
SELÇUK &
İZMİR

TO
AYDIN

Atatürk Yolu

M. Aksoy Sok.

Cemali Dağyaran Sok.

Turizm Sok.

Minare Sok.

Ergene Sok.

Friday Market

Leylak Sok.

Okul Sok.

Enginler Sok.

Gençlik Cad.

Topalı Sok.

Taşhan Bul.

Müjgan Sok.

Ünlü Sok.

Sevinç Sok.

Bahçırganı Sok.

Mustafa Yaran Sok.

Arın Sok.

Kublay Sok.

Zeki Aydın Sok.

Dolu Sok.

Candan Sok.

Adnan Menderes Bul.

Öztürk Sok.

TAXI

Kalender M. Sok.

Taksim Sok.

Çevre Yolu

50 Yıl Cad.

Rılat Sok.

Burç Sok.

Özgür Sok.

Avcı Sok.

Public Beach

İsmet İnönü Bul.

Sağlık Cad.

Atatürk Bul.

K. Arıkan Cad.

Sabucalı Sok.

Haci Hatice Hanım Camii

Kahramanlar Cad.

Zafer Sok.

Sönmez Sok.

Barlar Sok.

San Sok.

Gök Sok.

Kaynak Sok.

Kışla Sok.

Bozkırı Sok.

Castle

Kale Hamamı

Günçş Sok.

TO
SÖKE

Fisherman Harbor

Barbaros Hayrettin

Kervansaray Bul.

Belediye Hamamı

Aslanlar Cad.

Altın Sok.

Uğurlu Sok.

Yıldırım Cad.

Sabri Mumcu Cad.

Town Hall

Liman Cad.

Kıbrıs Cad.

Anıt Sok.

Güzel Sok.

Soysa Sok.

İteri Sok.

Passport Police

Güvercinada Cad.

Bezirgan Sok.

Aydınlık Sok.

İmam Sok.

Tepe Sok.

Şüpün Sok.

Güvercin Sok.

Serçe Sok.

Doğan Sok.

Sülün Sok.

Kartal Sok.

Şahin Sok.

Kuğu Sok.

Kelebek Sok.

Eğrim Sok.

İçli Sok.

Basın Sok.

Mehmet Işık Cad.

Bozaniçal Ali Sok.

Küçük Bey Ramazan Sok.

Harbor

Genoese Castle

Güvercinada

Aegean Sea

Public Beach

TO KADINLAR PLAJI
(LADIES' BEACH, 2km)

TO ■ (350m)

N

⚡ PRACTICAL INFORMATION

Tourist Office: 13 Liman Cad. (☎614 11 03; fax 614 62 95), corner of Liman Cad. and Güvercin Ada Sok. Open May-Oct. daily 8am-5:30pm; Nov.-Apr. M-F 8am-5:30pm.

Travel Agencies: Ekol Travel with **WorldSpan,** Kıbrıs Cad., 9/1 Buyral Sok. (☎614 92 55 or 614 55 91; fax 614 26 44). Cheap flights, ferry tickets, temporary baggage storage, room search, message board, car rentals, and emergency help finding English-speaking doctors. 15% *Let's Go* discount on ferry tickets. Open daily May-Nov. 8:30am-10pm; Dec.-Apr. 8:30am-5:30pm.

Banks: Several dot the waterfront area. **Türkiye İş Bankası,** on the corner of Atatürk Bul. and Liman Cad., offers a 24hr. V/MC/Cirrus **ATM.** Open M-F 9am-12:30pm, 1:30-5pm. **Koç Bank,** by the police station on Atatürk Bul., has a V/MC **ATM.** Open M-F 8:45am-5:30pm. Both offer **currency** and **traveler's check exchange.** Koç doesn't charge for changing cash, but both banks charge hefty fees for traveler's checks.

English Language Bookstore: Kuydaş Kitabevi, 8/B İnönü Bul. (☎614 18 28; fax 614 26 83), sells newspapers, magazines, guidebooks, novels, CDs, and cassettes. Cement reading patio in back and modern Turkish art exhibits on the 2nd floor. Staff speaks little English. Open daily 9am-midnight. For cheaper stuff including an intriguing used book collection (half the cover price) and a huge selection of postcards, try **Art Kitabevi,** 57 Sağlık Cad. (☎614 64 54), near the intersection of Sağlık Cad. and Barbaros Cad. Open daily 8:30am-12:30am.

Hamam: Kaleiçi Hamamı (☎614 12 92). Follow signs behind the PTT. Bath and massage $16.25; tea or coffee included. Both sexes bathe together. Open daily 7am-10pm.

Police: Headquarters, 6 Atatürk Bul. (☎614 13 82), and **Tourist Police** (☎614 10 22) are in the same building, past the *kervansaray* walking with the sea on your left.

Hospital: Kuşadası Devlet Hastanesi, 30 Atatürk Bul. (☎614 10 26 or 614 16 14), on the waterfront, past the police station, with the sea on the left. Little English spoken.

PTT: (☎614 33 11 or 614 15 79), across from the *kervansaray*, on Barbaros Hayrettin Paşa Bul. Open daily 7am-11pm. **Phones** available 24hr. **Currency** and **traveler's check exchange** open 8:30am-midnight. **Postal code:** 09400.

⚡ ACCOMMODATIONS

Most budget accommodations are located along Kıbrıs Cad. and near Yıldırım Cad.

▨ **The Golden Bed Pansiyon,** 4 Aslanlar Cad. (☎614 87 08; fax 612 66 67; email goldenbed_anzac@hotmail.com; www.kusadasihotels.com/goldenbed). Off Yıldırım Cad. Turn right onto Uğurlu Sokak as you walk up the hill away from the harbor. Owned by a Turkish-Australian couple, this newly renovated pension offers marvelous views of Kuşadası harbor from the balconies and rooftop terrace. Rooms are light and refreshing. Common areas freshly tiled and painted. Free transportation to and from Ephesus; taxi from *garaj* paid. Laundry $2 per kg. Hamam 25% off. Internet $1.50 per hr. Nightly chicken and fish BBQs ($5). Breakfast $2. $5 per person; $6 with balcony.

▨ **Hotel Sammy's Palace,** 14 Kıbrıs Cad. (☎612 25 88; mobile ☎(532) 274 21 29; fax 612 99 91; email sammy@superonline.com; http://abone.superonline.com/~hotelsammyspalace). Ideal for the fun-loving, group-loving backpackers always up for a rip-roaring late night complete with belly dancing in the hotel common room/bar/dance hall (free nightly in summer). 32 well-furnished, carpeted, peaceful rooms, all with bath and most with balcony, make recuperating from the festivities enjoyable as well. Satellite TV and free movie showings in common room. Free transportation to and from Ephesus. Cab fares from *garaj* paid by Sammy. Internet access $4 per hr. Laundry $2 per kg. Hamam discount. Dinner and breakfast on rooftop $6.50. Breakfast alone $3.25. Roof $2.50; dorms $5; singles $11.50; doubles $16. 10% *Let's Go* discount.

Liman Otel, Kıbrıs Cad. Buyral Sok. No. 4 (☎614 77 70; fax 614 69 13). On the waterfront, past the tourist office, with the sea on your right. Entrance in rear. A slightly more fashionable hotel that still manages to cater to the backpacker and budget traveler. Owner "Mr. Happy," a backpacker himself, provides a dorm room on the roof for his most frugal guests, inexpensive rooms with no view for those travelers who sacrifice scenery for savings, and beautiful seaside rooms for vacationers who want it all. Terrific location. A/C in all rooms except dorm. 10% discount on any bus ticket. Free transport to and from bus station and Ephesus. Internet $1.50 per hr. Laundry $2 per kg. Breakfast $1.50. Dorm $4; interior room $5; rear room $16; harbor-side room $19.50.

Hotel Sezgin, 15 Kahramlar Cad., Zafer Sok. (☎614 42 25; fax 614 64 89; email sezgin@ispro.net.tr; http:freeyellow.com/members8/hotelsezgin). Owner Sezgin heartily aims to please travelers, especially backpackers, with free transportation to and from the bus station, the Samos ferry, and Ephesus. Organizes a day trip to Priene, Miletus, Didyma, and Altınkum beach. Also 15% off tickets to Samos. Great water pressure, and satellite TV. Internet access $2 per hr. Laundry $2.50 per kg. Lounge and bar. Nightly fish, chicken, and beef BBQ ($5) with belly dancing at the weekend dinners ($1 per person). Breakfast included. Singles $8; doubles $14; triples $20. *Let's Go* readers stay 3 nights and get the 4th night free.

Önder Camping (☎618 15 90 and 618 1518). 15min. walk north of town on Atatürk Bul. (walk with sea on your left). Swimming pool. Laundry $2.50 per load. Tents $5. Space for tents $1. Caravans $4. Electricity $1. 10% discount at on-site restaurant.

Yat Camping (☎618 15 16). See directions to Önder. Swimming pool. Laundry $1.60 per load. Offers tents ($5 per person) and space for tents ($1.60). Caravans $2. Cars $1. Electricity $1. 10% discount at on-site restaurant.

FOOD

Yuvam Ev Yemekleri ve Mantı Evi, Camikebir Mah., 7 Kaleiçi (☎614 94 60). Behind the post office. Turn left at Yapı Kredi as you walk away from the sea, and take the 1st right. Similar to Avlu Restaurant, but slightly smaller with more atmosphere. Thursday is homemade *mantı* night $2. Okra $1.50. Meat dishes $2. Open daily 8am-10pm.

Avlu Restaurant, 15 Cephane Sok. (☎614 79 95). The 1st left off Barbaros Hayrettin Paşa Bul. as you walk away from the sea. A standard *lokanta* with no menu, just a display of the day's dishes to choose from. Decor isn't fancy, but food is fresh and prices are low. Meat dishes $1.25-1.60 per serving. Large selection of vegetarian dishes $1.20 per serving. *Tatlı* (dessert) $.80. Open 8am-11pm.

Seyhan Restaurant, 63 Sağlık Cad. (☎614 79 85). A slightly higher-end restaurant with wicker chairs, tablecloths, and a location great for people-watching. Huge selection and menu in 4 languages. English or Turkish breakfast $4; shrimp cocktail $2.50; excellent *sebzeli güveç* (vegetable stew) $5.75. Open Apr.-Sept. daily 9am-midnight.

Çınaraltı Restaurant (☎614 33 32 or 614 62 81). Take the dolmuş heading to Selçuk, and ask to be left off at Çınaraltı. Serves exceptional Turkish fare on a foliage-covered patio. *Pancar salatası* (beet-root salad; $1) and various fish and meat dishes, including their specialty, *Çoban Kavurma* (a mixture of grilled meats; $3.20).

SIGHTS

Kuşadası's best-known sights are its shopping areas and its numerous sparkling beaches. While the **Grand Bazaar** and **Barbaros Hayrettin Paşa Bul.** are, contrary to the claims of shop owners, expensive places to shop, it doesn't cost anything to browse the carpet and jewelry stores.

BEACHES. Unfortunately, Kuşadası's clean and sandy beaches are extremely overcrowded. **Kadınlar Plajı** (Ladies' Beach), just 3km from the city, is easily accessible by dolmuş from Adnan Menderes Bul. or the otogar *(20min., in summer every 3min. 7am-midnight, $.50)*. Expect to pay to enjoy the sun. *($1.60 for beach chair, with umbrella $1.20 extra.)*

DILEK NATIONAL PARK. A nature reserve just 26km from Kuşadası, this is the best place for swimming, walking, and picnicking. It contains four beaches and houses over 30 animal species. While overnight camping is not permitted in the park, Dilek offers daytime canyon hiking (6km from entrance gate), **sandy beaches** (İçmeler beach, 1km from the gate), and **sand-and-pebble shores** (Aydınlık Beach, 5km from the gate; Karvakı beach, 7km from the gate). Don't leave without seeing **Zeus Mağarası** (Zeus's Cave), a small cave opposite the sea, 100m outside the park entrance. Once rumored to be the site of hidden treasure, the cave is full of water bubbling up from the ground. *(Park open daily 8am-8pm; extended hours in July-Aug.; off-season 8am-5pm. $1.20 per person; $1.60 per motorcycle; $8 per car.)*

PIGEON ISLAND. A trip to Kuşadası would be incomplete without a visit to **Güvercinada** (Pigeon Island), the jutting peninsula housing the birds that are Kuşadası's namesake. Roam around the 14th-century Genoese castle, which the Ottomans turned into a military outpost in the 19th century, and enjoy a glass of *çay* at any of the various tea houses at this old lookout point. *(A 10min. walk from the tourist office with the sea on your right.)*

KUŞADASI MUSIC FESTIVAL. Kuşadası hosts this annual contest during which Turkish pop bands vie for bubble-gum glory. For tourists, this means free concerts in the last week of June. 2000 performers included Emrah, Edip Akbayram, and Ajda Pekkan. Sexy Turk Tarkan performed in 1999.

🎵🎤 ENTERTAINMENT AND NIGHTLIFE

The nighttime music and madness of the appropriately named **Barlar Sokak** ("bar street") literally spills out into the streets so brightly lit, it might as well be daytime. The side streets behind the PTT, like **Tuna Sokak**, house another host of roofless bars with live European and Turkish rock. The combination of dozens of discos and no weekday cover charge makes for easy club-hopping.

Heaven, 13 Sakarya Sok. (☎613 24 56). Behind the PTT, is one of the largest, most popular music clubs. Decorated in a mock Roman style with vines, a columns, and a few authentic remains, Heaven offers live Turkish pop in its inner open-air courtyard every night from 1-4am. Beer $4; cocktails $7.25. $8 cover only on Sa (one domestic drink included). Open June-Sept. daily 9pm-4am.

Adı Meydanı, 18 Kaleici Bahar Sok. (☎614 34 96). Behind the PTT. A romantic nighttime spot, including open-air courtyard with lamp-lighting, fireplaces, and attractive stone walls. Live traditional Turkish music every night (9pm-2am). The most popular dish is Brain Salad ($1.60), but there are plenty of more standard options too. Mixed grill $5.50. Beer $1.50-2.50. Open daily 7pm-2am.

The Green Bar, 33 Tuna Sok. (☎612 45 62). Behind the PTT. Mammoth banana trees adorn this small roofless bar. Live Irish music nightly at 11pm. Cocktails $5. Beer $1.50-2.50. Wine $1.60 per glass. Open daily 4pm-4am.

Ecstasy, 8 Sakarya Sok. (☎612 81 90). Across from Heaven, a disco with sleek decor and plenty of polished steel. "Underground" music along with videos on a large screen. Beer $3.25; *rakı* $5; mixed drinks $6.50-8. Cover F-Sa $8. Open daily 11pm-4am.

Another Bar, 10 Tuna Sok. Behind the PTT. A disco similar to Ecstasy's, with plenty of tables amid trees in a roofless courtyard. Live groups perform nightly 11pm-1am, followed by DJ spins until 4am. Cover F-Sa $7.50-8. Open May-Sept. 9:30pm-4am.

Jimmy's Irish Bar (☎612 13 18). The first bar on the right on Barlar Sok. The best of several Irish bars in town, Jimmy's fills even in the afternoon when the competition is dead quiet. Wait until 1am for partyers to dance on the tables. "Sheep Brain" (Archers, Grenadine, and Baileys), "Sperm of Barmen" (Archers, Baileys, and Vodka), and other mixed drinks $5. Cider $5. Large *Efes* $3.25. Open daily 2pm-5am.

The Log Cabin Irish Bar (☎612 42 44), on Barlar Sok. Crowded, but with enough space for jigs. Cocktails $5. Imported beers $5. Local beer $3. Open May-Oct. daily 9pm-4am.

PRIENE, MILETUS, AND DIDYMA

These three ancient sites, arranged in a line along the coast towards Bodrum, make an excellent daytrip from either Selçuk or Kuşadası. While organized guided tours often seem like a canned experience, they are the best option if you aim to visit all three sites in one day, most likely the easiest way overall. The transportation hub for the three cities is **Söke**, easily reached from Kuşadası or Selçuk by dolmuş or on any Bodrum-bound bus. From Söke, **dolmuş** run to **Miletus** (45min., every hr. 10am-4pm, $1.60), **Priene** (20min., every 30min. 7:30am-6:30pm, $.80), and Didyma (1hr., every 10min. 7am-10pm, $1.75).

Priene, set amid beautiful forested slopes, and Miletus, in the center of a vast plain, outdo Didyma for quantity, but not quality. Though Didyma's ruins include only one temple, it was one of the largest and grandest of the ancient world.

PRIENE (GÜLLÜBAHÇE)

Open daily in summer 8am-7pm.; in winter 8am-5pm. $1.60.

Though Priene was a leading member of the Panionic League, which controlled the Aegean coast after the decline of the Hittite empire, it lingered in the shadow of its neighboring economic rival, Miletus. The city's population never exceeded 5000. While its neighbors excelled in commerce, Priene devoted its resources to religion and sports. The city's ruins, on a plateau before the walls of Mt. Mycale, overlook the wanderings of the River Meander. Uphill from the dolmuş stop, ancient walls encircle the ruined city. From the main entrance, a path leads to what was once the main avenue of ancient Priene. Ahead and on the left is the **prytaneum**, the vaulted hearth of the city's sacred flame. Brought from Athens by the first settlers, the flame was extinguished only when the city was invaded. It was here that diplomats were received, heroes and athletes rewarded, and city administrative matters discussed. Beyond the prytaneum is the unmistakable **bouleterion,** or Senate House, a well-preserved, elegant auditorium. Sacrifices were offered on the inner chamber's huge marble altar to mark the opening and closing of Senate sessions. Only the foundation of the altar remains.

Walk uphill (to the right) from the prytaneum. On the raised platform to the left is the **upper gymnasium,** the older of Priene's two educational and physical training facilities. A little farther and on the right is the **Sanctuary of the Egyptian Gods** where Egyptians, who arrived in Priene to trade, worshipped the gods Isis, Serapsis, and Anubis. Large congregations convened up the hill a bit farther in the **theater.** The front row retains five **thrones of honor** with dignified bases carved to look like lions' paws. In front of the theater and beside the upper gymnasium stands a **Byzantine Church,** built in the 6th century AD with the stones of previous structures. Climb up the hill behind the church and continue with the church on your left to reach the **Temple of Athena,** an edifice that reflects the height of Hellenistic architecture. Alexander the Great financed the project, and Pytheos, the architect whose *chef d'œuvre* was the Mausoleum of Halicarnassus (one of the Seven Wonders of the Ancient World; p. 221), designed it. The temple retains largely intact front steps, interior floors, and five complete columns. The path that runs along the backside of the temple takes you to the remains of the **private houses** of Priene, unusually well-preserved examples of pre-Roman domestic architecture.

Exit the Athena Temple from the front, turn right on the stone path, and you'll approach the **Alexandreion,** where Alexander the Great is believed to have resided while liberating Miletus. Later, the house became a sanctuary devoted to him. Beyond is the **Temple of Cybele** where mostly poor residents worshipped.

Backtrack toward the Temple of Athena, and the spacious **agora** will be on your right. Women were allowed here only if accompanied by men, either their husbands or slaves. At the center, a public temple once hosted official ceremonies and sacrifices. Beyond the agora is the 3rd-century BC **Temple of Olympic Zeus.** From below the temple, you can gaze down on the **stadium** and **gymnasium,** with the names of young athletes inscribed on their walls. On either side of the main hall are small rooms once used for bathing and exercise.

MILETUS (MİLET)

☎ *(256) 875 50 38 or 875 52 56. Site and museum open daily in summer 8am-5:30pm; in winter 8am-5pm. $1.60.*

Now surrounded by arid plains, Miletus once sat upon a thin strip of land surrounded by four separate harbors. Envied for its prosperity and strategic coastal location, the city was destroyed and resettled several times. Eventually, it suffered the same fate as its Ionian neighbors—the silting of its harbors. For centuries, Miletus was a hotbed of commercial and cultural development. In the 5th century BC, the Milesian alphabet was adopted as the standard Greek script. Miletus later became the headquarters of the Ionian school of philosophers, including Thales, Anaximander, and Anaximenes. The city's leadership, however, faltered in 499 BC, when Miletus headed an unsuccessful Ionian revolt against the Persian army. The Persians retaliated by wiping out the entire population of the city, massacring the men and selling the women and children into slavery.

Today, the site's main attraction is the **theater,** which sat 15,000 and was originally at the water's edge. Clearly visible from the Priene-Didyma highway, the strikingly well-preserved structure dates from Hellenistic times, though most of the visible portion was constructed by the Romans. The remaining portions of Miletus are marshy most of the year, sometimes even in the summer. To the right of the theater as you enter the site is a restored Selçuk **kervansaray.** The footpath meandering to the right of the theater leads to the largest Roman baths in Anatolia, the **Faustina baths,** erected by the wife of Roman Emperor Marcus Aurelius. Visible beyond the baths is the dome of the 15th-century **Ilyas Bey Complex,** which included mosques, *medreses,* and baths, among other unidentified buildings. Further along the road past the baths are the north and south **agoras.** Today, only the pediment on which the gate to the south agora stood is visible, the grand entrance having been moved to Berlin's Pergamon Museum in 1905. Just north of the **south agora** is the **bouleuterion,** where the government assembly met. From the front of the bouleuterion, the **Sacred Way** runs past the **Nymphaeum, Hellenistic Gymnasium, Ionic Stoa,** and **Capitol baths** on the right, and the **north agora** on the left, to the **Delphinium,** the sanctuary of Apollo Delphinus. The temple, whose priests were all sailors, was first constructed to honor Apollo, who supposedly transformed himself into a dolphin and led the Cretans to Miletus.

Beyond the structures that border the Sacred Way lie a few isolated remains. Standing at the north end of this avenue, with the theater to your left, you can see the early 16th-century **Dervish Lodge** to the right, where followers of the Muslim mystic Mevlana studied. The **Inn of Fleas** is to the left. Though the name is not the original one, it is apt for the *kervansaray*-style structure today. Farther to the left is the **synagogue,** built in the Roman Period. North is where the two white marble lion-statues used to sit, nobly surveying the harbor known as the Bay of Lions. There is a small, rather underwhelming **Archaeological Museum** about 500m before the main entrance, featuring sculpture from the site. Even this fragment gives a good impression of the city's former wealth and beauty.

DIDYMA (DİDİM)

Open daily in summer 8am-7pm; in winter 8am-5pm. $1.60.

Ancient Didyma was the site of a sacred sanctuary to Apollo and an oracle that brought in most of the city's fame and wealth. The first Didyma oracles date from about 600 BC, 100 years before the Persians destroyed the sanctuary. It lay deserted until Alexander the Great's arrival, which supposedly inspired the arid spring miraculously to flow anew. The present sanctuary was begun during the 2nd and 1st centuries BC, but the original plans, like those for Alexander's empire, proved too ambitious and were never completed.

The **temple** at Didyma ranked as the 3rd-largest sacred structure in ancient Asia Minor, after the Temple of Artemis at Ephesus and the Temple of Hera on Samos. Virtually nothing remains of either of the latter two buildings, making the sanctuary at Didyma the best surviving example of colossal temple architecture. Many of its individual marble slabs weigh more than 1000kg. During the Roman period, the unfinished temple attracted pilgrims from all over ancient Greece. A church was

constructed on the site in 385 AD after Emperor Theodosius I outlawed the consulta-
tion of pagan oracles, but it suffered extensive damage from an earthquake in 1500.
The sacred road that ran from Miletus to Didyma ended at the temple gates. The statues that once lined the final stretch were carried away by the British in 1858 and have
been replaced by souvenir shops.

Inside the main gate rests the famous bas-relief of a giant **Medusa head,** once part of
an ornate frieze on the temple's exterior. The building's size is only apparent from the
stairway to the main façade. All that remains of the more than 100 columns are the
bases and lower sections. To transport these mammoth chunks of marble, the
Greeks constructed long shafts of stone leading to the temple site, lubricated them,
and then slid the building materials over the slippery surface.

In front of the temple is the spring that the priestesses supposedly tapped when
receiving prophecies from Apollo. Begin in the forecourt at the **Hall of Twelve Columns**
and continue to the **Hall of Two Columns,** where visitors waited for pronouncements.
From here, 22 steps lead down to the **sanctuary.** The southeast corner of the **temnos**
(the sacred area around the temple) has traces of another **sacred fountain** as well as
the foundations of a temple that housed a bronze statue of Apollo.

ALTINKUM BEACH   ☎256

Didim's sandy and clean Altınkum Beach is among the most crowded and touristed
beaches in Turkey. If you can find a spot, relax near the calm turquoise surf. If not,
idle the day in a large *çay* garden, browse through the souvenir shops, and soak up
the nightlife in the many discos and bars along the beach.

From **Söke,** the region's local transportation hub, board the Altınkum-bound
dolmuş (1hr., every 15min. 7am-9pm, $1.75). The dolmuş travel toward the sea along
Atatürk Bul. and stop at Altınkum Meydanı, 20m from the main entrance of the
beach. **Sultan Ferry** (☎412 95 49), moored at the far right end of the beach as you face
the water, runs to **Bodrum** (1¾hr.; M, Th 10:30am, returns 5:30pm; one-way $10,
round-trip $13). Sultan departs only with 80 or more travelers. The **Alibey Ferry** (☎813
14 79), right next to Sultan, sails to Bodrum regardless of demand (2hr.; Su, Tu-F
9am, returns 7pm; one-way $8, round-trip $13).

Altınkum has numerous small pensions. Reservations are recommended during
the summer. **Tüles Pansiyon,** 407 Sok. No. 12, has rooms with bath, balcony, and carpet. A kitchen, family room, and laundry service are available to guests as well.
(☎813 10 39. Breakfast $1.60. $5 per person.) **Villa Motel,** 17 Karakol Cad., is a little
closer to the action, just 200m from the shore and to the left of Altınkum Meydanı. All
rooms have phones, and some have tubs. Enjoy live Turkish pop nightly 9pm-2am in
the cafe, or request a tune in English. Guest kitchen. Rates vary depending on the
season. (☎/fax 813 18 73 or 813 38 01. Breakfast and dinner included. $10 per person.)

Big Ben, 20 Yalı Cad. (☎813 40 01), on the waterfront to the left of the Altınkum
Meydanı entrance, offers Turkish, English, and Chinese cuisine.

PAMUKKALE AND APHRODISIAS REGION

PAMUKKALE (HIERAPOLIS)   ☎258

Whether as Pamukkale ("Cotton Castle") or ancient Hierapolis (Holy City), this village has been drawing the weary to its thermal springs for more than 23 centuries.
The Turkish name refers to the surface of the shimmering, snow-white limestone,
shaped over millennia by calcium-rich springs. Dripping slowly down a vast mountainside, mineral-rich waters foam and collect in terraces, spilling over cascades of
stalactites into milky pools below. Legend has it that the formations are solidified
cotton (the area's principal crop) that giants left out to dry.

Overshadowed by natural wonder, Pamukkale's well-preserved Roman ruins and
museum have been massively underestimated and unadvertised; tourist brochures

over the past 20 years have mainly featured photos of people bathing in the calcium pools. Aside from a small footpath running up the mountain face, the terraces are all currently off-limits, having suffered erosion and water pollution at the feet of tourists. Although not open for bathing, the site is still worth a visit. It is best to spend the night and see the sights thoroughly, rather than rush the trip and return to Kuşadası or Marmaris the same day.

▣ TRANSPORTATION

Buses to Pamukkale stop in Cumhuriyet Meydanı in the center of **Pamukkale Köyü (village).** Most direct buses come from Kuşadası and pass through Selçuk (3½hr.; daily May-Aug. 9:15, 9:30, 9:45am; return 5pm; $5), but the more common route is through Denizli (see **Denizli: Transportation,** p. 212). **Dolmuş** run between Denizli and the beginning of the Pamukkale walking path, where Atatürk Cad. meets Mehmet Akif Ersoy Bul. (25min., every 15min. 6:45am-11pm, $.50). Otherwise, a Pamukkale pension can arrange free pick-up from the Denizli otogar.

▣ ORIENTATION AND PRACTICAL INFORMATION

Pamukkale is roughly divided into two areas. **Pamukkale Köyü,** at the foot of the white mountain, is home to many hotels and restaurants. The **Pamukkale site** encompasses the mountain itself, the calcium-rich **pools,** and the ruins of Hierapolis. From Cumhuriyet Meydanı, the central square in the village, take Atatürk Cad. past the bus company offices and up to Mehmet Akif Ersoy Bul. From here, a path heads up the mountain. Vehicles may ascend by continuing along Mehmet Akif Ersoy Bul. as it winds uphill to the site, tracing the course of an ancient road.

Tourist office: (☎272 20 77; fax 272 28 82). At the top of the hill, within the site. Open May 15-Sept. 15 daily 8am-noon, 1:30-6:45pm; in winter M-F 8am-noon, 1-5pm.

Tourist police: (☎272 29 09). At the top of the hill, within the site gates. Open 24hr.

Pharmacy: Denizli Eczanesi (☎272 29 20), Cumhuriyet Meydanı. Open daily 7am-10:30pm.

Banks: There are currently **no banks** or **ATMs** in Pamukkale.

PTT: One is located within the site (☎272 21 21; open daily 8:30am-7pm) and another is within the village on Yavuz Selim Cad., 300m from Cumhuriyet Meydanı (☎272 28 52; open M-F 8:30am-12:30pm, 1:30-5:30pm). **Site postal code:** 20285. **Village postal code:** 20280.

▣ ACCOMMODATIONS

All of the places listed below have swimming pools filled with Pamukkale thermal water, and offer free pickup from the Denizli bus station.

▨ **Koray Hotel,** 27 Fevzi Çakmak Cad. (☎272 23 00 or 272 22 22; fax 272 20 95). Rooms with carpet and bath all face a beautiful inner courtyard, where guests can relax and eat their meals by the pool under the grapevines. TV, salon, bar, and glassed-in rooftop restaurant for winter dining. Internet $1.20 per hr. Laundry $6.50. Unlimited dinner buffet $5. Breakfast buffet included. Singles $12; doubles $18.

▨ **Meltem Motel,** 9 Kuzey Sok. (☎272 24 13 or 272 21 57; fax 272 24 14; email meltemmotel@superonline.com.tr). Just outside Cumhuriyet Meydanı. With a warm welcome to backpackers, Meltem offers satellite TV with stereo sound for nightly movie showings. Owner Ali Baba takes guests on daily trips to the red springs, his "secret waterfall," and a nearby mud bath for a "magic massage" ($12). Blue tiled rooms all have bath. Direct view of Pamukkale mountain from restaurant/lounge on top floor. Internet $1.60 per hr. Laundry $4. Breakfast $2. $5 per person; dorm $4.

Venüs Hotel, 16 Hasan Tahsin Cad. (☎272 21 52). Gleaming white walls and polished bathrooms lend the rooms an air of freshness. All have vine-adorned balcony. Laundry $5.75. Dinner $5.50. Breakfast included. Singles $8; doubles $13; triples $21.

Dört Mevsim Hotel, 19 Hasan Tahsin Cad. (☎272 20 09). Follow the signs for Venüs Hotel and continue 20m. Rooms in this quiet, removed setting overlook a pool and lush flowers. Easygoing owner Hasanali organizes a daily trip to Aphrodisias for groups of at least 3 people ($10). Laundry $2.50. Fantastic *saç kebap* dinners $5. Breakfast $1.60. Camping $1.60. $5 per person.

Coşkun Pension-Camping-Restaurant, 37 Mehmet Akif Ersoy Bul. (☎272 25 54). On the left-hand side of the road as you approach Pamukkale. An unglamorous but active camping spot close to the entrance of the Pamukkale site. Home-cooked *gözleme* available at the outdoor restaurant. Live trout cooked fresh ($2.50). Small fee for laundry. Communal showers for campers. Breakfast $2.50. Space for tent $3.25; room with bath $6.50 per person; caravan with electricity $8.

🎭🎵 FOOD AND ENTERTAINMENT

Most of the pensions serve excellent dinners, making dining elsewhere unnecessary. The large buffet at the Koray Hotel is particularly impressive. Pamukkale's nightlife is definitely not as raging as that on the coast, but you can still find places to get a drink after dinner and dance into the early hours.

Konak Sade (☎272 20 02). On Atatürk Cad., just up the hill from Cumhuriyet Meydanı, on the left. An extensive establishment with traditional Turkish salon on the upper level. Poolside terrace seating with a view of cornfields and the Pamukkale mountain. Chicken grill $2.50; *Konak Sade kebap* $3.65; plenty of ice cream flavors for dessert $2. Free swimming for diners. Open daily 7:30am-2am.

Pamukkale Cafe-Bar-Restaurant, 13 Cumhuriyet Meydanı (☎272 21 90 or 272 22 86). Features 5 fixed menus: 2 are vegetarian $3.25; the other 3 include wine and either fish ($5), chicken ($5), or kebap ($5.75). A la carte dining also available. Meat, chicken, or cheese sandwiches $1.30. Open daily 9am-midnight.

Gürsoy Aile Restaurant, 3 Atatürk Cad. (☎272 22 67), in Cumhuriyet Meydanı. Simple outdoor dining. The house special is *gürsoy kebap* ($3.25), but salads, omelettes and pasta dishes ($1.60) will satisfy vegetarians. Fish $2.50. Open daily 7am-midnight.

Han Restaurant, 11 Cumhuriyet Meydanı (☎272 27 92), next to Gürsoy Aile. Seating on a porch under thick foliage. Specializes in kebap dishes. *Adana kebap* $2.30; eggplant in tomato sauce $1; mixed potato salad $1. Open daily 24hr.

Paşa Disco and Bar, 1 Mehmet Akif Ersoy Bul. (☎272 21 47), where Atatürk Cad. meets Mehmet Akif Ersoy Bul., across from the entrance to the Pamukkale site. Turkish tunes reverberate with the overhead flashing lights. Plenty of seating. Beer and soft drinks $1.60. Open daily 9pm-2am.

Harem Disco and Bar (☎272 22 52). On Atatürk Cad., uphill from Cumhuriyet Meydanı. A basement disco with modest dance space and carpet-covered sofas. A sign over the door reads *Damsız girilmez,* which means no entrance (for men) if not accompanied by a woman. Don't worry–it doesn't apply to tourists. Beer $1.60. Open daily noon-2am.

👁 SIGHTS

MOUNTAINSIDE BATHS. A favorite getaway spot for vacationing Romans almost 2000 years ago, the warm baths at Pamukkale still bubble away. Elegant, shallow pools at the top of the hill (near the road that separates the site from Hierapolis) gradually deepen farther down the slope. The terraces located near the center of the formation are the most intricately shaped. All of these are off-limits for bathing due to overuse. However, a narrow walkway leading down the face of the slope still allows shoeless visitors to touch the thermal waters. The Pamukkale Termal, beyond the Hierapolis Museum, is the only place where visitors can still swim in the thermal waters (see **Sacred Spring,** below). *(Site open 24hr. $5.50.)*

HIERAPOLIS MUSEUM. Directly across the street from the top of the walking path that leads up the mountain stand the stately archways that once formed the **city bath.**

The bath's glossy marble interior has been converted into the spectacular Hierapolis Museum, which houses the finds unearthed by Italian archaeologists. (☎272 20 34. Open Tu-Su 8am-5pm. $1.60.)

RUINS OF HIERAPOLIS. Just past the PTT is a wire fence, with an opening 50m up. From here you can walk to the right to explore the **nymphaeum**, a fountain temple dedicated to the Nymphs, and the remains of the 3rd-century **Temple of Apollo.** Next to the temple is the **Plutonium** (a.k.a. *Cin Deliği*, or Devil's Hole), a pit emitting toxic carbonic acid gas, now marked by a foreboding "Danger: Poisonous Gas" sign. Carved into the side of the mountain, the enormous **Grand Theater** dominates the vista. The theater is one of the best-preserved in Turkey; many carved stage decorations and much of the 25,000 person seating area remain intact.

Down the road to Karahayıt (to the left if you face the theater) are the north **city gate,** the ruins of a 5th-century Christian **basilica** dedicated to St. Philip, martyred here 1000 years ago, and a **necropolis,** holding some 1200 tombs and sarcophagi. The tombs vary considerably in size and architectural style. These plots were prime real estate; it was believed that proximity to the hot springs and vapor-emitting cracks would ease one's trip to the underworld. (The ruins extend downhill, starting from the rear of the Pamukkale Termal.)

SACRED SPRING. Don't leave Pamukkale without a heavenly dip in the sacred fountain at the **Pamukkale Motel Termal.** Warm, fizzy waters bubble at the spring's source, now blocked off to prevent divers from disappearing into its depths. On the pool's floor rest the remains of Roman columns, toppled by the earthquake that created the spring. Alongside the pool are cafes (beer $2; soft drinks $1.60; sandwiches $1.20) and souvenir shops. (☎ 272 20 24. Pool open daily 8am-8pm, until 6pm in winter. $5 for 2hr. Free just to browse.)

OTHER SIGHTS. Four kilometers beyond the vehicle entrance to the Pamukkale site is **Karahayıt** (Red Source). Visitors can view the red spring free of charge and swim in the hot spring waters in a pool nearby. ($1.60 per person.) Karahayıt accessible by the "Karahayıt-Pamukkale" dolmuş, which leaves from Denizli and pass by the bottom of the footpath entrance to the Pamukkale site. (Every 15min. 7:30am-10pm, $.70.) 15km beyond Karahayıt are the **mud baths of Gölemezli.** The mud baths are free and always open. However, they are accessible only with a guided tour. The Meltem Motel offers daily tours that visit the baths.

DENİZLİ ☎258

Fourteenth century North African traveler Ibn Battuta called Denizli "a most important town," and today Denizli has no qualms about being the Aegean region's fastest growing city after İzmir. Garbage-strewn streets and perpetual construction work around the outskirts of town give a bad first impression, but pleasant restaurants and parks line Atatürk Bul. and İstiklâl Cad. An overabundance of chicken statues commemorate Denizli's ties to the poultry industry. While some travelers may prefer to move on to Pamukkale right away, others who wish to spend only an afternoon in Pamukkale may opt to visit as a daytrip and spend the night in Denizli, a regional transportation hub.

◩ **TRANSPORTATION.** The otogar and *gar* (☎268 28 31) sit across from one another on busy İzmir Bul., at the eastern end of town. **Buses** run to: **Ankara** (6hr., 12 per day 7am-1am, $13); **Antalya** (5hr., 15 per day 4:30am-2am, $7.30); **Bodrum** (5hr., 5 per day 9:30am-9pm, $8); **Bursa** (8hr.; 7:30, 11:30pm; $12); **Cappadocia (Nevşehir)** (10hr., 4 per day 1:30-8:30pm, $14.50); **Didim (Didyma)** (4hr., 4 per day 6:30am-3pm, $5); **Fethiye** (4hr., 3 per day 9:30am-5:30pm, $5); **İstanbul** (10hr.; 7 per day 8:30am-11pm, express after 8:30pm; $16); **İzmir** (4hr., 30 per day 4:50am-1am, $6.50); **Konya** (6hr., 9 per day 10:30am-12:30am, $10.50); **Kuşadası** (4hr., take any İzmir bus and get off at Selçuk for a dolmuş, $3.25); **Marmaris** (4hr., 9 per day 5am-8:30pm, $6.50); **Nazilli** (1hr., take any İzmir bus, $2.50); **Selçuk** (2hr., take any İzmir bus, $3.25); **Söke** (3hr., take any Didim bus, $4). For **Aphrodisias**, take an İzmir bus to Nazilli, then a minibus to Karacasu, then a dolmuş or taxi to Aphrodisias. **Pamukkale** (30min.; summer every 30min., winter every hr. 7am-6:30pm; $.75). Alternatively, call ahead to a pension in Pamukkale for free pickup. **Trains** run to **İstanbul** (14hr.; 5:30pm; seat $7, sleeper $10); **İzmir** (6hr., 4 per day 5am-3pm, $4). 20% student discount with ISIC card.

■⁊ ORIENTATION AND PRACTICAL INFORMATION. There are **tourist offices** in the *gar* and otogar (☎268 65 39. Open M-F 8am-noon, 1:30-5:30pm; in winter until 5pm). A small 24hr. **police** station (☎241 89 20) is in the otogar, and a larger 24hr. station (☎241 89 21) is on Atatürk Bul. about 50m north of Delikliçınar Meydanı (turn right at the top of Atatürk Cad. onto Atatürk Bul.). A **PTT** is on Atatürk Bul. 30m beyond the police station. (☎241 01 49. Open daily 7am-11pm.) For medical assistance, go to the **Pamukkale University Hospital,** 42 Doktorler Cad. (☎241 00 37; fax 264 92 57), the best private hospital in the area. A **pharmacy, Atik Eczane,** is just outside of the otogar. (☎262 00 67. Open M-Sa 8am-8pm.) **Postal code:** 20100.

⌐⌐̈ ACCOMMODATIONS AND FOOD. Denizli Pansiyon, 1993 Sok. No. 14, is about 1km out of town in a pleasant residential neighborhood. Tidy rooms, all with bathroom, encircle a shady courtyard with a marble fountain. Free transportation from the otogar, and to Pamukkale. Daily trips to Aphrodisias ($8) can be followed by a relaxing swim at **Salda Lake** (additional $5). (☎261 87 38; mobile ☎(532) 410 39 99; fax 264 49 46. Large breakfast included. Homemade Turkish dinner $4. $8 per person.) **Altın Pension,** Topraklık Mah., 633 Sok. No. 4, is a convenient 20m behind the otogar, and offers utilitarian rooms with bath and telephones. Some have TVs. (☎264 54 72 or 242 76 02. Laundry $2.50. Breakfast $1.20. Singles $10; doubles $14; triples $21.) For a more cushy experience with bath, TV, A/C, and the occasional balcony, head to the 2-star **Yıldırım Hotel,** Santral Garaj Uzere, 632 Sok. No. 13, located conveniently behind the otogar. Ask to see a couple rooms first, since size varies substantially. (☎263 35 90 or 264 50 75; fax 263 35 90. Laundry $3.25. Breakfast included. Singles $16; doubles $29; triples $35; prices slightly negotiable.)

Grab a tasty kebap, *lahmacun* ($.80), or the generous "Special Kervan" mixed plate ($3.65) at the local chain, **Kervan Kebap,** 101 Atatürk Bul. (☎261 62 22), 300m beyond the PTT heading away from Delikliçınar Meydanı, or 8 Çaybaşı Condağan Parks Karşısı (☎263 07 45), just off Mimar Sinan Cad. before it intersects Atatürk Bul. (Both open daily 8:30am-10pm.) The name says it all at **İstanbul Fast Foods,** Çınar Mah., 106 Atatürk Bul., just before Kervan Kebap, underground on a side street. Inexpensive pizza ($1.60) and hamburgers ($.80) are popular items on their limited menu. Complete the evening with a game of pool on one of three billiard tables. (☎265 74 46. Open daily 9am-9pm.) The posh **Denizli Evi-Restaurant,** 10 İstiklâl Cad., on the right side after passing the Yeni Ulu Çınar Camii on Delikliçınar Meydanı, serves excellent meals. Balcony seating is available. (☎263 14 42. Cold dishes from $1.60; filet mignon $4. Open 8am-midnight.)

GEYRE (APHRODISIAS)   ☎256

Aphrodisias's extensive ruins are surrounded by tobacco fields and framed by the majestic Baba Dağ mountain range. Still very much under excavation, the site is expected by some archaeologists to eclipse Ephesus in grandeur after another 50 or 60 years. The site's stadium is remarkably intact and impressive, and the museum is unquestionably better than its counterpart in Ephesus.

The city has had nearly as many different names as the goddess Aphrodite, its Classical namesake, had lovers. Before its stint as the center of Greco-Roman worship of the goddess of love and fertility, Aphrodisias was named Ninoe, probably for Aphrodite's antecedent, the Akkadian goddess of love and war. It was later known as Lelegonpolis, Megalopolis, and Plasara until it became the center for the cult of Aphrodite. The rise of the Byzantine Empire saw the city's temples converted to churches, and the name to Stavropolis (City of the Cross), and later, Caria, from which the nearby modern village of Geyre probably takes its name.

AEGEAN COAST

Aphrodisias was well known as a center for astronomy, medicine, and mathematics, but above all as a showcase for sculpture. Chiseled from the famed white and bluish-gray marble quarried in the nearby foothills, the finer statues in the Roman Empire were often influenced by the Aphrodisian school of sculpture, which is believed to have operated from the first century BC to the end of the 5th century. Under excavation since 1961 by a team from New York University, the modern site contains an enormous theater, an odeon, numerous temples, and the best-preserved Roman stadium in the ancient world.

⌨⃣ TRANSPORTATION AND PRACTICAL INFORMATION. The best way to see the ruins is to take a daytrip from Pamukkale. When there is sufficient tourist interest, one bus leaves daily at 9:30am, picking up guests of the various hotels in Pamukkale. The bus departs Aphrodisias at 2:30pm (2hr., round-trip $10). However, many hotels make their own trips if there is enough interest. It is also possible to take a **dolmuş** to **Nazilli** from **Aydın** (45min., every 30min. 6am-midnight, $1.60) or **Denizli** (45min., every 30min. 7am-10pm, $2.50), catch a dolmuş from Nazilli to **Karacasu** (30min., every 10min. 6:30am-8pm, $2), and take another dolmuş from Karacasu onto Aphrodisias (10min., every 30min. 7:30am-11pm, $.50). Karacasu is known for its beautiful red pottery, and artists sell their wares for around $.40 per piece about 500m from the dolmuş stop. The **jandarma** is between the turnoff from the main highway and the entrance to the Aphrodisias site. (☎ 448 80 05. Open daily 8am-4pm.) The nearest **PTT** is in Geyre. **Postal code:** 09374.

▐▐ ACCOMMODATIONS AND FOOD. Since Aphrodisias can be visited as a daytrip, there's not much reason to stay in town. The **Aphrodisias Hotel-Restaurant,** operated by Mestan Gökçe Bey (who speaks Turkish, French, and English), is 2km from the Aphrodisias entrance, beyond Chez Mestan. This more elegant hotel offers clean rooms with bath, central heating in the winter, and rugs on the tile floors. All rooms have balconies. (☎ 448 81 32; fax 448 84 22. Singles $20; doubles $25; triples $30; camping $5.) The **restaurant** serves up a traditional Turkish plate ($6). Meals are held on the rooftop in winter and in the garden below in summer.

▣ THE RUINS OF APHRODISIAS. At the entrance, the dirt road to the left leads to the enormous and still acoustically sound **theater,** built in the first century BC. On the theater's *proskenion* (horizontal slab running above the columns) is a dedication, "to the people of Aphrodisias," from Gaius Julius Zoilos, a freed slave who financed the building's construction. Further along the road and on the right, a number of columns mark the remains of the **agora.** The looming structure at the bottom of the hill is **Hadrian's Bath,** equipped with a sauna, frigidarium, and changing rooms. Farther down the road to the right is the **odeon,** once graced by an extraordinary marble mosaic stage, used for concerts and political meetings. The 9 columns in front of the odeon form a court which archaeologists christened the **Bishop's Palace** because of the religious artifacts and statues unearthed there.

The highlights of a visit to Aphrodisias are the three magnificent structures located at the back of the site. The soaring Ionic columns of the **Temple of Aphrodite** mark the original home of a famous statue of the goddess. Sculpted nearly 2000 years ago, the statue was similar in appearance to the many breasted Artemis of Ephesus. So far, only copies of the original have been unearthed. The grand structure with elegant spiral-fluted Corinthian columns and beautiful floral reliefs on its pediment is the **tetrapylon,** the gateway into the ancient city. The name, which means "four gateways" in Greek, refers to the four rows of four columns that comprise the structure. The ancient 30,000 seat **stadium** is one of the best-preserved of its kind ever excavated. Even the marble blocks that once marked the starting line for foot races are still in the central arena. The first three rows of seats were removed and replaced with a tall wall to protect the eager Roman audiences from the violent animal hunts and wrestling matches.

The new **museum,** located near the site entrance, displays a breathtaking collection of Roman-era sculpture. It's surprising that these treasures have not been carted off to İstanbul or elsewhere. Among the highlights are the large statues of Aphrodite, her priests, and a satyr carrying the child Dionysus. (☎ 448 80 03. Site and museum open daily in summer 9am-6:30pm; in winter 8am-5pm. Site $4; museum $4.)

AYDIN   ☎256

Aydın was once home to Tralles, an important Roman scholastic town. Today, despite its palm-lined boulevards and intriguing variety of mosques, Aydın is perhaps more worthwhile as a base from which to explore the ruins of Nyssa than as an attraction in itself.

⌷ TRANSPORTATION. Buses connect Aydın to: **Bodrum** (2½hr., 7 per day 4am-5pm, $5.75); **Denizli** (2hr., every 30min. 6am-midnight, $4); **Fethiye** (5hr., every hr. 8:30am-1:30am, $8); **İstanbul** (11hr., 8 per day 9am-3am, $16); **İzmir** (1hr., every 30min. 6am-11:30pm, $4); **Kuşadası** (1hr., every 10min. 6am-10:30pm, $2); **Marmaris** (2½hr., every hr. 5am-2:30am, $5); **Nazilli** (45min., every 30min 6am-midnight, $1.60); **Söke** (45min., every 30 min. 6am-8pm, $2). For **Pamukkale**, take a Denizli bus and switch to a dolmuş at the Denizli otogar. From the *gar* at the intersection of Adnan Menderes Bul. and Gençlik Cad., **trains** run to: **Denizli** (3hr., 4 per day 12:15-9:40pm, $2); **Söke** (1hr.; 9:40am, 12:30pm; $.85); **İzmir** (Basmane station; 3hr., 6 per day 6am-5:53pm, $2). **İstanbul** can be reached via Denizli, and **Selçuk**, via İzmir.

✦ ORIENTATION. The center of Aydın stretches along **Adnan Menderes Bulvarı**, which runs north-south on a long hill (800m). At the bottom of the hill (the southern end), Adnan Menderes Bul. meets **Denizli Bulvarı**. The **otogar** is located on Denizli Bul. Restaurants, shops and banks line Adnan Menderes Bul. At the top of Adnan Menderes Bul. (the northern end), **Gazi Bulvarı** runs east-west. From the west, Gençlik Cad. meets Adnan Menderes Bul. 100m south of Gazi Bul.

⚐ PRACTICAL INFORMATION. The **tourist office** is on Aydın Denizli Yolu, the large highway beside which the otogar is located. It sits diagonally from the otogar on the southeast corner of the roundabout. Staffers speak some English and distribute helpful Aydın maps. (☎ 211 27 71; fax 211 28 61. Open July-Sept. M-F 8am-noon, 1:30-5:30pm; Sa-Su 9am-6pm; Oct.-June M-F 8am-noon, 1-5pm.) Several 24hr. V/MC **ATMs** and a **TC Ziraat Bankası** are at the intersection of Adnan Menderes Bul. and Gençlik Cad. The **police** (☎ 225 25 06 or 225 25 07) are on Aydın Denizli Yolu, 500m past the tourist office in the direction opposite the otogar. The local **hospital**, the **SKK Hastenesi** (☎ 212 92 22), is also on Aydın Denizli Yolu (which becomes İzmir Bul.), 500m from the tourist office in the direction of the otogar. Turn left at the intersection of Adnan Menderes Bul. and Gençlik Cad. and walk about 50m to the **PTT** (open daily 8am-11pm). **Postal code:** 09000.

⌂ ACCOMMODATIONS. Most accommodations are on Adnan Mederes and Gazi Bul. The **Orhan Hotel**, 63 Gazi Bul., is a 20-minute walk from the bus station, or a short taxi ride. Orhan has clean, large, nicely furnished rooms with TV and private bath. Some rooms have terraces overlooking the bustling streets below. (☎ 212 17 13; fax 225 17 81. Breakfast included. Singles $13; doubles $19.50; triples $28.) The **Baltacı Otel,** 3 Sok. No. 17, is to the right on Gazi Bul. after you walk up Adnan Menderes Bul. Take your 1st right just after Ramazan Paşa Mosque. Baltacı offers spacious rooms with slightly worn-out furniture and old but tidy bathrooms. (☎ 225 13 20 or 225 13 21; fax 225 13 21. Breakfast included. $11.50 per person.) A short walk from the bus station is **Otel Özlü**, 77 Adnan Manderes Bul., a two-star hotel with TV, phone, and bath in every room. Half the rooms come with A/C. The carpeted terrace has a panoramic view. (☎ 213 29 88; fax. 225 33 71. Breakfast included. Singles $18; doubles $28; triples $36.)

A E G E A N   C O A S T

[icon] FOOD AND ENTERTAINMENT. Adnan Menderes Bul. is full of enticing ice cream parlors and vendors selling *dondurma*, the gooey wonder that is Turkish ice cream ($.50-1.25 for a cone). Notable among these sweet shops is the posh, air-conditioned **Öz Süt**, 91/A Adnan Menderes Bul. (☎212 73 99. Open daily 8:30am-1am.) Plenty of restaurants offering Turkish cuisine also line this street. **Kervan Kebap ve Pide Salonu**, 46/A Adnan Menderes, a few doors up the hill from Kervansaray, is the place to go for Turkish pizza with meat or cheese ($1) and perhaps egg on top ($.30 extra). *Şiş kebap* costs $2. (☎213 36 94. Open daily 8am-11:30pm.) **Kervansaray**, 36 Adnan Menderes Bul., serves standards like *Iskender kebap* ($2), *çorba* ($.80), and tasty rice pudding ($1). (☎212 88 79. Open daily 7am-11pm.)

[icon] SIGHTS. The **Süleyman Bey Camii** is next to the *gar* (train station) at the intersection of Adnan Menderes Bul. and Gençlik Cad. Notable for the *muqarnas* (stalactitesque decoration) on its two outer vaults, the mosque also boasts detailed floral brushwork and arabesques that grace the central dome. The **Ramazan Paşa Camii**, 1 block north of the Süleyman Bey Camii, at the intersection of Gazi Bul. and Adnan Menderes Bul., witnessed the meeting held on May 22, 1919, that began the Turkish War of Independence (see **The Cult of Mustafa Kemal**, p. 16). This mosque has simple stained-glass windows and a central dome finished with ornate leaf-like gilding from Turkey's Baroque period.

Tralles, an ancient city known in Roman times for its wealth, lies just north of Aydın. Today, little remains of Tralles; the most prominent features are the **Üc Göz** (Three Arches), which were once part of the gymnasium's vaults. The ruins offer a spectacular view of Aydın and the surrounding mountains. To get to Tralles, either catch the dolmuş to **Topyataga** (15min., every 15min. 7am-11pm, $.50) from the corner of Adnan Menderes Bul. and Denizli Yolu. Once there, walk the 1km uphill.

The artifacts missing from the site of Tralles can be viewed in the **Aydın Archaeological Museum.** On display are coins, busts of such figures as Athena, and an eclectic mixture of 18th- and 19th-century Ottoman clothing, including headdresses. To reach the museum, turn left at the intersection of Adnan Menderes Bul. and walk about 500m. Make a right onto 20 Sok., and the museum will be on the right. *(Museum open daily 8am-noon, 1:30-5:30pm. $1.25, students $.75.)* The Aydın Lisesi, 300m past the PTT on Gençlik Cad., hosts the town's annual **traditional dance festival,** which draws international children's dance teams to perform in late June.

[icon] DAYTRIP FROM AYDIN: NYSSA. About 30km from Aydın lies ancient Nyssa (in Turkish, *Nysa*). Once home to such thinkers as the Stoic philosopher **Apollonius,** Nyssa now boasts some fairly intact ruins. The most striking is the large **theater,** on the main road 50m past the entrance gate. In Roman days, theater-goers passed through **vomitoria** on both sides before going to their seats. South of the theater, near the site entrance, are the poorly preserved **library** and the **gymnasium.** The **stadium,** built to accommodate 30,000 spectators, is situated at the bottom of the ravine. Seats at the northern end are visible. Across the road from the theater, a circuitous dirt path leads down into this large ravine and through a 115m-long **tunnel,** which used to channel the city's water supply. Walking through to the other side brings you back to the main road. Continue and you'll pass the recognizable remains of nine **vaulted shops** on your left and the less recognizable remains of the **market basilica** directly across from the shops. Signs point the way to the **bouleterion,** the smaller theater whose entrance gates are still intact. The **agora,** farther up from the bouleterion, contains impressive remains of ancient drainage gullies and three standing Ionic columns. Beneath a thin layer of dirt in the excavated corner of the agora are remnants of the original mosaic floor. The ruins of a Roman bathhouse lie beyond the agora and bouleterion, but as there is no path leading to it, the bath is best viewed from across the ravine, just after passing by the ticket office. *(☎351 27 26. Open daily 8am-7pm. $1.60. To reach Nyssa from Aydın, take the dolmuş to Nazilli from the otogar and ask to be dropped at Sultanhisar (30min., $1.20). From this small village you can walk up 3km to Nyssa. In scorching summer months, a taxi is a good option for the journey up, but the walk down is relatively easy 20min. descent. The dolmuş returning to Aydın can be caught from the north side of the highway, across from the arrival spot.)*

BODRUM PENINSULA

BODRUM ☎252

Known as the "Bedroom of the Mediterranean," Bodrum comes to life at night. Streaks of colored light emerge from pulsing dance clubs, playing on the yachts filling the harbor. The streets fill with foreign visitors bargaining for goods and choosing from among hundreds of bars and restaurants. Not far from this excitement, a quieter side of town can easily be found. Locals amble through whitewashed arches overrun with bougainvillea. Once the ancient city of Halicarnassus, Bodrum is known for the 4th-century BC funerary monument to King Mausolus, whose tomb was so magnificent that it was declared one of the Seven Wonders of the Ancient World. The king's memory lives on in the word "mausoleum."

While Bodrum is notorious for its nightlife, the surrounding Acadian Peninsula is famous for its silica beaches, lush forests, secluded swimming coves, and ancient ruins. As multitudes of Turkish jet setters, international yachtsmen, backpackers, and package tourists agree, it is easy to get sucked into Bodrum's daily rhythm of sun, shopping, sight-seeing, and water sports. All of these innocent activities are but a prelude to the bacchanalian delights that begin once night falls.

▛ TRANSPORTATION

Flights: The Bodrum Airport is about 45min. out of town. Buses to the airport depart from the otogar ($5). The **Turkish Airlines Office,** 208 Neyzen Tevfik Cad. (☎313 31 72), is open daily 9am-5pm. International flights go through İstanbul. To **İstanbul** and **Ankara** (1hr., 4 per day 6:10am-9:15 pm, $90).

Buses: The otogar is on Cevat Şakir Cad. Some companies also have offices along Neyzen Tevfik Cad. Companies serving Bodrum include: **Ulusoy** (☎313 01 66 or 313 01 67), **Kamil Koç** (☎316 66 32 or 316 06 50), and **Pamukkale** (☎316 13 69).

Destination	Company	Duration	Times (daily)	Price	Students
Ankara	Pamukkale	11hr.	5, 9pm	$15.50	
Ankara	Ulusoy	11hr.	8:30pm	$21.50	$18.50
Antalya	Kamil Koç	8hr.	9:30am, 10pm	$13	$12
Antalya	Pamukkale	8hr.	9:45am, 10:15pm	$12	
Bursa	Pamukkale	10hr.	noon, 7:30pm, 9pm	$13	
Denizli	Pamukkale	5hr.	noon, 9pm	$6.30	
Fethiye	Pamukkale	5hr.	7:30, 9:45am, 12:30, 10:30pm	$7	
İstanbul	Kamil Koç	12hr.	8:45am, 8, 10pm	$21	$19
İstanbul	Ulusoy	12hr.	7, 8, 9pm	$26	$22
İstanbul	Pamukkale	12hr.	noon, 9pm	$21	
İzmir	Pamukkale	4hr.	2am-6pm	$7	
Kalkan	Pamukkale	7hr.	12:30pm	$9.60	
Kaş	Pamukkale	7½hr.	12:45am, 10:15pm	$10	
Konya	Pamukkale	10hr.	5pm	$16	
Köyceğiz	Pamukkale	3½hr.	7:30, 9:45am, 12:15, 8:30pm	$5	
Kuşadası	Pamukkale	2½hr.	2am-6pm	$6	
Marmaris	Pamukkale	3hr.	9:30am-4:30pm	$5	
Milas	Pamukkale	1hr.	2am-6pm	$1.80	
Pamukkale	Pamukkale	5hr.	8:30, 10:30am, 3:30pm	$7	
Selçuk	Pamukkale	3hr.	2am-6pm	$8	
Side	Pamukkale	10hr.	12:45am, 10:15pm	$13	
Yalova	Pamukkale	11hr.	noon, 7:30, 9pm	$14.50	

Dolmuş: From the otogar to: **Marmaris** (3hr., every hr. 7am-8pm, $6); **Milas** (45 min., every hr. 7am-9pm, $1.20); **Muğla** (25min., every hr. 7am-8pm, $3).

Ferries: Tickets sold through travel agents. **Bodrum Express Lines** (☎316 40 67 or 316 10 87; fax 313 00 77) has offices in the otogar and near the castle. Walk past the castle on the right towards the sea; the office will be on the left. All ferries and hydrofoils run May-Sept. from the end of the jetty, past the office. To: **Kos** (1½hr.; daily 9am, return 4:30pm: arrive at the jetty 30 min. early for passport check); **Datça** (M, W, F 9am, return 4:30pm). Children under 11 free. Call for off-season schedule changes.

Hydrofoils: Bodrum Express Lines, (☎316 10 87 or 316 40 67; fax 313 00 77). To: **Dalyan** (2½hr., including 1½hr. coach transfer from Gelibolu to Dalyan; Th, Su 8am, return 6pm; $45 including lunch, Dalyan river cruise, and entrance to Kaunos); **Gökova,** a.k.a. the Bodrum-Gelibolu day cruise, (1¼hr.; Th, Su 8am, return 6pm; $38); **Kos** (15min.; daily 9am, return 4:30pm; $21, round-trip $24); **Marmaris** (2hr., coach transfer from Gelibolu to Marmaris included; Th, Su 8am, return 5:30pm; $24, round-trip $29, open return $39); **Rhodes** (2¼hr.; Sa 8:30am, return 4pm; $43, round-trip $48, open return $63).

Rentals: Botur Agency (☎313 90 52), on Cevat Şakir Cad. Rents cars ($36-96 per day); mopeds ($14-72 per day). **Avis** (☎316 23 33 or 316 19 96); **Budget** (☎316 3078); **Hertz** (☎316 1053).

⚡ ORIENTATION

Streets in Bodrum are marked by small blue signs, though it is often easier to navigate using landmarks. The main streets in town radiate from the Castle of St. Peter *(kale)*. **Cumhuriyet Cad.**, the main commercial drag, runs along the beach, twisting slightly inland to allow room for a small beach before returning to the sea. Ferries and yacht cruises depart from the breakwater and **Kale Cad.**, which runs from the left of the castle and ends at a mosque. **Belediye Meyd Cad.**, the street to the left of the mosque (when you're facing inland) turns into **Neyzen Tevfik Cad.**, the western harbor coastal road. From the mosque, **Türkkuyusu Cad.** curves slightly westward and **Cevat Şakir Cad.** heads straight inland. The ever-popular **Atatürk Cad.** stems to the right off of Cevat Şakir Cad.

🛈 PRACTICAL INFORMATION

TOURIST AND FINANCIAL SERVICES

Tourist Office: 48 Barış Meydanı (☎316 10 91; fax 316 76 94), at the foot of the castle. Pension information and room listings. Free brochures with maps. Open Apr.-Oct. daily 8:30am-5:30pm; Nov.-Mar. M-F 8am-noon, 1-5pm.

Travel Agencies: Botur, 24/A Cevat Şakir Cad. (☎316 90 52). Open 9am-10:30pm. Organizes bus trips to: **Pamukkale** and **Ephesus** (2 days; W, Sa 7:30am; return Th, Su 8pm; $45 includes overnight stay in a 4-star hotel); **Dalyan and Kaunos** (12½ hr.; Th, Su 7:30am, return 8pm; $20). **Village tour** (daily; 11am, return 4pm; $8).

Consulate: UK, Kıbrıs Şehitleri Ca. no. 421 1B (☎317 00 93/4), in Konacik. A 15min. bus ride from Bodrum. M-Th 9am-12:30pm, 2:30-4:30pm.

Currency Exchange: At the PTT from 8:30am-midnight. Most exchange booths along the harbor on Kale Cad. and along Cumhuriyet Cad. do not charge commission.

ATMs: Cirrus/Plus/MC/V ATMs located throughout the shopping areas. **Türkiye İş Bankası** (☎316 10 12), on Cevat Şakır Cad., is about halfway between the bus station and the castle. Open M-F 9am-12:30pm, 1:30-5:30pm.

LOCAL SERVICES

English Language Bookstores: A 24hr. **book fair** is located across from 06 Lokanta. Open from late June-Aug. **Sistem** (☎316 83 00). Open daily 10am-3am.

Laundromats: Mainly on Türkkuyusu Cad., Cevat Şakir Cad., and Atatürk Cad. $4 per load. Most open daily 8am-10pm.

Hamam: A new hamam has recently been built in a convenient location across from the otogar. Open M-Sa 8:30am-midnight. For another hamam (☎316 11 59), walk inland on

Bodrum

⬥ ACCOMMODATIONS

Aşkın Pansiyon, 5″
Dönen Pansiyon, 1″
Emiko Pansiyon, 4″
Melis Pansiyon, 2″
Otel Kilavuz, 6″
Sevin Pansiyon, 3″

TO MILAS AND GÖLKÖY

N

200 yards
200 meters

Dervis Görgün Cad.

Mumtaz Ataman Sok.

Omurga Dere Sok.

Aremis Cad.

Üçkuluyar Cad.

Üçkuluyar Cad.

Cunhuriyet Cad.

TO MORE BEACHES

Halikarnas Disco

Kumbahçe Bay

MARKETS

Cevat Sakir Cad.

Atatürk Cad.

Adliye Cad.

Dr. G. Cad.

Huseyin Özsoy Nafız Cad.

Sanat Okulu Cad.

BEACH

Kulcüoglu Sok.

Ali Baba Cad.

Türkkuyusu Cad.

Fuça Cad.

Stadium

Dr. Alim Bey Cad.

1

2

TAXI

3

Belediye Meyd Cad.

Kaşışkale Cad.

Bodrum Castle

Geren ce Sok.

Turgut Reis Cad.

West Harbor

Hamam Sok.

Mausoleum

Ferry Dock

Neyzen Tevfik Cad.

Aegean Sea

Antique Theatre

Kıbrıs Şehitleri Cad.

Kanlıdere Sok.

Turkish Airlines

Firkateyn Sok.

Afer Paşa Cad.

TO PENINSULAR BEACHES AND GÜMBET

AEGEAN CO

Cevat Şakir Cad., turn right onto Atatürk Cad., and turn left at the sign for the hamam, which will be on the right. Open for men Su-Tu, Th-F 8:30am-6pm; W, Sa 8:30am-noon. For women W, Sa noon-6pm. $6.

EMERGENCY AND COMMUNICATIONS

Police: 50 Barış Meydanı (☎316 10 04). At the foot of the castle, next to the tourist office. Open 24hr. **Emergency Police:** (☎316 12 15).

Pharmacies: Especially prevalent on Cumhuriyet Cad., Cevat Şakir Cad., and Atatürk Cad. All open daily 8:30am-8pm. All post the nighttime on-duty pharmacy; call 118 to find out which one is open 24hr. for that day.

Hospital: Bodrum Devlet Hastanesi (☎313 14 20 or 313 21 27), Kıbrıs Şehitleri Cad., uphill from the amphitheater. Public. Open 24hr. **Private Bodrum Hospital** (☎313 65 66). Walk inland on Cevat Şakir Cad., take a left onto Artemis Sok., turn left onto Kulcuoğlu Sok., take the 3rd right, and then make the 1st right. English spoken. Open 24hr. Or try the brand spanking new **Universal Hospital** (☎317 15 15) in Konacik.

Internet Access: Palmiye Internet Cafe (☎313 91 84; fax 313 91 81; email palmiye1@efes.net.tr), on Neyzen Tevfik Cad. From the mosque in front of the castle, walk along Neyzen Tevfik Cad. for 300m; the cafe will be on the right. 9 computers with internet access ($3 per hr.), frozen yogurt ($1-2), and fruit juice bars ($1-2). Open M-Sa 10am-midnight, Su noon-midnight. Other internet cafes can be found throughout Bodrum. Prices range from $1.50-3 per hr.

PTT: (☎316 12 12), on Cevat Şakir Cad., 4 blocks from the otogar (when heading towards the castle). *Poste restante*, international phone, and faxes. Open daily 8:30am-midnight. **Postal code:** 48400.

◪ ACCOMMODATIONS

Pensions are plentiful in Bodrum but may require some advance planning. All rates rise in the high season when *pansiyons* do not have to compete for customers. Single travelers *(tek kişi)* are often given double rooms and may have trouble finding a place in the high season; call ahead in the summer. Cheap pensions cluster behind the bank and to the right of the castle as you face inland.

☒ **Otel Kilavuz,** No. 50 Atatürk Cad. (☎316 38 92; fax 316 2852). From the otogar follow Cevat Şakir Cad. towards the castle, turning left onto Atatürk Cad. Walk 3 blocks and turn left onto Adliye Sok. This modern hotel has a garden, a pool, and a bar. Each of the 12 rooms has a large bathroom, phone, and art on the walls. Singles $12; doubles $16. Prices drop in off-season.

Emiko Pansiyon, Atatürk Cad., 11 Uslu Sok. (☎/fax 316 55 60; email emiko@turk.net). From the otogar, follow Cevat Şakir Cad. towards the water, turning left onto Atatürk Cad. After 50m, turn right down the alley marked with a sign for the Emiko Pansiyon; it's the 2nd building on your left. Run by Emiko, a lovely Japanese woman fluent in English, this *pansiyon* offers 8 simple rooms with hardwood floors and bath. Guests enjoy breakfast under the shade of grape leaves on the white-washed patio. Guest kitchen. Breakfast $2. Laundry $3. Singles $15; doubles $20.

Dönen Pansiyon (☎316 40 17). Walk inland from the taxi station on Türkkuyusu Cad.; the *pansiyon* is 3 blocks down on the left. Run by a friendly family, it has 14 lovely rooms, some with bath. Breakfast included. Laundry available. Singles $10; doubles $12; triples $15.

Aşkin Pansiyon (☎313 31 67). Following Cevat Şakir Cad. from the otogar towards the castle, turn left onto Atatürk Cad., right down a passageway about 20m past the sign for Emiko, and then left down a corridor with the *pansiyon*'s yellow sign. The rooftop terrace has a splendid view of the sea. 10 basic rooms, some with bath. Discos nearby, so ask for a room at the back if you crave quiet. $8 per person.

Sevin Pansiyon (☎316 76 82), on the left side of Türkkuyusu Cad. when heading inland from the taxi park. 27 modern rooms with comfortable mattresses and unique carved doors. All rooms with bath. Breakfast included. Laundry $3. Doubles $18.

Melis Pansiyon (☎316 05 60 or 316 14 87). From the harbor, walk down Türkkuyusu Cad. past the Sevin Pansiyon on the right. 15 large, cheerful rooms, all with bath. Breakfast $2.50 only during high season. Singles $9; doubles $11; triples $15.

☕ FOOD

Cheap eats in Bodrum consist of the usual kebap stands (kebap and chips $3) and the small cafeteria-style joints on Cevat Şakir Cad. (meals $2). Steaming corn on the cob ($.50) is sold from small carts along the main streets, and wherever you turn, the doughy beginnings of fresh pizzas ($6-8) are being tossed in the air.

🍴 **Tarçin** (☎313 87 50). Turn onto Atatürk Cad. from Cevat Şakir Cad. and turn left into the 2nd alleyway. Tarçin is 30m down, at the back of a grape-filled courtyard. Serves sumptuous homemade dishes that make use of the Bodrum market's colorful selection of fresh fruits and vegetables in an intimate setting ($4-9). Open M-F 8am-6pm.

🍴 **Sandal** (☎316 35 59). Turn onto Atatürk Cad. from Cevat Şakir Cad. and walk 5 blocks. Go straight at the Babil center spice exchange. For those craving the taste of the east, Sandal offers authentic Thai food *al fresco*. Munch on *pad thai* under the thatched roof while listening to sultry jazz tunes. Dinner around $9. Open M-F 10am-1am.

Paradise Garden. Turn onto Atatürk Cad. from Cevat Şakir Cad. and walk until you see the large white spice exchange. Turn right. The restaurant is on your left. Eat pizza and grilled meat ($3-$5) under the shade of large cyprus and cedar trees. For a refreshing treat, have a glass of freshly squeezed orange juice ($2.50). Open daily 8am-midnight.

06 Lokanta, 115 Cumhuriyet Cad. (☎316 83 83), near the 24hr. book fair. A popular meeting spot in the hub of the action on Cumhuriyet Cad. Regional Turkish specialties in an elegant atmosphere perfect for people watching. For a bargain, try the homemade vegetable soup ($2). A variety of hot dishes ($4-5) and vegetarian options. Open 24hr.

Golden Gate (☎313 11 32). From Cevat Şakir Cad., turn left onto Atatürk Cad. The restaurant is 300m on the left. Look for its red pagoda draped with colored streamers. Friendly and relaxed atmosphere where devoted regulars sip the cheapest beers in Bodrum ($.50). Entrees—whether Turkish, Chinese, or Italian—come with soup, bread, starters, salad, potatoes, vegetable, rice, and fresh fruit ($4-8). Open daily 9am-3am.

Karadeniz Patisserie, on Cumhuriyet Cad., is a nocturnal sweet tooth's dream. Serves freshly baked sweets, breads, and pastries. 4 apricot cookies for $.30; apple tart $2; cakes $4. Open 24hr.

👁 SIGHTS

THE RUINS OF HALICARNASSUS. The ruins of ancient Halicarnassus, once one of the largest Mediterranean cities in the ancient world, are Bodrum's best-known attraction. Unfortunately, most of the remains were either destroyed, buried beneath the modern town of Bodrum, or shipped to London. The old **city walls** and what remains of the **theater** are still partly visible. Names, barely visible on the weathered stone steps, pay tribute to those who helped to build the theater. The **mausoleum,** one of the Seven Wonders of the Ancient World, once rose to a height of 50m. A rectangular foundation, stone pedestal, and 36 Ionic columns supported the sepulchral chamber. Covered with a pyramid-shaped roof, the mausoleum was crowned by a statue of Mausolus driving a horse-drawn chariot. Crusaders demolished the structure to fortify the Castle of St. Peter. Today the mausoleum site houses a small porch with reconstructions of the mausoleum's friezes and an open-air museum with columnar fragments. To see the real goods, head to London's British Museum. *(To reach the theater, head towards Gümbet on Kıbrıs Şehitler Cad. To reach the mausoleum's remains, turn onto Kirkateyn Sok. from Neyzen Tevfik Cad. Theater and mausoleum open Tu-Su 8am-noon, 1-5:30pm; closes at 5pm in the off season. $2, students $1.)*

222 ■ BODRUM PENINSULA

THE CASTLE OF ST. PETER. Sandwiched between Bodrum's two bays, the castle stands watch over the rocky peninsula and the crashing waves below. Crusaders from the Knights of St. John constructed Bodrum's formidable castle during the 15th and 16th centuries. It was built over the ruins of an ancient acropolis and incorporated material from the nearby Mausoleum of Halicarnassus. A trans-national effort, the **English, French, German,** and **Italian towers** bear the names of the nations responsible for their construction. Despite their extensive fortifications, the Crusaders's towers were no match for Süleyman the Magnificent's forces, who overpowered the knights in 1523. Under Ottoman rule, the castle's importance waned, and in 1895 it was converted into a prison. The fortress now houses a museum with maritime and cultural exhibits.

The walls of the castle offer an escape from Bodrum's busy streets. Turquoise and amber peacocks parade under flowering trees and bushes. From the towers it is possible to see the entire city as well as some of the neighboring bays. Picnickers will enjoy the peace and quiet.

After walking up the stone ramp past a series of gates, enter the castle's lower courtyard where an **amphora exhibit** graces the left wall. Amphoras, two handled clay jars with rounded bases, were used to carry the wine and olive oil that was traded across the Mediterranean sea. Opposite the wall is an attractive church which became a mosque under the Ottomans. The **chapel** now houses a model of a sunken vessel and other shipwreck artifacts. Continue onwards to the **Museum of Underwater Archaeology,** featuring remnants of the oldest shipwreck ever discovered. The ship sank in the 14th century BC, carrying glass shipments for trade between Egyptian and Anatolian ports.

Stroll uphill into the **French Tower,** in which rest the **remains of a 4th-century BC Carian Princess.** Gaze into the princess's reconstructed face, view the intact skeleton, and marvel at this noblewoman's gold jewelry. Less macabre than it sounds, this exhibit is worth the extra price.

Head past the **Ottoman toilets** to the **Snake Tower,** home to pottery artifacts, and traverse a stairwell leading to the **Gatineau Tower,** which affords a spectacular view of Bodrum. Once upon a time, this tower acted as a dungeon and torture chamber, as proven by the skeletons found during excavation work. Don't leave the castle without a visit to the **German Tower,** replete with banners, stuffed deer heads, and a chandelier reminiscent of the Middle Ages. Most spectacular, however, is the **English Tower,** whose walls are decorated with Turkish banners, English armor, weapons, and engravings. A new exhibit featuring another ancient shipwreck contains such valuables as Nefertiti's seal and a page from the oldest book in the world. Enjoy medieval music and sample a glass of red or white wine ($1) or grape juice ($.60). *(The most central landmark in Bodrum. From the harbor walk left for 300 ft. The entrance to the castle is on the left.* ☎ *316 25 16. Open Tu-Su 8am-noon, 1-5pm. $4.80, students with ID $2.40. Carian Princess and Glass Wreck open Tu-F 10am-noon, 2-4pm. $1.60.)*

NOT A MUSEUM. Follow in Donna Karan's footsteps and head to Ali Güven's shop, Çarşı Mah., Kosophan Sok. (☎ 313 21 16), located off Cumhuriyet Cad., about two blocks from the harbor. Ali's famous sandals are a bit pricey ($150-200), but it is a treat to watch the master craft personalized shoes for his customers, including Bette Midler and Mick Jagger. Also available are hundreds of varieties of handmade leather wallets and hand bags.

🎵 ENTERTAINMENT

Bodrum, a.k.a. the "Bedroom," is a wild flesh-pot whose excesses seem to bring out everyone's extremes. Loud, exciting discos and calm, sophisticated bars are merely the foreplay to what happens later. All of the following except for Halikarnas Disco are located on Cumhuriyet Cad. For a wild taste of England in Turkey, hop over the western ridge of Bodrum to Gümbet, where more discos and bars can be found glittering in the night (30min. walk or 10min. dolmuş ride; dolmuş leave the otogar every 10 min.; $.40).

CLUBS

▨ **Halikarnas Disco,** Z. Müren Cad. At the end of Cumhuriyet Cad., 1km from the center of town. This famed open-air disco juts out into the ocean, where its strobe lights reflect off the sails of nearby yachts. The club's dressed-to-be-seen clientele makes serious moves under the gaze of spectators who pay to sit in the VIP seats. Daily shows featuring 25 performers, great music, and a celebrity-style entrance tunnel make this club the definitive Bodrum experience. $18 cover charge includes 1 local drink. Beer $3; cocktails $6.

▨ **Hadi Gari** (☎ 313 80 97). Next to the luminous castle, the oldest disco in Bodrum fuses elegance and funkiness. Stylish customers get down under twinkling white lights on the large outdoor dance floor. Others recline on plush rose and silver cushions in the softly lit interior. Offers an unbeatable view of Bodrum's colorful nightlife. Beer $3; *rakı* $3.60; cocktails $4-8. Restaurant by "day" (6pm-midnight), dance club by night (midnight-4am).

▨ **Greenhouse** (☎ 313 09 11). A much-favored dance bar that extends onto the beach, offering a laid-back atmosphere. Enthusiastic international and Turkish DJs. Everyone ends up here at some point. Beer $1.80; *rakı* $3; cocktails $5. Open daily midnight-5am.

▨ **M&M Club** (☎ 316 27 25). For the sleek elite and those who want to dish out the $12 cover, the M&M is known for its VIP treatment and excellent music. Dance on water aboard its moonlight yacht ($25 per person) under the glow of its giant steel octopus, while admiring the views of the harbor. Beer $2.40; cocktails $4-8. Open 8pm-5am.

Temple (☎ 316 17 21). A popular club where ferocious dancers and sly socializing fill the dance floor. Elegantly dressed twenty-somethings sip drinks in the club's dark wooden interior. Beer $2; *rakı* $2; cocktails $3-6. Open daily 7pm-5am.

White House (☎ 316 40 84). Not to be confused with the one in Washington, D.C., although Bill Clinton might approve of the antics in this pulsating club. An ultra-intense light system illuminates the animated Brits dancing inside and playing on the busy patio. Beer $1.80; *rakı* $2.50; cocktails $3-7. Open 3pm-5am.

Varil! (☎ 367 16 09). Fashionable, swiveling hips and bright garbage cans electrify this Turkish pop club. Owned by a famous İstanbul designer. Drinks $3.60. Open 9pm-4am.

BARS

Karşı (☎ (532) 256 44 17). Sexy bartenders and an enticing and diverse crowd make for a sultry evening of intrigue and alluring glances. The bar loudly dispenses underground, jazz, blues, and pop. Beer $3; *rakı* $3; cocktails $4-8. Open daily 10am-5am.

Sensi (☎ 316 68 45). For a riotous ride in bar craziness, join the mostly-British crowd at Sensi, where table dancing, karaoke, and wig-wearing 70s nights keep this joint quaking. For those who dare, drown your cares in an alcoholic fishbowl ($18). Beer $1.80; *rakı* $2; cocktails $3.60-5. Open daily 5pm-5am.

Körfez Bar (☎ 316 59 66). If Bodrum's repetitive techno-pop has given you an ear blister, head to this den of folk rock. Down-to-earth customers socialize under the watchful eye of Jim Morrison posters. Beer $1.80; *rakı* $2.40; cocktails $3-5. Open 8am-5am.

Fasıl Bar. Cozy upstairs room with excellent live Turkish music. Cover $5; beer $3.00; *rakı* $3.60; cocktails $4-7. Open 10pm-4am.

Ora Bar (☎ 316 39 03). A swanky candle-lit interior with the feel of a castle. A lively, polished crowd sways and socializes to rock and pop. Beer $2.40; *rakı* $3; cocktails $4-6. Open 7pm-4am.

Scotman. Grab a rustic wooden bench at this beachfront dive that bubbles with good cheer and frothy beer ($1.60). *Rakı* $2.40; cocktails $3. Open 8pm-5am.

Red Lion (☎ 316 37 48). For action-packed swigs, touch down at this combination dance and sports bar, where animated crowds watch games on ample TV screens while nodding to house music. Beer $1.80; *rakı* $3.60; cocktails $4-6. Open 4pm-5am.

Karya Otel (☎ 313 31 57). Take a much-needed break from Bodrum's discos and unwind at this friendly Cumhuriyet Cad. favorite. Enjoy the refreshing breeze from the sea while sipping coffee or a more exotic concoction with the locals. Great for people watching. Non-alcoholic hot and cold drinks $1; beer $1.20; cocktails $3. Open 24hr.

AEGEAN COAST

DAYTRIPS FROM BODRUM

The Bodrum Peninsula is an extremely popular Turkish vacation spot. Small villages mingle with coastal vistas and offer a more laid-back alternative to the excitement of Bodrum. Explore the peninsula's greener northern coast or drier, sandier southern coastline. Several of the peninsula's beaches have recently been awarded the European Blue Flag, an environmental award given to communities that keep their beaches especially clean and safe. All dolmuş to these beaches, which are marked by signs on their front window, depart from Bodrum's otogar.

BLUE JOURNEYS. Cevat Şakir Kabaağaç, a writer living in Bodrum between the World Wars, wrote the book *Mavi Yolculuk* ("Blue Journey"), detailing his sailing excursions along Turkey's then-uninhabited southern Aegean coast. These days, tour boats skirt the front of the castle seeking to recreate his journey with trips bound for the beaches on the southern coast of the peninsula. Although hardly as adventurous as those described in Kabaağaç's book, these tours are fun alternatives to the tourist throngs plaguing the beaches around the city. Itineraries for the tours vary widely; check the tour schedule at the dock. Popular destinations include the **Akfaryo**, or aquarium, for an early afternoon swim in the turquoise bay; **Kara Ada** (Black Island), where visitors can apply the special orange clay from deep within a cave that is reputed to restore youthful beauty *($.60 entrance fee)*; and **Deveplajı** (Camel Beach), where the trained dromedaries wait to offer rides *($4 for 10min.)*. **Lover's Bay** and **Rabbit Bay** offer more swimming. In the high season, Blue Journeys also include **Orak Island**, which has some of the best swimming spots on the peninsula. There aren't cheap accommodations in any of these locales, so stick with daytrips. *(Daily 9-11am, return 5-6pm; $12, lunch included.)*

GÖLKÖY AND TÜRKBÜKÜ. Calmer than the southern coast, the northern end of the peninsula offers swimming docks that stretch into the clear water. The quiet shores of Gölköy and Türkbükü draw sophisticated Turkish tourists and their yachts. *(Dolmuş depart frequently for both beaches: 20min., 8am-midnight, in Gölköy the dolmuş stops in front of the town's main grocery store, $1.)*

GÜMÜŞLUK (ALSO CALLED MINDOS). The Turkish name means "silvery," referring to ancient silver coins that were discovered in the area. Near the beach lie the sunken ruins of ancient **Mindos**, a 4th-century BC port impregnable even to Alexander the Great. The site, accessible through daily dives, consists of a 3m-thick city wall and a Roman basilica. Take a boat to **Rabbit Island,** a tiny peninsula 100m from shore that nurtures the fuzzy creatures. *(Take a dolmuş from the Bodrum otogar: 40min., 24hr. in high season, $1.40. For information on dives, contact the Aegean Prod Dive Center (☎316 07 37), on Neyzen Tevfik Cad., for more info.)*

BİTEZ. Recently awarded a Blue Flag in honor of its pristine environment, this narrow beach is popular with the British package tourist. Seaside bars have built pontoon docks over the water where you can order drinks while you sunbathe. Windsurfing is quite popular here, with several places offering instruction and rentals. *(Take the dolmuş: 20min., 24hr. in the high season, $.80. Windsurfing $15 per day.)*

YAHŞI. Also awarded a Blue Flag, the sand paradise of Yahşi is the longest beach in Bodrum. Flanked by surfers, sunbathers, and olive and tangerine trees, the turquoise waters offer a more serene warmth than other beaches in the area. *(Take a dolmuş: 30min., every 15min. 7am-5pm, $1.)*

BAĞLA. Famous for its deep clear water, Bağla's lovely beach is close to many great camping areas. *(Take a dolmuş: 40min., every 30min. 7am-5pm, $1.)*

TURGUT REİS. Named after the famous Turkish pirate and scourge of 16th-century European shipping, Turgut Reis, 18km from Bodrum, is the most accessible point on the west coast of the peninsula. Dolmuş follow a road that was once an ancient trading route. Popular with tourists who prefer relaxing on the beach to dancing in discos, it is usually fairly crowded. The numerous pensions in town fill up quickly in July and August. If you're up for a walk through fruit-laden groves, follow the small road near the Turgut Reis otogar north 4km for the more isolated and enjoyable Kadıkalesi beach. *(Take a dolmuş: 40min., every 15-30min., $1.)*

MİLAS ☎252

No longer the thriving capital of the ancient kingdom of Caria, Milas snoozes about 30 minutes from the action in Bodrum and about an hour and a half from the throngs of tourists in Kuşadası. Come to Milas for a calmer and a more restful village atmosphere. There are no loud nightclubs here—just Ottoman mansions on cobblestone roads, wide pedestrian boulevards for evening strolls, and a Tuesday market with fresh produce, quality leather shoes, and spices galore. Milas is also a convenient base from which to visit Labranda (20km away). Dolmuş service to Labranda is expected in 2001.

🖃🏧 TRANSPORTATION AND PRACTICAL INFORMATION. The newly opened **Milas Bodrum International Airport** (☎523 01 29 for reservations and ticketing) is on the outskirts of the town on the road to Bodrum. From Milas, the airport is only accessible by taxi. Call **Turkish Airlines** (☎513 37 14 or 513 37 15; fax 513 37 17) or see **Bodrum: Flights,** p. 217, for information about flights, prices, and times. **Buses** run to: **Ankara** (10hr.; 9, 10pm; $16.25); **Bodrum** (1hr., every hr. 5am-midnight, $1.60); **Denizli** (4hr.; 12:15am, 5, 7:30pm; $8); **İstanbul** (12hr., 3 per day 8:30-11pm, $21); **İzmir** (3hr., every hr. 5am-7pm, $8); **Selçuk** (2hr., every hr. 5am-7pm, $6.50); **Söke** (1hr., every hr. 5am-7pm, $3.25). To get to town from the otogar, take a free *servis* shuttle offered by the bus companies. Frequent **dolmuş** head to **Bodrum** (1hr., every 10min. 7am-8pm, $1.60) from the otogar. Dolmuş to **Güllük** (30min.; every 30min. 7:30am-9pm, 10pm; $1.20) and **Euromos** (15min., Yenice-bound dolmuş every 30min. until 6pm, $.70) leave from Cumhuriyet Meydanı.

Atatürk Bul. and Cumhuriyet Cad. meet at Cumhüriyet Meydanı, the roundabout in the center of town. Running perpendicular to them are İnönü Cad. (towards the museum) and Müştak Bey Cad. Services include: 24-hour V/MC **ATMs** at several banks on Cumhuriyet Cad.; the **police,** up Atatürk Cad. past Hotel Sürücü.; a small **hospital** (☎512 10 07), on Hastane Cad. past the ancient **Baltalı Kapı** (stone gate). To get there, walk up İnönü Cad. and bear right at the fork in the road, turning right onto Hastane Cad. Numerous **pharmacies** lie along Cumhuriyet Cad. For the **PTT** (☎512 28 37), follow İnönü Cad. from Cumhuriyet Meydanı and turn left up the first street after the fork. (Open M-Sa 8:30am-5pm.) **Postal code:** 48200.

🛏 ACCOMMODATIONS. Hotels in Milas are primarily on Atatürk Bul. and Cumhuriyet Cad. For an aesthetic experience at a reasonable price, **Sürücü Otel,** 10 Atatürk Bul., is 50m past the Kalbur Restaurant as you walk away from Cumhuriyet Meydanı. Big windows, balconies in the rear overlooking the mountains, telephones, TVs, spacious rooms, and lobby will lend you some luxury. (☎512 40 01. Breakfast included. Singles $13; doubles $19.50; triples $24.50.) The best budget option is **Hotel Turan,** 26 Cumhuriyet Cad., past the Kibris Patisserie on the right as you walk away from Cumhuriyet Meydanı. In spite of a bit of peeling paint and hospital-like corridors, Turan's clean rooms are comfortable enough with phone and TV. (☎512 13 42. Breakfast $1.60. Singles $8; doubles $13; triples $16.25.)

🍴🎭 FOOD AND ENTERTAINMENT. Enjoy a classy dinner lit by understated chandeliers at **Kalbur,** 47/A Atatürk Bul., 50m from Cumhuriyet Meydanı on the right. Try the *tavuk şinitsel* (chicken schnitzel; $2.50) or *mantı* (homemade ravioli in yogurt sauce; $2.50). (☎513 47 27 or 512 60 17. Open daily 8am-midnight.) For a quicker bite, grab freshly-made *gözleme* ($1.80) at the **Botanik Gözleme and Cafe,** 32/B Atatürk Bul., down the street from Kalbur, before Sürücü Otel. Enjoy casual outdoor seating on plastic chairs. (☎512 60 83. Open daily 7am-midnight.) To reach the year-old **Çetin Lokantası,** 15 Haciliyas Egemenlik Cad., walk one block away from Cumhuriyet Meydanı on Müştak Bey Cad., turn right, and continue

100m. Serves kebaps ($1.25), *pide* ($.80), *köfte* ($1.25), and soup ($1) in its small dining room. (☎513 55 24. Open daily 7am-10pm.) For dessert, savor baklava ($.80), slices of cake ($1), Turkish cookies ($2.85 per kg), and fresh lemonade ($.50) at **Kibris Patisserie,** 8 Cumhuriyet Cad. (☎512 16 98), 50m from Cumhuriyet Meydanı. The large park framing this intersection is a bit scraggly in the daytime, but attractive at night, making the **Park Büfe,** right beside Cumhuriyet Meydanı, just the place to stop for a drink. (Tea $.15; cola $.65. Open 8am-midnight.)

■ **SIGHTS.** Bright homes dot Milas's winding lanes between Cumhuriyet Cad. and İnönü Cad. The archaeological museum, **Milas Müzesi,** Hayıtlı Mah., 6 Köprülüler Cad., is on the segment of İnönü Cad. that runs parallel to Cumhuriyet Cad. This one-room repository contains finds from Milas and nearby Iasos, including a golden diadem, mouth, and eye covers from a grave in Beçin, displayed right on their owner's skull. (☎512 39 73. Open Tu-Su 8:30am-5:30pm. $1.60, students $1.)

Across the street from the museum, stroll in the wonderful floral garden of the **Ulu Camii,** a stone mosque built in 1398. Other Islamic architectural sites include the striking **Firuz Bey Camii,** built in 1394, and the *camii* built by Orhan Bey in 1330.

The most important ancient site is the **Gümüşkesen,** or silver purse, uphill past the point where Kadıağa Cad. becomes Gümüşkesen Cad. This monumental, well-preserved Roman tomb has intricate geometric stone work inside its pyramidal roof. It is believed to date to the 2nd century AD, but the mysterious lack of inscriptions makes more precise dating difficult. A hole in the raised floor of the structure permitted mourners to pour libations into the burial chamber below.

If time permits, stay for the deals at Milas's famous **Tuesday market.** Look out for leather goods, carpets, crafts, and fine lacework. To get to the market area, walk from Cumhuriyet Meydanı to the end of Cumhuriyet Cad. and turn left at Eti Bank.

LABRANDA (LABRAYNDA)

Because Labraynda is located 20km up a steep, winding road in ill-repair, it is not accessible by dolmuş or taxi. Currently the site can be reached by private car, but for most travelers the best way to see it is with a package tour. Some travelers hitch rides on dump trucks heading to a calcium deposit further in the mountains, but this is not advisable. A dolmuş service is expected in 2001, which will make the commute much easier. The road to the site starts across the highway from the otogar. Site open 8am-8pm. $1.60, $.75 for students with ISIC.

A rough ride over loose stones and thick dust serves as a 45-minute rite of passage to this sanctuary of Zeus. One of the least visited sites of ancient Caria, Labraynda was an important religious center devoted to **Zeus Stratios** (a.k.a. Zeus Labraundos), a version of the god peculiar only to this sanctuary but attested to in inscriptions from as far away as Athens. The site is unique since its well-preserved ruins, dating to the 7th century BC, precede the Romans. The cult of Zeus Stratios flourished into a cosmic affair complete with oracular signs, banquets, and baths. Today, the flowering terraces of Labraynda provide rich fodder for the honeybees of local villagers and spiritual vistas for lucky travelers.

There are a couple ways to enter. If you encounter a wooden gate, don't be discouraged: just call out and someone will let you in. Directly to the left of the site entrance is **andron A,** where all-male banquets venerating Zeus were held during the reign of Idrieus, the brother of Mausoleus. Behind the *andron* are the **oikoi,** homes for the priests in charge of maintaining the site and cult records. Walk through the 4th-century BC **Temple of Zeus,** marked by the remains of Ionic columns, to come face to face with a round, chair-like object used during the worship of Zeus. Behind the temple is an oddly shaped *stoa* with raised relief work. About 2m below and 25m ahead, an impressive **stairway** leads to the remnants of the ancient **agora,** where the four open windows on the left once housed shops. On the right stand the **Doric house** and **Byzantine church.** Behind the church is one of the most unique finds at Labranda—the domain of the ancient **fish oracle.** Archaeologists speculate that the

ARCHAEOLOGICAL OBSTACLES One often hears that Turkey has better Roman ruins than Italy and better Greek ruins than Greece. While sites are not so simply ranked, this statement isn't far off the mark. Not only are the better exposed treasures—Ephesus, Aphrodisias, Bergama—dazzling, but much lies still underground, waiting for sufficient funding to come to light. Unfortunately, a number of obstacles stand so firmly in the way that many discoveries will have to remain buried indefinitely. Funding is, of course, the biggest and most long-standing problem. The vast majority of current excavations in Turkey receives funding from international sources: Germans work at Bergama, Americans at Aphrodisias, Austrians at Ephesus, and so forth. The minimal Turkish funding remains largely private; *Efes* beer has generously funded the excavation and restoration work at Assos. The Turkish government, however, has lately created a huge impediment to increased archaeological research. Within the last year it has declared that all substantial ruins excavated must be restored, presumably in the interest of generating tourist sites like those at Ephesus and Bergama. As one can imagine, this requires a serious diversion of funding and energy. Instead of undertaking new excavations and bringing more to scholarly attention, archaeological teams must now spend their limited money on new marble and special architects. While the thought of having completely restored archaeological sites everywhere in Turkey may be attractive, in reality these new tourist attractions will have come at a considerable cost.

columns mark where the priests tempted jewel-bedecked fish with bait. If the fish accepted the offerings, the oracle was favorable.

For the complete Labranda adventure, climb the hill behind the Temple of Zeus (there's another gate here, but simply pass through) and follow the circuitous path to the exceptionally well-preserved **tomb.** The front chamber of this vaulted structure was once the final resting place of Idrieus' children. In the back lay the man himself and his two wives. On the way out ask the guide to show you the stone emblazoned with the ax of Zeus Stratios, the focus of the site's cult.

EUROMOS

From Milas take a dolmuş marked "Yenice" (15min., every 30min., $.70). Dolmuş going back to Milas from Söke or Yenice are the best bet for getting home. Site open 8am-7pm. $1.60.

The ancient city of Kyromos became known as Euromos when Caria came under Hellenistic influence in the 4th century BC. A shrine dating from as early as the 6th century BC was dedicated to Zeus and local god Stratios. Hidden in silvery olive groves, about 50m from the highway, the 2nd-century AD **Temple of Zeus** is a prime example of Roman-era temple architecture, featuring exquisite Corinthian columns. The still-unfluted columns indicate that the temple was never finished. Wealthy residents, whose munificence is recorded, unusually, on the columns themselves, financed the construction of the elaborate supports.

Notice the intact **architrave,** or stone lintel, running across the top of the columns. A walk around the back of the temple toward the unfinished supports reveals a stone engraved with a double ax, the symbol of Zeus Stratios, and the remains of a decorative lion head on the **sima,** or gutter. Rain water used to run out of the animal's mouth to the ground. The temple contains the remains of the altar and a curious upright pillar decorated in raised relief, a remnant of the door that led to the sacred inner shrine. Unfortunately, the temple's excellent state of preservation has been marred by shoddy, cement reconstruction work around the foundation. With your back to the length-wise fluted columns, you will see the hilltop remains of the ancient wall enclosing what were the **agora, theater,** and **baths.** Ask the guard to point out the 10,000-seat theater, hidden by grass and olive trees. A keen glance from above reveals a column on the other side of the modern highway; this is part of the ancient *agora* now covered by fields and crops.

AEGEAN COAST

AKYAKA (BAY OF GÖKOVA) ☎252

Sitting at the tip of the Bay of Gökova, the serene village of Akyaka is surrounded by a sandy beach and rich pine forests. The undeveloped land around the bay is perfect for camping and exploration. Gökova's river delta, set aside as conservation land, teems with aquatic life, including fish, turtles, and ducks. On the other side of the bay is the island of Sedir, whose white sand is said to have been shipped from Egypt 2000 years ago for Cleopatra and Marc Antony's honeymoon.

▐▌ TRANSPORTATION AND PRACTICAL INFORMATION. Since Gökova lies on the Muğla-Marmaris road, any **bus** heading there can drop you off. **Dolmuş** to **Marmaris** (10am, 6, 11pm; $1.60) and **Muğla** (every ½hr. 7am-10pm, $1) leave from the Akyaka dolmuş stop, across from Belediye Park, near the Belediye building.

Navigation can be tough in Akyaka. Though small, the town is not at all compact, and street names are rarely used. The main road, **Atatürk Cad.**, begins uphill from the town (where minibuses going to and returning from Muğla and Marmaris stop) and winds its way down and curves left. After the curve the pharmacy **Gökova Eczanesi** is on the right side of Atatürk Cad. The owner will open it after hours if medication is urgently needed. (☎ 243 53 00; after hours ☎ 243 57 99. Open daily 8am-9pm.) Also on Atatürk Cad., the very helpful **Mepar Tour Office** functions as the tourist office and travel agent, distributing free maps and providing an English-language book exchange. (☎ 243 55 51, fax 243 55 56. Open daily 7:30am-9:30pm.) There are **no banks or ATMs** in the town, but it is possible to change money at the jewelery store next to Mepar Tours (open daily 9am-9pm). The **PTT,** 100m down from Mepar, on the left, offers basic mail and phone services. (☎ 243 51 42. Open daily 8am-6pm.) **Postal code:** 48650.

Farther down Atatürk Cad., a small road on the left leads to the **National Forest** picnic and camping area. Atatürk Cad. continues for 2km to **Çinar Beach,** which is less crowded than the Akyaka public beach. The roads to the left before the *jandarma* and PTT run downhill to Akyaka's **public beach** and waterfront. The beach and the waterfront road has a few restaurants, cafeterias, bars, and souvenir shops.

▐ ACCOMMODATIONS. Because many pensions in Akyaka cater to (mostly Turkish) families, they often have kitchens or apartment-style layouts. Rooms are scarce in summer, so call ahead. Just five minutes from the beach, the **Murat Pension,** 14 Karanfil Sok., is reachable by turning left off Atatürk Cad. before the *jandarma,* walking all the way down the hill and turning left again across from the bars and restaurants; the pension is at the end of the road, on the left behind iron gates. Murat offers seven lovely rooms with wooden floors, a 3rd-floor guest kitchen, and mosquito-net windows; baths are shared. (☎ 243 52 79. Closed Nov.-Apr. Sept.-Oct. $5 per person; May-Aug. $6.50 per person.) On Atatürk Cad. across from Mepar Tours, **Server Pansiyon,** has six apartments (for 3-4 people) with modern bath, fully equipped kitchen, incredible stained wood ceilings, and tile floors. (☎ 243 54 97; fax 243 55 70. $25 per apartment per night.) To reach Akyaka's campground, **Gökova Orman Kampı,** go down Atatürk Cad. past the PTT and *jandarma* 400m to the left-side gates (always open) that lead to the picnic and camping area. There's overnight camping farther up in the forest. The campground has communal showers, toilets, electricity, and a restaurant. Bring your own gear. (☎ 243 50 35. $3.25 per tent or caravan with up to 4 people; bungalow $25.)

▐▐ FOOD AND ENTERTAINMENT. Akyaka's culinary offerings include plenty of steak and kebap ($3) places in the village center, fresh fish in picturesque settings by the river, and standard variations on Turkish and European cuisine in seaside cafeterias. Nightlife is easygoing. The scenery at **Halil'nin Yeri** is downright gorgeous, especially with the warm lamplight in the evenings; water babbles, ducks quack, and tall green reeds blow right next to your table. To get there from the Marmaris-Muğla road, turn left downhill after the pharmacy and walk 200m. (☎ 243 51

73. Cold dishes $1.50; grilled meats $3-4; fresh fish $11-22; wine $8-20 per bottle. Open daily 11am-1am.) The casual atmosphere and outdoor seating at **Mavi Sofra-2**, Nergiz Sok., is lovely on a summer night. From Atatürk Cad., turn left before the *jandarma*, follow the road downhill, and turn right at the bottom. (☎243 59 31. Tomato or eggplant kebap $4; steak $5; *pide* $2.50. Open daily 10am-3am.) Next to the Umut Restaurant, the **Caretta Bar** is a rustic, friendly bar playing Turkish and foreign music for a mostly local Turkish crowd. (☎243 59 31. Beer $1.20; *rakı* $2; cocktails $3.25. Open May-Oct. daily 8pm-2am.) The **Tropix Bar,** across from Caretta, is a hip rock 'n roll joint with comfortable bamboo chairs and outdoor seating. (☎243 50 72. Beer $1.25; Japanese *sake* $5. Open daily noon-2am.)

🎦 **SIGHTS.** Enjoying the public beach, with its secluded swimming coves, is Akyaka's main pastime. The beach extends from the right of the pier to the entrance of the pine-laced National Park ($.70). The beach's sandbar extends nearly 100m into the gulf. Ask at Mepar Tours for information on guided and unguided visits, including daily boat trips to nearby islands, jeep safaris to Gökova Bay and small villages, walking tours, and a river bird-watching trip.

AEGEAN COAST

GREEK ISLANDS

RHODES RODOS

> **RHODES CODES. 0241** for the northern half of the island; **0244** south of Kolymbia on the east; **0246** south of Kalavarda on the west.

Though Rhodes is the undisputed tourist capital of the Dodecanese, its sheer size shelters the centuries-old customs, natural resources, and serene escapes of the interior and smaller coastal towns. Sandy beaches stretch along the east coast, jagged cliffs skirt the west, and green mountains freckled with villages fill the interior; resort towns dominate the north. Kamiros, Ialyssos, and Lindos show the clearest evidence of the island's classical past, while medieval fortresses slumber in the City of Rhodes and in Monolithos.

CITY OF RHODES   ☎0241

The winding streets of the City of Rhodes blend medieval and Hellenistic architecture in stone and pebbles. The City of Rhodes was born in 408 BC when three city-states combined; it has been the island's capital for 20 centuries. The City of Rhodes's twisty layout and charming harbor have made it one of the most beautiful cities of the ancient world, and it remains regal today. Remnants of the 14th-century occupation by the Knights of St. John—a surreal palace and the grand fortress surrounding the Old Town—still lend the city a note of strangeness.

◤🛈 ORIENTATION AND PRACTICAL INFORMATION

The city is divided into two districts: the **New Town,** stretching to the north and west, and the **Old Town** below it, within the medieval fortress walls. All international and most domestic ferries use the **Commercial Harbor** outside the Old Town. **Mandraki,** the New Town's more traditional Greek island waterfront, docks private yachts, hydrofoils, and excursion boats. Beaches are to the north, beyond Mandraki, and along the city's west coast. The tourist office, both bus stations, and a taxi stand are in **Pl. Rimini,** beneath the fortress's turrets at the junction of the Old and New Towns. To get there from the small fishing and excursion boat-lined Mandraki, head a block inland keeping the park on the New Town side to your left. The New Town is a mecca for nightlife; **Orfanidou** has been popularly dubbed **Bar Street.** Schedules for ferries, Dolphins, and buses are at the EOT. Summer moped rental places are common throughout town, but the bumpy cobblestone Old Town roads are dangerous on a moped, especially since locals drive extremely fast. Be careful.

Ferries serve: **Agios Nikolaos,** Crete (1 per week, 6200dr); **Haifa,** Israel (36hr., 1 per week, 33,500dr); **Iraklion,** Crete (1 per week, 6200dr); **Kalymnos** (1-2 per day, 4300dr); **Kastellorizo** (3 per week, 2000dr); **Kos** (2-3 per day, 4000dr); **Leros** (1 per day, 4700dr); **Limassol,** Cyprus (17hr., 1 per week, 20,500dr); **Mykonos** (1 per week, 6800dr); **Paros** (1 per week, 6900dr); **Patmos** (1-2 per day, 5400dr); **Piraeus** (1-4 per day, 9000dr); **Samos** (2 per week, 6500dr); **Santorini** (1 per week, 5100dr); **Sitia,** Crete (1 per week, 5950dr); **Symi** (4 per week, 2000dr); and **Thessaloniki** (1 per week, 14,600dr). Most ferries have student discounts. Daily excursions from Mandraki Port go to: **Kos** (round-trip 14,000dr); **Lindos** (2hr., 1 per day, round-trip 5000dr); and **Symi** and **Panormitis Monastery** (round-trip 4000dr). **Bus** stations lie on opposite sides of Papagou at Pl. Rimini. The **East station** is served by **KTEL** (☎27 706, 75 134; fax 24 268), with service to: **Archangelos** (14 per day 6:50am-11pm, 600dr); **Faliraki** (20 per day 6:50am-9pm, 450dr); **Kolymbia Beach** (8 per day 8:15am-7:30pm, 600dr); **Lindos** (13 per day 8:30am-6pm, 1000dr); and **Pefkos** (6 per day

8:15am-6pm, 1100dr). The **West station** is served by **RODA** (☎26 300), and runs to: **Kalavarda** (9 per day 5am-9:20pm, 600dr); **Kalithea** and **Calypso** (34 per day 6:45am-11pm, 450dr); **Kamiros** (1 per day 1:30pm, 1000dr); **Monolithos** (1 per day, 1400dr); **Paradisi Airport** (27 per day 5am-11:30pm, 450dr); **Petaloudes** (9:30 and 11:10am, 1000dr); and **Theologos** (13 per day 5am-9:20pm, 420dr). Find **taxis** (☎27 666) in Pl. Rimini, and rent a moped from **Mandar Moto**, Zephiros 3 (☎34 576, 30 665), in the Old Town. Take Sokratous to Pl. Hippokratous and continue on Aristotelous until Pl. Evraion Martiron. (Mopeds 4000-7000dr per day. Open 8am-11pm.)

Collect incredibly helpful advice, brochures, and lodgings from the **Greek National Tourist Office (EOT)** (☎23 255/655), up Papagou a few blocks from Pl. Rimini at the intersection of Makariou. (Open M-F 7:30am-3pm.) Many **banks** are in the New Town, few in the Old Town; **ATMs** are widespread throughout both. **Ionian Bank,** Pl. Symi 4 (☎27 434), offers currency exchange. (Open M-Th 8am-2pm, F 8am-1:30pm, Sa 8:30am-1pm.) The **police** (☎23 294), on Eth. Dodekanission, 1 block behind the post office, are open 24hr; the **Tourist Police:** (☎27 423 or 23 329), in the GNTO building, speak English. The 24hr. **Port Authority** and Central Harbor Master (☎22 220 or 28 888), are on Mandraki just left of the post office, and have complete boat schedules. **Minoan Palace,** Ir. Polytechniou 13 (☎20 210), at corner of G. Efstathiou in the New Town, has **internet access** for 1000dr per hr., minimum 30min. (Open 9:30am-2am.)

ACCOMMODATIONS

Pensions are scattered about the narrow pebbled paths around Omirou Street in the quiet, charming Old Town, the preferred resting place for most travelers. Mike himself will treat you to a cheap room, Greek hospitality, and his own live renditions of familiar songs at **Mama's Pension,** Menekleous 28, off Sokratous, directly above Mike's Taverna. (☎25 359. Dorms 2500dr per bed; doubles 6000dr.) Animated Stathis welcomes all—travelers, tourists, families—to quiet, spacious rooms at **Pension Stathis,** Omirou 60. (☎24 357. French, Italian, and English spoken. Nightly folk music from nearby theater. Laundry 1200dr. Dorms 2500dr; singles 6000dr; doubles 6000-8000dr.) **Apollo Rooms,** Omirou 28C, is a great budget accommodation with a courtyard ideal for meeting fellow travelers; just grab any room if the owners are absent. (☎32 003 or 63 398. Simple rooms with shared baths 2500dr.) The bunk beds of **Hotel Andreas,** Omirou 28D, are ideal for families or groups. Laundry, international telephone, and internet access in rooms are included. (☎34 156; fax 74 285. Doubles 7000dr, with bath 9000dr; triples with bath 12,000dr; quads with bath 14,000dr.) The New Town is rather charmless, but affordable pensions dot the narrow streets of Rodiou, Dilberaki, Kathopouli, and Amarandou. A nice couple owns the **New Village Inn,** Konstantopedos 10. The open-air corridors lead to exceptional rooms around a tiled courtyard. (☎34 937. Singles 5000dr; doubles 8000dr.) **Hotel Capitol,** Dilberaki 65-67, has quiet, spacious rooms with private baths in the character-rich old home of Rhodes's mayor. (☎62 016 or 74 154. Singles 7000dr; doubles 8000dr; triples 12,000dr; quads 14,000dr.)

FOOD

In the Old Town, the food tends to be mediocre, the waiters aggressive, and the prices high. The New Town cafes are similarly overpriced, but a burgeoning expat community has brought with it a sophisticated international palate. Try the exquisite traditional Greek food in giant-size portions at **Yiannis,** Sokratous-Platonos 41, just off Sokratous away from the New Town. Post-meal, relax with a complementary offering of watermelon. (*Stifado, keftedes,* or special *mousaka* 1100-1800dr. Elliniko plate feeds three, 2800dr. ☎36 535. Open 10am-midnight.) The covert location makes the gastronomic gem that is **L'Auberge Bistro,** Praxileous 21, even more worthwhile. From the synagogue, walk south on Perikleous; take your 1st right, then 2nd left. (Pair of starters 600-1200dr; entrees 1800-2500dr. ☎34 292.) The local grilling house **Niohorio,** I. Kazouli 29, serves the basics; carnivores will love it. (*Gyros* 250dr, *souvlaki* 1200dr, sausages 600dr, meatballs 600dr. ☎35 116. Open noon-midnight.)

NIGHTLIFE AND ENTERTAINMENT

Nightlife focuses around Militado street, off Apellou in the Old Town. The streets are so stuffed with partiers that walking is nearly impossible; trying to get into bars is no easier. The atmosphere is friendly, as the locals all seem to know each other. The **Cafe Havana/Theater Bar,** 9 Militadou (☎0944 314 724 or 0932 278 587), one block south of Sokratous, does double duty: try the stinging *Scorpio* (1500dr).

The only thing skeezier than New Town cafes are the Romeos of **Bar Street** (as Orfanidou is known), their hands slithering indiscriminately around unsuspecting women. Nightlife here is neither shy nor tame. Popular bars and clubs are scattered throughout the New Town, but crowds flock to Bar Street; full bars sell expensive drinks, while empty bars will cut deals. The three rooms of the **Colorado Pub,** Orfanidou 57 (☎75 120), cover all moods. Live bands, a smashing club atmosphere, and a mellow pub, are all smashed together here; there's a 1500dr cover charge. **Scorpio,** Orfanidou 28 (☎22 109), has one of the liveliest dance floors until the wee hours of morning. Take advantage of their specials like 4 shots of tequila for 1000dr. Entrance 1500dr. Walk the plank to enter the bizarre, Disneyesque piratescape of **The Blue Lagoon,** 25 Martiou 2 (☎76 072). It opens at 8:30am, just in time for your morning poolside beer; don't miss the Blue Lagoon Special (1800dr). **La Scala,** a sprawling complex southwest of town by the beachside Rodos Palace Hotel in Ixia, is the king of Rhodes's nightclubs, accompanied by covers fit for royalty. Strap on your heels and shorten your skirts if you hope to fit in. Watch for special party nights. **St. Francis Church** (☎23 605), at Dimokratias and Filellinon, echoes with sublime weekly organ recitals (W 9pm). Nearby **Rodon** shows new flicks and subtitled classics (1200dr).

SIGHTS

Few islands are known for a sight you'll have to imagine; Rhodes is one of them. The wonder of the ancient world, called the **Colossus of Rhodes,** a 35m bronze statue of Helios astride the harbor entrance at Mandraki, leaves no earthly trace today. Legend has it that the Colossus toppled in a 237 BC earthquake. Two bronze deer are now frozen right where a colossal foot would have crushed them. A new Colossus is in the works, in an effort to make Rhodes a worldwide wonder again.

OLD TOWN. The streets of the Old Medieval Town (constructed by the Knights of St. John) are now labeled with bronze plaques and packed with the touristy stores of the poor imitation of the site's former Ottoman bazaar. Upon conquering the island, the Knights redecorated the capital city, replacing Hellenistic ruins with medieval forts and castles. The tall, square, hilltop tower, attributed to Grand Master Pierre d'Aubusson, marks the entrance to the **Palace of the Grand Master.** With 300 rooms, moats, drawbridges, huge watchtowers, and colossal battlements, the palace survived a long Ottoman siege in 1522, only to be devastated in 1856 by the explosion of 300-year-old ammunition in a depot across the street. The citadel was restored (and embellished) by 20th-century Italians determined to outdo the Knights; many floors now bear mosaics taken from Kos. The two outstanding exhibits on the north and southwest sides of the ground floor use archaeological findings and visual aids to tell a detailed version of Rhodes's extensive history. *(☎23 359, 75 674, 34 719. Open Tu-Su 8am-7pm, M noon-7pm. 1200dr, students 600dr.)* For a bird's-eye view of the fortified city, take the guided walk along the city walls. *(Open Tu and Sa 2:45-8pm. 1200dr, students 600dr.)*

Dominating **Pl. Argykastrou** with its beautiful halls and courtyards, the former **Hospital of the Knights** has been reborn as an **Archaeological Museum.** Its treasures include the exquisite first century BC *Aphrodite Bathing* and the 4th-century *Apollo.* *(☎27 674. Open Tu-Su 8:30am-2:30pm. 800dr, students and seniors 400dr.)* The **Avenue of the Knights,** or Ipoton, slopes uphill near the museum, and was the main boulevard of the city 500 years ago. A Byzantine fountain burbles at the center of Pl. Argykastrou. The 14th-century **Palace of Armeria,** now the **Archaeological Insti-**

tute, is on the right side of the *plateia*. Connected to the palace is the **Museum of Decorative Arts.** *(Open Tu-Su 8:30am-2:40pm, 6:45pm in the summer. 500dr.)* **Pl. Museum** is after the low archway; to its left is the **Church of St. Mary,** an 11th-century Byzantine building that became a Gothic cathedral by the time the Knights of St. John were through with it. Most of its frescoes were obliterated when the Ottomans converted it into the Enderoum Mosque. The Italians then re-converted the mosque to a church; it's now an **icon museum.** *(Open Tu-Su 8:30am-3pm. 500dr, students 300dr.)* The **Inn of the Tongue of England** is a 1919 copy of its 1483 predecessor, destroyed in a defensive battle; the Order of the Knights of St. John of Jerusalem consisted of seven different religious orders, called "tongues" because each spoke a different language. Their inns are named for the home country of their language. To the right inside Eleftherias Gate, at the base of the Mandraki, is the contemporary collection of the **Municipal Art Gallery.** *(Open M-Sa 8am-2pm. 500dr.)* Behind the ruined 3rd-century BC **Temple of Aphrodite** in Pl. Symi stands the 16th-century **Inn of the Tongue of Auvergne,** with an Aegean-style staircase on the facade.

Evidence of the city's Ottoman era is clearest in **Pl. Kleovoulou.** A walk down **Orfeos,** better known as the **Plane Tree Walk,** passes a large **clock tower,** to the highest viewpoint in the Old Town. In Ottoman days, the Old Town housed Muslims and Jews, while Christians lived outside its walls. Climbing the tower leads you to a small cafe. *(Open 9am-11pm. 1000dr includes a drink at the bar.)* The 19th-century **Mosque of Süleyman,** below the clock tower. The site's original mosque was built after Sultan Süleyman the Magnificent captured Rhodes in 1522. You can view the mosque from its exterior or from the clock tower. The **Turkish library** opposite the mosque houses 15th- and 16th-century Persian and Arabic manuscripts. *(Open 10am-1pm and 4-7pm. Donation expected.)* The 250-year-old baths and **hamam** in Pl. Arionos are worth a peek. *(☎27 739. Open Tu 1-6pm, W-F 11am-6pm, Sa 8am-6pm. 500dr.)* **Pl. Martyron Evreon** (Square of the Jewish Martyrs) lies at the heart of the old Jewish Quarter. Jewish refugees from the Spanish Inquisition added a Spanish flair to Old Town architecture. In 1943, 2000 Jews were taken from this square to Nazi concentration camps. Down Dossiadou is the **Shalom Synagogue,** restored by the 50 Jewish survivors of the war. Ask Lucia (who lives above it) to contact the caretaker, Mr. Soviano, to get in. *(Services F 5pm; dress modestly.)*

NEW TOWN AND MANDRAKI. If you're not blinded by the flashing display of consumer culture, you'll find stately Italian architecture throughout the modern business district. The bank, town hall, post office, and National Theater are among the Mussolini-inspired stone buildings presiding over wide Eleftherias. Opposite them is the majestic **Governor's Palace** and a cathedral built by the Italians in 1925. The cathedral replicates St. John's Church, leveled in an 1856 explosion. Three defunct **windmills** stand halfway along the harbor's pier. The **Fortress of St. Nicholas,** at the end of the pier, guarded the harbor from 1464 to the end of the Second World War. Opposite the cemetery is **Villa Kleovoulos,** which housed author **Lawrence Durrell** during his appointment with the Foreign Office from 1945-1947. Named after Süleyman's admiral, who died trying to capture Rhodes from the Knights of St. John in 1522, the **Mosque of Mourad Reis** recalls the Ottomans. The small, domed building inside is his mausoleum. Turbans indicate men's graves, flowers indicate women's. Greece's only **aquarium,** also a marine research center for the Dodecanese, shows creatures of the Aegean depths at the northern tip of the island. *(☎27 308 or 78 320. Open 9am-9pm. 600dr, students 400dr.)*

⬛ DAYTRIPS FROM THE CITY OF RHODES

Excursion boats trace the beach-filled coast from the City of Rhodes to Lindos, leaving the city in the morning and returning in the afternoon; it's a great way to escape the crowded beaches of the western coast. The boats make several stops, including Faliraki. Schedules and prices are posted at the dock along the lower end of the Mandraki (starting at 3500dr). **Waterhoppers** (☎38 146) and **Dive Med Centres** (☎61 115) offer **scuba diving** lessons and trips to Kalithea (lessons 12,000dr; non-diving passengers 6000dr), as well as trips for certified divers. **Rodini Park** is a forested area with streams, trails, a restaurant, and some small, harmless animals left over from the park's days as a zoo. Bus #3 runs to the park regularly. The snorkeler's heaven of **Kalithea,** 10km south of the City of Rhodes, has a deserted spa at the beach cove's meager snack bar (not-so-fresh cheese pie 350dr; soda 250dr).

FALIRAKI Φαλιρακη. Faliraki, 15km south of the City of Rhodes, ain't for the faint of heart. Beach bunnies hop between the sand and the bars all day long. The bars—named for alcohol-induced impotence (e.g. The Brewer's Droop) and advertising wall-to-wall foam parties—attract a wild crowd and pack the city's rooms. With each sunset, the sunburned masses migrate inland from the beach to uniformly priced beer (600-700dr) at jumping bars on Ermou; later, a second exodus flees to popular dance clubs. **Jimmy's Pub** (☎85 643) inland on Ermou, is a British bar with Guinness on tap; additional stimuli include soul music and TVs throughout the bar. Head on up to the cover-free club above it, popular after midnight. **The Brewer's Droop,** a few doors down from Jimmy's Pub, serves up daily movies, frozen margaritas (choose from banana, pineapple, melon, or strawberry; all 1500dr), and the occasional frozen orgasm ("screaming" or "multiple"). The bass starts bumping after midnight when pub crowds migrate to clubs. The most convenient option for Ermou indulgers is **Sinners,** a popular stop-over for house and techno music's biggest names. (Cover 2000dr, includes one drink.) Big, new, posh, and friendly **Millennium,** set back in a shopping center on the City of Rhodes-Faliraki, is quickly becoming Faliraki's most popular dance club. (Cover 1800dr includes a drink. ☎86 603.) *(There are two main bus stops, one on the City of Rhodes-Lindos road (14 per day, 450dr) and one on the waterfront to Lindos (14 per day, 800dr). Faliraki is a base for boat trips to Kos (11,000dr), Lindos (4000dr), and Symi (5000dr). Ermou is the main thoroughfare connecting the beach with the City of Rhodes-Lindos highway.)*

LINDOS Λινδος. With whitewashed houses clustered beneath a castle-capped acropolis, Lindos is perhaps the most picturesque town on Rhodes; writers, poets, painters, and professors congregate here. Charm like this hasn't remained a secret, however, and in summer, the streets of Lindos make the City of Rhodes look like a desert island. The crowds, astronomical prices, room shortage, and notorious heat make Lindos better outside July and August. Lindos is pedestrian-only: all traffic stops at **Pl. Eleftherias,** where you'll find **bus** and **taxi** stations. Buses to and from Lindos fill quickly, so arrive early. Past the **Telebank** 24-hour **ATM, Acropolis** street leads through the eastern part of town and up to the acropolis. **Apostolou Pavlou,** another main street, runs perpendicular to Acropolis just past the **Church of the Assumption of Madonna,** whose stone belfry rises above the middle of town. Lindos's ancient **acropolis** stands on sheer cliffs 125m above town, caged by scaffolding and the walls of a Crusader fortress; from the tip-top of the acropolis, the lowest point in the city is visible. Excavations between 1902 and 1912 yielded everything from 5000-year-old Neolithic tools to a plaque inscribed by a priest of Athena in 99 BC that lists the dignitaries who visited Athena's Temple—Hercules, Helen of Troy, Menelaus, Alexander the Great, and the King of Persia. The winding path up to the acropolis is veiled in lace tablecloths sold by local women, making for a surreal, frilly ascent. Right before the final incline, don't miss the ancient Greek *trireme*, which Pythokreitos carved into the cliffside as a symbol of Lindos's tie to the sea. The staircase-strewn, daunting 13th-century **Crusader castle** looms over the site entrance. The arcade, built around 200 BC at the height of Rhodes's glory, originally consisted of 42 columns laid out in the shape of the Greek letter Π. The large stone blocks arranged against the back wall upheld bronze statues long since melted down. The remains of the **Temple of the Lindian Athena,** built by 6th century BC tyrant Kleoboulos, appear at the top of the steps. The building is one of the few ancient temples with inner walls still fairly intact; colonnades flank both sides. Kleoboulos's tomb, inscribed with his timeless maxim, "Nothing in excess," is across the way. At the southwest foot of the acropolis are the remains of the **ancient theater.** As you leave the castle, make a U-turn to your left to reach the imposing **Doric Stoa,** whose 13 restored columns dominate the entire level. Donkey rides to the acropolis aren't worth the fare (1000dr one way), as the ten minute walk isn't strenuous. A cave called the **Voukopion,** on the north side of the rock face (visible from the donkey path), may have been used for special sacrifices that could not be performed in the acropolis. The cave probably dates from the 9th century BC, and was later transformed into a sanctuary for Athena by the Dorians. (☎31 258. Open M 12:30-6:40pm, Tu-Sa 8am-6:40pm. 1200dr, students 600dr. Ask for the free pamphlet on the history and explanation of the layout.) (*Buses run to: Faliraki (16 per day 7am to 7pm, 9500dr); Kolymbia Beach (3 per day, 700dr); Pefkos (9 per day, 300dr); City of Rhodes (16 per day, 1000dr); and Calypso (3 per day, 750dr). Excursion boats from Rhodes depart at 9am and return at 5pm, hitting City of Rhodes and Turkey, among other pit stops, as they travel along the coast. Pallas Travel, on Acropolis, has a free map, exchanges currency, and arranges excursions. (☎31 494; fax 31 595. Open M-Sa 8am-11pm, Su 9am-1pm and 5-10pm, in summer.)*)

EPTA PIGES. Eleven kilometers south of Faliraki, just before Kolymbia, a road to the right leads down 3km to Epta Piges. Constructed by Italians seeking potable water for nearby Kolymbia, the aqueduct now delights thrill-seekers, who slide through 150m of pitch-black tunnel. Laughers and shriekers alike end up in a large, picturesque freshwater pool; if the destination sounds nicer than the journey, take the path next to the tunnel that is used to return from the pool. A streamside taverna with peacocks sits at the entrance before the tunnel. (*Ask a Lindos/Archangelos bus driver to let you off at the tunnel.*) Continue inland past Epta Piges to visit the 13th- and 15th-century frescoes of the Byzantine **Church of Agios Nikolaos Fountoucli,** 3km past Eleousa. (*Three buses per day stop at Eleousa on the way to the City of Rhodes.*)

KAMIROS. Though the smallest of the three ancient cities of the Rhodian State, Kamiros far surpasses Ialyssos and the City of Rhodes in intricacy and preservation. People have lived here since Mycenaean times, but after a devastating earthquake in 226 BC, the city was reconstructed with a Hellenistic layout and design. The cistern on the north side of the temple dates to the 5th or 6th century BC, and the stone stoa (shaped like the Greek letter Π) is from at least the 2nd century. Visit the precinct of Athena Kamiras on the acropolis to sense the city's checkerboard layout. (*Take a bus from Kamiros to the City of Rhodes (2 per day 10am, 1:30pm; 1100 dr).* ☎40 037, 75 674. Open Tu-Su 8am-6:40pm. 800dr, students 400dr, EU students free.*)

VALLEY OF BUTTERFLIES. Seven kilometers inland from the village of **Theologos, Petaloudes,** or the **Valley of Butterflies,** is a popular visiting spot with or without the company of the little fluttering guys. During the summer, Jersey tiger moths flock to the valley's Styrax trees, attracted to their resin (also used to make incense) and the area's unique shadiness. While lounging away their final days in the trees, the moths fast, living only on water and body fat to conserve energy for rigorous mating sessions. After the deed is done, they die of starvation. The valley is accessible from an entrance next to an old mill, or from the main entrance farther uphill. The trail winds around a stream that collects in lily-covered pools and glides under little bridges. Avoid clapping and stomping to force the moths to fly, as other foolio visitors do: noise interrupts the moths' action. (☎81 801. 750dr, students half price.)

KOS KWS

The booming nightclubs and packed bars of modern Kos gloss over the past and live in the now. Famous figures in literature and medicine have lounged on these beaches: **Asclepius,** god of healing; **Hippocrates,** father of modern medicine and the Hippocratic oath; the poet **Theocritus,** and his teacher **Philetas.** In ancient times, Kos was a major trading power with a population of 160,000—eight times that of today. An episcopal seat of the Byzantine Empire, the island became a pirate target. The Knights of St. John arrived in 1315, seizing control and turning Kos into an outpost. Since then, it's passed under Italian, German, and British governments. Rivaling the City of Rhodes in numbers of visitors, Kos draws a young, loud, intoxicated crowd. Don't be dismayed by the raucous bars and mammoth hotels along the lengthy stretches of golden beach: there are also beautiful escapes.

GREEK ISLANDS

KOS TOWN

☎ **0242**

In Kos Town, the minarets of Ottoman mosques spike above grand Italian mansions, the massive walls of a Crusader fortress, and scattered ruins from the Archaic, Classical, Hellenistic, and Roman eras. The combination of ancient, medieval, and modern makes Kos a historian's paradise by day, while its bars make it a dissipated hotspot by night. It's one of the most expensive towns in the Dodecanese, and package tours leave very few rooms for independent travelers.

■ ☑ ORIENTATION AND PRACTICAL INFORMATION

The dignified walls of the **Castle of the Knights of St. John** overwhelm the vista as ferries pull into the harbor of Kos Town. Walk left (facing inland) from the harbor to reach the **Avenue of Palms,** also known as **Finikon,** framed by the stately trees. Continuing along the waterfront past the Palms leads to **Vassileos Georgios** and the rocky beach alongside it. Turn right onto the Palms, follow it to the next corner of the fortress, and you'll come upon **Akti Koundouriotou,** another waterfront street that wraps around the harbor. The city bus station, boats to Turkey, travel agencies, restaurants, and Kos's thriving nightlife are all here. Branching inland off Akti Koundouriotou are the town's main arteries: **El. Venizelou** leads through a row of travel agencies into the shopping district, and **Megalou Alexandrou,** a few blocks down, heads to **Pl. Palaiologou,** the ruins of ancient Kos Town, and the inland villages. The town's other sandy beach begins near the end of Akti Koundouriotou.

Ferries run to: **Kalymnos** (1¼hr., 1-3 per day, 1400dr); **Leros** (2½hr., 1 per day, 2100dr); **Patmos** (4hr., 1-2 per day, 2800dr); **Piraeus** (11-15hr., 2-3 per day, 7500dr); and **Rhodes** (4hr., 2 per day, 3400dr). One per week goes to: **Kastellorizo** (4300dr); two per week go to: **Nisyros** (1700dr) and **Symi** (2500dr). Ferries also go to: **Tilos** (2 per week, 1900dr). Boats run to **Bodrum, Turkey** every morning (10,000-13,000dr round-trip). Turkish boats leave in the afternoon and return the next morning (8000-13,000dr round-trip). Since travel is international, prices aren't regulated by the Greek government. The **Port Authority** (☎26 594) is at the corner of Megalou Alexandrou and Akti Kountouriotou. Visitors leaving with Turkish boats requiring an overnight stay also need a visa (3000dr). **Buses** (☎22 292, fax 20 263) leave from Kleopatras near the inland end of Pavlou behind the Olympic Airways office. M-Sa to: **Asfendiou-Zia** (40min., 3 per day, 350dr); **Kardamena** (45min., 6 per day, 600dr); **Kefalos** and **Paradise** (1hr., 6 per day, 800dr); **Marmari** (35min., 11 per day, 300dr); **Mastihari** (35min., 5 per day, 550dr); **Pyli** (30min., 5 per day, 350dr); and **Tigaki** (30min., 12 per day, 350dr). Sunday schedules are reduced; schedules are listed at the stop. Buy tickets on the bus. **Local buses** leave from Akti Koundouriotou 7 (☎26 276), on the water. To: **Asclepion** (15min., 16 per day); **Lampi** (25 per day); and **Thermae** (20min., 9 per day). Fares cost 150-250dr. **Taxis** (☎22 777 or 22 333) are near the inland end of the Avenue of Palms. Rent a quality bike at **George,** P. Tsaldari 3 (☎28 480), near the port authority. (Mopeds 2500-5000dr per day, bikes 500-1000dr. Open 8am-8pm.) **Greek National Tourist Office,** on Akti Miaouli in the same building as the tourist police, provides maps, brochures, and schedules. (Open M-F 8am-8:30pm, Sa 8am-3pm.) There's a **National Bank** (☎28 167), behind the Archaeological Museum, one block inland from the water on A.P. Ioannidi. (24hr. **ATM.** Open M-Th 8am-2pm, F 8am-1:30pm.) For **emergencies,** call ☎22 100; **ambulances,** call ☎22 300; for **general information** call ☎132. The 24hr. **police** (☎22 100), on Akti Miaouli in the big yellow building by the castle, speak some English; the **tourist police** (☎22 444) are in the same place. (Open 7:30am-2pm.)

▐ ACCOMMODATIONS

Hotel vacancies are rare in summer, so start searching for rooms early. Most inexpensive places are on the right side of town if you're facing inland. It's better to seek your own room, since Kos's dock hawks are notoriously bad. The aroma of fresh jasmine from the garden won't smother you nearly as much as Sonia and Alex's hospitality will at ▨ **Pension Alexis,** Herodotou 9. If rooms are full, the proprietor will set you up with a mattress and sheets on the patio or cut you a deal at his elegant Hotel Afendoulis. View-friendly verandas and common baths. Prices are flexible, especially if you're carrying *Let's Go*. Try Sonia's famous feta omelette for breakfast (1000dr). Take the first right off Megalou Alexandrou, on the back left corner of the first intersection. (☎28 798 or 25 594. Doubles 5500-7000dr; triples 7500dr.) Traditional wood-paneled rooms surround a central courtyard at **Hotel Afendoulis,** Evrilpilou 1, right down Vas. Georgiou practically on the beach. All have private baths. Ask about the cheaper cellar rooms. (☎/fax 25 321 or 25 797. Breakfast 1000dr. Doubles 7500-9000dr.) **Kos Camping** is 3km southeast from the center and accessible by public transport, in a shady, well-maintained setting right across from the beach. (☎23 910 or 23 275. Mini-market, bar, laundry facilities, cooking room, rental assistance, and security boxes. 1750dr per person. Your own tent 800dr, rental 1000dr. Buses run every 30min.)

🍴 FOOD

The fruit and veggie **market** in Pl. Eleftherias, on Vas. Pavlou, inside a large yellow building with a picture of grapes over the doors, is touristy and expensive; mini-markets have cheaper fruit. (Open M-F 7am-9pm, Sa 7am-6pm, Su 10am-2pm.) A true diamond in the rough, ▧ **Ampavris,** on E. Georgiou, is a rare authentic restaurant. Take the road past the Casa Romana; it's about a 15min. walk from town. (Stuffed flower buds 900dr, entrees 1000-1800dr. ☎25 696.) **Hellas,** Psaron 7, at corner of Amerikis, serves huge portions of tasty Greek dishes in a service-friendly atmosphere. (Lamb *kleftiko* 1500dr, *moussaka* 1200dr. Vegetarian options. Open noon-1am.) If you're looking for that hidden local taverna, seek out **Andonis Taverna,** on the corner of Amerikis and Paleo Polemiston, with its excellent traditional dishes and large portions. Hospitality reigns; try the *mekri meze* for 1700dr, which serves two. (Main dishes 1500-2000dr. ☎25 645.) **Nick the Fisherman,** Averof 21, at the corner of Alikarnasou, brings daily catches straight to your plate at the best *psarotaverna* in town. Ask for Larry's friendly service. (Mussels 1600dr, sea-urchins 1600dr; entrees from 1500-2000dr. Open 8am-midnight.)

🎵 NIGHTLIFE

Most bars are in two districts. The first is around **Exarhia** (a.k.a. **Bar Street,** between Akti Koundouriotou and the ancient *agora*, around **Vas. Pavlou**). Beers are 800-1000dr, cocktails 2000dr. Most places open at 9pm, fill by 11pm, and rock until dawn. The second district, waterfront **Porfiriou,** is cheaper and more subdued, but equally drunken. **Orfeas** (☎25 713), on the corner of Fenaretis and Vas. Georgiou, shows American movies (2000dr). Kitsch (peanut-vending machines) meets de rigeur (elegant candles) at ▧ **Fashion Club,** Kanari 2, by the dolphin statue rotary. This is Kos's most ostentatious club, but it's not nearly as pretentious as the bouncers would have you think. (2500dr cover includes a drink. No cover for the cafe in front. ☎22 592.) The former bathhouse of ▧ **Hamam Club** (☎28 323) near the *agora*, next to the taxi station in Pl. Diagoras, now soothes you with aural massage: live, outdoor acoustic sets play until midnight over a hopping dance club floor. Enjoy crazy drinks made by an equally nutty barman in one of the one-time private bathing rooms. Opposite the beach, **Heaven,** on Zouroudi, has a cabana theme. A big, loud, popular outdoor disco. (2000dr cover includes first drink and is sometimes waived early in the evening. W night foam parties. ☎23 874.)

👁 SIGHTS

The run-down field of ruins bounded by Nafklirou, Hippocrates, and the waterfront was the **Roman agora;** it's now dominated by a population of sunbathing cats. The remains of a **Temple of Aphrodite** and the more impressive 2nd-century AD **Temple of Hercules** lie beside two Roman roads: the **Cardo** (axis), perpendicular to Grigoriou, and the **Decumana** (broadest), parallel to Grigoriou and intersecting Cardo. Nearby, you'll find an ancient gymnasium, a Roman swimming pool, and an early Christian basilica built over a Roman bath. At the end of the Decumana, the wood-sheltered 3rd-century AD **House of Europa** has a mosaic floor depicting Europa's abduction by that mean bully Zeus. The **odeum,** a well-preserved Roman theater, lies across the street. The 3rd-century AD **Casa Romana,** uncovered by an Italian archaeologist in 1933, is down Grigoriou. The meager ruins of a **Temple of Dionysus** stand opposite the Casa Romana. *(Open 24hr. Free.)*

Invading Knights of St. John built the massive 15th-century **castle.** The once-movable bridge marks the connecting entrance from the Square of Hippocrates, and linked the island castle to the mainland. Destroyed by an earthquake in 1495, the fortress was rebuilt by Grand Master Pierre d'Aubusson. In the 16th century, elaborate double walls and inner moats resisted Ottoman raids; now, it's a fantastically preserved example of medieval architecture. *(Take the bridge from Pl. Platanou across Finikis. ☎28 326. Ask for the helpful pamphlet available at the door. Open Tu-Su 8am-2pm. 800dr, students 400dr.)* The gigantic **Plane Tree of Hippocrates,** allegedly planted by the great physician 2400 years ago, has grown to an enormous 12m diameter in Pl. Platanou. It's alluring to envision Hippocrates teaching and writing beneath its noble foliage; it's deflating to realize that the tree is only 500 years old. A spring beside it leads toward an ancient sarcophagus used by the Ottomans as a cistern for the **Hadji Hassan Mosque.** Behind the tree, is the monumental **Town Hall,** originally the Italian Governor's Palace. The most impressive Ottoman structure is the **Defterdar Mosque** in Pl. Eleftherias. Nearby, on Diakou, is the abandoned art deco **Synagogue of Kos,** in use until the Second World War. The city's Byzantine **Greek Orthodox Cathedral** looms large on the corner of Korai and Ag. Nikolaou. Near the Casa Romana are the ruins of an even older (5th century BC) and more striking Hellenic mansion. *(Open Tu-Su 8:30am-2:30pm. 600dr, students and seniors 300dr.)*

Hellenistic and late Roman sculptures dominate the island's finds at the **Archaeological Museum.** A celebrated statue, found at the Kos Odeon and presumably of Hippocrates, stands in the northwest room. A 2nd-century AD Roman mosaic in the central courtyard depicts Hippocrates and a colleague entertaining the god Asclepius. Statues of Dionysos, Artemis, and Aphrodite occupy the North room and Atrium. *(In Pl. Eleftherias. ☎28 326. Open Tu-Su 8:30am-3pm. 800dr, students 400dr.)*

◪ DAYTRIPS FROM KOS TOWN

ASCLEPION Ασκληπειον. The ancient sanctuary of **Asclepion** devotes itself to the healer god. In the 5th century BC, **Hippocrates** opened the world's first medical school here to encourage the development of a precise medical science. Combining priestly techniques with his own, Hippocrates made Kos the foremost medical center in ancient Greece, and many present-day doctors travel here to take their Hippocratic oaths. Carved into a hill overlooking Kos Town, the Aegean, and Asia Minor, the second- and third-century BC complex contained three levels. A sacred forest of cypress and pine trees still adjoins the site. Inside, you'll find 2nd-century AD Roman baths. The three stacked levels, called *andirons*, remain: the lowest holds a complex of 3rd-century AD Roman baths and a preserved cistern. Climb the 3rd-century BC steps to the remarkable second *andiron* and the elegant columns of the 2nd-century AD **Temple of Apollo** and the 4th-century BC **Minor Temple of Asclepius.** The 60-step climb to the third *andiron* leads to the forested remnants of the **Main Temple of Asclepius** and an overview of the site, Kos Town, and the Turkish coast opposite. *(4km west of Kos Town. Take the bus in summer (15min., 16 per day), or a moped. Follow the sign west off the main road, and go as straight as you can. Taxis are 500dr. ☎28 763. Open June-Sept. Tu-Su 8am-7pm. 800dr, students 400dr.)*

RURAL KOS. Claustrophobes will be pleased at how quickly Kos Town's urban fracas gives way to pastoral landscapes north of town. The island's northern reaches stretch out flat, with bike-laned roads. Pedal along the main road east of town past a sandy, crowded stretch, on the way to the stinky hot springs of **Empros Thermae,** near the road's end and marked by several parked bikes and a Cantina. **Lampi Beach** is at the northernmost tip of the island. A nude beach lies between touristy Tigaki and Marmari. *(Buses run to Empros Thermae (9 per day), Lampi (34 per day), Marmari (10 per day), and Mastihari (4 per day).)* The main road from Kos Town heads 9km southwest to modern **Zipari** and the ruins of the early **Christian Basilica of St. Paul.** From there, a twisting road winds through the green foothills of the Dikeos Mountains to **Asfendiou,** five small, deserted settlements that you can hike without encountering a soul. *(Buses from Kos Town go to Asfendiou (40min., 3 per day, 350dr).)* Continue up this road to **Zia,** a delightful, refreshing little village in the forests of Mt. Dikeos with to spectacular island views and some quality wandering. **Ag. Georgios,** in the center of town, also accommodates incredible 13th and 14th-century frescos. South of **Lagoudi,** one of the prettiest of the five villages, the road becomes a narrow mule path and the hills grow wilder. Uphill 8km, you'll come to the compact **Pyli** ruins, with 14th-century frescoes in a Byzantine church-within-a-castle. *(Buses run from Kos Town (30min., 5 per day, 350dr).)* Hills, ravines, and the occasional pasture roll across southern Kos, which is edged by the best **beaches** on the island. Among the beaches stretching to Kardamena, **Camel** is mildly busy and beautiful; **Paradise** is popular; and, farther north, Hawaiian-flavored **Magic** is empty and enticingly blue. *(The bus lets off at any of the beaches.)* A few oceanside ancient columns distinguish **Kefalos,** Kos' ancient capital; head to the surrounding beaches, like picturesque **Limionas,** where you can swim and then sample a delicious harborside meal beside a sunset view at **Limionas** restaurant. (Open 10am-11pm.) A gorgeous, deserted beach stretches along the coast to **Mastihari.** ◼ **Agios Theologos,** 4km west of Kefalos, is one of the island's quietest and most drop-dead-gorgeous beaches; tiny, boulder-strewn **Kastri Island** is a short swim from the shore. Walk for an hour on the dirt path that branches to the right from the Kefalos bus stop to get there; you'll likely have the beach to yourself.

SAMOS SAMOS

Although it is perhaps the most beautiful and definitely the most touristed island in the northeast Aegean, Samos remains less frenetic than some of its island siblings, with a more adult crowd. Many see Samos as a stepping-stone to Kuşadası and the ruins of Ephesus (p. 193), but this green island has birthed architects, sculptors, poets, philosophers, and scientists. Pythagoras, Epicurus, Aesop, and Aristarchus (who called the sun the center of the universe 1800 years before Copernicus) all grew up playing on Samos's sandy beaches. The residents here cherish their sumptuous local red wine, *kokkino krasi,* more than anything else. In summer 2000, wildfires devoured much of the lush greenery on the east side of the island. Touristed areas escaped significant damage, and visitors during 2001 will likely not see any damage around Samos Town. Ancient sites around Pythagorion remain intact, showing the fires' path only in the charred brush nearby.

VATHY (SAMOS TOWN) BAQN ☎ 0273

This is one of the northeast Aegean's most appealing port cities, where palm trees shade quiet inland streets, an engaging archaeological museum stands across from a garden, and red roofs speckle the neighboring hillside of Vathy.

◼◪ **ORIENTATION AND PRACTICAL INFORMATION.** Samos Town unfurls around a crescent-shaped waterfront. **Pl. Pythagoras,** identifiable by its four large palm trees, consists of cafes, taxis, and a giant lion statue. Turn onto the side streets between the port and Pl. Pythagoras to hit the most densely packed pension neighborhood on the island. Heading along the waterfront away from the port, past Pl. Pythagoras, will take you to the **Municipal Gardens,** circled by the town's public amenities and the archaeological museum. **Ferries** go to: **Chios** (5hr., 4 per week, 2690dr); **Fourni** (2hr., 5 per week, 1800dr); **Lesvos** (8hr., 1 per week, 4090dr); **Mykonos** (6hr., 4 per week, 5100dr); **Naxos** (6hr., 4-7 per week, 4900dr) via **Paros** (4370dr); and **Piraeus** (12hr., 2-3 per day, 6700dr) via **Ikaria** (2100dr). Ferries to **Kuşadası, Turkey,** leave from Samos Town daily (1¼hr.; 8:30am and 5pm; 10,000dr for a one-way morning departure, 9000dr for a one-way afternoon departure, 11,000dr return for a daytrip). Turkish entrance **visas** must be purchased at the Turkish border by Americans ($45), British (UK£10), and Irish (IR£5), *if* they are planning to stay for more than one day. **Buses** follow the waterfront past Pl. Pythagoras, turn left onto Lekati, and go one block to the **station**. To: **Avlakia** via **Agios Konstantinos** (7 per day), **Heraion** (3 per day), **Pythagorion** (12 per day), and **Tsainadon** via **Kokkari** and **Lemonakia** (9 per day). **Taxis** (☎ 28 404), are available 24hr. in Pl. Pythagoras. Rent a moped at **Pegasus** (☎ 61 831 or 62 047), near the dock (mopeds around 5000dr; cars around 12,000dr; open 8:30am-10pm). There's a **tourist office** (☎ 28 530 or 28 582), on a side street one block before Pl. Pythagoras (open July-Aug. M-Sa 8:30am-2pm). There's a **National Bank** on the waterfront just beyond Pl. Pythagoras, with a 24hr. **ATM** (open M-Th 8am-2pm, F 8am-1:30pm). The **police** and **tourist police** (☎ 22 100), are after Pl. Pythagoras on the far right of the waterfront, facing inland; they speak some English. Check email at **Net Cafe** (☎ 22 535), on the waterfront past Pl. Pythagoras (500dr per 30min; open 9am-midnight).

⌐¡ ACCOMMODATIONS. It is advisable to call ahead during the high season. If you arrive and all the beds listed below are filled, try the pensions around **Ionia** or ask a travel agent. The cool, traditional rooms of **Pension Trova,** Kalomiris 26, have the occasional bath and balcony. Turn right at the end of the ferry dock and walk 100m along the waterfront to take a left onto E. Stamatiadou before the Hotel Aiolis. Take the second left onto Manoli Kalomiri and wrap uphill around the bend to hit Kalomiris. (☎ 27 759. Singles 4000-6000dr; doubles with bath 5500-8000dr.) Simple, 70s-era rooms center around an elegant courtyard at **Pension Avli,** Areos 2. Turn right at the end of the ferry dock, walk 100m along the waterfront, and take a left onto E. Stamatiadou before the Hotel Aiolis. Take the second right onto Manoli Kalomiri and the second left onto Areos. (☎ 22 939. Doubles 6000-7000dr. Open summer only.) The compulsively neat rooms of **Pension Dreams,** Areos 9, have fridges and baths. Some rooms' balconies rival your backyard in size. (☎ 24 350. Singles 5000-6000dr; doubles 5000-7000dr; triples 6000-7500dr.)

⌐¡⌐ FOOD AND NIGHTLIFE. Gourmands will find their time well-spent in savoring sweet Samian wine, served at all of the island's nearly indistinguishable restaurants, which otherwise offer a standard spate of traditional meals. **Gregory's,** just past the post office heading inland, is a local favorite. (Entrees 1500dr. Open noon-2:30pm and 7pm-midnight.) Similarly priced and more conveniently located is **Christos** (☎ 24 792), in Pl. Nicolaos behind Pl. Pythagoras, with outdoor seating for optimal people-watching. The most popular bar is **Escape,** a five-minute walk on the way to the Pythagoras Hotel. Come 3am, all taxis head out of town to the **Totem** discotheque. On a mountainside outside town, it escapes noise regulations.

⌐ SIGHTS. The phenomenal **Archaeological Museum** sits behind the municipal gardens. Its broad collection looks at Samos' past glory as a commercial and religious center for worshiping Hera. Finds from ancient Heraion, the temple of Hera, and other local digs are enshrined in two recently renovated buildings full of informative notes; you'll find more proof of Heraion's bygone splendor here than at the crumbled remains at the site. The first building houses intricate Laconian ivory carvings of mythological notables, and awesome statues like a colossal 5m **Kouros** from 560 BC. There's also the stunning **Geneleas group.** A nearly life-size votive offering depicting a family, it's named after its sculptor; it once graced ancient Heraion's Sacred Way. An exhibit on Hera-worship shows off remarkable offerings made to the goddess. Objects from Ancient Egypt, Cyprus, and the Near East testify to the island's extensive early trade. In the last room, a case of gorgeously nightmarish **protomes** (cauldron handles) is not to be missed. (☎ 27 469. Open Tu-Su 8:30am-3pm. 800dr, seniors and students 400dr, EU students free.) In July and August, Samos hosts fine classical and jazz concerts featuring Greek artists as part of the **Manolis Kalomiris Festival.** Contact the tourist office for a schedule of events.

The best way to keep in touch when you're traveling overseas is with **AT&T Direct®** Service. It's the easy way to call your loved ones back home from just about anywhere in the world. Just cut out the wallet guide below and use it wherever your travels take you.

For a list of AT&T Access Numbers, tear out the attached wallet guide.

AT&T

Italy ● 172-1011	**Russia (Moscow)** ▶▲●755-5042
Luxembourg + ..800-2-0111	(St. Petersbg.)▶▲● ..325-5042
Macedonia ● ..99-800-4288	**Slovakia** ▲ ..00-42-100-101
Malta 0800-890-110	**South Africa** ..0800-99-0123
Monaco ● 800-90-288	**Spain** 900-99-00-11
Morocco 002-11-0011	**Sweden** 020-799-111
Netherlands ● ..0800-022-9111	**Switzerland** ● 0800-89-0011
Norway 800-190-11	**Turkey** ● 00-800-12277
Poland ▲● ..00-800-111-1111	**Ukraine** ▲ ....8◆100-11
Portugal ▲ 800-800-128	U.A. Emirates ● 800-121
Romania ●......01-800-4288	**U.K.**.............0800-89-0011

FOR EASY CALLING WORLDWIDE

1. Just dial the AT&T Access Number for the country you are calling from.
2. Dial the phone number you're calling.   *3.* Dial your card number.

For access numbers not listed ask any operator for **AT&T Direct®** Service.
In the U.S. call 1-800-331-1140 for a wallet guide listing all worldwide AT&T Access Numbers.
Visit our Web site at: **www.att.com/traveler**
Bold-faced countries permit country-to-country calling outside the U.S.
- ● Public phones require coin or card deposit to place call.
- ▲ May not be available from every phone/payphone.
- + Public phones and select hotels.
- ◆ Await second dial tone.
- ▶ Additional charges apply when calling from outside the city.
- † Outside of Cairo, dial "02" first.
- ✕ Not available from public phones or all areas.
- ✔ Use U.K. access number in N. Ireland.

When placing an international call *from* the U.S., dial 1 800 CALL ATT.

EMEA   © 8/00 AT&T

Italy ● 172-1011	**Russia (Moscow)** ▶▲●755-5042
Luxembourg + ..800-2-0111	(St. Petersbg.)▶▲● ..325-5042
Macedonia ● ..99-800-4288	**Slovakia** ▲ ..00-42-100-101
Malta 0800-890-110	**South Africa** ..0800-99-0123
Monaco ● 800-90-288	**Spain** 900-99-00-11
Morocco 002-11-0011	**Sweden** 020-799-111
Netherlands ● ..0800-022-9111	**Switzerland** ● 0800-89-0011
Norway 800-190-11	**Turkey** ● 00-800-12277
Poland ▲● ..00-800-111-1111	**Ukraine** ▲ ....8◆100-11
Portugal ▲ 800-800-128	U.A. Emirates ● 800-121
Romania ●......01-800-4288	**U.K.**.............0800-89-0011

FOR EASY CALLING WORLDWIDE

1. Just dial the AT&T Access Number for the country you are calling from.
2. Dial the phone number you're calling.   *3.* Dial your card number.

For access numbers not listed ask any operator for **AT&T Direct®** Service.
In the U.S. call 1-800-331-1140 for a wallet guide listing all worldwide AT&T Access Numbers.
Visit our Web site at: **www.att.com/traveler**
Bold-faced countries permit country-to-country calling outside the U.S.
- ● Public phones require coin or card deposit to place call.
- ▲ May not be available from every phone/payphone.
- + Public phones and select hotels.
- ◆ Await second dial tone.
- ▶ Additional charges apply when calling from outside the city.
- † Outside of Cairo, dial "02" first.
- ✕ Not available from public phones or all areas.
- ✔ Use U.K. access number in N. Ireland.

When placing an international call *from* the U.S., dial 1 800 CALL ATT.

EMEA   © 8/00 AT&T

◪ BEACHES. Most of the northern coast of Samos is easily accessible from the road to **Karlovassi**. Built on a peninsula 10km west of Samos Town is the eminently visitable northern village of **Kokkari**. **Lemonakia Beach,** 1km west of Kokkari next to Tsamadou, and the wide white beach west of **Avlakia** are both alluring. Kokkari, Lemonakia, and Avlakia are reachable from Samos Town though the irregular KTEL bus service (7-9 buses per day). Infrequent buses (1-2 per day) shouldn't deter you from the splendid beaches of southwest Samos. A couple kilometers west of the peaceful red-roofed hamlet of **Marathokampos** is the spacious beach at **Votsalakia**. A bit farther is an even better beach at **Psili Ammos**.

◪ DAYTRIP FROM VATHY: POLYKRATES' PROJECTS. The ancient city of Pythagorion (Πυθαγορειο), once the island's capital, thrived during the 6th century BC under the reign of **Polykrates the Tyrant**. Herodotus reports that Polykrates undertook the three most daring engineering projects in the Hellenic world, among them the **Tunnel of Eupalinos**, 1500m up the hill to the north of town, in fact an underground aqueduct that diverted water from a natural spring to the city below. It may owe its misnomer to its size, which just fits a person. About 200m of damp cavern are open to visitors. To reach the tunnel, walk back inland from the bus stop in town and follow the signs. The 20min. walk to the tunnel entrance passes minor ancient ruins, rolling hills, and grazing goats. (☎61 400. Open Tu-Su 8:45am-2:45pm, last entrance 2:15pm. 500dr, students 300dr, EU students free.) Polykrates' 40m deep **harbor mole** (rock pier) still supports the modern pier. Blocks, columns, walls fragments, and entablatures are strewn throughout Pythagorion like Lincoln Logs after a floorquake—the presentation in the small **Archaeological Museum** is no different. Half the collection fits in the building, and many pieces are haphazardly scattered on the sidewalk in front. (☎61 400. Open Tu-Su 9am-2:30pm. Free.) The ruined **Castle of Lycurgus**, on the south side of town, was built in the beginning of the 19th century by Lycurgus, a Samos native and leader in the Greek War for Independence. The **Church of the Transfiguration** is a pale blue variation on classic Orthodox architecture. (A bus from Samos Town arrives at Pythagorion every hour (20min., 280dr). The beach town of Pythagorion, 14km south of Samos Town, sits atop the ancient city of the same name.) Polykrates' magnum opus is in **Heraion** (Ηραιον; EAR-ion). Seven centuries of pilgrims worshipped Hera on Samos when Polykrates began enlarging the temple. Eventually, 134 columns supported the 118m-long, 58m-wide 530 BC version of the Temple of Hera; a 525 BC fire wrecked it. A lone standing column remains of the once-majestic colonnade; casts of the Geneleas group, now in the Samos Museum, accompany it. Walk along the beach to return to the temple. If you can't enter through the beachside back gate, a path brings you inland to the main road and main entrance farther along the beach, past two houses. Follow custom: wrap up in your finest toga and carry along a jug of libations on this path, which runs close to the ancient Iera Odos (Sacred Way) from Pythagorion to the temple. (The bus from Pythagorion (10min., 3 per day, 250dr) stops in Heraion Town. ☎95 277. Open Tu-Su 8:30am-3pm. 800dr, students 400dr.)

GREEK ISLANDS

MEDITERRANEAN COAST

Alternately chic, garish, and remote, Turkey's Mediterranean coast stretches along lush national parks, sun-soaked beaches, and pine forests. Natural beauty and ancient ruins have made the western Mediterranean one of the most touristed regions in Turkey. While increasingly over-run with pushy touts, Armani sportswear and mega-hotels, the western coast also caters to the backpacker circuit. By day, travelers take tranquil boat trips, hike among waterfalls, and explore submerged ruins; by night, they exchange stories over *Efes*, dance under the stars, and fall asleep in seaside *pansiyon*s and treehouses.

HIGHLIGHTS OF THE MEDITERRANEAN COAST

HACK your way through an Amazonian forest to find ruins of an ancient city overrun by crabs, turtles, birds, and lizards in **Olimpos** (p. 279).

HIKE up a rocky path through the enchanting **Butterfly Valley** and spend the night in a campsite surrounded by countless nocturnal Jersey Tiger Butterflies (p. 268).

DISCOVER the eternal Promethean flame—the **Chimaera** of Mt. Olimpos (p. 280).

PEER through the clear Mediterranean waters to see the staircases and walls of the sunken city of **Kekova** (p. 277).

VISIT the Mediterranean's only seal colony in the **Blue Caves** near Kaş (p. 277).

WITNESS stunning **Saklıkent Gorge** on a rafting trip along its icy stream (p. 264).

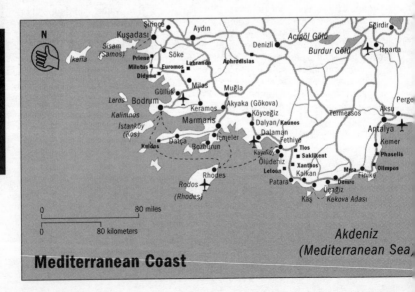

Mediterranean Coast

MARMARİS COAST

MARMARİS ☎252

Marmaris contains all the shameless beach town necessities: eclectic tourist shops, seaside restaurants, expensive yachts, a boisterous beach front, and decadent nighttime festivities. Rumor has it that Marmaris derives its name from Süleyman the Magnificent's order to "hang the architect" *(mimarı as)* of the local fortress. Exactly what was so distasteful about this understated castle is hard to say, as throngs of appreciative international tourists swarm to the landmark each summer. In ancient times, Marmaris was one of the Caria kingdom's most important seaports, connecting Anatolia with Rhodes and Egypt. Marmaris's natural harbor hosted the naval campaigns of both Süleyman the Magnificent in 1522 and Lord Nelson in 1798. Today, boats set off from Marmaris for hidden coves at the foot of pine-blanketed cliffs and the Greek island of Rhodes.

⊏ TRANSPORTATION

Buses: To reach the otogar (☎412 30 37), walk down Ulusal Egemenlik Bul. from the statue and make a sharp right onto Mustafa Münir Elgin Bul. The station is on the left, around the corner from the shopping center. Bus companies include: **Varan** (☎412 09 79); **Kamil Koç** (☎412 80 76 or 412 06 30); and **Pamukkale** (☎412 55 86).

Inter-city dolmuş: From the hub at the Tansaş Shopping Center to: **Bozburun** (1½hr.; high season noon, 2, 5pm; low season noon; $2.40); **Dalaman** (2hr., 7:30am-10pm, $3); **Fethiye** (4hr., 7:30am-10pm, $6); **İçmeler** (10min., 7am-1am, $.50); **Köyceğiz** (1hr., 7:30am-10pm, $2); **Milas** (2½hr., 9am-5pm, $6); **Muğla** (1hr., 9am-5pm, $1.80); **Ortaca** (1½hr., 7:30am-10pm, $2.40). **Kalkan** and **Kaş** can be reached from Fethiye, and **Dalyan** can be reached from Ortaca.

Local Dolmuş: Two main inner-city dolmuş routes both start at Tansaş Shopping Center. One heads straight down Ulusal Egemenlik Bul. to **Beldibi**. The other turns right onto Atatürk Cad. before weaving down backstreets to **Armutalan**.

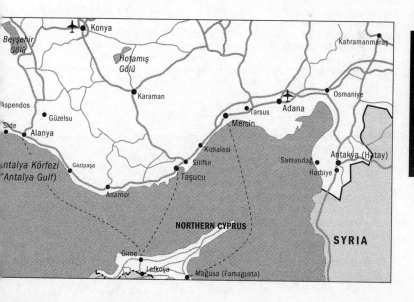

BUS SCHEDULE

DESTINATION	DURATION	FREQUENCY/TIME	PRICE
Ankara	11hr.	9:45am, 9, 10pm.	$25
Antalya	7hr.	11pm	$10
Adana	16hr.	2:15pm	$15
Bodrum	3¾hr.	summer 8:30am-5:30pm; winter 8:30am-2:30pm	$4
Datça	1¾hr.	summer 9am-9pm; winter 10am-8pm	$4
Erzincan	24hr.	7:30pm	$22
Eskişehir	10hr.	7:30pm	$14
Göreme (Cappadocia)	14hr.	10:30am	$16
İstanbul	12½hr.	9am, 6, 9pm	$20-23
İzmir	4½hr.	5:15am-3am	$9
Kayseri, Sivas	12hr.	10:45am	$14
Konya	10hr.	7pm	$14
Kuşadası	5hr.	June 15-Sep. 15 10:45am	$9
Pamukkale	4½hr.	8:15am-5:15pm	$6

Catamarans: To **Rhodes** (1hr.; May-Oct. daily, Nov.-Apr. Tu and F; 9:15am, return 4pm; round-trip $35, open return $55-60). Make reservations one day in advance with any travel agency.

Hydrofoils: To **Rhodes** (1hr.; May-Oct. daily 9:45am and 4:30pm, return 3pm; $40-60). Contact **Yeşil Marmaris** (see below).

Ferries: Leave for **Rhodes** only when there are enough cars (1½hr.; $20, round-trip $25). Contact Yeşil Marmaris. There's more to pay: $10 port tax, then $10 to get out of Greece, $10 more to get back into Turkey, and the cost of another $45 Turkish visa if required for your country.

 ## ORIENTATION

From the bus station, outside of town on Mustafa Münir Elgin Bul., take a dolmuş ($.40) or taxi ($3) to the town center on **Ulusal Egemenlik Bul.,** where the **Tansaş Shopping Center,** bus offices, and the dolmuş hub can be found. Located across from a large school at the intersection of Ulusal Egemenlik Bul. and the sea, the **Atatürk Statue** is a good reference point. Facing the water at the monument, turn left down **Kordon Cad.** to reach the tourist office and harbor. **Barlar Sok.** (Bar Street) and the **castle** are also to the left. **Atatürk Cad.** and **Uzunyalı Cad.** run from the right of the statue. Atatürk Cad. leads to the popular waterfront walkway and public beach before veering right and becoming **Kemal Seyfettin Elgin Bul.**

 ## PRACTICAL INFORMATION

TOURIST AND FINANCIAL SERVICES

Tourist Office: (☎412 72 77 or 412 10 35), 250m along Kordon Cad. on the border of the old city. English-speaking and very helpful. A/C. Open in summer daily 9am-6pm; in winter M-F 8am-5:30pm. **Yeşil Marmaris** (☎412 64 86 or 412 64 88), on the harbor, 30m from the tourist office can book catamaran trips to Rhodes (see above).

Budget Travel: Interyouth Hostel, Tepe Mah., 42 Sok No. 45 (☎412 36 87; fax 412 78 25; email interyouth@turk.net). They'll help find cheap airline, bus, and boat tickets and arrange jeep and moped rentals. Able to suggest many scenic trips. Offers an extraordinary Backpacker's Cruise on the hostel's 2 beautiful yachts ($200 for 5 days with English- speaking guide, all-inclusive).

Consulates: UK (☎412 64 86 or 412 64 87; fax 412 50 77), in the Yeşil Marmaris office building on the harbor, around the corner from the tourist office. Open M-F 7:30am-noon, 2:30-5pm.

Banks: Several with **ATMs** on Kemal Seyfettin Elgin Bul., Atatürk Cad., and Kordon Cad. Most open daily.

LOCAL SERVICES

English-Language Bookstore: Deveda Şi Kitabevi (☎ 412 20 34), on the harbor. New and used books. Open 11:30am-1am. The Marmaris Gymnasium, opposite the Atatürk statue, hosts a **book fair** from mid-June to Nov. offering books in many languages.

Laundromats: Marina Laundry (☎ 413 08 45). On Haci Mustafa Sok., near Bar Street. Open daily 9am-11pm. The **Interyouth Hostel** in the bazaar also offers laundry service to non-guests ($5 per load).

Hamam: Sultan Hamam (☎ 413 68 50 or 412 41 42; fax 413 68 51), straight inland from the Atatürk statue, in the basement of a building on the right side of Ulusal Egemenlik Cad. Full service $17; drinks $1; **fitness room** with stationary bikes, free weights, and basic weight machines $3 per hr. Open daily 8am-midnight. **Armutalan Turkish Bath** (☎ 412 07 10) offers free pick-up from your hotel, saunas, jacuzzi, swimming pool and cafe. Full service $17.

EMERGENCY AND COMMUNICATIONS

Police: (☎ 412 14 94), on 49 Sok., inland off Kordon Cad., 3 blocks from the tourist office, close to the PTT. Little English spoken.

Pharmacies: located on every other block throughout the city.

Hospital: Public Devlet Hastanesi (☎ 413 44 56), on Datça Yolu Üzeri. From the Atatürk statue, walk 500m up Ulusal Egemenlik Bul., turn left on Datça Cad., and continue

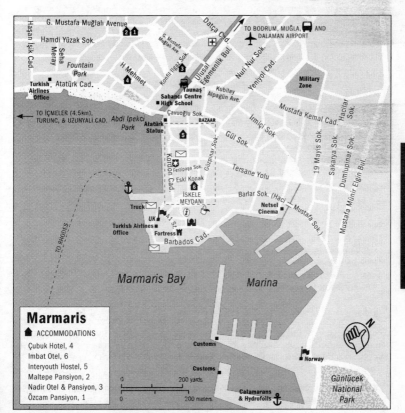

Marmaris

🏠 ACCOMMODATIONS

Çubuk Hotel, 4
Imbat Otel, 6
Interyouth Hostel, 5
Maltepe Pansiyon, 2
Nadir Otel & Pansiyon, 3
Özcam Pansiyon, 1

MEDITERRANEAN COAST

900m uphill. **Private Ahuhetman Hospital** (☎ 413 14 15). **Esen Sağlık Medical Center** (office ☎ 413 13 16; mobile 0532 321 39 11; home 413 37 71; fax 413 13 16), on Kemal Seyfettin Elgin Bul. Follow Atatürk Cad. until it changes to Kemal Seyfettin Elgin Bul.; the Center is on the right, opposite Diana Travels and McDonald's. English-speaking doctors and nurses. 24 hr. emergency and non-emergency treatment.

Internet Access: Internet Cafe (☎ 413 72 37), on the Yat Limanı. Follow Barbados Cad. (along the harbor) past Barlar Sok. $4 per hr. Open daily 9am-2am. The air-conditioned **Interyouth Hostel** in the bazaar offers access for $4 per hr.

PTT: (☎ 412 12 12), on Fevzipaşa Cad., off Kordon Cad. Currency exchange 9am-10pm; phone service 8am-midnight; direct money transfer 8:30am-12:30pm, 1:30-5:30pm. Package pickup around the corner. There's also a postal truck outside the tourist office on the waterfront. Open daily 8am-11pm. **Postal code:** 48700.

▉ ACCOMMODATIONS

Interyouth Hostel, Tepe Mah., 42 Sok. No. 45 (☎ 412 36 87; fax 412 78 23; email interyouth@turk.net). Located deep within the bazaar. From the Atatürk statue, take the first left, turn right inside the bazaar. The youth hostel is on the right. Hospitable managers take care of guests and non-guests alike. Not to be confused with the other Interyouth Hostel at Kemeraltı Mah., 14 İyilikataş Mevkii. Book exchange, internet access ($4 per hr.), international phone, laundry ($6). Sunset cruises every other night in the summer ($10). Can arrange cheap travel. Breakfast in the terrace bar and nightly spaghetti dinners (7:30pm, free for guests). 4-night cruises $200 per person. Dorms $5; private room $13. $1 discount for ISIC, HI, and IYTC holders.

Nadir Otel and Pansiyon, Kemeraltı Mah., 56 Sok. (☎ 412 11 67 or 412 18 06), next to the rocky outcrop behind the Tansaş Shopping Center. All rooms with TV and balcony. Ask for the side away from the shopping center. Laundry $.60 per item. The hotel has 24 doubles with bath. Singles $12; doubles $17. Breakfast included. The *pansiyon* offers 20 rooms, some with bath. $5 per person. Breakfast not included.

Maltepe Pansiyon, 64 Sok. No. 7 (☎ 412 16 29 or 412 84 56). Walk 400m down Ulusal Egemenlik Bul. from the Atatürk statue, turn left on G. Mustafa Muğlalı Cad., and turn left again 25m from Eet Cafe. Friendly family management. 18 simple rooms with bath and colorful rugs. Terrace with TV. Breakfast $1.80. Free use of washing machine and kitchen. Singles $6; doubles $12; triples $18; quads $24.

Özcan Pansiyon, Kemeraltı Mah., 3 Çam Sok. (☎ 412 77 61), next to Maltepe. 17 tidy rooms with balconies, most with bath. Communal kitchen. Colorful outside patio/bar. German spoken. Owner runs 2 boat trips to sites around Marmaris. Laundry and international phone. Breakfast $1.80. $6-7 per person; off-season $5.

Çubuk Hotel (☎ 412 67 74). Head down Atatürk Cad. from the statue and turn right on the 1st street after the park; the hotel is on the left under a yellow concrete awning. 27 carpeted rooms with bath, phones, balconies, and A/C. Breakfast included. Doubles $14 for 1 person, $19 for 2 people; off-season $12 for 1, $15 for 2.

İmbat Otel, 5 Eski Çarşı Sok. (☎ 412 14 13 or 413 63 20). Facing the tourist office, take a sharp left into the bazaar; the İmbat Otel will be on the left. Carpeted rooms close to the bars and clubs. Run by the amiable "Rakı Man," who occasionally indulges his guests in this Turkish drink of delight. Little English spoken. Breakfast $2. Free tea, coffee and soda for guests. Laundry $6. 18 rooms. $5 per person.

◖ FOOD

Marmaris is chock-full of busy and pricey eateries. For cheap fare, try the several small restaurants in the bazaar area or the fast food-style kebap places on almost every corner (chicken, meat, and vegetable kebaps $3-5). Or carbo-load with a baked potato slathered with toppings ($2-4) at the stands along Atatürk Cad.

◪ Kervansaray Restaurant (☎ 412 64 84). From the statue, head straight on Ulusal Egemenlik Bul., turn left on Datça Yolu, and take another left on Yunus Nadi Cad.; the restaurant is on the first corner on the right. For $12, feast on a large meal, with Turkish wine or beer and enjoy live Turkish music, wrestling, and traditional folk dances. The finale features the most famous male belly dancer in Marmaris. Ask at the Interyouth Hostel for more information, as groups often go from there. Open daily Apr.-Oct.

Marmaris Turkish Kitchen (☎412 40 60). In the bazaar on the left, 1 block past the PTT. Simple Turkish cooking served al fresco. Salads $1.80, omelettes $3, meat $3-$7. Everything comes with a huge spherical piece of delicious Turkish flat bread.

Eet Cafe Mozart, Org. Muğlalı Cad. #1-2-4 (☎413 87 64). Head straight down Ulusal Egemenlik Bul. and turn left on the street after Tansaş Shopping Center; this charming Dutch cafe/patisserie/restaurant is on the right. Serves European fare (fish and chips wrapped in newspaper; $8.50). The chef is open to creating new dishes. Turkish breakfast $2; English breakfast $3; apple tart $3; croissants $1. Open 8:30am-12:30am.

Internet Cafe (☎413 72 37). Yat Limanı, (for directions, see **Internet Access**, p. 246). Breezy patio and colorful antique-filled interior. Turkish dishes and vegetarian options $2-5; moist homemade cakes and cookies $1.50. Open daily 9am-2am.

👁 SIGHTS

BEACHES. Only 1500m away from the tourist office, **Günlücek National Park** offers a small, quiet beach and picnic tables set against a lush forest with fragrant frankincense trees. (Follow the harbor road past the marina and across the wooden footbridge, or catch a dolmuş from in front of the Tansaş Shopping Center: 5min., every 15min., $.40.) While the lively, crowded beach in Marmaris ($2.50 per person) is great for skin toasting, ice cream licking, and playful frolicking, quieter and prettier beaches in the area are accessible only by boat. Pleasant **İçmeler beach** is an exception. (Dolmuş from the front of Tansaş Shopping Center or anywhere along Atatürk Cad.: 10min., every 5min. 8am-1am, $.50. Alternatively, catch the water dolmuş to İçmeler from the waterfront next to the tourist office: 20min., in summer daily 7am-7pm, leaves when there are enough customers, $4.)

BOAT TRIPS. Water dolmuş going to **Turunç Beach** depart from the waterfront behind the Atatürk statue. (45min., daily in summer, every hr. 7am-7pm, $1.) In high season, daily boat trips to **Dalyan** and **Kaunos** feature **Turtle Beach** and **mud baths** (see Dalyan and Kaunos, p. 237). (Buy tickets from the boats moored on the waterfront across from the bazaar. Only in summer; 9:30am, return 7pm; $18 per person; lunch included.)

Full-day boat tours stop at **Paradise Island Beach,** the **Akvaryum (aquarium),** several phosphorous caves, and the popular **Turunç Beach.** They continue to the **Gölenye Springs,** whose waters reputedly cure intestinal ills; the less-crowded **Kumlu Buk Beach,** near the remains of a fortress; and the tiny village of Keçi, in the heavily-wooded Nimara Peninsula, which offers spectacular views of the surrounding coastline. ($10-15 per person; lunch included.) For those in search of a longer voyage, the Interyouth Hostel in the bazaar offers a 4-day boat trip exploring the rugged coast line from Marmaris to Fethiye ($200 per person).

The fine sand beaches of **Kleopatra's Island,** a.k.a. Sedir Adası, are a good daytrip. Legend has it that Marc Antony imported the white sand from the Red Sea some 2100 years ago in an attempt to get Cleopatra into the sack. Those less romantically-inclined suspect that fossilized plankton make the sand so white. (The island can be reached by boat or through an organized tour arranged by any travel agency. A bus will pick up people at 10:30am at a planned meeting place and drive 20min. to Çamlı village, from where a boat will depart for the island. 45min., in summer 17 per day from 10:30am, return 7pm.)

Travelers should also consider renting a motorbike (inquire at the Interyouth Hostel) and spending a day exploring the archeological sites dotting the Bozburun Peninsula. (About $30 for 1 day.)

OLD TOWN. Meandering through this area of Marmaris rewards the explorer with local color and spectacular views. Small whitewashed buildings cluster on the hill surrounding the castle. Narrow stone passages reveal local children, cats, colorful gardens, and stunning vistas of the sea. The old town is a relaxing place to spend the afternoon wandering.

MEDITERRANEAN COAST

CASTLE. A lush garden complete with peacocks and turtles fills the inner court-yard of the castle, while the paths along the ramparts offer panoramic views of the Marmaris harbor. Built in 1522 by Sultan Süleyman, Marmaris's castle was used as a base for the successful campaign against the Crusaders camped out on Rhodes. The castle now exhibits artifacts from 3000 BC onwards and an **ethnography room** of Ottoman material culture. Another room displays changing art collections. *(From the tourist office, take the street to the right, turn left into the bazaar, and then turn right down the narrow alley after the Sultan Restaurant; the castle is at top of the stone stairs. Open Tu-Su 8:30am-noon, 2-5:30pm. $1.20, students $.60.)*

🎵 ENTERTAINMENT

It is hard to tell which is hotter in Marmaris: the burning sun or the blazing night-life. 11pm is showtime for Barlar Sok., Uzunyalı Cad., and Barbados Cad. (the har-bor), when bars and clubs kick into high gear. Loud, bright, and contagious music and neon lights spill onto the street.

To reach **Barlar Sok.** (Bar St.), take the left road next to the tourist office (when facing the office), turn left into the bazaar at the next corner, and walk straight. Let the music and lights be your guide. **Uzunyalı** is on the opposite side of Marmaris, right on the waterfront. **Barbados Cad.** is the pavement along the harbor. Most bars and clubs have no cover. Unless otherwise noted, all are open daily year-round. At bars with both indoor and outdoor seating, drinks are usually cheaper outside.

CLUBS

Backstreet (☎412 40 48). On Bar St. An open-air tropical oasis. Ultra-hip dancers groove to international rock and pop, while onlookers chill under palm trees along a tiny creek. Beer $3.00; *rakı* $3.50; cocktails $4-8. Open May-Sept. 9am-4am.

Greenhouse (☎412 50 71). Halfway down Bar St. Known for its excellent cutting-edge music and comfortable setting, this bright turquoise air-conditioned dance club and bar is a Marmaris favorite. Beer $2; *rakı* $3.50; cocktails $5-10. Open 9pm-5am.

The Beach Club (☎412 11 88). 50m before Cheers on Uzunyalı. Famous for its cabana-like exterior decorated with fluorescent surfboards and zebra-print bar stools, plus an out-door bar painted with tropical fish. Inside, the sophisticated surroundings reverberate with the top-notch electronic sounds of hip-hop, house, and Top 40. Beer $1.20-2; *rakı* $2; cocktails (which have a "never say when" philosophy) $5. Open in summer daily 8am-4am; in winter Sa-Su 8am-4am.

Cheers (☎412 67 22). On the beach at the far end of Uzunyalı. An outrageously fun disco "theme park" featuring *Grease* and *Saturday Night Fever*. A mega sound system blasts 60s and 70s music. Keep an eye out for Travolta-impersonating patrons reveling in those summer nights. Beer $1.80; *rakı* $3.60; cocktails $4-6 (try the special "fish-bowls" and you'll be swimming home, $20). Open Apr.-Oct. 8am-4am.

BARS

Mavi Bar (☎412 01 97). On Barbados Cad. This simple yet elegant bar with small can-dlelit tables hosts live Turkish and Mediterranean folk music for a mostly Turkish crowd. Beer $1.20; *rakı* $1.80; cocktails $4. Open 9am-1am.

Magic Garden Bar. On the right at the beginning of Bar Street. This colorful refuge offers a great place to talk and people-watch. Sit at bright green terrace tables under a canopy of grapes. Contemporary music. Cider $3.50. Special mixed drinks $5. Open midnight-2am.

Reggae Bar (☎413 65 05). On Barbados Cad., near the Escape Bar. Caribbean bar filled with Bob Marley paraphernalia. Clientele jams to reggae and sips tropical concoc-tions under the Hawaiian-style thatched roof. Beer $1.80; *rakı* $1.80; cocktails $3-5. Open Mar.-Nov. 9am-2am.

Escape Bar (☎412 74 17). On the right at the far end of Bar St., is a cheaper, casual alternative to the flashy nightclubs. Dart boards and surfing posters cover the brick walls; the pool table is ready for action. Friendly backpackers swap travel stories with yacht owners. Beer $1.50; *rakı* $2.30; cocktails $2-4. Open 8pm-2:30am.

İÇMELER
☎252

The next cove west of Marmaris, İçmeler is quickly becoming as crowded as its more famous neighbor. The full-blown concrete conglomerate of tall luxury hotels and neon-signed restaurants now runs all the way down to the beach. If you can overlook the prevailing package-tour feel of the place, İçmeler's beach is slightly better than the one in Marmaris. You'll also find some quiet, laid-back pensions a pleasant distance from the mammoth beach-front resorts. Frequent dolmuş service to Marmaris, only 10 to 15 minutes away, makes İçmeler a feasible alternative to lodging in Marmaris while staying within reach of its bars and clubs.

⊏ TRANSPORTATION. Dolmuş run to **Marmaris** from the beach on Kayabal Cad. or from İnönü Cad. (every 15min. 7am-1am, $.75). Dolmuş boats travel to **Marmaris** (20min., in summer daily 7am-7pm, departs when full, $5) and **Turunç beach** (40min.; in summer every hr. 10am-1pm, return 2 and 4:30pm; $1).

◼◪ ORIENTATION AND PRACTICAL INFORMATION. Dolmuş and buses enter İçmeler via **Atatürk Cad.** (later **İnönü Cad.**), passing Agua Life water park on the left and turning left down **Kayabal Cad.** and **Cumhuriyet Cad.** Further towards the shore, both run parallel to the beach. Any street to the left off Kayabal Cad. leads first to the residential area with a few *pansiyons*, then to the huge hotels, and finally to the beach. **Kenan Evren Cad.**, which ends at the beach, links Kayabal Cad. and Cumhuriyet Cad. As streets are very poorly marked, you may want to get a map from the Marmaris tourist office.

There is no tourist office in İçmeler, but maps are available in the Marmaris office and from vendors in Marmaris. A more than adequate number of **currency exchanges** and **ATMs** dot Cumhuriyet Cad. and Kenan Evran Cad. There is a **pharmacy** on Kenan Evran Bul., one block from the beach. A small **health clinic, Sağlık Ocağı,** is on 51 Sok., off İnönü Cad., around the corner from the PTT (☎455 36 98. Open M-Sa 8:30am-noon, 1-5:30pm). The **police station** (☎455 23 55) is at Kayabal Cad., 72 Sok. No. 3. The **PTT** is on İnönü Cad. (☎455 34 60. Open in summer 8am-10pm; in winter 8:30am-12:30pm, 1:30-5:30pm.) **Postal code:** 48720.

⌐ ACCOMMODATIONS. The *pansiyons* located in the residential section between Kayabal Cad. and Cumhuriyet Cad. are the most quiet and cost-effective options in İçmeler. To reach the **Bellevue Hotel,** between 68 and 59 Sok., turn onto Cumhuriyet Cad. off İnönü Cad. and walk toward the water. This hotel, which has a beautiful pool and garden bar, offers modern rooms with carpet, A/C, phone, and bath. (☎455 26 96. Breakfast included. Doubles $25. Prices may vary with seasons.) To get to **Leydi Pansiyon,** turn left off İnönü Cad. (when heading towards Kayabal Cad.) onto 49 Sok. and follow the signs; the *pansiyon* is two blocks down on the left. Surrounded by a garden, the Leydi provides communal bath, kitchen and rustic rooms with dark wood. (☎455 22 44. 8 rooms. $5 per person.) To reach **Ekince Pansiyon,** head down Kayabal Cad. away from İnönü Cad., passing the Yorkshire Lass Restaurant on the left. The *pansiyon* has 11 simple rooms with bath (☎455 45 92. Doubles $15; triples $22. 40% off in winter.)

◪◪ FOOD AND ENTERTAINMENT. Along the beach, İçmeler's dining tends toward the pricey, but there are some smaller restaurants that offer good food at a much lower cost. Take a seat at the **Yorkshire Lass Restaurant, a.k.a. Captain Bullshit's Place,** 33/A Kayabal Cad., about 300m from the intersection of İnönü Cad. and Kayabal Cad. Join Jimmy, Ibo, and Ali—all of whom are more than eager to chat—for an entertaining and tasty meal. The restaurant serves a smorgasbord of Turkish, English, and Chinese food. (☎455 51 70. Hamburgers $2; 3 course Chinese dinner $7. Open daily 8am-about midnight.) The **Küçük Ev,** or Little House, 36 Kayabal Cad., on the right leaving the dolmuş stop is a popular restaurant with outdoor seating. It dishes out delicious, affordable kebaps ($3), veggie pizza and *meze* ($1.20-$3), and desserts ($2). (☎455 21 11 or 455 28 14. Open daily 8am-midnight.) To reach the

Erden Café and Bar, head from the bus station down along the shore about 75m; the Erden will be on the left. Located on the beach, this popular hangout offers great views and simple, decently priced food. (Sandwiches $1; spaghetti $4; drinks $1.)

İçmeler's nightlife is not as mighty as Marmaris's, but there are a few popular places well worth checking out. Beware that the music has to be turned down at 1am. The buccaneer's dance bar of choice for "ay ay mating," is **Korsan.** Coming from Marmaris, turn left on Cumhuriyet Cad., and turn left again at the Channel. A tropical fantasy, this wild dance bar is filled with waterfalls, life-sized pirates, and a stylish crowd nodding to alternative music. (Beer $1.80; *rakı* $3.60; cocktails $4-6. Open daily 5pm-5am.) One block further away from Marmaris, on a parallel street, the **Heaven Bar** features European music and a relaxed clientele. (Beer $1.80; *rakı* $2.50; cocktails $4-6. Open daily 8am-2am.) To reach **Deniz Kapısı** (☎455 30 17), walk straight out of İçmeler from the dolmuş stop. Immediately before the sharp curve in the road, Deniz offers cocktails ($6), food, karaoke, free use of its beach, and, on Thursdays and Sundays, a **Full Monty Show.**

🕿 **SIGHTS.** İçmeler's **beach** tends to be cleaner and slightly less crowded than those at Marmaris. Be forewarned—you will have to pay $1 for your seat. Water sports include the perennial favorites: **parasailing** (10min., $30), **banana boats** (15 min. ride $6), and **paddle boats** ($7 per hr.). Equipment is available on the beach or by calling **Mar-Bas Water Sports** (☎455 30 58 or 455 30 59), in the Mar-Bas Hotel on the right side of the beach. Boat lovers can rent a high-powered **speed boat** ($40-$60 per hr.). **Diving centers,** including the **European Diving Centre** (☎455 47 33; fax 455 47 34), near the Paloma Beach Hotel, offer underwater recreation for all ages and skill levels. ($70 per day; equipment, lunch, and pick-up/drop-off services included.) **Boat trips** run to **Dalyan** and **Kaunos** (daily 9am-7pm, $20, lunch included), and, closer to home, the bays around İçmeler (10am-5pm, $6-10). Ask at the harbor for details.

BOZBURUN
☎252

Bozburun lies in a small valley surrounded by the rocky dry hills of the Datça Peninsula. Set against the harbor, Bozburun is a peaceful place for strolling along the waterfront, watching shipwrights assemble the skeletons of embryonic yachts and just enjoying the motion of the ocean. While locals prefer to jump off the rocks into the sea, timid tourists may prefer the small beach to the right of the harbor.

🖪 🖪 **TRANSPORTATION AND PRACTICAL INFORMATION.** It's easiest to get to Bozburun from Marmaris. Catch a dolmuş opposite the round Pamukkale office on Ulusal Egemenlik Cad. or at the rather distant otogar (**to Bozburun:** 1 hr.; 10:30am, noon, 2:30, 5, 7pm; leaving **from Bozburun:** 6:30, 8:30, 10am, noon, 4:30pm). Dolmuş depart opposite the mosque, about a block inland from the harbor. In the low season, bargain (hard!) for a taxi from Marmaris to take you to Bozburun and wait to drive you back (there are no taxis in Bozburun).

There are **no banks** or **ATMs,** but most shops will change money. The **jandarma** (state police; ☎456 20 02), to the right of the mosque when facing inland, is open 24hr. The **PTT** is next to the mosque (open from 8am-8pm). **Postal code:** 48710.

📷 **ACCOMMODATIONS AND FOOD.** Bozburun's *pansiyons* are located on a small dirt road that runs to the left of town as you face the sea. **Pembe Yunus Pansiyon,** 75m farther along the shore from Yılmaz, has a communal kitchen and 20 elegant rooms with floral drapes and bathrooms. Ask for the newer rooms near the cliff. (☎456 21 54 or 456 22 11. Breakfast included. $12 per person.) Surrounded by a lush garden, the two-building **Yılmaz Pansiyon,** 391 İskele Mah., looks out onto the sea. Facing inland, walk 50m along the harbor. Guests enjoy its ten rooms, most with bath, as well as its communal kitchen. (☎456 21 67. Breakfast $3. $5 per person.) The **Suna Pansiyon,** immediately next door to the Yılmaz, offers seven clean rooms, some with blue tile floors and lace curtains. (☎456 21 19. Breakfast included. Singles $8; doubles $12.

To reach the **Old Sailor,** go straight towards the harbor from the dolmuş stop. This friendly restaurant dishes up gorgeous views as well as savory vegetarian Turkish starters ($1.50), grilled fish and meat ($6), and sticky baklava ($1.50). For cheap meals, try the selection of Turkish "home food" and seafood in a pleasant outdoor setting at **Kandil Restaurant.** Head right at the waterfront, walk through the square with a small Atatürk statue; the restaurant is straight ahead. (☎456 22 27. Omelettes $2; steak $4.80; şiş $3.20; seafood salads $4-5. Open 8am-midnight.) **Gül Cafe Bar,** is about 25m from Kandil Restaurant. Sip cappuccino ($.75) and nibble fresh crepes ($2.50) at this classy restaurant. (☎456 26 60. Open 9am-11pm.)

DATÇA

☎252

With its tranquil small-town atmosphere, Datça offers a more restful experience than the flashing disco balls and wild throngs of Bodrum and Marmaris. The dirt road to Datça twists along the mountainous Datça peninsula, providing occasional glimpses of an emerald string of deserted bays. The road to Datça along the slim, rugged Datça peninsula may be a bit terrifying, with sharp turns and sheer drops, but determined visitors brave the hair-raising ride for the town's hospitality, laid-back nightlife, and beaches that are both less crowded and more beautiful than those at Bodrum and Marmaris. Small bars line the harbor, where boats lie waiting to depart to the ancient Dorian city of **Knidos** at the tip of the peninsula.

▐ TRANSPORTATION

Buses: Buses leave from the **Pamukkale** office (☎712 33 02 or 712 42 069), close to the harbor. Open daily 5:30am-noon, 2pm-midnight. All buses traveling inland stop in **Marmaris** (1½hr., 8 per day 6am-6:30pm, $3.60). See **Marmaris: Orientation and Practical Information** (p. 244) for destinations beyond Marmaris.

Ferries and Seabuses: Ferryboat Association (☎131 01 15). On the street past the bus station on the left. To **Bodrum: ferries** (2hr.; June M, W, F 9am and 5pm; July-Sept. daily 9am and 5pm; $10, round-trip $17; children under 5 free); **seabuses** (35 min.; June M, W, Sa-Su 8:30am and 4:30pm; July-Sept. daily 8:30am and 4:30pm; $16, round-trip $19). **Ulusoy** offers shuttles from its office to the dock (minibuses leave 30min. before departure; free). Contact **Seher Tour** (☎712 24 73 or 712 87 89; fax 712 38 60; winter ☎712 30 17; fax 712 24 70) for boats to the Greek island **Symi** (9am, returns 3pm; $16 including port tax; 10 people min.).

Moped rentals: (☎712 29 15), on the left side of the road to Marmaris, past the police station and PTT. $20 per day including helmets. Open daily 8am-5pm.

✴▐ ORIENTATION AND PRACTICAL INFORMATION

Since street names are rarely used in Datça, all directions below are given from the main square where stands the stump of what used to be a large tree. Facing the shops that block the beach, the main road extends to the left towards Marmaris. To the right, it leads to the harbor, making a sharp left towards the marina.

Tourist office: (☎712 31 63; ☎/fax 712 35 46). From the stump, follow the main road towards Marmaris and turn left before the police station; the office is on the right. English spoken. Open in summer 8:30am-noon, 1-7pm; in winter 8am-noon, 1-5pm.

Bank: Türkiye İş Bankası (☎712 32 72) and others offer **currency exchange.** Open M-F 9am-12:30pm, 1:30-5:30pm. Datça's main road has 3 Cirrus/Plus/MC/V ATMs.

Laundromat: A small laundromat is located 1km up the main road towards Marmaris.

Hamam: (☎712 94 69). With your back to the beach, walk away from the stump onto a small road and turn left after 3 blocks; the hamam is 1 block on the left. Clean and simple. $15. Open daily 7am-10pm.

Police: (☎712 37 92). On the left side of the road to Marmaris, across from the school.

Pharmacy: (☎ 712 30 92). On the right side of the main road towards the harbor. Open daily 8am-9pm.

Hospital: Devlet Hastanesi (☎ 712 30 82). Follow the main road to Marmaris and turn right on the street after the PTT.

PTT: (☎ 712 26 04). Located next to the government center and near the police station. *Poste restante*, fax, and currency exchange. Postal window open daily 8:30am-5:30pm. International phone service daily in summer (mid-May to mid-Sept.) 8am-midnight; in winter 8:30am-6pm. 8 phones outside open 24hr. **Postal code:** 48900.

▚ ACCOMMODATIONS

Reservations are recommended for the high season (July and August) when room prices usually rise. There are no set reception hours, but you can usually find the owners in nearby stores. While not the norm, Visa and MasterCard can be used.

▨ **Tunc Pansiyon** (☎ 712 30 36). From the main road towards Marmaris, turn left on the small Buxerolles St. Tunc is on the left. A fancy pension with tiled floor, plants, and a stylishly decorated eating area with satellite TV. 22 tidy, modern rooms with large windows and bath. Friendly management. English spoken. Communal kitchen and laundry (prices vary). Breakfast included. $8 per person.

Aşkin Pansiyon (☎ 712 34 06 or 712 25 17). On Buxerolles, across from Tunc Pansiyon. Look for the bright yellow sign. 22 charming rooms with bath and hot water. During July and Aug., pick fresh grapes from the vines surrounding the terrace and communal kitchen. Little English spoken. $7 per person.

Mandalina Pansiyon (☎ 712 49 95). On the right side of the main road towards the harbor. Owners can be found in the neighboring restaurant. 8 large, airy rooms with balcony, great bathrooms, and hot water. Modern communal kitchen. Eat breakfast in their tranquil garden restaurant ($3.50). $5 per person.

Antalyı Pansiyon (☎ 712 38 10; fax 712 21 28). On the left side of the road towards Marmaris. Large marble hallways with grand mirrors and colorful rugs. 14 polished rooms with bath, hot water, and balcony. Communal kitchen, TV, and splendid views of the sea from the terrace. Owners can be found in the nearby furniture store. $8 per person, with breakfast $10, with A/C $12.

Tuna Pansiyon (☎ 712 39 31 or 712 20 14). On the main road across from Antalyı Pansiyon, 25m from Kumluk Beach. 17 simple rooms with balcony, bath, and hot water. Some have lovely views of the garden and beach. Communal kitchen and eating area. Owners can be found in nearby grocery store. No English spoken. Doubles $17; triples $25. Off-season: doubles $10; triples $17.

Huzur Pansiyon (☎ 712 30 52 or 712 33 64). Turn left on the side street across from the bus station and follow the signs. The *pansiyon* will be on the right. Clean rooms with panoramic views and lace curtains. Good *pansiyon* for families. Communal kitchen. Breakfast included. Singles $10; doubles $14; triples $18.

Ilıca Camping (☎/fax 712 34 00). On Taşlık Beach. From the harbor, turn right and walk 150m along the shore. Water sports and grills on the beach. Attached restaurant serves beer ($.80-$1.60). Tents $5 per person; 2-4 person bungalows $8 per person.

◖ FOOD

Travelers can buy fresh food from the small markets on the main road (pine and thyme honey are local specialties) and cook in the communal kitchens of the *pansiyons*. Most of the smaller and more traditional restaurants are located towards the harbor, before the curve of the main road. The larger and more touristy restaurants, offering views and a wider selection of food options, are at the harbor.

▨ **Kemal Restaurant** (☎ 712 20 44). Towards the harbor on the right side of the main road. Excellent homemade Turkish food in a comfortable, classy setting. Look for pink flowered tablecloths. Vegetarians can enjoy the çorba (soup; $1.20). Others can savor the köfte ($3) or şiş ($3.60) amid original oil paintings for sale. Open M-Sa 8am-10pm.

Karaoğlu Garden House (☎ 712 30 79). Head towards the harbor and turn left onto a narrow road with a sharp incline across from the bus station; the restaurant is on the right after the road descends. Its spacious terrace offers a superlative 180° view of the beach and harbor. Sip wine and savor their specialty of lamb in a clay pot ($7). Vegetarian dishes ($2-3).

Linman Restaurant (☎ 712 38 53). On the main road to the harbor, on the right side of the curve. Open-air windows overlook the harbor and Taşlık beach. Casual, open interior surrounded by natural stone. Ottoman food and extensive wine list. Octopus salad ($1.50), mezes ($1.50), shrimp soufflé ($8), and vegetarian specials ($5).

Yasu Meyhane/Tavern (☎ 712 28 60). On a hill across from the Knidos taxi stand. Look for the lighted daisy sign. Eclectic restaurant in an old building overlooking Taşlık Plaji. Chicken dishes ($4-7) and a generous vegetarian selection. Live music most nights. More of a bar after 11pm. Open 10:30am until the last customer leaves.

Nokta Patisserie (☎ 712 32 05 or 712 81 55). On the left side of the road as you walk away from the center square and towards Marmaris. Close to the police station. This cheerful restaurant offers home baked cookies and breads ($.50-$1). A colorful array of fruit, crème, and chocolate cakes also available for purchase ($8 per cake).

👁 SIGHTS

People come to Datça for its serene beaches and for the impressive remains of the ancient city of **Knidos,** about 30km west of Datça proper (see below). In Datça, **Kumluk Plaji,** hidden behind the stores along Atatürk Cad., tends to be crowded with tourists staying at the vacation complexes nearby. The prettier and less-frequented **Taşluk Plaji** lies to the right of the ships docked at the harbor.

As befits a coastal town, Datça hosts a July 1st **Sea Festival.** Young men fearlessly ascend a greasy mast in order to capture the Turkish flag. During the **Culture and Music Festival,** held in late summer (call the tourist office for dates), pop singers and Turkish folk dancers entertain crowds at the harborside amphitheater. Datça also hosts an annual **almond festival** in mid-July. Nut growers from all over the peninsula come to Datça to have their produce judged. As the peninsula's almonds are renowned for their flavor, the judges have an enviable task.

🎵 ENTERTAINMENT

Lacking the lights and special effects of that of Bodrum and Marmaris, Datça's animated nightlife consists of small family-run bars perfect for talking and people-watching. For a more mellow evening, join the locals in a leisurely stroll along the harbor or play tavla (backgammon) in one of the many tea houses.

Sunrise Bar (☎ 712 95 18). A harbor favorite. Under the twinkling white lights and green foliage, small tables and chairs sprawl right up to the moored boats. Tourists, sailors, and fishermen discuss sea travels. Beer and rakı $1.20; cocktails $4-6. Open 8am until customers leave.

Eclipse Bar (☎ 712 43 10). At the harbor, on the left side of the main road. Hip, young Turks, backpackers, and surfers vigorously socialize with each other and the cool owner. Casual atmosphere with alternative music. Beer $1.60; rakı $1.80; cocktails $4-6. Food served too ($1.20-2). Open noon-4am. Closed in winter.

Marın Bar (☎ 712 84 38 or 712 37 04). On the right along the harbor. This glittering open-air disco/bar is surrounded by faux-Classical statuary, blue lights, and American movie posters. Customers bust a move to reggae and Turkish pop. Beer $1.60; rakı $1.80; cocktails $4-6. Open 9am-3am. Closed in winter.

Gitanes. From the harbor, head towards Taşlık Beach. At the "Fish Restaurant" sign, turn right up the small hill; Gitanes is on the left. Bass-heavy music fills this funky candlelit disco-bar though the music gets quieter after 1am. Original artwork on the walls. Beer $1.50; rakı $1.20; cocktails $4-8. Open 8pm-4am. Closed in winter.

⚐ DAYTRIP FROM DATÇA: KNIDOS

Visiting Knidos can easily turn into an all-day affair. Taxis happily make the journey (1hr. each way) for a hefty $48. A cheaper option is to take a boat tour from Datça (daily 9am-6:30pm; $12, with lunch $14). In addition to Knidos, boats often stop for swimming along the southern bays of the peninsula. Call Burak Tour (☎712 37 74; mobile ☎526 21 76; fax 712 30 33) for more information. Knidos site open daily 8am-7pm. $2, students free.

During the 4th century BC, the port town of **Knidos**, located at the tip of the Datça Peninsula where the Aegean and Mediterranean meet, was a member of the six-city Dorian League. An artistic and intellectual center of the ancient world, Knidos was home to Sostratos, designer of the Pharos lighthouse at Alexandria (one of the Seven Wonders of the Ancient World) and of the astronomer Eudoxus, who calculated the earth's circumference.

Undoubtedly the most impressive feature in Knidos was the now-lost naked **statue of Aphrodite** by Praxiteles. This work was so beautiful that it drew tourists from afar even in ancient times, yet it was so scantily clad that it was rejected by the inhabitants of the island of Kos. Despite this crowning monument's absence, Knidos still has enough interesting ruins to make the trek there worthwhile.

Knidos's stone terraces make exploration of the site slightly confusing. Stick close to the marked arrows. To the left past the entrance booth is the grass-filled site of the ancient **agora**, a small **Byzantine church** complete with mosaic floor remains, and the Temple of Dionysus. Ascending about 350m higher into the terrace allows you to view the **base** of the ancient **Aphrodite statue.** The holes where the temple's 11 columns rested are still visible. A slight descent past the boxy gateway onto the **Corinthian temple** built by Stratos reveals fallen Corinthian capitals. Nearby are the remains of the **sundial** used by Eudoxus in the 4th century BC.

The two most impressive artifacts at Knidos are the large **Byzantine church** at the center of the site (near the Corinthian temple) and the looming remains of the **theater** which seated 4500 to 8000 spectators. The church displays extensive mosaic floor tiling and stones with Christian decoration. The curious blocks laced with Arabic inscriptions date from the 6th century and record the presence of Arabic seafarers in Knidos.

KÖYCEĞİZ   ☎252

Home to various endangered species of birds, turtles, and rare gum-producing liquid amber trees, Köyceğiz is a peaceful town located at the northern tip of tranquil Köyceğiz Lake. Locals gather around the cool natural springs that bubble from the ground, talking as their children play in the water. From its shores, the weary traveler can enjoy a quiet swim or a boat trip to the rejuvenating **Sultaniye hot springs,** the ruins of **Kaunos,** or **Turtle Beach.**

⚐ TRANSPORTATION

The otogar is located on Köyceğiz's main street, Atatürk Cad. To get to the center from the otogar, take a dolmuş (5min., every 10-15min., $.40). **Kamil Koç** (☎262 42 94 or 262 42 08) offers service to: **Ankara** (11hr., 7:30pm, $15.70); **Dalaman** (20min., 8am-10pm, $.85); **Fethiye** (2hr., 8am-10pm, $3); **İstanbul** (13hr., 7pm and 8pm, $19). **Pamukkale** runs to: **Bodrum** (3½hr.; 10:45am, 12:30, 2, 4:30pm; $6); **Bursa** (10hr., 8pm, $15); **İzmir** (5hr., 9am-5:30pm, $6); **Kaş** (4hr.; 9:30am, 12:30, 4:30pm; $6); **Marmaris** (45min., 8am-8pm, $2); **Ortaca** (20min., every 20min. 6am-midnight, $1.20), from which **Dalyan** and **Dalaman** are accessible. Dolmuş to **Ortaca** leave from the dolmuş stop, located one block inland from the tourist office on Atatürk Cad. (every 30 min. 6am-9pm, $.80).

⚐ ORIENTATION AND PRACTICAL INFORMATION

The **tourist office** opposite the mosque on Atatürk Cad., provides maps and accommodations listings. English spoken. (☎262 47 03. Open in summer M-F 8:30am-7pm, Sa-Su 9am-6pm; in winter M-F 8:30am-noon, 1:30-5pm.) The **hospital, Devlet Hastanesi,** is located to the left down a side street opposite the bus station. (☎262

47 18. Open 24hr.) Look for the blue sign with the large "H." To reach the **police station** (☎262 21 74), turn left (with your back to the lake) in front of the central mosque on Atatürk Cad. There is a **bank** with an **ATM** on the left side of Atatürk Cad. as you enter town. For the **PTT**, turn left at the same mosque, then make the first right. (☎262 46 60. Open 8:30am-noon, 1:30-6pm.) **Postal code:** 48800.

ACCOMMODATIONS

Tango Pension (☎262 32 10; fax 262 43 45), on Ali İhsan Kalmaz Cad. Turn right at the water, walk 100m along the waterfront, and follow the signs inland to the bright peach-colored *pansiyon* surrounded by a tropical garden. 18 large, modern rooms with bath and balcony, and a dorm room. Friendly and helpful owners. Lively atmosphere. Laundry $5. Windsurfing $6 per hr. Internet $3.50 per hr. Transportation to waterfall $.80 each way. Daily boat trips (10am-7pm) to Turtle Beach, Dalyan, Kaunos, and mud baths $7. Breakfast $2; dinner $4. Dorms $4; otherwise $7 per person.

Alila Hotel (☎262 11 50 or 262 11 51). Walk one block past the mosque. The Alila is on the left. A luxurious lakefront hotel with beautiful sculptures and carved wooden ceilings. The spacious rooms have panoramic views of the lake. Garden terrace and swimming pool. Breakfast included. 4 course dinner $6. Singles $11; doubles $17. A/C $4.

Otel Flora (☎252 4976; fax 262 38 09; email alp-giray@hotmail.com). On the lake. From the center of town walk 150m; the Flora is on your right. An environmentally conscious hotel, the Flora offers 16 clean, modern rooms. Set in a beautiful garden with frankincense trees. Breakfast included. Delicious 5 course dinner $4. $8 per person.

Fulya Pension (☎262 23 01), next door to the Tango Pension. 17 cheerful doubles and triples, all with bath. Pink hallways! $5 per person, with breakfast $6.

FOOD

Ali Baba (☎262 31 66). From the tourist office, walk inland 2 blocks; the restaurant is on the right. Delicious homemade Turkish cooking in a charming setting (full meal $2). Open daily 8am-10pm.

Peunguen Pide Salonu (☎262 34 17), on Fevzipaşa Cad. Enjoy fresh-baked *pide* ($.40-$1.20) and eclectic decor—bright movie posters and a fish tank. A local hangout.

Çiçek Restaurant (☎262 30 38), located on Atatürk Cad. near the mosque and tourist office. Serves delicious cold vegetarian Turkish dishes ($1.50 each). Grills $3; omelettes $2.80; beer $1.20.

Şamdar Restaurant (☎262 49 71). On the lake, to the right of the tourist office (when facing the lake). Look for the elegant peach and turquoise building. Breezy outdoor restaurant with delicious food. Meze $1-3; grills $4-5.

Eskimo Ice Cream (☎262 36 59). From the tourist office walk left along the water. Turn inland when you come to the horseshoe-shaped fountain. The Eskimo is on the left. This local secret serves delicious homemade ice cream in flavors galore ($1).

SIGHTS

There's a tiny **beach** near the campground, 900m away from town, but swimming stops are included in most boat trips. Boats depart daily from the dock opposite the tourist office for the nearby **therapeutic mud baths; Turtle Beach,** where limited swimming hours (8am-8pm) help ensure the turtles's right to privacy; the ancient Lycian city of **Kaunos;** and the **Sultaniye thermal springs,** where therapeutic waters reaching 40°C reputedly alleviate stress and rheumatism (open 6am-10pm; admission $.80). The boat trips last from about 10:30am to 7pm and cost $10 with lunch. Another option is the hour-long moonlight cruise around Lake Köyceğiz (10pm, $2). Catch a boat at the dock or call travel agencies such as **Özay Tourism** (☎262 18 22; fax 262 18 19), across from the mosque (open 9am-7pm), or **Şahin Boat** (☎262 25 01; fax 262 43 45), at Tango Pension (open 24hr.). Tango also offers a three-hour **trek** which includes a one-hour jeep ride, lunch, and swimming (9am-7pm, $6).

MEDITERRANEAN COAST

A small but spectacular waterfall lies about 7km away from Köyceğiz along the uphill road to Muğla. Located 10 minutes from the yellow Arboretum sign on the central road, this pristine waterfall is the perfect spot for daydreaming and sunbathing. To get to the waterfall, take a dolmuş heading to Marmaris or Muğla and ask to be let off near the Arboretum sign (\$.50). Şahin offers a jeep service to the waterfall (1:30-4:30pm, \$1.80).

DALYAN AND KAUNOS (CAUNUS)   ☎252

The placid, cobblestoned village of Dalyan overflows with pleasant restaurants and tacky souvenir shops. The town seems to have grown naturally out of the breezy river beside it. Lycian rock tombs built into the nearby cliffs are visible from Dalyan's harbor, and thick reed beds teeming with wildlife are just minutes away. A short trip downstream leads to the ancient city of Kaunos and the tranquil Turtle Beach, where endangered sea tortoises are struggling to survive. The Dalyan shore has recently been declared a natural reservation.

No one is quite sure about Kaunos's origins. When it became fashionable to have one's city founded by a hero or a god, early residents invented a son of King Miletus, Caunus, and claimed that he established the city in 3000 BC. Kaunos appears both as a Lycian and a Carian settlement in the course of history, but the Caunian language, beliefs, clothing, and way of life were distinct from those of their neighbors, the Lycians and the Carians. Kaunos had a reputation for being unhealthy; contemporary scholars believe that the marshy land was infested with malaria-carrying mosquitoes. Still, the city served as a major commercial harbor until the end of Byzantine rule, when silting rendered the harbor unusable.

▛ TRANSPORTATION

Buses: While Dalyan has no otogar, frequent city buses run to Ortaca (20min., every 15min., \$.40). From Ortaca, **Kamil Koç** (☎284 31 26, in Ortaca ☎282 20 45) and **Pamukkale** (☎284 20 82; in Ortaca ☎282 51 76) send buses to: **Ankara** (12hr.; 8pm, 8:30pm; \$14.50); **Antalya** (5hr., every hr. 8:30am-11:30pm, \$8.40); **Bodrum** (4hr., 7 per day 10:30am-7:30pm, \$7); **Bursa** (10hr., 5:30pm, \$14.50); **Fethiye** (1¼hr., every 30 min. 6am-midnight, \$2.40); **İstanbul** (14hr.; 5:30, 6:30, 7pm; \$22); **İzmir** (5hr., 7am-1:30am, \$10); **Kaş** (4hr., 3pm, \$7.30); **Kuşadası** (6hr., 11:30pm, \$11); **Marmaris** (1½hr., 8:45am-9:45pm, \$2.40); **Pamukkale** (4½hr.; 12:15, 1:45, 5:45pm; \$7.30).

Dolmuş: The dolmuş from **Ortaca** stops in front of the mosque. A new dolmuş line now runs directly to **Marmaris** and **Fethiye** every morning at 10, 11am, and noon (\$1.80).

✳❼ ORIENTATION AND PRACTICAL INFORMATION

The open area with a turtle statue and mosque is a good reference point. Facing the river, walk left along Maraş Sok. to find plenty of *pansiyons*, restaurants, and a few bars. Maraş Sok. is closed to vehicles from 8pm to 7am to allow pedestrians a pleasant evening stroll.

Tourist Office: (☎284 42 35). Tough to find. With your back to the turtle statues, head into the passageway across Maraş Sok., which is surrounded by 2 ice cream parlors. Provides maps, accommodations listings, and information in 7 languages. Open 8:30am-noon, 1-6pm; in winter 8:30am-noon, 1-5:30pm.

Boat tours: Offices are located behind the turtle statue. The 12 Island Tour travels to local bays and islands, passing by Göcek (9am-6pm, \$28-32 per person, with lunch). Less expensive tours travel to Bacardi Bay and other local bays for swimming (10am-6pm, \$12 per person). The most popular tours cover the ancient city of Kaunos, mud baths and hot springs, and Turtle Beach (10:30am-6pm, \$12 per person, with lunch).

Banks: Several branches with 24-hour **ATMs** in the town center, on the road to Ortaca.

Laundromat: (☎284 44 18), on Maraş Sok., across from Dalyan Camping. \$5 per load. Open 8am-midnight.

Police: (☎284 20 31), on J. dur Karakol Sok., off Maraş Sok.

Pharmacy: (☎284 25 09). Open 8am-8:30pm.

Medical Assistance: Sağlık Ocağı (☎284 20 33), on 130 Sok. near the river. Follow Maraş Sok.; turn right at the Çelik Apart Hotel sign. Open 8:30am-noon, 1:30-5:30pm.

Internet Access: There is an internet cafe one block past the tourist office on the same small alley ($1.20 per hr.). The Fruit Bar (see **Food,** below) also offers internet access for $1.50 per hr. The connection may be erratic.

PTT: (☎284 21 21). Offers **currency exchange,** *poste restante,* fax, and international phone service. Open 8am-midnight. **Postal code:** 48840.

ACCOMMODATIONS

Many small family-run *pansiyons* line Dalyan's main street, Maraş Sok, but make sure your room comes with mosquito-netted screens in the summer. Most offer amenities such as pools, air conditioning, gardens, and views of the rock tombs. Bargaining for the rate may be worth your while.

Kristal Pension (☎284 22 63 or 284 31 53; fax 284 27 43). From the turtle statue, walk down Maraş Sok.; make the 2nd left onto 10 Sok., and continue 1 block. Marble floors, garden pool, and a gorgeous terrace. 20 clean rooms with bath and screens. Great family atmosphere. Breakfast included. Singles $7; doubles $14.

Gül Motel Pension (☎284 24 67; fax 284 48 03). Across from the Kristal Pension. Plant-filled entryway, Ottoman-style tea room, and attractive breakfast terrace. 20 large, clean rooms with bath. The owner will make special Turkish dinners (guests choose the menu) on request. Breakfast $2. Singles $6; doubles $12, with A/C $16.

Aktuş Pansiyon (☎284 20 42 or 284 22 73). On Maraş Sok. 15 charming rooms with bath and fans. Rooms have a chalet-like atmosphere, some with great views of the rock tombs. Doubles $12, with A/C $18; triples $19.

Dönmez Hotel (☎284 21 07). From the turtle statue, turn right onto Maraş Sok. Take the 2nd right, and the hotel is on the left, past the pasta restaurant. This spacious hotel surrounds a courtyard and fountain. Offers simple air-conditioned rooms and a swimming pool. Breakfast on the terrace, complete with views of the rock tombs. Doubles $17.

Dalyan Camping, 106 Maraş Sok. (☎/fax 284 41 57). About 350m from the turtle statue. Turn off where the road begins to bend. Do not be discouraged by the entrance; a clean campsite with views of the rock tombs and acropolis lies beyond. Modern bathrooms with hot showers. Swimming available. Laundry $4 for 5kg. Large fish dinner $6. Breakfast $1.20. 2-person tent $4; 2-person bungalow $8; caravan $8.

FOOD

Many restaurants along Maraş Sok. offer knockout views of the river. They serve nearly identical Turkish and European menus of *meze* ($1-4), omelettes ($4), grills ($7-10), and other standard fare. For do-it-yourself eats, visit the open-air market in front of the PTT. (Open Su 8am-8pm.)

Niobe Restaurant. Take the first left off of Maraş Sok., the restaurant is the 2nd on the left. Offers healthy vegetarian food including such favorites as vegetable *şiş kebaps* ($1.50) and vegetarian pasta ($2.80).

Dalyan Cafe (☎284 32 78). About 60m along Maraş Sok. Enjoy an incredible selection of *gözleme* (crepes) amidst Turkish rugs and traditional low tables. Experiment with fillings like banana, kiwi, cheese, or meat ($1.20-1.80) and watch your meal created before your eyes. Open 7am-2am.

Station Pasta House (☎284 46 50). Across from Pembe restaurant. For a little taste of Italy, this small restaurant with red checkered tablecloths serves pasta dishes ($2-4) and pizzas ($2-4). Try the vegetable lasagna ($3). Open 10am-11pm.

Fruit Bar (☎284 41 64). On Maraş Sok. A cheerful bar where customers can indulge in their wildest fruit fantasies. Fruit pizzas ($6); crêpes ($2.50); banana split ($6); melon ice cream ($3); shakes and fresh juices ($1-3). For a refreshing drink, try the fresh fruit and yogurt drinks ($2). Open 9am-midnight.

◉ SIGHTS

Carian **rock tombs,** dating from the 4th century BC, lie opposite the river. Dalyan's other notable sights are best seen on a boat tour. After passing the rock tombs, the boats visit the ruins of ancient **Kaunos.** From the drop-off point at the base of the acropolis, a 600m dirt path leads up to the admission gate and site.

From the gate, an enormous Roman bath lies on the left. Behind the bath, a well-preserved, rounded nave marks a 5th-century **church,** one of the oldest in the area. Walk down the path behind the church toward the remains of a first-century BC **Doric temple** and a recently-discovered **fountain,** where ancient customs information was recorded. Further down the path, the **theater** once held 5000 spectators. (☎284 28 45. Open in summer 8am-7pm; in winter 9am-5pm. $1.80, students free.)

The boat tour continues along a circuitous path through reed beds to **İztuzu Beach.** The beach is only open from 8am-8pm in order to allow endangered loggerhead turtles to lay their eggs by night. Bring at least $4 to rent beach chairs with umbrellas, since sunbathing with towels on the turtles' resting area is forbidden (see **Save the Sea Turtle,** p. 461). The Kaunos/Turtle Beach tours also stop at local **mud baths** and **thermal springs.** After coating yourself with the restorative mud, relax in the 40°C thermal baths, whose curative powers supposedly extend to arthritis, wrinkles, and stress. (Open 7am-7:30pm. $.80.)

♫ ENTERTAINMENT

Crazy Bar (☎284 47 00). On Maraş Sok., fairly close to the town center. This disco bar has a groovy cave-like interior complete with fake moss, plants, rocks, and flashing colored lights. Lots of room to shake your booty. Plays techno-pop, house, and Turkish pop. Beer $1.20; *rakı* $1.60; cocktails $3.60. Open 7pm-3am.

Albatross Bar (☎284 30 37). On Maraş Sok. Outdoor seating and interior Ottoman-style room. An excellent spot for people-watching while sipping a beer. Good selection of rock, blues, and jazz, with occasional live performances. Beer $1.20; cocktails $3. 10% discount for *Let's Go* readers. Open 7pm-2am.

Nektar Bar (☎284 20 70). On Maraş Sok. An open-air "Secret Garden Bar" complete with lush banana trees, waterfalls, and a twinkling disco bar. Entertain yourself and a new-found friend with a game of backgammon. Plays 60s, 70s, and 80s music. Beer $1.20; *rakı* $1.80; cocktails $2-6. Open 24hr.

DALAMAN ☎252

Dalaman's only attraction is its airport. After landing there, travelers would be wise to move right along out of town.

◪ TRANSPORTATION. The airport isn't even all that close to the city; to get there, take a taxi (10-15min., $6-11, try to bargain). **İstanbul Airlines** (☎692 54 02) flies to **Germany, Britain,** and **İstanbul** on the weekends. Call for other destinations. **Turkish Airlines** (☎692 54 99) flies to **İstanbul** and **Ankara** (both destinations: 1hr.; 6:10, 10:20am, 7:15, 9:30pm; $71, students with ID $64).

The **otogar** is at the intersection of **Kenan Evren Bul.** and **Atatürk Cad.,** the town's main thoroughfare. **Pamukkale** (☎692 28 20) offers a 10% student discount on some routes. Buses run to: **Ankara** (10hr., 8:15 pm, $14.50); **Antalya** (5hr.; noon, 1am; $7.30); **Bodrum** (4hr., 6am-5pm, $7); **Bursa** (7hr., 8pm, $16); **Fethiye** (1hr., every 30min. 7:30am-midnight, $1.80); **İstanbul** (13hr., 6:15pm, $20); **İzmir** (5hr., 6:45am-1:30 am, $10.80); **Kalkan** (2½hr.; 3, 3:30, 4pm; $6); **Kaş** (3hr.; 10:15am, 2:15pm, 3am; $7); **Marmaris** (1½hr., 7:30am-6:30pm, $4.80); **Milas** (2hr., every hr. 7am-7:30pm, $6); **Pamukkale** (5hr.; noon, 1:30, 5:30pm; $9); **Selçuk** (4hr., 5:30am-1am, $10.80). To get to the dolmuş stop from the otogar, take a left on Atatürk Cad. and walk 300m down on the right past the *jandarma*. **Dolmuş** run to: **Fethiye** (1hr., every hr. 7am-8pm, $1.45); **Marmaris** (1½hr., every hr. 8am-8pm, $.50); **Muğla** (3hr., every hr. 7am-7pm, $2.40); **Ortaca** (for **Dalyan;** 20min., frequent, $.40).

7 PRACTICAL INFORMATION. The **police station** (☎692 58 88) is across from the otogar. The **hospital** is on Kenan Evren Bul. before the intersection with Atatürk Cad. (☎692 50 26. Open 24hr.) Dalaman's large **PTT,** 3 Sok. No. 20, off Atatürk Cad., offers *poste restante*, international phone calls, and fax. (☎692 40 08. Open daily 8:30am-noon, 1:30-6pm.) **Postal code:** 48770.

ACCOMMODATIONS AND FOOD. Don't be fooled by the pricey hotels and pensions that line Kenan Evran Bul. on the way to the airport. Several cheap and attractive pensions are located in the town's central area. **Yılmaz Pension,** Cengiz Topel Cad., 2 Sok., 10/1, a wonderfully pink pension surrounded by a lush garden, has eight large carpeted rooms and shared bathrooms. (☎692 55 11. Singles $5; doubles $10.) **Çelik Pansiyon,** Atatürk Cad., 9 Sok. No. 6, next to Yolcu pension, has four carpeted rooms, some with bath. (☎692 58 76. Breakfast $1.20. $5 per person.) **Yolcu Pension,** Atatürk Cad., 9 Sok. No. 8, has four bedrooms, a pleasant terrace, and a shared kitchen. Follow Atatürk Cad. from the central roundabout about 100m, turn left onto 9 Sok., and take the first right. (☎692 58 90 or 692 24 96. Breakfast included. $6 per person; price may be negotiable.)

For eats, try **Dalyan Restaurant** (☎692 31 04), about 150m down Atatürk Cad. from the bus station. Under a grape-covered terrace, this restaurant serves such Turkish staples as *çorba* ($3), kebaps ($4), and *pide* ($1.75).

GÖCEK
☎252

A tiny, beautiful village on a sparkling bay, Göcek caters mostly to wealthy yacht owners. Think "Lifestyles of the Rich and Famous," minus Robin Leach. However, even the non-rich and anonymous can enjoy exploring this relaxed seaside town.

TRANSPORTATION AND PRACTICAL INFORMATION. Göcek is about 1km off the Dalaman-Fethiye road. The town's one main road, **Atatürk Cad.** (İskete Mah.) runs from the gas station on the Dalaman-Fethiye road to the main square (with a statue of Atatürk at its center). This street is lined with restaurants, boating and tourist shops, and some *pansiyons*. With your back to the statue, the harbor is on the left and the dolmuş hub and otogar are on the right.

To get to Göcek, take any **bus** between Dalaman and Fethiye and get off at the gas station. Buses from Dalaman to Fethiye pass by every 30 minutes (20min., $1). Reach the **hospital** (☎645 11 77), with an English-speaking doctor, by turning your back on Atatürk, walking down Atatürk Cad., taking the first right and then the first left. To reach **Okyanus Internet Café,** turn left at the harbor and walk 25m. ($2 per hr. Open 8am-midnight.) The **PTT** is in the main square. (☎645 14 63. In summer 8am-10pm; in winter 8:30am-noon, 1:30-5pm.) **Postal code:** 48310.

ACCOMMODATIONS, FOOD, AND ENTERTAINMENT. The **Dim Pansiyon** is on the right side of Atatürk Cad., about three blocks away from the harbor. This beautiful *pansiyon* offers 13 large rooms with bath, a kitchen, pool, and garden bar. (☎645 12 94. Breakfast $1.80. Doubles with A/C $17.) Walk down Atatürk Cad. 50m from the Dalaman-Fethiye road to the **Zelga Hostel.** This laid-back establishment has a cozy, air-conditioned terrace bar and 10 simple rooms. (☎645 18 75. Doubles $17.) **Ünler Pansiyon,** also on Atatürk Cad., has 16 large rooms with dark wood and screens. (☎615 11 70. Breakfast included. Rooms $12, with A/C $19.)

The popular **Anatolian Restaurant,** on Atatürk Cad., is decked out in full Anatolian style with mud walls, a straw roof, water pipes, and floor seating. (☎645 19 74. *Meze* $1.20; grills $4-8; vegetable casserole $3; glass of wine $1; open 8am-1am.) The **Magic Marina,** on the harbor, is a lively bar with a huge chessboard. (☎645 11 67. Beer $1.60; *rakı* $2-3; cocktails $3-8. Open 8am until the last customer leaves.) **Dr. Jazz,** on Atatürk Cad., is an elegant social jazz bar that opens onto the harbor. (☎645 17 29. Beer $1.20; cocktails $3-8. Open 8:30am-midnight.)

SIGHTS. There is not much to see in Göcek, so most people just come to relax. There are daily boat trips to the nearest **beach** (7km away) and other nearby bays (9:30am-4pm, $14 per person with lunch).

FETHİYE COAST

FETHİYE ☎252

A big town with a small-town feel, Fethiye rests peacefully on a harbor surrounded by pine forests and mountains. Its inexpensive *pansiyons* and nearby islands make Fethiye a popular stop on the Mediterranean backpacker circuit. Most visitors take daytrips to Ölüdeniz, Butterfly Valley, Karaköy, or Saklıkent Gorge during the day and later on enjoy Fethiye's winding streets and low-key nightlife.

Fethiye rests on ancient Telmessos, founded in the 5th century BC. Telmessos was ruled by the Persians until it joined the Lycian Federation in the 4th century BC. From then, the list of its rulers runs the familiar gamut, including Alexander the Great, the Ptolemies, the Romans, and the Byzantines. The city was called Meğri, "the far city," after its inclusion in the Ottoman Empire in 1424. In 1934, the city was renamed "Fethiye" in honor of a martyred fighter pilot, Fethi Bey.

TRANSPORTATION

Buses: The otogar is on Ölüdeniz Cad. Buses running along the coastal road can drop off passengers anywhere, so there's no need to wait for a bus to a specific destination. **Ulusoy** (☎612 37 37), **Kamil Koç** (☎612 06 36 or 614 19 73), and **Pamukkale** serve Fethiye. To: **Alanya** (6hr.; 2:30pm, 2:30am; $9); **Ankara** (9hr.; 10, 10:30, 11pm; $19); **Antalya** (4hr.; 2:30pm, 2:30am; $7); **Bodrum** (5hr., 5 per day 8:30am-4pm, $8); **Bursa** (10hr.; 5, 9:30, 10:30pm; $14.50); **Çanakkale** (12hr., 12:15pm, $17); **Cappadocia** (13hr., 6pm, $14.50); **Eskişehir** (7hr.; 9:30, 10:30pm; $12), **İstanbul** (13hr., 7 per day 5pm-11:30pm, $24); **İzmir** (6½hr., 5:30am-12:30am, $10.80); **Kaş** (2hr., 4am-5:30pm, $3.60); **Marmaris** (2½hr., 12:30-6:30pm, $4.80); **Pamukkale** (4½hr.; 9:30am, noon, 3:15, 4:30pm; $6); **Selçuk** (6hr., 6:15am-12:30am, $10.80).

Dolmuş: From the dolmuş stop near the intersection of Hastane and Atatürk Cad. to: **Çalış Beach** (5min., every 5min. 7am-1am, $.40); **Ölüdeniz** (20-25min., every 10min. 7am-9pm, $1); **Saklıkent** (45min., every 30min. 7am-7pm, $2). Dolmuş run to **Kayaköy** from the main dolmuş station on Atatürk Cad. (40min., every hr. 7am-7pm, $1.20). **Dolmuş boats** to **Çalış Beach** leave from the waterfront to the right of the main harbor (every 20min. 9:30am-8pm, every 30min. 10pm-midnight; $2).

Taxi: (☎614 44 77). On Atatürk Cad., across from the Atatürk head. 24hr. service.

Mopeds: Abalı Rent (☎614 95 36). Between the antique theater and the entrance to the old town. Prices start at $20 per day. Open 8am-midnight.

ORIENTATION

The otogar is 2km from the center of town, on the way to Ölüdeniz. If there are no *servis* shuttles to the town center, leave the terminal, cross the street, and wait for a dolmuş heading to Fethiye (about 10min., frequent, $.40). The dolmuş runs on the main street, **Atatürk Cad.**, past a mosque, PTT, and the Atatürk head. Facing the PTT, the harbor, tourist information office, and old town are on the left. The ritzy **Çalış Beach** is to the right along **Sedir Sok.**, which becomes **Akdeniz Cad.** Çarşı Cad. runs behind Atatürk Cad. on the other side of the bazaar.

PRACTICAL INFORMATION

TOURIST AND FINANCIAL SERVICES

Tourist Office: 1/A İskele Meydanı (☎/fax 614 15 27). Past the PTT. English spoken. Map and lodging info. Open daily 8:30am-5pm; in winter M-F 8am-5pm.

Travel Agencies: Fetur (☎614 20 34 or 614 24 43; fax 614 38 45; www.fethiye-net.com). 50m past the tourist office on Fevzi Çakmak Cad. Arranges flights and daily tours. Open daily 9am-5:30pm. **Garfield Tourism and Travel Agency** (☎614 93 12 or

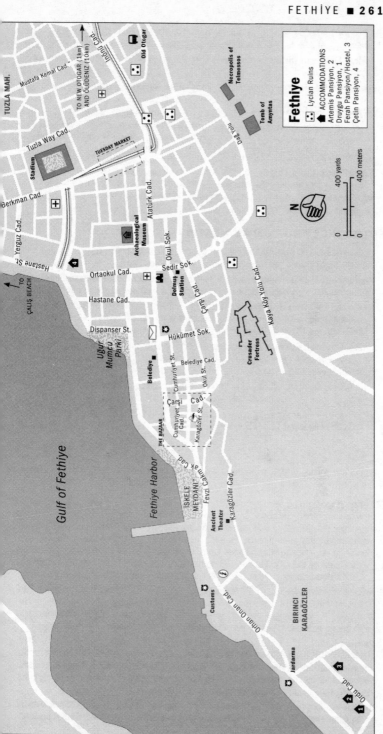

Gulf of Fethiye

Fethiye Harbor

Fethiye

614 93 13; fax 614 25 93), along the harbor on Fevzi Çakmak Cad., offers 3-day back-packer yacht cruises ($119 in high season; B.Y.O.B.).

Diving: European Diving Center (☎614 97 71; fax 614 97 72) offers beginning and advanced scuba dives ($60).

Banks: On Atatürk Cad., facing the PTT. 24hr. **ATMs. Money exchange** 8:30am-5:30pm.

LOCAL SERVICES

English-Language Bookstore: Imagine Bookstore (☎614 84 65), on Cumhuriyet Cad., sells books, maps, and music. Air-conditioned. Open 9:30am-midnight.

Laundromat: (☎612 56 32). On Çarşı Cad. $4.50 per load. Open daily 8:30am-9pm.

Hamam: (☎614 93 18). In the middle of the old town, opposite the Car Cemetery Bar. Soak up history at this 400-year-old bath. $12 per person. Open 6am-midnight.

Market: Along the canal about 500m from the tourist office. Vendors sell clothes, fresh vegetables, and fruit. Held Tu 7am-7pm.

EMERGENCY AND COMMUNICATIONS

Police: (☎614 10 40). Around the corner from the tourist office, near the ancient the-ater. A larger branch (☎614 13 09) is on Atatürk Cad., across from the PTT.

Pharmacies: Many on Atatürk Cad., including **Kestepli Eczanesi Pharmacy** across from the mosque. A very helpful pharmacy can be found right next to the public hospital.

Hospitals: ▉**Letoon Hospital** (☎612 54 84), on Patlanak Mahaller Cad., has English-speaking doctors. Open 24hr. The public **Devlet Hastanesi** (☎614 40 17 or 614 40 18) is near the PTT at the intersection of Atatürk and Hastane Cad.

Internet Access: Internet Café, on Atatürk Cad. next to Imagine Bookstore. $1.80 per hr. Open 9am-midnight. Other internet cafes dot the city. The Ferah Pansiyon also offers internet access to guests.

Post Office: On Atatürk Cad., 500m from the tourist office. *Poste restante*, international phone calls, money exchange, and fax. Most services 24hr. **Postal code:** 48300.

▐ ACCOMMODATIONS

Cheap *pansiyons* can be found on and around Fevzi Çakmak Cad. Some excellent pensions on Karaözler Ordu Cad. are well worth a brief and scenic walk from the city. Quality varies widely in Fethiye—if you find a place on your own, ask to see a room before you check in.

▉**Ferah Pansiyon,** 2. Karagözler Ordu Cad. No. 21 (☎/fax 614 28 16; email ferahpension@hotmail.com). Call for free pickup from the otogar. A 10-minute walk or a 3-minute dolmuş ride ($.20) from Atatürk Cad. (Get off at the *jandarma*, walk up the hill opposite the bay, and take the 1st right; the hostel is on the left.) One of the best hos-tels in Turkey. 9 clean and spacious rooms, most with bath, and one terrace dorm room with a view of the bay. Laundry $3. Free use of a nearby pool. Discount at nearby hamam. Home-cooked dinner $5. Breakfast included. Dorms $3.60; $10 per person.

▉**Artemis Pansiyon** (☎612 49 80; fax 612 50 13). Down the street from the Ferah Pan-siyon, on the right. 14 bright rooms with balconies and bath. Beautiful terrace with har-bor view. The multilingual owners used to work as chefs in a 5-star İstanbul hotel and now create gourmet meals for guests. Breakfast included. Singles $8; doubles $14.

Pension Çetin, 100 Cad. Dolgu Sahası DSİ Yanı (☎614 61 56; fax 614 77 94). When facing the PTT, head right on Atatürk Cad. and turn left onto Hastane Cad.; a sign for the pension is 100m down on the right side of street. 18 large and comfortable rooms with wood paneling, bath, and balconies. Very friendly and helpful owner. Conveniently close to the Tuesday market. Breakfast included. $15 per room.

Druygu Pension (☎614 35 63). Just past the Artemis Pension. 10 simple, comfortable rooms, all with bath. Harbor view from the terrace. Breakfast included. $5 per person.

FOOD

Çarşı Cad., in the pleasant old town, oozes with great dining possibilities. Options near the harbor have views, but tend to be pricier. On the boardwalk of Çalış Beach (up Hastane Cad. away from the mosque) are restaurants, bars, and cafés.

Meğri Lokantası, Cumhuriyet Mah. 13/A Çarşı Cad. (☎614 40 74; fax 612 04 46). Near the harbor, off Atatürk Cad., right before the curve in the road. Enormous selection of sumptuous Turkish fare. *Soğuk* (cold) *meze* $1.40; *şiş* $3.60. Open all night.

Meğri Restaurant (☎614 40 47). In the main square of the bazaar. A sister establishment of the Lokantası, this large outdoor restaurant specializes in fresh fish. Fish $4-7; *meze* $2. Open 9am-1am.

Birlik Restaurant. Walk along the harbor until you reach Hastane Cad. Offers delicious Turkish food, cafeteria style, for unbelievably low prices. A favorite with local men. Vegetable dishes $.30; meat dishes $1; dessert $.30.

Yörükoğlu (☎612 20 64). On Çarşı Cad. This small, friendly restaurant serves huge, savory "Turkish burritos" ($2) and makes tortillas before your eyes. Open 8am-1am.

Sedir Restaurant, 3 Tütün Sok. (☎614 10 95). From Atatürk Cad., turn onto Çarşı Cad. and make another left before the curve in the road. Elegant outdoor seating. Tasty wood-fired pizzas $4-6; grills $4.80. Open 7am-midnight.

Rıhtım Pastanesı, Cumhuriyet Mah. 13/3 Çarşı Cad. (☎612 38 31). These people must be in league with the local dentists. A huge selection of international pastries and Turkish classics like baklava. Try a sampling of dozens of mini-tarts. Open 7am-2am.

👁 SIGHTS

RUINS. The road north into Fethiye ascends steep hillsides thick with pine trees and loud with the shrill chirps of crickets. Isolated from the rest of Asia Minor, this region fostered the development of an insulated Lycian culture in ancient times. Believed to be the descendants of a pre-Hittite Anatolian people, the Lycians remained independent until the Persians gained control in 545 BC. The **necropolis** that remains is the most concrete remnant of Lycian culture. The facades of the cliff-hewn tombs replicate Greek temples down to the pediments, porticoes, and cornices. The tombs themselves are thought to be replicas of Lycian homes. The most notable find at the site is the 4th-century BC **Tomb of Amyntas,** reached by a 200-step climb. You can enter the other tombs as well, though to reach them you must clamber around the rocks. From the necropolis, the remains of the **Fethiye Tower,** built by the Knights of St. John of the Templar, are visible. *(Follow the tiny roads behind Çarşı Cad. to the left and uphill to the rock tombs. Necropolis open 24hr., illuminated at night. $1.20.)*

ARCHAEOLOGICAL MUSEUM. Fethiye's museum contains Lycian artifacts from neighboring digs. Upon entering, be sure to check out the display on ancient dress and weaving techniques. Of particular note are the **Stelae of Music** in the back room, a trilingual stele from Letoon that helped crack the Lycian dialect, and an unbelievable 19th-century **Greek wooden door** carved with elaborate floral decorations. *(Located 1 block from the Devlet Hastanesi on Atatürk Cad., towards the bus station. ☎614 11 50. Open Tu-Su 9am-5pm; in winter 8:30am-5pm. $1.20.)*

OUTDOOR ACTIVITIES. An evening stroll on the hillside roads above Fethiye offers a fantastic view of the surrounding hillsides, the sea, and yachts in the marina. Eventually, the dirt roads wind into a quiet farming village. For something completely different, one- or three-day **boat trips** to nearby islands include the riotous booze cruises for "backpackers and free-minded travelers." **Twelve-island tours** usually stop at Göcek Island for a quick swim, continue to the resort town Göcek, then on to Flat Island, and finally to the Dock-Yard Island (where the ruins of an Ottoman dockyard can be seen). Other stops include **Cleopatra's Bath** (where bath-

MEDITERRANEAN COAST

ing in the spring is said to make you look ten years younger), the Step Cave, and *çay* at **Somanlık Bay.** The Ölüdeniz-Butterfly Valley tour stops first by **Butterfly Valley** and continues to the famous beach at Ölüdeniz (see p. 266). There are also trips to Turtle Beach and Dalyan-Kaunos, which include a mud bath ($18; see p. 256). Call a travel agency for details (see **Travel Agencies,** p. 260). *(Boats depart 10am, return 6:30pm; $11-18; lunch and tea included.)*

Check with a travel agent for **horseback riding** trips to Ölüdeniz and Kayaköy. *(3hr., leaves when there are enough people, $15.)* **River rafting trips** on the Dalaman River are another favorite pastime of Fethiye visitors. *(Daily 8am-6pm. Lunch included. $72.)*

🎵 ENTERTAINMENT

Despite its large size, Fethiye's nightlife is relatively quiet. The bars and clubs are located in the old town. For a taste of package tour pizzazz, head down to the string of lively bars along Çarşı Beach.

▨ Ottoman Bar (☎612 11 48). On the right, before Maman Sok. runs into Çarşı Cad. Fit for a pasha: fragrant smoke drifts from the large selection of water pipes (try the apple-apricot flavor). The relaxed crowd lounges outdoors in cushion-lined booths when not dancing. Water pipe $3.60; beer $1.80; *rakı* $2. Open daily noon-3am.

Car Cemetery Bar, 33 Hamam Sok. (☎614 11 81). Across from the old hamam in the old city. Have a cold beer amid deceased car parts. Cocktail names like "orgasm," "slippery nipple," and "blow job" will be sure to spice up your evening. Beer $1.80; *rakı* $2; cocktails $4-6. Open 10am-4am.

The Music Factory (☎617 51 72). On Hamam Sok., is a tourist favorite. A pumping metallic cage with 2 levels of flashing dance floors and stylish, thrashing bodies. House and dance music. Beer $1.80; *rakı* $2; cocktails $2-6. Open daily 5pm-5am.

Yes Bar (☎614 92 89). On Cumhuriyet Cad., above the English bookstore. Enjoy free melon with your drink and watch buff waiters dance with their mirror reflections. Yes—yes—oh—yes! Alternative music. Beer $1.20; *rakı* $3; cocktails $4-6. Open 8pm-4am.

🏞 DAYTRIPS FROM FETHİYE

SAKLIKENT GORGE

To get to Saklıkent Gorge from Fethiye, grab the Saklıkent dolmuş, opposite the mosque and near the intersection of Hastane Cad. and Atatürk Cad. (45min., every 30min., $2). Otherwise, most travel agents along Fethiye's marina would be delighted to offer you a package tour ($15). A third choice is to catch a dolmuş tour ($4) from the main dolmuş station in Fethiye (located opposite the sea on Çarşı Cad., behind the petrol station). These depart at 10am and return at 6pm, going to Saklıkent, Tlos, and Yaka Park (home of a fish-farm restaurant).

Ice-cold water gushes in from natural springs to flood this 18km-deep canyon, leaving in its wake incredibly smooth, white stone walls and stone terraces. Occasional patches of sunshine illuminate striking views of the mountains above the raging rapids. Enter the opening of the gorge and battle rushing water and slippery-smooth surfaces, going as far into the gorge as you feel comfortable. Claustrophobes should run for their lives. There are ill-fitting plastic shoes for rent in the gorge ($1) and at the River Tree Bar outside the gorge ($.50; $1 if you lose them). Sneakers or other shoes with good traction are a better bet. *(Gorge open in summer 8am-8pm. $1.90. Given the challenging nature of the excursion, Let's Go does not recommend going deep into the gorge alone.)*

A number of local restaurants cater to the hungry adventurer. **Saklıkent,** past the wooden bridge in the mouth of the gorge, serves traditional Turkish food at low Ottoman tables on beautiful patios built over the rushing water. (☎636 85 55. *Köfte* $2.80. Open 7am-8:30pm.) **Kayıp Cennet,** over the bridge in Paradise Park, serves up a huge buffet of cold *meze*, a main course of fish or chicken, and watermelon for dessert. It also has nifty Ottoman-style seating on small islands in the river. (☎636 84 06 or 636

87 77. Buffet $4; drinks extra. Open 24hr.) **River Bar** (☎636 87 67) offers full lunch plates (salad, trout, and fries $6; omelettes $1.20) and popular treehouse **camping** (free for customers; toilets and showers available; $1 per person; caravan with electricity $4). The bar also offers **internet** service and **rafting** expeditions. Sleep for free on cushioned riverside platforms at the neighboring **Kanyon Restaurant** (☎659 00 89); beer is discounted for those who spend the night. River rafting and *rakı* don't mix.

TLOS

Many Fethiye travel agencies offer daily tours to Tlos, which usually include Saklıkent Gorge (see Travel Agencies, p. 260). Alternatively, Saklıkent-Yaka Park-Tlos daytrip dolmuş depart from the dolmuş station in Fethiye (10am, return 6pm; $4; bring your own lunch). A third option is to catch any Saklıkent-bound dolmuş from Fethiye (30min., every 20min., $2); ask to be let off near Tlos. Trek 4km uphill from the yellow sign. Open 8am-7pm. $1.20.

One of the six major cities of the Lycian Kingdom, Tlos is now home to an eclectic mixture of Lycian, Roman, Byzantine, and Ottoman ruins. Its prominent **castle** is visible from kilometers away. At the entrance to the site, ignore the sign for the castle (20m from the entrance booth). Instead, start at the theater and bath at the back of the ruins and work your way up to the castle. With a seating capacity of 5000 in its heyday, the **theater** still has several intact entrances, including one leading to the stage. Continuing down the road, take a left at the hamam sign and walk for about 20m. On the right is a well-preserved but still fairly unexcavated **Roman bath,** whose high arches once supported a bath and sports center.

Back on the main road and to the left, a large **stadium** stands with arched entryways through which Roman gladiators once rushed in anticipation of bloody duels. Continue back toward the castle sign and ascend a small mountain to see 7th-century BC **rock tombs** and well-preserved **Lycian Sarcophagi** with inverted boat-shaped lids. The tombs' corrugated roofs replicate the style used by the Lycians in the roofs of their own homes. A hike up to the **castle-fortress** is rewarded by an incredible view of the valley, the old horse stables, and the rest of the site. Far in the distance, the gorge appears as a massive crack in the mountains.

A favorite place to stop is **Yaka Park Restaurant,** 2km up the road from the Tlos ruins. Fish ($4.50) and chicken ($4) meals are served at shady tables over falling water. Be sure to tour the fish farm and the twisting waterways that wind through the enormous outdoor eating area, full of those very fish you're about to eat. (☎636 87 67. Open 8am-10pm.) Dolmuş pass the restaurant before arriving in Tlos. Across from the ruins is the **Belleforo Restaurant.** (Meal $3. Room with breakfast $5, with breakfast and dinner $8.) Or try the speckled trout, a local specialty, at the **Tlosaile Restaurant** next door.

KAYAKÖY

Dolmuş leave for Kayaköy from in front of the mosque in Fethiye (30min., every hr. 7am-8pm, $1.20). Roaming the abandoned town takes about 3 hours. (Open 9am-6pm. $1.50; free after 6pm.)

Deserted and desolate, the abandoned village of Kayaköy looms eerily over a quiet agricultural valley some 10km from Fethiye. Built in the beginning of the 18th century, Kayaköy was inhabited by 2500 Orthodox Greeks until the 1923 population exchange (see **The Treaty of Lausanne,** p. 16). Kayaköy was abandoned and the newly-arrived Muslims refused to move into the village, some say out of respect for those who, like themselves, were forced to leave their homes. Others suggest that the Muslims disliked the style of Kayaköy's two-story houses, which had a first floor reserved for animals and the bath outside of the house. Each house was built on the hill, so that its shadow would not fall on another house. The doors, windows, and roofs were taken by the Muslims to help build new houses down the road, leaving Kayaköy a haunting shell of what it once was. The Turkish Ministry of Culture made the ghost town a historical monument in the mid-1980s when commercial interests threatened to turn Kayaköy into a holiday village. If sponsors put out, there are plans to build a library and restore some of the houses and the two Greek Orthodox churches.

MEDITERRANEAN COAST

Three popular **hikes** can be made from Kayaköy. A 2-hour hike to **Ölüdeniz** winds through cool pine forests, with views of the Blue Lagoon. Signs about every 100m direct hikers. The lovely and less touristed **Cool Water Bay,** another popular trek, takes between 45 minutes and 1½ hours. **Gemiler Beach,** a 2½-hour hike, passes an exquisite hidden monastery. For trekking advice, ask at the popular **Çavuşoğlu Motel and Restaurant** (☎(258) 616 67 49), which has great *mezes* ($1.50), pizza ($2.40), and grills ($4.60). Crash in one of their 14 colorful rooms with bath ($18 per room), or bring a tent and camp free in the garden by the swimming pool. Next door, the **İstanbul Restaurant** (☎616 73 82) serves tasty *böreks* ($1.20), french fries ($1.20), soups ($1.20), and various meat dishes ($3; open daily 7am-midnight).

ÖLÜDENİZ   ☎252

This famous Turkish Riviera retreat caters to both the hippie and glitzy beach town crowds. Although posters of the partially enclosed beach hang on the walls of most Turkish hotels, no picture can convey the sheer beauty of Ölüdeniz's enticing beach and lagoon. Ölüdeniz has been bitten hard by the tourist bug, and it suffers from the usual symptoms of commercial package tours and resorts. However, the excellent campsites and the variety of exciting outdoor activities still allow visitors to appreciate the area's glorious natural beauty. Ölüdeniz is well placed for daytrips to the Butterfly Valley and nearby bays, and it has become a popular paragliding spot for amateurs and professionals alike.

TRANSPORTATION AND PRACTICAL INFORMATION

The best way to reach Ölüdeniz is via Fethiye. Dolmuş conveniently stop on the main pebble beach before a curve in the main road. The lagoon and some campgrounds are on the right (when facing the water). To the left along the waterfront is a string of bars, restaurants, other campsites, and paragliding companies.

Dolmuş: In summer, dolmuş run to **Fethiye** (25min.; every 10min. 7am-1am, return every 15min.; $3). Dolmuş stop in Fethiye near the petrol station on Çarşı Cad. or at the mosque near the intersection of Atatürk Cad. and Hastane Cad. (see p. 260).

Tourism Cooperative: (☎617 04 38 or 617 01 45; fax 617 01 35), in the small wooden building on the left just up the Fethiye road. Helps with rooms and offers valuable information about boat trips and paragliding. English spoken. Open daily 8:30am-11pm.

Travel Agencies: Living Force (☎/fax 616 67 91; open 8am-11pm), **Traveler's World** (☎617 00 45; fax 617 00 54; email cemgurk@hotmail.com), and **Adventura** (☎617 03 14; fax 617 03 78), all on the main road along the waterfront, offer tours. Trips to **Camel Beach,** the **Blue Caves,** and **Butterfly Valley** ($9; see p. 268); jeep safaris to **Saklıkent Gorge, Tlos, Patara, Xanthos,** and a local mudbath ($30; see p. 264); and boat service to **Dalyan-Kaunos** ($20; see p. 256). Adventura also offers **paintball** (9:30am-1:30pm, 2:30-7:30pm; $24 includes 50 balls) in a pine forest near Kayaköy; **horseback riding** (8:30am-noon, 4:30-7:30pm; $16); **diving** ($67); and **river rafting** (8:15am-9pm; $72, meals included). Traveler's World can also book flights.

Currency Exchange: At larger campsites, some stores, and the Tourism Cooperative.

Hamam: Sultan Hamam Club Belcekiz (☎617 00 77), on the waterfront. Bath and drink $15. Open 9am-9pm.

Police: Jandarma (☎617 00 55 or 617 01 27), 50m toward the lagoon entrance.

Pharmacies: Several along the main road of Hisarönü.

Medical Assistance: Lykia Medical Service (☎616 69 30). Walk 1 block up the road to Fethiye, turn right, and continue 100m. **Esnaf Hospital** (☎616 65 17 or 616 65 13), near Lykia Medical. English spoken. Both open 24hr. Fethiye's **Letoon Hospital** also keeps an ambulance here and offers emergency service.

Internet Access: In the back of **Buzz Bar,** on the waterfront next to Traveler's World. $2 per hr. Open 10am-10:30pm. **Ölüdeniz Camping, OBA Camping, Crusoe's Bar** (see below) offer access for $1.50 per hr.

PTT: (☎617 01 08), next to the police station. Offers international phone calls and basic mail services. Open Apr.-Oct. 8:30am-9pm. **Postal code:** 48340.

ACCOMMODATIONS

Campsites offer backpackers a laid-back community atmosphere, but **Hisarönü,** the village uphill from the beach, is growing in popularity for its cheap pensions and hi-tech discos. Dolmuş from Fethiye to Ölüdeniz stop here. It is also possible to find a room in one of Ölüdeniz's many hotels for about $8 per person. Ask at the Tourism Cooperative for information on local hotels and bookings.

Ölüdeniz Camping (☎617 00 48; fax 617 01 81; email oludenizcamping@superonline.com). 1km along the road to the lagoon entrance (turn right from the dolmuş stop). Call for free pick-up. Not to be confused with Ölüdeniz Pension. A backpackers' mecca, with 40 bungalows, a small beach, market, restaurant, and bar. Famous peach ice cream cocktails. Internet access $1.50 for 30min., $2.50 per hr. Beer $1.20. 2-for-1 drinks 7-9pm. Turkish breakfast $2. English breakfast $3. Bungalows $5 per person; double bungalows with showers $8; tents $3 per person, with own tent $1.60; spot in the large treehouse $2; caravans with electricity $5.

OBA (☎617 04 70; fax 617 05 22; email obamotel@superonline.com). Follow the road to the main beach and turn left at the OBA sign; OBA is on the right. This large and friendly campsite is another popular option for backpackers. Laundry $5 per load. Internet access $2.50 per hr. International calling available. Excellent bar and restaurant with a special vegetarian menu (meals $3-7; beer $1). 31 bungalows. $5 per person, with shower $6; mosquito-netted bed in the large treehouse $2.40; rooms $7-9.

Deniz Camp, Hostel, and Beach Chalet (☎/fax 617 00 45; email cemgurk@hotmail.com). To the left of the exit road when facing the water, behind Buzz Bar. Enjoy rustic bungalows or rest under the olive grove. Experienced guide Anthia Gurkan can reserve plane and bus tickets and arrange trekking and paragliding. Laundry $5 per load. Tidy bungalows $8 per person; caravans $7, with electricity $8; tent $6.

FOOD

Food, drink, and revelry cost a pretty penny in Ölüdeniz, especially along the boardwalk, but the quality and service usually match the prices. You can always opt to grab a meal at your campsite.

Hippie Shake (☎617 06 60). From the boardwalk, turn left at the only street that intersects the waterfront strip and walk 10m. *Muesli* $2.40; spicy chicken and tabouli pockets $3; burgers and salads $2-4; delicious shakes, smoothies, and desserts $2-3.

Sugar Shack/Help Bar (☎617 04 98), to the left on the boardwalk. This funky combination bar and snack shack has mouth-watering specials, sizzling fajitas, and "funky and fruity cocktails" ($3). Salads $3-4; pasta dishes $5; a mean chocolate cake $2.40. Beer $1.45; cocktails $2-6. Basketball, punching bags, and foosball (free). Open 9am-2am; kitchen closes at 11pm.

Our Place (☎616 69 19). In Hisarönü, on the Fethiye dolmuş route. A delicious and unique selection of vegetarian cuisine. The menu changes every night. Swimming pool, bar (beer $1.20), and a cozy reading area with couches and used books in English. Soup $2; salads $2; main dishes $4-8; outstanding desserts $2-3. Open 11am-3am.

Kum-Tur/Kumsal Pide (☎617 00 58; fax 617 03 77). Left of the dolmuş stop, at the end of the boardwalk. One of the oldest restaurants in Ölüdeniz. Traditional Turkish food at good prices. Quiet eating area in the shade. Salads $1.60; *pide* $2-4; seafood $3-6.

SIGHTS

Its marvelous pebble beach aside, Ölüdeniz's main attraction is the **Blue Lagoon,** an idyllic peninsula of beach cradled in wooded hills and lapped by shining, clear water. Take a blissful, quiet dip in these waters, especially on weekday mornings and evenings when crowds are thinner. Enter from Tabiat Park, on the right of the road from Fethiye, where potable water, bathrooms, and showers are available. It's a 20-minute walk to the tip or a $6 taxi ride from the dolmuş station. *(Park and lagoon open 6:30am-9pm. $1.20, cars $4.80.)*

 The next best thing to swimming in the Blue Lagoon is to see it from above by tandem **paragliding.** There are plenty of offices on the boardwalk, including **Sky Sports Paragliding** (☎617 05 11; fax 617 03 24; email skyosman@hotmail.com), which will show you their video and set you up for one of several daily flights. Passengers are driven to the top of Baba Dağı and given take-off and landing instructions. (Flight time varies with conditions, but the whole experience usually takes about two hours and costs $130. You may have to book a day in advance.) Experienced solo pilots can usually get transportation to the top of the mountain from paragliding companies ($8; another $8 to fly from the mountain). Paragliding is not without risk; stick to companies that seem reputable and safe.

 Ölüdeniz is a great base for daily boat excursions. **St. Nicholas Island,** which once housed a thriving Greek community, now offers swimming, a spine-tingling view of the coast, and the remains of a Byzantine basilica. For other tours to places such as **Camel Beach,** the **Blue Caves,** and **Butterfly Valley,** see **Travel Agencies,** p. 266.

♫ ENTERTAINMENT

Ölüdeniz's nightlife focuses on the waterfront, where stores and restaurants burn the midnight oil and a few bars and clubs stay open into the wee hours.

 Crusoe's Bar (☎617 01 75). A very happening bar-disco overlooking the water. Dance to hip-hop and other tunes or enjoy a drink in the "cabana." Large-screen TVs show major sports events and one English-language movie per night (9pm, free with drink). Air-conditioned interior has a pool table. Internet access $1.50 per hr. Beer $2; cocktails $5. Open 2pm-5am.

 Buzz Bar/Buzz Snacks. On the left side of the boardwalk. Chill at this bar or snack at the adjoining café. Great view of the water. Internet access and daily specials. Beer $2; cocktails $3-5. Open 10am-2am.

 Tonoz Beach Club Bar/Barcelona Night Club/Vault Bar/Chillout Cafe & Restaurant (☎617 05 88). On the street past the Hippie Shake. A massive block-long complex. The Vault Bar advertises nightly English-language films, except Sa, when they "party too hard and can't bother." The mellower may sip wine ($2.40 per glass) by the pool.

 Banana Club/Bar. 175m past the Tonoz Beach Club (when heading away from the beach). This tropical dive offers billiards ($4), a sauna (free with drinks), a pool table, darts, a pool, and plenty of strange banana concoctions ($2-6) that keep customers singing along to pop music.

▣ DAYTRIP FROM ÖLÜDENİZ: BUTTERFLY VALLEY

Small wooden dolmuş boats heading to Butterfly Valley leave from the beach to the right of Ölüdeniz (45min.; 11am, 2, 6pm; return 8am, 1, 5pm; $3 each way). Fancier yacht tours will also take you on a daytrip that includes Butterfly Valley for a much higher price.

Almost indescribably beautiful, this tiny turquoise bay near Ölüdeniz is home to waterfalls and several species of butterflies, including the nocturnal orange and black Jersey Tiger butterfly. After the daytrippers leave, an inviolable silence settles over Butterfly Valley, with only the rolling surf and the occasional strains of a backpacker's guitar to lull visitors to sleep in their treehouses.

From the entrance to the valley, proceed up the rocky path leading to the 2 **waterfalls** (follow the blue dots). Though the journey can be made in 25 minutes, most visitors take more time as they relish the butterflies and flowers along the way. Since some stones can be slippery, it's best to wear shoes with good traction. (*$1, students $.50.*) More experienced hikers may opt to take the rocky path up to the quiet, traditional mountain village **Faralya**. The journey is steep and considered risky. *Let's Go* recommends that those who choose to take this route proceed with caution and not go alone. The hike can take 30 minutes to an hour each way.

Should you decide to spend the night, you can camp on the beach ($1.60 per tent) or rent a mattress in either the 20-person or 35-person treehouse ($3 per person). There is also a Greek home with beds ($3 per person). All accommodations have toilets and showers. Food is readily available at the local eatery ($5 per plate). The **Rock Café**, built into the sides of the cliffs, serves juices ($1.50) and stronger drinks. Water can be pricey, and since the stream water should be avoided, it is best to bring your own.

PATARA ☎242

Though this tiny, relaxing village has quiet streets and cozy restaurants, its seemingly endless (13mi.) beach is its main attraction. On the way to their daily beach worship, visitors marvel at the imposing ruins that lie peacefully among seaside hills. The seat of the Roman governor of Lycia and the site of an oracle of Apollo, Patara was an important port before its harbor silted up. It was also the birthplace of St. Nicholas, more affectionately referred to as Santa Claus.

▐ ▐ TRANSPORTATION AND PRACTICAL INFORMATION

Pamukkale offers **bus** service from Fethiye (1hr., every hr. 7am-7pm, $2). From the bus stop at the Antalya-Patara fork, take a dolmuş into town (2km, $.60). From town, another dolmuş runs to the nearby beach (10min., every 30min. 8am-6pm, $.50). From the dolmuş station (☎843 51 17 or 843 51 18), **dolmuş** run to: **Fethiye** (1hr.; 9:15, 10, 11am, 5pm; $3); **Kalkan** (30min., every hr. 8:45am-6:30pm, $1.40); **Kaş** (1hr., every hr. 8:45am-6:30pm, $2.40); **Saklıkent Gorge** and **Xanthos** (10am-4:30pm, $6). Call **Patara Taksi** (☎843 50 56; from the beach ☎843 52 52) for **taxis**. To **Xanthos** $12; **Letoon** $14.

Kirca Travel (☎843 52 98; fax 843 50 34; email kircatravel@superonline.com), run by the same family as the Flower Pension, offers transport to the airport ($40) and Letoon ($10) as well as treks into the mountains ($26). **St. Nikolas Travel** (☎843 53 08; fax 843 50 24), across from St. Nikolas Pension, offers a variety of boat trips to all the classic Turkish Riviera destinations, including **Kekova, Myra, Ölüdeniz, Butterfly Valley, Kalkan,** and the **islands.** Tours depart from the office ($18-25 per person; barbecue, lunch, and wine included). They also offer daily 15km **canoe trips** on the Xanthos River (10am-5pm, $14.50 per person) and trips to **Saklıkent Gorge, Tlos, Letoon,** and **Xanthos** (daily 9:30am-6pm, $14.50; see p. 264 and p. 271). **Han Horse Riding** (☎843 51 60), next to the PTT, offers horseback trips along the river and the beach. (Depart 7am, 10am; return 5pm, 8pm; $32 per horse.)

A helpful nurse takes the place of a health center. The **PTT** (☎843 52 20), near the dolmuş station in the town-center, has international **phones** and **currency exchange** (open 8:30am-12:30pm, 1:30-8pm; in winter 8:30am-5:30pm). **Postal Code:** 07975.

▐ ACCOMMODATIONS

Several affordable pensions line the road leading into the village center.

Flower Pension (☎843 51 64; fax 843 50 34). 200m before the centrum. Turn right off the main road onto a small dirt road marked by 5 *pansiyon* signs. 11 rooms with colorful woven rugs, bath, screens, balcony, and mosquito nets. Free use of laundry machine. Delightful garden and eating area. Homemade Turkish dinner $3.60. Breakfast included. Singles $9; doubles $12.

Akay Pension (☎ 843 50 55 or 843 51 72). On the right off the main road from Fethiye. A green and pink building next door to the Flower Pension. A wonderful *çay* room and 12 clean rooms with bath and mosquito nets. Homemade Turkish dinners. Breakfast included. Singles $8; doubles $12; triples $14.

Hotel Mehmet (☎ 843 50 32; 843 50 78). Take a right up the hill as you come into town. The hotel is about 200m on the left. A simple, clean room with bath, fan, and balcony. Small garden with refreshing swimming pool. Internet access $1.50 per hr. French, German, and English spoken. Breakfast included. Doubles $20.

Paradise Pansiyon (☎ 843 51 90). Behind the Akay Pension. This simple pension offers 8 rooms with bath, mosquito netting, and a fan. Free laundry. Dinner available. Breakfast included. Singles $8; doubles $12.

Medusa Camping (☎ 843 51 93). Across from the dolmuş station. Look for the hand-painted green sign. Communal kitchen, clean showers, and toilets. Bring your own tent or caravan. $2 per person; electricity $.80.

◖▮ FOOD AND ENTERTAINMENT

▨ **Bistrot** (☎ 843 51 08 or 843 52 31). In the town center under the Otlu Market sign and on the right. This cozy eatery serves up southern Turkish cuisine under a lush grape arbor. Try the *içli köfte* (mixed meat, flour, and spices; $6), the *Adena aşuresi* (a custard-like dessert with raisins and cinnamon; $2), and their special drink, *boğma* ("The Bomb"; $6), to keep you going all night long. Open 8am-3am.

Seker Restaurant. Walk down the main road about 10m past the dolmuş station. Eat grilled fish ($4) or BBQ chicken ($6) under the watchful gaze of the stuffed tropical parrots hanging from the roof of this lively restaurant. Free fresh fruit at the end of every meal. Some of the cheapest beer in town ($.75).

Ayşe's Pancake House (☎ 843 20 71). In the center of town. A family business run by the delightful Yasemin and her mother. Specializes in *gözleme* of every variety, including banana-chocolate ($1.40-1.60). They also serve *mantı*. Open 8am-1am.

Gipsy Bar (☎ 843 50 09). Across from the dolmuş station. For a late-night game of pool or a little dancing to current hot tunes. Beer $1.20; *rakı* $1.60. Open 9am-4:30am.

Voodoo Bar. On the left along the main street. A small flower-engulfed refuge. Spend the evening talking over rum ($3.20) or a beer ($1.25). Open 9am-2am.

SANTA'S PRE-ARCTIC DAYS
Santa Claus, a.k.a. St. Nicholas, was born in Patara in 270 to a wealthy wheat trader. As a young man he won a reputation as a hopeless do-gooder. On one of his journeys, he came across a landlord who had murdered three boys and pickled their bodies. At this sight, he graciously brought the boys back to life. Along with hundreds of other Christians, St. Nicholas was martyred during the reign of the emperor Diocletian after becoming bishop of nearby Myra. He remained unknown in Europe until the 13th and 14th centuries, when the Dutch coined the term *Sinterklaas*. His association with gifts comes from a time when he dropped a bag of gold into the window of a house inhabited by three poor sisters, providing them with dowries and saving them from resorting to prostitution. These days, jolly old Saint Nick's cheeks might not be quite so rosy. The Roman Catholic Church took away his sainthood in 1969 and excised his feast day from the church calendar, claiming that his miraculous works and acts of piety were nothing but old wives' tales. St. Nicholas's church and grave are near the village of Demre (see p. 278), and an orthodox service is held there every year on the anniversary of his death, December 6, 343. The Archaeological Museum in Antalya houses some of his relics (see p. 285).

⊙ SIGHTS

Patara's beautiful, calm beach is a nesting ground for the shy loggerhead turtle (see **Save the Sea Turtle,** p. 461), but during the day it's licked by a pleasant surf and is not exceptionally crowded. The nearby Lycian archaeological site is somewhat hidden in the grass, and is considered unimpressive except for a few high points. The **Mettius Modestus arch,** built in 100 AD, rests on the right of the road to the beach. A half-covered **amphitheater** lies farther in the field to the right, and a **necropolis** with numerous sarcophagi surrounds the gate. The ruins of Roman baths, a Christian basilica, the **Baths of Vespasian,** and a theater lie along the path from the gateway to the sea. *(The beach and ruins require a $3 ticket that can be used for a week. Both open 8am-8pm. Wear good shoes to the beach or your soles will sizzle.)*

✚ DAYTRIPS FROM PATARA

LETOON

The best ways to get to Letoon are by taxi from Patara ($20) or daily tours with companies from Ölüdeniz (see p. 266) or Patara (see p. 269). Dolmuş from Kaş can drop visitors off about 2km from Letoon ($3.20). Site open 9am-7:30pm. $1.20, students $.80.

A lesser-known but impressive archaeological site close to Patara, Letoon was a Lycian religious sanctuary whose ruins date from the Roman and early Byzantine periods. The Lycians founded this site in honor of Leto, who, after giving birth to Zeus's illegitimate children, Artemis and Apollo, came here to escape the wrath of Hera, Zeus's jealous wife. Leto and each of her children have a temple at the site. The central **Leto temple** bears only the marks of the thick Ionic columns that once stood there. **Mosaics** of Apollo's lyre and Artemis's bow and arrow decorate the floor of the **Temple of Apollo.** The **church** behind the temples also bears mosaic floors and a Greek-inscribed tablet that was used to decipher the Lycian language. The large **theater,** opposite the temples, is marked by a remarkably well-preserved entrance pediment, and the outer part of the other entrance is adorned with a row of 16 detailed theater masks representing Dionysus, Silenus, a satyr, a girl, and a comic old woman.

XANTHOS

To get to Xanthos, take a Fethiye-bound dolmuş or bus from Patara (15min., $1), Kalkan (1½hr., $1.50), or Kaş, get off at the village of Kirik, and walk uphill. Otherwise, take a taxi ($20) or tour from Patara (see p. 269). Site open daily 6am-7:30pm. $1.20, students $.80.

Most notable for its **rock tombs,** the ruins of the ancient Lycian capital of **Xanthos** are perched above the Eşen River, 85km from Fethiye and 22km from Kalkan. In the 6th century BC, the Lycians gathered everything they owned for a last stand against the Persians. When all hope was lost, they set the city on fire and fought to the death. Years later, the Romans fortified Xanthos in exchange for support of their Anatolian campaigns. Xanthos was a diocese during the Byzantine era.

As you climb the road to Xanthos, check out the **Roman city gate,** dedicated to Emperor Vespasian. At the end of the well-preserved **theater,** located to the left past the postcard shop and admissions kiosk, stands the 6th-century BC Lycian **Tomb of the Harpies,** a misnamed structure whose women are presumably Sirens conveying souls to the Isles of the Blessed. The remains of the **acropolis** and a Byzantine church are visible from the theater. The 5th-century BC Xanthian **Inscribed Pillar,** the largest known Lycian inscription, stands across from the theater in the **agora** area. Its 250 lines in the Lycian language, describing Lycian battles in the Peloponnesian Wars, are followed by 12 lines of satire in Greek. Walk 200m through the parking lot to a **Byzantine basilica,** with several large, beautifully-colored floor mosaics buried beneath a layer of sand.

KALKAN   ☎242

More than just a beach town, tiny Kalkan is a surprisingly sophisticated mini-metropolis that serves as a lovely base for some unique tours and exploration. Like many small Mediterranean towns, this picturesque seaside village has steep cobblestone streets speckled with pleasing pensions, varied and inviting restaurants, and small shops teeming with spices, carpets, and jewels. If Kalkan's small, rocky beach on the harbor disappoints, head 3km toward Kaş for the exquisite sand and surf of Kaputaş Beach.

▐ TRANSPORTATION

Buses, dolmuş, and taxis stop on a hill above the shopping district and harbor.

Buses: Kamil Koç (☎844 34 34) and **Pamukkale** (☎844 33 46) serve Kalkan. To: **Ankara** (10hr., 9pm, $18); **Antalya** (4½hr., 7:15am-6pm, $3); **Aydın** (7hr.; 9:30am, 9:30pm; $10); **Bodrum** (6hr., 9:30am, $10.80); **Bursa** (11hr., 7:30pm, $17); **Dalaman** (3hr.; 8:15, 9:30, 10am, 9:30pm; $5.40); **Dalyan** (3¼hr.; 8:15, 9:30, 10am, 10:15pm; $6); **Eskişehir** (9½hr., $13); **Fethiye** (1½hr., 9:30am-9:30pm, $3.60); **İstanbul** (12hr.; 7, 8pm; $23); **İzmir** (8hr.; 9:30, 10am, 9:30, 10:15pm; $15); **Kaş** (30min., 7:15am-6pm, $1); **Kemer** (4¼hr., 7:15am-6pm, $3); **Köyceğiz** (3½hr.; 8:15, 9:30, 10am, 10pm; $6); **Marmaris** (4½hr., 9:15am, $8.40); **Olimpos** (4hr., 7:15am-6pm, $3); **Selçuk** (7hr.; 9:30, 10am, 9:30, 10:15pm; $12).

Dolmuş: From the stop uphill from the PTT to: **Kaputaş Beach** (15-20min., every 30min., $.60); **Kaş** (every 30min., $1.20); and **Patara** (frequent, $1.40).

Taxis: (☎844 31 00). Taxis cluster around the bus stop uphill on the main road.

▓❼ ORIENTATION AND PRACTICAL INFORMATION

Kalkan is on the main road between Fethiye and Kaş. The road downhill passes the PTT and banks before becoming **Hasan Altan Sok.** and entering an area with shops and pensions. The two roads that break off from it, sloping down to the harbor, are good places to look for pensions and restaurants.

Travel Agencies: ABI Travel (☎844 26 94; fax 844 26 95; www.kalkan.org.tr/kalkan/alinda), is one of the 1st offices on the right when entering the main shopping district. The English-speaking staff helps with **canoe trip** tickets and plans daytrips to the area's small islands and sites, including **Saklıkent Gorge** and **Tlos, Xanthos** and **Letoon,** and the **sunken city of Kekova.** They also **rent cars** ($50 per day; cheaper for 6 days or more). Backpacker discounts available. Open Apr.-Oct. 8:30am-11pm. **Kalamus Specialty Tours** (☎844 33 42), right before ABI, specializes in tailor-made treks and tours dedicated to showing visitors "the real heart of Turkey." These include daily tours of nomad villages to learn about Lycian archaeology, local architecture, religion, culture and crafts, nature, and photography ($30, lunch included). Open 9am-midnight.

Bank: TC Ziraat Bankası (☎844 34 26), on the left side of the main road when coming from the bus stop, has a V/MC/Cirrus **ATM.** Open M-F 8:30am-noon, 1:30-5:30pm.

Pharmacy: (☎(542) 433 48 12), uphill from the bus stop. Open 8am-8pm.

Hospital: Tuana Medical Center (☎844 22 44), up the road and to the right before the dolmuş stop on Kalamar Cad. English-speaking doctors available. Open 24hr.

Internet Access: Kalamus Specialty Tours (see above). $1.20 for 45min.

PTT: (☎844 32 30 or 844 32 21). On the left side of the main road, 25m past the dolmuş station. Has **currency exchange,** fax, and *poste restante.* Open in summer 8am-midnight; in winter 8:30am-7pm. **Postal Code:** 07960.

ACCOMMODATIONS

Öz Pansiyon (☎844 34 33 or 844 22 22). 25m from the turnoff to Kalkan from the Kaş road. Öz is on the left, just over the rainbow. 25 modern rooms with bath, screens, and balcony. Breakfast included. Singles $10; doubles $14, with A/C $20. V, MC.

Çelik Pension, 9 Yalıboyu Mah. (☎844 21 26). To the left off the main road from the bus stop. 9 very clean rooms, most with balcony, bath, and screens. Breakfast served on a beautiful, flower-shaded rooftop. For quiet, ask for a room away from the noisy discos. Singles $10; doubles $14; triples $20.

Numrun Pansiyon (☎844 31 62). On Nolu Sok., across from Belgin's Kitchen. A small, clean *pansiyon* with large simple rooms, some with harbor views. Breakfast included. Doubles $13, with A/C $16.

FOOD

Foto'nun Yeri (☎844 34 64). Head downhill from the bust stop and turn right. The restaurant is on the right. Gorgeous shady terrace with red tile roof, dark wood, cushions and low tables, and climbing morning glories. Meals cooked before your eyes. *Gözleme* $2; *mantı* $3; *menemen* (omelette) $3. Open 8am-midnight.

Belgin's Kitchen, 1 Yalıboyu Mah., 2 Nolu Sok. (☎844 36 14 or 844 36 80), down the main shopping street and off to the right. Carpets, low couches, and a relaxed terrace create a pleasant atmosphere. Friendly, family-run business. *Mantı* $4; stuffed grape leaves $2; *çorba* $1.40. Also serves trout ($6), yogurt and honey ($3), and rice pudding. Live traditional Turkish music every night. Open 10am-midnight.

Özgür Restaurant (☎844 25 69). Across from Foto'nun Yeri. A cozy and relaxed spot with a breezy upstairs terrace. Try the delicious *gözleme* and fresh melon juice. Omelettes $3-5; *çorba* $1; pasta $3; terrific beer $1.60. Open 9am-midnight.

Odak Restaurant. On the left immediately past the dolmuş stop. This small restaurant boasts a beautiful terrace with a panoramic harbor view. Enjoy free bread and cheese with every meal. Pizza $.80-$3; casseroles $3.50; desserts $1.20.

SIGHTS

Kalkan has a small but decent beach located to the left of the marina (when facing the water). Even better is **Kaputaş Beach,** a wonderful sandy cove with excellent views of the islands, located 15 minutes away by dolmuş. Be prepared for a steep hike between the dolmuş drop-off and parking at the top of the cliff down to the water. Kalkan is also a good place from which to embark on any of the standard boat tours along the Mediterranean coast (see **Travel Agencies,** p. 272).

ENTERTAINMENT

Moonlight Bar (☎844 30 43). Head downhill from the bus stop and turn left before the shopping district. A popular nightspot with excellent music and a stylish crowd, the Moonlight Bar promises you "the stars." Outdoor tables and an indoor dance floor. Spectacular view of the water. Beer 1.60; *rakı* $2; cocktails $6. Open noon-6am.

Yalı Cafe-Bar (☎844 34 90). Down Yalıboyu Mah. Where the British bop to their own pop. Outside seating, upstairs *çay* room and terrace. Bright bar and dance floor. Happy hour 6-10pm (buy 2, get 3). Beer $1.60; cocktails $4-5. Open 1pm-3:30am.

Halat Cafe-Bar (☎844 37 57). Off the main road, above the mosque and next to the fountain. Loud but classy joint churns out Euro and Turkish pop tunes (take requests). Billiards $3.20 per hr. Beer $1.20-1.60; *rakı* $2; cocktails $6. Open 7pm-4am.

Alternative Terrace Bar and Restaurant. On the hill next to the Moonlight Bar. This hip bar with an artistic twist offers "the best view in town," "wicked desserts," and the standard selection of beer, *rakı*, and cocktails at reasonable prices.

KAŞ COAST

KAŞ   ☎242

The serpentine road from Kalkan to Kaş passes glittering inlets dotted with pebble beaches. Sandwiched between sea and mountains, cosmopolitan Kaş is refreshingly hassle-free. Its pleasant streets are lined with inexpensive, hospitable places to stay, excellent restaurants, and laid-back bars. A peninsula curves around from one side of the town's harbor, creating a calm, rock-lined lagoon ideal for swimming. Kaş is the place to take a boat trip, soak in a little Roman and Lycian history, dance to a hodge-podge of American folk, blues, rock, and Turkish pop, or simply lounge on the waterfront, cocktail in hand. Kaş hosts a national arts festival every year for three days at the end of June. Turks from around the country come to enjoy the professional dance, music, and art displays.

▣ TRANSPORTATION

Buses: The otogar, uphill on Atatürk Cad., is serviced by **Kamil Koç** (☎836 19 49) and **Pamukkale** (☎836 13 10). To: **Ankara** (11hr., 8:30pm, $19); **Antalya** (3hr., every 30min. 8am-10pm, $5.40); **Aydın** (6½hr.; 7, 10pm; $10.80); **Bodrum** (7hr., 9am, $10.80); **Bursa** (12hr., 7pm, $18); **Dalaman** (3hr.; 7, 10pm; $7); **Fethiye** (2hr., 6 per day 9:30am-10pm, $3.60); **İstanbul** (15hr., 4 per day 6-8pm, $24); **İzmir** (9hr.; 9:30am, 7, 9:30, 10pm; $16); **Muğla** (5hr.; 7, 10pm; $9); and **Selçuk** (8hr.; 9:30am, 7, 9:30, 10pm; $13). To get to **Olimpos**, take any Antalya-bound bus.

Dolmuş: From the otogar to: **Kalkan** (40min., every 30min. 9am-6pm, $1.20); **Kaputaş Beach** (20min., every 30min. 9:30am-7:30pm, $1.20); **Patara** (1hr., every 30min. 9am-6pm, $2.40); **Saklıkent** and **Xanthos** (10am, returns 6pm; $9.60); **Xanthos** (1¼hr., every 30min. 9am-6pm, $3.20).

Taxis: (☎836 19 33).

Car Rental: Ali Baba Rent-a-Car (☎836 25 01; fax 836 32 25). On Hastane Cad. Motorbikes from $12 per day; cars $35-60 per day. Open 8am-midnight.

✦ 🛈 ORIENTATION AND PRACTICAL INFORMATION

Most of the activity centers around the small harbor along the main street, **Cumhuriyet Cad.** At its west end near the mosque, Cumhuriyet Cad. intersects **Hastane Cad.** before becoming **Atatürk Cad.** At its east end near the Atatürk statue, Cumhuriyet Cad. intersects **Çukurbağlı Cad.** (also known as Şübe Sok.), which leads to the PTT. From the Atatürk statue, **Hükümet Cad.** passes above the harbor to the two beaches. The street going uphill behind the tourist office—the one with most of the souvenir shops—is **Uzun Çarşı Cad.**

Tourist Office: 5 Cumhuriyet Meydanı (☎836 12 38; fax 836 16 95), to the left as you face the back of the Atatürk statue. A very helpful, English-speaking staff distributes local maps. Open daily 8am-noon, 1-7pm; in winter M-F 8am-5pm.

Travel Agencies: Nearly all agencies offer tours to **Kekova**. Tour prices vary slightly, so shop around before buying a ticket. **Bougainville Travel**, 10 Çukurbağlı Cad. (☎836 37 37; fax 836 16 05; email bougainville@superonline.com), has a friendly staff and offers **diving** courses, **kayaking** trips to Kekova ($40; see p. 277), and **jeep safaris** to **Saklıkent Gorge** (9am-6pm, $41 with lunch; see p. 264). Open daily 8:30am-10pm. **Simena Tours**, 1 Elmalı Cad. (☎836 14 16), down the street from the otogar, books airline tickets and arranges popular daytrips to **Kekova** and **Saklıkent Gorge**. It also plans **canoe tours** of Xanthos on Xanthos River (9am-6pm, $24 with lunch; see p. 271) and trips to **Gömbe**, a traditional village in the mountains near a lake (10am-6pm, $20 with trout lunch). Open 9am-8:30pm. **Dolce Vita Travel Agency** (☎836 16 10), next to the tourist office, offers friendly and professional service to all the popular sites.

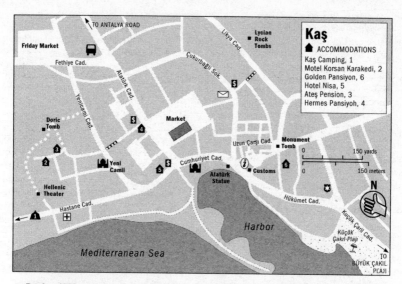

Banks: ATMs are sprinkled throughout the harbor area and on Atatürk Cad. **Türkiye İş Bankası** (836 15 60) is on Atatürk Cad. Open 8:30am-noon, 1:30-5:30pm.

English Bookstore: Galileo Bookstore, 7 Topçu Sok. (☎/fax 836 34 20), just uphill from the Red Point Bar, offers new and used books in many languages. Open daily 10am-midnight. **Cafe Merhaba** (☎836 18 83), on the corner opposite the PTT, has a great selection of international periodicals. Open 9am-11:30pm.

Laundromat: Habessos Laundry (☎836 12 63), on Uzun Çarşı Antik Sok., across from Galileo Bookstore. Wash and dry $5 per load, with ironing $7.40. Open 8am-midnight.

Hamam: (☎836 30 62), at Hotel Hera on Hükümet Cad. Full service $15.

Police: (☎836 10 24), across the entrance to Küçük Çalık Plaj (Little Pebble Beach).

Hospital: Private (☎836 11 85), before the campground on Hastane Cad. From the tourist office, head 500m past the mosque. **Munise Ozan** (☎836 41 42), next to Ali Baba Rent-a-Car on Hastane Cad., offers free public health services and has a certified tourism doctor.

Internet Access: Internet Cafe (☎836 28 45), on Çukurbağlı Cad. $3.60 per hr. Open daily 8:30am-midnight. **Magic Com. Internet Cafe** (☎836 27 24), 2 stores down from the Internet Cafe. $1.20 per hr. Open daily 8:30-midnight.

PTT: (☎836 14 50 or 836 14 78), on Çukurbağlı Cad. Walk 50m up from the Atatürk statue. *Poste restante* available. Open daily 8:30am-midnight. **Currency exchange** desk open 8:30am-5pm. 24hr. international phones. **Postal Code:** 07580.

ACCOMMODATIONS

Since pensions tend to jack up their prices in the high season, the search for inexpensive accommodations in July and August will test your haggling abilities. There are many budget *pansiyons* on the side streets to the right of Atatürk Bul. (when heading from the otogar to the waterfront). If you've got some extra cash, the pensions and hotels on the hill on the other side of town, many of which have beautiful water views and easy beach access, are worth the money.

Motel Korsan Karakedi, 17 Yenicami Sok. (☎836 18 87; fax 836 30 86). Walk east along Hastane Cad. towards the theater, turn right on Yeni Cami Cad., and turn left after the mosque; the motel is on the left. 13 beautiful rooms, with bath, fan, and balcony. Some with sea views. Swimming pool and terrace with TV and bar. English spoken. Breakfast included. Singles $7; doubles $14.

Hermes Pension, 2 İmdi Cad. (☎836 32 22). On the right 1 block in from Atatürk Cad. when walking toward the water from the otogar. Clean, airy, pleasant rooms, all with large bath, tile floors, and balcony. Nice neighborhood. Little English spoken. Breakfast served on terrace with view of the water. Singles $9; doubles $14; triples $16.

Ateş Pension, Yeni Cami Cad. No. 3. (☎836 13 93). On the right side of town, near the Motel Korsan Karakedi. Once you make it to the top of the hill, follow the numerous spray-painted signs that start around the mosque. A popular backpacker hangout with simple rooms, some with bath and balcony. Ottoman style reading area on the rooftop terrace. TV and CD player. Dinner $3.50. Breakfast included. Singles $7; doubles $14.

Golden Pension (☎836 17 36). On the left side of the harbor when facing the water. In the lively, older part of town near most of the good bars and restaurants. Walk uphill to the monumental Lycian sarcophagus and turn right. Backpackers flock here for large rooms and terraces with views. Breakfast $1. $10 per room, with toilet $12.

Hotel Nisa (☎836 35 81). On Hastane Cad. A lively hostel with 20 simple rooms, all with bath. International phone and fax, safe deposit, laundry ($4), TV and stereo, and a communal kitchen. Breakfast $2. Doubles $12.

Kaş Camping (☎836 10 50). On Hastane Cad., 100m past the theater. Beautiful view, hills, shade, grass, and unreliable hot water. Great terrace for meals. Breakfast $2. Tents $2 per person; 10 double bed bungalows $10; caravan with electricity $6.

◖ FOOD

Spaghetti House. Turn left at the tourist office. Walk straight for 25m and take another left. This gourmet Italian restaurant offers a fantastic selection of pasta and salad at reasonable prices. Savor creamy *tiramisu* at one of the small outdoor tables. Salads $1.20; pasta $2-4; dessert $2. Open 10am-1am.

Don Quixote. In the town's main square. This lively restaurant is a great place to relax and people-watch. Enjoy large salads ($1.20), pizzas ($2-4), fruit, honey, and yogurt ($2.20), and burgers ($3). Open 8am-1am.

Dolphin Cafe and Bar. Elegant restaurant next to the Blue House, with a spectacular 2-story terrace and view of the harbor. Outdoor seating. Specializes in seafood $4-8. Delicious *meze* ($2) and large salads ($3). Open noon-1am.

Chez Evy, 2 Terzi Sok. (☎836 12 53). Up the street and around the corner from the Red Point Bar. If you've got some extra cash, Chez Evy is *the* place to savor exquisite French food in Turkey. Magnificent jasmine-enclosed garden and beautiful Ottoman reclining areas provide an ideal setting for enjoying mushroom-cheese crêpes ($4), a hearty portion of broiled lamb ($12), or salad *niçoise* ($5). Open M-Sa 8am-2am.

The Blue House (☎836 21 71). Next to the Golden Pension. For a little extra money, dine in this extraordinary, antique-filled house. A small, beautiful terrace overlooks the harbor and town. Especially pleasant at night. Soups $1.20; vegetable dishes $1-2; chicken and other grills $4-9.

Corner Cafe. Across the street from the PTT. Small but friendly cafe serves yogurt with honey ($2.50), flavored rice ($2.50), salads ($2), pastas, kebaps, and fresh fruit-juices. Open 8am-midnight.

◖ SIGHTS

The Kaş shoreline is a mixture of white jagged rocks, surrounded by foaming surf, and with small pebble coves. To the left of the main square, dozens of swimming docks provide the perfect place from which to dive. The entrance to **Küçük Çalık Plajı** (Little Pebble Beach) is atop the hill on Hükümet Cad., 200m left as you exit the tourist office. More determined sunbathers and swimmers frequent the less-crowded **Büyük Çalık Plajı** (Big Pebble Beach), 15 minutes down the road to the left.

The most impressive of the town's historical sites is the **Hellenistic theater,** just past the hospital on Hastane Cad. The only intact ancient structure in Kaş, the solitary theater overlooks the sea and the Greek island of Kastellorizo. On special occasions the town hosts various concerts and performances here. Follow the path behind the theater 50m to the 4th-century BC **necropolis** with Doric tombs. Up Uzun Çarşı Cad. behind the tourist office, there's a free-standing **Monument Tomb,** also from the same era. Kaş houses a famous **Friday market** behind the otogar, selling everything from fresh produce to clothing and household items (8am-8pm).

The **Blue Caves,** 15km from Kaş, are home to the Mediterranean's only **seal colony.** Swim in the morning before the sea becomes rough. **Doves Cave,** 2km past Kalkan, can be reached only by water. Opposite this grotto, the wide **Güvercinlik Cave** spouts a cold underwater stream. The nearby town of **Kemer** is saturated with tourists. Though it falls somewhat short, it does offer one of the few Mexican restaurants on the Turkish Mediterranean, a multitude of overpriced, under-occupied hotels, nice beaches, and a pleasant mall-type pedestrian shopping area. To escape the tourist jumble, rent a motorbike and lose yourself in the views and villages between Kaş and Kekova.

♫ ENTERTAINMENT

Red Point Bar (☎836 16 05). On Uzun Çarşı Antik Sok. Look for the small red sign. Situated on a quiet side street, this is reputed to be the hottest bar in town. Hit this perpetually packed club for a beer ($1.60), rakı ($2.20), or cola ($1). Dance the night away or talk at the outdoor tables. Open until 3am.

Bacchus (☎836 43 78). Across from the Golden Pension. Silvery trees and shimmering, moonlit flowers fill this aromatic garden bar. American folk music. Beer $1.20; rakı $1.80; cocktails $2-5; espresso $1.20; ice cream $1. Open 8am-3am.

Hi Jazz Bar (☎836 11 65). Across from Chez Evy. Head uphill and turn left after the Red Point Bar. Simple and elegant, this softly-lit bar with photos of jazz artists offers a refreshing break from the usual Mediterranean nightlife scene. Run by a friendly New York City taxi driver. Beer $1.60; rakı $2; cocktails $2-6. Open noon-3am.

Deja Vu Bar. Facing the harbor, turn left at the Atatürk statue and walk 75m uphill. Deja Vu is on the right. Throughout the night, laid-back blues and rock flow from the depths of this hip bar. Sit on the terrace and sip some of the cheapest beer in Kaş ($.75). Vodka $1.20; cappuccino $1.20. Open daily 6pm-3am.

Deep. Across from the PTT. Decorated with hand-made trees, dangling colored lanterns, mosaics, and plush couches. Beer $1; rakı $1.50; cocktails $2-5. Open 4pm-2:30am.

⚑ DAYTRIP FROM KAŞ: THE SUBMERGED CITY OF KEKOVA

Off the coast near Üçağız, the Lycian city of Kekova lies submerged under the clear Mediterranean waters. During the eras of Hellenistic and Arab control, the city served as a lookout post and refuge from marauding pirates. From craggy Kekova Island, one can see through calm water to the underwater walls and staircases that collapsed in an earthquake. If the waters are exceptionally smooth, it may be possible to spot an amphora or two. Above sea level on Kekova Island, a motley assortment of doors and walls still bear evidence of long-gone floors and ceilings. The highlight of the trip is the partially submerged Lycian sarcophagus near the village of Kale. **Swimming or snorkeling among the ruins is forbidden.** *(Trips from Kaş, often on glass-bottom boats, cost around $30 including a gourmet lunch. Kekova can also be visited by sea kayak ($35). Kayaking allows for the best views of the ruins, a pleasant lunch in Üçağız (a small coastal village difficult to get to by other means), and some hearty exercise. Inquire at Bougainville Travel in Kaş for more details (see p. 274). It's best to visit in the morning when the area is not as crowded, and the sea is calmer and clearer. Kekova is also reachable from Demre (see below).)*

MEDITERRANEAN COAST

DEMRE AND MYRA ☎242

The ancient ruins of Myra stretch high into the dry cliffs. The mixture of Lycian rock tombs, sculptures, and a Roman theater is truly awe-inspiring. The offerings of nearby Demre, unfortunately, are not. Its rather drab establishments alternate with unfinished concrete buildings along dusty, hot streets. On the road down from the Beydağları Mountains to Kaş, Demre was once an important member of the Lycian League, and St. Paul is said to have stopped here in 61 AD on his way to Rome. Demre was the diocese of St. Nicholas, better known as **Santa Claus** (see **Santa's Pre-Arctic Days**, p. 270). The kind-hearted saint, born in Patara (60km west of Demre), became the Bishop of Myra in the early 4th century. In addition to Santa, the town has a nearby calm beach and cold springs accessible by car.

▐▄ TRANSPORTATION AND PRACTICAL INFORMATION. Demre's layout is fairly simple. Take a left at the otogar exit and walk 100m to reach the T-junction with the town's main street. To the left 300m is the Church of St. Nicholas. The ruins of Myra are 3km straight from the T-junction. From the otogar, **buses** run to: **Antalya** (3hr., every 20min. 6:45am-7:45pm, $3); **Fethiye** (3¼hr., every hr. 9am-10pm, $4.65); **Kaş** (1hr., every 30min. 8:30am-10pm, $1.40). **Myra Otogar Taksi** has **taxis** (☎871 43 43) at the otogar. Other services include: **banks** and an **ATM** on Noel Baba Cad., including a **Türkiye İş Bankaşı** on the way to St. Nicholas Church (open 11am-5:30pm); a **police station** (☎871 42 21), near the otogar; and a **PTT** (☎871 55 19), 200m to the right of the T-junction (open 8:30am-6pm). **Postal code:** 07570.

▐▀▌ ACCOMMODATIONS AND FOOD. ▓ **Kent Pension,** in a bright green building 2.5km up the road to Myra, has 10 clean, comfortable rooms with 24-hour hot water and garden-side bungalows with bath. The pension also provides motorbike rental ($5 per day); tours of Kekova with visits to several bays, the Blue Caves, and a shipyard (10am-6pm, $20 without lunch); and shuttles to the beach and cold springs. (☎871 20 42. Dinner $3.50-6. Breakfast included. Singles $11; doubles $13; triples $16; 2-person bungalows $11.) Another option is **Hotel Kiyak,** Merkez Girişi PK 65, a salmon-pink hotel across from the Kekova Pension and near the traffic roundabout. Its 24 large, modern rooms have balconies, bath, phone, and TV. The hotel also organizes Kekova tours ($18) and "mountain safaris," with visits to a waterfall, lakes, and a hamam ($20). (☎871 45 09; fax 871 20 93. Breakfast included. Singles $8, with A/C $14; doubles $18, with A/C $23.)

Demre's dining options are sparse. Inquire about evening meals at pensions, which typically provide reasonable quality and ample portions. Otherwise, you can find a cheap meal along the main road towards St. Nicholas Church. **İpek Restaurant,** near St. Nicholas Church, dishes out Turkish specialties. (☎871 54 48. Hot *meze* $1.60-1.80; *pide* $1.60. Open 6am-1am.) To satisfy a sweet tooth, **Inci Pastanesi** across from the İpek restaurant sells pastries. (Open 8am-11pm.)

▣ SIGHTS. Myra was one of the most important cities in the Lycian League, a federation that included 70 cities, including Xanthos, Patara, Olimpos, and Tlos. Myra was divided into three areas: the **sea necropolis** in the southwest part of the site, the **acropolis** area and its surrounding walls, and the **river necropolis.** The **rock tombs** built into the sea and the river necropolis are of particularly high quality. Some tombs are stylized to imitate wooden beams, and many still have slight traces of color. The river necropolis is less touristed than the sea necropolis, since it requires an arduous climb over thorny, brambled cliffs. The site's other major highlight is a **theater** with 35 consecutive rows of seats and a still-intact stage. Stone tablets engraved with theater mask reliefs lie scattered about the structure. The theater was destroyed by a devastating earthquake in 141 AD, but was later rebuilt and modified to host gladiatorial games. *(Open daily in summer 8am-7:30pm; in winter 8am-5:30pm. $1.15, students $.70.)*

Demre's other major attraction is the **Church of St. Nicholas,** thought to be built on the site of the famous saint's tomb (see **Santa's Pre-Arctic Days,** p. 270). An annual Orthodox service takes place in the theater on December 6, the anniversary of St. Nicholas's death. The current structure, which dates from the 8th century, suffered centuries of neglect until the Russian Tsar ordered its repair in the 19th century. Later lost under debris and shifting sand from the Myras River, the church remained hidden until 1956. Excavations since 1989 have uncovered many new rooms and treasures, including tombs from all periods of the church's history and Byzantine frescoes crafted after the Arab invasions of the 11th century.

Scholars have generally agreed that the tomb of St. Nicholas is located in the southern nave of the church. In 1087 Italian merchants broke into the tomb and hastily took the remains to Bari, Italy, leaving behind only those that appear in the **Antalya Museum** (see p. 285). The Turkish government's efforts to bring St. Nicholas back to the church have fallen on the deaf ears of Vatican officials for the last 20 years. *(Open daily in summer 8am-7:30pm; in winter 8am-5pm. $2.80, students $1.85.)*

OLİMPOS

☎242

Enchanting Olimpos is a true backpacker's town, one of the few budget spots along the Turkish Riviera. Olimpos brings travelers closer to the heavens by giving them the chance to sleep in a treehouse and make a nighttime ascent of the Chimaerea, where a naturally-occurring flame has burned since ancient times. Roman and Byzantine ruins are close enough to the beach that visitors can partake in nearly simultaneous cerebral and solar stimulation, but the ruins are remote enough to give a sense of forested isolation. But beware: like Homer's Lotus-Eaters, travelers have been known to extend their stays indefinitely.

TRANSPORTATION AND PRACTICAL INFORMATION

To get to Olimpos from Antalya, take a Kaş- or Demre-bound bus and ask to be let off at Olimpos. From Kaş, take an Antalya-bound bus. **Buses** stop at a rest station on the main road. From there, **dolmuş** run down the 10km dirt road that leads to the treehouses (15min., every hr. 9:30am-6:30pm, $1.15), dropping passengers off at the pensions of their choice. Olimpos has **no PTT, pharmacy, bank,** or **police station.** Many pension owners accept US dollars, offer international phone calls, and arrange tours that include trekking or rafting. **Postal code:** 07350.

ACCOMMODATIONS

The Turkish government has classified Olimpos as a *"sit,"* or archaeological site, banning the use of concrete. This means no asphalt roads (hence no direct bus service) and no cement building foundations, a potential kiss of death to tourism. Resourceful Olimpians have turned *sit* into gold, building back-to-nature treehouse **pensions,** which line the dirt road to the beach and ruins. Unfortunately, the question is not whether there are bugs, but rather how many and of what kind. Most places also offer *pansiyon* rooms and sturdy bungalows for an inflated price. Prices are generally standardized. (Treehouses $7 per person; bungalows $10 per person; rooms $13 per person.) All prices generally include breakfast and dinner.

Şaban Pansiyon (☎ 892 12 65). A relaxed, welcoming, family-run pension. The dinners alone make a stay here worthwhile. 24hr. service to Antalya airport $42. Camping $6.

Carreta Carreta. Across the road from Şaban. This tiny pension has some of the largest, best-quality, and sturdiest treehouses in Olimpos.

Kadir's Yörük Treehouses (☎892 12 50; fax 892 11 10; email treehouse@superonline.com.tr). The first pension at the bottom of the road. More like a sprawling Ewok village than a pension, Kadir's is a post-adolescent summer camp. Guests can watch movies, play volleyball, and chill. At night, Kadir's bar becomes the focus of nightlife. Beer $1.15; cocktails $2.35. Laundry $4.65 per load. 45 treehouses.

Türkmen Camping (☎892 12 49). Offers treehouses and sparkling showers, a clean kitchen, and brand new bungalows.

Green Point Camping (☎825 71 82; fax 825 70 94). About 1km up the beach from Olimpos. Great campground with clean toilets and shower. 100m from Çıralı beach. 1-person tent $3.50; 2-person tent $5.90; 2-person caravan with electricity $15.

👁 SIGHTS

▓**CHIMAERA.** During the 2nd century BC, Olimpos's proximity (7km) to this perpetual flame inspired the residents to worship Hephaestos, god of fire and the forge. They believed the flame to be the breath of the Chimaera, a mythical beast that was part lion, part goat, and part serpent. Geologists have yet to produce a better explanation, but they suspect natural methane gas plays some role. In past centuries, the flame was even brighter than it is today; according to ancient reports, ships navigated by it. Chimaera is best seen at night, and bus tours leave Olimpos at 9:30pm (2½hr., $2.80); ask a pension owner for details. Wear sturdy shoes and bring a flashlight since reaching the flame requires a tricky 20-minute uphill hike through unlit mountainous terrain.

RUINS. The ruins at Olimpos are a jumbled pastiche of everything from ancient temples to crumbling walls of medieval castles. Follow the road from the pensions to the beach. The ruins tend to be overgrown with vines and dry bushes, and inhabited by **snakes** and **scorpions,** so be very cautious when exploring the site. About 10m beyond the entrance booth, you can cross the dry river bed to reach a row of tombs and one of the crumbling arches. If you continue on the main path, about 40m further a small path leads off to the left, climbing uphill to a rather large but unimpressive archway. Beyond the archway it is easy to get lost in overgrown orange groves and reeds. The sign at the beginning of the pathway reads simply "temple."

On the other side of the road across the stream are the decrepit **theater** and **medieval walls.** Though it is not unusual to see locals at the stream swimming and drinking, tourists should avoid doing so. If you continue along the main path once more, you will reach the beautiful beach, where the best-preserved group of ruins looms over the water on a rocky cliff to the right. *(Open when staffed. $2.80, students $1.85. Hold onto your ticket stub, as it will be good for multiple entry to the beach and site.)*

"YES, PLEASE" The Turkish language is replete with multi-purpose expressions. One particular favorite is *"çok güzel,"* literally "very beautiful," which can be used in reference to pretty much anything one finds agreeable. Another is *"buyurun,"* from the verb *buyurmak* meaning "to order" or "to command." *"Buyurun"* is a prompting word used in a number of different contexts. A waiter bringing food might use it to express "here you are," or a shopkeeper might use it to express "what can I do for you?" The possibilities are endless. Sadly, the linguistic wizard charged with teaching English to generations of Turks decided that there was a direct English translation of *"buyurun"*: specifically, "yes, please." Not only does "yes, please" make no sense in the contexts in which it is so often used by Turkish restaurateurs and hawkers, but the equivalent Turkish *"evet, lütfen"* is equally nonsensical. When you think you'll turn murderous the next time you hear "yes, please," keep in mind that the speaker is trying to find the equivalent of a friendly and welcoming—and untranslatable—expression.

ANTALYA GULF COAST

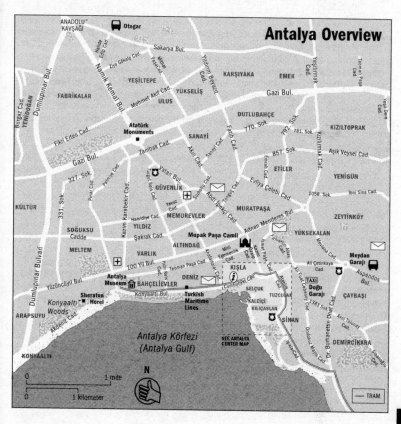

Antalya Overview

PHASELIS

On the road between Antalya and Olimpos, the ancient city of Phaselis is a combination of beaches, Roman ruins, and pine groves. Situated around three natural harbors, the city was founded around 690 BC as a colony of Rhodes. Its location made it a strategic port on the shipping routes between Greece and Syria. It declined only in the Byzantine period as Alanya and Antalya grew in prominence.

From the parking lot near the water, pass through the aqueduct to arrive at the **military harbor.** A second harbor lies to the left, encircled by an uncrowded pebble beach. The town's main road runs to the right, and on the right side of the road, you can amble through the **Roman baths.** The decomposing **theater** is 100m down the road and up a short hill on the left. At the end of the 150m Roman road, you will arrive at the third harbor, now a **sandy beach.** *(Buses from either Antalya or Olimpos pass the turn-off for Phaselis (frequent, about $1). The ruins are about 3km (30min.) from the highway, and the tree-lined roads make the walk bearable in summer. Pay at a booth 2km up the road from the site. Open May-Oct. 7:30am-7pm; Nov.-Apr. 8am-5:30pm. $4, students $2.50.)*

ANTALYA ☎ 242

Capital of the so-called Turquoise Riviera and linked by air with Munich, Moscow, and Amsterdam, Antalya is a city of many faces. This busy metropolis encircles Kaleiçi ("inside the fortress"), the crescent-shaped old city that brims with cobblestone streets, Ottoman houses, tourist businesses, and carpet dealers. At Kaleiçi's heart, pricey eateries and cutting-edge nightclubs line the ancient walled harbor that once sheltered Roman ships and now welcomes luxury yachts.

Antalya's size might overwhelm the casual visitor, but the city offers something for everyone. Beaches, ruins, waterfalls, an outstanding museum, and restaurants serving Turkish regional specialties and the international flavors of *chez* McDonald's make this place one of the most cosmopolitan in the country. The Antalya Altın Portakal ("Golden Orange") Film Festival held in the fall is a huge affair, screening both international and Turkish titles.

▐ TRANSPORTATION

Flights: Antalya International Airport, 15km from town (domestic flight info ☎ 330 30 30; international flight info ☎ 330 36 00). **THY** (☎ 243 43 81 or 243 43 82), has an office on Cumhuriyet Cad., next door to the tourist office. Open M-F 8:30am-8pm, Sa-Su 8:30am-5:30pm. Buses run between the THY office and Antalya Airport in summer (10 per day 4:45am-2:30am, $3). Flights to **İstanbul** ($61, students $51; round-trip $79, students $61) and various foreign cities including **Lefkoşa** ($180, students $130; round-trip $360, students $260).

Buses: If you find yourself confused trying to find a company that travels to your destination, try **Kamul Koç.** If they do not serve, they'll be able to point you in the right direction. The otogar has 24hr. luggage storage. $2 per bag per day.

Dolmuş: Antalya has 2 dolmuş hubs. **Doğu Garaj** sends dolmuş to **Lale** and **Lara Beaches.** To get here from Atatürk Cad., turn right on Ali Çetinkaya Cad., walk 1 block, and turn right at the Start Hotel. The **Meydan Garajı,** at the intersection of Mevlâna Cad., Aspendos Bul., and Ali Çetinkaya Cad., 1½km from the city center, has dolmuş to **Perge** and **Aspendos.** Dolmuş to the **museum** and **Konyaaltı Beach** run along Antalya's main roads, Konyaaltı Bul. or Işıklar Cad. Most dolmuş trips cost around $.30.

BUS SCHEDULES

DESTINATION	DURATION	FREQUENCY/TIME	PRICE
Adana	12hr.	8pm-midnight	$16
Alanya	2hr.	7pm-midnight	$4
Anamur	4hr.	7pm-midnight	$6
Ankara	8hr.	7am-midnight	$9.50
Antakya	13hr.	5:30pm	$14
Bodrum	8hr.	8:30am-11:30pm	$15
Demre	3hr.	every 20min. 5:30am-8pm	$2.50
Fethiye	5hr.	every hr. 8am-11pm	$6
Göreme (Cappadocia)	10hr.	8:30, 10pm	$16
İstanbul	12hr.	6:30am-11pm	$17
İzmir	8hr.	9am-midnight	$10
Kaş	3hr.	every 30min. 8am-10pm	$4
Kayseri	11hr.	8:30pm	$12
Marmaris	7hr.	8:30am-11:30pm	$9.50
Mersin	10hr.	8pm-midnight	$9.50
Olimpos	1¼hr.	every 20min. 5:30am-8pm	$1.50
Pamukkale	4hr.	9am-11:30pm	$7
Taşucu	9hr.	8pm-midnight	$8.50
Trabzon	17hr.	5pm	$23

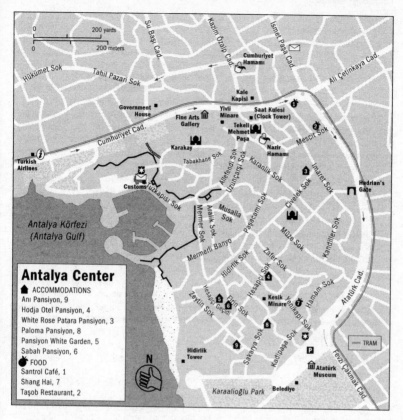

Antalya Center

🏠 ACCOMMODATIONS
Anı Pansiyon, 9
Hodja Otel Pansiyon, 4
White Rose Patara Pansiyon, 3
Paloma Pansiyon, 8
Pansiyon White Garden, 5
Sabah Pansiyon, 6

🍴 FOOD
Santrol Café, 1
Shang Hai, 7
Taşob Restaurant, 2

Trams: A new tram system runs from the Antalya Museum along Cumhuriyet Cad., then down Atatürk Cad. to the stadium (every 20 min., $.25). Blue signs mark tram stops.

Vehicle Rental: Available from many agents in Kaleiçi, who require a valid driver's license and minimum age of 21. Daily fees start at $32 for a car, $16 for a scooter.

◼ ORIENTATION

In 1997, Antalya gave birth to a gargantuan orange **otogar,** replete with fountains, several **ATMs,** cafes, A/C, and labyrinthine bathrooms with seat toilets. Unfortunately, this wonderland is 4km out of town at **Anadolu Kavşağı,** the intersection of Namık Kemal Cad. and Dumlupınar Bul. Gray buses ($.40) run from outside the otogar to the city center, near **Kaleiçi,** the old city. **İşıklar Cad.,** at the intersection of **Kazım Özalp Cad.** and **Cumhuriyet Cad.,** is marked by a brick-red fluted minaret and a stone clock tower. Hostels, restaurants, and historically important ruins and buildings, are located in this area. The two beaches are on the outskirts of town.

◼ PRACTICAL INFORMATION

TOURIST, FINANCIAL, AND LOCAL SERVICES

Tourist Office: (☎ 241 17 47), on Cumhuriyet Cad., to the left of the red fluted minaret and past the military complex. Helpful, English-speaking staff distributes free maps. Open M-F 8am-7pm, Sa-Su 9am-7pm; in winter M-F 8am-5pm, Sa-Su 10am-5pm.

Travel Agencies: Most pensions will organize tours for you, though they charge a commission unless they run the tours themselves. Try **Akay Tur,** 54 Cumhuriyet Cad. (☎243 17 00; fax 241 98 47). From the clock tower, head 50m west along Cumhuriyet Cad., climb the stairs on the right, turn left, and look for the signs. Offers well-run tours to: **Perge, Aspendos, Side,** and **Manavgat** (9am-6pm, $35); **Köprülü Kanyon** (9am-6:30pm, $35, including lunch); **Termessos** and **Upper Düden Waterfall** (9am-3pm, $25). Due to heat, this tour is not available July-Aug. **Medraft,** near the THY office on Cumhuriyet Cad., offers many tours as well.

Consulates: UK, Dolaplıdere Cad. Pırıltı Sitesi, 1st fl. (☎247 70 00; fax 824 67 03). **The Turkish Republic of Northern Cyprus (TRNC),** Kışla Mah. 35th Sok. Dörteldemir Apt. 11 PK 633 (☎248 98 47).

Banks: For cash transfers, go to **Koç Bank,** opposite Hadrian's Gate on Atatürk Cad. Banks, many with **ATMs,** are clustered about the main streets outside Kaleiçi.

English-Language Bookstore: Owl Bookshop, Barbaros Mah. 21 Akarçeşme Sok. (☎243 57 18), off Hesapçı Sok., 500m into the old city from Hadrian's Gate. Turn left at the Alp Paşa Restaurant. A cat named Pythagoras lurks among back issues of *Harper's,* the *New Yorker,* and an excellent selection of books. Open daily 10am-8pm.

Laundromat: Yıkama Laundry, 28 Tabakhane Sok. (☎241 11 74), beside the Anı Pansiyon. Wash and dry $5. Open 8am-11pm. Mysteriously, **Öz Ünaller Rent A Car,** 43 Hesapçı Sok. (☎248 93 72; fax 248 42 89), beside the Kesik Minaret, also has a laundry service. 5kg $4; ironing $.40 per piece. Open daily 8am-8pm.

Hamams: Cumhuriyet Hamam (☎244 49 98). From the clock tower, head 1 block north and turn right. $7 per person. Open daily 5am-2am. **Nazır Hamam,** in Kaleiçi, near the Tekeli Mehmet Paşa mosque. Bath, massage, and scrub $7. Open for men Su, F 10am-5pm; for women M-Th, Sa 10am-5pm; for couples daily 5pm-midnight.

EMERGENCY AND COMMUNICATIONS

Tourist Police: (☎/fax 243 10 61). Face the water and turn left on a little street left of the Atatürk bust at the harbor. Little English spoken.

Hospital: The closest hospital to Kaleiçi is the private **Akdeniz Sağlık Vakfı Hastanesi,** 17 Ali Çetinkaya Cad. (☎247 90 01 or 247 90 02; fax 247 90 03), on the left side of Cumhuriyet Cad., 400m past the intersection with Atatürk Cad. There is also the **Özel Interhospital,** Kiziloprak Mn 933 Sok. Medyan PTT arkasi (☎311 50 00).

Pharmacies: Many are located on Atatürk Cad., opposite the old city walls.

Internet Access: Natural Internet Cafe (☎243 87 63; fax 243 87 64), in the shopping area on Cumhuriyet Cad., downstairs and west from the Atatürk statue. $1 per hr.

PTT: To get to the **main branch** (☎243 45 79), head west on Cumhuriyet Cad. and take the 1st major right onto Anafartalar Cad. Open daily 8:30am-5:30pm for stamps, *poste restante,* and **currency exchange. Telephones** and **internet** also available.

Postal code: Antalya has a number of postal codes. Kaleiçi's is 07100. Mail sent *poste restante* should be addressed 07000.

▌ ACCOMMODATIONS

The best place to stay is within the ancient walls of **Kaleiçi,** which contain over 200 pensions and hotels on its winding streets. Unless otherwise stated, all include private shower and breakfast. Bargaining may help, especially for students.

▨ La Paloma Pansiyon, Kılıçarslan Mah., 60 Hesapçı Sok. (☎244 79 24; fax 244 79 25). A beautiful new *pansiyon,* offering gorgeous rooms with spotless tile showers, air conditioning, and comfortable beds. Guests eat a mouth watering breakfast poolside in the Mediterranean-style courtyard. Well worth the splurge. Singles $20; doubles $35.

Sabah Pansiyon, Kaleiçi Kılıçarslan Mah., 60 Hesapçı Sok. (☎247 53 45; fax 247 53 47). A popular backpackers' hangout with a pleasant courtyard area. Organizes cheap tours. Vegetarian and regular dinners $3.50; beer $.80. Laundry $4 per load. Bike/scooter rental $20 per day; car rental $24 per day. Singles $6; doubles $8, with bath $13, with A/C $18; roof, couch, or floor $3; camping $2.50-3.

Anı Pansiyon, 26 Tabakhane Sok., Hesapçı Sok. (☎247 00 56). Understated and luxurious, the elegant Anı has large windows, high ceilings, and wooden furniture in a converted Ottoman home setting. Singles $12; doubles $19.

Hodja Otel Pansiyon, Kılıçarslan Mah. 37 Hesapçı Sok. (☎248 94 86; fax 248 94 85). Wonderfully spacious, Hodja has large central hallways, elegant Ottoman paintings, and 12 rooms with bath. Staff speaks English. Singles $9.30; doubles $19; quads $38.

White Rose Patara Pansiyon, Barbaros Mah., 4 Civelek Sok. (☎242 70 50; fax 247 39 51). Family-run pension with spacious, modern, comfortable rooms. Colorful *kilims* in the halls and relaxed garden area for breakfast. Singles $12; doubles $14.

Adalya Tesisleri (☎719 96 35). By the entrance to Lara Beach. Accessible by dolmuş on Atatürk Cad. Tantalizing views of oil tankers. 34 basic bungalow rooms with 2 bunks each go for $2. The "camping" option consists of being given a tent (you can't bring your own) to pitch on concrete platforms. 3-person tents $7; 4-person tents $10.50.

⬤ FOOD

Try not to pay the "tourist price." The restaurants around the old city arch tend to have nice atmosphere, but overpriced, overrated food. Near the harbor, prices rise in direct proportion to the quality of the view, and the best and cheapest meals are often found in cheap dives a few blocks from the walls of Kaleiçi.

Taşob Restaurant. Facing away from the water, turn left off of Atatürk Cad. onto Mescit Cad. Taşob is on the right. The best kebaps in Antalya, served sizzling with fresh, warm flatbread ($2.50). Turkish clientele attests to the quality. *Meze* $1.20.

Shang Hai Chinese Restaurant. If you're tired of kebaps, try this family-run locale that offers cheap, high-quality Chinese food. Nice atmosphere. Try the homemade noodles.

Santral Cafe and Patisserie. Yum, yum, yum! Superlative tea and pastries ($.30-.50). Also serves cakes, tarts, and ice cream. Outdoor seating.

👁 SIGHTS

▥ THE ANTALYA MUSEUM. This museum is one of Turkey's best. Winner of the 1988 European Museum of the Year Award, it presents exhibits ranging from prehistoric times to the founding of the Turkish Republic.

To the left of the entrance is the **Hall of Natural History and Prehistory,** which contains various ancient objects and an example of a **pithas burial,** a skeleton resting in a huge smashed urn. Just past this display, excavations of Phrygian settlements feature some amazingly detailed metalwork from the 7th and 8th centuries BC.

Around the corner is one of the museum's highlights, the newly refurbished **Salon of the Gods,** with large 2nd-century statues of Zeus, Aphrodite, Athena, Artemis, Hermes, and Dionysus, as well as their Egyptian sidekicks Serapis, Isis, and Horus. The **Salon of Small Objects and Underwater Remains** to the right houses several silver and ivory Phrygian statuettes excavated from 8th-century tombs. A blue-lit glass case nearby is littered with "underwater findings," mainly barnacle-encrusted earthenware salvaged from 3rd-century shipwrecks. The gem of the collection is a magnificently painted Grecian urn, mysteriously labelled the "Tibet Crater." To the left of the Salon of the Gods is the **Hall of Emperors,** home to 2nd-and 3rd-century Roman marble busts from Perge (see **Perge,** p. 286). The **Hall of the Cemetery Culture,** the next room, contains seven beautifully carved sarcophagi.

The adjoining **Icon Hall** displays a small but exceptional collection of Orthodox Christian **icons.** Beyond the Hall of Cemetery Culture lies the **Mosaic Salon,** which contains a Seleucid floor mosaic and smaller 6th-century Byzantine works. The **Hall of Money and Jewelry** contains a few of the **world's first coins,** minted between 640 and 630BC by the Lydians. These were forged from white gold, or electrium, under the last Lydian king, Croesus. The **Ethnography Salon** displays daily implements of Ottoman and Bedouin life. Check out the elaborate wooden ceiling display near the exit. (*2 Konyaatı Bul., about 2½km from town along Cumhuriyet Bul., which changes its name to Konyaaltı Bul. Dolmuş labeled "Konyaaltı/Liman" head along this street,*

MEDITERRANEAN COAST

stopping at the large "D" signs ($.30). Ask to be let off when you see the yellow museum signs before the dolmuş heads downhill to the beach. The tram also runs from Kaleiçi to the museum ($.25). ☎241 45 28. Open in summer Tu-Su 9am-6pm; in winter 8am-5pm. $6, students $4.50.)

OTHER SIGHTS. Near the entrance to Kaleiçi, at the intersection of Cumhuriyet Cad., stands the symbol of Antalya, the unique red-tinted **Yivli Minare** (fluted minaret). Dating from the 13th century, this minaret was constructed by the Selçuk Sultan Alaeddin Keykubad. Down Atatürk Cad., on the right, stand the three adorned arches of **Hadrian's Gate,** built in 130 AD to commemorate the emperor's visit. Through this gate, about halfway down Hesapçı Sok., is the **Kesik Minare** (Broken Minaret). The mosque traces Antalya's history: it was once a Roman temple, then a domed basilica, and, finally, a Selçuk mosque. At the far end of Hesapçı Sok. is the **Hıdırlık Tower,** believed to have been built as a lighthouse in the 2nd century.

Kaleiçi, a charming district with serpentine streets and old buildings, is a great late afternoon stroll. Founded as Attaleia in the 2nd century BC by King Attalos II of Pergamon, this area is still fortified by Greek, Byzantine, and Selçuk walls.

Antalya's two large and placid beaches, **Lara** and **Konyaaltı,** are both accessible by dolmuş (to Lara from the Doğu Garaj, to Konyaaltı from Konyaaltı Bul.; $.30). Konyaaltı is free, while Lara charges $.50 for admission and $3.50 for an umbrella and two chairs. On the way to Lara, stop off at the **Lower Düden Waterfall,** a cascade that tumbles 20m into the sea. The spectacular **Upper Düden Falls,** about 10km from Antalya, is included in most half-day tours of Termessos (see p. 288).

🎵 ENTERTAINMENT

Whether you're looking for an elegant dance club or a more rowdy bar, there's no shortage of nightlife in Antalya. **Cinemas** generally show English-language films with Turkish subtitles. **Oscar,** Zafer Sok., along Atatürk Cad., shows Hollywood blockbusters and other foreign films ($3.50).

Club Alley, above the harbor, is easily identified by the intense green laser it shoots out across the water at night. The be all and end all of nightlife for Antalya's young and wealthy. 8 independently-owned bars encircle a central bar in this spacious outdoor establishment. The evening begins with mellow hip-hop, while bass-heavy dance beats pick up the pace as the night wears on. Beer and *rakı* $6; cocktails $10. Cover Su-Th $8.15, F-Sa $11.65. Open 8pm-4am.

Club 29 (☎241 62 60 or 247 59 37). Along the harbor after Denizcinin. Megabass Euro, Turkish, and American pop blast from all directions while underwater flood lamps illuminate the sea. On weekends, young Turks pack the floor until daybreak. Cover M-Th $9, F-Sa $11. Beer $3.50; *rakı* $4.65. Open 11pm-4am.

Yelken Cafe Bar Sells the cheapest beer on the harbor. For a low-key drink with friends, this place should do you good. Beer $1.15.

Denizcinin Köşesi (Fisherman's Corner), 1 Yat Limanı (☎247 53 29). Along the harbor. This popular bar spins a range from oldies to contemporary pop music. Beer $1.85; *rakı* $2.25; cocktails $5.85; pizza $5-6. Open 9am-5am.

Tequila Mexico Bar, 24 Yat Limanı (☎243 41 15). Near the bazaar. This fortress-like bar looms over Antalya's quiet harbor. Festively decorated, it has nightly music, with live Latin tunes W, F-Sa. Beer and *rakı* $3.50. Corona $7; tequila $5. Open 7pm-3:30am.

🏛 DAYTRIPS FROM ANTALYA

PERGE

Dolmuş run from Meydan Garajı in Antalya to Aksu ($.35). Ask to be let off at Perge, which is a 2km walk from the highway; beware the hot summer sun. Daily tours also visit both Perge and Aspendos ($25-27, admission and lunch included). Talk to your pension owner or contact Akay Travel Service (see Antalya: Travel Agencies, p. 284). Site open daily May-Oct. 7:30am-7pm, Nov.-Apr. 8am-5:30pm. $4.

The extensive remains of ancient Perge (16km from Antalya) make it easy to imagine what life was like in this prosperous town of over 100,000 inhabitants. The city was supposedly founded by Greek heroes after the Trojan War, but it didn't earn its place in history until it sided with the omnipotent boy-wonder **Alexander the Great** when he stormed through Asia Minor.

The 12,000-seat **stadium,** along the road uphill to the site, once hosted wild beast fights and athletic events. The wall at the far end protected spectators from the bloodier incidents. For all this danger, however, the victor only took home a measly bottle of olive oil. Against the opposite hill is a theater featuring fine reliefs of Dionysus, the god of wine and merriment.

The official site entrance is the **Roman gate,** once two stories high and covered with a marble façade, located beyond the theater and the stadium. Niches inside the gate mark where statues once stood. Past the Roman gate are the ruins of the Emperor **Hadrian's Gate.** The city-state of Perge primarily worshipped Artemis, the huntress, but because the townspeople used both the Greek and Latin languages, large stones also bear the name Artemis's Roman name, Diana. A large **agora** is on the right. Here, shops were arranged by trade and inspected by officials known as *agoranomas.* Noteworthy are the intricate black and red mosaic floors of the shop right before the main *agora* complex. The marble columns still standing originally connected to the shops by wooden roofs, forming a covered portico.

Opposite the *agora* lie the remains of the **athletic complex** and **bath.** Passing through the remains of a large swimming pool and exercise area, enter the bath, a series of three rooms. The first was known as the *frigidarium* (for cold water), the second *tepidarium* (for warm water), and finally the *caldarium* (for hot water). A stroll through the multi-room complex reveals marble floors and scant bits of marble wall tiling. Under the brick vaults in the last room, fires were built to keep enormous pots of water boiling. The rising steam heated the room and water. The hot water would then pass to the warm room, then the cold room as the heat was lost, finally ending up outside in a large water basin known as the *nymphaeum.* Up ahead, two imposing 3rd-century BC Hellenistic towers mark the beginning of the long, colonnaded avenue. In ancient times, water flowed along the street from here into a fountain dedicated to **Emperor Septimus Severus.**

ASPENDOS

From Antalya, take the bus from Meyden Garaji to Serik ($1), a town located beyond Perge and Aksu but on the same road. Dolmuş run to Aspendos from the Serik otogar ($.35). Site ☎ (242) 735 74 43. Open May-Oct. 7:30am-7pm; Nov.-Apr. 8am-5:30pm. $4.50.

Aspendos's magnificent ▨ **theater,** built by the architect Zeno under the reign of Marcus Aurelius (161-180 AD), owes its remarkable state of repair largely to the Selçuks, who restored it as a *kervansaray.* Aspendos arguably has the most magnificent remaining Roman theater in Asia and the single most memorable monument on Turkey's Mediterranean coast. Upon visiting it in 1909, the archaeologist D.G. Howarth wrote, "You may have seen amphitheaters in Italy, France, Dalmatia and Africa; temples in Egypt and Greece; palaces in Crete; you may be sated with antiquity or scornful of it. But you have not seen the theater of Aspendos."

It takes little imagination to envision the ancient tragedies and comedies, the coarse Roman plays, the gladiatorial duels, and mock naval duels for which the theater was filled with water. The acoustics are stunning: send a friend to the back row and she'll be able to hear anything you say with just a little projection.

When Atatürk visited Aspendos, he was so impressed by the remains that he declared it would be used again as a theater. The annual **Aspendos Opera and Ballet Festival** (☎ (242) 248 00 08) is still held here in late June and early July, and performances continue for most of the summer; call for details. A **Folk Festival** in early July, run by the Folk Dance Music Youth Society, İstanbul Folklore (☎ (216) 410 24 47 or 410 24 48), features dance companies from Western and Eastern Europe and parts of Asia. Another highlight is the **Mevlâna Sema Ritual,** a whirling dervish exhibition, followed by Turkish folk dancing. Admission prices vary. Opposite the old Selçuk mosque area is a small museum housing Roman theater tickets and pictures of Atatürk's visit. If you're not pooped yet, head farther uphill along the road past the theater to see the extensive remains of Roman **aqueducts** dotting the landscape. The rest of ancient Aspendos has not yet undergone excavations like those at Perge and Side, and so most of the city lies in a state of uninspiring decay.

TERMESSOS

*Due to the severe heat, the ruins of Termessos are not accessible in July and Aug. Getting to Termessos is easiest with a half-day tour from Antalya (10am-3pm, $25). For more info see Antalya: **Travel Agencies,** p. 284. Buses running to Korkuteli can stop at the entrance of Güllük Dağı National Park, from which it is a grueling 10km (2hr.) climb to the ruins. Taxis make the trip for $5 each way. Arrange for the cabbie to wait for you. Visitors should be aware of the dangers of heatstroke (see p. 50). Wear good hiking shoes and pants for the bramble-covered mountainous terrain. Park open daily 8am-5pm. $2.*

On a mountaintop surrounded by rocky crops and dense undergrowth, ■**Termessos** wins the grand prize for best location of an ancient city. Termessos was famed for its wildlife and the valor of its Pisidian residents, who withstood Alexander the Great's attack in the 4th century BC. The site is now a collection of well-preserved buildings, including a magnificent theater and a unique water-storage system.

Near the parking lot at the site entrance stand the high stairs and impressive doorway of the **Temple of Artemis.** With the temple on the right, walk up the path past the **city walls,** built in stepwise fashion and now crumbling under the weight of spreading tree growth. About 500m up is the large **gymnasium-bath complex,** where remains of columnar façades sit opposite arches used for water collection. Continue up to reach the **well** and a flat valley area where the **Senate hall** and magnificent **theater** stand. The sheer rocky cliffs and mountains that surround the theater provide a backdrop that once complemented and amplified the staged drama.

A bit farther lies the **Grave of the Hero** and five enormous underground **cisterns** used for rainwater collection. The **Corinthian temple** is now little more than a tall structure with a few Corinthian capitols. Climb down the opposite mountain through the ancient necropolis, whose face is strewn with well-preserved stone **sarcophagi** and **rock tombs.** In contrast to the house-shaped structures of the Lycians, the tombs constructed by the Pisidian inhabitants of Termessos were delicately etched in rock, sometimes decorated with mask façades.

Near the entrance to Güllük Dağı Park is the small **Flora and Fauna Museum,** which contains some stuffed animals and dried plants from the region, as well as photos, Ottoman wares, and treasures excavated from Termessos.

DÜDEN

In Turkish, the term *düden* means the point at which an underground river hits daylight for a brief moment. Glimpse two such moments near Antalya in the Upper and Lower Düden Waterfalls. At the Upper Waterfall, accessible by dolmuş ($.50) or on a day tour from Antalya (see **Antalya: Travel Agencies,** p. 284), torrential cascades rush over leafy greenery before plunging into the calm Mediterranean. Visitors can take the refreshing path that leads directly behind the falls. *(Site open 7am-7:30pm. $.50.)* The less impressive Lower Falls, located en route to Lara Beach, can be reached via the Lara dolmuş from Antalya ($.35).

KÖPRÜLÜ KANYON

*Akay Tours offers daily trips from Antalya for around $35. Medraft, whose service is a bit more expensive ($52 per person), also offers an optional speedboat exploration of the canyon at the base of the river ($30 for 20min.). See **Antalya: Travel Agencies,** p. 284.*

An organized rafting tour to Köprülü Kanyon falls far short of the ideal encounter with nature; however, it may be the safest way to see the canyon. After the two-hour bus ride from Antalya to Köprülü, tourists are dropped near the mouth of the canyon where they can choose to ride the rapids in a two-person kayak or an eight-person boat. By the end of the day, passengers will have taken in breathtaking views of the natural setting and paid a pretty penny for it.

SİDE

Side (SEE-deh) contains all the necessary ingredients for a complete Mediterranean coast vacation: Hellenic ruins, parasailing, an illustrious museum, beautiful sandy beaches, and the self-proclaimed "best" disco in Europe. It's Mediterranean-style one-stop shopping—bargain for leather goods in the crowded pedestrian streets, study up on ancient history in the 7th-century Roman ruins, and make coconut oil libations to the sun god Ra.

The early history of Side will likely never be fully uncovered. According to the residents themselves, the city was colonized by Greeks, who, immediately upon arrival, forgot their mother tongue and instead began speaking a strange, barbarian language. All inscriptions that date before the 3rd century BC are written in a unique and still undeciphered script. Alexander the Great conquered Side in 334 BC and destroyed the Persian Empire in 331. Side later prospered under Roman and Byzantine rule, but, as a result of increasingly ferocious Arab raids and a 10th century conflagration, the population was moved to Antalya.

▐▊ TRANSPORTATION

Side's **otogar** (☎ 753 12 86 or 753 42 44), 1km from the tourist center, is a very peculiar place: there are bus companies but very few buses. Theoretically, buses leave from Side's otogar to: **Ankara** (10 per day 9am-10:45pm, $16); **Bodrum** (10:45am, 9:45, 10pm; $16); **Bursa** (5 per day 10:45am-11pm, $14); **Eskişehir** (5 per day 10:45am-11pm, $13); **İstanbul** (8 per day 9am-9pm, $21); **İzmir** (7 per day 9am-10:30pm, $16); and **Marmaris** (9:30am, $16). You're best off buying your ticket in advance, to ensure that the bus knows to stop in Side en route. Entering Side, you may get dropped at the otogar, but it's more likely that buses will leave you at a gas station marking the highway turn-off in **Manavgat**, from which dolmuş run to the Side otogar ($.60). From the otogar, a ridiculous-looking red tractor-drawn carriage makes the run to town ($.16). The Manavgat otogar offers a better selection of buses departing the region, and it can be reached by dolmuş from Side (every 5 min. 6am-midnight, $.60). Frequent **buses** run from Manavgat to **Alanya** (every 30min. 6am-7pm, $3) and **Antalya** (every 20min. 6am-11pm, $2).

▆▊ ORIENTATION AND PRACTICAL INFORMATION

The helpful Side **tourist office** is past the otogar and Luna amusement park, toward the highway. You can snag brochures and a list of Side's 200 pensions and 150 hotels. (☎ 753 12 65. Open June-Aug. daily 8am-5pm; Sept.-May M-F 8am-5pm.) The **Side Internet Cafe**, marked by a logo-ed surfboard, is on Small Beach Street. (☎ 753 23 99. $1.60 per hr. Open daily 9am-midnight.) In the event of a **medical emergency**, dial ☎ 753 12 21. Other services include: the **hospital**, across from the tourist office, just off the main street between Side and the highway; the **jandarma** (☎ 156), which has jurisdiction over Side and may respond faster than the police; and a small **PTT**, in the center of town, which offers no services beyond the post and a **money exchange**. A larger PTT is near the beach west of Side, past the hospital. (Both open 8am-midnight for all offered services.) **Postal code:** 07330.

▐▌ ACCOMMODATIONS

Pettino Pansiyon (☎ 732 99 72; fax 753 12 72). Turn left at the Jungle Bar in the middle of town to get to this pleasant, breezy spot. 13 comfortable rooms encircle an arboreal courtyard and bar, where wooden decor adds to the Amazonian ambiance. Breakfast $3. $9.70 per person.

Sidemara Motel (☎ 753 10 83). Along the eastern beach. One of the best deals in town. Around a petite garden, clean rooms offer phones, shiny baths and plenty of elbow space. 50m from the sea, Sidemara also has an "American Bar" (for those who can tell the difference). Breakfast $1.60. Singles and doubles $8; triples $10.

Hanımeli Pansiyon (☎ 753 11 00), near the Hermes Restaurant on the western side of the peninsula, boasts one of the lovelier courtyards in Side. 12 rooms located in a beautiful old Ottoman mansion. Ocean or garden view. Breakfast included. Rooms $23.

Yaşa Motel (☎ 753 40 24; fax 753 14 44). On Turgut Reis Cad., next to the parking lot. Near the sea, Yaşa has a charming, if oddly decorated, courtyard. 30 clean, comfortable rooms of varying quality. Breakfast included. Singles $8-12; doubles $16-20.

Beach House Hotel (☎ 753 10 59 or 753 16 07). On the small eastern beach. Located over an ancient Roman villa (hence the "Beach House"), this upper-scale hotel has 20 rooms (with fan and phone) that have been graced by the likes of Simone de Beauvoir. Ocean-view balconies, a terrace bar, and a garden over ancient ruins may inspire you to write your breakthrough novel as well. Breakfast included. Singles $13; doubles $19.

Yakamoz Pansiyon (☎ 753 19 81). To the right just before the tourist colony entrance. Though wood-panelled rooms are clean and quiet, the seaside pension asks too much for its unsightly exterior. Better deals are on the other side of the entrance gate. Breakfast included. Singles $12.50; doubles $22.50; triples $27.50.

Rasel Pension (☎ 753 18 75 or (533) 410 68 85). On the right side of the road to the tourist colony (heading away from the otogar). Follow the sign inland to 17 bungalow rooms set up like a summer camp, with virtually no tourist clients. Works if you're looking to pitch a tent or find a cheap sleep near the beach. Watch the waves from the raised platform bar, a popular meal-stop for nearby beach-goers. Breakfast included. Rooms $8 per person. Tents $8.

🍴 FOOD

No coastal resort would be complete without seafood and a kickin' nightlife. Fine seafood is proferred throughout the city, and slightly pricey restaurants line the waterfront. For savory, affordable Turkish food, try **Uğur Lokantası** (☎ 753 36 54) on Orkide Sok., where $4 will get you salad and a mean stuffed pepper. For finer dining, hit the **Soundwaves Restaurant** (☎ 753 10 59), next to the Beach House Hotel. On a picturesque seaside terrace, meat and chicken meals run $5-8, with a slightly pricier seafood menu. Next door, the **Soundwaves Patisserie and Cocktail Bar** is a great lunch spot and serves up a solid cheeseburger ($2.50).

👁 SIGHTS

While chugging past Side's ancient ruins and arches in a little red tractor, one gets the feeling of traveling through time. Further, a Roman footpath is being cleared along the right-hand side of the paved road, so visitors can retrace the footsteps of ancient Side's residents. The **nymphaeum,** a memorial fountain at the entrance to Side, once had a marble façade depicting punishments administered to those who committed sexual sins or who sinned against the gods. Ironically, the Side of today is as loose as it gets—get down, get dirty; chances are your neighbors are naughtier than you. The 2nd-century **theater** of Side, which seated 25,000, boasts its role as one of "the largest and most imposing Greco-Roman ruins in Asia Minor." Though 10 years ago the amphitheater was sturdy enough to house the Moscow Circus, today's entrance fee only allows you to walk a 50m fenced-off strip dividing the crumbling upper and lower *cavea,* or seating area. *(Open daily 8am-midnight. $4.)* The rather unimpressive ruins of two **agora** lie scattered behind the theater. A bit further down the road in the direction of the otogar, ancient **Roman baths** have been converted into an excellent ▦ **Archaeological Museum.** A visit to Side is incomplete without seeing this revamped bathhouse, which now houses sarcophagi, marble reliefs, ancient columns, and a breathtaking array of marble statues. *(Open Tu-Su 8am-noon, 1-5pm. $4.)* At the end of the tiny peninsula, parts of the **Temples of Athena and Apollo** have been re-built, making for a spectacular photo spot. Located in a field of razed ruins, the temples' standing columns were repaired and hoisted under the finance and care of an American businesswoman. Beautiful beaches extend on either side of the peninsula. To the west, wide, flat stretches make popular sunbathing spots while to the east, some tourists unfurl sleeping bags on the sand near wooden shacks.

🎵 ENTERTAINMENT

Oxyd Disco. 3km west on the highway outside of Side (taxi $9). The best disco in the area. The bizarre combination of styles—ranging from the Hittite fortress exterior to the industrial piping of the upper dance floor to the space-age rigging over the main dance floor—actually manages to work in this outdoor shrine to postmodernism. A good DJ, fashionable Turks, 2 bars, and an ingenious interior design. Cover $10.50, includes unlimited domestic drinks. Foreign drinks run about $4. Open 11pm-4am.

The Light House. On the water. With a fleet of B-52s cleared for takeoff and plenty of Sex On The Beach to be had, this place is ground zero for mindless carousing. Through the ancient ramped entrance is a giant, open-air, waterfront dance floor with multiple bars. Cover $12, includes indigenous drinks. Guys must bring a girl. Open until 4:30am.

Barracuda Bar and Cafe (☎ 753 27 24), **Stones Bar** (☎ 753 36 69), and **Temple Bar** (☎ 753 27 24). All beyond the temple. This side-by-side triumvirate of small dance-bars blasts an uninteresting mix of Turk and Euro-pop with enthusiastic gusto. Straggling dancers wave around on small dance floors, though patrons are mostly table-side bar-hoppers. Beer $1.60; *rakı* $2.40; cocktails $6. Open 11am-3am.

Denizati Disco (☎ 753 21 49). By the waterfront PTT. Tasteful hip-hop/house/Turko-pop complemented by a strobe light and smoke machine Beer $1.60; *rakı* $3; cocktails $7. Open 7pm-5am.

Blues Bar (☎ 753 11 97). A well-kept secret on Mosque Street, this tastefully decorated bar plays a broader selection than its name suggests. Cavernous interior with an out-doorsy ambiance. Houses a winter bar with fireplace. Serves up a tasty Bloody Mary ($4). Beer $1.60. Open 11pm-3am.

🔳 DAYTRIP FROM SIDE: MANAVGAT WATERFALLS

Four kilometers north of Manavgat, a set of small falls in a pleasant, shaded area has become a popular escape from the midday heat. Bring a picnic or sip cold drinks purchased from one of the overpriced cafes. Be forewarned: on a hot day, the crowd at the falls can make Side look like a ghost town. If you're just looking for some solitude, try wandering up the road along the river north of the falls. (To get to the falls from Side, first take a dolmuş to the Manavgat otogar ($.60) and from there catch another dolmuş to the falls (Manavgat şelalesi; $.60). Day-long tours from Antalya to Perge and Aspendos usually include a visit to the falls ($.40).)

EASTERN MEDITERRANEAN COAST

ALANYA ☎ 242

Inching westward along the Mediterranean, Alanya marks the starting line for Turkey's marathon of coastal debauchery. Swarms of Nordic tourists discovered Alanya sometime in the 1980s, rendering the once-idyllic seaside town a maze of apartotels, palm trees, restaurants, shops, and beautiful Scandinavians. Looking beyond the tacky façade, Alanya rightfully deserves its tourist boom; miles of gorgeous blue-flag beaches, monuments of Selçuk grandeur, and nights of inebrious clubbing mix together for some undiluted vacation fun.

🔳 TRANSPORTATION

Buses: From the otogar to: **Adana** (9hr., every 1½hr. 7:30am-9pm, $13.50); **Anamur** (3hr., every 1½hr. 7:30am-9pm, $5); **Ankara** (8hr., 6 per day 10am-11pm, $14.50); **Antalya** (2hr., every 1½hr. 7:30am-9pm, $4); **İstanbul** (14hr., 5 per day 8:30am-7:45pm, $20); **İzmir** (10hr.; 10:30am, 6:30, 9pm; $14); **Konya** (4hr., every hr. 7am-11pm, $9); **Mersin** (8hr., every 1½hr. 7:30am-9pm, $11); **Side** (1hr., every 30min.

7:30am-9pm, $2.60); **Taşucu** (6hr., every 1½hr. 7:30am-9pm, $9). The otogar has luggage storage that extorts $1.60 for 20min.

Ferries: Fergün Shipping Co. Ltd. (☎511 55 65; fax 511 53 58), 50m north and uphill from the Kızıl Kule on Atatürk Cad. Sells seabus tickets for **Girne** (W, F 6am; return Tu, Th 4pm; one-way $25, students $20, ages 4-12 $15, under 4 free; round-trip $40, students $30, ages 4-12 $25, under 4 free). Office claims to be open 24hrs.

☀🛈 ORIENTATION AND PRACTICAL INFORMATION

Atatürk Cad., dotted by hotels, restaurants, banks, and ATMs, runs along the city's east-west axis; the water borders the south. The **otogar,** one block from Atatürk Cad., is on the western side of town. Dolmuş ($.40) head from the otogar down Atatürk Cad. to within a few blocks of the harbor *(liman)* and İskele Cad., home to dozens of restaurants, bars, and clubs. The peninsula is the best landmark in town. The kitschy harbor is bunched about beneath its eastern flank, while on the western side, Güzelyalı Cad. runs along an only slightly less touristy strip with beaches and restaurants but fewer hotels. The tourist office stands at the intersection of Damlataş Cad., İsmet İnönü Cad., and Güzelyalı Cad., marking the city's center of gravity, with excellent beaches and affordable accommodations.

Tourist Office: (☎513 12 40; fax 513 54 36). Located next to the Damlataş Cave, at the intersection of Damlataş, İsmet İnönü, and Güzelyalı Cad. Offers an unattended table of free maps and brochures. Open M-F 8:30am-6pm, Sa-Su 9:30am-4pm.

Travel Agency: 2000 Tours, 34/1 Damlataş Cad. (☎512 56 79). Offers Jeep Safari adventure tours through the Taurus Mountains ($25 per person; stops at old Turkish villages and Dim Creek) and historical Perge-Aspendos-Side tours ($25 per person).

Pharmacies: Many line Damlataş Cad., which runs parallel to and south of Atatürk Bul.

Hospital: Besides the numerous, well-advertised international clinics catering to tourists, the **Devlet Hastanesi** (☎513 48 43) provides general medical treatment.

Internet Access: Cafes line Atatürk Cad.; try **My My Donose Chatroom,** the one closest to the Red Tower. $1.20 per hr. Open daily 10am-1am. Away from the harbor, head to **Eksen Internet Cafe** by taking a left at the Foto Yunus sign on Damlataş Cad. $.80 per hr. Open daily 10am-1am.

PTT: Main office, in the middle of Atatürk Cad. Postal services, fax, and telegraph open 24hr. **Currency** and **traveler's check exchange** daily 9am-11pm. **Postal code:** 07400.

🏠 ACCOMMODATIONS

Alanya is awash in hundreds of hotels and pensions. Condominium-like "apartotels" are popular, especially among the European tourists who account for the lion's share of Alanya's visitors. Good deals can be found on Bebek Sok., near the tourist office and Alanya's famed Cleopatra Beach. Night owls might try İskele Cad., whose hotels are a stumble and crawl from the frantic nightlife.

Sunway Hotel, 2 Bebek Sok. (☎511 18 80; fax 512 75 72). Big with the Nordics, and a great deal. Offers a rooftop terrace, small lobby bar, and rooms with private bath, balcony, and phone. Breakfast included. Room fan $2.40. Singles $8; doubles $16.

Hotel Marina, 80 İskele Cad. (☎513 43 21; fax 513 96 11). Well located (by the Red Tower). Cheap, attractive rooms with balconies overlooking the harbor. Breakfast included. Singles $10; doubles $15; triples $20.

Mola Otel, 8 Bebek Sok. (☎513 30 21). They call him Şişman Amca (Uncle Fatso). The hotel's congenial proprietor, that is, who relishes the endearing nickname from his days of Ankara ice-cream vending. "Fatso's place" offers 26 comfortable, basic rooms in the heart of Alanya. Breakfast included. Singles $12.50; doubles $20. Room fan $1.60.

Kalyon Hotel, 123 Atatürk Cad. (☎513 43 92; ☎/fax 513 44 76). North of the tourist office. Its exchange services, international newspapers, and pool make it feel like a classy hotel despite the low price. Breakfast included. Singles $10; doubles $18.

Baba Hotel, 6 İskele Cad. (☎513 10 32). The 30 rooms are somewhat worn, but bathrooms are surprisingly clean. Singles $6, with bath $10; doubles $7, with bath $12.

◉♫ FOOD AND ENTERTAINMENT

Those looking for relatively expensive European food will find themselves in the right place, as the outdoor restaurants along the west beach and near the harbor carry plenty of steak and schnitzel. Recently administered stringent regulations shut down many of Alanya's shabbier eateries, making meat-eating a non-hazardous activity once again. In short, you can trust the *döner*. In the nightlife sector, flashy Alanya exudes its share of loud music and disco-light wattage. The most posh and worthy clubs line Rıhtım Cad., along the harbor below Atatürk Cad.

Musti's Restaurant and Cafe Bar, 7 Bebek Sok. (☎ 511 02 76). Across from Mola Otel, beneath the apartotels of the same name. Away from the chaos of main streets, this small restaurant is run by friendly, fiery management and presents an eclectic menu of Euro-Turko and specialty dishes. The Chicken Bombay special is to die for ($6). Open daily 8:30pm-midnight.

Cafe Sedir Restaurant, 4 Güzelyalı Cad. (☎ 512 38 76). Down the street from the tourist office. Nightly overflowing crowds make Sedir hard to miss. The fame is well-earned; the polyglot menu fills a 3-ring binder with over 30 house specials, meat and chicken dishes, grills, steaks, salads, and sandwiches ($4-6).

Bistro Bellman. On Rıhtım Cad., by the bungee crane. This restaurant by "day" (6pm-11pm), club by "night" (11pm-3am) is the place to be seen. Frequent theme parties and a hip crowd animate the dance floor, where hips swivel to techno remixes of otherwise cheesy pop. Nordic tourists vie for majority dominance screaming to chants of "Do we have Sweden/Norway/Denmark in the hoooouuse?!" If you tire of watching the sexy bartenders and sleek patrons, divert your eyes to the big screen TVs that flank the massive sitting space. Or, go bungee jumping. Beer $2.50; cocktails $5-6.

James Dean Bar. Next door to Bistro Bellman, where everybody aspires to that "rebel-without-a-cause" suave. Mellow beginnings have tourists sipping cocktails until the mostly pop selection (expect Madonna) inspires dancers to get their groove on. Beer $2.50; cocktails $4-6. Open 9pm-4am.

Zapf Hahn. In the same cluster. An uninspired Top 40 selection and aimless light show attempt to make up in quantity for what they lack in quality. The giant, open-air dance floor sheltered by a corrugated metal canopy, is like a post-apocalyptic pirates' cave gone wild. Beer and *rakı* $2.50. Open until 4am.

◉ SIGHTS

Most of Alanya's sights cluster on the peninsula. Known in ancient times as Coracesium, Alanya gained notoriety as a pirate cove until the Roman General Pompey destroyed the town's huge fleet in 67 BC. Marc Antony later conferred the city upon Cleopatra as a gift, resulting in many a souvenir shop being named in her honor. Many of the city's great structures date from the 13th century, when the city fell under Selçuk control and was renamed **Alaiye** in honor of Sultan Alaeddin Keykubad. Alaiye fell to the Ottomans in 1471.

SELÇUK SIGHTS. The **Kızıl Kule (Red Tower),** built in 1226 under Sultan Keykubad's reign, is spectacular. The 30m high octagonal structure constructed from red, kiln-baked brick served as the city's first line of defense from seaborne attack; soldiers could shoot arrows at ships from five levels while drawing water from the giant cistern built into the tower's spire. The strategic location on the harbor now affords spectacular views of the surrounding area. The Kızıl Kule also houses an Ethnographic Museum, with the usual array of old carpets and costumes. *(Tower open Tu-Su 8am-noon, 1:30-5:30pm. $1.65, students $.70.)*

A magnificent 200m walk behind the castle walls from the tower will take you to the only remaining Selçuk-era **tersane** (shipyard) in Turkey. This nursery for Keykubad's navy has five chambers, all open to the sea; munitions were stored in the nearby *tophane* (arsenal).

İÇ KALESİ (FORTRESS). At the top of Alanya's headland is the fortress which houses a mint, a Byzantine-era monastery, a church, and a cistern. The walls are still mostly intact, and in one corner stands the *Adam Atacaği* ("place for throwing people"). Now surrounded by bars, this platform is the spot from where the condemned were once heaved onto the jagged cliffs and the sparkling sea below. Today, instead of gawking at prisoners, tourists arrive in the early evening to watch the twilight over the ocean. Had the condemned prisoners taken the time to appreciate their plummet, they could have enjoyed one of the most beautiful views in the Mediterranean. The fortress is also worth seeing after dark, when Alanya's lights sparkle like jewels below, and many a car parks at this quintessentially romantic spot. *(You can either trudge the 3km to the top or take a dolmuş from the north end of İskele Cad. or opposite the tourist office (every hr. 7am-8pm, $.30). Fortress open daily 8am-5:30pm. $2.80, students $1.85.)*

CAVES. Damlataş Cave, discovered by accident while blasting stones in 1948, is a two-story affair replete with eerie stalactites and stalagmites. The 90-100% humidity inside the cave does wonders for asthma, but the unending flow of tourists that pass through makes it impossible to gaze in solitary awe at the strange workings of Mother Nature. *(Follow the signs along Güzelyalı Cad. in the direction of the peninsula. Open daily in summer 10am-8pm; in winter 10am-5pm. $1.20, students $.60.)*

Far more impressive is Alanya's **Dim Cave,** located 9km northeast of town. Three hundred and sixty meters long, with heights between 10-15m, Dim Cave is an absolutely awesome tangle of limestone-dissolved stalactites and stalagmites. Carbonic acid rainwater continues to drip along the interior, aiding the unearthly formations. Unfortunately, no dolmuş run to Dim Cave, so access is either by tour group, car, or taxi. *(Open 9am-8pm. $2.40).* The nearby **Dim Creek** is becoming a wildly popular tourist stop, where visitors swim in the absolutely frigid water. Picnic spots and restaurants are set up along and actually in the river, with floating raft eateries and waiters wading barefoot to serve. The best pick is probably **Ada Piknik Motorcu Şevketin Yeri,** where chicken, fish, or meat meals ($3-6) are served on carpeted, pillowed rafts. Further down the creek, a 9m high bridge makes for an adrenaline-surging plummet to the icy water below.

OTHER SIGHTS. Alanya also has a decent **museum** with exhibits from local Bronze Age excavations to 19th-century Ottoman *kilims*. *(The museum is located across from the tourist office. Open Tu-Su 8am-noon, 1:30-5:30pm. $1.15, students $.70.)*

You can always go **bungee jumping** from the massive crane in the harbor for $50. (Open 4pm to 2am.) Relax during the day at the beautiful **Grand Alanya Büyük Hamam** (☎511 33 44) on Damlataş Cad., where $16 will get you a sauna, jacuzzi, shock pool, *kese*, and 90min. creamed massage (same-sex masseur). There's a separate woman's hamam, for those uncomfortable with the co-ed thing, and a "vitamin bar" awaits post-scrub indulgence.

ANAMUR ☎324

Anamur is a city of many faces. The least attractive of these is the one facing the bus station, so don't be discouraged when you arrive; this is the city center, heavy on dust and concrete. Most visitors stay near the prettier beaches at the İskele (dock), Anamur's tourist district. A laid-back town of 60,000, Anamur is isolated enough that it hasn't been exposed as heavily to the tourist debauchery that has hit the coast further west. For the most part, it's still a popular vacation spot for Turkish families, and pleasant pensions, uncrowded beaches, and a vigorous nightlife make a stay here relaxing and enjoyable. The nearby ruins of ancient Anemurium and the well-preserved Mamure Kale offer more than just a day at the beach.

◪ TRANSPORTATION

Buses: The **otogar** is about 1km downhill from the main square, easily identifiable thanks to—all together now—an Atatürk statue. Buses travel to: **Adana** (6hr., 9 per day noon-midnight, $8); **Alanya** (3hr., 8 per day 9am-midnight, $5); **Ankara** (10hr., 5 per day 7am-11pm, $16); **Antalya** (5hr., 8 per day 9am-midnight, $8); **İstanbul** (16hr.; 2:30, 5pm; $21); **İzmir** (13hr., 3pm, $19); **Konya** (6hr., 5 per day 7am-11pm, $12);

Mersin (5hr., 9 per day noon-midnight, $6); **Side** (4hr., 8 per day 9am-midnight, $6); **Taşucu** (3hr., 9 per day noon-midnight, $5). Dolmuş run from behind the otogar to the town center (*şehir merkezi*; $.40) and İskele (every 20min. 7am-1am, $.65), contrary to claims of taxi drivers, who charge $7 for the trip.

Ferries: This past winter, **Fergün Maritime** began operating ferries to Northern Cyprus from the Anamur İskele as well. Ferries depart to **Girne** (F, Su 6pm; return F, Su 4pm; one-way $22, students $21; round-trip $40, students $38; group discounts available).

✈🚌 ORIENTATION AND PRACTICAL INFORMATION

Tourist Office: (☎814 35 29; www.anamur.gen.tr), on the 2nd floor of the otogar. Provides free maps, directions, and a list of accommodations. You may be hard-pressed to find an English-speaker. Open M-F 8am-noon, 1-5pm.

Banks: Several near the main square. **Akbank**, on the road to Atatürk's left, has a Cirrus/Plus/MC/V **ATM** and cashes **traveler's checks** without commission. Open M-F 9am-12:30pm, 1:30-5:30pm. On the İskele side of town, a four-language Cirrus/Plus/MC/V **ATM** is next to the Fergün booth.

Pharmacies: Near the main square.

Hospital: (☎814 10 86).

Internet Access: Idea Internet Cafe, on the 2nd fl. of an apartment building, down the road from the main square, walking with Akbank on your right. $1 per hr. Open daily 8am-midnight. **Number 1 Internet Cafe,** behind Eser Pansiyon on the İskele side of town $1 per hr. Open daily 10am-1am.

PTT: (☎814 10 01), a block downhill and on the right. Offers phone coins, telegraph, and fax, but no money exchange. Open daily 7am-11pm. **Postal code:** 33640.

🏠📷 ACCOMMODATIONS AND FOOD

Anamur's İskele area has more than a dozen pensions with similar facilities (private showers, balconies, breakfast) and fixed prices that are rarely obeyed to the letter (singles $8; doubles $10; triples $12; breakfast $1.60). The best is ◼ **Eser Pansiyon.** Run by two retired English-speaking schoolteachers and their charismatic son Tayfun, the pension has 11 charming rooms, internet access ($2.50 per hr.), a beautiful garden, and a shaded rooftop terrace. (☎814 23 22. Breakfast included. Singles $7.30; doubles $11.30; triples $16.) Another option is **Hotel Bella Roma,** down the street. Its 18 rooms (four with A/C) are equipped with private bath and spacious balconies. (☎816 47 51. Singles $9.70; doubles $13.75, with A/C $20; triples $16, with A/C $23.) For greater indulgence, try **Hotel Dolphine,** 17 İnönü Cad., which offers modern but charmless rooms with A/C, TV, shower, minibar, and phone. (☎814 34 35; fax 814 15 17. Breakfast included. Singles $10.50; doubles $19; triples $24.) Popular with Turkish youth, **Pulla Camping** (☎827 11 51), about 1½km from Mamure and accessible by the Mamure dolmuş, sits atop a gorgeous sandy beach. With electricity, toilets, hot showers, and a restaurant, this isn't exactly roughing it. Bring your own tent and stash up to four people for $4.65.

Restaurants and street food vendors line İskele's main drag, İnönü Cad. It's easy to find good *gözleme* ($.70). **Turtle's Pizza** serves cheap, tasty food including excellent *kumpir* (baked potato stuffed with a Russian salad and peas; $2). At the base of the İsekele, **Kap Anamur** (☎814 23 74) boldly advertises a 1 million lira ($1.60) menu, made up of your standard Turkish fare with *kumpir*-style bonuses.

👁 SIGHTS

ANEMURIUM. Nineteenth century travelers stumbled upon the ruins of Anemurium 1200 years after Arab raids forced out the city's inhabitants. The city reached its height during the early Roman period, 500 to 600 years after its founding in the 4th century BC. It became an episcopal see (area under the authority of a bishop) during the Byzantine period and existed in relative wealth and peace until a massive 6th-century earthquake. Arab raids emptied the town just decades later.

The paved road uphill through the ruins leads past a fabulous pebbled **beach** with bamboo umbrellas. The remains include Roman aqueducts, city walls, baths, a gymnasium, an *odeon*, an amphitheater, a *bouleterion*, and several churches. The renowned **necropolis,** Asia Minor's most impressive city of the dead, bursts with 350 tombs carved from gray limestone blocks. Most feature a sarcophagus room and a frescoed antechamber that served as a chapel. Some colored mosaics survive in the nearby **Necropolis Temple.** Most of the city's houses are still being excavated from under the sand dunes, which until recently concealed the remains of a giant **oil lamp factory.** Some 700 terra-cotta oil lamps were unearthed all in one lot, indicating that they were about to be shipped elsewhere.

The drive from Anamur to Anemurium, along the base of the Cilician Mountains, passes through hillsides crammed with hundreds of glass greenhouses, home to the city's famous banana trees. The shores behind the ruins hide some of Anamur's most beauteous beaches. If you're looking for near-isolation and don't mind a 1½km trek to the beach, you can take a taxi directly from the otogar to the ruins ($14) and stay at either of two tiny, idyllic pensions. **Anamuryum Ören Pansiyon** offers three clean doubles with bucolic views, a shared bathroom, washing machine (free), and kitchen. (☎835 11 91. Breakfast included. $5 per person.) Next door, **Alper Pansiyon** offers spacious rooms in a family home. Use of the tidy bathroom, kitchen, and terrace is free. Call ahead. (☎835 11 13. Breakfast $2.50. One double and two quads. $5 per person.) *(Dolmuş stop at the turn-off for a 2km hike to the ruins, with a new service running dolmuş all the way through at 11am and 4pm. Some İskele hotels and pensions, Eser and Dolphine among them, occasionally organize fishing boat excursions to Anemurium. A taxi will also take you there, wait for you, and take you back for an official $17, but try bargaining. Site open daily 8am-8pm. $2.50.)*

MAMURE KALE. Dramatically jutting out into the sea, this *kale* is one of Anatolia's most impressive castles. A nearby stream feeds the 10m-wide moat encircling the structure and leading to the sea. While there are no sea monsters, those who fall in will have to ward off hordes of little turtles. Today the remains are a veritable playground for all ages; navigate labyrinthine, wildflower-choked rooms, clamber up spiral staircases, and peer through narrow windows at the sea. Come nightfall, Mamure's lights dazzle. *(Dolmuş ($.30) run at least every 30min. from both the city center and the İskele area. You can also walk along the shore to the castle, though that involves swimming across a small creek. Open 8am-8pm. $2.50, students $1.50.)*

OTHER SIGHTS. Softa Kale is built atop a home to many a grape-arbored summer villa. If you're pressed for time, skip the trip because Softa is not that impressive; the ruins, which are in shambles, are frequented only by your occasional sheep flock. *(Dolmuş continue 12km past Mamure/Bozdoğan to Softa/Bozyazı, but the castle isn't accessible by car. Wear pants and comfortable hiking shoes, as you'll have to climb.)* For cavefans, the **Köşekbükü Cave** offers an impressive array of stalactites and stalagmites about 20km east of the İskele. A taxi will take you there for about $24, a price unworth the haul unless you really have a subterranean fetish.

■ NIGHTLIFE

When the sun goes down, İnönü Cad. comes to life. The music is turned up, lanterns and strings of lights illuminate the streets to near-daylight brightness, car traffic ceases, and the sidewalks overflow with food vendors, souvenir hawkers, and pedestrians looking to enjoy a cool evening. Many peaceful beachfront cafes and tea gardens metamorphose into bopping joints where singing crowds dance until dawn. The nightlife here is characterized by cheap *Efes* ($1.90 per pint), live music, and a cheery atmosphere. **Yakamoz Bar** features dancing, a good selection of Turkish pop, live music, and a young crowd. (Beer $1.80, but beware of the nuts since you'll get charged for them.) The **Zeyno Bar** has İskele's best live music (mostly pop) which draws a large, lively crowd. (Beer $1.70.)

The blood-red castle 1km outside of İskele, on the road in from Anamur proper, is the **Apollo,** one of the best discos on the Mediterranean. The castle walls contain an open-air dance floor animated by an excellent selection of Western and Turkish pop and a dazzling light display. This very slick, spacious club also accommodates extensive seating areas and an excellent bar. (Beer $2.40; *rakı* $3. Cover $6, includes one drink. Open 10pm-4am.)

TAŞUCU
☎324

While storming the Turkish Mediterranean, tourists have overlooked Taşucu, mercifully leaving it free of Benettons, leather dealers, and resort hotels. Though Taşucu is neither a cosmopolitan center nor the seat of glorious ancient civilizations, the small, friendly town is worth visiting for free beaches with pleasant boardwalks and cheap transportation to Northern Cyprus.

TRANSPORTATION. From the otogar, **buses** head to: **Adana** (3hr., 9 per day 7:30am-11pm, $5); **Alanya** (6hr., 8 per day 10am-1am, $8); **Anamur** ($3hr., 8 per day 10am-1am, $5); **Ankara** (8hr., 5 per day 9:30am-11:30pm, $12); **Antakya** (6hr.; 8:30am, 1:30, 7:30pm; $8); **Antalya** (8hr., 8 per day 10am-1am, $10); **İstanbul** (15hr.; 4, 9:30pm; $20); **Konya** (4hr., 5 per day 9:30am-11:30pm, $7.20); **Mersin** (2hr., 9 per day 7:30am-11pm, $3); **Side** (7hr., 8 per day 10am-1am, $9.60). **Dolmuş** run to **Silifke** (20min., every 15min., $.40). The **PTT**, across from the dock, and several ferry boat offices sell tickets for the seabus and ferry to **Girne (Kyrenia), Northern Cyprus.** Unless you are into patronizing the underdog, stick with **Fergün Denizcilik Şti. Ltd.** (☎741 23 23 or 741 37 11), which owns the largest, fastest, and most reliable of the fleets. The **seabus** has daily departures (2½-5hr. depending on weather; 11am; $23, round-trip $42; students $1.60 discount). Arrive in the morning to make sure your chosen vessel will sail, and then secure a ticket. The **ferry** leaves daily at midnight (6hr.; $18, round-trip $32; students $1.60 discount).

ORIENTATION AND PRACTICAL INFORMATION. Most of the town occupies a narrow strip between the highway and the sea. Lined with banks and restaurants, the 200m-long main commercial strip links the **harbor** and ferry docks at the western end of town to the **otogar** at the opposite end. **Sahil Cad.** runs east of the otogar, passing inviting beaches on the right and affordable accommodations on the left. Further east, the beaches get better and more crowded.

A **Türkiye İş Bankası,** near the harbor, has a V/MC/Cirrus/Plus **ATM.** The two-story building complex down the road from the PTT houses at least three **internet cafes,** all of which charge about $1 per hour and stay open 10am-midnight. In a **medical emergency,** call the Sağlık Ocağı (☎741 44 88). The **PTT** is open daily 8am-11pm. No exchange services are available on weekends. **Postal code:** 33900.

ACCOMMODATIONS AND FOOD. Sahil Cad., running east along the sea, has many sunny, similarly priced seaside pensions. **Meltem Pansiyon,** 75 Sahil Cad., all the way down Sahil Cad., is among the best. Its 17 immaculate rooms vary in design; some have A/C, 12 have private kitchenettes, and all have insect screens for the windows—a much-needed commodity in this part of Turkey. (☎741 43 91. Breakfast $1.60. Singles $8, with A/C $13; doubles $11.30; triples $21.) Closer to the otogar on Sahil Cad., the brand-new, German-run **Dilara Pansiyon** offers seven rooms with bath. (☎741 52 74. Breakfast included. Singles $6.40; doubles $13.) Near the otogar, where the sign points in the direction of Mersin, **Tuğran Pansiyon,** 3 Sahil Cad., offers 16 rooms (six with A/C) with balconies and showers. (☎741 44 93; fax 741 26 92. Breakfast $2. Singles $13; doubles $20.) Taşucu's seafood is both fresh and affordable. Small joints serving decent, cheap kebap and seafood are easy to find. For finer dining, the **Denizkızı Restoran,** overlooking the harbor right across from the dock, serves good *ızgara* (grilled meats; $3) and fish ($8).

SİLİFKE
☎324

Caught between the beach towns of Kızkalesi and Taşucu, Silifke has gracefully declined participation in the Mediterranean tourist pageant. Seleucus, one of Alexander the Great's generals and successors, founded the city in the 3rd century BC. In 1190 AD, the German Emperor Frederick Barbarossa drowned near the town while leading a band of Crusaders from Germany to the Holy Land. Today, Silifke offers a number of famed sights and transportation to many regional destinations.

TRANSPORTATION. Buses run to: **Adana** (2½hr., every 15min. 6am-7:30pm, $4); **Alanya** (6hr., 9 per day 9:30am-1:30am, $8); **Anamur** (3hr., 9 per day 9:30am-

1:30am, $5); **Ankara** (8hr., 5 per day 9:45am-11:30pm, $12); **Antakya** (7hr.; 6:30, 8:30pm; $6); **Antalya** (8hr., 9 per day 9:30am-1:30am, $10); **İstanbul** (16hr.; 3, 4:30pm; $19); **Kızkalesi** (30min., every 15min. 6am-7:30pm, $.60); **Konya** (4hr., 6 per day 7:30am-3pm, $8.40); **Mersin** (1½hr., every 15min. 6am-7:30pm, $2); **Side** (7hr., 9 per day 9:30am-1:30am, $10). **Dolmuş** head to **Taşucu** (15min., every hr. 7am-7pm, $.35).

⬛🔃 ORIENTATION AND PRACTICAL INFORMATION. Most of Silifke's facilities and businesses lie on the southern side of the Göksu River. **İnönü Bul.**, which passes the Temple of Jupiter and the center of town, runs from the **otogar** at its eastern end to a T-junction with **Menderes (Mut) Cad.** A right turn onto Mut Cad. leads across a stone bridge to the river's northern bank.

The well-stacked and helpful **tourist office** has a bookshelf of surprisingly tasteful Turkey brochures, maps, and other goodies. After crossing the bridge, hook a right on Atatürk Cad. and take a left at Turim Kredi Kooperatif. (☎714 11 51; fax 714 53 28. Open M-F 8am-noon, 1-5pm.) In a **medical emergency,** call the **Devlet Hastanesi** (☎714 11 59). The **PTT** is on Menderes Cad., right before the bridge, and offers standard postal services. (Open daily 7am-11pm.) **Postal code:** 33960.

▞▟ ACCOMMODATIONS AND FOOD. For a cheap, comfy sleep, the **Arisan Otel Pansiyon**, 89 İnönü Cad. exudes college-dormitory cool. Three floors of a former apartment building serve as spacious, clean *pansiyon* rooms with fans or A/C and telephones. (☎714 33 31. Breakfast included. Singles $6.40, with A/C $8; doubles $14.50, with A/C $19. Group discounts negotiable.) For the comfort-seeker, the two-star **Otel Ayatekla** provides more upscale accommodations with TVs, minibars, and remote-controlled A/C. (☎714 39 23; fax 714 87 03. Breakfast included. 24 rooms. Singles $14; doubles $28; suites $40. V, MC.)

Fine dining is difficult to come by in Silifke, and finding restaurants open after dark proves challenging. *Lokanta* are mostly clustered around the otogar and the intersection of Mut Cad. and İnönü Bul. Packed around lunchtime, **Gözde Restaurant** serves up decent Turkish food, including a number of vegetarian *mezes* for about $3. Walking with Akdeniz Hotel on your left, make your first right after the taxi stand. At night, the wood-paneled 2nd floor of the **Pıknık Gazino,** on İnönü Bul., blasts live music from a stage that features the flattened remains of an antelope nailed to the wall. (☎714 35 66. Beer $2.40. Open 9pm-3am.)

🔲 SIGHTS. Silifke's most prominent sight is the **kale** (fortress) on the hill, 180m above town. The 15-minute trek to the top starts at the road near the intersection of Mut Cad. and İnönü Bul. Occupied by Armenians, Crusaders, Karamanoğlu, and Ottomans, the 800-year-old structure with still-intact double walls affords a great view of Silifke. One of the town's most striking features is the **water cistern,** or *tekir ambarı* ("striped granary"), which supplied the town's water in Byzantine times. A spiral staircase descends 12m to the bottom. On İnönü Bul. in the middle of town are the remains of a 2nd-century **Roman temple** to Jupiter, which the Byzantines converted to a basilica in the 5th century. Though only one column still stands, the fallen columns at least provide close-up views of the Corinthian crown. Silifke's **Stone Bridge** dates back to the Roman period, 77-78 AD, though it looks spiffy now after a series of 19th- and 20th-century repairs.

On the road to Mersin, the town of **Narlıkuyu** houses some of Silifke's most eminent sights. One visit to the hilltop town can (quite literally) take you to the pits of hell and back. The **Hell Chasm** is Corycian cave formed by a stream-eroded ceiling collapse. According to mythology, Zeus defeated the monstrous, fire-breathing Typhon and hurled him into this pit before imprisoning him in Mt. Etna for all eternity. Today, a little platform juts out over the frightening 128m precipice. The similarly formed **Chasm of Heaven,** the largest of the Corycian caves, is more hellish than its infernal neighbor. A footpath of 452 excruciating stairs descends to Typhon's Cave entrance, marked by a small chapel built in honor of St. Mary in the 5th or 6th century AD *(Chasms open 8am-7pm. $2.40, students $1.60.)*

At the bustling chasm-side restaurant, a small corridor marks the entrance to the awesomely beautiful **Asthma Cave.** With an entrance of 80 winding stairs, this 200m long cave is still dark and slick, so be sure to wear sturdy shoes. *(Open 10am-*

5pm. $.35.) Across the street, the **Temple of Zeus** commemorates the god's victory over Typhon. The original HelleDoric order temple was converted into a Christian basilica in the 5th century. *(Hop the Mersin bus in Silifke (every 15 min.), and make it clear that you wish to get off at the Narlıkuyu junction. From here, the hike uphill is about 2.5km. While Let's Go does not recommend hitchhiking, somebody will probably offer you a ride up. On the way back, cross the main highway at the base of the hill and head downhill to the bus stand, where the Mersin-Silifke bus swings by once every 30min. ($.60).)*

The ancient city of Olba (now **Uzuncaburç**) is 30km north of Silifke, without public transport. For history buffs, a trip provides rewarding ruins that have outlived Hellenistic, Roman, and Byzantine times. Remains include a temple to Zeus, tombs, a theater, city gate, and 22m-high tower, after which the city is named.

KIZKALESİ

☎324

Legend holds that once upon a time, a king built a castle on the island off the coast to protect his daughter from the untimely death prophesied for her. She lived in splendid near-isolation until a snake, unintentionally hidden in a fruit basket sent by the king's adviser, fulfilled the prediction with a poisonous nibble. A lovely story, but the Maiden's Castle (Kızkalesi), and its counterpart on the shore, were actually built to protect the Armenian city of Corycus from foreign invaders. Today, these "obstacles" provide the *raison d'être* for the town's tourist industry.

The majority of visitors to this small resort town are Turks on a short holiday from nearby cities. German tourists and a smattering of Americans stationed at İncirlik base make up much of the rest. Despite the unchecked hotel construction brought on by the recent tourist boom, Kızkalesi still remains fairly small, and it offers hedonistic beaches and a vibrant nightlife. The nearby sites of Kanlıdivane and Adam Kayalar also make fine daytrips, allowing the dilettante archaeologist to leave Kızkalesi with something more than memories of sun, sand, and beer.

▐▜ TRANSPORTATION AND PRACTICAL INFORMATION. Nearly all of Kızkalesi's sleeping, eating, and nightlife establishments line the 1km strip of waterfront. **Buses** run through Kızkalesi en route to **Mersin** or **Silifke** (supposedly every 15min., $.80). While there's no official tourist office, the **New Göreme Travel Agency,** Mavi Deniz Cad., 4 Belediye Sok. (☎523 22 21), on the highway, provides free info and maps, while putting in a good word for their own tours. There are **no banks** in Kızkalesı; the nearest ones are 25km away in either Erdemli or Mersin. Other services include: the **police** (☎523 22 21); **Kızkalesi Eczane** (☎523 2850); a medical clinic, **Sağlık Ocağı** (☎523 21 39); and the **PTT,** located behind the Belediye building, with a string of public phones outside (open M-F 8:30am-12:30pm, 1:30-5:30pm; Sa 8:30am-1pm). **Postal code:** 33790.

▌ ACCOMMODATIONS. Kızkalesi has an astounding number of hotels and pensions, and it is impossible to walk the streets without being hounded by eager cries of "yes, please!" and *"pansiyon?"* Though rooms generally cost $14 ($18 with A/C), the best value can be found on the main street running from the beach to the highway. The **Best Motel,** 2 Plaj Yolu No. 6, has 12 large but simple rooms cooled by ceiling fans. (☎523 20 74 or 523 25 23. Breakfast $1.60. $11.30 per room.) **Ro.e Hotel,** 2 Plaj Yolu, offers 18 spacious rooms, six of which have A/C. (☎788 55 92. Breakfast included. $16, with A/C $24.) For sheer comfort worth far more than its asking price, try the **Yaka Hotel.** Its 16 well-furnished rooms boast telephone, A/C, minibar, and even coffee/tea machines. The owner, Yakup Kahveci, is also a head-honcho of regional tourism and a geyser of information. (☎523 24 44. Breakfast included. Singles $20; doubles $30.) Further from the beach, **Sahil Motel,** Mavi Deniz Mah., 2 Plaj Yoluhirişi, is an excellent value. The 21 no-frills rooms are "cooled" with electric fans. (☎523 20 59. Breakfast $2. Singles, doubles, and triples $12, with A/C $17; quads with A/C $19.20.) Next door to Yaka, the quiet, homey **Hotel Rain** offers 19 rooms with A/C and a killer open buffet breakfast. (☎523 27 82. Breakfast included. Singles $16; doubles $29.) For 15 nicer, mid-range rooms, try the **Inka Hotel.** All rooms are clean, and have Mediterranean balcony views. (☎523 21 82; fax 523 26 73. Singles $18, with A/C $24; doubles with A/C $29.)

MEDITERRANEAN COAST

▓▆ FOOD AND ENTERTAINMENT. Almost all the hotels and pensions have full-fledged restaurants that bring in live singers and lively, table-dancing crowds. Price and quality are consistent with those of their rooms. Other options include **Cafe Rain,** on the beach, which serves snacks and full meals, from spaghetti to schnitzel to 12 kinds of pizza. (☎523 2234. Excellent vegetarian *tava* $2.65; cocktails $2.50.) The camouflage netting and Confederate flag hint at the presence of American servicemen. Afterwards, hit the adjacent **Oxyd Disco,** where a cavernous interior pulsates with eclectic music, from Turko-pop to techno. (☎533 260 88 97. Cocktails $3-5. Open 10pm-3:30am.) Try the **Honey Restaurant and Bar** (☎523 24 38), whose owner, Erdoğan, claims credit for introducing *tartuni* (minced meat adorned in a wrap; $1) to Kızkalesi. The mixed Turkish-German menu of this tastefully and unassertively hip restaurant features a "$3 Ottoman pan" with beef, onions, garlic, and tomatoes. Cheap *lokanta* are on the other side of the highway.

▓ SIGHTS. The **sea castle,** about 150m from the shore, is Kızkalesi's main attraction. Non-swimmers can catch frequent boats to and from the castle ($3.20). Alternatively, large paddle boats ($4) and smaller "sea bicycles" ($1.60) are rented out on the beach. The walls of the castle reflect the influence of many civilizations, from the Armenians to the Crusaders. Inside, there are ramparts and chambers worth exploring, but its novelty as an island castle is its real attraction. The **land castle,** made partially of pieces salvaged from the ancient city of Corycus, is surrounded by an empty moat. Breaches in the walls afford beautiful views of the water. *(Open daily 8am-7pm. $2.40, students $1.60.)*

In the rugged "Devil's Glen" valley, 7km north of town, hikers can find the eerily majestic **Adam Kayalar,** a set of 13 Roman reliefs of humans from the 1st and 2nd centuries carved into the face of the valley. The descent is a bit steep, so wear sneakers or boots. The most interesting place near Kızkalesi is the ancient city of **Kanlıdivane** ("Bloody Crazy"), named for its rust-colored soil and rocks. The chasm in the center, over 90m wide and 60m deep, is believed to be the final resting place of criminals and outcasts who were hurled to the bottom. The red-rock and shattered buildings give the feeling of walking amidst a lost Martian civilization, rendering Kanlıdivane as spooky as it is fascinating. *(Open daily 8am-7pm. $1.60.)*

Getting to either Adam Kayalar or Kanlıdivane can be difficult; public transportation doesn't service either site. A bus from Kızkalesi can drop you 3km from Kanlıdivane ($.60). The walk is mostly uphill and unpleasant on hot days. While *Let's Go* does not recommend hitchhiking, someone will probably offer you a lift as you trudge up the hill. Hiring a taxi to Kanlıdivane costs $24, to Adam Kayalar $29. With enough tourists, one of the local travel agencies will organize expeditions. On an off day, they may provide a ride that will cost less than a taxi. **Öztop's Rain Travel Agency** (☎532 27 84; email oztoprain@superonline.com), owners of the eponymous cafe and hotel, will also organize a 60km tour of local sights (Heaven and Hell Chasms, Adam Kayalar, Kanlıdivane, Uzuncaburç) for $12 per person.

MERSİN ☎324

A small fishing village 150 years ago, Mersin has blossomed into a mid-sized cosmopolitan city in response to Adana's need for a Mediterranean port. With almost as many construction projects as department stores, Mersin's sound and fury epitomizes Turkey's explosive, Western-modeled urbanization. Mersin is not much of a tourist town, and its brief history has left it no monuments more impressive than the towering Merit Hotel. Travelers will mostly find the city useful as a dock from which to catch a ferry to Northern Cyprus.

▐ TRANSPORTATION

Flights: The **Turkish Airlines (THY)** office (☎233 02 74) and countless travel agencies with THY banners can book flights from the nearby Adana airport.

Buses: The busy otogar is located 1½km from the city center. To: **Adana** (1hr., express, very frequent, $1.60); **Ankara** (7hr.; daily midnight, F-Sa 2:30pm; $15); **Antalya** (6hr.;

11pm, midnight; $10); **İstanbul** (13hr., 6pm, $25); **İzmir** (13hr.; 7am, 6, 7pm; $17); **Konya** (5hr., 7am-6pm, $10); **Nevşehir** (5hr.; 9, 10am, 5pm; $8); **Trabzon** (17hr.; 2, 7pm; $18). To reach the waterfront from the otogar, take a left at the exit, turn right at a T-junction, and take another left at the next main street. From there, head west (walk with the water on your left). Alternatively, dolmuş run from outside the otogar ($.80).

Trains: To reach the *gar* (☎231 12 76), walk 1km from the city center along İsmet İnönü Bul., with the water on your right. Then follow the rotary 200m away from the shore. To: **Adana** (1hr., express trains daily every 30min. 6am-10:30pm, $1); **Ankara** (17½hr., 5:45pm, $9); **İstanbul** (19½hr.; Tu, Th, Sa 7:30pm; $9.30); **Kayseri** (16½hr., 4:20pm, $4.80); **Konya** (7hr.; Tu, Th, Sa 7:30pm en route to İstanbul; $3.60). 20% student discount, 40% handicapped discount. Buses are faster and more reliable, though the station hosts a pleasant *çay* garden.

Ferries: Turkish Maritime Lines (☎233 98 58), about 1km, with the water on your right, from the city center along İsmet İnönü Bul. Ferries depart from the harbor building located on a small road that forks off to the right after Atatürk Park. To **Mağusa, Northern Cyprus** (10hr.; M, W, F 10pm; $24, students with ID $21). Tickets must be bought the day of departure.

⚡🛈 ORIENTATION AND PRACTICAL INFORMATION

Mersin's center stretches along the waterfront, which marks the city's south side. It consists of pedestrian-dominated streets between **Cumhuriyet Meydanı,** next to the municipality building, and **Gümrük Meydanı,** where the **Ulu Camii** (Great Mosque) stands as an unpleasant testament to the hideous misuse of concrete. **İsmet İnönü Bul.** is the wide road that runs east-west along the waterfront, while the narrower **Atatürk Cad.** runs parallel to it through the city center.

Tourist Office: (☎238 32 71), near the harbor building, has an English-speaking staff that provides free maps and information. Open daily 8am-noon, 1-5pm.

Consulates: Northern Cyprus (☎237 24 82 or 237 24 83). Walk 800m west of the city center along Atatürk Cad. and follow the road 100m as it curves right. The consulate is at the first intersection. Visas can be obtained on arrival in Mağusa, but the consulate will be happy to field any questions. Open M-F 8am-1pm, 2-4pm.

Hospital: Devlet Hastanesi (☎336 39 50), has plans to revamp, though current hospital facilities are reliable. Anglophone doctors.

Internet Access: World Internet Cafe, off Atatürk Cad. Head west towards the Northern Cyprus consulate and take a left just before the lights. $2.50 per hr. Otherwise, try the **Internet Cafe** at the entrance to Atatürk Park, which has similar prices.

PTT: on İsmet İnönü Bul., right next to the "4-star" Mersin Oteli (uncomfortable, expensive rooms with tacky furniture) on the eastern end of Gümrük Meydanı. Open daily 8am-7pm. If APS (express mail) just isn't fast enough, try **UPS** or **DHL;** both have offices further down İsmet İnönü Bul., towards the tourist office. **Postal code:** 33100.

🏠🍴 ACCOMMODATIONS AND FOOD

Mercifully, air-conditioning is a standard feature of Mersin's hotels, which are mostly clustered together on Soğuksu Cad. The best deal is **Hotel Savran,** 46 Soğuksu Cad., whose clean rooms have TV, phone, bath (and tub!), A/C, and a celestial blue touch. (☎232 44 73. Breakfast included. Singles $13; doubles $23.) Right next door, **Hotel Hitit** offers similar lodgings with less impressive baths and no breakfast for the morning grumbles. (☎231 64 31. Singles $11; doubles $16; triples $24.) **Gökhan Hotel,** 20 Soğuksu Cad., is the classiest two-star hotel you'll ever see. With a jazzy bar, open buffet breakfast, and sophisticated lounge, Gökhan's rooms are worth far more than their asking price. (☎231 62 56. Fridge in room. Singles $20; doubles $35; triples $45.) For the committed budget traveler, the **Ak Hotel,** 90 Kuvayi Cad., just across from the Merit Hotel, provides worn rooms, some with balcony and/or private shower. (☎336 21 70. $5 per person.)

There are a variety of good, cheap eateries in the town center. Wash down the local specialty *tantuni* (minced meat, onions, lettuce, tomatoes wrapped up like a tortilla) with *şalgam*, a carrot-juice drink similar to *ayran* (can be made sweet or salty). At **Yaprak Tantuni**, on Atatürk Cad., the tasty wraps ($2) make up for what the shabby sitting space lacks. The small, outdoor cafes on Atatürk Cad. serve fresh fish ($2.50). **Kukla Kebap**, on Adnan Menderes Bul., about 4km west of the city center, serves some of the best *İskender kebap* in town ($3.50). For a break from seafood and Turkish cuisine, discover **Bella Roma**, located near the internet cafe about 500m west of the city center on Atatürk Cad. The posters in this Italian restaurant pay homage to Botticelli, Puccini, and Sophia Loren, among others. Choose from a wide variety of pasta dishes ($3-5) or dig into a pizza ($3).

◐ 🎵 SIGHTS AND ENTERTAINMENT

A relatively young city, Mersin doesn't have much history to draw on. The only "sight" is the rather generically-named **Museum,** on Atatürk Cad., just west of Cumhuriyet Meydanı. It displays a pretty standard set of archaeological curios from local excavations. *(Open daily 9am-noon, 1-5pm. $1.25, students $.75.)*

If the Mediterranean climate is too much for you (and you don't have breasts), head to the male-only **5 yol hamam** (Beşyol hamam), about 500m north of the *gar* and 500m east of the Merit Hotel ($2.50; massage and scrub add $3.50). Take a pleasant stroll amidst *çay* gardens and fishing boats in **Atatürk Park,** which lines the waterfront through the center of town. $1 will get you a scoop of sweet-smelling, roasted nuts. Chug around the harbor in a pleasure boats ($2.50).

In the "Nightlife? Who needs a nightlife?" department, Mersin's center shuts down after dinner. The daytime crowds head west a few kilometers to Adnan Menderes Bul., which meanders along the seaside. The area is filled with bars, *çay* gardens, restaurants, and an outdoor movie theater. You can catch the blue Poscu dolmuş in front of the PTT and ask to be let off at the Hilton; a short walk along the water leads to some decent restaurants. Otherwise, a cab ride should cost $3-4.

ADANA   ☎ 322

Turkey's sixth largest city is appropriately named after Adanus, the Greek god of weather. The average June-August temperature is 100°F, with high humidity and a persistent hot wind that seems to issue from a giant invisible hairdryer. If you visit in these months, the weather will probably occupy most of your waking thoughts. Modern Adana is an agricultural town, wealthy because of its pivotal role in the Turkish textile industry. Its famous *Adana kebap* (spicy minced lamb and herbs, flattened into strips and grilled) tantalizes the eager tastebuds of locals and tourists alike. The nearby US military base at İncirlik does its part for the local economy; Adana has a large otogar and many hotels, and its airport is a stopping point between Northern Cyprus, Antalya, and the Middle East. The city is home to several interesting historical sights and some modern attractions as well. The new Sabancı Merkez Camii, the second largest mosque in Turkey and in the greater Middle East, dominates Adana's skyline, looming proudly behind the glittering Roman bridge. In July 2000, Adana's proximity to an earthquake zone narrowly saved it from being chosen as the site of a nuclear power reactor.

▣ TRANSPORTATION

Flights: The airport is 4km west of the city center on highway E-5. Frequent buses and dolmuş run to the airport from the stop on Ziya Paşa Cad., across from Hotel Kaza ($.80). The **Turkish Airlines,** 1 Stadyum Cad. (☎454 15 45), on a side street off Atatürk Cad., is across from Atatürk Park. Open M-F 8:30am-5:30pm, Sa 8:30am-noon. To: **Ankara** (2 per day; $50, students $45); **Antalya** (2 per day; $82, students $55); and **İstanbul** (3 per day; $140, students $59). **Cyprus Turkish Airlines** (☎363 15 41 or 363 13 75; fax 363 13 75; www.kthy.net), on Çakmak Cad. across from İnönü Park. Flights to **Ercan** (M-F 5:30pm, Sa 6:50am; $65, students a whopping $2 less).

Buses: The larger companies usually offer free *servis* shuttles between their central offices on highway E-5 (near Akbank) and the otogar (45min.-1hr. before departure),

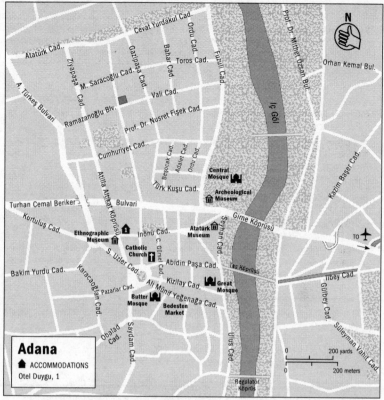

Adana

▲ ACCOMMODATIONS
Otel Duygu, 1

where the godawful squeaking puppets of roaming vendors will decidedly drive you insane. To: **Ankara** (6hr., 4 per day 8am-1pm, $12); **Antakya** (3½hr., 9 per day 8:30am-7pm, $5); **Antalya** (9½hr., every hr. 9am-10pm, $15); **İstanbul** (12½hr., every hr. 9am-11pm, $20); **İzmir** (14hr.; 10:30am, 5pm, midnight; $17); **Kayseri** (6½hr.; 12:30, 4pm, midnight; $7); **Konya** (6½hr., 7 per day 8:30am-midnight, $11); **Mersin** (1½hr., every 30min., $2.50) via **Tarsus** (45min., $1.25). A small dolmuş station on the E-5, by the river and in front of the Sabancı Merkez Cami, services local towns.

Trains: The handsome, old-fashioned *gar* is located on İstasyon Cad.; head down Atatürk Cad. past Atatürk Park, and make a left. To: **Ankara** (7½hr., 1:15pm, $7); **Diyarbakir** (11hr., 4:20pm, $20); **Elazığ** (10hr., 8:40am, $20); **Gaziantep** (6hr., 4:50am, $3.50); **Mersin** (2hr., 29 per day 4:45am-11pm, $1).

◾ ORIENTATION

Adana has few street signs. The **E-5 highway** runs from the center of town past the oto-gar, located 5km away, and continues along the Mediterranean coast. In town, the landmarks on the E-5 are the big Akbank building, the overpass, and the minarets of the new Sabancı Merkez Camii beside the river. **Atatürk Cad.**, which changes its name to **Saydam Cad.** after passing **İnönü Cad.**, houses the tourist office, several hotels, a large Atatürk statue, the main PTT, and Atatürk Park. To get to the center of town from the **Merkez Otogar** (bus station), take an E-5 dolmuş from across the road (every 5min., $.40). Be sure to cross the road, because destination plates are the same in both directions. The dolmuş exits the E-5 about 1km before the Akbank, one block short of the overpass. Disembark here and head for **Kurtuluş Meydanı** (Liberation Square), across from **İnönü Cad.** If you take a taxi, make sure the meter is on ($6-8).

⚡ PRACTICAL INFORMATION

Tourist office: (☎363 14 48 or 363 12 87). On Atatürk Cad., this is the garish peach building next to Akbank. English-speaking staff offers those gigantic "yes-I'm-a-tourist-and-can't-fold-a-map" type maps. Open M-F 8am-6pm.

Consulates: US (☎453 91 06), on Atatürk Cad., at the corner of Atatürk Park.

Banks: The landmark **Akbank** on the corner of T. Cemal Beriker Bul. and Atatürk Cad. Great currency exchange rates. Like most banks in Adana, has V/MC/Cirrus/Plus **ATM.**

Currency Exchange: *Döviz* bureaus cluster around Saydam Cad., to the right as you exit the tourist office; try **Yüksek Dövis** (☎563 02 66; fax 563 19 36).

English-Language Bookstore: Yolgeçen Kitabevi, on Atatürk Bul. near the *gar*, sells day-old copies of *USA Today* and the *International Herald Tribune.*

Pharmacies: These pepper the town; try **Ünlü Eczanesi** (☎363 37 75), across the street from the Ethnographic Museum.

Internet Access: Duck into Çakmak Plaza (on Çakmak Cad.), your regular shopping mall, for a taste of home and some hard-core A/C. On the top floor, the **Electrocom** and **Online Internet Cafes** are scrunched between Pizza Hut and Pizza Han. $1 per hr.

PTT: The main PTT is past the Atatürk statue on Atatürk Cad. Open 24hr., with standard stamp, fax, and telegraph services. There's a smaller 24hr. PTT opposite the *gar* on İsta-syon Cad. **Currency exchange** 8am-5pm. Another small PTT is on İnönü Cad. Open daily 8am-5pm. **Postal code:** 01122.

🏠 ACCOMMODATIONS

If you're looking for cleanliness and comfort at a low price, Adana is not the place for you. Apart from the several 5-star hotels ($65-100), most of Adana's two-star facilities cater to businessmen or other non-tourists. If sticky nights and the lullaby of a ceiling fan sound unappealing, then you're better off forking over some extra cash or staying elsewhere.

Otel Mercan, 5 Ocak Meydanı, Melekgirmez Çarşısı (☎351 26 03). Clean and plush for its class. All rooms have showers and A/C. Singles $12; doubles $18; triples $25.

İpek Palas, İnönü Cad. No. 89 (☎363 35 12; fax 363 35 16), A bit fancier with private showers, telephones, ceiling fans, and TV. Spacious rooms, but ask for the quieter and cooler ones not facing the street. Not cool enough? Try shaving your head at the hotel's barber. Breakfast $1.60. Singles $13; doubles $23; triples $29.

Otel Duygu, 14 İnönü Cad. (☎363 15 10). Refurbished and reaching for its 3rd star, Duygu offers beautiful rooms with A/C, telephone, TV, and sparkling private baths. Gorgeous room decorations fit for a Hollywood set, with billowing curtains. Breakfast included. Singles $20; doubles $32; triples $45.

Hotel Gümüş, İnönü Cad. No. 87. Right next door to İpek Palas. Small yellow rooms without A/C capture Adana's burning spirit. Shared *à la turka* toilets. No breakfast service. Singles $7; doubles $11; triples $16.

🍴 FOOD AND ENTERTAINMENT

⊠ Küçük Ev Restaurant (☎363 56 87). Off Çakmak Cad., next to the massive Yimpaş shopping center. This food is divine! Beyond the wood-paneled entrance to this former mansion, Ümran Kaçmaz and her team of "chefs" prepare an unbelievable array of home-cooked foods. A lunchtime selection of 28 meals and dinner palette of 12 includes *sarma* (stuffed grape leaves), *dolma* (stuffed zucchini), and various eggplant specialties (main courses, $1.50-2.50). Ideal for vegetarians, this "little house" is a delightful break from the region's easy, greasy meat dishes, though those are offered as well. Open M-F 7:30am-8:30pm; open Saturdays in winter.

Yeni Onbaşılar (☎363 20 84). On Atatürk Cad., opposite the tourist office and above the Yaza Merhaba clothing store. The most recommended *kebapci* in town, Yeni serves

Here's your ticket to freedom, baby!

**Wherever you want to go...
priceline.com can get you there for less.**

- Save up to 40% or more off the lowest published airfares every day!

- Major airlines serving virtually every corner of the globe.

- Special fares to Europe!

If you haven't already tried priceline.com, you're missing out on the best way to save. **Visit us online today at www.priceline.com.**

up Adana's spicy specialty ($2), along with a popular şiş piliç (chicken şiş; $2.80). Open daily 11am-10:30pm.

Capino Cafe, 158 Çakmak Cad. (☎363 00 46). Adana's answer to McDonald's, serving up *Adana kebap,* pizza, burgers, and *çöp şiş,* all for under $2.

Bizarre Cafe (☎359 20 67). On the edge of Ocak Meydanı. Far from a misguided claim, the name is quite apt. Pass a mural of muscle-bound waitresses to admire the central fish tank. Burger and fries $2.

Ecem Chicken, 38/B Abidinpaşa Cad. (☎351 12 01), stands by its specialty. Try the chicken breast ($1.80) or the *kaşarlı* (a chicken and cheese dish; $1.60).

■ SIGHTS

Walking east along the E-5 toward the river, you will pass the huge **Sabancı Merkez Camii** (Central Mosque), the second largest mosque in both Turkey and the Middle East (Ankara houses its superior). Financed by the famous Turkish multi-millionaire and businessman Sakıp Sabancı, the mosque is one of many local projects under the Sabanci hand (check out the Hilton being built nearby). Though the mosque lacks historical importance, its sheer beauty merits visitors, particularly under the nightly glow of spotlights.

Just before the mosque is Adana's **Archaeological Museum,** one of the few of its kind in this region that's worth any attention. On display are Hittite sculptures, Roman jewelry, Bronze Age pottery, and coins from various eras. Particularly fascinating are works from the nearby Çukurova excavation, and a sunny courtyard of old sarcophagi. (☎454 38 55. *Open Tu-Su 8:30am-noon, 1:30-5pm; $1.60.*) Leave the museum, turn right, and follow the river to the small **Atatürk Museum,** located in an old mansion commemorating a March 15, 1923 visit. The museum features an eerie life-sized waxwork of the Turkish statesman. (*Open Tu-Su 8am-noon, 1-5pm. $1.60, students $.80.*) A 5-minute walk past the museum lies the famous **Roman bridge,** built by the Roman architect Auxentus in the 4th century. Continue past it for 5 minutes and turn right at the government building to reach the 19th-century **clock tower.** On the right before the clock tower is a park, and just beyond it, the **Ulu Camii** (Great Mosque), built by Halil Bey in 1507 and enlarged in 1541. Halil is buried inside, though current restoration prevents visitors from entering.

Continuing on toward Saydam Cad. leads to **Yağ Camii** (Butter Mosque), an unusual structure that was converted from a church in 1501. Note the roof tiles, more common on Greek mansions than on mosques. The **Catholic church,** home to the city's small Christian community, is down the road to the right, 50m past the Atatürk statue and then down some narrow streets. Press the buzzer for entrance into this charming building. The paintings lining the hall depict St. Paul's (Saul's) vision on the road to Damascus and important events in the life of Christ. Just off İnönü Cad. (follow the sign) is a small **Ethnographic Museum** displaying pistols, coins, and old handmade *kilims.* (*Open Tu-Su 8am-noon, 1:30-5pm. $2.*)

On the outskirts of old Adana (toward the residential areas) lies an enormous, man-made **lake** and nearby dam. By day, sun-drenched beaches and tea gardens draw carloads of picnickers. Nightfall brings some of Adana's only worthwhile entertainment, as flashy **amusement parks** line the road to innumerable lakeside restaurants and bars. Many of the eateries offer boat-top dining; for about $12 per person, small boats will ship patrons out to a tiny lake island and back.

From opposite the tourist office, a white dolmuş marked "Cemal Paşa" on top and "Göl" on the destination board will take you all over Adana before stopping at the lake (every 10min., $.50.)

▶ DAYTRIP FROM ADANA: TARSUS

Buses and dolmuş frequently run the Adana-Mersin route, and all stop in Tarsus (45min., every 30min., $1.85). Catch a dolmuş in Adana by the Merkez Camii or a bus at the otogar.

With over 100,000 inhabitants, Tarsus is not much of a break from the noise and filth of Adana or Mersin. Yet for many, the city's history makes it a must-see. Located about 30 minutes west of Adana, the city was both the **birthplace of St. Paul** and the ancient capital of Roman Cilicia in about 63 BC. **Antony and Cleopatra** groupies who have been retracing the couple's rendezvous points along the eastern Mediterranean will also be interested to learn that the couple reportedly "met" here in 41 BC. Across from the massive Atatürk statue in the center of town is **Cleopatra's Gate**, a beautiful arch that once marked the ancient city's entrance. Today, the arch is trapped in a traffic circle, but a vibrant imagination can fill in the gold and cavalcade that once greeted Cleopatra's arrival. Her departure made up in gossip what it must have lacked in glory; the ancient town's exit is marked by a less impressive arch near the Eski Cami, called **Kancık Kapısı** ("Bitch Gate"). A few blocks from the major thoroughfare in town is a small courtyard where **St. Paul's Well** is located. Of the now-adorned well, only the round stone slab remains from about 20 AD, when the epistler supposedly struck the watering hole. *(Courtyard open 8am-5pm, $1).* Following Atatürk Cad. toward the waterfalls, you'll find on your right the **Roman Road Excavations.** You too can play archeologist and explore the emerging artifacts and fascinating ruins (but watch out for unmarked ditches!). The **archeological museum,** housed in an old *medrese* near the center of town, seems to have had all its artifacts removed to another museum, except for some fragmentary sarcophagi in the small courtyard. However, the guard will still try to extract the admission fee. *(Open Tu-Su 8am-noon, 1-5pm. $1.25, students $.75.)*

Overnight options in Tarsus are limited to the four-star hotel by the waterfall ($80) or two in-town options. At **Hotel Zorbaz,** the conspicuous pink building in the center of town, gaudy purple doors mark reasonably clean and spacious rooms with *à la turka* toilets. (☎622 21 66. Singles $7.30; doubles $11.30; triples $16.) The nearby **Cihan Palas Otel** has sunny bedspreads in more sterile rooms with phone, TV, and tiled baths. (☎624 16 23. Singles $12; doubles $22.70.)

Tarsus' pleasant but unimpressive **Şelale** (waterfall) lies on the edge of town. Tea gardens and restaurants make it a good lunch stop, particularly to try Tarsus' special "cup holder" *lahmacun*, which are shrunken versions of the original. The **Şelale Hasbahçe Restaurant** (☎622 49 23) serves *ızgara* (grilled meats; $3) and a local coffee specialty called *Tarsusi.*

ANTAKYA (HATAY) ☎326

In Antakya, site of the ancient city of **Antioch,** the throngs of tourists diminish, as does the Mediterranean resort atmosphere. Antakya offers sprawling markets in the old sections of town, manicured tea gardens, and the world famous Hatay Museum. It was in Antioch that Christianity received its name; St. Peter's Grotto is half-hidden in a cave on the south side of Mt. Stauros, 2km from town.

Seleucus I Nicator, one of Alexander the Great's chief generals, founded Antioch in 300 BC and domineered Asia from here. The population swelled to 500,000, but growth was tumultuous. Internal strife, the neighboring Persian and Roman Empires, and a catastrophic earthquake in 148 BC all threatened the city.

Even before Antioch fell to the Romans in 64 BC, this prominent Silk Road stop acquired a reputation for vice and decadence. By 42 BC, equipped with brandnew city walls, an acropolis, amphitheater, courthouse, baths, and aqueducts, Antioch was the third-largest city in the Roman Empire and a center of science and commerce. As Christianity grew, so did religious philosophy. Around 40 AD, the Apostle Peter gathered the first Christian congregation here, converting Antioch and renaming it Theopolis (City of God). Only after losing 200,000 lives in a devastating 6th-century earthquake did the city enter a hopeless decline. Although Justinian rebuilt the city, later marauders trashed his good work, and Antioch's splendor was reduced to ruins. The crumbling walls along the surrounding mountain ridge give a nod to the city's former glory. At the end of WWI, Hatay province became a part of France's Syrian protectorate, and it was only reattached to Turkey in 1939.

▌▘ TRANSPORTATION

Buses: To: **Ankara** (10hr., 6 per day 10am-10pm, $13.50); **Antalya** (14hr., 10 per day 9am-6:15pm, $13.50); **İstanbul** (16hr., 8 per day 2:30-6pm, $19); **İzmir** (16hr., 4 per

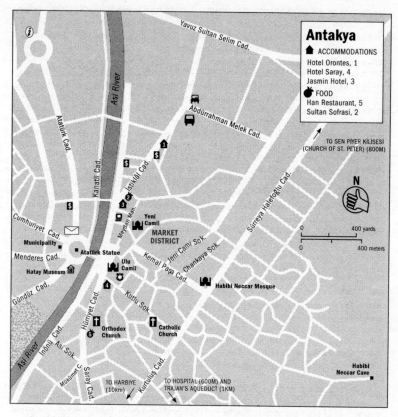

Antakya

♠ ACCOMMODATIONS
Hotel Orontes, 1
Hotel Saray, 4
Jasmin Hotel, 3
♠ FOOD
Han Restaurant, 5
Sultan Sofrasi, 2

day 12:30-7pm, $19); **Kars** (23hr., 3pm, $21); **Kayseri** (8hr.; 9am, 8:30pm; $10); **Mersin** (6hr., 10 per day 9am-8pm, $5); **Trabzon** (20hr., 3:30pm, $18). **International buses: Aleppo** (3-4hr., 4 per day 9am-6pm, $8) and **Damascus** (9hr.; 9:30am, noon; $15). See **Border Crossing: Syria**, p. 309.

Dolmuş: To **Gaziantep** (3hr., every ½hr., $4). Across from the otogar, regional and local dolmuş leave for **Harbiye** (20min., every 10min., $.50) and **İskenderun** (30min., every 15min., $1.25).

⬛🛈 ORIENTATION AND PRACTICAL INFORMATION

The **Asi River** divides Antakya, with the otogar, commercial center and hotels on the eastern side. Across the river is the Atatürk statue rotunda, with the PTT, the museum, and tourist information nearby. From the otogar, the center of town is 700m along **İstiklâl Cad.** The museum is visible from here, straight across the river.

Tourist Office: 47 Atatürk Cad. (☎216 06 10). Vaglige Beginde. Inconveniently located at the far northwest side of town. From the PTT walk 15min. down Atatürk Cad. to the west corner of the park. Open M-F 8am-noon, 1:30-5:30pm.

Banks: Türkiye İş Bankası, one of the many banks in town, has a branch on İstiklâl Cad., halfway between the center of town and the otogar. Another is just down Hürriyet Cad. from the Saray Hotel. Both offer **currency exchange** and 24hr. V/MC/Cirrus/Plus **ATMs.** The otogar and the exchange office on İstiklâl Cad., across from Vakıf Bank, provide Syrian pounds at more favorable rates (see **Border Crossing: Syria**, p. 309).

English-Language Bookstore: Ferah Koll. Şti., past Nuri Restaurant. Open 7am-9pm.

Pharmacy: Among the many pharmacies is **Gazipaşa Eczanesi** (☎214 97 04), just down Hürriyet Cad. from the Saray Hotel. Open M-Sa 8:30am-7:30pm.

Hospital: Devlet Hastanesi (☎214 54 30), at Bagri Yanikda, 4km from town. Dolmuş run from town center ($.30). Taxi $4.

Internet Access: Over 40 outlets, all around $1.25 per hr. Some close at 10pm if quiet. **Superonline Internet Cafe** (☎214 51 08), **Ay-Isigi House** (☎216 35 08) and **Can Bilgisayar** (☎216 45 20) are all on the museum side of the river, toward the tourist office. On the hotel side of the river, **Mavera** (☎213 56 26) is in the arcade where Kemal Paşa Cad intersects with İnönü Cad. **Data-Net** (☎215 12 15), on Huriyet Cad. 15, is close to Hotel Saray.

PTT: In the center of town. Mail service daily 8:30am-6pm. 24hr. phone service. **Postal code:** 31000.

▌ ACCOMMODATIONS

Most accommodations are mid-range or above in Antakya.

▨ **Jasmine Hotel,** 14 İstiklâl Cad. (☎212 71 71). Shared bathrooms, rooftop patio, and lawn furniture. Rooms open into a central atrium. Singles $5; doubles $8; triples $10.

▨ **Hotel Saray,** 3 Hürriyet Cad. (☎/fax 214 90 01), the best of the middle range choices, offers a pleasant breakfast salon and new rooms with bath. Breakfast included. Singles $14; doubles $17; triples $25. Add $5 per room for A/C.

Hotel Orontes, 58 İstiklâl Cad. (☎214 59 31; fax 214 59 33). Spotless yet nondescript. Rooms have A/C and TV. Breakfast included. Singles $31; doubles $44; triples $55.

◖▌ FOOD AND ENTERTAINMENT

Among the specialties of the region are hummus and *içli köfte*, often known as *oruk*, a spicy bulgur wheat and red pepper stuffed with seasoned lamb and pine nuts. *Ekşi aşı*, a variation on *oruk*, is covered in tomato sauce. For dessert, *künefe* (or *peynirli kadayıf*) is a baklava-style pastry stuffed with white cheese. Much of this Syrian-influenced Turkish cuisine is unavailable in the rest of Turkey.

In the third week of July, Antakya hosts a four-day **music festival,** during which marching bands, DJ carts, and traditional singers fill the streets with howling crowds well past midnight. The beautifully restored **Antik Beyazıt Hotel,** Hukumet Cad. 4, is a must-see. Across İstiklâl Cad. from Hotel Divan is Antakya's red-light district; avoid flashing neon lights and anything labeled 'gazino.'

▨ **Sultan Sofrasi,** 18 İstiklâl Cad. (☎213 87 59), has no peer in town. Sample *mumbar*, *aşur* and *sultan sarma* in air-conditioned comfort. Open 7am-10pm.

▨ **Anadolu Restaurant,** 50/C Hürriyet Cad. (☎215 15 41). 10min. down the street from the Saray Hotel. Popular among locals, Anadolu serves vegetarian *meze* and excellent hummus. Outdoor seating. Cheaper than Sultan. Full meal $5-6. Open 10am-midnight.

Han Restaurant (☎214 17 16). On Hürriyet Cad. Despite the external appearance, Han has a smashing upper level with a grove of fruit trees. A great place to spend the day ordering drinks and reading. Try *cacık* (garlic yogurt with cucumbers). Full meal $5-6. Open 10am-midnight.

'46 Edem Dondurma (☎214 53 36). On Atatürk Cad., 100m from the center of town. Serves your favorite fruit flavors as well as 3 varieties of *dövme* ice cream: plain *(sade)*, chocolate *(çikolata)*, and the heavenly pistachio *(fıstık)*. Dövme ("beaten") is pounded, kneaded, and stretched to a thick, gooey consistency.

▨ SIGHTS

HATAY MUSEUM. Except for the ruins of the ancient walls, earthquakes and marauders have destroyed much of Antioch's ancient splendor. Only the breathtaking and world-renowned Hatay Museum hints at the magnificence of the ancient city. The museum houses one of the world's best collections of **Roman mosaics,** assembled by an archaeological team from Princeton University, the British Museum, and the Chicago Oriental Institute. Painstakingly pieced together from thousands of tiny tiles, these huge mosaics depict images with near-photographic precision. Highlights are a 2nd-century wild boar hunt ('A Pig Hunt in Calydonia'), the striking 'Personification of Soteria,' the small, priapic hunchback mosaic ('The Happy Hunchback'), and a scantily clad man running in horror from an enormous levitating eye radiating farm implements ('Evil Eye'). The most imposing mosaic is the giant 5th-century hunting scene on the floor; climb the spiral staircase for a complete view. An air-conditioned salon houses coins, jewelry and mounted heads. Sarcophagi fill the garden outside. *(Open Tu-Su 8:30am-noon, 1:30-5pm. $3.50, students $2.)*

ST. PETER'S CHURCH (SEN PİYER KİLİSESİ). Founded by the Apostle Peter, who preached here with Paul and Barnabas, this church (a.k.a. St. Peter's Grotto) was built into a cave so that services could be conducted in secret. The original congregation here coined the term "Christianity" to describe their new religion.

The hillside above the church, riddled with the remains of tunnels, natural caves, and bits of Antioch's city walls, has been a holy place since pagan times. A path zigzags 200m to a high relief of a veiled figure, alternately described as a windblown Mary or as the Syrian goddess of Hierapolis flanked by Charon, boatman of Hades. *(To reach the church walk 20min., take the erratic city bus #6, or take a taxi ($2.20). Open Tu-Su 8am-noon, 1:30-4:30pm. $1.25. There is no regular mass here; check with the Antakya Catholic Church (☎ 215 67 03). Relief open Tu-Su 8am-noon, 1:30-5:30pm. Free.)*

DAYTRIP FROM ANTAKYA: MONASTERY OF ST. SIMEON

To reach the site, follow the sign south off the Antakya-Samandağ road just past Karaçay. The road heads uphill 4km before forking right at a white shrine. A track leads a few kilometers farther to the monastery. The Antakya-Samandağ dolmuş (1hr., every 15min., $2) will drop you at the turn-off, if you ask, or at Karaçay, where you can hire a taxi (round-trip $10).

Samandağ, about 30km southwest of Antakya, is a Mediterranean resort popular with Turkish and Syrian tourists. The seaside area, though more appealing than the dreary town, is heavily polluted. Between Samandağ and Antakya lies the **Monastery of St. Simeon Stylites** (the Younger), where Simeon sat on a pillar for 25 years. Driven by the ascetic impulse that characterized Syrian Christianity in the 4th century, Simeon imitated the better-known Simeon the Elder, whose ruined basilica and eroded column are across the border in Syria. He retreated to a deserted mountaintop and chained himself atop a 13m pillar to live the rest of his life in penitent solitude. This isolation did not last long, as he soon attracted crowds of pilgrims, to whom he delivered sermons against the rampant vice of Antioch. A monastery, whose foundations are still intact, was built around the remains of his pillar.

BORDER CROSSING: SYRIA

The overland crossing at Bab al-Hawa on the Aleppo-Antakya road takes less than 30min. each way. Obtain your Syrian visa in advance from your home country or at the Syrian embassy in Ankara (see p. 357). In theory, only travelers from countries without Syrian embassies can purchase border visas; otherwise they can cost up to $100 at the border. Three-month double-entry visas cost $61. Any passport with evidence of a trip to Israel will be refused a visa or entry.

Several Antakya bus companies, including **Has**, offer service to **Aleppo** (3-4 per day, $8). Avoid Öztur, which uses substandard buses without air conditioning. Allow 4-5 hours for the journey and border formalities. The border has two stops on each side. At one stop on the Turkish side, you will have to leave the bus and go through passport control. Passport control and luggage searches are slower on the Syrian side, sometimes as long as 1½ hours. Remember to bring a pen to fill out the Syrian immigration card. The bus ride to Aleppo deposits you in a slightly different world; be ready for erratic transportation and dingier budget accommodations.

The Syrian currency is the Syrian pound (S₤). Because the official exchange rate (at the time of publication, US$1=S₤64.9) is somewhat less than the black market rate, change money in Antakya, where it's legal to exchange at the better rate.

CENTRAL ANATOLIA

Central Anatolia fosters the traditional spirit of Turkish culture. While the Aegean and Mediterranean Coasts (a.k.a. the "Turkish Riviera") have evolved into a crescent of tourist sites and Eurobeaches, and the Black Sea Coast feels somehow like Eastern Europe, the essence of traditional Turkey is alive and well in the dry, windy mountains of Central Anatolia. The astonishing landscapes and improbable natural formations of Cappadocia are some of the most fascinating in the world, not only for their unearthly aesthetic, but because they represent the tumultuous religious history of the region. The proximity of Cappadocia, an ancient Christian stronghold, to Konya, Turkey's most conservative Islamic city, hints at the area's diversity. Unique for its land and its faiths, Central Anatolia also houses the modern Republic's secular bastion at Ankara and the ruins of a 4000-year-old Hittite capital at Boğazkale. A vibrant culture, welcoming atmosphere, and inspiring landscape characterize these windswept plains of Turkey's heartland.

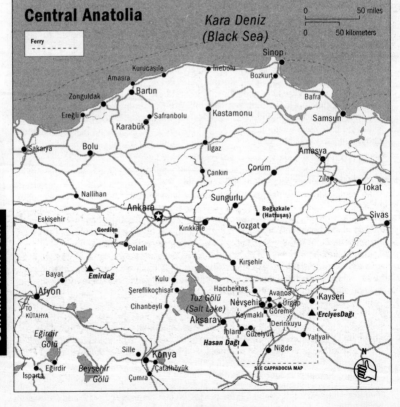

CAPPADOCIA

Cappadocia's enchanting landscape remains unparalleled in history and mystery. Ten million years ago, violent eruptions from the volcanic Mt. Erciyes (3916m) and Mt. Hasan (3268m) covered the underlying plateaus with 100-120m of **tufa,** a soft stone made of lava, ash and mud. Rain, wind, and flooding from the Kızılırmak River shaped the tufa into a striking landscape of cone-shaped monoliths called *peribaca* ("fairy chimneys"), which are grouped in valleys and along gorge ridges. Chunks of hard basalt trapped on the surface of the prehistoric sludge often protected the underlying tufa from wind erosion, thus forming bouldered caps on many of the fairy chimneys.

Cappadocia's unique landscape has long been a hotbed of religious activity. From about 525 BC, the fire-worshipping Zoroastrian Persians revered the region's Erciyes Dağ and Hasan Dağ as holy mountains. Early Christians also found inspiration in Cappadocia; by the 4th century, it was a major center for Christian philosophy and civilization. Hiding from Romans, Iconoclasts, Sassanids, and Turks, these hardy Christians carved beautifully frescoed churches and colossal underground cities into the pliant tufa. Throughout Cappadocia's staggering moonscapes, stairs, windows, and sentry holes have been carved into the rock. Many of these "troglodyte dwellings" are still used as houses, storage rooms, or stables, while others have been converted to hotels and bars.

Visitors today are both captivated by the genius of ancient civilizations and inspired by pristine hikes through Cappadocia's bizarre geology, which is sometimes compared to the Grand Canyon on acid. Most travelers reside in the touristic and convenient towns of Göreme and Ürgüp. For a more authentic touch, villages like Güzelyurt, Üçhisar, Mustafapaşa and Ihlara may tempt you to abandon your life plans and become a local shepherd or hiking guide.

If you can only spare a day or two, it is probably easiest to stay in Göreme, visit the spectacular **open air museum,** and then see the highlights of Cappadocia on one of the local companies' full-day tours.

GETTING AROUND CAPPADOCIA

During high season, a dolmuş follows the Ürgüp-Göreme-Çavuşin-Zelve-Avanos circuit (June-Sept. leaves Ürgüp M-F every other hr. 10am-6pm; returns from Avanos M-F every other hr. 9am-5pm). Dolmuş also run frequently between Ürgüp and Mustafapaşa, and Ürgüp and Ortahisar. In winter, most connections within Cappadocia must be made via Nevşehir, from which buses depart every 30min. for all major Cappadocian towns. Transportation within this region costs between

$.60 and $2.50. Most visits to southern Cappadocia must be made through Aksaray. Buses from Nevşehir to Ankara stop in Aksaray (every hr., $2.50 to Aksaray).

Car rentals start at about $30 per day, though prices skyrocket to about $50 for automatics. **Europcar** (☎341 34 88 or 341 43 15) in Ürgüp rents automatics with A/C for $90 per day. Rental agencies in Göreme and Ürgüp rent **bicycles** ($3 per hr. or $14 per day); **mopeds** ($8 per hr. or $20 per day); and **motorcycles** ($50 per day).

Guided tours of Cappadocia's major sites are run through agencies in Göreme (see **Travel Agencies**, p. 314) and Ürgüp (see **Travel Agencies**, p. 321). These agencies typically provide a day-long tour of the region including bus, lunch, and admission to all the sights ($30). Multiple-day tours are planned for outdoors enthusiasts.

NEVŞEHİR   ☎384

Nevşehir serves as Cappadocia's transportation hub, and even "direct" transport will probably entail a bus switch in Nevşehir. The city is unimpressive to the tourist's eye and a tiresome 2km walk from the otogar. However, Nevşehir's quiet local flavor is visible everywhere: blue-uniformed school children meander the roads as side-street shop owners gossip across clothes racks and backgammon boards.

⌐ TRANSPORTATION. Buses leave the otogar for: **Adana** (4hr.; 9am, 1:30, 4:30pm; $7.50); **Alanya** (12hr.; 11am, 7, 9pm; $17.50); **Ankara** (4hr., 11 per day 9am-8pm, $7.50); **Antalya** (10-11hr.; 11am, 7, 8, 9pm; $15); **Bodrum** (14hr., 8:30pm, $18.75); **Bursa** (9hr., 6:30pm, $13.75); **İstanbul** (10hr., 5 per day 7:30-9pm, $15); **İzmir** (12hr.; 7:30, 9:30pm; $15); **Kayseri** (1½hr., 11 per day 7am-7pm, $2.50); **Konya** (2½hr., 4 per day, $6.25); **Marmaris** (14hr., 8pm); **Mersin** (5hr.; 9am, 1:30, 4:30pm; $7.50). **Dolmuş** leave from the otogar to **Aksaray, Üçhisar, Niğde, Göreme, Ortahisar, Ürgüp, Avanos,** and **Kayseri** (M-Sa every 30min. 7am-7pm, Su every hr. 7am-7pm; off season M-Sa every 30min. 7am-5pm, Su every hr. 7am-5pm; $.75).

■*■*■ **ORIENTATION AND PRACTICAL INFORMATION.** The two main streets in Nevşehir are the east-west Atatürk Ave., and, perpendicular to it, **Lale Cad.** Lale Cad. runs uphill to the right of the otogar before intersecting Atatürk Ave.(called **Yeni Kayseri Cad.** east of the Lale Cad. intersection). The Nevşehir Belediye (municipal) buses from Ürgüp and Göreme stop on Lale Cad. before reaching the otogar. The city's redeeming features are the markets and bazaars off Atatürk Cad. Turn left off any of the side streets and temporarily lose yourself among the locals.

The helpful staff of the **Tourist Office,** 14 Yeni Kayseri Cad. (☎ 213 36 59), one block west of the town's Atatürk statue, offers free maps and brochures, as does **Rock City Travel Agency** (☎ 212 06 03), on the far east of Atatürk Ave., across from the Nevşehir Museum. The organized staff and Anglophone owner handle anything from airplane tickets to $15 guided day tours of Cappadocia. The Nevşehir **hospital** (☎ 213 12 00), next door to the tourist office, is the town's main facility for medical emergencies. Restaurants, pharmacies, shops, a tea garden, several **ATMs,** and a **PTT** (open M-F 8:30am-12:30pm, 1:30-5:30pm) line Atatürk Ave.

■*■*■ **ACCOMMODATIONS, FOOD, AND ENTERTAINMENT.** OtelNisa,35Yeni Kayseri Cad., just off Atatürk Bul., has TVs and private showers in its rooms, some with balcony views. (☎ 213 58 43 or 212 61 68; fax 213 58 43. Breakfast included. Singles $8; doubles $15; triples $18.) Nearby, family-run **Hotel Seven Brothers,** Kayseri Cad., 23 Tusan Sok., has TVs and private baths in each of its 48 rooms. (☎ 213 49 79 or 212 81 78; fax 213 04 54. Breakfast included. Singles $10; doubles $16.) **Şems Otel,** on Atatürk Bul., has well-furnished rooms with private showers. (☎ 213 35 97; fax 213 08 34. Breakfast included. $10 per person.) At the western end of Atatürk Ave. there are scatterings of questionable hotels with dirt-cheap rooms ($2-3).

Turkish "fast food" peppers Nevşehir's streets, where you can grab decent kebap, *döner,* and *lahmacun* for under $3. Fly by local favorite **Şirin Döner** on Atatürk Ave. (☎ 212 44 95) for some tasty to-go. Nightlife in Nevşehir is as non-existent as virgins in a Trabzon "hotel"; spend your time getting massaged, scrubbed, and scraped instead at the **Damat İbrahim Paşa Hamam,** 43 Camikebir Cad. (☎ 213 26 58), where $10 buys a divinely complete hamam experience. The hamam is part of the larger Damat İbrahim Paşa mosque-bath-*medrese* complex, completed in 1727.

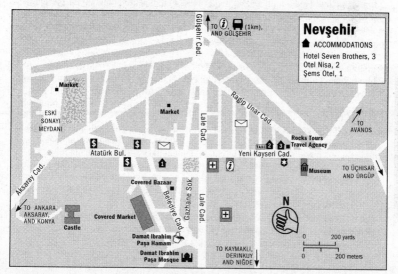

GÖREME   ☎384

The village of Göreme is indisputably the capital of Cappadocia's backpacker scene. Scores of tour groups operate out of Göreme, but the city's industry caters largely to the independent traveler. Surrounded by picturesque fairy chimneys, Göreme offers tourists no fewer than 50 pensions, mostly cave dwellings carved into the soft tufa. Its central location really makes it the best base for exploring Cappadocia, and the glorious Open-Air Museum is only a short walk away. Despite the tourist traffic, Göreme has retained some of its small-town charm; apple *çay* offerings abound and an extended stay will probably earn you local friends. Be forewarned that visitors have been known to stay permanently in the majestic area; "once you've tasted Göreme's water, you're bound to come back," foretells one local adage. The staggering number of foreign brides (locals say around 200) who've settled here suggests a different allure....

⬅ TRANSPORTATION

Buses: Göreme's otogar is in the center of town. Buses travel via **Nevşehir** to: **Alanya** (13hr.; 7:15, 7:30, 8pm; $16); **Ankara** (4hr., 14 per day 7am-8:30pm, $8); **Antalya** (10hr., 5 per day 7:15-9pm, $15); **Bodrum** (14hr.; 7:30, 9, 10pm; $20); **Bursa** (10hr.; 5:30, 7:30pm; $16); **Eğirdir** (8hr., 8:30pm, $13); **Fethiye** (13hr., 6 per day 7:30-9pm, $19.50); **İstanbul** (11hr., 8 per day 6:30-8:30pm, $16); **İzmir** (11hr.; 6:30, 7:30, 8pm; $16); **Kayseri** (1hr., 13 per day 7am-6:30pm, $3); **Konya** (3hr., 8 per day 8am-8:15pm, $7.30); **Marmaris** (14hr., 5 per day 7-8pm, $20); **Mersin** (5hr.; 8am, noon, 3pm; $8); **Olimpos** (12hr., 4 per day 7:30-9pm, $19); **Pamukkale** (10hr., 4 per day 7-9pm, $14); **Selçuk** (13hr., 6 per day 6:30-9pm, $19).

✳🛈 ORIENTATION AND PRACTICAL INFORMATION

Finding your way around Göreme is not difficult. The main road, heads out west toward Nevşehir and northeast toward Çavuşin. The otogar, just off the main road, is at the eastern end of the town center. A smaller, cobblestone road runs south from the town center. At the eastern end of town, a road up to the Open-Air Museum breaks off from the main road, heading southeast up a hill. Restaurants are mostly located near the main road, and *pansiyons* are everywhere.

Tourist Office: (☎ 271 25 58; www.wec-net.com.tr/belediye/göreme). In the otogar, this cooperative provides info on all of Göreme's lodgings. Doing your own research here will acquaint you with Göreme's myriad pensions. Additionally, **Backpacker Information** (on your left as you exit the otogar; ☎ 271 27 36) can help "the independent traveler" organize an itinerary, and offers $10 per day (for lodging and transportation) hostel-based connections through Cappadocia and Turkey's western coast.

Tours: Zemi Tours (☎271 25 76; fax 271 25 77), on the left side of the road leading from the otogar to the Open-Air Museum, and **Neşe Tours** (☎ 271 25 25 or 271 26 43; fax 271 25 24; www.prizma.net.tr/İnesecafe), next to the Internet Cafe, are reputable and affordable. Zemi, in addition to full and multi-day tours ($30-150), offers a unique 2-day Ihlara Gorge Camping Trip ($50 per person) with tents, beds and meals provided. **Kapadokya Balloons** (☎271 24 42; fax 271 25 86; www.kapadokyaballoons.com), with an office next door to Cafe Dociş, offers breathtaking 90min. balloon tours, a.k.a. "aerial nature walks," through the Cappadocian landscape. Professional and multilingual pilots Kaili and Lars fly as high as 700m and low enough to pick flowers. Balloons fly for 1½hr. with 8 or 12 passengers Apr.-Oct. daily at dawn, weather permitting. $230 per person; book at least two days before.

Banks: Two are next to the Open-Air Museum. Open daily 9am-5:30pm. There is an **ATM** in the center of Göreme, across from the otogar and to the left.

Laundromat: (☎271 25 79), behind the otogar, across from the Göreme Belediye Handicrafts Market. Wash and dry $7, with ironing $6. Open daily 9am-8pm.

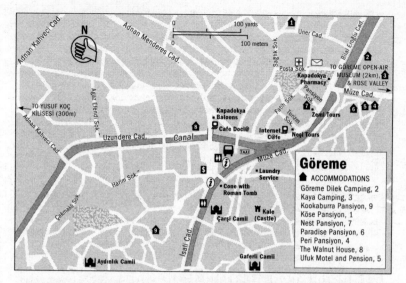

Göreme

▲ ACCOMMODATIONS

Göreme Dilek Camping, 2
Kaya Camping, 3
Kookaburra Pansiyon, 9
Köse Pansiyon, 1
Nest Pansiyon, 7
Paradise Pansiyon, 6
Peri Pansiyon, 4
The Walnut House, 8
Ufuk Motel and Pension, 5

Pharmacy: Kapadokya Pharmacy (☎271 21 37), on the main road near the hospital. Open daily 8am-8pm.

Medical Assistance: The **Göreme Sağlık Ocağı Hospital** (☎271 21 26), near the PTT, is actually a Community Health Clinic, but it also serves medical emergencies.

Internet Access: Cafe Doci@ (see p. 316) and Internet C@fe. **Internet Cafe** (☎271 25 25). Next door to Nese Tours, across from the bus terminal. A quiet place to check email. Offers a printer, non-alcoholic drinks, daily newspapers and weekly magazines. English-style keyboard to preserve your sanity. $4 per hour. Open 8am-10:30pm.

PTT: Though many street-side stores offer PTT services (money exchange, stamps, phone cards), the official post office is on the main road just after the turn-off for the Open-Air Museum. Offers the best exchange rate in town. Open daily 8:30am-12:30pm and 1:30-5:30pm. **Postal code:** 50180.

▼ ACCOMMODATIONS

Under Göreme's government, all pensions have fixed minimum prices for non-dormitory rooms: $5 per person, with bath $7, and up to $10 for a single. Establishments designated as starred hotels may charge higher rates. Hit the tourist office (see above) for more complete comparative information on all of Göreme's accommodations, most of which will pick you up if you call ahead.

Köse Pansiyon (☎271 22 94; fax 271 25 77). Just behind the PTT. Makeshift Ottoman divans, vine-covered ceilings, swimming pool, ying-yang murals, and helpful Scottish-Turkish owners make Köse the backpacker's mecca. Breakfast $2. Vegetarian and 4-course dinners $4. 2 dorm rooms with mattresses on the floor ($4 per person; bring your own sleeping bag, if possible) and 13 rooms, some with private bath.

Peri Pansiyon (☎271 21 36; fax 271 27 30). On the right walking east on the road to the Open-Air Museum. Lounge on the sunny, floral courtyard. Tame atmosphere, but close to the action at **Flinstone's**. Four-course dinner ($5) on the wood-panelled *kilim*-ed terrace. 7 cave rooms. Friendly management also offers non-tufa rooms to suit your taste. Singles $7, with bath $10; doubles $20. Cave rooms: singles $10, luxury caves $25.

Kookaburra Pansiyon (☎271 25 49). Take a left on the 1st dirt road behind Orta Mah. and fork left to reach Kookaburra. 10 attractive rooms, some with private showers and stunning views. Charming decor adds old Turkish flair. $3 breakfasts and a cave bar.

Paradise Pension (☎/fax 271 22 48; www.hitit.co.uk/paradise/). An excellent pension. Next door to the Flinstone's Cave Bar. Big with the Aussie crowd. 2 dorm-style fairy chimney rooms, each with 5 beds and shared bath. 9 smaller rooms, some with private bath. Laundry $6, Turkish breakfast $2.

Ufuk Motel and Pension (☎271 21 57; fax 271 25 78; www.ufukpension.com.tr/). Next door to Paradise on Göreme Open-Air Museum Way, offers 4 cave rooms, 3 with private showers. 11 regular rooms, some with private showers. Garden, wood, and *kilim* furnished dining terrace. Laundry $4. Complete dinner $6.

The Walnut House (☎271 25 64; fax 271 22 35). Across from the otogar, is a real steal in comfort and luxury. Arched ceilings, a *kilim*-ed sitting room, and homemade meals give this place an authentic Turkish flair. Central heating in winter. All rooms have bath and telephone. Singles $14; doubles $20; triples $28. V, MC.

Nest Pansiyon. Off the main road behind Zemi Tours. This new, small pension offers a respite for the harried traveler. Clean rooms, rose-canopy garden, and swimming pool.

Göreme Dilek Camping (☎271 23 96). Across from Peri Pansiyon. Vast, floral campsite and pool snuggled among phallic rocks. Campsite $4.50 per site; tents $3 per person, tent rentals $8; caravans $10.

Kaya Camping (☎343 31 00; fax 343 39 84). Walk 5-10 min. uphill from the museum. A superb vista of the opposite valley. Kitchen, pool, and private showers. The environmentally aware will enjoy its solar power. $3 per person; $1.50 per tent.

🎨🎵 FOOD AND ENTERTAINMENT

🍴 **Orient** (☎/fax 271 23 46). A highly-recommended local favorite opposite the Yüksel Motel and Cafe Doci@ featuring delicious Turkish food and atmosphere. Charming furniture complements the wood floors and cave atmosphere of this restaurant and bar. The sizzling *sac tava* is a must-try house specialty ($4). Entrees and vegetarian dishes $3-4. 5-course daily special $5. Open 7:30am until crowds leave, usually 1am.

🍴 **Cafe Doci@** (☎271 29 03; www.indigoturizm.com.tr/cafedoci@). To the left as you exit the otogar on the road toward Nevşehir. Run by young entrepreneurs Arman and Haluk, whose flawless English has an Australian twang. Mammoth burgers ($3), good beer ($3- $5), and good times make this a young backpacker's hotspot. Blaring Ameri/Euro pop draws nightly crowds. A big-screen TV offers American channels and movies during the day. Internet $2 per hr. Opens 8am for breakfast and closes when the partying ends, usually around 2 or 3am.

Flinstones Bar (☎271 22 48). A revamped cave at the turnoff for the Open-Air Museum. "*Raki* is the answer; I don't remember the question." Partyers at this "Backpacker's Underground Pub" can hit the stocked bar or sprawl out on the *kilims* with a few friends and a hookah. Fans of Britpop will delight in the DJ's discerning taste. Beer $2. Open until the party ends around 3am.

Pacha Bar (☎271 23 40). Well-situated in the middle of Göreme's central promenade and marked by celestial murals, Pacha is often the busiest bar in town. Enjoy beer ($2) or mixed drinks ($3) at the bar or on cushioned benches. Open until business ends.

Cappi Restaurant (☎271 20 79 or 271 29 05). Across the street from the turn-off to Museum Way, this Cappadocian pizza joint is classy but affordable. An appetizing selection of both Italian pizza and Turkish pide (about $5) served in a handsome, wood-paneled interior or at outdoor tables.

🔅 SIGHTS

GÖREME OPEN-AIR MUSEUM

From Göreme village, follow the Open-Air Museum Way about 2km east, walking uphill. Open year-round 8am- 5pm. $5.25.

Stroll through the remains of eras past in Göreme's impressive Open-Air Museum. With seven Byzantine churches, a convent, and a kitchen/refectory, the Open-Air Museum is a delight to history, art, and religion buffs. In the 4th century, St. Basil founded one of the first Christian monasteries here, setting down religious tenets that influenced the teachings of St. Benedict and, subsequently, the entire Western monastic tradition. Monasticism ended in the 15th century under Turkish rule. From then until the 1923 Population Exchange, the Greeks and Turks used the old churches to store apples, potatoes, and hay. Today, the remains offer tourists an array of Cappadocia's most spectacular frescoes.

ST. BASIL CHURCH. The empty tufa ditches underfoot were once graves in this early Christian monastery. Though only saints could be buried inside monasteries, the wealthy could pay their way into monastic burials and thus (supposedly) to paradise. If you use a flashlight and magnifying glass, the artist's fingerprints are just visible on the church's 10th-century frescoes.

ÇARIKLI KİLİSE (SANDAL CHURCH). Çarıklı Kilise earns its name from the footprints below the church's back wall, supposed molds of Jesus' feet. The church itself dates back to the 11th century, rendering the holy footprints but a popular myth.

YILANLI KİLİSE (DRAGON CHURCH). To the right of the entrance, note the area's best-preserved fresco, of St. George slaying the dragon. This building is also known as St. Onuphrius church after its fresco of the hermaphroditic-looking figure of St. Onuphrius. One popular legend claims that the Egyptian girl Onophirios was so beautiful that she could not drive away all the men seeking to ravish her. She prayed for assistance and was granted a long white beard and moustache, which solved all her problems. Another tale tells of St. Onuphrius, who belonged to a 4th-century commune of Egyptian hermits. When a certain St. Paphnutius visited the commune, he was impressed by the moral fervor and self-control of Onuphrius, who is therefore depicted with a beard to represent wisdom. The seemingly full breasts show the artist's technique for depicting strong soldiers; similar "breasts" can be found on many fresco figures, including Jesus.

KARANLIK KILISE (DARK CHURCH). Light filters through a tiny window in the narthex, preserving a set of breathtaking frescoes. By far the most impressive artwork in the museum, its walls depict a number of scenes of Jesus, including His birth, entrance to Bethlehem, Transfiguration, Crucifixion and Resurrection. The dome also houses a rare fresco of a teenage Jesus. *($10; watch your head walking in)*

OTHER SIGHTS

NEARBY CHURCHES. A ticket to the Open-Air Museum will also admit you to a number of nearby churches. The first, **Tokalı,** is right outside the museum's entrance and contains three smaller churches and a chapel. Behind the Tokalı Church, about 250m from the entrance, are the **Church of Mother Mary** and the 10th-century **Church of St. Eustathios.** Aynalı is across from Kaya Camping, 600m uphill from the museum entrance. To reach **Saklı** and **El Nazar,** hike 500m uphill to the right from the museum's entrance. Unless you really have a fresco fetish and don't mind asking around for a key, these last churches may not be worth the hike.

KARŞIBUCAK YUSUF KOÇ KİLİSESİ. If you're up for a half-hour's diversion while in Göreme, the Karşıbucak Yusuf Koç Kilisesi is a pleasant visit. Enjoy reasonably well-preserved frescoes as well as a terrific view of Göreme and the surrounding area. *(Keeping the canal on the left, head west of the bus station, and take a right on the dirt road just beyond Ottoman House. The second left off this road leads up a hill and left to the church—follow the sign. Free.)*

⚠ HIKING

Cappadocia's breathtaking landscape is a hiker's seventh heaven. It's best to start early, as the midday sun can be brutal. Though most of the hikes are moderate, safe, and accessible, *Let's Go* recommends hiking with partners, tour groups, or guides to hit all sights, stay safe, and navigate trickier areas. Women traveling alone should especially consider these options, as long, empty trails may cause unease and detract from the hike. Wear hiking boots and long pants to protect your legs from prickly shrubbery.

SUNSET POINT. Some of the best hikes can be found by straying off the road that leads to the Open-Air Museum. To reach Sunset Point, follow the road about 1km past the museum, take a left on the dirt road by Kaya Camping, turn left again at the next paved road and walk for about 3km. The entrance fee ($.60) is a bit criminal, as there are better, free views. But from here, you can descend into the **Kırmızı Vadi (Rose Valley)**, whose bizarre, multi-colored rock formations make this one of the area's better hikes. The complete Rose Valley hike is 14km long, but there are points of ascent and exit about 3 and 7km into the trek. For the shorter hikes, transportation arrangement (taxi or tour group is your best bet) is necessary, since dolmuş don't pass by. The full hike, wandering off the paths and getting lost from time to time, will bring you to Çavuşin in an hour or two. Take the Avanos-Nevşehir bus or the Avanos-Zelve-Göreme-Ürgüp minibus back to Göreme (every 30min. until 6pm; weekends every hr.). A taxi from Çavuşin to Göreme costs roughly $5.

PIGEON VALLEY. Pigeon Valley can be reached by following the canal west of the otogar. This destination earns its name from the birdhouses carved into its cliffs. According to local folklore, humans and fairies lived together peacefully in the valley until a human and a fairy fell in love. The forbidden romance sparked a war that drove the fairies from the valley forever, transforming them into pigeons. As a gesture of reconciliation, guilt-ridden humans built birdhouses to lure the fairy-pigeons back. The birdhouses also serve a more practical purpose, as the bird droppings are used as fertilizer, particularly for Cappadocia's famous wine and pekmez-making grapes. Pigeon Valley is a confusing hike, as roads become paths, paths become streams, and streams disappear quite frequently. Just be persistent, respect the many gardening patches, and you'll eventually wind up in Üçhisar.

LOVE VALLEY. Located to the north of Göreme, this gorge is affectionately known as "Penis Valley" because of the phallic rock formations that would give even Grade A porn stars a complex. To get there, take a left on the dirt road at the onyx factory on the road to Göreme. Walk about 400m and descend on the right into the valley. You're best off hiking the valley's center, as tufa may crumble underfoot. When in doubt, follow the creek heading northeast and after a couple of hours you'll inevitably end up in Çavuşin. About 1km into the hike, a small ridge divides the valley in two; steer left and the ■ looming penises are hard to miss.

ÜÇHİSAR

Üçhisar's hidden treasure is its mesmerizing twilight; the "Ancien Village Walking Road" winds in a horseshoe to the town's **kale** (castle), offering visitors a calming panoramic view of the valley and its sunset.

■■ TRANSPORTATION AND PRACTICAL INFORMATION. The Göreme-Nevşehir bus (every 30min., $.70) stops at the road junction less than 1km away from the gigantic fort, which gives the town its name (Üçhisar means "fort on the tip"). No commercial traffic runs through the tiny town center, where you can find the **Üçhisar Eczane** (pharmacy; ☎219 25 00).

⌐ ACCOMMODATIONS. Üçhisar's accommodations are generally grouped either in the town square (walk down the Ancien Village Walking Road, turn left onto any side street and turn left again into town) or on the road toward the *kale*. Down the road from the town center, walking with the taxi stand on your left, is the **Erciyes Pansiyon.** Enjoy warm, family ambiance under the shade of cherry trees. All 12 rooms come with private bath. Try the homemade *pekmez.* (☎219 20 90. Breakfast included; $8 per person.) Right in the center of town, the **Anatolya Pension** offers 13 cute rooms overlooking a petite vegetable garden. All rooms have bedside maps, terra-cotta lamp covers and tile baths clean enough to eat off. (☎214 23 34. Breakfast included; $20 per person.) **Le Jardin de 1001 Nuits,** on the cobblestone street below the *kale*, has numerous shower-equipped fairy chimney rooms. A comely restaurant complements the hotel. (☎219 22 93; fax 219 25 05. Breakfast included. Singles $6, with nice view $12.) **Ahbab Konağı,** on the other tip of the horseshoe, across from the *kale*, has dark wood floors, impeccable white sheets, a stone terrace with jacuzzi, and wine faucets (woo hoo!). Splurge while you can. (☎219 30 20; fax 219 30 21; email asen@alfa.gen.Tr. $30 per person, breakfast included. With dinner $40. V, MC, AmEx.)

📷📀 **FOOD AND ENTERTAINMENT.** At the ▧**Oase Cafe & Bar,** below the *kale*'s valley façade, nightfall is a spectator event. Outdoor tables and a charming mix of Turkish and Texas-style decor makes this the perfect spot to sip a beer with the sinking sun. (☎219 27 60; email oase_cafe_bar@email.com. Beer and *rakı* $1.60; internet access $1 per hr.) Under a sprawling canopy of trees in the town center, the **Centre Café and Restaurant** is one of the only places in Central Anatolia where you'll find hot dogs on the menu ($1) in addition to your standard Turkish meat meals ($2-4). (☎219 21 11.) The **Duyurgan Winery,** to the right on the same road, produces some of Cappadocia's best wines. Enjoy free wine tasting and a free tour of the winery. (☎219 29 79; fax 219 23 46. 8am-8:30pm.)

🔘 **SIGHTS.** The Üçhisar **kale,** used as a castle until the 14th century, is now Üçhisar's only commercial tourist attraction. Looming high above Cappadocia, it makes for a great climb. (Open 9am-7:30pm, $2). Üçhisar is also the starting point of a number of good hikes, including Love Valley (see **Hiking,** p. 318). Head toward Göreme and turn left on the dirt road at the onyx factory. Walk about 400m and descend on the right into Love Valley—you'll be in Çavuşin in a couple of hours.

UNDERGROUND CITIES: KAYMAKLI AND DERİNKUYU

By dolmuş, Kaymaklı and Derinkuyu are about 30min. and 45min. from Göreme, respectively, with a connection in Nevşehir. From Göreme, dolmuş run to Nevşehir (every 30min. 6:30am-7pm, $.50) and then go to Kaymaklı ($.60) and Derinkuyu ($.80). Both sites open daily 8am-5pm. Each site $3.75.

Although Cappadocia contains almost 30 **underground cities** carved from *tufa,* Kaymaklı and Derinkuyu are the largest. The earliest written mention of Hellenic communities in Derinkuyu and Kaymaklı appears in Xenophon's *Anabasis,* which dates them to at least the 4th century BC. Some think the cities began as cave dwellings that were later used by the Hittites for storage and ambushes. Between the 5th and 10th centuries, the Byzantines expanded them into full-fledged cities that shielded people from Iconoclast and Sassanid raids (see **Christianity and the Byzantine Empire** p. 8).

These underground complexes were designed with mind-boggling ingenuity. Low and narrow passages, easily blocked off by massive millstones, hindered prospective invaders. Wineries consisted of a tub-like area for grape-stomping and a chute that carried the juice into another tub for fermenting. The holes drilled in some pillars suggest that the underground inhabitants enforced strict discipline by chaining and torturing transgressors. It was forbidden for anyone to leave while the cities were occupied, lest their departure give away the hideouts. Strangely enough, no evidence of a permanent settlement has been conclusively found in either Derinkuyu or Kaymaklı.

Derinkuyu, 45m deep with a 55m well, is slightly more impressive than Kaymaklı. With eight levels open to the public, Derinkuyu has sizable rooms and halls, good lighting, and relatively easy access. Kaymaklı, smaller than Derinkuyu at 35m below ground, boasts a more complex structure. The village has been built around the underground city, so residents could enter storage areas through tunnels in their courtyards. It was common for underground cities to use tunnels for intercity water transport. Rumor has it that a similar Cappadocian tunnel, used for escape rather than carrying water, runs the 9km between Kaymakli and Derinkuyu.

In both sites, red arrows lead down, blue arrows up. Although all explorable areas are lit, a flashlight may come in handy. Stick to the marked and lighted areas, and you'll be safe. If you wish to stray from the herd, just remember that these cities were designed to foil potential trespassers, who would fall to their deaths from sudden drops hidden behind corners.

CENTRAL ANATOLIA

ÇAVUŞİN-ZELVE

The provincial village of Çavuşin may lack Göreme's glory, but it teems with authentic flavor. About 2km down the road from Göreme (heading toward Zelve), this inviting town offers road-weary travelers a glimpse of village life. Tourists in Çavuşin may stumble upon a local wedding, be invited to eat *manti* (Turkish ravioli) in a villager's home, or simply enjoy close proximity to the area's best hikes. Çavuşin's old village originally consisted of Greek dwellings hewn into the surrounding cliffs, made uninhabitable by erosion and earthquakes. These deserted buildings and *tufa* houses, around which the new village is clustered, make for some rewarding exploring. The worn cliffs and caves, which provide extraordinary valley views, are best to climb with hiking boots. Both the Ürgüp-Avanos minibus and the Göreme-Avanos bus pass through Çavuşin.

While better as a daytrip from Göreme or Ürgüp, Çavuşin does have a number of good *pansiyons*. The newly-renovated **Turbel Motel** offers sizeable rooms with nifty log-beam ceilings and one of the most splendid panoramas of the area: a sprawling green valley to one side and the haunting old village to the other. Accommodating francophone owner, Mustafa Kaygisiz, organizes camping trips in the Taurus Mountains. (☎532 70 84; fax 532 70 83. Dinner $5. Breakfast included. Singles $10; doubles $18.) The **Green Motel**, up from the main road and just past the town square has pricey rooms with bath and a sitting room with Ottoman decor (☎532 72 28; singles $20, doubles $30). A campsite is also available for $5 per tent. For more affordable respite, the nearby **Panorama Pansiyon** (☎532 70 02) offers secluded and comfortable rooms with shared bath for $6.50. Dinner at the adjacent Panorama restaurant costs $4.

The under-visited 5th-century **Church of St. John the Baptist,** the oldest known church in Cappadocia, can be reached by following the town's main road past the old village and climbing either the hill or the tufa and rocks. The sweaty climb is worth the view, even though the frescoes are barely visible. The 10th-century **Çavuşin Church,** on the main road beside the turn-off to the village (look for the steps leading up to the rock face), has some well-preserved frescoes. (Open daily 8am-5pm. $2.)

The **Zelve Open-Air Museum,** (open daily 8am-5:30pm; $4) consisting of churches and homes carved into three deep valleys, will appeal more to the adventurer than to the art history fan. There are very few surviving frescoes, but the complex of tunnels and caves provides hours of gleeful (if tricky) climbing, burrowing, and exploring. The dull way to reach the museum is to take the Ürgüp-Avanos minibus one stop from Çavuşin. With a extra hour or two, you can follow the main road past Çavuşin, take a right up the dirt road behind the pottery shop and continue to climb for a magnificent ridge walk (beware the heights). Alternatively, descend into **Paşabağ Valley** (**Monk's Valley,** marked by the street-side shopping 1.5km west of Zelve Museum), which is punctuated by mushroom-shaped rock formations and unique three-headed chimneys.

ÜRGÜP   ☎384

Ürgüp emerges from a pastiche of rock formations, early Christian dwellings, and old Greek mansions. Tourists will appreciate Ürgüp's organized information network, central otogar, and proximity to noteworthy villages and points of interest. With fewer pansiyons and neo-hippies than Göreme, Ürgüp appeals to those independent travelers who tirelessly flee from the commotion of booming tourism.

▊ TRANSPORTATION

Buses: English-speaking **Aydın Altan** of **Nevtur** (☎341 43 02) will answer bus-related questions. To: **Adana** (5hr., 3 per day 8am-3pm, $8); **Alanya** (14hr., 4 per day 6-10pm, $18); **Ankara** (5hr., 5 per day 7am-5:30pm, $8); **Antalya** (11hr., 3 per day 6-8pm, $15); **Bodrum** (14hr., 7pm, $19); **Eskişehir** (8hr., 7pm, $11); **Fethiye** (15hr., 3 per day 6-8pm, $19); **İstanbul** (12hr., 4 per day 6-8pm, $16); **İzmir** (12hr., 6:30pm,

$16); **Konya** (4hr., 6 per day 8am-7pm, $6); **Kuşadası** (13hr.; 6:30, 7:30pm; $18); **Marmaris** (15hr., 7pm, $19); **Mersin** (5hr., 3 per day 8am-3pm, $8); **Pamukkale** (10hr., 7pm, $15); **Side** (13hr.; 7, 8pm; $15); **Selçuk** (13hr., 6:30pm, $18).

Rental Agencies: Several are near the otogar. Bikes $5-10 per day; mopeds $15-20 per day; cars from $30 per day. Roads are reasonably tame and organized in this area, though only skilled stick-handlers may conquer the hills without stalling.

✴🛈 ORIENTATION AND PRACTICAL INFORMATION

The main square, marked by a bath house and an Atatürk statue, is 20m down **Güllüce Cad.** from the otogar. This road forks uphill into two smaller roads, both near accommodations. Intersecting **Güllüce Cad.** in the main square is **Kayseri Cad.**

Tourist Office: (☎341 40 59). Inside the garden on Kayseri Cad. Follow the signs all over the city. Grab maps and brochures, or drop your bags while you explore. Run by English- and German-speaking Zeki Güzel. Open daily Apr.-Oct. 8am-7pm; Nov.-Mar. 8am-5pm. Alternatively, fork left at the hamam and walk up to the **Turkish Airlines Office,** which doubles as a classier tourist office. Arrange plane tickets, get info, or simply cool off in the stone building that was once Ürgüp's prison. Open 8am-5pm.

Travel Agencies: The reliable and affordable **Erko Tours** (☎341 32 52; fax 341 37 85; www.erkotours.com.tr), in the otogar, gladly organizes tours of Cappadocia. Upscale and professional **Argeus Tours** (☎341 46 88; www.argeus.com.tr) also operates out of the Turkish Airlines Office. $70 for all-inclusive day tours.

Hamam: Tarihi Şehir Hamamı (☎341 22 41) at the fork in the main square. Co-ed, so bring a friend to this steamy one-room complex. Complete bath with massage (male masseur), *kese* (exfoliating scrub), and sauna. $8 per person. Open daily 7am-11pm.

Pharmacies: Several near the otogar; walk toward the hamam and **Eczane Ürgüp** (☎341 44 52) is on the left, sandwiched between carpet shops.

Medical Assistance: Call the **hospital** (☎341 40 31), off Kayseri Cad. just behind Tourist Information. The **Cappadocia Health Center,** 28 Dumlupınar Cad. (☎341 54 27 or 341 54 28; fax 341 34 92), offers more private, out-patient clinical care.

Internet Access: Asia Teras (see **Food,** p. 322).

PTT: (☎341 80 12). Turn right out of the tourist office and take the first right uphill. Open daily 8:30am-7pm; in winter 8am-5pm. Offers telephone services, stamps, fax, telegraph, and a **currency exchange** that's closed noon-1:30pm. **Postal code:** 50400.

◤ ACCOMMODATIONS

▨ **Hotel Surban** (☎341 47 61 or 341 46 03; fax 341 32 23). Fork right at the hamam and trudge up the steep hill. Spacious, *kilim*-ed lounge and bar, parking space, cave restaurant, and ping-pong table make Surban ideal for groups, and lots of fun. Rooms with private bath and towels. Singles $10; doubles $20; triples $30.

Bahçe Hostel (☎341 33 14; fax 341 48 78). Across the street and uphill from the hamam. Once known as Ürgüp's only backpacker hostel. Less bohemian than it once was, but its inviting cave bar/disco remains. Rooms are spacious but unspectacular; some with private bath for an extra buck. Singles $7; doubles $10; triples $15.

Hotel Elvan, İstiklâl Cad., 11 Barbaros Hayrettin Sok. (☎341 41 91; fax 341 34 55). Downhill from Hotel Akuzun, to the left off the hamam. Maternal Fatma Hanım will boil medicinal teas for her diarrheal guests. Tidy rooms with private baths. Singles $15; doubles $20; triples $30. V, MC.

Hotel Asia Minor (☎341 46 45; fax 341 27 21; http://members.xoom.com/asiaminor10/index.htm). Behind the Atatürk statue. A beautiful 150-year-old Greek mansion with an attractive breakfast garden, and frescoes adorning lobby walls. Breakfast included. $30 per person; doubles $40. $5 student discount.

Türkerler Otel, Camping and Swimming Pool (☎341 33 54). Fork right at the mosque, climb up the hill and steer left at the next fork. Pitch a tent for a couple of bucks on the environs of this tiny pension. Call ahead to check if the swimming pool is in fact filled, and cut a price with the laid-back owners (Turkish business at its best). If camping's lost its novelty, patrons can check into the on-grounds hotel or pension.

▐ FOOD

Han Çırağan (☎341 25 66). Between the hamam and the Harem Disco. Heavy with Turkish spirit, this restaurant is in a 300-year-old *kervansaray* whose rooms are still used by merchants in horse-drawn carriages. Try the filling Han Çırağan special of *döner* with cheese, mushroom, carrots, and peppers ($4). The bar and winery next door specialize in all-you-can-drink "Turkish nights," where the din of *kanun, saz,* and merriment echo through the cave ($12 per person). Did we mention all-you-can-drink?

Şömine Cafe (☎341 84 42; fax 341 84 43). In the center of the town square, on the second level across the Atatürk statue. With a multilingual menu and professional service, Şömine caters largely to the tourist scene. Try the house specialty, *testi kebap,* a dish of lamb, tomatoes, onions, and garlic roasted in a clay pot. After 6 hours, the pot is broken to reveal a delicious meal for two ($8) Other entrees $2-4.

Asia Teras (☎341 38 39; email asiateras@hotmail.com). 20m to the left when exiting the tourist office. Billiards ($2 per hr.) and internet access ($2.50 per hr.), along with mediocre American food (burgers $1-1.50). Beer $1; *rakı* $2. Open 10am-midnight.

Mikro Restaurant (☎341 20 68; fax 341 32 39). A local favorite, serving unbeatable Turkish food, with main courses running about $4. Lucky patrons will catch *mantı* night, when the home-cooked Turkish ravioli leaves everybody smiling.

▐ ENTERTAINMENT

Cappadocia is one of Turkey's major viticultural regions, with its center in Ürgüp. Uphill to the right behind the Atatürk statue, the renowned **Turasan Winery,** supplier of 60% of Cappadocia's wines, offers free tours and tastings in its rock-carved wine cellar. Buy cheap wine here (most bottles $2.50-4) or splurge on the more robust '89 vintage ($7.50) or the extra-special '97 Kalecik Karası ($15). (Open 8am-8pm. Tours available until 5pm.) Several wine shops around the main square also offer free tastings. In the late September, the Ürgüp **wine festival** brings eager competitors from France, Italy, Argentina, and the USA, among others.

If you find yourself still energized after a day of boozing and trooping through Ürgüp's narrow cobblestone streets, put on your dancing shoes.

▐ Prokopi Pub Bar (☎341 64 98). Right in the town square. Popular with tourists, this hip bar plays an excellent selection of electronica, dance beats, and American and Brit pop. Dance floor for the inspired or intoxicated. Beer $2.50; *rakı* $3; mixed drinks $4-6. Open until the party dies, usually around 3am.

Bar Barium. Next to the Star Disco. This popular venue features funky mirrored walls and a solid mélange of Turkish and American pop. Beer and *rakı* $2.50. Open until 4am.

Harem Disco. At the foot of the road to the winery. Turkish and European techno blast in a candlelit cave complete with a fireplace and disco ball. Open daily until 4am.

Armağan Disco. Across from the Kapadokya Market (under the "Born To Be Free" sign). Usually free from tourist hordes, Armağan blares disco tunes and Turkish pop, which are occasionally interrupted by a belly-dance act. Upstairs, several (relatively) quiet stone-cut rooms with divans and carpets sometimes host live traditional music. Beer and *rakı* $2.50. Open until 5am.

▐ DAYTRIP FROM ÜRGÜP: SOĞANLI

Getting to the valley on your own isn't easy: a taxi may cost up to $50 and tour companies, which are only marginally cheaper, don't spend much time here. Public transportation only goes to Mustafapaşa. The cheapest way to visit Soğanlı is to rent a scooter in Ürgüp and brave the Turkish roads with nothing but a crash helmet between you and certain death ($20, an additional $2.50 for gas). Valley open daily 8:30am-5:30pm. $1.

About 40km south of Ürgüp, the **Soğanlı valley** is one of the few places in Cappadocia where beauty remains untarnished by tourism. Thanks to its remote location, you can probably have the place to yourself.

There are about 150 stone churches in the valley, but most have been filled in, destroyed, or converted into birdhouses. The five major churches, all dating from the pre-Ottoman era, are decorated with aged and desecrated frescoes which have not been granted Göreme-style renovations. The **Geyikli Kilise** (Church of the Deer) is at the intersection of the valley's branches. Heading right, you should first see the **Karabaş Kilise** (Dark Church), notable for the darkened halos that hover over the saints. Down the road is the **Yılanı Kilise** (Snake Church) which has a fresco depicting St. George slaying the dragon. Above the stream, **Kubbeli Kilise** (Domed Church), the largest and most impressive church in the valley, is distinguished by the only rock-carved dome in Cappadocia. The **Tahtalı Kilise** (Wooden Church), at the end of the left valley road, is accessible by a narrow set of stone steps; inside one can just make out a fresco of Christ's descent into hell. Taking either of the two paths through the valley allows you to make a complete circuit in an hour.

Pleasant stops between Ürgüp and Soğanlı include **Damsa Dam**, 5km beyond Mustafapaşa, the only beach environment you're likely to find in Central Anatolia ($.25 per person, $.60 per car). Further down the road, near Cemil, the **Keşlik Monastery** contains a blackened church, a refectory, and a monastery ($.60).

MUSTAFAPAŞA ☎384

With fascinating moonscape valleys, old Greek houses, and Orthodox churches, Mustafapaşa appeals most to hikers and architecture enthusiasts. Formerly known as Sinassos, this friendly village was home to Greeks and Turks alike until the population exchange of 1923. Currently, 96 old Greek houses are under protection by local government and not open to tourists. However, visitors will still be fascinated by the unique mix of Greek and Selçuk architecture; poke around the village and you're likely to get some guidance in seeking out preserved frescoes.

⌨ TRANSPORTATION AND PRACTICAL INFORMATION. Dolmuş make the 5km run from Ürgüp's otogar to Mustafapaşa (9 per day; M-F 8:15am-6:15pm, return 7:45am-5:45pm; $.65 each way). Dolmuş stop in Mustafapaşa's square, where a shop labeled "Information" sells postcards and trinkets while doubling as the tourist office. (Open daily June-Aug. 8:30am-7pm; closed in winter.) On the wall to the left of the door, an imaginatively scaled diagram (be sure to read the labeled distances) indicates the location of the closest sites. Alternatively, walk uphill from the town square and turn left for the small, outdoor wooden cabin for **Tourist Information** and keys to the locked churches (see Sights). In **medical emergencies,** call the **Sağlık Ocağı** clinic in nearby Ürgüp (☎ 343 33 64). Around the corner from the tourist office, take the path to the left for the **PTT.** (Open M-F 8am-12:30pm, 1:30-5:30pm; Sa 8am-12:30pm.) **Postal code:** 50420.

⌨ ACCOMMODATIONS. Hotel Pacha, a former Greek mansion, has a beautiful terrace restaurant, with *kilims*, a fireplace, couches, and a bar. The hotel serves five-course dinners for $5.50. (☎ 358 50 04; fax 353 53 31; email pachahotel@hotmail.com. 11 rooms. Breakfast included. $7.50 per person.) The **Monastery Pension,** downhill and to the left from the dolmuş stop, was once a Greek monastery. The cave bar supplies the only appreciable nightlife in Mustafapaşa. (☎ 353 50 05. Breakfast included. 13 rooms. $6 per person.) **Hotel Cavit,** restful and accommodating, offers 10 clean, little rooms and a vine-covered terrace for those fabulous Turkish breakfasts. (☎ 353 51 86. Breakfast included. $9.70 per person.) The massive **Hotel Sinassos** provides opulence at an affordable price. A breathtaking domed restaurant, disco ball, and swanky reception spell luxury. (☎ 353 54 34 or 353 51 26. Large, comfortable rooms with private bath $15 per person.) **Paşa Camping,** next door to Aios Vasilyos church, boasts bathrooms, shower facilities, and even a make-shift disco. (☎ 353 50 18. $1 per person, $1 per tent, $6 per caravan.)

◨ **SIGHTS.** Mustafapaşa's most beautiful sight is the **Gömede Valley,** whose entrance is a mostly uphill 2km hike from the center of town. Few pains have been taken to make it accessible to hikers; after climbing the cobblestone road from town, turn right onto the dirt path and walk to a paved road. Follow the steep downhill trail (by the water dispenser) to the bottom and up again, then turn right on a dirt path. The valley hike is a moderately difficult 7km trek past pigeon houses and abandoned cave dwellings. On the way, you may see the 1200-year-old **Kara Ala Kilise** ("black white church"), named for the striking dichromatic contrast of its frescoes. You can also explore the more spacious **Tavşanlı Kilise** and the recently discovered **Kimistavros Kilise,** whose ceilings are carved with 1100-year-old crosses. (Valley open daily in summer 8am-6:30pm; in winter 8am-5pm. $1.50.)

Access to Mustafapaşa's two most famous churches requires a key from Tourist Information and a preposterous fee of $7.30. Northwest of the old fountain in the square, a gravel road leads downhill 1km past the Paşa Restaurant to the 7th-century Byzantine **Aios Vasilyos Church.** The visible portion of Aios Vasilyos is an uninspiring stone cubicle the size of a closet, but two flights of stone stairs lead down to a magnificent subterranean church. Because it's carved into the side of the valley, windows let in enough daylight to illuminate some of the frescoes. One such window, the only one accessible from the ground, served as a sentry post: the church could be sealed off by rolling an enormous boulder in front of this window. Closer to town, 50m downhill from the town square, **Aios Costantinos-Heleni Church** has an exterior more impressive than the barren inside

Much closer to the center of town is **Monastery Valley,** featuring the **Aios Stephanos Kilise, Aios Nikalaos Kilise,** and the **Sinasos Kilise.** The hike itself is just a few kilometers, though without arranged transportation you'll probably have to hike out and back to the entrance. For a taste of regional flavor, try the **Şarap Farbrikası** winery. Here you can take a free tour and sample local wines.

AVANOS   ☎ 384

The banks of the nearby wine-colored Kızılırmak, Turkey's longest river, have been providing the potters of Avanos with red, iron-rich clay for centuries. Roughly a hundred workshops crowd the area, especially in the cobblestoned Old Town. With workshop signs emblazoned with names like Chez İsmail, Chez Barış, Chez Celebi, and, alarmingly, Chez Rambo, the town clearly caters to its many foreign visitors. Watch the potters at work or try your own hand at the giant, foot-powered wheels. If clay is your thing, Avanos is close enough to Cappadocia's major tourist centers to make it an easy daytrip, and it is vibrant and distinct enough to merit an extended visit.

◨◪ **TRANSPORTATION AND PRACTICAL INFORMATION.** To get to Avanos, take the Ürgüp-Göreme-Çavuşin-Zelve-Avanos **dolmuş** (departs Ürgüp M-F every other hr. 9am-5pm, $.80) or the Göreme Belediye **buses** (M-F, every 30min. 8am-7pm, $.30). Both stop at the otogar. For more transportation info, see **Getting Around Cappadocia,** p. 311. The **tourist office** is across the river from the otogar. Take a right after crossing the bridge into town and walk 100m. (☎511 43 60. Open M-F 8am-noon, 1:30-5:30pm; closes at 5pm in winter.) Just after crossing the bridge, an uphill stone path on the left leads to the well-marked Old Town, where most of the ceramics studios and a few of the pensions and cafes can be found. The town square, past the tourist office, is marked by several terra-cotta statues (the town's Atatürk monument is located less prominently on a nearby corner). **Kirkit Voyages** (☎511 32 59, 511 54 40 or 511 45 42; fax 511 21 35; www.kirkirt.com), across from the tourist office, specializes in guided horse tours (2hr. tour $8; half-day tour $24; or 10-day camping trips) and rents French mountain bikes ($20 per day). The **Alaadin Hamam,** a block to the left after you cross the bridge, is one of Cappadocia's better-equipped bath houses, with a cold, marble "shock pool" for a pre-steam dip. (☎511 50 38. $8; open 8am-2am.) The **PTT** is just past the square. (Open daily 8am-5:30pm.) **Postal code:** 50500.

▛▟ ACCOMMODATIONS AND FOOD. The **Sofa Hotel**, just across the bridge into town and up the first hill on the left, offers a small tea garden, a 60-person restaurant fit for royalty, and 34 beautiful rooms with puffy, floral bedspreads. (☎511 44 89 or 511 51 86; fax 511 44 89; www.hotels.wec-net.com.tr/data/sofa. Singles $16; doubles $32.) **İlhan's Guesthouse,** 1 Zafer Sok., next door, has six homey rooms with bath. (☎511 48 28. $8.50 per person; 15% discount for *Let's Go* readers.) The **Kirkit Pension** offers lodgings in a restored Ottoman stone house behind Kirkit Voyages. (☎511 31 48 or 511 32 59; fax 511 21 35. 15 rooms; $9 per person, with bath $11 per person.) On the bank of the Kızılırmak, behind the Ziraat Bankası and next to the mosque, **Mesut Camping and Restaurant** (☎511 35 45) charges $5 per tent.

Atatürk Cad. is full of fine restaurants in both the old and new town. The ▨ **Sarıkaya** dining experience includes "Turkish banquets," folklore narrations, music, and dancing, all in a massive restaurant carved into a hillside cave ($12 per person; fixed menu). The **Köşk Mantı Evi,** next to Kirkit Voyages, specializes in *mantı* (Turkish ravioli; $3) and showcases traditional Turkish music in a cozy cave atmosphere. Town favorite **Tuvanna Restaurant** (☎511 44 97; fax 511 26 32) serves Italian-style pizza ($2.50) and spaghetti meals ($3-4), along with an assortment of Turkish cuisine. It's also one of the few places you'll find a ▨ non-Turkish toilet while wandering the streets of Avanos, so have a seat. Many small, decent *kafeteriya* line the river. After dark, tourists and locals alike duck into the **Kervanhan,** in the Old Town near the square. The DJ plays Turko-pop and belly dancing music until 4am. (Beer $3; *rakı* $4.) Just up the street is the predominantly Turkish **Labirent,** offering more of the same. (Beer and *rakı* $3. Open until 4am.)

▨ SIGHTS. In the town square, a clay monument commemorates **pottery** and the other crafts that give Avanos its distinctive character. A trip to Avanos is not complete without a visit to **Chez Galip** and its quirky ▨ **hair museum,** one block up from the town square. Shoppers at the pottery studio wielding a *Let's Go* book can get raging discounts on the beautiful handiwork (consult his assistant). Non-consumers can wander to the hair museum; perhaps the strangest sight in Cappadocia, this cavernous hall in the largest and most renowned of Avanos's pottery shops has been set aside for Galip Körükçü's collection of women's hair. The collection, begun in 1979, now numbers over 100,000 locks and has an entry in the *Guinness Book of World Records*. Each lock of hair is pinned to a wall or ceiling, giving the cavern an unsettling organic feel. Every year, ten locks are chosen, and their former owners are given a two week long paid vacation in Avanos, which includes pottery making, carpet weaving, and horseback riding. Good luck, Rapunzel. (☎511 42 40; fax 511 45 43; www.chez-galip.com; email chzgalip@tr-net.net.tr. Open daily 8:30am-9:30pm; in winter 8:30am-6pm.)

NİĞDE   ☎388

Niğde's dusty streets swarm with university students, strolling arm in arm. Islamic architecture dominates the town's backdrop of restaurants, bookstores, and pastry shops. Niğde comes alive every Thursday on market day, when fruits and vegetables are sold in the shadows of Selçuk mosques. Architecture aside, this quotidian lifestyle is none too appealing for tourists, most of whom skip the city entirely and head straight to the Eski Gumeşler Monastery.

▛ TRANSPORTATION. Niğde's otogar, on **Emin Erişeğil Cad.,** provides connections to: **Adana** (3hr., very frequent 8:30am-2:30am, $5.60); **Aksaray** (1½hr., 6 per day 8am-4:30pm, $1.50); **Ankara** (5hr., 9 per day 6am-6:30pm, $10); **Antalya** (10hr., 3 per day 7:30-10:30pm, $13); **Erzurum** (10hr.; 5:15, 9:30pm; $16); **İstanbul** (11hr., 3 per day 9:30am-7:30pm, $20); **İzmir** (12hr.; 7, 7:30pm; $16); **Kayseri** (1½hr., frequent 6am-10:30pm, $4); **Konya** (3hr., 5 per day 9am-7:30pm, $7.50); **Mersin** (3hr., frequent 9am-2:30am, $5.60); **Nevşehir** (1hr., 7 per day 9am-7pm, $3); **Trabzon** (13hr., 9:30pm, $19).

⊞ ORIENTATION AND PRACTICAL INFORMATION. Turning right out of the otogar leads to **Bankalar Cad.**, named for its abundance of **banks** and **ATMs.** Turn left to reach **Atatürk Meydanı**, the town's central square, marked by a statue and a government building. From here, head east on **İstasyon Cad.** past banks and shops to the Thursday market. Services include the **tourist office** (☎232 34 01; theoretically open M-F 8am-noon, 1:30-5:30pm) just off the square, and the modern **hospital** (☎232 22 20 or 232 22 24), two blocks west of the square, where you'll find Anglophone doctors. **Internet access** is the lifeblood of a college town. **Accent.com** is on the right side of Bankalar Cad., next to Akbank. (☎232 99 80; www.accentcafe.com. $1.50 per hr.) The smoky **Cafe Internet Klas-2,** across from the Ak Medrese, also caters to mouse-happy surfers. (☎213 35 53 or 233 22 62. $1.60 for 2hr.) **Klas,** part 1, is just around the corner. The **PTT,** about 100m down the road from Atatürk Meydanı offers stamps, telegraph, and fax services. (Open M-F 8:30am-12:30pm, 1:30-5:30pm.) **Postal code:** 51100.

⊞ ACCOMMODATIONS AND FOOD. From ritzy to ramshackle, Niğde's accommodations run the entire comfort gamut. The glitzy **Hotel Evim,** in the center of town, wears its three stars with pride; it has a restaurant and currency exchange in the lobby and provides fully loaded rooms with TV, phones, bathtubs, and balconies. (☎232 35 36 or 232 21 51; fax 232 15 26. Breakfast included. Singles $38; doubles $45.) Silky blue bedspreads soothe tired backs at **Otel Şahin,** where clean, spacious rooms come with phone and TV. (☎232 09 51; fax 232 09 53. Breakfast included. Singles $12; doubles $24.) **Otel Nahita** has 30 rooms with phones and balconies plus a ragin' disco bar that fills with local students on weekends. (Hotel ☎232 53 66. Singles $8; doubles $12. Bar cover $1.60, includes one drink.) Conserving cash and don't mind a twinge of dinge? Try **Bilge Pansiyon,** one block up from the otogar, above Sümerbank. Two floors of dorm-style rooms (bunk-beds galore) share a hall bathroom. (☎213 47 42. $4 per person.)

Niğde doesn't have a remarkable culinary arsenal. **Bor Cad.,** running south of Atatürk Meydanı, is littered with small *lokantas*, dominated by the Sultan "fast-food" chain. Flashy white decor sparkles inside local favorite **Saruhan** (☎232 21 72), where suspiciously slimming mirrors will whet your appetite for their incredible *döner*, kebap, and *pide* ($2-4). For the Bohemian side of Anatolia, check out the numerous student-frequented cafes and *okey* salons near the end of Bor Cad. The *çay* garden is particularly pleasant. For a university town of 60,000, Niğde's nightlife is severely lacking, though the most tragically hip meet at **Cafe Şamdan,** one block down from the old Bor Garaj on the right, which runs an esoteric category of its own: a "Fast Food, Breakfast, and Chips Salon." Live music (from Turkish folk to Western pop) graces the cafe's mostly college crowd.

⊞ SIGHTS. The most compelling sight in Niğde is actually 9km from the city. The **Eski Gümüşler Monastery** is one of Cappadocia's larger and better-preserved *tufa*-carved structures. Discovered in 1963, the monastery was active in the middle Byzantine era and contains some of the best-preserved frescoes dating back to the 10-12th centuries AD. The three apses depict scenes from the life of Jesus, while the main church features a rare mosaic of a smiling Virgin Mary. Crypts and storage pits dot the courtyard like moon craters, while the upper chambers and the caves outside the monastery make for some fun exploring. (*Dolmuş run between Niğde's otogar and Gümüsler; 15min., $.40. Monastery open 8am-noon, 1:30-6:30pm. $2.*)

Back in town, the **Alaeddin Camii,** built by the Selçuks in 1223, sits atop a hill near the clock tower. One local story about the mosque claims that one of the architects, sick with unrequited love, designed the eastern portal so that the morning summer light creates the outline of a girl's crowned head. Trying to see the head is likely to strain your imagination; recuperate at the *çay* garden next door.

While in Niğde, be sure to check out the **Süngür Bey Camii,** south of the Alaeddin Camii. The mosque has been modified by so many different rulers over the centuries that it has come to possess elements of several different architectural styles. The **Ak Medrese,** a block away, is worth visiting if you have nothing better to do. Built in 1409, this Selçuk style *medrese* earns its name from the white marble inscriptions above the portal (*Ak* means "white"). Niğde's **Archaeological and Ethnographic Museum** was closed for renovations at the time of publication but is expected to re-open in the summer of 2001.

IHLARA ☎382

The Ihlara Valley, tucked away between rolling green hills, is one of Central Anatolia's most famous hiking sites. As one approaches Ihlara, a massive gorge (100m deep, 200m wide, and 14km long) suddenly heaves into view, cleaving the surrounding sea of green. Peace-loving Christians found this valley an ideal hideout from nomadic raiders, and now 105 churches and countless dwellings remain carved into the canyon walls. The serene village of Ihlara rests at the southern end of the canyon and makes for the best point of entry into this hidden world.

TRANSPORTATION AND PRACTICAL INFORMATION

Package tours from Göreme and Ürgüp run to the valley, and may be the best option for solo travelers. Dedicated pioneers can catch the Ankara bus in Nevşehir (1hr., every hr. on the hr., $3 to Aksaray), hop off at Aksaray, and take a bus to Ihlara (1hr.; 11am, 2, 6pm; $.75). Get off near the turnoff for the valley entrance, where the pensions are, to avoid walking to the center of town at the bottom of a steep 1km hill. In an emergency, call the **police** (☎451 20 08). The 24-hour **Eczane pharmacy** (☎453 75 41) is in the town square, on the right side of the road to Derinkuyu. The **hospital** (☎453 70 06) serves standard medical needs. The tiny **PTT** is on the ground floor of the *belediye* building at the turnoff for the valley. It offers standard **phone cards,** stamps, and **telegraph services,** but no money exchange. (☎453 71 00. Open 8:30am-12:30pm, 1:30-5:30pm.) **Postal code:** 68570.

ACCOMMODATIONS AND FOOD

Ihlara's pensions line the road that forks left at the valley entrance. Many pensions will run you to the valley entrance or to Selime in the morning. The only food served outside the pensions is at the excellent **Ihlara Restaurant** (lunch $2-4), near the official entrance to the gorge, and at a cluster of second-rate eateries around the square (*pide* and *kebap* $1.50-3).

Akar Motel (☎453 70 18; fax 453 75 11) offers 10 motel rooms and 8 smaller, homier pension rooms with bath and balcony. Both are clean and comfortable. Breakfast included. Dinner $3-4. Singles $9.70; doubles $19.

Bişginler Ihlara Pansiyon (☎/fax 453 70 77) has spacious rooms with balconies, hot water, and toilet. Free car or tractor excursions to Hasan Dağ with a *saç tava* picnic and Turkish music. Cozy restaurant-lounge serves *saç tava* at dinner for $2. 12 rooms. Breakfast included $8; campers $6; tents $2.50.

Pansiyon Anatolia (☎453 74 40; fax 453 74 39) has a campsite and 15 small rooms, some with showers and balconies. A pleasant, if mysterious, floral smell lingers in the halls. Breakfast $2.50; dinner $2-4. Bed $5; tent $3. Closed in winter. V, MC.

Aslan Camping, Restaurant, and Pension (☎457 30 33) marks Ihlara Valley's 3km point, in the town of Belisirma. Pitching a tent in the valley is illegal, so overnight hikers can party around the Aslan bonfire instead. Restaurant patrons camp for free, otherwise $3.20 per tent (rentals available). Nearby pension with 22 rooms charges $8 per person, breakfast included.

HIKING THE VALLEY

Most people visit the valley on a guided tour from Göreme or Ürgüp. These tours usually hike 3 of Ihlara's 14km, starting at the Ihlara entrance and ending in Belisirma, where a restaurant and campsite mark an official exit point. Continuing north, another official entrance/exit point is halfway into the valley, in Yaprakhisar (the Aksaray bus also passes through here). The full 14km hike ends in the town of Selime, through which the last Aksaray-Ihlara bus passes at 5:30pm. To reach the valley's official entrance from the town square, head 1km uphill toward Aksaray (a sign marks

"Ihlara Valley 2km") and take the first main intersection to your right. A paid parking lot and Ihlara Restaurant mark the official entrance, where 400 stone stairs bring you down the gorge to the frescoed rock churches. You're best off hiking until Belisırma with the river on your right, as most of the stone churches will be on your left. To hike the opposite way (south, from Selime to Ihlara), take the 7 or 7:30am Aksaray bus and get off at Selime. Ask the locals to point you to the valley entrance (vadı girişi). Depending on your pace and the amount of exploring you do, the 14km hike takes about six hours. The flat and well-worn path involves a few scrambles among the boulders north of Belisırma, and rainy-day hikes can be dangerous on the slick rocks. Hiking alone is ill-advised. (Open 8am-7pm. $2.50.)

The Ihlara Valley consists of 14km along the north-south Melendiz River, which runs from Selime to Ihlara village. Sixteen of the valley's 105 churches are open to visitors, and most of these are within 1km of the official valley entrance in Ihlara. The first one you are likely to see is **Ağaçaltı Kilise** (Church Under the Trees), at the base of the stairs leading into the valley. Spectacular blue and white angels encircle the Christ figure on the well-preserved dome. Another 30m south past the Ağaçaltı (to the right after descending the entrance stairs, away from Belisırma) lies the **Pürenliseki Church**, whose faded walls enclose the many martyrs of Sivas. The **Kokar Kilise** (Odorous Church), 70m farther along, celebrates biblical stories with colorful frescoes and ornate geometrical ceiling crosses.

Sümbüllü Kilise, 100m down river from Ağaçaltı Kilise, is noteworthy for its rock facade and five deep, arched bays separated by pillars. Cross the bridge opposite the Sümbüllü Kilise, and walk up the stairs 70m down river to find the **Yılanlı Kilise** (Snake Church), named for a display of Satan's serpents. Having seen Yılanlı Kilise, you're better off back-tracking, crossing the bridge, and making your way to Belisırma with the river on your right. The walk is on the whole more pleasant, and you're liable to find a few more churches. From Belisırma to Selime, walk downstream, keeping the river on your left for the clearest path.

GÜZELYURT

About 13km east of Ihlara, pristine hikes, unequaled hospitality, and fresh sights await travelers in the small town of Güzelyurt, situated on the edge of a rolling, green valley. Its friendly home-run pensions and unspoiled charm welcome visitors to life in a true, traditional Turkish "köy." Don't be fooled by the serene surroundings; mysterious underground cities, horseback riding programs, and nearby hikes are sure to keep you busy.

■■ ORIENTATION AND PRACTICAL INFORMATION. Buses to Güzelyurt leave Aksaray (5 per day 11am-6:30pm, return 7:30am-5:30pm; $1.10). Unfortunately, dolmuş don't run between Ihlara and Güzelyurt, but a taxi will take you there for about $6. In the direction opposite Niğde, follow the gaze of Atatürk's left eyeball, and 50m from the town square, you should see **Sibel Eczane**, the town's **pharmacy** (☎451 26 76). It is run by the forthcoming and pleasant Sibel, one of the town's only English-speakers. The **PTT**, a beige building on top of a hill, is situated on the outskirts of town, 10 minutes from the square. Follow the road toward Niğde and take a right just before the sign denoting the boundary of Güzelyurt. (Open M-F, 8:30am-12:30pm, 1:30-5:30pm.) **Postal code:** 68500.

▌ ACCOMMODATIONS. There are few places to stay in Güzelyurt. **Otel Karballa,** behind the bust of Atatürk, is housed in a beautiful 19th-century monastery built by the local Greek population evicted in the 1923 population exchange (see **The Cult of Mustafa Kemal,** p. 16). Linked with the French sporting club UCPA, Karballa offers fantastic equestrian programs, hikes to Ihlara and other valleys, mountain biking excursions, and a valley-view swimming pool (activities $16 per person). Meals are served in the refurbished refectory once used by the monks. (☎451 21 03 or 451 21 04; fax 451 21 07; www.kirkit.com; email karballa@hotmail.com. Dinner $10. Breakfast included. Singles $26; doubles $34.) Cozy **Günalp Pansiyon** (☎451 20 76), past the road to the monasteries, offers 5 rooms, breakfast, and genuine Turkish hospitality for $8 per person. **Nalbantoğlu Pansiyon,** which you can find through the town's grocer of the same name, overlooks Güzelyurt's ranch, lake and enchanting sunset. (☎451 21 69. 3 rooms; $8 per person.) **Kardelen Pansiyon** (☎451 22 55), behind the unmarked blue door next to the pharmacy, and **Halil Pension** (☎451 27 07) are small family pensions that offer bed, breakfast, and dinner for $12. To get to Halil, walk 300m down the road to the pharmacy and take a left on Kayabası Sok. The pension is behind a white gate 200m down the road on your left.

⬛ SIGHTS. Exploring Güzelyurt's unspoiled sights makes for a regular Tom-and-Huck adventure. Walking down the town square with the Atatürk bust on your left, a sharp right downhill points toward the monasteries. Off this road, signs mark two **underground cities**, which don't charge admission and are much smaller than the great cities of Kaymaklı and Derinkuyu. A series of light bulbs lines the narrow tunnels and chambers, where exploration is very do-it-yourself: bring a flashlight. A third underground city in the center of town is kept locked for safety issues, and the key floats about among villagers. Down the hill from the underground cities, a $2.40 ticket will get you into Monastery Valley and a courtyard with the Camii and Sivişli Churches. The paradoxically named **Camii Kilise** (Mosque Church) was originally built in 385 as the Church of St. Gregory of Nationtus. It sported many beautiful frescoes, all of which were whitewashed or stolen when the church was converted into a mosque in 1923. The mosque is seldom used for worship, but villagers are still resistant to the proposal of restoring the frescoes and converting the mosque into a museum. Call out if the door is locked, and someone will arrive to open it. *(Open 10:15am-8:30pm.)* Across the path from the Camii Kilise and up a very steep set of badly formed stone steps is the **Sivişli Kilise** (St. Anargiros Church), formerly a pilgrimage site, with a dome and four columns all carved out of rock. For a fantastic view of the village and valley, climb the stairs to the left of the church.

Monastery Valley itself is a splendid little hike that runs about 4.5km and features over 50 churches and monasteries carved from stone. Follow the steep path to enter the valley; if you hike to the end (about 1hr.), you'll emerge next to the old Greek village of Siurihisar, at which point you're best off hiking back in order to avoid a ludicrous cab fare. *(Valley open 8am-7pm.)*

AKSARAY

☎382

Aksaray has seen Assyrians, Hittites, Persians, and Alexander the Great, all of whom wisely moved on once their business was done. In 1470, the Ottomans forcibly transplanted many of the city's residents in order to boost the Muslim population of İstanbul. Most travelers will wonder why Aksarayans didn't jump at the opportunity to leave. A few Selçuk and Karamanoğlu sites aside, noisy and large Aksaray has nothing to offer the traveler but a bus station with connections throughout Cappadocia and the rest of Turkey.

⬛ TRANSPORTATION. To get to the main square from the otogar, turn left out of the building, make the first left, and walk for 5 min. **Buses** run to: **Alanya** (12hr., 8pm, $11); **Ankara** (3hr., frequent 6am-6:30pm, $5); **Antalya** (11hr., 8pm, $10); **Güzelyurt** (1hr., 5 per day 11am-6:30pm, $1); **Ihlara** (1hr., 3 per day 11am-6pm, $.60); **İstanbul** (9hr., frequent 8-10pm, $10); **İzmir** (11hr., 7:30pm, $11); **Kayseri** (2½hr., frequent 5:30am-7pm, $4.25); **Konya** (2hr., frequent 6am-6:15pm, $4.25); **Nevşehir** (1hr., every hr., $2); **Niğde** (1½hr., 6 per day 8am-5pm, $1.50). Nevşehir-Konya and Nevşehir-Ankara buses stop at the Mobil station on the ring road, 2½km from the center of town. Either take a taxi ($5), or walk (ask for the *şehir merkezi*).

⬛ ORIENTATION AND PRACTICAL INFORMATION. The **tourist office** (☎212 50 51 or 212 35 63) is on the left a few blocks past the main square. The easiest way to get there is to turn right as you exit the Ulu Camii park. (Supposedly open M-F 8am-5pm.) A number of **banks** and **ATMs** are around the square, but none offer currency exchange. To change money, head over to any of the *döviz* offices (change bureaus) across from the mosque; try **Cakarlar Döviz & Altin.** (☎214 24 24; fax 214 22 23.) The **police** can be reached at ☎212 66 50 or 212 11 85. Aksaray is home to a large, quite modern **hospital** (☎212 91 00, 213 10 43, or 213 52 07), at the entrance to town. The two **internet cafes** charge $1.50 per hour; one is 100m up the road from the otogar toward the main square, and the other is 50m from the main square toward the tourist office. To find the **PTT,** take a right before the square, walk a few minutes to the park, and turn left—it's across a small side street from the camii. From here, the office, marked by a large roof antenna, should be visible. (Open daily 8:30am-12:30pm, 1:30-5:30pm.) **Postal code:** 68200.

▐▝▟ ACCOMMODATIONS AND FOOD. Rooms in Aksaray can be very cheap, often for good reason. Women traveling alone and unmarried couples may have some difficulty finding accommodations. The ones listed here are among the less questionable. To get to **Otel Ihlara** turn left out of the otogar, cross the street, and take another left on a small dirt street; the hotel is in a large, unmarked blue building. It offers large, clean rooms with phones, fridges, and bath. (☎213 32 53; fax 213 18 42. Breakfast included. Reserve in advance. Singles $10; doubles $12. Student discounts available.) **Aksaray Pansiyon** has large, clean rooms, a wicker-roofed terrace, a sunny TV salon, and a kitchen. Exit the otogar by the Pension Çakmak, cross the street, and continue down the opposite road. (☎212 41 33. Breakfast $2.50. Singles $6.50; doubles $11; triples $16.) If you choose to avoid the city center, you can camp at **Ağaçlı Turistik Tesisleri**, which is accessible only by a $7-8 round-trip taxi ride. (☎215 24 00. $4 per person; $3 to park a camper.)

The center of town is replete with unremarkable, cheap *lokantas*. The **Golden Apple Pastanesi** (☎213 67 65) is a pastry shop buzzing with the music of teenagers' cell phones and adorned with funky ceiling art. It features Turkish preserves such as *kuru pasta* (stuffed cheese pastries; $4 per kg) and *susamlı peynirli* (salt-covered pastries), along with ice cream and a selection of sweets.

▨ SIGHTS. The **Zinciriye Medresesi,** built in the Karamanoğlu period, is a museum of artifacts from the diverse inhabitants of Aksaray's past. Works of the Hittites, Greeks, Romans, Byzantines, Selçuks, and Ottomans are on display, including a Hittite stone marker, a 3rd-century Roman eagle sculpture, and a cannon from WWI. To get there, head away from the otogar past the city square, turn right, and walk downhill. (Open Tu-Su 8am-noon, 1:30-5:30pm. Free.) Built by the Karamanoğlu in the early 15th century, the **Ulu Camii,** across from the PTT, remains one of the town's religious centers. The **Eğri Minare** (Crooked Minaret), five minutes further up the main road and on the right, was built with red bricks in the 13th century (Selçuk period). Its 92 stairs cannot be climbed because the structure is leaning. The street below is partially cordoned off in anticipation of any steel rope failure. Rumors claim that this crooked minaret inspired Pisa's famous tower.

HACIBEKTAŞ   ☎384

> I have rained with the rain and I have grown as grass.
> I have guided aright the country of Rum;
> I was Bektaş, who came from Khurasan.
> ——Hacı Bektaş Veli

Over seven centuries ago, a Sufi named **Hacı Bektaş Veli** warned a shepherd not to lead his sheep onto a certain hill, where the wolves would certainly decimate his flock. The shepherd scoffed at the warning and left his herd grazing unattended for a few moments, when, lo and behold, the sheep were killed by marauding wolves. When the suspicious shepherd found the remains of his flock, he demanded eyewitness testimony to confirm that wolves were to blame. Suddenly, at the behest of Hacı Bektaş Veli, five large rocks on the hill made their way over to the shepherd and affirmed that wolves had indeed killed the sheep.

Five kilometers from those stones of lore is a village of about 8000 that takes its name from its most romanticized inhabitant. Although the details of Hacı Bektaş

Veli's birth and death are unclear, his progressive beliefs inspired a dervish order, the **Bektaşı,** that continued to spread his teachings and to exert religious and political influence in both the Ottoman Empire and in modern Turkey (see **Sufism,** p. 27). Hacıbektaş hosts a **festival** every year from August 16-18 to honor its Sufi namesake. The town has attracted followers for centuries, and today the festival draws thousands of pilgrims from all over Turkey.

▣ ☏ TRANSPORTATION AND PRACTICAL INFORMATION. The T-junction where **Atatürk Bul.** (which becomes **Nevşehir Cad.** after the museum) runs up against **Hacı Bektaş Veli Bul.** forms the center of town. Marked by a statue of the great Sufi master, this intersection also serves as the local bus stop. A number of bus companies have booths nearby. Buses leave for: **İstanbul** (5:30, 8pm; $15); **İzmir** (6pm, $15); **Kırşehir** (8:30am, 2, 6pm; $1.25); **Konya** (8, 9am; $6); **Mersin** (12:30, 3:30pm; $7.50); **Nevşehir** (noon, 4:45pm; $1.25).

Services include: the **tourist office** (☎441 36 87; open M-F 8am-noon, 1:30-5:30pm); a **pharmacy** (☎441 36 58), opposite the museum; a **hospital** (☎341 30 15 or 341 35 85), down Nevşehir Cad., on the left; the **PTT,** on Atatürk Bul., between the museum and town square (open daily 8am-12:30pm, 1:30-5:30pm). **Postal code:** 50800.

�⌂ ACCOMMODATIONS AND FOOD. The **Hotel Hünkar,** in the complex of shops opposite the museum, offers 16 basic but serviceable rooms. A mysterious wall-sized photograph of a ski lodge dominates the lobby. (☎441 33 44. Singles with bath $8.) Even more basic is the **Fuat Baba Pensiyon,** down Hacı Bektaş Veli Bul., about 1km from the museum. (☎441 30 70. Singles $5, with bath $7.)

Many eateries in the center of town serve standard food ($2) in rooms decorated with a curious combination of portraits of Hacı Bektaş Veli and soft-core porn.

▣ SIGHTS. The ▣ **Hacıbektaş Müzesi,** at the end of Atatürk Bul., includes the lodge of the Bektaşı dervishes and the Sufi's tomb. It is centered around three main courtyards, and Anglophone visitors can listen to a recorded walking tour. The mostly unremarkable first courtyard contains the ticket booth and the Three Saints Fountain, built in 1902. Pass through the Door of the Three at the end to enter the second courtyard, dominated by a rectangular pool with a lion-shaped fountain. The **Aş Evi** (dervish kitchen), through the first door on the right, contains a number of cooking utensils, including a massive black cauldron. The second door on the right leads to the small but exquisite **Tekke mosque.** The series of rooms on the left includes the **Ceremonial Hall,** where Bektaşı ritual ceremonies were held. The nine-vaulted ceiling represents the nine levels of the celestial path. Enter the third courtyard through the Gate of the Six, where you'll pass a corner commemorating Atatürk's visit here in 1919. Filled with the graves of dedicated dervishes, the courtyard has two main buildings which house the dead. To the right, under the shade of the 700-year-old **Wish Tree,** stands the mausoleum of the second greatest Bektaşı, Balım Sultan, who was responsible for spreading the order into Europe. It is said that God will grant the wishes of those who tie ribbons to the tree. The antechamber of the main building is the tiny room (*çilehane*), where dervishes meditated to achieve communion with God. The main chamber, called the Forty Saints area, displays a number of the order's prize possessions. Hacı Bektaş Veli's opulent coffin is in a small room that has been adorned with hand-painted motifs. Doorways in the museum are tiny not because the Bektaşi are unusually petite, but because short entrances make visitors bow humbly before God. Like the Tekke Mosque, this building is holy ground; visitors should dress conservatively and remove their shoes, though it is not necessary for women to wear headscarves. In the Sufi tradition, stepping directly on a doorway's threshold is disrespectful, so try to take wide bounds when you enter. (*Museum open Tu-Su 8:30am-noon, 1:30-5:30pm. $1.25.*)

KAYSERİ ☎352

Even though Kayseri (pop. 500,000) is easily Cappadocia's largest metropolis, wide streets and large public spaces save the city from claustrophobia and over-crowding. In spite of Kayseri's accumulation of fascinating attractions over the course of its 6000-year history, foreign visitors (though welcome) are unusual here. Despite its Westernized appearance, the city is culturally and religiously con-servative; entertainment is scarce, and female tourists should keep prudent dress in mind. With few tourist traps, this renowned carpet center could be your one-stop shop for cheaper buys than those in İstanbul.

Originally the capital of an independent Cappadocia, the city was renamed Cae-saria under the reign of the Roman emperor Tiberius Caesar (AD14-37). Like most other cities in Anatolia, it then passed from the Romans to the Byzantines, and later to the Selçuks. Kayseri (a derivative of the town's Roman name) blossomed under Selçuk rule. As an important post along trade routes, Kayseri amassed the wealth that financed such 13th-century monuments as the Hunat Hatun Complex and the Gevher Nesibe Tibbiyesi, the world's first medical university.

◧ TRANSPORTATION

Flights: Erkilet Airport (☎338 33 53), 90km northeast of Kayseri down Sivas Cad., is the most organized in Cappadocia. To **İstanbul** (1hr.; daily 9:55am, 9pm; $84, stu-dents $67). Buy tickets from the **THY Office**, 1 Yıldırım Cad. (☎222 38 58; fax 222 47 48), which also offers an airport shuttle to the city for $1.60 (call ahead to arrange).

Buses: From the otogar (☎336 43 73), on Osman Kavuncu Cad. to: **Adana** (5hr., fre-quent 7am-1am, $8); **Aksaray** (2½hr., frequent 9am-5pm, $5); **Ankara** (4½hr., every hr. 7am-2am, $8); **Antalya** (12hr., frequent 5-11:30pm, $11.50); **Bursa** (10hr.; 6:30, 7:30pm; $13); **Erzurum** (9hr., frequent 7-11pm, $13); **İstanbul** (11hr., frequent 9am-10:30pm, $17); **İzmir** (12hr., frequent 6pm-midnight, $17); **Konya** (5hr., frequent 8am-6pm, $8.20); **Kuşadası** (14hr., 6pm, $16); **Mersin** (5hr., frequent 7am-midnight, $8); **Nevşehir** (1½hr., every hr. 7am-2am, $3); **Sivas** (2hr., express, every hr., $5); **Trabzon** (14hr., frequent noon-midnight, $15). Minibuses to **Ürgüp** leave from a stop on Osman Kavuncu Cad., near Düvenönü Meydanı (1½hr., every 2hr. 8am-6pm, $2.50).

Trains: Kayseri's *gar* (☎231 13 13), at the end of Hastane Cad., sends daily trains to: **Adana** (6½hr.; 2:20, 4:40pm; $5); **Ankara** (8½hr.; midnight, 1, 4, 4:30am; $5); **İstan-bul** (22½hr.; 4, 4:40am; $7); and **Kars** (17hr., 4:40pm, $7), among others. Buses are faster and more reliable.

✸ ORIENTATION

The **otogar** is on **Osman Kavuncu Cad.** which meets **Park Cad.** and **İnönü Bul.** at **Düvenönü Meydanı.** From Düvenönü Meydanı, Park Cad. leads to the massive **kale**, a Roman-era stone fortress which dominates the center of town. To the right is **Nazmi Toker Cad.**, known as **Bankalar Cad.** for its many banks, where a massive underpass crosses Park Cad. Kayseri's second main square, marked by the clock tower, is **Cumhuriyet Meydanı,** where Park Cad. meets Sivas Cad. and **Seyyid Burhanettin Bul.** heads away from the fortress, past the Hunat Mosque Complex and the tourist office to the **Döner Kümbet** (Revolving Tomb), the **Archaeological Museum,** and the **Seyyid Burhanettin Türbesi** (tomb).

⊘ PRACTICAL INFORMATION

Tourist Office: 61 Kağnı Pazarı (☎222 39 03 or 231 92 95; fax 222 08 79), next door to the Hunat Hatun Complex. English-speaking staff will gladly inundate you with maps and brochures. Open daily 8am-5pm.

ATMs: Sprout all over **Bankalar Cad.**, where you'll get lira for your V/MC/Cirrus/Plus.

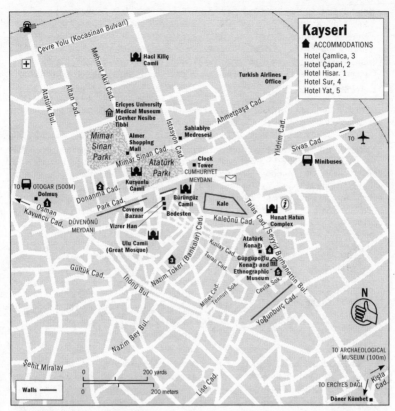

Kayseri

♠ ACCOMMODATIONS

Hotel Çamlica, 3
Hotel Çapari, 2
Hotel Hisar. 1
Hotel Sur, 4
Hotel Yat, 5

Hospitals: Erciyes Tıp Fakultesi Hastanesi (☎437 49 01 or 437 4902), **Özel Gülhane Sağlık Merkezi,** 24 Kiçikapu Cad. (☎222 48 54 or 222 48 35), and **Hunat Sağlık Merkezi** (☎221 06 00), next to the Hunat Hatun Complex. All have **ambulance services** and English-speaking doctors. In an emergency, call ☎336 27 50.

Internet Access: There are a number of Internet cafes in the residential area north of Sivas Cad. and east of the THY office. Slow access costs around $2.50 per hr.

PTT: On Sivas Cad. in Cumhuriyet Meydanı. 24hr. phones. Poste Restante. telegraph, fax, and **currency exchange** 8:30am-5pm. **Postal code:** 38000.

▌ ACCOMMODATIONS

Since Kayseri is not a backpackers' town, the fancy hotels and even the cheaper, spartan ones tend to be overpriced. Most hotels will negotiate a discount for business groups, but rarely for students. Hotel prices rise about 25% in the winter, as most visitors (whether businessmen or skiers) come with snowfall.

Hotel Yat, 14 Talas Cad. (☎232 73 78 or 232 35 95). Definitely the most postmodern joint in town. The name is a play on words: *yat* means both "go to bed" and "yacht" (hence the nautical decor). The 8 balconied rooms are bright and colorful, with orange phones and blue and green walls. Singles $13; doubles $28. Add $2 for bath.

Hotel Çamlıca, Bankalar Cad., 14 Gürcü Sok. (☎232 34 93 or 232 23 54; fax 231 43 44). Bright lounge, tacky palm-tree murals and 70s posters will make you feel like one of Charlie's Angels. Your mission? To conquer the shared *à la turka* toilets at the end of the hall. Breakfast included. Singles $11, with shower $13; doubles $23, with shower $24.

Hotel Çapari, 12 Donanma Cad. (☎222 52 78; fax 222 52 82). On the street parallel to and 1 block north of Park Cad. Like the other red-carpet, mid-range, 2-star hotels in Düvenönü Meydanı, Çapari has a restaurant, rooftop sauna, and well-furnished rooms with TV and phone. Breakfast included. Singles $30; doubles $50; suites $75. V/MC.

Hotel Hisar, 24 Osman Kavuncu Cad. (☎336 66 44). Bare rooms and dark halls have a strangely charming quality. Free laundry facilities. Singles $8; doubles $14; triples $22.

Hotel Sur, 12 Talas Cad. (☎222 43 67; fax 231 3992). Inside the old town walls, by the Ethnographic Museum. Central location and 2-star comfort. Singles $18; doubles $29.

🍴 FOOD

Kayseri is the present-day capital of Turkish cold cuts. This is the place for *pastırma* (spicy, salted, sun-dried beef or veal with garlic, pepper, and parsley; $4 per kg), *sucuk* (extremely spicy, well-salted beef sausage resembling a long, thin salami; $3 per kg), and *salam* (salted Turkish salami, similar to *sucuk* but less spicy). Inexpensive picnic fare is also easy to find, as the many bread shops sell loaves of fresh bread for about $.20. Vegetarians might consider the specialty cheese, *tulum peyniri*, or *bal* (honey; $2.50-3.25 per jar), both sold at most food stores. For dessert, try Kayseri's special *kaymaklı ekmek kadayıfı* (fluffy, honey-saturated bread topped with sweetened cream; $1.50), which is not as unbearably sweet as many Turkish desserts. Many inexpensive restaurants can be found on the back streets parallel to Bankalar Cad. Kayseri is not a city that parties until dawn; even most of the restaurants shut down by 10 or 11pm.

🍴 İskender Kebap Salonu (☎231 27 69 or 222 69 65). On Millet Cad. behind the fortress. Overwhelmingly recommended by locals, this glossy 3-story restaurant serves an unbeatable meal of *İskender kebap* (thin layers of butter-soaked meat blanketing *pide* bread and served with yogurt) and a tall, foaming *ayran* for just $3.50. Placemats explain the history of *İskender kebap*, for those devoted meat historians.

🍴 Divan Pastanesi (☎222 39 74). An incredible string of pastry shops. The best one is just around the corner from İskender Kebap Salonu. Cases of sweets, breads, and pastries hug the sleek glass and metal furniture. Open M-Sa 7:30am-10pm, Su 7:30am-9pm.

Dinçerler Et Lokantası, around the corner from İskender, serves excellent *tavuk çöp şiş* (cubes of chicken grilled on wooden skewers), *piliç, köfte,* or *ızgara köfte* ($3).

Avcılar İskender, 10A Park Cad. (☎222 70 45). Between Düvenönü and Cumhuriyet Meydanı. Serves first-rate *köfte* and *piliç şiş* ($3) with delicious *kuru fasulye* (pinto beans; $1.50). The 2nd-floor dining room has nice street views.

👁 SIGHTS

GEVHER NESİBE TİBBİYESİ. In May 1993, NASA named a newly discovered mountain on Venus after the Selçuk princess Gevher Nesibe Sultan in recognition of her contribution to modern science. When she died of tuberculosis in 1204, her elder brother, Giyasettin Keyhüsrev Sultan, commissioned a medical center in her name. The **Gevher Nesibe Tibbiyesi** opened in 1206 to become the world's first medical school and the most technologically advanced hospital. The hospital treated everyone for free, and patients, doctors, and medical students were admitted regardless of religion. Today its two seminaries house the **Erciyes University Medical Museum,** where you can take a tour of a 13th-century operating room, mental ward, clinic, and hospital. Considering the many difficulties of running a large-scale, pre-electric hospital, the scope and scale of the facility are impressive. The skylight in the *ameliyat hane* (operating room) concentrates maximum sunlight on the operating table. The equally well-planned *hamam* managed to heat both halves of the building during Kayseri's snowy winters. Perhaps most remarkably, the *akıl hastanesi* (mental hospital) is equipped with one of the earliest known P.A. systems: sound vents in the upper corners of the stone cells enabled a single person upstairs to address all the patients at once. This seminary is not without a tomb of its own—look out for the low-flying sparrows when descending the stairs to the **Gevher Nesibe Sultan Mescidi ve Sandukası** (little mosque), where the princess is interred. Other alcoves are dedicated to relevant quotations from the Koran ("Whoever saves one life has in a way resurrected us all") and hospitals founded by Turkish women (from Gevher Nesibe to Valide Sultan in 1845). Atatürk's last brushes with the medical world are also memorialized, including a photo of a syringe, labeled (in Turkish), "The last injection of *extrait hepatique* administered to Atatürk before his death by Dr. M.K. Berk." *(From Park Cad., cut north across Atatürk Parkı and Mimar Sinan Parkı. Open W-Su 8am-5pm. $1.25, students $.75.)*

HUNAT HATUN COMPLEX. Early in the 13th century, Alâadin Keykubad, Sultan of the Anatolian Selçuks (1219-1237), captured the Alanya fortress from its Persian ruler, Kir Vart. One of the conditions of Vart's surrender was that his daughter Hunat ("lady" in Persian) Mahperi Hatun would become the sultan's wife. After her marriage, Lady Hunat (as she is redundantly called in English) converted to Islam and commissioned the **Hunat Hatun Complex** (Külliyesi), made u⸝ of the **Hunat Hatun Camii, Türbe** (tomb), **Medrese**, and ▧ **Hamam.** The mosque, built in 1238, is the largest in Kayseri. Dress conservatively (women with head scarves), and remove your shoes before climbing the stairs to the tomb, the domed stone chamber containing three coffins. The engraved coffin is that of Lady Hunat herself; beside her rests her grandson, Selçuk Hatun. The occupant of the coffin closest to the entrance is a mystery. The still-functioning hamam has excellent facilities, separate for men and women. *(In the center of town, across from the kale. ☎ 231 58 05. Hamam open daily 8:30am-5:30pm. Bath $2.50; massage and scrub $2.50.)*

GÜPGÜPOĞLU KONAĞI AND ETHNOGRAPHIC MUSEUM. Built in the 15th century and later expanded, the **Güpgüpoğlu Konağı** is a beautifully preserved 1419 Ottoman mansion. Stroll through the replica kitchen, sitting room, and bride's room, where mannequins in period dress evoke a sense of the life and times of the Ottoman upper crust. Converted into the **Ethnographic Museum,** the rest of the mansion houses a significant collection of coins, guns, costumes, and household objects, mostly from the Ottoman period. In the summer, Turkmen nomads set up camp on the mountains, along the roads up to **Erciyes Dağı,** where they raise woolproducing sheep away from the hot climate of lower altitudes, which often makes their sheep sick. When cold weather sets in, they sell the sheep in the city and either move on or return to their home villages. *(Staying inside the old city walls, head south from the kale about 150m, just beyond Hotel Sur. Güpgüpoğlu Konağı ☎ 222 95 16. Museum ☎ 222 21 49. Open Tu-Su 8am-5pm. $1.60.)*

ARCHAEOLOGICAL MUSEUM. The first of two halls in this small, fascinating museum displays objects from the Early Bronze Age, along with treasures unearthed from nearby Kültepe, a 6000-year-old settlement that peaked as an Assyrian trading colony (2500-1750 BC). Among the pottery and metalwork are some tablets bearing the earliest writing found in Anatolia, dating to the Neo-Hittite Period. The centerpiece of the second hall is the Heracles (Hercules to the Greeks) Sarcophagus, a large marble tomb depicting the 12 labors of Heracles. *(Head down Talas Cad., turn left at Kışla Cad., and follow the signs to the museum. ☎ 222 21 49. Open daily 8am-5pm. $1.)*

CITADEL. First built by the Byzantines in the 6th century, and improved upon by the Selçuks, the massive **kale** is Kayseri's most distinctive landmark and houses its most budget-friendly bazaar. Replete with countless jewelers and cobblers, the *kale* is connected to the even larger, centuries-old covered markets nearby. The oldest, which was built in 1497, is the **Bedesten bazaar,** near the Ulu Camii. It is connected to the **Vizier Kervansaray** (Vezer Han; 1723) which still bustles with wool traders and other craftsmen.

MOSQUES. West of the fortress, past the bazaar, the **Ulu Camii** (Great Mosque, a.k.a. Camii Kebir or Sultan Cami), constructed in 1134, is Kayseri's oldest mosque. Built on 42 stone pillars by Melik Mehmet Gazi Danişmendoğulları, this mosque's minarets stand 46m high. In the northwest corner of Atatürk Parkı, the **Kurşunlu Camii** (built in 1585) is the only piece of architecture in Kayseri designed by hometown hero Mimar Sinan Eseri (1492-1588), Turkey's most famous architect (see **Ottoman Architecture,** p. 23). Though far smaller than the city's other major mosques, the delicate arches and graceful design are clearly the products of a great master. Next to the *kale*, the immense and beautiful **Bürüngüz Camii** is a 20th-century imitation of the Blue Mosque in İstanbul. As with all mosques, visitors ought to dress conservatively (women preferably with head scarves), remove their shoes before entering, and speak softly while inside.

TOMBS. One of Kayseri's distinguishing features is its wealth of preserved Selçuk tombs. Probably the most interesting is the 13th-century **Döner Kümbet** (Turning Tomb), on a traffic island down Talas Cad. on the way to Erciyes, south of the *kale*. The 12-sided, cone-roofed tomb does not revolve, but it is said that the pure of heart will see it slowly rotating early in the morning. Don't rush to beat the roosters; the surrounding traffic will make you dizzier than a clean soul ever could. Though visitors are not allowed inside the tomb, they can peer through a metal grate in the wall to the uninteresting, empty space.

The sacred **Seyyid Burhanettin Türbesi** was built in the early 13th century for Burhanettin Tirmizi (1165-1244), the first *mevlevi* at Hunat Hatun Medrese. This five-star tomb includes two separate and heavily trafficked prayer rooms for men and women. Inside you'll find the teacher's enormous sarcophagus under a gargantuan chandelier and a beautiful dome decorated with rows of Selçuk floral designs. *(Turn left at the Döner Türbesi to find the tomb nestled in a little park. Remember to leave your shoes by the door or carry them in a bag. Women may want to wear a head scarf.)*

🎒 DAYTRIPS FROM KAYSERİ

SULTAN HAN. The 13th-century Sultan Han, Turkey's second largest *kervansaray*, served as a safe haven for traveling merchants during the Selçuk period (see **Selçuk Architecture and Decorative Arts,** p. 22). Built in 1255 by Vizier Celeddin Karatay, the building now echoes with the incessant calls of bats from the great hall, replacing the murmurs of road-weary travelers and traders. After walking through the old guest quarters and hamam, notice the intricate snake patterns on the *eyvans* (arches) of the mosque in the courtyard. Be sure to climb the stairs to check out the roof and the dome over the great hall. *(Sultan Han is about 45km from Kayseri, and less than 1km from the Kayseri-Sivas highway. To get there, catch one of the hourly Kayseri-Sivas buses and ask to be let off at Sultan Han ($3). To return to Kayseri, flag down the Sivas-Kayseri minibus at about 20min. past the hour. Open Tu-Su 9am-1pm, 2-6pm. $.60.)*

ERCİYES DAĞI (MT. ERCIYES). The snow-capped heights of hulking Erciyes Dağı are clearly visible from Kayseri and serve as a perpetual reminder of the volcanic fury that shaped the Cappadocian landscape. At 3917m, the mighty (now extinct) volcano is the tallest mountain in Central Anatolia. From late October through March, skiers flock to the 2215m-high **Tekir Yaylası** (ski track), equipped with two chair lifts, two teleskis, and three beginner's lifts. The accessible part of the mountain runs from the ski base to a point 2770m high and offers sports fans a ski altitude of about 550m. and heavenly conditions on the few trails Erciyes offers. *(Lifts open daily 8am-5pm. $2 to the top. Day pass $15; ski rentals $12.)* The **Sağlık Ocağı** first-aid clinic (☎342 20 31) caters to winter emergencies. The **Kardelen Restaurant and Disco Bar** (☎342 21 01) at the ski base, is open year-round, though summer meal selections are limited to piles of meat. A true winter hot spot, Kardelen never loses its party spirit; the neon disco downstairs pulsates even when sheep are the only passers-by.

In the summer, hiking groups trek the mountain from the ski base up. While experienced mountaineers may climb the west face to the summit (eight hours up; three down), the melting snow and falling rock render this a dangerous route. Alternatives include a shorter, eight-hour hike to the mountain's bowl and back or a tougher south-side climb to the summit. In any case, be sure to wear sturdy boots and dress in layers. To get to Erciyes, take the Kayseri-Develi dolmuş (every hr. 7am-9pm, $.80), and ask to be let off at **Kayak Evi** (☎342 20 31; fax 342 20 32), the year-round hotel at the base of the ski slopes. *(In summer $10 per person; hot-water turned on only for groups; no meal service. In winter $35 per person includes bath and meals.)* Groups can call ahead and speak with Veysel, the hotel's Turkish- and German-speaking ski instructor, to arrange a guided hike ($15 per person). Independent travelers may have problems with logistics, and a trekking tour arranged elsewhere ahead of time may be the best way to attack Erciyes.

KONYA AND ENVIRONS

KONYA   ☎332

Come, come again and again! Come be you unbeliever, idolator or fire worshipper. Whoever you are and whatever your condition come! Our hearth is not the threshold of despair. Even if you have fallen a hundred times, come!
        —Celeddin-i-Rumi

Konya (pop. 675,000) brims with the lingering flourishes of the Selçuk dynasty, evoking a world of whirling mystics and hushed prayers in sacred candlelit mosques. The city has long played host to spiritual visionaries. In Roman times, when it was called Iconium, a visit by St. Paul initiated the city's gradual transformation into a Byzantine Orthodox patriarchate. After the Selçuks of Rum invaded and made it their capital in the 11th century, Konya's churches were replaced with the greatest mosques of the era. In 1228, the great Persian poet Celeddin-i-Rumi, known to many Turks simply as Mevlâna ("our master"), moved to Konya with his family from their home in Afghanistan. Rumi's poetry and life inspired the now-famous Sufi order known for its Whirling Dervishes. Today, Muslims often stop in Konya to visit Mevlâna's tomb before embarking on the *hajj* to Mecca.

Despite a large student population, Konya remains one of Turkey's most religiously conservative cities. Konya University, with 45,000 students, has had a huge effect on the city's tolerance, although staunch conservatism remains. Women should wear long skirts and baggy shirts, and women traveling alone should cover their hair with a traditional headscarf. Shorts are not recommended for men or women. More information concerning women in public is below in the listings.

▐ TRANSPORTATION

Flights: Konya's airport is about 20km out of town. Buses link the PTT and the airport every hr. ($3). Turkish Airlines flies to İstanbul (1hr.; daily 7am; $65, students $50).

Trains: Konya's modest railway station is 2km from the town center on Ferit Paşa Cad. To **İstanbul** (13hr.; daily 5:45, 9pm; $10). To get to town from the *gar*, take a city bus (5min., every 30min., $.70), or catch a dolmuş on Ferit Paşa Cad. (frequent, $.60).

Buses: The otogar (☎235 46 49 or 235 46 47) is on A. Hilmi Nalcacı Cad. **Özkaymak** (☎352 29 98) and **Aksel** (☎234 1106) service Konya.

BUS SCHEDULES

DESTINATION	DURATION	FREQUENCY/TIME	PRICE
Adana	5 hr.	6:30am, midnight	$12
Afyon	3 hr.	10am, 1, 3:30, 11pm, midnight	$7
Alanya	5 hr.	9am, noon, 4pm, 12:30am	$8.50
Antalya	6 hr.	9, 11am, 4pm, midnight	$10
Aydın	8 hr.	9pm	$12
Bodrum	12 hr.	11am, 7:30pm	$15.70
Bursa	7 hr.	9am, 2pm, midnight	$12
Denizli	6 hr.	7:30am-11:30pm	$10
Erzincan	10 hr.	8pm	$17

DESTINATION	DURATION	FREQUENCY/TIME	PRICE
Erzurum	12 hr.	8pm	$19
Göreme	3 hr.	9am-6pm	$9
Isparta	4 hr.	9, 11am	$8.50
İstanbul	12 hr.	10am-midnight	$17
İzmir	8 hr.	10am, 1, 3:30, 11pm, midnight	$12
Kayseri	5 hr.	8, 10pm, midnight	$10
Malatya	10 hr.	10pm, midnight	$15.70
Marmaris	13 hr.	10pm	$15.70
Mersin	4 hr.	6:30am, midnight	$9.50
Milas	9 hr.	7:30, 11am, 7:30pm	$16
Muğla	10 hr.	10pm	$16
Sivas	8 hr.	8pm	$13

Local Transportation: A **Light Railway** connects Konya University, the otogar on A. Hilmi Nalcacı Cad., and Alaaddin Tepesi. Tickets can be purchased at any of the many stops along the route ($.30, students $.20).

Taxi: Stations are located throughout the city, mostly near the main tourist sites like Mevlâna Müzesi and Alaadin Tepesi.

✴🛈 ORIENTATION AND PRACTICAL INFORMATION

Konya's main street runs between the turquoise-domed **Mevlâna tomb** and the circular **Alaaddin Bul.**, which embraces **Alaaddin Tepesi** (Alaaddin Hill), actually a prehistoric burial mound. The section of road closest to the Mevlâna Müzesi and tomb is called **Mevlâna Cad.**; the other half is **Alaaddin Cad.** Most of Konya's sights, hotels, and restaurants are in this area.

Tourist office: 65 Mevlâna Cad. (☎351 10 74; fax 350 64 61). Across from the Mevlâna Müzesi. Look for a green sign. English-speaking staff member usually available. Take advantage of their free city and regional maps, but take their accommodation and carpet shop advice with a grain of salt. Open M-F 8am-noon, 1:30-5:30pm.

Banks: On either side of Alaaddin Cad. Most have **ATMs**.

Luggage storage: At the otogar. $3 per bag. Open 6am-10pm.

Hamam: (☎353 00 93). Across from the PTT, behind Şerafettin Cad. Open for men daily 6am-midnight, for women daily 7am-9pm. $5.

Police: (☎322 28 16). On Ferit Paşa Cad. Open 24hr.

Hospital: State-run **Nunune Hastanesi** (☎235 45 00), is on Hastane Cad. The receptionists don't speak English, but most doctors do. **TIP Medical Faculty** (☎323 26 00) is on the outskirts of town.

Internet Access: Cafe Internet, Büyük Ihsaniye Mah. Isaniye Cad. Birlik Ap. No. 5 (☎321 60 31). Uncomfortable atmosphere for women. $.60 per hr. Open 9am-10pm.

PTT: (☎352 02 55), on Alaaddin Cad., to the left while facing Alaaddin Tepesi. Postal services open daily 8:30am-5pm. Phones: 8:30am-11pm. **Postal code:** 42000.

▌ ACCOMMODATIONS

Most of the hotels and pensions are tucked away in alleys off Mevlâna Cad. Room rates are high, but prices tend to be negotiable. Hot water is often only available upon request. Otel Derviş and its neighbor Mavi Köşk Oteli, which are fine for groups of 2 or more, are the standard backpacker haunts. Women traveling alone should spend the extra money and stay in the nicer hotels along the main streets.

Otel Derviş, Mevlâna Cad., 11/C Bostan Çelebi Sok. (☎350 24 81; fax 351 16 88), a block from Mevlâna Müzesi. Head down Mevlâna Cad. toward the museum, and turn right down an alley 2 blocks before Hotel Dergâh. 11 clean rooms with bath. Singles $8, with bath $10; doubles $12-18; triples $20-24.

Konya

▲ ACCOMMODATIONS

Hotel Dergâh, 3
Mavi Köşk Oteli, 4
Otel Çeşme, 2
Otel Derviş, 5
Otel Şems, 1

CENTRAL ANATOLIA

TO ☐ (2.5KM)

Üçler Cemetery

Koyunoğlu Museum

Kerimler Cad.
Topraklık Cad.
Aksaray Cad.
Sanhasan Cad.
Durak Fakih Cad.
Oyaloğlu Cad.
Köprübaşı Cad.
Anafartalar Sok.
Nazımbey Cad.
Servet Sok.
Mevlâna Tekke
Selimiye Camii
Selimiye Cad.
Menguç Cad.
Mevlâna Cad.
Ayanbey Sok.
Aziziye Camii
Sırçalımescit Cad.
İstanbul Cad.
BAZAAR
Türbe Cad.
Karaman Cad.
Mevlâna Cad.
Tevfikiye Cad.
Baba Sultan Sok.
Gülistalar Sok.
Heper Sok.
Şerafettin Cad.
Şerafettin Camii
Altınbay Sok.
Mecidiyeler Sok.
Sultan Veyet Cad.
Latif Sok.
Borsalı Sok.
Şems Sok.
19 Mayıs Sok.
Şems Sok.
Şems Mosque
Sina Sok.
Abdullah
Salim Sok.
Mazbardabalık Sok.
Alaaddin Cad.
PTT
Sahip Ata Cad.
Vali İzzet Bey Cad.
Archaeological Museum
Ankara Cad.
Tile Museum
Sırçalımedrese Cad.
Ethnographic Museum
Furkandede Cad.
Karatay Medres
Selçuk Pavillion
Alaaddin Camii
Alaaddin Tepesi
Alaaddin Bul.
Mümine Hatun Sok.
Sabit Sok.
Sultan Şah Cad.
Bus Office
M. Muzaffer Cad.
Lavrende Cad.
Hastane Cad.
✚
Ince Minare Medrese
İnce Minare Sok.
Mücellimbaşı Sok.
Abdülaziz Paşa Cad.
Atatürk's House
Kadı İzzettin Sok.
Saf Fahri Sok.
Nasreddin Hoca Sok.
Çadıran Sok.
Sait Paşa Cad.
Sultan Cem Cad.
Kazım Karabekir Cad.
Atatürk Cad.
Ambereis Cad.
Vatan Cad.
Millet Cad.
N
400 yards
400 meters
0
0
TO ✚ (500M)
Ferit Paşa Cad.
Atatürk Stadium

Otel Şems, Şems Cad. No. 8 (☎353 54 53). Quiet modern hotel on a side street. Ride the elevator to your basic room with clean beds and shower. A better option for women traveling alone. Bargaining can save you lots. Singles $25; doubles $37.

Mavi Köşk Oteli, Mevlâna Cad., 13 Bostan Çelebi Sok. (☎350 19 04), next to Otel Derviş. 9 rooms with TV, some with bath. Singles $12; doubles $15-24; triples $16-24.

Hotel Dergâh, 19 Mevlâna Cad. (☎351 11 97 or 351 76 61; fax 351 01 16), next to the tourist office. Convenient location. This 2-star hotel features 86 simple rooms with phones and bath. Breakfast included. Rooms $16-30.

Otel Çeşme, İstanbul Cad., 35 Akifaşa Sok. (☎351 24 26). Follow Mevlâna Cad. toward Alaaddin Tepesi on Mevlâna Cad., turn right on İstanbul Cad. and take the 1st left; the hotel is on the right. 25 small, spotless rooms with TV and bath. Singles $16; doubles $22; triples $28; quads $36.

🎭🎵 FOOD AND ENTERTAINMENT

Konya's specialty is *fırın kebap*, a chunk of oven-roasted mutton served unceremoniously on a *pide*, sometimes under the alias *tandır kebap*. Konya is also renowned for its Turkish pizza, here called *etliekmek*. There are plenty of cheap eats on Konya's backstreets, but the atmosphere might be uncomfortable for women traveling alone. Women should choose restaurants that advertise a family *(aile)* section. Unsurprisingly, alcohol is hard to find in this conservative burg.

Köşk Konya Mutfağı (☎352 85 37). With the tourist office on your left head toward the Mevlâna Müzesi, turn right on Topraklık Cad., then turn right on Menguş Cad. A bare brick wall and plastic Coke sign conceal a 150-year-old house that serves terrific food. Specialities include *gebzeli çöp kebap* (*kebap* with eggplant; $2), *çöp şiş,* and *etli yaprak sarması* (meat-stuffed grape leaves with yogurt; $1.50).

Şifa Lokantası, 56 Mevlâna Cad. (☎352 05 19), will fill you up for $2-3. Vegetarian options. Caters to tourists and families. Open daily 7am-10:30pm.

Deva Restaurant, 68 Mevlâna Cad. (☎354 27 40). Smaller and less touristy. Free deliveries. Has a comfortable *aile* (family) section. Meals $2-3. Open daily 7am-11pm.

Hotel Şahin, 39 Mevlâna Cad. (☎251 33 50). One of the few bars in Konya. Beer $1.60; vodka $4 per shot; whiskey $6 per shot. This dimly lit establishment is closed to single women. Open until 2am.

Ankara Pastanesi. Turn left from Alaaddin Cad. onto Alaaddin Bul.; the cafe is on the left. Try the delicious milk puddings. Frothy instant coffee provides a quick caffeine fix.

📷 SIGHTS

Konya's museum is dedicated to recalling its Selçuk glory days. The city's architectural riches showcase such classic Selçuk designs as carved loops and swirls, luminous tiles, octagonal or decagonal floor plans, and flowing quotations from the Koran. To read more about Selçuk architecture, see **Selçuk Architecture and Decorative Arts,** p. 22. There is great religious significance of these sights; for tips on visiting Muslim holy places, see **Visiting Mosques,** p. 33.

MEVLÂNA MÜZESİ. Mausoleum, museum, and monument in one, the **Mevlâna Müzesi** (a.k.a. the **Mevlâna Tekke**) is marked by its tower of light blue tiles, erected over a century after Rumi's death. Inside the well-touristed mausoleum lie the turban-domed sarcophagi of Rumi, his father, his oldest son, and his closest disciples. The original site of the museum was a rose garden planted by the sultan for Rumi's father. Later, Sufis who joined the Mevlevi order lodged in the chambers here. In 1926 the dervish lodging became an archaeology museum, and in 1954 it was restored as the Mevlâna Museum.

Enter through the "Door of the Dervishes," passing the ticket window. To the immediate right, in front of the kitchen pavilion, is the **Wedding Night Pool,** named for the day of Rumi's death, the night of his union with his Creator. Every year on that date the dervishes would gather around the pool and perform whirling

"I WAS RAW, then I got cooked, and finally got burnt," - Rumi
Mevlâna Celeddin-i-Rumi, the greatest of all mystical Persian poets, made his home in 13th-century Konya after leaving his native Balkh (now part of Afghanistan) during the Mongol invasion. Following in his father's footsteps, Rumi became a highly respected traditional Islamic scholar and was the head of a *medrese*, a theological school. When Rumi was about 37 years-old, he met **Şems of Tabriz,** a 60-year-old wandering Sufi master from Iran. Şems purposely shattered Rumi's dependence on intellect as the only means for knowing God and, in doing so, revealed Rumi's own source of divinity and the power of love. The two men became inseparable and went into week-long periods of **sohbet,** mystical conversation and merging. Şems mysteriously disappeared in 1248 (he was purportedly murdered by envious members of Mevlâna's entourage). Rumi expressed the wrenching experience and revelations that resulted from this spiritual consummation in spontaneous and ecstatic poetry, music, and dance. Above all, Rumi considered love the greatest guide on the mystical path. His passion-filled poetry of flaming hearts, moonlit gardens, and grievous longing is an account of the meeting, loss, and fervent mystical union of Rumi with Şems, Rumi with God, and Rumi with his true divine self as they all become interchangeable in their spiritual positions of Lover and Beloved.

Rumi's most famous poems were compiled into *Divan-i-Şemseddin-i-Tabriz* (1870 pages, 42,000 lines of poetry) and his later work of lyricism and stories, *Mathrawi* (25,618 couplets). His verses have inspired centuries of readers throughout the Middle East, South Asia, Africa, and the West. After Rumi's death on December 17, 1273 (called his "Wedding Night" with the divine), his disciples founded the Mevlevi Order (see **Mevlevi Order,** p. 27), known abroad as the "Whirling Dervishes" because of their meditative ceremonial dance, or **sema.** For English-speaking readers, Coleman Barks provides an evocative English translation of Rumi's poetry. Anne-Marie Schimmel's *I am Wind, You are Fire* is an excellent introduction to Rumi's life and teachings.

rituals. Today, visitors pray here and drink the sacred water. To the left stands a **fountain** given to the site in 1512 by Sultan Yavuz Selim. The Mevlâna museum and mausoleum is straight ahead. In the first small room, the **reading room,** dervishes recited and copied the Koran. Some verses, written in extraordinary Arabic, Persian, and Turkish calligraphy, hang on the walls. In the hushed and colorful main hall, approximately sixty **tombs** hold the bodies of Rumi's family and friends. Male disciples are buried in the tombs capped with turbans; those without turbans hold female disciples. The color of the turban indicates the status of the person buried in the tomb: green means that the person was a family member and white indicates a friend. Bigger turbans represent chiefs of the dervishes. The dervishes used the four-piece gold and silver **Nişan Taş** displayed along the left wall to collect April rainwater, believed to have medicinal properties. To the left of the bowl is a famous line from one of Rumi's poems written in Arabic, Persian, and Turkish: "Either be as you appear, or appear as you are." The two large tombs at the end of the hall hold Rumi and his son. The beautiful black silk cloth with gold embroidery that covers the sarcophagi was given by Sultan Abdülhamid II in 1894. Rumi's father is buried in the wooden sarcophagus next to these two tombs.

The next room was constructed in the 16th century for the dervishes' **whirling rituals.** Musicians performed on the raised platform, and men watched on the lower platform to the right. Women watched from upstairs. Now the space houses prayer rugs used by Rumi, crystal chandeliers with ornate marble lattices, Rumi's clothing, and the *serpuş* (hat) of Şems, Rumi's most beloved mentor.

The next room houses manuscripts from the 12th-19th centuries. Among them are old editions of Rumi's work, copies of the Koran (one of which fits into a tiny silver pillbox), examples of rich Islamic miniatures, and several specimens of calligraphy. A box holds part of Mohammed's beard. There are also two strings of prayer beads, used by dervishes for group prayer: assembled on the floor in a circle, the dervishes rotated the large elliptical balls in turn with their prayers.

In the **kitchen pavilion,** across the courtyard from the museum, wax models illustrate the dervishes' daily life. The wax figures show dervishes cooking and eating, all in meditative silence, discussing theological questions, and whirling in a trance. The single figure in the small room to the left is a *Nevniyaz* (dervish candidate). Candidates sat in a room in the kitchen and prayed for three days. If the dervishes agreed to let him train, he underwent an initiation known as the "1001 days of suffering," in which he had to successfully complete 18 kinds of services, ranging from toilet cleaning to food serving. If he found his shoes in his cell when he woke up in the morning, he continued his service; if they were gone, he had to leave quickly and quietly. Fortunately for the model, his shoes are still there.

Every year from December 10-17, Konya celebrates Rumi's extraordinary life. The festivities include one of the few opportunities to see whirling dervishes perform. The celebration is popular, so reserve rooms in advance. *(Museum open M 10am-5:30pm, Tu-Su 9am-5:30pm. $3. The building is considered a holy place. The staff will lend those wearing shorts a sarong to wrap around their legs. Shoes must be removed and carried. Women should cover their heads. Head scarves are provided at the door.)*

NEAR THE MEVLÂNA MUSEUM. The **Selimiye Camii,** completed in 1587, stands next door to the Mevlâna Müzesi. Konyans gather to pray here under a beautifully decorated tomb and crystal chandeliers that hang almost within arm's reach. The design on the mosque's carpet mimics the one on the dome above.

Aziziye Camii, three minutes from the Mevlâna Tekke, was built between 1671 and 1676 at the behest of Sultan Mehmet IV's bookkeeper and renovated in 1867. The mosque's design is a mix of 17th-century Baroque and 18th-century Rococo.

ŞERAFATTİN CAMİİ AND MAUSOLEUM OF ŞEMS. Across from the PTT on Mevlâna Cad. stands the impressive Şerafattin Camii, whose Selçuk mosaic tiles and classic Ottoman minaret suggest the periods of its construction (13th century) and restoration (17th century). If you walk out behind the Şerafettin Camii down the small street past a hamam and into a small park on the left, you will come to the Mausoleum and Mescid of Şems of Tabriz. The Selçuk-style mausoleum, supposedly built on the site where Şems's murdered body was found, contains his wooden catafalque. The attached room was also used as a *Şemshane,* a place where the dervishes would practice their meditative ceremonial dance *(sema).*

ALAADDİN CAMİİ. The Alaaddin Camii stands atop **Alaaddin Tepesi,** a hill that may well conceal countless as-yet undiscovered layers of human history stretching back to the Bronze Age. Closer to the surface are a park and some quiet tea gardens, crowned by the 13th-century Alaaddin Camii. One of Konya's oldest fixtures, it was built when the region was newly conquered, and its Syrian Selçuk architecture shows the influence of non-Islamic cultures. Recently renovated, the mosque now has iron beams that span the *eyvans* (arches) and columns that emerge gracefully from the floor. The visually eloquent *mihrab* (prayer niche), covered in inscriptions and multicolored tiles, compensates for the lack of external decoration. Tiny stones are stuck in crevices along the outside wall of the mosque, facing the Selçuk Pavilion. Visitors pick up a small stone from the area, make a wish or say a prayer, and then throw the stone at the wall. If it sticks, the prayer will be answered or the wish will come true. *(Mosque open daily 9:30am-5:30pm.)*

KARATAY MEDRESE AND TILE MUSEUM. This 13th-century school for teaching the Koran and Shar'ia Law to young Selçuks was built by Emir Celâleddin Karatay, a close friend of the Mevlâna and a "voice of reason" to counter Rumi's spiritual and poetic ecstasy. The *medrese* has rather logically become a **tile museum,** since the interior itself is a marvelous example of Selçuk tilework. A tile-covered dome hovers over a square central pool. The now-empty pool, which was open to the sky, reflected the stars at night. Students measured the reflections to learn the distances between stars. The inside of the dome is covered with an pattern of interlinked stars, though age and decay have destroyed the upper tiles. Displays include tiles from Kubadâbâd Palace, near Beyşehir Lake, and ceramic plates from Konya. *(On Alaaddin Bul.* ☎ *351 19 14. Open daily 9am-noon, 1:30-5:30pm. $1.40.)*

OTHER MUSEUMS. Konya's **Stone and Woodwork Museum** is in the **İnce Minare Medrese** (Medrese of the Slender Minaret). The highlight is a massive stone portal whose arch is engraved with Arabic script and bas-relief plants. The minaret from which the *medrese* took its name was struck by lightning in 1901 but has since been rebuilt. Inside are works from the Selçuk, Karamanoğulları, and Ottoman periods, including winged angels and double-headed eagles carved in stone. The woodwork exhibit features carved doors and window shutters, *yazma* stamps, and a ceiling. *(On Alaaddin Bul., next to McDonald's.* ☎ *351 32 04. The museum was closed at the time of publication. Regular hours are daily 9am-noon, 1:30-5:30pm. $1.40.)*

Konya's **Archaeological Museum** contains artifacts from prehistoric times to the Byzantine era. One of the 3rd-century Roman sarcophagi on display illustrates the labors of Hercules. Ancient toiletries include Roman ivory combs and toothpicks. *(On the small Şuhip Ata Cad., about 7 blocks south of Alaaddin Tepesi. Open Tu-Su 9am-noon, 1:30-5:30pm. $1.40, children and high school students free.)*

Turn left out of the Archaeological Museum gates to get to the **Ethnographic Museum,** displaying ornate embroidery, clothing, jewelry, metal hats, and hunting equipment that includes a small metal contraption used to make deer noises. *(*☎*351 89 58. Open Tu-Su 9am-noon, 1:30-5:30pm. $1.40.)*

🚍 DAYTRIP FROM KONYA

SİLLE. Sille, 8km away, can be visited in one morning. Visitors come to see the **Aya Elena Kilisesi,** a 4th-century Christian church decorated by more recent frescoes. (Open Tu-Su 9am-4pm. $1.) The two caves facing the church were inhabited at one point. *Sille-bound bus #64 leaves the municipal bus stop (on Alaaddin Cad., across from the PTT) every 30min. ($1), stopping in the middle of Sille's main street, distinguished by the stores and standard-issue Atatürk bust. The PTT is ahead and around the corner (open M-F 8:30am-12:30pm, 1:30-5:30pm), and the church lies 50m past the PTT on the main road.*

ÇATALHÖYÜK. The neolithic town of Çatalhöyük, dating back to the 8th millennium BC, vies with Jericho for the coveted title of "World's First City." Near the town of Çümra, 50km south of Konya, the 9000-year-old town is touted as the most important archaeological site in Turkey. Çatalhöyük was inhabited by between 5-10,000 people for 1000 years, and was one of the largest and most complex settlements of its time.

Archaeologist James Mellaart discovered the site in 1958. The most sensational objects from Çatalhöyük are the **female figurines,** particularly one of an ample, naked woman, seated on a throne of leopards, who appears to be giving birth. Archaeologists have found carved female breasts that have **vulture beaks** within them. Some conclude that the town was a matriarchal society that worshipped the Mother Goddess, but not enough evidence has been found to support the theory.

Çatalhöyük families lived in compact mud-brick houses which were used for cooking, sleeping, and religious worship. When family members died, they were buried under platforms in the house. About every 100 years, residents would fill in the house and build a new one on top of it, eventually forming a mound 20m high.

The enormous site is slowly being excavated by an international team. Archaeologists eagerly await discoveries about and insight into the ancient culture's art, symbolism, mythology, textiles, use of pottery, metals, and wood, and domesticated plants and animals. Although the most important finds have been whisked to Ankara's **Museum of Anatolian Civilizations** (see p. 363), the site offers a unique, interactive experience. If you visit the site between July and mid-September, you can watch the excavation in progress and talk with the many archaeologists and other workers. At other times, a guard will show you around. The site includes a laboratory, a museum, and a replica of a Çatalhöyük house. *The easiest way to get to*

CENTRAL ANATOLIA

Çatalhöyük is to take a dolmuş from Konya's otogar to Çümra (45min., 6-7 per day 9am-6pm, $.75), from where a taxi can take you the remaining distance (10min.; $20, try to bargain).

WESTERN ANATOLIA

EĞİRDİR   ☎246

This small, conservative, ex-fishing town in the Central Taurus mountains is surrounded on three sides by Turkey's fourth largest lake, Eğirdir Gölü (540 sq. km), a beautiful body of water whose color shifts with the strength of the wind, rippling from hues of jade to tones of gray. The lake yields innumerable carp and bass, and in the fall, orchards fill with golden delicious apples.

█ TRANSPORTATION

Trains: The *istasiyon* (☎311 46 94) is 2km west of downtown, off 2nd Sahil Yolu. To: **Ankara** (8hr., 6pm, $6); **İstanbul** (13hr., 5:30pm, $8); **İzmir** (10hr., 9:30pm, $7). Schedules change frequently, so call ahead. Station open daily 6am-noon, 5-7pm.

Buses: The otogar (☎311 40 36) is south of town center. To: **Ankara** (6hr.; 10:45am, 12:30pm; $15); **Antalya** (2½hr., 8am-6pm, $7); **Cappadocia** (7hr.; noon, 8:30, 11:30pm; $12); **Isparta** (30min., 8am-6pm, $1.20); **İstanbul** (10hr., 7:30pm, $14.50); **İzmir** (7hr., 4 per day 10am-4:30pm, $8.40); **Konya** (4hr., every hr. 8am-8pm, $8). Frequent **local buses** and dolmuş (7am-10pm, $.25) leave from behind the mosque, across from the otogar. One runs to **Yeşilada** (1.5km) and the other to the train station and the 3 beaches.

█ ORIENTATION

The city consists of a peninsula jutting into the lake, **Eğirdir Gölü,** and two islands connected by bridges to the mainland. The city center, marked by a walk-through minaret, a marketplace, several restaurants, and pensions, is on the mainland. The **otogar** sits directly between the minaret and the lake shore. The closer island, little more than a floating *çay* garden, is called **Canada** (JAHN-ah-dah), which means "soul island" or "life island." Most of the town's pensions are on the more bulbous **Yeşilada** (Green Island), which is connected to Canada, eh.

To reach the lake, walk straight from the otogar past the Hizir Bey Camii on the right, and follow the road as it curves left onto **2nd Sahil Yolu.** This street runs past the **PTT** and the **tourist office** to a **soldiers' casino** *(askeri gazinosu)* and several pensions before hitting **Yazla Plajı, Altıkum Plajı,** and **Bedre Plajı. Yenimahalle Cad.** begins beside the otogar, 100m south of the archway, and continues past the modern hospital on to Konya.

█ PRACTICAL INFORMATION

Tourist Office: 2nd Sahil Yolu No. 13 (☎311 43 88; fax 312 20 98). From the otogar gate, walk straight and follow 2nd Sahil Yolu as it curves up and to the left. English spoken. Open M-F 8:30am-6pm.

Banks: Türkiye İş Bankası, on 2nd Sahil Yolu, before the PTT (when walking from the town center) has a V/MC/Cirrus/Plus **ATM.** Several other ATMs dot the town center.

Luggage Storage: At the otogar. $1 per bag. Open roughly 6am-8pm.

Police: (☎311 53 63), on 2nd Sahil Yolu, 20m past the PTT.

Pharmacy: (☎311 22 01), across from the police station. Open 8am-midnight.

Hospital: (☎311 47 90), on Yenimahalle Cad. Turn left out of the otogar and walk 300m. Open 24hr. The health center, **Sağlik Ocağı** (☎311 48 55 or 311 64 90), is next to the hospital. Open M-F 8am-5:30pm. Both have English-speaking doctors.

PTT: (☎311 45 90), on 2nd Sahil Yolu on the way to the tourist office. Information and *poste restante* daily 8am-11pm. Fax and express mail M-F 8:30am-12:30pm, 1:30-5:30pm. **Postal code:** 32500.

⌐ ACCOMMODATIONS

Eğirdir has some excellent pensions scattered on the mainland and on Yeşilada. Since most don't have singles, they will make single travelers pay for double occupancy during high season (June-Sept.). To save $2-3, let pension representatives at the otogar bid on you with their rivals. Bargaining is acceptable.

⊠ Lale Pension, Kale Mah, 6 Sok. No. 2 (☎312 24 06; fax 311 49 84). Exit the otogar and head right to the large yellow signs leading to Lale, 2min. from the shore. Backpackers clamber for 9 clean rooms with hardwood floors and bath. The mountaineer owner offers sage advice on trekking, boat trips, and other outdoor activities. Enjoy the astounding terrace view. Laundry $3. Dinner $6.50. Breakfast $3.50. $15 per person.

⊠ Köşk Pension-Restaurant, 37 Yazla Mah. (☎311 43 82 or 311 63 50). At the top of 2nd Sahil Yolu, 800m from town. Free car service to and from town and the beaches; call for pick-up or meet the driver at the Tuborg/Pepsi sign across from the otogar. Most of the 17 rooms have showers and lake views. Owned by the local Pepsi distributors, Köşk features a free "Pepsi Tur" every Sunday, which shuttles guests in a Pepsi truck 70km south to the scenic Çandır Canyons (9am-9:30pm). Boat tours also available. Singles $6-10; doubles $12-20.

Choos Choos Pansiyon (☎311 49 26; fax 311 67 64). On Yeşilada Mah. The newest pension on the island, offering clean modern rooms overlooking the lake. Breakfast $2.50. Singles $7; doubles $14.

Altınkum Plajı Camping (☎311 48 57), Altınkum Plajı. Roughly 2km past the tourist office. Bear right at the "major junction" sign after Köşk. *Plaj*-bound dolmuş leave from across the otogar (every 15min.). Camp on Eğirdir's best-loved beach and enjoy electricity, hot showers, and phone. Small tents $2; large tents $4; cement shell $6; small double occupancy concrete hut with shower and toilet $10.

⌖♫ FOOD AND ENTERTAINMENT

Eğirdir cooks make a mean fish. The local specialities are *sazan* (carp), usually served whole; *levrek* (bass), generally filleted and fried in a light tomato flavored batter; and *karides* (shrimp). All of these are available at the lake-front pension-restaurants of Yeşilada.

Kervansaray Restaurant (☎311 63 40; fax 311 63 90) serves more luxurious meals. Offers a wine list and an extensive menu including *ızgara çeşitler* (mixed grill; $5) and fish ($4-10), all served on a lakefront terrace. *Levrek* comes in a light, crisp tomato batter that must be tasted to be believed ($2.60). Open 9am-midnight.

Big Fish Restaurant (☎311 44 13). Veer left as you enter Yeşilada; Big Fish is on the right facing the water. Airy and colorful restaurant with a lovely view and scrumptious, fresh fish dishes ($2-9). Open 7am-midnight.

Disco Bar, near the bazaar, is the town's after-hours social center. Off-duty soldiers, university students, and tourists pack the small dance floor, drink from the full bar, or sit outside on the terrace in the cool night air. Beer or *rakı* $2.

⌐ SIGHTS

BEACHES. The small **Yazla Plajı,** originally a retreat for secondary-school teachers, is now open to the public. Past the Köşk Pension at the top of the hill, signs point to Eğirdir's finest beach, **Altınkum Plajı** (Golden Sand Beach), 1½km farther along 2nd Sahil Yolu. *($.40; parking $.80; dolmuş from town center $.25.)* Some 11km farther is the less-crowded **Bedre Plajı.** While there are no real beaches on Yeşilada, you can clamber down the rocky shore and swim wherever you like for free.

WISE ASS Nasrettin Hoca is a fabled 14th-century Ottoman wise man, born in a village near Eğirdir. Spouting wisdom still quoted by Turks today, he traveled the land with his talking blue donkey. One day he arrived at the mosque unprepared for his sermon, and asked the audience if they understood what he was going to tell them. When they all replied "no," he told them that if they didn't understand, there was no point in telling them, and he sat down. The following week when he asked the same question, they all replied "yes." Since they knew what he was going to say, he told them there was no point in saying it, and sat down once again. By the third week, half of the audience said "yes" and the other half said "no," to which Hoca bowed politely and asked those who knew to tell those who did not. Turks often consider these vignettes not merely interesting, but uproariously funny. Apocryphal Nasreddin Hoca comics often appear on plastic *ayran* cups, most accompanied with English subtitles.

Pisidia Tours (☎311 53 62; fax 311 58 58) runs tours and parties on Lake Eğirdir on a small yacht. The boat's skipper, the enterprising Turko-Australian Aydın Akdüz, lets backpackers sleep on board or camp out on deck under the stars for $4-6.

OUTDOOR ACTIVITIES. Eğirdir will not disappoint nature lovers or adventurers. **Paragliding** ($40), which offers aerial views of the glorious lake, is brand new (check with the tourist office for information). Pensions often organize fishing trips, camping, and other watersports. Other possibilities include trekking and wind surfing. Prices are negotiable.

Warm hospitality and gorgeous views make the village of **Akpınar Köyü** a popular trekking destination. The trek takes about two hours. Twenty-seven kilometers east of Eğirdir lies the 1½km long **Zindan Cave**, which once served as a Roman temple dedicated to Eurymedon. Explorers should bring a flashlight. Near the village of Sağrak, 40km southeast of Eğirdir, stands the ruined Pisidian city of **Adada,** now consisting of an ancient temple's fallen columns, sarcophagi, and an amphitheater. Coins have been found here dating to the first century BC. Only 25km south of town, **Lake Kovada National Park** teems with wildlife that draws butterfly collectors in the spring. Avid walkers can follow a popular stretch of the **King's Road,** by which Lydian rulers once traveled from Ephesus to Babylon. The trail passes through the Çandır Canyons near Lake Kovada. (*Many pensions can be coerced into running excursions to these sights, especially if you get a group to conspire. Otherwise the only other way is by taxi, which wait at the sites and drive you back to Eğirdir. Ask your pension owner to help negotiate prices: Zindan $40; Adada $35; National Park $40.*)

OTHER SIGHTS. Poised atop an archway in the town center is one of two **walk-through minarets** in the world. Built by the Selçuks in the 13th century, it is part of the **Hızır Bey Camii.** Walking under the arch is considered good luck.

AFYON
☎272

Surrounded by vast fields of innocuous-looking poppies, Afyon ("opium") is a leading producer of the world's opium, grown here legally for pharmaceutical use. Afyon is proud of its role in the War of Independence, when Atatürk made his headquarters here. If you delight in views, a climb to the towering Hittite fortress will likely be the highlight of your stay. However, modern-day Afyon is a rather nondescript town, so it's best to stop just long enough to see the sights and try some *lokum* (Turkish delight) before getting on your way again.

TRANSPORTATION. Afyon's otogar is on the eastern edge of town along **İsmet İnönü Cad.** To reach the city center, take dolmuş #2, opposite the otogar on İsmet İnönü Cad., to **Bankalar Cad.** ($.20). **Buses** to: **Alanya** (6½hr., 10 per day 8am-1am, $10.50); **Ankara** (3hr., 25 per day 5:30am-3:30am, $6.50); **Antalya** (4½hr., 25 per day 7am-1am, $7.50); **Aydın** (5hr., 13 per day 11am-12:30am, $8, via **Denizli**); **Bodrum** (7hr., 2 per day 10:15pm-midnight, $10); **Bursa** (4hr., 13 per day 11:30am-3:30am, $10); **Datça** (8hr., 11, 11:30am, 11:45pm, 12:30am; $13.75); **Denizli** (3hr., 13 per day

11am-12:30am, $6.50); **Eskişehir** (2¼hr., 11 per day 8:45am-1am, $4.25); **İstanbul** (7hr., 15 per day 11am-12:30am, $13); **İzmir** (5hr., 30 per day 8:30am-3am, $7); **Kayseri** (8hr., 2 per day 6pm-midnight, $16); **Kuşadası** (service only in summer; 7½hr., 5 per day 11am-3am, $10); **Kütahya** (1½hr., 9 per day 7:30am-11:30pm, $3); **Konya** (4hr., 15 per day 12:30pm-3:30am, $8); **Marmaris** (8hr., 5 per day 10:30am-1:30am, $11.25). Depending on the bus company, students may receive a 10% discount.

The *istasyon*, in the northeast corner of town, sends trains to: **Adana** (11-15hr.; 1:10am, 5:40pm; $2-5); **Denizli** (5-6hr.; 5:55pm, midnight, 2am; $2.50); **Eskişehir** (3-4hr.; 5:10am, 3:50, 11:10pm,; $1.75); **İstanbul** (Haydarpaşa station; 8hr., 8 per day 8:10am-3:30am, $4.50); **Konya** (5hr.; 1:10, 3:50, 9:30pm; $2.50); **Kütahya** (2hr., 5 per day 8:25am-1:20am, $1.50). Prices and travel times vary by train. Students and seniors receive a discount. To get to town from the *istasyon*, follow Ordu Bulvarı 2km to Hükümet Meydanı.

▚🔢 ORIENTATION AND PRACTICAL INFORMATION. Bankalar Cad. runs from the İmaret Camii in the south to **Hükümet Meydanı** and the tourist office in the north. In between lie most of Afyon's banks, hotels, and restaurants. **Ulu Camii** and the **Mevlevi Camii** sit to the west, where the fortress rises imposingly over the city.

The **tourist office** is on Bankalar Cad. (☎215 65 25; fax 213 26 23. Open daily 8am-noon and 1:30-5:30pm.) As the name suggests, there are numerous **banks** along Bankalar Cad.; the T. C. Ziraat Bankası has an **ATM** and **changes money** and **traveler's checks.** (Open M-F 8:30am-noon and 1:30-5pm.) For bathing, İmaret Camii's 700-year-old **hamam** is the clear choice. (4 Kurtuluş Cad. ☎215 97 07. Open 6am-midnight. Women $1; men $1.50.) The **hospital** (Afyon Devlet Hastanesi, Atatürk Cad.) can be reached at ☎212 08 02, and the **police emergency number** is 155. Reach **Doğuş Internet Cafe** by turning off Bankalar Cad. onto Dumlupinar Cad. at the PTT. (Dumlupinar 2 Cad., Ersaraç Apt. No. 24/A. ☎215 57 20. $1 per hr. Open daily 8:30am-midnight.) The **PTT**, also on Bankalar Cad., has phones and a currency exchange that cashes traveler's checks. (Postal window open 8am-7pm; exchange open 8:30am-noon, 1:30-5pm.) **Postal Code:** 03000.

▛ ACCOMMODATIONS. The cheapest of Afyon's hotels is the **Otel Lale,** 23 Bankalar Cad. Conveniently located across from the İmaret Camii, Lale offers small, simple rooms above the puttering mopeds of Bankalar Cad. (☎215 15 80. Singles $5.50, $5 for students; doubles (the only rooms with toilet and shower) $10.50, $8.50 for students; triples $15, $13.50 for students.) **Otel Kafadar,** 2 İmaret Camii Cad., offers basic rooms, some with gorgeous mosque views. The hotel has a Turkish toilet and shower on each floor. (☎215 28 36. Singles $3; doubles $5.50, $4 for students; triples $8, $6.50 for students.) Though 2km from the center of town, the **Otel Karaca,** on Ambaryolu Çıkışı directly opposite the otogar, offers the comforts of a fine hotel at a budget-friendly price. Its bright rooms come with TV, bath, and breakfast. (☎215 28 51; fax 213 04 37. Singles $13; doubles $20.)

▛▟ FOOD & ENTERTAINMENT. Shops throughout the city display the local Turkish delight (*lokum*) and sausage (*sucuk*). For a cheap meal, dine on *pide*, *lahmacun*, or *döner* (all under $2) anywhere along Bankalar Cad. Slightly more upscale, the white tableclothed **İkbal Lokantası,** 21 Uzun Çarşı Cad. (☎215 12 05), serves up tasty three-course meals for under $6. İkbal is about 20m down Üzün Çarşı Cad., a side street off Bankalar Cad. **Sinema Günleri** in the Afyon Belediyesi Kultur Merkezi, shows English-language movies with subtitles for the homesick, but is closed from June-Aug. (☎212 09 67. $2.25, students $1.75.)

◙ SIGHTS. Afyon owes its old name, *Afyonkarahisar* ("The Black Fortress of Opium"), to the mighty rock that dominates the city. A hike up the 500 or so steps to the top of the **fortress** affords a thrilling view of the surrounding area, though some report danger of being mugged in the heights. The panorama is especially striking at sunset, when the call to prayer echoes from all 80 of the city's mosques. The route to the fortress passes Afyon's most striking mosques, the Mevlevi Camii and the Ulu Camii. Be warned, though: the walk from the center of town to the fortress can take over an hour. To get there, take Üzün Çarşı Cad., which meets Bankalar Cad. across from the Otel Oruçoğlu. After a few blocks, bear right onto Köprübaşı Cad. at the small roundabout. Köprübaşı Cad. becomes Yukarı Pazar Cad as you walk uphill. Turn left at the POLİS sign and walk up the steps to the **Mevlevi Camii,** originally the site of Afyon's *mevlevihanesi* (dervish meeting place). The *Mevlevhanesi* was established in the 13th century by Sultan Veled, Celeddin-i-Rumi's son (see **I Was Raw,** p. 341). Return to Yukarı Pazar Cad. and continue heading uphill to the **Ulu Camii** (Great Mosque). The Ulu Camii showcases Selçuk mosque construction, with a flat timber roof supported by a forest of more than 40 wooden columns, each capped with a carved *muqarna* (stalactite-shaped) capital. Pray that a guardian caretaker will show up to unlock the doors. Signs at the mosque show the way to the first of the castle's steps.

Back in the center of town, the **İmaret Camii** stands at the southern end of Bankalar Cad. This late Selçuk/early Ottoman mosque provides an oasis of profound silence in this noisy part of town. Near Hükümet Meydanı, in the otherwise peaceful Anıt Park, the emotionally charged **Victory (Zafer) Monument** celebrates Turkish independence. Just across the street, the **Victory Museum** (*Zafer Muzesi*) exhibits weapons, photographs, and other souvenirs of the War of Independence. Most descriptions are in Turkish, but certain museum officials speak limited English. (☎ 212 09 16. *Open daily 8am-noon and 1:30-5:30pm. Free.*) Afyon's archaeology museum (*Arkeoloji Müze*) is on Kurtuluş Cad. (☎ 215 11 91. *Open Tu-Su 8:30am-noon and 1:30-5pm. $1.50, students free.*

KÜTAHYA   ☎ 274

Since the 16th century, Kütahya has been renowned as a center of legendary ceramic artistry. The entire city—mosques, hotels, fountains, and yes, even the bus station—is tiled with intricate patterns of blue and white. Students from Dumlupınar University help keep the city young, and Kütahya's wide-open square with numerous internet cafes and shops creates a busy street scene. But away from the city center, families still live in aging Ottoman houses and women laboriously wash their rugs in the street. Close to Kütahya rest the dramatic ruins of Aizanoi, an ancient Roman city with a spectacularly well-preserved temple.

▐ TRANSPORTATION

Kütahya is a regional capital sprawled at the base of large hills. The **otogar,** better known as the *çinigar* (tile-station) for its elaborate tile decorations, is about 1km out of town, northeast of the center on **Atatürk Bul.** Much more convenient, however, is the bus **terminal** on Afyon Cad. just off the main square (Belediye Meydanı). All buses leaving the otogar also stop at the centrally located *terminal* about 5min. after their departure.

> **Buses:** To: **Afyon** (1½hr., 6 per day 9:30am-7:30pm, $2.70); **Ankara** (4½hr., 10 per day 8am-2am, $8); **Antalya** (6hr.; 11am, 12:30pm, 1:30am; $10); **Bodrum** (7½hr., 1:30am, $13.75); **Bursa** (2½hr., 7 per day 8:15am-3:30am, $7.50); **Denizli** (4½hr., 2 per day 1:30am-7:30pm, $8.75); **Eskişehir** (1½hr., every hr., $1.50); **İstanbul** (6hr., 9 per day 6am-1:30am, $12.50); **Konya** (5hr., 4 per day 11am-1:30am, $10); **Mersin** (10hr., 11am, $16). Buses no longer run to Kayseri.

✦▐ ORIENTATION & PRACTICAL INFORMATION

Coming into town, the central junction is **Belediye Meydanı,** a roundabout whose center is a giant ceramic fountain. Starting perpendicular to Atatürk Bul. and running northwest, **Adnan Menderes Bul.** leads to several hotels and ceramics outlets. Across the roundabout from Atatürk Bul. and leading southwest is Kütahya's main drag, **Cumhuriyet Cad.,** featuring numerous banks, hotels, and restaurants, as well as the **PTT** and the **Ulu Camii.** The Dönenler Camii and Kütahya's museums are in the neighborhood of the Ulu Camii; from here, winding streets lead uphill to some Ottoman houses and the fortress.

Tourist Office: A booth is on Belediye Meydanı, providing excellent maps of the city and colorful brochures describing its many attractions. Open M-Sa 9:30am-12:30pm and 1:30-6pm. For more comprehensive information, see the Tourism Director's office (☎223 19 62), inside the Vilayet Building on Belediye Meydanı.

Hospital: ☎223 60 53. Across from the Vilayet Bina, a 5min. walk up Afyon Cad.

Internet Access: There are many internet cafés in Kütahya. For a fast connection try **Gence İnternet,** at Asım Gündüz Cad., No. 11 (☎223 53 63).

PTT: On Cumhuriyet Cad. Telephones and a **currency exchange.** Open 24hr. **Postal code:** 43000.

ACCOMMODATIONS

The best cheap places are scattered around Belediye Meydanı.

Otel Gönen (☎224 77 99 or 224 78 00; fax 224 78 01), Menderes Buhran, Belediye Meydanı. In the main square. All rooms with private shower, toilet, and TV. Singles $19, $13 for students; doubles $29, $23 for students.

Hotel Yüksel, 1 Afyon Cad. (☎212 01 11). Friendly management. Singles $8, $6 for students; with shower and TV $11, $8 for students; doubles $10, $8 for students; with shower and TV $13, $10 for students.

Otel Benli, 4 Cumhuriyet Cad. (☎216 13 77). Centrally located, but you share a Turkish toilet. The rooms are not the cleanest. Singles $5, $4 for students; doubles $7, $6 for students; triples $10, $9 for students.

FOOD

Cheap kebap restaurants line Cumhuriyet Cad. and Lise Cad., by the roundabout.

Hisar Çaybahçesi, in the *kale* (castle), below the Döner Gazino restaurant. For a unique *çay* experience, order the *semaver* (samovar), an elegant teapot-like device which brews tea over hot coals ($1.25 for 2 people).

Döner Gazino, at the top of the *kale*. Take dolmuş #2 to save a half hour's walk uphill from Belediye Meydanı. There is no better place to spend a late afternoon in Kütahya. Housed in what was once the fortress's central turret, this slowly revolving restaurant provides striking sunset views and refreshing *çay* ($.35). Food is reasonably priced.

Gaziantep Sofrası (☎224 39 60). Walk on Menderes Bul. away from the square and take a right at the corner with the Diamond Gardens Bilardo Salonu. Stands slightly above other restaurants with its wooden exterior and delicious food. A hearty meal of *ayran, lahmacun, kebap,* and *baklava* costs about $3.

SIGHTS

People come to Kütahya to see **tiles.** Though the tile industry had withered to one artisan early this century, today, it seems like everyone makes tiles. Shops selling local ceramics are concentrated along Atatürk Bul. on the way to the otogar and along Menderes and Abdurahman Kasa Bul. near the roundabout. Every July, Kütahya celebrates its craft for three weeks at the Dumlupınar Fuarı, Turkey's largest **handicrafts fair.** The fairground is 2km outside of town along Atatürk Bul.

Kütahya's mosques and museums are clustered at the end of Cumhuriyet Cad., about 1km uphill from Belediye Meydanı. Closest to town is the 14th-century **Dönenler Camii** (on Cumhuriyet Cad.), one of the few remaining *mevlevihanesi* (dervish meeting places) in all of Turkey. In dervish services, musicians sat on the platform encircling the central chamber while dervishes revolved on the floor below. Today Dönenler Camii functions only as a mosque. Though covered by

CENTRAL ANATOLIA

thick green carpet, a trap door in the center of the floor leads to a sacred well. For a token donation of about $.25, the mosque's guardian will show you the well and offer you a (dingy) glass of the water—it is said that those who drink from it are headed for heaven. More likely than not, they're headed for stomach problems.

Further along Cumhuriyet Cad. lies **Ulu Camii** (Great Mosque), originally built in 1410 but renovated in the 17th century by master architect Sinan. The mosque's *medrese* houses Kütahya's **archaeological museum**, at Börekçiler Mahallesi, on Ulu Camii Cad. Here, gaze at works ranging from the late Myosen and Paleolithic eras to the Ottoman period, including artifacts from **Aizanoi** (see p. 350). (☎223 69 90. Open Tu-Su 9am-5pm; $1.50. Students free.) Kütahya's more impressive ▨ **Tile Museum** *(Çini Müzesi)* has found a home behind the Ulu Camii on Gediz Cad. The museum displays works from *çini* masters, some dating from as early as the 14th century. (Open Tu-Su 9am-noon, 1:30-4:30pm. $1.50, students free.) For real history buffs, the **Kossuth Museum** at Börek Mahallesi, Macar Sokak commemorates Lajos Kossuth (1802-1894), one of the leaders of the Hungarian freedom movement. (☎223 62 14. Open Tu-Su 9am-noon, 1:30-5pm. $1.75, students free.)

No visit to Kütahya is complete without a stop at the sprawling **kale,** where the breathtaking view of the plain and distant mountains compensates for the schlep. To get there, either walk uphill along Ertuğrul Gazi Cad. from the Ulu Camii and then bear left onto Kale Sok., or take dolmuş #2 from Cumhuriyet Cad. and ask to be let off at the *kale* ($.25). The dolmuş will stop at the base of a short cobblestone path that ends at the top.

Kütahya's most striking **Ottoman houses** line Germiyan Sok., reached by taking a left off Menderes Bul. just after it intersects with Kapan Cad. In order to preserve Kütahya's crumbling architectural heritage, the Turkish Ministry of Culture recently allotted money to purchase and restore five antique houses.

Recover from all that walking at one of Kütahya's baths. The 700-year-old **Küçük Hamam,** at 65 Cumhuriyet Cad. near Küçükpark tea garden, houses an elegant marble interior and sauna. (Open 6am-11pm; $1.75, students $1.50.) Built in 1549, **Balıklı Hamam** has twin domed hot-rooms and separate rooms for men and women. (☎223 43 54. $1.75, students $1.50.) To get to Balıklı Hamam, walk along Cumhuriyet Cad. and turn right onto Balıklı Cad., near Küçükpark. The hamam is about 200m up Balıklı Cad. on the left at #65.

▨ DAYTRIP FROM KÜTAHYA: AIZANOI

The ruins of Aizanoi lie in and around the small town of Çavdarhisar. Buses leave the Kütahya otogar (1½hr., 12 per day 6am-2am, $1.50), stopping at a BP gas station in the center of Çavdarhisar. Ask for the return schedule when you buy your ticket. From the bus stop, walk about 1km west on the road to Emet and Aizanoi, over a small bridge. Site open daily 8am-noon, 1:30-5:30pm. $1, students free.

The walk to Aizanoi passes through a rural peasant agricultural community, providing a glimpse of Anatolian country life. This ancient Roman city, which features an unusual 2nd-century temple to Zeus, lies in scenic ruin against a backdrop of rolling countryside. Follow the Emet and Aizanoi road to the **old baths,** on the right near the mosque. The baths feature beautiful mosaic floors that are currently being restored. Continuing along the road, cross one of the town's two surviving Roman bridges to the **Temple of Zeus.** Friendly and charismatic guard Nazım Ertaş will unlock the gate of the cool and vast barrel-vaulted **chamber,** which rests directly beneath the temple of Zeus. Research suggests that the chamber may have served as an oracle or simply as a storeroom for grain. Such a giant cellar is unusual for Roman temple architecture and remains unparalleled in Asia Minor.

The uneven road on your left as you approach the temple leads to the remains of the city's **marketplace.** The round building housed a food market and the colonnaded street in back was once lined with covered shops.

Back on the main road, walk past the temple and take the next right onto a winding farm path. Continue past the remains of the **gymnasium** and bath to the **stadium** and **theater** complex. The larger of the two venues, the stadium once held athletes and their cheering audiences; today you may find a shepherd and his flock resting among the rubble. Next to the stadium, the theater remains reasonably well-preserved, despite some earthquake damage. Aizanoi is the only known ancient city in which the stadium and the theater were combined into one facility.

If you're hungry, stop for a bite at **Tan-Pa Lokantası** (☎ (274) 351 30 07), right in front of the BP gas station. While you wait for a bus back to Kütahya, you can fill up here on decent *köfte*, rice, vegetables, and *ayran* for $3.

ESKİŞEHİR ☎222

Most travelers stop over in Eskişehir en route from İstanbul to Ankara or Konya. Though founded over 3000 years ago, Eskişehir, or "Old City," now offers little more than the hustle and bustle of a modern industrial city. Residents here must live with the constant roar of fighter jets from the nearby air force base; people here might mistake the rare tourist for NATO personnel. Eskişehir also is home to *Anadolu Üniversitesi* (University of Anatolia), the country's largest with 60,000 students. Visitors come for the thermal baths or for the meerschaum (*lületaşı* in Turkish) produced exclusively in the area. Nearby villages mine the soft, white mineral, which craftsmen carve into tobacco pipes and other objects. Although Eskişehir is a transportation gateway into Central Anatolia, most travelers prefer to spend their time and money elsewhere.

 TRANSPORTATION. To get to town from the otogar, take any bus and ask for **Köprübaşı,** the central district ($.35, $.25 for students). The bus will stop near a large outdoor TV screen at the intersection of İsmet İnönü Cad. and Cengiz Cad. **Buses** run from the otogar to **Afyon** (2½hr., every hr., $4); **Alanya** (7hr., 8 per day 11:30am-1:30am, $14); **Ankara** (3hr., every hr. 5am-3pm, $7); **Antalya** (6hr., 8 per day 10:30am-1:30am, $11); **Aydın** (7hr.; 12:30pm, midnight; $15); **Ayvalık** (8hr., 5 per day 11am-11pm, $13); **Bodrum** (11hr., midnight, $16); **Bursa** (2½hr., 10 per day 6am-3:45am, $7); **Çanakkale** (7½hr., 7 per day 10am-1:30am, $12); **Datça** (12hr., 11pm, $19); **Denizli** (5hr., 4 per day 2:30pm-midnight, $9); **Fethiye** (7hr., 10:30pm, $15); **İstanbul** (6hr., every hr. 5am-2am, $10); **İzmir** (6hr., every hr., $13); **Kütahya** (1¼hr., every hr., $1.50); **Marmaris** (11hr., 11pm, $16). Students discounts are roughly 20%, depending on the bus company.

 Trains leave Eskişehir's *istasyon* for **Ankara** (2½hr.; 9-12 per day 5:30am-3:30am; $7, students $6); **İstanbul** (Haydarpaşa station; 4hr.; 10-14 per day 4am-1am; $10, students $8); **İzmir** (11hr.; 7:35am, 10pm, 12:55am; $7, students $5); **Konya** (8hr.; 4:45am, 2:15, 11:56pm; $6, students $5; end of the line is **Karaman**). To reach the city center from the *istasyon*, turn left and follow İstasyon Cad. until it intersects with İsmet İnönü Cad; turn right here and walk about 1km to the center of town.

 ORIENTATION AND PRACTICAL INFORMATION. Navigation in Eskişehir is tricky, since streets are rarely labeled and have the habit of changing names at intersections. **İsmet İnönü Cad.** becomes **Sivrihisar Cad.,** which runs parallel to the river and leads to a number of hotels. **İki Eylül Cad.** crosses the river and runs several blocks before turning left. **Hamamyolu Cad.,** parallel to İki Eylül Cad., passes by thermal baths, restaurants, and a park. To get there, take the 2nd left as you walk on Köprübaşı Cad. away from the intersection of Sakarya Cad. and Sivrihisar Cad.

 The **tourist office,** on the ground floor of the Municipal Building (*Vilayet Binasi*) on İlk Eylül Cad., provides colorful brochures about all parts of Turkey except Eskişehir; maps of the city, however, are available. (☎ 230 17 52; fax 230 13 68. Open daily 8am-5:30pm.) Among the numerous travel agencies is **Sedef Turizm,** 1 İlk Eylül Cad. (☎ 230 30 71; fax 231 31 67). There are a number of **banks** in the city square and on Sivrihisar Cad., including a Yapı ve Kredi with two **ATMs. Eskişehir Hastanesi (hospital),** Çifteler Cad., ☎ 237 48 00; staffers speak little English. The **PTT** is on İlk Eylül Cad. near the tourist office; there is also one at the otogar.

CENTRAL ANATOLIA

ACCOMMODATIONS AND FOOD. Otel Divan, 5 Sivrihisar Cad., offers the best value in town, with a central location and pleasant rooms with communal toilets and showers on each floor. (☎ 232 00 31. Singles without TV $7; doubles with TV $15.) Further down Sivrihisar Cad., the **Otel Çiçek,** 29 Sivrihisar Cad., provides sparser accommodations at better prices. (☎ 234 40 56. Singles $5; doubles $10.) There are no showers, but it's a short walk to the **Yeni Hamam** ($1.50) on Köprubuşı Cad. **Has Hotel Termal,** 7 Hamamyolu Cad. (☎ 231 91 91), features its own thermal bath, is clean, well-located, and has a friendly management. A pricier option is the ▧ **Hotel Arslan,** 107 Yunusemre Cad. (☎ 231 09 09; fax 231 50 18), with well-equipped singles ($23) and doubles ($38); prices may be negotiable.

Finding **cheap eats** is no problem in Eskişehir, as both İlk Eylül Cad. and İsmet İnönü Cad. are lined with restaurants and shops selling *döner* with *ayran* for $1 or less. Before you leave, stop by one of the town's sweet shops and try the local *nuga helvası,* a fluffy yet chewy confection peppered with walnuts.

▧ SIGHTS. Meerschaum crafts can be found at the otogar or throughout the city; two well-marked shops lie off of İki Eylül Cad. In late September, Eskişehir celebrates its prized craft at the **International White Gold Festival.** If you have some time to kill, visit the **Archaeology Museum** *(Arkeoloji Müzesi)* on Hasan Polatkan Cad., where you may have the unique experience of having an entire museum to yourself. (Open daily 8:30am-noon, 1:30-5pm. $1.25, students free.) To get there, walk down İki Eylül Cad. to Seyh Sahabettin Cad. Follow Seyh Sahabettin Cad. to the next intersection and bear right onto Lise Cad.; the museum is about 500m down on your right. Rest your travel-weary bones at Eskişehir's **thermal baths,** said to cure rheumatism, fractures, and kidney stones. A good soaking costs $1.50 at both the Has Hotel Termal (see above) and the Yeni Kaplua Termal, 5 Hamamyolu Cad. (☎ 231 15 01). The Yeni Kaplua Termal offers a 20% student discount.

NORTH-CENTRAL ANATOLIA

ANKARA ☎ 312

Rising from the Anatolian plains, Ankara is unquestionably the seat of the Turkish Republic. Located at the intersection of two Eurasian trade routes, the city was first founded as Ankuwash over 3200 years ago by the Hittites. Legend has it that Ankara was next ruled by the great Phrygian King Midas. Subsequently occupied by Lydians, Galatians, Augustan Romans, Byzantines, and Selçuks, Ankara eventually fell into Ottoman hands. Then known as Angora, the sleepy village was populated mainly by long-haired goats. In 1923, after the Turkish War of Independence, Atatürk built this planned, modern city overnight, more or less from scratch. The curtains of the new nation's Opera House hastily went up, the Painting and Statue Museum was constructed and filled with contemporary Turkish art in just 18 months, and swampland was dredged to make way for the garish Gençlik Park. Today, Ankara is an administrative metropolis of parks, tree-lined boulevards, and embassies; it is also the nation's premier college town, which contributes to a vibrant nightlife in parts of town such as Kızılay. The Museum of Anatolian Civilizations may be the best museum in Turkey, and one can only begin to understand Atatürk's pivotal place in the national consciousness after a visit to his mausoleum, the Anıtı Kabır. Ankara is a convenient base for securing visas for Eastern Europe, the Middle East, the former Soviet republics, and Central Asia.

⚓ GETTING THERE

Flights: *Havaş* buses (every ½hr. 4am-11:30pm, $5) to Esenboğa Airport (☎398 00 00) leave from Hipodrom Cad. (next to the train station). Major carriers serving Ankara include: Aeroflot, Air France, Alitalia, Austrian Airlines, British Airways, Canadian Airlines, Delta, Iberia, JAL, KLM, Lufthansa, and Swissair. **Turkish Airlines (THY),** 154 Atatürk Bul., Kavaklıdere (info and reservations ☎419 28 00; sales ☎468 73 40 or 468 73 41), offers direct flights to: **Adana** (1hr., 3 per day, $68); **Antalya** (1hr., 3 per day, $70); **Bodrum** (1¼hr., 5 per day, $82); **Dalaman** (1¼hr., 4 per day, $82); **Diyarbakır** (1½hr., 2 per day, $68); **Erzurum** (1½hr., 2 per day, $68); **İstanbul** (1hr, 15 per day, $82); **İzmir** (1¼hr., 12 per day, $82); **Sivas** (1hr.; M, Th; $59); **Samsun** (1hr., daily except Sa., $59); **Tokat** (1hr., Tu, $59); and **Trabzon** (1¼hr, 3 per day, $68). Prices and schedules subject to change. Students under 24 and travelers over 65 receive a 25% discount; travelers under 12 receive a 50% discount. It's best to buy tickets 2 days in advance. The private travel agencies between Kızılay and Kavaklıdere are convenient ticket vendors. THY open M-F 8:30am-8pm, Sa-Su 8:30am-5:30pm.

Buses: The **terminal** (a.k.a. AŞTİ or otogar), 5km west of Kızılay in Söğütözü, is the westernmost stop on the Ankaray subway line. Take any train to Kızılay. To get to Ulus from there, transfer to the Metro line and ride 2 stops north to Cumhuriyet Cad., about 400m west of the equestrian statue. Dolmuş ($.60) and city buses ($.50) run from the otogar to Ulus, stopping at Hisarparkı Cad., in the middle of the cheap hotel area. A taxi for the same trip should cost about $6.75; to Kızılay, $8. Scores of bus companies connect Ankara with nearly every point in Turkey. Ask for smaller destinations; chances are that there's a bus going there. For major cities, **Varan,** 34/1 İzmir Cad., Kızılay (☎418 27 06 or 224 00 43), and **Ulusoy,** 18/A İnkılâp Sok., Kızılay (☎419 40 80 or 224 01 72 or 286 53 30), offer safer, faster, and more comfortable transportation. There are no longer direct bus routes to **Afyon, Kemer,** or **Side,** which are instead served by the İzmir bus (for Afyon) and the Antalya bus (for Kemer and Side). Prices and schedules subject to change. Student discounts sometimes available upon request.

BUS SCHEDULES

DESTINATION	DURATION	FREQUENCY/TIME	PRICE
Adana	7hr.	22 per day 9:30am-midnight	$12
Alanya	7½hr.	21 per day 7am-1am	$20
Antalya	7hr.	34 per day 7am-12:30pm	$13
Bodrum	12hr.	11 per day 7:30-10:30pm	$16.50
Çeşme	9hr.	11:30pm	$16.50
Eskişehir	3hr.	33 per day 7am-10:30pm	$4
Fethiye	8hr.	3 per day; 2 at 9:30pm, 1 at 10pm	$20
İstanbul	5½hr.	150 per day 6:30am-1:30am	$15
İzmir	8hr.	65 per day 7am-12:30am	$13
Kayseri	5hr.	40 per day 7am-1am	$8
Konya	3hr.	75 per day 6am-11pm	$8
Kuşadası	9hr.	10 per day 9am-midnight	$15
Kütahya	4½hr.	11 per day 8am-midnight	$10.50
Marmaris	10hr.	6 per day 9am-11:30pm	$15
Polatlı (for Gordion)	1 hr.	every 30min. 7am-9:30pm	$1.50
Samsun	7 hr.	20 per day 8am-midnight	$10
Sivas	6½ hr.	15 per day 9am-midnight	$12
Sungurlu	3 hr.	12 per day 8:30am-7:30pm	$10

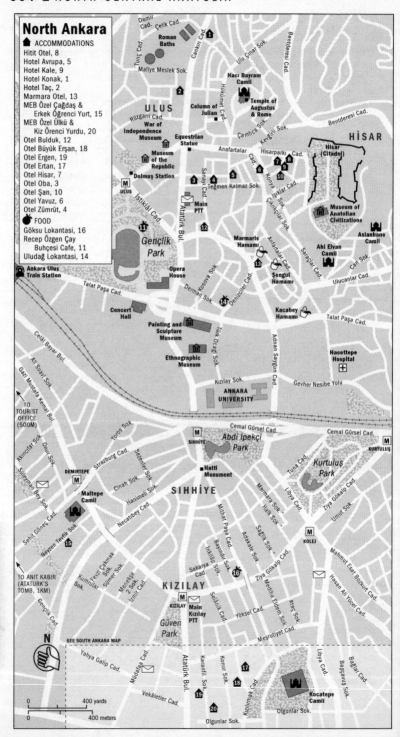

North Ankara

🏠 ACCOMMODATIONS
Hitit Otel, 8
Hotel Avrupa, 5
Hotel Kale, 9
Hotel Konak, 1
Hotel Taç, 2
Marmara Otel, 13
MEB Özel Çağdaş &
    Erkek Öğrenci Yurt, 15
MEB Özel Ülkü &
    Kiz Örenci Yurdu, 20
Otel Bulduk, 12
Otel Büyük Erşan, 18
Otel Ergen, 19
Otel Ertan, 17
Otel Hisar, 7
Otel Oba, 3
Otel Şan, 10
Otel Yavuz, 6
Otel Zümrüt, 4

🍎 FOOD
Göksu Lokantasi, 16
Recep Özgen Çay
    Buhçesi Cafe, 11
Uludağ Lokantasi, 14

TO
Yahya Galip Cad.
TO
ANIT KABIR
(ATATÜRK'S TOMB,
1.5KM)

Meşrutiyet Cad.
KIZILAY
Vekâletler Cad.
Mustafa Kemal Cad.
Müdafaa Cad.
Karanfil Sok.
Konur Sok.
Selâni Sok.
Kızılırmak Cad.
Libya Cad.
Başçavuş Cad.
Bağlar Cad.

TO NATIONAL
LIBRARY (2KM)
SEE NORTH ANKARA MAP

Olgunlar Sok.
Dilgunlar Sok.
Kocatepe
Camii

İsmet İnönü Bulvarı
BAKANLIKLAR

Akay Cad.

Parliament
(Büyük Millet
Meclisi)

Güvenlik Cad.
Havuzlu Sok.
Dikmen Cad.

Büklüm Sok.
Bade Sok.
Tunus Cad.
Besteker Sok.
Tunalı Hilmi Cad.
Bardacik Sok.
Hacıyolu Sok.
Akyüz Sok.
Yaprak Sok.
Bülbülderesi Cad.
Başak Sok.
Bağlayan Sok.

N

Ömür Sok.

Paris Cad.
Tandoğan Cad.
Şimşek Cad.
United
States
Germany
Italy
Bulgaria
Egypt
France
Atatürk Bul.

Büklüm Sok.
Bülten Sok.
Tunalı Hilmi Cad.
Büyükelçi Sok.
Kennedy Cad.
Esat Cad.

Elçi Sok.
Hoşdere Cad.
Alidede Sok.
Tomurcuk Sok.
Treboğlu Sok.
Selimiye

Yazanlar Sok.
KAVAKLIDERE
Kuveyt Cad.
Güven Sok.
Gelincik Sok.
Yeşilyurt Sok.
Kıbrıs Sok.

Güvenlik Cad.
Güneş Cad.
Meneviş Sok.

Abay Kunanbay Cad.
Billur Sok.
Güniz Sok.
Kuğulu
Park
Binnaz Sok.
Iran
Tahran Cad.
Nenehatun Cad.
Reşit Galip Cad.

Poland

Switzerland
Çelebi Sok.
Romania
Israel
Portugal
New Zealand
Brazil
Bükreş Sok.
Farabi Sok.
Alaçam Sok.
Jordan
Finland
Pakistan
Netherlands

Gelibolu Sok.
Cinnah Cad.
Noktalı Sok.
Kırantin Sok.
İran Cad.
Budak Sok.
GAZIOSMANPAŞA
Attar Sok.
Filistin Sok.
Canada
Australia
Iraq
Turan Emeksiz Cad.

Segmenler Park

Refik Belendir Sok.
Hoşdere Cad.
Kuzgun Sok.
Mesnevi Sok.
Dedekorkut Sok.
Russia
Büzümcük Sok.
Kuloğlu Sok.
Karyağdı Sok.
İlişkip Cad.
And Sok.
Atatürk Bulvarı
Şehit Ersan Cad.
Çankaya Cad.

India
Greece
Japan
ÇANKAYA
Kader Sok.
Şairler Sok.
Kırlangıç Sok.
Kırçiçeği Sok.

UK
Atatürk Country
Residence Museum
Presidential Palace
(Cumhurbaşkanlığı
Köşkü)
Petek Sok.
Koza Sok.

Botanical
Gardens
Pilot Sok.
Cinnah Cad.
Mexico
Atakule
Tower
Piyade Sok.
Abdullah Cevdet Sok.
11 Sok.

0   400 yards
0   400 meters

**South
Ankara**

■ ACCOMMODATIONS
Hilton Hotel, 7
M.E.B. Özel Ülkü & Kiz
   Örenci Yurdu, 2
Otel Büyük, 3
Otel Ergen, 1
Otel Ertan, 4
Sheraton Hotel, 6

● FOOD
Daily News Café, 8
Hacı Arif Bey Lokantasi, 5

DESTINATION	DURATION	FREQUENCY/TIME	PRICE
Tokat	6 hr.	10 per day 9am-11pm	$10.50
Trabzon	10 hr.	9 per day 7:30am-8:30pm	$15
Tehran, Iran	36 hr.	M,W, and F 7pm	$35

Trains: The train station *(Ankara Ulus Station)* is connected to Gazi Mustafa Kemal Bul. via a long underground tunnel doubling as a covered market. Follow this tunnel past the last platform to Gazi Mustafa Kemal Bul. The Maltepe Ankaray stop will be about 300m to the left. Alternatively, walk the 1½km up Cumhuriyet Bul. to Ulus Sq. Students and travelers over 60 receive a 20% discount. **Sivas** is served by the Malatya train.

TRAIN SCHEDULES

DESTINATION	DURATION	FREQUENCY/TIME	PRICE
Adana	12 hr.	8:15pm	$9, students $7
Afyon	7 hr.	6:35pm	$7, students $5.50
Diyarbakır	23 hr.	M,W,F,Sa 6:50am; Tu,Th,Su 7:40pm	$10, students $8
Erzurum	22 hr.	2 per day 9am-6:25pm	$9, students $7
Eskişehir	3 hr.	10 per day 8am-11:30pm	$2-31
İstanbul (Haydarpaşa)	6½-9½ hr.	7 per day 8am-11:30pm	$4-35
İzmir (Basmane)	15 hr.	6:10, 6:35, 7:10pm	$9, students $7
Kars	27 hr.	6pm	$9, students $7
Kütahya	7 hr.	2 per day 6:10-7:10pm	$6, students $4.50
Malatya	19 hr.	7:25pm	$6.75
Sivas	12 hr.	6:50am, 6:08, 7:40pm	$5.50, students $4

▐ GETTING AROUND

Local Buses: Buses come in 3 flavors: red and green (both government-run), and blue (private). Buy tickets for red and green buses from booths near major bus stops or from street vendors. On the blue buses, pay the conductor after boarding. Tickets on all buses cost $.50, students $.30.

Local Dolmuş: Hubs near Hacı Bayram Camii and at the intersection of Denizciler Cad. and Adnan Saygun Cad. $.35-.60, depending on distance. Student fare available.

Subway: Ankara's new, clean subway system provides possibly the fastest and easiest way to get around the city. The east-west Ankaray line (stations marked by a white "A" on a green background) connects the bus station to Dikimevi, with stops in Tandoğan, Maltepe, Kızılay, and the Colleges (Kolej). The north-south Metro line (white "M" on red background) also stops in Kızılay, running north from there to Sıhhiye, Ulus, and the northwestern suburbs. 5-ride passes $2.50, students $1.50. 6:15am-midnight.

Car Rental: Hertz, 138/B Atatürk Bul., Kavaklıdere (☎468 10 29; fax 468 19 26), and **Avis,** 68/2 Tunus Cad., Kavaklıdere (☎467 23 13; fax 467 57 03), both have airport offices and are more expensive. Both open daily 9am-7pm. **Best Rent A Car,** Büklüm Sok., No. 89/9, Kavaklıdere (☎467 00 08; fax 467 02 05). Rents Fiat Şahin (from $45 per day) and Escorts (from $73 per day). Open M-Sa 8am-7:30pm, Su 8:30am-6pm. **Alara Rent A Car,** 1/A Güniz Sok., Kavaklıdere (☎426 54 75; fax 426 52 63), rents Fiat Şahins (from $30 per day) and air-conditioned Toyotas (from $84 per day). Prices include unlimited mileage and insurance. Open M-Sa 8:30am-7pm.

◤ ORIENTATION

The city's main street, **Atatürk Bul.,** runs north-south. At its north end, the **Ulus** precinct consists of dusty cement apartments and crowded markets, all centered around a colossal equestrian monument to Atatürk. To the east of Ulus rises **Hisar** (Citadel), a traditional Anatolian village scattered with upscale restaurants and crowned by the 9th-century **Ankara Fortress** *(Ankara kale).* Ulus and Hisar comprise **Eskişehir** (Old City) and include most of the sights and the cheapest hotels. A couple of kilometers south of Ulus along Atatürk Bul. is **Sıhhiye,** a commercial neighborhood distinguished mostly by its giant Hittite reindeer. Further south along Atatürk Bul. is **Kızılay,** the center of **Yenişehir** (New City), bustling with bookstores, bars, *kebap* houses, and students from the six nearby universities. West of Kızılay is **Maltepe,** a district full of grim nightclubs and cheap student dorms. **Kavaklıdere, Çankaya,** and **Gaziosmanpaşa,** south of Kızılay, represent the stately side of Ankara: lush residential areas of embassies, ministries, five-star hotels, and night clubs. Bus #613 runs the length of Atatürk Bul. from the Atakule tower to the equestrian statue in Ulus. In addition, a new **subway system,** the **Ankaray suburban railway line,** runs east-west from its center in Kızılay. The bus terminal (**AŞTİ** on the signs, otogar to locals) in **Söğütözü** is 5km west of Kızılay, at the westernmost Ankaray subway stop. The railway station *(gar)*, on **Cumhuriyet Bul.**, is 1½km southwest of Ulus Square.

⑦ PRACTICAL INFORMATION

TOURIST AND FINANCIAL SERVICES

Tourist Offices: 121 Gazi Mustafa Kemal Bul. (☎ 231 55 72). Directly outside the Maltepe stop on Ankaray (from Kızılay, take the train headed toward AŞTİ). The friendly, English-speaking staff provides free city and country maps and can serve as your interpreter to the tourist police (☎ 303 63 53). Open daily 9am-5pm. The airport tourist office (☎ 398 03 48) offers similar services. Open 24hr.

Embassies: Bulgaria, 124 Atatürk Bul., Kavaklıdere (☎ 426 74 55; fax 427 31 78). Visa applications M-F 10am-noon. **Egypt,** 126 Atatürk Bul., Kavaklıdere (☎ 426 10 26; fax 427 00 99). **Greece,** 9-11 Ziaürrahman Cad., Gaziosmanpaşa (☎ 436 88 60; fax 446 31 91). Visa applications M-F 9:30am-noon. **Iran,** 10 Tahran Cad., Kavaklıdere (☎ 427 43 20; fax 468 28 23). Visa applications M-F 3-5pm. **Iraq,** 11 Turan Emeksiz Sok., Gaziosmanpaşa (☎ 468 74 21; fax 468 48 32). Visa applications M-F 10am-3pm. **Israel,** 85 Mahatma Gandi Cad., Gaziosmanpaşa (☎ 446 29 20; fax 426 15 33). **Jordan,** 18A Mesnevi Dede Korkut Sok., Aşağı Ayrancı (☎ 440 20 54; fax 440 43 27). **Lebanon,** 44 Kızkulesi Sok., Gaziosmanpaşa (☎ 446 74 85; fax 446 10 23). **Northern Cyprus,** 20 Rabat Sok., Gaziosmanpaşa (☎ 437 60 31; fax 446 52 38). **Russia,** 5 Karyağdı Sok., Çankaya (☎ 439 21 22; fax 438 39 52). **Syria,** 40 Sedat Simavi Sok., Çankaya (☎ 440 96 57; visa department ☎ 440 17 21; fax 438 56 09) Visa applications M-F 8:30-9:30am. For embassies of **Australia, Canada, New Zealand, South Africa,** the **UK,** and the **US,** see **Consular Services in Turkey,** p. 40.

Banks: You can't throw a stone in Kavaklıdere, Kızılay, Maltepe, Ulus, or Sıhhiye without hitting a bank branch. All large banks offer **currency exchange,** but only major banks such as **Akbank** (no commission) and **Garanti** will cash **traveler's checks.** Change offices *(döviz)* along Atatürk Bul. offer slightly better rates (but no traveler's checks). 24hr. **ATMs** can be found on virtually every street corner. **Türkiye İş Bankası, Yapı ve Kredi, Pamukbank,** and **Garanti Bankası** accept V/MC/Cirrus/Plus/Eurocard; Vakıfbank and Akbank also accept AmEx.

Wire Transfers and Moneygrams: Western Union, 27 Meşrutiyet Cad., Kızılay (☎ 419 88 58). Open M-Sa 9am-5pm. Western Union services also at **MNG Bank,** 84 Uğur Mumcu Cad., Gaziosmanpaşa (☎ 447 66 50). Open M-F 9am-6pm. AmEx cardholders can send and receive moneygrams at Koçbank by the statue in Ulus Meydanı.

LOCAL SERVICES

Lost Property: Kayip Eşya offices in Esenboğa (☎ 398 05 50), the **main otogar bus terminal** (☎ 224 10 10 or 224 01 78), **city municipal buses** (☎ 384 03 60), and the **Head Security Office** *(Emniyet Müdürlüğü,* ☎ 303 06 06), İskitler Cad.

Library: National Library *(Millî Kütüphane),* Bahçelievler (☎ 212 62 00; fax 223 04 51; www.mkutup.gov.tr). Take the dolmuş ($.35) to Balgat from Kızılay's Güvenpark and ask to be let off at the Millî Kütüphane. Entry to this multi-level, marble, CD-ROM-equipped library will be easier if you have either a form from your embassy (for foreigners living in Turkey) or a research permit, obtained from the Turkish Embassy in your home country. Study salons open M-F 9am-8:30pm, Sa-Su 9:30am-6:30pm; stacks open M-F 9am-noon, 1:30-4:30pm.

English Language Bookstores: Most bookstores in Kızılay offer a range of Penguin Classics, Steven King, and nonfiction. **Dost Kitabevi**, has the best selection, with a branch in Kızılay, 11 Karanfil Sok. (☎425 24 64; open M-Sa 9am-10pm, Su noon-7pm) carrying English language newspapers and magazines. **Tahran Kitabevi**, 19/A Selânik Cad., Kızılay (☎417 25 50) carries a range of magazines (*The Economist*, *Newsweek*, *Bride*, etc.) and many hard-to-find books about Turkey. Open M-Sa 9am-12:30pm, 2-7pm. **Turhan Kitabevi**, 8/B Yüksel Cad., Kızılay. From spring to fall, the **open-air book market** on Olgunlar Sok. sells a haphazard collection of back-issue US magazines.

Turkish-American Association (Türk-Amerikan Derneği): 20 Cinnah Cad., Kavaklıdere (☎426 26 44; fax 468 25 38; Programs Dept. ☎426 26 48). Cinnah Cad. branches off from Atatürk Bul. south of Bakanlıklar. Take any bus from Atatürk Bul. heading toward Çankaya or Gaziosmanpaşa. Offers Turkish and English classes, art exhibits, ballroom dances, concerts, and a lecture series. Monthly bulletin with events schedule. Small selection of US magazines in the **Graphica Cafe** (tea $.35). Open daily 9am-8:30pm.

Laundromat: Self-service **Ekspres Çamaşır** (☎419 32 32, ext. 272), in Kızılay in the Beğendik shopping mall under the Kocatepe mosque. Go up the first set of motorized ramps and take a right; exit the main shopping area through the corridor and turn left. Wash and dry $3.75. Free locker storage. Open daily 9:30am-9pm. **Bora Çamaşer Yıkamatik**, 16/A Dumlupınar Cad., Cebeci (☎363 42 43), is closer to Ulus. Follow Cemal Gürsel Cad. to the Kurtuluş Ankaray stop, turn left and go underneath the train overpass. From here turn right onto Gerher Nesibe Yolu and then left onto Dumlupınar Cad. Wash and dry $3.75. Open daily 8am-9pm.

Hamams: Şengul Hamamı, 3 Acıçeşme sok., Ulus (men's section ☎311 03 63; women's section ☎310 22 98), down a small side street off Denizciler Cad., about 200m from the Marmara Otel. Nearly 600 years old, with pool and sauna. $4; massage $1.50. Students 20% off. Open daily 5:30am-11pm. **Karacabey Hamamı**, 101 Talat Paşa Cad., Ulus (☎311 84 47), has a stately wooden antechamber. $3.75; *kese* and massage each $1.25. Open daily 6:30am-11pm. The **Marmara Hamamı** (☎324 25 27), 17 Denizciler Cad., next door to the Marmara Otel in Ulus, has a sauna and a spacious central room. $5; massage $2, $3 for hotel guests. Open daily 5am-10pm. Separate women's hamam right around the corner (open 8am-6:30pm).

EMERGENCY AND COMMUNICATIONS

24-Hour Pharmacy: Listings of on-duty (*nöbetci*) pharmacies in the *Hürriyet* daily paper (same page as movie listings). On-duty establishments have a sign in their windows.

Hospital: Bayındır Tıp Merkezi, Kızılırmak Mah. #3-3A, 28th Sok., Söğütözü (☎287 90 00), is Ankara's best private hospital. Centrally located, brand-new **Bayındar Kilnik**, 201 Atatürk Bul. (☎428 08 08), Kavaklıdere, is smaller but offers all services. **Hacettepe Üniversitesi Tıp Fakültesi Hastanesi** (☎310 35 45), Hasırcılar Cad., Samonpazarı and **Ankara Üniversitesi Tıp Fakültesi Hastanesi** (☎319 21 60), Tıp Fakültesi Cad., Dikimevi, are the largest university hospitals.

Internet Access: Most of Ankara's internet cafes are in Kızılay, though connection speed and ambiance vary. **Internet Center Cafe**, 107 Atatürk Bul. (☎419 27 54; fax 425 79 27), on the 3rd floor of the Engürü İş Hanı, is one of the best. Fast connection. Color printing, photocopying, scanning. $1.25 per hr. Open daily 9am-11pm. Nearby **Intek Internet Cafe**, 47/1 Karanfil Sok. (☎417 17 72), offers speedy connections for $1.50 per hr. Tea, coffee, and other snacks Open daily 8am-midnight. **İrde Internet Cafe**, 31 Selanik Cad., 2nd fl. (☎419 68 56), offers great connections for $1.50 per hr.

PTT: In **Ulus**, on Atatürk Bul., just south of the equestrian statue. Open 24hr. In **Kızılay**, on Atatürk Bul. just off Kızılay Square. Open M-Sa 8am-8pm; Su 8:30am-12:30pm, 1:30-5:30pm. In **Kavaklıdere**, on Cinnah Cad. just off the Kavaklıdere roundabout. Open daily 8:30am-12:30pm, 1:30-5pm. In the **train station** on Talat Paşa Cad. Open daily 7am-11pm. All offer full services. **Postal code:** 06443.

ACCOMMODATIONS

KIZILAY

Though slightly more expensive, the lively, student-oriented Kızılay is more pleasant than the dustier, noisier Ulus. Ulus is nearer to most of the sites, but Kızılay is the cultural downtown.

Otel Ertan, 70 Selânik Cad. (☎418 40 84 or 425 15 06). Going south along Atatürk Bul., take the 4th left after McDonald's onto Meşrutiyet Cad., then the 3rd right onto Selanik Cad. Garden in front. Great value on a peaceful street, yet close to the Kızılay nightlife. 20 rooms, all with shower, toilet, and TV. Singles $15.50; doubles $24.50.

Hotel Ergen, 48 Karanfil Sok. (☎417 59 06 or 417 59 07; fax 425 78 19). Going south along Atatürk Bul., take the 4th left after McDonald's onto Meşrutiyet Cad., then take the next right. Two-star Ergen has 48 rooms, well-furnished with private bath. Most have TV. No hot water 2-8pm. Singles $28, students $24; doubles $40, students $30.

Otel Büyük Erşan, 74 Selânik Cad. (☎417 60 45 or 417 60 46; fax 417 49 43), across from Otel Ertan. True to its name, 3-star "Big Erşan" has 85 rooms, each with toilet, shower, TV, and refrigerator. The hotel has a retro feel, like something out of a 60s movie. Singles $26; doubles $38; triples $57.

M.E.B. Özel Ülkü Kız Öğrenci Yurdu, 61 Karanfil Sok. (☎419 37 15 or 419 30 67; fax 419 36 49), between Akay Cad. and Meşrutiyet Cad. This girls' dormitory provides clean, safe lodgings and a cafeteria. 24hr. hot water. Open July-Sept. Breakfast $3. Singles $12, with bath $16; doubles $24, with bath $32.

MALTEPE

Just west of Kızılay, Maltepe is home to a few cheap student dorms. Though somewhat removed from the sights, it is still relatively close to the Kızılay action and escapes the chaotic bustle of Ulus.

M.E.B. Özel Çağdaş Erkek Öğrenci Yurt, 15 Neyzen Tevfik Sok., Maltepe (☎232 29 54 or 232 29 55). From the Demirtepe Ankaray stop, walk 100m along Gazi Mustafa Kemal Bul. with the Maltepe mosque on your right (back toward Kızılay). A set of stairs just past the mosque leads to Neyzen Teufik Sok.; walk uphill until you see the dorm on your left. Most rooms share a bath. Dormitories serve as a co-ed hostel from July-Aug., but only accept male students at other times of the year. Singles $10; doubles $20.

Hitit Öğrenci Yurtları, 96 Gazi Mustafa Kemal Bul. (☎231 02 81 or 231 07 91), on the left as you walk from the Maltepe Ankaray stop back toward Kızılay. This dorm offers lodging to male guests at the unbeatable price of $30 per week. Rooms for 1, 2, 4, or 6 people. Shared bathrooms. Prices drop for stays of a month or longer.

ULUS

Ulus is packed with cheap hotels, some more squalid and Dickensian than others. The highest concentration is by the market, east of the equestrian statue.

■ Hotel Kale, Anafartalar Cad., 13 Alataş Sok. (☎311 33 93 or 310 35 21). From the statue, follow Anafartalar Cad. toward the Citadel; bear right before it becomes Hisarparkı Cad., and take the 3rd left onto Şan Sok. Hotel Kale is about 150m ahead at the intersection of Şan Sok. and Alataş Sok. Near the center of Ulus, but a quiet distance from any major thoroughfare. 32 rooms with TV, toilet, and shower. Singles $16, students $13; doubles $29.50, students $24.50; triples $39, students $34.

Otel Zümrüt, 16 Şehit Teğmen Kalmaz Cad. (☎309 15 54 or 309 01 17). From the statue, follow Atatürk Bul. south; take the 2nd left onto Teğmen Kalmaz Cad. All the advantages of a larger hotel at an unbeatable price. Singles $7, with shower $10.50; doubles $12, with shower and toilet $17; triples $17, with shower and toilet $21.

Otel Hisar, 6 Hisarparkı Cad. (☎311 98 89 or 310 81 28). Walk east from the equestrian statue. Offers simple rooms and Hisar views. Singles $6.50; doubles $11.

Otel Bulduk, 26 Sanayi Cad. (☎310 49 15, 310 49 16, or 310 49 17). Walk south from the equestrian statue along Atatürk Bul., take the first left after the PTT, then turn right onto Sanayi Cad. Bulduk is on the right. 68 quiet rooms, all with TV. Singles $13, with bath $16.50; doubles $23, with bath $28; triples $36. 15% student discount.

Hotel Taç, 35 Çankırı Cad. (☎324 31 95 or 324 31 96). North of the statue, Atatürk Bul. becomes Çankırı Cad., a busy, noisy, well-lit street. Lodging here is closer to the Roman ruins and slightly more expensive than elsewhere in Ulus. 35 clean rooms, some with private showers. Singles $8, with shower and toilet $11.50; doubles $16.50, with shower and toilet $19.50.

Hitit Otel, 12 Hisarparkı Cad., (☎310 86 17; fax 309 69 39). Walk east from the equestrian statue toward the Citadel; the hotel will be on the right. This more expensive 44-room hotel is one of Ulus's nicer offerings. All rooms with private bath and TV, and most with great views of the Citadel. Singles $30, students $20; doubles $45, students $32; triples $65, students $50.

CAMPING

D.S.İ. Kampı Campground, Bayındır Barajı (☎372 27 31), on the Samsun Yollu Üzeri about 15km from Ankara. By car, take the road to Samsun, past Kayaş; this state-operated campground is on the right. Dolmuş leave the Ulus hubs on Denizciler Cad. and Bentderesi Cad. ($.30). Gas station and cafe nearby. Free use of toilets, showers (24hr. hot water), and laundry. $1.50 per day. Open May 1 until it gets too cold (about Sept.).

🍴 FOOD

The main culinary neighborhoods are Kızılay (mid-range), Gençlik Park (cheap), Hisar (upscale, touristy), and Kavaklıdere (upscale, trendy). In addition, just southeast of the Atakule Tower, **Hoşdere Cad.** lays claim to many good restaurants, as does Ahmet Mitat Sok., the side street one block south. For comprehensive supermarkets selling food, rugs, furniture, electronics, watches, shoes, linens, toys, cosmetics, and life insurance, head to **Gima,** with branches on Atatürk Bul. (next to the PTT) in Kızılay and on Anafartalar Cad. in Ulus, or **Beğendik** (open 9am-10:30pm), under the Kocatepe mosque in Kızılay (at the south end of Mithat Paşa Cad.). The **Migros** chain (look for the *MMM* symbol) restricts itself to standard supermarket wares and has branches on Celâl Bayar Bul. in Maltepe and on Uğur Mumcu Cad. in Çankaya. In addition, small, hyper-specialized food stores line the streets of Kavaklıdere, Kızılay, and Ulus.

KIZILAY

Some of Kızılay's streets have been turned into pedestrian zones bustling with a student crowd in restaurants, bars, and cafes. It's hard to go wrong here; just follow the crowds and avoid fast food joints. Numerous shops on **Olgenlar Sok.** sell Kızılay's cheapest meal, the $.75 *döner*. A couple blocks farther from Atatürk Bul., Bayındır Sok. has some better and more expensive restaurants.

Göksu Restaurant, 22/A Bayındır Sok. (☎431 22 19), is one of the classier places in the neighborhood, with excellent Turkish and European food at mid-range prices (decent filet mignon $4.50). The desserts are particularly delicious. Sit outside on the glass-enclosed patio or inside among the exaggerated but elegant reproductions of Hittite reliefs, while waiters in bowties attend to your needs. Open daily noon-midnight.

Körfez Lokantası, 24 Bayındır Sok. (☎431 14 59). Specializes in Black Sea seafood ($7-12). *Kiliç* (swordfish), *barbunya* (red mullet), *karides* (prawn), and other dishes available depending on the season. Open daily 11:45am-midnight.

Cafe M, 42 Selânik Cad. (☎419 36 65). Cell-phone toting collegiate hipsters aplenty. Try M's banana split ($2) or the *tiramisu* ($1.50). Open daily 7am-10:30pm.

Cafe Tenedos, 29/A Kızılırmak Cad. (☎419 34 50), at the intersection of Kızılırmak Cad. and Selânik Sok., west of the Kocatepe mosque. Live quality jazz from Sept.-June. Pleasant patio, wooden interior. Ginger peach soda $2. Open daily 9am-midnight.

ULUS

Since Ulus isn't a particularly compelling neighborhood for restaurants, the quickest and easiest option is to grab a *döner* or *kebap*.

⬛ Uludağ Lokantası, 54 Denizciler Cad. (☎309 04 00; fax 312 18 19; www.uludagkebap.com.tr). This is possibly the best restaurant in Ankara. Though fairly upscale, the food is reasonably priced. *Özel Uludağ Kebap* $3.50, *Ekmek Kadayıfı* (Turkish sweet pastry with cream) $2.

Tapi Tavuk, 23/A Şehit Teğmen Kalmaz Cad. (☎309 38 16; fax 309 18 15; order in 311 21 11). Decent, inexpensive food in a down-to-earth environment. Chicken is their specialty. *Tavuk Şiş* $2.50, *Tavuk köfte* $2.

HİSAR

To get to Hisar's several good restaurants, climb the steps at Hisarparkı Cad. until you reach the citadel walls. Inside lies naught but a confusing labyrinth. Instead, bear right and follow the road uphill to the southern gate (restaurant signs will aid you along the way). Inside, several high-class (read: not kebap joints) but reasonably-priced Turkish restaurants are clustered around the main square.

⬛ Kale Washington, 5-7 Doyran Sok. (☎311 43 44; fax 324 59 59). On the square just to the left, offers tasty fare on an open-air, canopied terrace (*patlican salatası* (eggplant salad) $2.50, entrees about $6). Their delicious *crème caramel* ($1.50) comes with a unique square spoon. Open noon-midnight.

Zenger Paşa Konağı, 13 Doyran Sok. (☎311 70 70). A combination restaurant and museum in a restored Ottoman house. Don't leave without trying the delicious *gördeme* crepe specialty ($1). Open daily 11am-midnight.

Hisar Kule Lokarta (☎301 78 99). With even better prices than its Hisar rivals, this restaurant offers excellent food and stunning views from the roof tower. *Patlıcan salatası* $1, *meze* $1.50. Open 9am-2am.

KAVAKLIDERE AND GAZIOSMANPAŞA

Embassy employees favor the several upscale establishments lining Arjantin Cad., the road leading uphill to the right of the Sheraton Hotel. For less expensive, kebap-style dining, look for Hoşdere Cad., south and east of the Atakule Tower.

⬛ Daily News Cafe, 1 Arjantin Cad. (☎468 45 13). Spend a relaxing afternoon here and escape the news blackout with a free copy of the English-language *Turkish Daily News*. The interior is decorated only with newspapers. Sauteed chicken with white wine sauce $6.50. Live music F-M 7:30pm-10:30pm. Open daily 9am-midnight.

⬛ Hacı Arif Bey, 48 Güniz Sok. (☎467 00 67; reservations ☎467 57 67; fax 428 44 44). Directly opposite the home of former Turkish President Süleyman Demirel, this large restaurant serves food fit for a king. *İskender Kebap* $3.50; *Peynirli künefe* $1.50.

Dolmax, Tunalıhılmı Cad., Büklüm Sok. (☎467 52 52; fax 428 27 17). Combination restaurant and doll shop has to be seen to be believed. Excellent food served in surroundings of surreal, endless shelves of dolls. Chicken fried rice with chef's sauce, $5.50.

Karacaoğlu Atatürka, 30 Arjantin Cad. (☎467 33 44). Authentic and reasonably priced Turkish food (with a few twists) in a classy environment. Outdoor terrace in summer. Mushroom *mantı* $3.50, sesame chicken $4.75. Open daily 11:30am-10:30pm.

Kristiansen, 24 Arjantin Cad. (☎466 13 46). The Danes provide a unique and welcome respite from standard cafe fare with an array of salads ($5), *smørrebrød* (open-faced sandwiches $6), and spectacular Danish pastries ($2). Photographs of Danish families and Atatürk reflect the Turkish-Danish co-ownership. Open daily 8am-11:30pm.

Dönen Restaurant (☎440 74 12), atop the Atakule tower in Çankaya. Serves trout ($11) and *ızgara* ($8) as the guests slowly revolve on a giant mechanized disc. Overpriced food may be justified by the best view in Ankara. Open daily 10am-1am.

🎵🎭 ENTERTAINMENT AND NIGHTLIFE

KIZILAY

Like so many other aspects of the city, Ankara's nightlife is centered in Kızılay, where dozens of bars and multipurpose cafe-bars cover a few city blocks. Manic dancers should be warned, however, that Kızılay's nightlife is of the chat-over-a-beer and listen-to-live-music variety. Pub life is centered on **İnkılâp Sok.** and the even livelier **Bayındır Sok.**, two and three blocks east of Kızılay Sq. Roam the traffic-free streets as you pick the crowd you want to hang with. **S.S.K. İşhane** (Life Insurance Office Building), on the corner of Ziya Gökalp Cad. and Selânik Cad., is the center for bars and clubs. This entire cement block throbs with the bass-kicking sounds from small live music bars. Kızılay's bar prices are fairly uniform: a pint of *Efes*, the local favorite, goes for $1.10-1.50; mixed drinks from $3-4.

Brothers Bar, 61 Selânik Cad. (☎419 41 26). At the far end of Selânik Cad., just past the Ertan Hotel. Mellow music and mood. Young musicians play acoustic renditions of Turkish tunes while the large collegiate crowd sings along. Open daily 11am-midnight.

Zx Bar Disco, 14/A Bayındır Sok. (☎431 35 35). Packs a 3-floor Turkish pop punch: disco downstairs, live music upstairs, and a bar in the middle of it all. Beer $1.50. Open daily noon-12:30am.

Nil Bar, 19/C Bayındır Sok. (☎431 07 73), and the **Alesta Bar,** 19/B Bayındır Sok. (☎431 12 04), open onto the street next door to each other. Pleasant outdoor tables and deafening cover bands playing a mix of Turkish and American rock inside. Beer $1.50. Both bars open daily 9am-midnight.

Gölge Bar, 1-2-3 S.S.K. İşhanı (☎434 09 78). Literally "Shadow Bar," *Gölge*, is well-known to the city's youth. Live bands play heavily distorted covers of English rock, from the Rolling Stones to the Cure. The club's dark, smoky space and cheap beer ($1.50) attract an equally nonuniform crowd. Live music nightly, with 2 bands F and Sa. Cover required only after 9pm on F and Sa ($2.50, includes a beer). Open daily 1pm-4am.

Blues Cafe & Bar, 19/16 Bayındır Sok. (☎432 42 46), on the 2nd floor of the building on the corner of Bayındır Sok. and Sakarya Cad. Makes up for its lack of live music with a well-chosen soundtrack of American blues and rock. Wooden benches arranged around the dark, cozy space are stamped with such names as Bob Marley, Pink Floyd, and Jimi Hendrix. Open daily 11am-12:30am.

May Day Club, Beş Evler Cad., Gençler Birligi Sporklubu Yanı. Open only in the summer, when it becomes the place to see and be seen in Ankara for hard-core clubbing.

Metropol Sanat Merkezi Movie House, 76 Selanik Cad., Kızılay (☎425 74 78), offers six screens of artsy and pop films, mostly American ($3.75, students $2.50).

Kızılırmak Movie House, 21 Kızılırmak Sok., Kızılay (☎425 53 93), **Derya,** 57 Necatibey Cad., Sıhhiye (☎229 96 18), and **Megapol,** 33 Konur Sok., Kızılay (☎419 44 92) also play British and American films. For listings, check the *Turkish Daily News* or pick up a flyer from any theater.

KAVAKLIDERE

If the mellow/metalhead schizophrenia and pricey lifestyle of Kızılay is getting you down, head to the less crowded, posh bars and clubs scattered around Kavaklıdere, Gaziosmanpaşa, and Çankaya. Bars are spread throughout the residential area and can be hard to find. Güvenlik, Farabi, and Üsküp (a.k.a. Çevre) Cads. contain several nightspots, while **jazz bars** on Abay Kunanbay Cad., uphill from the McDonald's on Tunali Hilmi Cad., feature live Turkish music most nights.

Süleyman Nazif Club, 97 Güvenlik Cad. (☎468 57 83). Dance floor with Turkish and Euro techno, where a young, mostly-Turkish crowd lets loose, and a calmer upstairs lounge. Open W-Sa 10pm-2am.

Marilyn Monroe, 54/A Büklüm Sok. (☎467 12 12). Enjoy the Marilyn decor while sipping an *Efes* with the mainly Anglo-American expat crowd. Terrace open in summer. Restaurant attached. Open 10am-midnight.

The North Shield, 111 Güvenlik Cad., Kavaklıdere (☎466 12 66; fax 468 86 91). One of the most popular bars in the area. The mixed crowd at this faux-Scottish pub favors older folk, but includes the weekend student surge. The only place in Ankara where you can spend $250 on a single glass of 52-year-old malt whiskey. Local beers $4, imports $6.50; whiskies $6.50 and up, up, up. Open daily noon-1am.

Likya, SOA/4 Tunus Cad., Kavaklıdere (☎426 27 23), draws a carefully dressed student crowd with its soundtrack of American and European pop tunes. Hair gel recommended. On Thursday the DJ spins all from tango to techno. *Efes* $3. Open daily noon-2am.

No Name Club, 16/2 Çevre Sok. (☎467 80 37; fax 467 70 39). Plays Turkish pop and "Turkish underground" to a young and frenetic crowd. DJ from 10:30pm until 2am; live music from 11:30am-2am. Beer $5, *rakı* $6.50. On Friday and Saturday $24 cover for a table, $12 cover to stand. Open 10:30pm-2am. Closed June 15-Sept.15.

Batı Cinema, 151 Atatürk Bul., Kavaklıdere (☎418 83 23; $3.50, students $2), also plays British and American films. For listings, check the *Turkish Daily News* or pick up a flyer from any theater.

Open-air cinema. On the roof of the Kavaklıdere Sheraton (☎468 54 54), with nightly 9:30pm screenings for $7 (summer only). Another place to catch up on American flicks. There's no popcorn, but there is a **bar** (first drink on the house, additional cocktails $3).

ULUS

Most of the clubs, cafes, discos, and movie houses are elsewhere in Ankara, but there are still some diversions in Ulus. **Gençlik Park** is crammed with cheap restaurants and also contains a garish **amusement park** and an artificial lake with rental pleasure boats ($.75 per ½hr.). This can be a rather depressing place, but it's at its best in the early evening, when the lights first come on. Smoke a *nargile* ($2) at the **Kecep Özgen Çay Bahçesi tea house.** (Park open in summer 9am-midnight. Tea house open 7am-midnight.) From November until mid-June, the terra cotta pillared **State Opera and Ballet House** (*Devlet Opera ve Balesi*), Atatürk Bul. Opera Meydanı holds daily performances. Performance schedules are posted on the bulletin board outside the opera house or available at the tourist office. (☎324 22 10 or 324 20 10. Tickets $5 and $10, students 50% off.) The nearby **Presidential Symphony Orchestra Hall** (*Cumhurbaşkanlığı Senfoni Orkestrası Konser Salonu*), 38 Talatpaşa Bul., has concerts F 8:30pm and Sa 11am. (☎310 72 90. Tickets $3 or $5; 50% student discount.) **Akün Cinema,** 227 Atatürk Bul., shows American films in the original English (☎427 76 56; $3.50, students $2).

⬛ SIGHTS

▨ **MUSEUM OF ANATOLIAN CIVILIZATIONS (ANADOLU MEDENIYETLERI MÜZESI).** Arguably Ankara's most important sight, this museum, at the foot of the Citadel, won Europe's Museum of the Year Award in 1997. This restored 15th-century Ottoman building houses a collection of astoundingly old artifacts tracing the history of Anatolia from a 6th millennium BC bone and obsidian razor to Ottoman pottery. The museum's greatest strength is its organization—a U-shaped corridor leads visitors chronologically through the development of human technology, art, and religion. The museum is small enough that a visitor can browse the entire collection without getting "museum feet;" quality, rather than quantity, is the key. Larger artifacts (statues, wall sections, etc.) are kept in the central room. Some of the greatest hits include artifacts from Çatalhöyük, the blockbuster of all Neolithic sites; perfectly preserved Hittite bull vessels; original gate figures from Boğazkale; and a life-size reproduction of King Midas's tomb at Gordion. Equally impressive is the room of 3300-year-old hieroglyphic tablets. An underground section, including ancient coins, opened four years ago. English labeling is reasonably extensive, but if you want more time to absorb Anatolia's rich history, the photo-packed catalogue ($10) explains all. *(2 Gözcü Sok. Walk to the top of Hisarparkı Cad., turn right at the Citadel steps (without climbing them), and follow the Citadel boundaries to a set of steps leading up to the entrance. ☎ 324 31 60; fax 311 28 39. Museum open Tu-Su 8:30am-5:30pm. $3, students $2; on Monday, $6.50, students $5.)*

ATATÜRK'S MAUSOLEUM (ANIT KABİR). Upon Atatürk's death, Turkey held an international contest to select a plan for his **mausoleum.** The winner, Emin Onat, designed the simple, monumental, Hittite-influenced **Anıt Kabir.** It took nine years to complete and now covers 750,000 sq. meters near Tandoğan Square.

At the mausoleum entrance, six unhappy statues of men and women represent the grief of the Turkish nation upon its father's death. Twenty-four lions, paired Hittite-style and symbolizing power, line the broad stone promenade leading to the mausoleum. Across the vast courtyard is the tomb of İsmet İnönü, first prime minister of the Republic and Atatürk's close friend. The mausoleum complex has no fewer than nine towers and two giant victory reliefs, a museum, and a **hall of honors.** Objects on display include Atatürk's 1936 **Lincoln sedan,** his rowing machine, his tie clips, and numerous ceremonial gifts and plaques he received as Turkey's head of state. An excellent series of photographs commemorates Atatürk's career and social life. Other photographs taken after his death show **cloud formations** shaped like his profile, suggesting that even the sky mourned his loss. In the Reform Tower, the **Cinevision salon** shows non-stop period documentaries, including some very moving posthumous propaganda films with Chopin soundtracks. "Tell us heavens, tell us flag, clouds, birds, mountains—where is Atatürk now?" Wrap up your tour with a stop at the gift shop for your favorite Atatürk paraphernalia: Atatürk post cards, CD-ROMs, plaques, clocks, and photos. *(Anıt Cad. Take the Ankaray line to Tandoğan and follow the Anıt Kabir signs along Anıt Caddesi. The unmarked entrance is guarded by two soldiers. It's a 10-minute uphill walk from the gate to the mausoleum entrance. ☎ 231 79 75. Open M 1:30-5pm, Tu-Su 9am-5pm. Free.)*

HİSAR. On a high hill overlooking the city, the original, pre-republican hilltown of Ankara remains more or less unchanged. Called Hisar (Citadel) for its imposing Byzantine walls, this network of narrow, twisting streets is full of merchants and craftsmen of every variety. It's probably the best place in town to go looking for carpets or *kilim.* At the very top of the hill, the eastern tower *(Şark Kulesi)* and the northern tower *(Ak Kale)* offer excellent views. The towers are tricky to find, however; the easiest way is simply to follow any street leading uphill. Buy shoes, sheets, and Superman outfits on Çıkrıkçılar Sok., which runs just southwest of the citadel, downhill from the entrance to the Museum of Anatolian Civilizations.

MOSQUES. The immense **Kocatepe Mosque** looms just east of Kızılay on Mithat Paşa Cad. Completed in 1987, this facility is billed as a 16th-century mosque using 20th-century technology: glowing green digital clocks indicate prayer times. Constructed with dazzling white stone, it shines as one of the world's largest mosques. The stunning stained-glass-and-tiled interior contains a model of the mosque at Medina—a present from King Fahd of Saudi Arabia in 1993. Kocatepe is particularly striking at night, when moths sleep on the white flagstones overlooking the illuminated city and the enormous, round crystal chandeliers inside are lit. After your visit, you can do a little shopping at the Beğendik supermarket and mall—ultra-modern, air-conditioned, and directly underneath the mosque.

Downhill and south of the citadel's towers, the small, 13th-century **Aslanhane Mosque** (Ahi Şerafettin) bears witness to Ankara's Selçuk legacy. Inside, wooden pillars with Corinthian capitals stretch from the ornate floor to the wooden ceiling, while Selçuk *faïence* tiles adorn the mosque's alcove. One of Ankara's most important mosques, the **Hacı Bayram Camii,** among the Roman ruins, is built alongside the tomb of dervish saint Hacı Bayram Veli. To get there, go east from Ulus's equestrian statue on Anafartalar Cad. and take a left at the first major intersection.

ROMAN RUINS. Compared to the Classical ruins of the Aegean and Mediterranean coasts, Ankara's Roman remains are less than impressive. If this is your last and only opportunity to see a piece of Rome, however, you may want to check out the **Roman Baths (Roma Hamamı)**, a five-minute walk up Çankırı Cad. from the equestrian statue in Ulus. Built by the Emperor Caracalla (212-217), these baths were in continuous use for 500 years. Little can be seen today except the well-excavated foundations. The many brick piles supported the floors of the baths and allowed heated air to circulate and warm the tiles. Column capitals, statues, and other fragments are arranged around the grass. (Open Tu-Su 8:30am-12:30pm, 1:30-5:30pm. $1.50, students free.)

The inner sanctum of the **Temple of Augustus and Rome (Ağustos ve Roma Mabedi)** lies in overgrown ruin directly adjacent to the Hacı Bayram Camii. Romans built the temple in 25 BC on the site of earlier temples to Cybele the Anatolian fertility goddess, and the Phrygian moon god. Later converted to a Byzantine church, the site became holy to Muslims in the 15th century when Hacı Bayram Veli, a dervish saint, was buried here. Guests can ask the guardian of the dervish tomb to unlock the temple gate. To the south toward the vegetable market, the lonely **Column of Julian (Julianus Sütünü)**, built in honor of the emperor's 4th-century visit, is now crowned by an immense stork's nest. (Follow Hükümet Cad. past the fork leading to the Hacı Bayram Camii and take a left.)

OTHER SIGHTS. At the southernmost end of Atatürk Bul. lie the grounds of the **Presidential Mansion (Cumhurbaşkanlığı Köşkü)**, Çankaya, still the home of Turkey's head of state. While you can't tour the current quarters, if you come to the entrance at 5 Ziaürrahman Cad. and leave your passport at the guardhouse, you will be given a tour of **Atatürk's "country residence,"** which dates back to times when Çankaya was still well outside the city. The residence, preserved as Atatürk left it, displays a much more human side of the man than Anıt Kabir. (Expect to encounter a heavy security presence. Your best bet is to proceed directly to entrance #5. ☎ 468 63 00. Open Su 1:30-5pm.)

West of the Presidential Mansion on Çankaya Cad. is the **Atakule Observation Tower.** Enter the mall below and make your way to the central courtyard, where you'll find the tower elevator ($1.25). From the tower's observation deck you can see past Ankara to the farmland and mountains beyond. Just outside the tower is the Botanical Park, one of Ankara's better picnic spots and a favorite of the city's young couples. Housed in a tiny greenhouse within the park are the pleasant, if not particularly exotic, **Botanical Gardens.** (Bus #613 runs from the equestrian statue in Ulus to the Atakule Tower via Kızılay and Kavaklıdere. Park open daily am-sunset. Free.)

OTHER MUSEUMS. North of Kızılay, just off Atatürk Bul. between Sıhhiye and Ulus, two of Ankara's less inspiring museums stand side by side, looking out across the city. Unfortunately, both were closed for renovations at the time of publication. The **Ethnographic Museum** (Etnografya Müzesi) displays clothing, calligraphy, woodwork, a model room from a dervish lodge, and a golden tuğbu tree rendered by Sultan Mahmud II's daughter, Adile. (Due to reopen in early 2001. ☎ 311 30 07 or 311 95 56. Open Tu-Su 8:30am-12:30pm, 1:30-5:30pm.) Next door, the **Painting and Statue Museum** (Resim ve Heykel Müzesi), commissioned by Atatürk, documents the development of modern Ottoman and Turkish painting, from its birth over 160 years ago through its Cubist and Naive periods to the present day. Over the stairs in the front hallway, two giant oil paintings depict a wolf leading the first Turkic peoples to Anatolia from Central Asia and Atatürk leading the nation upwards from the ashes of the Ottoman Empire (see **Modern Turkish Art,** p. 23). (Painting and Statue Museum closes for renovation every July-Aug. However, modern Turkish art exhibits are on display on the ground floor of Mimar Arif Hikmet Galerisi and the Güzel Sanatlar Galerisi). ☎ 310 20 94. Open Tu-Su 9am-noon, 1-5pm. To get to both museums, climb the steps from Atatürk Bul. to Talat Paşa Cad., passing overhead. Head east for about 400m; the museums will be on the hill to your right.)

In Ulus, the first and second Grand National Assembly buildings have been converted into separate, but very similar, historical museums. The First Assembly building, a.k.a. the **War of Independence Museum** (*Kurtuluş Savaşı Müzesi*, 14 Cumhuriyet Bul.), is preserved exactly as it was in the early 1920s. Paintings and photographs tell the story of Turkey's fight for independence, and several rooms are filled with photographs of each member of the original assembly. Next door is the Second Assembly building, or the **Museum of the Republic** (*Cumhuriyet Müzesi*). Used by the Assembly from 1924 until 1960, this museum is most dramatically distinguished from its partner by an assembly hall full of wax politicians listening attentively as a waxen Atatürk waxes loquacious in his famous Great Speech. Also on display are a few of İsmet İnönü's personal effects, as well as stamps and money used by the republic, including now-inconceivable one-lira notes from the 1930s. None of the museum's descriptions a re in English, but an English language brochure is available at the front desk. *(The museums are west of the equestrian statue, toward the Metro stop on Cumhuriyet Bul. War Museum is at #14. ☎ 310 71 40; $1.50, students $1. Museum of the Republic is at #22. ☎ 310 53 61. $1.50. 65 and over $.80. Both museums open Tu-Su 8:30am-noon, 1:30-5pm.*

▓ DAYTRIP FROM ANKARA: GORDION

*Unfortunately, reaching Gordion can be somewhat difficult. Buses and trains run to Polatlı, the nearest town of any size. Non-express trains from Ankara to Eskişehir usually stop here once or twice a day (2hr., $4). Currently, only the **Baysal bus company** (☎ 224 05 42) links Ankara's otogar to Polatlı (1hr., every ½hr. 7am-9:30pm, $1.50). From Polatlı's bus station, take a service bus into the town center at the train station. A dolmuş leaves from there to Gordion (and adjacent Yassıhöyük) every day but Su (20min., 2 per day 8:30am-3pm, $.75). More likely, you will be forced to hire a taxi ($15-25 round-trip, including an adequate 1hr. waiting time). Some find it cheaper to strike a deal with a local who has a car.*

About 100km west of Ankara lie the ruins of the ancient city of Gordion, where the Phrygians established their capital in the 8th century BC. The Phrygian King Midas, who ruled here, has been immortalized in Greek mythology as the man who greedily wished that everything he touched would turn to gold, with the distastrous result that even his food and drink became golden and inconsumable. Taking pity on the starved, thirsty Midas, Dionysus granted a cure. Centuries later, after the fall of the Phrygian empire, Alexander the Great would once again make Gordion famous when he sliced the Gordion knot in half with his sword, thus fulfilling the prophesy that he who successfully untied the knot would rule Asia.

Over 80 burial mounds surround Gordion. About a quarter of them have been excavated over the past 40 years by an archaeological team from the University of Pennsylvania. The most impressive of these towering earth mounds is the **Royal Tomb,** which contained a perfectly preserved "log cabin" made of juniper trunks— one of the oldest standing wooden structures in the world. Inside the cabin lies the intact body of a man in his 60s. Ankara's Museum of Anatolian Civilizations (see p. 363) displays a replica of the tomb. The scale of the tomb can only be understood by traveling the narrow passage to the center of the mound (not recommended for claustrophobics). To get in, ask the attendant at the **museum** across the street. Renovated in 1999, the museum contains fairly well-labeled examples of Bronze Age, Hittite, and Phrygian pottery, as well as photographs documenting the excavations. (Museum open daily 8:30am-5:30pm. $3.50, students free.) The **acropolis,** built and rebuilt during the 8th and 7th centuries BC, stands a good 15-minute walk to the southwest of the museum. To get there, follow the main road through the nearby town until you see signs pointing out the site. Today, the acropolis is likely only exciting to scholars, but a visit does provide an indication of the settlement's considerable size. The complex of mounds is covered with a maze of randomly disintegrating walls, a few still towering to suggest the city's former glory. The Phrygian gate building is the largest monumental fortification in Central Turkey.

BOĞAZKALE ☎ 364

Put your Greco-Romans and Turks back on the shelf—welcome to Hittite country. Nowhere in the world is the former glory of the 4000-year-old Indo-European civilization more evident than in its ruined capital, Hattuşaş. The ancient city is on the outskirts of present-day Boğazkale, just over 200km east of Ankara and 30km off the Samsun highway. Situated 1000m above sea level, in a gorgeous pastoral setting, the real mystery of Boğazkale is why it isn't visited more. With dramatic natural landscapes, unusual ruins, and hospitable accommodations, Boğazkale's stock is perhaps the most undervalued on the Turkish tourism market.

The 8km loop passing through the Hattuşaş Hittite ruins makes for a beautiful hike through a wild landscape of cliffs and valleys. If you're in a hurry, you can take a taxi or beg for a lift from site personnel. Three kilometers northeast of the site is Yazılıkaya, an open-air temple that contains bas reliefs of 100 of the 1000 or so Hurrian gods. Back on the main road, Boğazkale's small but impressive museum maintains a collection of the site's artifacts. In the last week of June, Boğazkale (along with the regional capital Çorum) hosts a Hittite cultural festival.

▐▌ TRANSPORTATION AND PRACTICAL INFORMATION

Short of renting a car, the easiest way to get to or from Boğazkale is via **Sungurlu.** Dolmuş leave from Boğazkale's town square (25min., when full 7am-5:30pm, $.75). If you're going from Boğazkale to a smaller destination that may not be served by Sungurlu's small otogar, ask the dolmuş to drop you at the **Mavı Ocak Tesisleri** restaurant and gas station, 2km from Sungurlu on the main Sungurlu-Çorum/Samsun highway. It is a frequent rest stop for buses along the highway. The two-lane road from Sungurlu is Boğazkale's only real street, which runs past the museum and a few hotels before ending abruptly in the town square. Near the museum, across from the Aşıkoğlu Hotel, a separate road branches off and heads toward Hattuşaş, Yazılıkaya, and two hotels (the Kale and Başkent). At the site, locals will offer to drive you around, but if you have at least a half day, it's best to see the sights on foot. The town square contains **pharmacies,** bakeries, markets, and the **PTT** (open M-F 8:30am-noon, 1-5:30pm). There is also a **T.C. Ziraat Bankası** that **exchanges traveler's checks.** While there are currently **no ATMs** in Boğazkale, there are several in Sungurlu. Next to the Aşıkoğlu Hotel, the **Boğazkale İlce Sağlık Ocağı** (☎ 452 20 07) is a 24-hour **clinic. Postal code:** 19310.

▐▌ ACCOMMODATIONS AND FOOD

The area's only restaurants are in the pensions. Outside of that, your only hope is sustenance from the bakery and the grocery store.

▨ **Hattuşaş Pension and Restaurant** (☎ 452 20 13; fax 452 29 57). The only hotel in the Cumhuriyet Meydanı. 9 clean, spacious rooms, 2 with private showers and most with a view. The friendly English-speaking owner, Ahmet Baykal, is an excellent source of information. Breakfast $1.50. Singles $7; doubles $12; children under 12 free. V, MC.

Kale Motel and Restaurant (☎/fax 452 21 89). On the road to the Yazılıkaya Hittite temple. Take a right out of the Boğazkale museum and another right at the Petrol Ofisi gas station. The motel is 700m up the hill, on the left, and is a 5-10min. walk from Yazılıkaya. All rooms have baths and great balcony views. Hilltop camping. Breakfast included. 13 rooms. Singles $6; doubles $10. Camping $2 per tent (bring your own); caravan $3. *Let's Go* discount 25% with a student ID.

Başkent Motel Camping (☎ 452 20 37; fax 452 25 67). On the road toward the Yazılıkaya temple. 18 comfortable, decorated rooms with bath and views. Başkent's campground has all the advantages of a hilltop location. Singles $11; doubles $22; camping $4.50 per tent (bring your own); caravan $4.50, with electricity $6.

Aşıkoğlu Hotel and Restaurant (☎ 452 20 04; fax 452 21 71), across from the museum, is Boğazkale's upscale, newly-renovated, modern hotel. All rooms have their own bath. Breakfast included. Hotel singles $30, motel $20; hotel doubles $40, motel $30. Camping $2.50 per tent; caravan $2.50.

CENTRAL ANATOLIA

🏛 THE HITTITE SITE

Expect to spend a full day exploring Yazılıkaya and Hattuşaş. For more information on the Hittites, see **From Hittites to Hellenes,** p. 6.

Beginning in 1600 BC, the great Hittite kings occupied Hattuşaş for four centuries, competing with Egypt for control of the fertile lands and trade routes of Mesopotamia. They conquered Syria (14th century BC) and battled Pharaoh Ramses II (1285 BC). At the same time, they ruled their civilization with a sophisticated legal code. The Hittite Empire ended around 1200 BC when Hattuşaş was burned, though historians still aren't sure exactly who destroyed the city. It may have been the Kashka people, vengeful vassals from the Black Sea, or perhaps the "Sea People," invaders from the Greek islands.

The site has two **ticket kiosks,** one at Hattuşaş and one at Yazılıkaya. To get to the Hattuşaş kiosk, follow the road uphill toward the Başkent and Kale motels and then turn right at the Hattuşaş sign. Bring plenty of water and **start early** before the heat sets in. From the **Hattuşaş** ticket office, signs point to **Yazılıkaya,** about 3km east. *(Both sites open daily 8am-7pm; in winter 8am-6:30pm. $2. The ticket is valid for both Hattuşaş and Yazılıkaya. Since Hattuşaş isn't near any restaurants, you may want to pack a lunch.)*

HATTUŞAŞ. The Hattuşaş road runs from the ticket kiosk in a 7km loop following the city walls. Walking the loop in a counter-clockwise direction, you'll first pass the **Büyük Mabet,** a temple dedicated to the weather god Hatti and the sun goddess Arinna. Today, visitors enter through the *propylon*, or processional entrance, which originally consisted of three (a holy number to Hittites) doors separated by two pools of water. Guards standing in recesses would lay bridges down to admit worshippers. At the Büyük Mabet entrance you'll find salesmen hawking miniature Hittite figures and souvenirs ($4.20).

Farther in are the quarters of the priests, musicians, scribes, and soothsayers, as well as the temple's warehouses, where thousands of cuneiform tablets documenting commerce were found in 1907. Downhill from the temple were the offices of Assyrian merchants. Here, archaeologists found a parallel text in Akkadian and Hittite hieroglyphics that allowed scholars to translate Hittite. The smooth round holes bored into many of the stones originally held bronze rods that kept the stones together. Also, note the individual shrines to the sun goddess and the weather god, to the right of the entrance. These adjacent rooms, the spiritual heart of the temple, were built of special granite from a quarry over 30km away.

Up the hill, the right fork of the road passes the Hittite kings' ruined summer castle, **Yenicekale,** and then winds steeply up to meet the city walls. On the right is the *Aslanlıkapı*, or **Lion's Gate,** consisting of two crumbling doorways framed by lion statues. Note the grooves about a foot above the ground for the hubs of entering chariot wheels. A photographic computer reproduction posted nearby shows what the gate might have looked like in the 13th century BC. Follow the restored city walls running atop the embankment up the hill to the **Yer Kapı,** or "Ground Gate." Popularly known as the *Sfenksli Kapı*, or **Sphinx gate** (1250m above sea level), it was guarded by four sphinxes until one was taken to Berlin and another to İstanbul. Only one remains, as the fourth one has been missing since the city's discovery. The most intriguing feature here is the 71m-long tunnel leading from inside the city walls to the outside. It was once suggested that the tunnel served a military function, allowing for surprise exits in times of siege. However, scholars now agree that it had a ceremonial function. To get a sense of the wall's overwhelming size, walk though the tunnel, take a left, and walk about 100m along the wall to the corner staircase. Once on top, you can walk back toward the gate, the city's highest point. From here, you can observe several razed *mabet* (temples) and a Byzantine church, now little more than giant blueprints marked out by limestone blocks. The plum tree to your left as you pass through *Sfenksli Kapısı* marks the point where the cuneiform and hieroglyphic-inscribed Boğazkale tablets, now in Ankara, were excavated (see **Museum of Anatolian Civilizations,** p. 363).

Moving eastward and downhill along the wall, the next place of interest is the *Kralkapı*, or **King's Gate.** The giant figure is a reproduction; the original is in the Museum of Anatolian Civilizations. Originally believed to be the gate's namesake king, this fellow is actually a war god carrying a battle axe to symbolically defend the gate. Farther along, two cuneiformed chambers lie 50m apart on the right side of the road, on either side of the now-dry Sacred Pond. **Chamber 2,** much more remarkable and well-preserved than unstriking **Chamber 1,** was commissioned around 1200BC by King Shuppiluliuma II, the last king of Hattuşaş. The enclosed cult chamber contains a relief of the king holding a symbol with an inscription mentioning a "divine earth road," the symbolic entrance to the underworld. Just across the road is **Nişantaş,** a rocky mound whose eastern side bears a badly weathered 10-line hieroglyphic inscription, believed to be a narration of the deeds of Shuppiluliuma II. Last on the tour, and worth skipping if you're short on time, is the **Büyük Kale,** a ruined complex of archives, offices, and royal apartments linked by courtyards. This was the main fortress of the Hittite kings, and it contained most of their documents. Archaeologists found 8000 cuneiform tablets here, including a treaty between Hattuziliz II and the Egyptian Pharaoh Ramses II.

▓YAZILIKAYA. The temple of Yazılıkaya is best visited between 11am and 1pm, when the figures carved into the rock are illuminated by the sun directly overhead; shade from the towering grotto easily obscures the bas-relief deities at other times. While in later days the Hittites built large temples at this site, the holy shrine was originally only a series of narrow ravines in the rock (Yazılıkaya means "inscribed rock" in Turkish). These ravines contain reliefs of gods and goddesses on parade. Goddesses appear in profile, wearing long, trailing robes; gods, most wearing kilts, face forward, and their rank can be inferred by the number of horns on their hats. The deities' names are often inscribed over their heads, preceded by an oval ("god" in hieroglyphics).

To the left, **Chamber A** consists of a long, snaking procession of gods and goddesses, increasing in rank toward the head of the procession. Archaeologists suggest that this gallery was used to celebrate the Hittite New Year in the spring. While Hittites had over 1000 deities, most of them were adopted from pre-Hittite peoples native to the area. On the left wall, 42 male gods form a long line, at the back of which are the 12 gods of the underworld; 21 goddesses face them on the right wall. On the far wall, the sculpture culminates in the marriage of the Hittite's two most powerful deities, **Teshub,** the storm god, and **Hepatu,** the sun goddess. Teshub is standing on the backs of two lesser gods, while Hepatu stands on a lion. To the right of Hepatu is a two-headed eagle, a symbol first used by the Hittites. Facing the procession of deities to the right of the entrance stands the famous 2.6m high relief representing King Tudhaliya IV (c. 1250-1220 BC), astride two mountains and under a winged sun disk. His name appears in hieroglyphics in the bouquet-like object in his right hand. The relief's peculiar white and rubbery surface is the result of a latex reproduction procedure employed by a French archaeologist. Unfortunately, latex is not meant to be used for the reproduction of outdoor reliefs, and the king's now-damaged image will disappear in 20-30 years. **Chamber B,** accessible via a narrow passage to the right of the site's entrance, contains better-preserved but less extensive reliefs. On the right wall, a relief of 12 sword-carrying gods might represent the 12 months of the year. Carved into the left wall is the relief of a sword, its hilt formed by 4 lions and its pommel in the shape of Nergal, god of the underworld. This chamber may have been used for the death rites of King Tudhaliya IV, who appears to the right of the sword. The niches carved into the rock were most likely used for sacrificial animal offerings.

BOĞAZKALE MUSEUM. Dolmuş from Sungurlu pass directly in front of the modest Boğazkale Museum, which features an excellent collection of Hittite bureaucratic paraphernalia, including stone stamps, clay contract envelopes, and cuneiform deeds on stone tablets. Photographs document the progress of the dig, and a large map of the site is very helpful. Unfortunately, labels and explanations are not in English. The front desk sells the informative *Guide to Boğazköy* by Kurt Bittel for $5. (☎ 452 20 06. *Open daily 8am-5:30pm. $1.25.*)

SUNGURLU ☎364

Sungurlu is a necessary connection on the way to Boğazkale. From the main highway, **Lise Cad.**, between the otogar on the right and a large playing field on the left, runs toward the center of town, passing the large, green **Gençlik Park** before intersecting **Cengiztopel Cad.**, marked by Hotel Fatih. Buses to Sungurlu stop either on the main highway or at the otogar, which sits just off the highway across from a Petrol Ofisi gas station. **Buses** leave the otogar for: **Amasya** (4hr., 9 per day, $7); **Ankara** (3hr.; 13 per day 7:15am-8pm; $4.80, students $3.50); **Antalya** (10hr.; 6, 7, 8pm; $13, students $11.50); **Bodrum** (10hr.; 6:30pm; $13.50, students $12); **Fethiye** (10hr.; 7pm; $13.50, students $13); **İstanbul** (9hr.; 8:30pm; $13, students $12); **İzmir** (10hr.; 8pm; $13, students $12). For other destinations, you may wait at one of the highway rest stops and hop on a bus en route (ask at the otogar for more info). Despite the claims of local taxi drivers, **dolmuş** do head to **Boğazkale,** from next to Hotel Fatih and Gençlik Park (30min., leaves when full 8am-6pm, $.65). A private taxi is $8 for a one-way trip to Boğazkale, $24-32 for a full tour of the ruins.

Among the numerous banks, a **Türkiye İş Bankası** that **cashes traveler's checks** and has a V/MC/Cirrus/Plus **ATM** is within sight of the Hotel Fatih. (Open M-F 9am-12:30pm, 1:30-5:30pm.) **Gözde Internet Cafe,** a lengthy walk down Çorum Cad. at 100 yıl hal içi No. 40 (☎365 20 40), charges $1 per hr. The **hospital** (Devlet Hastanesi) can be reached at ☎311 80 07. **Postal code:** 19300.

You can crash at **Hotel Fatih,** 24 Cengiztopel Cad., which offers 15 sunny rooms, most with a view and bath; a toilet *alla turca* is on each floor. (☎311 34 88. Singles $8, with shower $12; doubles $16, with shower $22; triples $24.) In the center of town, across from the Türkiye İş Bankası, is the simple but functional **Otel Ferhat,** 3 Baykal Sok., with 17 basic rooms and one lucky toilet *alla turca* per floor. (☎311 80 67. Singles $4.50, with bath $5.50; doubles $9.50, with bath $11.) On the outskirts of Sungurlu, about 1km from the town center, the **Hitit Motel** offers 23 large, clean, bungalow-style motel rooms, each with TV and bath. Hitit also has a large pool and restaurant. (☎311 84 09; fax 311 38 73. Singles $17; doubles $25.) You can find a decent meal at **Birand Restaurant,** inside Özel İdare İşhanı. Follow Lise Cad. past the intersection with Cengiztopel Cad. and take the next right onto Çorum Cad. The restaurant is 100m down on the right. The comprehensive menu includes *dolma* ($1.50) and cold *mezes* ($1.25). (☎311 99 16. Open daily 6am-11pm.) Crunchy *leblebi* (roasted chickpeas), a regional specialty, are available at dozens of shops throughout town.

TOKAT ☎356

And the inhabitants live in luxury, and all their property is planted with vines; and there is a multitude of women who make gain from their persons, most of whom are dedicated to the goddess. There, on account of the multitude of prostitutes, outsiders resort in great numbers and keep holiday.
 —Strabo, Geography

Situated in a valley surrounded by rocky hills, the modern city of Tokat is quieter and more conservative than its history would suggest. Step away from the noisy bustle of Gaziosmanpaşa Bul. to find an old city of crumbling Ottoman houses and winding cobblestone streets, where tourists draw crowds of curious children. Tokat's handful of first-rate sights make for a brief but enjoyable stay, especially when combined with the spectacular caves at nearby Ballıca.

Ancient Tokat, or Comana Pontica as Strabo knew it, was the notorious site of a debauched cult dedicated to the Anatolian mother goddess known appropriately as Ma. Annual orgies were held in honor of the goddess, presided over by the priesthood, the temple courtesans, a throng of wild flagellants, and Linda Tripp.

Near Tokat in 47 BC, Julius Caesar delivered a crushing defeat to Pharnaces II, the King of Pontus, who had dared attack the Roman provinces of Armenia, Cappadocia, and Galatia. Caesar's and Pharnaces' troops clashed between Tokat and Zile, resulting in a Roman victory that inspired Caesar's *"Veni! Vidi! Vici!"* Since then, Tokat has seen Byzantines, Selçuks, Mongols, and Ottomans come and go.

⌐ TRANSPORTATION

Flights: The small airport is about ½hr. away. Tickets to Ankara can be purchased at the **THY office**, 206/4 Gaziosmanpaşa Bul., 2nd fl. (☎214 72 54; fax 212 41 69), opposite the Kent Bank. Open M-Sa 8:30am-12:30pm, 1:30-4pm; open until 7pm in summer. Flights on Tu at 2:20pm; $58, 25% student discount.)

Buses: Metro, Tokat İtimat and **Topçam** have offices at Cumhuriyet Alanı and at the otogar, near the north end of Gaziosmanpaşa Bul., about 2km from Cumhuriyet Alanı. To: **Adana** (9hr.; 4 per day 1:30-8pm; $16, students $14.50); **Afyon** (10hr.; 2 per day at 9pm; $19, students $17.50); **Alanya** (13hr.; 2 per day at 2pm; $22.50, students $21); **Amasya** (1¾hr., 10 per day 7:30am-9:30pm, $3); **Ankara** (6hr.; 7 per day 7am-12:30am; $13, students $11); **Antalya** (12hr.; 2 per day at 2pm; $21, students $19); **Aydın** (11hr.; 2 per day at 3pm; $19, students $17.50); **Denizli** (12hr.; 2 per day at 3pm; $21, students $19); **Diyarbakır** (10hr.; 4 per day 9-11pm; $19, students $17.50); **Erzincan** (4hr., midnight, $9.50); **Erzurum** (8hr., midnight, $14.50); **İstanbul** (12hr.; 10 per day 9:30am-9:30pm; $19, students $17.50); **İzmir** (14hr.; 2 per day at 4pm; $22.50, students $21); **Kayseri** (5hr.; 4 per day 1:30-8pm; $9.50, students $8); **Malatya** (6hr.; 2 per day at 11pm; $14.50, students $13); **Marmaris** (16hr.; 2 per day at 3pm; $24, students $22.50); **Mersin** (12hr.; 2 per day at 8pm; $16, students $14.50); **Samsun** (4hr.; 10 per day 7:30am-10pm; $8, students $7); **Sivas** (1½hr., 10 per day 7:30am–6pm, $3); **Trabzon** (12hr.; 4 per day 3-10pm; $16, students $14.50). To get to town from the otogar, take one of the free *servis* shuttles offered by the bus companies. Otherwise, turn left from the bus company offices, walk 400m to a roundabout, and take another left onto Gaziosmanpaşa Bul.

Local Transportation: You can probably walk everywhere you want to go in town, but dolmuş ($.30) and local buses ($.25) run along Gaziosmanpaşa Bul.

◼◪ ORIENTATION AND PRACTICAL INFORMATION

Mountains and jagged promontories surround the town on three sides, crowned at one point by a **kale** (fortress). The main street, **Gaziosmanpaşa Bul.**, runs north-south, passing through **Cumhuriyet Alanı,** a large plaza that is the town's center.

Tourism Office: A tourist information kiosk is on Gaziosmanpaşa Bul., next to the Gök Medrese. Open M-F 9am-12:30pm, 1:30-6pm; Sa-Su 9am-1:30pm, 2-6:30pm.

Banks: A handful of banks with **ATMs** line Gaziosmanpaşa Bul. **Akbank** (☎214 15 95) **cashes traveler's checks at no commission** and accepts V, MC, Cirrus, Plus. Open M-F 9am-12:30pm, 1:30-5:30pm. **TC Ziraat Bank** (☎214 32 50) also cashes traveler's checks. Open M-F 8:30am-noon, 1:30-6pm.

Hamam: Tarihi Ali Paşa Hamamı (see p. 373).

Hospital: Devlet Hastanesi (☎214 54 00). Ardola Sok., south of the main square on the road to Sivas.

Pharmacies: along Gaziosmanpaşa Bul., among them the **Eczane** at No. 79 (☎214 10 73). Open daily 8am-7pm.

Internet Access: 75 Yil Internet Merkezi (☎212 52 98), behind the Meridyen shopping center, in the car park area. Walk south from Cumhuriyet Alanı and take the 2nd left after passing the Latifoğlu Konağı. $1.25 per hr. Open daily 9am-midnight.

PTT: In Cumhuriyet Alanı. *Poste restante* and other services daily 8:30am-6pm. **24hr. phones. Postal Code:** 60000.

⌐ ACCOMMODATIONS

▧ **Hotel Çağrı,** 92 Gaziosmanpaşa Bul. (☎212 10 28). Outside Cumhuriyet Alanı, near Türkiye İş Bankası. Inexpensive, clean, and cozy rooms with TV, neatly prepared beds, and faux mahogany furniture. 13 rooms, 8 with bath. Singles with bath $9.50; doubles $12, with bath $14.50; triples $17.50, with bath $21. 15% student discount.

Hotel Taç, 1 Vakıf İşhanı (☎214 13 31; fax 212 03 14), across Gaziosmanpaşa Bul. from the Taş Han. 35 spacious pink and white rooms, most with TV. Nice views of the Taş Han and fortress. Breakfast $1.25. Singles $9.50, with bath $12; doubles $16, with bath $22.50; triples $22.50, with bath $29. 20% student discount.

Otel Plevne, 83 Gaziosmanpaşa Bul. (☎214 22 07 or 212 88 56), just off Cumhuriyet Alanı. 18 large, basic rooms, 16 with TV and bath. Laundry service. Breakfast included. Singles $8, with bath $11; doubles $16, with bath $22.50; triples $24, with bath $32.

Hotel Yeni Çinar, 2 Gaziosmanpaşa Bul. (☎214 00 66 or 213 19 29; fax 213 19 27). Near the Türkiye İş Bankası. Probably the highest-quality hotel in the center of Tokat. Brand-new with fully-equipped rooms with TV, minibar, and bath. Attached is an excellent restaurant (*Tokat kebap* $3; cola $.50). Breakfast $1.25. Singles $25, students $24; doubles $40, students $36; triples $56, students $48.

◖ FOOD

Though famous for its wines, Tokat is no culinary capital. The two local specialties are *Tokat kebap* (skewered lamb, potatoes, and eggplant; $4), and *çokelekli* (pita bread filled with crumbled cheese and lamb or potatoes; $.80). Inexpensive restaurants line Gaziosmanpaşa Bul. and its neighboring streets. Vegetarians tired of *çokelek* can try *nohut* (stewed chickpeas) at many of the restaurants, but beware of uninvited chunks of lamb that sometimes turn up.

 Meridyen Cafe, 49 Gaziosmanpaşa Bul. (☎214 18 00), on the top (6th) floor of the Meridyen shopping center. Enjoy an excellent meal and the best view in Tokat from the outdoor terrace tables at this evening student hangout. *İskender kebap* $3; *ayran* $.40. Open daily 10am-10pm; kitchen closes at 9pm.

Bulvar Restaurant, 111 Gaziosmanpaşa Bul., opposite the Otel Taç. Serves the best *Tokat kebap* in town ($3.50), washed down with a bottle of local water ($.25), said to cure kidney, gall, and intestinal miseries. Open 6am-midnight.

Gaziantep Sultan Restaurant (☎212 81 81). Just off Cumhuriyet Meydanı, in the Ulaşioğlu İş Merkezi. The formal atmosphere is surprising for a small town like Tokat. Go for the house specialty *Sultan kebap* ($3). Open 6am-11pm.

◖ SIGHTS

GÖK MEDRESE (BLUE SEMINARY). The most widely visited sight in Tokat, the *medrese* now serves as the town's **museum.** It owes its name to the brilliant tiles that once decorated the entire exterior but are now only visible in the central courtyard. The enamel on these tiles uses a formula so distinct that modern-day enamel technology has never been able to reproduce it. The *medrese* was built in the 1270s by the **Mu'in al-Din Süleyman** (a.k.a. "Butterfly"), a Rasputin-like adviser to the Sultan Kiliç Arslan IV. Mu'in al-Din fluttered craftily around Kiliç Arslan until, no longer able to bear his lust for power, he had the sultan strangled at a banquet in 1264 and appointed himself regent to the underage successor. "Butterfly's" remains are reportedly in the Gök Medrese's collection of sarcophagi.

The museum focuses on artifacts unearthed at the Hanözü, Sebastopolis, and Maşat Höyük archaeological digs between Tokat and Zile. In the calligraphy gallery, note the 7½ meter-long Ottoman diploma required of all tradesmen, listing the owner's every credential from family background to school performance to completed pieces. Other intriguing items on display include local rugs and *kilims*, an exhibit on the making of *yazma* (cloth decorated with woodblock prints), and a wax model of the martyr Christina, whose waxy serenity is offset by the faithfully reproduced bloody gash across her throat. The *medrese* also houses the **Kırkkızlar Türbesi** (40 Girls' Mausoleum) which has 20 coffins painted the color of cotton candy. Museum staff claim that the interred bodies are those of Mu'in al-Din Süleyman and his closest relatives. *(Across from the fortress on Gaziosmanpaşa Bul. Open Tu-Su 8:30am-noon, 1-4:30pm. $1.50, students free.)*

OTTOMAN HOUSES. On Gaziosmanpaşa Bul. (☎214 36 84), a few blocks south of Cumhuriyet Alanı (stand with your back to the PTT and take a right) is the splendid **Latifoğlu Konağı**, a richly decorated 19th-century Ottoman family mansion that is one of Turkey's finest. The sign is easier to see when coming from the north, but the large white house is unmistakable. Enter through the garden. *(Open Tu-Su in summer 8:30am-noon, 1-5pm; rest of year 8:30am-noon, 1-4:30pm. $1.50, students free.)* The hilly, stone-paved **Sulu Sokak** to the west of the Ali Paşa Camii brims with equally nice, though less well-maintained, Ottoman homes. *(Walk toward Cumhuriyet Alanı from the Taş Han and take a right just before passing Ali Paşa Camii.)*

TARİHİ ALİ PAŞA HAMAMI. You can't avoid the 425-year-old hamam in Cumhuriyet Alanı. Intentionally or not, its roof sings a glorious architectural ode to the human breast. The roof is made of two giant side-by-side domes, while the smaller domes are studded with nippled glass bulbs. Across the street, Ali Paşa, the hamam's founder, is buried in the garden of the black-domed mosque bearing his name. *(Women 6am-5pm; men 5pm-11pm. Bath $2.25; kese $1.25; massage $1.25.)*

TAŞ HAN. This *kervansaray*, next door to the Gök Medrese, was built in the 17th century for Armenian merchants. Once a major stop on the Silk Route, the Taş Han, at the time of publication, was being converted into a hotel.

OTHER SIGHTS. At the summit of the hill, at the top of Sulu Sok., in his home at 26 Sofyon Mah., ■ **Duran Atılgan** (☎ 212 04 37) operates a **zurna** shop. These incredibly loud, strident oboe-like woodwinds are used in Turkish folk music. Altıgan, a self-taught virtuoso, performs on request. He'll even sell you a *zurna* ($30-100). *(His house is a bit hard to find; ask passers-by for "Duran Amca" or simply the "zurnacı.")* North of here, the old **fortress** presides over the city. Not much remains, but it has a nice view, and if you climb up during the call to prayer, the town's *müezzins* create a peculiar acoustic effect. *(Head north from Cumhuriyet Alanı; past the museum, you'll see a yellow sign marked "kale." The trip is either a 30min. walk or a $1.50 taxi ride.)*

⚡ DAYTRIPS FROM TOKAT

■ **BALLICA MAĞARASI (CAVES).** A new paved road 25km from Tokat winds up White Mountain *(Akdağ)* 1916m to the entrance of the Ballıca Mağarası. Stalactites and stalagmites of awe-inspiring size have been forming on the marble and limestone walls of these giant caves since the Pleistocene Era, at a rate of 1cm every 400 years. Evidence suggests that some of the caves had human inhabitants in the Hittite period. Ballıca is made up of eight vast chambers that are unseasonably cool in the summer and warm in the winter. Descending hundreds of stairs into a horizonless landscape of jagged and bulbous green rock, punctuated only by the dripping of water and the chattering of bats, visitors have ample opportunity to indulge in *Journey to the Center of the Earth* fantasies. Although there is no English explanation of the caves inside, the paths are very well marked, and it is impossible to get lost. A friendly, English-speaking guide (or *Rehber*) can lead you around for the modest fee of $.75 per person. A thorough tour of the caves takes 1-3 hours. The caves are a popular stop for elderly asthmatics who believe the air within will help their breathing. *(Open daily 8am-8:30pm. $.75.)* A cafe just outside the entrance offers lovely views of the surrounding hills (tea $.20; cola $.50; bottled water $.25). *(Tur 2000 buses leave daily for Ballıca from their office at 225 Niksar Yolu Kavşağı, opposite the Yavşaroğlu Düğün Salonu (1hr. each way, Sa-Su 11am, $2.50). Tur 2000 may be willing to arrange group trips on weekdays. Alternatively, groups might want to spend $25 to hire a taxi to Ballıca and back. Another option is to catch a public bus to Pazar from Tokat's Cumhuriyet Alanı (1hr., $2) and take a taxi to the caves ($5) from in front of the PTT.)*

Travelers who go through Pazar might want to stop at an old **kervansaray** and the **Belediye İşhanı Sosyal Dayanışma Vakfı**, a blanket and *kilim* school. The school is in the back of the building across from the Belediye Hotel on Pazar's main road; turn toward the PTT and the entrance will be on the left. The students and faculty don't speak English, but will display their wares, serve you free tea, and let you try your hand at *kilim* weaving. *(☎ 261 20 01. Open M-F 8:30am-12:30pm, 1:30-5pm.)*

KAT. Budget travelers with ailments of the body, heart, or mind should check out the **healing spring** in Kat. The local tradition is to make a wish in the glade beside the spring, tie a handkerchief to a branch, and drink the spring's water. The area's greatest attractions, however, are the fresh *kiraz* (cherries) sold by farmers at absurdly cheap prices ($.25 per kg). While there's no real reason to sleep here, the site offers a clean, 8-room hotel. (Singles $8.75; doubles $17.50.) *(Dolmuş run hourly from the minibus station, just behind the Gaziosmanpaşa Lisesi (school), off Gaziosmanpaşa Bul. (daily, 45min., 7am-5:30pm, $.75). A taxi from Tokat to Kat is $25. Entry to the park costs $.50; access to the spring waters $1.25; to drink and bathe in a private room $7.50.)*

SİVAS ☎ 346

A thriving outpost in the dry expanse of Anatolia, Sivas was founded by Hittites in 1500 BC. The city saw the successive rule of Assyrians, Persians, Romans, and Byzantines before flourishing under the control of the Selçuk Sultanate of Rum. Sivas still bears the marked imprint of the Selçuk architectural style. In modern Turkish history, Sivas is renowned as the site of the Sivas Congress of September 1919, during which Atatürk sought to fortify Turkish resistance against Allied attempts to partition Anatolia. The traveler arriving at the outskirts of the city would never guess that hidden among the blocky cement-and-glass cityscape are the intricate geometric patterns of some of the most interesting Selçuk monuments in Anatolia. Sivas is also an important center for the production of *kilims*.

▐ TRANSPORTATION

The easiest way to get into town from the otogar is to take one of the many free *servis* buses to the bus company offices in Hükümet Meydanı; ask the driver for the *şehir merkezi* (city center).

Buses: Sivas Huzur (☎223 11 88), on Atatürk Bul., is reputable and drops their listed price 10% for tourists. To: **Adana** (8hr., 1:30pm, $11); **Afyon** (10hr., 4pm, $18); **Amasya** (3½hr., 2 per day 8am-5pm, $8); **Ankara** (6½hr.; 8, 9am, 1:30pm, midnight, 12:30am; $10); **Antalya** (13hr., 6:30pm, $18); **Bursa** (11hr., 7pm, $18); **Eskişehir** (9hr., 7pm, $15); **İstanbul** (12hr.; 9am, 5.30, 7.30, 9:30pm; $20); **İzmir** (13hr., 4pm, $17.50); **Kayseri** (2hr., 2 per day 1:30-6:30pm, $5); **Konya** (8hr., 6:30pm, $15); **Mersin** (8½hr., 1:30pm, $13); **Samsun** (5½hr., 8am-5pm, $10); **Tokat** (1½hr., 4 per day 8am-5pm, $3).

◆▐ ORIENTATION AND PRACTICAL INFORMATION

The city is centered on **Hükümet Meydanı,** the square containing the tourist office and most Selçuk sights. **Atatürk Bul.,** where most of the banks, hotels, and restaurants are located, runs southeast from here toward the new **otogar,** 3km south of the city. **İnönü Bul.** heads southwest from the square toward the train station.

Tourist Office: (☎221 35 35), inside the Valilik building in Hükümet Meydanı; ask the police officer inside for the *"turizm danışma."* Provides a decent city map and brochures. Open M-Sa 8:30am-noon, 1:30-6:30pm.

Banks: Approaching the main square along Atatürk Bul., turn left into Belediye Sok. for **Sekerbank, Ziraat, İş Bankasi, Emlak,** and **Halk.** Additional branches line Atatürk Bul.

Laundromat: Ms. Çiti Laundry, Hikmet Işık Cad., Adliye Arkası (☎223 04 50), directly behind the Valilik building. Wash and dry $2.75. Open daily 8am-8pm.

Hamam: Kurşunlu Hamamı, 23 Arap Şeyh Cad. (☎223 24 88), is Sivas's oldest. Follow Atatürk Bul. from the city center and turn right after Otel Ergin; the hamam is on the right, about 300m ahead. Bath $2; *kese* $1; massage $2. Open daily 4:30am-11pm.

Hospital: (☎221 60 20), north of Hükümet Meydanı. The Kizilay 24hr. private clinic is more convenient; you pay $11 for a consultation. Turn left off Atatürk Bul. into Belediye Sok.; it will be on the first left corner.

Internet Access: Sivas has many cafes scattered throughout its center. Closest to the Otel Madımak are **Speed Bilgisayar,** Gasiosmanpaşa Cad., 6 Erzcan Apt. (☎224 91 78); **Okyanus Cafe** on corner of Belediye and Hiknet Isit Cad, or **Gold Internet Cafe** (☎224 01 83) on Kepener Cad. All are $1 per hr. and close between 11pm-midnight according to demand. For those staying in one of the 4 hotels on Kursun Cad. the **Blue Moon Cafe** (☎221 33 49) is opposite Hotel Fatih.

PTT: In Hükümet Meydanı. Open 8:30am-12:30pm, 1:30-5:30pm. **Postal code:** 58030.

ACCOMMODATIONS

Most of Sivas' hotels are on Atatürk Bul. There is a cluster close to Hükümet Meydanı, and another 1km further away around Kursun Cad. A local directorate grades hotels and controls prices, but hotels may still negotiate.

Yavuz Otel (☎225 0204), on Atatürk Cad., is clean and roomy, if you can brave hallucinogenic carpets and wallpaper.

Otel Akgül, 17 Atatürk Bul. (☎221 12 54), strikes a good balance between quality and cost. Rooms away from Atatürk Bul. are quieter. Like all hotels of its class in town, its listed prices are: singles $9; doubles $15; triples $21. Add 40% for shower in room.

Otel Madımak (☎221 80 27), on Eski Belediye Sok., is a rebuilt 2-star hotel and one of the nicest in Sivas, despite its tragic history (see **Sights,** below). 38 rooms with TV, bath, upholstered chairs, and elegant two-toned furniture. Quoted prices: singles $20; doubles $36; triples $50.

Sultan Otel (☎221 29 86), on Eski Belediye Sok. Singles $17, $13 per extra person.

FOOD

A number of decent, cheap restaurants are off Atatürk Bul. near the PTT (Aliagacami Sok.). **Liquor** stores are rare. There is one opposite Otel Madımak and another **(Kalkan)** on Hiknet Isin Cad. Both close at midnight. If you're bar-bound, **Akalan** is on Belediye Cad., but only admits couples. Beer is $1.50. Open till midnight.

Niyazibey İskender, 4 Eski Belediye Sok. (☎221 34 94), next door to the Madımak Otel, stands above the rest. The interior is complete with flowers, wooden columns, glass chandeliers, and $3 *iskender kebap*. Open M-Sa 8am-11pm, Su 8am-9:30pm.

Büyük Merkez Lokantası, 13 Atatürk Bul. (☎223 64 34). This 3-floor restaurant is popular among locals. Swiftly serves up *kebaps* ($2.10), *börek* ($.90), and a wide variety of local dishes. Open daily 4:30am-midnight.

Hacı Osmanoğulları Aile Et Lokantası, 6/506 Meydan İş Merkezi Aynalı Çarşı (☎224 75 90). On the top floor of the high-rise at the north end of Atatürk Bul. Nice view and a classy atmosphere. *Izgara* $2.10; soups $1.25. Open daily 8am-11pm.

SIGHTS AND ENTERTAINMENT

Fortunately for the tourist, most Selçuk architecture in Sivas is crammed around the central square. For historical background, see **The Great Selçuk Sultanate,** p. 9.

KALE CAMİİ. This small mosque was built in 1580 during the reign of Sultan Murat III. Its well-preserved frescoes and chandelier of drooping glass teardrops earn it a reputation as the most beautiful Ottoman mosque in Sivas. *(Head along İnönü Bul away from the city center to the first building on the left.)*

SELÇUK SIGHTS. A few steps east across the path from the Kale Camii is the **Bürüciye Medrese,** founded in 1271. To the left of the entrance is the tiled *türbe* of the Iranian founder. The tomb's heartfelt inscription reads, "This is the tomb of the humble, homeless servant Muzaffer. May God forgive his sins." Particularly striking is the incredible detail of the interlocking patterns around the doorway.

Follow the cobblestone path farther away from Hükümet Meydanı. On the right is the 13th-century **Çifte Minareli Medrese.** Two red-brick minarets with flecks of remaining blue tile flank the extensive relief of the gateway. Directly opposite is the **Sifaiye Medrese,** built in 1217 under Selçuk Sultan Keykavus I as a hospital, medical school, and asylum, and converted into a *medrese* in 1768. The courtyard with four *eyvans* (vaulted recesses) now functions as a kind of motley bazaar-cum-tea-garden. Above the large *eyvan* at the end of the courtyard opposite the entrance are two reliefs: on the left a bearded man surrounded by solar rays and on the right a woman with braided hair. Don't overlook Sultan Keykavus's enameled *türbe* in the southern wall of the courtyard (to the right when you enter).

Separate from this complex is the **Ulu Cami,** the oldest mosque in Sivas, built in 1196. The interior is a forest of columns (50 in all, arranged in 11 rows). The red-brick minaret was added in the 13th century. *(From the Sifaiye Medrese, return to İnönü Bul., continue walking away from the city center, and after the park ends take the 2nd left onto the wide Cemal Gursel Cad.; the Ulu Camii is 500m ahead.)* Follow the yellow signs to the **Gök Medrese,** or Blue Seminary, which was built for the Selçuk vizier Sahip Ata Fahreddin Ali in 1271. You may be permitted to climb the unnerving wooden staircase to the top of one of the minarets, where there's a view past the city's boundaries to the craggy steppes beyond. *(Open daily 7:30am-noon, 1:30-6:30pm. $.90, students $.60.)*

OTEL MADIMAK. For a taste of recent Turkish history, head over to the Otel Madımak. *(2 Eski Belediye Sok., near the PTT.)* On July 2, 1993, a group of Turkish Alevi intellectuals gathered here for a symposium to honor a 16th-century Ottoman poet, hanged for writing against repression. Among the group was the late Aziz Nesin, Turkish translator of Salman Rushdie's *Satanic Verses.* Nesin's arrival sparked riots in Sivas. Angry mobs chanting religious slogans broke through police gunfire, set fire to the hotel, and surrounded the blaze to prevent rescue squads from entering or controlling the situation. The hotel burned to the ground, killing thirty-seven, though Nesin himself managed to escape by ladder. Though there is no memorial of what happened, the stepped-up police presence every July 2 reveals just how clearly the event lingers in the city's memory (see **Alevi,** p. 31).

ATATÜRK CONGRESS AND ETHNOGRAPHIC MUSEUM. This museum commemorates the historic council that took place here in 1919. After skipping town in foreign-dominated İstanbul, Atatürk landed in Samsun and proceeded to Amasya and Sivas, organizing meetings with leaders from across Turkey in preparation for the War of Independence and the foundation of the Republic (see **The Cult of Mustafa Kemal,** p. 16). The ethnographic items have English labels, but the extensive descriptions of the Sivas Congress are only in Turkish. *(In the city center, across İnönü Bul. from the Selçuk buildings. Open Tu-Su 8am-noon, 1:30-5:30pm. $1.25, students free.)*

▶ DAYTRIP FROM SIVAS: BALIKLI KAPLICA

Take a bus from Sivas's old bus station to Kangal ($1.50), and from the main square (with a large mosque and an Atatürk statue) take a dolmuş the rest of the way (9am-5pm, less frequent after 3pm; $.60). After 5pm dolmuş drivers raise prices. On quieter days, skilled negotiation can yield a $5 round-trip by taxi which includes an adequate hour in the baths.

For a surreal adventure into the realm of bizarre sanatoriums, take a trip out to Balıklı Kaplıca, at first glance just another Turkish hot spring. Ah, but look closer! The bubbling, selenium-rich waters are the world's only habitat for several species of friendly, **flesh-eating fish.** These fish (designated by the management as drillers, suckers, and dressers), along with the healing properties of the water, have made the spring one of the foremost treatment centers for psoriasis, a non-transmittable skin disease. Patients frustrated with the ineffectiveness of conventional medicine flock here to consume untold gallons of water and submit to the care of the "doctor fish." It's worth a dip, even for those who don't suffer from psoriasis.

The spring offers two types of pools: "normal" pools for tourists and other casual visitors ($.75 per day paid upon entry to the park), and *tedavi* (treatment) pools for those with skin ailments ($10 per day). An usher wards tourists away from the treatment pools, so only intentional exfoliation or a morbid interest in it will ensure a dip here. While the tickle of tiny bites may feel a bit peculiar at first, you'll soon get used to the fish as they mysteriously hone in on patches of dry, dead skin. (Pools open daily 7am-noon, 2-7pm). In the nearby stream, the more imposing "doctor snakes" are said to combat St. Anthony's fire, another skin ailment. These snakes are small, harmless and, in fact, rarely encountered.

It's not worth staying overnight in Balikli Kaplica (☎469 11 51), but there are a few options if you're in a pinch: the overpriced **Unsallar Hotel** (☎457 30 36; unsal@alnet.net; singles $33; doubles $58); the nearby **pansiyon** (singles $25; doubles $30); the *baraka*, or shed (singles $15; doubles $20); and the nearby campground ($5 per tent). There's food at the site's **market** and decent **restaurant,** also run by Unsallar. (*Tavuk ızgara* $2.10; *biber dolmasi* $1.75)

BLACK SEA COAST

Along the shores of the Black Sea, the heat of Anatolia gives way to soft sea breezes and tall fir forests descending from high hills to the edge of the sea. The relative brevity and raininess of its summer season may have left the area untouched by international tourism, but come vacation, many Turks make a bee-line for the beautiful ports of Amasra and Sınop, and the refreshing, sandy beaches in Ünye and Çaka. Traveling between towns often requires hours of transit in a crowded dolmuş, careening treacherously around the one-lane mountain Black Sea road with marvelous views. Where forests thin out, fields of tobacco and cherries alternate with sloping pastures nibbled by grazing cattle. *Yaylas* and high-altitude villages provide a welcome retreat to escape the summer heat.

In ancient times Phoenician and Greek traders established colonies in the few spots where the sheer cliffs break to form natural harbors. The ancient trading posts of Sinop, Trabzon, and Amissos (now Samsun) were all pivotal links on the Byzantine Silk Road. Later, the area was a refuge for the Commenus dynasty as the Ottomans encroached upon Constantinople. After World War I, Mustafa Kemal landed at Samsun to begin the Turkish War of Independence. Until recently, NATO naval bases dotted the coast, staring down Soviet fleets on the horizon. Commerce with Georgia and other former Soviet republics has brought new prosperity, but has also led to a marked increase in prostitution in and around Trabzon.

HIGHLIGHTS OF THE BLACK SEA REGION

VISIT ancient **Sumela Monastery** (p. 409), beautifully carved into a cave on the side of a sheer cliff and frescoed with the vivid blues and golds of Byzantium.

TURN the clock back centuries as you visit the brilliant restored Ottoman mansions of **Safranbolu** (p. 379), and discover why the town is on the UNESCO World Cultural Heritage List.

INVESTIGATE the enchanting **Çoruh Valley,** a bizarre cultural crossroads, where you can admire the breathtaking facade of Öşk Vank *kilise* (p. 419).

TREK THROUGH the towering, snow-capped **Kaçkar Mountains** (p. 419), led by a local expert, into the *yayla*s (high plateaus) and crater lakes.

LOSE YOURSELF in the tranquil beauty of **Amasya** (p. 393) and explore the mysterious cliff tombs of the Pontic Kings.

BASK in the sun and dine on fabulous seafood at the untouristed beaches of **Amasra** (p. 383).

DIVE into the crystal-clear waters of **Sinop** (p. 388), the northernmost point in Turkey.

WEST OF TRABZON

The Black Sea highway offers one of the most beautiful drives in the world. Coastal jewels like Amasra, Sinop, and Ordu combine a natural sense of peace with a liberal and friendly population. From Samsun to Trabzon, the Black Sea coast is relatively heavily populated and traveled. West of Samsun, however, lies a different landscape and rhythm. While travel between Samsun and Trabzon is easy, with numerous buses and dolmuş connecting towns along the way, the Black Sea road is in poorer condition and is less often traveled. **The ride is dangerous,**

THE BLACK SEA FERRY For travel in either direction along the Black Sea coast between **İstanbul** (p. 86), **Zonguldak, Sinop** (p. 388), **Trabzon** (p. 403), and **Rize** (p. 410), the Black Sea Ferry provides the most novel, hassle-free, and direct route. In the past it has also stopped at **Giresun** (p. 400), and service may resume there in the future.

Tickets are sold at Turkish maritime lines offices in each city's harbor area. In İstanbul, make purchases at the Karaköy terminal. The quality of on-board lodging ranges from A/ 2 (comfortable, with a two-person bunk) to B/4 (crowded, with four people) to airline-style seats ("Pullman seats"), which are the cheapest. Fares from İstanbul run as follows:

CLASS	TO SAMSUN	TO TRABZON	TO RIZE
A/2	$34	$59	$60
A/4	$27	$44	$45
B/2	$31	$52	$53
B/4	$24	$39	$40
Seat	$13	$17	$18

The ferries leave İstanbul Mondays at 2pm, from the dock at Sarayburnu, a five-minute walk along the shore from the Sirkeci train station. Boarding starts at 1pm. The boat docks at Samsun around 4pm on Tuesday and at Trabzon about 8am on Wednesday. The return trip leaves Trabzon on Wednesdays at 7pm, hits Samsun at 9am on Thursday, and reaches İstanbul Friday at 1pm.

Though costly, food and drinks are sold on board (the purser on the main deck sells the required restaurant vouchers). A better bet is to bring your own groceries. There are also a few small markets near the pier entrance at Samsun.

If the seas are rough (which is rare in the summer), bring along Dramamine or other over-the-counter motion sickness medications. Even if the ride rocks and rolls, however, the hauntingly beautiful nighttime seascape and the unusual mode of travel make it worthwhile.

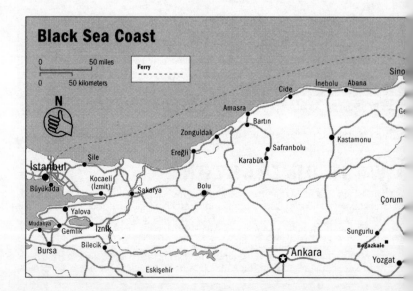

Black Sea Coast

partly because of traffic and partly because of the road conditions. Despite these drawbacks, those who decide to travel on the coastal road rather than via the inland transport hub of Kastamonu will be rewarded with small fishing hamlets, spectacular cliffs jutting straight into the sea, and countless fjords. The spectacular vistas and rich cultural traditions make this a side of Turkey not to be missed.

SAFRANBOLU   ☎ 370

Safranbolu's atmosphere turns back the clock to a 19th-century Ottoman town. The elegant wooden houses have been well-preserved and restored, and ongoing construction is confined to Yeni Safranbolu, the new town, 2km away. The restoration began in 1975, and today, many of the houses are converted to hotels or *gezi evleri* (houses open to visitors). The town was placed on the UNESCO World Cultural Heritage List in 1994 in recognition of its extensive preservation efforts.

▐ TRANSPORTATION

Buses: While direct buses do travel to Safranbolu, you may have to take a dolmuş from the steel manufacturing town of Karabük, 8km away (15min., frequent, leaves when full, $.45). Safranbolu itself is served by **Ulusoy** (☎ 712 66 44), **Güven** (☎ 725 21 45), and **Avrupa** (☎ 712 43 15), which have offices around New Safranbolu's town square. Buses leave from New Safranbolu to: **Adana** (9hr., 3:30pm, $18); **Amasra** (2hr., 8:15am, $4); **Ankara** (3hr., 15 per day 5am-6pm, $9); **Antakya** (15hr., 6:30pm, $20); **Bursa** (9hr., 7pm, $15); **Giresun** (9hr., 7pm, $18); **İstanbul** (7hr., 17 per day 7am-11:30pm, $14); **İzmir** (12½hr., 3 per day at 8:30pm, $18); **Ordu** (8hr., 6pm, $17); **Rize** (14hr., 6pm, $22); **Samsun** (6hr., 5pm, $14); and **Trabzon** (13hr., 6pm, $20).

Taxis: Metered taxis between the old and new town cost about $3.

▐ ▐ ORIENTATION AND PRACTICAL INFORMATION

Safranbolu has two very distinct sections: the beautiful old town, called **Çarşı**, and the largely uninteresting new one, called **Yeni Safranbolu** or Kıranköy. The heart of

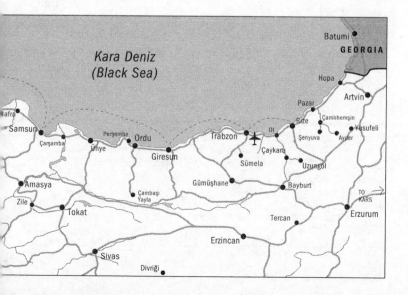

Çarşı and its center of transportation is the main square, **Çarşı Meydanı.** If you stand in the square and look towards the old baths, you will see three streets. On the extreme left, Kastamonu Yollu leads to the Çarşı Pansiyon. The next street, **Akın Sok.,** runs to the Cinci Han, an old *kervansaray.* To the right, **Yukarı Çarşı Sok.** leads to the Arasna, the site of the tourist office and a number of touristy shops. Behind you, **Hilmi Bayramgil Cad.** runs to the new town.

Tourist Offices: The government-run tourist office, **Turizm Danışma Müdürlüğü,** 5 Arasta Sok. (☎/fax 712 38 63), in the Arasta Bazaar, offers maps. Open 8:30am-6pm.

Banks: TC Ziraat Bankası, behind Cinci Han, has an **ATM.** Open M-F 8:30am-noon, 1-5pm; **currency** and **traveler's check exchange** closes at 4:30pm.

Hamam: The 250-year-old **Tarihi Cinci Hamamı,** in the center of Çarşı, is large and clean. Separate sections for men and women. Bath $3; *kese* $.75; massage $1.20. open for men 6am-11pm, for women 10am-8pm.

Hospital: (☎712 11 87), in the new town, near Kaya Erdem Cad., behind the Kız Sağlık Meslek Lisesi.

Internet Access: Only available in New Safranbolu. Try **Cyberland Internet Cafe,** Yavuz İshanı, İnönü Mah., Kaya Erdem Cad. $.80 per hr. Open 10am-11pm.

PTT: On Hamamönü Sok., near the Çarşı Pansiyon. Open M-Sa 8:30am-12:30pm, 1:30-5:30pm. A bigger PTT, on Sadri Artunç Cad., is in Bağlar towards New Safranbolu. Open 8am-11pm. **Postal code:** 78600.

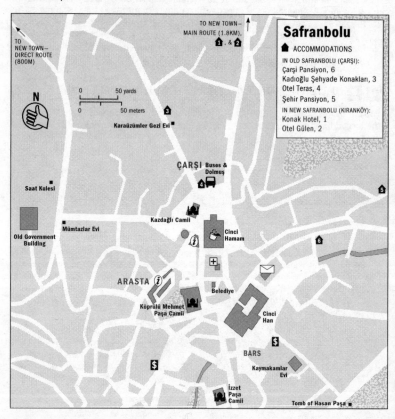

Safranbolu

ACCOMMODATIONS

IN OLD SAFRANBOLU (ÇARŞI):
Çarşı Pansiyon, 6
Kadıoğlu Şehyade Konakları, 3
Otel Teras, 4
Şehir Pansiyon, 5
IN NEW SAFRANBOLU (KIRANKÖY):
Konak Hotel, 1
Otel Gülen, 2

ACCOMMODATIONS

Safranbolu is popular year-round, and accommodations tend to fill up on weekends. If possible, make reservations a few days in advance. New Safranbolu is a hilly 2km road from Çarşı, though frequent dolmuş ease the pain.

OLD SAFRANBOLU (ÇARŞI)

Otel Teras, Çarşı Meydanı, 4 Mescit Sok. (☎725 17 48). Conveniently located directly off the main square in a magnificent Ottoman house. 6 decorated, clean, modern rooms with bath and TV at reasonable prices. Breakfast included, served on a pleasant terrace. Singles $16; doubles $24; triples $32.

Çarşı Pansiyon, 1 Bozkurt Sok. (☎725 10 79). East of the small PTT office. A great budget option, Çarşı has 12 simple rooms, 4 with private bath and 2 with Ottoman-style floor mattresses. Breakfast included. Singles $14; doubles $24; triples $32.

Şehir Pansiyon, Akçasu Mah. No. 10 (☎712 19 70). Beyond Çarşı, heading 100m uphill on Akçasu Sok., just past the Dağdelen Camii. 8 rooms, 3 with bath, and 4 with hill views. Breakfast included. Singles $14; doubles $24; triples $32.

Kadıoğlu Şehzade Konakları, 24 Mescit Sok., Hacıhalil Mah. (☎725 27 62; fax 712 56). All modern rooms with bath, telephone, and TV. Breakfast included. Singles $19; doubles $32; triples $40.

NEW SAFRANBOLU

Otel Gülen, 2 Utku Sok., Ulu Camii Karşısı (☎725 10 82). From the roundabout in New Safranbolu heading towards Çarşı, take the 2nd right onto Cumhuriyet Cad.; the hotel is about 200m ahead. An incredible bargain. Stay in an authentic Ottoman house with a splendid rustic interior at rock-bottom prices. Charismatic owner offers 9 rooms, 4 with bath. Singles $3; doubles $6.50; triples $9.50.

Konak Hotel, 4 Sağlık Sok. (☎725 24 85), on the left as you walk 150m from the roundabout towards Çarşı. 12 comfortable, clean, renovated rooms, 5 with bath and TV. Breakfast $1.25. Singles $12; doubles $24; triples $32.

FOOD

Safran Ocakbaşı (☎712 10 76), Çarşı Meydanı, Hamamönü Sok. Serves good food in a clean restaurant at reasonable prices. *Kanat* (wing) *şiş* $1.30. Free *ayran*.

Karaüzümler Gezi Evi Kafeterya, Hacı Halil Mah., Mescit Sok No. 20 (☎725 14 49). Up the road from Otel Teras. This museum-house serves 5 varieties of *gözleme* ($1), with *dolma* ($1.50) and *erik suyu* ($.80), in a lovely garden or inside in the Ottoman salon.

Kadıoğlu Şehzade Sofrası, 8 Arasta Sok. (☎712 50 91; fax 712 56 57). On the main square. Though a bit touristy, it's one of the places where you can try *kuyu kebap* ($3), made by hanging a whole lamb in a specially prepared underground pit and roasting it for hours and *Safranbolu bükme* (sweet dessert; $2). Decor includes Ottoman couches, low tables, and a bubbling fountain. Open 8am-11pm.

Merkez Lokantası, 1 Yukarı Çarşı (☎725 14 78). Join locals for cheap, ambiance-free meals. *Köfte* $1.50; *Yayla Çorba* (soup) $.60. Open daily 6am-7pm.

Çevrikköprü Tesisleri (☎737 24 61; fax 737 21 19), about 6km from Safranbolu on the road to Kastamonu. Take one of the hourly dolmuş from Çarşı towards Yörük Köyü and ask to be let off at the restaurant. They specialize in *kuyu kebap*. The meat is particularly tender (250g portion $3). In addition to *gözleme*, baklava, and *pide*, they also have a pool full of live trout ($2). Open 9am-midnight.

Boncuk Cafe (☎712 20 65). In the Yemeniciler Arastası. Safranbolu's quietest spot for tea ($.30) or coffee ($.80), but it is as touristed as the rest of the Arastası.

🔍 SIGHTS

OTTOMAN ARCHITECTURE. Safranbolu's highlight is unquestionably its architecture. Traditional wooden mansions are characterized by an overhanging second floor and highly ornate ceiling decorations. Their complex floor plans were designed to maximize comfort and to keep men and women separated. To see the architecture up close, take a peek inside the fancier hotels or visit the *gezi evleri*, restored houses that accept visitors for a small fee.

The best place to start is **Kaymakamlar Evi** (Governor's Residence; ☎712 66 78), the local museum. Enter through the courtyard, where the animals were originally kept. The house has three knockers. Each would indicate the gender of the caller to the members of the household, so a resident of the same sex could answer the door. Various tools and utensils are on display in the courtyard, including wooden cone *frustums* used for making *ayran*. Upstairs, the elaborate construction and decoration of the home attest to the complexity and grandeur of Safranbolu's Ottoman houses. One of the most unusual features is the *döner dolabı*, a rotating cabinet set in the wall between the kitchen and the dining room that allowed female residents to serve food to male guests without showing themselves. After your tour, sip tea ($.25) the garden. *(To get to the house from the square, walk along Akın Sok. to the Cinci Han; Kaymakamlar is on the little street past the TC Ziraat Bankası and behind the Cinci Han. $.80, students $.40. Open in summer 9am-9pm, in winter 9am-5pm.)*

Kileciler Evi, at the intersection of Akpınar Sok. and Sışayanın Sok., 300m down Manifaturacılar Sok., heading away from the Cinci Han and main square, is worth the walk. This house boasts a gorgeous exterior, trellised balcony, and restored interior. *(☎712 82 00. Open M-F 9am-7pm, Sa-Su 9am-8pm. $.80, students $.40.)*

Other *gezi evleri* include the **Karaüzümler Gezi Evi,** on Mescit Sok. past the Otel Teras. Though more worn than Kaymakamlar, the rough, unfinished, wood-reinforced façade of the this 97-year-old building is an interesting change from the flat white of other mansions. *(Open 9am-10pm. $.70, students $.30.)* On Hükümet Sok., high on a hill past the Tahsin Bey Konağı, the Mümtazlar Evi has an interesting octagonal room on the top floor, as well as a tea garden (tea $.25; cappucino $1.25) with a great view. *(☎712 63 59. Open 8:30am-midnight. $.80.)*

OTHER SIGHTS. Walk up the narrow broken street past Kaymakamlar Evi to reach **Hıdırlık Tepesi,** a lookout point with fantastic views of Safranbolu in all its antiqued glory. Hıdırlık Tepesi houses the **tomb of Hasan Paşa,** an Ottoman notable exiled to Safranbolu in 1843. Peek through the tiny barred slit to see his elaborately carved wooden tomb and the hundreds of coins thrown in by visitors. Also visit the grave of **Candaroğlu Hıdır Paşa,** who conquered Safranbolu in 1358.

Uphill from the Mümtazlar Evi is the old government building, or **Hükümet Binası,** a 19th-century structure that's prettier from a distance. On Manifaturacılar Sok. past the Cinci Han, the **İzzet Paşa Camii,** built in 1796, verges on a Baroque excess of decorative squiggles. The more central 17th-century **Köprülü Mehmet Paşa Camii,** across from the Cinci Han, is less exciting, but its courtyard opens onto the very touristed **Yemeniciler Arastası,** the shopping arcade that houses the tourist office. An oval-shaped complex, this was once home to Safranbolu's famous shoe industry. Today, cafes and gift shops crowd the intimate arcade.

🎵 ENTERTAINMENT

Most of Safranbolu's hopping nightlife centers around the Cinci Han.

■ **Beyaz Ev Pub,** 18-20 Pazar Yeri (☎712 52 53). Behind the Cinci Han. A friendly environment, great live music, and *Efes* draft beer ($1.50) make this a great place to spend an evening. Be sure to sign their guestbook—a collection of compliments, witticisms, and poems by foreign patrons in various stages of intoxication. Live guitar and *saz* music W and F-Sa. Open daily 11am-2am.

Arasna Bar, Arasta Arkası Sok., No. 4 (☎712 41 70; fax 725 30 82). On the ground floor of the Arasna Hotel, this bar hosts an enthusiastic crowd on Friday and Saturday, when live music plays from 10pm. Beer $1.75.

Hangar Disco and Bar (☎712 67 27). In Pazar Yeri, behind the Cinci Han. A compact, crowded dance floor in Old Safranbolu's only disco. Beer $2. Cover $3 from 1pm-6pm, $4 from 7pm-3am; first drink and munchies included. Open 1pm-2am.

Turku Cafe Bar, 22 Pazar Yeri (☎725 46 66). Next to Hangar Disco. Live Turkish folk music W and F-Su 9pm-1am. Beer $1.50. Open 11am-2am.

AMASRA   ☎378

Today, along with Sinop, Amasra (pop. 6300) is one of the region's most lovely coastal towns. Over 3000 years of trade and fishing have left Amasra the same quiet beach getaway that Queen Amastris was looking for in the 4th century BC when she founded the town on the site of Sesamos, an ancient Miletian port. Its natural beauty is as striking as that of its namesake: craggy cliffs rise above snaking shorelines, rocky islands, and rich blue waters. Far from the urban grind, Amasra's beautiful coast, excellent seafood, and unerringly spectacular sunsets make it one of the best places on the Black Sea to catch your breath and kick back for a few days. Amasra is also a good base for beach daytrips in nearby Bozköy.

⌷ TRANSPORTATION. The main transport hub closest to Amasra is **Bartin,** 16km south, accessible by **dolmuş** (every ½hr. 7:30am-9pm; $.80, students $.60). Most major buses pass through Bartin. **Özemniyet** (☎315 10 56) and **AS74** (☎315 17 63) provide direct **bus** service from Amasra to: **Afyon** (8½hr., 7pm, $19); **Ankara** (4½hr., 8 per day 5:30am-1am, $9.50); **Bodrum** (17hr., 7pm, $24); **Bursa** (8hr.; 10:30am, 5pm; $13); **İstanbul** (8hr., 7 per day 6:30am-11:30pm, $13); **İzmir** (13hr., 5pm, $21). **Minibuses** run to **Bartin** and **Cide** (2½hr.; 7, 11am, 2:30, 7pm; $3, students $2.50).

⛴⛴ ORIENTATION AND PRACTICAL INFORMATION. Amasra sits on a peninsula that juts out into the Black Sea, forming two harbors. The western harbor is known as **Küçük Liman,** the eastern one as **Büyük Liman. Küçük Liman Cad.** runs along the western harbor by the hotels before winding left into the fortress. There is a small square on the western harbor, surrounded by the PTT and a number of hotels and restaurants. **Çekiciler Cad.** (the woodworking market) runs east from Küçük Liman Cad. across the peninsula towards the eastern harbor.

In the square, **Türkiye İş Bankası** has an **ATM** and **exchanges currency** and **traveler's checks.** (Open M-F 9am-12:30pm, 1:30-5:30pm.) While there is **no tourist office** in town, the **Belediye Bina** (municipal building) has a reception desk which can be of assistance. A wonderful English-language resource is the **Aydın Eczanesi,** a pharmacy (☎315 23 23) next door to the PTT. Friendly pharmacist Aydın Söğüt, his wife, and his daughter can help with minor currency exchange and, of course, **medical assistance.** (Open daily 8:30am-midnight.) Other services include: the **Devlet Hastanesi** (state **hospital,** ☎315 21 98), though there are no 24-hr. pharmacies; **IZO Internet Cafe** on Kum Mah., Barış Sok. No. 3/A (open 9am-midnight; $.90 per hr.); and the **PTT,** on the square by the western harbor, which has a currency exchange (open in summer 8am-11pm; rest of year 8am-5pm). **Postal code:** 74300.

⌂ ACCOMMODATIONS. In the summer, make reservations in advance. Toward the center of town, the ▪ **Otel Belvü Palas,** 20 Küçük Liman Cad., has 15 large, clean rooms with whitewashed walls, many with stunning views and all with bath. (☎315 12 37. Singles $13; doubles $25.50; triples $38.50; quads $51.) The **Nur Turistik Pansiyon,** Küçük Liman Mah. Çamlık Sok. No. 3, along the waterfront road, offers 17 rooms, eight with waterfront views. (☎315 10 15. Singles $8; doubles $16; triples $24.) **Paşakaptan Oteli,** 1 Çamlık Sok., next door to Nur Turistik, has 20 large, well-furnished rooms, 10 with bath, and 15 with harbor views. (☎315 10 11. Singles $9.50; doubles $19; triples $29; quads $38.50.) Across the peninsula, on the eastern harbor, is the small **Amasra Oteli,** 49 General Mithat

Ceylan Cad, which offers eight comfortable, carpeted rooms, six with bath and two with sea views. (☎315 17 22; fax 315 30 25. Doubles $19; triples $24. Discount for longer stays.) Next door is the larger, more glamorous **Otel Timur,** 57 Çekiciler Cad., sporting marble hallways, hardwood floors, and 18 rooms with immaculate bath, six with sea views and TV. (☎315 25 89; fax 315 32 90. Breakfast included. Doubles $24; triples $32.)

🖾🖾 **FOOD AND ENTERTAINMENT.** The restaurants along Amasra's western harbor dish out the port's unsurprising specialty, fish. The large and luxurious 🖾 **Canlıbalık Restaurant,** 8 Küçük Liman Cad., recognized as the town's best, provides an open-air setting with great harbor views and friendly, professional staff. (☎315 26 06. *Barbun* fish $3; *mezgit* fish $2.50; *rakı* $1.25. Open noon-midnight.) Near the Timur and Amasra hotels, overlooking the fishing boats in the eastern harbor, **Çeşm-i Cihan Restaurant,** 21 Büyük Liman Cad., serves a wide variety of tasty fish (from $3) and *Efes* ($1.25) on an outdoor terrace. (☎315 10 62. Open 11am-midnight.) **Liman Restaurant** (☎315 23 48), at the far end of the Büyük Liman Cad., at the end of the harbor, serves *alabalık* (trout; $4), *çupra* fish ($5), and *rakı* ($1.25). **Kale Altı Kafeterya,** Çekiciler Cad. No. 37, is in the middle of the artisan/carpenter's road, serves excellent *gözleme* ($1.25). (☎315 19 21. Open 8am-1am.) Next to the Canlıbalık, **HAN Bar,** Küçük Liman Cad. No. 17, has live Turkish music every night. (☎315 27 75. Tuborg beer $1.30, *rakı* $2. Open 10am-3am.) **Beden Altı Disco-Bar,** on Büyük Liman Cad. at the end of the harbor, is an outdoor **disco** adjacent to Liman Restaurant, and is Amasra's only nightclub. ($1.50 cover includes a drink. Beer $1.25. Open in summer 9pm-1am.)

🖾 **SIGHTS.** Amasra is above all a place to relax. If you must see sights, you can't do much better than the local **woodworking craft and artisans' market** on Çekiciler Cad. One of the more interesting stores here is **Ecem Müzik,** 30 Çekiciler Cad., a small shop with a wide variety of Turkish musical instruments, including wooden *saz* starting at $48. (☎315 22 64. Open in summer 9am-9pm.)

Although the town was fortified as far back as the 3rd century BC, the **citadel** that today stands around a few houses dates from the 9th century AD. Start your tour by following Küçük Liman Cad. from the western harbor left through the fortress gates. You'll arrive at an ancient Roman **bridge** connecting the large island of **Boztepe** to the mainland. Turn right onto Kemere Sok. before the bridge and walk uphill to the **Fatih Camii,** Kale İçi Mah., Camii Önü Sok., a ruined 9th-century Byzantine church that was converted into a mosque when Sultan Mehmet II conquered Amasra in 1460. Pass through another gate a little further ahead to reach a **lookout point** atop the fortress walls on the right. Strings of lights affixed to a billboard outline the silhouette of Atatürk on one side and of Sultan Mehmet the Conqueror on the other. A bit further on lies another neglected Byzantine **church.** The frescoes inside have faded to the point of being barely visible.

The town **museum,** Kum Mah. Çamlık Sok., closed for renovations for the last 3 years, has miscellaneous items from the Hellenic through Ottoman eras, including a collection of Ottoman pistols. Outside, ancient columns and tablets with Hellenic, Roman, early Christian, and Ottoman inscriptions suffer daily rains. (☎315 10 06. Open Tu-Su 8:30am-5:30pm. $1.50, students $1.25.)

If you're looking for something a bit wilder than Amasra's semi-urban beaches, head to nearby **Bozköy,** 15km away, a secluded beach with fine sand, clean blue waters, and dramatic green cliffs. The beach houses a cheap campsite. (Open July 1-Sept. 15. $2 per tent.) Bozköy can be reached via minibus (25min., leaves when full 10am-7pm, $.75), or by taxi (about $16.) Two kilometers further east is the small town of **Çakraz,** with a more developed but still beautiful beach lined with cafes and a few reasonable hotels. Minibuses from Amasra stop in both Bozköy and nearby Çakraz. Be aware that neither Bozköy nor Çakraz is protected by a bay like Amasra's. Some consider these "open beaches" to carry a greater safety risk.

İNEBOLU
☎366

A half an hour west of Abana, İnebolu (pop. 9500) lies on a long rocky beach, divided by a small river. It is the center of the regional fishing industry, and for tourism purposes serves primarily as a Turkish vacation resort and a coastal connection from Kastamonu. A large number of wooden Ottoman houses still stand in the town, though many have fallen into disrepair.

▐ TRANSPORTATION. Metro (☎811 49 60) and **Kastamony Özlem** (☎811 39 30) run **buses** from the **otogar** to: **Ankara** (6hr., 8 per day 5am-8pm, $9.50); **Bursa** (8hr.; 6:15, 6:30pm; $14); **İstanbul** (9hr., 5 per day 9am-8pm, $15); **İzmir** (13hr., 6:30pm, $27); **Kastamonu** (1¾hr., 4 per day 8am-9:30pm, $2). **Minibuses** leave the otogar for: **Abana** (every ½hr. 9am-5pm; $1.50, students $1.25); **Kastamonu** (1 ¾hr., 12 per day 6:30am-6pm, $1.50); **Sinop** (3hr.; 2:45, 4:45pm; $6.50, students $5.50). Minibuses also stop at the Petrol Ofisi on the coastal road.

▞▐ ORIENTATION AND PRACTICAL INFORMATION. The coastal road is known as **Zafer Yolu** to the east of the river and as **İsmetpaşa Cad.** to the west. **Cumhuriyet Cad.** runs inland from the PTT past businesses to a few old wooden houses.

There is a **tourist office** in a wooden hut on the coastal road, 200m east of the river, staffed by a German-speaking woman. (Open daily June-Sept. 11am-7pm.) Many banks, including an **Akbank** (open M-F 9am-12:30pm, 1:30-6pm) with an **ATM** and **currency exchange,** line Cumhuriyet Cad. Other services include: **pharmacies** on Cumhuriyet Cad; the **hospital** (☎811 31 94); **internet access** at **Internet Cafe,** Boyran Mah., 71/B Şarmin Apt., next to Sahil Pansiyon (☎811 57 50. $1 per hr.); and the **PTT,** on the coastal road near the river. (Open daily 8am-11pm; airmail M-F 8:30am-5:30pm). **Postal code:** 37500.

▐ ACCOMMODATIONS. Closest to town, **Sahil Pansiyon,** 63 İsmetpaşa Cad., about 400m west of the bridge and up a flight of stairs, offers family-style living in a quiet location. The six clean rooms have common kitchen and Turkish toilet; top floor rooms have a splendid sea view. (☎811 43 98. $4.25 per person.) The rest of the accommodations lie along the beach. Call ahead in summer. The **Huzur Motel,** 8 İsmetpaşa Cad., right across from Sahil. It has 16 beachside rooms, 11 with Turkish toilets, 5 with Western toilets. (☎/fax 811 46 52. Doubles $11; triples $13.50.) The **İnebolu Yakamoz Tatil Köyü,** Bayram Mah., İsmet Paşa Cad., 500m west of the town center. 56 rooms, all with bath. (☎811 43 05 or 811 31 00.) Motel doubles $16; five-person suites $24; bungalow triples with wooden interior, bunk beds and fridge $13; ytong triples (concrete units) with kitchen $16.)

▐ FOOD. The best establishment in town, the **Gazi Denizcilik Restaurant** on İsmetpaşa Cad., serves a wide variety of fish (*kalkan* $6.50; *barbun* $5) and *pide* ($2.50) on its seaside terrace. (Open Apr.-Nov. 8am-2am.) Also excellent, the **Şehir Restaurant,** on the second floor of the building next to the PTT, has the same owners, menu, and prices, but is open year-round. Try the *Palamut* fish ($3) or *rakı* ($1.25). (☎811 40 72. Open 6am-2am.) For a simpler dining experience, try the **Huzur Pide Salonu,** next to the Huzur Motel. (*Pide* $1.25; *ayran* $.40; *mantı* ($1.60). (☎811 57 64. Open June-Sept. 9am-11pm.)

ABANA
☎366

Situated a half hour east of İnebolu and 2½ hours west of Sinop, Abana (pop. 3000) is a small town whose pebble beach is popular with campers. As it has one of the only campsites around, Abana is a must for those tenting their way along the coast. Those arriving at the end of July can enjoy the annual **Abana Culture and Art Festival** (☎564 10 08), featuring concerts, art exhibitions, and sports tournaments.

▐ TRANSPORTATION. There is no otogar, so all **buses** stop near the bus company offices in the square. Buy bus tickets either from **Kastamonu Özlem** (☎564 24 24) or **Soner Turizm** (☎564 20 20) for: **Ankara** (7hr., 8:45pm, $11); **İstanbul** (10hr.; 2 buses each at 8:30am and 6:30pm; $16, students $13.50); **Kastamonu** (1½hr.; 2 per day at 6:30pm; $3, students $2.50); **Safranbolu** (6hr.; 5am; $11, students $9.50); **Samsun** (6hr.; 5am; $11, students $9.50); **Zonguldak** (7hr.; Th and Su 9:30am; $11, students $9.50). **Minibuses** service: **İnebolu** (½hr.; 8am, 12:30, 2:30pm, then depends on demand; $1.25, students $1); **Sinop** (2½hr.; 5, 9:15am, 5pm; $5.50, students $4.50).

✦⁊ ORIENTATION AND PRACTICAL INFORMATION. Hilmi Uran Cad., the town's main street, extends east from the central square, **Cumhuriyet Alanı**. Services include: a **tourist office** in a small booth on the square (open June-Sept. 8am-midnight); a **TC Ziraat Bankası** with an **ATM** on Hilmi Uran Cad. (open M-F 8am-noon, 1:30-5:30pm); the **hospital** (☎564 11 25); **internet** access at **Beyaz Saray (White House) Internet Cafe**, Merkez Mah., Cumhuriyet Alanı, just off the main square, facing the sea (open 9:30am-1am; $1.25 per hr.); and the **PTT**, next door to the bank (open M-F 8:30am-12:30pm, 1:30-5:30pm). **Postal Code:** 37970.

⌘ ACCOMMODATIONS. Otel Bora, Tahsin Coşkun Cad., directly in Cumhuriyet Alanı, offers the best value with eight rooms overlooking the square. (☎564 12 60. $6.50 per person; discount available.) **Otel Saraçoğlu**, Cevizlik Cad. No. 1, is a new hotel just off Çeşme Sok., to the left of the Atatürk statue. (☎564 26 75. 22 tidy rooms, three with bath. Singles $6.50; doubles $11; triples $14.50, with bath $16; quads $19.) From the square, follow the signs 200m west along the coastal road to **Sahil Pansiyon**, 23 Sahil Cad., a hospitable, family-run place on the seaside with seven quad rooms, four baths, a kitchen, and sea views. (☎564 15 41. $4.50 per person.) Next door to the Sahil Pansiyon is **Ümit Pansiyon**, 24 Sahil Cad. Six rooms, all with bath, are of better quality than Sahil's, but they cost more. (☎564 11 07. $8 per person.) Along the coastal road east of the square is a cluster of bungalow villages. **Doğan Güneş Camp Cafe**, 600m east of the town center, is a seaside campsite with a cafe (beer $1, cola $.60), cold water showers, and toilets. (☎564 30 82. Campsite open June-Sept. $4 per tent or caravan.)

⌑⌂ FOOD AND ENTERTAINMENT. Abana's food is rather unspectacular. The **Köseoğlu Restaurant**, 1 Merkez Mah., in the center of town, has decent fish (*kalkan* $6; *Çiniköp* $4.50) with *rakı* ($1.25) and *Revanı* dessert ($.70). (☎564 11 74. Open 6am-1am.) Nearly next door, **Ümit Ocakbaşı**, 10 Hilmi Uran Cad., serves *kıymalı pide* ($1.50) and pizza ($3) with cola ($.70). (☎564 24 29. Open in summer 8am-2am; in winter 8:30am-9pm.) **Beyaz Saray Restaurant**, Merkez Mah., Kamil Demircioğlu Cad., just off the main square by the sea, has great views, but is perhaps better for an evening drink since the menu is somewhat limited. (☎564 28 40. *Mezgit* fish ($2), *Izgara köfte* ($2), *rakı* ($1.25). Open noon-2am.)

As for entertainment, the town's three main activities are swimming at the beach, sipping tea at the beach, and climbing the nearby hills to look out over the beach. After a day at the beach, head along the coastal road past the campsites to the cluster of **bars** and *çay* gardens which offers live Turkish pop music nightly.

KASTAMONU ☎366

An administrative center for the Romans, Byzantines, Selçuks, and Ottomans, Kastamonu (pop. 57,000) is still an outpost of activity in the sparse green mountains. As it is the region's transportation hub, travelers headed to Ankara or the nearby coast will most likely pass through here. Kastamonu has many wooden Ottoman houses and old Islamic monuments, and its flowing river and surrounding lush countryside make for a relaxing setting.

▤ TRANSPORTATION. Metro (☎214 27 27) and **Kastamony Özlem** (☎214 12 12) provide **bus** service to: **Ankara** (4hr.; 9 per day 5am-midnight; $9.50, students $8); **Bursa** (8hr.; 6:30pm; $17.50, students $16); **Konya** (8hr., 10pm, $16); **İstanbul** (8hr.; 7 per day 10am-11pm; $16, students $14.50); **İzmir** (14hr.; 6:30pm; $27.50, students $24). **Soner Turizm** (☎212 13 34) runs **minibuses** to **Abana** (1½hr., 10 per day 10:30am-7:30pm, $3). **Doğuş** (☎214 17 98) runs buses to **Cide** (2½hr.; 8am, 3, 4:30pm; $1.50). **Demirkaya** (☎214 49 46) goes to: **İnebolu** (1hr., 15 per day 10:30am-7:30pm, $2.50) and **Sinop** (3 hr., 5pm, $6.50).

⚡🗺 ORIENTATION AND PRACTICAL INFORMATION. The main road, the north-south **Cumhuriyet Cad.**, runs parallel to the river that bisects the town. It also passes through **Cumhuriyet Meydanı,** the town's central square. **Belediye Cad.,** which runs west from the river, is home to a number of cheaper hotels and restaurants.

The **Tourism Office and Müdürlüğu** (Directorate), 15 Nasrullah Meydanı, adjacent to the Nasrullah Camii, distributes brochures. (☎212 10 62. Open M-F 8am-noon, 1:30-5:30pm). **Internet access** is available at **Alem Internet Cafe,** Topçuoğlu Mah., İzbeli Sok. No. 3, on a side street off Cumhuriyet Cad. (☎212 84 02. Open 9am-1am. $1 per hr.) A speedy connection is also available at **Efenet Internet Cafe,** 67-68 Nasrullah İş Merkezi. Walk south along the river and take the second right after Belediye Cad.; it's on the bottom floor of the shop-filled building on the left. ($1 per hr.) Other services include: several **banks** in Cumhuriyet Meydanı, including a **Türkiye İş Bankası** with an **ATM** (open 9am-12:30pm, 1:30-5:30pm); the 500-year-old **Araba Pazarı Hamamı,** 80 Belediye Cad., at the end of Belediye Cad. (☎214 57 09; hamam $2.50, *kese* $2, massage $1.75; men's section open 5:30am-11pm, women's section open 8am-5pm); the **hospital** (☎214 10 53); and the **PTT** in Cumhuriyet Meydanı (open daily 8:30am-5:30pm). **Postal code:** 37200.

⌐ ACCOMMODATIONS. The **Otel Selvi,** 10 Banka Sok., has 54 comfortable rooms, 40 with bath and most with TV. Turn onto Belediye Cad. from Cumhuriyet Cad. and then take the first left. The owner speaks excellent English. (☎214 17 63; fax 212 11 64. Singles $6.50, with bath $10; doubles $11, with bath $17; triples $16, with bath $25.50.) The rest of the hotels are on Cumhuriyet Cad. and can be noisy. The **Otel İdrisoğlu,** 25 Cumhuriyet Cad., has 28 older rooms with private bath and TV. (☎214 17 57; fax 214 79 66. Singles $12, students $11; doubles $19, students $17.50; triples $25.50, students $22.50.) The cheapest joint in town is the **Otel Ilgaz,** 4 Belediye Cad., off Cumhuriyet Cad., which has 16 very basic rooms, a shared squat toilet, and old shower on each floor. (☎214 11 70. Doubles $8; triples $9.50.)

⌂ FOOD. Kastamonu has a number of good, inexpensive kebap spots scattered around the square. Many serve the local specialty, *etli ekmek* (minced, spiced meat sandwiched between crispy layers of *pide*). The **Uludağ Pide ve Kebap Salonu,** 19/D Cumhuriyet Cad., serves great *İskender kebap* ($3) and *ayran* ($.30). (☎214 11 96. Open 7am-10:30pm.) Across the river, the comfortable **Kardelen Kebap,** 32 Plevne Cad., provides savory *mercimek çorba* (lentil soup; $.70) and tasty *etli ekmek* ($1.50). (☎212 25 29. Open daily 6:30am-11pm.) After dinner, head to the centrally located **Şengün Pastanesi,** 17/B Cumhuriyet Cad., to sample the local specialty, *sepetçoğlu şekerleme* (a dry, flaky confection; $2.50 per kilo), or the delicious *çekme helva* (a white, cube-shaped sweet). (☎214 23 65. Open 5am-11pm.)

▣ SIGHTS. Kastamonu's main attractions are its varied examples of Islamic architecture. In a square near the Otel Selvi is Kastamonu's largest mosque, the **Nasrulla Kadi Camii,** built in 1506. The splendid **Nasrullah Fountain,** in front of the mosque, bears the inscription "The guest who drinks water from the fountain can't keep himself from coming here again." Opposite the Nasrullah Camii is the **Aşır Efendi Han,** which is now a commercial and shopping center. From here, follow Belediye Cad. to the top and turn left, so that you are opposite the otogar. On the left is the **Yakup Ağa Külliyesi,** a deserted complex that includes a mosque, *medrese,* and kitchen, all built in 1547. Bear right at the fork onto Atabey Sok. towards Kastamonu's oldest mosque, the squat, 13th-century **Atabey Camii,** 500m uphill and well behind the Aşır Efendi Han. A little further uphill, bear right onto Kale Sok., a narrow street that leads to the city's **castle,** a well-preserved complex with a commanding view of the city and surrounding hills. First constructed by the Byzantines, it achieved its ultimate girth under Tamerlane, when the Central Asian conqueror took the city from the Ottomans in 1402.

The **ethnographic museum,** in the Liva Paşa Konağı on Cumhuriyet Cad., adjacent to the Sağlık Müdürlugu (Health Directorate), contains a variety of craft-related exhibits in a well-restored three-floor Ottoman house. (☎214 01 49. Open Tu-Su

8:30am-noon, 1:30-5pm. $1.50, students $.75.) To get there, start from Cumhuriyet Meydanı, walk south along the river 200m and take the second right; the museum will be on the left.

SİNOP
☎ **382**

Sinop takes its name from Sinope, a mythical nymph who spurned the advances of the thunderbolt-hurling god Zeus. Hoping to lure her into his Olympian sack, he offered to grant her a single wish. Thwarting the horny Olympian's plans, she asked for eternal virginity. Zeus, bound to his promise, isolated her on the tiny mountainous peninsula where modern Sinop now slumbers, a town yet to be deflowered by tourists.

With its somewhat removed northern location, Sinop's crystal-clear waters and long, sandy beaches are possibly the cleanest in Turkey. Sinop's natural harbor and peninsula have provided shelter to sailors since ancient times. This is among the most beautiful and enjoyable towns to visit along the Black Sea coast.

█ TRANSPORTATION

The town's main street, **Sakarya Cad.**, runs from the city center southwest past the **otogar** toward the mainland. The larger bus companies don't serve the treacherous road between Sinop west to Amasya; local companies pick up the slack.

Buses: Sinop Bırlık (☎ 261 17 33) and **Sinop Barış** (☎ 261 51 63) run from the otogar to: **Ankara** (9hr.; 3 per day at 9pm; $16, students $14.50); **Bursa** (10hr.; 2:30pm; $12, students $11); **Giresun** (6hr.; 8pm; $12, students $11); **İstanbul** (11hr.; 9am, 7pm; $28, students $24); **İzmir** (18hr.; 2:30pm; $28, students $24); **Kastamonu** (3hr.; 6 per day 10am-7pm; $8, students $6.50); **Ordu** (6hr., 8pm, $9.50); **Rize** (10hr., 8pm, $14); **Samsun** (3hr.; 10 per day 7am-8pm; $8, students $6.50); **Trabzon** (8hr.; 8pm; $13, students $11); **Ünye** (5hr.; 8pm; $9.50, students $8).

Minibuses: These run westward along the coastal road to **Abana** (2½hr.; 8am, 5:45pm; $5.50, students $4.50) and **Inebolu** (3hr.; 8am, 5:45pm; $6, students $5).

█ █ ORIENTATION AND PRACTICAL INFORMATION

The Sinop peninsula juts northeast into the Black Sea. In the center of town at a large roundabout, **Sakarya Cad.** intersects **Atatürk Cad.**, which runs south towards the harbor and a large square, **Uğur Mumcu Meydanı.**

Tourist office: (☎ 261 52 98). Stand in the square with your back to the PTT and turn left; the office is off the road on the right. Open July-Sept. daily 8am-8pm.

Pharmacies: On Sakarya Cad.

Hospital: Atatürk Hastanesi (☎ 261 45 10). Open 24hr.

Internet Access: FVT Internet Cafe, Aşıklar Cad. No. 31, on the main coastal road. Open 9am-midnight. $.80 per hr.

PTT: In Uğur Mumcu Meydanı. Open 8:30am-11pm, full mail services until 5pm. 20 phones, available until 11pm. **Postal code:** 57000.

█ ACCOMMODATIONS

A popular vacation spot for young Turks, Sinop has plenty of reasonably priced rooms, mostly next to the fortifications along the quiet waterfront. Yuvam Belediye Plajı and Karakum Plajı are two of many campsites.

▨ **Otel Meral,** 19 Kurtuluş Cad. (☎ 261 31 00). 20 simple, large, sunny rooms, 3 of which have private bath. Rooms on higher floors have stunning harbor views. Solar-powered hot water. Singles $6.50, students $5, with bath $9.50; doubles $12, students $9.50, with bath $19; triples $16, students $14.50; quads with bath $24.

Uğur Aile Pansiyon, 4 İskele Cad. (☎261 59 47). Along the waterfront. A budget-friendly place with 9 large rooms, 2 with a great view, common baths, kitchen, and free laundry. English spoken. Restaurant on the harbor offers good fish. Singles $8, students $6.50; doubles $13, students $9.50; triples $14.50, students $13; quads $19, students $16.

Otel Denizci, 13 Kurtuluş Cad. (☎261 09 04). Lovely family-run hotel. 10 rooms, 5 with baths. Check on the pigeons through a door between the 2nd and 3rd fl. Free laundry. Singles $5, with bath $8; doubles $9.50, with bath $16; triples $14.50, with bath $19.

Karakum Tatil Köyü (☎261 26 94; fax 261 26 93). This vacation village on Karakum beach is 2km west of the town center along the coastal road. You can make the trip via the regular dolmuş ($.30) or on foot (30-35min.). Breakfast is included at the hotel, bungalows, and apartment villas. **Hotel:** has 18 simple rooms, all with bath and sea views. Singles $9.50; doubles $19; 2-room suites $32. **Bungalows:** 2-person $22.50; 4-person with kitchen $45. **Apartment villas:** 3-person with kitchen $34. **Campsite:** $4.80 per tent or caravan (open June-Sept.).

Gazi Piknik ve Mesire Yeri (☎260 23 87). Set in a forest by the beach. Turn right from the otogar on Sakarya Cad. and walk 100m; the campsite is on the left. Sinop's largest, cheapest, closest campsite. $4 per tent or caravan. Electricity $.50. Student discount.

🍴🎵 FOOD AND ENTERTAINMENT

There are several excellent fish restaurants in the port. Follow the waterfront past the tourist office to the cheap restaurants serving *mantı* and *gözleme*. After a day at the beach, Sinop vacationers play backgammon and *erikriç* (a local version of the game played with tiles) at the waterfront cafes on Kıbrıs Cad.

🍴Balık Restaurant, 1/B İskele Cad. (☎260 33 68). Near the port next to the fortress. Possibly the best fish restaurant in town. Serves fresh crab ($.50 per crab). *Rakı* $1.25. Open in summer 9am-4am; in winter 9am-midnight.

Saray Restaurant, 18 İskele Cad. (☎261 17 29), on the port waterfront, is the runner-up. Select your own fish from the kitchen. Salmon $4. *Rakı* $1.50. Open in summer 9am-4am; in winter 9am-midnight.

Burç Cafe (☎260 32 19). Atop the citadel's tower. A great place to have tea ($.25) and enjoy the view. Live *saz* performances nightly at 9pm. Open Apr.-Oct. 8am-midnight.

Diogenes Bar, 5 İskele Cad. (☎261 57 21), across from the Uğur Restaurant. Behind the large black door lies Sinop's most vibrant bar. Beer $1.25. Open in summer 8pm-4am; in winter 5pm-midnight.

Teleskop Disco. On Karakum Beach, 1km west of the town center and slightly uphill from the coastal road. Head here after a few cups of tea. DJs spin Turkish and foreign dance music. Beer $1.20. Open 9:30pm-very late.

👁 SIGHTS

BEACHES. Beach-goers have a number of options in Sinop's clear, fresh waters. **Akliman Halk Plajı,** 12km from town on the western coast, is long, beautiful, and uncrowded. *(Dolmuş leave from Uğur Mumcu Meydanı. 20min.; every 30min. M-F 8am-6pm, Sa-Su 8am-10pm; $.50.)* The **Gazi Piknik ve Mesire Yeri** has a small, quiet beach, usually populated by camping families. *($.50.)* The nearby **Yuvam Belediye Plajı,** next to the Orman company, is free. The crowded and overdeveloped **Karakum Plajı** draws a younger crowd of sun-seekers. *(A ½hr. walk or brief dolmuş ride ($.30) northeast from Uğur Mumcu Meydanı along Kıbrıs Cad. $.35.)* **Boat tours** leave from the port ($7 per hr.).

FORTIFICATIONS. Sinop's fortifications date from 770 BC, when the port was settled by Miletian colonists. What stands today is a mish-mash of Pontic and Ottoman renovations. Some remains stand near the otogar, but the walls by the harbor at the end of Atatürk Cad. are much more impressive.

MUSEUM. Most notable for a large Hellenistic sculpture of a deer strangely unconcerned about being devoured by lions, the museum also houses a sizable collection of Greek, Roman, and Ottoman coins, early Bronze Age pottery, and various amphorae. Upstairs is a collection of 19th-century Greek Orthodox icons, including several beautiful Annunciations and a vicious St. George slaying the dragon. Also upstairs is a beautiful exhibit on Ottoman calligraphy.

Behind the museum lie the remains of the **Temple of Serapis,** dating to the 4th century BC. Serapis is associated with Asclepius, god of medicine, healing, and dreaming. There is also a memorial to Ottoman soldiers who died after an 1853 surprise Russian attack on the Ottoman navy in Sinop Harbor. *(At the eastern end of Sakarya Cad. Open Tu-F 8am-noon, 1:30-5:30pm; Sa-Su 9am-noon, 1:30-5:30pm. $1.50.)*

SELÇUK SIGHTS. Sinop's two oldest Islamic monuments are the 13th-century rectangular Selçuk **Alaaddin Camii** and **Pervane Medresesi,** next to each other on the north side of Sakarya Cad. The *medresesi* now houses a school, but you can get a peek of the courtyard. Sultan Keykubad built the high-walled mosque—with a single large dome and two small flanking domes—after the Selçuks seized Sinop in 1214. The mosque's *mihrab* is a spectacular example of Selçuk calligraphy in gold and marble. The *medresesi* was built in 1262 after the second sacking of the city.

OTHER SIGHTS. One kilometer from the city center is the **Seyit Bilal Türbesi,** the Selçuk-built tomb of a Muslim martyr. Seyit Bilal was leading an armada to attack Constantinople when a storm forced him into the Byzantine-controlled port of Sinop, where he was decapitated. Legend has it that after his execution, he walked from the city center, at that time located near the Alaaddin Camii, to the site of his tomb—all the while carrying his newly severed head under his arm. While the tomb and its accompanying mosque aren't particularly striking architecturally, the site is exceptionally holy for Sinopean Muslims. *(From the intersection of Sakarya Cad. and Atatürk Cad., continue heading uphill with your back to Sakarya Cad.)*

Abandoned and deteriorating rapidly, the extensive ruins of **Balatlar Kilisesi,** a 7th-century Byzantine church, retains some beautiful frescoes of the evangelists and various saints. *(Near the intersection of Radar Yolu and Kemalettin Sami Paşa Cad., 1km northeast of the museum. To get there, walk uphill from the intersection of Atatürk Cad. and Sakarya Cad. towards the Seyit Bilal Türbesi, but take the right fork after the jandarma road sign.)*

SAMSUN ☎ 362

The largest city on Turkey's Black Sea coast, Samsun is known as the "City of the 19th of May," (or *On Dokuz Mayıs*). This date is inscribed all over the city, marking the day that Atatürk first came ashore on Anatolian land, initiating the movement toward the Turkish War of Independence. The event is celebrated annually at the 19th of May Youth and Sports Festival. Samsun also hosts an annual folk dance festival in mid July. Much of Samsun's architecture was destroyed in an 1869 fire, but occasional Ottoman houses still stand amidst modern construction.

▐▀ TRANSPORTATION

The **otogar,** on **Atatürk Bul.,** the coastal road, is about 2km east of Cumhuriyet Meydanı, the town's main square.

Flights: THY office, 8 Kazımpaşa Cad. (☎435 23 30; fax 431 82 60). *Servis* buses run to the airport 1½hr. before each flight, returning to the office after arrivals. The 23km trip costs $20-25 by taxi. To **Ankara** (45min., Tu-F and Su 7:30pm; $58) and **İstanbul** (1hr.; daily 6, 10am; $82). 25% discount for students and travelers over 65.

Buses: If arriving in town, ask to be let off at Cumhuriyet Meydanı, where all the bus companies have offices. 10-20% student discount, depending on the company.

BUS SCHEDULES

DESTINATION	DURATION	FREQUENCY/TIME	PRICE
Adana	12hr.	7, 10:30pm	$15
Alanya	17hr.	5:30pm	$21
Amasya	2½hr.	6 per day 8:30am-5pm	$4
Ankara	6½hr.	15 per day 9am-midnight	$16.50
Antalya	15hr.	5:30, 6:30pm	$24
Bodrum	19hr.	6:30pm	$20
Bursa	13hr.	7pm	$15
Giresun	3½hr.	7:30pm	$5
Hopa	10hr.	8:30am	$14.50
İstanbul	12hr.	9 per day 7:30am-11pm	$24
İzmir	16hr.	5, 6pm	$26
Kayseri	8hr.	9am, 3pm, midnight	$11
Malatya	10½hr.	9:30pm	$11
Marmaris	21hr.	8, 9:30pm	$20
Mersin	12hr.	7, 10:30pm	$13
Ordu	3hr.	7:30, 10pm	$4.50
Rize	8½hr.	5 per day 8:30am-midnight	$13
Sivas	5hr.	5 per day 9am-9:30pm	$9
Tokat	4hr.	5 per day 9am-9:30pm	$8
Ünye	1½hr.	7:30am, 11pm	$2.50

Trains: On Atatürk Bul., 700m east of Cumhuriyet Meydanı (☎223 50 02 or 223 22 93). To **Sivas** (8hr.; Su-M, W, F 8:20am; $4-5.50) and **Amasya** (2½hr., daily 7pm, $1.25-2).

Ferries: East (Tu 8pm) to **Trabzon** (12hr., $3.50-40) and **Rize** (17½hr., $5-42). West (Th 6:30am) to **İstanbul** (30hr., $13.50-50). The westward boat stops at Sinop and Zonguldak for ½hr. each. The dock is 1km west of Cumhuriyet Meydanı. Walk or dolmuş on Atatürk Bul. ($.30). Buy tickets at the **Alemdarzade office** (☎445 16 05; fax 445 16 04), on the 1st floor of the red building inside the port gates. Open M-Sa 8am-6pm.

✈🛈 ORIENTATION AND PRACTICAL INFORMATION

The journey to town, easier by taxi ($4.50) or dolmuş ($.35), reveals Samsun's tacky industrial sprawl. Kazımpaşa Cad. leads west of the main square to Saat Kulesi Meydanı. The brick-paved streets surrounding this square are home to budget accommodations and restaurants. Further inland running parallel to the shore is **Gazi Cad.**, and further inland still is **Çiflık Cad.** (a.k.a. **İstiklâl Cad.**). Finally, even further uphill, but still running parallel to the shore, is **100 Yıl Bul.**

Tourist Office (☎431 12 28), across Atatürk Bul. from Cumhuriyet Meydanı. Helpful staff speaks English; office has A/C. Open Apr. 15-Sept. 15 8am-7pm; Sept. 15-Apr. 15 8am-noon, 1:30-5pm.

Travel Agencies: Kar Tur, 5/B Kazımpaşa Cad. (☎431 10 26; fax 431 30 60). Deals with tour bookings, ticket sales for THY and other airlines, and Ulusoy bus tickets.

Banks: Many with **ATMs** on Gazi Cad., running parallel to Atatürk Bul., 2 blocks inland.

English-Language Bookstores: Furtan Kitap Kırtasiye, Kale Mah., İstiklâl Cad. No. 35 (☎432 97 97). English-language newspapers and magazines Open M-Sa 9am-8pm, Su 10am-7pm. **Dünya Kitabevi,** 60 Şevketiye Cad. (☎239 08 49; fax 233 97 53), on a side street off İstiklâl Cad. Periodicals include the *Wall Street Journal, USA Today, Time,* and the *Economist.* Open M-Sa 8:30am-9:30pm; Su 11am-8pm.

Laundromat: Nurpak Kuru Temizleme, 56/B Bahariye Cad. (☎234 53 67), on a side street off İstiklâl Cad. Turn off İstiklâl Cad. when you reach the Lee Cooper store. Wash and dry $1.25 per kg. Open 8am-midnight.

Pharmacies: Many are in and around Cumhuriyet Meydanı.

Hospitals: Devlet Hastanesi (☎230 33 00); **19 Mayıs Üniversitesi Hastanesi** (☎457 60 00); **Büyük Anadolu Hastanesi** (☎435 17 85).

Internet Access: CEN NET Internet Cafe, İstiklâl Cad. No. 99. (☎231 26 49). $.80 per hr. Open 9:30am-11:30pm. There are slower connections, but a more central location, at **Karteksan Internet Cafe,** 4/1 Orhaniye Geçidi, (☎431 83 07; fax 431 64 33), 150m down Mevlevihane Cad., a street running east from Cumhuriyet Meydanı. $1.50 per hr. Ping-pong $.80 per hr. Open 8am-11pm.

PTT: On Kazımpaşa Cad. Mail services 8am-noon, 1-5:30pm. Telephone services available 24hr. **Postal code:** 55060.

▶ ACCOMMODATIONS

Most of Samsun's budget hotels are conveniently located just west of the Cumhuriyet Meydanı, along the roads leading to the Saat Kulesi (Clock Tower) Meydanı. For more upscale hotels, head to the establishments in Cumhuriyet Meydanı itself.

Divan Otel, Necipbey Cad., 20 Meserret Sok. (☎/fax 431 36 71), offers more comforts. 22 clean rooms with bath, colorful carpets, towels, and soap. Singles without TV $8; doubles with TV $16; triples with TV $19.

Otel Necmi, Kale Mah., 6 Bedestan Sok. (☎432 71 64; fax 432 20 29). Near the PTT, in the midst of the clothes bazaar. A good budget option. 17 small but clean rooms. Each of the 5 floors has a toilet and shower. Singles $8, students $6.50; doubles $13, students $11; triples $19, students $17; quads $25.50, students $22.50.

Deniz Otel, Kale Mah., 42 Bankalar Cad. (☎431 58 78). Around the corner from Divan. 20 basic, sunny rooms. Each of the 4 floors has a shower and toilet, and the 4th and 5th have a lovely sea view. Singles $10, students $9.50; doubles $17.50, students $13; triples $22.50, students $16.

◖ FOOD

▨ Körfez Restaurant, Körfez Mah. No. 15, Kurupelit (☎457 52 91 or 457 53 29). Körfez is 13km west of the Samsun town center. Take a minibus marked "Atakent-Kurupelit-FAKÜLTE" (15min., $.30), which departs when full from the dolmuş hub on Atatürk Bul., near the Büyük Hotel. A taxi costs $11. Widely recognized as serving among the best *pide* dishes in Turkey, Körfez sits on the sea, with a splendid view of Samsun's entire coastline. Try the *Karışık Yumurtalı pide* ($3) with a *Şeftali Su* (apricot juice; $1).

Oskar Restaurant, Belediye Meydanı (☎431 20 40). Near the watch tower, this large establishment with a pleasant wooden interior serves *kuzu tandir* (oven roasted lamb; $3) and *Beğendeli Kebap* ($2.50).

Cumhuriyet Lokanta, Saathane Meydanı Şeyhhamza Sok. No.3, 3rd fl. (☎43 21 65). This excellent restaurant, owned by Bülent Kaptan (former president of Samsunspor Football Club), serves a tasty *kara lahana dolma* (vegetable dish; $1.50) and a variety of kebaps (from $1.25).

İtimat Balık Lokantası, Cumhuriyet Cad. No. 64-66 (☎420 05 24). 300m east of Cumhuriyet Meydanı. Head here for an excellent fish meal. The atmosphere is better in the evenings. Salmon $5, *Efes* $1.50.

♫ ▤ ENTERTAINMENT AND NIGHTLIFE

Samsunspor Football Club plays from late August until May at the **On Dokuz Mayıs Stadium.** Tickets are available at the stadium the day of the match ($1-3).

Konak Sinemasi (Cinema) (☎431 24 71), İskur Hanı. Just above the northeast corner of Cumhuriyet Meydanı. Shows the latest Hollywood films, with Turkish subtitles.

Ata Kum Beach, 6km west of the city center. Since Samsun's beaches are better left unvisited, take a dolmuş here for a relaxing dip.

C Bar (☎ 233 35 97). Dr. Damil Cad. 300m down İstıklâl Cad., on a small side street by the Turkmaz Ayakkabı shoe store. A kicking combination bar/club. Tuborg beer $2.25. Open daily 9pm-4am.

Collo Disco, Atatürk Bul. No. 629 (☎ 432 49 99). Adjacent to the Büyük Samsun Oteli. Though pricey, this is one of only a handful of quality clubs along the Black Sea. Beer $4. $4 cover includes one drink. Open F and Sa, 9pm-4am.

👁 SIGHTS

Samsun's most important cultural site, the **Atatürk Museum,** is located near the coast, behind the big fountains, just off Cumhuriyet Meydanı. It displays photographs of the national hero and a number of his personal effects. While not nearly as extensive as Ankara's museum at Ant Kabir, the small collection nevertheless offers a glimpse into his life. *(Open Tu-Su 8am-noon, 1-5pm. $1.25, students $.75.)*

Samsun's **Archaeological Museum** contains a well-preserved Roman floor mosaic depicting a battle between the Tritons and the Nereids. The museum also features an extensive exhibit on the excavation of pre-Roman İkiztepe, including a dramatic display on the ancient practice of skull surgery. Most exhibits have explanations in English. *(☎ 431 68 28. Open Tu-Su 8am-noon, 1-5pm. $1.50, students $.75.)*

On the north side of Cumhuriyet Meydanı stands the **Gazi Museum,** which features the bedroom Atatürk lived in, as well as artifacts, in a well-preserved house. *(☎ 435 75 35. Open Tu-Su 8am-noon, 1-5pm. $1.50, students free.)*

AMASYA   ☎358

Towering cliffs, a quiet river, carved rock tombs, and stately Ottoman houses are all part of Amasya's fortuitous meeting of human and natural architecture. In older areas, the town's pedestrian streets and waterfront houses suggest something like a Turkish Venice, despite the rugged surroundings. Today, Amasya is a quiet town, famous for its apples and beautiful setting.

The birthplace of the geographer Strabo (roughly 63 BC), Amasya was the capital of Pontus, a kingdom of Greek-speaking Persians that arose after the death of Alexander the Great. After a series of costly wars with the Romans, the city was razed by Pompey in 64 BC. Rebuilt as a provincial capital, the town flourished under the Romans and Byzantines before falling in 1071 to the Selçuks, who left a legacy of Islamic monuments. Under the Ottomans, who arrived in 1391, Amasya became a theological and cultural center, with 18 *medresesi* by the 18th century.

⌐ TRANSPORTATION

Buses: Arriving buses stop either at the city center or the **otogar,** 3km northeast of town (otogar information ☎ 218 80 12). The larger bus companies provide a free *servis* shuttle to the city center. Otherwise, to get to the center, take any of the city buses ($.30, students $.25) or dolmuş ($.35, students $.30) that stop across the street from the otogar. Dolmuş run to the otogar from behind the Atatürk statue in the main square. A taxi costs $2.50. Otherwise, turn left at the otogar's exit and follow the road straight to the city center. Buses run from the otogar to: **Adana** (10hr.; 4 per day 11am-8pm; $19, students $16); **Alanya** (14hr.; 3 per day at 3pm; $22, students $19); **Ankara** (5½hr.; 7 per day 8:30am-12:30am; $9.50, students $8); **Antalya** (12hr.; 3 per day at 3pm; $22, students $19); **Bursa** (11hr.; 3 per day 6:30-8pm; $19, students $16); **Denizli** (12hr.; 2 per day at 4pm; $19, students $16); **Diyarbakır** (12hr.; 4 per day 7:30-11:30pm; $19, students $17.50); **Erzurum** (9½hr.; 9:30pm; $19, students $16); **İstanbul** (10hr.; 9 per day 9:30am-11:15pm; $19, students $16); **İzmir** (14hr.; 4 per day at 5pm; $22.50, students $21); **Malatya** (8hr.; 6 per day 7:30pm-midnight; $13, students $11); **Marmaris** (15hr.; 2 per day at 4pm; $22.50, students $19); **Mersin** (same bus as .dana; 11hr., 4 per day 11am-8pm; $19, students $16); **Samsun** (2hr.; 8am, 11:30pm; $3); **Sivas** (4hr., 12 per day 8am-11:30pm; $3); **Tokat** (1¾hr., 12 per day 8am-11:30pm; $3); **Trabzon** (8hr.; 5 per day 5-10pm; $13, students $11).

Trains: The *gar* (☎218 12 39), on the north bank, is about 2km west of the main square. To get to town, take one of the dolmuş ($.35) or buses ($.30) that stop across the street. Alternatively, turn left out of the station, cross the first bridge, and take another left onto Mustafa Kemal Paşa Cad., which becomes Atatürk Cad. and runs through the center of town. To **Samsun** (3hr.; daily 4:55am; Tu, Th, Sa, Su 2pm; $1.25) and **Sivas** (5½hr.; M, F, Su midnight; $2.25). 60% discount for students and travelers over 60.

✦♄ ORIENTATION AND PRACTICAL INFORMATION

Amasya is divided by the **Yeşilırmak (Green River)**, which runs roughly east-west. The **north bank,** home to Ottoman houses and the cliff tombs of the Pontic Kings, is the older part of town. The tourist office and most restaurants and hotels lie on the **south bank,** either on **Mehmet Paşa Cad.,** the road running immediately along the river, or the more substantial **Atatürk Cad.,** running parallel one block farther south. The city center *(şehir merkezi)*, which sits between these two roads, is a large plaza with an Atatürk monument.

Tourist Office: (☎218 74 28). Opposite the Yimpaş supermarket in a kiosk along the river's south bank; little English spoken. To get here, turn right from the main square when facing the river. Open Apr. 15-Sept. 15 M-F 10am-noon, 2-6pm; Sa-Su 1-6pm. Closed in the off-season. Tourism director's office on Atatürk Cad. (☎218 50 02).

Banks: Many with **ATMs** line the south bank of the river. **Yapı ve Kredi,** just across the street from the PTT, cashes **traveler's checks** and has a V/MC/Cirrus/Plus **ATM.** Open M-F 9am-12:30pm, 1:30-5pm. **TC Ziraat Bankası,** on Siyat Paşa Bul., will also change traveler's checks. (☎218 41 53). Open M-F 8:30am-6pm.

Hamams: Mustafabey Hamamı (☎218 34 61), just off Mehmet Paşa Cad., 50m east of the tourist office. Divides its single 550-year-old dome between the sexes. Bath $2 for men, $1.50 for women; *kese* $1.25. Open for men 5-11pm, for women 11am-5pm. The 13th-century **Yıldız Hamamı** (☎218 15 94) is across from the Zümrüt Otel on Hazeranlar Sok. Married couples can enter a private bathing area. Bath $2 for men, $1.50 for women; *kese* $1.25; massage $.70. Open daily 5am-midnight.

Hospital: Devlet Hastanesi (☎218 40 00).

Internet Access: Nokta Internet Cafe (☎218 89 73), next to the Yimpaş grocery on Yavuz Selim Meydanı, 10 Belediye Dukkanlar. $.75 per hr. Open daily 9am-midnight.

PTT: On Mehmet Paşa Cad., 100m west of the main square. Open daily 8:30am-12:30pm, 1:30-5pm. Phone card sales and services 8am-11pm. **Postal code:** 05100.

▌ ACCOMMODATIONS

Though the two Ottoman inns along the river are more expensive than most lodgings in Amasya, their beautiful views and traditional decor make them worth the extra expense. Reservations are recommended during July and August.

▨ **İlk Pension,** Gümüşlu Ñah., 1 Hitit Sok. (☎218 16 89; fax 218 62 77), down a small side street off Mehmet Paşa Cad., near the Yimpaş supermarket and across the street from the tourist office. Restored by its architect-owner, the 180-year-old pension offers 6 large, decorated rooms, 5 with private bath. Breakfast $3. Singles $17-34; doubles $25-45. 10% student discount. 25% discount for architects 45 years and older(!).

▨ **Emin Efendi Pension,** Hatoniye Mah., 73 Hazeranlar Sok. (☎212 08 52; fax 212 18 95), on the north bank of the river. Cross over the bridge by the PTT, turn left, and continue 300m. The 5 Ottoman-style rooms, most with shared bath, all have a magical view of the river. Dinner $15. Breakfast $3. Singles $22; doubles $33; triples $39.

▨ **Yuvam Pansiyons 1** and **2,** 24/1 Atatürk Cad. (☎218 13 42; fax 218 34 09; email ariecz@superonline.com), to the left of the main square when facing the river. The **first** is an apartment building with 14 clean but unremarkable rooms, 11 with bath. Singles $9.50, with bath $11.50; doubles $16, with bath $19. The **second** *pansiyon*, farther from the town center but more comfortable, is only open if there are enough guests. Singles $13; doubles $26; triples $38. Camp in the garden: $4 per tent; $6.50 to use their single tent; $13 for the 2-person tent. Both *pansiyons* have kitchens and washing machines ($4 per load), and offer a 10% student discount.

Yalıboyu Otel, 19/D Ziyapaşa Bul. (☎218 70 29). Each sparkling room in this brand new hotel offers TV and private bath. Excellent rooftop restaurant (*Amasya kebap* $2.50; *Efes* beer $1.50). Singles $16, students $13; doubles $29, students $25; triples $40, students $37.

Zümrüt Otel, 28 Hazeranlar Sok. (☎218 26 75; fax 212 35 54), on the way to the Emin Efendi Pension. Offers 12 cheap rooms with TV and fridges. 4 with river views, 9 with showers. Access to kitchen. Breakfast included. $9.50 per person, students $8.

☐ FOOD

Amasya's several kebap and *pide* restaurants are filled all day with locals escaping the sun, sipping tea, and taking in the scenery. If you're in more of a do-it-yourself mood, stock up at **Yimpaş,** a supermarket just across the street from the tourist office. (Open daily 8am-10pm.)

Amasya Şehir Derneği Restaurant, 1 Karşıkaya Mah., 1 Tevfik Hafiz Sok., Vilayet Önü (☎218 10 13), in the Öğretmen Evi (teachers' hostel) on the north riverbank, across the bridge from the Atatürk statue. A great terrace just above the river, although the menu is somewhat thin. *Kuzu dolma iç pilav,* $3. Open daily 11am-midnight.

Ocakbaşı Restaurant, 5 Ziya Paşa Cad. (☎218 56 92). Face the river from the PTT; turn left on Ziya Paşa Cad. (along the river). Serves standard Turkish dishes in an outdoor plaza. *Lahmacun* $.50. Open daily in summer 6am-midnight; rest of year till 10pm.

☐ SIGHTS

THE MUMMIES AND THE ARCHAEOLOGICAL MUSEUM. This museum has an impressive collection of artifacts spanning the history of the region. Note the stunning arabesques on the original door of the Selçuk Gök Medrese and the grisly mummified remains of Mongol rulers and their children, on display in the old Selçuk *türbe* (tomb). (*Just past the Sultan Beyazıt Mosque on Atatürk Cad. Open Tu-Su 8:30am-noon, 1:30-5:30pm. $1, students $.50.*)

PONTIC TOMBS. Carved out of the cliffs north of the city are the now-empty **Kralkaya mezarları,** the tombs of the Pontic kings. Though the graffiti-covered tombs are less impressive up close than from below, a climb up offers beautiful panoramic views of the valley and city. At the same site you'll also find the scanty ruins of the palace of the Pontic kings, known as the **Kızlar Sarayı,** or Palace of the Maidens. The site draws its name from the harems that were a part of the palace complex. (*Cross the bridge by the PTT and follow the yellow signs up the hill to the Kralkaya mezarlan. Open daily 8:30am-8pm. $1.50, students $.75.*) If you really catch tomb fever, head to the **Aynalı Mağara** (Mirror Cave), a few kilometers northeast of town. As the tomb is not enclosed, you can walk all the way around it to see how it was completely cut away from the rock. Unfortunately, graffiti takes a good deal away from the site. (*It's a substantial walk on foot; from the south bank, follow Mehmet Paşa Cad. east past the tourist office, then cross the river at the next bridge, and follow Zubeyde Hanım Cad. to a large roundabout with signs to the tomb. Alternatively take a $4 round-trip taxi from town.*)

FORTRESS. The ancient 3rd century BC *kale* looms high above the city. It was renovated first by the Ottomans and again in the 1980s. The extensive ruins and spectacular views of the entire gorge are worth the long and steep hike. (*From Zubeyde Hanım Cad., on the north bank, follow signs marked "Kale." The walk from the city center takes about 45min.-1 hr.; if you're in a hurry, catch a cab for about $4 one way.*)

OTTOMAN HOUSE MUSEUM (HAZERANLAR KONAĞ). This museum, on the north side of the river, is one of Amasya's best-preserved Ottoman houses, along with the İlk and Emin Efendi *pansiyons.* These houses are characterized by wooden or half-timber exteriors and upper floors that extend out over the street.

Inside, the complicated floorplans often provide separate stairways and quarters for men and women. Decoration consists of geometrically carved wooden ceilings, and, in the restored houses, *kilims*, carpets, and embroidered cushions. The basement houses a gallery of Turkish modern art. *(Open M-F 8am-noon, 1:30-5:30pm.)*

YILDIZ HATUN MEDRESESİ. This **Birmarhane,** or insane asylum, 20m east of the tourist office, was built in 1308 by the Mongol Sultan Olcaytuas as a hospital, asylum, and medical school. The intricately carved doorway and other features of the building look remarkably Selçuk, revealing the extent to which the Mongols incorporated the architectural styles of the peoples they conquered. Doctors continued to be trained at the Bimarhane up until the 19th century. Today, the building houses a music conservatory.

MOSQUES. Follow the river a short way west from the PTT to the **Sultan Beyazıt II Camii.** Amasya's largest Islamic monument, the mosque was completed in 1486 by Sultan Beyazıt II's eldest son and heir apparent Ahmet, who lost the throne in 1513 to his younger brother. The side areas of the mosque were used as dervish quarters, a feature which disappeared from Ottoman architecture after about 1500. From here, continue west on Atatürk Cad., past the archaeological museum to the Selçuk **Gök Medrese Camii** (Blue Seminary Mosque). The blue tiles that gave the mosque its name *("gök"* means "sky") are now mostly gone, and the spectacular carved door has been moved to the archaeological museum. Still, the intricately carved Selçuk doorway is worth a look. The mosque was built in 1267 by Şerafettin Torumtay, governor of Amasya. He and his family now lie buried on the mosque grounds, in the aptly named **Tomb of Torumtay.** Across the street is the splendid Ottoman ▧ **Yörgüç Paşa Camii,** with striking sections of red stone and pristine frescoes. The intimate interior marks a change from the vast vaulted spaces of the larger mosques. East along the river, past the tourist office, is the early Ottoman **Mehmet Paşa Camii,** a sprawling complex that houses a Koranic school for girls.

ÜNYE
☎452

Ünye, 95km east of Samsun, is a charming town with good beaches and a seaside promenade. Several good pensions, restaurants, camping areas, and nearby hiking options make it worth a day's visit. Visitors during the last week in July can enjoy annual art, folklore, and dance festivals.

◪ TRANSPORTATION. The **otogar,** 1km east of the town center, offers a regular dolmuş connection, but **buses** generally stop at their offices downtown. **Ulusoy** (☎323 61 47), **Metro** (☎323 57 74), and **Eray** (☎324 61 57) run buses to: **Afyon** (12hr., 5 per day 5-7pm, $17.50); **Alanya** (18hr., 5 per day 4-7:30pm, $25.50); **Amasya** (4hr.; 5:30, 7, 8pm; $8); **Ankara** (9hr., 5 per day 9am-10:30pm, $12); **Antalya** (16hr.; 3:30, 4, 9:30pm; $24); **Bodrum** (20hr., 4:30pm, $25.50); **Bursa** (13hr., 6 per day 4-9pm, $21); **Çanakkale** (22hr.; 4:30, 6pm; $27); **Eskişehir** (10hr.; 6, 9pm; $16); **İstanbul** (12hr., 9 per day 11am-11pm, $21); **İzmir** (18hr.; 4, 5:30, 8:30pm; $24); **Kayseri** (9hr.; 5, 9pm; $16); **Malatya** (10hr., 7pm, $18); **Marmaris** (21hr., 7:30pm, $27); **Sivas** (7hr., 7pm, $11); **Tokat** (6hr., 7pm, $9.50). 10-20% student discount, depending on the company.

▦ᚱ ORIENTATION AND PRACTICAL INFORMATION. The center of town is **Cumhuriyet Meydanı,** a small square along the coast marked by an Atatürk monument. The **tourist office,** 7 Ünye Spor Lokalı Halı Saha Yanı, is about 500m east of the town center, on the coastal road. (☎323 49 52. Open daily M-Sa 8am-6pm; in winter 8am-noon, 1:30-5:30pm.) There is a **Türkiye İş Bankası** with an **ATM** on the coastal road, just east of the main square. (Open M-F 9am-12:30pm, 1:30-5:30pm.) You can reach the **hospital** at ☎323 98 53. **Internet access** is available at **Inter Point Internet Cafe,** Hükümet Cad., Cezmi Sider İshanı. (☎323 22 33. $.80 per hr. Open 9am-midnight.) Also try **Millennium Net Cafe,** 21/4 Belediye Cad., Hannadar İşhanı, 3rd fl. (☎ 323 99 53. $1 per hr. Open 10am-11pm.) To reach the **PTT,** on Belediye

Cad., from the tourist office, cross the street and turn right at the dolmuş stop. (Mail services 8am-5:30pm. Telephone services until midnight.) **Postal code:** 52300.

⌐ ACCOMMODATIONS. 🔲 **Otel Güney,** 14 Belediye Cad., in the heart of Cumhuriyet Meydanı, offers 22 clean, comfortable rooms, 14 with bath. (☎323 84 06. Breakfast included. Singles $9.50, with bath $11; doubles $11, with bath $13.) Just outside Cumhuriyet Meydanı, **Otel Burak,** 4 Belediye Cad., offers 14 simple rooms with bath. (☎324 52 16. Singles $9.50; doubles $14.50; triples $25.50. 10% student discount.) The cheapest joint in town is the **Otel Çınar,** 22 Hükümet Cad., down a side street behind the Findikkale bus office in the center of town. The 14 small rooms all come with bath. (☎324 85 48. Singles $4.50, students $4; doubles $8, students $6; triples $12, students $9.50). Even better, take a dolmuş heading west along the coastal road to one of the cheap pensions or beachside campsites that offer Ünye's brand of mellow coastal living. About 1km from the town center, the first place the dolmuş passes is the **Belediye Çamlık Moteli,** which tempts travelers with 13 large, villa-like rooms with bath, a beautiful sea view, and a cool, pine tree setting. (☎323 10 85 or 323 13 33. Doubles $12; quads with kitchen $20.) Another 1km further west are **Gülen Camping** (☎324 73 68), and, next door, the bigger, better-equipped **Uzunkum Camping,** 62 Atatürk Mah. Uzunkum features showers, toilets, hot water, electricity, a large private beach, and a restaurant. (☎323 20 22. Small tents $5; large tents $6.50; caravan $8. Trout $3; *meze* $1.50. Open May-Oct.)

⌂ FOOD. In town, sample the magnificent fish dishes at the 🔲 **Park Restaurant,** 6 Devlet Sahil Yolu Üzeri, on the waterfront opposite the town square. Try the *kalkan* ($6) or *levrek* ($6) Black Sea fish. Reservations are a good idea in summer. (☎323 30 53. Open daily 8am-1am). Adjacent to the Çamlık Hotel, the **Çamlık Restaurant,** 1km west of town, occupies a lovely tree-lined spot overlooking the sea. (☎323 11 75. Trout $3. Beer $1.25.)

🔳 SIGHTS. Ünye's most important sight is the **Çaleoğlu fortress,** a Byzantine castle about 5km south of town. From the tourist office, head 300m inland along Niksar Cad. to the dolmuş hub, and ask the drivers about the *kale.* Dolmuş drop you off 2km downhill from the castle (8am-9pm, $.30). Another option is to take a taxi straight to the castle ($6.50). The road leads to the base of the castle, where you'll see a **Pontic tomb** carved into the rock and have an impressive view of the surrounding green hills. A steep and narrow path leads to the top; unfortunately, it is lined with stinging, unfriendly plants and is slippery when wet.

Ünye's best **beach** is aptly named *Uzun Kum* ("long sand"), stretching for over a kilometer, about 4km west of the town center (dolmuş $.30).

If cleanliness is next to godliness, you can't go wrong with Ünye's **hamam,** once a 700-year-old **Byzantine church.** The church itself isn't much to look at, but who opens their eyes during an exfoliating massage? (8 Hükümet Cad. Open for men daily 4am-noon; for women noon-5pm. Hamam $2.50; *kese* $1.50.)

Boat tours leave from the dock in the center of town. Tickets are available at **Şahmer Turizm** (☎634 50 54 or 324 22 09; ½hr., in summer every ½hr. 8-11pm, $1.50.) The **Asarkaya National Park,** 6km southeast of Ünye, has good picnic facilities and hiking trails in the woods overlooking the sea. To get there, take a dolmuş from the hub opposite the tourist office ($.40, 7am-9pm).

ORDU   ☎452

Despite an 1883 fire that destroyed much of its historic architecture and the hasty departure of its Greek and Armenian communities after the War of Independence, the city is today a vibrant and flourishing urban center, and it makes a good base from which to visit the glorious *yayla*s (highland plateaus) that rise up farther inland. Along with Giresun, Ordu is the center of the local hazelnut *(fındık)* industry, producing vast quantities of chocolate and hazelnut candy. At the end of June or in early July, Ordu hosts the Golden Hazelnut Festival *(Fındık Şenliği),* a

THE VOLKSWAGEN BEETLE FESTIVAL Some things are universal. The Turkish word for Volkswagen driver, "VosVoscu," implies a certain friendly openness. Started five years ago by Beetle fanatic and *yayla* expert Enis Ayar, the long-haired, energetic owner of Ordu's Ayışığı Cafe, the July festival brings *VosVoscu* together in Ordu's beautiful countryside. Though it varies from year to year, the general plan of each year's festival is the same. After congregating in Ordu, scores of Beetles, which Turks call *Kaplumbağa* (turtles), come from all over the country, and sometimes as far as Greece, and proceed to the highlands, where they camp, hike, and drive in a large loop that takes them inland to the 3100m lake, Karagöl, and then back out to Giresun. The 2000 festival included a high-altitude outdoor concert by the Ankara-based "Fanfare" classical music group. The festival offers fantastic opportunities to relax, hike, eat fresh trout, meet dozens of friendly people, and ogle Mr. Ayar's four converted Beetles: one normal, one jeep, one pick-up truck, and one limousine.

lively week-long festival that includes theater, singing contests, and folk dance (information ☎225 01 33). Perhaps the most important event is the Volkswagen Beetle Festival in July (see **The Volkswagen Beetle Festival,** above).

▐ TRANSPORTATION. Dolmuş (line #2) run to and from the **otogar** ($.30), 1km east of the city center. To walk from the otogar to the city center, turn left and follow the highway for 15-20min. Alternatively, take a taxi ($3). **Metro** (☎214 12 30) and **Ulusoy** (☎214 16 54) **buses** run to: **Afyon** (13hr.; 8 per day 2pm-8:30pm; $22.50, students $19); **Alanya** (20hr.; 2, 3pm; $29, students $26); **Amasya** (6hr.; 5:30pm; $9.50, students $8); **Ankara** (9hr.; 4 per day 9:30am-9pm; $17.50, students $14.50); **Antalya** (19hr.; 3 per day 2-8pm; $25.50, students $24); **Bodrum** (22hr.; 3pm; $27, students $24); **Bursa** (15hr.; 5 per day 2:30-7:30pm; $25.50, students $22); **Diyarbakır** (18hr.; 5:30pm; $21, students $19); **Elazığ** (13hr.; 5:30pm; $19, students $17); **Erzincan** (12hr.; 10am; $19, students $17); **Erzurum** (8hr.; 2pm; $16, students $14); **Eskişehir** (12hr.; 3 per day 3-7:30pm; $21.50, students $19); **İstanbul** (14hr.; 5 per day 6-8pm; $27, students $22.50); **İzmir** (18hr.; 3 per day 4-8:30pm; $29, students $24); **Konya** (12hr.; 1, 5:30pm; $24, students $21); **Malatya** (12hr.; 5:30pm; $17.50, students $15); **Marmaris** (18hr.; 6pm; $27, students $24); **Rize** (4hr.; 11:30am; $8); **Samsun** (3hr.; every hr. 9am-9pm; $5.50, students $4.50); **Sivas** (9hr.; 5:30pm; $14.50, students $12); **Trabzon** (3hr.; every hr. 8am-midnight; $5.50, students $4.50); and **Tokat** (7hr.; 5:30pm; $13, students $11).

▐▐ ORIENTATION AND PRACTICAL INFORMATION. Ordu lies along the coastal highway **Atatürk Bul.** From the waterfront city center, which is marked by an Atatürk statue, **Hükümet Cad.**, lined with shops and restaurants, runs inland toward the PTT and the museum. Cobblestone Sırrı Paşa Cad. is pedestrian-only. **Boztepe**, a majestic hill 8km away, overlooks the entire coast. Forest and sea meet at **Kiraz Limanı**, a harbor 2km west of the city center.

The helpful **tourist office**, 117/A Atatürk Bul., is in the city center and has an English-speaking staff. (☎223 16 08. Open M-Sa 8am-noon, 1-5pm; in winter closed Sa.) Next door, **Çotanak Tur Seyahat Acentası,** 112 Atatürk Bul. (☎225 20 54; fax 214 15 49), sells THY tickets and other travel services. **Banks** with **ATMs** are on Hükümet Cad. **Internet access** is at the six-computer **Comuf Internet Cafe**, Süleyman Felek Cad., 58 Kayserilioğlu Sok., along the highway, about 200m west of the city center and opposite the Pikola Cinema. (☎241 63 88; fax 225 29 94. $1 per hr. Open daily 8:30am-midnight.) Other services include: **pharmacies** on Hükümet Cad.; the **hospital** (☎225 01 80; open 24hr.); and the 24-hour **PTT**, 100m up Hükümet Cad. from the coast. (Mail services 8:30am-12:30pm, 1:30-5:30pm.) **Postal code:** 52100.

▐ ACCOMMODATIONS. Ordu's best value, **Otel Kervansaray,** 1 Kazim Karabekir Cad., in the middle of the town square, offers 38 basic rooms, most with bath. With your back to the Atatürk monument, walk left; the hotel's sign is to the right, across the street and behind the *Belediye Binası* (municipal building). (☎214 13 30. Singles $5, with bath $6.50; doubles $8, with bath $12; triples $9.50, with bath $14.50.) About 200m further east along the coast lies the better-quality, 64-room **Turist Hotel**, 134 Atatürk Bul. Sunny rooms overlooking the sea suffer from the noise from the coastal road; a recently renovated section offers quieter choices. All rooms have bath and TV. (☎214 91 15; fax 214 19 50. Breakfast included. Singles $13, new section $14.50; doubles $24, new $26; triples $34, new $35.50.)

◯̈ FOOD. Across from the Atatürk Monument, all-purpose cafe-bar-restaurant-art gallery-cinema ⬛ **Ayışığı** (☎223 28 70), 1 Atatürk Bul., serves delicious local specialties such as *Boztepe kebap* (chicken and *köfte* with peppers, potatoes, garlic, and yogurt; $3) and sauteed mushrooms ($1.40). Run by charismatic Enis Ayar, founder of the Volkswagen Beetle Festival, the restaurant proudly declares *"aile salonumuz yok!"* ("We have no family room!"). The cinema is open only in winter ($1.25). On a pier across from the Turist Hotel, **Mıdının Yeri (Midi) Restaurant**, 55 İskele Üstü, offers sea views and a wide selection of Black Sea seafood, including *alabalık* (trout) with salad from $4. (☎214 03 40. Open 8am-1am.) **Bulvar Cafe**, Atatürk Bul. No. 98, just west of the main square, offers a wide-ranging English-language menu. (☎223 02 76. Spaghetti $1.50; pizza $2.) Atop the towering Boztepe hill, the **Boztepe Restaurant-Cafe** has fantastic coastal views and a limited menu of *köfte* ($2) and *Ayran* ($.50). The 8km taxi ride will cost $6-7. (☎223 14 96. Open 9am-2am.) The better **Boztepe Restaurant-Cafe** was closed for renovation at the time of publication. Ordu is world famous for its **hazelnuts** and **chocolates**, exported from its Sağra factory to the rest of Europe. At the **Sağra Nuthouse**, 95 Süleyman Felek Cad. (☎212 13 24), you can sample delicious sweets (1kg of assorted hazelnut chocolates $5).

▣ SIGHTS. The **Ordu Paşaoğlu Konağı** and **Ethnografy Museum** (☎223 25 96), housed in a gorgeous 19th-century mansion, are past the PTT in the Selimiye Mah., at the intersection of Taşocak Cad. and Erkoçak Sok. The first floor contains the standard assemblage of carpets, swords, and traditional dress, while the second floor has been decorated in traditional Ottoman fashion. (Open daily 9am-noon, 1-5pm. $1.50, students $1.) The **Pikola Sinema**, 52 Atatürk Bul., on the coast about 100m west of the Atatürk monument, shows subtitled American films. (☎225 09 71. $3, students $2.50.) **Ordu Cinema**, Düz Mah., Yıldırım Cad. No. 6, also shows films in their original language with subtitles. (☎214 11 71. $2.50, students $2.) Unfortunately, Ordu's two main cinemas close during the summer.

Saray Hamam, Hükümet Cad. No. 49, between the PTT and the Ethnografy Museum, offers *kese* ($1.25) and bath ($2). (☎223 30 43. Open 5am-11pm, women only Sa 10am-5pm.) The **Belde Hotel**, Kirazlimanı Mevkii, 1km west of the town center, opens its **pool** to non-guests. (☎214 39 87. M-F $5, Sa-Su $6.50.) When night falls, settle into the rhythm of the Black Sea and stroll along the **Kordon** (shoreline), where vendors sell boiled corn, sweets, and nuts.

There are **rock tombs** 10km inland from Ordu, in **Bübenköy** and **Dellikkaya**. Dolmuş run from 8am-3pm (1½hr.). A taxi should cost about $12. Twenty kilometers west along the coast is a well-situated Greek church, **Yason Kilisesi.**

▟ DAYTRIP FROM ORDU: ÇAMBAŞI AND TURNALIK YAYLAS. A visit to Ordu is not complete without a stop in the pristine mountain highlands of Çambaşı Yayla (1850m), 2½ hours south of the city. A seemingly endless skyward climb up broken mountain roads leads to this cool, misty paradise with flowering alpine pastures, rocky crags, and icy mountain streams. Three minibus companies have service to Çambaşi, of which the best is **Çambaşı Seyahat**, 2 İsmet Paşa Cad. (☎214 47 02). The minibus leaves when full to Turnalık Yayla (1¾hr., 6:30am-7pm, $1.50) and Çambaşı Yayla (2hr., 6:30am-7pm, $2.50), the two main towns in the highlands. To get to the office, follow the coastal road east from the center of Ordu and turn right at the small river. After the second bridge, turn left onto Zübeyde Hanım Cad., bear left onto İsmet Paşa Cad., and finally take the first right.

NATAŞAS The world's oldest profession is legal in Turkey, and trafficking in prostitutes from the former Soviet Union (hence their Turkish name: the *Nataşas*) has increased dramatically since 1989. Turkish brothels are supposed to be officially licensed and regulated by health and social service authorities. A 1990 law was passed that set the penalty for abducting or raping a prostitute to be equal to that for crimes against any other woman.

Unofficial estimates suggest there may be around 100,000 prostitutes in Turkey. Many women have been abandoned to the brothels after having incurred the scorn of their families. However, a large number have also slipped in unannounced from the former Soviet states. These women may often be the victims of what has grown into a billion-dollar trafficking in women's bodies. Pimps lure desperate former-Soviet-bloc women under the pretense of offers of employment, marriage, or modeling. These women are frequently abused, threatened, drugged, and raped by pimps who hold their passports and demand that they work to repay the "debt" they have accrued for being taken abroad. As illegal immigrants, they are often left with no political recourse, and their life expectancy averages a grim 35 years.

The best of Çambaşı Yayla's selection of basic hotels is the ■ **Ulus Otel,** with 17 comfortable rooms, two with their own sink, shower, and squat toilet. A restaurant is attached. (☎844 23 63 or 214 99 88. Singles $8; doubles $12; triples $16.) If Ulus is full, proceed to the **Otal Doğan,** which has four clean rooms, orthopedic beds, a shared shower, and squat toilet. (☎844 23 03. Singles $8; doubles $16; triples $24.) Those wishing to camp can proceed 3km past Çambaşı Yayla, either on foot or via minibus, to **Ertaş** (☎214 19 69 or 844 20 10), a restaurant, campground, and trout fishery set in a spectacular valley. Ertaş provides three-person tents for $8 per person (price is the same if you have your own tent) and serves up fresh-grown trout with style ($4 per kg). Twenty-five kilometers beyond Ertaş lies a huge crater lake, **Karagöl,** at an altitude of 3100m. The trip takes about two hours by car, but may require a 4WD vehicle and partial access by foot. There are no hotels in Turnalık Yayla, but if you bear left at the fork marked *"Vos Vos Kampı"* and continue walking 2km, you'll reach a **free campground** on the bank of a stream. If you follow the road through the campground for another 10 minutes, you'll come to a series of refreshing mountain pools. The **Belde Otel** in Ordu has a six-room lodge called the **Turnalık Dağ Evi,** in **Çelikkıran** (1600m), a 2km (½hr.) walk from Turnalık. A *servis* bus makes the two-hour trip from the hotel in Ordu ($32). Enjoy hikes, fishing, and horseback riding. (☎214 39 87. Breakfast $3. Singles $12; doubles $16.)

GİRESUN ☎454

This beautiful coastal city (pop. 75,000) proudly emphasizes its independence and differences from its grittier neighbor, Trabzon. With its excellent hotels, beaches, nightlife, and nearby *yaylas*, Giresun is a delightful place to spend a couple of days. There is a public circumcision *(sünnet)* festival here in July, but more interesting (depending on your taste) is the Giresun Aksu festival, held every May 20th. This elaborate pagan fertility ritual, said to have originated in Hittite days, heralds spring and the sowing of new seeds. Participants pass under several iron trivets and circumnavigate the nearby island, throwing 15 stones overboard to symbolically cast away the sorrows of the past.

▐ TRANSPORTATION. Ulusoy, 3 Alparslan Cad. (☎216 44 44; open daily 6:30am-9pm), behind the Belediye Binası; **Metro,** Alparslan Cad. No. 5 (☎216 63 63); and **Fındıkkale,** Gazi Cad. No. 5 (☎216 28 28), offer service to: **Alanya** (20hr.; 12:30pm, 1pm; $29, students $27); **Ankara** (11hr.; 5 per day 8am-8:30pm; $16, students $14.50); **Antalya** (18hr.; 6:30pm; $26, students $24); **Bodrum** (21hr.; 1:30pm; $29, students $24); **Bursa** (15hr.; 4 per day 5pm-2am; $24, students $22.50); **Diyarbakır** (20hr.; 2:30pm; $24, students $22.50); **Erzurum** (10hr.; 4 per day at 2pm; $16, students $14.50); **İstanbul** (15hr.; 9 per day 4-7:30pm; $24, students $21); **İzmir** (18hr.; 5

per day 3:30-3pm; $29, students $26); **Marmaris** (20hr.; 4:30pm; $27, students $25.50); **Samsun** (4hr.; every hr. 8am-8:30pm; $5.50, students $5); and **Trabzon** (2hr.; departing constantly; $3.50, students $3). Dolmuş near the square run east to Tirebolu and Trabzon and west to Ordu, usually departing when the vehicle fills up.

■▪ ORIENTATION AND PRACTICAL INFORMATION. Giresun slopes upward from the coast, covering the hills behind it. The town center, near the water, is the **Atapark.** Running uphill from here is **Gazi Cad.**, the town's main street, where most of the hotels, restaurants, cafes, and banks can be found. The **otogar** is on the coast 3km west of the city center on **Atatürk Bul.** It can be reached by free *servis* shuttles provided by the bus companies or by frequent dolmuş.

The **tourist kiosk,** with helpful maps and brochures, is in the Atapark. (☎216 30 07. Open M-Sa 8:30am-6pm.) Also try the **Director of Tourism** (*Türizm Müdürlüğü*) at Gazi Cad. No. 72, who speaks English. (☎212 31 90. Open M-F 8am-noon, 1-5pm.) There are several **banks** on Gazi Cad.; a **TC Ziraat Bank** and a **Türkiye İş Bankası** with **ATMs** are on the square. (Open 8:30am-5:30pm.) **İnanç Internet Cafe,** Suat Akgün Sok., 2nd fl., can be reached by walking 200m up Gazi Cad, on a small side street on the left. (☎214 03 69. Open 9:30am-midnight. $.75 per hr.) The **Devlet Hastanesi** (**hospital;** ☎216 10 30) and the **PTT** lie about 1km uphill on Gazi Cad. (Open 8:30am-12:30pm, 1:30-5:30pm. 24hr. telephone service.) **Postal code:** 28100.

▪ ACCOMMODATIONS. The best budget bet is the ▪ **Otel Bozbağ,** 8 Eski Yağcılar Sok. To get there, walk one block east from the main square, then turn right. Bozbağ offers 33 bright rooms, half with baths, and a quiet location. (☎/fax 216 12 49 or 216 24 68. Breakfast $1.25. Singles $6.50, with bath $8; doubles $11, with bath $14.50; triples with bath $19.) The ▪ **Er-Tur Hotel,** Osmanağa Cad., Çapulacılar Sok. No. 8, is an absolute bargain. Walk east from the main square and bear right onto a small street. The 25 wonderful, clean rooms all have bath and TV. (☎216 17 57; fax 216 77 62. Singles $10; doubles $20.50; triples $30.) Cheaper options lie near the top of the hill, including **Kılıç Otel,** 12 Çınarlar Sok., which has 21 quiet rooms with tidy beds. Each of 3 floors shares a toilet and shower. (☎216 19 52. Singles $3, students $2; doubles $6, students $5; triples $9.50, students $7.)

▪▪ FOOD AND ENTERTAINMENT. The ▪ **Tibor Restaurant,** 4/4 İncedayı Sok., is one of the fancier places in town. Walk up Gazi Cad., take the first right, and then the first left; Tibor is on the roof of the building on your right. All dishes come with delicious *mısır ekmeği* (cornbread). Go for the *Barbun Buğlama ve Tavası* (steamed striped mullet with cornflour; $4). (☎212 28 78. Open 11am-3pm, 6-11pm.) **Deniz Lokanta,** Hacı Miktat Mah., Aplarslan Cad. No. 1, is one block east of the main square. This pleasant restaurant holds an excellent reputation among locals and accepts major credit cards. (☎216 11 58. *Tavuk şiş* $1.50, *Ayran* $.30. Open 6:30am-11pm.) For dessert, head to the **Balkaya Pastanesi** (☎216 13 15), Gazi Cad., No. 67. Founded in 1932, this landmark serves a tasty *Fındıklı* (hazelnut) biscuit ($.30) and the *Hindistan Cevizli* ($.30).

People come from many surrounding towns for the trendy beach club atmosphere at ▪ **Aretias Disco-Bar,** Teyyaredüzü Mah., Atatürk Bul., No. 1. Take a dolmuş from the town center; tell the driver "Aretias." (Cover $2. Beer $1.50; *rakı* $2. Open 8:30pm-2am; Sa is the best night.) To reach **Yaman Beach,** tell the dolmuş driver "*Yaman plaj.*" Enjoy live music nightly in a low-key atmosphere. (Tuborg beer on tap $1.50.) Up the hill, the **Adı-Yok Cafe,** 32/B Gazi Cad., Turkish for "no-name cafe," is the local youth hangout. Student bands play against a backdrop of old vinyl records glued to the walls and ceiling. (☎216 69 51. Tea $.40; coffee $.90; cappuccino $1.20. Open 8am-1am.) Up the street, **Seranad Bar,** 57 Gazi Cad., features live music every night. (☎212 45 44. Beer $1.50; *rakı* $1.80. Open noon-3am.)

▪ SIGHTS. The main place of interest in Giresun is the city **museum,** housed in the 18th-century Gogora church. It opened as a museum in 1988. Follow the coastal road about 1½km from the Atapark and turn right on a road leading uphill. The dome retains a fresco of Christ. The most interesting items in the collection are the illuminated Korans and old photographs of Giresun. (☎212 13 22. Open M-F 8am-5pm; Sa-Su 8am-noon, 1-3pm. $1.50, students $1.)

Architecture buffs will enjoy the perfectly preserved Catholic church, now housing the Çocuk kütüphane (children's public library), Çınarlar Mah., Cemal Gürsel Cad. No.44, located opposite the Öğretmen Evi. This 19th-century church became a children's library in 1967. (☎216 25 16. Open Tu-Sa 8am-noon, 1-5pm.)

Follow the signs from Gazi Cad. to the **kale** on the eastern headland, more popular now for its view and its çay garden than for the state of its medieval ruins. The climb to the top is steep but relatively short.

Giresun's harbor is the home of the Black Sea's only habitable **island**, with a few crumbling ruins dating from the same period as the castle. Today, it is inhabited only by flocks of sea birds. In summer, boats offer 1½-hour trips around the island and the rest of Giresun's harbor. The 7pm tour is perfect for enjoying the stately Black Sea sunset. (Daily June-Aug.; 7, 9pm; $1.75.)

Dolmuş leave from Giresun's square for **Kümbet Yayla**, a cool highland paradise (54km, 2¼hr.; 7:30am-4pm; $2). There is constant service ($1.50) to and from the town of **Dereli** to Kümbet. The hotels and restaurants in Kümbet will do for a night.

TİREBOLU   ☎454

The small seaside town of Tirebolu (pop. 17,000) is dominated by the walls of the scenic but otherwise unremarkable **Castle of St. John**, a 14th-century Genoese outpost. In the 20th century, the castle has become yet another tea garden. Tirebolu's real attraction, however, lies simply in its relaxed pace. At night, colored lights illuminate the oceanside walkways where locals and visiting Turkish families enjoy lively conversation and late-night çay.

▐▀▐ TRANSPORTATION AND PRACTICAL INFORMATION. Tirebolu has two main streets: the **coastal highway** and, paralleling the highway about 100m uphill, **Gazipaşa Cad.** Two bridges link the roads, one about ½km west of the castle and one just east of it. Most of Tirebolu's few banks, shops, and services are spread along Gazipaşa Cad.'s winding route.

Buses stop next to the western bridge at the bus and dolmuş lot. **Ulusoy** (☎441 40 62 or 441 29 57) and **Metro** (☎411 49 52), across from the lot, sell tickets to: **Ankara** (11hr.; 4 per day 9am-7:30pm; $16, students $14.50); **Antalya** (20hr.; noon; $29, students $27); **Erzurum** (8hr.; 3:30pm; $11, students $9.50); **Giresun** (45min., frequent, $1.50); **İstanbul** (16hr.; 10 per day 11:30am-9pm; $22.50, students $20); **Samsun** (5hr.; every hr.; $8, students $6); and **Trabzon** (1½hr.; frequent; $3, students $2). For a comparable price, dolmuş to Giresun and Trabzon depart from the same lot or from various points on Gazipaşa Cad.

Türkiye İş Bankası, halfway up Gazipaşa Cad., can exchange traveler's checks and cash. (☎411 41 04. Open M-F 8:30am-12:30, 1:30-6pm.) There's also a **TC Ziraat Bank** with an **ATM** on Gazipaşa Cad., near the PTT. (☎411 20 35. Open M-F 8:30am-6pm.) The **police station** (☎411 30 00 or 411 40 19) is in the dirt lot across from the castle. The **hospital**, Tirebolu Devlet Hastanesi, is on the downhill and eastern end of Gazipaşa Cad. (☎411 42 78. Open daily 8am-4pm, 24hr. for emergencies.) The hospital houses Tirebolu's best **pharmacy**. (☎411 48 66. Open daily 8am-9pm.) For fast internet access, try **ESO NET Internet Cafe** on Amiral Şükrü Okan Cad. No. 98, which is the main coastal highway. ($1.25 per hr. Open 9am-midnight.) The **PTT** is located on Gazipaşa Cad., just above the westerly bridge.

▐▀▐▌ ACCOMMODATIONS, FOOD, AND ENTERTAINMENT. Since Tirebolu has only one functioning hotel, you'd be better off staying in Trabzon or Giresun. In a pinch, your only option is **Otel Huzur**, Gazipaşa Cad No. 15., Çintaşı Mah., next to the Çintaşı Camii, a 10-min. walk uphill from the town center. The six rooms share a shower and a squat toilet. Request hot water for your shower. (☎411 40 93. Singles $4.50; students $4; doubles $9.50, students $8; triples $14.50, students $12.) Although there are no great **camping** spots in Tirebolu, some campers set up on the beach east of town.

The standard kebap and *pide* joints on Gazipaşa Cad. are often on a reduced menu. You can also stock your room with fresh fruit, breads, cheese, and other inexpensive goodies from Tirebolu's many markets. Cherries and hazelnuts, both regional specialties, come into season in the summer.

In Tirebolu's afternoon heat, it's hard to resist joining the kids who jump off the castle rocks into the water. Feel free, or head to the **beach** just east of the castle.

In the evening (and late into the night during the summer), the çay patios flanking the castle shift into high gear. The dimmest and most surreal of them is perched on what was once the Castle of St. John. It's somewhat sad to see this monument given over to plastic chairs, Pepsi, and loud pop music, but the view is splendid, and you may get a peek at small-town Turkish teen romance.

TRABZON ☎462

Trapezus, Trebizond, Trabzon: this city has a rich history and the names to prove it. In its current incarnation, Trabzon sees itself as a city on the move, leading the eastern Black Sea region into the 21st century. Since the collapse of the Soviet Union and the reopening of Turkey's northeastern borders, Trabzon has resumed its role as an important trade and transport hub for Russia, Georgia, Armenia, Azerbaijan, and Iran. The cell phones, traffic, and new concrete edifices of the region's most recent boom are now accompanied by thousands of immigrants who came west chasing riches and opportunities. Their entrepreneurial ranks include the prostitutes that ply the area between the city's central square and Russian bazaar. Trabzon is also the place to start organizing trekking tours to the stunning Sumela Monastery and the tranquil Kaçkar Mountains to the south.

Trabzon's history as a commercial port and hilly refuge dates back to the ancient Greek colonists of Miletus, who dubbed their new community Trapezus. During the Greek and Roman periods, Trapezus grew to a commercial center of international scope. Under Alexius Comneni, who sought refuge here from the Crusaders during the sack of Constantinople, the city reached its heyday as the capital of the Trebizond Empire. His dynasty became the longest-lived, and one of the wealthiest, in Greek history; its rulers lived off the profits of trade and local silver mines. The kingdom held out against the Ottomans until 1461 (even longer than Constantinople), when Mehmet the Conqueror seized it. Under Ottoman rule, the churches were converted to mosques, and Islam became the dominant religion. Trabzon was invaded by Russian forces in 1916, but reclaimed by the Turks in February 1918. The city has been growing ever since, and, with nearly 1.5 million busy residents, it shows no signs of looking back.

▐ TRANSPORTATION

Flights: The airport is a 10min. drive east of the Atatürk Alanı. Dolmuş leave constantly from next to the Hotel Horon, just off the Atatürk Alanı. You can also catch the airport-bound dolmuş along the coastal highway. **THY's main office** (☎321 16 80 or 321 34 46; fax 326 64 34) is at the southwest corner of Atatürk Alanı. To **Ankara** (1½hr.; 5:50, 10:05am, 7:30pm; $68, students $54) and **İstanbul** (2hr.; 5:40, 9:40am, 7:20pm; $85, students $63). **İstanbul Airlines (Hayayollari),** Maraş Cad., Kazazoğlu Sok., Sanat İşhani No. 9/1 (☎322 33 46 or 322 38 06; fax 321 64 45), offers slightly better fares. To **İstanbul** (Tu 11:50am, Th 4:50pm, Fri 8:30pm, Sa 11:50am; $71, students $54). **Azerbaijan Airlines (Hava Yollari),** 35 Maraş Cad., 3rd fl. (☎326 24 97; fax 326 60 29), flies weekly to **Baku** (1hr.40min., Su. noon, $277 round trip, students $239).

Buses: The inter-city bus terminal (information ☎325 23 43) is 3km east of the main square and easily accessible by dolmuş. **Ulusoy** (☎325 22 01 or 325 21 60) and **Metro** (☎325 72 86) are 2 reliable firms serving: **Ankara** (12hr., 7 per day 7:30am-8pm, $25); **Bursa** (17hr., 4 per day noon-2pm, $33); **Erzurum** (6hr., 6 per day 7am-6pm, $12); **Giresun** (2hr., every hr. 6am-11pm, $4.50); **İstanbul** (18hr., 10 per day 11am-7:30pm, $33); **İzmir** (23hr., 3 per day 10am-4pm, $40); **Kayseri** (12hr., 2 per day 11:30am-3pm, $21); **Rize** (1¼hr., every 15min. 6am-9pm, $3); **Samsun** (6hr., every hr. 6am-11pm, $13); **Tirebolu** (2hr., every hr. 6am-11pm, $5). Depending upon the company, students may receive a 25% discount.

International buses: Currently, 3 companies provide service to **Georgia. Göktaş** (☎325 04 11 or 325 51 40), **AST/Buse** (☎325 69 82), and **Nuhoğlu** (☎325 48 12) run buses to: **Ardahan** (8hr., 6pm, $15); **Posov** (10hr., 6pm, $20); **Batumi** (5hr., 6pm, $10); **Kutais** (6hr., 6pm, $15); and **Tbilisi** (12hr.; 6pm; $30, students $25). Both **AST/Buse** and **Nuhoğlu** provide service to **Baku, Azerbaijan** (2 days; 6pm; $50, students $40). Depending on political conditions, **AST/Buse** also provides service to **Yerevan, Armenia** (24hr.; 6pm; $40, students $35). Travelers are advised to obtain the relevant visas in advance; see **Consulates**, p. 404, for information.

Dolmuş: Trabzon's dolmuş are, in fact, ordinary-looking 4-5 person cars, but, like dolmuş elsewhere, the final destination is listed above the windscreen. Most dolmuş lines originate in the main Atatürk Alanı, but you can hop on anywhere ($.40, students $.30).

Ferries: The **Turkish Maritime Lines** office (☎321 70 96 or 321 20 18) is just inside the gate at the base of İskele Cad. (which curves down behind Hotel Anıl). From early June–late Aug., a ferry plugs along between Trabzon, Samsun, and İstanbul. For schedule and rates, see **The Black Sea Ferry**, p. 378. Open M-F 8am-5pm.

International Ferries: To **Russia:** All year long, the "COMETA" sea-bus ferry follows the Trabzon-Sochi route to Russia (12hr., 5pm, $50-$100). **Sarı Tur** (☎326 44 84) sells tickets for the two ferries, "Appolonia" and "Karden," which link Trabzon and **Poti, Georgia** (Tu and F; 10hr.; evening departure; $30 one-way, $50 round-trip).

✈ ORIENTATION

Trabzon descends from the hills to the sea, spreading over nearly 10km. Luckily, almost all of the city's hotels, restaurants, and services are concentrated around **Atatürk Alanı**, the main square, just uphill and west from the city's central port. **Kahramanmaraş (Maraş) Cad.** runs west out of Atatürk Alanı, leading past banks, the PTT, and a few historical sites before ending just below the ancient **Aya Sofia.** Running parallel to Maraş Cad. are the pedestrian-only **Kunduracılar Cad.** and charming **Uzun Sok. Gazipaşa Cad.** is the short main road between Atatürk Alanı's western edge and the coastal highway, **Sahil Yolu**, which leads to the inter-city **otogar,** 3km east. To the west, it passes a stretch of tea gardens and amusement parks.

ⓘ PRACTICAL INFORMATION

TOURIST, FINANCIAL, AND LOCAL SERVICES

Tourist Office: Ali Naki Effendi Sok., No. 1. Opposite the southeast corner of Atatürk Alanı, adjacent to the Hotel Nur. (☎321 46 59). Brand new and well-equipped government tourist office, with some English spoken. Open in summer daily 8am-5:30pm; in winter closed on weekends.

Travel Agencies: Afacan Tour, 40/C İskele Cad. (☎321 44 39 or 321 58 04; fax 321 70 01), 100m from Usta Hotel. Open in season 7:30am-6pm. Offers tours of: **Sumela** (daily 10am-4pm, $4.50); **Uzungöl** (Sa-Su 9am-7pm, $12); **Ayder** (Su 9am-7:30pm, $8); **Karaca Cave and Zigana** (Sa 9am-6:30pm, $12 with lunch). Both agencies open daily in season 9am-7pm. Off-season hours at both are irregular. **Usta Tour,** 4 İskele Cad. (☎326 18 70; fax 326 18 71), across from the northeast corner of Atatürk Alanı and adjacent to the Usta Hotel complex. Tours of **Sumela** (Tu and Th 11am-6:30pm; $6.50, students $5.50); **Uzungöl** (W and Sa 9am-6:30pm; $8, students $7); **Ayder Yayla** (Su 9am-7pm; $11, students $10). Open in season 8:30am-5:30pm.

Consulates: Georgian Consulate, 20 Gazipaşa Cad., 2nd fl. (☎326 22 26; fax 326 22 96). Quite far down Gazipaşa Cad., approaching the sea. Visas are usually processed the day of demand. Transit visas $15; 2-week visas $40; one-month visas $50. Open M-Sa 9am-12:30pm, 2-6pm. **Iranian Consulate,** Kızıl Toprak Sok. No. 3 (☎326 76

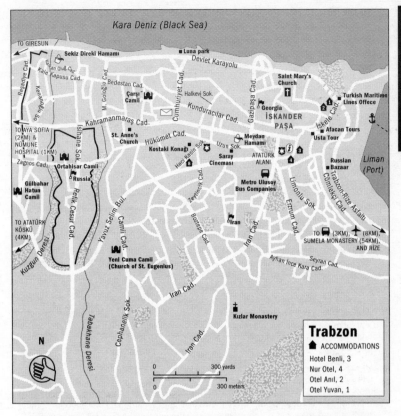

Kara Deniz (Black Sea)

Trabzon
⚓ ACCOMMODATIONS
Hotel Benli, 3
Nur Otel, 4
Otel Anıl, 2
Otel Yuvan, 1

50). Just off Boztepe Cad. (Open M, Th, and Sa 8am-1pm, 3-5pm; Su 8am-1pm.) Allow 2 days. Westerners may be told to seek visas from the Iranian Embassy in Ankara. **Russian Consulate,** Orta Hisar Mahallesi, Refik Cesur Sok. No. 6. (☎326 26 00; fax 326 26 01). US and other Western citizens should generally obtain visas at the Russian Embassy in Ankara. Open M-F 9am-1pm, 3-5pm.

Banks: Trabzon's larger banks are along Maraş Cad., just west of Atatürk Alanı. For traveler's checks try **Akbank** or **TC Ziraat Bank** (☎326 71 13; open M-F 8:30am-5pm).

English-language Bookstore: D+R, 17/C Uzun Sok. (☎321 98 55). Located just over a block down from the southwest corner of Atatürk Alanı, this cafe/bookstore/music store carries the *Turkish Daily News, International Herald Tribune, Financial Times,* the *Guardian, The Economist, Time, Newsweek,* and English tabloids. Open daily 10am-9pm. **Kitap Kırtasiye,** Uzun Sok. No. 3/A (☎326 20 34). Closer to Atatürk Alanı than D+R. Stocks similar publications. Open M-Sa 7am-8:30pm, Su 10am-6pm.

Laundry: Pak Çiti Laundry, Cumhuriyet Mah., Zeytinlik Cad. No. 18/B (☎326 13 51). From Atatürk Alanı, walk down Uzun Sok. until you reach Zeytinlik Cad., then turn left. $4 per load. Student discount available. Open M-Sa 8am-8pm.

EMERGENCY AND COMMUNICATIONS

Police: Trabzon is split into 6 police districts, each with its own telephone number. The best option is to call ☎155. A tourist police office (☎326 30 77) is next to the Kibris Restaurant on the east side of Atatürk Alanı. Open daily 8am-5pm.

Hospital: Trabzon's best hospital is the **K.T.U. Farabı Hastanesi** (Karadeniz Teknik Üniversitesi Tıp Fakultesi; ☎325 30 11 or 377 50 00). Take any dolmuş marked K.T.U.

Another option is the private **Özel Karadeniz Hastanesi** (☎229 70 70). **Nümune Hospital** (☎230 22 97) is 2km west of downtown at the intersection of Maraş Cad. and Faik Dranaz Cad. Take a dolmuş marked "*Hastane*" or "*Nümune*" to the *Nümune Durağı*. There are numerous **pharmacies** on Gazipaşa Cad.

Internet Access: In Atatürk Alanı, try **World Internet Cafe** (☎323 11 34), located on the 2nd floor of the building adjacent to McDonald's. Open daily 9:30am-1am. Also surf at **Limit Internet Cafe** (☎323 28 94), inside the Corner Hamburger and Pizza joint on the east edge of Atatürk Alanı. $2 per hr. Open daily 7am-11pm. **IPEK Internet Cafe,** Maraş Cad., İpekyolu İs Merkezi No. 60 (☎323 31 50), on the 2nd floor of an outside flight of stairs, is pleasant, clean, and managed by a friendly woman. $1.25 per hr. Open daily 8am-11:30pm.

PTT: West down Maraş Cad. Open 8:30am-5:30pm. Telephone services open 24 hr.
Postal Code: 61020 (downtown only).

■ ACCOMMODATIONS

While Trabzon seems to have more hotels per square kilometer than any other city in the world, only a few are off the prostitution circuit. The hotels below have managements dedicated to keeping them safe and free of *Nataşas* (see p. 400).

■ **Otel Anıl,** Güzelhisar Cad. No. 10 (☎326 72 82 or 326 72 83). Adjacent to Otel Yuvan, 50m off İskele Cad. A welcoming oasis of peace and cleanliness. 36 big rooms have carpeting, tiled baths, hot water, and TV. Breakfast included. It's a good idea to reserve during the busy summer months. Singles $13; doubles $21; triples $30.

■ **Hotel Nur,** Meydan Camii Sok. No. 10 (☎323 04 45 or 323 04 46; fax 323 04 47). Off Atatürk Alanı, opposite the İskender Paşa Camii, next to the tourist office. Very friendly, helpful management. 15 large, clean rooms, all with shower, toilet, and TV. Fresh watermelon always available at breakfast. Singles $13; doubles $22.50; triples $35.

Hotel Yuvan, Güzelhisar Cad. No. 10 (☎/fax 326 68 23 or 326 68 24). Adjacent to the Otel Anıl, 50m off İskele Cad. This simple, good-value hotel has shower, toilet, and TV in every room. French-speaking management. Singles $10; doubles $16; triples $20.

Hotel Benli (☎321 10 22). Across from İskender Paşa Camii, adjacent to the tourist office and Hotel Nur. Provides basic rooms in a safe, older hotel. Each floor has a squat toilet and old shower. 41 rooms. Singles $4, students $3; doubles $8, students $6.50.

◖ FOOD

Trabzon's local cuisine is a melange of standard Turkish fare, fresh Black Sea fish, and corn, potatoes, and peas from the fertile highlands south of the city. Atatürk Alanı supports a dazzling array of restaurants, from tasteful dining rooms to late-night upper-story beer halls. Even McDonald's has hauled up another pair of its corporate arches. A **fruit and vegetable market** lies 1.5km west of the square along Maraş Cad. (open daily 6:30am-9pm). Cheese, bread, and other basics are cheapest at the **Tan-Şa Supermarket** on the southwest corner of Atatürk Alanı.

Kebabistan, Maraş Cad. No. 30 (☎321 86 51), opposite the Zorlu Grand Hotel. Among the cleanest and best in Trabzon. *Vali kebap* ($4); *ayran* ($.40). Open 11am-11pm.

Güloğlu Restaurant, Atatürk Alanı No. 4/E (☎321 53 32). A recently-renovated kebap and *lahmacun* salon. Enjoy the A/C while you indulge in the *Sarma Beyti Kebap* ($2) and finish with a 6-piece portion of delicious baklava ($1). Open 6am-11pm.

Tad Pizza and Burger (☎321 12 38). On the northeast corner of the main square, opposite the Belediye (municipality) building. Good for a break from kebap and *ayran,* but the hamburgers ($1) might be better called *köfte* burgers. Tad also has a $1 salad bar and serves a curiosity called *aşure,* a fruity pudding ($1). Open 7am-11pm.

Petek Restaurant, Taksim Meydanı No. 5 (☎323 30 34). Just off Atatürk Alanı, 100m up from McDonald's, this brand new restaurant serves the tasty *Kanşik Petek kebap* ($4) with an *ayran* ($.30). Open 6am-11pm.

HALLUCINOGENIC HONEY In the 5th century BC, Cyrus of Persia recruited a ragtag troop of jack-booted Greek thugs to pillage various villages in Asia Minor. Among the 10,000 Greeks was Xenophon, who recorded their misadventures in the *Anabasis*. On the march home, the booty-laden horde happened upon an enormous swarm of bees whose hives brimmed with honey. This particular pillage, however, had payback: some of the soldiers who sampled the nectar ended up unconscious or ill. Those who consumed the ambrosia in moderation reported fantastical visions (who knows what the bees were seeing). The morning after, the entire legion woke up with a wicked hangover and some rich but embarrassing stories. After enduring a few days of rehab and detox from the deleterious effects of too many mind-altering substances, the iron-hearted Hellenes were marching west to Trabzon. And you thought you were tired when you rolled into town...

Ev Mamülleri, Gazipaşa Cad. No. 11/A (☎326 24 20). Situated midway down Gazipaşa Cad., walking toward the sea. Without a doubt the best pastry house in Trabzon. Make sure to taste the delicious *laz börek* ($1.25). Open 7am-midnight.

👁 SIGHTS

AYA SOFIA. Today a restored and beautified museum (meaning the walls have a few placards), Aya Sofia has a history as complex as the city itself. The site originally held a temple of Apollo (117-38) and then a basilica. Comnenian Emperor Manual I (1238-1263) commissioned the construction of the edifice you see today. Orthodox Christians claimed the basilica for the next 200 years, decorating its interior and exterior with frescoes and reliefs. Upon the 1461 Ottoman seizure of Trebizond, the church became a mosque. The Turks briefly used the building as a hospital and munitions depot during part of World War I. A 1960s restoration project uncovered some of Turkey's best frescoes. Though most of the paintings are crumbling, many still show discernible images. Frescoes in the main hall and the auxiliary rooms are dedicated to the life of Jesus. One lesser-known detail lies on the outer wall of the east side, where carved engravings show sailboats from the Comnenian Period. These are attributed to Genoans and Venetians who pined for their distant homelands. The lovely garden outside the main building may well be the most peaceful spot in Trabzon. *(To reach the Aya Sofia, either take a dolmuş from Atatürk Alanı, or, from the old city, take a dolmuş along the coastal highway; ask the driver for Aya Sofia and walk 2 blocks uphill. Museum open Tu-Su 9am-5pm. $1.50, students free.)*

ATATÜRK KÖŞKÜ (ATATÜRK'S VILLA). Atatürk Köşkü was built at the turn of the century by a wealthy Greek. The elegant white villa only actually housed "Father Turk" twice, but it is nevertheless a popular museum. *(Take a yellow dolmuş marked "Çamlık" or a bus marked "köşk" ($.20) southwest into the spectacular hills that overlook the city. Open 8am-7pm, in winter 8am-5pm. $1.25, students $.75.)*

OTHER RELIGIOUS SITES. St. Anne's Church stands as the oldest existing Christian structure, dating from the 7th century, when the Byzantine Emperor Basil I ruled Trebizond. To get there, start from the square and take Maraş Cad. west past the PTT and down an alley on the left (Mısırlıoğlu Aralığı). The church is closed for restoration. Further down Maraş Cad., take a left on Fatih Camii Sok. and walk uphill about 300m. There lies one of the city's treasures, **Fatih Camii,** also known as **Ortahisar Camii.** This mosque was once the cathedral of the *Panagia Chrysokephelos*, the Golden-Headed Virgin. Once a favorite of the Comneni rulers, it was converted to a mosque by Mehmet in 1461, when the floors were carpeted and the exquisite but idolatrous mosaics were covered in plaster. A small portion of the original mosaic remains intact on the east side of the mosque, since it is non-figurative and therefore not offensive to Muslim worshippers.

To reach **Gülbaharhatun Camii,** the Mosque of the Spring Rose, go south from Maraş Cad. to Uzun Cad. Walk west until you reach the south side of **Atapark,** a verdant spot with relaxing tea gardens. Gülbaharhatun mosque was built in 1514 by the Ottoman Sultan Selim I in honor of his mother, Ayşe Gülbahar, who is buried in an impressive **tomb** to the left of the ornate mosque. Just up the road on Amasya Sok. is the birthplace of Süleyman the Magnificent.

KIZLAR (GIRLS') MONASTERY. This monastery was used by the Greeks until the 1923 **population exchange** (see p. 16). Most interesting is the main chapel, a cave on the south side where scholars claim Mithraic (ancient Persian sun god) ceremonies were held. Weathered frescoes still decorate the chapel walls. The lookout point 100m below the entrance to the monastery makes a great picnic spot. At daily prayer times, you can hear echoing calls to prayer from dozens of mosques. (The monastery is a 2km walk up Iran Cad. from Atatürk Cad to Böztepe. One can also take the bus marked "Böztepe." The monastery was closed for renovation at the time of publication.)

🎵 ENTERTAINMENT

Football. Trabzon is a football town, and adored **Trabzonspor,** the blue-and-burgundy colored local team, plays regularly from late August to late May. The stadium is about 5km east of downtown, on the seaside Spor Cad. Prices vary with the matches, but average about $4 for sheltered seats and $1 for open ones.

Saray Sineması, Kasım Oğlu Çıkması No. 15 (☎321 00 06). About 500m west of Atatürk Alanı. Take the 4th left off Uzun Sok. and look up to the left. It shows Hollywood films with Turkish subtitles, and, unlike most places, doesn't show pornography. Most shows start around 8:30pm. $3.50, $2.50 for students.

Magicworld: Cosmic Bowling and Billiards, Maraş Cad., İpek Yolu İş Merkezi (☎323 33 11), at the basement level, in the mall opposite the Zorlu Grand Hotel. Escape the hectic Turkish rhythm surrounded by 5 lanes, 6 pool tables, and a sparkling new cafe and restaurant. Bowling for 2, $4.50; billiards, $4. Open 10am-midnight.

Amusement Park. Trabzon's long seaside terrace makes for a pleasant stroll. At the west end lies an amusement park, featuring not the most impressive rides and a video arcade. Free; $.60 charge for individual rides.

Russian (Rus) Bazaar, Çömlekçi Mah., begins near the Otel Anıl, at the top of the hill, and continues down to the sea. Shoppers can find anything. Open daily 8am-7pm.

Sekiz Direkli Hamam, Pazarkapı Mah. (☎322 10 12). Located a worthwhile 2km west of the main square. Walk along Maraş Cad. and bear right on İslahane Sok., well before the walls of the old city. Walk down İslahane for 150m, then bear left on Kalkan Oluğ Cad. for 50m. The hamam will be on your right, on Hamam Sok. Rejuvenate yourself with a scrub and massage. Bath $4.50, kese $5.50. Constructed by the Selçuks around 1073 BC and used until 1916, it was renovated eight years ago with marble and wood paneling. (Open daily 4:30am-11pm. Th 8am-5pm reserved for women only. A taxi from the main square costs $2.50.)

Meydan Hamam, Maraş Cad. No. 3 (☎321 38 23), just off Atatürk Alanı. Less beautiful than Sekiz Direkli, but better located. Kese $1.25, massage $1.50, bath $3.50. Open for men 5am-10:30pm, women 9am-5pm; separate sections for men and women.

🌙 NIGHTLIFE

Kibris Restaurant. On the top floor of a building on the east side of Atatürk Alanı. A great place for a pint of Efes; the food is not as spectacular. Open 10am-midnight.

Şişman Restaurant (☎322 34 45), on the top floor of a building on Maraş Cad., just off Atatürk Alanı. Its outdoor tables provide a scintillating vantage point for gawking at the hustle and bustle below while nursing a rakı ($1.25) or Efes ($.90). Open 9am-1am.

English Pub, Zorlu Grand Hotel, Maraş Cad. No. 9, 2nd fl. Unwind in plush armchairs in Trabzon's best hotel. Rakı $2. Open 5pm-2am.

Efulim Club and Restaurant, Kunduracılar Cad., Ofluoğlu İş Merkezi, 2nd floor (☎326 92 88). Enjoy live music in elegant surroundings. *Efes* $2. Restaurant open noon-6pm. Club open 8am-1am. Bar open until 2am.

High Life Disco, Gazipaşa Cad. Head toward the sea; the disco is on the right 20m before the bridge. A favorite among area students and free of *Nataşas*.

Façuna Night Club (a.k.a. Façino), Grand Hotel Zorlu, Maraş Cad. No. 9, top floor. Drinks may be pricey (*Efes* $4), but the big floor of this fashionable hotel club ranks high among Trabzon's slim pickings. Open Sept.-June F-Sa 9pm-2:30am.

▐ DAYTRIP FROM TRABZON: SUMELA MONASTERY

The monastery and adjoining national park are accessible by dolmuş or private tours (see Trabzon: Travel Agencies, p. 404), which run from June through September. Dolmuş start loading up by Trabzon's Russian Bazaar about 8am, leaving as they fill. It's tough to find one after 11am. The ride to the park from Trabzon takes one hour. Tours tend to rush; they'll generally consist of a ½hr. hike through the park to the monastery (park admission $1.50, students $1) and a lunch of fresh trout ($3) at the Sumela Restaurant. If you bypass the tour option, there are two trails up to Sumela, so ask locals at the top for directions down the alternate route via the ruins of the Santa Barbara Chapel.

Nowhere else in northwestern Anatolia is the region's Byzantine legacy so breathtakingly combined with the jagged, forested landscape than at Sumela Monastery. Approximately 45km southwest of Trabzon, high in the mountains, Sumela was founded in 385 AD by two ambitious Athenian monks who, according to legend, were visited by the Holy Virgin in a dream. Sumela's structures were built into a cliffside cave which provides natural protection from the elements and contributes to its astonishing beauty. The monastery reached the height of its glory in the late Middle Ages, when it had 72 rooms, an immense library, five fully frescoed chapels, and a refectory, much of which can still be identified. The inner chapel is a spectacular treat even for those wearied by the tourist-track's parade of Byzantine imagery. The three layers of frescoes portray scenes from the Old and New Testaments, as well as enthroned Byzantine emperors. Though tattooed with Turkish, Greek, and English graffiti, the frescoes remain unique and impressive. A fire 60 years ago destroyed all of the monastery's wooden structures, many of which are currently being renovated. At the moment, the restoration team outnumbers visitors. Take advantage of the solitude and stick your head out of a monk's bedroom window. Savor glimpses of the panorama that Sumela's lucky devotees enjoyed for centuries until the 1923 Greco-Turkish population exchange (see **The Treaty of Lausanne,** p. 16). In addition to the usual junk, the park gift shop sells dynamite picture-postcards (2 for $1) of Sumela before the fire.

EAST OF TRABZON

Pitched in battle against industrial modernization, Anatolia's traditions have retreated from its Black Sea shores to the snowy Kaçkar mountain peaks. An elevated waterside freeway is the harbinger of growing commerce, population, and tourism. A recovering economy, political stabilization, and improving relations with neighboring Caucus states are bringing previously unknown comforts to the region. While beautiful swimming spots must be shared with an influx of Turkish visitors, stunning Kaçkar treks and forested, windswept highlands can still be enjoyed alone.

Along the sea and in the northwestern Kaçkars, rain falls more days than it doesn't. In the drier northeastern Kaçkars, cascades have carved out tremendous ravines and canyons of orange and yellow bedrock. After hundreds of years, the Hemşin people continue to make their homes here, where they retain autonomous traditions and belief systems. There, *yayla* (highland plateaus) grace the mountainsides, standing as meeting grounds for Hemşin peoples from all over Europe.

UZUNGÖL   ☎462

If you hear exhausted Trabzon urbanites proclaiming *çok güzel!* and looking wist-fully inland, they're probably talking about Uzungöl (pop. 3000). A gorgeous and serene retreat, the village and its wooden lodges surround a long trout-filled lake in the lush mountains 98km from Trabzon (via Of and Çaykara). The tiny popula-tion is equally divided between cash-crop agriculture and burgeoning hotel man-agement. Uzungöl's signature dishes are its farm-fed trout followed by *sütlaç* rice pudding. Its soaring landscape, lovers' bridge, and lakeside mosque make this vil-liage a regional highlight.

■᛫ ORIENTATION AND PRACTICAL INFORMATION. Though frequently snowbound in winter, Uzungöl's cool moist summers draw visitors via hired tours (see **Trabzon: Tourist Agencies,** p. 404) and dolmuş, which depart from Trabzon's **Rus Pazari** (Russian Bazaar) and the Rize highway dolmuş lot. All journeys change vehicles at either **Of** or **Çaykara,** where a second tariff is required (total $4). In peak season (June-Aug.) and on weekends, direct services are available ($3).

Dolmuş stop in the village center (by the big mosque at the edge of the lake) or 1km further down the road, where **Uzungöl Pansiyon** and the **İnan Kardeşler** complex are spread along the lake's far end. From either of these stops, dolmuş leave Uzungöl for Trabzon or Rize (morning-4pm). Both outgoing tour buses and locals appear willing to stop for hitchhikers. All government services and most of the shops are by the mosque. Uzungöl has an extremely basic **PTT,** a **police station,** a rudimentary **health clinic,** and hardware stores.

᛫᛫᛫ ACCOMMODATIONS, FOOD, AND ENTERTAINMENT. ■Özkan **Tesisleri** (☎656 61 97 or 656 62 80), on the mosque end of the lake, has a cozy com-munal fireplace and a large TV with a Eurosport bent. Campers can pitch tents upstream from the dam free of charge. Next cheapest is a $12 triple room above the **Uzungöl Lokantasi** restaurant by the bridge, followed by the **Kardeşle Uzungöl Pansiyon,** on the main road at the far end of the lake. (☎656 61 29; $6 per person with bath and breakfast.) Remaining options are all excellent and include free breakfast and views. The **İnan Kardeşler** offers chalet-style log cabins with immac-ulate hot water showers, seat toilets, porches with wooden furniture, and stacks of warm blankets. (☎656 60 74. Dinner $3. Singles $12; doubles $24; triples $42.) **Motel Taşustu** (☎656 17 67) starts from $10 also and offers a huge elevated balcony. **Motel Sezgin** has its own trout farm. Ask to feed the fish. (2-trout dinner $2.50. $11 per person.) **Aygün Dinlenme Tesisleri** (☎656 60 42 or 656 65 23), includes breakfast, and has two-bed A-frame bungalows for $25; 3-person accommodation $40; or 2-story, seven-bed version for $75. More expensive are the new **Hotel Onal** and **Hotal Keleş** (☎656 63 21), each with $15 singles or $25 with 3 meals daily, the latter with daily folk dancing (July-Sept.) from 8pm. Otherwise evening options include relax-ing by a fire or challenging the local sharks to eight-ball at **Motel Sezgin Bilardo.**

The **İnan, Sezgin,** and **Özkan** all have similar fare for about $3-5 per meal; other-wise eat with the locals at **Alabalik Lokantas,** with its customized bread cupboards. Alcohol is not sold in Uzungöl. Instead, walk, talk, eat, and hike in some of Tur-key's most resplendent environs. Check with **İnan** or **Özkan** for preferred routes (see **Trekking in the Kaçkars,** p. 419).

RİZE   ☎462

Rough-and-tumble but friendly, this provincial port town (pop. 54,000) serves as the easternmost major business center on the Black Sea coast. Rize is populated with Turks, Azerbaijanis, and Georgians, and it's had a lengthy history under the region's succession of keepers. Unfortunately, most of the city's demographic, historical, and architectural diversity has been mowed down as Rize joins its coastal compatriots in a concrete race for modernization. It is the high tech tea capital of Turkey, a booming entertainment mecca, and the administrative center for the surrounding Kaçkar hills.

TRANSPORTATION AND PRACTICAL INFORMATION

Rize is best explored from its central **Belediye Parkı,** with adjoining **Cumhuriyet Cad.** and **Atatürk Cad.** containing most essential services. Dolmuş and minibuses stop on the coastal highway; head one block inland and turn right to hit Belediye Parkı.

Buses: Ulusoy (☎217 45 45), at the northwest corner of Belediye Parkı, runs from the dolmuş lot on the main highway to: **Ankara** (14hr., 5:30pm, $17); **Erzurum** (6hr., 7:30am, $5); **Giresun** (4hr., very frequent 8:30am-10pm, $5); **İstanbul** (18hr.; 11:30am, 3:30, 6pm; $22); **Samsun** (8hr., very frequent 8:30am-10pm, $9); **Trabzon** (1½hr., very frequent 8:30am-10pm, $2.50). The **Artvin Express** (☎212 09 05; 4hr., 4 per day 11am-4pm, $7), which departs from the lane next to Hotel Akarsu, serves **Yusufeli** (8hr., 8am, $10) and **Van** (14hr., 9pm, $12). Dolmuş, the best bet for closer destinations, leave from the big lot on the highway.

Tourist Office: (☎213 04 07) In the T. C. Rize Valiliği building, 5 blocks west of town. The director Atilla Karahasanoglu can arrange English-speaking advisors. The **tourist information booth** (10am-6pm) is more convenient, in front of the museum and west of the **Belediye Parkı. Ritur Travel Agency** (☎217 88 48; email i.h.yildiz@ihlas.net.tr), is at the northwest corner of Belediye Parkı. General manager Köksal Bey speaks fluent English. Ritur runs trekking and rafting expeditions. Open 8am-5pm. For more info on trekking, see **Trekking in the Kaçkars,** p. 419.

Police: (☎213 03 74), next to the Hotel Kaptanlar on the main highway.

Pharmacies: Numerous pharmacies line the south side of Belediye Parkı.

Hospital: The state hospital (☎231 04 91) has 24hr. service.

Internet Access: Rize has six cafes. The cheapest ($1 per hr.) are in the **Belediye Parkı.** Open 8am-11pm. The most novel is seaside in Luna Park.

PTT: On the south side of an open area 25m off the southwest corner of Belediye Parkı. Open daily 8:30am-5:30pm; mail service closed 12:30-1:30pm. **Postal Code:** 53100.

ACCOMMODATIONS

The majority of Rize's hotels cater to mobile businessmen's needs: low price, proto-cleanliness, a TV lounge, and a touch of prostitution. While most of these places offer a good night's sleep under $10, women traveling alone should probably avoid them. Better options include:

Hotel Akarsu (☎217 17 79). Just west of Belediye Parkı, this is a secure family (*aile*) place with clean, standard singles ($4) and doubles ($7).

Hotel Efes (☎214 11 11), Atatürk Cad. Highly recommended. Singles $8; triples $20.

Kaçkar Hotel. Slightly more expensive, this hotel includes a faux-marble entrance, bathtub, TV, and rooftop restaurant. Singles $20; doubles $30.

Keleş Hotel (☎217 46 12), has a top-floor restaurant which is a local favorite. Singles $20; doubles $30.

Hotel Asnur, (☎214 17 61), and the 4-star **Hotel Dedeman** (☎223 44 44), start at $60 per double, but deals can be struck during the off-season with General Manager Ercan Turhan at riz~fercan@dedeman.com.tr.

FOOD

Rize's highest concentration of *pide* and *kebap* joints is on the north side of Belediye Parkı, stretching east along Cumhuriyet Cad. These Turkish mainstays cost $2-5. Don't leave without trying the local specialty, *meşhur kuru fasülye* (lamb with cooked beans in sweet tomato sauce), made especially well at **Kandıl's,** 5/A Çanakkale Cad. (☎217 28 13). To get there, turn off Cumhuriyet Cad. when coming from the garden. **Müze Kafeterya,** with a veranda and view, offers bland western food and traditional *mulama* (cheese melt dip) and *lahana* (vineleaf parcels). Rize's moneyed young chat in this well-kept, cushioned Ottoman building and on its sea-view balcony. Open 9am-10:30pm. The highly regarded **Mis Lahmacun** specializes in $.50 Turkish pizza and a fast-food candor. Closer to the square, the big and modern **Arı Market** offers a selection of Western goods.

🔆 SIGHTS

Tea is the primary focus of most visits to Rize, and the best place for the *çay* connoisseur and casual enthusiast alike is the **Tea lab,** featuring Ministry of Agriculture greenhouses, laboratories and a rose-scented *çay* garden. At dusk, locals lounge here on patio furniture, gazing over the valley and out to sea. For your sip of the good life, hike up the road between the PTT and the main mosque, bearing right at an intersection. Taxis will drive up for $2. To see a *çay* production line, take the *"İslampaşa"* dolmuş ($1) to the last stop to reach a small tea factory that offers **free tours** solely in Turkish.

The **Rus Pazarı,** east of town, sells everything from Armenian *kilim*s to plastic Stalin pins and three-way flashlights. Take in a windswept view of the city from the **Rize Kalesi,** a small stone fortress built on a 160m hill. The *kale* is visible from a block west of the square. One kilometer east of **Belediye Parkı** on the water is **Luna Park,** with dollar rides, and **Ayder Dugun Salonu,** with a waterside cocktail bar and rotunda. The top-floor nightclub of the **Dedeman Hotel** (taxi $4 each way) offers coastline panoramas, free live music and a chance to watch the Rize elite at play.

GEORGIAN FRONTIER

Though years of mutual suspicion simmer, economic liberalization is opening the Black Sea route between Rize and Georgia's beachside frontier city of Batumi. Overlanders to Armenia must also use this route since direct land crossings with Turkey remain closed.

HOPA. Hopa is the last town of note before the border at Sarp. Public transport terminates in a dolmuş lot on the highway, close to the PTT. ▧ **Otel Huzur,** Cumhuriet Cad. 25, is the best choice (☎(466)351 40 95 or 351 43 82. Crisp singles $11. $5 per extra bed.) Manager Huseyin Demir will store luggage for travelers making daytrips into Georgia. More expensive are **Hotel Cihan** (☎351 48 97) and **Ustabas** (☎351 57 84), which charge $15 per person for marginally better rooms than those at Huzur. Fine dining may not be far away, but it hasn't arrived yet. Numerous diners line the main highway, most east of Hotel Huzur. Catch a glimpse of Rize at play nightly after 11pm at **Paparazzi Disco** (☎351 33 65), on Yen Yol Uzeri. Techno kicks off at midnight; beware the $2.50 beer.

THE GEORGIAN BORDER. This is a bilaterally simple border crossing, involving transit times of less than an hour. The border is open 24 hours, with both countries performing a double check of papers. Normally, only vehicles are searched. Turkish procedures are straightforward and free, while Georgia accounts for any hard currency entering and leaving the country and charges US$3 each way, providing a receipt. Note that Georgian officials may attempt to extract an additional $5 on the Georgian side of their offices just inside the gates of the compound. Polite passive resistance may be effective since officials seem unlikely to pursue tourists if they walk past with the locals. Georgian taxis to Batumi are $5-10 for 15km, while $1 minibuses are slow to fill. This process is exactly reversed when returning to Turkey from Georgia. Turkish minibuses often refuse the short trip to Hopa, hoping for a longer fare to Rize. Some travelers choose to break the cartel by walking away and flagging down the first vehicle to pass.

HEMŞİN VALLEY

Moving east from Rize, the Kaçkar mountains become steeper and more lush, and their inhabitants become distinctly Hemşinli (see p. 32; p. 415). Diverse flora and fauna in the lower valleys give way to grassy *yaylas* (highlands) and sweeping views higher up. At every altitude, locals and their visiting relatives do their best to make travelers feel at home, pointing them in the right direction for anything from short walks through the hazelnut trees to longer treks over some of the most striking peaks in the Kaçkar Dağları. Plentiful rainfall characterizes this region, so bring waterproof gear and sturdy footwear. Stinging nettle undergrowth necessitates long trousers and sleeves (see **Trekking in the Kaçkars,** p. 419).

Two roads reach the valley. From Pazar itself, it's 17km inland to **Hemşin,** a scenic but otherwise unremarkable town. Instead, take the second road 5km east of Pazar and follow a raging river 21km up to Çamlihemşin. Here the left-hand fork crosses the river and winds up to the rapidly expanding tourist retreat of **Ayder,** while the right leads to the little-touristed **Çamlihemşin Valley** and the handful of scattered buildings comprising **Şenyuva.**

ŞENYUVA VALLEY

Şenyuva's character is slow, sleepy and secluded. Elderly men sit drinking tea and dogs sleep undisturbed on the winding gravel roads. The loudest noise is that of the river cascading through the valleys. Şenyuva offers a first-hand lesson in both contemporary and traditional Hemşin life, and makes an excellent base for trekking excursions.

From Rize or Trabzon, catch a morning dolmuş to Çamlihemşin and continue straight up the valley rather than turning left over the bridge to Ayder. Usually this means hitching, taking a private taxi or walking the 5km to the valley's only lodge, ▩ **Otel Doğa** at Ortankoy. (☎651 74 55. $7 per person; $11 with breakfast and dinner.) Hand-built by İdris Duman, a local who left the valley for 40 years and learned English and French on his travels, Doğa offers a spacious living room (the TV gets the BBC), warm beds, hardwood floors, and thunderous rapids. Trekking, camping, and luggage storage is available. Two major *yaylas* are accessible from this hotel (see **Trekking in the Kaçkars,** p. 419). Check with Doğa about accommodation options any higher up the valley.

Zilkale (Bell Castle), a 10km walk up the main valley road, makes a pleasant daytrip. Most likely a minor Armenian or Genoan trading post, this ancient fortress pops into view after about 8km. About 300m up the road from Hotel Doğa stands the impressive **Ortank Kiprisi Bridge,** built by Hemşin peoples over 200 years ago. Across the road from Hotel Doğa, a gravel track leads to **Orton,** offering exhilarating views of the whole valley.

CLEAR WATER, MURKY POLITICS

Before the Hemşinli (and *way* before the nation of Turkey), the Fırtına ("Storm") River made its mad rush down the Şenyuva Valley to the Black Sea. But this little river is scheduled for a big change from open air to hydroelectric pipeline, under a government proposal and against local sentiment. Valley residents and thoughtful expatriots suspect something less than beneficence in the motives for the project, which would add to a national energy supply already 30% in excess of what Turkey actually uses. Construction projects in the region are notorious for padding the pockets of contractors with government (and sometimes mafia) connections rather than benefitting those who end up living next to a dusty stream-bed. Matters are further complicated by what some local Hemşinli and Laz residents see as a new threat to their cultural independence by a profoundly nationalist government. A functional river supports traditional life, they say, just as hydroelectric power supports an industry blind to all but the most recent past. The struggle continues against what the Turkish government sees as just another necessity of true modernization.

AYDER
☎ 464

Twenty kilometers up the left-hand fork at Çamlihemşin, the road rises to Ayder, a Hemşin summer village with big ambitions. The rustic wooden houses of this mist-shrouded village are surrounded by lush forests, open *yayla*, and, increasingly, the concrete totems of the tourist trade. On the far side of the valley, a slender brook fed by melting mountain snow rushes over crags to join a roaring stream on the valley floor. During high season, busloads of tourists make the trip to breathe fresh mountain air and dip into piping-hot spring water. This influx can mean crowds, but it also makes Ayder a prime spot for watching Hemşinli festivities unfold as urban exiles return home. The party kicks off the last weekend in May, with the dancing and mingling of the Ayder Festival. Bring a good raincoat and selective vision. Unbridled development has overtaxed Ayder's resources, and the town, empty nine months out of the year, can barely cope with the summer influx.

🚍 TRANSPORTATION AND PRACTICAL INFORMATION

Ayder consists of two sections: **Birinci Ayder** (First Ayder) and **İkinci Ayder** (Second Ayder). Dolmuş stop in the former, home of most of the tourist spots, including hotels, restaurants, hot springs, stores, and the tiny **PTT**. İkinci Ayder, 500m uphill, has some new hotels, many summer villas, and cow pastures. Dolmuş between Ayder and Çamlihemşin ($1) are frequent in summer, but irregular in winter. Ayder charges a $.50 **admission fee** for private vehicles, which is collected in a booth 4km from the center of town. At the center of town, by the shops, is a small **PTT**. (Open daily 8:30am-5:30pm.)

🏠 ACCOMMODATIONS

Because of their proximity to the hot springs, few hotels have shower facilities. Most average about $10, but you may get a break early in the season, when prices often haven't been adjusted for inflation. Reservations might be necessary during peak season, and some hotels may not open until the end of June. All offer views. ▣ **Otel Yesilvadi** (☎ 657 20 50) is the most impressive of these. At $3 per person or $7 with shower, it offers verandas, a fully-equipped kitchen, and an engaging staff. **Çağlayan Hotel** is a few steps up the hill from lower Ayder and one step up from true asceticism. Its owner (the great-grandson of the founder) combines an English-speaking welcome with Hemşinli authenticity. (☎ 657 20 73. Singles $6; doubles $12.) Slightly more upscale but similarly rustic, **Hotel Saray,** toward the lower end of lower Ayder, occasionally hosts late-night fêtes in its dining room. (☎ 657 20 01 or 657 20 02. 15 bathless doubles $15.) **Otel Ayder,** the big, white, institutional building at the lower end of the main road, has six sterile doubles. (☎ 657 20 39. Singles $8; doubles with bath $13. Open June-Sept.) Down the hill from the Saray, **trekking guide** Adnan Pirikoğlu runs the **Pirikoğlu Pensiyon** with dorm-style doubles and shared hot water showers. (☎ 657 20 21. $10 per person.)

The **Kardelen Pansiyon** is secluded 2km up the road, above Hoşdere, in the cluster of buildings above the Ayder *yayla*. Muhammet Önçırak leaves his İstanbul home every June to run this peaceful 5-room pension that many travelers use as a base for their treks (see **Trekking in the Kaçkars,** p. 419). Before climbing into the Kaçkars, consult the military-issue map hanging on his wall. (☎ 657 21 07. $5 per person. Open June-Aug.) Nature lovers and those strapped for cash can camp for free in the area around his house.

🍴 FOOD

Ayder is a good place to try the Hemşinli mountain specialty *muhlama*, a melted mix of cheese, butter, and corn flour that looks like mashed potatoes and behaves like fondue. Fresh bread replaces a spoon. **Dört Mevsim** ("The Four Seasons"), between Birinci Ayder and İkinci Ayder, makes the specialty especially well ($3). Beer, cognac, and *rakı*, among others, are also available. (Open 8am-midnight.) **Pirikoğlu Lokantası** serves equally wholesome meals. The owner, Adnan Pirikoğlu, is a guide who leads mountain groups (see p. 420) while his brother cooks the local specialty *katneraç* (soup made of corn flour, milk, and butter; $2). Full meals are about $4. (☎657 20 21. Open daily May-Oct. 6am-11pm.)

A late dinner at **Nazlı Çiçek**, just before the bridge above lower Ayder, provides the best opportunity to see traditional local dancing (apart from August weekends on the *yayla*). They also serve a hearty breakfast ($2). A handful of small markets can be found near the bridge.

🔍 SIGHTS

Ayder's local 🔲 **hamam,** below the road by the bridge, is a government-funded natural hot spring housed in the largest and most sophisticated edifice in town. Men (see **The Hamam,** p. 34) might want to wear their own shorts rather than the mildewed pairs provided ($.50). Women can wear bathing suits or a large shirt. Either way, locals will engage you in frank conversation, rarely enjoyed beyond the hamam walls. Water temperatures are close to scalding, but a gradual immersion is rewarding (and safe). The time limit is one hour. Locals swear by the curative properties of the hot water and suggest that swallowing it in large doses resolves all stomach problems—those wary of dysentery and giardia would be wise to decline. (Apr.-Oct. 15 daily 7am-8pm. Regular bath $2.50, private tub $9.)

Minibuses also run past İkinci Ayder to the *yayla* of **Avusor** (5km, $1.50), **Lower Kavron** (7km, $2.25), and **Upper Kavron** (12km, $2.25). These are popular trekking bases on the shoulder of 3932m **Kackar Dagi.** Only Upper Kavron has facilities, a workers' cottage and diner; otherwise bring your own. Unless the weather is clear in Ayder, thick fog and cold make this visit inadvisable.

THE HEMŞİNLİ

The origins of the Hemşinli people are heavily disputed, but it seems most likely that they are descended from an Armenian tribe that immigrated to the Kaçkar Mountains about 500 years ago, living in virtual isolation until 200 years ago. Although nominally and linguistically Turkish, the Hemşinli still maintain an independent and unique culture. The best-known markers of Hemşinli culture are the colorful dress of the women and the beauty of their breathtaking *yayla*, the summer villages that rest above the tree-line.

When it's not *yayla* season, traditional Hemşinli live with many people in large homes, depending on cow husbandry and corn cultivation for their livelihoods. During Ottoman rule, the Hemşinli lived in peace, sharing the Kaçkar region with Armenians and Greeks, and absorbing elements of Islam into their lifestyle, albeit a somewhat looser Islam that still allows for some occasional drinking, dancing, and all-out shenanigans. Hemşinli traditionally live on a yearly cycle that follows the seasons. Their winter villages are usually built low in the hills with access to a river, and, as the weather gets warmer, they relocate to higher and higher grass-covered *yaylas*. The traditional house structure (*konak*) is divided into three levels made of stone or wood. The basement level is for animals, the second level for family living, and the top level for drying grass.

Out of economic necessity, Hemşinli families have begun a slow urban migration. Today, many villages are primarily comprised of elderly people, and many of the palatial hillside *konak* are all but empty. The city-dwelling Hemşinli have made a name for themselves as bakers, sweet-shop owners, and master chefs. The diaspora generally returns in full festive force each summer to enjoy the clean air of the *yayla* and to reestablish familial and cultural bonds. Some Hemşinli predict that there will be an increase in the number of people returning permanently to the villages, but that remains to be seen.

ARTVİN ☎466

Artvin is stapled onto a mountainside, overlooking the vast Çoruh River Valley. Chiseled into the western slope is a nameless 5km series of switchbacks that lead from the otogar station up to the town above. The rarefied Artvin air sustains a beleaguered mix of military men, college students, shopkeepers, and prostitutes.

▐ TRANSPORTATION

The **otogar** is five steep kilometers from the center of town, near the fortress at the base of the river valley. Local dolmuş ($.80), free shuttle buses, the municipal bus (every 30min., $.50), and taxis ($3) all run from the otogar up to the town center on İnönü Cad.

Flights: The **THY office,** in the Hotel Karahan, sells tickets leaving from Erzurum, Trabzon, and Kars. Open daily 8am-5pm.

Buses: Artvin Express (☎212 13 76 or 212 15 20) has an office next to the enormous municipal building halfway up İnönü Cad. To: **Ankara** (17hr., 2 per day 11:30am-2:30pm, $19); **Erzurum** (4hr.; 6, 10am, 1, 5pm; $6); **Hopa** (2hr., every hr. 7am-1:30pm, $2.50); **İstanbul** (22hr., 2 per day 10am-12:30pm, $24); **Kars** (5hr., 2 per day 11:30am-noon, $5); **Rize** (3hr.; 7:30, 10, 11:30am, 12:30pm; $5); **Trabzon** (5hr.; 7:30, 10, 11:30am, 12:30pm; $6); **Yusufeli** (2½hr.; 10am, noon, 2:30, 5pm; $2.50); Dolmuş from Hopa run to the Georgian border at Sarp.

✦▐ ORIENTATION AND PRACTICAL INFORMATION

Hotels, restaurants, banks, tea houses, and shops line **İnönü Cad.,** the main street, which runs downhill from town.

Tourist Office: (☎212 30 71), in Cami Meydanı ("Mosque Square"), on the uphill side of Hotel Karahan. Head uphill at the taxi stand across from Kaçkar Oteli and take the 1st right; the office is at the far end on the 2nd floor. Run-down but amicable. One English speaker and glossy brochures. Open daily 8am-noon and 1:30-5:30pm.

Banks: Akbank, across from the Artvin Express office. Changes cash and American Express traveler's checks. Open 8:30am-4:30pm.

Hamam: (☎212 11 58), appropriately located on Hamam Sok., by the Kaçkar Hotel. Women should make an appointment in advance rather than wrestle with the random gender schedule. Bath $2.50; massage $1.50; scrub $1. Open daily 6am-10pm.

Pharmacy: Six pharmacies are scattered on İnönü Cad., taking turns to be open 24 hr.

Hospital: (☎212 15 32), on the main winding road above the town center.

Internet Access: Multiple options exist and connections are fast. Heading up İnönü Cad., **Casper Internet Cafe** will be on your left on the 2nd floor. Open daily 10am-midnight. Further along are **Sis** and **Arge** cafes, which offer identical services.

PTT: Halfway up İnönü Cad. Cash and card phones. Open 24hr. **Postal code:** 08000.

▐ ACCOMMODATIONS

Hotels are indifferent to tourists; most are either expensive or involved in prostitution (or both). Many are still safe and clean, with *Nataşa* encounters rising as prices fall (See **Nataşas,** p. 400).

▨ **Hotel Ugrak** (☎212 65 05). Though a bit worn, this hotel is your best bet for value. It is a bit removed from the late-night scene, with secluded top-floor rooms. $5 per person.

▨ **Kaçkar Oteli** (☎212 33 97), on Hamam Sok., just uphill from Çağdaş. From İnönü Cad. follow the steps under the hotel's red sign. Run-down, but spacious rooms with showers and seat toilets. $8 per person.

Hotel Karahan (☎212 18 00), on Cami Meydanı. From İnönü Cad. enter under the sign and walk up three flights. Though Karahan is the best hotel in town, its rates are not justified. All rooms have TV, bath, phone, and balconies with panoramic views. Bar, restaurant, and in-house travel agency. Singles $40; doubles $50.

Hotel Çağdaş (☎212 33 33 or 212 48 50), on İnönü Cad, under a big yellow sign 100m downhill from the PTT. New, wood-paneled rooms have showers and seat toilets. Most rooms are occupied almost entirely by the bed. Doubles $24.

🍴 FOOD

Artvin's ugly *rakı*/gambling/*Nataşa* scene has a reputation for getting rowdy at night, so don't venture out alone. Any establishment termed a *Casino* is probably tapping that market.

⊠ Hanedan Restaurant (☎212 72 22), on İnönü Cad., near the town center. The watering hole for Artvin's elite, Hanedan has a bar with views of the valley. Meal and beer $3. Open daily 8am-11pm.

Nazar Restoranı (☎212 17 09), at the lower end of İnönü Cad. Decorated with bizarre posters. A bar and precipitous balcony complement the cheap, excellent food, including delicious *meze*. Open daily 10am-midnight.

Çağdaş Gazinosu has occasional live Turkish music after 8pm. Because of the Russian clientele, prices are higher. Open daily 9am-midnight.

Restaurant Asya (☎212 66 62), has a nightclub feel, with low lights, live music, and locals. Beware: a belly dance may cost a cool $50.

Saklıca Restaurant. This real bargain is also the best hidden. Enter the narrow stairway opposite Karahan Hotel and turn left. Be sure to eat upstairs, where the menu is better. Vegetarian options include *fasulye pılaki* (green beans in olive oil; $1.50). $2 per meal.

👁 SIGHTS

The town's calendar is dominated by the annual **Kafkasör Festival,** held at the end of June in Kafkasör *yayla* (10km above Artvin). Thousands of visitors are lured by wresting and bloodless bullfights, where prime bulls go head to head in a lengthy shoving match, and the owner of the winning animal is publicly honored. Unfortunately, folk-dancing and traditional arts are less visible than they once were. Artvin rooms are difficult or impossible to find over the festival weekend—the best and most popular option is to camp in the peaceful forests and open grasslands around the *yayla*. A 15th-century Georgian citadel at the base of the valley is now an army base closed to visitors. You'll find the best view of Artvin from above.

YUSUFELİ
☎466

Yusufeli lies 9km off the main Artvin-Erzurum road, offering solace from the urbanization and illicit commerce of its larger neighbors. On the drive inland from Artvin, the Çoruh River narrows as the valley walls steepen into dry, crumbling spires and cliffs. Yusufeli is Turkey's white-water rafting capital. Yusufeli a Tekkale (6km up the valley) makes a relaxing base for walks, hikes, and treks in the upper Çoruh Valley or the Kaçkars. Even a day or two is enough to see a few of the valley's Georgian churches.

🚍 🏛 TRANSPORTATION AND PRACTICAL INFORMATION. The tourist center of Yusufeli is the rectangular area enclosed by four streets named after Turkish politicians: **Enver Paşa Cad., Fevzi Çakmak Cad., Mustafa Kemal Cad.,** and **İnönü Cad.** Most hotels occupy the upstream end of İnönü Cad., the central street that passes the **otogar** lot, **pharmacies,** and some decent dry restaurants.

BLACK SEA COAST

Artvin Express, in the otogar lot, runs to: **Ankara** (18hr., noon, $19); **Artvin** (2hr., 10 per day 6am-5pm, $2.50); **Bursa** (22hr., 9am, $24); **Erzurum** (3hr., 2 per day 9-11am, $3.50); **Hopa** (2½hr., 9am, $5); **İstanbul** (20hr., 10am, $24); **Rize** (4½hr., 9am, $6); **Trabzon** (6hr., 9am, $7). Dolmuş head from the otogar up the Çoruh and Barhal valleys, with prices set according to distance ($1.50 to Tekkale; $2.50 to Sarigol).

A small **hospital** (☎811 20 15) and **police** station are also centrally located. **Akin Cafe** on Ersis Cad. has internet access. The **PTT** is on İnönü Cad. at the downstream end of town. **Postal code:** 08800.

ꘌꘌ FOOD AND ACCOMMODATIONS. Yusufeli's better hotels are all close to each other on İnönü Cad. There's not much variety, but all establishments listed are clean and quiet. The **Hotel Çiçek Palas** (☎811 21 02) and the **Hacioğlu Oteli** (☎811 35 66), both just off İnönü Cad., offer basic, peaceful rooms. (Singles $6; doubles $10.) While the more homely Hacioğlu has hot showers, **Çiçek Palas** has a common stove. The **Barhal Hotel** (☎811 31 51), overlooking the Bahol River from a courtyard about 20m upstream on İnönü Cad, offers sterile rooms with river views. (Singles $6; doubles $10; triples $15.) The owner, Sırali Aydur, runs the Mountain Sports Club. To reach **Greenpeace Camping,** cross the bridge by the Barhal Hotel, turn right, take another right at the T-intersection, and turn left. The grounds offer secluded campsites in a garden, cold shower, and light meals. ($1-2 per night. Open mid-June-mid-Sept.) Dolmuş are infrequent; many travelers hitchhike.

The ■ **Mavi Köşk Restorant** (☎811 23 29), off İnönü Cad., has delicious food, patio dining, and a well-stocked bar. (Full meal about $3.50. Open daily 8am-1am.) One of the more popular meeting places is **Çınar Lokantası** (☎811 23 65), which overlooks the river beneath the Barhal Hotel. Its menu includes grilled meat, fresh trout, *rakı*, and vegetarian *meze* (Full meal with beer $3.50. Open daily 9am-midnight.) Also popular with the locals is **Mahsen Restaurant** (☎811 20 08).

THE ÇORUH VALLEY

The Çoruh River winds its way towards Yusufeli through a stunning, arid valley, meandering past trout farms, fruit trees, and sleepy villages. For travelers with time, the following villages offer a window into the Hemşin way of life.

◪ BASES FOR EXPLORING THE ÇORUH VALLEY

TEKKALE. About 6km up the paved road from Yusufeli, Tekkale makes an excellent base for hikes up tributary streams to the area's numerous abandoned **Georgian churches** and *yayla*. Longer hikes lead up past the spring snow line to the peaks and freezing lakes of the southeastern Kaçkars. Dolmuş run to Tekkale only in the afternoon ($1.50). Some travelers choose to hitchhike. Taxis are about $5.

BARHAL. From Tekkale, a side road climbs up towards remote Barhal (also accessible by a separate road from Yusufeli). Dolmuş head to Barhal at sporadic times in the late afternoon and early evening. At the south of town, the **Barhal Pension** (☎(466) 826 20 31) has new wooden rooms occupying the second floor of a house. (Dinner and breakfast included. $10 per person.) At the town center, essentially a small cluster of markets and *çay* houses, the road splits right 4km to the **Karahan Pension,** 50m uphill from the **Barhal Kilise** (see **Daytrips in and Near the Çoruh Valley,** below). Ask locals for directions. Run by Mehmet Karahan, the Karahan offers great lodging for those visiting the church or trekking into the Kaçkars. Its wooden loft has a large, airy deck where meals are served. (Breakfast and dinner included. $12 per night.)

SARIGOL. Sarigol serves as a launch point for rafting trips. Its tiny tree-lined main street deserves a couple of hours just to visit the carpentry shop, the supply depot, the tea houses, and the long verandas where elderly men play cards. Ask rafting guides to plan a meal break here.

🏛 DAYTRIPS IN AND NEAR THE ÇORUH VALLEY

Hand-drawn maps of the area can be found at Cemil's Pension in Tekkale or at the Çinar Restaurant in Yusufeli.

BARHAL KILISE. A number of tough but beautiful day and multi-day hikes criss-cross the ridges bounded by Tekkale, Yusufeli, and Barhal. From the center of Barhal, the road splits left to various *yayla*, and right 4km to **Barhal Kilise**, 50m before the Karahan Pension. Barhal Kilise, an amazingly well-preserved 10th-century Georgian church, now serves as the town's mosque and is usually locked. Its main attractions are exterior carvings of small crosses, a lion, and a bird. Across from the church and up the slope, a dilapidated fortress provides spectacular views.

DÖRTKILISE AND BAYIRKILISE. From Tekkale, follow the road to Yusufeli 7km to **Dörtkilise** ("Four Churches"). Only one of the original four churches still stands, and the ruins of the other three have been scattered. The remaining church is a hauntingly beautiful place to spend the evening, and the ground outside makes for a prime campsite. To the right of the church, a small path winds steeply up the valley wall 2km to **Bayırkilise**. At an altitude of 1650m, this minor Georgian church offers spectacular views. From here, it's a generally level 5km hike north to the small village of **Elecumle**. To complete a loop back down to Tekkale, cut down the switchback path to the road and head the 9km into town. This loop makes for a long day; some may want to catch a ride part way up or down the road. If you have camping equipment (see **Trekking in the Kaçkars,** p. 419) you can continue on from Elecumle up to the high-altitude lakes, **Küçük Göl** (2850m) and **Büyük Göl** (2900m). The climb passes through the *yayla* and villages of **Kusana** and **Salent**. A trail also ascends from Büyük Göl about two hours up to an awesome 3300m pass, and then descends five hours through **Modut** village to the road to Barhal (15km).

GEORGIAN CHURCHES. A number of isolated **Georgian churches** and striking spots can also be found in the **Tortum Valley,** which holds the road from the Yusufeli turn-off up to the immense Tortum Dam and Tortum Lake on the way to Erzurum. Unfortunately, transportation anywhere except along the main road is minimal and expensive. A full-day taxi costs $80-100; try to find other travelers. Whatever your mode of transport, the roads offer breathtaking views of the mountainsides.

İŞHAN KİLİSE. A pilgrimage to **İşhan Kilise**, 35km from Yusufeli, is worthwhile only for the road's awesome mountainscapes and deep ravines. To get there, take the highway east from Yusufeli to the gas station. Follow the signs first to Erzurum, then bear left toward Olur. Ten to 15km down the road, a sign points left to İşhan Kilise, which is located in a mountain village 5km up the unpaved road. Begun in 730 and finished three centuries later, the church was enhanced with a Byzantine dome in 1200 before its stewardship passed back into Georgian hands. The immense Gothic church is decorated with deteriorating frescoes depicting the apostles and the visions of Zachariah.

ÖŞK VANK KİLİSE. Back down on the highway south to Erzurum, turn off to **Çamlıyamaç** for the **Öşk Vank Kilise** (50km from Yusufeli), one of the most beautiful Georgian churches anywhere. The well-preserved façade of this airy church features carvings of angels, patrons, and animals. Above the entrance, note a colorful band of frescoed faces next to the image of what may be Öşk Vank itself. Another 25km south towards Erzurum is the **Hahokilise,** just outside the town of **Bağbaşı**.

TREKKING IN THE KAÇKARS

There are innumerable opportunities for outdoor activity in the Kaçkar Mountains, and a few months would still not be enough to satisfy a dedicated hiker. Since treks lead through villages and *yayla*, they are seldom too remote. The terrain ranges from lush, deciduous rainforest in the foothills along the Black Sea coast to arid, eroding steppes further southeast in the Artvin and Çoruh Valleys. There are trails above the tree line in all of the Kaçkar regions, affording spectacular views, glacial lakes, and snow well into the spring.

The main obstacle to trekking here is the lack of any high-quality maps. Matters are complicated by poor trail maintenance, thick afternoon Kaçkar fog and stinging nettle undergrowth. Nonetheless, if you have trekking experience and don't mind taking time to decode local maps, directions, and advice, trekking without a guide can be profoundly rewarding.

An easier option is a guided tour. Prices range according to personal needs, group size, trip duration, and the professionalism of the company. Treks are best undertaken from late June (after the snow melts) through September. Only Adnan Pirikoğlu in Ayder offers organized trekking in winter. Phone ahead. A small advance payment will allow guides to purchase the necessary supplies.

Either way, striking the right balance between responsible trekking and local custom can be tricky, especially in Turkey's increasingly threatened Kaçkar wilderness. The general rule of thumb is simply to leave the site the way you found it (or cleaner). All solid human waste should be buried, and all trash and food scraps packed out. You may also need to remind your guide of the importance of frequent stops for **water.** At high altitudes, stay warm and hydrated, and ascend less than 1000 ft. per day. (see **Environmental Hazards: High altitude,** p. 50).

🏃 TREKKING AGENCIES

TRABZON. Usta Tour (☎ (462) 326 18 70; fax 326 18 71) has numerous package deals, organized to the last detail by the local mountaineering group. Options include daytrips to Uzungöl or Zigana, Karaca Cave, and seven-day tours of the Pontic Alps regions. They also offer a three- to four-day mule trek to *yayla* and crater lakes in the western Kaçkar Mountains. Call or fax with questions or reservations. Small groups of four to eight can be accommodated upon arrival.

RIZE. RI-TUR Travel Agency (☎ (464) 217 14 84; fax 217 14 86; email i.h.yildiz@ihlas.net.tr), which operates the town's tourist office and sells international IATA tickets, runs a huge range of regional programs. These can be jointly arranged with international travel agencies so that trips begin and end in İstanbul. The tours are expensive. The 13-day trans-Kaçkar trips ($776) include the *yaylas* of Yukarı Kavron (the highest peak in the Kaçkars) and a rafting trip on the Çoruh River. Various week-long hiking or trekking packages run about $400-500. Small groups can be accommodated more cheaply with personal transportation and guides ($80 per day). RI-TUR's partner organization in İstanbul is **Interopa Travel** (email interopa@escortbet.com).

ŞENYUVA. The Doğa Hotel (☎ (464) 651 74 55), a riverside lodge in the heart of Hemşin country, is one of the best options in the region for budget travelers seeking help before going their own way. The helpful **İdris Duman** can arrange many daytrips or provide advice about two to four day treks that you can do independently. His treks head into the *yaylas* of the western Kaçkars. He can arrange trips to the Pokut and Elevit *yaylas* above Şenyuva that include camping or overnight stays in high-elevation lodges. Despite the wet summer weather, this is a great deal. Travelers are welcome to store supplies and equipment at his lodge.

AYDER. Besides **Türkü Tourism,** which has a lodge in Ayder, there are two other inexpensive and reliable options. At the lower part of town, Adnan Pirikoğlu of **Hotel Pirikoğlu** (☎ 657 20 21) leads treks for $50 per day (no matter how many people) and gives advice about all things mountainous. The town relies on his kind guidance to help confused English speakers. His favorite is a five-day circuit of the Kaçkars (a very good deal), which includes eight crater lakes, the highest summit (Yukarı Kavron; 3037m), lower and upper Kavron *yaylas*, Jicemekçur *yayla*, and Denizgölü, a very deep volcanic lake. Adnan can provide equipment for two people; otherwise bring your own. He will gladly plan smaller trips for travelers free of charge, and he will store extra gear in his hotel.

Also in Ayder, **Muhammet Önçirak** runs the **Kardelen Pension** (☎ (464) 657 21 07), a base for trekking trips. As a member of Turkey's Mountaineering Group, he is a great resource for budget travelers hoping to trek cheaply in the Kaçkars. When asked how much he charges for trekking guidance, he responds, "In exchange for a bottle of *rakı*." Muhammet has a rare topographic map of the region.

YUSUFELİ. Trekkers are drawn to Yusufeli for its dry weather and rafting. Though self-guided trekking takes a little more effort (and research), there is an excellent guide service at **Barhal Hotel,** run by Sirali Aydin, head of the local Skiing-Rafting-Mountain Sport club. (☎ and fax 811 38 93). A three-hour rafting trip down from Sarigol over 20km of medium rapids costs $20 per person ($30 if your group has fewer than 4 people). Check water flow at Yusufeli before committing. The trip downstream from Yusufeli to the Sukausumu gasoline station contains grade V rapids and is for experienced rafters only.

EASTERN ANATOLIA

Welcome to Eastern Turkey, a secret kept even from its own people. Racial and political faultlines traverse this part of the world. Fortunately, tensions have subsided somewhat and once again, one of the world's richest anthropological and historical regions welcomes visitors. Snowy peaks and thundering cascades, the Silk Road and shimmering Van Gölü, hauntingly beautiful Ani and Paşa Palace will, more often than not, be enjoyed without another traveler in sight. After checking passports, once-twitchy police now share apricots and çay with travelers. Hotel keepers remember your name, and Eastern Anatolians will consider you their *misafir* (guest) and offer you the utmost hospitality. This is an Eastern Turkey in transition. Internet now allows you to cultivate lifelong friends here. Massive public works programs are returning wealth to the region and Kurdish music and poetry is slowly surfacing after statewide sanctions. Almost no Turks raised in the western part of the country have ever been to Eastern Anatolia, having been taught that the region is war-torn, remote, and impoverished. This negative image of Turkey's frontier lands has also permeated much of the world, leaving the area untouched by all but the most intrepid of travelers. However, the region offers some of Turkey's most astonishing beauty, both natural and man-made.

Situated neatly on a time-worn crossroad, Eastern Anatolia has been the stomping ground of Hittites, Hurrians, Urartians, Assyrians, Persians, Romans, Byzantines, Arabs, Armenians, Mongols, Selçuks, Ottomans, Russians, Kurds, and Turks. In an unending game of musical chairs, push-pull power plays have privileged each civilization separately, leaving behind a heterogeneous legacy of occupation, construction, and war. Eastern Anatolia's pivotal role in contentious and explosive world politics has continued through the 20th century. The Armenian slaughter of 1915 occurred largely within Turkey's eastern border territory, and its ramifications continue to influence world politics from European Union membership negotiations to American congressional lobbies (see **Armenians,** p. 30).

HIGHLIGHTS OF EASTERN ANATOLIA

EXPLORE the surreal toppled statuary heads upon the man-made summit of **Nemrut Dağı** (p. 443) at dusk and dawn. This grandiose timeless monument of Commagene King Antiochus I stands sentinel over are more recent one, the massive Atatürk Dam.

VISIT the Işak Paşa Sarayı in **Doğubeyazıt** to discover the beauty and elegance of the ancient Kurdish palace (p. 432), flanked by breathtaking *Agri Dagi* (Mt. Ararat)

SWIM in the silky waters of **Lake Van,** make pilgrimage by boat to the most beautiful surviving Armenian structure in Anatolia (Akdamar Church; p. 436), then swim in crystal clear Nemrut Golu, within a 3000 meter volcanic crater, all in a day.

JOURNEY to **Şanlıurfa,** the City of Prophets, to see the birth cave of Abraham and the cave that saw Job's body consumed by worms (p. 444).

WANDER Under the shadows of nearby military watchtowers, wander through magnificent **Ani,** the ancient capital of the Armenian Empire (p. 430).

ERZURUM   ☎ 442

Despite its extremely harsh climate, Erzurum, perched at 1950m on an elevated plateau, is a crossroads for travelers coming north from Van, south from Artvin, or east from Central Anatolia. The city is also a good base for several daytrips, including Pasinler's hot springs and Palondöken's ski resort area.

Travel in Eastern Turkey should be approached with caution. Travelers should be updated on all consular advisories and travel warnings (see **Southeastern Turkey**, p. 46), and should be very careful to follow all relevant rules and laws. That said, tensions in the region have decreased significantly over the past two years, and no tourist should avoid Eastern Turkey solely on safety grounds. The unpredictable nature of travel in Eastern Anatolia requires that travel schedules be flexible. Aside from large luxury buses, arrival and departure times for transportation should be considered tentative.

Let's Go does not recommend that **women** travel alone to Eastern Turkey. Even with a head scarf and long, concealing clothes, women may be considered fair game for wandering eyes and forward flirtations, though the constant accompaniment is almost all benign. To avoid unwanted advances, dress very conservatively, memorize some key phrases, and stay in the more expensive hotels (see **Women Travelers**, p. 68).

Many empires have fought for this strategic city linking trade routes between Iran and Anatolia. Early 13th-century Arz ar-Rum ("Land of the Romans"), as Erzurum was called by the Arabs and the Turks, prospered under the Selçuk Sultans. After the Mongol invasions, Ottoman Sultan Selim I seized the city in 1515. Russia even had its turn, occupying Erzurum in 1829, 1878, and again during WWI.

Erzurum has a rich history as a garrison town; armed soldiers have walked the city streets and dined in its cafes for over 1500 years. More recently, Erzurum has become a college town, with a young liberal student population challenging the conservatism of one of Turkey's most old-fashioned and religious cities.

▐ TRANSPORTATION

The **otogar** is 3km west of downtown. Most major bus companies provide free shuttles to the town center, and taxis (all have meters) cost approximately $2-3. The main **dolmuş** lot is a short walk northwest of Gürcü Kapı, but heading there directly means navigating a maze of side-streets—it's easier but longer to go all the way north on İstasyon Cad. and follow the outer loop around.

Buses: Laid out like a miniature international airport, the **otogar** has 4 cardinal wings: one each for arrivals and taxis and 2 for departures. Not many of the major bus companies operate this far east, and the ones that do, including **Ağri** (☎218 69 34), **Dadaş** (☎218 27 88), and **Ulusoy** (☎234 24 06), have scaled-back service. Shop around; look at the bus you'll be taking whenever possible.

BUS SCHEDULES

Destination	Company	Duration	Times (daily)	Price
Adana	Ağri	17hr.	11am and 3pm	$17.50
Ankara	Dadaş	12hr.	7:30am, 7, 8:30pm	$17.50
Antalya	Dadaş	21hr.	10:30am	$23.50
Doğubeyazıt	Ağri	4hr.	11am, 12:30, 2:30pm	$6
Erzincan	Dadaş	2½hr.	10am, 2:30, 5pm	$3.50
İstanbul	Dadaş	18hr.	noon, 4, 6pm	$21
İzmir	Dadaş	22hr.	10am, 2:30, 5pm	$20
Malatya	Ağri	10hr.	11am, 3, 4:30pm	$12
Şanlıurfa	Ağri	15hr.	4:30pm	$16.50
Sivas	Dadaş	6hr.	10am, 2:30, 5pm	$11.50
Trabzon	Ulusoy	5hr.	8am, 1, 6pm	$10, students $8

Trains: Eastbound trains (M, W, F, Su 9:29am; Tu, Sa 3:31pm) to: **Karasu** ($1, students $.80) and **Kars** ($2.50, students $2). Westbound trains (M, Tu, Th, Sa 11:23am and W, F, Su noon) to: **Ankara** ($10, students $8); **Erzincan** ($2.50, students $2);

Eastern Anatolia

Black Sea

Expressway

GEORGIA

Batumi
Hopa
Posof
Artvin
Ardahan
Çıldır
Giresun
Rize
Akyaka
Leninakan
(Gümrü)
Trabzon
Ayder
Kars
Yusufeli
Ani
ARMENIA
Uzungöl
Sankamış
Yerevan
Gümüşhane
Bayburt
Pasinler
Iğdır
Mt. Ararat
(5122m)
Tercan
Erzurum
Ağrı
Erzincan
Doğubeyazı
Maku
Divrigi
Muradiye
Waterfall
Tunceli
Bingöl
Lake Nemrut
Lake
Van
IRAN
Muş
Tatvan
Van
Hoşap
Castle
Elazığ
Bitlis
Akdamar
Malatya
Nemrut
Dağı
Batman
Hasankeyf
Siirt
Kahta
Diyarbakır
Şırnak
Hakkari
Adıyaman
Şanlıurfa
Mardin
Nusaybin
Habur
Zakhü
TO GAZIANTEP
Harran
Tigris
IRAQ
Akçakale
SYRIA
N
0   50 miles
0   50 kilometers

Eskişehir ($12.50, students $10); **İstanbul** (Haydarpaşa station; 12hr.; $15, students $12); **Kayseri** ($7.50, students $6); **Sivas** ($5.50, students $4.50). Durations vary.

Dolmuş: Dolmuş and minibuses leave from the **Gölbaş Semt Garajı,** 1km northwest of Gürcü Kapı, to destinations as far as Trabzon, Erzincan, and Kars (generally 9am-6pm). Buses are often faster and more comfortable, and not much more expensive.

ORIENTATION AND PRACTICAL INFORMATION

Gürcü Kapı (Georgian Gate) is the center of the old city. From here, **İstasyon Cad.** heads down to the **gar** while **Menderes Cad.** runs 750m uphill to intersect with **Cumhuriyet Cad.** Most establishments are around Cumhuriyet Cad. and Menderes Cad.

Tourist Office: (☎218 56 97; fax 218 54 43), on Cemal Gürsel Cad., near the university. The director Muhammet Yoksuç speaks excellent English. Open daily 8am-7:30pm.

Banks: The best place to change money is at **TC Ziraat Bankası** on İstasyon Cad. at Gürü Kapı, 50m from Hotel Polat. No commission. Other banks line Cumhuriyet Cad.

Hamam: Erzurum's finest hamams are the combined male and female establishments at **Kirkcesme** (☎218 23 41), Ayazpaşa Cad. Kirkcesme Sok. 5., a short walk from Hotels Sefer and Polat after crossing İstasyon Cad. Women $2; open 8am-5pm. Men 2.50 plus $1 for a scrub; open 5:30am-11pm.

Pharmacies: On Hastaneler Cad. and next to the Hotel Kosh on Mumçu Cad. Open 24hr.

Hospitals: The hospital complex stretches along the well-named Hastaneler Cad.

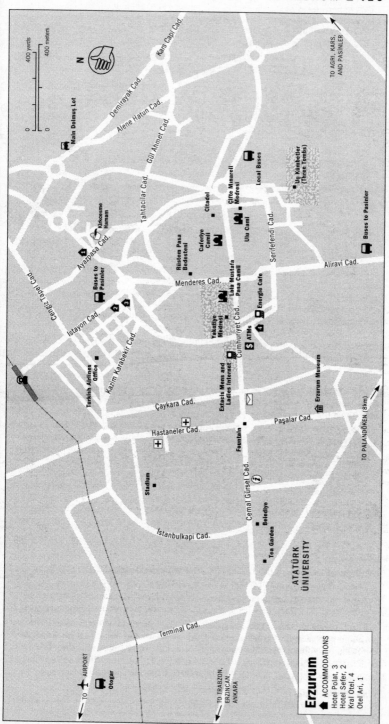

Erzurum

ACCOMMODATIONS
Hotel Polat, 3
Hotel Sefer, 2
Kral Otel, 4
Otel Ari, 1

Internet Access: Bengisu Internet Cafe, 50m up İsmet Paşa Cad, the side street by the PTT. **Energie Cafe** is in a lane opposite Hotel Kamal. Open 24hr. **Extacis Mens and Ladies Internet,** on Cumhuriyet Cad., is open 8:30am-1am.

PTT: The main branch lies on Cumhuriyet Cad., 300m west of Menderes Cad. 24hr. international cash phones. **Postal codes:** 25000, 25100, and 25200.

ACCOMMODATIONS

Cheap is not best in Erzurum; for a little extra, you can enjoy the best hotels in town, assigned stars by the Ministry of Tourism. They typically include breakfast.

▨ **Hotel Polat,** 4 Kazim Karabekir Cad. (☎218 16 23). The tired exterior hides new rooms with TV, phone, and hot water bath. Beware low ceilings in the quieter 6th-floor rooms. Singles $12; doubles $18; triples $24.

▨ **Otel Ari,** Ayazpaşa Cad. 22 (☎218 31 41), Central and clean. The best value. $5 per person.

Kral Otel, 18 Erzincan Kapı (☎218 77 83), will be a 4-star hotel by 2002. In the meantime, ask for their superb renovated rooms at cheapie prices. Singles $18; triples $30.

Hotel Sefer (☎218 67 14; fax 212 37 75), diagonally across from Polat at the corner on İstasyon Cad. A step up in price rather than value. Though noisy at times, the rooms are excellent. Singles $20; doubles $30; triples $33. V, MC.

FOOD

Possibly Eastern Turkey's most remarkable restaurant is the ▨ **Erzurum Evleri,** off Cumhuriyet Cad. in a side alley called Yuzbasi Sok. Traditional *kilim* pillow seating and an Ali Baba cave-like interior complements superb *Iran* soup, vine leaf *yapa sarma,* crock pot *guvec,* and kebap. (☎233 20 31. Open 9:30am-11:30pm.) Since 1928, ▨ **Güzelyurt,** 54 Cumhuriyet Cad., has been among Erzurum's finest, with starched tablecloths and great service. (☎218 15 14. Open 11:30am-midnight.)

The student population also supports a modest cafe scene on the downhill half of Cumhuriyet Cad. **Salon Asya,** at 27 Cumhuriyet Cad., 50m downhill from Menderes Cad., is a popular kebap and *lahmacun* spot. (☎212 12 43. Open 5am-1am.) Erzurum's dining rooms are on Gürcü Kapı and along Cumhuriyet Cad. **Donerci Canbaba** at No. 18 (☎234 30 13; open 7:30-midnight), **Donerci Hacibey** (☎218 32 80), and **Ziyade,** across and downhill from Salon Asya stand out, with full meals at about $4. Have dessert and tea at **Pado,** at 13 Cumhuriyet. (Open until midnight.) Night owls wolf down dessert at **Serender Palisseria,** 32 Cumhuriyet Cad. (☎218 56 45. Open till 1:30am.) A large fruit and vegetable **market** operates daily from dawn to dusk at Gürcü Kapı, 50m in on İstasyon Cad.

SIGHTS

Though they cover almost 4000 years of history, most of Erzurum's major sights can be explored in about five hours. Starting from the eastern side of the downtown area at the corner of Cumhuriyet Cad. and Tabriz Kapı, you can travel westward (towards the PTT) to the *camii,* the castle, museum, and the *kervansaray.*

ÇİFTE MİNARELİ MEDRESE. In 1253, Hüdavend Hatun, the daughter of Sultan Alaeddin Keykubad, commissioned this Koranic school, the most lauded of Erzurum's sights. Its twin fluted minarets are tiled in blue and provide the inspiration for the school's name, "The Twin Minaret *Medrese.*" The rooms that flank the entrance portal on the upper and lower levels were once inhabited by students of the religious school. The Ministry of Tourism recently renovated the courtyard, constructing a high-class *çay* garden where locals and tourists alike find refuge from the summer heat. In back lies the **Hatuniye Türbesi,** the tomb of Hatun.

ULU CAMİİ. Built in 1179 by Melik Mehmet, one of the city's Saltıd rulers, this Selçuk mosque has a dramatically different architectural style from the neighboring Çifte Minareli *Medrese*. Dim lighting, internal columns, and an unusually low ceiling create a somber, reverent ambiance. An ingenious dome of layered wooden slats lies before an impressive skylight adorned with *muqarnas* (decorative element on mosque walls). A recent restoration has revitalized prayer traffic, so remove your shoes as you enter.

KALE. In the 5th century, Emperor Theodosius II built this citadel at the city's highest point (about 2000m). With each war, the fortress was demolished, then rebuilt and fortified by the winning side. Inside are cannons with Russian and Ottoman inscriptions, a *mescit* (small mosque) from the 12th century that looks like a *kümbet* (tomb), and a clock tower. The clock tower provides splendid views of Erzurum and the vast landscape beyond. Bring a flashlight to explore the dark, steep stairway that climbs to the top. *(From Ulu Camii, head directly north across the street, and walk upwards. Open daily 8am-5:30pm. $.50.)*

OTTOMAN MOSQUES. Continue west on Cumhuriyet Cad. to two Ottoman mosques: the **Caferiye Camii** (1645) and the **Lala Mustafa Paşa Camii** (1563). Lala Mustafa Paşa, the conqueror of Cyprus, commissioned this mosque during his reign over Erzurum. Next door is the **Yakutiye Medrese,** in a large city park where a good cross-section of Erzurum's population wiles away the summer afternoons. Lion reliefs and ornate geometric designs decorate the school's west entrance. Today, the *medrese* contains the city's best **museum.** Ethnographic exhibits are displayed in former student rooms. Features include Ottoman arms, ornaments, ceramics, dervish costumes, and manuscripts. *(Museum open daily 8:30am-5pm. $1.)*

RÜSTEM PAŞA KERVANSARAY. Because Erzurum was such an important intercontinental trading city, Süleyman the Magnificent's Grand Vizier funded the construction of this *kervansaray*, which served as a travelers' rest stop. Today it houses the **Rüstem Paşa Bedesteni,** a jewelry market with a focus on obsidian, a black volcanic stone mined in Oltu, 150km away. Obsidian is often crafted into *tesbih* (prayer beads or worry beads). Prices for the beads start at $5 and rise quickly.

ERZURUM MUSEUM. A mammoth skeleton along with two millennia of coins, pots, and other antiquities await the intrepid visitor who walks uphill along Pasalar Cad. *(Open Tu-Su 8am-5pm. $1.50, students $1.)*

⚑ DAYTRIPS FROM ERZURUM

PASİNLER. A fortress and hot springs tempt travelers to wander about 38km east of Erzurum to **Pasinler,** where 14th-century **Hasan Kale** towers over the town. Originally an Armenian structure, the fortress was rebuilt by the Uzon Hasan (1433-1478), ruler of the White Sheep, a Turkmen tribal federation. On arrival, plan a 40-minute round-trip hike from the town. Although still impressive, it steadily crumbles from neglect and disuse, but affords a view of the four hot-spring hamams on the other side of the highway below. Two are notable: **Sifali Banyölü Otel** (☎661 32 16), which offers private room baths for $3 per hour, and the two-star **Hotel Kale,** starting at $3.50 for Roman bath, sauna, and gym. Private rooms are $5 per hour.

The town center is the **Sehitler Parki** and Cumhuriet Cad., joined to the highway by Milli Egemenlik Cad. and Belediye Cad. At the Hasankale end of town, Belediye Cad. contains the Erzurum Coach stop, **Aymer Hypermarket, Sanko Bilardo Internet Cafe,** and the best restaurants: **Hajibaba Lok., Saray Lok.** (☎661 47 00), and **Ozlem Lok.** (☎661 34 84). *(Pasinler Beledesi shuttles between Erzurum and Pasinler (every 45min.). It loops through town and can be hailed at the bus stop on İstasyon Cad., opposite Hotel Sefer, or from 500m south of Cumhuriyet Cad.)*

TERCAN. The ideal place to break the 2½-hour journey between Erzurum and Erzincan is at Tercan. The splendid **Mama Hatun Türbesi,** built in 1182, holds the remains of Mama Hatun, a Selçuk princess who helped Saladin conquer this portion of Anatolia. In each of the eight half-circles that form the structure's outer walls, a lesser member of the nobility is buried. At the center is a *mihrab* atop a vaulted tomb. If it is open, head through the door and down the steps to see the sarcophagus, covered in green felt. Above it, the prayer room is still used by pilgrims and pious Muslims, especially women. Nearby is a recently renovated *kervansaray* whose doors are usually locked. *(Buses between Erzurum and Erzincan, which stop at the petrol station in Tercan, are frequent but not always on time ($4 to either city).)*

PALONDÖKEN. Palondöken, 10km of Erzurum, is home to some of Erzurum's best **ski slopes.** In winter, frequent transportation connections are available, but a taxi is your only option in summer ($19 round-trip). The **Dedeman Hotel** (☎ (442) 316 24 14), right on the slopes, is rated four stars and has a price to match.

ERZINCAN   ☎446

Very little of ancient Erzincan remains in the city's modern incarnation. In 1939 the city suffered one of the most devastating earthquakes in Turkish history, in which more than 30,000 people were killed. The subsequent 1993 quake (plus a few in between) destroyed most of the buildings of historical interest. Erzincan has recovered rapidly, and commercial and civil industry are exploding throughout the downtown area. The result is an energetic town with efficiently organized avenues, clean pavements, and wide open public spaces.

Altıntepe, "the Golden Hill" is a very important Urartian (ancient Anatolian) site, discovered in 1938 during the construction of the eastern portion of the Turkish railroad (see **From Hittites to Hellenes,** p. 6). Believed to have been constructed between the 7th and 8th century BC, Altıntepe was once a substantial palace and temple. Resist the taxi temptation and take a $.40 dolmuş from diagonally opposite the otogar. Though *jandarma* presence is low, visitors will be cordially removed from the sight if seen. The five-minute ascent offers the intrepid a magnificent view of the valley from battlements, platforms, and tumbled columns.

▐ TRANSPORTATION. The **otogar** is at the far eastern end of town, where E-80 briefly turns south. This small, new station boasts a tiny **PTT** and connections to almost everywhere in Turkey. **Buses** travel to: **Adana** (Ağri, 12hr., 5 per day, $20); **Andara** (Dadaş, 10hr., 9am, 1, 8pm; $17.50; **Antalya** (Dadaş, 19hr., 1 per day, $25); **Doğubeyazıt** (Ağri, 7hr., 3 per day, $10); **Erzurum** (Dadaş, 2½hr., every hr., $5); **İstanbul** (Dadaş, 15hr., 5 per day, $25); **Kayseri** (6hr., $13); **Malatya** (Ağri, 7hr., 4:30pm, $11); **Konya** (11hr., $12); **Sivas** (Dadaş, 4hr., 9am, 12:30pm; $15); **Trabzon** (Ulusoy, 6hr., 3 per day, $13). **Dolmuş** and **minibuses** leave from the dolmuş stop diagonally opposite the otogar. This is the best way to get to **Altintepe** ($.40 each way). Longer dolmuş journeys can be extremely slow compared to buses.

▐▐ ORIENTATION AND PRACTICAL INFORMATION. All travelers' needs, including major **banks** with **ATMs, 24-hour police assistance,** and the **hospital,** are on or near the intersection of **Fevzipaşa Cad.** and **Urdu Cad.** After this intersection, Fevzipaşa Cad. becomes **Halitpaşa Cad. Dunya Internet Cafe** (☎224 24 42) is on the 2nd floor next to Anil's Restaurant. (Open 9:30am-midnight. $1 per hr). Leaving the otogar, turn right into Urdu Cad. where the **PTT** is 150m on the left.

▐ ACCOMMODATIONS. Many hotels have sprouted up on the 2km stretch of Fevzipaşa Cad. The following hotels are all close to the otogar, and all offer more or less the same amenities. ▧ **Otel Karakaya,** 40B Fevzipaşa Cad., boasts a lounge with a fish tank and plush Victorian furniture. This dark and pious establishment does have some windowless front rooms; insist on the back. (☎214 36 73. Singles $8; doubles $12; triples $16.) For a little extra, try the new **Hotel Hanedan,** 34/B Fevzipaşa Cad. (☎224 24 04. Singles $10; $5 per extra person.) On the south side of the street, the **Otel Kervan** ($6 per person) is closest to the otogar. One block west across the boulevard is the well-presented **Kiliçlar Oteli,** 14 Fevzipaşa Cad. (☎212 16 41. Same prices as Hanedan). The quietest is the well-concealed **Mete Hotel,** İnönü Mah. 5/ Sok. (☎214 74 05), in an alley off Fevzipaşa Cad.

FOOD. Dozens of *kebapçis* and *salonus* line Fevzipaşa Cad. Near Otel Kervan, the **Oba Restaurant**, Fevzipaşa Cad. 54, serves good grilled chicken. (☎223 34 25. Full meal $3-4. Open 1pm-1am). Try the fresh *şiş kebap* (full meal $5-8) at **Doy Doy Restaurant** (☎212 23 60). To arrive there, head west on Fevzipaşa Bul. until you reach the open pavilion, then turn left onto the unmarked Subat St. Walk four short blocks; the restaurant is on your right. Local favorite **Derya Restoran**, 21/C Fevzipaşa Cad., offers $2 kebap. (☎223 77 17. Open until midnight.)

KARS
☎474

The poverty of Kars contrasts sharply with the haunting beauty of the rugged steppe that envelops it. Yet this contrast and that of the brutal winters and dusty summers only add to Kars's old-world charm. Horse-drawn carts drive alongside automobiles, and vendors set out their varied wares on poorly paved streets. In the town center, a few stately 19th-century buildings founder, submerged under smog, dust, and other hastily built dwellings. Recent public works (fountains, malls, and manicured lawns) promise better times ahead for Kars. Unfortunately, because the key commercial routes to the east bypass the city, those opportunities are limited. Kars has numerous interesting historical relics, all dwarfed by the magnificence of the Armenian ruins at Ani, just 48km to the west.

TRANSPORTATION

Flights: THY, 80 Atatürk Cad. (☎212 38 38). To **İstanbul** ($68; daily 11am, $50) via **Ankara.** An airport dolmuş ($2) leaves from here 2hr. before flight time. Also sells **IATA** international tickets. İstanbul Airlines flies directly to İstanbul (M, Th 12:30pm; $60).

Buses: Doğu Kars (☎223 33 33), across from the bus station, **Kafkas Kars** (☎223 29 55) and the new **Kars Turgutreis** (☎223 60 38) serve the area. Buses run to: **Ankara** (9, 10, 11am, noon, 5pm; $16) via **Sivas** ($12); **Erzurum** (15 per day, $4); **İstanbul** (9:30, 11:30am, 1pm; $25); **İzmir** (11am, $25). Only **Kars Turgutreis** serves **Van** (8am, $12). All companies have a free shuttle bus from their main office to the new otogar, leaving 1hr. before the bus departs.

Trains: The **Doğu Ekspresi** leaves daily at 8:30am for İstanbul's Haydarpaşa station. It stops en route in **Erzurum, Erzincan, Sivas,** and **Ankara.** Prices to İstanbul range from $8 to $25, depending on class. The **Karma Treni** leaves for **Erzurum** daily at 1pm.

Dolmuş: Eski Otogar, the old bus station 2 blocks east of town center, has become the minibus and dolmuş lot to local destinations. A minibus or 2 leaves for **Trabzon** ($12) and **Yusufeli/Artvin** ($6) daily. Doğubeyazıt cannot be reached directly. Dolmuş leave for **Iğdır** (every hr. 6am-5pm, $4), where you can connect to other destinations. Dolmuş depart when full to **Sarikamis** (6am-5pm, $1.50), **Selim,** and **Ardahan.**

ORIENTATION AND PRACTICAL INFORMATION

Kars was occupied by Russia from 1877 through 1920, and the town's architecture and layout bears an unmistakable Russian imprint. All the main streets run north-south and east-west, forming blocks and straight, long avenues. **Halıt Paşa Cad.** runs west from the old bus station past cheap hotels, restaurants, and shops. It passes **Kasım Paşa Cad.,** which forbids automotive traffic, then **Atatürk Cad.,** which has restaurants, airline offices, tourist information, and many banks. To the north the **Kars Kale** towers over the city. To the south of the city, train tracks mark the end of city life. The new **otogar** is 3km east of town and the airport 6km to the east.

Tourist Office: (☎212 68 17). The office is in a gray building on the corner of Karadağ Cad. and Atatürk Cad. in the downtown business district. Open 8:30am-5:30pm daily. Photocopied city maps, glossy brochures, and Ani applications (see **Ani,** p. 430).

EASTERN ANATOLIA

Banks: Türkiye İş Bankası, on the corner of Halıt Paşa Cad. and Atatürk Cad., cashes traveler's checks. Open 9:30am-12:30pm, 1:30-5:30pm. Many other banks downtown change cash and have 24hr. Cirrus/Plus/MC/V **ATMs.**

Police and **Tourist Police:** (☎212 47 00).

Hospital: (☎223 12 02 or 223 12 03), on Gazi Ahmet Muhtar Paza Cad (C.A.M.P Cad.), while **pharmacies** are on almost every block.

Internet: Fisilti, 42 G.AMP. Cad. (☎223 81 84). $1 per hr.

PTT: Main branch on Ökül Cad. between Karadağ Cad. and Faıt Bey Cad. Located with Turk-Telekom. Both open 24hr.

▌▐ ACCOMMODATIONS AND FOOD

Most hotels in Kars are clean, comfortable, and noisy. **Hotel Kervansaray,** 204 Faık Bey Cad. (☎223 19 90), and neighboring **Hotel Nursuray** (☎223 13 64), are super budget options, centrally located with basic rooms, clean sheets, and shared baths. Back rooms are quieter. (Showers $1. $4 per person.) Another good bet is **Hotel Yılmaz,** 146 Küçük Cad., perhaps the quietest hotel in town. Here rooms are well maintained, with TVs and phones. (☎212 51 74. Singles $11; doubles $20.)

As with hotels, the food in Kars is cheap and acceptable, with a couple of splendid exceptions. **Ocakbaşı Restoran,** 176 Atatürk Cad. (☎212 00 56), serves delicious soups, *tavuk dolma* (chicken, hazelnut, and melted cheese) and *Kunëfe* (a birdsnest of hazelnuts, cheese, and honey) for dessert. Standard kebap and *lokanta* cuisine is readily available. Vegetarians may find eating in Kars a challenge. Kars is known for its *Kaşar* (meaning "kosher") yellow cheese. **Salon Sema Piknik,** 9 Faık Bey Cad., is one block east of the Hotel Kervansaray. Vegetarians can ask for *Kaşarli pide,* a sort of cheese-*pide*-pizza with some vegetables and egg, at this upbeat salon-style eatery. (☎223 21 18. Full meal $3. Open daily 8am-10pm.) A lunchtime crowd always gathers at **Cafe Kristal,** 181 Atatürk Cad., for its cheerful atmosphere, tasty cuisine, and good *döner kebap* (☎223 22 67. Full meal $3.50. Open 8am-10pm.) At the top of the pedestrian mall, **Antep Pide,** 119 Atatürk Cad. (☎223 07 41), serves an economical Turkish lunch. **Grand Malatya Restaurant and Pastene,** 68 Atatürk Cad., serves a great variety of desserts from its bakery (☎223 17 31; desserts $1; open 8am-9pm), as does the **Baklava Salönü** on Atatürk Cad.

◉ SIGHTS

Kars has numerous worthwhile sights. Take a picnic to the north side of the town, where **Kars Kale** overlooks the city. It was constructed by either the Armenians or the Selçuks in 1152. After Tamerlane destroyed the building in 1386, Sultan Murat III had it reconstructed in 1579. (Open daily 9am-6pm. Free.)

Most of the other key sights are nearby. On the right during the ascent is the **Church of the Apostles,** built by the Bagratid King Abas and repaired by the Ottomans. Today the church stands abandoned and usually locked. The 12 apostles are still visible, carved in relief on the lower section of the dome. North of the church is the **Taş Köprü,** a stone bridge that dates from the 15th century. The **Muradiye Hamamı** ($2 per person) steams at the foot of the bridge. Open as early as 5am, the service alternates between men and women; the schedule changes each day, so check the sign over the door (*"erkek"* is men, *"kadın"* is women).

Kars's **museum,** a 20-minute walk from town, is definitely worth a visit. It features local pottery from 5000 BC to the present as well as Urartian jewelry, photos from local sites, and two tall wooden doors from a church with an interesting eagle relief. Upstairs are *kilims,* old metalworks, weaponry, and ornate embroidered dresses. (Open 8:30am-5:30pm. $1.50.)

▐▌ DAYTRIPS FROM KARS: THE ANCIENT CITY OF ANI

Because of its sensitive border location, all visitors to Ani must obtain a permit. The application process is a complex song-and-dance that begins with a form in the tourist office, which is then stamped by tourist police before a final presentation at the museum where

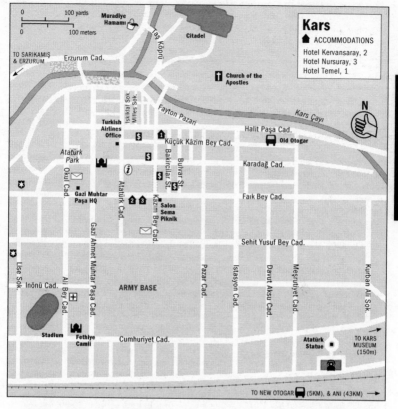

Kars
♦ ACCOMMODATIONS
Hotel Kervansaray, 2
Hotel Nursuray, 3
Hotel Temel, 1

permits are issued for $1. Passports are required at each point; however, they need not be presented in person. No public transportation runs between Kars and Ani. Taxis carry up to 4 for $33. Larger groups can negotiate a minibus or take a dolmuş ($8 per person) organized through the tourist office. Drivers usually take passengers through the entire permit process (8am-4pm). Çelil Ersözoğlu (☎ 223 63 23; cell 0532 226 39 66) is a helpful English-speaking tour guide and usually the dolmuş driver. Otherwise, Ani Tour (☎ 223 99 90), in the old bus station, officially offers a similar package deal, though service varies with demand. Staying overnight at Ani is illegal, as is straying, pointing cameras towards Armenia, or climbing Ani's southern fortress (with Turkish flag atop). Ani is a triangular plateau wedged southward into the junction of the Alaçay and Arpaçay river canyons, on the west and east, respectively. Armenia lies visibly on the east bank of the Arpaçay. Visitors enter through the Aslan Kapısı (Lion's Gate), in the middle of the 10m tall, 2500m long walls, built in 972. The Lion's Gate is the last remaining of the original seven gates along this double wall. Heading left from the entrance and walking clockwise makes a 3km circuit that touches all the ruins.

Among ruins, the ancient city of Ani is a colossus. Spread over 5 square kilometers, it swarms with Turkish military and is shadowed by Armenian watch towers. The 45km ride to Ani is spectacular: wild horses graze over the green landscape dotted with purple and yellow mountain flowers. On a clear day, Mount Ararat (5137m) rises formidably in the background behind the distant ruins.

The name Ani comes from the name of the Persian goddess Anahid, who was worshipped by the Urartians at this site. King Ashot III (952-977) chose this spot for the capital of Bagratid Armenia. Christian Ani prospered on trade, growing to rival Constantinople. The Byzantines took control in 1045, followed by the Selçuks in 1064. Power traded hands repeatedly between Armenians and Byzantines, until the city was seized two centuries later by the Mongols, who left their mark upon the city's architecture. Harsh weather destroyed many of the great buildings, leaving only the most majestic as a testament to past greatness.

The **Church of the Holy Redeemer,** built in 1034, is the first step along the southeast path. It was hit by lightning in 1957, and is now just a half-shell with massive piles of rubble. On the west side there is a relief of an angel resting over an Armenian cross. Continue south and pass an 11th-century Selçuk **hamam,** and then head down the slope to find one of the three **Churches of St. Gregory (Tigorn Honents)** that gazes over a ledge onto the Arpaçay River. Among its fascinating frescoes, the east wall depicts major events in Armenian religious history, including the trial and torture of St. Gregory the Illuminator, who brought Christianity to Armenia. The opposite walls reveal scenes from the life of Christ. Down the valley over a slim path past the Silk Road sign stand the remains of the **Covenant of the Virgins,** from which you can see Armenia and an old bridge across the Arpaçay River. Walking farther south leads to the largest building in Ani, the domeless **Cathedral of Virgin Mary,** built from 939 to 1001 and designed by Titridates, who previously had collaborated in the restoration of İstanbul's Aya Sofia after earthquake damage. The Selçuks converted the cathedral to a mosque during their reign, but under Christian leaders it reverted to its role as a church. A passage to the left of the altar leads up to a private room; bring a flashlight for safe exploration. Farther southwest lies the **Menüçehir Camii,** built in 1072 and said to be the first mosque in Anatolia. Its climbable minaret bears the uniquely non-Selçuk inscription of Allah's name. From the mosque's window are views of the river and Armenia.

Above the mosque, the 4th-century **citadel** still acts as a strategic location for Turkish soldiers and is often off-limits. The rotunda-style **Church of St. Gregory (Abighamrets),** lying northwest of the citadel, has an interesting six-niche design inside. In the center of the plateau is the **Church of the Holy Apostles,** once converted into a *kervansaray* and now mostly rubble. Note the variety of Islamic geometric designs and *muqarnas* (stalactite ornamentations). To the northwest is the third **Church of St. Gregory,** built by the Armenian king Gegik I, and the **Selçuk Palace.**

DOĞUBEYAZIT   ☎472

Turkey's portion of the Silk Road ends at Doğubeyazıt. This is a frontier town, a bit rough around the edges, that worries little about its looks. Having long outgrown its tiny main street, DoĞubeyazit pulses with the roar of traffic to Iran. On either side, the town is flanked by marvels that ensure its place on the map: **Ağri Dağ** (Mount Ararat) and the **Işak Paşa Palace.**

▐ **TRANSPORTATION.** Visitors arrive either at the **otogar,** at the east end of town, or the **dolmuş stop,** at the other end of the same street. **Buses** depart from the otogar for western locations including **Ankara** (18hr., 2 per day, $25), and **İstanbul** (2hr., 2 per day, 22hr., $25). However, service is limited and indirect. **Minibuses** run to **Erzurum** (4hr., every hr., $8) via **Ağri** ($6). **Bus tickets** can be purchased at **Meteor Tourism** (☎312 35 05), on the corner of Çarşi and Güven Cad. At the far west end of Belediye Cad., near the dolmuş stop and above the *çay* house, stands the **THY office,** 5 Meyramane Cad. (☎312 67 72. Open daily 7am-8pm.) **Dolmuş** leave for **Van** (3hr., $5) via **Çaldiran** ($3) and **Kars** (4hr., $6) via **Iğdir** ($2).

▐▌ **ORIENTATION AND PRACTICAL INFORMATION.** Belediye Cad. has all the necessities. **Turan Demirhan** (☎311 39 74; email turandemirhan@hotmail.com) offers free tourist information in English, and organizes all tours from his travel agency at Büyük Agri Cad., 2nd fl., near the BP sign. Cheap hotels are clustered near the east end of town, and the **PTT** and **banks** are near the middle. **Currency exchange** is available at **Turkiye İş Bankası.** (Open 8am-12:30pm, 1:30-5:30pm.) V/MC/Cirrus **ATMs** are prevalent throughout town. A large **supermarket** can be found at the junction of Rifki Baskaya Cad. and Guven Cad. Three **internet cafes** line Carsi Cad., including **Omega** (☎312 75 48) and **Klas** (☎312 49 18), the latter doubling as a *biliardo salonu* (pool hall). The **PTT** is open daily from 8:30am-5pm, with 24-hour phones (note: Türk Telekom cards will not function). **Postal code:** 04400.

WORLDWIDE CALLING MADE EASY

The MCI WorldCom Card, designed specifically to keep you in touch with the people that matter the most to you.

MCI *WORLDCOM* WORLDPHONE.

1·800·888·8000

J. L. SMITH

www.wcom.com/worldphone

Please tear off this card and keep it in your wallet as a reference guide for convenient U.S. and worldwide calling with the MCI WorldCom Card.

HOW TO MAKE CALLS USING YOUR MCI WORLDCOM CARD

> **When calling from the U.S., Puerto Rico, the U.S. Virgin Islands or Canada** to virtually anywhere in the world:
1. Dial 1-800-888-8000
2. Enter your card number + PIN, listen for the dial tone
3. Dial the number you are calling :
   Domestic Calls: Area Code + Phone Number
   International Calls:
   011+ Country Code + City Code + Phone Number

> **When calling from outside the U.S.,** use WorldPhone from over 125 countries and places worldwide:
1. Dial the WorldPhone toll-free access number of the country you are calling from.
2. Follow the voice instructions or hold for a WorldPhone operator to complete the call.

> **For calls from your hotel:**
1. Obtain an outside line.
2. Follow the instructions above on how to place a call.
   Note: If your hotel blocks the use of your MCI WorldCom Card, you may have to use an alternative location to place your call.

RECEIVING INTERNATIONAL COLLECT CALLS*

Have family and friends call you collect at home using WorldPhone Service and pay the same low rate as if you called them.
1. Provide them with the WorldPhone access number for the country they are calling from (In the U.S., 1-800-888-8000; for international access numbers see reverse side).
2. Have them dial that access number, wait for an operator, and ask to call you collect at your home number.

For U.S. based customers only.

START USING YOUR MCI WORLDCOM CARD TODAY. MCI WORLDCOM STEPSAVERS℠

Get the same low rate per country as on calls from home, when you:

1. **Receive international collect calls to your home** using WorldPhone access numbers

2. **Make international calls with your MCI WorldCom Card** from the U.S.*

3. **Call back to anywhere in the U.S. from Abroad** using your MCI WorldCom Card and WorldPhone access numbers.

* An additional charge applies to calls from U.S. pay phones.

WorldPhone Overseas Laptop Connection Tips —
Visit our website, www.wcom.com/worldphone, to learn how to access the Internet and email via your laptop when traveling abroad using the MCI WorldCom Card and WorldPhone access numbers.

Travelers Assist® — When you are overseas, get emergency interpretation assistance and local medical, legal, and entertainment referrals. Simply dial the country's toll-free access number.

Planning a Trip?—Call the WorldPhone customer service hotline at 1-800-736-1828 for new and updated country access availability or visit our website:

www.wcom.com/worldphone

MCI WorldCom Worldphone Access Numbers

Easy Worldwide Calling

MCI *WORLDCOM.*

The MCI WorldCom Card.
The easy way to call
when traveling worldwide.

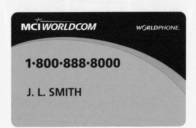

MCI WORLDCOM   WORLDPHONE.

1·800·888·8000

J. L. SMITH

The MCI WorldCom Card gives you...

- Access to the US and other countries worldwide.
- Customer Service 24 hours a day
- Operators who speak your language
- Great MCI WorldCom rates and no sign-up fees

For more information or to apply for a Card call:
1-800-955-0925

Outside the U.S., call MCI WorldCom collect (reverse charge) at:
1-712-943-6839

COUNTRY	WORLDPHONE TOLL-FREE ACCESS #
Argentina (CC)	
Using Telefonica	0800-222-6249
Using Telecom	0800-555-1002
Australia (CC) ♦	
Using OPTUS	1-800-551-111
Using TELSTRA	1-800-881-100
Austria (CC) ♦	0800-200-235
Bahamas (CC) +	1-800-888-8000
Belgium (CC) ♦	0800-10012
Bermuda (CC) +	1-800-888-8000
Bolivia (CC) ♦	0-800-2222
Brazil (CC)	000-8012
British Virgin Islands +	1-800-888-8000
Canada (CC)	1-800-888-8000
Cayman Islands +	1-800-888-8000
Chile (CC)	
Using CTC	800-207-300
Using ENTEL	800-360-180
China ♦	108-12
Mandarin Speaking Operator	108-17
Colombia (CC) ♦	980-9-16-0001
Collect Access in Spanish	980-9-16-1111
Costa Rica ♦	0800-012-2222
Czech Republic (CC) ♦	00-42-000112
Denmark (CC) ♦	8001-0022
Dominica+	1-800-888-8000
Dominican Republic (CC) +	
Collect Access	1-800-888-8000
Collect Access in Spanish	1121

COUNTRY	ACCESS #
Ecuador (CC) +	999-170
El Salvador (CC)	800-1767
Finland (CC) ♦	08001-102-80
France (CC) ♦	0-800-99-0019
French Guiana (CC)	0-800-99-0019
Germany (CC)	0800-888-8000
Greece (CC) ♦	00-800-1211
Guam (CC)	1-800-888-8000
Guatemala (CC) ♦	99-99-189
Haiti +	
Collect Access	193
Collect access in Creole	190
Honduras +	8000-122
Hong Kong (CC)	800-96-1121
Hungary (CC) ♦	06*-800-01411
India (CC)	000-127
Collect access	000-126
Ireland (CC)	1-800-55-1001
Israel (CC)	1-800-920-2727
Italy (CC) ♦	172-1022
Jamaica +	
Collect Access	1-800-888-8000
From pay phones	#2
Japan (CC) ♦	
Using KDD	00539-121♦
Using IDC	0066-55-121
Using JT	0044-11-121

COUNTRY	ACCESS #
Korea (CC)	
To call using KT	00729-14
Using DACOM	00309-12
Phone Booths +	
Press red button ,03,then*	
Military Bases	550-2255
Luxembourg (CC)	8002-0112
Malaysia (CC) ♦	1-800-80-0012
Mexico (CC)	01-800-021-8000
Monaco (CC) ♦	800-90-019
Netherlands (CC) ♦	0800-022-91-22
New Zealand (CC)	000-912
Nicaragua (CC)	166
Norway (CC) ♦	800-19912
Panama	00800-001-0108
Philippines (CC) ♦	
Using PLDT	105-14
Filipino speaking operator	105-15
Using Bayantel	1237-14
Using Bayantel (Filipino)	1237-77
Using ETPI (English)	1066-14
Poland (CC) +	800-111-21-22
Portugal (CC) +	800-800-123
Romania (CC) +	01-800-1800
Russia (CC) + ♦	
Russian speaking operator	
	747-3320
Using Rostelcom	747-3322
Using Sovintel	960-2222
Saudi Arabia (CC)	1-800-11

COUNTRY	WORLDPHONE TOLL-FREE ACCESS #
Singapore (CC)	8000-112-112
Slovak Republic (CC)	08000-00112
South Africa (CC)	0800-99-0011
Spain (CC)	900-99-0014
St. Lucia +	1-800-888-8000
Sweden (CC) ♦	020-795-922
Switzerland (CC) ♦	0800-89-0222
Taiwan (CC) ♦	0080-13-4567
Thailand (CC)	001-999-1-2001
Turkey (CC) ♦	00-8001-1177
United Kingdom (CC)	
Using BT	0800-89-0222
Using C& W	0500-89-0222
Venezuela (CC) + ♦	800-1114-0
Vietnam ♦	1201-1022

KEY

Note: Automation available from most locations. Countries where automation is not yet available are shown in *italic*

(CC) Country-to-country calling available.

- ♦ Limited availability.
- ★ Not available from public pay phones.
- ♦ Public phones may require deposit of coin or phone card for dial tone.
- ♦ Local service fee in U.S. currency required to complete call.
- ▶ Regulation does not permit Intra-Japan Calls.
- + Wait for second dial tone.
- ■ Local surcharge may apply.

Hint: For Puerto Rico and Caribbean Islands not listed above, you can use 1-800-888-8000 as the WorldPhone access number.

ACCOMMODATIONS AND FOOD. The early tourist boom of the 1990s brought a plethora of hotels to Doğubeyazıt, most of which are now empty. A cluster of enjoyable, very cheap hotels lies around the far east end of Belediye Cad. Of these, the best value are ■ **Hotel Tahran,** on Küçük Agri Cad., and ■ **Hotel Kenan** (☎312 78 69), on Emniyet Cad. (Breakfast included. Doubles $15.) The cheapest available options include **Hotel Saruhan** (☎311 30 97), **Hotel Yayla,** and **Hotel Erzurum** (☎312 50 80), all along Çarşi Cad. (Singles $5; doubles $9.) Slightly more expensive is the **Hotel Urartu,** just off Çarşi Cad. near the center of town. (☎312 72 95. Doubles $22.) At the top end, the best value is at the new **Hotel Ararat.** (☎312 49 88. Doubles $27.) A pricey stay at the **Hotel Grand Derya** includes breakfast and dinner. (☎312 75 31. Doubles $55.) Near the Palace (see **Sights,** below), visitors can now stay at **Murat Camping.** Nestled beneath the ruins, guests can camp with access to toilets, hot showers, the restaurant, and traditional evening entertainment. (☎312 34 34. Camping $3 per night; double rooms with views $5 per person.) Murat and his brother Sayim Sahin also double as Mt Ararat guides (☎(542) 710 00 67).

Near the hotels, three restaurants, serving *lokanta*-style food, receive local acclaim. The **Dorya Restaurant,** opposite the PTT. (☎311 53 09. $3 per meal.) Equally good is **Tad Lokantası,** 134 Carsi Cad. (☎312 44 30), serving kebap and *asure* (regional Turkish pudding; $.60).

SIGHTS. Aside from the spectacular view of Mt. Ararat, most visitors come to Doğubeyazıt to see the **Işak Paşa Palace.** The road runs 6km from the Hotel Saruhan to the palace's rock ledge, making for a peaceful 1-1½ hour walk or a $6 taxi ride. In 1685, a local Kurdish chief built the palace using tariffs extracted from Silk Road travelers who passed nearby. The intricacy and beauty of the structure shows taste and nobility, beginning with an ornate entranceway covered in relief work and *muqarnas* (stalactite ornamentation). From the southwest corner to the left, walk past the giant holes in the ground that once held a garrison. The large entranceway with lion reliefs leads to the **harem,** the **master's chamber,** and the **kitchen.** A nearby hole in the ground is the archetypal "loo with a view," a squatting toilet that allowed the ruler to gaze at the kingdom. Starting again at the outer courtyard, the northwest corner has an eight-sided **türbet,** a **mosque,** and a **sarcophagus.** Up the hill and beyond the mosque is an earlier mosque and Urartian fortress. *(Open daily 6am-5:30pm. $2, students $1.)*

There are several other sites in the Doğubeyazıt area, including the supposed spot where **Noah's Ark** landed **(Uzengili).** One of the world's largest **meteor craters** is 39km from Doğubeyazıt and 5km off the road to Iran. To avoid the hike, most travelers take a taxi ($30) or join a tour. Options include five days in the surrounding areas for $150 per person or tours into Iran. Two-to-three day **horseback riding** expeditions cost $60 per person and include all meals. The route can incorporate **hot springs, Fish Lake,** and **Uzengili.** For all of the above, contact Turan Demirhan (☎311 39 74). **Memet Arik,** Belediye Cad., No. 6 (☎312 67 72; fax 312 77 76), runs regional tours, taking in all the highlights. Pickups can be arranged.

DAYTRIPS FROM DOĞUBEYAZIT. Movement on **Mt. Ararat** is subject to military restrictions, given the current tensions with Armenia. The first **permits** are now being offered to foreign climbers. At present, climbers require a military clearance from *Genel Kurmay Baskanligi* military headquarters in Ankara. Though a formality, regional approval in Ağri and local military permission cause delay. With the correct papers, climbers pass the two military road blocks and climb to 4200m on day one, then reach the summit early the next morning. Equipment can be rented in Doğubeyazıt. Upon invitation of a local, tourists without a permit can be escorted as high as 2500m. For more info, call Murat (see above).

In both directions, the **Iranian border** is far easier than it has been in previous years. A letter of invitation must be processed through Tehran, which takes least a week. The border is 35km east of Doğubeyazıt. There is an Iranian Consulate four hours west, in Erzurum. Alcohol, drugs, playing cards and pornographic material are likely to complicate matters with Iranian officials.

VAN
☎432

The waters of Lake Van are a magical reflecting pool, turquoise by day, fiery red at sunset, and quicksilver after dusk. The high alkaline content of the lake is useful for cleaning clothing but highly irritant to open wounds. For 3000 years, Lake Van and its environs have been Eastern Turkey's most vibrant and fascinating cultural center. In approximately 800 BC, the Urartian Kings established their capital here, building impressive citadels and canals all over the region. Van's strategic location on the Silk Road *(Ipek Yol)* ensured prosperity and power for those who ruled it. Following the Urartians came the Assyrians, Persians, and Armenians, before the Selçuk and then the Ottoman Turks came to power during the 14th century.

Van's history has always been one of political strife and ethnic upheaval. It was here, in the 1880s, that both the first organized Kurdish rebellion and the first Armenian moves for independence manifested themselves. Armenia's alliance with Russia triggered the forced exile and slaughter of 1.5 million Armenians (see **Armenians**, p. 30). Today, over one million people are estimated to live in the greater Van area, and the population is (apart from the army and government officials) almost entirely made up of ethnic Kurds.

⌐ TRANSPORTATION

Travelers arrive at the **airport** (5km south) or the bus station (1½km north of the city). The **otogar** is 2½km from the town center. Frequent dolmuş marked "İskele-Otogar" go to town ($.30). An airline bus usually meets flights at the airport. Otherwise, walk 300m to the main road for a $.40 dolmuş to avoid the $10 taxi.

Flights: THY (☎216 10 19) has direct daily flights to **Ankara** (10:15am, 2:50pm) and **İstanbul** (noon). **İstanbul Airlines** (☎217 12 29) has 3 direct flights to İstanbul per week. Both offices are on Cumhuriyet Cad., south of K. Karabekir Cad.

Buses: Van's otogar services most destinations in Turkey. **Best Van** (☎214 2881), **Van Seyahat** (☎216 14 03), and **Van Gölü** (☎216 33 33) have ticket offices at the corners of K. Karabekir Cad. and Cumhuriyet Cad. Most companies have free transport to the bus station 30min. before departure. To: **Ankara** (18hr., 8 per day, $25); **Antakya** (18hr., 1 per day, $20); **Diyarbakır** (6hr., 6 per day, $11); **Erzurum** (6hr., 4 per day, $11); **İstanbul** (25hr.; 8am, 1pm; $36); **İzmir** (25hr., 3 per day, $37); **Malatya** (11hr., 6 per day, $13); **Şanlıurfa** (10hr., 2 per day, $13); **Trabzon** (12hr., 1 per day, $20).

Dolmuş: Dolmuş leave 4 times daily in the morning from 200m west of Beş Yol. to: **Doğubeyazıt** ($4); **Çaldıran** ($2); and **Erçis** ($3).

✴🚻 ORIENTATION AND PRACTICAL INFORMATION

Cumhuriyet Cad. runs the length of downtown, containing all the traveler's needs between the Atatürk statue (north) and the tourist information center (south).

Tourist Office: (☎216 20 18 or 216 36 75), across from the Asur Otel in a yellow building marked "Turizm Müdürlüğü." They offer brochures and a map, but speak minimal English. (Open M-F 8am-noon, 1:30-5:30pm). For more complicated questions, go to the **Buyuk Asur Hotel** (☎216 37 53), across the road, where Remzi Bozbay (mobile ☎(542) 784 64 30; email rb_asuroteli@hotmail.com) speaks English, offers tourist information, and arranges tours to all sites in the region.

Banks: **Türkiye İş Bankası** and **Vakıf Bank** on Cumhuriyet Cad. exchange **traveler's checks** across the street from each other near the PTT. Both open 8am-noon, 1:30-5:30pm. **ATMs** line the main avenue.

Internet Access: On Cumhuriyet Cad., **Cafe Net** is upstairs at No. 71/1, **Bra-Net** is in the Ozgul Centre opposite Hotel Buyuk Asur, while **Mavi** (☎214 83 04) features A/C and lies 50m from the tourist office. $1 per hr. All open 8:30am-midnight.

Medical and Emergency Services: The **Devlet Hastanesi** (state hospital) is 300m south of Beş Yol on İskele Cad. Ambulance service available.

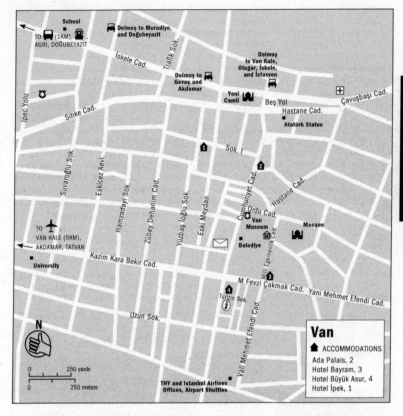

Van

🔺 ACCOMMODATIONS
Ada Palais, 2
Hotel Bayram, 3
Hotel Büyük Asur, 4
Hotel İpek, 1

PTT: (☎214 34 90). On Cumhuriyet Cad. near Sok. 6. Large PTT with *poste restante* service and a row of 15 Türk Telekom phones. **Mail service** open 6am-11pm; **phone service** available 24hr. **Postal code:** 65100.

ACCOMMODATIONS

Van's 1990s tourist boom created many now-empty hotels, most of which charge surprisingly low rates as a result. The cheap hotels stand together, 200m south of the Atatürk statue, tucked into Eski Sumerbank Sok., off Cumhuriyet Cad.

Ada Palas (☎216 22 34) is the best of these. $1.60 per person.

Hotel İpek, Cumhuriyet Cad., Sok. 1, No. 3 (☎216 30 33). West of Cumhuriyet Cad. Sok. 1, in the heart of the market district. Though basic, some rooms have showers, but share a bath. Singles $2.50; doubles $5; triples $7.50. With shower add $3.

Hotel Büyük Asur, Cumhuriyet Cad. and Turizm Sok. #5 (☎216 87 92). This affordable hotel is a traveler's hub and a major step up in quality. All rooms have large beds and are well furnished, with 24hr. hot water showers. The lobby boasts a breezy breakfast deck and a traditional *kilim*-pillow lounge. Singles $12; doubles $16; triples $24.

Hotel Bayram, Cumhuriyet Cad. #1/A (☎216 11 36). Comparable and just 30m from Büyük Asur, Bayram has quiet, newly furnished rooms with tiled bath and shower. Singles $11; doubles $22; triples $33.

Camping along Van's lakeshore is not ill-advised, but, as always, check first. In places like **Edremit**, 12km southwest of Van, there are several official campgrounds that charge $1-2 to set up a tent. Camping on **Akdamar Island** is prohibited, but **Ayanis Kale** makes a fantastic campsite. Though difficult to get to, the northeastern shoreline of Lake Van is perfect for camping and swimming with its isolated rock beaches.

FOOD

Kurdish cuisine has sadly disappeared from restaurant menus, leaving behind standard Turkish fare. Breakfast consists of delightful, fresh honey and *oltu peynir* (local white cheese with herbs) and is served in many *kahvaltı salonu* (breakfast houses) downtown. Van is a fairly dry city, but alcohol can be found in some small grocery stores; look for the *Efes Pilsen* beer signs. The best options are **Ginar Lokantasi** and **Sultan Sofra**, both on Cumhuriyet Cad.

- **Merkez Et Lokantasi** (☎216 97 01), on the busy corner of İskele Cad. and İpec Yolu. This is Van's best, and worth the 1km trip from town. An artificial waterfall and stunning gas station location complements dishes like *sarma beyti* (spicy garlic mince rolls). Meal and soft drink $4. Open 8am-11pm.

- **Cinar Restaurant** (☎214 66 06), behind the Bayram Hotel. Cinar has a broad menu, a pleasant upstairs location, and the best food on the street. The kitchen closes at 9pm.

  Erol Kardeşler Kahvaltı Salonu, Sok. 8 on Cumhuriyet Cad. This is the best breakfast house in town, serving thoroughly fresh *oltu peynir*, honey and butter, omelettes, hot sweet milk, tomatoes, and yogurt. Open from 5am.

SIGHTS

Van is a good base for an array of interesting sights. Astonishing natural beauty provides a backdrop for a unique blend of Urartian, Armenian, and Kurdish influences. If time is short, give priority to **Akdamar Church, Hoşap Castle, Van Kale** and **Çavuştepe Fortress** (see **Daytrips from Van,** below).

After the Russians destroyed the old city of Tuşba, the local Kurds and their Turkish rulers built the new city of Van 5km to the south. Consequently, Van's center offers nothing of historical importance aside from the **Van Museum.** The ground floor contains prehistoric finds from Tilkitepe as well as Urartian helmets, textile tools, bronze belts, and cremation bowls. The inner courtyard has large stone carvings of lions and Urartian inscriptions. Upstairs is a *kilim* collection and a gallery called the "Genocide section," which presents a misleading portrayal of the slaughter of Turks by Armenians and omits any mention of the Armenian genocide. *(Open 8am-noon, 1:30-5:30pm. $1.50, students $1.)*

Carpet and **kilim** sellers here are the primary distributors for western Turkish dealers, and thus they are in a position to offer the same quality found in tourist areas for up to 70% less. Here, **Sene Kilim,** crafted by Kurdish villagers in Northern Iran and Southeastern Turkey, are easy to find. As always, do not purchase carpets at high prices unless claims of age and rarity can be authenticated.

DAYTRIPS FROM VAN

A well-planned daytrip can incorporate Hoşap Castle, Lake Van, and a visit to Akdamar Church, arguably the pearls of the Van region.

AKDAMAR CHURCH AND OTHER ARMENIAN CHURCHES

Akdamar Church is 50km west of Van on an island 5km off the coast. Dolmuş headed for Gevaş will take you the additional 9km to the boat dock for Akdamar if you clear it with the driver before you board. Dolmuş depart from Van, 400m north of Cumhuriyet Cad. on K. Karabekir Cad. (every hr. if full 6am-5pm; Gevaş $1, Akdamar $1.50). Frequent ferry service from the boat dock allows for convenient transportation to the site (daily every 30min.; or when full. 6am-sunset; $3, student $2). When the boat is slow to fill, passengers can split the $30 total and leave promptly.

AKDAMAR the **Church of the Holy Cross,** on Akdamar Island, is a highlight of any visit to Van. The derivation of the name *Akdamar* is traceable through Armenian folklore. The Princess Tamara had fallen in love with a peasant boy on the mainland. Every night she would light a candle on the island, whereupon he would swim out to profess his love. Her father, the king, caught wind of this forbidden love, became very angry, and locked his daughter in the castle. One night the king put the candle on a boat and moved it around the lake. The boy swam in endless circles, and with his last drowning gasp, shouted "Aght Tamara, Aght Tamara!" ("Oh Tamara!").

For more than two millennia, Armenians flourished in the Van region. Here they built villages, churches, and castles, of which little remains; most of their creations have been either razed or converted to mosques. Some scholars argue that Van Armenians are actually descendents of the Urartians, but cultural and linguistic differences make this unlikely. The Armenian kingdom first united in 95 BC under Tigranes the Great, and thrived until it was eclipsed in 1071 by the Selçuks.

A major architectural and artistic feat, Akdamar is built of sandstone and topped with a characteristic domed ceiling. All evidence of the accompanying palace has long disappeared. The attached monastery remained active until it burned down in the 20th century.

The surviving reliefs on the outside of the church describe human evolution, as well as Armenian and Christian religious history. These artistic representations once doubled as decorations and as a teaching tool for the community. Beginning in the west, **King Gagik** holds a model of the church, standing next the Bible-clutching **Jesus.** The four Apostles sit in the apse of each outer wall of the church. From the feet of the Apostle on the western wall begins a **vine scroll** depicting bible stories around the entire building. Every figurine's eye sockets originally had jewels that were stolen long ago. The **frescoes** inside are largely dilapidated, though it is clear that the dome's ceiling once depicted the miracle of creation, and the walls displayed the life of Christ. The monastery foundations lie just to the south of the church, while the Turkish flag to the east marks where the castle once stood.

On an island 20km east of Akdamar, there is a 13th-century Armenian church called **Çarpanak Kilise.** Akdamar boats will negotiate the trip but only for larger groups. At İskele Harbor in Van, you can rent boats (2hr. each way, $60). Twenty kilometers over a dirt track lie the ruins of **Yedi Kilise** (Seven Churches).

URARTIAN FORTRESSES

HOŞAP CASTLE. Sixty kilometers south of Van on the road to Hakkari, the Hoşap Castle is one of the greatest Kurdish castles in all of Turkey. Built in 1643 by Lord San Süleyman of the Mahmudites, the castle was funded by the taxation of travelers en route from Anatolia to northwest Iran. After the erection of his magnificent castle complex, Süleyman chopped off the hands of the architect to prevent him from building another of equal beauty. The walls are made of a mixture of dirt and pigeon eggs. The entrance gate has two reliefs of chained lions, denoting the gladiatorial matches between animals and men that took place within the castle walls. The upper level contains royal rooms, the harem, and a hamam, all with a view of the valley and the village below. *(For travel details see Çavuştepe (below). Open 8am-5pm. If the doors are locked, wait for the caretaker in the village below. $1.50, students $1.)*

VAN KALE. Van Kale, an ancient Urartian fortress towering high on rock bluffs, was constructed by King Sarduri I (840-830 BC). Known as Tuşba to the Urartians, it formed the center of a vast kingdom.

Start at the far north near the car park and *çay* garden. The large stone slabs near the fishery are ancient **Urartian piers.** Up the hill on the west side lies the locked **burial chamber** of King Argishti I with inscriptions on the wall. The gate can be unlocked by the caretaker. The king is buried deep in a carved cave with connecting rooms that held the garrison and supplies. Walking up the hill 150m brings you to a flat area that was once the site of the **temple of sacrifice.** The drainage ditch you see was for collecting the animal blood. Pass the **Ottoman palace** to the south end of the fortress, then stumble down a steep rocky hill at the west wall to reach the **burial chambers** of Urartian kings Menua I and Sarduri I. The top of the rock bluff, now bearing the remains of an Ottoman mosque and castle, offers a view of Van. Today, in **Tuşba** village, burial mounds stand as monuments to the cultural decimation that the area has suffered. The two **Selçuk mosques** have been rebuilt; the southern one is still in use. The one with the peculiar minaret is what remains of the **Ulu Camii** built by the Persian-influenced Black Sheep Turcomans. *(Dolmuş depart from Beş Yol. (every 20min., $.30). Kale $2, students $1. Open 24hr., but escorts at night are recommended. A walking tour will demand at least 2hr.; add an extra hour if you plan to visit the old city off the western slopes.)*

TOPRAKKALE, ÇAVUŞTEPE, AND AYANIS. Built in 735 BC by Rusa II, Toprakkale (Toprak Castle) is just 4km southeast of Van. At the time of writing, access to Toprakkale was prohibited, as it is in a military zone. **Mehir Kapısı's rock niche,** a Urartian site between the bluff and the castle, may be open to visitors.

Çavuştepe (formerly Sardurihinili), 25km south of Van, was once a sprawling, three-part castle more than 850m long and 80m high. Built in 764 BC by Sarduri II (764-735 BC), Çavuştepe commanded a strategic position in the Gürpınar Valley until the Scythians destroyed it in the 7th century BC. The temple grounds contain a **sacrifice stone** and a **cuneiform inscription.** The deep holes near the Turkish flag acted as a large **water cistern.** *(Open 8am-6pm. $1.50, dolmuş $4.)*

Thirty-three kilometers northeast of Van, on the edge of the lake, lurks the little-known fortress of **Ayanis.** Built about 2400 years ago by Rusa II and since buried, it is now the focus of archeological excavation, though so far only the temple and the castle spire have been fully uncovered. The drive out to Ayanis is bumpy and strikingly beautiful, passing many a tantalizing empty beach. *(Only one dolmuş leaves for Ayanis village daily from Van, returning the next morning. Therefore, options are either to organize a private car or camp overnight. Head 21km northeast of Van on İpek Yolu (the Silk Road highway) toward Muradiye, turn left at the sign for Alaköy, and follow the gravel track for 12km.)*

TATVAN AND ENVIRONS

An uninspiring town in a stunning location, Tatvan hugs the eastern end of Lake Van and offers a launch point for a trip to Turkey's other Nemrut, a breathtaking series of lakes (Nemrut Gölü), and hot springs within an inactive volcanic crater. Set back from the water, Tatvan's services are all along its main thoroughfare, centered around Tatvan Park and the main dolmuş lot opposite.

The best option among the mid-range accommodations is ▧ **Hotel Altilar,** Cumhuriyet Cad. No. 164, which offers clean rooms. (☎827 40 96; $10 per person.) Apart from the flagship **Hotel Kardelen** (☎827 95 00; singles $18, doubles $35), most are bare-bones budget stuff. The best dining is actually 2½km out of town, along the north shore of the lake. **Supan Adabağ Restaurant** has fresh tasty kebap ($3) and a breezy view of the lake denied to downtown Tatvan diners.

Nemrut Gölü is a geographic marvel only 15km from Tatvan. Inactive since 1440, this volcano formed Lake Van by closing its outflow. Now its eerie crater hides a series of crystal-clear lakes at 3050m above sea level. The 90-minute taxi ascent costs $30 and includes two hours in the crater. The road is just barely navigable by two-wheel drive traffic. Hitching is not only dangerous, but also unrewarding, as the route offers no services and traffic flow is unpredictable. As the road clears the crater lip, the lakes of Nemrut unfold. Half a kilometer into the crater, road signs indicate left to the large lake (Büyük Gölü) and should be followed if time is limited. Turning right leads to a series of smaller lakes (less suited to swimming), cozy campsites, and hard-to-locate hot springs. The route to the big lake is 2km, after which vehicles must stop 50m from the water's edge. Swimming here surpasses that in Van. Don't be perturbed by the possible encounter with seasnakes.

VAN'S NORTH COAST

Driving the remote north coast of Lake Van is a highlight of Turkey's southeast, though the main thoroughfare, transport and hitching options are limited. The recent detente in regional tensions have meant that travel restrictions have been lifted and the road is open 24 hours. The Tatvan (west) end of this route contains most of the important sites. First is **Ahlat**, with its famed **Selçuk tombs** *(kümbets)* and **Hasan Padisah's mausoleum.** Next is **Adilcevaz Kef Fortress,** a further 26km east to the Göldüzü turnoff. Turn away from the lake here, travel 3km to the village of Aydınlar, and continue further 6km up to **Sarısu** (taxi $10), with incredible lake views from the shoulder of Mt. Suphan at 2500m. Only extremely fit walkers should consider the 5-hour Suphan ascent, with a small freezing crater lake at the 4053m summit. Otherwise, pass Erciş and continue 70km to the Van-Doğubeyazıt road (Rte. 975), with **Muradiye Şelale** (waterfall) just 17km north (6km north of Muradiye). The sign for the waterfall is only visible from the Van direction, and the falls are 300m from the road. Cross the old steel suspension bridge to walk down to the pools below the falls. *(Open 24hr. Free. Camping permitted.)*

DİYARBAKIR (AMED)   ☎412

The hard-core travelers' litmus test is Diyarbakır. To the outsider, it grants little concession. Two million citizens, half refugees, are submerged within a timeless cacophony of commerce, cooking, and the echo of car horns. They ply their trades within black basalt city walls that amplify the commotion and the merciless summer heat. To Kurds, this place by the Tigris is Amed, their proxy capital. For a nation that has never had its own country, those walls offer sanctuary within a sea of perceived repression and injustice. On the surface, Kurds and Turks embrace as brothers. Yet while Kurds cannot carve out a land for themselves, dreams simmer like the horizon. After 5000 years and 26 civilizations, Amed has time on its side.

⌐ TRANSPORTATION

Flights: THY (☎228 84 01) has flights to **Ankara** (daily 10:25am, 7:40pm; $60) and **İstanbul** (daily 9:40am, 9:30pm; $80). Check for other indirect routes to these cities.

Bus: The otogar is 4km from town, accessible by dolmuş in front of the hotels on Kilbris Cad. To: **Adana** (8hr., 17 per day, $6); **Ankara** (14hr., 8 per day, $17); **Antakya** (9hr., 3 per day, $8); **Doğubeyazıt** (13hr., 4 per day, $22); **Erzurum** (10hr., 2 per day, $16); **Gaziantep** (5hr., 20 per day, $3); **İstanbul** (19hr., 9 per day, $20); **İzmir** (19hr., 2 per day, $20); **Kahramanmaraş** (6hr., 3 per day, $3.50); **Kars** (15hr., 1 per day, $24); **Konya** (15hr., 3 per day, $14); **Malatya** (5hr., 3 per day, $6); **Mersin** (9hr., 20 per day, $6); **Şanlıurfa** (3hr., 20 per day, $6); **Trabzon** (15hr., 4 per day, $22); **Van** (7hr., 4 per night, $13). **Mardin** minibuses leave from the Melek Ahmet and Gazi Cad. intersection (1 hr., $3).

Taxis: Avoid taxis in Diyarbakır, where the meters spin like a roulette wheel.

◼✷🔊 ORIENTATION AND PRACTICAL INFORMATION

Tourist Office: Diyarbakır is ill-prepared for tourists. The official Tourist Office is in the basement of the **Dağ Kapisi** (☎221 21 73) and can offer you a brochure. Filling the gap are English-speaking part time guides who can connect you to anything you need. **Esat Kahraman** runs **Bianca Travel Agency,** 22 İnönü Cad. (☎223 14 25). Also contact the well-traveled **Ubeydullah Calisir,** nicknamed 'Japonali' (☎229 22 71; mobile ☎0535-259 34 66), who enjoys helping tourists find their way without obligation.

Banks: Every major bank lines Gazi Cad. from the İnönü Cad. intersection towards the center of town. Open 9am-5:30pm. **ATMs** available 24hr.

Hamam: Diyarbakır's oldest hamam is closed indefinitely. Remaining options are Turkish baths attached to the larger hotels. Hotels Dedeman, Turistik, Demir and Kervansaray have pools that charge $8 for a dip. Men can use the city pool just outside the Dağ Kapisi on the way to the Hotel Dedeman for $1.50.

Police: On Gazzi Cad. next to Hasan Paşa Hani. open 24 hr.

Pharmacy: Akdeniz Eczane, 11/A Kibris Cad. (☎222 56 68). Open 8am-6:30pm. Part of a rotating pool of pharmacies that remain open 24hr.

Hospital: Devlet Hastanesi, outside the city walls. Turn left 200m on Yusef Azizoğlu Cad.

Internet Access: The city's 20 cafes are wonderfully concealed, and the joy of discovery compensates for slow connections and daily power outages. For **Number 1 Computer Internet House,** cross from the hotels on Kibris Cad, traverse the dolmuş lot, then walk 200 meters left down Selim Amca Sofra Sal. **Gotum Cafe** (☎223 13 14) is in Ofis Camii Sok. Kupik Apt 6. Both open 8am-midnight. $1 per hr.

Post Office: The main PTT is on the corner of İnönü and Vilayet Cad. Postal services open 8:30am-noon, 1:30-5:30pm.

ACCOMMODATIONS

Diyarbakır has an excellent range of accommodations, concentrated on İnönü, Kibris and Izzet Paşa Cads. However, because positive word of mouth has little impact upon the post-Gulf War tourism trickle, many lower-end proprietors range from indifferent to outright unfriendly.

Aslan Palas, Kibris Cad. 21 (☎221 12 27). With TV, private bath, and A/C, this is the top choice. Singles $7; doubles $11; triples $16.

Otel Surkent, Izzet Paşa No. 19 (☎221 66 16). Basic, airy rooms have real bathrooms. $4 per night.

Ozbal Hotel (☎222 27 02), off Izzetpaşa Cad. on Nebioglu Sok. The cleanest cheap option. Shadowing by other buildings kills any view but keeps daytime temperatures down. Communal shower. $3 per person.

Ertem Palas (☎223 04 00), next door to Özbal, has better rooms, but check the cleanliness of the communal facilities first.

Hotel Grand Kervansaray (☎228 96 06) is wildly expensive, but its history, architecture, and watermelon in the fountains makes it definitely worth a stop.

FOOD

Traditional food reigns in Diyarbakır; a forlorn Burger King loiters beyond the city walls. Speak to locals about the dishes that are heat-labile and best avoided (dairy, pre-cooked, undercooked and reheated).

Sarmasik Ocakbasi, 31 Kibris Cad. (☎224 25 97). The best in town. Try *guvec,* delicious crockpot of lamb and vegetable. Full meal and drinks, $3. Open 24hr.

Tuccarlar, Ticaret Merkezi Kat 1, 5th fl. (☎228 90 21). It has city views, breezes, great alternatives to kebap (*semiz otu* yogurt, pepper, and juicy *bostane* salad each $1), and live traditional music until 1am.

Journalists Club, opposite Tuccarlar and disguised as a *çay* garden, happily serves tourists *Içli köfte* (crumbed meat and vegetable ball) and *kie-mumbar* (intestine stuffed with minced meat and vegetable).

SIGHTS

Within the walls of the old city, all major sites can be seen in two hours, preferably in the cooler hours. Start at the Selçuk **Ulu Camii,** then have tea in the restored camel market across the road. The **bazaar,** like the camel market, winds down after 6pm. The 5½km wall has five gates and 16 towers. **Meryamana Kilisesi** is a 3rd-century Aramaic Church, now lying in ruins. Nearby, the **Grand Kervansaray Hotel** offers a drink stop and beautiful pool ($8 per dip). Next is the restored home of **Cahit Sitki Taranci** and, finally, just south of town is **Atatürk's house** and the **Ducle bridge,** built in 1065.

MARDİN
☎ **482**

Travelers lured by Deyrul Zafarin Monastery will discover there is much more to Mardin. Though a perennial hotbed of Kurdish separatist activity, this frontier town lies dormant again, allowing tourists a glimpse of one of Turkey's most intriguing populations. A 10,000 year heritage has woven a patchwork of different cultures together in this upper Mesopotamian city. Even today, Syrian Orthodox goldsmiths and Muslim copperworkers beat out their trade side by side.

EASTERN ANATOLIA

⬛ TRANSPORTATION AND PRACTICAL INFORMATION. Mardin clings to a rocky hill on the border of the Syrian Desert. The east-west highway runs 500m below the main street, **Birinci Cad.** From the central Atatürk statue, **dolmuş** stops are located 1km in both directions at either end of Birinci Cad. From these, a *servis* bus will shuttle you to intercity buses around town. Services include: the **tourist office,** set back from the main highway (follow the yellow signs left and up the hill); **banks** on Birinci Cad. with 24-hour **ATMs** (open 9am-5:30pm); the **police** on Yeni Sehir Cad. (open 24hr); **Devlet Hastanesi** (state hospital), next to the PTT on Meydan Cad; the **Yakamos Internet Cafe;** and the **PTT,** on the corner of İnönü and Vilayet Cad. (open 8:30am-noon, 1:30-5:30pm.) **Postal code:** 47000.

⬛ ACCOMMODATIONS, FOOD, AND SIGHTS. Quality rooms are almost impossible to find, but **Hotel Bayraktar,** in the center of town, diagonally across from the Atatürk statue, offers decent, quiet rooms with cold showers and old beds. (☎212 16 45. $12 per person.) **Hotel Bilen** is cheaper ($5 per person).

Beyond the numerous *lokantasi* that dot the main street, fine dining options are well concealed in Mardin. Superb and priced accordingly, **Cag Et Lokantasi** (☎212 65 55), 500m off the main thoroughfare on Sosyal Sigorta Hastanesi Yani, goes to great lengths to preserve Mardin's unique cuisine. Try *Icli Kofta, kiya lamacun, cacik* cucumber yogurt, and the local sweet coffee called *mirra.* Ask to sample (not for sale) Mardin's local wine from the Monastery. The **Tabibler Lokantasi,** in SSK Is Hani Kat. 4 (☎212 59 01) serves traditional food and booze.

The **Mardin Museum,** on Cumhuriyet Meydanı, is housed in an 1895 building constructed by the patriarch of Antakya, Ignatius Bentham Benni. It boasts a collection spanning 4000 years of Mardin culture. *(☎21 16 64. Open Tu-Su 8:30am-noon, 1-5pm. $1.)* On Birinci Cad. is the **Kirklar Kilesesi.**

⬛ DAYTRIP FROM MARDİN: DEYRUL ZAFARIN MONASTERY. This monastery is the key reason to visit Mardin. In 451, the Monophysitic congregation of the Syrian Orthodox Church (Jacobites) split from the Byzantine Church after the Council of Chalcedon's debate about the true nature of Christ. It served as the seat of the Syrian Orthodox church from 493 to the 1920s. The hardy Mardin Christian community has dwindled from 2000 to 200 over the past 30 years. The church still uses Aramaic, Jesus' language, as its liturgical tongue. Services are held daily, led by one of the three remaining monks. *(2.4km east of town. Town buses go to within 1500m (a 40min. walk); buses may detour for an added fee. Taxis $9. Open dawn to dusk. On weekdays, the monks tend to be more hospitable than on weekends, when masses of Turkish tourists descend. Though a few basic cells are available for visitors to stay in, those with a specific religious interest are preferred.)*

In **Kiziltepe,** 25km south of Mardin, the 13th-century **Ülü mosque** with *mihrab* reliefs and a beautiful portal is a fine example of Artukid architecture. The **Oztoprak Hotel** has just opened. ($12 per person.) Those with private transport should detour to **Casagi Konak,** halfway between Diyarbakır and Mardin and 5km east along the Dicle River. This forested canyon is perfect for swimming and camping.

MALATYA
☎ **422**

Malatya (pop. 400,000) is Turkey's apricot capital and birthplace of Turkey's second president, İnönü. It lies in a fertile basin, shadowed by a barren range that points the way to the magnificent Nemrut Dağı ruins. While most approaches are unremarkable, the journey from the south (Adana or Maraş) is characterized by cascade carved gorges. Don't be fooled by the fashion and outdoor çay gardens, as Malatya remains firmly adherent to Islamic social custom. Unmarried couples promenade rarely, and you'll find neither alcohol nor nightclub. While tourists are still somewhat unexpected here, the town remains friendly and hospitable.

⌐ TRANSPORTATION

Most travelers arrive in Malatya's palatial **otogar,** 3km west of town. **Dolmuş** connect this station with downtown, passing the train station on the way.

Flights: Cem Tour, 11/1 Galleria İş Merkezi (☎ 322 66 66; fax 322 84 44), just west of the main square, sells **THY** tickets. Bus service meets each flight and departs from multiple downtown locations 2hr. before departure, sometimes for a fee. THY flies daily at 7:30pm to both **Ankara** ($60) and **İstanbul** ($80). 25% student discount.

Buses: Regular dolmuş link the town center and the **otogar** ($.20). A taxi costs $2-3. To: **Adana** (6hr., 3 per day, $9); **Adıyaman** (3hr., 6 per day, $6); **Ankara** (10hr., 6 per day, $18); **Diyarbakır** (4hr., 3 per day, $6); **Erzurum** (8hr., 3 per day, $10); **İstanbul** (16hr., 6 per day, $20); **Kahramanmaraş** (30min., 3 per day, $3); **Kayseri** (5hr., 2 per day, $9); **Konya** (10hr., 2 per day, $16); **Mersin** (7hr., 4 per day, $10); **Van** (9hr., 2 per night, $12). Companies offer shuttle service from downtown ½hr. before departure.

Trains: The **station** (☎ 324 77 70) is located 1km west of the statue on Atatürk Cad. The İstanbul-Ankara line and the Adana line run to Malatya. To: **Adana** (2 per day, $2); **Ankara** ($4.50, $7 express); and **İstanbul** (2 per day, 1st class $8, 2nd class $6).

✳▐ ORIENTATION AND PRACTICAL INFORMATION

The town's main street, **İnönü Cad.** (a.k.a **Atatürk Cad.**) runs parallel to the highway that links Ankara to Van. Blue buses run the length of this road. The town square is crowned with a statue of **İnönü,** Atatürk's successor. Hotels, restaurants, banks, and the PTT are all within a five-minute walk from the İnönü statue.

Tourist Office: Vilayet Binası Kat. 1 (☎ 324 25 14 or 323 30 25), on the 1st floor of the town hall. English spoken by Kemal and Sabrı. If the office is closed, try the çay garden in the rear of the building. Open M-F 8am-noon, 1:30-5:30pm. Tours to **Nemrut Dağı** depart daily at 11:30am from behind the town hall, in the parking lot next to the tea garden. The $30 fee includes summit lodging at the **Guneş Motel,** dusk then dawn at the site, 2 meals and transport. Transport-only deals can also be arranged. Hitching or local transport is not advisable due to the remoteness of this location.

Travel Agencies: Cem Tour (see "Flights") offers more expensive tours ($150-$250), though these may be longer and include the Atatürk Dam, Huran and Old Ufa. Ragop speaks English. Open daily 8am-8pm.

Banks: Many major banks scatter around the main square. All are open M-F 8am-noon, 1:30-5:30pm. **Traveler's checks** can be exchanged at **Vakifbank** and **TC Ziraat.** Local businessmen often give better rates with less hassle.

Hospital: The state-run **Devlet Hastanesi** (☎ 321 89 84) and the more impressive **Turgut Özal Hastanesi** (☎ 341 06 60), 3km towards Nemrut, both offer 24hr. care.

Post Office: The main **PTT** (☎ 322 54 94) is 30m down a small alley off the northwest corner of the main square. Open 8am-noon, 1:30-5:30pm; 24hr. card phones are here and along İnönü Cad. **Postal code:** 44000.

ACCOMMODATIONS AND FOOD

Among Malatya's budget picks, **Park Otel**, 17 Atatürk Cad., 100m east of the square, has 24hr. hot water. The back rooms are quieter except during the call to prayer. (☎321 16 91. Singles $8; doubles and triples $12.) Claustrophobes should avoid **Otel Ozen**, PTT Cad. 18 (☎321 1770), unless $7 doubles suppress symptoms. **Otel Tahran**, along PTT Cad. has, simple, dark rooms, private bath, hot water, phones, and a communal kitchenette. (☎324 36 15. Singles $5; doubles $8; triples $12.) Mid-range **Hotel Yeni Sinan**, 6 Atatürk Cad., is centrally located with quiet back rooms and an airy upstairs lobby. (☎321 29 07. Singles $15; doubles $18.) Slightly pricier is the **Malatya Büyük Otel**, 151 Yeni Camii Karş, north of the statue, past the fountain and the mosque. Pricier, but you get A/C and fridge. (☎321 14 00. Breakfast included. Singles $17; doubles $25; triples $32.)

▨ **Mangal Vadisi** (☎326 22 00), on Kisla Cad., offers "cook-your-own" Anatolian food; enjoy lunch here with the local businessfolk. Beyond this, locals recommend **Lokanta**, 29 Postahane Cad., next to Hotel Tahran. It serves high-quality food, including rice *pilav* and grilled chicken. (☎325 99 88. Full meal $3-4. Open daily 7am-10pm.) **Birinci Pastanesi**, on Fuzuli Cad., halfway to the museum, has tasty desserts. (☎322 19 52. Open daily 7am-1am.)

SIGHTS

Aside from its convenient proximity to Nemrut Dağı, Malatya has some sights of its own worth exploring. Its famous fresh and dried *kaysısı* (apricots) are purveyed in the fantastic **apricot market**. Apricot, raisin, and nut enthusiasts should walk east from the Malatya Büyük Hotel, asking locals for directions. Malatya has numerous outdoor restaurants and *çay* gardens, the largest of which is **Kernek**, 500m behind the İnönü statue. Here, one can promenade with the locals or dine at the **Kernek Selalesi ve Park Restaurant**, which offers cheap food, a view over the entire park, and a water garden.

In the **bazaar** district, sprawling north from the Malatya Büyük Otel, vendors peddle everything from head scarves to metal work. In addition, a roving bazaar sets up tables in different city neighborhoods every day, offering local clothing and perishable goods. The **kilim and carpet bazaar** is on İnönü Cad., opposite the statue, with cheaper carpets than in western Turkey. Near the Malatya Büyük Otel, dusty male travelers can enjoy a Turkish bath in the 125-year-old **Belediye Hamam**. (Bath $2; *kese* $4. Open daily 5am-9pm.) Women can go to the similarly-priced **Saray Palace**, 100m behind the Belediye building. Just over 10km away, the town of **Battalgazi** and apricot groves now cover what would have once been **Eski Malatya** (old city of Malatya). Now only the **city walls** and the 13th-century **Ulu Camii** remain. The ancient Hittite site of **Aslantepe** can be reached 4km northeast of the city; contact the tourist information office upon arrival.

NEMRUT DAĞI

Accessible from Malatya (see p. 442), Kahta, Adiyaman, and Şanlıurfa (see p. 444). The site is at the base of a cone-shaped pile of rocks, at the bottom of which are three terraces on the north, west, and east. Open during daylight hours. $3.50, students $2. The Malatya road ends 100m below the eastern terrace, while the road from Kahta ends in a parking lot 1km from the summit. Beside the parking lot is Nemrut Kafeteria, offering 24hr. food, drinks, and a bathroom. Allow at least 2hr. to explore the site, including the walk up. Rough winds can cause chills and dehydration: bring layers and water.

Upon the highest peak in the region (2150m), Commagene King **Antiochus I** ordered the construction of a 75m pyramid of rubble, flanked by massive statues, their heads long since decapitated by earthquakes (most recently 1938) and time. At dawn and dusk, solitude and silence prevails on this impressive funerary monument, the calm broken only by the whipping of a constant wind.

A HEAD OF HIS TIME

Antiochus's tomb lies buried beneath a man-made mountain of rubble, guarded by towering stone statues. Locked for centuries inside the peak of Mount Nemrut, this burial site, described as the eighth wonder of the ancient world, was discovered in 1881. Since then it has continued to thwart archaeologists and modern investigative technology, with its delicate structure likely to collapse and crush any attempt to burrow towards its possible secrets and treasures.

The site holds relics dating back to the Commagene kingdom, a border kingdom which managed to fend off the Romans and Persians encroaching from either side between 162 BC and 72 AD. The kingdom was greatest under Antiochus, who is best remembered for installing a brand new pantheon of syncretic gods like "Apollo-Mithras" and "Zeus-Oromasdes." He commissioned 10m high statues of these gods in their honor; they are seen bestowing the divine mandate upon a 10m statue of himself. The Herculean labor of constructing this shrine from six-ton stone blocks (not to mention a 75m tall peak (now eroded to 50m) of crushed rock now thought to hide the tomb itself) leads archaeologists to think it may rival Tutankhamen's for wealth and majesty.

Meanwhile, the collection of 3m tall stone heads continues to attract visitors to the site. These gargantuan amputata, fallen from the shoulders of crumbled statues, recall Shelley's "Ozymandias" or its precursor, Horace Smith's "On a Stupendous Leg of Granite, Discovered Standing by Itself in the Deserts of Egypt, with the Inscription Inserted Below." But *this* king has so far clung to his treasures through both might and wile: he put not just heavy bricks in the way, but also Turkish bureaucrats. Denied access to the tomb itself, archaeologists have contented themselves with interpretation of the site's sandstone reliefs, among them, possibly the worlds first horoscope, dating precisely to Antiochus' coronation in 109 BC. Distressingly, these carvings have recently begun to deteriorate. Propped-up statues have toppled again under the weight of winter snow. In addition, visitors run amok over the barricade-free site. Though there is talk of restoration efforts, locals are sceptical. Only five years ago, a toppled head was restituted for the ludicrous sum of 6 million lira ($10,000). Locals offered to complete the same task with 20 tourists, ten minutes, and a blanket, but to no avail. Perhaps red tape is the one thing that will ensure Nemrut remains as it is for decades to come.

Antiochus broke away from the Seleucids in the wake of Alexander the Great's death. He created specific plans for the construction this egomaniacal monument, made up of nine towering figures of the king surrounded by deities and animals on east and west terraces. Careful observation can match fallen heads to the torsos above. The figures mirror each other from north to south: Lion, Eagle, Apollo, Tyche (Fortuna), Zeus, Antiochus, Hercules, Eagle, and Lion. This juxtaposition of man and god was arranged to demonstrate the king's relation to these deities.

If you plan a trip to Nemrut Dağı, you will need to stay in a nearby town. Malatya (p. 442) and Şanlıurfa (p. 444) are probably the better options, as they are pleasant cities in their own right. Kahta and Adiyaman are reasonable bases as well. The bus company **Adiyaman Ünal** (☎ (416) 216 11 12) arranges fast day tours to Nemrut Dağı from Adiyaman. Nemrut closes from first snowfall (Nov.) until mid-April, though winter walking tours can be arranged. *Jandarma* clear the site after dusk and enforce a non-climbing policy on the unstable rubble pyramid.

ŞANLIURFA
☎ 414

Though officially known as Şanlıurfa (Glorious Urfa), it is *Peygamberler Şehri* to Muslims, or the City of Prophets. Urfa is a place of pilgrimage, being the putative birthplace of Abraham and the home of the prophet Job. Oozing history, the town lures travelers into its tantalizing side streets. To the south, the endless chaotic splendor of the bazaar produces enough sensory stimulus for days of wandering.

Urfa is more timeworn than civilization itself, with Biblical references and archaeological finds dating back 4000 years. From 1370 BC, the Hittites called this city Uras, which collapsed with the fall of Hattuşaş (see **Hattuşaş**, p. 368), under the authority of nearby Carchemish. Hegemony quickly passed from the Assyrians to Alexander the Great, upon whose death the whole region became part of a Seleucid province in 806 BC. Seleucus I Nicator named Urfa Edessa, making it the capital of his small empire, which survived until 132 BC, when Urfa became Orhai, an independent kingdom of local Aramaens. Four centuries later, after Orhai had become one of the first Christian kingdoms, it was conquered by the Romans.

The Romans were stretched here, with the Persians frequently wresting control of the city before it fell to the Arabs in 637 AD. Relative peace held until the end of the 10th century, when power changed hands again in battle between Turks, Arabs, Armenians, and Byzantines. In 1098, during the first Crusade, Baldwin I set up a short-lived feudal state in Edessa. A vengeful Selçuk *emir* Nur-ed Din of Aleppo, burned the city to the ground, sold its citizens into slavery, and destroyed all its churches and monasteries. Selim the Grim captured the city in 1516, but it was not incorporated into the Ottoman Empire until as late as 1637.

Urfa's economy has boomed with the Southeast Anatolian Project's (GAP's) Atatürk Dam, which, to the chagrin of those downstream, controls the flow of the Euphrates (Firat) River. Despite oppressive summer heat (up to 50°C by day), the city is a fascinating destination for both travelers and pilgrims, meriting a couple of days for sightseeing and a daytrip the nearby ancient city of **Harran**.

⌐ TRANSPORTATION

The otogar is 1½km from the town center. Take a taxi for $4-5, or stop any dolmuş and mention your preferred hotel ($.20), as all listed are on the main route. Some bus companies have free shuttle service to the otogar.

Flights: THY (☎ 215 33 44), on Atatürk Cad., next door to Şan-Med Hospital, has flights to **Ankara** ($60) and **İstanbul** ($80) 4 days per week. 25% student discount. A $1 shuttle bus transports passengers to the airport 2hr. before departures.

Bus: Urfa's otogar is a bustling transport hub. To: **Adana** (5hr., 17 per day, $6); **Ankara** (12hr., 8 per day, $17); **Antakya** (6hr., 3 per day, $8); **Diyarbakır** (3hr., 20 per day, $6); **Doğubeyazıt** (16hr., 4 per day, $22); **Erzurum** (15hr., 2 per day, $16); **Gaziantep** (2hr., 20 per day, $3); **İstanbul** (17hr., 9 per day, $20); **İzmir** (17hr., 2 per day, $20); **Kahramanmaraş** (3hr., 3 per day, $3.50); **Kars** (20hr., 1 per day, $24); **Konya** (12hr., 3 per day, $14); **Malatya** (6hr., 3 per day, $6); **Mardin** (4hr., 5 per day, $6); **Mersin** (3-4hr., 20 per day, $6); **Trabzon** (15hr., 4 per day, $22); **Van** (12hr., 4 per night, $13). **Dolmuş** and **minibuses** leave from the same parking lot.

✷⁊ ORIENTATION AND PRACTICAL INFORMATION

Roads from Diyarbakır (north), Mardin (east), and Gaziantep (west) all meet above the city (Mustafa Kemal Pasa Fountain). From here **Atatürk Cad.**, changing to **Sarayönü Cad.** and **Dıvan Cad** run south across the *Karakoyun deresi* (river) through the center and the old part of town before splintering around the fortress.

Tourist Office: 23m from the doors of the Hotel Edessa (opposite Hasan Pasa Camii), the state tourist office (☎ 215 24 67) is heralded by marble steps and a sr. all sign. Locals are oblivious to its existence. They organize a $17 Harran taxi tour as required. Open M-F 8am-noon, 1:30-5:30pm. **Tourist police** are nearby on Gol Cad.

Tourist Agencies: Local English teacher Özcan Aslan runs **Harran and Nemrut Tours** (☎ 215 15 75; mobile ☎ 0(542) 761 30 65; fax 215 11 56). Look for a big yellow canvas sign above the footpath next to the Şan Med Hastenesi, down from İpekpalas Oteli. Open daily 8am-7.30pm. Özcan offers short Harran tours in the morning or evening (3-4hr.; $8 per person, min. $32 for entire dolmuş). His Nemrut Dağı tour includes Atatürk Dam, Kahta, Karakus tumulus, the Roman bridge, Arsemia, and Yeni Kale (9am-11pm, dusk at Nemrut; 1am-1pm, dawn at Nemrut; either option $30 per person, 2 person min.). Sunset/sunrise option includes 2 meals and overnight in Kevansaray Hotel for $50 per person. Mardin tour (6-9pm) visits Deyrul Zafaran Monastery ($25 if there are

4 people or more). The 2-day option adds Nuysaibin, Jacob's grave, Medyat, Hasankeyf, Batman, food, and lodgings ($60).

Banks: Those with **ATMs** are concentrated around Fuar and Sarayönü Cad. **Mutlu Doviz** and **Altin** exchanges, opposite the Art Gallery, are open M-F 9am-6pm, Sa 9am-1pm.

Hamam: Urfa's oldest hamam is the **Vezir,** just opposite the PTT. Entry $2. Open 11am-5pm for women, 6-11pm for men; hours fluctuate with demand.

Police: Across from Golbaşı Park. **Tourist police:** (☎ 215 60 80). Open 8am-6pm.

Hospital: The **Özel Şan-Med Hastanesi** is a good private hospital at the center of town (☎216 27 72, 216 36 16, or 215 43 48). V, MC. Also downtown, the state-run **Devlet Hastanesi** is on Hastahane Cad., though it's rarely used by travelers.

Post Office: The main **PTT** is located between the Şan-Med Hospital and the bazaar. Open daily 8am-noon, 1:30-5:30pm. Services include *poste restante* and 24hr. card telephones. **Internet** services are also available here. **Postal code:** 63200.

ACCOMMODATIONS

Urfa's daytime heat persists through the night, so A/C is seriously worth considering in summer. If you elect to go without, make sure to buy bottled water for the night. Because Urfa's visitor flow varies, attempt to bargain prices down Oct-May.

- **Hotel Ugur Palas,** Koprubasi Cad, is a budget dream. The owner is reputable and the rooms are clean, with shared bath. $4 per person.

- **Valiligi Konuk Evi** (☎ 215 93 77), on Vali Fuat Bey Cad. Not as budget-oriented as other Urfa options, but with only 6 rooms, this exquisitely restored mansion books out in advance. Staff wear traditional dress and the restaurant is affordable. Singles $22; doubles $40; suite $50.

- **Hotel İpek Palas,** 4 Şanmed Hastanesi Arkası (☎ 215 15 46). Behind the Şan-Med Hospital on Atatürk Cad., in the town center. Clean, quiet rooms with A/C, private hot showers, TV, and phones; cheaper rooms have fans. Singles $12; doubles $18; triples $24.

- **Otel Doğu,** 131 Sarayönü (Atatürk) Cad. (☎ 215 12 28). With echoing halls and stark, clean rooms, Doğu is a nice choice if you don't need A/C. Back rooms are quieter. Singles $6; double $8; triples $10.

- **Safak Oteli,** on Gol Cad., is the ultimate budget experience. $3.50 per person.

- **Hotel Bakay,** Asfalt Cad., 24 Atlas Sinamasi (☎ 215 89 75), is friendly and popular with Turkish groups. Singles $15; doubles $25.

FOOD

Renowned for its culinary wonders, Urfa's steaming kitchens have a downside: traditional preparation techniques conspire with the weather to leave numerous unwary tourists locked in their latrines. Many foods, especially meats, can quickly become infested with bacteria in the sweltering heat. Local specialties include *patlıcanlı kebap* (aubergine and meatball on a skewer) and *domatesli kebap* (meatball and tomato on a skewer). Another specialty is *içli köfte* (a deep-fried mutton and rice ball), not to be confused with *çiğ köfte*, raw meat with bulgur.

- **Sultan Sarayi Restaurant** (☎ 316 37 50). 3km north along Atatürk Cad., set among parkland. Catch the dolmuş marked 'Karakopru' ($.20), and get on at the university. Those with kebap-fatigue should order *lebeni* (yogurt and wheat), spicy *bostona* salad, and chicken *pirzola* ($3 with drinks) before 10:30pm.

- **Gulizar Konuk Evi** (☎ 215 05 05). By the Ulu Camii. Walk 20m up Irfaniye Sok. from Sarayonu Cad. Brand new, and open for 3 meals a day until 10pm.

- **Güney Lokantası,** 17 Köprübaşı (☎ 313 22 37), across from Hotel İpek Palas. is one of the few welcoming places for vegetarians in the city. They offer about 3 dishes with absolutely no meat, including *fasulye* (beans with red sauce) and *bamya* (okra in tomato-oil sauce). Full meal $2-3. Open 6am-midnight.

HOLY CARP! In a cave in Urfa, the prophet Abraham was born in secrecy at a time when King Nemrut had decreed that all children should be put to death. Abraham was fully cognizant of having escaped Nemrut's wrath, and at age 10, seized with monotheistic fervor, he began smashing the city's pagan idols. Nemrut, infuriated with Abraham, fashioned a giant slingshot from two tall pillars on a hill, from which he rained firebrands down on the boy below. God took pity on Abraham and called on nature to protect him: "O fire, be gentle to Abraham, keep him safe and the fuel cool." A rose garden sprang up around Abraham, the fire became water, and the burning wood turned into fish in the ponds. The pillars, carp, and cave can still be seen today. You can feed the fish, considered sacred, with sacred fish food for $.30.

Hotel Edessa has the only Western menu in town, including stroganoff or curry ($4), spaghetti ($2), and crème caramel ($2), in addition to local dishes.

Cardaklı Kösk Restaurant (☎ 217 10 80), next to the Edessa, offers traffic-free views of the floodlit fortress.

Çay gardens abound in Urfa. Beneath the floodlit fortress, **Gölbaşı** gardens encircle the sacred fish lakes. North of town, **Guresh** and **Millennium Cay Bahesi** flank each other on Atatürk Bul. with **Temigun Bahesi** just before the main stadium.

👁 SIGHTS

A walking tour of Urfa starts on Atatürk Cad. past the post office. Cross the road and visit Urfa's oldest **hamam,** the **Vezir,** then continue around the corner for a cold glass of *biyanbali* from **Serbetci Abdullah** (☎216 77 99), the best source in town. Make sure you visit the **Ulu Camii,** built between 1170 and 1175. It is on the right as one walks towards the fortress. The mosque has a beautiful courtyard and a Byzantine bell tower that now serves as a minaret. The engaging *Imam* Muhammed Guhadaroğlu enjoys guiding visitors *($1 donation).* The first mosque on Göl Cad. is the late Ottoman **Haşon Paşa Camii.** Behind it lies the large **Mevlid Halil Camii,** which houses the supposed **birth cave** of the prophet Abraham. There are separate entrances for men and women; women are able to forge all the way back into the sacred cave, while men may only look through a barred fence, praying in the proper direction. *(Dress respectably.)*

The fantastic **bazaar** begins at the far south end of Atatürk/Sarayönü/Dıvan Cad. Enter any portal for a surreal adventure in the tiny alleys that stretch for kilometers. Each is disorienting, filled with the sounds of machinery and the smell of spices. If you want to leave, ask for **Gölbaşı,** the large park near the pools of sacred carp. **Davlet Guzel Sanatlar Gallery** is worth a look. *(Free. Open 8am-5pm.)*

The entrance to the city's **citadel** is marked by **Corinthian columns,** constructed in 242 BC, from which, according to legend, Nemrut shot firebrands at Abraham. *(Open daily 8am-6pm. $2, students $1.)* There are two entrances: the stairway on the front wall in the blazing sun and a cave walkway lit by lamps, 50m east. On top, the view is spectacular. 3km south of the bazaar is **Eyyüp Peygamber,** which contains the cave where Job lived for 7 years in physical torture. *(Take an "Eyyübe" dolmuş from Atatürk Cad., across from the tourist office (every 5min., $.20.) Open daylight hours. $1.)*

Urfa's **Fine Arts Museum** is on Atatürk Cad. near Kara Meydanı. More of an art school than a gallery, the museum is one of Urfa's old Ottoman houses. One hallmark is the "bearded arch," which ripples upward to a sharp point, like an inverted beard. *(Open M-Sa 8am-noon, 1:30-5:30pm; July-Aug. M-F. Free.)* The **Archaeological Museum** houses everything from reliefs to jewelry, and on the 2nd floor you'll find Christian icons from the **Ancient Church of the Twelve Apostles,** now the **Fırfırlı Camii.** *(Walk on Nusrat Cad. west for 500m; it's on the right. ☎ 313 15 88. Open daily 8:30am-noon, 1:30-5pm. $2, students $1.)* From the carp pools at the southern end of the town, walk 1km north on Vali Fuat Bey Cad. to reach the mosque/church. For Turkish-dubbed western movies, **Emek Aile Sinemas** can be found 50m from Sarayonu Cad. on Fuar Cad. *(Showings M-F 2:15, 8:45pm; Sa-Su and holidays 3:45pm.)*

🔁 DAYTRIP FROM ŞANLIURFA: HARRAN

Harran lies 44km from Şanlıurfa, toward the Syrian border. Documents dating from approximately 2000 BC mention Harran. Even more astounding is its continuous occupation from 5000 BC through to the Mongol invasion in 1260 AD. Supposedly, Abraham married here, and his family moved to Harran for a sojourn on their way to Palestine. Harran was home to a religious group known as the **Sabians** in the later centuries of the first millennium. Worshippers of the sun and moon, the Sabians' society granted equality to men and women, and the **citadel** that stands at the site is supposed to be the remains of a temple to the god of the moon. Further exploration of the site reveals an ancient castle, the oldest Islamic university, and the supposed site of Abraham's family's house. There is a half-buried underground tunnel and a nearly intact 4km town wall. The **Ulu Camii,** built by the Umayyads in the 8th century, displays an odd square minaret.

Today the town's inhabitants live in peculiar **beehive-shaped houses,** which are both cool and economical to construct. Youths will often pester and offer to guide; women traveling alone should be wary. Four-hour tours cost $10 per person, while full day tours incorporate **Sogmatar** and the ruins of **Jethro City** ($20 per person; see **Şanlıurfa: Travel Agencies,** p. 445). Local transport (Akcakale minibus heading south from Urfa; $1) leaves visitors 10km from the village on the main road. Taxis manipulate this fact, and locals in vehicles may charge similarly. There are two small *lokantasi* on the edge of the Harran site, but nothing at Sogmatar.

GAZİANTEP   ☎342

The largest city in southeast Turkey has a rich heritage dating back to the Stone Age. Yet apart from its fortress, floodlit at night upon a man-made hill, this heritage is giving way to a veneer of modernity. Today, Gaziantep competes with its neighbors for preeminence in trade and industry. At night, locals flock to Centenary Park, complete with water gardens, bike tracks, shopping, and a cinema. Beyond the city, a fertile plain of pistachios, olive trees, and vineyards extends in all directions. Gaziantep is a crossroads town for travelers heading west to the Mediterranean coast, south to Antakya and Syria, or east to Van. The Turkish Grand National Assembly granted the town its epithet *Gazi* (war hero/veteran) in 1921 for its resistance to foreign occupation during the War of Independence.

⬛ TRANSPORTATION

Buses: The otogar is a palatial structure 3km north of town. Regular minibuses ($.40) run from İstasyon Cad. at the waterway. **Hidayet Turizm** (☎328 96 96) is one of many companies with offices here. To: **Adana** (2hr., 6:30am-2am, $5); **Ankara** (10hr., 50 per day 7:30am-midnight, $13.50); **Antalya** (14hr., 10 per day, $16); **Erzurum** (4 per day, $15); **İstanbul** (16hr., 6:30am-9pm, $17); **İzmir** (16hr., 2 per day 4-7pm, $19); **Kars** (23hr., $21); **Kayseri** (8hr., $10); **Mersin** (6hr., 40 per day, $6); **Sivas** (3, 5, 8pm; $11); **Trabzon** (20hr., 6 per day, $18); **Van** (6, 9pm, midnight; $14).

Trains: There are 3 rail routes out of Gaziantep. The service to the west (Tu, Th, Sa 9:30am) runs 2hr. to tiny Narli to meet the **Adana-Elazig Express** to **Adana** (6 hr.), **Konya** (14hr.), and **İstanbul** (27hr.). A daily 2:45pm service leaves for Narli to meet the **Diyarbakır Express**, via Malatya and Elazig. A daily service runs east along the Syrian border to a dead end at **Nusaybin** (10hr., 7am), 50km beyond Mardin.

ORIENTATION AND PRACTICAL INFORMATION

Gaziantep has a disorderly street plan, centered upon its **Antep Kalesi fortress** and divided by a park-lined waterway, **Allenben Deresi. İstasyon Cad.** crosses the waterway before intersecting with **Atatürk Bul.** to the right and **Eski Saray Cad.** to the left.

Tourist Office: A large information office (☎230 99 60) in 100 Year Park. Uzguy Çinkay speaks English. Regional info, maps, brochures. Open M-F 8am-noon, 1:30-5:30pm.

Banks: All major banks have **ATMs** and line Atatürk and Eski Saray Cad. Open 8:30am-noon, 1:30-5pm.

Hamam: 2 of the city's better hamams are in the shadows of the fortress. **Naip** and **Pasa** both admit women by day, before switching to male-only clientele after dusk.

Police: The main headquarters are across the Parki on Aksöy Bul. and 4 Cad.

Hospital: Devlet Hastanesi (public, ☎220 93 37). **Sani Konukoğlu Tip Merkezi** (☎220 95 00) provides care at international standards. Most convenient is the private clinic **Özel Hayat Hastenesi** at 17 İstasyon Cad. It sees patients for $25.

Internet Access: The **Eksen Internet Cafe**, 14 Atatürk Bul., 1st fl. (☎231 41 48), 100m from İstasyon Cad. (open 8am-midnight).

Postal code: 27000

ACCOMMODATIONS

Gaziantep offers more affordable hotel options than nearby Kahramanmaraş. Try **Hotel Petek,** Karagöz Cad. 1/D. (☎231 19 82. Singles $10; doubles $16.) **Bulvar Palas Oteli,** at 11 İstasyon, has clean, simple rooms and a bizarre foyer reminiscent of the Addams Family. (☎231 34 10; singles $7; doubles $11; triples $16). The **Otel Ada Palas** (☎231 33 22) on Gümrük Cad., off Eski Saray Cad., charges $4 per person.

For a slightly more expensive option, start with the **Hotel Büyük Murat**, which has larger rooms than **Hotel Gulluoğlu**. Both are on Eski Saray Cad., on either side of Postane Sok. Both offer dimly-lit rooms; ask for one away from the busy front. (Singles $13; doubles $20; triples $30 with TV and private bath.)

FOOD AND ENTERTAINMENT

Wander 500m along Eski Saray Cad. from İstasyon Cad. to ▧ **Cavusoğlu** (☎231 30 69) or the less pretty ▧ **Cagdas** (☎234 40 00), one block off to the left on Uzun Carsi 14. Both offer quality kebap and baklava for $3 per person. (Both open 9am-11pm.) Tucked off İstasyon Cad. on Sayi Ahmet Sok. is quiet **Sadirvan** (☎231 81 88). Visitors to the Anthropological Museum can relax at the nearby **Fuar Restaurant** (☎323 69 69) and sample *alinazik*, a combination of local yogurt dip and kebap. Beware the rapidly mounting bill. The uncontested baklava master is ▧ **Güllüoğlu** on Suburcu Cad. 20. (☎231 22 82. Open 7am-8:30pm.)

Next door is **Dedikodu,** Gaziantep's favorite **disco,** though ravers would prefer **Taj Mahal,** 3km out of town. Walking from town along the Parki offers outdoor drinking, light dining, and live music, ideal for evenings. After passing the tourist office, look for **Birecikliler Yardimlasma** (☎232 88 81), under the bridge, and **Pegasus.** Just before the mosque is **Incilipmar Sofrasi** (☎234 26 57), with an attached antique shop. Between the mosque and Fevzi Cakmak Bul. is the youthful **Rainbow** (☎338 88 77), run by Eylem Yilmaz. It has nightly music and traditional potato *yufka* cooked on a plate in a nearby tent. The best of the west can be found in the space-age **Begendik** arcade on İstasyon Cad. Its third floor restaurant offers the last profiteroles, lasagna, and donuts before travelers dive into the Anatolian heartland.

SIGHTS

Day visitors should target Gaziantep's **Archeological Museum** (☎231 11 71), just beyond the stadium on İstasyon Cad., and if possible, the **Ethnographic Museum** (☎230 47 21), on Hamfioğlu Cad. in the Bey district. *(Both are open Tu-Su 8am-noon, 1-5pm.)* **Duluk** village, one of Anatolia's earliest habitations lies 10km north. It contains an archaeological site with Hittite and Roman influences, blended in underground stone churches and mausoleums. Take a minibus from İstasyon Cad. ($1.50) and sit in the village *çay* house until a bus returns. Taxis from town cost $8 but are unlikely to wait the hour required to explore the site.

Three key sites lie outside Gaziantep. **Belkis (Zeugma)** is just off the Şanlıurfa road, 10km from Nizip village. Hellenistic, Roman and Byzantine influences are combined in a series of villa remnants, many of which will flood with the construction of the Birecik Dam. Check with locals to establish what remains visible after water levels stabilize. **Yesemet** is a field of Hittite statues, progressively excavated over the last 100 years. It is a two-hour detour from the town of Ishlahiye. **Rum Kale,** 25km from Yazuveli, requires an additional day to visit. This late-Hittite castle is said to have held St. John's biblical manuscripts. Rising water levels from a nearby dam are likely to flood the approaches to Rum Kale, so inquire at tourist information about access first.

NORTHERN CYPRUS

Along the shores of Northern Cyprus, seductive sunsets and slooooow sailboats reveal the island's easy, breezy attitude. Many civilizations have swept through Cyprus' remote lands, leaving history fans a gold mine of ruins to explore, from medieval castles to mosque-made-cathedrals. Lazy, hazy days hide a racy secret: come nightfall, harbor-side casinos bubble with crowds of tourists and hard-core gamblers alike. Since the prohibition of casinos in Turkey a few years ago, Northern Cyprus has become a honeycomb for gambling bees. Even if you're not into the extravagant casino thing, Cyprus' quiet Mediterranean beaches, legendary mountains, and magical ruins still merit a few days' visit from mainland Turkey.

Travelers in Northern Cyprus need not feel intimidated by the heavy military presence, which actually grants the island a sense of security. In the cities policemen lackadaisically direct traffic as blue-beret-wearing UN peacekeepers cruise the streets. Military bases swallow everything from fields to monasteries. Sentries and shepherds walk side by side, and sometimes the sentries *are* the shepherds.

Turkey is the only country that recognizes the "Turkish Republic of Northern Cyprus," which comprises 37% of the entire island. Though officially proclaimed on November 15, 1983, it was more or less established by the 1974 Turkish military action (variously known as the "peace operation" or "invasion" depending on the speaker's point of view). The government of Northern Cyprus, a parliamentary democracy on the British model, is led by President Rauf Denktaş. The official language is Turkish and the official currency is the Turkish lira. Most of the 175,000 residents are Turkish Cypriots, though about 40,000 are immigrants from the Turkish mainland. A few hundred Brits and Germans also live here, with a number of bonus Brits dropping in on their holiday homes in the summer. About half the population speaks English, and many older residents speak Greek.

HIGHLIGHTS OF NORTHERN CYPRUS

EXPLORE the fairy-tale beauty of the 10th-century **St. Hilarion Castle** (p. 462), a paradisiacal summer house of the ages, coveted as an ancient and modern-day battle prize.

REVISIT Cyprus's royal past in the ghostly halls of **Girne Castle** (p. 460), the dwelling place of the notorious Lusignan ruling family, whose eerie dungeon caged the victims of court politics and intrigues.

JOURNEY among thick cypress groves and silver olive trees to discover the glorious, restored **Bellapais Abbey** (p. 462), whose elegantly crafted cloisters command a majestic view over the sea.

TOUR the extensive ruins that stood preserved in sand in ancient **Salamis** (p. 472) for 1000 years, and gawk at the strange Royal Tombs near **Mağusa** (p. 468).

ESSENTIALS

MONEY

Northern Cyprus uses the same currency as Turkey, the lira. For exchange rates, see p. 42. Due to high inflation, all prices are quoted in US dollars, which are widely accepted for large payments like hotels and car rentals. Many places, particularly along the northern coast, will quote prices and accept payments in British sterling (pounds). Credit cards are generally not accepted on the island, and some ATMs don't take foreign cards, so carrying cash is your best bet.

GETTING THERE

The international boundary that divides Cyprus remains nearly impossible to cross. Visitors can enter Northern Cyprus from Southern Cyprus for a maximum of one day, but they cannot cross the Green Line in the other direction. One-day passes are available on the southern side of the Green Line, but only with stringent restrictions (borders close at 5pm; see p. 465 for more information on the Ledra Palace crossing). Upon entering Northern Cyprus from any other country, ask the immigration official to stamp a separate visa and not your passport if you have future plans to visit the south or mainland Greece. The easiest way to enter Northern Cyprus is **via sea or air** from Turkey. The best place to catch **ferries** from mainland Turkey is Taşucu, which sends seabuses (2½hr.) and ferries (5hr.) to Girne every day. Less frequent ferries also travel to Girne from Alanya and Anamur, and 3 night ferries per week (10hr., rather uncomfortable travel) embark from Mersin to Mağusa. Turkish air carriers are the only ones that fly into Northern Cyprus; flights run between Lefkoşa's Ercan airport (☎231 46 39) and most major airports in Turkey. You can get more information from **Cyprus Turkish Airlines'** head office in Lefkoşa. (☎392 228 39 01; email info@kthy.net; www.kthy.net.)

TOURIST SERVICES

Tourist offices in Northern Cyprus have odd hours, usually scheduled around the noontime heat. An administrative office in Lefkoşa, along with branches in Girne and Mağusa, offers piles of brochures and city maps. Northern Cyprus' touristic press network is actually quite impressive; get your hands on "The Premier Tourist Guide to Northern Cyprus," where you'll find every phone number you could possibly need, plus a number of "pick-me" hotel and restaurant ads.

EMERGENCIES

As with government-sector Turkish hospitals (*Devlet Hastane*), initial emergency medical treatment is free.

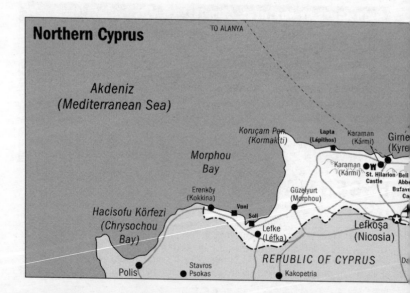

Northern Cyprus

TO ALANYA

Akdeniz
(Mediterranean Sea)

Koruçam Pen.
(Kormakiti)

Lapta
(Lápithos)

Karaman
(Kármi)

Girne
(Kyre

Morphou
Bay

Karaman
(Kármi) St. Hilarion Bell
Castle Abbe
Bufave
Ca

Erenköy
(Kokkina)

Güzelyurt
(Morphou)

Vuni
Soli

Hacisofu Körfezi
(Chrysochou
Bay)

Lefke
(Léfka)

Lefkoşa
(Nicosia)

REPUBLIC OF CYPRUS

Polis

Stavros
Psokas

Kakopetria

Da

EMERGENCY NUMBERS IN NORTHERN CYPRUS. These 24-hour phone numbers can be dialed from any phone in Northern Cyprus. At card-operated public phones you can dial them without inserting a card. At coin-operated phones, you must insert a coin, but it will be returned to you after the call.

> **Police:** ☎ 155 (in Karpaz dial 381 23 25)
> **Ambulance:** ☎ 112
> **Forest fire:** ☎ 177
> **Fire:** ☎ 199

TRANSPORTATION

Exercise extreme caution when driving in Northern Cyprus. Winding roads, reckless drivers, and scores of tourists unfamiliar with driving on the left-hand side of the road all provide less-than-optimal road conditions. See **Road Safety,** p. 47.

If you want to see much at all of Northern Cyprus, you will have to resign yourself to renting a car. There is efficient dolmuş service between the three major towns of Mağusa, Lefkoşa, and Girne, and it is relatively easy to reach Lapta, Güzelyurt, and Lefke as well. However, many of Northern Cyprus's finest attractions, such as St. Hilarion Castle, Bellapais Abbey, and the Karpaz Peninsula are miles away from the nearest dolmuş route. Most rental companies will not rent vehicles for fewer than 3 days, and they charge around $35 per day for Renaults and $50 per day for Nissans with A/C and automatic transmission. In theory, you need to be 25 years old and have a UK or international driver's license to rent a car. In practice, anyone with a driver's license of any kind can rent a car. Students should make it clear that they are not at any of the island's English-speaking universities; these students have a well-earned reputation for reckless driving that has caused most rental agencies to refuse them service (see **The Hazards of Being a ZZ-Driver,** p. 471). While Mağusa and Girne are far better bases for island exploration, Lefkoşa offers a number of affordable rental options. Gas costs around $.95 per liter. For more information, contact the **Rent-A-Car Association,** based in Girne (☎ 815 22 72).

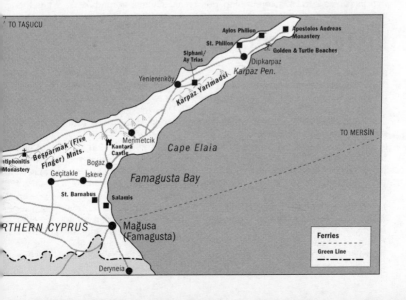

NORTHERN CYPRUS

The void left by adequate public transportation has been eagerly filled by armies of taxi drivers with fleets of Mercedes-Benz cabs. Northern Cypriot taxis have no meters. Instead, drivers have little booklets that list the prices of various destinations on the island. Always agree on a price before you get into the cab. In general, expect to pay $4 for 5km, $7 for 10km, $11 for 15km, and $13 for 25km. You can also get a full-day chauffeured tour of the island for $75-100. It never hurts to bargain. If you don't take out the maximum possible collision insurance, many agencies require a hefty cash deposit (see **Car Insurance,** p. 68).

KEEPING IN TOUCH

Because Northern Cyprus is not recognized by the international community, it is treated as a province of Turkey for the purpose of postal communication. Mail sent to Northern Cyprus passes first through Mersin, and is then shipped to the island. Thus, to send letters to Northern Cyprus, use the postal code "Mersin 10, Turkey." A sample address is: Chloe K. <u>TEE</u>, Dome Hotel, Girne, Northern Cyprus, Mersin 10, Turkey. The "TRNC" has its own internationally accepted stamps.

You can call Northern Cyprus the same way you'd call a province in Turkey. From abroad, dial 90 (Turkey) as the country code, followed by **392,** the **phone code** for Northern Cyprus. Phonecards from mainland Turkey don't work in Northern Cyprus' pay phones, but post and telecommunication offices sell "TRNC" phonecards. In theory, international operators are accessible via TRNC phone lines, though in practice, American calling cards (e.g AT&T, MCI) do not work.

HANDY TIDBITS

Electricity in Northern Cyprus operates on 240 volts, with plugs to reflect the island's British flavor. Most outlets are English standard plugs, though occasionally you'll find Turkish standard plugs. Appropriate adapters are necessary for electrical appliances.

Cuisine is similar to that of Turkey, though there are number of Cypriot specialties. Particularly, *hellim* cheese (usually made from goat's milk and later boiled) is wildly popular and delicious, with a salty, mozzarella-ish flavor and consistency. Myriad *mezes* and local desserts complement the island's palette, and are certainly worth a touch of gluttony.

Like much of mainland Turkey's southern coast, **temperatures** in Northern Cyprus can soar to "way-too-freakin'-hot" (read: summer around 34°C). When the mercury's pushing 40, follow the Cypriots and flee the midday heat (11am-4pm).

HISTORY AND CULTURE

ANCIENT CYPRUS

The remains of round stone dwellings indicate that Cyprus has been continuously inhabited since roughly 7000 BC. Cyprus's deposits of copper ore made it an important mining and trading center in the Bronze Age. Indeed, linguists are unsure whether *Kypros*, from which the word "copper" is derived, first referred to the island or to the metal itself.

Regular visits from Mycenaean traders from 1400 to the mid-12th century BC led to the adoption of the Greek language, written notation for commerce, and Hellenistic architectural influences that are still visible today. The **Phoenicians** shared political control with the Greeks until the **Assyrians** washed up in the 7th century BC and dominated the island for 100 years. After the waning of Assyrian power, the Egyptians and then the Persians ruled the island, in the face of much Cypriot resistance. **Alexander the Great** absorbed Cyprus into his growing empire, but after his death in 323 BC, Ptolemy claimed the island for Egypt, forcing the last royal family of Salamis to commit suicide. Rome annexed Cyprus in 58 BC, and the Apostle Paul introduced Christianity to Cypriots in 45 AD. Cyprus became the first country in the world to be ruled by a Christian.

BYZANTINE AND OTTOMAN RULE

Roman civic thought, Greek philosophy, and Greek Orthodox tradition melded in Cyprus during the centuries of Byzantine rule. In 1191, **Richard the Lionheart,** en route to Jerusalem, overran the island. King Richard sold Cyprus to the **Knights Templar,** who returned the gift to Richard; he in turn sold it to Guy de Lusignan, a minor French noble. The **Lusignan Dynasty** (1192-1489) brought European feudalism, Gothic architecture, wealth (for the nobles), and a suppression of cultural and religious freedom. In 1489 the **Venetians** annexed the island. However, in 1570, following a two-month siege, Nicosia surrendered to the Ottomans. Famagusta's fall a year later marked the start of the **Ottoman period** in Cyprus.

Under Ottoman rule, feudalism was abolished, peasants were granted land, and the Orthodox Church flourished. As the Ottoman Empire waned in the 19th century, **Britain** found itself defending Ottoman territories against Russian expansionism. In July of 1878, tired of nursing the "sick man of Europe" without compensation, British forces landed at Larnaka and assumed control of Cyprus. Britain set a deal with Turkey whereby the island's excess revenue paid off Ottoman war loans.

CYPRUS IN THE 20TH CENTURY

INDEPENDENCE. After World War II, with the end of the British Empire, **General George Crivas** and **Archbishop Makarios** founded the **EOKA** (National Organization of Cypriot Fighters) an underground Greek movement seeking *enosis*—union with Greece. When the United Nations vetoed the Greek request to grant Cyprus self-government in 1955, General Crivas and the EOKA initiated a round of riots and guerrilla attacks against the British government, attempting to foster popular resistance to colonial rule. In response to increased EOKA activity, the underground **Volkan** (Volcano) group, under the leadership of now-President of Northern Cyprus **Rauf Denktaş,** founded the **TMT** (Turkish Resistance Organization). TMT was a paramilitary organization designed to fight the *enosists* and to push for **taksim,** or partition of the island between Greece and Turkey. British, Greek, and Turkish foreign ministers finally agreed in 1959 to establish an independent Cypriot Republic. On August 16, 1960, Cyprus was granted independence, becoming a member of the UN and the British Commonwealth.

ANNEXATION. The new **constitution** stated that a Greek Cypriot president and a Turkish Cypriot vice-president were to be elected, and that the Greek to Turkish ratio in the House of Representatives would be 70:30. In 1959, Archbishop Makarios became the Republic's first president, and **Fazıl Küçük,** the Turkish Cypriot leader, became vice president. In 1963, Makarios proposed 13 constitutional amendments which implied greater autonomy. When the Turkish government threatened military force in response, renewed violence broke out between the EOKA and TMT, ending in the division of Nicosia along the Green Line. In February 1964, the UN dispatched a "temporary" peacekeeping force that remains today.

In 1968, Makarios and Küçük were both re-elected by an overwhelming majority, although in the years following they were subject to several coup plots. Intermittent violence exploded into an international affair in 1974 when the Greek Cypriot National Guard, assisted by the military **junta** in Greece, overthrew Makarios and replaced him with **Nikos Sampson,** a notorious gunman known for shooting up ethnically mixed neighborhoods in Lefkoşa and pushing for immediate *enosis*. Five days later the Turkish army invaded Cyprus from the north to protect Turkish Cypriots. A half-century after the foundation of the Turkish Republic, the 1923 "population exchange" between Greece and Turkey was repeated in bloody microcosm on Cyprus as families that found themselves on the wrong side of the battle line fled their homes. With the declaration of the Turkish Federal State of Cyprus (TFSC) in early 1975, *taksim* was effectively achieved.

In November 1983, the North declared itself the independent Turkish Republic of Northern Cyprus (TRNC), which only Turkey has recognized. In 1992, the UN reduced their peacekeeping mission significantly. **Glafkos Clerides,** former head of the conservative Democratic Rally (DISY), became head of the Republic of Cyprus in 1993. The re-election of Denktaş in the North helped the negotiation process, and resolution may be possible in the near future. Turkey has threatened to seek unification with Northern Cyprus if the Republic of Cyprus joins the European Union. In early August 1997, Turkey and Northern Cyprus had already agreed to work toward partial defense and economic integration. The agreement, which incensed the Greek government, came just five days before UN-sponsored talks between the two sides were supposed to yield greater cooperation.

WHAT'S TO COME. Periods of tension alternate with periods of relative calm, but there are still threats to future good relations. The announcement in March of 1998 that the EU is considering the Republic of Cyprus as a potential member state has catalyzed a host of questions as to the future of the island's separate peace. Although Turkey is now a full candidate for membership in the EU, questions have arisen about the political status of Northern Cyprus in the event of the Republic of Cyprus's gaining admittance into the EU.

Though only Turkey has recognized the new state, the self-proclaimed "Turkish Republic of Northern Cyprus" (TRNC) has established trade relations in Europe and with several Arab states. Led by Rauf Denktaş, the TRNC lags far behind the Republic of Cyprus economically, but it is significantly more prosperous than the Turkish mainland. In recent years, the island has seen the arrival of thousands of lower-income settlers from Turkey.

GIRNE AND THE NORTH

GIRNE (KYRENIA)

The Mediterranean rests affectionately beside Girne, separated from the city by the 500m of remnants of the bordering walls. Fish restaurants, bars, and open-air cafes rim the semi-circular harbor created by the wall. Girne also oozes Britishness, and a small but growing community of British expats lives harmoniously with Turkish Cypriots and transient tourists. You can bet on horse and dog races broadcast live from the U.K. at the Dome Hotel Casino, stay in the Lord Kitchener room at the aptly titled Nostalgia Hotel, shop for Earl Grey tea at any local grocery store, and pay for your fried liver and onions in sterling instead of lira at one of the many British pubs. This town is ideal for those looking to spend some time sipping cold drinks and doing little else. Don't let the lethargic pace fool you, though: in and around Girne, there are treasures for more vivacious spirits to discover.

▐ TRANSPORTATION

Ferries: Tickets for the **Fergün Ferries** can be bought in the main square office (☎ 815 33 77; open M-F 8am-6pm, Sa 8am-2pm) or at the new harbor, at least 1hr. before departure. Dolmuş run from the new harbor to the main square (supposedly every 30min., $.75). Alternatively, exit the port gates on the right, continue 500m down the road, take a right at the main intersection onto İskenderun Cad., and walk about 1½km. Fast daily **seabuses** to: **Alanya, Turkey** (3hr.; Tu, Su 4pm; $45, round-trip $60; students $40, round-trip $50), and **Taşucu, Turkey** (2½hr.; daily 9:30am; $29, round-trip $56; students $27, round-trip $53). **Slower ferries** also run to **Taşucu** (5hr.; daily 11:30am; $17, round-trip $33; students $16, round-trip $30). Expect to pay an additional tax of $10 for trips to Alanya and $9 (students $6) for Taşucu. Ferries rarely depart on time.

Dolmuş: From the parking lot off the square, dolmuş run to: **Acapulco Beach and Resort** (5 per day 9:30am-5pm, $.80); **Lapta** (every 15min. 7am-7pm, $1) via **Karaoğlanoğlu** ($.75); **Lefkoşa** (every 15min., $1.35); and **Mağusa** (every 15min., $2.40).

Taxis: Stands are on every street corner. Trips within town, including the new harbor, officially cost $4. There should be a list of standard fares. You can also hire your own personal cab for a whole day for $100. Bargaining is worthwhile.

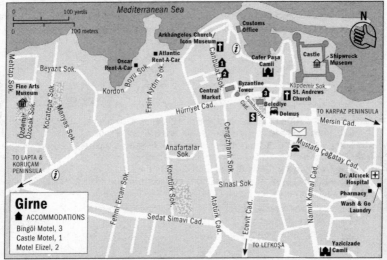

Car Rental: Among many agencies, **Atlantic** (☎815 30 53; fax 815 56 73), in the Dome Hotel, has Renaults (Apr.-June $25 per day; June-Oct. $23; Nov.-Mar. $16), Jeeps (Apr.-June $27 per day; June-Oct. $34; Nov.-Mar. $22), and a range of automatics with A/C (Apr.-June $30 per day, June-Oct. $37, Nov.-Mar. $24). Insurance included. 3-day min. Open daily 9am-7pm. Across the street, **Oscar** (☎815 22 72) offers much the same, with a range of Jeeps. Automatic cars and those with left-side steering available, but automatic, left-side steering vehicles are a rare commodity.

✴ ORIENTATION

A wide, grassy mall fills the coast from the harbor to the **Dome Hotel,** a rambling white plaster colonial institution that marks Girne's center of gravity. About 200m along the mall from the Dome, the **old harbor,** now used only by pleasure boats, is where most of the hotels and upscale restaurants are located. At the far end of the mall rises the massive **Kyrenia Castle.** Turn inland at the castle walls, make a right, and walk uphill to reach a roundabout and modern fountain which mark the **main square,** Girne's overland transportation hub, with dolmuş and taxis galore. From here, **Cumhuriyet Cad.,** which becomes **İskenderun Cad.,** leads towards the **new harbor,** 2km from town, where ferries from Turkey arrive. Behind the main square and to the left runs **Hürriyet Cad.,** the main drag, lined with shops and a few hotels. The streets to the right lead to the seafront; the nearest streets lead to the old harbor.

⁊ PRACTICAL INFORMATION

TOURIST, FINANCIAL, AND LOCAL SERVICES

Tourist Office: (☎815 21 45). In the stone ruins at the harbor entrance, 500m past the intersection of Hürriyet Cad. and Fehmi Ercan Sok. Free city maps of Girne, Lefkoşa, and Mağusa. Open M-F 8am-6pm; Sa-Su 8am-2pm.

Travel Agencies: May be a solution to Northern Cyprus' transportation dilemma. The best is **Kaleidoskop Turizm** (☎815 1818; email kaleidos@kktc.net), in the main square behind the bank. Congenial English- and German-speaking manager, Irene Raab, can arrange just about anything. Local sightseeing tours run $30 to see Salamis, Mağusa, Güzelyurt, or the like. **Apple Tour** (☎815 54 99; fax 815 18 94), just nearby on Ecevit Cad., can arrange half-day tours of the sights near Girne for $30.

Banks: MC/V/Cirrus/Plus **ATMs** are on Hürriyet Cad., near the castle. **Vakıfbank,** in the main square, cashes **traveler's checks.** (Open M, Th 8:30am-12:30pm, 2:15-4:15pm;

Tu, W, F 8:30am-12:30pm.) Banks open M-F 8am-noon. **Exchange offices** are scattered along the street leading from the Atatürk statue left and up to Hürriyet Cad.

Expatriates' Notice Board: In front of PTT. Info on events, apartment rentals, and more.

English-Language Bookstore: Green Jacket Bookshop, 20 Temmuz Cad. (☎/fax 815 71 30), roughly 1½km from town. From the main square, walk to the end of Hürriyet Cad. and continue for 700m on the coastal road; it's on the left across from the petrol station. A random selection of novels, non-fiction, and history/guidebooks on Cyprus. Open M-F 9am-1pm, 3:30-6:30pm; Sa 9am-1pm. **BBD** news agents on Hürriyet Cad. near the square have a small selection of British newspapers.

Laundromat: Wash and Go Laundry (☎815 18 23). Walking with the hospital on your left, pass the national archives to the 2nd town center. It's on your right. One load $4.80; two loads $8. Dry cleaning $3-5. Open M-Sa 8:30am-1pm, 3-6:30pm.

EMERGENCY AND COMMUNICATIONS

Police: (☎815 20 14 or 815 21 25). On the road immediately beside the castle, just off the harbor and behind the Harbor Club.

Pharmacies: Güven Eczane (☎815 24 09), across from the hospital.

Hospital: Dr. Akçiçek Hospital (☎815 22 66 or 815 22 54), on Cumhuriyet Cad., roughly 100m past the PTT. Clinicians occupy the cottage-like left side, while "Acil" marks the emergency entrance to your standard big, white hospital. Anglophones easily available, as in all of Girne.

Internet Access: The cheapest is **Cafe Net,** well-advertised and located across the street from the *jandarma.* Charges $1.60 per hr. Open daily 10am-10pm. **Cafe Online** (☎815 64 28), in the plaza where Hürriyet Cad. and Fehim Ercan Sok. meet. $2.40 per hr. Open M-Sa 10am-6pm. **VIP Net,** where Hürriyet Cad. and Sedat Simavi Cad. converge. $1.80 per hr. Open Su-F 2pm-1am.

Telephones: In the main square, by Cumhuriyet Cad. TRNC phonecards only. The **Telekomunikasyon Dairesi,** opposite the PTT, sells 200-unit cards ($5.25). Open M, Su 8am-1:30pm, 3:30-5pm; Tu-F 8am-1pm; Sa 8am-12:30pm. Office closed? Head to the PTT.

PTT: Just off the main square, on Cumhuriyet Cad., offers standard mail services including parcels, stamps, and *poste restante.* Open in summer M 7:30am-2pm, 3:30-6pm; Tu-F 7:30am-2pm, 4-6pm; Sa 8:30am-12:30pm. In winter M-F 8am-1pm, 2-5pm; Sa 8:30am-12:30pm. Parcel office open M, W, F 9-11:30am.

▌ ACCOMMODATIONS

Accommodations in Girne fall into three classes. The European tourist-oriented hotels, many on the sea, charge over $20 per person for gluttonous luxury. If you're going to be splurging on lodgings at all in the course of your Cypriot travels, this is the place. Some of the cheaper hotels and pensions, in the $10-15 range, are dingy, while others can be quite nice. The third group, the $2-3 pensions and dormitories, are not suited for tourists.

▨ **Castle Motel,** 1 Bafra Sok. (☎815 39 42). From the main square, head west one block on Hürriyet Cad., take a right at the taxi stand, and follow the road until you see the sign. Dwarfed by gigantic beds, the clean rooms are equipped with TV, minifridge, private showers, and high-tech electric fans. Lovable decor, fully stocked bar, and surprisingly beautiful floral baths. Breakfast included. Singles $11.30; doubles $22.60.

Set Pension (☎815 38 45). Just inland from the old harbor. Vast, wooden rooms with TV and minifridge situated in a gorgeous old English mansion. Overlooks neighboring arboreal stone courtyard/restaurant. Lavish ambiance (including Japanese hall lamps) eclipses that "just another pension" feel. Breakfast $2. Singles $13; doubles $19.50.

Motel Elizel, 3 Bafra Sok. (☎815 47 74 or 815 82 83; fax 815 82 81). Across from Castle Motel. Friendly staff and spacious, clean (but unimpressive) rooms, some with balconies. Breakfast $2.40. $10 per night.

THOSE LOONY LUSIGNANS Girne's castle stands as a giant monument to the Lusignans, French nobles who took control of Cyprus during a 12th-century crusade. The Lusignans proved that even Crusaders could have dysfunctional families. Raymond de Lusignan's wife, the lovely Countess Melusine, was said to turn into a serpent from the waist down every Saturday before eventually becoming the dragon that now haunts her castle in Poitou.

Peter I, arguably the greatest of the Lusignan kings (1358-1369), went off to Egypt to recruit soldiers and funding for the Crusades, after having seduced his favorite mistress, Lady Jeanne d'Aleman. Peter was later assassinated and dismembered by mutinous barons while in bed with the famed beauty, Lady Echive de Scandelion.

John II ruled Cyprus from 1432 to 1458 under the domineering influence of his unscrupulous and ambitious second wife, Helena Palaeologa. The couple had only one child (Carlotta), but John's mistress, Marietta of Patras, bore him a son, who would later become King James II. Never one to leave an offense unreturned, Helena bit off Marietta's nose in a fit of jealousy.

Carlotta fared much worse. Widowed, then orphaned, then remarried to the insipid nonentity Louis of Savoy, she managed in her loneliness to grow quite "close" to her half-brother James. The Lusignan High Court, sensing James was a threat to the purity of the line, poisoned the friendship and drove James to Cairo where his dynamic ways won the support of the Mamluk Sultan, who lent him a fleet to help him claim the Cypriot crown from his half-sister. In 1460, James took the entire island except for the castle of Girne, in which Carlotta withstood his attacks for four years.

Bingöl Motel, 6/A Ziya Rızkı Cad. (☎815 27 49). On the main square, across from Set. Comfortable but basic rooms with private showers. Ask for the bigger rooms up top. Breakfast included. Singles $11; doubles $22.

Soli Residence (☎815 88 70; fax 815 87 80). In the town center, next to the otogar. Run like a huge youth hostel, Soli offers 60 suites with 2 bedrooms, sitting space, kitchen, bath, TV, phone, and A/C around swimming pool. Washing machine and cleaning service. Breakfast included. Singles $18; doubles $28. 20% discount Aug.1-Oct.1.

🔲 FOOD

The harbor, lined with tiny seafood restaurants, is the most obvious place to dine. The standard $7.50 fish and chips combo makes a pleasant enough dinner when accompanied by twilight harborside views. In and around the square, a number of small eateries, such as **Dedem** (☎815 33 94), serve typical Turkish food at typical Turkish prices ($2-3). It's best to avoid the fish in these establishments; stick to your *döner* and *çeşit ızgara* (mixed grill). **Supermarkets** are a good source for inexpensive picnic food.

Set Ristorante Italiano (☎815 60 08). Adjoining the pension of the same name. Unbeatable ambience and great, affordable food. Set in a Romeo-and-Juliet-esque stone courtyard with draping vines and flowers, this candlelit dining experience is complete with classical music and pasta in all its incarnations. Veggie menu, pizzas and specialty dishes. Starters $3.20; main meals $5-7. Open 6-11pm.

Girne Taverna "Paşa Bahçe Restaurant" (☎815 27 99). On Türkmen Sok., down the street from the Telecommunications office. Serves wildly delicious (though pricey) meals in a garden of grape vines and palm trees. House special kebap ($9.80) roasts for 4 hours in the afternoon for an unforgettable meal. Alternatively, a 15-variety Cypriot *meze* special costs $8. Other meals run about $8-12.

Ella's Cafe Bar (☎815 20 16), a "London style cafe and sandwich bar" across the street from Dome Hotel. A great change from standard eateries, Ella's offers homemade cakes and Girne's greatest Nescafe. Calling ahead will score you a packed lunch for daytrips and take-outs. Sandwiches $4; Nescafe $2.40.

The Grapevine. 200m up Ecevit Cad. from the main square. Away from the beauty and bustle of the harbor (but unfortunately next to a gas station), this terraced restaurant serves filling fish and steak dishes ($7-12). Well-stocked bar with $1.20 pints of *Efes*.

SIGHTS

GİRNE CASTLE. Built by the Byzantines with material plundered from the ruins of a now nonexistent Roman city, the massive castle, Girne's preeminent sight, was later fortified by the Lusignans. In the 15th century, Queen Carlotta, the last true monarch of the Lusignan dynasty, held out here for four years during the siege led by her illegitimate half-brother, the future James II (see **Those Loony Lusignans,** p. 459). After the Venetians rebuilt some of the walls and added several towers, the Turks took the fortress in 1570 without firing a single cannon.

A number of the chambers in the well-preserved castle have been set aside for special exhibits and the castle's six museums. The **Shipwreck Museum,** across the large, open courtyard, contains the remains of a ship that dates back to the time of Alexander the Great (300 BC). The ship and some of the cargo, including 400 wine amphoras from Rhodes and more than 9000 blackened almonds (the crew's main dietary staple), are on display. The amusing **Lusignan dungeons,** according to the posted sign, "have been brought back to their former gruesome role as a place to torture or imprison undesirables." Fortunately, these "undesirables" are plaster mannequins and not unmannered tourists. In one room, an anatomically correct Turk is stretched out on the rack. In another, you can peer two stories down through a raised grating at a languid, scantily clad Lady Jeanne, mistress to King James. The queen threw her here when she gave birth to James's illegitimate son. Other sights in the castle worth a visit are the Byzantine **St. George Church,** exhibits related to the excavation of nearby Neolithic and Bronze Age sites, and the Venetian and Lusignan towers. *(The castle is just east of the old harbor. Open daily in summer 9am-7pm; in winter 9am-4:45pm. $4, students $.50.)*

BEACHES. The north coast beaches, some of the finest in Cyprus, draw thousands on a good weekend. Most charge a small fee (usually around $2.40) and sit awkwardly below monolithic, multi-storied resorts or "bungalow-style" condo developments. **Kervansaray,** the best of the area's free beaches, lies near the village of **Karaoğlanoğlu,** several kilometers west of Girne. *(To get there, take a taxi (about $6) or the Girne-Lapta dolmuş ($.35) from the main square and get off at the "Güler's Fish" sign on the right.)* A mostly German and Turkish crowd of sun-bathers and hedonists bake at the popular **Acapulco Beach,** about 4km east of town. The beach stretches along the choice **Acapulco Resort,** where comfortable bungalows surround a tantalizing casino nightlife. *(Take a minibus from town ($.80) or hire a cab ($8). $2.40.)* **Sunset Beach** is along the road to Lapta, 6km past the turnoff for Kervansaray. This smaller beach, which also charges $2.40, is an ideal base for **Sea Nest Water Sports** (☎851 19 86). Rent windsurfers ($12 per hr.), sailboats (Lasers; $12 per hr.), canoes (1-person canoe $2 per 30min., 2-person $4), and 2-person motor boats ($2 per 30min.).

MARINE TURTLE CONSERVATION PROJECT. Not just another pretty stretch of sand, **Alagadi Beach** is the headquarters of the Northern Cyprus Marine Turtle Conservation Project. Initiated in 1992 by Glascow University and the Society for the Protection of Turtles in Northern Cyprus, the project, staffed mostly by university students from the UK, aims to study and protect the **green and loggerhead turtles.**

To avoid alarming the turtles, a maximum of eight to 10 visitors can accompany the patrols each night (9pm-dawn) to observe the females nest. Arrange a visit in advance. Lying on the beach at night, you will have the opportunity to stare at a night sky unlike anything near a big city. And when a patrol locates a nesting site, there's a real treat of watching a turtle patiently lay her eggs, flop awkwardly back to the water, and then glide gracefully out of sight. *(Alagadi is a 15min. drive east of*

SAVE THE SEA TURTLE The beaches of Northern Cyprus are one of the few remaining nesting sites of the green and loggerhead sea turtles. These remarkable and elusive creatures have been on the earth for nearly 100 million years, but they have been brought to the brink of extinction by human (often tourist-related) pollution of the beaches and predation of nesting sites by foxes and dogs. The green turtle is classified as endangered, the loggerhead as vulnerable. There is still insufficient data on these creatures as most of their 60 to 120 year life-span is spent at sea, but it is estimated that every year there are 300 to 500 nesting female green turtles and 200 nesting female loggerheads in Cyprus. Sunbathers on Cyprus's beaches should follow a few guidelines. Stay away from the beaches from dusk to dawn. Do not drive on the beaches, since tire ruts can be impassible barriers for hatchlings struggling to reach the sea. Stay close to the water, as nests—normally buried further up the beach—can be disturbed by fires, umbrellas, or anything else that might alter the temperature of the sand in which the offspring are incubating. Finally, do not leave any litter on the beach. For more information about the sea turtles of Northern Cyprus, contact Kutlay Keço, the president of the Society for the Protection of Turtles (SPOT) at the Grapevine Restaurant (☎815 24 96) in Girne or visit the website of the Marine Turtle Conservation Project at www.seaturtle.org/mtrg/.

Girne. Since there is no public transportation, you'll have to drive or hire a taxi ($10 each way; try to bargain). The night on the beach is free, but a $12 donation will get you a T-shirt and $24 will allow you to adopt a turtle. Flash photography is not permitted on the beach.)

OTHER SIGHTS. **Arkhángelos Church** contains an interesting **Icon Museum** (☎815 53 13). Mostly from the last two centuries, icons line the ground floor and three-tiered balcony. From the upper balcony you can look across at the magnificent altarpiece depicting Christ in a large golden chalice, surrounded by levitating angel heads. *(Open 9am-1pm, 2-4:45pm. $1.60, students $.40.)* Girne's **Fine Arts Museum,** a seaside stone cottage that once belonged to an English governor, lies 1km down the street from the Dome Hotel. Two salons of European paintings (including the requisite oils of windmills and nursing mothers) give way to several gabled rooms of yellow porcelain Chinese horses, red and gold dragons, and Mt. Fuji fire screens. *(Open daily 9am-1pm, 2-4:45pm. $1.60, students $.40. Because of the intervening military zone, you have to take a circuitous route to get there: walk along Hürriyet Cad., turn right on Kocatepe Sok., and pass the military hospital. The well-marked museum is on the left.)*

🎵 ENTERTAINMENT

Beach-going, moseying, and nap-taking are Girne's most popular entertainment activities for those who aren't into the gambling scene. The peace-loving community has recently passed laws banning loud music late at night, killing the club scene. Nevertheless, the western end of the old harbor has a number of lively bars and casinos that are open all night.

Cafe 34, in the old harbor, is the bold loner of loud-ish, pulsating music. It earns highest marks for Cyprus' best brandy sour and its tasteful indoor and terraced outdoor drinking areas, which become jammed with hip Turks and Turk Cypriots on Friday and Saturday nights in high season. *Rakı* and beer $1.80; brandy sour $3. Open 10pm-2am.

Shenanigans "must be time for a pint" Irish Pub (☎815 45 21), around the corner from Set, reverberates with laughter and conversation. Patrons lounge on the couches or at the bar, alternately filling and killing their pints. Beer $1.90. Open 6pm- "closing."

Zeus Cafe. Conspicuously advertised along the harbor. Serves up good pub grub and live English music. Beer $1.90; brandy sour $2.40. Open until 2am.

Sunset Beach (☎821 83 30). Equipped with an **outdoor disco** teeming with local youth on summer weekends. Open M-Sa 11pm-3:30am, or later, depending on the crowd.

NORTHERN CYPRUS

DAYTRIPS FROM GİRNE

ST. HILARION CASTLE

If St. Hilarion Castle looks like something out of a fairy tale, it's because it is: St. Hilarion served as Walt Disney's inspiration when he designed the castle for *Snow White and the Seven Dwarves*. It sprawls across a mountain peak 10km north of Girne. Built in the 10th century over the site of an early monastery, St. Hilarion, together with **Bufavento** and **Kantara** castles, formed part of the Byzantines' early warning system against raiders. After some renovations in the 12th and 13th centuries, the Lusignans transformed it into a glamorous palace of unfettered luxury. Though the castle was abandoned by the Venetians when they conquered the island in 1489, it has endured quite well. Centuries later, in 1964, the Turkish TMT used the castle as a stronghold and garrison from which to push the cause of *taksim* (see **Cyprus in the 20th Century**, p. 455).

While simply gazing upon the castle from a distance is enough to inspire dreams of magic looking-glasses and evil women with self-esteem issues, closer exploration reveals that St. Hilarion kicks the crap out of Disneyan imitations. The castle's walls blend into the mountainside, concealing the tunnels, courtyards, and chambers that make up the steep climb to the top. From the high **Tower of Prince John**, you can gaze out towards Girne far below and look down at where, in the 14th century, a deluded Prince John of Antioch hurled his Bulgarian bodyguards, suspecting them of treason. Climb 360 steps to the elevated upper ward, where you can walk along the castle's outer walls. *(In summer, open daily 9am-5pm; winter 9am-1pm, 2-4:45pm. $3.30, students $.40.)* Walking to the castle is prohibited since a military base is on the way, and photos can be taken only after passing military property. The road up has spectacular views, though twisty, cliffside roads are not for the faint of heart. Dolmuş don't head up to St. Hilarion, so either rent a car or take a taxi ($24 round-trip from Girne; one-hour stop at the castle included).

BEYLERBEYİ (BELLAPAIS ABBEY)

This tranquil hillside village 6km east of Girne contains one of Northern Cyprus' most notable sights, the stunning Gothic **Bellapais Abbey** (a corruption of the French name *Abbaye de la Paix*, or Abbey of Peace). Building began in the late 12th century on a home for Augustinian monks fleeing Jerusalem. Plundered by the Genoese, sacked by the Turks, and snatched by the British (for road-building materials), these days the abbey basks in restored beauty. Thirty-meter cypress trees tower above the delicately arched cloisters and silvery olive groves. Inside, flying buttresses support the majestic remains of vaulted roofing and romantic stone balconies. Illuminated for artistic performances, Bellapais' nocturnal beauty will take your breath away. *(Abbey open daily 8am-7pm. $3.30, students $.40.)* The **Kybele Restaurant**, inside the abbey's courtyard, overlooks the sea and serenades guests with baroque and classical music. It serves tasty, if slightly pricey food, and features a wine house. (☎815 75 31 or 815 75 33. Fish *şiş* $9; local wines $7-8 per bottle. Open 11am-11pm.) The village itself is worth a stroll if you have the time. **Erol's Restaurant** (☎815 36 57), in neighboring Ozanköy, 1km from Bellapais on the main road towards Girne, serves stellar Cypriot cuisine, with 24 types of Cypriot *meze* ($4) and vegetarian *şiş kebap* ($4). This popular restaurant often fills up, so reserve in advance. Since there is no public transportation to either village, your options are to either hire a taxi ($6.20 one way) or to rent a car and follow the signs east out of town.

KARAOĞLANOĞLU

Four kilometers west of Girne, and stretching about 2km along the coastal road, the village of Karaoğlanoğlu offers lovely beaches and excellent accommodations, including some luxurious villas. Karaoğlanoğlu can be reached via the dolmuş to Lapta ($.40) or a taxi ($4). The **PTT** (open daily 8am-1pm, 2-5pm) and a **police station** are in the center of town; head to Girne for other services.

The accommodations in Karaoğlanoğlu will leave you wondering why the rest of Northern Cyprus charges so much more. ■ **Silver Waves** offers well-furnished, beach-front apartment rooms with A/C. To get there, follow the signs for the Top Set Hotel, but instead of taking a right into the hotel's parking area, head straight toward the sea. Some rooms come equipped with kitchenettes and/or A/C. (☎822 24 18 or 822 32 08; fax 228 26 12. Continental breakfast $2.40. $9 per person.) The **Şendiniz Hotel** has well-furnished rooms with bath, most with A/C. A number of two-level duplex rooms with balconies and A/C are also available. To get there, follow the signs from the main road. (☎822 24 01; fax 822 22 30. Breakfast included. Singles $10; doubles $20; duplex rooms $24.) For something a bit more posh, try the **Mountain View Hotel & Bungalows,** marked by a series of conspicuous signs to the sea. Plush rooms with A/C, phone, and TV encircle the pool and bar area. (Breakfast $6. Singles $30; doubles $24; triples $21.)

The **Address Restaurant and Brasserie,** 13 Alı Aktaş Sok., makes for some fine seaside dining. Shrimp, *börek*, and cocktails run about $3, while a full fish or meat dinner ranges $7-10. (☎822 35 37. Open daily 12:30-3pm, 7-11pm.) Just within town limits as you head in from Girne, the **Pegasos Restaturant** offers a pretty standard menu backed by a strong bar and excellent conversation. (Open 11:30am-midnight.) On the other end of town, **Planter's Bar & Bistro,** 159 Karaoğlanoğlu Cad., serves European and Italian food ($12), with occasional live music. (☎822 22 19. Open 6:30pm-when customers leave.)

LAPTA (LÁPITHOS)

The town of Lapta, with its narrow, snake-like roads, covers the base of the mountains, growing in the cracks and sprouting on the jagged bluffs. Once a predominantly Greek village, it's now home to settlers from Paphos. Hotel-owned beaches and casinos provide most of the entertainment. Like many tourist spots, Lapta is separated into two distinct sections, one for locals and the other for visitors.

⟐⟐ TRANSPORTATION AND PRACTICAL INFORMATION. Dolmuş depart from the town square for **Girne** (frequent 7am-7pm, $.80). The **police station** and **PTT** (open M-F 8am-1pm, 2-5pm) are on the main road at the base of the mountain. Just a few hundred meters to the north and technically outside of the municipality borders is the tourist-oriented strip of seaside Lapta, marked by convenience stores, restaurants, discos, and expensive hotels.

⟐ ACCOMMODATIONS. The best deal is **Blue Song Bungalows,** about 100m east of the gaudy Celebrity Hotel and next to a convenience store with the same name. A perfect place to unwind, Blue Song offers four cabin-like bungalows. (☎821 83 92 or 825 21 96. $22 per night; $132 per week.) Providing basic facilities, **Büyük Kent** is located 100m up the alley from the town square. Frequented almost exclusively by locals. (☎821 85 55. Doubles $8, with breakfast $11.)

⟐⟐ FOOD AND ENTERTAINMENT. Hilltop Restaurant (☎821 88 84), by the old monastery, about halfway uphill to the springs, has a pleasant (if fenced-in) view of the valley below. A relatively tourist-free atmosphere and the sumptuous *kleftigo* (lamb roasted in a pot for 3hr.; $5 with chips and salad) make this place a winner. Hilltop also serves a Cypriot specialty: meat and tomatoes seasoned with dried *molehiya* (mint) leaves ($5). **Ali Paşa,** on the water, is a favorite among the Brits. European and Turkish offerings include several vegetarian options. (☎821 89 42 or 821 83 29. Lunch $2-3; dinner $5-7.) At **Başpınar** (☎/fax 821 86 61), perched above town by a spring, enjoy the house specialty, a goat dish cooked in a clay pot (Su and W; $6), and views of Lapta. Vegetarians should ask for the *moussaka* (eggplant with rice and yogurt; $7.20) or try some of the 20 *meze* dishes.

Students and young locals frequent the **Golden Bar,** on the beach by the Marmaris Hotel, for its good mix of music (European, American, and Turkish; sometimes live) and a fun clientele. (Beer $2; cocktails $2.50-4.) **Sunset Disco** (see **Girne: Enter-**

tainment, p. 461), a short drive away, is also popular. As for the "nightclubs" on the beach: let their run-down exteriors divert you to other stomping grounds.

🔲 **SIGHTS.** Fresh from an afternoon at the beach, hire a taxi ($2.40) to drive up to the **Başpınar** ("headspring"), which has supplied the town's water for over 3000 years. The view is the real attraction, and the walk downhill (30-45min.) allows you to chase the sun as it dives below the horizon. The brown **mosque** to the left (from the vantage point of the spring) was, like many mosques in Northern Cyprus, formerly an Orthodox church. To the right, a gray Orthodox **monastery** seems to occupy its own island. To get to either of these sites, you'll have to navigate a winding set of narrow roads. You may pass three or four wonderfully restored **Greek houses** with fruit gardens, the handiwork of local poet-cum-businessman-cum-politician Doğan Boransel. (Houses $200-$350 per week.)

LEFKOŞA AND ENVIRONS

LEFKOŞA (NORTH NICOSIA)

Sounds of construction and urban traffic dissolve into the shouts of children at play and machinery hums in scattered shops along the **Green Line.** A series of oil-drums, barbed wire, steel, and concrete barricades forms a sort of poor man's Berlin Wall, around which the Turkish and Greek Cypriot communities co-exist. Tourists wander the streets, gliding between Lefkoşa's older sights while casting a curious eye over the historically and politically salient divide. The mostly residential Lefkoşa lacks Cyprus' coastal appeal, so unless you appreciate the more honest face the town presents, a daytrip from a more comfortable base in Girne or Mağusa is probably your best bet.

Though it was founded in the 3rd century BC, Lefkoşa did not become the capital of the island until the 10th century AD, when Arab raids forced the Byzantine inhabitants to build a secure inland fortress. In the 12th century, the prosperous city was conquered by Roman Catholic Crusaders, and 200 years later it fell to the Venetians, who built the present city walls. Despite the added defenses, the Ottomans captured the city in 1570, and the arrival of the Turks marked the beginning of the island's modern ethnic conflict. In 1964, the Green Line was established to separate the Greek and Turkish sectors of the city, and ten years later the division was further cemented following the Turkish invasion. **The Green Line is considered a military restricted zone, and photography of it is prohibited.**

▐ TRANSPORTATION

Flights: Ercan airport, 17km from town, is serviced only by Turkish carriers. Taxis from the airport cost $16; be sure to fix the fare in advance. **Cyprus Turkish Airlines** (☎227 38 20 or 228 39 01) has an office on Atatürk Meydanı. Open M-F 8:30am-1pm, 2:30-5pm; Sa 9am-2pm. All Cyprus Turkish Airlines offices have timetables listing all flight times. Flights to: **Adana** (45min.; M, W, Su 4pm; F 3:30pm, 4pm; round-trip $120); **Ankara** (1hr.; daily at noon; $102, round-trip $135; students $62, round-trip $124); **Antalya** (1hr.; Su-F; $100, round-trip $130; students $60, round-trip $120); **Dalaman** (1¼hr.; W 5pm, Su 8:30am; $100, round-trip $130; students $60, round-trip $120); **İstanbul** (1½hr.; frequent daily flights; $110, round-trip $145; students $66, round-trip $132); **İzmir** (1½hr.; flights M, Th-Sa; $110, round-trip $145; students $66, round-trip $132). 5 flights per week to **Stansted, London**, via Antalya (4hr.; $250, round-trip $300; students $166, round-trip $300), and 2 per week to **Heathrow, London**, via İzmir (4hr., round-trip $316).

Buses and Dolmuş: From the otogar, buses run to: **Lefke** (every hr. 7am-6:30pm, $1.60); **Güzelyurt** (en route to Lefke); **Girne** (every 15min. 7am-7pm, $1.40); **Mağusa** (every 30min. 7am-7pm, $2). To get to **Ercan Airport,** ride the **Paşaköy** dolmuş and ask to be

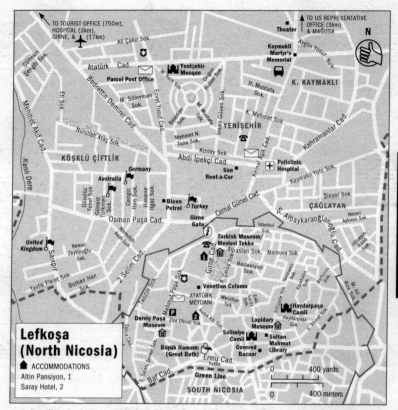

Lefkoşa (North Nicosia)

▲ ACCOMMODATIONS
Altin Pansiyon, 1
Saray Hotel, 2

let off at the airport (1, 2, 4, 4:30pm; $1). Additionally, dolmuş from the town square run the **Lefkoşa-Girne** route (7am-5:30pm, $1.85).

Car Rental: Bicen Petrol, 61 Bedrettin Demirel Cad. (☎223 38 53 or 227 16 80), at the gas station near the roundabout just past the Turkish embassy, rents Renaults and Nissans for a 3 day minimum ($28 per day). **Sun Rent-a-Car,** 10 Abdi İpekci Cad. (☎227 87 87), has jeeps ($50 per day) and automatic Nissans ($55 per day). Open M-Sa 8:30am-6pm, Su 8:30am-3pm.

✴ 🛈 ORIENTATION AND PRACTICAL INFORMATION

To get to town from the **otogar**, follow **Kemal Aşık Cad.** south for 1km (15min.; walk with the otogar on your right) to **Girne Gate** and the old city walls. From there, **Girne Cad.**, the main street, runs to the main square, **Atatürk Meydanı,** and continues to the **Green Line.** If you arrive from the south at the **Ledra Palace** crossing, walk 500m up the street to a roundabout with a Turkish **victory monolith** in the middle. Follow the city walls to Girne Gate.

Tourist Office: Lefkoşa houses Northern Cyprus' Ministry of Tourism (☎228 96 29), inconveniently situated at the extreme northwest of the city on Bedrettin Demirel Cad., 2km from Girne Gate. Deals mostly with administration, though it has an impressive array of brochures and booklets. Welcomes drop-ins. Open M 9am-6pm, Tu-F 9am-5pm; in winter M-F 8am-5pm. A smaller office (☎227 29 94) is more conveniently located just inside Girne Gate, in the stone structure in the middle of the road. English-speaking staff provides free maps. Open M 9am-4pm, Tu-Sa 9am-2pm.

Embassies: Turkey (☎227 23 14), at Bedrettin Demirel Cad., has a full embassy in Northern Cyprus. Open M-F 9am-noon. The following countries have "representative offices," offering some consular services: **Australia,** 20 Güner Türkmen Sok. (☎227 73 32; open Tu, Th 8:30am-12:30pm); **Germany,** 28 Kasım Sok. No.15 (☎227 51 61); **UK,** 29 Mehmet Aleif Cad. (☎228 70 51 or 228 38 61; open M, W, F 9am-1:30pm; Tu, Th 9am-1:30pm, 2:30-5pm); **US,** 6 Saran Sok. (☎225 24 40; open M-F 8am-1pm, 2-3:30pm), 3km out of town. For more information, you can contact the **Foreign Affairs Office** in Lefkoşa (☎227 23 31 or 228 76 47).

Currency Exchange: Several *döviz* offices along Girne Cad. Open M-F 8am-1pm, 2-4pm. **Banks** close at noon, but the large ones in Atatürk Meydanı reopen from 3:30 until nighttime. **TC Ziraat Bankası,** on the corner across from the smaller tourist information center, changes traveler's checks. Open M 8am-4pm, Tu-F 8am-1:30pm. **ATMs** are near Atatürk Meydanı; the one outside **Türkiye İş Bankası** takes foreign cards, including Cirrus/V/MC.

English-Language Bookstore: Rüstem Kitabevi, 26 Girne Cad. (☎228 35 06), just beyond Atatürk Meydanı in the direction of the Green Line. Open since 1937, it has collected a delightful number of Penguin and Oxford paperbacks as well as a wide array of fiction, non-fiction, and books on Cyprus. Open M-F 8am-6pm, Sa 8am-2pm.

Police: (☎228 33 11), on Girne Cad. close to Atatürk Meydanı.

Hospital: (☎228 54 41 or 223 2441). **Burhan Nalbantoğlu Devlet Hastanesı** (say that in one breath) is 3km from the town center on the road to Girne, roughly 700m from the Victory Monument. Look for the *Hastane* sign.

Telephones: Kontürlü Telefon (metered phone) offices pepper the Old City streets. Your cheapest bet ($.80 per minute to the US) is across the street from tourism office, facing Özner Taxi. **Pembe Telefon,** 30m right of the PTT, also has metered booths and sells phone cards. Open M-F 7:30am-2pm, 3:30-5:30pm. The **Government Telecommunications Department** is on Arif Salim Cad., halfway between Girne Gate and the otogar.

Post Office: (☎228 5448 or 228 59 82), on Sarayönü Sok., offers standard postal services, plus speedy APS delivery. From Girne Gate, take a right off Atatürk Meydanı. Open M 7:30am-2pm, 3:30-6pm; Tu-F 7:30am-2pm, 4-6pm; Sa 8:30am-12:30pm.

▝▘ ACCOMMODATIONS AND FOOD

Budget travelers may have difficulties finding suitable accommodations in Lefkoşa. The few hotels geared toward tourists ask US$20-40 per person and lack charm, while the many pensions generally cater to locals who can't afford apartments. For a roof and a clean bed, one of the best deals is the **Altın Pansiyon** (☎228 50 49), on the right side of Girne Cad. as you enter the gate, which offers 23 tidy if cell-like rooms with shared bath ($11). Inexpensive **restaurants** crowd the area near the Girne Gate; typical Turkish fare such as *döner kebap* goes for around $3.50. For a shift in routine, try **Cafe Palace,** marked by the massive yellow umbrellas in Atatürk Meydanı, just below the luxurious **Saray Hotel** ($70). Serves up burgers (including veggie) in addition to your standard *döner* plate. (☎227 1045. Burgers $1.50; with fries $2.50.) **Havuzbaşı Restaurant,** is pressed against a cement wall constituting part of the Green Line. It specializes in non-stop live music and affordable kebap-type meals. (☎228 4004. *Meze* $.80; meal $3; massive *rakı* bottle $9. Open 8am-3am.) Slightly nicer and more expensive joints are near the Selimiye Camii and in the New Town. The classier **Moyra Restaurant,** 32 Osman Paşa Cad., near the Tourism Administrative Office, specializes in a Cypriot menu complete with *şeftale köfte* (meat wrapped with intestines) and the to-die-for *katmer* dessert. (☎228 68 00. Meals $9; cocktails $4.)

◉ SIGHTS

The **Selimiye Camii/St. Sophia Cathedral** is a bizarre sight: a seemingly ancient cathedral looming in the shadow of its two soaring minarets. Despite the *sec-*

cade (prayer rugs) and Islamic calligraphy, the saints carved in the arches above the door and the flying buttresses show that it was once a Roman Catholic cathedral. Refurbished by the Ottomans in 1570, it was originally built in the Gothic style in 1326 by French architects at the behest of Queen Alix of Champagne. From Atatürk Meydanı, with Girne Gate at your back, continue down Girne Cad., looking left for the twin minarets. Beside it is the **Bedesten,** the 14th-century Orthodox Cathedral of St. Nicholas. Ottomans respectfully converted it first into a covered market and then a barn. Next door is the Bedesten's modern successor, where fruit, vegetables, and surprisingly tasteful souvenirs are available at decent prices.

With your back to the Selimiye Camii, head straight for a block and take a left to get to the 700-year-old **Büyük Hamamı,** once part of a 14th-century church. Since the time of the building's construction, Lefkoşa has risen about 2m, leaving the hamam slightly subterranean. *(Open daily 8am-10pm. Bath, exfoliation, and massage by professional male masseur $15.)* Just a dice throw away is the **Kumarcılar Hanı** (Gamblers' Inn). Formerly for 17th-century traveling merchants, it now houses Northern Cyprus's Antiquities Department, along with a small restaurant. *(Open M-F 8am-2pm.)* A block or two to the east and beyond the Selimiye Mosque is the Gothic-era **Haydarpaşa Camii,** once a Lusignan church and today a gallery. Face the Green Line and follow it to the right to the **Derviş Paşa Museum.** *(Open M 9am-2pm, 3:30-7pm; Tu-Su 9am-7pm. $1.80, students $.40.)* The former mansion of a notable 20th-century Cypriot newspaper owner, it has been converted into an unimpressive ethnographic museum displaying clothing and household goods. The **Mevlevi Tekke,** near the tourist office, once a Sufi *tekke,* is now a small Turkish museum housing life-size models of whirling dervishes and Islamic artifacts. *(Open M 7:30am-2pm, 3:30-6pm; Tu-F 7:30am-2pm. $3, students $.40.)*

░ DAYTRIP FROM LEFKOŞA: LEFKE (LÉFKA)

On the road stretching from Güzelyurt to Gemikonaği, on the far western rim of Northern Cyprus, lies a patch of Mediterranean coastline short-shrifted by most tourists. The area around Lefke has neither Girne's beaches nor Lefkoşa's history, but it does contain the ruins of Soli and Vouni. It offers a rural reprieve from low-rise, whitewashed cityscapes and from the last stubborn reminders of modernity.

SOLİ. Ancient Soli first attracted Assyrians around 700 BC and was later populated by Greeks. It is said to derive its name from Solon, the Athenian law-maker. The city changed hands, was razed, rebuilt, and abandoned after the Arab raids of the 7th century. Soli's two principal attractions, the **Roman theater** and the **basilica,** were built in the early 3rd and early 5th centuries AD, respectively. The stones that originally made up the 4000-seat theater were shipped off to Port Said in the 19th century to aid in the construction of the Suez Canal. Today's theater is a restored version of the original, located up a set of steep stairs. Christianity has a distinguished history in Soli, since St. Mark was reportedly baptized here. The large 4th-century basilica bears an amazing number of intricate floor mosaics. *(To get to Soli, follow the main road from Güzelyurt (this is the same road that heads west from Lefkoşa). Without turning off to Lefke (the sign points left to Lefke University), continue straight and follow signs to the ruins. If traveling by bus, buy a ticket to Lefke and ask the driver to drop you off at the turn; from there, the hike is about 2-3km. A taxi from Lefke costs $3 (one-way). From Lefkoşa a taxi runs $40. Renting a vehicle is easier, though more expensive considering the 3-day minimum. Soli is open daily 8am-7pm. $3.25, students $.80.)*

VOUNI. Formerly a hilltop palace of 130 rooms, Vouni was built by the Phoenician King of Marion in order to watch over Soli. Abandoned after a 380 BC fire, Vouni offers little more than a courtyard and a pair of cisterns, though the view of the Mediterranean and Güzelyurt Bay is stunning. According to locals, stolen gold was transported from pirate ships up to the palace via the cistern's tunnels.

The **Liman Restaurant & CMC Pub** is posted on the main road eastbound, just past the Lefke turn-off. Located across from the monstrous copper slag-heaps and mining equipment left over from the **Cyprus Mining Corporation (CMC)**, this restaurant serves a friendly plate of fish and chips ($7) from 10:30am-midnight. Hearing that Cyprus was an "island of copper," an American geologist started the mine in 1917. The entire operation was shut down during the Turkish invasion in 1974. Masks, mining helmets, and WWII-era curios fill the space along the walls. *(The 2nd most popular destination near Lefke (in a popularity contest of two sights), Vouni lies 10km west along the road leading to the Soli ruins. The road to the ruins is a treacherous one with endless blind curves and thousand-foot drops. Delicate-stomached travelers should take a taxi and close their eyes (one-way from Lefke $8, from Lefkoşa $40), or skip the trip altogether. Ruins open daily 10am-5pm. $3.25, students $.80.)*

MAĞUSA AND THE KARPAZ

MAĞUSA (FAMAGUSTA, GAZİMAGUSA)

The sea around Mağusa is separated from the city by a vast port—a port you may have already encountered disguised as the anonymous "seaport in Cyprus" where Shakespeare set his great tragedy ■ *Othello*. In Shakespeare's time, Mağusa was still the world's richest, wildest, most cosmopolitan, and glamorous city, *the* trading post between Christian West and Muslim East—a sort of agglomeration of modern-day New York, Paris, and Hong Kong. Every language could be heard in the streets, from Greek to French, Norse to Persian, Georgian to Amharic. Mağusa itself was, in addition to a point of transit, a supplier of countless luxury exports including filigree cloth, lace, wine, crystals, indigo, saffron, and gum mastic.

Stories hold that two Nestorian Lachas brothers, the city's richest merchant-princes, held banquets at which tables were piled with precious stones intended as party favors. Both the hearth and the kitchen stoves were fueled with fragrant sandalwood logs that perfumed guests and meal alike. The funds poured into hunting, jousting, and the procuring of women gradually earned Mağusa, even by the 14th century's none-too-rigorous standards, a reputation for depravity. St. Bridget of Sweden was especially gloomy in her indictment of "the new Gomorrah." Presumably unnerved, the citizens of Mağusa began church-building with their typical zeal. At one point 365 churches stood within the walls. Only 17 remain.

Crumbling and time-worn monuments to Mağusa's wonder years are scattered about the old city, ringed by the massive city wall. The center of the world no longer, Mağusa seems to have developed a quirky sense of irony at its own fall from grace. A ramble through the old town can take you past a gag shop, a reggae-themed restaurant, or a UN office-cum-barber shop. In the shadow of former greatness, Mağusa nonchalantly goes about its business. If you're in town around June 27-July 19, you can catch the exceptional **International Famagusta Culture, Art, and Tourism Festival**, which draws musicians, dancers, actors, and artists from all over the world. Performances ranging from reggae concerts to choirs to ballets are held in splendid venues such as the Othello Castle and the Salamis Theater.

▬ TRANSPORTATION

Buses: Run from the poorly organized otogar to: **Dipkarpaz** (2hr.; 1, 4pm, return 5:30am; $1.60); **Girne** (1¼hr., every hr. 7am-8pm, $1.80); **Lefkoşa** (1hr., every hr. 7am-8pm, $1.60). There are also buses out to the villages on the Karpaz Peninsula.

Dolmuş: From the Victory Monument roundabout to **Lefkoşa** (every 30min., $1.60). **Virgo Trans,** on the left as you head towards the otogar, runs to **Girne** (every hr. 7:30-9:30am, 6:30pm; $1.45).

Ferries: Although faster, cheaper, more comfortable sea-buses to Taşucu are available from Girne, **Turkish Maritime Lines** (☎363 59 95, 366 57 86, or 363 67 86; fax 366 78 40) operates ferries to **Mersin** (10hr.; Su, Tu, Th 10pm; $24, students with ID $21).

The office hides outside the old city walls, through Canbulat Bastion on Bülent Ecevit Cad. (follow the signs to *Kıbrıs Türk Denizcilik Bilet Satış Merkezi*). Open in summer 7:30am-2pm, 3:30-6pm; in winter 8am-1pm, 2-5pm. Buy tickets from the port agency.

Car Rental: The petrol station on the left just beyond the otogar rents Renaults ($30 per day). **Deniz Rent-A-Car** (☎378 81 47 or 378 82 98), based at the Mimoza Beach Hotel, 9km north of Mağusa, rents Renaults ($27 per day, with A/C $35) and automatic, air-conditioned Suzukis ($52). 3-day min. for both.

✹🛂 ORIENTATION AND PRACTICAL INFORMATION

Buses stop on the Lefkoşa road (Gazi Mustafa Kemal Bul.). Disembark and turn right; a 250m walk leads to the imposing and vaguely frightening **Victory Monument,** where Atatürk's stern visage emerges from a tower of suffering Turk Cypriots. Behind it are the old city walls. Follow the road outside the walls 500m to the tourist office. The sea is 400m farther away. On the left is the **Canbulat Bastion** and past it, the port where **ferries** arrive. The vacated **Maraş,** now a military zone, lies to the right. The museums, old churches, and Othello Tower are all within the old city.

Tourist Office: On Fevzi Çakmak Bul. Free city maps. English spoken. Open M 7:30am-2pm, 3:30-6pm; Tu-F 7:30am-2pm, 3-6pm; Sa-Su 9am-6pm.

Banks: Türkiye İş Bankası, between the Lala Mustafa Paşa mosque and the Namık Kemal Museum, has one of the city's few V/MC/Cirrus/Plus **ATMs.**

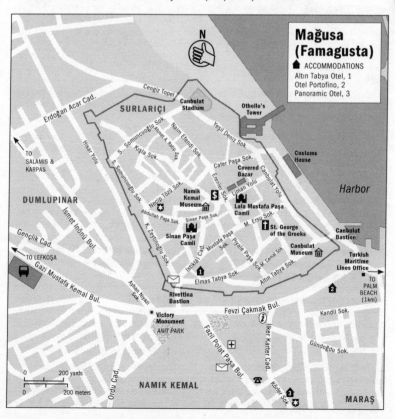

Mağusa (Famagusta)

▲ ACCOMMODATIONS
Altın Tabya Otel, 1
Otel Portofino, 2
Panoramic Otel, 3

Laundromat: Tözun temizleme (☎366 48 48). Stay right as the road forks 50m south of the Victory Monument rotary, and the cleaners will be on the right after another 50m. Thorough wash and dry for $4 per 4kg. Open M-F 8am-1pm, 2-6pm; Sa 8am-2pm.

Police: (☎366 53 10 or 366 53 21), on İlker Karter Cad.

Hospital: The **Mağusa Devlet Hastanesi** (☎366 53 28), on Fazil Polat Paşa Bul., is unmistakably white and yellow.

Phones: 60 Fazil Polat Paşa Bul. With the tourist office on your left, go left at the first major intersection. 2 card phones; sells phonecards on-site. Open daily 7:30am-8pm.

Internet Cafe: Cafe Net, next to TC Ziraat Bankası. Stay left as the road forks 50m south of the Victory Monument rotary, away from the city wall. $2 per hr.

PTT: Pass the tourist office (on your left) and turn left on the 1st street before the Victory Monument. Open M 7:30am-2pm, 3:30-6pm; Tu-F 7:30am-2pm. The smaller branch in the bastion, near Land's Gate, has no phones. Open M 9am-noon, Tu-F 9am-6pm.

ACCOMMODATIONS

Panorama Hotel and Restaurant (☎366 58 80; fax 366 59 90), next to the main PTT, is the cheapest deal in town. Enjoy breakfast in the terrace garden ($1.80) or wood-paneled eating room. 10 clean rooms with shared bath. Buy some peace for $9 per person.

Otel Portofino, 9 Fevzi Çakmak Bul. (☎536 43 92 or 536 43 93). By the tourist office. Recently renovated. Loaded rooms with TV, phone, tubs, A/C, and hair dryers. Some have an ocean view. Hotel bar. Breakfast $5. Singles $20; doubles $35; triples $50.

Altın Tabya Otel, 7 Kızılkule Yolu (☎366 53 63 or 366 25 85). Just to the right as you enter the old city. 18 stuffy rooms with ceiling fans and balconies, 14 of which have private baths. Oddly enough, a vast sitting room usurps the majority of hotel space. Breakfast included. Singles $14.50; doubles $23; triples $29.

FOOD

Cafes of varying quality pepper the old city. Liman Yolu, which leads between Namık Kemal Museum and Lala Mustafa Paşa mosque all the way to the wall by the port, has a number of fine restaurants.

Cyprus House Restaurant and Art Gallery (☎366 48 45). Across from the phone office. Serves a special steak filet with chips and salad ($7) and octopus ($5) in a tastefully decorated terrace garden. The art gallery features antique pots and pans, pastoral watercolors, and Dalí-esque oils. Live music Tu and Sa nights. Open 11am-3pm, 6pm-until stragglers stumble home. V, MC.

Desdemona Kebap & Meze Sarayı, 10m towards the Othello Castle from Canbulat Bastion. Serves *meze* meals—20 different hot and cold appetizers, as well as a kebap main course. A full *meze* ($9) is enough for two; coffee included. Tack on salad, bottled water, and fresh fruit for $13 total.

Viyana Kebap House, 19 Liman Yolu (☎366 60 37). Across from the Lala Mustafa Paşa Camii. Serves decent kebap in a gorgeous grape bower around a fountain, where you can avoid the restaurant's unsightly interior. *Adana kebap* $2.50.

SIGHTS

Though the old town is relatively small, it possesses an impressive number of medieval constructions in varying states of disrepair. The waterfront is consumed by the unattractive seaport. However, beautiful beaches are not a long walk away.

OTHELLO'S TOWER. Named in honor of Shakespeare's tragic figure, the castle itself has nothing in common with the story but the name itself. Nonetheless, this massive fortification, where Venetians imprisoned the last of the Veronese ruling family for 11 years, makes for some fascinating exploration. Originally built in the

THE HAZARDS OF BEING A ZZ-DRIVER If you are a young backpacker in Northern Cyprus, you will most likely be confused for a student at the English-language Eastern Mediterranean University in Mağusa. The EMU's international student body of 11,000 consists mostly of affluent mainland Turks and native Turk Cypriots. Large minorities of Pakistani, Sudanese, and West Africans come to EMU as an affordable and relatively close-to-home alternative to the universities in their own countries. A small minority of students from Britain and other English-speaking countries make up the rest. Being identified as an EMU student is generally not a good thing. Purportedly there to get an education, most students are more interested in Northern Cyprus's recreational attractions. Rental agencies are reluctant to rent cars to local students, and the mainland Turks who drive over in their Mercedes-Benz or BMWs are required to bear a special license plate that begins with the letters "ZZ." The notorious "ZZ-driving" refers both to the license plates and to the less-than-straight lines traced by these often inebriated students. Casino and bar-side streets pulsate with car-stereo music as teenagers cruise by in a motorcade of flashy cars. They're an affable bunch to associate with, but student backpackers might avoid a few cold shoulders from Cypriots if they make it clear that they are in fact students from overseas.

12th century, the tower is Mağusa's oldest standing building. In the 15th century, the Venetians transformed it into an artillery stronghold, reportedly on the advice of a young visitor named Leonardo da Vinci. The large courtyard is still occasionally used for delightful open-air performances, especially during the cultural festival. *(In the northeast corner of the old city. The tower is hard to miss. Head down to the waterfront and follow the city wall north. Open daily 10am-5pm. $2.40, students $.80.)*

LALA MUSTAFA PAŞA MOSQUE. The Lusignans originally dubbed this Gothic edifice (Mağusa's largest house of God), **St. Nicholas' Cathedral.** When the Ottomans captured Mağusa, they removed all the statuary and representational stained glass, slapped down some carpets, erected the minarets, and—*voila!*—the gorgeous Lala Mustafa Paşa Mosque. *(In the center of town, on Liman Yolu Cad. As the largest building in town, it is visible from a distance. Small donation expected.)*

BEACHES. The beaches around Mağusa are among the largest and most beautiful on the island. **Palm Beach,** beneath the large hotel of the same name, is the closest. From Canbulat Bastion, follow the sea 1km north. A large stretch of sand extends north of Salamis, where beaches are mostly owned by one hotel or another, but are nevertheless hospitable to non-guests. Exemplary, and free, **Mimoza Beach,** 9km north of Mağusa, rife with tourists and young people and welcomes non-residents of the commendable three-star **Mimoza Beach Hotel** (singles $34; doubles $50). Some quieter beaches lie up the coast towards the Karpaz Peninsula.

CITY WALLS. Though impressive, the **city walls** and surrounding **moat,** the result of 20 years' labor by 16th-century Venetians, fell somewhat short of their intended purpose; after a vicious year-long siege, the city fell to the Ottomans in 1571. For a spectacular view and an idea of the thickness of the walls, climb the ramps to the **Rivettina Bastion.** The **Canbulat Museum,** inside the **Canbulat Bastion,** houses a small collection of odds and ends that includes Bronze Age, Venetian, and Ottoman artifacts, Venetian maps and charts drawn up to plan the city's defense, a 16th-century hand-printed Koran, and the tomb of the Ottoman commander for whom the museum is named. *(The Rivettina Bastion is immediately left of the entrance to the old city. The Canbulat Bastion is in the southeast corner of the city: from the entrance to the old city, take a right and follow the wall. Canbulat Museum open daily 8am-7pm. $2.40, students $.60.)*

OTHER SIGHTS. Facing the entrance of the Lala Mustafa Paşa Mosque, go right for a few blocks to reach the 15th-century **Church of St. George of the Greeks,**

which combines Gothic and Byzantine styles. Its original domed roof was destroyed in the Ottoman invasion; cannonball marks are still visible on some walls. On the other side of the Lala Mustafa Paşa Mosque, stands the **Church of St. Peter and St. Paul,** complete with flying buttresses. It was built by a 14th-century merchant from the profits of a single business transaction and later converted to the **Sinan Paşa Mosque.** Across the road, a car park infringes on the site of the **Venetian Governor's Palace,** but enough of the walls and ruined staircases still stand to clamber around in. Next to Sinan Paşa Mosque is the **Namık Kemal Museum.** The Ottoman poet Namık Kemal (1840-1888) was exiled to this building from 1873 to 1875 for criticizing the sultan. The upper story contains first editions, photos, letters, and Kemal anecdotes. *(Open M-F 8am-2pm. Free.)* Outside is the **Dungeon.** Head away from Othello's Tower and the sea to pass, on the left, the twin chapels of the **Knights Templar** and the **Knights of St. John of Jerusalem,** which are usually kept locked. Next, go straight to the 14th-century **Nestorian Church,** a.k.a. **Church of St. George the Exiler.**

DAYTRIP FROM MAĞUSA: SALAMIS

Legend has it that Salamis, one of the nine ancient cities of Cyprus, was founded in the 11th century BC by **Teucer,** a hero in the *Iliad* and famed father of the Trojan people. The town was at one time the capital and richest city on the island. The oldest anecdote about Salamis appears in the 5th book of Herodotus, who writes that in 502 BC, the Persian of Amathus decapitated Onesilos of Salamis and hung his head over the city's gates. A swarm of bees moved in to the hollowed head and filled it with honeycomb. Interpreting this as a pro-Onesilos gesture by the gods, the Amathusians made yearly sacrifices to their former Salamisian enemy. After Arabs sacked Salamis in the 7th century, it was left covered in sand until its excavation 1000 years later. It was thus spared the looting of the rowdy Middle Ages.

Eight kilometers north of Mağusa, Salamis is divided in two by the road that leads up the Karpaz Peninsula. To the east, between the road and the sea, lie the mostly Roman remains of the ancient city, which include the well-preserved **gymnasium** and the semi-circular **theater.** To the west lies the **necropolis of ancient Salamis** and, further down, the **tomb** of and **museum** in honor of **St. Barnabas.**

The Dipkarpaz bus, leaving from the Mağusa otogar can drop you at the signposted turn-off for the ruins (1, 4pm; $.80). Getting back might be more of a challenge, as the return bus only comes by very early in the morning (5:30am). There will probably be no cabs waiting outside the ruins, but you will be sure to find one at the **Mimoza Beach Hotel,** which is a pleasant half-hour walk north of Salamis, along the beach. Cab rides to and from the ruins should cost about $5.

ROMAN SALAMIS. To the right of the entrance stands Salamis' best preserved building, the **Palaestra** (gymnasium), built by the Emperors Trajan and Hadrian after an earthquake destroyed the city in 76 AD. It was constructed by slaves who transported the columns in small wooden boats from Turkey, Greece, and Italy. The Palaestra's swimming pool is surrounded by beautiful marble statues, whose heads, unfortunately, the statues' heads were pilfered for use as garden ornaments in the 16th and 17th centuries. Beside the Palaestra lie the elaborate baths, comprised of the **sudatorium** (sweating room), the **caldarium** (hot water baths), and the **frigidarium** (cold rooms). In the central *sudatorium,* a fresco fragment depicts Hylas, Hercules's lover, refusing the water nymphs. The *sudatorium* in the southeast corner of the structure contains a couple of surviving mosaic fragments.

To the left, wander through the labyrinth of corridors and ruined walls that were once residences and public buildings. Take the opportunity to marvel at the Roman fascination with temperature control—under many floors, air vaults supported by 2m pillars of terra-cotta tile are exposed. These **hypocausts,** connected by air ducts to outer furnaces, were stoked day and night by slaves. Nearby is the **theater,** built during the reign of Augustus. The original seating capacity was 15,000. The lower seats are original; the nose-bleed seats are 1960s replicas. The theater was used for gladiator shows and bawdy plays. Today it is only occasionally used, usually during the **Mağusa Cultural Festival.** Ask at the entrance of the ruins about upcoming events. From the theater, follow the paved road and bear left at the fork to find other ruins which haven't weathered the centuries quite as well. Just beyond the **late city wall** to the south is the 2000-year-old **agora.** It is surrounded by a wrecked colonnade at the end of a 48km stone aqueduct. The city also contains a **Temple of Zeus,** with a podium that affords a view of the *agora,* and three basilicas. Two of them, **St. Epiphanios** and **Kampanopetra,** both have some interesting mosaics and views. The third with baptismal basins has no name. *(Site open daily during daylight hours. $3.20, students $.40. Visitors can drive through the ruins, maneuvering around ancient columns like a timorous bull in a china shop. Stop-and-go touring (with a car) will take a good 90min.; the sights are too spread out to see all of them by foot.)*

CHRISTIAN SALAMIS. The St. Barnabas Monastery, officially the **St. Barnabas Icon and Archaeological Museum,** is 400m up the road from the Necropolis. Some claim that St. Barnabas was a Cypriot Jew from Salamis, educated in Jerusalem, who returned to Cyprus with St. Paul in 45 AD to help spread Christianity. St. Barnabas and St. Paul were initially ill-received in Paphos, where Paul was bound to a pillar and beaten. When he converted the Proconsul to Christianity, however, Cyprus became the first nation with a Christian ruler. In addition to working with Paul, Barnabas was a scribe, who used to carry a copy of the Gospel of Matthew. Since he had accepted Christianity, the Jews eventually stoned Barnabas to death for being a traitor. Some 430 years later, St. Barnabas appeared in a dream to Archbishop Anthemios of Salamis, revealing his grave's location. After having the grave opened, the Archbishop took the martyr's remains, identifiable by the Gospel that he carried, to Emperor Zeno in İstanbul. Suitably impressed, Zeno commissioned the building of the Monastery of St. Barnabas and granted autonomy for the Church of Cyprus.

The church, which owes its Greek Orthodox appearance to the renovations of Archbishop Philotheas in 1756, houses a fabulous collection of 19th- and 20th-century icons. Now an archaeological museum, the monastery contains a well-arranged and labeled array of artifacts, from 9000-year-old rocks to what might be the only 2600-year-old toys you will ever see—tiny horse-drawn chariots with real turning wheels. Finally, 150m from the monastery is the chapel **tomb of St. Barnabas.** If it is locked, get the key from the custodian. The actual body of St. Barnabas has since been moved to Jerusalem. *(Open daily 9am-7pm. $.80, students $.40.)*

THE NECROPOLIS OF SALAMIS. Covering about 7 square kilometers, the site consists of the small, indoor **Royal Tombs Museum** and a series of excavated tombs, dating from the Bronze Age to the Byzantine period. Without a car, getting to these scanty ruins is burdensome, and most visitors won't cover all of the razed ruins. The entombed kings and nobles have long ago disintegrated and their grave treasures are scattered among faraway museums, but you can peer through the windows at the skeletons of several royal horses unearthed near the surface of the tombs. Accessible from this yard is the stone mausoleum, oddly called **St. Katherine's Prison,** dating from 700 BC. It has yielded countless archaeological curiosities, including an ivory-panelled throne and a bronze cauldron decorated with griffins, now in a southern Cyprus museum. Following the dirt road that passes the ticket booth for another 50m south, you will reach the **Necropolis of Cellarka,** the densest concentration of tombs. *(As you head away from Mağusa, take a left about 500m before the turn-off to Roman Salamis. The ticket office is a short distance up a small dirt road veering off to the left. Driving to the tombs and walking around shouldn't take more than half an hour. Open daily 8am-sunset. $3.20, students $.40.)*

KARPAZ PENINSULA

The Karpaz is Northern Cyprus' most remote region, comprised of arid, gently sloping hills covered with shrubs, wildflowers, and the occasional olive and mulberry grove. It is believed that Teucer, the founder of Salamis, first landed in Karpaz (near Yenierenköy), later one of the largest baronies under the Lusignans.

A narrow, paved road meanders from Girne along Cyprus' northern coast before turning inland. Traversed by the occasional flock of sheep, this curvy route is popular with tourists; you'll feel like the star of an SUV commercial. A dirt-road turnoff just after Esentepe brings you to the unspoiled **Antiphonitis Church**, which houses a number of beautiful, 12th-century frescoes. Continuing down the coast, you'll reach the gorgeous, 10th century **Kantara Castle.** Perched 610m above sea level, Kantara is one of the three Byzantine mountain castles (St. Hilarion and Bufavento being the other two), and it offers majestic views of the sprawling peninsula. Supposedly a castle of 101 rooms, legend holds that the person to discover the 101st will enter paradise. (*Accessing Kantara can be a pain; a good five hours is requisite whether you take the coastal route, the inland road from İskele, or the more direct one from Boğaz (not for those afraid of heights). Time permitting, this castle-lover's paradise absolutely merits a visit. (Open daily 9am-5pm. $1.60, students $.40)*

Once inland, follow the highway north and you'll hit the small town of **Yenierenköy**, a pleasant road stop that offers one of the peninsula's better accommodations. With friendly management and an English-speaking proprietor, the **Theresa Hotel** sits 7km past the town, next to the 16th-century Therisos church. It offers 18 comfortable rooms with clean baths, hot water, electricity, and balconies. (☎374 4266. Breakfast included. Singles $15; doubles $18.) A seaside restaurant serves fish with the sunset for about $4 per person. A few kilometers after the hotel, a marked turnoff to Sipahi will bring you to the 6th-century **Basilica of Ay Trias,** where breathtaking mosaics sprawl beneath columnar ruins. Before Dipkarpaz, signs will mark a side road to the **Eleousa Monastery,** 1½km from the main road. While the site is an unimpressive ramble, the neighboring **Elusa Manastırı Pansiyon** offers five enormous (albeit basic) rooms with private bath and shaded restaurant ($6 meals) for Karpazian stragglers. (☎855 85 53. Singles $11; doubles $16.)

The highway splits at **Dipkarpaz,** the largest village on the peninsula, where 400 of the 3000 inhabitants are Greek Cypriots. Before reaching the town, you'll pass the seaside **Blue Sea Hotel,** which offers 11 well-kept rooms without A/C or fans. (☎372 23 93. Breakfast included. Singles $15; doubles $20; triples $30.) Nearby **Livana Hotel and Restaurant** has a Peter Pan-ish ambiance, though similar prices can buy you incomparable luxury. Eight treehouse-style bungalows have double beds with mosquito netting and *à la turka* outhouses. Not into the Tarzan thing? Try the 14 indoor rooms (nine have private baths), which are genuinely unimpressive, but livable. (☎372 23 96. Breakfast included. Singles $14.50; doubles $21.)

The fine white sands of **Turtle Beach,** along the road past Dipkarpaz (fork right after the Atatürk statue, at the coffee shop), are among the last in the Mediterranean frequented for egg-laying by the endangered **loggerhead** and **green turtles.** In July and August, the turtles frantically paddle sand to dig holes as deep as 1m where they lay eggs. You can crash here at the **Sea Turtle Beach Restaurant & Bar Bungalows,** where an array of wooden bungalows and tents makes for a summer-camp feel. (☎372 21 30. Singles $8; doubles $13; tent rental $13; tent owners camp free.) Neighboring **Golden Beach,** which earns its name from the flaxen hues of the sand at sunset, offers similar bungalow lodgings.

The peninsula's real claim to fame is the Greek Orthodox **Apostolos Andreas Monastery,** at the tip of Zafer Burnu, approximately 25 poorly paved kilometers from Dipkarpaz. Some Christians believe that St. Andreas traveled to Palestine on a ship navigated by a half-blind captain and struck a rock where the monastery now stands, bashing open a magical spring that restored the captain's sight. A lush, chandeliered church with a gilded apse remains for visitors to pray and light candles. *(Open during daylight hours. Free.)* Just behind the church, the meditative can find solace by sitting on the rocks by the Mediterranean. Across the parking lot, stout, white **municipal-owned rooms** (☎372 23 96) with private bath are rented out for $10 per person; you can get keys and info from the monastery's guards. If you're intent on seeing the very tip of Northern Cyprus, a 5km stretch of road leads from the monastery to **Zafer Burnu**. The view is unbeatable, but its rocky, nightmarish road has left many a visitor desperately pumping a car jack.

Forking left at Dipkarpaz will bring you to **Ayios Philon** and **Aphendika**. The former is a 4th-century religious complex touched by a 12th-century Byzantine church. Aphendika contains the ruins of three 6th-century basilicas destroyed by subsequent Arab invasions. Don't flip a coin at the road fork; if you're pressed for time, veering right will bring you to more impressive sights and beaches.

Doing all this without a car is downright impossible. However, you can catch the Karpaz flavor by hopping one of the **buses** from Mağusa, which often leave at 1pm and 4pm, stopping briefly in Yenierenköy. The bus from Dipkarpaz leaves for Mağusa every morning at 5:30am. The problem with this is that the sights on the Karpaz are so spread out that a single bus trip will do you very little good. Most **taxis** won't go lower than about $50 for a trip that includes a stop at the monastery. **Prestige Tours** on Hürriyet Cad. in Girne offers a $40 full-day tour every Thursday, visiting Kantara, some churches, a beach, and Apostolos Andreas.

NORTHERN CYPRUS

PHRASEBOOK AND GLOSSARY

PRONUNCIATION

Turkish words are spelled with an adapted Roman alphabet. The language is phonetic; each letter has only one sound that is always pronounced distinctly. Nouns are the same in singular and plural. Words are usually accented on the last syllable; special vowels, consonants, and combinations include:

TURKISH	ENGLISH
c	*j* as in jacket
ç	*ch* as in check
ğ	lengthens adjacent vowels
ı / I	(no dot on the "i") *i* as in cousin
i / İ	*ee* as in peace
j	*zh*, like the *s* in pleasure, or *j* as in French *jadis*
ö	*ö* as in German *könig*, or *eu* as in French *deux*
ş	*sh* as in short

TURKISH	ENGLISH
u	*oo* as in boot
â	dipthong of *ea*, or faint *ya*
ü	*ew* as in cue; the French *tu*
ay	*eye* as in pie
ey	*ay* as in play
oy	*oy* as in toy
uy	*oo-ee* as in phooey

TURKISH PHRASEBOOK

GENERAL		
ENGLISH	TURKISH	PRONUNCIATION
Hello.	Merhaba.	mehrhaba
Goodbye (during the day).	İyi günler.	eee-YEE goon-lehr
Goodbye (in the evening).	İyi akşamlar.	eee-yee ak-SHAM-lahr
Good night.	İyi geceler.	eee-yee geh-jeh-LEHR
What's up/What's new?	Ne haber?	nah-behr?
How are you?	Nasılsın?	nah-sil-sihn?
May it come easy. (greeting to someone who is working)	Kolay gelsin.	koh-lay gehl-seen
Do you speak English?	İngilizce biliyor musun?	een-gul-EEZ-je beel-ee-YOR muh-SUN?
I don't speak Turkish.	Türkçe bilmiyorum.	Toork-che BEEL-mee-YOR-uhm
I am learning Turkish.	Türkçe öğreniyorum.	Toork-che ok-OO-yohr-um
I don't understand.	Anlamadım.	ahn-luh-mah-dim
Where are you from?	Nerelisin?	nehr-eh-LEE-sin?
I am American.	Amerikalıyım..	am-ehr-eh-KALi-yim
I am English.	İngilizim.	EEN-geh-leez-im
I am Irish.	İrlandalıyım.	ihr-lan-DAHLi-yim
I am Australian.	Avustralyalıyım.	ah-vu-STRAHLi-yim
I am from New Zealand.	Yeni Zelandalıyım.	yenih zeh-lan-DAHLi-yim
I am South African.	Güney Afrikalıyım	GUH-ney afri-KALi-yim
I am Canadian.	Kanadalıyım.	kahn-ah-DAHLi-yim
I am Scottish.	İskoçyalıyım.	Ihsk-oCHYAHli-yim.
My name is...	İsmim...	Ees-meem...
yes/no/maybe	evet/hayır/belki	eh-veht/hyer/behl-kee

GENERAL

ENGLISH	TURKISH	PRONUNCIATION
Please	Lütfen.	loot-fahn
Thank you.	Teşekkür ederim.	tesh-ekur edeh-rim
Pardon me.	Pardon.	par-dohn
What time is it?	Saat kaç?	sa-at ka-ch
May I help you?/Go right ahead.	Buyrun.	boy-RUHN
You're welcome/It's nothing.	Bir şey değil.	beer shey dee-eel
What is...	...ne?	neh?
I am a student.	Oğrenciyim.	OH-ren-jee-yeem
How old is...?	...kaç yaşında?	kach yash-in-dah?
who?	kim?	keem?
when?	ne zaman?	neh-zah-mahn?
yesterday/today/tomorrow	dün/bugün/yarın	doon/boogoon/yahr-un
One minute!	Bir dakika!	bee-dak-ka
I'm hungry.	Acıktım.	ach-ik-tim
I'm sorry.	Özür dilerim.	oz-oor deel-er-im
Where is the bathroom?	Tuvalet nerede?	too-walet nehr-e-de?
Help!	İmdat!	EEM-daht!
Police	polis	po-LEES
Can I buy you a drink?	Sana içki ısmarlayabilirmiyim?	SA-na eech-ki us-MAR-lee-ah-BEE-leer-mee-im?

IN A RESTAURANT

ENGLISH	TURKISH	PRONUNCIATION
Do you have food without meat?	Etsiz yemek var mı?	eht seez yemek vahr mi?
I am a vegetarian.	Vejetariyanım.	vej-e-tar-iyan-im
Do you have eggplant salad?	Patlıcan salatası var mı?	paht-lee-jan sahlatasi vahr mi?
Check, please.	Hesap, lütfen.	hesahp, lootfen
I want a glass of water.	Bir bardak su istiyorum.	beer bahr-dak soo eest-eee-yor-uhm
Can I have the salt/pepper?	Tuz/biber alabilirmiyim?	tooz/beeber/ahl-a-bee-leer-meey-um?
What's in...	...neler içinde, acaba?	neh-lehr eech-een-deh, a-jah-bah?
Are you open/closed?	Açık/kapalı mısın?	a-chik/kah-pah-li misin?
I didn't want...	...istemedim.	eestemedim
Compliments to the chef	Ellerine sağlık	ehleh-rih-neh sah-lihk

AILMENTS

ENGLISH	TURKISH	PRONUNCIATION
I need a doctor.	Doktora ihtiyacım var.	dohk-tor-ah eeh-tee-ya-cum vahr
My stomach hurts.	Midem ağrıyor.	mee-dehm ahr-EE-yor
My tooth aches.	Dişim ağrıyor.	dee-sheem ahr-ee-yohr
Where is a pharmacy?	Eczane nerede?	ej-ZAH-ne neh-reh-de?
I am looking for a dentist.	Dişci için arıyorum.	DEESH-jee ahr-ee-yor-uhm
I have a sore throat.	Boğazım ağrıyor.	bo-AH-zuhm AH-ree-yohr
I have diarrhea.	İshalım var.	EES-hahl-um vahr
I have a cold.	Nezlem var.	nehz-lehm vahr
I have a headache.	Başım ağrıyor.	bash-uhm ahr-ee-yor
I want medicine.	İlaç istiyorum.	eee-lach-i ee-stee-yohr-uhm

DIRECTIONS

ENGLISH	TURKISH	PRONUNCIATION
Where is...?	...nerede?	nehr-eh-deh?
I am looking for...	...için arıyorum.	eecheen ahr-ee-yohr-uhm

DIRECTIONS		
ENGLISH	**TURKISH**	**PRONUNCIATION**
left/right/straight	sol/sağ/doğru	sohl/sa-a/doh-oo
straight (said only to a taxi driver)	düz	dooz
I am going to ...	...ya gidiyorum.	...yah geed-EE-yohr-uhm
Turn left.	Sola dön.	sohl-ah dohn
one-way street	tek yön	teyk yohn
How far is it to...?	...a ne kadar uzakta?	...a neh kahdahr oozakta?
Where is the bus station/airport/ferry?	otogar/hava limanı/feribot nerede?	oh-tow-gahr/hah-vah lumahnu nehr-e-deh?
I'm going to...	...'a gidiyorum	...ah gee-dee-yohr-uhm
I'd like to get off.	Inecek var	EEN-ehjeck vahr
What time does it leave?	Saat kaçta kalkiyor?	sah-at kach-tah kahlk-ee-yohr?
Can I make a ticket reservation?	Rezervasyon yapabilir miyim?	reh-sehrVAH-seeyon yap-a-bee-leer mee-yim?
How long does it take?	Ne kadar sürür?	neh kahdahr SuOOR-oor?
Which bus goes to...?	...a hangi otobüs gider?	...a hahn-gee oto-boos GEE-dehr?
When is the next bus?	Sonraki otobüs kaçta kalkıyor?	sohn-rah-kee oto-boos kach-tah kahlk-EE-yohr?
Can I get out here?	Burada inebilirmiyim?	boor-ah-dah een-eh-bee-leer mee-yum?
Where does it leave from?	Nereden kalkar?	neh-reh-dehn kal-kar?
Slow down, please.	Yavaş lütfen.	yah-vash loot-fahn

IN A HOTEL		
ENGLISH	**TURKISH**	**PRONUNCIATION**
Is there an available room?	Boş odanız var mı?	bosh odaniz vahr mih?
single room/double room/triple room	tek/çift/üç kişilik	tehk/cheeft/ooch keesheeleek
Can I see it?	Bakabilirmiyim?	buk-ah-beel-EER mee-yeem?
Can we camp here?	Burada kamp yapabilirmiyiz?	boor-ah-dah kamp YA-PA-bee-leer-mee-iz?
Is there hot water?	Sıcak su var mı?	sijak soo vahr mi?
Is there a room with a shower?	Duşlu oda var mı?	DOOSH-lu odah vahr mi?

AT THE MARKET		
ENGLISH	**TURKISH**	**PRONUNCIATION**
Can I have _____ ?	Ben _____ alabilirmiyim?	ben _____ ala-beel-EER mee-yeem?
apple/pear/squash	elma/armut/kabak	elmah/armout/kabak
peach/banana/onion	şeftali/muz/soğan	shef-tali/mooz/sohan
How much is...?	...ne kadar?	neh kah-dar?
...is too expensive	...çok pahalı	chok pa-haa-li
No way! Impossible!	Hayır! İmkansiz!	hay-ir! eem-kahn-sizh!
Flattery will get you nowhere.	Yavşayarak bir yere varamazsın.	yahv-sha-YAR-ak beer yereh varah-mahsin

NUMBERS		
ENGLISH	**TURKISH**	**PRONUNCIATION**
zero	sıfır	si-fihr
one	bir	beer
two	iki	ee-KEE
three	üç	ooch
four	dört	durt

NUMBERS		
ENGLISH	TURKISH	PRONUNCIATION
five	beş	besh
six	altı	altih
sevn	yedi	ye-DEE
eight	sekiz	SEH-kuz
nine	dokuz	doh-KOOZ
ten	on	ohn
eleven	on bir	ohn beeer
twelve	on iki	ohn eekee
thirteen	on üç	ohn ooch
fifteen	on beş	ohn besh
twenty	yirmi	yeer-mee
twenty-one	yirmi bir	yeer-MEE beer
thirty	otuz	OH-tuhz
thirty-five	otuz beş	OH-tuhz besh
forty	kırk	kuhrk
forty-three	kırk üç	kuhrk ooch
fifty	elli	ahy lee
sixty	altmış	ahlt-mish
seventy	yetmiş	yeht-mish
eighty	seksen	sex-ahn
ninety	doksan	dohk-sahn
one hundred	yüz	yooz
one thousand	bin	been
million	milyon	meel-yohn
billion	milyar	meel-yahr
one and a half	bir büçük	beer booch-ook
one half	yarım	yahr-um
one quarter	çeyrek	chey-rehk

TIME AND HOURS		
ENGLISH	TURKISH	PRONUNCIATION
open	açık	ach-uk
afternoon	öğleden sonra	oy-leh-dehn sohn-rah
night	gece	ge-je
closed	kapalı	kap-ah-LIH
morning/evening/yesterday	sabah/akşam/dün	sah-bah/aksham/doon

WORDS AND PHRASES		
ENGLISH	TURKISH	PRONUNCIATION
beautiful/good/delicious	güzel	goo-ZEHL
bad/good	kötü/güzel	koh-too/goo-zehl
sad/happy	üzgün/mutlu	ooz-GOON/moot/LOO
hot/cold	sıcak/soğuk/	sijak/soh-ook
big/little	büyük/küçük	BOO-yook/KOO-chook
Cheers!	Şerefe!	she-reh-FEH
Bon Appetit!	Afiyet olsun.	Ah-FEE-yet ohl-sun
I love you.	Seni seviyorum	sehn-EEE sehv-EE-yohr-uhm
I want to dance.	Dans etmek istiyorum	dahns et-meck ee-STEE-yohr-uhm
Are you a pimp?	Pezvenk misin?	pehs-seh-vehnk mih-sihn?
I accept bribes.	Rüşvet alırım	roosh-veht AL-lih-rihm

WORDS AND PHRASES		
ENGLISH	**TURKISH**	**PRONUNCIATION**
I am not interested in you.	Seninle ilgilenmiyorum	sehn-ihn-leh eel-gee-LEHN-mee-yohr-uhm
Shame!	Ayıp!	Ahy-uhp
Go away!	Haydı git!	hah-dee, git
red/orange/yellow/green	kırmızı/turuncu/sarı/yeşil	kihr-mih-zih/tuh-RUN-suh/sar-ih/yeshil

GLOSSARY

ada: island

ağa: a minor noble in the Ottoman empire, modern usage refers to a person of local import

agora: marketplace or meeting area of an ancient Roman city

Ağustos: August

aile: family

Akdeniz: Mediterranean Sea

altın: gold

anahtar: key

apse: curved recess at the altar end of a church

Aralık: December

architrave: a wooden or stone lintel (beam) resting on columns.

at: horse

ayran: salty yogurt drink

bakkal: grocery

baklava: try it; you'll like it

balık: fish

bamya: okra

banka: bank

bay: man (as it is written on public bathrooms)

bayan: woman (see above)

bayram: holiday

bedesten: bazaar

belediye: municipal

bema: under Byzantines, flat part of altar; under ancient Greeks a raised platform or podium

bend: dam

bent: dam

benzin: gasoline

bey: a minor Ottoman title, it follows the first name as an honorarium

beyaz peynir: lit. "white cheese," similar to the Greek feta cheese

bilet: ticket

börek: a pastry with fillings, usually cheese

borstal: a British school for delinquent boys providing therapy and vocational training

boş: free, unoccupied

bouleterion: meeting place for local government in ancient Rome.

burada: here

caliph: lit. successor: the civil and religious head of the Muslim faith

camekan: a disrobing room of a *hamam*

cami: (sometimes "*camii,*" depending on modifier) mosque

Cuma: Friday

Cumartesi: Saturday

cumhuriyet: republic

cuneiform: wedge-shaped ancient inscriptions used by the Hitties, Assyrians, Persians, etc.

çarşaf: a bedsheet, or the full-length dress worn by religious Turkish women

Çarşamba: Wednesday

çarşı: market

çay: tea

çeşme: fountain

çiçek: flower

çıkış: exit

çorba: soup

dağ: mountain

deniz: sea

Denizyolları: Turkish Maritime Lines

devlet: state

Dikkat!: Careful!

doktor: doctor

dolma: lit. "stuffed," usually refers to peppers or tomatoes stuffed with rice or meat

dolmuş: shared taxi system, often confused with minibuses, which serve the same function

dolu: full

domates: tomato

döner: thinly shaved meat from a skewer

durak: stop

dürüm: sandwich of döner wrapped in a thin flour tortilla

eczane: pharmacy

Ege Deniz: Aegean Sea

Ekim: October
eski: old
et: meat
Eylül: September
exedra: semicircular niche
exonarthex: a transverse vestibule preceding the facade in a Byzantine church
eyvan: domed side chamber of an Ottoman religious building
ezan: Muslim call to prayer
faïence: A general term used to refer to various kinds of glazed earthenware and porcelain
gar: train station
garaj: small bus station
gazete: newspaper
gazeteci: journalist
ghazi: warrior for the Islamic faith
giriş: entrance
göbek taşı: lit. navel stone; the platform in the middle of the hot room of a *hamam*
göl: lake
gözleme: crêpe-like pancake with fillings
gümüş: silver
gün: day
hamam: Turkish bath
han: inn, usually in towns; also a title of a prince or a ruler
hanım: polite form of address for women, it attaches to the 1st name; analogous to "Bey"
hastane: hospital
hava alanı: airport
Haziran: June
hicri (hijra): the Muslim dating system, wherein time is measured from 622, the date of Mohammed's flight from Mecca to Medina
hisar: fortress
hoca: teacher in charge of religious instruction.
hürriyet: freedom, liberty
ızgara: grill; grilled food
içecekler: beverages
içki: alcoholic beverages
imam: prayer leader at a mosque
imaret: charitable house for travelers, often attatched to a medrese
indirim: sale/discount
isim: name
iskele: ferry/dock or jetty
istasiyon: train station
istiklal: independence
iwan: also eyvan, a vaulted or domed recess open on one side
jihad: purification, struggle with one's self

kaaba: shrine at Mecca containing a sacred black stone
kaftan: long robe or tunic
kahve: coffee
kale: castle, citadel
kapı: gate
kaplıca: developed hot springs
Karadeniz: Black Sea
Kasım: November
kervansaray: hotel located along a trade route
kese: exfoliatory scrub in a *hamam*
khan: respectful title, refers to lords or members of nobility (Mongol derivation)
kilim: tapestry weave mat
kilise: church
kitap: book
köfte: spiced meatballs
köşk: pavilion, kiosk
köpek: dog
kufic: thick, angular Arabic script attributed to the scholars of Kufa
kümbet: tomb or mausoleum
lahmacun: often called Turkish pizza, it is bread topped with ground meat and spices
liman: harbor
lokanta: restaurant
lokum: Turkish Delight
makarna: pasta
mahalle: district or neighborhood or a larger municipality or postal area
mantı: stuffed pasta, similar to ravioli
Mart: March
Mayıs: May
medrese: İslamic theological school teaching Islamic law (Shar'ia)
mescit: a prayer hall without a mimber; not used for the Friday prayer
Mevlana: lit. "master," Sufi spiritual leader; often used to refer to Rumi
meydan: town square
meze: appetizers—little salads and spreads that precede a full meal
mihrab: a niche elaborated into an ornate portal, it indicates the direction of Mecca and therefore of prayer
mimar: architect
mimber: The hooded dais reached by long stairs from which the Friday prayer is conducted
minare: Turkish for minaret; tall spires flanking mosques from which the call to prayer is issued
muezzin: mosque officer responsible for the call to prayer

APPENDIX

muqarna: decorated transitional element between walls and vault, often with a stalactite appearance

müze: museum

namaz: pen-air mescit or camii, especially for the army

naos: a temple or the cella of a temple

nargile: hookah

narthex: narrow vestibule along the west side of a church

nave: the principle, lengthwise aisle of a church

necropolis: cemetery

nehir: river

nöbetçi: on duty

Nisan: April

nymphaeum: temple of the Nymphs, an ornamental fountain with statues

Ocak: January

oda: room

orada: there

otel: hotel

otobüs: bus

otogar: bus station

öğrenci: student

pancration: an athletic contest involving wrestling and boxing

pansiyon: typical accommodation.

patlıcan: eggplant

park yeri: car park

Pazar: Sunday

Pazartesi: Monday

Perşembe: Thursday

pide: not to be confused with pita bread, pide is bread filled with cheese or meat

polis: police

proscenium: a raised platform in front of the stage-building used by Roman actors

PTT: post office (Posta Telefon Teleğraf)

Ramazan: The Muslim month-long fast

saat: hour or time

sağ: right

salata: salad

Salı: Tuesday

saray: palace

sarhoş: drunk

satrap: lit. "protector of the country," a governor under the ancient Persian Empire

saz: long-necked, fretted, stringed instrument used in Turkish folk music

sebze: vegetable

Selçuk: the first Turkish state in Anatolia (11th-13th centuries)

sema: a dervish ceremony

sima: the gutter of a classical building

sol: left

squinch: support, usually in the shape of an arch.

su: water

Sufi: an adherent to one of the mystical branches of Islam; sects include Mevlevi, Bektaşi and Naqshbandi

sultan: lit. "power," the ruler of the Ottoman Empire

süt: milk

stelae: narrow stone slab set upright bearing writing or decoration; used as a grave marker

stoa: a colonnade or unattached portico

şadirvan: fountain

şarap: wine

şehir merkezi: city center

şerefe: balcony of a minaret, also used in drinking as a toast ("To your health")

Şubat: February

tatlı: lit. "sweet," usually refers to dessert

tavla: backgammon

tekke: Sufi lodge

Temmuz: July

THY: Turkish Airways (Türk Hava Yolları)

TML: Turkish Maritime Lines

transept: the "wings" of a church, perpendicular to the nave

tufa: soft rock

tuğra: the seal of a sultan

türbe: freestanding tomb

tuvalet: toilet

ulema: Ottoman religious intelligentsia

umma: Muslim community

Valide Sultan: The mother of the sultan

vezir: Vizier, the chief advisor to the Sultan, responsible for managing state affairs

yabancı: foreigner

yalı: ornate wooden house along the Bosphorous

yasak: forbidden, prohibited

yayla: flat grassy highland area

yeni: new

yer: room/place

ylyecekler: food

yok: indicates a lack of something

yol: road

INDEX

A

Abana 385
Abbasid Caliphate 10
Abdul Mecid 123
Abdülaziz 14
Abdülhamid II 15, 124
Abdülmecid I 14
Abkhazia 32
Abraham, the Prophet 444
  birthcave of 447
Academy of Fine Arts 23
accommodations 55
Achilles 148, 166
Acropolis, Pergamon 177
Adada 346
Adalar. See İstanbul,
  Prince's Islands, Adalar.
Adam Atacaği 294
Adam Kaylar, Kızkalesi 300
Adana 302–305
Adanus, god of weather
  302
address abbreviations 68
adhan 26
Adrianople. See Edirne.
Aegean Coast 164–229
aerogrammes 57
Afyon 346–348
Afyonkarahisar, old Afyon
  347
Ahmed Cemal Paşa 15
Ahmet, Sultan 103
AIDS 52
aile 55
air travel 64
airports
  İstanbul 82
  İzmir 182
  Adana 303
  Ankara 352
  Antalya 282
  Kars 429
  Kayseri 332
  Şanlıurfa 445
  Van 434
Aizanoi, ruins of 350
Akbil 84
Akçay 170
Akdamar Church, near Van

436
Aksaray 329
Akyaka (Gökova) 228
Alaeddin Keykubad,
  Selçuk sultan 335, 426
Alaiye, ancient Alanya 293
Alanya 291–294
Albanians 125
alcohol 48
Aleppo, Syria 309
Alevi 31
Alexander Sarchophagus
  109
Alexander the Great 166,
  393, 444, 454
  birth of 193
  slicing the Gordion knot
    366
  the teaching of 169
Alexandria 8
  library of 179
Ali, nephew of Muhammed
  27
Allah 25
alphabet (Turkish) 17
Altınkum Beach 192, 209
alternatives to tourism 72
altitude, high 50
Amasra 383–384
Amasya 393–396
Amathus 472
American Express 43
American Red Cross 49
Amyntas, tomb of 263
Anıt Kabır 363
Anadolu Hisarı 80
Anahid, Persian goddess
  431
Anamur 294–297
ANAP 18
Anatolian Civilizations
  Museum, Ankara 363
Androclus 193
Anemurium, Anamur 295
Ani 30, 430
Ankara 352–366
Antakya 8
Antalya 282–286
Antalya Museum 279, 285
Anthemius of Tralles 101
Antioch. See Antakya.

Antiochus I 443
Antony. See Cleopatra.
ANZAC 147, 148
ANZAC Day 148
Aphrodisias. See Geyre.
Aphrodite, statue of 254
Apollo 188, 271, 407, 444
Apollonius, 216
Apostolos Andreas
  Monastery 474
apricot markets, Malatya
  443
apse 21
Aquarium 247
Aqueduct of Valens 115
arabesk 24
Archaeology Museum
  İstanbul 109
Arians 9
Armenia 430, 432
Armenians 30, 121, 298,
  299, 397, 434
  churches 432, 436
  religious history of 432
Artemis 188, 193, 196, 271
arts 20–24
  Byzantine 21
  Greco-Roman heritage
    20
  Islamic art and
    architecture 22
  modern Turkish art 23,
    365
  Ottoman architecture 23
  Ottoman decorative arts
    23
  Selçuk architecture 22
Artvin 416–417
Arz ar-Rum (Erzurum) 423
Asclepion
  Kos 238
  Pergamon 178
aşıks 24
Aspendos 287
Ass. See Booty
Assos. See Behramkale.
Assyrians 454
Asya 81
Atatürk
  Battle of Gallipoli 147
  cloud representations of
    364

conversion of Aya Sofia
101
last brushes with
medical world before
death 335
mausoleum of 363
reform agenda of 16
the '36 Lincoln sedan of
364
unflattering comic strips
of 115
War of Independence 16
ATMs 44
au pair 73
Augustus 196
Auspicious Event 111
Avanos 324
Avrupa 81
Aarup
Aya Sofia 21
İstanbul 80, 101
İznik 162
Trabzon 407
Ayanis Fortress, near Van
438
Aydın 215–216
Ayder 414–415
Ayder Festival 414
Ayvalık 171–173

B

Bagratid Armenia 430, 431
Bahçeli, Develt 19
Balıklı Kaplıca 376
Balım Sultan 331
Balat 118
Balkan Wars 15
Ballıca Mağarası 373
ballet 363
banks 42
Barbarossa, Emperor
Frederick 124, 298
bargaining 45
Barhal 418
Basil I 407
basilica 21
Basilica of Saint John 200
beaches
İnebolu 385
Abana 385
Akçay 170
Altınkum Beach 192, 209
Amasra 384
Anamur 294
Antalya 286

Bodrum 224
Bozcaada 167
Camel Beach 268
Datça 253
Eğirdir 345
Girne 460
İçmeler 250
İztuzu Beach 258
Kaş 276
Kaputaş Beach 273
Karaoğlanoğlu 462
Kervansaray 460
Köyceğiz 255
Mağusa, Northern
Cyprus 471
Marmaris 247
Samos 241
Sinop 389
Tirebolu 403
Behramkale (Assos) 169–
170
Bektaşi 28, 331
Bellapais Abbey. See
Beylerbeyi.
Bergama 8, 174–179
Beyazit Camii 112
Beyazit I 159
Beyazit II 112, 142
Beyazit Külliyesi (Beyazit
Complex), Edirne 142
Beylerbeyi Palace 129
Beylerbeyi, near Girne 462
Beylik Period 12
bible stories 437
bisexual travelers 70
Black Sea Coast 377–421
Black Sea Ferry. See
ferries.
Black Sheep Turkomans
438
Blue Caves 268, 277
Blue Mosque 23, 102
Boat Trips 247
Bodrum 217–225
body language 33
Boğazkale 366–369
book bazaar, İstanbul 110
booty 107, 170
foreign brides 314
shaking 258
Sultan Got Back 106
Talking Ass 346
teenage wives 167
Tom Jones 144
booze cruises 263
Boransel, Doğan 464
border crossings

Bulgaria 143
Georgia 412
Greece 144
Syria 309
Bosphorus 81
Bozburun 250
Bozcaada (Tenedos) 167–
169
Brighton Beach 147
bullfights 417
bungee jumping 294
Bursa 137–159
butterflies, Jersey Tiger 268
Butterfly Valley
near Ölüdeniz 268
Büyükada 130
Byzantine architecture 21
Byzantines 101
Byzas 80

C

Caesar, Julius 166
calcium pools 209
Calligraphy Museum,
İstanbul 112
calling cards 58
camping 56
Şenyuva Valley 413
Abana 385
Akyaka 228
Altınkum Beach 192
Ankara 360
Bergama 176
Boğazkale 367
Bozcaada 168
Çavuşin-Zelve 320
Çeşme 191
Çoruh Valley 419
Datça 252
Eğirdir 345
Edirne 141
Foça 181
Göreme 316
Kaş 276
Kuşadası 205
Mt. Uludağ 159
Olimpos 279
Ölüdeniz 267
Pamukkale 211
Patara 270
Saklıkent Gorge 265
Sinop 389
Ünye 397
Van 435
Yusufeli 418
Çanakkale 148–151
Çanakkale Memorial 148

Cappadocia 311–337
car insurance 67
car rental 67
Caria 213, 225
Carian rock tombs 258
Caricature Museum
  (Karikator ve Mizah
  Müzesi) 115
cash cards 44
Castle of St. John 402
Çatalhöyük 343, 363
Caunus. See Dalyan and
  Kaunos.
Çavuşin-Zelve 320
çay 33, 412
CDC 49
Çeşme 189–192
  Film Festival 189
Centers for Disease
  Control (CDC) 49
Central Anatolia 310–376
Chalcedon, Council of 441
charter flights 62
children and travel 71
churches, Greek
  Ag. Francis, Rhodes 232
  Ag. Nik. Fountoucli,
    Rhodes 235
  Christian Basilica of St.
    Paul, Kos 239
  Kos Greek Orthodox
    Cathedral 238
  of the Transfiguration,
    Samos 241
Churchill, Winston 147,
  148
Çiçek Pasajı 121
Çiller, Tansu 19
Çirağan Sarayı 125
Circassians 32
circumcision 118
circumcision festival,
  Giresun 400
Cirrus 44
Cleopatra 293
  Antony's token of love
    for 179
  honeymoon with Marc
    Antony 228
Cleopatra's bath 263
Clerides, Glafkos 456
climate 39
Cold War 17
Colossus of Rhodes 232
Column of Constantine
  103

Comana Pontica. See
  Tokat.
Comneni Dynasty, Trabzon
  403
Constantine 8, 80, 103
Constantine Monomachus
  102
consulates
  Adana 303
  Antalya 284
  Bodrum 218
  Edirne 140
  İstanbul 89
  İzmir 184
  Marmaris 244
  Mersin 301
  Trabzon 404
contraceptives 53
Coracesium. See Alanya.
corruption 413
Çoruh Valley 418–419
Cotton Castle 209
Council of Nicaea 9
Council Travel 61
credit cards 44
Crivas, General George
  455
Crusaders 248
Crusades 80, 101, 222,
  298, 459
customs 33
Cybele, mother goddess of
  Anatolia 182, 193
Cyprus 18, 451–475
Cyprus Mining Corporation
  (CMC) 468
Cyrus II 7

D

Dalaman 258
Dalyan and Kaunos 256–
  258
Damlataş Cave 294
Daniel in the Lion's Den
  208
Dardanelles 144
Darius 7
Datça 251–253
dehydration 50
Delphic Oracle 193
Demre and Myra 278–279
dengbeys 25
Denizli 212
Denktaş, Cypriot President
  Rauf 451, 455, 456

Derinkuyu 319
derviş 27, 122, 337, 348
dervish meeting places,
  mevlevihanesi 349
devşirme system 12
devil's footprint 174
diarrhea 51
Didyma (Didim) 208
dietary concerns 71
Dikili Taş (Egyptian
  Obelisk) 103
Diocletian 8
Dionysus 254
disabled travelers 70
diseases 51–52
  food- and water-borne 51
  insect-borne 51
Divan 106
Divan Yolu 23, 112
documents and formalities
  39
Doğubeyazıt 432
Dolmabahçe Palace 123
dolmuş
  etiquette 66
  travel 65
Dorian League 254
dorms 56
dress 33
drinks 36
driving 67
driving permits 67
drugs 48
Dumlupınar University 348
Durrell, Lawrence 233

E

Eğirdir Gölü 344
earthquakes 102
Eat me! 376
Eceabat 144
Ecevit, Bülent 19
Ecumenical Council 194
Edirne 138–143
Efes (Ephesus) 193–197
Efes (Ephesus) 7
Eğirdir 344–346
Egyptian Spice Bazaar
  (Mısır Çarşısı) 110, 117
electric current 53
elevation, high 50
email 59
embassies
  Northern Cyprus 466

Turkey 39
emergencies 49
emergency medical
   services 50
Empress Zoe 102
Enver Paşa 15
EOKA, Cyprus 455
Ephesus. See Efes.
Erbakan 19
Erdogan, Tayyib 19
Erzincan 428
Erzurum 422–427
Eski Cami, Edirne 142
Eski Gümüşler Monastery
   326
Eskişehir 351
etiquette 33
Eudoxus 254
eunuchs 106
Euromos 227
European Union 19
   Cyprus and 456
Eurymedon 346
Evren, Kenan 18
exchange rates 42
exhaustion, heat 50
Eyüp Camii 119

F

fairy chimneys 311
Faliraki, Rhodes, Greece
   234
Famagusta. See Mağusa.
Faralya 269
Fatih Camii, İstanbul 116
Fatih Mehmet. See
   Mehmet the Conqueror.
Fazilet (Virtue Party) 19
Fazilet Party, 115
ferries 63
   İstanbul 84
   İzmir 184
   Black Sea 378
   Samsun 391
   Yalova 160
festivals 37–38
   Mağusa Cultural Festival
      473
   Samos, Manolis
      Kalomiris 240
   traditional dance
      festival, Aydın 216
Fethiye 260–264
fez 17
Fez Travel 65

Film, Festival 282
financial matters 42
fish oracle 226
Five Pillars of Islam 25
flesh-eating fish 376
Florence Nightingale's
   chambers, İstanbul 129
Foça 179–182
folk music 24
food 35
football. See futbol.
Four Seasons Hotel 95
Fourth Crusade 101
frostbite 50
futbol 34, 132, 408

G

Galat Mevlihane 122
Galata Tower 122
Galen 178
Gallipoli 122, 144–151
   battlefields of 147–148
   Brighton Beach 147
   Çanakbayırı 147
   Çanakkale 148–151
   Eceabat 144
   Gelibolu 146
   Kilitbahir 148
   Lone Pine Memorial 148
   New Zealand Memorial
      148
GAP Project 445
gay travelers 70
gecekondus 75
Gelibolu 146
Genoese 202
Geogian Frontier 412
Georgia 32, 377
Georgian churches 417,
   418, 419
getting around 64–67
Gevher Nesibe Sultan,
   Selçuk princess 334
Geyre (Aphrodisias) 213–
   215
giardia 52
Gibson, Mel 150
Giresun 400–402
Girne (Kyrenia) 456–461
Giyasettin Keyhüsrev
   Sultan, Selçuk prince 334
Glanz, Derek, author 23
glossary, Turkish-English
   476
GO25 card 42

Göcek 259
Gök Medrese (Blue
   Seminary)
   Sivas 375
   Tokat 372
Gökova. See Akyaka.
Golden Horn 81
Gomorrah 468
Gordion 7, 366
Gordion knot 7
Göreme 314–317
Göreme Open-Air Museum
   316
Grand Bazaar (Kapalı
   Çarşısı) 110, 119
Greek Orthodox
   Patriarchate 118
Green Line (Cyprus) 452,
   455, 464
Gülhane Park 104
Güllübahçe. See Priene.
Güvercinada Island 206
Güvercinlik Cave 277
Güzelyurt 328

H

Haci Ahmet, Selçuk
   architect 188
Haci Bektaş Veli 28, 330
Hacıbektaş 330
Hadrian 138, 196
Hagia Sophia. See Aya
   Sofia.
hair museum 325
hajj 26
Halicarnassus 221
hamam 34, 131
han 11
handicrafts 349
harassment 69
Harem Girls 104
Harran, near Şanlıurfa 448
Hatay museum, Antakya
   308
Hatay. See Antakya.
Hattuşaş 368
Hattuziliz II 368
Hatun, Hunat Mahperi 335
hazelnut 397
head scarves 19
healing spring 373
health 48–53
   heatstroke 50
   sexually transmitted

diseases 52
women 52
heatstroke 50
Hellenistic Era 8
Hellespont. See
Dardanelles.
Hemşin 32, 409
Hemşin Valley 413, 415
Hemşinli 413, 415
hepatitis A 51
Hepatu 369
Hera 271
Hercules 444
Herodotus 472
Heybeliada 131
Hierapolis. See
Pamukkale.
high altitude 50
hijra 26
hiking
Belgrade Forest,
İstanbul 126
Çambaşı Yayla 399
Cappadocia 317
Çoruh Valley 418
Eğirdir 346
Erciyes Dağı 336
Gömede Valley 324
Hemşin Valley 413
Ihlara Valley 327
Kaçkars 419
Köyceğiz 255
Monastery Valley 329
Soğanlı 322
Turnalık Yayla 399
Hikmet, Nazım 24
Hippocrates
med school 238
plane tree of 238
Hippodrome 103
Hisar, Ankara 364
Hisarönü 267
hitchhiking 66
Hittites 6, 366
HIV 52
Hoca, Nasrettin 24, 346
holidays 37
Homer 7
honey 117, 252
Hopa 412
horseback riding 269, 433
hostels 55
hot springs 414
hot-air ballooning 314
Hüdavend Hatun 426
hypothermia 50

I

Iasos 226
Ibn Battuta 212
İbrahim Paşa Sarayı 111
İbrahim the Drunkard 114
İçmeler 249–250
Iconoclasm 9
identification 41
Idrieus 227
Ihlara 327–328
Iliad 7
immunizations 49
İncirlik, US military base
302
İnebolu 385
İnegöl Köfte 152
İnönü, İsmet 17
insurance 53
International Driving
Permit (IDP) 67
International Efes Festival
196
International Student
Identity Card (ISIC) 41
International Teacher
Identity Card (ITIC) 42
International White Gold
Festival 352
International Youth
Discount Travel Card 42
internet 59
Isador the Younger 101
Işak Paşa Palace,
Doğubeyazıt 432, 433
İşhan Kilise 419
ISIC 41
İskender kebap 152
Islam 25–28
Isodorus of Miletus 101
İstanbul 75–136
accommodations 90–96
Aksaray-Lâleli 116
Anadolu Hisarı 127
Arnavütköy 125
Asian Bosphorus 129
Askeri Müzesi 122
Bebek 125
Belgrade Forest 126
Beşiktaş 123–125
Beyazıt 112–115
Beylerbeyi 129
buses 85
camping 96
Caricature Museum
(Karikator ve Mizah

Müzesi) 115
Çengelköy 129, 130
common transportation
routes 87
Eminönü 117
Emirgan 127
entertainment 131–132
Eyüp 118
Fatih 115
Fener and Balat 118
food 96–100
getting in and out 82
history 80
İstiklâl Caddesi 121
Jewish quarter 118
Kariye Camii 119
Moda 127
nightlife 133–136
orientation 81
Ortaköy 125
practical information
88–90
Prince's Islands, Adalar
130
Saraçhane Park 115
Sariyer 126
sights 101–130
Sultanahmet 101–111
Taksim 120
Taksim and Beyoğlu 120
tramvay 85
Üsküdar 128
Yedikule 120
Zeyrek 115
İstanbul University 110
ITIC 42
İzmir 7, 182–187
İznik 161–163

J

Jacobites 441
James II, King 459
Janissaries 12, 111
Jericho 343
Jersey Tiger butterfly 268
Jews 31, 121, 182
jihad 26
Job 118
worm cave of 447
Julius Caesar 370
Justinian I 101

K

Kızıl Kule, Alanya 293
Kızılay 358, 361

Kaş 274–277
Ka'aba 102
Kaçkars 419
Kadesh, Treaty of 109
Kafkasör Festival 417
Kalkan 272–273
Kamiros, Rhodes 235
Kangal 376
Kapalı Çarşısı 110
Karagöz (shadow theater) 124, 158
Karamanoğlu 298, 330
Kariye Camii 119
Karaoğlanoğlu 462
Karpaz Peninsula 474
Kars 429–430
Kastamonu 386
Kastellorizo 277
Kaunos. See Dalyan and Kaunos.
Kavaklidere 361, 362
Kayaköy 265
Kay-Khosrow I 11
Kaymakli 319
Kayseri 332–336
Kekova, submerged city of 277
Kemal, Namık 15, 24, 472
Kemal, Yaşar 24
Kemer 277
kervansaray 11
    Edirne 140
    Sultan Han 336
Keykavus I, Selçuk Sultan 375
Kiliç Arslan IV 372
Kilitbahir 148
Kir Vart, Persian ruler 335
Kızkalesi 299–300
Kleopatra's Island 247
Knights Templar, Cyprus 455
Konya 337–343
Köprülü Kanyon 288
Koran 25
Kos 235–239
    Asclepion 238
    Asfendiou 239
    central 238
    Kefalos 239
    southern 239
Kos Town, Kos 236
Köyceğiz 254–256
Kuşadası 202–207
    Music Festival 206

Küçük, Cypriot President Fazıl 455
Küçük, Fazıl 455
külliye 23
Kültepe, 335
Kurds 18, 29, 433
    folk music 25
Kütahya 348–350
Kyrenia. See Girne.
Kyrenia Castle 457
Kyromos. See Euromos.

L

Labranda (Labraynda) 226
Lajos Kossuth 350
Lala Mustafa Paşa, Erzurum 427
language 32
language schools 73
Lapta (Lápithos) 463
Lausanne, Treaty of 16
Laz 32
leather goods 116
Lefke (Léfka) 467
Lefkoşa (North Nicosia) 464–467
leisure 34
Lelegonpolis 213
Lepanto, battle of 13
lesbian travelers 70
Lesbos 169
Leto 188, 271
Letoon 271
Lindos, Rhodes, Greece 234
literature 24
Lone Pine Memorial 148
Lusignan Dynasty, Cyprus 455, 459, 460
Lycian League 278
Lycian sarcophagi 265
Lycians 263, 271, 277
Lydians 7, 188
Lysimachus 8, 175

M

Mısır Çarşısı. See Egyptian Spice Bazaar.
Ma, Anatolian mother goddess 370
Mağusa (Famagusta) 468–471

Mahmut I 102
Mahmut II 14, 111
mail 57
Makarios, Archbishop 455
malaria 51
Malatya 442–443
Mamure Kale, Anamur 296
Manisa 187
Manual I, Comnenian Emperor 407
Manzikert, battle of 10
Marcus Aurelius 186, 208
Mardin 444
Marmaris 243–248
MasterCard 43
Mausoleum of Halicarnassus 7, 221
McDonald's 343, 362
Mecca 26
Medic Alert 50
medical assistance 49
Medina 26
Mediterranean Coast 242–309
Medusa head 209
meerschaum 352
Megalopolis 213
Mehmet II. See Mehmet the Conqueror.
Mehmet the Conqueror 101, 103, 104, 121, 151, 167, 403
meler 249
mermer 188
Mersin 301–302
Mevlâna Müzesi 340
Mevlâna. See Rumi, Mevlâna Celaleddin.
Mevlevi 27
Midas, King 7, 366
mihrab 22
Mihrimah Camii 128
Milas 225
Miletus (Milet) 208
Military Museum (Askeri Müzesi) 122
minare 22
minber 22
Minoans 7
minority travelers 29-32, 71
misnomer, Gate of Felicity a.k.a. White Eunuch's Gate 106
Model Mugging 46

Modern Turkish Art 128
Monastery of St. Simeon 309
money 42
Monophysitism 9
moonscapes 311
mopeds 66
mosaics 21
  Antakya 308
  Aya Sofia 102
  Kariye Camii 119
  Kos 237
  Letoon 271
  Mosaic Musuem, İstanbul 111
  Rhodes 232
mosques 22
  Defterdar, Kos 238
  Hadji Hassan, Kos 238
  Mourad Reis, Rhodes 233
  Süleyman, Rhodes 233
mosquitoes 51
Mother Goddess 343
Motherland Party (ANAP) 18
motorcycles 66
mountains
  Ararat 431
  Baba Dağ range 213
  Beydağlari range 278
  Bülbül Dağı 200
  Cilician 296
  Erciyes Dağı 311, 336
  Hasan Dağ 311
  Pagus 182
  Pion 195
  Stauros 306
  Taurus 344
  Uludağ 152
movie theaters
  İstanbul 132
  Ankara 362
Mu'in al-Din Süleyman 372
müezzin 26
Muhammed 25
Murat I 138, 142, 170
Murat III 375
Müren, Zeki 24
Museum of Anatolian Civilizations 363
music 24
musical instruments 384
Mustafa III, tomb of 117
Mustafa Kemal. See Atatürk.
Mustafapaşa 323

Muvatellish, Hittite King 109
Mycenaeans 454
Myra. See Demre and Myra.

N

NASA 334
Nataşas 400
National Pact 16
National Parks
  Akyaka National Park 229
  Dilek National Park 206
  Lake Kovada 346
NATO 17
Naval Museum, İstanbul 124
nave 21
Necropolis Church, Anemurium 296
Necropolis of Telmessos 263
Nelson 243
Nemrut Dağı 443
Nero 194
Nesin, Aziz 24
Nestorian Lachas brothers, Cyprus 468
Nevşehir 312
New Zealand Memorial 148
Niğde 325
Nicaea. See İznik.
Nicene Creed 9
Nicopolis, battle of 156
Nicosia. See Lefkoşa.
Nika Revolt 80, 101, 103
Ninoe, the goddess 213
Nizam-i-Cedid 14
Noah's Ark 433
Northern Cyprus 451–475
  essentials 451–454
  getting there 452
  history 454–456
  keeping in touch 454
Nur-ed Din of Aleppo, Selçuk emir 445
Nyssa 216

O

obsidian 427
Öcalan, Abdullah 18, 29, 46
Odyssey 7
older travelers 69
Olimpos 279–280
  Blue Lagoon, Ölüdeniz 268
Ölüdeniz 266–268
opera 363
opium 346
Oracle of Delphi 103
Orak Island 182
Ordu 397–399
Orhai, independent Armenian kingdom of 445
Osman Hamdi Bey 23, 109
Osman, founder of the Ottoman dynasty 12, 152
Osmanlı 152
Otel Madımak 24, 376
Othello 468, 470
Ottoman
  architecture 23, 382, 395
  art 23
  history 12
Ottoman houses 350
Ottoman Public Debt Administration 15
outdoors 56
Özal, Turgut 18
özgun 24

P

packing 53
Painting and Statue Museum (modern Art), Ankara 365
palace treasury 107
  emeralds 107
  gold 107
Pamuk, Orhan, 24
Pamukkale (Hierapolis) 209–212
Panionic League 207
pansiyon 55
Paphos, settlers from 463
paragliding
  Eğirdir 346
  Ölüdeniz 268
parasailing
  İçmeler 250
  Side 289
parasites 52
Pasinler 427
passports 40
Patara 269–271

patriarchates 9
Pausanias, the ancient traveler 193
pensions 55
Pergamene Empire 175
Pergamon. See Bergama.
Perge 286
Persians 208
Perwer, Şivan 25
Peter, the Apostle 306, 309
Pharnaces II 370
Phaselis 281
Philetaerus 175
phrasebook 482
Phrygians 7, 366
pickle juice 156
Pierre Loti 119
Pillars of Islam 25
pirates
  Barbarossa 124
PKK 18, 29, 46
Plasara 213
Pliny the Younger 170
PLUS 44
Polatlı 366
politics 18
  ANAP (Motherland Party) 18
  European Union 19
  Virtue Party 19
  Welfare Party 19
polygamy 16
Polykrates, tyrant 241
Pompey 8, 293, 393
Pontic Kings 8
Pontic tombs 395, 397
Pontus 8, 393
pop music 189
Population Exchange 16
Porcelain 106
Porte 13
poste restante 57
pottery 325
Praxiteles 254
Priapus 200
Priene 207
prison 95
prostitution 101, 116, 377, 400, 416
Ptolemy 8, 454
Pytheos 207

Q

qibla 22

Queen Amastris 383

R

rafting 417
  Köprülü Kanyon 288
  Saklıkent Gorge 265
  Yusufeli 417
Ramazan (Ramadan) 26, 37
Ramses II 6, 109, 368
Rashidun 27
Red Cross 49
Reis, Piri 146
relics 107
rental cars 67
City of Rhodes 230–233
Rhodes 230–235
  Epta Piges 235
  Kamiros 235
  Mandraki 233
  Valley of Butterflies 235
Richard the Lionheart 455
rivers
  Alaçay, Ani 431
  Arpaçay, Ani 431
  Asi River, Antakya 306
  Cayster River, Ephesus 193
  Çoruh 417
  Göksu, Silifke 298
  Kızılarmak 311
Rize 410–412
rock tombs
  Dalyan and Kaunos 258
  Tlos 265
Romans 8
Roxelana 13
Rumeli Hisarı 80, 126
Rumi, Mevlâna Celaleddin 11, 27, 208, 337, 340, 341
Rüstem Paşa Camii 117
Rüstem Paşa Kervansaray 427

S

Sabancı Merkez Camii, Adana 304
Sabians 448
Sack of Constantinople 103
Sadberk Hanım Müzesi 126
şadirvan 22
safety 45

Safranbolu 379–383
saints
  Barnabas 473
  Cyril 9
  Demetrios 201
  John 201
  Nicholas 269, 270, 278, 279
  Paul 8, 193, 305, 337, 473
  Peter 306
  Philip 212
  Simeon 309
Saklıkent Gorge 264
Saladin 427
Salamis 472–473
Salat 26
Saltıd Rulers 426
Samos 239–241
  beaches 241
  Heraion 241
Sampson, Nikos 455
Samsun 390–393
Sanaat 24
Sandal Church 317
Şanlıurfa 444–448
Santa Claus 269, 270, 278
Sarapis, Egyptian Grain God 196
Sardis 188
Sarlmsaklı Beach 174
Sart. See Sardis.
satrapies 7
Schliemann, Heinrich 164
scuba diving
  Fethiye 262
  İçmeler 250
  Kaş 274
  Ölüdeniz 266
Sea Peoples 7
seal colony, Kaş 277
security 45
Sedir 228
Selçuk 197–200
Selçuks
  Alanya 293
  Kayseri 332–336
  Konya 337–343
  Sivas 375
  Tokat 370–373
Seleucus I 8, 306, 445
self defense 48
Selim I 12, 408, 423
Selim II 25, 142
Selim the Grim
  tomb of 116
Selim the Sot 13

Selimiye barracks 129
Selimiye Camii, Edirne 142
sema 342
Şems of Tabriz 341, 342
Şenyuva Valley 413
Septimus Severus 103
Serapis 390
Sesamos. See Amasra.
Seven Ecumenical
  Councils 9
Seven Sleepers, cave of
  197
seven wonders of the
  ancient world
  Colossus of Rhodes 232
sexually transmitted
  diseases 52
Seyit Bilal 390
Şeytan Sofrası 173
Shabadah 25
shadow theater. See
  Karagöz.
Shakespeare 468
Shi'ism 10, 27
Side 289–291
Silifke 298
Silk Route 11, 373, 434
Sille 343
Sinan 23, 119
  Aya Sofia rennovation,
    İstanbul 101
  Aya Sofia, İznik 162
  Mihrimah Camii 128
  Rüstem Paşa Camii 117
  Selimiye Camii, Edirne
    142
  Süleymaniye Külliyesi
    114
  tomb of 115
Sinop 388–390
sirens 179
Şirince 200
Şivan
Sivas 373–376
Sivas Congress 374
skiing
  Mt. Uludağ, near Bursa
    159
Smyrna. See İzmir.
Soğanlı Valley 322
soccer. See futbol.
Softa Kale, Anamur 296
Söke 228
Soli 467
solo travel 69
Solomon, King 101

Solon 467
Sostratos 254
specific concerns 68–72
Spoonmaker's Diamond
  107
sports 34
St. Anne's Church,Trabzon
  407
St. Basil Church 317
St. George 317
St. Hilarion Castle 462
St. Nicholas Island 268
St. Peter's Church 309
STA Travel 61
standby 62
Stavropolis 213
STDs 52
Straatoğlu, Derek, actor 23
Strabo, geographer 370,
  393
Stratos 254
street addresses 68
street children 48
studying abroad 72
Stylites, Saint Simeon of
  309
Sufism 27–28, 122, 330,
  467
Süleyman the Magnificent
  13, 104, 152, 182, 187,
  243, 408
  tomb of 114
Süleymaniye Külliyesi
  (Süleymaniye Complex),
  İstanbul 114
Sultan Han 336
Sultanahmet Camii. See
  Blue Mosque.
Sultanate of Coke
Sultanate of Rum 11
sunburn 50
Sungurlu 369
Sunni 10
sunscreen 50
synagogues 208
  Kos 238
  Shalom, Rhodes 233

T

Taş Han 373
Taşucu 297
Talat Pasa 15
Tamerlane 430
Tantalus 188

Tanzimat 14
tariqa 27
Tarkan 24
Tarsus 305
taverna 24
taxes 45
tea labs, Rize 412
teach English 73
Tekkale 418
tekke 27, 467
telephones 57
Telmessos, ancient city of
  260
Temo, musician 25
Temple of Aphrodite 214
Temple of Artemis 7, 193,
  200
Temple of Athena 207
temples
  Aphrodite, Rhodes 233
  Apollo, Kos 238
  Aprodite, Kos 237
  Asclepios, Kos 238
  Dionysus, Kos 238
  Hera, Samos 241
  Hercules, Kos 237
  Lindian Athena, Rhodes
    234
Tenedos. See Bozcaada.
Tercan 427
Termal 160
terrorism 46
Teshub 369
Teucer 472
Thales 208
Theodosius I 103
Theodosius II 8, 427
thermal baths 352
thermal springs
  Bursa 157
  Dalyan and Kaunos 258
  Kos 238
  Köyceğiz 255
  Pamukkale 211
  Termal 160
  Vekamp, near Çeşme
    192
thieving Brits 193, 209, 462
thieving Germans 208
Thomas Cook 43
Thrace 138–144
Thutmosis III 103
Tiberius Caesar 332
Tigranes the Great 8, 437
Tile Museum 342
Tiled Pavilion (Çinli Köşk)

109
tiles
  İznik 163
  Kütahya 349
time zones 59
tipping 45
Tirebolu 402
Titridates 432
Tlos 265
TMT, Cyprus 455
Tokat 370–373
Tom 144
Topkapı Palace (Topkapı
  Sarayı) 104–108
  Archaelogical Museum
    104
  Church of Divine Peace
    104
  Imperial Mint 104
Tortum Valley 419
Trabzon 403–408
Trabzonspor 408
trains 63, 65
Trajan 196
Tralles, ancient city of 216
transportation
  cars 67
travel agencies 61
traveler's checks 43
Trebizond. See Trabzon.
treehouse pensions,
  Olimpos 279
trekking agencies 420
trekking. See hiking.
TRNC (Turkish Republic of
  North Cyprus) 455
True Path Party 19
Truva (Troy) 7, 164–167
Tuşpa 7
Tudhaliya IV, King 369
tufa 311
Tulip Period 14
Tunnel of Eupalinos 241
türbe 22
Turkish Airlines (THY) 62,
  64
Turkish baths (Hamam) 34
Turkish film 123
Turkish Riviera 266
Turkish Touring and
  Automobile Association
  67
Turkish War of
  Independence 16
Turkish-Islamic Synthesis
  doctrine 32

Turkmen nomads 427
türkü 24
Turquoise Riviera 282
Turtle Beach 247
turtles 461
  Girne 460
  İztuzu Beach 258
  Karpaz Peninsula 474
  Patara 271
  Turtle Beach 255
Tuşba, village of 438
Twelve-island tours 263
Tyche 444
typhoid fever 52

U

Üç Şerefeli Cami, Edirne
  142
Üçhisar 318
ulema 14
Ulu Cami
  Bursa 156
Ulus 359, 360, 363
Umayyads 448
UN 468
Underground Cistern 111
underground cities 319
UNESCO 379
Universities
  İstanbul University,
    Beyazit 112
  Bosphorus University
    125
  Marmara University,
    İstanbul 103
  University of Anatolia,
    Eskişehir 351
Ünye 396
Urartian Fortress 437
Urartians 428, 430, 431,
  434
Urfa. See Şanlıurfa.
Ürgüp 320–322
Uzungöl 410

V

Valley of Butterflies,
  Rhodes 235
valuables, protecting 48
Van 434–437
Van Gölü 434
Vathy, Samos 239
  daytrips 241
Vestal Virgins 197

Viagra, Turkish 117
Viaud, Julian Marie 119
Virgin Mary 201, 409
  house of 200
Virtue Party (Fazilet) 19
Visa 43
Volkan, Cyprus 455
Volkswagen Beetle
  Festival, Ordu 398
volunteering abroad 73
Vouni 468

W

waterfalls
  Düden, near Antalya 288
  Muradiye, near
    Doğubeyazit 433
Western Union 44
whirling dervishes. See
  derviş.
White Sheep, The 427
wilderness 56
windsurfing
  Çeşme 192
wine 167, 322
Winston Churchill,
  quotation 118
women 17, 28
women travelers 68
  health 52
Wonders of the Ancient
  World 7
  Mausoleum of
    Halicarnassus 20
  Temple of Artemis 20,
    193
wonders. See seven
  wonders of the ancient
  world
woodworking market 384
work permit 73
Worker's Party of
  Kurdistan. See PKK.
World Cultural Heritage
  List 379
World War I 147, 148

X

Xanthian Inscribed Pillar
  271
Xanthos 271
Xerxes 7

Y

Yıldız Parkı Complex 124
Yalova 159
Yassıhöyük.See Gordion.
yaylas 56, 413, 417
Yazılıkaya 367, 369
Yeşil Türbe, Bursa 156
Yerebatan Sarayı
  (Underground Cistern)
  111
Young Ottomans 15
Young Turk Revolution 15
Yunuş Emre 11
Yusufeli 417

Z

zakat 26
Zelve. See Cavuşin-Zelve.
Zeus 271, 388
Zeus Stratios 226
Zindan Cave 346
Zoroastrians 311
zurna 373vb

MAP INDEX

Aegean Coast 165
Adana 303
Antakya 307
Antalya Center 283
Antalya Gulf Coast 281
Black Sea Coast 378-379
Bodrum 219
Bursa 155
Bursa Overview 152
Çanakkale 149
Central Anatolia 310
Central İstanbul 78-79
Eastern Anatolia 424
Edirne 139
Ephesus 195
Erzurum 425
Fethiye 261
Gallipoli Peninsula 145
Girne 457
Göreme 315
İstanbul 76-77
İstanbul Overview 81
İzmir 183
Kapadokya (Cappadocia) 312

Kars 431
Kaş 275
Kayseri 333
Konya 339
Kuşadasi 203
Lefkoşa (North Nicosia) 465
Mağusa (Famagusta) 469
Marmaris 245
Mediterranean Coast 242-243
Nevşehir 313
North Ankara 354
Northern Cyprus 452-453
Northwestern Turkey 137
Safranbolu 380
Selçuk 199
South Ankara 355
South of the Golden Horn 113
Sultanahmet and Süleymaniye 92-93
Topkapı Palace 105
Troy Site Plan 166
Tünel and Taksim 97
Turkey viii-ix
Turkey: Regions xv
Van 435

INDEX

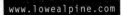

If I had my life
to live over again,

I would relax. I would limber up. I would take more chances.

I would take more trips.

I would climb more mountains, swim more rivers, and watch more sunsets.

I would go places and do things and travel lighter than I have.

I would ride more
merry-go-rounds.

Excerpt from Nadine Stair, 85 years old / photo> John Norris

Lowe alpine

technical packs & apparel

Will you have enough stories to tell your grandchildren?

<u>Yahoo! Travel</u>

DO YOU YAHOO!? ™